The Hong Kong Filmography,
1977–1997

The Hong Kong Filmography, 1977–1997

A Reference Guide to 1,100 Films Produced by British Hong Kong Studios

JOHN CHARLES

Foreword by Tim Lucas

McFarland & Company, Inc., Publishers
Jefferson, North Carolina, and London

The present work is a reprint of the illustrated case bound edition of The Hong Kong Filmography, 1977–1997: A Complete Reference to 1,100 Films Produced by British Hong Kong Studios, *first published in 2000 by McFarland.*

LIBRARY OF CONGRESS CATALOGUING-IN-PUBLICATION DATA

Charles, John, 1965–
The Hong Kong filmography, 1977–1997 : a complete reference to 1,100 films produced by British Hong Kong studios / by John Charles; foreword by Tim Lucas.
p. cm.
Includes bibliographical references and index.

ISBN 978-0-7864-4323-9
softcover : 50# alkaline paper ♾

1. Motion pictures — China — Hong Kong — Catalogs. I. Title.
PN1993.5.C4C425 2009 016.79143'75'0952 — dc21 00-38003

British Library Cataloguing-in-Publication data are available

On the cover: Faye Wong in *Chung King Express*, 1994
(Miramax Films / Photofest)

Manufactured in the United States of America

McFarland & Company, Inc., Publishers
Box 611, Jefferson, North Carolina 28640
www.mcfarlandpub.com

To Richard Akiyama and Sanney Leung.
Thanks for your help and friendship.

Acknowledgments

The author wishes to thank the following individuals (listed alphabetically), whose assistance aided greatly in the creation of this book: Jian Ai, Richard Akiyama, Jeff Briggs, Diana Bringardner, Damon Brittingham, Evans Chan, Jerry Chan, William Connolly (Martial Arts Movie Associates), Frank Djeng (Tai Seng Video Marketing Inc.), Wei Hu, Fran Kloepfer, Shelly Kraicer, Gere LaDue, Ryan Law (Hong Kong Movie Database), Sanney Leung, Tim Lucas, Ian McDowell, Ken Mei, Susie Modjallal, Marc Morris, Ron Murillo, K.M.D. Sartori, Jeff Segal, Helen Soo (Tai Seng Video Marketing Inc.), Marc Walkow, Miles Wood, and Tim Youngs (Another Hong Kong Movies Page).

Foreword

The heavy title of the even heavier book in your hands brings to mind a flurry of images that are, ironically, lighter than air. To most Americans, Hong Kong cinema is the unparalleled realm of action choreography, ranging from the mesmerizing Bruce Lee films of the early 1970s, and the dazzling and often hilarious stuntwork of Jackie Chan, to John Woo's ballistic ballets of desperate (but unfailingly cool-looking) men squeezing off sparks from a gun in each hand. However, as John Charles proves in this ambitious critical survey, the whole of Hong Kong cinema is infinitely more varied.

It's a simplification, perhaps, but it seems to me that every ten years, the muse of cinema shines brightest at a different latitude and longitude: In the '20s, it was Germany; in the '30s, America; in the '40s, England; in the '60s, France—and so on. From the late '80s throughout the last decade of the 20th century, that bright light was unquestionably emanating from Hong Kong.

At a time when most international film markets were either depressed, defunct, or coasting on direct-to-video porn, and when Hollywood films seemed inseparable from their merchandising and amusement park ride potential, Hong Kong commanded the world's attention as a hotbed of ideas and invention—a celebration of the grand diversity and pageantry of movie-making.

There was room for everything: action, comedy, horror, eroticism, mythology, historical drama, contemporary love stories, even (for lack of a better phrase) art cinema. And for every film that was imported to U.S. screens, there were others whose content seemed at odds with Western sensibilities, such as comedies built around stories of rape, murder and cannibalism.

Long before U.S. distributors wised up and started importing Hong Kong films to American screens, the cognoscenti had discovered them on videotape. For a time, it seemed that the most popular movies among North American film buffs were *A Better Tomorrow, Bullet in the Head, The Armour of God,* and the outrageous *Sex and Zen*—movies that had not yet received a legitimate release, either theatrically or on tape. One of these cutting edge tapeheads was a young videostore clerk named Quentin Tarantino, who recognized the untapped commercial potential of Ringo Lam's 1987 *City on Fire* and proceeded to tap it—as the blueprint for his 1992 screenwriting and directorial debut, *Reservoir Dogs.*

What was most remarkable about this exciting period of discovery was that Hong Kong gave the world, seemingly overnight, a whole new galaxy of movie stars: Jackie Chan, Chow Yun-fat, Brigitte Lin Ching-hsia, Jet Li, Gong Li, Maggie Cheung, Tony Leung Chiu-wai, Michelle Yeoh, Yuen Biao, Amy Yip, and many others, whose past careers could then be investigated and enjoyed at our leisure. Every last one of these actors and actresses had the charisma, the glamour, and perhaps equally importantly, the distance one associates with the stars of vintage Hollywood. They also had great directors, like John Woo, Tsui Hark, and (my favorite working director of the moment) Wong Kar-wai, whose collective works were informed by such disparate filmmakers as Jean-Pierre Melville, Sergio Leone, and Woody Allen.

In recent years, as Hong Kong has returned to Chinese rule, much of its native talent has been lured away to different parts of the world. Today, John Woo, Jackie Chan, Chow Yun-fat, and many other HK artists are making films in Hollywood. Sammo Hung is starring in a CBS series, Maggie Cheung is making films in France, and with the release of *Tomorrow Never Dies*, Michelle Yeoh has become a Bond girl. Therefore, the two decades chronicled between the covers of this hefty tome essentially bracket the phenomenon of Hong Kong cinema in its entirety.

The author of this reference work is John Charles, who has been a valued contributor to my magazine

Video Watchdog since the early 1990s. Giving John a regular forum in which to share his knowledge of Hong Kong cinema has been one of the privileges of my professional life, and it is a joy for me to witness this grandscale fulfillment of his passion for the subject.

John has studied not only HK cinema, but the languages native to Hong Kong and Mainland China as well, and this makes him more sensitive than most reviewers to the nuances that elude translation, the ones closest to a movie's heart. He is equally alert to dubbing gaffes, re-edits, missing footage, inept subtitling, flat mono compressions of stereo soundtracks, and all the other blemishes and birthmarks that can make even a great movie seem mediocre. Consequently, John's reviews delve into the soul, as well as the style, of these films—and they do it with sensitivity, humor, and intelligence.

In the past several years, as the cult following of Hong Kong cinema has grown around the world, numerous books have been published on the subject: historical overviews, collections of interviews, and hastily written booklets of popcorn-like reviewlets. John's labor of love is the first serious, in-depth, critical guide to Hong Kong cinema in English. I have no doubt that it will be greeted as the definitive work on the subject, and hold that distinction for some time.

Tim Lucas
Cincinnati, Ohio
July, 1999

CONTENTS

PREFACE

Welcome to **The Hong Kong Filmography, 1977–1997**, a comprehensive collection of reviews covering 1100 films released during this 21-year period. Thanks to the success of Bruce Lee and Jackie Chan, Hong Kong cinema has attained a measure of popularity in mainstream American circles, but nothing beyond action and kung fu films have really broken through. This is a shame, as HK filmmakers have far more to offer than just remarkable action choreography and potentially fatal stuntwork. One of my goals with this book was to reveal the many "hidden" pleasures available to adventurous film fans, while also providing more seasoned viewers with information on other productions that might appeal to them. Consequently, this book embraces all of Hong Kong's output: romance, comedies, thrillers, mysteries, fantasies, sex films, dramas, children's features, horror, and science fiction, as well as the expected action and kung fu extravaganzas.

The late 1970s saw the emergence of a special period in HK cinema. Young filmmakers (many of whom cut their teeth in the West) like Tsui Hark, Ann Hui On-wah, and Patrick Tam Kar-ming revitalized the industry at a time when audiences were tiring of the old formulas and old approaches. This book covers the start of this "New Wave," continues on through the late '80s and early '90s (a golden period for HK cinema, which saw production slates and theater attendance rates at peak levels), and concludes at the end of 1997.

As I write this in the summer of 1999, the future of the industry is shrouded in uncertainty. Massive, well-organized VCD piracy has caused box-office revenues to take a huge tumble and that, coupled with a major shift in audience preference towards megabuck Hollywood "event" movies, has left HK cinema teetering on the brink of disaster. In an attempt to lure viewers back into theaters showing local fare, studios have begun utilizing American-style computer generated special effects in films like **The Stormriders** (1998) and **Gen-X Cops** (1999). While both features enjoyed box-office success (particularly the former, which might have gone on to become the region's all-time champion, had its receipts not been cut short by the widespread availability of several pirate video versions), it is too early to tell if this approach will insure continued success—or simply buy a little more time.

Writing a book on Chinese cinema, be it Hong Kong, Taiwan, or Mainland China, can be a daunting task as far as names go. For example, what should one choose: Andy Lau? Andy Lau Tak-wah? Andy Lau Tak Wah? Lau Tak-wah? Lau Tak Wah? Liu De Hua? Liu De-hua? Liu Dehua? Obviously, some choices have to be made, and I have opted, in the majority of cases, to use a combination of the performer's Cantonese and English names. Hence, in this case, the listing would be Andy Lau Tak-wah. Performers from outside of HK, like Taiwanese actress Brigitte Lin Ching-hsia and Mainland star Gong Li, are listed by their Mandarin names or by a combination of Mandarin and English where applicable. There are a few exceptions to this rule; Taiwanese actress Yeh Yu-ching, for example, is better known by her Cantonese name, Yip Yuk-hing, so she is listed as Veronica Yip Yuk-hing. I list each actor's name in the same form throughout the book, regardless of how it appears in the credits.

One could argue that a writer's opinion should be stated succinctly enough in his or her review that a numerical score is not really necessary. I do not entirely disagree with that, but I provide ratings as an additional feature for those who seek to compare the opinion of the writer with their own, or simply want a quick evaluation of the movie in question. The ratings scale ("10" being the highest and "1" the lowest) is based on the quality of the film and its entertainment value. Anything with a rating of "5" or higher is worth seeing, in my opinion. A film that scores lower than "5" might be worthwhile to fans of the director or stars but even they had best approach it with low expectations. A bad movie is a bad movie and, while some are much more entertaining than others, they have still been given a failing grade.

The English subtitles on Hong Kong films are not something that many companies devote much time to. Consequently, if you are just starting to watch these movies via their original HK release editions, you have noticed many strange sentences filled with substantial syntactical and semantic errors. A few unfortunate films are rendered all but incomprehensible by shoddy translation. Nevertheless, you should not let bad subtitling deter you from watching a movie.

A number of video release entries in the text are followed by the notation "Poor Subtitles." This is not a comment on the translation but on the simple readability of the subs, which on some non-letterboxed releases are substantially cropped on the sides or occasionally drop off the bottom of the screen. Such problems vary from monitor to monitor, depending on the amount of overscan the unit has. Again, in the vast majority of cases, this is not meant to discourage one from viewing a film, but I felt that the potential viewer should still be alerted to this anomaly in advance. Entries marked "Tiny Subtitles" or "No Subtitles" are self-explanatory.

While I have been able to see a large number of HK films in a variety of formats, it was impossible for me to see every version of every movie. Consequently, there may be a few entries that do not carry the warning of "Poor Subtitles" or "No Subtitles" when they should. However, I am confident that the vast majority of listings here are properly annotated.

Unless otherwise noted, the character names appearing in the reviews are the ones used in the English subtitles. These can differ from version to version; Chow Yun-fat's character in **The Killer**, for instance, is called "Jeffrey" in the original HK edition but is "John" in the U.S. laserdisc and DVD releases.

In some reviews, the music credit simply says "Not original." I have used this when a large percentage or even 100 percent of the music in a movie has either been obtained from a library track company (like DeWolfe in the U.K.) or has been recycled from other sources.

In addition to the common English titles, I have also included the phonetic Cantonese and Mandarin (pinyin) titles for the sake of comparison. Many Chinese titles do not translate well into English but the differences can be quite fascinating, so I feel that they merit inclusion. In most cases, the Chinese titles are far more imaginative and singular than the largely generic English handles.

While this book is about Hong Kong cinema, I have journeyed slightly beyond these parameters and included a handful of Mainland productions and approximately two dozen of Taiwanese origin. These films are sometimes incorrectly listed as being from HK and, while I do not want to perpetuate this error, I felt they should be included because they feature participation by major HK entertainment figures, either in front of or behind the camera. These ringers are each identified by their place of origin in the body of the review.

John Charles
Guelph, Ontario
July 1999

The Films

1. Abbot of Shaolin

(1978; Shaw Brothers) ★: 6/10. *Siu lam ying hung bong* (Cantonese), *Shao lin ying xiong bang* (Mandarin): "Shaolin Hero Gang." Cinematographer: Yu Chi; Music: Not Original; Writer: Ngai Hong; Producer: Mona Fong Yat-wah; Action Director: Tang Te-hsiang; Director: Ho Meng-hua. Cast: David Chiang Da-wei (Chi San), Lo Lieh (Pai Mei), Lily Li Li-li (Wu Mei), Norman Tsui Siu-keung (Chi-lung), Jamie Luk Kim-ming (Lin). 2.35:1. No official domestic video release. 85 minutes. Also known as **A Slice of Death** (US title).

David Chiang has a rare outing as a Shaolin monk in this average Shaw Brothers period film. After Shaolin Temple is destroyed by Ching forces, monk Chi San vows to rebuild the structure and restore the Shaolin teachings. He travels south, impressing many with his superb kung fu, which inspires rich benefactors to aid him financially and various martial artists (including Norman Tsui and Jamie Luk) to beg for his instruction. However, the Ching forces, under the leadership of Taoist chief Pai Mei (Lo Lieh, in his signature white-haired villain role) and a powerful Tibetan lama, are in pursuit. There is some good technique on display here, but the episodic plotting takes the edge off of the drama, and the final duel between Chiang and Lo is short and perfunctory. The stock soundtrack includes the famous "shower murder" cue from **Psycho**! The character names cited above are from the English dubbed version.

Above the Law *see* **Righting Wrongs**
Above the Law II: The Blonde Fury *see* **The Blonde Fury**

2. The Accident

(1983; Woo's Film Production H.K. Co.) ★: 5/10. *Che wan* (Cantonese), *Che hun* (Mandarin): "Car Spirit." Cinematographer: Lu Cheng; Music: Not Original; Producer: Wu Chi-chung; Writer-Director: Liu Piu-lun. Cast: Kent Cheng Chuk-see (Fatty Cheng), Ma Bo-ming (Siu-ching), Ngai Dik, Wei Chiu-wah, Fung Chou. 1.85:1. VHS: World Video. 90 minutes. Also known as **Blood of the Black Dog**.

More silly than scary, this independent horror thriller is still not without interest and should appeal to those fascinated by the eastern counterparts of traditional western horror tenets. Kent Cheng plays a struggling blue collar worker who saves a young girl named Siu-ching from being hit by a toy car thrown from the window of a skyscraper. Not long afterwards, while trying to get medicine for her mother during a violent rainstorm, Siu-ching is hit and killed by a drunk driver. Her restless spirit proceeds to haunt the parties responsible for the crime and those unlucky enough to be around them (one man is burned alive by exploding toy cars!). When Siu-ching's mother dies of grief, the hauntings become even more frequent and intense, leading the remaining two people involved in the accident to enlist the aid of a female Taoist. In an uncomfortably realistic scene, she sacrifices a black dog and uses its blood as the main source of power in a ritual to vanquish Siu-ching's spirit. However, the demon proves more powerful (and crafty) than expected.

Like many of the lower budget HK horror thrillers, **The Accident** presents its horror sequences with great gusto, which almost compensates for the lack of technical polish; and the finale serves up an interesting amalgam of Christian and Tao methodology. In spite of his star billing, Cheng is only a supporting player and disappears around the midpoint. The patchwork soundtrack includes cues swiped from **Sorcerer** (1977), **Star Trek: The Motion Picture** (1979), and **Raiders of the Lost Ark** (1981).

3. Aces Go Places

(1982; Cinema City Co.) ★: 7/10. *Jui gaai paak dong* (Cantonese), *Zui jia pai dang* (Mandarin): "Best Partners." Cinematographers: Yip Pak-ying, Ho Ming, Arthur Wong Ngok-tai, Chow Kin-ming; Art Director: Wong Chui-man; Music: Sam Hui Koon-kit; Writer: Raymond Wong Pak-ming; Producers: Karl Maka, Dean Shek Tien; Action Direction: Hong Kong Action Stunt; Director: Eric Tsang Chi-wai. Cast: Sam Hui Koon-kit (King Kong), Karl Maka (Albert Au, aka Kodojak), Sylvia Chang Ai-chia (Superintendent Ho), Dean Shek Tien (Gigolo Joe), Chen Sing (Mad Max), Tsui Hark (Belligerent Man Backstage), Cho Tat-wah (Hua), Lindzay Chan Ling-chi (Ballerina), Raymond Wong Pak-ming (Priest), George Lam Chi-cheung (Ambulance Driver). Dolby Digital (DVD only). 2.35:1. VHS: Montevideo (Dubbed), Tai Seng (Poor Subtitles). Import LD: Golden Cinema City. Import VCD: Mei Ah. Import DVD: Universe. 83/93 minutes. Also known as **Mad Mission: Diamondfinger** (Montevideo title).

This action/comedy broke box office records and made the fledgling Cinema City studio a major player in the HK movie industry, on par with giants Golden Harvest and Shaw Brothers. Notorious thief King Kong makes off with a fortune in Mafia diamonds, framing fellow robber "White Glove" for the deed. The HK police call in harried Albert Au (who has been on King Kong's tail for ages) from America to help them, pairing the bald detective with the department's premiere female cop, hot-tempered Superintendent Ho. The latter finally manages to nab King Kong and, after much coercion, the thief agrees to help Albert retrieve the diamonds and arrest White Glove. In the process, Albert manages to tame his ferocious partner, but he and King Kong must fend off both White Glove *and* another thug called Mad Max while trying to figure out where KK's (now) deceased partner hid the stones.

Actor-singer Sam Hui split from his brothers, Michael and Ricky, and Golden Harvest to go solo at Cinema City, and the substantial success of **Aces Go Places** brought him even greater fame. He is ably supported by Sylvia Chang and (especially) Karl Maka, whose gift for physical comedy makes him a perfect foil. The car chases and stunts mostly just induce yawns nowadays, some of the best gags and situations are lifted from old Hollywood films, and the editing is something less than great, but the appeal of the premise (reminiscent of '60s European caper films) and the performers remains...and don't forget that incredibly catchy theme! One of the most memorable bits (where King Kong and Albert take turns being strangled by a rope) would later be copied in the horror-comedy **Return of the Demon**. *Aces Go Places* was followed by four sequels and **97 Aces Go Places**, a disastrous attempt to revive the series eight years after the last "official" entry. Atlas International's English dubbed version runs ten minutes shorter and sacrifices most of the movie's charm.

4. Aces Go Places II

(1983; Cinema City Co.) ★: 6/10. *Jui gaai paak dong daai hin san tung* (Cantonese), *Zui jia pai dang da xian shen tong* (Mandarin): "Best Partners Show Their Stuff." Cinematographers: Abdul M. Rumjahn, Peter Ngor Chi-kwan, Johnny Koo Kwok-wah, Arthur Wong Ngok-tai; Art Director: William Cheung Suk-ping; Music: Sam Hui Koon-kit, Teddy Robin Kwan; Writer: Raymond Wong Pak-ming; Producers: Karl Maka, Dean Shek Tien; Action Director: Lau Kar-wing; Director: Eric Tsang Chi-wai. Cast: Sam Hui Koon-kit (King Kong), Karl Maka (Albert Au, aka Baldy), Sylvia Chang Ai-chia (Superintendent Nancy Ho), Yasuaki Kurota (Bull), Cho Tat-wah (Hua), Tsui Hark (Mr. F.B.I.), Charlie Cho Cha-lei (Wong), Raymond Wong Pak-ming (Priest), Eric Tsang Chi-wai (Fattie), Billy Lau Nam-kwong (Gunman). Dolby Digital (DVD only). 2.35:1. VHS: Montevideo (Dubbed), Tai Seng (Poor Subtitles). Import LD: Golden Cinema City. Import VCD: Mei Ah. Import DVD: Universe. 88/102 minutes. Also known as **Mad Mission Part 2: Aces Go Places** (Montevideo title).

A Clint Eastwood lookalike named "Filthy Harry" is hired (by a Henry Kissinger lookalike, no less!) to liquidate King Kong and Albert. But the duo also have other things to worry about: KK is framed for a bank robbery by a cute Eurasian girl he's fallen for, and Albert's relationship with Superintendent Ho is on the rocks. KK and Albert end up being framed again by the girl (for a jewelry store heist this time) and must help the police nab the true culprits or be committed to an asylum by Albert's conniving boss! That fate, however, may be more desirable than the one that awaits them: wired with time bombs, they must face off against Filthy Harry's heavily-armed robot.

The stunts are a lot more spectacular this time out, but too much time is devoted to KK and Albert's romantic travails, which are not especially amusing. Still, the rest is quite entertaining (particularly the climax, in which KK combats the robot with a barrage of miniature artillery), and Tsui Hark is great in a supporting role as a mental patient who thinks he's an F.B.I. agent. The dubbed version is missing a considerable amount of footage and is not a desirable way to see the movie.

5. Aces Go Places III: Our Man from Bond Street

(1984; Cinema City Co.) ★: 6/10. *Jui gaai paak dong lui wong mat lim* (Cantonese), *Zui jia pai dang nu huang mi ling* (Mandarin): "Best Partners: Her Majesty's Secret Order." Cinematographers: Bill Wong Chung-bo, Yiu Yau-hung; Music: Noel Quinlan; Writer: Raymond Wong Pak-ming; Producers: Karl Maka, Dean Shek Tien; Action Director: Corey Yuen Kwai; Director: Tsui Hark. Cast: Sam Hui Koon-kit (King Kong), Karl Maka (Albert Au, aka Baldy), Sylvia Chang Ai-chia (Nancy Ho), John Sham Kin-fun (Albert's Superior), Peter Graves (The Man from Bond Street), Jean Marchent (James), Richard Kiel (Big Goon), Ricky Hui Koon-ying (Puffer Fish), Cho Tat-wah (Hua), Charlie Cho Cha-lei (Tso), Lowell Lo Kwun-ting (Subway Driver). Dolby Digital (DVD only). 2.35:1. VHS: Thorn-EMI (Dubbed), Tai Seng (Poor Subtitles). Import LD: Golden Cinema City. Import VCD: Mei Ah. Import DVD: Universe. 85/96 minutes. Also known as **Mad Mission Part III: Our Man from Bond Street** (Thorn-EMI title).

As the title suggests, the spy genre is the target this time, and the result ended up being the most financially successful film of the series. While in Paris, King Kong is kidnapped by a certain British secret agent, named James. His mission: secretly help the government locate "The Star of Fortune," one of the Crown Jewels, which has recently been stolen. In a highly unlikely twist, it is hidden in a vault at the HK Police Headquarters, meaning that KK will have to steal the rock from right under his friend Albert's nose. Albert, meanwhile, is in the midst of his usual domestic problems with Nancy (the couple now have a mischievous, chrome-domed baby boy appropriately named "Baldy Jr."), and KK is able to use the pretense of setting his buddy up on a date as a way of giving himself an airtight alibi. KK grabs the stone but eventually deduces that his new partners are not who they claim to be.

Produced on a much grander scale than the first two features, **Aces III** is a characteristically uneven effort. As with part 2, the sequences depicting the marital strife between Albert and Nancy are tiresome and consist almost exclusively of tired situations from old sitcoms. However, the absurdly elaborate robbery set pieces (which feature a lot of unconvincing but ambitious special effects) and spy movie send-ups are fun, particularly cameos by Peter Graves (from the **Mission Impossible** TV series), Sean Connery lookalike Jean Marchent, big Richard Kiel ("Jaws" in **The Spy Who Loved Me** and **Moonraker**), and a dead ringer for "Oddjob" (the bowler-throwing villain from **Goldfinger**, originally played by Harold Sakata). Even "Queen Elizabeth" and "Ronald Reagan" put in an appearance. The awful dubbed version deletes nearly 20 minutes from the original and adds extra, unfunny footage revolving around Graves' character. Director Tsui Hark has a cameo.

6. Aces Go Places IV

(1986; Cinema City Co.) ★: 7/10. *Jui gaai paak dong chin lee gau cha poh* (Cantonese), *Zui jia pai dang qian li jiu cha po* (Mandarin): "Best Partners: Going a Thousand Miles to Save the Police Woman." Cinematographer: Sander Lee Kar-ko; Art Director: Suzy Cheung Kai-san; Music: Tony Lo Tung-ni; Writers: Karl Maka, Ringo Lam Ling-tung; Producers: Karl Maka, Dean Shek Tien; Action Director: Chu Kai-sang; Director: Ringo Lam Ling-tung. Cast: Sam Hui Koon-kit (King Kong), Karl Maka (Albert Au, aka Baldy), Sally Yeh Chian-wen (The Professor's Daughter), Sylvia Chang Ai-chia (Nancy Ho), Cho Tat-wah (Hua), Kwan Tak-hing (Police Hockey Team Coach), Shih Kien (Interpol Hockey Team Coach), Roy Chiao Hung (The Professor), Ronald Lacey (Leader of the Villains). Dolby Digital (DVD only). 2.35:1. VHS: Tai Seng (Poor Subtitles). Import LD: Golden Cinema City. Import VCD: Mei Ah. Import DVD: Universe. 88/90 minutes. Also known as **Mad Mission 4: You Never Die Twice** (Dubbed version).

Uncharacteristically violent as these films go, **Aces IV** still manages to emerge as one of the better entries, despite the dark tone of some scenes and impersonal direction by Ringo Lam (who has stated in interviews that he helmed the film only as a favor to Karl Maka, who gave Lam his start with **Esprit d'amour**). This time, King Kong, Albert, and Baldy Jr. must travel to New Zealand to save Nancy (inexplicably called "Sylvia" in the subtitles) when she is kidnapped by a gang of criminals (led by Lacey, reprising his Nazi villain from **Raiders of the Lost Ark**!). In exchange for her life, the thugs demand an experimental prism which is the key component in a device designed to transform regular mortals into supermen.

At a brisk 88 minutes, **Aces IV** gets off to a running start and rarely stops to take a breath, serving up all manner of chases, stunts, and physical gags. Sally Yeh adds comic flare as KK's not-so-bright girlfriend, and it is a gas to see Cho Tat-wah and Kwan Tak-hing (who co-starred in many vintage **Wong Fei-hung** films) share the screen once again. Reportedly, the references to **Raiders of the Lost Ark** are deleted from the dubbed version (which, for a change, actually runs slightly longer than the HK cut).

7. Aces Go Places V: The Terracotta Hit

(1989; Cinema City Co.) ★: 5/10. *San jui gaai paak dong* (Cantonese), *Xin zui jia pai dang* (Mandarin): "New Best Partners." Cinematographer: Paul Chan Chung-chau; Art Director: Vincent Wai Kai-san; Music: Richard Lo Sai-kit, Teddy Robin Kwan; Writer: Tsang Kwok-chi; Producers: Karl Maka, Richard Cheung Kuen; Action Director: Lau Kar-wing; Director: Lau Kar-leung. Cast: Sam Hui Koon-kit (King Kong), Karl Maka (Albert Au, aka Baldy), Leslie Cheung Kwok-wing (The Brother), Nina Li Chi (The Sister), Conan Lee Yuen-ba (The Chinese Rambo), Melvin Wong Kam-sun (Thug), Ellen Chan Ar-lun (Ellen), Danny Lee Sau-yin (Prisoner from Hong Kong), Roy Cheung Yiu-yeung ("The Murderer King"), Cho Tat-wah (Wah), Ha Chi-chun (Female Communist Agent #1), Fennie Yuen Kit-ying (Albert's Niece), Maria Cordero (Woman in Window), Mark Houghton (Blonde Thug), Deborah Grant (Deborah). Dolby Digital (DVD only). 2.35:1. VHS: Tai Seng (Poor Subtitles). Import LD: Golden Cinema City. Import VCD: Universe (Poor Subtitles). Import DVD: Universe. 102 minutes.

Sylvia Chang is missed and the story is ill-conceived, but the all-star cast and action sequences keep one moderately interested in this, the last and least of the original **Aces Go Places** films. King Kong and Albert part ways following a disagreement while on a job in Thailand. We then jump ahead to three years later: Brother and sister thieves swipe a priceless antique sword (called "The Chinese Excalibur") from some rival criminals, framing KK and Albert for the snatch. Pursued by the HK police, Mainland operatives (led by Conan Lee as "The Chinese Rambo"), and the original gang of criminals (who also have dozens of terracotta statues in their possession), "The Best Partners" are forced to put aside their differences and figure a way out of the mess. Things get especially hairy, however, when they are grabbed by the Mainland's National Security forces and tossed into a Beijing prison.

As with **Aces IV**, there are stretches where the film starts taking itself too seriously. The scenes set at the prison (which is run by Roy Cheung, sending up his **Prison on Fire** role) are too close to the real thing to be funny and not effective enough as drama to make us care any more about the characters. While the previous film was not seriously marred, **Aces V** doesn't really recover until the big action setpiece in the final reel, which unfolds in a warehouse filled with terracotta statues (some of which are not what they seem). This was followed by **97 Aces Go Places**, an ill-conceived attempt to revive the series with a new cast.

Actress *see* **Center Stage**

8. The Adventurers

(1995; Win's Movie Production) ★: 6/10. *Daai mak him ka* (Cantonese), *Da mao xian jia* (Mandarin): "The Great Adventurer." Cinematographers: Arthur Wong Ngok-tai, Ardy Lam Kwok-wah; Art Director: Luk Chi-fung; Music: Teddy Robin Kwan; Writers: Ringo Lam Ling-tung, Yip Kong-yam, Sandy Shaw; Action Director: Lam Moon-wah, Producer Director: Ringo Lam Ling-tung. Cast: Andy Lau Tak-wah (Wai Lok-yan), Jacqueline Wu Chien-lien (Crystal), Rosamund Kwan Chi-lam (Mona), Paul Chun Pui (Ray Lui), David Chiang Da-wei (Shang), Ben Ng Ngai-cheung (Dog), William Ho Kar-kui (General Buboei), John Ching Tung (Major Bodar), Victor Wong Chi-keung (Uncle Nine), George Kee Cheung (Tung), Phillip Ko Fei (Wah), Parkman Wong Pak-man (Officer Cheng), Wong Kam-kong (Military Officer). 1.85:1. VHS/LD: Tai Seng. Import LD/VCD/DVD: Mei Ah. 107 minutes.

Director Ringo Lam fashions a revenge saga here that is reminiscent of his earlier films but lacks the narrative focus and larger-than-life characters found in his best work. Yan is a young fighter pilot seeking to avenge his sister and parents, who were murdered in 1975 by Ray Lui, now a billionaire involved in arms smuggling. Working in tandem with Shang, a CIA operative who spirited him out of Cambodia when he was a child, Yan journeys to Thailand, where he gets involved with Lui's mistress. Yan then goes to San Francisco, where he falls for and marries the gangster's daughter, Crystal. Once Yan has gained Lui's trust, he accompanies his father-in-law to the secret base of a Cambodian dictator so that the CIA can pinpoint and destroy it with an air strike.

While moderately engrossing, **The Adventurers** cannot help but pale in comparison to Lam's previous two thrillers, **Full Contact** and **Burning Paradise**, which unfolded in exotic, amoral worlds filled with uneasy loyalties and brutal violence, all presented with considerable style and verve. With its episodic plot and conventional presentation, there is little here that possesses the same kind of impact. Lau and Wu make an engaging couple, though one can't help being reminded of their pairing in the superior **A Moment of Romance**, on which Lam served as Associate Producer. To the director's credit, this film sports some well-staged action sequences, and the location work in The Philippines and San Francisco (the latter segments featuring US-based actors Victor Wong and George Kee Cheung) gives the enterprise an impressive sweep, at a time when spiraling costs and plummeting box office receipts forced HK filmmakers to curtail such luxuries.

9. Adventurous Treasure Island

(1996; Chang-Hong Film and Video Co.) ★: 2/10. *Wong gam do lik him gei* (Cantonese), *Huang jin dao li xian ji* (Mandarin): "Golden Island Adventures." Cinematographer: Yu Kwok-bing; Art Director: Jason Mok Siu-kei; Music: Mak Chun-hung; Writer: Candy Cheng; Producer: Mark Wu Dan; Action Director: Yuen Bun; Directors: Herman Yau Lai-to, Ha Sau-hin. Cast: Kok Siu-man (Chu Si-ting), Sik Siu-lung (Siu-lone), Ng Man-tat (Chu Yi-shing), Vivian Hsu Ruo-hsuan (Siu-sin), Jackson Liu Hsiu-hsien (Captain Hook), Wong Yat-fei (Uncle Fai), Emily Kwan Bo-wai (Teacher), Shing Fui-on (Cop). 1.85:1. VHS: Tai Seng. Import LD/VCD: Universe. 92 minutes.

Bizarre is the word for this low-budget Taiwanese children's fantasy starring the pint-sized duo of Sik Siu-lung (the kung fu whiz kid) and Kok Siu-man (the fat comic relief kid and the most obnoxious child star in Chinese cinema). When a video game falls from the heavens and into his hands, Chu Si-ting takes it home and gives it a whirl. Just when things are getting good, he is sucked inside his TV set, along his with big brother, Chu Si-man. They land in some weird, alternate universe that is filled with kung fu fighting pirates trying to steal a key from Siu-lone, the leader of Treasure Island. After watching Si-ting best Siu-lone in a kung fu match, the evil pirate Captain Hook tries to get the boy to help him destroy the island. Meanwhile, Mr. and Mrs. Chu have also been brought to this strange world and are being held prisoner on the pirate ship. Si-man and cute island girl Siu-sin convince Siu-lone to try and rescue the captives and defeat the pirates once and for all. Though enjoyably odd at first (particularly the allusions to **Peter Pan**), tedium soon takes over, and the attempts at humor rarely rise above the desperate.

An Affair in Nanjing *see* **The Christ of Nanjing**

10. The Age of Miracles

(1996; United Filmmakers Organization) ★: 3/10. *Ma ma faan faan* (Cantonese), *Ma ma fan fan* (Mandarin): "Grandmother and Fan-fan." Cinematographer: Henry Chan Chun-kit; Art Director: Ringo Fung Kai-fai; Music: Clarence Hui Yuen, Chiu Chang-hei; Writers: On Sai, Lam Ngoi-wah, Ella Chan Bo-wah; Producer/Director: Peter Chan Ho-sun. Cast: Alan Tam Wing-lun (Fan), Anita Yuen Wing-yee (Mrs. Sheung), Eric Tsang Chi-wai (Uncle Wei), Jordan Chan Siu-chun (Sheung Chun), Christine Ng Wing-mei (May), Teresa Carpio (Moon), Roy Chiao Hung (Death), Manfred Wong (Pig Head), Kelly Chan Wai-lam (The Policewoman). 1.85:1. VHS: Tai Seng. Import LD/VCD/DVD: Fitto Mobile. 100 minutes.

With her son about to perish from a 106 degree fever, a desperate Mrs. Sheung tells the heavens that she is willing to have a decade taken off of her life if the boy is allowed to live. Miraculously, she gets her wish, and Death (Roy Chiao, looking quite dapper in a white suit and hat) leaves the child on Earth. The film then picks up a few years later, with Fan now a grown man and his mom 68 years old and feeling that her number is just about up. After more than three decades of living with his mother, Fan is ready to immigrate to America with his wife, but the old lady will not hear of him leaving her behind. Adding to the misery is the return of Moon, Fan's obnoxious daughter, and the woman's multiracial brood of children. Feeling unloved, Mrs. Sheung disappears on a four day bus tour, with Death constantly at her side. When the time finally comes for the man in the white suit to take her away, Mrs. Sheung pleads her case and is given back those ten lost years. This changes her outlook on everything, transforming the woman from a stubborn old crone to a helpful, sympathetic friend. There is just one catch: Mrs. Sheung has been discovered half dead in the very field where she made her case to Death ten days earlier.

Buried under a layer of very unconvincing old age make-up, Anita Yuen still manages to project a variety of emotions and expressions, giving a highly satisfying and convincing portrayal. However, the script alternates between heavy-handed, artificial sentiment (heightened by a multitude of cheesy, fantasy-oriented computer generated shots of stars, blooming flowers, schools of fish, etc.) and strained comedic asides featuring broad, unlikeable characters. The end result is simply wearisome and far from the uplifting experience the filmmakers clearly intended. **He Ain't Heavy, He's My Father** (which Peter Chan co-directed with Lee Chi-ngai) proffers a much more astute and entertaining look at old age, integrated into a far more interesting storyline.

11. Ah Fai the Dumb

(1997; Cameron Entertainment/The Young Filmmakers) ★: 3/10. *Tin choi yue baak chi* (Cantonese), *Tian cai yu bai chi* (Mandarin): "Genius and Idiot." Cinematographer: Cheung Tung-leung; Art Director: Suzy Cheung Kai-san; Music: Violet Lam Man-yee; Writer: Raymond To Kwok-wai; Producer: Tong Hing-chi; Action Director: Kuk Hin-chiu; Director: Derek Chiu Sung-kei. Cast: Eric Kot Man-fai (Fai), Andy Hui Chi-on (Little Ping), Athena Chu Yan (Minmin), Ada Choi Siu-fan (Jody), Law Kar-ying (Uncle Ying, aka Iron Pen), Law Koon-lan (Millie), Almen Wong Pui-ha (Eddie's Wife), Joe Junior (Pang Chin), Lau Yee-tat (Newspaper Vendor). 1.85:1. VHS: Tai Seng. Import LD/VCD/DVD: Mei Ah. 101 minutes.

Ah Fai is a hyperactive, 27-year-old simpleton everyone makes fun of, much to the chagrin of his long-suffering mother. When the woman receives an offer of marriage and the chance to move to Hawaii, she reluctantly accepts, leaving Fai in the care of her old flame, fortune teller Ying. One day, Fai falls off the roof of a building and, miraculously, only receives a concussion. While operating on him, doctors discover a huge tumor in his head and remove it. Not only does Fai make a full recovery, his I.Q. rises dramatically and he even develops ESP. Now the sensation of Temple Street, Fai quickly parlays his talent into wider fame and fortune. However, he has become a cruel and unfeeling person in the process, and the condition has started to reverse itself, leaving him facing the prospect of becoming an idiot again.

Viewers put off by comedian Eric Kot's shameless mugging had best avoid this vapid production, which finds him devouring the scenery in the opening half and even overplaying the character *after* he has become more intelligent. In addition to being half-baked, the narrative is burdened with unnecessary subplots that are no more believable than the main storyline. Prior to the accident, Fai isn't so much retarded as simply an obnoxious twit; after the accident he's just a different kind of twit. It is difficult to care about his fate either way.

12. Ah Kam

(1996; Golden Harvest/DACA Entertainment) ★: 4/10. *Ah Gam dik koo si* (Cantonese), *A Jin de gu shi* (Mandarin): "Ah Kam's Story." Cinematographer: Ardy Lam Kwok-wah; Art Director: Yank Wong Yan-kwai; Music: Yoshihide Otomo; Writers: Chan Man-keung, John Chan Kin-chung; Producers: David Lau Kar-fu, Catherine Hun Kar-chun; Action Director: Ching Siu-tung; Director: Ann Hui On-wah. Cast: Michelle Yeoh Chu-kheng (Kam), Sammo Hung Kam-po (The Chief), Satoshi Okada (Sam), Jimmy Wong Kar-lok (Long), Mang Hoi (Copy). 1.85:1. VHS: Tai Seng. Import LD/VCD: Mei Ah. 95 minutes.

A seemingly ideal vehicle to showcase Michelle Yeoh Chu-kheng's dramatic and athletic talents, **Ah Kam** starts off as a fascinating behind-the-scenes look at the HK filmmaking process, begins to go askew midway, and is then fatally undermined by a disastrous third act. Kam is a dauntless young stuntwoman seeking to win the respect of "The Chief," a crusty, battle-scarred action director (seemingly modeled after Ching Siu-tung, who served as stunt co-ordinator on this film). This portion of the film, which concentrates on their blossoming father-daughter relationship and the day-to-day stresses of trying to make a living in a cutthroat business, is engrossing throughout. However, invention fails the screenwriters at this point, and the plot spirals into listless melodrama. Kam gets into a bad relationship, rejoins the troupe, and then must look after Long, The Chief's young brat of a son, when the old man is killed in a skirmish with triads. The child (and Jimmy Wong, the actor portraying him) are so unrelentingly obnoxious, it soon becomes impossible to sympathize with Kam (who suffers in silence for so long you want to reach into the screen and shake her), her situation, or her seeming inability to extricate herself from it. While fans of Yeoh (who gives a studied, low-key performance that is among her best to date) should definitely go the whole nine yards, other viewers will probably come away from the experience more satisfied if they just skip the second half. There are brief appearances by the likes of Cho Wing (as a Mainland triad gang-leader), Richard Ng Yiu-hon, Damian Lau Chung-yan, Kent Cheng Chuk-see, Crystal Kwok Kam-yan, Rain Lau Yuk-tsui, and Yip Wing-cho. Yeoh was badly injured while executing a leap from a highway overpass onto a moving truck and, in time-honored HK fashion, outtake footage of her being taken away in an ambulance runs under the closing credits.

13. Alan & Eric Between Hello and Goodbye

(1991; Movie Impact) ★: 3/10. *Seung sing goo si* (Cantonese), *Shuang cheng gu shi* (Mandarin): "A Story of Twin Cities." Cinematographer: Jingle Ma Cho-shing; Art Director: Ben Luk Man-wah; Music: Richard Lo Sai-kit; Writers: Barry Wong Ping-yiu, Lee Chi-ngai; Producers: Eric Tsang Chi-wai, Peter Chan Ho-sun; Director: Peter Chan Ho-sun. Cast: Alan Tam Wing-lun (Alan Tam), Eric Tsang Chi-wai (Eric), Maggie Cheung Man-yuk (Olive Cheung), Blackie Ko Shou-liang (Pierre), Barry Wong Ping-yiu (Alan's Boss), Paul Fonoroff (Hairy Keung), Michael Dinga (Alan's Agent). 1.85:1. VHS: Tai Seng (Poor Subtitles). Import LD/VCD: Ocean Shores (Poor Subtitles). Running time unknown.

There are few surprises to be found in this heavy-handed drama which is a far cry from the films its director would be noted for later on. Childhood friends Alan and Eric are separated for several years but reunite when the latter returns to HK from San Francisco. The pair open a chicken farm together and Eric falls for Olive Cheung, a flighty girl he meets one day at the dog pound. After standing Eric up one evening, she makes their second date but promptly ignores him once she meets Alan. A bad storm destroys the chickens, but Alan's gig as a restaurant entertainer gets him a high-powered agent and a recording contract. Dejected by Olive's love for Alan and his lack of success in life, Eric signs on with the crew of a fishing boat. Alan's meteoric success sours his relationship with Olive, however, and Eric becomes seriously ill from all of the time he spent at sea.

An inauspicious debut for talented director Peter Chan, **Alan & Eric** is clearly the work of someone eager to make his mark. The trouble is, everything from the performances to the dialogue here seems forced and artificial, and the inevitability of the narrative makes for tedious viewing. The whole enterprise ends up seeming like an ego trip for Alan Tam and Eric Tsang, who even play characters named after themselves. A key scene unfolds at the headquarters of Impact, the production company that backed the film.

14. All About Ah-Long

(1989; Cinema City Co.) ★: 4/10. *A Long dik goo si* (Cantonese), *A Lang de gu shi* (Mandarin): "Ah Long's Story" or "Ah Lang's Story." Cinematographer: Horace Wong Wing-hang; Art Director: Raymond Chan Kam-ho; Music: Lo Tai-yau, Richard Lo Sai-kit; Writers: Ng Man-fai, Philip Cheng Chung-tai; Producer: Raymond Wong Pak-ming; Action Directors: Ching Siu-tung, Yuen Bun; Director: Johnny To Kei-fung. Cast: Chow Yun-fat (Long), Sylvia Chang Ai-chia (Sylvia), Wong Kwan-yuen (Porky Yeung), Ng Man-tat (Dragon Ng). Dolby Digital (DVD only). 1.85:1. VHS: Tai Seng. Import VCD: Mega Star. Import LD: Golden Cinema City. Import DVD: Universe. 95 minutes.

Chow Yun-fat won the Best Actor prize for his convincing work in this otherwise mawkish melodrama, which takes its cues from **Kramer vs. Kramer**. Former motorcycle racer-turned-construction worker Long and his unruly young son Porky haven't much money but live happily. Out of the blue, the child's mother, Sylvia, returns after a long absence. Now a successful executive, Sylvia unknowingly hires her son for a commercial she is producing, and this exposure to Porky engenders maternal feelings. Flashbacks reveal that a pregnant Sylvia broke up with Long after she caught him with another woman. Told by her mother that her baby was born dead, Sylvia left for America and a new life. Long begins making rather pathetic attempts to woo her back, but it doesn't take long for Sylvia to decide that his low income and brutish nature are a bad influence on the boy. She wants to take the child back overseas, but Porky resists and decides to stay with Long who, in an effort to better his situation, has re-embarked on his racing career.

Far too heavy-handed and cliched to be involving, there is not one honest or genuine moment to be found here. The shallowness of the writing is also made evident by the fact that the film relies on several feel-good, music video-style montages to make up for the fact that it is lacking in any real character development, and the tragedy injected into the final reel is unforgivably calculated. Although the scenario requires him to be an undisciplined and impolite child, Wong Kwan-yuen is so shrill and obnoxious, he simply annoys. HK audiences warmed to **All About Ah-Long**, making it one of the most successful films of the '80s, but it seems doubtful that many Western viewers will share that sentiment.

15. All for the Winner

(1990; Golden Harvest/Paragon Films) ★: 7/10. *Do sing* (Cantonese), *Du sheng* (Mandarin): "Saint of Gamblers." Cinematographers: Jimmy Leung Chi-ming, Chan Yuen-kai; Art Directors: Raymond Lee King-man, Lau Man-yu; Music: Lowell Lo Kwun-ting; Writer: Jeff Lau Chun-wai; Action Director: Corey Yuen Kwai; Producer-Directors: Corey Yuen Kwai, Jeff Lau Chun-wai. Cast: Stephen Chiau Sing-chi (Shing), Ng Man-tat (Blackie Tat), Sharla Cheung Man (Yee-mong), Sandra Ng Kwan-yu (Ping), Paul Chun Pui (Hung Kong), Corey Yuen Kwai (Fishy Shing), Vincent Wan Yeung-ming (Billy), Sheila Chan Sak-lan (Ying). 1.85:1. VHS: Tai Seng. Import LD/VCD: Star Entertainment. 101 minutes.

Conceived merely as a low budget attempt to cash in on the success of the Chow Yun-fat hit **God of Gamblers**, this jubilant little sleeper went on to out-gross it at the box office and made Stephen Chiau Sing-chi a superstar in the process. Mainland hick Shing arrives in HK and drives his Uncle Blackie crazy until the latter learns that Shing has powers allowing him to see through solid objects. Ever the gambling man, Blackie realizes that his nephew's gifts could make him rich beyond his wildest dreams. Word soon gets out about Shing, and he finds himself caught between HK gambling master Hung Kong and his Taiwanese counterpart, Chan Chung, both of whom want him to represent them in a forthcoming competition. The latter manages to get Shing first, prompting Hung to try and knock him off. The attempt fails, but Shing has fallen head-over-heels for his boss' beautiful bodyguard, Yee-mong, and is unable to play when she is taken hostage by Hung's men.

The film just spins its wheels during the portion covering Shing's depression over the loss of his love, but the remainder is engaging fun. As per genre regulations, the buffoonery is bracketed with plenty of shootouts and hand-to-hand combat. Chiau and Ng play off each other as well as any comic team around, and the big card game finale offers up a terrific climactic twist. In addition to the expected preponderance of scatological gags, there's a great send-up of **A Better Tomorrow**, and Chiau also does a couple of wicked Bruce Lee imitations! In spite of its name, **God of Gamblers II** is actually the follow-up to *this* film, while **The Saint of Gamblers** is the "official" sequel.

16. All Men Are Brothers: Blood of the Leopard

(1993; HK Film Entertainment Production Co.) ★: 3/10. *Sui woo juen ji ying hung boon sik* (Cantonese), *Shui hu zhuan zhi ying xiong ben se* (Mandarin): "Waterside Story: True Essence of a Hero." Cinematographer: Joe Chan Kong-hung; Art Director: Chung Yee-fung; Music: William Woo Wai-lap; Writer: Johnny Lee King-kai; Producer: Wilson Tong Wai-shing; Action Directors: Hon Chun, Ching Kwok-leung; Director: Billy Chan Wui-ngai. Cast: Tony Leung Kar-fai (Lin Chung), Elvis Tsui Kam-kong (Ru Chi-shen), Joey Wang Tsu-hsien (Lin's Wife), Lam Wai (Lu Chien), Lau Ching-wan (Tso Wu), Wu Ma (Prime Minister), Lau Shun (Kao), Sin Lap-man (Kao, the Junior), Austin Wai Tin-chi (Opposition Commander). 1.85:1. VHS/LD: Tai Seng. Import LD/VCD: Mei Ah. 96 minutes.

A lumbering remake of Ching Kong's 1972 Shaw Brothers classic **Pursuit** (itself an adaptation of a classic Chinese sword-play story generally known in English as "All Men Are Brothers"), this independent production is certainly among the lesser entries in the recent crop of period fantasies. Upright military officer Lin Chung befriends Ru Chi-shen, an obnoxious, alcoholic monk with incredible martial arts abilities. The two soon become inseparable, practicing their kung fu at every opportunity. When Lin is framed by a jealous colleague, he faces a military tribunal but is saved by Ru before the soldiers transporting him can carry out orders to slay their prisoner *en route*. When his wife and loyal friend, The Prime Minister, are murdered, Lin plots his revenge, but intentionally alienates Ru in order to save him from what will be certain death.

Far too much of the running time is given over to dull court intrigue and conventional male bonding sequences between Lin and Ru. Elvis Tsui gives one of his most vivid and charismatic portrayals, but even he cannot make up for the one dimensional stoicism of Tony Leung Kar-fai's character or Sin Lap-man's unbearable performance as the main villain's incessantly whiny (and seemingly retarded) son. In addition, most of the action is clumsily staged, with ample cuts utilized in an attempt to improve the less-than-fluid choreography.

17. All of a Sudden

(1996; Mandarin Films) ★: 4/10. *Ging bin* (Cantonese), *Jing bian* (Mandarin): "Fear Change." Cinematographer: Yu Kwok-ping; Art Director: Jason Mok Siu-kei; Music: Mak Chun-hung; Writer: Candy Cheng; Producers: Nancy Wong Kit-chen, Victor Yeung Kar-on, Tong Yen-hou; Action Director: Chu Kai-sang; Director: Herman Yau Lai-to. Cast: Irene Wan Pik-ha (Ho-yee), Simon Yam Tat-wah (Tsui Chin-tung), Alfred Cheung Kin-ting (Lam), Dayo Wong Chi-wah (Mak). 1.85:1. VHS: World Video. Import LD/VCD: Fitto Mobile. 97 minutes.

One of the sleaziest Category IIB films in memory, **All of a Sudden** is notable only as the softcore debut of former teen star Irene Wan. When a naked woman falls to her death in an apparent suicide, her husband, Tsui Chin-tung, seeks vengeance. His target is rich businessman Lam Kwok-chui, with whom his wife was having an affair. Disguising himself as a robber, Tsui intends to assault Lam, but ends up driving away with the man's wife, Ho-yee, and their young child. Blackmailed by a disreputable neighbor into demanding a ransom for the woman, Tsui complies, and a drop off is set up. Despite the fact that Lam provides only a tiny percentage of what was demanded, Tsui decides to let Ho-yee go free anyway. Naturally, after this betrayal, Ho-yee is suspicious of her husband, particularly when the brakes on her car give out for no reason. Returning to Tsui, the two of them begin an affair of their own and plot how to deal with Tsui.

Playing out exactly like one of the many direct-to-video softcore mystery thrillers appearing on American video store shelves every week, **All of a Sudden** is able to retain viewer interest through its baser elements, but that is not a good enough reason to endure the poor scripting and unbelievable scenario (though the film remains somewhat above average by director Herman Yau's standards). Dayo Wong provides weak comedy relief as the flaky investigator on the case.

18. All the Wrong Clues (...For the Right Solution)

(1981; Cinema City Co.) ★: 7/10. *Gwai ma ji doh sing* (Cantonese), *Gui ma zhi duo xing* (Mandarin): "Zany Wiseguy." Cinematographer: Bill Wong Chung-bo; Art Director: William Cheung Suk-ping; Music: Teddy Robin Kwan; Writers: Raymond Wong Pak-ming, Roy Szeto Cheuk-hon; Producers: Karl Maka, Dean Shek Tien; Director: Tsui Hark. Cast: George Lam Chi-chung (Yoho), Teddy Robin Kwan (Chief Inspector Robin), Karl Maka (Ah Capone), Kelly Yiu Wai (The Femme Fatale), Eric Tsang Chi-wai (The No. 1 Killer, aka Popeye), Cho Tat-wah (Gang Boss), John Sham Kin-fun (Piano Player). 1.85:1. VHS: Tai Seng. Import LD: Golden Cinema City. There is no DVD for this film. Import VCD: Mega Star. 98 minutes.

After his first three films flopped at the box office, Tsui Hark signed on at Cinema City for this highly commercial comedy and wound up with his first hit. Set in the 1930s, **Clues** is a slapstick farce spiced up with some creative visual touches that foreshadow the trademark look Tsui's pictures would develop later in the decade. Broke private eye Yoho inadvertently gets himself in the middle of a case involving the notorious mobster Ah Capone(!), who plans to swindle an old millionaire out of his stocks. Along the way, Yoho crosses paths with various damsels and dames, while getting a little help on the side from his childhood buddy, pint-sized Chief Inspector Robin.

A good portion of the gags fall flat, but the local variations on Western cinema standards (silent comedy, Warner Brothers gangster pictures and cartoons, etc.) are fun, the cast is spirited, and the presentation highly energetic. Eric Tsang appears in a great recreation of Bruce Lee's destructive cameo from the James Garner vehicle, **Marlowe**. Co-star Teddy Robin Kwan helmed the sequel, **All the Wrong Spies**, while director Tsui Hark stepped in front of the camera for a supporting role.

19. All the Wrong Spies

(1983; Cinema City Co.) ★: 7/10. *Ngoh oi Ye Loi-heung* (Cantonese), *Wo ai Ye Laixiang* (Mandarin): "I Love Ye Loi-heung," "I Love Ye Laixiang," or "I Love Fragrance of the Night." Cinematographer: Johnny Koo Kwok-wah; Art Director: Hai Chung-man; Music: Chris Babida; Writer-Producer: Raymond Wong Pak-ming; Director: Teddy Robin Kwan. Cast: George Lam Chi-cheung (Yoyo), Teddy Robin Kwan (Inspector Teddy Robin), Brigitte Lin Ching-hsia (Bridget), Paul Chun Pui (Fat Chick), Tsui Hark (Tora Hiroshima), Joe Junior (Joe), Shing Fui-on (Soldier), Anders Nelsson (The American). Dolby Digital (DVD only). 1.85:1. VHS: Tai Seng. Import LD: Golden Cinema City. Import VCD: Mega Star (No Subtitles). Import DVD: Mega Star. 102 minutes.

This follow-up to the popular **All the Wrong Clues** unfolds during World War II, with various parties out to get their hands on plans for the atomic bomb. Bumbling detective/resistance fighter Yoyo is ordered to get the plans from a defecting Jewish scientist, who stole it from the Nazis and seeks to sell it to the Americans. When police commissioner Fat Chick snatches the formula, Yoyo goes into partnership with Inspector Robin to swipe it, but they are beaten to the punch by cat burglar Bridget. The pair then decide to put the grab on Japanese envoy Hiroshima, who is supposed to receive the formula from Chick, and have Yoyo take his place. The ruse works, but Yoyo discovers that Bridget (who just happens to be his old flame) is now Chick's fiancée, which complicates things considerably.

With its clever allusions to **Casablanca** and recycled Three Stooges and Marx

Brothers sight gags, **All the Wrong Spies** is an amusing send-up of both the Hollywood thrillers and comedies of the era. The various chases and wire-enhanced stunts offer a gleeful marriage of traditional caper comedy slapstick and HK-style action choreography. And remember: The password is "I Am Woman."

20. All-Mighty Gambler

(1991) ★: 5/10. *Do wong ji juen* (Cantonese), *Du wang zhi zun* (Mandarin): "Most Respected Gambling King." Cinematographer: Mok Chat-yun; Music: Not Original; Writer: Cheung Ming-wai; Producer: Tsui Lung; Director: Wilson Tong Wai-shing. Cast: Chin Siu-ho (Yan Chi-yung), Norman Tsui Siu-keung (Chu Chi-ang), Ellen Chan Ar-lun (Ice Chan), Chen Kuan-tai (Tai), Yip Wing-cho (Fat Bill), Henry Fong Ping (Feng), Tai Po (Tai's Son), Johnny Wang Lung-wei (Wai), Fung Hark-on (Thug), Michael Chan Wai-man (Fat Bill's Enforcer), Lo Lieh (Low), Billy Chow Bei-lee (Billy). 1.85:1. VHS: World Video (Poor Subtitles). 96 minutes.

One of several productions that followed in the wake of **Casino Raiders** and **God of Gamblers**, this minor actioner opens with triads Chu and Yan stealing millions in gambling money for their boss, Tai. After skimming some off the top for themselves, they turn over $3.8 million. Seductive female gambler Ice Chan returns to HK from America with the intention of getting revenge on Tai, who murdered her father a few years earlier. Aware that Chu and Yan are the man's bodyguards, she decides to make a play for Yan as a way of getting close to her target. However, Ice genuinely falls in love with him and ends up making an unsuccessful attempt on Tai's life, without Yan's knowledge. Meanwhile, Tai enlists the services of Chu and Yan to fleece another affluent gambler, but it soon becomes obvious that the pair are victims of a plot hatched within their own gang.

Strictly a formula affair, the film lacks urgency, flair, and credibility, but a charismatic turn by Chin Siu-ho and the terrific cast of veteran martial arts stars at least keep it watchable.

21. All's Well, Ends Well

(1992; Regal Films Co./Mandarin Films) ★: 4/10. *Ga yau hei si* (Cantonese), *Jia you xi shi* (Mandarin): "Family Has Happy Affairs." Cinematographer: Kin Lee Kin-keung; Art Director: Raymond Chan Kam-ho; Music: Violet Lam Man-yee; Writers: Vincent Kok Tak-chiu, Tessa Choi Ting-ting; Producer-Director: Clifton Ko Chi-sum. Cast: Stephen Chiau Sing-chi (Shang Foon), Leslie Cheung Kwok-wing (Shang So), Maggie Cheung Man-yuk (Holliyok), Teresa Mo Shun-kwan (Leung Mo-shang), Raymond Wong Pak-ming (Moon), Sandra Ng Kwan-yu (Ching), Loletta Lee Lai-chun (Foon's Girl), Sheila Chan Sak-lan (Sheila), Kwan Hoi-shan (Grandfather), Tommy Wong Kwong-leung (Brother Kwong), Clifton Ko Chi-sum (Annoyed Karaoke Patron), Vincent Kok Tak-chiu (Japanese Businessman). 1.85:1. VHS: Tai Seng. Import LD/VCD/DVD: Mei Ah. 100 minutes.

A box office smash, this all-star New Year's comedy isn't nearly as funny as it should have been, being content to rely almost entirely on its cast to keep the audience watching. The thin, barely cohesive plot concerns a group of bizarre love affairs undertaken by members of the same family: Husband Raymond Wong cheats on dimwitted Sandra Ng by seeing Miss HK contestant Sheila Chan; butch biker babe Teresa Mo and effeminate Leslie Cheung go from adversaries to unlikely lovers; and hip disc jockey Stephen Chiau falls for Maggie Cheung, who lives her life entirely through the movies (unfortunately for Chiau, it is never the *same* movie). Wong quickly begins to miss Ng, and Chiau turns into a drooling idiot after getting bashed on the head.

There are far too many throwaway scatological gags, and very few fresh concepts. On the other hand, there are mildly amusing parodies of **A Chinese Ghost Story** and **Misery**, and Maggie Cheung gets to imitate Madonna, Julia Roberts in **Pretty Woman**, and Demi Moore in **Ghost**. The film gained some pre-release notoriety when triads stole part of the negative and demanded a ransom. **All's Well, Ends Well, Too** and **All's Well, Ends Well '97** followed.

22. All's Well, Ends Well '97

(1997; Mandarin Films) ★: 4/10. *97 Fung yau hei si* (Cantonese), *97 Gu you xi shi* (Mandarin): "'97 Family Has Happy Affairs." Cinematographer: Tam Chi-wai; Art Director: Nelson Cheung Hok-yin; Music: Not Original; Writers: Raymond Wong Pak-ming, Vincent Kok Tak-chiu; Producer: Raymond Wong Pak-ming; Action Director: Chin Kar-lok; Director: Alfred Cheung Kin-ting. Cast: Stephen Chiau Sing-chi (Kung), Roy Chiao Hung (Father), Christine Ng Wing-mei (Yinsu), Jacqueline Wu Chien-lien (Shenny), Francis Ng Chun-yu (Little Fei), Raymond Wong Pak-ming (Old Fei), Christy Chung Lai-tai (Suen), Amanda Lee Wai-man (Karen Kam), Gigi Lai Chi (Gigi), Emil Chow Wah-kin (Long), Alfred Cheung Kin-ting (Mental Patient). 1.85:1. VHS: World Video. Import LD/VCD/DVD: Mei Ah. 92 minutes.

Raymond Wong's semi-annual New Year's comedy extravaganza features a multitude of stars (and almost as many Pepsi plugs) but only a handful of chuckles. Brothers Old Fei and Little Fei decide to play a trick on their layabout sibling, Kung, by convincing him that he has won $31 million in the Mark Six lottery. However, when Kung bashes his head, he pulls a fast one on them by pretending to be retarded, thus shaming his brothers into looking after him. Love also figures into everyone's life: Kung has the hots for Suen, who is pulling the same insanity stunt to protect her now-single mother from dishonest men; Old Fei's homely wife, Yinsu, acquires newfound confidence when she pursues a handsome photographer named Long; Little Fei can't get enough of Karen, a rude, black leather-clad hooligan, when he really should be dating pretty Beijing native, Shenny; and the brothers' father has his eye on Suen's mom.

Star watchers will have a field day (in addition to those listed above, there are a multitude of cameos in the final reel), but the humor is very strained; the minute or so of outtakes running under the end credits offer more laughs than the feature! While the plotting in films of this nature is usually slapdash, this one barely even bothers to resolve the various story threads and is poorly directed to boot. Watch **Eighth Happiness** instead.

23. All's Well, Ends Well, Too

(1993; Mandarin Films) ★: 3/10. *Fa tin hei si* (Cantonese), *Hua tian xi shi* (Mandarin): "Happy Event in the Flower Fields." Cinematographer: Sander Lee Kar-ko; Art Directors: Ring Lee Chi-keung, Hai Chung-man; Music: James Wong Jim, Mark Lui Chung-tak; Writers: Joe Ma Wai-ho, Raymond Wong Pak-ming, Clifton Ko Chi-sum; Producers: Raymond Wong Pak-ming, Ronny Yu Yan-tai; Action Director: Tony Leung Siu-hung; Director: Clifton Ko Chi-sum. Cast: Leslie Cheung Kwok-wing (David Copper Feel), Sam Hui Koon-kit (Chow Tung), Raymond Wong Pak-ming (Lam Ka-sing), Teresa Mo Shun-kwan (Jinx), Ricky Hui Koon-ying (Lady Chow), Sandra Ng Kwan-yu (Gut), Rosamund Kwan Chi-lam (Snow White), Ng Man-tat (Snow White's Father), James Wong Jim (The Magistrate). 1.85:1. VHS: Tai Seng. Import LD/VCD/DVD: Ocean Shores. 85 minutes.

Consisting almost entirely of jokes that are either uninspired, overly broad, or too telegraphed to be amusing, this Lunar

New Year's period farce falls distressingly flat—in spite of its all-star cast. Penniless scholar Lam Ka-sing marries into the vulgar Chow family, much to his eternal regret. Soon after fleeing the Chow household, Lam inadvertently saves the life of master swordswoman Jinx. In the meantime, the Chow siblings, Tung and Gut, throw a party for their ailing mother (played by Ricky Hui, no less), who refuses to accept medical attention until Lam returns home. Tired of being locked in the house by her overbearing father, Snow White dresses as a man and goes out for a night on the town, meeting and falling for magician David Copper Feel (yuk, yuk). Meanwhile, Snow White's dad mistakes Tung for David, convinces him to marry his daughter (whom he mistakenly believes to be pregnant), and is then unable to call off the arrangement when he realizes Tung is the wrong suitor. Meanwhile, Gut catches a glimpse of David in drag and decides that he is her dream lover, while Tung discovers Jinx's finer qualities.

This all-too-typical Raymond Wong mishmash features a multitude of lame sight gags "punched up" with cartoon sound FX, silly anachronisms (like "Frog Pagers," 7-11 outlets, and credit cards), a parody of **Basic Instinct** (which was very successful in HK), and just about every possible cross-dressing joke that Wong and co-writers Clifton Ko and Joe Ma could come up with. The end result is far more grating than congenial and a real waste of some talented players. As with the other two entries in this dismal "series," it is clear that the performers had a great time clowning around on the set, but precious little of their fun is communicated to the viewer. **All's Well, Ends Well '97** came next.

24. Always on My Mind

(1993; United Filmmakers Organization/Topping Time Films) ★: 7/10. *Cheung chin foo chai* (Cantonese), *Qiang qian fu qi* (Mandarin): "Money Grabbing Husband and Wife." Cinematographer: Ardy Lam Kwok-wah; Art Director: Fong Ying; Music: Joseph Chan Wing-leung; Writer: James Yuen Sai-sang; Producer: Claudie Chung Chun; Director: Jacob Cheung Chi-leung. Cast: Michael Hui Koon-man (Chang Yau-wai), Josephine Siao Fong-fong (Yin), Cherie Chan Siu-ha (Sze, aka Susanne), John Tang Yat-kwan (Chung), Simon Lui Yu-yeung (Chang's Assistant), Joe Junior (Poon), Jacob Cheung Chi-leung (Himself). 1.85:1. VHS: Tai Seng. Import LD/VCD: Mei Ah. 104 minutes.

Comedian Michael Hui stars in this atypical Jacob Cheung (**Cageman**) film, which is surprisingly effective thanks to its star's comedic abilities and some shrewd satire. With his eccentric wife and lovelorn kids driving him crazy, TV News anchorman Chang Yau-wai already has enough trouble on his hands. One day, during a broadcast, he suffers a painful stomach ache and must be helped off-camera. A visit to the doctor reveals the worst: He has intestinal cancer. Faced with only three months to live, Yau-wai concocts a scheme that will leave his family financially sound. While out on a remote assignment, the now-fearless reporter apprehends an armed criminal single-handedly. The upper management promptly fires him but, when an overwhelmingly positive response comes in from the public, Yau-wai is rehired with a 200% raise and absolute freedom to say whatever he wants on the air. Not wanting to hurt his family, he tells them that his cancer is just a hoax put on to garner ratings. As the days pass, Yau-wai becomes a bigger and bigger celebrity, receiving all manner of lucrative endorsement offers. A cancer specialist then reveals that there is a 50/50 chance of recovery if Yau-wai agrees to an operation. The newsman must now decide what is more important: leaving his family secure or taking the chance and possibly dying even sooner.

While Yau-wai is a television anchorman, Hui still plays the role very much like his signature put-upon every man, right on down to the staccato delivery. It is a wonderful characterization, and, complimented by Josephine Siao's equally fine work as the man's apprehensive wife, the film's gradual shift from comedy to drama is more credible and affecting than one would expect. James Yuen's script initially seems to be going down the usual hackneyed, well-worn path towards overblown melodrama. Fortunately, it soon takes a couple of unexpected turns, and the points it makes about the media and the public's blind willingness to follow whatever is dictated to them are intelligent and plausibly put forth.

American Dragon *see* **Guns of Dragon** [*sic*]

25. An Amorous Woman of Tang Dynasty

(1984; Shaw Brothers) ★: 8/10. *Tong chiu ho fong nui* (Cantonese), *Tang chao hao fang nu* (Mandarin): "Uninhibited Liberated Woman of Tang Dynasty." Cinematographer: Ardy Lam Kwok-wah; Art Director: Raymond Lee King-man; Music: Jim Shum Sing-tak; Writers: Chun Tinnam, Eddie Fong Ling-ching, Yau Kongkin; Producer: Mona Fong Yat-wah; Action Director: Tony Leung Siu-hung; Director: Eddie Fong Ling-ching. Cast: Pat Ha Man-chik (Yu Hsuan-chi), Alex Man Chi-leung (Tsui Po-hou), Tom Poon Chun-wai (Yung), Cheung Kwok-chu, Lam Hoi-ling, Kong To. 1.85:1. VHS/LD: World Video (Poor Subtitles). Import LD: Ocean Shores (Poor Subtitles). 102 minutes.

One of the most significant and offbeat HK adult films, **An Amorous Woman of Tang Dynasty** is a period softcore drama with a decidedly feminist perspective and sexual encounters that are always relevant to the story. Taoist priestess/poetess Yu Hsuan-chi possesses a yearning to experience aspects of life that go beyond the traditional parameters of her station. While associating with the upper echelon of society, she also carries on a torrid relationship with roving swordsman Tsui Po-hou. Hsuan-chi (a highly intelligent woman who chose to become a priestess in order to be independent) and Pohou (a man who chose to be an assassin rather than live a mundane life) are a seemingly ideal match, but he eventually leaves her to resume his travels in the martial world. In the meantime, Hsuan-chi earns the reputation among the townsfolk of being amoral, because of the sexual relationship she carries on with her maid, Lu Chiao. Po-hou returns but soon abandons her again, prompting Hsuan-chi to take up with other men. However, when she discovers that Chiao has been impregnated by a man whose identity she refuses to divulge, Hsuan-chi's actions lead to tragic consequences.

Amorous Woman (Eddie Fong's directorial debut) is filled with beautiful imagery, and the regal staging seems inspired more by Japanese cinema than traditional HK fare. In a film well-acted by all, it is Pat Ha who gives the standout performance: cold yet passionate, determined yet vulnerable. Her daring work, combined with the intelligent screenplay and meticulous production, rank this far above the flood of period sex films that followed the creation of the Category III rating in 1989. Fong's original cut of the film runs over an hour longer but is not currently available for viewing.

26. Ancient Chinese Whorehouse

(1994; Long Shong Pictures H.K./Golden Power Productions) ★: 5/10. *Ching lau sap yi fong* (Cantonese), *Qin lou shi er fang* (Mandarin): "Qing Twelve Story Building." Cinematographer: Poon Takyip; Art Director: James Cheung Yingwah; Music: Mak Chun-hung; Writer: Ng Man-fai; Producer: Wang Ying-hsiang; Action Directors: Cheung Wah, Lai Keung-kuen; Director: Ivan Lai Kai-ming. Cast: Yvonne Yung Hung (Miss Ng), Kent

Cheng Chuk-see (Kong), Ching Suet-ngan (Siu-ching), Dick Lau Dik-chi (Yat), Yuen King-tan (Sister Bamboo), Elvis Tsui Kam-kong (The Prince), Shing Fui-on (Chin). 1.85:1. VHS: World Video. Import LD/VCD: Universe. 96 minutes.

One of the better entries in the period sex genre, this offers up some enjoyably base humor and bizarrely enticing eroticism, which helps to counteract distasteful scenes of torture and rape. The main plot centers around Siu-ching, a young maiden who reluctantly sells herself to a brothel for five years in order to raise money to bury her recently deceased father and pay off his debts. After she initially refuses to perform her duties, the madam of the establishment, Miss Ng, sentences her to a dip in the "magic cup" (a boiling tub of eels!). Siu-ching, understandably, changes her mind, and is aided in her transition by kind worker Yat, who harbors an obvious affection for the girl. Various subplots fill out the remainder of the running time: When a competitor brings in a Caucasian hooker from overseas, the virginal master carpenter Kong tries to boost business by creating wild sexual props like the "Tai Chi Bed" and new positions like the "Super Shooter;" Yat and Siu-ching try to mend their relationship after a misunderstanding arises from her use of a powerful aphrodisiac; the top-heavy Sister Bamboo finds herself without clients after accidentally smothering one with her enormous breasts; and Miss Ng concocts a plan to trap a killer rapist (Elvis Tsui) who has been preying on the local working girls. The bizarre highlight has to be Yat and the white girl doing it on a *giant chicken* sex chair (a prostitute is called a *kai* or "hen" in Cantonese slang)! For more in the same vein, try the **Sex and Zen** films and **Yu Pui Tsuen III**.

27. Angel

(1987; Molesworth) ★: 7/10. *Tin si hang dung* (Cantonese), *Tian shi hang dong* (Mandarin): "Angel Operation." Cinematographer: Sander Lee Kar-ko; Art Director: Leung Yui-man; Music: Richard Lo Sai-kit; Writer-Producer: Teresa Woo San; Action Director: Tony Leung Siu-hung; Directors: Raymond Leung Pan-hei, Tony Leung Siu-hung, Ivan Lai Kai-ming. Cast: Moon Lee Choi-fung (Moon), Elaine Lui Siu-ling (Elaine), Hideki Saijo (Saijo), Yukari Oshima (Madam Yeung), Alex Fong Chung-sun (Alex Fong), David Chiang Da-wei (John Keung), Yeung Kwan (Head of the Cartel), Hwang Jang-li (Chan), Lam Chung (Torture Victim). 2.35:1. VHS: Arena/Xenon (Dubbed), World Video (Poor Subtitles). LD: Winson Entertainment. 93 minutes. Also known as **Iron Angels, Midnite Angel** (Arena/Xenon title).

A surprise hit that spawned two official sequels and scores of imitations, **Angel** is a superior girls-with-guns action fest that is almost stolen by its colorful villainess. When International Police torch their opium fields, a drug cartel gets revenge by brutally murdering the officers who headed up the mission. In response, the authorities enlist help from the Angel Organization and its top agents, Saijo, Moon, and Elaine. Stealing a shipment of drugs as a reprisal, the Angel team (working in conjunction with American DEA agent Alex Fong) invoke the wrath of the ferocious Madam Yeung, who has just assumed control of the cartel by murdering her boss. This results in a series of battles between the two forces which climaxes with Saijo being buried alive inside an armored car while Moon and Elaine take on Yeung and her forces in the drug storage warehouse.

Produced on an ambitious scale for its budget, the film includes location work in Japan and Thailand, adding to the storyline's James Bond overtones. The action is not as constant as some of the later **Angel** imitations but is appropriately fierce and well-choreographed. Moon Lee and Elaine Lui give appealing performances, but Japanese dynamo Yukari Oshima all but walks away with the film as the cackling, cheerfully sadistic Yeung. A terrific martial artist, Oshima possesses such great screen presence that you cannot take your eyes off of her. Although **Angel** won her a cult following, she has not been used as effectively in any of her later movies, several of which paired her up with Moon Lee. Lee, Lui, and Alex Fong returned for the first follow-up, the aptly titled **Angel II**. Avoid Arena/Xenon's **Midnite Angel**, a dubbed and mediocre quality rendition which opens with an unrelated Moon Lee fight sequence lifted from **Angel III**.

28. Angel II

(1988; Molesworth) ★: 6/10. *Tin si hang dung II jo foh fung gaau lung* (Cantonese), *Tian shi xing dong II zhi huo feng jiao long* (Mandarin): "Angel Operation II: Fire Phoenix Flood Dragon." Cinematographer: Nico Wong Man-wan; Art Director: Chan Tak-hei; Music: John Wong Sai-cheung, Tang Siu-lam; Producers: Teresa Woo San, Raymond Leung Pan-hei; Action Director: Stanley Tong Kwai-lai; Writer-Director: Teresa Woo San. Cast: Moon Lee Choi-fung (Moon), Elaine Lui Siu-ling (Elaine), Alex Fong Chung-sun (Alex Fong), Nathan Chan Ting-wai (Peter Kam), Gary Siu Yuk-lung (Marco), Kharina Isa (Kharina). 2.35:1. VHS: World Video (Poor Subtitles). Import LD: Ocean Shores (Poor Subtitles). 94 minutes. Also known as **Angels** (UK video title), **Iron Angels II**.

The first sequel to **Angel** finds Moon, Elaine, and Alex jetting off to Malaysia for a well-deserved vacation. There they encounter Peter Kam, an old friend of Alex, who has accumulated great wealth through his palm oil business, along with a stellar reputation as a philanthropist. However, he is also the leader of a fascist army that plans to overthrow the country's government. The Angel Team learns of his activities and are ordered by their superiors in America to take him out. The mission is a difficult one, not only for Alex but also for Elaine, who has fallen in love with the handsome entrepreneur.

Not as exciting as its forerunner, and lacking as formidable an antagonist as Yukari Oshima, **Angel II** still possesses much of the original's appeal. The action scenes are sparse until the prolonged climactic battle, which unfolds in the jungle. The gunplay is staged with gusto, and Moon Lee has a sensational hand-to-hand bout with one of the enemy commanders. Malaysian actress Kharina Isa, the new addition to the series, is little more than a pretty mannequin. Regardless, it would be her and not Elaine Lui who would join Lee and Fong in **Angel III**. "Flood Dragon" in the Chinese title is a term that people who lived around the Yellow River used to indicate a sudden rise in the water level ("The Flood Dragon is rising").

29. Angel III

(1989; Molesworth) ★: 5/10. *Tin si hang dung III moh lui mut yat* (Cantonese), *Tian shi xing dong III mo nu mo ri* (Mandarin): "Angel Operation III: Last Days of an Evil Woman." Cinematographer: Nico Wong Man-wan; Art Director: Horace Ma Kwong-wing; Music: John Wong Sai-cheung, Tang Siu-lam; Action Director: Tang Tak-wing; Writer-Producer-Director: Teresa Woo San. Cast: Moon Lee Choi-fung (Moon), Alex Fong Chung-sun (Alex Fong), Kharina Isa (Kharina), Ralph Chen Cheng-gui (Kwai), Mark Steinborn (Mark, aka "Mr. Computer"), Katy Hickman (The Blonde). 2.35:1. VHS: World Video (Poor Subtitles). Import LD/VCD: Ocean Shores (Poor Subtitles). 91 minutes. Also known as **Iron Angels III, Return of the Iron Angels**.

Elaine Lui did not return for this, the last of the official **Angel** movies, and her dynamic presence is sorely missed. Moon Lee is once again in terrific form and Alex Fong does some impressive kickboxing, but this entry remains a step down from its predecessors. A terrorist group (headed up by Qaddafi, no less!) is eliminating various dignitaries, so Moon and Alex are each given separate assignments: She will infiltrate the killers by impersonating a Japanese assassin they have recruited, while he will scour Bangkok for leads with the aid of local contact Kwai. Moon is able to get inside the terrorist base, but her cover is eventually blown and she barely escapes with her life. Alex's travels, meanwhile, land him in the middle of Thailand's kickboxing competitions (a digression that makes about as much sense as any of the storyline here). The Angel team learns that the killers plan to wipe out the dignified guests at an important garden party, prompting Alex and Kwai to strap on some handy rocket packs(!) and fly to the rescue.

While the **Angel** films were never meant to be anything more than mindless fun, this one is just too foolish and slapdash for its own good. **Angel III** does serve up what is arguably the best fight sequence in the trilogy: Moon Lee single-handedly battling a dozen guards in the terrorist fortress. It's an exhilarating sequence and goes a long way in making this entry's many shortcomings more palatable.

30. Angel Enforcers

(1989; Grandwell Film Production) ★: 5/10. *Wong ga fei fung* (Cantonese), *Huang jia fei feng* (Mandarin): "Royal Flying Phoenix." Cinematographer: Cheung Hoi; Music: Not Original; Writers: Edmund Leung Yiu-ming, Lai Lun; Producers: Chan Man-ching, Ma Tak; Action Director: Phillip Ko Fei; Director: Ho Chi-mou. Cast: Sharon Yeung Pan-pan (Zhou), Cheung Kwok-leung (Dei), Ha Chi-chun (Female Crime Boss), Dick Wei (Assassin), Woo Fung (Uncle Deng), Cho Tat-wah (Joe Tso), Charlie Cho Cha-lei (Zhao), Tai Po (Paul), Phillip Ko Fei (Ko), Mark Houghton (Thug), Mike Abbott (Thug). 1.85:1. VHS: Tai Seng. 90 minutes.

One of the first of many girls-with-guns features that followed in the wake of **Angel**, this brisk cheapie has so much going on action-wise that aficionados should be more than pleased with it. One of HK's most unsung action movie heroines, Sharon Yeung, toplines as Zhou, a supercop out to arrest a butch female crime boss (who dresses in white three piece suits and wields a riding crop!). In addition to this case, she and her fellow officers must defend themselves from an assassin with an axe to grind: One of Zhou's colleagues fatally shot the man's best friend (another killer) in the line of duty, and the assassin is now targeting everyone involved in the incident.

Forget the connect-the-dots plotting and enjoy the enthusiastically staged gunplay and Yeung's incredible acrobatics. Woo Fung and Cho Tat-wah put in supporting appearances as (what else?) bumbling senior officers, and Charlie Cho provides some dubious comic relief as a low-life who gets his just desserts in novel fashion (he is raped by two male porn stars!). Director Ho Chi-mou is actually prolific schlockmeister Godfrey Ho, who also goes by the Cantonese names Ho Chi-keung and Ho Chun-sing. Most of the music has been stolen from **Halloween II**, **The Hidden**, **A Nightmare on Elm Street**, **Phantasm**, **Near Dark**, and various Tangerine Dream albums.

31. Angel Force

(1990; Hatract Films/Ying Feng Film/Chun Wah Film and TV) ★: 5/10. *Tin si dak ging* (Cantonese), *Tian shi te jing* (Mandarin): "Angel Special Cop." Cinematographer: Cho On-sun; Music: Not Original; Writer: Lee Chung-lai; Producers: Chin Kei, Chin Chang-lung, Kwok Nan-hung; Action Director: Yuen Bun; Director: Wah San. Cast: Moon Lee Choi-fung (Mone), Wilson Lam Chun-yin (Lin Chen-fei), Hugo Ng Toi-yung (Little Vietnam), Lung Fong (Lon), Johnny Wang Lung-wei (Poison Owl), Shing Fui-on (Thug). 1.85:1. VHS: World Video (Poor Subtitles), SYS/Youngtze (Dubbed). LD: World Video (No Subtitles). Import LD: Star Entertainment (No Subtitles). 86 minutes.

After a slow start, this action cheapie delivers more than its fair share of **Rambo**-style jungle combat. Martially skilled cops Mone and Chin-fei are assigned to create a special task force for a mission in Burma. Their objective: rescue an important hostage being held by the vicious renegade general, "Poison Owl." When Chin-fei is badly wounded by a would-be assassin, Mone takes command, leading her troops into the proverbial "heart of darkness." However, Poison Owl is not the only enemy she has to worry about.

Directed in run-of-the-mill fashion by Wah San (best known in the West for his wild sci-fi thriller **Super Infra-Man**, released in America by Joseph Brenner as simply **Infra-Man**), **Angel Force** offers up only the most rudimentary genre elements, but it is efficient enough to hold one's interest. Hugo Ng gets the best role as "Little Vietnam," the requisite disturbed vet, who comes up with an inventive variation on the oft-imitated "shoot the hostage" bit from **The Big Heat**. Moon Lee evidently made this right after finishing **The Nocturnal Demon** (also 1990), as she sports much the same silly haircut her character had in that film. For some reason, the subtitles (which are extremely tiny and faint) are done entirely in lower case. The soundtrack includes music lifted from **A Nightmare on Elm Street 2: Freddy's Revenge**.

32. Angel-Hunter

(1992; Flaming-Star International Co.) ★: 3/10. *Lui gaau fung wan chi che gaau yap cham* (Cantonese), *Nu jiao feng yun zhi xie jiao ru qin* (Mandarin): "Girls' School Turbulent as Evil Cult Invades." Cinematographer: Li Hsin-yeh; Art Director: William Yam Wai-leung; Music: Michael Lai Siu-tin; Writer: Raymond Cheung Man-wai; Producer: Dean Shek Tien; Action Director: Yuen Bun; Director: Sun Chung. Cast: Vivian Chow Wei-man (May), Lau Ching-wan (Jack Chow Man-kit), Carrie Ng Kar-lai (Sister Man Ying), Anthony Wong Chau-sang (Kwok, aka The Bishop), Ng Man-tat (Professor Cheung), Wong Kam-kong (Lee Pang-sing). 1.85:1. VHS: World Video. Import LD: Golden Cinema City. 97 minutes.

This ill-conceived thriller spent a year on the shelf before appearing in theaters for a one week run. When a school girl commits suicide, guidance counselor Jack Chow Man-kit becomes convinced that heretics are responsible. The dead girl's troubled friend, May, is lured into joining a church run by The Bishop, a seductive, Jim Jones-type figure. Jack teams up with the eccentric Professor Cheung to try and obtain videotape footage of the group performing a black mass (which mainly consists of drugs, sex, and atmospheric lighting)—a plan that falls apart when Jack is drugged and sleeps with May. The experience puts a dent in his convictions, but his resolve returns when he sees what is happening to May, and when his boss (who just won an election, thanks to financial contributions from The Bishop) threatens to blackmail him with video footage of he and May having sex.

There is merit in the premise: After the Tianamen Square massacre in 1989, many HK residents felt very unsure about the future, and it is quite plausible that some would fall victim to false promises of love and security. However, the storyline here is merely silly, and what little credibility there is goes right down the drain when Ng Man-tat's character shows Lau Ching-wan and Vivian Chow "secret footage" of a satanic sacrifice...and it's a clip from Robin Hardy's **The Wicker Man** (1973)! Anthony Wong and Carrie Ng are well cast as the villains, and their gleefully evil performances provide partial compensation.

33. Angel of the Road

(1993) ★: 3/10. *Ma lo tin rite si* (Cantonese), *Ma lu tian shi* (Mandarin): "Road Angel." Cinematographer: Wilson Chan Pui-kai; Art Director: Raymond Lee King-man; Music: Lowell Lo Kwun-ting; Writer: Chan Ching-cheung; Action Director: Tony Leung Siu-hung; Producer-Director: Barry Chung Man-keung. Cast: Max Mok Siu-chung (Ming), Loletta Lee Lai-chun (Maggie), Roy Chiao Hung (Maggie's Father), Alex To Tak-wai (Tony), Ronald Wong Pan (Half Day), Ng Man-tat (Mong), Alex Fong Chung-sun (Rango), Chen Kuan-tai (Ming's Father). 1.85:1. VHS: Tai Seng. Import LD/VCD: Mei Ah. 89 minutes.

Showcasing HK formula filmmaking at its dullest, this flatly directed drama (another imitation of **Off Track** and **A Moment of Romance**) does not possess so much as an ounce of style or creativity. It concerns the exploits of drag racer Ming, who is forced to make a living as a delivery van driver for a triad-run company. Despite his low social position, Ming hopes to win the affections of Maggie, a young student from the right side of the tracks, despite heady opposition from the girl's father and her rich, snobby boyfriend, Tony. In the meantime, Ming and his buddies run into trouble with a rival triad gang (led by a smirking Alex Fong) when they try to branch out and start their own business.

No surprises here and precious little of interest. Even the racing scenes and car chases are blandly staged. Max Mok and Loletta Lee do deserve a measure of credit, however, for still being able to convincingly play teenagers, even though both are well past that stage in life.

34. Angel of Vengeance

(1993; New View Film Co.) ★: 1/10. *Miu gaai sap saam mooi* (Cantonese), *Miao jie shi san mei* (Mandarin): "Thirteen Little Sisters of Temple Street." Cinematographer: Chan Yen-shan; Writer: Lau Sung-pai; Producer: Lau King-sam; Action Director: Cheung Chung-kwai; Director: Robert Lau Chung-pak. Cast: Yukari Oshima (Lori), Chung Fat (Wang Pan), Alex Fong Chung-sun (Wu), Law Yui, Tse Ming-yin. 1.85:1. VHS: Tai Seng. Import LD/VCD: Universe. 84 minutes.

This insipid action cheapie is precisely the sort of enterprise that killed Yukari Oshima's career before it ever really got going. She plays Lori, a kung fu fighting tough girl out to rescue her sister from the mobster/slave trader Wang Pan. If his kidnapping of her sibling were not enough of a reason to kill him, Wang is also the individual who forced her father to commit suicide when she was still a child. When Lori is unable to overpower Wang's henchmen, she escapes and is given refuge by Betty Chien, a college student doing a paper on prostitutes. Powerless to check out brothels first hand, Betty enlists the aid of a young man to do it for her. When that doesn't work out, she disguises herself as a man. Guess who just happens to work at the whorehouse Betty goes to?

Poor direction, amateurish choreography, overwrought performances, leaden pacing, frightful comedy relief, shoddy production values…you name it, this one has it. If that were not enough, there are several instances of outright misogyny, making it an uncomfortably unpleasant experience as well. The soundtrack includes a cue lifted from Ennio Morricone's score for **The Thing**.

35. Angel Terminators

(1990; Grandwell Film Production) ★: 4/10. *Gwang tin wong ga jeung* (Cantonese), *Hong tin huang jia jiang* (Mandarin): "Rumble Sky Royal General." Cinematographer: John Yeung Hok-leung; Art Director: Leung Kar-ming; Music: Not Original; Writer: Yeung Kei; Producer: George Lai Hing-lun; Action Director: Chan Siu-lung; Director: Wai Lit. Cast: Sharon Yeung Pan-pan (Ida), Kenneth Tsang Kong (Ken Zheng), Kara Hui Ying-hung (Hon), Michiko Nishiwaki (Miss Nishiwaki), Carrie Ng Kar-lai (Carrie), Dick Wei (Sama), Shum Wai (Ben). 1.85:1. VHS: Tai Seng (No Subtitles). Import LD: Star Entertainment (No Subtitles). 92 minutes.

One of HK cinema's best martial artists, Sharon Yeung is invariably more impressive than the films she appears in, and this low-budget cop actioner is no exception. Kenneth Tsang plays a drug trafficker who returns to HK after an absence of several years, looking to retake his lost territory; Yeung is the gung-ho officer intent on bringing him down. Captured and turned into a heroin addict, Yeung is eventually able to get straight with the help of her loyal informant. Joining up with fellow cop Kara Hui, the pair launch a decisive assault on Tsang's mansion. Carrie Ng appears in a subplot as one of Tsang's old lovers, who becomes involved with him again in order to save the life of her debt-ridden husband.

There is well-staged and fairly inventive action here, and Yeung's final act is a real showstopper; but, more often than not, the proceedings are dreary and predictable. The terrible stock music (which often bears only a tenuous connection to what is unfolding onscreen) just makes matters worse. Produced in 1990, the film did not open in HK until October of 1992. As of this writing, only the Taiwan release from Long Shong Video has English subtitles. **Angel Terminators II** bears no direct relation to this production.

36. Angel Terminators II

(1993) ★: 4/10. *Foh jung* (Cantonese), *Huo zhong* (Mandarin): "Combustible." Cinematographers: Wong Chieh, Wong Kar-fai; Art Director: Choi Wei-wei; Music: Not Original; Writer: Lee Ho-kwan; Producer: George Lai Hing-lun; Action Director: Yuen Po; Directors: Wong Chun-yeung, Chan Lau. Cast: Sibelle Hu Hui-chung ("Big Aunt"), Moon Lee Choi-fung (Chitty), Yukari Oshima (Bullet), Wong Chi-yeung (Chin Bo, aka Brother Mad), Jason Pai Piao (Bao), Lo Lieh (Tiger Wan), Sophia Crawford (Blonde). 1.85:1. VHS: Tai Seng. Import LD: Star Entertainment. 93 minutes.

Aside from continuing the "girls with guns" theme of its forerunner, this low-budget actioner bears no connection to *Angel Terminators*. Upon finishing her prison sentence, tough girl triad Bullet rejoins her old friends, including Chitty, who looks like a good girl but is a black belt fighter who can more than take care of herself. Bullet's activities are monitored with justified suspicion by her police officer father and his tough female partner, "Big Aunt." The main plotline doesn't really kick in until the second half. While helping out her friend May, who is being blackmailed into working as a prostitute, Bullet steals some jewels belonging to vicious triad Chin Bo. The gangster takes May and another friend hostage, demanding the return of the gems as payment for their release. When the exchange goes wrong, the criminals murder their hostages and the courier, setting the stage for a definitive gun battle.

While below average, the film still finds its stars in good form. Yukari Oshima is amusing as the attitude-heavy Bullet (who wears pants with the word "Slut" literally written all over them!); Sibelle Hu is at home in her trademark "tough broad" persona; and Moon Lee gives 110% as per usual. However, the proceedings are blandly directed, and the fight choreography rarely takes full advantage of the leads' abilities. Lo Lieh makes a welcome appearance as Chitty's long-winded uncle.

Angels *see* **Angel II**

37. Angels' Project

(1993; SLG Film Productions) ★: 5/10. *Tin si kong lung* (Cantonese), *Tian shi kuang long* (Mandarin): "Angel Crazy

Dragon." Cinematographer: Lee Yao-tong; Music: Not Original; Writers: Lo Kin, Gary Chan Chi-sing; Producers: Lee Man-chi, Ng Kian-seng; Director: Cheung Ho-tak. Cast: Sibelle Hu Hui-chung (Chief Inspector), Moon Lee Choi-fung (Siu-fung), Benny Lai Wai (Chan Wai), Lung Fong (Inspector Tsui), Mark Houghton (Caucasian Thug). 1.85:1. VHS/LD: World Video. 89 minutes.

This passable action cheapie bears no direct connection to **Angel** or its sequels, though it sports the same stock music that seems to turn up in all of these like-named films. Sibelle Hu and Moon Lee play HK policewomen assigned to escort a prisoner named Susanna to Malaysia as part of a case involving a computer disc. Some time after turning the woman over to local authorities, they notice her making an escape attempt. The disc goes missing, but the women capture a small-time hood who has links to the key underworld figures involved. After Lee is injured in a car crash, Hu and her captive track Susanna, only to find her just as she is being murdered. At this point, the man reveals his true identity as an undercover cop, and he, Hu, and a recuperated Lee join together with government troops for a military-style strike on the villains' remote hideout.

The opening reel is dreadful and the action choreography is only average at best, but the leads are likable, the Malaysian scenery is nice, and the film kills time efficiently. Moon Lee's fans will no doubt be disappointed by her character's prolonged disappearance from the narrative.

38. Angry Ranger

(1991; Golden Harvest/Golden Way Films/Paragon Films) ★: 5/10. *Fo baau long zi* (Cantonese), *Huo bao lang zi* (Mandarin): "Explosive Ruffian." Cinematographer: Cheung Yiu-cho; Art Director: Oliver Wong Yui-man; Music: Sound Department Ltd; Writer: Chan Kam-cheung; Producer: Jackie Chan; Action Direction: Jackie Chan Stunt Team; Director: Johnny Wang Lung-wei. Cast: Ben Lam Kwok-bun (Peter), Sun Chien ("Big Circle" Han), Leung Yuen-ching, Jackie Lui Chung-yin, Wai Kwan-lung, Benny Lai Wai (Thug Buying Ice Cream). 1.85:1. VHS: Tai Seng (No Subtitles). Import LD/VCD: Universe. 90 minutes.

Just released from prison (a result of his involvement in a bloody gang fight), Peter returns home to find that the neighborhood has changed greatly in his absence. After a few beers too many, he offends local gang leader "AIDS" Lun (who was nothing but a small potato when Peter last walked the streets) and proceeds to destroy the hood's car. This initiates a series of increasingly violent tit-for-tat incidents between the two rivals. Another point of contention is the fact that Peter has started seeing Jane, who is the property of vicious gang leader "Big Circle" Han. Han, naturally, wants Peter dead, but instead of performing the deed himself, he frames Peter for the murder of another leader's man.

Films directed by Johnny Wang (a former Shaw Brothers kung fu star often cast as ruthless Manchu villains) tend to be decent, small-scale actioners that suffer from tediously formulaic and contrived plotting. This one is no exception, and some terrific action (courtesy of producer Jackie Chan's stunt team) is really about all it has to offer, unless you are a fan of Ben Lam (who does a satisfactory job in a rare lead role) or Sun Chien (who appeared opposite Wang in several Shaw productions).

39. Another Chinese Cop

(1996; World Perfect Production) ★: 3/10. *Chung gwok "O" gei chi huet seng ching yan* (Cantonese), *Zhong guo "O" ji zhi xie xing qing ren* (Mandarin): "China's 'O' Department: Bloody Lovers." Cinematographer: Pang Chun-wai; Writers: Lai Man-cheuk, Chui Fung-cheung; Producer: Lai Man-cheuk; Director: Lam Yee-hung. Cast: Anthony Wong Chau-sang (Li Shu-pei), Elvis Tsui Kam-kong (Hwa Chiang), Diana Pang Dan (Mindy), Billy Chow Bei-lee (Tai), Liu Tai-wai (Lin), Yuen King-tan (Chinny), Gabriel Wong Yat-san (Tortoise), Law Kar-ying (Li Tai-chu). 1.85:1. VHS: World Video. Import LD/VCD: Star Entertainment. Import DVD: China Star. 91 minutes.

A plodding mixture of comedy, drama, and standard police action elements, **Another Chinese Cop** stars Anthony Wong and Elvis Tsui as Mainland cops investigating the kidnapping of a millionaire by a couple (Diana Pang and Billy Chow) looking to get rich quick. The man turns up dead, a victim of the "Eagle Paw" (*sic*), a kung fu technique few can master. This revelation leads Tsui to suspect his old friend Chow, the country's martial arts champion (which earned him the nickname "Tysan" [*sic*]), who had once saved his life. Liu Tai-wai appears in a supporting role as a Hong Kong reporter who becomes the object of Tsui's affections.

The skimpy storyline contains all manner of superfluous digressions, and the film stops dead in its tracks for a couple of dull, badly staged song and dance numbers by Pang. The climax (which finds Tsui trying to deactivate a bomb) is particularly weak. Wong can do little to enliven his role, but Tsui gives a charming, understated performance as the noble half of the partnership. His sincere characterization is easily the best thing about this entirely forgettable enterprise.

40. Armageddon

(1997; Win's Entertainment/Flea Market) ★: 4/10. *Tin dei hung sam* (Cantonese), *Tian di xiong xin* (Mandarin): "Heaven Earth Great Ambition." Cinematographer: Horace Wong Wing-hang; Art Director: Alfred Yau Wai-ming; Music: Chan Kwong-wing; Writers: Gordon Chan Kar-seung, Vincent Kok Tak-chiu; Action Director: Bruce Law Lai-yin; Producer-Director: Gordon Chan Kar-seung. Cast: Andy Lau Tak-wah (Dr. Ken Tak), Anthony Wong Chau-sang (Chiu Tai-pang), Michelle Lee Kar-yan (Adele), Vincent Kok Tak-chiu (TC). Dolby Digital. 1.85:1. VHS: Tai Seng. Import LD/VCD/DVD: Carnival. 112 minutes.

It is a rare event when HK filmmakers produce a science fiction thriller, so it is especially sad when one as ambitious as this turns out to be such a disappointment. When a noted scientist is incinerated by a mysterious force at the precise moment that several satellites fail, "walking encyclopedia" Dr. Ken is called in to investigate. Authorities believe that the death of the man (an apparent instance of spontaneous combustion) and two others in his field may be the work of an enigmatic group called the "Brotherhood of Technology." The dead scientists were peers of Ken, who is the inventor of a revolutionary system called VOD, which greatly enhances the capabilities of one's TV set in regards to entertainment, internet access, etc. As VOD would put internet providers and video software manufacturers out of business, police suspect that these companies would like to see Ken put out of commission (i.e. dead) before it hits the market. When another man is reduced to ashes, Ken's team begins to explore different theories, but none of them can provide an explanation for the sudden reappearance of Ken's girlfriend, Adele, who was killed in an accident some time earlier.

While initially interesting, the developing mystery soon bogs down as the cast members cite various philosophies and religious precedents as explanations for what is unfolding, and a second act detour to Prague does nothing but add some attractive scenery. When a Caucasian messenger of God (or is he from the *other* place?) appears, the proceedings grow progressively sillier and culminate in an ending that can charitably be described as unsatisfying.

41. The Armed Policewoman

(1995; Cheung Sing Movie Co.) ★: 2/10. *Gau ng toh cheung nui ging* (Cantonese), *Jiu wu tuo qiang nu jing* (Mandarin): "'95: Armed Policewoman." Cinematographer: Nico Wong Man-wan; Art Director: Yiu Chi-hong; Music: Tsang Kwong-wah; Writer: Lee Chi-yin; Producer: Ma Tin-yiu; Action Director: Lam Man-wah; Director: Cheung Kon-man. Cast: Carrie Ng Kar-lai (Madam Chu), Valerie Chow Kar-ling (Ling), Ng Man-tat (Law Man-tat), Roy Cheung Yiu-yeung (Ng), Lau Siu-ming (Wong). 1.85:1. Import LD/VCD: Ocean Shores. 91 minutes.

In a bid to curb the rising crime rate, the HK police force decides to issue guns to a select group of female officers. Two of the candidates, the inept Madam Chu and hotshot rookie Ling, are chosen to be partners. On their first day out, they stumble across an arms cache belonging to triad leader Law Man-tat. Shortly thereafter, Chu's husband and son are murdered, so she accepts an assignment to go undercover as a lawyer to win Law's trust, as a prelude to getting revenge. Chu manages to crack open Law's safe and transmit incriminating evidence from a computer disc to her superiors, but is caught in the act. The gangster then straps a bomb to her and demands $10 million U.S. dollars in exchange for her life. Ling, meanwhile, has shacked up with her instructor, Officer Ng, and the two set out on their own to capture Law and save their friend.

A couple of competently staged action sequences and sincere performances by the leads are not nearly enough compensation for ludicrous plotting and a multitude of painfully unfunny comedy.

42. The Armour of God

(1987; Golden Harvest/Jadran Film/ Paragon Films/Artpic Company) ★: 6/10. (Both versions). *Lung hing foo dai* (Cantonese), *Long xiong hu di* (Mandarin): "Dragon Elder Brother, Tiger Younger Brother." Cinematographers: Peter Ngor Chi-kwan, Bob Thompson, Arthur Wong Ngok-tai, Cheung Yiu-cho; Art Directors: William Cheung Suk-ping, Eddie Ma Poon-chiu, Jonathan Cheung Hoi-kei; Music: Michael Lai Siu-tin (HK version), Michael Wandmacher (US version); Writers: Edward Tang King-sang, Roy Szeto Cheuk-hon, Lo Kin, John Sheppard; Producers: Leonard Ho Koon-cheung, Chua Lam; Action Directors: Jackie Chan Stuntmen Association, Lau Kar-wing, Brandy Yuen Chun-yeung; Director: Jackie Chan. Cast: Jackie Chan (Jackie), Alan Tam Wing-lun (Alan), Rosamund Kwan Chi-lam (Lorelei), Lola Forner (May), Bozidar Smiljanic (Bannon), Ken Boyle (Grand Wizard), John Ladalski (Chief Lama), Robert O'Brien (Witch Doctor), Kenny Bee, Bennett Pang, Anthony Chan Yau, Danny Yip, Clarence Fok Yiu-leung, Carina Lau Kar-ling (Singers). Dolby Digital (DVD only). 1.85:1. VHS: Tai Seng, Dimension (Dubbed, 88 minutes). LD: Image (Dubbed, 88 minutes). Import LD: Star Entertainment (No subtitles). Import VCD: Mei Ah, Mega Star. Import DVD: Mega Star. 88/98 minutes. Also known as **Operation Condor 2: The Armour of the Gods** (US title).

Jackie Chan almost lost his life when a stunt went wrong during the making of this Lunar New Year's actioner, which is one of the star's weaker 1980s efforts. Chan (who also directed) plays Jackie (aka The Asian Hawk), a soldier of fortune who travels the world in search of rare antiquities. A group of Satanic (but decidedly bumbling) monks kidnap his old girlfriend, Lorelei, and demand that he give them three pieces of "The Armour of God" (five artifacts from The Crusades that are reputed to have magical properties) in exchange. After borrowing the pieces in question from affluent collector Bannon, Jackie, his rock star friend Alan, and Bannon's daughter, May, infiltrate the monks' monastery. Inside they find Lorelei and affect an escape, but the girl has been brainwashed; when the opportunity arises, she steals the armor, drugs Alan, and returns to the monks with the artifacts and the rock singer as her prisoner. Returning to the monastery, Jackie single-handedly takes on the monks and their minions while trying to save his friends.

The film gets off to a decidedly shaky start via a throwaway action sequence set in Africa but shot in *Yugoslavia* and peopled with locals covered in black make-up. It was during this portion of the shoot that Chan leapt from a wall onto a tree, lost his footing, and fell about forty feet down, splitting his head open on some rocks (his skull is now held together by a piece of plastic, and there is a small hole on the right side of his head). Alan Tam is a colorless sidekick, the storyline is dull, and the big climactic stunt (which has Chan leaping off a cliff onto the top of a hot air balloon) is unconvincingly staged and poorly photographed to boot. Things pick up in the second half, though, thanks to some fine kung fu (particularly a wild bit in which Chan battles against some black amazons clad in dominatrix garb!) and the sort of playful staging that would make its 1991 sequel, **Armour of God II: Operation Condor**, so entertaining. The film (which premiered in Japan during the summer of 1986, six months prior to its HK bow) was released direct-to-video in America by Dimension Films in 1998 under the fraudulent title **Operation Condor 2: The Armour of the Gods**, even though it precedes the "original" by four years! This version has a new score, new English dubbing, and runs about ten minutes shorter. Incidentally, "The Losers," a band shown at the beginning of the film, is a send-up of Tam's hugely successful group "The Wynners." His partners, Kenny Bee and Anthony Chan Yau, also appear in the sequence, which is almost entirely cut out of Dimension's edition. Character names listed above are from the dubbed version.

43. Armour of God II: Operation Condor

(1991; Golden Harvest/Golden Way Films/Paragon Films) ★: 8/10. (HK version) ★: 5/10. (US version). *Fei ying gai waak* (Cantonese), *Fei ying ji hua* (Mandarin): "Flying Eagle Plan." Cinematographer: Arthur Wong Ngok-tai; Art Directors: Oliver Wong Yui-man, Eddie Ma Poon-chiu, Dominique Lo Kar-yiu; Music: Chris Babida (HK version), Stephen Endelman (US version); Writers: Jackie Chan, Edward Tang King-sang; Producer: Leonard Ho Koon-cheung; Action Direction: Jackie Chan Stuntmen Association; Director: Jackie Chan. Cast: Jackie Chan (Jackie), Carol Cheng Yu-ling (Ada), Eva Cobo De Garcia (Elsa), Shoko Ikeda (Momoko), Alfred Brel Sanchez (Adolf), Bozidar Smiljanic (Duke Scapio), Ken Lo Wai-kwong (Adolf's Guard #7). Dolby Digital (US version only), Sony Dynamic Digital Sound (US version only), Unidentified Stereo Process (HK LD and DVD only). 2.35:1. VHS: Tai Seng (No Subtitles), Dimension (Dubbed). LD: Dimension (Dubbed). Import LD/VCD: Star Entertainment (No Subtitles). Import VCD/DVD: Mega Star. 107 minutes (HK version), 92 minutes (US dubbed version). Also known as **Operation Condor** (US title).

This spectacular follow-up to Chan's 1987 blockbuster went 100% over budget and was in production for over a year, boasting location work in Spain, Morocco, The Philippines, and HK. Jackie is "Jackie," a soldier of fortune hired to find 240 tons of Nazi gold stashed decades earlier in a fortress beneath the Sahara desert. He teams up with Ada (a prissy historian), wandering tourist Momoko, and Elsa, the granddaughter of the German captain in charge of hiding the loot. The group is pursued by various Arab mercenaries and the forces of Adolf (Alfred Brel Sanchez, better known as Aldo Sambrell), the last living soldier from the original brigade, who is returning to the base to get the gold for himself.

While obviously patterned after **Raiders of the Lost Ark**, the film features several large-scale stunt sequences that are very much in the spirit of Chan's earlier work. The underground base (a huge, elaborately designed set that is still among the most imposing seen in a HK production) hosts the most impressive setpiece, which literally took months to film: Chan fights with two adversaries while all three are blown around in a giant wind tunnel! The broad, stereotypical Arab characters are an embarrassment, as is the fact that all three of the women constantly rely on Jackie to project them. However, such flaws are almost to be expected, as **Operation Condor** is the contemporary equivalent of the simple, unpretentious thrills found in the golden age of Republic serials. On that level, it more than surpasses its models and ranks among the best of Chan's modern-day adventures. Dimension's American version adds new opening and closing title sequences, while deleting about 17 minutes from the HK cut. The editorial changes reveal a complete lack of understanding of just why this film works. Not only has much of the comedy been removed, the action sequences have been condensed in spots! What was previously a rollicking action comedy with a consistently light tone now plays like a straight-forward adventure with an odd penchant for goofy asides. Stick with the original.

44. Arrest the Restless

(1992; Win's Movie Production) ★: 5/10. *Laam Gong juen ji faan fei jo fung wan* (Cantonese), *Lan Jiang zhuan zhi fan fei zu feng yun* (Mandarin): "Lam Kong Legend: Anti-Punk Squad Turbulence." Cinematographer: David Chung Chi-man; Art Director: Jason Mok Siu-kei; Music: Joseph Chow Kung-shing; Writers: Chan Man-keung, Sammy Tsang Kan-cheung; Producer: Stephen Siu Yeuk-yuen; Action Directors: Leung Man-hung, Chris Lee Kin-sang; Director: Lawrence Ah Mon. Cast: Charles Heung Wah-keung (Lam Kung), Leslie Cheung Kwok-wing (Teddy Pak), Vivian Chow Wai-man (Leung Siu-man), Deanie Yip Tak-han (Teddy's Mother), Paul Chun Pui (Ngan Tung), Guy Lai Ying-chau (Flash Pao), Alex To Tak-wai (Teddy's Buddy), Fruit Chan Kwoh (Whiz), Henry Fong Ping (Teddy's Boss), Ku Feng (The Master), Lee Siu-kei (Spunky). 1.85:1. VHS: Tai Seng. Import LD/VCD/DVD: Mei Ah. 112 minutes.

The success of the **Lee Rock** pictures led to this similarly handsome but largely uninteresting drama, which takes place in a period between those two films. When he makes an arrest that threatens to derail the kickbacks enjoyed by his superiors, Sergeant Lam Kung is demoted down to the juvenile crime unit. Rebellious but fair teenager Teddy Pak gets off on the wrong foot immediately with Lam, who continues to anger his superiors by arresting the sons of prominent government officials. The real enemy for both is psychotic drug dealer Sam Chow, whose parents protect him from prosecution. Teddy also has his hands full dealing with the troubles caused by his no-account, debt-ridden mother, who is constantly on the verge of being executed by loan sharks. When Chow and his men attack Teddy's girlfriend and murder another girl, Teddy is framed for the crime and only Lam can save him.

This film's costumes and art direction are so beautiful that one wishes they could have been used in support of a more interesting and original scenario instead of one with such a tedious inevitability to it. Leslie Cheung does good work as the young anti-hero of the piece, but movie mogul Charles Heung is colorless, while Deanie Yip and Paul Chun give overwrought performances in the sort of parts they have played more than once too often over the years.

45. As Tears Go By

(1988; In-Gear Film Production Co.) ★: 7/10. *Wong kok Ka Moon* (Cantonese), *Wang jiao Ka Men* (Mandarin): "Mongkok Carmen." Cinematographer: Andrew Lau Wai-keung; Art Director: William Cheung Suk-ping; Music: Danny Chung Teng-yat; Producer: Alan Tang Kwong-wing; Action Directors: Stephen Tung Wai, Benz Kong To-hoi, Tony Poon Kin-kwan; Writer-Director: Wong Kar-wai.; Cast: Andy Lau Tak-wah (Wah), Maggie Cheung Man-yuk (Ngor), Jacky Cheung Hok-yau (Fly), Alex Man Chi-leung (Tony), Ronald Wong Pan (Site), Lam Kau (Kung). VHS: World Video. Import LD: Mei Ah. Import VCD: Cameron Entertainment. 98 minutes.

Wong Kar-wai's directorial debut is a visually striking triad thriller/romance that pales somewhat in comparison to his later work. Gangster Wah is visited one day by his pretty cousin Ngor, who has come from Lantau Island to Kowloon to get medical treatment for a lung condition. The hot-tempered man and the timid girl have little in common and can barely communicate at first, but, gradually, they become more and more comfortable together. Wah's buddy, Fly, has a hair-trigger temper that constantly gets him into trouble, necessitating that Wah act on his behalf. It's clear that Fly is a timebomb whose days are numbered, but Wah steadfastly stands by him nonetheless. After vacillating for some time, Wah finally breaks down and visits Ngor on Lantau. The two begin a relationship that looks as if it will soon blossom into a full-fledged romance. However, Fly has once again gotten himself in trouble, and this time Wah's rescue of his friend enrages demented triad boss Tony. The gangster and his men severely beat and humiliate Wah and Fly, prompting the latter to accept what will almost certainly be a fatal assignment (silencing an informant in police custody before the man can testify in court) as a way of regaining face.

Inspired by **Mean Streets**, this is the most straightforward of Wong's movies thus far. While some of the director's trademarks are already in place (particularly his stylistically distorted action scenes), the film also utilizes traditional devices like "hit single" interludes (including a Canto cover of Berlin's "Take My Breath Away") to help sell its emotions and a storyline that rarely strays from genre conventions. Regardless, the high quality of the performances, Danny Chung's excellent score, and Andrew Lau's slick cinematography keep it consistently engrossing and very much worthwhile. Prints of HK origin have absolutely horrible English subtitles. The UK video version (on the Made in Hong Kong label) is much better in this regard but is also missing 17 seconds of violence, snipped by that country's censor board.

46. Ashes of Time

(1994; Scholar Films/Jet Tone Productions/Beijing Film Studio/Tsui Siu Ming Productions/Pony Canyon) ★: 10/10. *Dung che sai duk* (Cantonese), *Dong xie xi du* (Mandarin): "Evil East, Malicious West." Cinematographer: Christopher Doyle; Art Directors: William Cheung Suk-ping, Alfred Yau Wai-ming; Music: Frankie Chan Fan-kei, Roel A. Garcia; Producer: Chan Pui-wah; Action Director: Sammo Hung Kam-po; Writer-Director: Wong Kar-wai. Cast: Leslie Cheung Kwok-wing (Ouyang Feng), Tony Leung Kar-fai (Huang Yaoshi), Brigitte Lin Ching-hsia (Murong Yin/Murong Yang), Jacky Cheung Hok-yau (Hong Qi), Tony Leung Chiu-wai (Swordsman With Failing Eyesight), Charlie Yeung Choi-nei (The Girl), Carina Lau Kar-ling (Peach Blossom), Maggie Cheung Man-yuk (The Woman), Bai Li (Hong Qi's Wife), Lau Shun (Leader of Ouyang's Opponents In Opening Battle). 1.85:1. VHS/LD/DVD: World Video (Remastered for the English market). VHS/LD: World Video (Original Chinese market version). Import LD/VCD/DVD: Mei Ah. 98 minutes.

A film that absolutely requires multiple viewings to be fully appreciated, Wong

Kar-wai's period fantasy is a captivating character study filled with affecting performances, stirring music, and mesmerizing imagery. Difficult to summarize, it centers on the cynical, world-weary Ouyang Feng (aka "Malicious West"), whose interior monologues set up much of the narrative. After ten years of fighting, Ouyang has retreated from White Camel Mountain into the desert where he runs an inn and "solves problems" as a middleman for people with the right sum to offer. He is visited annually by Huang Yaoshi (aka "Evil East"), an old friend with similar views on life, who has taken up with the woman Ouyang spurned a decade earlier (played by a radiant Maggie Cheung, who is not credited). A year earlier, Huang promised to marry Murong Yin, the sister of swordsman Murong Yang, but later reneged. Now Yang has come to the inn seeking vengeance and engages Ouyang to kill his old friend. However, it becomes apparent to Ouyang that Yin and Yang may actually be the same person. A young girl, with nothing but a mule and some eggs, offers them to Ouyang in payment for wiping out the bandits who killed her brother, but the innkeeper balks and advises her to proffer sexual favors instead. An all-but-blind swordsman, needing money so that he may return home, is hired by some villagers to slay the horse thieves who have been tormenting them, but is slaughtered when his sight finally fails him. Skilled young fighter Hong Qi accepts the girl's offer and slays both her brother's killers and the remaining horse thieves, but, in spite of his great abilities, he cannot be a good husband to his long-suffering wife, whom he stubbornly refuses to bring along on his martial adventures.

Upon first viewing, much of the film seems overly oblique, with its non-linear presentation, myriad flashbacks, and preponderance of voiceovers, but one remains entranced by the sheer radiance of the visuals, the quality of the performances, and the enveloping, adventurous score. Upon second viewing, the relationships become clearer, and fresh possibilities emerge as doors open to reveal degrees of profundity and commentary on love and other human foibles that went previously unnoticed. Later viewings allow one to fully integrate the easily perceptible and more intellectually demanding pleasures into a unique and supremely stimulating whole. One of the main plot elements is a magical wine which causes one to forget the past, an ingenious device that allows Wong to alter the flow of events, interweaving them into and around the lives of the protagonists. While the wine does seem to work on the characters who consume it, the effect is disastrous: Huang cannot remember even his best friends, and Murong is pushed once and for all over the brink into insanity. The others are consumed by the memories of their loved ones and haunted by the wrongs they have done them. It is a pain that drives one man into both literal and spiritual exile and another to pursue a noble but, ultimately, lamentable death. The characters are consumed by loneliness and alienation, adrift in their own worlds save for fleeting contact with others who share their emotional burdens. In keeping with this predicament, the occasions where they do manage to connect physically (particularly in a beautifully realized sequence in which Brigitte Lin strokes a seemingly sleeping Leslie Cheung, with each using the occasion to fantasize about the lover they have lost) provide only fleeting comfort. The only person to emerge happy is the least complex: Hong. His exposure to Ouyang's cynicism leaves him a better person and reinforces a joy of life that the rest have lost and are seemingly incapable of recapturing.

While director of photography Christopher Doyle dazzles the viewer's eye with one gorgeous sandscape and unique tableau after another, **Ashes** does possess some recognizable roots in film history. Although presented with Wong's customarily stylized slow motion, Tony Leung Chiu-wai's battle against hordes of swordsmen is reminiscent of the combat found in Japanese samurai films, while the soundtrack offers up an accompaniment for this footage that would fit right into the spaghetti western of your choice. The swordsman and his affliction is also reminiscent of Cameron Mitchell's titular character in Sergio Corbucci's Italian western **Minnesota Clay** (1965), while Leung's last thought before death was echoed previously by one of the villains in the second entry of Toho's **Lone Wolf and Cub** series.

The film ended up going way over budget and schedule (Charlie Yeung's role was originally played by Joey Wang Tsu-hsien, but all of the latter's footage had to be scrapped when Wang was not available for reshoots) and then spent several more months in post-production while Wong and four editors cut and re-cut it (the director dashed off the much more economical **Chungking Express** during a brief break in the editing). Ironically, these delays caused it to arrive right at the end of the late '80s/early '90s swordplay cycle—which is fitting, as it redefines the parameters of that genre while also continuing some of the themes and character archetypes Wong broached in **As Tears Go By** and **Days of Being Wild**. The resulting hybrid is one of the most challenging and rewarding films to emerge from HK since the start of the New Wave, and a superb achievement. A parody of the same source material (Jin Yong's "The Eagle Shooting Heroes"), which also takes drastic liberties, was filmed concurrently with much of the same cast and crew(!) by Wong's partner, Jeff Lau Chun-wai, as **Dong Cheng Xi Jiu** and appeared in theaters over a year before this picture. Avoid World Video's English market version of **Ashes**, which is missing the bottom third of the picture!

47. Asian Connection

(Magnum; 1995) ★: 7/10. *Dak ging gap sin fung* (Cantonese), *Te jing ji xian feng* (Mandarin): "Special Police: Anxious Vanguard." Cinematographer: Ko Chiu-lam; Art Director: Jessy Lam Chak-chi; Music: Wong Bong; Writer: Wong Ho-wah; Producer: Yuen Chun-man; Action Director: Yuen Tak; Directors: David Lam Tak-luk, Yuen Tak. Cast: Danny Lee Sau-yin (Lee), Michael Chow Man-kin (Mike Chau), Jean Wang Ching-ying (Cheng Xiao-nan), Chen Sung-yung (Ma Jiu), Blackie Ko Shou-liang (Chen Jian-shui), Jack Gao Jie (Jiang Tian), Ricky Yee Fan-wai (Cheung Hung/Zhang Xiong), Jackson Liu Hsiu-hsien (Jiang's Man). 1.85:1. VHS: Tai Seng. Import LD/VCD: Star Entertainment. 96 minutes.

This efficient police actioner is another entry in a growing subgenre of films in which HK cops strike up an alliance with their Taiwan or Mainland counterparts in order to snare a major criminal, with conflicting procedures and clashing egos threatening to scuttle the operation. Danny Lee and Michael Chow play HK narcotics officers who lose five million in government money when a drug bust goes awry. Pursuing the thief (Ricky Yee) to Taiwan, they initially create havoc for their local counterparts (noted character actor Chen Sung-yung and **Iron Monkey**'s Jean Wang) before joining forces with them in their pursuit of the gangsters (Blackie Ko and Jack Gao) running the narcotics.

As far as procedural thrillers go, this breaks no new ground, but the characters are developed with greater care than usual for the genre and the plot offers enough twists and intrigue to keep the viewer attentive. Directors David Lam and Yuen Tak (who can be glimpsed briefly in the film) also stage some accomplished action scenes; in particular, two sensational chases through congested Taipei streets, and a railyard shootout that climaxes aboard a highjacked transport train. Like many recent productions, **Asian Connection** was shot with sync sound and offers a realistic mixture of Cantonese, Mandarin, and English dialogue. Interestingly, the format allows the viewer to discern that Danny

Lee's real voice, while perfectly adequate, is not the one heard in the Cantonese versions of **The Killer, Organized Crime and Triad Bureau**, and many other features.

48. Asian Cop—High Voltage

(1995; Movie Master International Film) ★: 5/10. *Go aat sin* (Cantonese), *Gao ya xian* (Mandarin): "High Voltage." Cinematographer: Chim Pak-hung; Art Directors: Reynaldo Atun, Fernando Estacio, Roger Gandae; Music: Anthony Lee Hon-kam, Marco Wan Ho-kit; Writer: Cindy Chow Fung; Producers: David Ng Tai-wai, Hung Wing-fai; Action Director: Donnie Yen Chi-tan; Director: Andrew Kam Yeung-wah. Cast: Donnie Yen Chi-tan (Chiang Ho-wa), Roy Cheung Yiu-yeung (Dick), Lily Lee Li-li (Jenny), Edu Manzano (Edu), Frankie Chin Chi-leung (Gray Bear). 1.85:1. VHS: World Video. Import LD/VCD: Universe. 90 minutes.

Aside from being lensed in The Philippines, this cop actioner offers nothing new to the genre, though it is executed with a modicum of style and serves up the requisite amount of mayhem. Hotheaded HK police officer Chiang Ho-wa travels to The Philippines on an extradition case. While there, he encounters none other than Dick, the ruthless criminal who murdered Chiang's wife. Partnered up with Edu, a local cop with a much more restrained, by-the-book style, Chiang instigates all manner of trouble, including a brawl in a nightclub. The duo learns that Dick is in cahoots with Cardosa, a respected rich man, and the pair are running a successful counterfeiting ring. However, Dick has plans to eliminate his partner and does so—framing Chiang for the crime in the process.

The fight sequences feature a fair amount of editing, but Donnie Yen's skills still manage to shine through most of the time, and Roy Cheung does a solid job as his adversary. Together they make this routine production more interesting than it has any right to be.

49. Assassin, The

(1993; Prosper Film Productions) ★: 5/10. *Saat yan je Tong Jaan* (Cantonese), *Sha ren zhe Tang Zhan* (Mandarin): "Killer Tong Jan" or "Killer Tang Zhan." Cinematographer: Chiu Fei; Art Director: Chan Siu-ha; Music: Jonathan Wong Bong-yin; Writers: Charcoal Cheung Tan, Szeto Wai-cheuk; Producer: Chan Kan; Action Directors: Benz Kong To-hoi, Stephen Tung Wai; Director: Chung Siu-hung. Cast: Zhang Fengyi (Tong Po-ka/Tong Chop), Rosamund Kwan Chi-lam (Yiu), Max Mok Siu-chung (Wong Kau). 1.85:1. VHS/LD: World Video. 81 minutes.

This offbeat entry in the period fantasy sweepstakes presents a definite change of pace, but its good points are almost negated by a weak and uninteresting storyline. The film opens with Tong Po-ka and his lover Yiu on the run from a throng of soldiers. Upon capture, Yiu is taken away and Tong is charged with kidnapping, having his eyes sewn shut as punishment. After enduring this torture for a time, he is forced to battle a group of other prisoners in a life and death match. As the winner, he is rechristened "Tong Chop," named the kingdom's chief assassin, and paired with neophyte killer Wong Kau. After numerous gory homicides (during which Tong frequently hacks his opponents into pieces), Tong finds himself unable to carry out his next assignment: the murder of a young child. Retreating from the world of martial arts, he reunites with Yiu, who now has a husband and son. In retribution for Tong's betrayal, the royal eunuch has Yiu's village burnt to the ground, prompting Tong to pick up his sword once more. In the interim, Wong has become the seasoned and ruthless killer that Tong once was, and now isn't above betraying his erstwhile friend in order to gain the post of top assassin.

Some period fantasies require multiple viewings in order to be fully comprehensible to non-Chinese speaking viewers, but **The Assassin** could easily be viewed and understood without subtitles. Although that may sound like a blessing after overly convoluted fare like **The East Is Red** and **Kung Fu Cult Master**, it is actually a liability. While director Chung Siu-hung's other films are quite drab, this one is filled with beautiful visuals and florid production design, and the action scenes offer an intriguing marriage of wire-enhanced acrobatics and the ultra-gory bloodletting found in Japanese samurai epics (the abundant carnage earned this the adults-only Category III rating). However, because of this extra care, the one-note screenplay and stock characters are particularly frustrating. Best known in the West for his fine performances in **Farewell, My Concubine** and **Temptation of a Monk**, Mainland actor Zhang Fengyi seems justifiably bored with this material, while Max Mok (sporting a silly heavy metal rocker wig) garners the most attention as the increasingly sadistic apprentice. As usual, Rosamund Kwan is relegated to the role of attractive scenery.

50. Au Revoir, Mon Amour

(1991; Golden Harvest/Paragon Films) ★: 5/10. *Hoh yat gwan joi loi* (Cantonese), *He ri jun zai lai* (Mandarin): "Will Mr. Sun Come Back." Cinematographers: Bill Wong Chung-bo, David Chung Chi-man, Peter Pau Tak-hei, Peter Ngor Chi-kwan; Art Directors: Eddie Ma Poon-chiu, Horace Ma Kwong-wing; Music: Anthony Lun Wing-leung, Chan Ming-to; Writers: Jerry Liu Wing-leung, Gordon Chan Kar-seung; Producer: Chua Lam; Action Director: Mang Hoi; Director: Tony Au Ding-ping. Cast: Anita Mui Yim-fong (Wu Mei), Tony Leung Kar-fai (Shen), Carrie Ng Kar-lai (Mrs. Wu), Hidekazu Akai (Lieutenant Noguchi), Kenneth Tsang Kong (Wu), Norman Tsui Siu-keung (Tieh), Chikako Aoyama (Woman at Japanese Embassy). Dolby Digital (DVD only). 1.85:1. VHS: Tai Seng (No Subtitles). Import LD/VCD: Star Entertainment (No Subtitles). Import DVD: Mega Star. 124 minutes. Also known as **Till We Meet Again** (Mega Star DVD title).

Shanghai, December 1941: The Japanese occupation of China has been in place for four years. One evening, five Japanese monks are murdered in the streets. Shen, a visitor to the city, learns that the killers were Chinese and hired by a Japanese man. Trying to get some answers out of the latter, Shen ends up in a life and death struggle with him but is saved by the intervention of Mei. The pair first met five years earlier, but their subsequent relationship came to an abrupt end when Shen left to fight for the revolutionary forces. Although she still harbors anger towards Shen, Mei soon falls in love with him all over again. She also has feelings for Noguchi, an honest and compassionate Japanese embassy official, who helps her smuggle Shen past the secret police to safety. Shen again leaves Mei to fight with the underground, even after he finds that she is now pregnant with his child. When Noguchi discovers that Shen has been killed during a raid by the secret police, he proposes marriage to Mei and she accepts. However, he is mistaken: Shen survived the attack and has been ordered to liquidate Noguchi and his love.

An absolutely gorgeous production—from the photography to the costumes—this is, alas, a shallow and aloof affair, more akin to a soap opera than the sweeping dramatic epic the filmmakers clearly aimed for. Anita Mui and Tony Leung Kar-fai are fine, as is boxer-turned-actor Hidekazu Akai (as one of the few sympathetic Japanese characters to be found in HK cinema), but their love triangle cannot compare at all to the one found in director Tony Au's **Dream Lovers**, and this film also lacks the passion so evident throughout that earlier work. **Au Revoir, Mon Amour** remains heartily recommended to those who admire HK cinema for its artistry; on this count, it is an undeniable success, offering up some of the most stunning visuals in memory. If only the screenplay possessed a comparable degree of proficiency.

51. An Autumn's Tale

(1987; D & B Films Co.) ★: 7/10. *Chau tin dik tung wa (Lau man daai hang)* (Cantonese), *Qiu tian de tong huo (Liu mang da heng)* (Mandarin): "An Autumn's Fairy Tale (Gangster Magnate)." Cinematographers: David Hayman, David Chung Chi-man; Art Directors: Christy Addis, Yank Wong Yan-kwai; Music: Lowell Lo Kwun-ting; Writer: Alex Law Kai-yui; Producer: John Sham Kin-fun; Director: Mabel Cheung Yuen-ting. Cast: Chow Yun-fat (Samuel Pang, aka "Figurehead"), Cherie Chung Cho-hung (Jennifer Lee), Danny Chan Pak-keung (Vincent), Gigi Wong Po-yi, Wong Man, Brenda Lo Yip-mei. 1.85:1. VHS: Tai Seng. Import LD: Mei Ah. Import VCD/DVD: Mega Star. 98 minutes.

After saving for two years, Jennifer Lee flies to New York City and moves into a less than elegant apartment building above her obnoxious but good-hearted cousin, "Figurehead." She had intended to meet up with her boyfriend, Vincent, so that they could study together, but he dumps her and heads off to Boston. Seeing that Jennifer is deeply saddened by the situation, Figurehead goes out of his way to cheer her up by redecorating the girl's apartment, getting her Broadway tickets, etc. He also soon falls in love with Jennifer but feels self-conscious because of his incessant gambling and lower class background. Jennifer, meanwhile, adores his company but does not feel that he is the kind of man she wants to marry. To make matters worse for Figurehead, Vincent has returned and seeks to reconcile with Jennifer.

Attractively shot on location, this is an affable romantic comedy/drama which is taken to another level by its talented leads. Chow Yun-fat, in particular, radiates earthy charm as the perpetually disheveled Figurehead; his lecture to Chung about how one must be positioned just the right distance away when adding salt to a dish is priceless. The story follows familiar patterns and, while the film vanishes rather quickly from memory, it is very pleasing while it lasts. One can easily see why it was such a major box office success. **An Autumn's Tale** also won the Best Picture, Best Cinematography, and Best Screenplay statues at The Hong Kong Film Awards.

52. The Avenging Quartet

(1993; Art Dragon Film Production Co.) ★: 4/10. *Ang hoi gung ying* (Cantonese), *Ba hai gong ying* (Mandarin): "Tyrant Sea Revolutionary Hero." Cinematographer: Wong Kar-fai; Art Director: Jon Hau Wing-choi; Music: Sherman Chow Ching-hung, Yeung Chi-cheong; Writer: Matt Chow Hoi-kwong; Producer: Chan Fai-lung; Action Director: Lam Moon-wah; Director: Siu Wing. Cast: Cynthia Yang Li-ching (Chin), Moon Lee Choi-fung (Feng), Michiko Nishiwaki (Sen), Yukari Oshima (Oshima), Waise Lee Chi-hung (Hsiong), Chin Kar-lok (Paul), James Ha Chim-see (Sen's Partner). 1.85:1. VHS: Tai Seng. Import LD/VCD: Universe. 96 minutes.

Girls-with-Guns fans are the only ones who will get much out of this mediocre effort, which brings together cult favorites Moon Lee, Cynthia Yang, Yukari Oshima, and Michiko Nishiwaki (all of whom are featured in the eye-catching theatrical poster). While the direction is a bit more stylish than usual for this sort of fare, and the periodic action scenes usually satisfy, the storyline is unforgivably puerile. Mainland policewoman Chin arrives in HK looking for her old boyfriend, Hsiong, who fled China seven years ago. When she is harassed by some drunk jerks one evening, Chin receives help from Feng, a spirited high society girl, and the two become friends. Hsiong, meanwhile, is in possession of an old Chinese painting wanted by some Japanese buyers. Planning to bilk them with a forgery, he accidentally discovers a document concealed behind the canvas which contains evidence of Japanese WWII atrocities. After Hsiong sticks her with the bogus painting, Oshima, the leader of the Japanese, teams up with her fellow countrywoman, Sen (who is Feng's evil sister-in-law *and* has a score to settle with Hsiong), to acquire the genuine article.

The four women finally share the screen for a knockdown brawl during the climax, but it is poorly handled, and the closing minutes are jarringly nasty, incorporating a wholly unnecessary rape and torture sequence. The resolution to the story is also far from satisfying and appears to have been concocted more-or-less on the spot. The female leads fare adequately, but talented martial artist Chin Kar-lok is wasted in a superfluous supporting role as a bumbling, comic relief cop. The Taiwan version runs four minutes shorter.

Avenging Warriors of Shaolin *see* **Shaolin Rescuers**

Awakening (1992) *see* **Mary from Beijing**

53. Awakening

(1994; Concept Link Productions) ★: 7/10. *Gwai mai sam hiu* (Cantonese), *Gui mi xin qiao* (Mandarin): "Ghost Bewitches Crux of the Heart." Cinematographers: Sung Kong, Chim Pak-hung; Music: Tommy Wai Kai-leung; Writers: Chung Kai-cheung, Lam Kei-to, Chung Ngoi-fung; Producers: Cha Fu-yee, Chung Kai-cheung; Director: Cha Chuen-yee. Cast: Anthony Wong Chau-sang (Liu Sheng-ming), Simon Yam Tat-wah (Lam Cho-wen), Anita Lee Yuen-wah (Dicky), Carman Lee Yeuk-tung (Fei-fei). 1.85:1. VHS: Tai Seng. Import LD/VCD: Ocean Shores. 92 minutes.

A blissfully eccentric horror-comedy that will annoy many viewers but tickle a select few, **Awakening** centers on Liu Sheng-ming, a crooked *feng shui* master who has amassed a sizable fortune deceiving the public. However, his little con game may soon be coming to an end. Answering a call to investigate ghostly activities in an apartment building, Liu runs into the exceedingly strange Lam Cho-wen, who blames the swindler for the death of his wife. Lam (who may also be a ghost himself) drives his target around the bend by using the same sort of tricks Liu employs to deceive his customers. Intent on exposing Liu as the fraud he is, Lam also begins hitting on the man's wife. Liu counters by taking up with the beautiful Fei-fei ... but she is definitely not what she seems.

The narrative is a bit of mess thanks to the atrocious English subtitles. However, it seems that director Cha Chuen-yee was not all that worried about coherence, being more interested in leaving viewers off-balance and slack-jawed; he succeeds! Seasoned movie psychopaths Anthony Wong and Simon Yam have a grand time hamming it up here and their congenial performances are half of the fun.

54. Banana Club

(1996; Martini Film Company/Mandarin Films) ★: 5/10. *Jing paai heung jiu kui lok bo* (Cantonese), *Zheng pai xiang jiao ju le bu* (Mandarin): "Legitimate Trademark Banana Club." Cinematographer: Tony Miu Kin-fai; Art Director: Vincent Lam Wai-sam; Music: Peter Kam Pui-tat, Kwok To-kai; Writers: Tessa Choi Ting-ting, Wong Ho-wah; Producer: Kimmy Suen King-on; Director: Jimmy Sin Chi-wai. Cast: Michael Chow Man-kin (Michael), Edmond Leung Hon-man (Edmond), Simon Lui Yu-yeung (Simon), Paulyn Suen Kai-kwan (Vee), Halina Tam Siu-wan (Mindy), Amanda Lee Wai-man (Mad), Alvina Kong Yan-yin (Banana Queen), Cheung Tat-ming (Station Director), Lau Yee-tat (Guitar Man). 1.85:1. VHS: Tai Seng. Import LD/VCD: Fitto Mobile. 93 minutes.

Inspired by a HK radio program, this formula comedy strives for cheap laughs and garners a few. Michael, Simon, and Edmond are the bored hosts of "Love Studio," a talk radio program with lower ratings than the weather report. Cancelled by their hyper station director, the three spend their final broadcast insulting callers and being obnoxious twits. The change in format is a hit and they are hired back, with the program now called "Banana Club" (after a certain male organ). The bulk of the film concerns their romantic travails: Michael falls in love with Vee, a frequent caller in love with a married man; Edmond is worried that he is becoming gay, a thought spurred on by Mad, a punkish girl who has lost interest in men; and Mindy, the mousey station secretary, is going to make Simon love her if it kills him. Will these screw-ups realize that the women of their dreams are right in front of their eyes? Is there really any doubt?

While this was never meant as an earnest look at romance, did the guys have to be such sexist jerks? They don't deserve an ounce of sympathy, and the film actually expects the audience to allot them some. The female characters are easily **Banana Club**'s one redeeming quality. Paulyn Suen and Halina Tam give bubbly, winning performances; Amanda Lee is amusingly brassy; and Alvina Kong is a scream, doing wicked parodies of sexpots Kong Suet-fa, Diana Pang Dan, and Lily Lee Li-li. They make this simple-minded exercise worth considering. Lots of familiar faces appear here in small roles, including Raymond Wong Pak-ming, Linda Wong Hing-ping, Christine Ng Wing-mei, Money Lo Man-yee, Emily Kwan Bo-wai, Julian Cheung Chi-lam, and Ben Lam Kwok-bun. The same year's **Top Banana Club** bears no direct connection to this production and takes the same premise in an entirely different direction.

55. Banana Cop

(1984; Cinema City Co.) ★: 4/10. *Ying lun pei pa* (Cantonese), *Ying lun pi pa* (Mandarin): "London England Balloon Guitar." Cinematographer: Ricardo Coll; Art Director: Hai Chung-man; Music: Violet Lam Man-yee; Writer: Poon Yuen-leung; Producer: Teddy Robin Kwan; Director: Leung Po-chi. Cast: George Lam Chi-chung (Inspector Edward Yip), Teddy Robin Kwan (Chiu Din-boh, aka Ping Pong Ball), Cherie Chung Cho-hung (Amy), Billy Lau Nam-kwong (Obnoxious HK Cop), Sarah Cresswell (Policewoman). 1.85:1. VHS: Tai Seng. Import LD: Golden Cinema City. Import VCD: Mega Star. 96 minutes.

In the wake of **All the Wrong Clues (...for the Right Solution)** and **All the Wrong Spies**, George Lam and Teddy Robin Kwan teamed up once again for this uneven comic outing, set and shot in England. Refined Scotland Yard Inspector Edward Yip (who has become almost fully Westernized over the years and cannot read or write Chinese) is dispatched to HK to bring back a diminutive convict named Ping Pong Ball, who has information needed to solve a homicide case. Knowing that he is as good as dead if brought back to Britain, Ball quickly gives Yip the slip, forgetting that half of HK's underworld wants his head too. He agrees to accompany Yip overseas but evades him once again not long after they arrive. Fleeing from another assassin, Ball meets and falls for blind school teacher Amy, while Yip becomes romantically involved with a white policewoman. After constantly giving Yip a hard time, Ball decides to work with him, and the pair attempt to get their hands on a pi pa case (a pi pa is a Chinese string instrument) filled with mob money.

In contrast to Lam and Kwan's pervious pairings, the storyline is muddled and dull, and the comedy is usually too reserved to really register. Director Leung Po-chi (who would go on to make other movies in the UK) makes good use of the local color—but not enough to make the film worthwhile.

56. Banana Spirit

(1992; Bojon Films Company) ★: 6/10. *Jing ling bin* (Cantonese), *Jing ling bian* (Mandarin): "Wild Spirit Changes." Cinematographers: Philip Ma Kam-cheung, Chow Kim-ming; Art Director: Louise Kwong Hoi-ming; Music: Chow Kam-cheung; Writers: Lo Kin, Gary Chan Chi-sing; Producer: Yip Wing-cho; Action Director: Brandy Yuen Chun-yeung; Director: Lo Kin. Cast: Francis Ng Chun-yu (Chic), Lam Ching-ying (Chen), Ngai Sing (Che), Tommy Wong Kwong-leung (Rabid Hsiung), Richard Ng Yiu-hon (Tang), Yip Wing-cho (Yeh). 1.85:1. LD: Network Kingdom. Import LD/VCD: Universe. 95 minutes.

This entertaining horror-comedy finds mortician Chic aiding his buddy Che on his job as a Taoist ghostbuster. Desperate to raise some money so they can pay off a debt to gangster Rabid Hsiung, the pair agree to help old master Tang in his quest to capture the elusive "Banana Spirit." While initially skeptical, the pair are soon convinced when confronted by a vicious demon. Their midnight excursion also awakens Muyung Yu-yu, the Banana Spirit herself, who takes the form of a model Chic is attracted to. After a passionate night together, Chic and Yu-yu become inseparable. The benevolent spirit helps him win a fortune at a gambling joint run by Hsiung and saves Chic's life when he is shot by robbers. Hsiung takes notice of Yu-yu's abilities and tries to force the spirit to use her powers for his benefit. During the subsequent struggle, Chic kills the triad, who then rises from the grave (looking like Jack Nicholson's "Joker" from **Batman**) and seeks vengeance. To make matters worse, Yu-yu can only exist on the earth for a limited amount of time, and it is running out quickly.

Some gratuitous nudity earned this the Category III rating, but it is considerably tamer than most other efforts with this classification. Likeable, moderately developed characters, above average scripting, and some amusing local horror elements help to make this one of director Lo Kin's better efforts to date.

57. The Banquet

(1991; Hitamin) ★: 7/10. *Ho moon ye yin* (Cantonese), *Hao men ye yan* (Mandarin): "Powerful Family Midnight Banquet." Cinematographers: Kin Lee Kin-keung, Lee Tak-wai, Horace Wong Wing-hang, Peter Pau Tak-hei, Ardy Lam Kwok-wah, Tam Chi-wing, Christopher Doyle, David Chung Chi-man, Andrew Lau Wai-keung; Art Directors: Ng Ching-mau, Ho Kim-seng, Ray Lam Chan-fai, Hai Chung-man, Eddie Ma Poon-chiu; Music: Lowell Lo Kwun-ting; Writers: Wong Jing, Szeto Wai-cheuk, Tsui Siu-ming, Tsui Hark, Clifton Ko Chi-sum, Gordon Chan Kar-seung, Eric Tsang Chi-wai, Barry Wong Ping-yiu, Tessa Choi Ting-ting; Producers: Dick Cho King-man, Jacky Pang Yee-wah, Tam Tak-cheung, Lam Wai-ha; Directors: Tsui Hark, Joseph Cheung Tung-cho, Clifton Ko Chi-sum, Alfred Cheung Kin-ting. Cast: Eric Tsang Chi-wai (Mario Tsang Siu-chi), Carol Cheng Yu-ling (Mimi), Richard Ng Yiu-hon (Siu-chi's Father), Sammo Hung Kam-po (Hung Tai-bo), Jacky Cheung Hok-yau (Hok-yau), Tony Leung Kar-fai (Leung), Rosamund Kwan Chi-lam (Gigi), Andy Lau Tak-wah (Himself), Teresa Mo Shun-kwan (Herself), David Wu Tai-wai (Jogger), James Wong Jim (Food Vendor), Kwan Hoi-san (Uncle Chicken Roll), May Lo Mei-mei (Waitress), Sandra Ng Kwan-yu (Waitress), Pau Hon-lam (Uncle Lotus Seed Bun), John Sham Kin-fun (Curly), Woo Fung (Old Man), Josephine Koo Mei-wah (Photographer), Maggie Cheung Man-yuk (Dancer), Carina Lau Kar-ling (Dancer/Woman at Dinner), Tony Leung Chiu-wai (Wai), Meg Lam Kin-ming (Servant), Wong Wan-si (Servant), Billy Lau Nam-kwong (Soccer Player), Teddy

Robin Kwan (Soccer Player), Lau Siu-ming (Wong), Joey Wang Tsu-hsien (Hok-yau's Wife), Fennie Yuen Kit-ying (Waitress), Simon Yam Tat-wah (The Gigolo), Eric Kot Man-fai (English Teacher), Jan Lam Hoi-fung (English Teacher), Lau Kar-leung (Master Lau, aka Uncle Nine), Karl Maka (Mak), Kara Hui Ying-hung (Servant), Anita Mui Yim-fong (Herself), Sally Yeh Chian-wen (Herself/Woman at Dinner), Michelle Lee Kar-yan (Li Kar-yan), Sylvia Chang Ai-chia (Herself), Anthony Chan Yau (Himself), Michael Hui Koon-man (Himself), Maria Cordero (Woman with Michael Hui), Chor Yuen (Man on Stairs), John Woo Yu-sen (Man on Stairs), Tommy Wong Kwong-leung ("Robbers"), Raymond Wong Pak-ming (Forty), Alan Tam Wing-lun (Prince in Dream), Mimi Chu Mi-mi (Party Guest), Stephen Chiau Sing-chi (Himself), Lawrence Ng Kai-wah (Party Guest), Gong Li (Herself/Waitress), Leslie Cheung Kwok-wing (Himself/Little B-Head), George Lam Chi-cheung (Prince Alibraba), Jamie Luk Kim-ming (Vassal), Gabriel Wong Yat-san (Vassal), Melvin Wong Kam-sun (Party Guest), David Chiang Da-wei (Party Guest), Waise Lee Chi-hung (Party Guest), Gloria Yip Wan-yee (Party Guest), Lee Hoi-sang (Man at Dinner), Ku Feng (Man at Dinner), Leung Kar yan (Man at Dinner), Ching Siu-tung (Man at Dinner), Yuen Woo-ping (Man at Dinner), Ti Lung (Waiter), Aaron Kwok Fu-shing (Little B-Head's Brother), Bill Tung Biu (Uncle Bill), Lydia Shum Tin-ha (Aunt Bill), Leon Lai Ming (Cook), Kenneth Tsang Kong (Waiter), Ng Man-tat (Cook), Loletta Lee Lai-chun (Girl at Table), Lowell Lo Kwun-ting (Cab Driver), Nat Chan Pak-cheung (Man Feeding Dog), Barry Wong Ping-yiu (Man at Table), Phillip Chan Yan-kin (Policeman), Feng Sing (Man at Table) ... and many more! 1.85:1. VHS: Tai Seng. Import LD/VCD: Mei Ah. 97 minutes.

Put together in record time to aid victims of flooding in China, this all-star comedy won't mean much to those just starting to watch HK films, but seasoned aficionados will have a ball. The flimsy plot centers around a battle between billionaires Mario Tsang Siu-chi and Hung Tai-bo to get the contract to rebuild Kuwait after the Iraqi invasion. As part of a plan to win favor with ruler Prince Alibraba (a staunch family advocate), Tsang tracks down his aged father (whom he hasn't seen in ten years) and tries to spruce him up in time for a lavish party he will be hosting for the prince. As an added impetus to get his way, Tsang claims that he has cancer and only a few weeks to live.

As one would expect from such a project, the writing and direction are uneven and a handful of serious dramatic sequences don't work at all. However, even if you only like a few of the stars, chances are this is worth your time.

58. The Bare-Footed Kid

(1993; Cosmopolitan Film Productions Co./Shaw Brothers) ★: 8/10. *Chik geuk siu ji* (Cantonese), *Chi jiao xiao zi* (Mandarin): "Bare Foot Kid." Cinematographer: Horace Wong Wing-hang; Art Director: Bruce Yu Kar-on; Music: William Woo Wai-lap; Writer: Yau Nai-hoi; Producer: Mona Fong Yat-wah; Action Director: Lau Kar-leung; Director: Johnny To Kei-fung. Cast: Aaron Kwok Fu-shing (Kuan Feng-yu), Maggie Cheung Man-yuk (The Proprietress), Ti Lung (Tuan Ching-yun, aka Tuan Nam), Jacqueline Wu Chien-lien (Lien), Paul Chun Pui (Hua), Kenneth Tsang Kong (Ke Hu-po), Wong Yat-fei (Kwai), Benny Lai Wai (Soldier). 1.85:1. VHS: Tai Seng (No Subtitles). Import LD/VCD: Star Entertainment (No Subtitles). 90 minutes.

A superior remake of Chang Cheh's **Disciples of Shaolin** (1975; released in America by World Northal as **The Invincible One**), this period kung fu drama is deceptively low-key for much of its running time but gradually builds to an emotionally potent climax. The titular character is the rather naive and thick-headed Kuan Feng-yu, who hasn't much in his favor, save for masterful martial arts abilities. Following the death of his father, Feng-yu seeks out the man's old friend, Tuan Ching-yun, finding him employed at The Four Seasons Weavers. A former capitol guard turned fugitive, Tuan acts as the protector of the business' beautiful and determined proprietress. High ranking official Ke Hu-po (the owner of a rival establishment) is determined to take control of Four Seasons and instructs his lackeys to do whatever it takes for this to happen. The men torch all of Four Seasons' inventory, prompting Feng-yu to seek revenge. Impressed by the lad's skills, Ke wins over the gullible Feng-yu with praise and gifts and hires him to be one of his elite fighters. Now a pawn in Ke's grab for power over the region, Feng-yu's gullibility inadvertently puts Tuan and his former employer in danger.

The martial arts choreography by Shaw Brothers veteran Lau Kar-leung is an intriguing combination of his old school approach and the newer, more stylized action popularized by Ching Siu-tung and Tsui Hark. Likewise, while the story is of an older vintage, it unfolds here with a more controlled and contemporary cadence, eschewing melodrama in favor of more subtle and realistic emotions. Aaron Kwok is a bit too broad as the wide-eyed innocent, but Ti Lung plays the part of the traditional hero with his customary nobility and provides the film with much of its heart and soul. Maggie Cheung and Jacqueline Wu have less interesting roles but still acquit themselves quite well. The Taiwan and British tape versions have English subtitles.

Battle of Champions *see* **God of Gamblers' Return**

59. Battle Wizard

(1977; Shaw Brothers) ★: 6/10. *Tian long ba bu* (Cantonese), *Tin lung baat bou* (Mandarin): "Eight Section Sky Dragon." Art Director: Johnson Tsao; Music: Not Original; Writer: Ngai Hong; Director: Pao Hsueh-li. Cast: Danny Lee Sau-yin (Tuan Yi), Tin Lei (Mou Wan-ching, aka Sing Yao-cha), Yuen Cheung-yan (Bandit), Norman Tsui Siu-keung (Royal Guardsman), Ha Ping (Woman). 2.35:1. No official domestic video release. 78 minutes.

Twenty years after his legs were amputated by Prince Tuan Ching-tun (using the Yang Chi technique, which allows one to shoot bolts of energy from the fingers), evil Wong Po-yen sets his sights on the man's son, Tuan Yi (a timid scholar with no martial arts ability whatsoever). While wandering the countryside, Yi meets up with maiden Cheung Ling-ar, who has an affinity for snakes and can use them as weapons (they burrow into the victim and eventually explode out of their skulls!). When they run into trouble, Ling-ar tells Yi to go on ahead and search for mystical swordswoman Mou Wan-ching (aka Sing Yao-cha), who is known for killing every man she encounters and is also a practitioner of Yang Chi. Since Yi alerted her to a forthcoming attack by some brigands, Wan-ching spares Yi's life, and he reciprocates when she is poisoned by a demon. Attacked by a giant snake, Yi is able to kill the creature by biting its throat and, by drinking the creature's blood, he is imbued with great martial prowess. His plans to marry Wan-ching, however, are scuttled when his father reveals the girl's true heritage. Complicating matters further is the return of Wong (using giant metal stilts that look like chicken legs), who captures Yi and Wan-ching, with plans to feed them to his kung fu fighting ape(!).

An enjoyable juvenile period kung fu fantasy based on Jin Yong's *Demi-Gods and Semi-Devils* (a 2000 page novel that also served as the basis for **Dragon Chronicles:**

The Maidens of Heavenly Mountain), **Battle Wizard** utilizes some props, opticals, and sound FX left over from the studio's incredible 1975 sci-fi extravaganza **Super Infra-Man** (released stateside by Joseph Brenner as simply **Infra-Man**), which also stars Danny Lee. In addition to the highlights noted above, watch for Wong's mutant henchman (who can run at high speed, has a giant claw and a steel head), a poisonous magic frog which renders anyone who consumes it invincible, deadly energy daggers, and an exploding head! While not as well-made or eye-opening as say **Holy Flame of the Martial World, Battle Wizard** holds much of the same appeal as that later film, and those who have a fancy for HK fantasies should definitely seek it out. A note about the print used for this review: The only available source was a bootleg video version released in Britain during the early '80s by a label called Hotline. Their tape (in English with Arabic and French subtitles) features all but illegible credits, heavy wear, and is obviously missing some footage. Thus, the running time listed above is just an estimate of what an uncut English print of this film might run.

60. The Beasts

(1980; Century Motion Picture & Distribution Co.) ★: 6/10. *Sahn gau* (Cantonese), *Shan gou* (Mandarin): "Mountain Dogs." Cinematographer: Bob Thompson; Art Director: Tony Au Ding-ping; Writers: Eddie Fong Ling-ching, Lee Tan; Producer: Vicky Leung Lee Siu-ha; Director: Dennis Yu Wan-kong. Cast: Chen Sing (Chan), Wong Ching ("Cousin"), Kent Cheng Chuk-see (Moe). 1.85:1. LD: Winson Entertainment. 90 minutes.

A well-produced combination of Wes Craven's exploitation hits **The Last House on the Left** (1972) and **The Hills Have Eyes** (1977), this brutal thriller concerns an ill-fated camping trip made by five teenagers (three boys and two girls). Deep in the woods and away from civilization, the kids run afoul of five seemingly in-bred psychos who rape one girl and savagely murder her brother. Four of them are arrested, but the girl is so badly traumatized by the attack that she must be confined to a padded room at a sanatorium. As she is unable to testify, the police cannot lay any charges and must release the suspects. Horrified by this miscarriage of justice, the father of the two victims heads out into the woods seeking vengeance, employing such nasty weapons as a bear trap and a wooden box with nails sticking out of each side.

The production credits offer up more surprises than the film, including several individuals who would become major players in the HK industry. Co-writer Eddie Fong Ling-ching later became the director of such distinguished features as **An Amorous Woman of Tang Dynasty, Cherry Blossoms** and **The Last Princess of Manchuria** while also authoring screenplays for his wife, fellow director Clara Law Cheuk-yiu. Popular actor/producer/director/composer Teddy Robin Kwan (**All the Wrong Clues ... For the Right Solution**), acclaimed future director Stanley Kwan Kam-pang (**Rouge, Center Stage**), and production designer/director Tony Au Ding-ping (**Dream Lovers**) also acquired early credits here. Well-photographed and possessing a palpably lurid and depraved atmosphere, **The Beasts** is a grim and disturbing work. However, as the storyline steadfastly adheres to the "eye for an eye/revenge for a rape" conventions, it ultimately adds little to the genre. The performances are passable but the characters are mundane, with only Kent Cheng's large, bald retard (who chums around with the villains but does not actually participate in their crimes) being anything out of the ordinary. In addition to the unsavory human depravity, there are several instances of cruelty to animals involving snakes and chickens which may be too much for some viewers. The character names listed above are from the English-dubbed version, which was released on video in the UK by Mercury prior to the "Video Nasties" debacle.

61. Beauty Investigator

(1992; New Treasurer Films Co.) ★: 3/10. *Miu taam seung giu* (Cantonese), *Miao tan shuang jiao* (Mandarin): "Beautiful, Lovely and Clever Inspectors." Cinematographer: Kwan Chi-kan; Music: Not Original; Writer: Chung Kai-cheung; Action Director: Ng Yuk-kui; Producer: Cheung Po-wing; Director: Lee Tso-nam. Cast: Moon Lee Choi-fung (Li Min-feng), Yukari Oshima (The Hitwoman), Melvin Wong Kam-sun (Wong), Sophia Crawford (Lisa), Billy Chow Bei-lee (Kinada), Shum Wai (Chui Wai), Chung Fat (Chung Fat), Tai Po (Little Ming). 1.85:1. VHS: Tai Seng (Subtitled or Dubbed). Import LD/VCD: Universe. 91 minutes.

This low rent action-comedy will only be of interest to diehard fans of Moon Lee and Yukari Oshima. Min-feng and Grace are two ambitious but inept policewomen assigned to go undercover as nightclub hostesses in order to apprehend a psychopath preying on girls in that profession. When Grace overhears a conversation, the pair become involved in a triad gang power struggle. Utilizing the services of a Japanese hitwoman, Brother Bee is hastening his rise to the top of the organization by eliminating all who outrank him, including his own father. While Bee is able to achieve his goal, he is targeted for termination by a Japanese gang that is out for revenge after having been cheated by him in an arms deal. When Grace tries to take Bee into custody, he kills her, prompting Min-feng to buy some illegal weapons (including a handy wrist rocket launcher!) and avenge her partner by slaughtering the triad and his cronies. The action sequences are only fair at best and insufficient compensation for the tired plotting and insipid comic relief. Rated Category III for a gratuitous shower scene featuring Sophia Crawford.

62. Because of Lies

(1995; Kelvin Films Co./FM Film Production Co.) ★: 3/10. *Gau man lung dik fong yin* (Cantonese), *Jiu wen long de huang yan* (Mandarin): "Nine Tattooed Dragon's Lie." Cinematographer: Gigo Lee Chi-hang; Art Directors: Lee Chi-keung, Ken Chiu Kin-san; Music: Tse Chiu-kwong; Writer: Ella Chan Po-wah; Producer: Henry Fong Ping; Director: Lee Kwok-lap. Cast: Simon Yam Tat-wah (Lung), Yu Li (Shirley Kee), Law Kar-ying (Ho Siu B), Kenneth Chan Kai-tai (Chris), Sheila Chan Sak-lan (Siu B's Girlfriend), Henry Fong Ping (Fong), Pau Fong (Doctor), Yip Wing-cho (Restaurant Boss). 1.85:1. VHS/LD: World Video. 85 minutes.

This trivial drama stars Simon Yam as a divorced, alcoholic triad with a young son. Constantly in trouble with the law, he is something less than an ideal parent. Yu Li is his beautiful neighbor, a success at business but not at love and burdened further by having to care for her mother, who is in the advanced stages of Parkinson's Disease. Yam tries to better himself by opening a restaurant and, as Li's relationship disintegrates, the two begin to grow closer together. When Yam's partner deserts him, his life falls apart and he disappears, prompting Li to go back to her sleazy fiancé. Naturally, circumstances ensue that will guarantee a different outcome.

While overwrought, the drama is still intermittently effective, thanks in no small part to persuasive performances by the two leads. However, in the final analysis the narrative contrivances and lack of credibility are too formidable for them to overcome.

63. Before Dawn

(1984; Wong's Film Productions) ★: 4/10. *Dai 8 dim* (Cantonese), *Di 8 dian*

(Mandarin): "Eighth Hour." Cinematographers: Johnny Koo Kwok-wah, Lee Tat-hung; Art Director: Lee Yiu-kwong; Music: Siu Fai; Writer: Chan Fong; Producer: Tong Ching; Director: Clarence Fok Yiu-leung. Cast: Deanie Yip Tak-han (Ka-pao's Mother), Loletta Lee Lai-chun (Margaret), Ku Feng (Margaret's Father), Jimmy Wong Shu-kei, Leung San, Yung Sai-kit (Ka-pao's Father). 1.85:1. VHS: Tai Seng (Poor Subtitles). 89 minutes.

Clarence Fok's fourth film directorial debut certainly bears little resemblance to his later work, though that is marred by the same lack of subtlety found here. This aggressively downbeat drama tells of troubled teen Mok Ka-pao, who is ashamed of the fact that his middle-aged mother is still working as a prostitute. His relationship with unstable, homosexual friend "Butterfly" gets him involved with some underworld types and, eventually, results in him selling himself. This causes great distress for his mother, who has been trying to bring him up as best she can. Ka-pao is attracted to cute schoolmate Margaret, but her home life is even worse, as she must endure a drunken, abusive father and a shrewish, ineffectual mother. When Butterfly is murdered by a psychotic client, the man frames Ka-pao for the crime and, while the boy is eventually cleared of guilt, the incident drives a permanant wedge between mother and son.

There are some effective moments here and Deanie Yip is very good, but the storyline is all over the place, touching on too many characters and subplots to do justice to any of them. The heavy-handed approach and distractingly lurid exploitation elements just exacerbate the problem.

Beggar Su *see* **Heroes Among Heroes**

64. Beginner's Luck

(1994; Long Shong Pictures/Power World Production) ★: 5/10. *Wan choi tung chi* (Cantonese), *Yun cai tong zi* (Mandarin): "Carry Fortune Kid." Cinematographer: Joe Chan Kong-hung; Art Director: Jon Hau Wing-choi; Music: Sherman Chow Ching-hung, Raymond Wong Ying-wah; Writers: Kent Cheng Chuk-see, Johnny Lee King-kai; Producer: Yu Shu; Director: Billy Chan Wui-ngai. Cast: Lau Ching-wan (Mark), Jacqueline Wu Chien-lien (May), Michael Chow Man-kin (Hark), Kent Cheng Chuk-see (Chow Sing-chi), Bowie Lam Bo-yee (Bowie), Lau Shun (May's Father), Ha Ping (Auntie Lan), Bobby Yip King-sang (Shark Sang). 1.85:1. VHS: World Video. 97 minutes.

An inconsequential but sporadically entertaining look at the average HK citizen's obsession with racetrack betting, this mild comedy benefits immensely from Lau Ching-wan and Jacqueline Wu's likeable performances. Mark is an upright guy but hopelessly addicted to gambling. He and his buddies, Hark and Bowie, spend most of their time cooking up hair-brained schemes to win at the track, while, May, Mark's ever-patient girlfriend, tolerates his antics. However, after ten years of Mark's promising to marry her and not following through, even she has had enough, and Mark must carry on his gambling in secret. When Hark gets in deep trouble with a triad loan shark, Mark uses money he had earmarked for his wedding to bail his buddy out. Naturally, May is furious and breaks off with him. Can Mark mend his ways in time to win her back? Of course. Will the film end with him betting everything on a long shot? What do you think?

The story is much too predictable and the dramatic complications are pretty feeble, leaving this one to coast along on charm alone; it almost succeeds. Trivia note: The movie Lau and Wu go to see is **Brotherhood**, which was also helmed by this film's director, Billy Chan.

65. The Beloved Son of God

(1988; Movie Impact) ★: 6/10. *Fei maau lau long gei* (Cantonese), *Fei mao liu lang ji* (Mandarin): "Travel Memoirs of the Fat Cat." Cinematographer: Wilson Chan Pui-kai; Art Director: Eric Lam Sai-kan; Music: Lo Kit; Writer-Producer: Kent Cheng Chuk-see; Director: Dick Cho Kin-nam. Cast: Kent Cheng Chuk-see (Fat Cat), Wu Ma (Ng), Maggie Cheung Man-yuk (Bibi Cheung), Lung Ming-yan (Lung), Billy Lau Nam-kwong (Violent Patient), Alvina Kong Yan-yin (Retarded Girl at Food Stand), William Ho Kar-kui (Ho Kar-kui), Shing Fui-on (Thug), Jamie Luk Kim-ming (Thug). 1.85:1. VHS: Tai Seng. Import LD: Ocean Shores. Import VCD: Mega Star. 94 minutes.

Talented character actor Kent Cheng takes center stage in this predictable sequel to **Why Me?** Though *Beloved Son* suffers from some of the same problems as its forerunner, it is a bit more successful. Cheng reprises his role as Fat Cat, a retarded man who is generally placid but is pushed over the edge one day by thugs. Shot by police, he spends the next three years in an asylum and then becomes the responsibility of social worker Bibi, who relocates him to a halfway house. While on an outing with Fat Cat, Bibi is hit by a car and taken away in an ambulance, leaving her confused charge alone and on his own. Lost on an island after accidentally boarding a ferry, Fat Cat is reluctantly taken in by Ng, a cranky old man who is constantly looking for ways to get rid of him. The two eventually begin to bond, and Ng grows to understand Fat Cat's positive qualities, as does the entire village. However, when Bibi discovers his whereabouts, she feels duty bound to take Fat Cat back to the city.

The film makes a convincing case about how the mentally deficient are ostracized and mistreated in HK, and that one must be patient and give them the care they deserve. However, everything about the film (from the dialogue to the performances) is a bit too overstated for it to be fully convincing.

66. Best Friend of the Cops

(1990; Kay's Productions) ★: 3/10. *Chu biu yat chuk* (Cantonese), *Zhu biao yi zu* (Mandarin): "A Bunch of Suckers." Cinematographer: Lau Hung-chuen; Art Director: Choi Hing; Music: David Wu Tai-wai; Writer: Joyce Mak Shun-ling; Producer-Director: Wong Wah-kei. Cast: Alex Man Chi-leung (Jen Chin-hsing), Jacky Cheung Hok-yau (Tsai Tzu-chiang), Paul Chun Pui (Pao Pu-ping), Jimmy Wong Shu-kei. 1.85:1. VHS: Tai Seng. Import LD: Golden Cinema City. 94 minutes.

This good natured but altogether forgettable comedy stars Alex Man as a disgraced cop turned con artist who systematically bilks a group of officers who are unaware of his past activities. Jacky Cheung co-stars as a drug addict with knowledge of Man's criminal past; but the best thing about this misfire is Paul Chun's performance as a petulant veteran who knows a rat when he smells one. His comic timing during the climactic card game (where he desperately tries to prove his hunch about Man's scheme) provides the only real entertainment to be found here. David Wu is credited with the score, though he was probably just the music editor, as most of the cues here are not original.

67. The Best of Best

(1992; Galaxy Films) ★: 5/10. *Fei foo jing ying ji yan gaan yau ching* (Cantonese), *Fei hu jing ying zhi ren jian you qing* (Mandarin): "Flying Tiger, Excellent Hero: Among People There Is Love." Cinematographer: Ng Kin-man; Art Director: Danny Yuen Ching-yeung; Music: Richard Lo Sai-kit; Writers: Leung Hung-wah, James Fung Shui-hung; Producers: Stephen Shin Kei-yin, Leung Hung-wah; Action Directors: Benz Kong To-hoi, Tony Poon Kin-kwan; Director: Herman Yau Lai-to. Cast: Jacky Cheung Hok-yau (Li

Man-kit, aka Dee), Ng Man-tat (Ball), Sammi Cheng Sau-man (Heidi), Paul Chun Pui (Hung Kwan), Carrie Ng Kar-lai (Hung), John Ching Tung (Tsuen), Victor Hon Kwan (Brother Nine Teeth), To Siu-chun (KK), Lee Siu-kei (SDU Instructor). 1.85:1. VHS: Tai Seng. Import LD/VCD: Mei Ah. 96 minutes.

Special Duty Unit officer Dee has a decidedly rocky relationship with his slovenly, alcoholic father, Ball, who accidentally killed Dee's brother twenty years earlier. While on a mission to take out some homicidal robbers, Dee rescues Heidi, the daughter of triad leader Hung Kwan. The two strike up a relationship, much to the chagrin of their fathers, who are old enemies. When Heidi refuses to stop seeing Dee, Kwan orders him eliminated, setting the stage for Dee to take the law into his own hands.

While largely undistinguished, this remains one of director Herman Yau's more entertaining efforts to date, thanks mainly to Ng Man-tat's vivid characterization and the promise shown by Sammi Cheng (making her film debut). As these films go, the action sequences are sparse and unimaginatively staged, save for a pair of impressive fire stunts.

68. Best of the Best

(1996; Golden Harvest/BOB & Partners Company/Everwide) ★: 6/10. *Fei foo hung sam 2 ji ngo hei bei tin go* (Cantonese), *Fei hu xiong xin 2 zhi ao qi bi tian gao* (Mandarin): "Flying Tiger Great Ambition 2: Arrogance Higher Than Heaven." Art Director: Cyrus Ho Kim-hung; Music: Lin Che-yeung; Writers: Manfred Wong, Candy Cheng; Producer: Manfred Wong; Action Director: Dion Lam Dik-on; Cinematographer-Director: Andrew Lau Wai-keung. Cast: Daniel Chan Hiu-tung (Chan Hiu-tung), Julian Cheung Chi-lam (Coolman Ho Chi-lum), Karen Mok Man-wai (Karen Kook), Roy Cheung Yiu-yeung (Eagle), Jerry Lam Hiu-fung (LoLo), Jason Chu Wing-tung (Hommie Chu Ka-choi), Amanda Lee Wai-man (Amanda), Annie Wu Chen-chun (Annie Ng Ching-yee), Damian Lau Chung-yan (Calvin Chan Lik-wang), Marianne Chan Miu-ying (Lily Yuen), Blackie Ko Shou-liang (Single Ball), Herman Yau Lai-to (Yuen Nam-sam). 1.85:1. VHS: Tai Seng. Import LD/VCD/DVD: New City. 107 minutes.

The Chinese title of this SDU action thriller passes it off as a sequel to **The Final Option**, though it is actually just another imitation of that Gordon Chan hit and has no connection. After some arms dealers decimate a SDU squad, another team of potential replacements is put through the brutal two week training period, under the command of Eagle (Roy Cheung, doing a much better job at playing the type of character Michael Wong undertook in **Option**). One of the trainees is Hiu-tung, a former patrolman who signed up after his partner was brutally murdered by a Vietnamese assassin. One of Hiu-tung's fellow candidates, Coolman, is openly hostile towards him, but Hiu-tung does not learn the reason why until his parents reveal a secret to him. For the final phase of their training, the men are sent to a deserted island for three days, only to run afoul of the Vietnamese arms dealers who killed Hiu-tung's partner.

As with the other entries in this subgenre, the first half is given over mostly to the training exercises, with the men's newly acquired skills put into play during the finale. The characters cover all of the usual stereotypes, but the action sequences are reasonably good and the film fulfils expectations. **Best of the Best** is of some note for addressing the fate of the Vietnamese being held in camps (who, by British agreement with Mainland authorities, had to be forcibly repatriated before HK returned to Chinese rule), though, like **Red Shield**, these refugees are largely depicted as savages, a sentiment that was in sync with most HK residents' view of them at the time.

69. Bet on Fire

(1988; Win's Movie Production) ★: 7/10. *Feng mo fung wan* (Cantonese), *Huo wu feng yun* (Mandarin): "Fire Dance Turbulence." Cinematographer: Tom Lau Moon-tong; Art Director: Carman Wan Siu-wai; Music: Romeo Diaz, Wong Chan; Writer: Manfred Wong; Producer: Jimmy Heung Wah-sing; Action Director: Stephen Tung Wai; Director: Joseph Cheung Tung-cho. Cast: Cherie Chung Cho-hung (Hung), Sharla Cheung Man (Man), Maria Cordero (Cat), Shing Fui-on (Madly), Paul Chun Pui (Tong Pun), To Lai-qui (Lovely), Wu Ma (Lau), Wong Jing (Bespectacled Sleazoid), Billy Lau Nam-kwong (V7 Guy #1), Stanley Fung Shui-fan (V7 Guy #2), Nat Chan Pak-cheung (V7 Guy #3), Charlie Cho Cha-lei (Charlie). 1.85:1. VHS: Tai Seng. Import LD/VCD: Ocean Shores. 95 minutes.

After her father is arrested and her mother is hospitalized with a heart ailment, pretty Mandy becomes a nightclub hostess in order to support her younger sister and pay for the operation their mother gravely needs. She learns the ropes from Hung, a seasoned B-Girl whose excessive drinking periodically lands her in the hospital. The two become close friends, watching out for each other while dealing with jealous co-workers and sleazy guests. When Hung loses all of her money in the 1988 stock market crash, she attempts suicide but is saved by Mandy's intervention. In order to help her, Mandy agrees to sleep with gangland boss Tong Pun, despite the fact that he and his men had previously raped Hung. Tong also refused to compensate Mandy's family when her father was imprisoned while trying to collect from one of Tong's debtors. When Mandy's father gets out of jail and discovers what has transpired, all hell breaks loose.

While this melodrama makes token attempts to present the life of HK clubgirls with a smidgen of verisimilitude, it is an exploitation movie first and foremost. On that level, it succeeds, thanks largely to an excellent performance by Cherie Chung and an effective one by Sharla Cheung (both in roles of greater depth than they are usually allotted). As the affluent villain ("You poor people dare struggle with me?"), Paul Chun adds some color with one of his customarily vivid characterizations. The violent finale is predictable but highly satisfying on an emotional level, which is where the film works best anyway.

70. A Better Tomorrow

(1986; Cinema City Co./Film Workshop) ★: 9/10. *Ying hung boon sik* (Cantonese), *Ying xiong ben se* (Mandarin): "The Essence of a Hero." Cinematographer: Horace Wong Wing-hang; Art Director: Bennie Lui Chi-leung; Music: Joseph Koo Kar-fai; Writers: John Woo Yu-sen, Chan Hing-ka, Leung Suk-wah; Producer: Tsui Hark; Action Directors: Blackie Ko Shou-liang, Stephen Tung Wai; Director: John Woo Yu-sen. Cast: Ti Lung (Sung Tse-ho), Chow Yun-fat (Mark Lee), Leslie Cheung Kwok-wing (Kit), Waise Lee Chi-hung (Shing), Emily Chu Bo-yee (Jackie), Kenneth Tsang Kong (Ken), Tien Feng (Mr. Sung), John Woo Yu-sen (Taiwan Police Chief), Shing Fui-on (Shing's Man), Tsui Hark (Audition Judge). Dolby Digital (DVD only). 1.85:1. VHS: Republic (Dubbed), Tai Seng. Import LD: Golden Cinema City. Import VCD: Mei Ah. Import DVD: Mega Star. 95 minutes.

In association with his longtime colleague Mark, gangster Sung Tse-ho has fashioned a successful counterfeiting operation—without the knowledge of his younger brother, Tse-kit, who has just graduated from the police academy. When their father is murdered as retribution for a deal gone awry, Tse-ho is double-crossed and sent to prison, and Mark is crippled while avenging his friend. In the interim, their empire is usurped by Shing, an ambitious underling who has little of Tse-ho's experience and none of his benevolence. Upon release, Tse-ho meets up again with Mark, and the two join forces to bring down Shing in order to protect Tse-kit, whose dogged pursuit of the crimelord has put his life in significant danger.

The most influential HK film of the 1980s, John Woo's glorious triad melodrama broke box office records and spawned a sequel, a prequel, and far too many imitations. Filled with superb, passionate performances all around, the film made a superstar out of Chow Yun-fat (unforgettable as the supercool triad who must regain his dignity after being crippled and enduring three years of abject humiliation). It also revived the career of former Shaw Brothers star Ti Lung (excellent as a honorable man caught in a predicament from which there is no deliverance) and got HK permanently cited as the gunplay capital of moviedom. Woo's apprenticeship with Chang Cheh shows through here in almost every scene: Following the structure of a traditional martial arts film, **A Better Tomorrow** carries on Chang's predominant themes of male camaraderie, the importance of honor, and the strength of true friendship to survive even the most adverse circumstances. It is a stirring piece of storytelling from a master craftsman that stands up to the test of time and multiple viewings. Mega Star released two DVD versions of the film; the first features substantial, inappropriate changes to the music track. The disc was later reissued with the original music tracks; that version carries a sticker that says "100% Original Music." Republic's abominable dubbed version (which also features some different musical cues) should also be avoided at all costs.

71. A Better Tomorrow II

(1987; Cinema City Co./Film Workshop) ★: 6/10. *Ying hung boon sik II* (Cantonese), *Ying xiong ben se II* (Mandarin): "The Essence of a Hero II." Cinematographer: Horace Wong Wing-hang; Art Director: Andy Lee Yiu-kwong; Music: Joseph Koo Kar-fai; Producer: Tsui Hark; Action Director: Ching Siu-tung; Writer-Director: John Woo Yu-sen. Cast: Ti Lung (Sung Chi-ho), Chow Yun-fat (Ken Lee), Leslie Cheung Kwok-wing (Sung Chi-kit), Dean Shek Tien (Lung), Kwan San (Ko Ying-pui), Emily Chu Bo-yee (Jackie), Kenneth Tsang Kong (Ken), Regina Kent (Peggy Lung), Shing Fui-on (Ko's Man), Lau Siu-ming (Inspector Wu), Lam Chung (Ko's Man), Lung Ming-yan (Chong), Ng Man-tat (Wong), Ken Boyle (Bearded Crime Boss). Dolby Digital (DVD only). 1.85:1. VHS: Tai Seng. Import LD: Golden Cinema City. Import VCD: Mei Ah (No Subtitles). Import DVD: Mega Star. 104 minutes.

Following the events depicted in the original, Sung Chi-ho (spelled "Tse-ho" in the previous film's subtitles) is offered a release from prison if he agrees to provide the authorities with information on his mentor, shipyard owner Lung. Sung's younger brother, police officer Chi-kit, has already gained Lung's confidence by romancing the man's daughter, Peggy. Out of fear for his brother's safety, Ho agrees to help. When a competitor out to take control of Lung's assets is murdered, Lung is convinced that he himself pulled the trigger and flees to New York City, where he goes insane following an attempt on his life. While Mark's twin brother Ken nurses Lung back to sanity and deals with extortion threats from the Italian Mafia, Chi-ho and Kit both find their lives on the line. After Lung magically returns to normal during a gun battle, he and Ken journey back to HK in order to even the score with Ko, the associate of Lung who betrayed him and stole his business.

There were reportedly two conflicting schools of thought at work in the creation of this sequel. On the one hand, John Woo sought to continue down the path he had established, centering events around the relationship between the Sung brothers. On the other hand, producer Tsui Hark and Cinema City partner Dean Shek saw the film as a perfect comeback vehicle for the latter, whose career had taken a downturn (Shek is even given star billing in the credits). The two sides apparently never reconciled their differences: Woo's cut was drastically reworked by Tsui, without any input from its director. This rift between the two former friends also led Tsui to take the job of helming **A Better Tomorrow III** himself, prompting Woo to film the story he had originally conceived for that film on his own as **Bullet in the Head**. The behind-the-scenes row is certainly evident in the final product, which lacks the emotional power of its forerunner and suffers from the inclusion of elements awkwardly celebrating the status the first film achieved (a former crony of Mark and Ho keeps "memorabilia" in a glass case and makes sketches of exploits he couldn't possibly have seen, while the kids hanging out in Ken's restaurant dress and act like Mark, just as happened in HK after the original was released). Also, the NYC sequences with Lung and Ken are far less interesting than the moments shared by Chi-ho and Chi-kit, and Shek's mad act is often ludicrously over-the-top. However, there are still some fine moments, courtesy of Ti Lung and Leslie Cheung (with the latter doing an excellent job of enhancing an underwritten part) and the justifiably famous guns-and-grenades finale serves up as visceral a charge as you will find in the genre.

72. A Better Tomorrow III

(1989; Cinema City Co./Golden Princess/Film Workshop) ★: 8/10. *Ying hung boon sik III: jik yeung ji gor* (Cantonese), *Ying xiong ben se III: tzu yang tsu gor* (Mandarin): "The Essence of a Hero III: Song of the Setting Sun." Cinematographer: Horace Wong Wing-hang; Art Director: Luk Chi-fung; Music: Lowell Lo Kwun-ting; Writers: Tai Fu-ho, Edward Leung Yiu-ming; Action Directors: Lau Hong-sai, Lau Chi-ho; Producer-Director: Tsui Hark. Cast: Chow Yun-fat (Mark), Anita Mui Yim-fong (Chow Ying-kit), Tony Leung Kar-fai (Cheung Chi-mun), Saburo Tokito (Ho Cheung-ching), Shih Kien (Chi-mun's Father). Dolby Digital (DVD only). 1.85:1. VHS: Tai Seng. Import LD: Golden Cinema City (114 minutes). Import VCD: Universe. Import DVD: Mega Star (114 minutes). 100/114/130 minutes. Also known as **Love and Death in Saigon**.

Tsui Hark's prequel to the previous films takes place in 1974, allowing him to have Chow Yun-fat reprise his "Mark" character from the original. When his cousin, Cheung Chi-mun, gets into trouble with the local authorities, Mark journeys to Saigon to bail him out of jail. The two set up a black market weapons deal with the beautiful Chow Ying-kit, using guns obtained from Chi-mun's contact, a Vietnamese army commander. Their arranged exchange turns out to be a trap from which the three barely escape alive. The trio plan to leave Vietnam and head back to HK, with Chi-mun's father in tow, but when trouble occurs at customs, Ying-kit must stay behind to act as a witness. Back in HK, Chi-mun and Mark open a car repair business. When Ying-kit finally does meet up with them, it is not long before her old boyfriend, mobster Ho Cheung-ching, appears as well. Ying-kit loves Mark but he intentionally shuns her, as he knows that Chi-mun has fallen for her. Ho feels so threatened by the two men that he tries to kill them with a bomb; when that fails, he merely warns them to leave HK or face certain death. Although she loves Mark, Ying-kit returns to Saigon with Ho, evidently planning to murder him as retribution for his actions. Mark and Chi-mun follow, planning to save her and kill Ho themselves. With the American troops pulling out of Saigon, the city is in chaos, making their task all the more difficult.

Very different in style and mood from Woo's films, Tsui's entry revolves around a strong female protagonist, something not seen in Woo's work. While Woo made icons out of Chow Yun-fat and Ti Lung, Tsui perfectly exploits Anita Mui's singular screen presence. The brotherly bond between Chow and Leung remains a key ingredient, but it is Mui (in a role that beautifully bonds the traditional femme fatale with the sort of forceful and resourceful woman rarely seen in this genre) who is the heart and spirit of the film, as both the object of affection and the most multifarious character. In a bit of elaboration that might not have gone over well with Woo, it is Ying-kit who not only teaches Mark how to wield a gun but even picks out his trademark overcoat and sunglasses! With Lowell Lo's superb, melancholy score perfectly complementing the emotions, this is superior melodrama, almost on par with the original, though those expecting the level of gunplay found previously will be disappointed. The soundtrack includes a cue recycled from **The Big Heat**. Taiwan prints run 130 minutes.

73. Beware of Pickpockets

(1981; Cinema City Co.) ★: 2/10. *Foon lok san sin woh* (Cantonese), *Huan le shen xian wo* (Mandarin): "The Merry Supernatural Nest." Cinematographer: Ho Ming; Art Director: Chuen Tai-yung; Music: Joseph Koo Kar-fai; Writer: Raymond Wong Pak-ming; Producer: Karl Maka; Director: Wu Ma. Cast: Dean Shek Tien (The Pickpocket), Wu Ma (The Superintendent), Karl Maka (Big Nose), Raymond Wong Pak-ming (Dishonest Diner), Liu On-lai, Cheung Kar-wai. 2.35:1. VHS: Tai Seng (Poor Subtitles). Import VCD: Mega Star. 90 minutes.

Here's **Oliver!** HK style, with Dean Shek doing one of the Chaplinesque turns he specialized in at the time. He plays a kind-hearted pickpocket who takes care of seven young orphan boys in a rundown church called "Fairyland." Karl Maka plays the bumbling beat cop on his trail, and Wu Ma is his equally incompetent superior: Both want Shek's head for the embarrassments he has caused them over the years. When faced with eviction for non-payment of rent, Shek tries to steal some jewels from his evil brother, Dog Lice.

While some viewers might enjoy the novelty of Cantonese musical numbers, the tired slapstick (with many pratfalls lifted directly from vintage Warner Brothers cartoons) and heavy-handed pathos are headache-inducing and will impress no one. The running time listed above is for the Taiwan video version, released by New Ship Film Enterprise Company. The Mega Star VCD carries the incorrect English title **Beware of Pickets**.

74. Beyond Hypothermia

(1996; Sanqueen/Milky Way Image) ★: 4/10. *Sip si 32 doe* (Cantonese), *She shi 32 du* (Mandarin): "Celcius 32 Degrees." Cinematographer: Arthur Wong Ngok-tai; Art Director: Bruce Yu Kar-on; Music: Ben Cheung Siu-hung; Writer: Szeto Wai-cheuk; Producer: Johnny To Kei-fung; Action Directors: Yuen Tak, Yuen Bun; Director: Patrick Leung Pak-kin. Cast: Jacqueline Wu Chien-lien (The Killer), Lau Ching-wan (Long Shek), Han Sang-woo (Yichin), Shirley Wong Sa-lei, Cheung Sung-kei. 1.85:1. VHS/LD: World Video. Import LD/VCD: Mei Ah. 85 minutes.

This violent thriller about a female assassin with a lower than normal body temperature (an interesting idea that is never explored to any significant degree) has a very promising opening third but goes astray, finally self-destructing with an utterly ludicrous finale. The nameless killer (who is friends only with a possessive Cambodian woman who passes along information about targets and the money she is to be paid) performs her hits with a professional, icy demeanor but finds that she must unwind afterwards by having a bowl of noodles at a food vendor's stand. This becomes a routine for her, and she develops an emotional attachment to Long Shek, the kindly vendor (who nicknames the woman "Pretty Ghost") whose company helps to bring a warmth and stimulation to her otherwise detached life. Pretty Ghost goes to South Korea for a job and eliminates the boss of a local syndicate, which sets the dead man's chief bodyguard, Yichin, on a bloody trail of vengeance. Yichin discovers the identity of the assassin's go-between, and the woman elects to betray Pretty Ghost, a decision made easy by the fact that the latter has announced her intention to retire.

Once again, Wu and Lau work well together, and the former very effectively conveys the gradual humanizing of her character. Unfortunately, as with the director's **Somebody Up There Likes Me**, agressively stylized visuals overwhelm the story, and the final reel is (to put it charitably) an ill-conceived mess that undermines the film to a fatal degree. Watch **On the Run** instead.

75. Beyond the Sunset

(1989; Dream Factory Film Co.) ★: 7/10. *Fei yuet wong fan* (Cantonese), *Fei yue huang hun* (Mandarin): "Fly Over the Sunset." Cinematographer: Kin Lee Kin-keung; Art Director: Yank Wong Yan-kwai; Music: Chan Wing-leung; Writers: Jacob Cheung Chi-leung, Chan Kam-cheung; Producer: Chung Man-keung; Director: Jacob Cheung Chi-leung. Cast: Petrina Fung Bo-bo (May), Cecilia Yip Tung (Pearl), Richard Ng Yiu-hon (Wong), Lowell Lo Kwun-ting (Allen), Alexander Roels (Derek). 1.85:1. VHS: World Video. Import LD/VCD: Universe. 115 minutes.

A strained relationship between mother and daughter is the basis of this drama, which served as a comeback vehicle for former child star Petrina Fung. Single mother May feels that she gave up everything to raise her daughter Pearl, only to have the girl go against her wishes when she grew up. Out of defiance, Pearl moved to America and married a man that she has not even introduced to her mother. Now, a number of years later, Pearl returns to HK, with her young son in tow, in order to try and patch things up.

The film tells about how children can forget their elders and depicts the maladroit gestures each party must make as they inch toward a reconciliation. The situations are overly familiar, but the film does an effective job of capturing the emotions of everyday characters, and the quality of the performances go a long way in selling the drama. Fung and Cecilia Yip (who can seem to do no wrong in any film) are very good, and comedian Richard Ng gives a natural, engaging turn as a shy, kindly swimming coach with a heart condition who becomes a companion for the lonely May. **Beyond the Sunset** won the Best Picture, Best Script, and Best Supporting Actress (Cecilia Yip) prizes at The Ninth HK Film Awards.

76. Big Bullet

(1996; Golden Harvest/Paragon Films) ★: 7/10. *Chung fung dui liu feng gaai tau* (Cantonese), *Chong feng dui nu huo jie tou* (Mandarin): "Emergency Unit: Angry Fire on the Streets." Cinematographer: Arthur Wong Ngok-tai; Art Director: Eddie Ma Poon-chiu; Music: Peter Kam Pui-tat; Writers: Susanne Chan Suk-yin, Joe Ma Wai-ho; Action Director: Ma Yuk-shing; Producer-Director: Benny Chan Muk-sing. Cast: Lau Ching-wan (Bill Zhu), Jordan Chan Siu-chun (Jeff), Cheung Tat-ming (Matt), Theresa Lee Yee-hung (Apple), Francis Ng Chun-yu (Yang), Anthony Wong Chau-sang ("Bird"), Yu Rongguang ("Professor"). Dolby Digital (DVD only). 1.85:1. VHS: Tai Seng. Import LD/VCD/DVD: Universe. 91 minutes. Also known as **EU Strike Force** (Singapore title).

Now that police procedural specialist Che-Kirk Wong has departed to Hollywood, one of his successors in the genre could turn out to be a man few would have placed at the forefront of HK filmmakers: Benny Chan Muk-sing. With the notable exception of his slick, trend-setting action-drama **A Moment of Romance** (1990), Chan's work has been uniformly lackluster, leading some to attribute the high quality of **Romance** to the production involvement of Johnny To and Ringo Lam. With **Big Bullet**, he finally displayed some genuine proficiency once again and transformed a potentially mundane cop actioner into a witty, economical, and consistently exciting thriller. In addition to impressing many HK critics, the film obviously struck a chord with Jackie Chan, who tapped him to co-direct his next movie, **Who Am I?** (1998). Lau Ching-wan stars here as Zhu, a distinguished but short-fused officer who is transferred to the "Emergency Unit" after decking his incompetent superior. When his friend and former superior Yang is killed during a mob hit, Zhu leads his ragtag team of EU subordinates way out of their jurisdiction and into direct conflict with the criminals. After a daring robbery of $9 million in US dollars from Interpol headquarters, the gang tries to get the money out of HK aboard a hijacked British transport craft, leading to an exciting battle both inside and *on top of* the plane.

Like Steven Tung's equally diverting **Fox Hunter** (1995), **Big Bullet** never strays beyond the bounds of its genre but does such a good job in every department that the cliches become amiable rather than tiresome. In contrast to the standard HK action star vehicles, this is peopled almost solely by character actors and comedians, all of whom turn in fine work. Lau Ching-wan is one of HK's busiest performers, specializing in offbeat characterizations in both comedies and dramas, and he does a first rate job as an action hero. One of HK's most promising new stars, Theresa Lee is marvellous as a spunky Canadian-born cop with a knack for computers, while Cheung Tat-ming and Spencer Lam provide some well-timed comic relief. The wittiest bit of casting, however, is the decision to have Jordan Chan (best known for his seemingly endless stream of roles as petty gangsters and *Generasian* X losers) play the requisite straight-laced, by-the-book cop in the group. It's a definite stretch for him but he's more than up to it. As the villains, Wong and Yu are more restrained than usual and are overshadowed by the heroes, which is the way it really should be anyway (name one recent Hollywood action film where the villain *didn't* outshine the hero). Dayo Wong Chi-wah puts in a characteristic appearance as a flaky informant, and actor/director Vincent Kok Tak-chiu appears briefly as an officer who keeps Zhu abreast of developments at headquarters.

77. Big Circle Blues

(1992; Big Business Movie Company) ★: 1/10. *Foh baau daai huen jai* (Cantonese), *Huo bao da quan zi* (Mandarin): "Fire Explodes the Big Circle." Cinematographer: Wong Wing-chung; Music: Not Original; Writers: Chan Hiu-bing, Fu Nam-ying; Producer: Cheung Wing-kit; Action Director: Lung Sang; Director: Chow Cheung. Cast: Michiko Nishiwaki (Show-yun), Mark Cheng Ho-nam (Wei), Wu Ma (Police Chief), Gary Siu Yuk-lung (Young). 1.85:1. VHS: Tai Seng (Poor Subtitles). 87 minutes.

Even the most undemanding action fans will have trouble making it through this turgid effort, which is inept on every level. After pulling a jewellery store robbery in HK, some ruthless Mainland thieves travel to Taiwan, where they plan to exchange the booty for cash. Their fence gives them far less than they are entitled to, prompting the criminals to raid and destroy one of the man's drug operations. Mark Cheng and Michiko Nishiwaki play squabbling cops on the crooks' trail, who must wade through a pile of corpses as the bandits rob and murder their way across the country, playing cross and double cross with the fence's men.

There is immoderate gunplay but absolutely no *elan*—and that, coupled with poor performances, awful stock music, feeble scripting, and glacial pacing make this one to definitely pass up.

78. The Big Deal

(1992; Joe Siu International Film) ★: 2/10. *Tan san fung chuk* (Cantonese), *Tou shen gu zu* (Mandarin): "Godly Theft Clan." Cinematographer: Wong Chit; Music: Not Original; Writer: Lee Ho-kwan; Producer: Joe Siu King-kai; Action Director: Yuen Cheung-yan; Director: Wong Chun-yeung. Cast: Moon Lee Choi-fung (May), Yukari Oshima (Sim-lan), Tommy Wong Kwong-leung (Lethal Weapon/Mad Bill/Fish Ball Vendor/Wan the Pimp), Sibelle Hu Hui-chung (Super Canon), Yuen Wah (Tee Tung-feng, aka "The Saint Hero"), Yuen Cheung-yan (Che Hai), Woo Fung (Inspector), Sophia Crawford (Saint Hero's Girlfriend), Gabriel Wong Yat-san (Taxi Driver), Isabella Chow Wang (Beauty with Deep Voice), John Wakefield (Guy with Calculator). 1.85:1. VHS: Tai Seng. Import LD/VCD: Universe. 96 minutes.

Those who have little tolerance for the unabashed silliness that characterizes the work of Wong Jing and Chu Yen-ping are advised to give this cheapjack comedy a wide berth. A graduate of the "anything for a laugh" school of humor, the film's enthusiasm is admirable, but the hit and miss ratio is much lower than comparable endeavours from Wong and Chu. May and Sim-lan are bickering thieves who are constantly driving their master, Che Hai, crazy with their non-stop fighting. Their paths cross with Super Canon (spelled like the copier company) and Lethal Weapon, two very unconventional police officers who are out to nab the notorious Saint Hero (who just happens to be an old student of Che Hai). All of the miscreants are after an invaluable painting and an ancient sword but seem more interested in making faces and knocking each other senseless with whatever is within reach. *The Big Deal* is strangely watchable for the lengths the director is willing to go in pursuit of even the cheapest laugh but never genuinely amusing.

79. The Big Heat

(1988; Cinema City Co./Film Workshop) ★: 8/10. *Sing si dak ging* (Cantonese), *Cheng shi te jing* (Mandarin): "Big City Special Police." Cinematographer: Horace Wong Wing-hang; Art Directors: Benny Lui Chi-leung, Raymond Chan Kam-ho; Music: Lo Tai-yau; Writer: Gordon Chan Kar-seung; Producer: Tsui Hark; Action Directors: Chu Kai-sang, Phillip Kwok Tsui, Wong Kwan; Directors: Andrew Kam Yeung-wah, Johnny To Kei-fung. Cast: Waise Lee Chi-hung (John Wong Wai-pong), Phillip Kwok Tsui (Kam, aka Tangerine), Joey Wang Tsu-hsien (Ada), Paul Chu Kong (Han Ching), Yung Sai-kit (Ho Ka-nin), Peter Lai Bei-tak (Peter Ng), Matthew Wong Hin-mung (Lun Kwok-keung), Ken Boyle (Wong's Superior), Roy Cheung Yiu-yeung (Ho's Man), Michael Chow Man-kin (Scarfaced Hood), Robin Shou Wan-bo (Hospital Assassin), Che-Kirk Wong Chi-keung (Gangster Who Gets Hand Blown Off). 1.85:1. VHS: Tai Seng. Import LD: Golden Cinema City. Import VCD: Megastar (Censored version). 98 minutes.

It is wholly fitting that this gritty, violent police actioner draws its English title from Fritz Lang's 1953 classic. Both are tough, exciting, and above average for the genre. Faced with quitting the force because of nerve damage that is retarding his reaction time with a gun, cop John Wong is resigned to his fate. However, he changes his mind upon learning that his ex-partner (who had previously saved his life) has been brutally murdered in Malaysia. Working with partner Kam, bumbling rookie Lun, and Malaysian cop Ong Chat-fu, Wong is able to deduce that affluent businessmen Ho Ka-nin and Han Ching are at the center of the case, which appears to be a blackmail attempt by Wong's associate that turned deadly. Ho's homosexual preferences have been captured on film, and his underworld dealings with Han will be compromised if the pictures are made public. The reason for this is that Han is blackmailing the man himself and will do anything to keep this fact from the police in order to keep his drug smuggling operation going. Wong and his men must face not only Han's gang of killers but also the roadblocks his power and connections put in front of them, including a high-ranking police official on his payroll.

Any film that opens with a power drill piercing a man's hand means business, and the villains of **The Big Heat** die the sort of horrible deaths rarely seen outside of slasher films. While the violence quotient and nihilistic presentation certainly increase the film's shock value, it still remains a compelling police procedural centered around a (then) timely issue: the 1997 handover to China. Han cites the occasion as the motivating factor behind his illegal activities (as one of his Russian partners puts it, "Selling drugs and capitalism together is the best way"). This is the movie that pioneered the famous "shoot the hostage in the leg" setpiece (later copied in **Speed**), which was sent up two years later in **Forbidden Arsenal** (with Waise Lee on the other end of the gun!). The VCD version is heavily cut. The soundtrack includes a brief bit of music lifted from John Carpenter's **Prince of Darkness**.

80. The Big Score

(1990; Grand March Movie Production Co.) ★: 6/10. *Juet kiu ji doh sing* (Cantonese), *Jue qiao zhi duo xing* (Mandarin): "Peerless Scam Artist All Stars." Cinematographer: Gigo Lee Chi-hang; Art Director: Jon Hau Wing-choi; Music: Lowell Lo Kwun-ting; Producer: Wong Tin-lam; Action Director: Wong Kwan; Writer-Director: Wong Jing. Cast: Danny Lee Sau-yin (Kung Ching), Joey Wang Tsu-hsien (Penny), Wong Jing (Soft), Lung Fong (Panther Wong), Anthony Wong Chau-sang (Ma Qun), Tang Shui-man (Ling), Agnes Aurelio (Female Assassin). 1.85:1. VHS: Tai Seng. Import LD/VCD: Universe. 106 minutes.

Wong Jing produced, directed, and co-starred in this action comedy, and his mark is all over it. Determined Inspector Kung Ching has spent three years trying to nail big time gangster Panther Wong. With the help of undercover cop Ma Qun, Kung is able to arrest him, but the gangster's men exact revenge by horribly crippling Ma and murdering his wife and young daughter. Furthermore, the computer disc and papers containing the evidence needed to make the case stand up in court are stolen, allowing Wong to go free. Hampered by a superior with a personal vendetta against him, Kung quits the force and joins up with Ma's old buddy Soft, a shifty gambler, to exact revenge. The gangster has a soft spot for snooty society dame Penny, whom he is blackmailing, so Kung turns on the charm and wins her over. Together the three friends hope to bilk Wong out of all his money, which would leave the gangster at the mercy of his merciless bosses.

In true Wong Jing fashion, **The Big Score** is all over the map, blending the requisite car chases and shootouts with uneasy shifts from gruesome violence to broad slapstick. Soft's unique talents at the gaming tables even allowed the film to ride the wave of success generated by the director's box office smashes, **Casino Raiders** and **God of Gamblers** (both 1989). There is also the usual quota of uniquely Cantonese humor, no better example of which can be found than in the way that Kung wins Penny over: He takes her to a particularly scummy restaurant and convinces her that their main dish is Penny's pet poodle! Works every time.

81. A Bite of Love

(1990; D & B Films Co.) ★: 5/10. *Yat aau OK* (Cantonese), *Yi yao OK* (Mandarin): "One Bite, OK." Cinematographer: Cheng Siu-keung; Art Director: Ringo Cheung Sek-wah; Music: George Lam Chi-cheung, Danny Chung Teng-yat; Writers: Leung Hung-wah, Cheng Siu-keung; Producer-Director: Stephen Shin Kei-yin. Cast: George Lam Chi-cheung (Duke Lee), Rosamund Kwan Chi-lam (Anna), Norman Tsui Siu-keung (Fung), Hui Siu-hung. 1.85:1. Dolby Stereo. VHS: Tai Seng. Import LD/VCD: Universe. 94 minutes.

The runaway success of Golden Harvest's horror-comedy **Mr. Vampire** (1985) resulted in an avalanche of sequels and imitations, with Hong Kong movie screens soon overrun by a veritable army of *gyonsi* (hopping vampires). This passable effort from D & B Films goes a different route, making light of European vampire conventions instead. The aristocratic Duke Lee prides himself on leading a more civilized lifestyle than his fellow bloodsuckers, dining only on animal blood. When oncoming bankruptcy threatens to put his British castle on the auction block, he finds some welcome diversion in the company of the beautiful Anna. His plans for romantic bliss are short-circuited by Anna's brother, a Triad heroin dealer suffering from a terminal illness. When the Duke uses his life-enhancing blood to save a mortally injured little boy, the gangster sees this as the ticket to regaining his health. Kidnapping Lee and the child, he uses their blood to revitalize himself but is later vampirized when the two unwilling donors make their escape. His inherently evil nature transforms him into a formidable adversary, who is more than a match for the weakened Duke and the skeptical Anna.

Granted a fairly sizeable budget, director Stephen Shin (**Black Cat I & 2**) was able to enhance the proceedings with some British location work, flashy opticals, sync sound recording, and a Dolby Stereo mix. Unfortunately, after an effective opening half, the proceedings start to flag under the weight of narrative contrivances (e.g., Anna meets up with an erstwhile Van Helsing in a laserdisc shop, where the climactic staking from **Fright Night** just happens to be playing on a store monitor!). *A Bite of Love* is an affable enough diversion overall, but Western horror mythos were sent up to better effect that same year in Jamie Luk Kim-ming's **Doctor Vampire**.

82. Black Cat

(1991; D & B Films Co.) ★: 5/10. *Hak mau* (Cantonese), *Hei mao* (Mandarin): "Black Cat." Cinematographer: Kin Lee Kin-keung; Art Director: Fu Chi-chung; Music: Danny Chung Teng-yat; Writers: Lam Wai-lun, Lam Dan-ping, Chan Bo-sun; Action Directors: Benz Kong To-hoi, Tony Poon Kin-kwan; Producer-Director: Stephen Shin Kei-yin. Cast: Jade Leung Ching (Erica/Catherine), Simon Yam Tat-wah (Brian), Thomas Lam Cho-fai (Allen Yeung). Dolby Digital (DVD only). 1.85:1. VHS: Tai Seng. Import LD: Ocean Shores. Import VCD: Ocean Shores, Mega Star. Import DVD: Mega Star. 95 minutes.

A blatant ripoff of Luc Besson's **La Femme Nikita**, this rather unpleasant actioner is even less satisfying than its overrated model. In her debut role, Jade Leung plays a vicious derelict who escapes from police custody while being transported to her trial. After being captured by a top secret agency and having a computer chip implanted in her brain (the "Black Cat" of the title, which is supposed to increase her potential but is soon forgotten after it is introduced), she is trained in all manner of assassination techniques and sent out into the field. After performing one hit, she is photographed by a wildlife protection officer (Thomas Lam). Although she has ample opportunity to kill the witness, Leung instead strikes up a relationship with him. Her ties to the agency begin to disintegrate when an old friend from Leung's past dies in a suspicious explosion and her lover becomes aware of what she does for a living.

Leung handles the physical aspects of the part well, but her character is not especially interesting and neither are her dramatic travails. As it follows the French film so closely, the storyline offers no surprises, save for a twist involving Lam's character that is laughably contrived. The sync sound recording here is actually a drawback, revealing the severe limitations of the caucasian performers. Some good action sequences, location work in Vancouver, New York, and Japan, and an invigorating score by Danny Chung provide partial compensation. A sequel followed the next year.

83. Black Cat 2: Assassination of President Yeltsin

(1992; D & B Films Co.) ★: 3/10. *Hak mau 2* (Cantonese), *Hei mao 2* (Mandarin): "Black Cat 2." Cinematographers: Cheng Siu-keung, Leung Lik-chi, Lee Chi-wah; Music: Chris Babida; Writers: James Fung Shui-hung, Sin Kam-ching, Ivy Lee Mo-king; Action Director: Tony Poon Kin-kwan; Producer-Director: Stephen Shin Kei-yin. Cast: Jade Leung Ching (Erica), Robin Shou Wan-bo (Robin). Dolby Stereo, Dolby Digital (DVD only). 1.85:1. VHS: Tai Seng. Import LD: Universe. Import VCD: Universe, Mega Star. Import DVD: Mega Star. 90 minutes.

This ambitious but frequently laughable follow-up opens with Jade Leung's assassin undergoing another operation to implant a new, experimental microchip into her brain. With her memory now wiped, the "B2" chip transforms her into a Terminator-like killing machine that can be switched off by remote control! She is teamed with fellow agent Robin Shou (who receives an "introduction" credit here, despite the fact that he had made a number of movies prior to this one) to track down and destroy AYO ("The Anti-Yeltsin Organization"), a terrorist group out to murder the controversial president (played by an almost dead-on lookalike). Several members of the opposition have been given a special radioactive drug to enhance their capabilities, and that foreign chemical element in their bodies allows Leung's enhanced senses to track them.

This one outdoes its predecessor in terms of action, presenting a James Bond-style ski chase in addition to the usual car chases and hand-to-hand combat. However, none of these sequences are particularly well-staged, being marred by choppy editing and/or silly wirework. The sci-fi twist added here was clearly inspired by **Terminator 2: Judgment Day** (there is even a battle in a steel mill), and it is merely silly, making the already shaky plotting even harder to swallow. While Leung's character was poorly developed last time out, she is nothing but a lovely prop here, striking poses with handguns while clad in chic, designer outfits. Unlike the original, which offered a mix of Cantonese and English dialogue, this one is dubbed in the former langauge. An expensive flop, **Black Cat 2**'s only lasting claim to fame is that it was the project that helped put D & B Films out of business.

84. Black Magic with Buddha

(1983) ★: 5/10. *Lo moh* (Cantonese), *Nao mo* (Mandarin): "Brain Magic." Cinematographer: Wong Wing-lung; Art Director: Ting Yuen-tai; Music: Not Original; Writer: Chiu Chi-kin; Producer: Gracy Wong Tong Kar-lee; Director: Lo Lieh. Cast: Chen Kuan-tai (Chin Ben), Candice Yu On-on (Annie), Lo Lieh (The Sorcerer), Man Yu-wah. 2.35:1. VHS: Tai Seng (Poor Subtitles). 94 minutes. Also known as **Black Magic with Butchery**.

An enjoyably silly horror thriller patterned after the Shaw Brothers' **Black Magic** films from the mid '70s, this low-budget entry was directed by veteran actor Lo Lieh (who also appears in a supporting role as a sorcerer), best known in the West for his lead role in the kung fu hit **Five Fingers of Death** (1972; aka **King Boxer**). In Indonesia to try and make his fortune, Chin Ben and a local guide stumble across a tomb that houses an ancient mummy. The man removes the corpse's brain and gives it to Chin, telling him that it possesses the power to grant him a wish—provided he feeds it an animal brain once a day. He also gives Chin a vial of holy water with which he can destroy the evil thing afterwards. Returning home, Chin sets about changing his life, but, as one might expect, the brain giveth and the brain taketh away. After he wishes for great wealth, Chin's wealthy sister is killed by the creature. He receives an inheritance but it is not as great a sum as he had hoped. Subsequently, Chin does not destroy the thing and neglects to feed it, prompting the brain to go on a rampage, possessing Chin's girlfriend and, later, Chin himself.

While a certain amount of the storyline was never really meant to be taken seriously, **Black Magic with Buddha** is compromised by its dimestore special effects and stock score, which consists largely of the same shock cue repeated over and over to unintentionally comic effect. Still, the proceedings are quite atmospheric, and the movie is definitely of interest to horror fans, who will revel in the enthusiastically applied gore and Eastern supernatural elements. In addition to the aforementioned track, music from **Phantasm** and **Alien** can also be heard.

Black Magic with Butchery *see* **Black Magic With Buddha**

85. Black Mask

(1996; Win's Entertainment/Film Workshop) ★: 5/10 (HK Version), ★: 4/10 (US Version). *Hak hap* (Cantonese), *Hei xia* (Mandarin): "Black Knight." Cinematographer: Cheung Tung-leung; Art Directors: Eddie Ma Poon-chiu, Bill Lui Cho-hung; Music: Teddy Robin Kwan, Ben Vaughn (the latter in US version only); Writers: Tsui Hark, Koan Hui-on, Teddy Chan Tak-sam, Joe Ma Wai-ho; Producer: Tsui Hark; Action Directors: Yuen Woo-ping, Kuk Hin-chiu, Dion Lam Dik-on; Director: Daniel Lee Yan-kong. Cast: Jet Li Lianjie (Tsui Chik), Lau Ching-wan (Detective Shek Wai-ho, aka "The Rock"), Karen Mok Man-wai (Tracy), Francoise Yip Fong-wah (Yeuk-lan), Patrick Lung Kong (Hung), Chung King-fai (Police Commissioner), Moses Chan Ho (701 Member), Henry Fong Ping (Tai), Anthony Wong Chau-sang (King Kau), Xiong Xinxin (Kau's Man), Lawrence Ah Mon (Operating Room Doctor). Dolby Digital. 1.85:1. VHS/DVD: Artisan (Dubbed). Import LD/VCD/DVD: Mei Ah. 98 minutes (HK version)/90 minutes (US version).

Adapted from a HK comic book, this Jet Li action thriller is bogged down by tiresomely overblown visuals, choppy editing, and a weak, uninteresting storyline. Squad 701 is a special combat team whose members have all undergone brain surgery to remove their nerves. As they can literally feel no pain, this gives them a tremendous advantage over opponents. However, after the experiment goes awry, the team members are ordered terminated. Several of them escape, one of whom now works as a librarian under the name Tsui Chik. All of HK's drug dealers have been brutally murdered by unknown assailants, save for one: King Kau. Before the police can protect him, Kau is seriously injured by Yeuk-lan, one of the Squad 701 soldiers and a confederate of Tsui. Having taken control of his fellow surviving 701 members, a madman named Hung plans to corner the world drug market, and Tsui (who has adopted a superhero persona and been nicknamed "Black Mask" by the press) is the only one powerful enough to effectively oppose him.

Never more than mildly diverting, **Black Mask** is so filled with clutter it is difficult to concentrate on anything else. There is no shortage of action, but the setpieces are awkwardly assembled and generally lack a sense of excitement or exhilaration, doing little to make the story any more engaging. The sequence in which Tsui and Hung battle in a room filled with poison gas is merely a more elaborate version of a similar fight in Li's **The Bodyguard from Beijing**, which was already a reprise of an identical battle in **Tiger Cage** (the latter was helmed by Yuen Woo-ping, who serves as action director here). Lau Ching-wan is wasted as a tough cop, nicknamed "The Rock," and Karen Mok's ultra-perky and emotional heroine seems better suited to an *anime*. Jet Li's charisma manages to shine through on occasion, but as a hero, Black Mask is stoic to the point of being almost entirely colorless. A shortened version was released to domestic theaters by Artisan Entertainment in 1999. The dubbing on that edition is a slight step above that given to the Jackie Chan films (Canadian-born Francoise Yip does her own voice), but the original soundtrack has been replaced with tiresome hip hop tunes that make the film even more of a strain. Original composer Teddy Robin Kwan is still credited on the Artisan version, despite the fact that his music is used only in the trailer and TV spots. Ironically, the American release contains a bit more violence than the HK print, which was cut to secure a IIB rating.

86. The Black Morning Glory

(1993; ERA Pictures/Gold Harbour International) ★: 5/10. *Dip ying ging ching luk ye jui gik* (Cantonese), *Da ying jing qing lu ye zhui ji* (Mandarin): "Repeat Shadow Frighten Love: Pursue Enemy in the Green Country." Cinematographer: Eric Chu Kwok-fai; Art Directors: Raymond Kwok Siu-keung, Eric Lam Yau-sang; Music: Johnny Yeung Kei-cheung; Writers: Joyce Cheung Lai-ling, Shirley Woo Suet-lai; Producers: Andrew Leung Chung-chu, Chan Hon-fai; Action Director: Cho Wing; Director: Casey Chan Laiying. Cast: Michelle Lee Kar-yan (Michelle Lam Man-ting/Fan Lin), Lau Sik-ming (Michael Fu Ka-kit), Lester Chan Chit-man (Ken Wong), Waise Lee Chi-hung (Tsao Wing), Woo Fung (Uncle Wu), Cho Wing (Kinju). 1.85:1. VHS: Tai Seng. 90 minutes.

In Japan to supervise a fashion show, Michelle Lam is murdered one evening by Fan Lin, an assassin who is her exact duplicate. The two knew each other as children but were separated when Lin was kidnapped and sold. Working from instructions provided by her Japanese client, Lin returns to the coastal island where she grew up, and steps into Michelle's shoes. Her mission is to retrieve a disc which Michelle's double-dealing boyfriend Ken needs to complete his end of a major counterfeiting deal. Michael, a lawyer/gardener who knew both Michelle and Lin as children, falls back in love with the mysterious woman, while his friend, Officer Tsao, suspects her of murder when the real Michelle's body is discovered by Japanese authorities.

Gorgeous Michelle Lee does a passable job in the dual role, but this modestly budgeted thriller fails to capitalize on the possibilities offered by its premise, and the final reel serves up one tired cliche after another. The English title refers to a new strain of morning glory that Michael has created. Lee would go on to play a hitwoman again the following year in **The Other Side of the Sea**.

87. The Black Panther Warriors

(1993; In-Gear Film Production Co.) ★: 2/10. *Hak paau tin ha* (Cantonese), *Hei bao tian xia* (Mandarin): "Black Panthers Rule the Sky and Earth." Cinematographers: Arthur Wong Ngok-tai, Jingle Ma Cho-shing, Gigo Lee Chi-hang, William Yim Wai-lun, Cheung Tung-leung, Eric Chu Kwok-fai; Music: Lowell Lo Kwunting; Writer: Sammy Tsang Kan-cheung; Producer: Rover Tang Kwong-chow; Action Director: Lau Sung-feng; Director: Clarence Fok Yiu-leung. Cast: Alan Tang Kwong-wing (Black Cougar), Brigitte Lin Ching-hsia (Ching-ching), Tony Leung Kar-fai (Mo Po, aka Black Jack Lover), Simon Yam Tat-wah (Chen Ren), Carrie Ng Kar-lai (Madam Rose, aka One Thousand Needles), Chen Mingchen (Chen), Dicky Cheung Wai-kin (Robert Parkinson), Yuen Wah (Bloody Wolf), Melvin Wong Kam-sun (Chu), Pau Fong (The Master), Lily Lee Li-li (Wet Nurse). 1.85:1. VHS/LD: Tai Seng. Import LD/VCD: Mei Ah. 90 minutes.

This all-star action-comedy disaster concerns a group of master thieves who have been recruited to steal a file from the police department. The prize: enough money to last the rest of their lives. After figuring out how to crack the building's intricate security system, leader Black Cougar (not "Black Panther," as per the title) tries to pull the job himself. He succeeds, but it is a set-up and he is captured. While the rest of the team fend off squads of hitmen and try to discover Cougar's whereabouts, the latter learns that his brother, Bloody Wolf, is responsible for the treachery.

The four minute long coming attractions trailer makes this look like one of the greatest action spectaculars ever committed to film, but don't be fooled: Even if it wasn't hobbled by one of the worst subtitling jobs ever, this would still be a major disappointment. With the story rendered so nonsensical, the viewer is left with little more than a handful of ultra-stylized (not to mention over edited) combat setpieces, painfully insipid comedy, and the attractive cast playing dress-up in a series of outlandish costumes. Alan Tang, Brigitte Lin, Carrie Ng, and Simon Yam manage to escape this debacle unscathed, but Tony Leung Kar-fai is embarrassingly over-the-top, and Dicky Cheung is absolutely unbearable as a computer whiz who turns into a drooling idiot unless he is sucking on a pacifier.

88. Black Rose II

(1997; CineMagic) ★: 3/10. *Hak mooi gwai yi git gam laan* (Cantonese), *Hei mei gui yi jie jin lan* (Mandarin): "Black Rose Befriends Golden Tulip." Art Director: Ben Lau Man-hung; Writer: Kei On (pseudonym for Jeff Lau Chun-wai); Producers: Kristie Yeung Sham Choi-man, David Lai Tai-wai; Action Director: Yuen Tak; Directors: Jeff Lau Chun-wai, Corey Yuen Kwai. Cast: Nancy Sit Kar-yin (Chuchu, aka Black Rose), Spencer Lam Sheung-yee (Lui Kei), Jan Lam Hoi-fung (Hui Chi-mo), Sandra Ng Kwan-yu (Sandra Suen May-tong), Desiree Lam Kee-wan (Yan-yan, aka Candy), Blackie Ko Shouliang (Dan), Bobby Yip King-sang (Loan Shark), Donnie Yen Chi-tan (Boxing School Owner). 1.85:1. VHS: Tai Seng. Import LD/VCD/DVD: Mei Ah. 92 minutes.

The law of diminishing returns is certainly in evidence with this follow-up to **92 Legendary La Rose Noire** and **Rose Rose I Love You**. The least of the three films, it is comprised of especially stale slapstick and more in-joke references that will mean little to those who lack a knowledge of 1960s HK entertainment. Center stage is given this time to veteran actress Nancy Sit, who made a very successful comeback in the mid '90s. Mousy delivery boy Chi-mo falls for cute dance instructor Yan-yan, but when he pursues the girl one day, she turns out to be the middle-aged Black Rose in disguise. The dotty superheroine imprisons Chi-mo in her home, alongside Lui Kei (who has been stuck there for thirty years), forcing the two to be her servants. Eventually, as a result of Lui's pleading, Black Rose rescues the real Yan-yan from loanshark Sandra (Sandra Ng doing another of her obnoxious butch caricatures), prompting the triad to lead her goons in a retaliatory attack on Rose's mansion.

The most imaginative and amusing aspect of the film is the opening credit sequence, which is presented in a most offbeat and enjoyable manner. However, Tony Leung Kar-fai's goofy Lui Kei caricature is sorely missed, and the various send-ups (including the Japanese hit **Shall We Dance?**) are less than inspired. A handful of chuckles emerge (thanks mainly to Black Rose's inept weapons, like "Killer Lipstick" and a lethal electrified pen that has to be plugged in to work) but not nearly enough to justify a viewing.

89. The Blade

(1995; Golden Harvest/Film Workshop) ★: 8/10. *Do* (Cantonese), *Dao* (Mandarin): "Sword." Cinematographer: Kam Sing; Art Directors: William Cheung Suk-ping, Bill Lui Cho-hung, Alfred Yau Wai-ming; Music: William Woo Wai-lap, Raymond Wong Ying-wah; Writers: Tsui Hark, Koan Hui-on, So Man-sing; Producer-Director: Tsui Hark. Cast: Zhao Wenzhou (On), Xiong Xinxin (Lung), Song Nei (Siu-ling), Moses Chan Ho (Iron Head), Valerie Chow Kar-ling (The Prostitute), Austin Wai Tin-chi (Master of Sharp Manufacturers), Ngai Sing (On's Real Father). 1.85:1. VHS: Tai Seng. Import LD/VCD: Mei Ah. 100 minutes.

The most intense and innovative swordplay film in memory, Tsui Hark's remake of the Chang Cheh classic **The One-Armed Swordsman** (1967) transmutes the courtly combat of traditional Chinese martial arts films into a wanton cotillion of feral conduct and primal slaughter. Zhao Wenzhou gives a forceful performance as On, a loyal and noble worker at Sharp Manufacturers, a respected sword manufacturing establishment. An overheard conversation about his father's actual fate, and his desire to avenge a noble monk's senseless death at the hands of some vicious hunters, sends him on a reckless, ill-fated quest for vengeance. When his right arm is lost in battle, On becomes a hopeless outcast in the martial world, where being crippled is far worse than being dead. His only chance now lies in the development of a new fighting technique which will compensate for his disability and give him the speed and power necessary to defeat his father's killer, the barbarous, tattooed Lung.

Filled with nightmarish images drenched in deep hues, shock cuts, and an incessant, pounding score, **The Blade** is a stark return to the brutality and cynicism of Tsui's early realist work, minus the conspicuous leftist political leanings (another kind of sword, the cross, plays a role here). In refreshing contrast to the genre norm, Tsui centers much of the film on the actions of strong female characters, notably a savage prostitute and the story's narrator, Siu-ling, whose commentary is used to provide a touch of humanity to this hellish world. The fight choreography is spectacular, with the combatants defying gravity through more traditional means (no overdone wirework here), and Zhao's considerable grace and swordsmanship is more apparent than ever before. All is not perfect, however. As an example of dazzling, virtuoso filmmaking, **The Blade** is a magnificent achievement, but it is also an oppressive and exhausting one, whose precepts are not always put forth in a clear and cohesive fashion (partially the fault of the subtitles, which are coherent but weakly translated). That said, this remains a portentous film which, like Wong Kar-wai's **Ashes of Time**, sets new standards and opens exciting new vistas in a seemingly played-out genre.

90. Blade of Fury

(1993; Grand March Motion Picture Co.) ★: 4/10. *Yat do king sing* (Cantonese), *Yi dao qing cheng* (Mandarin): "One Dagger Fallen City." Cinematographer: Lam Kai-san; Art Director: Yank Wong Yan-kwai; Music: Lowell Lo Kwun-ting; Writers: Charcoal Cheung Tan, Roy Szeto Cheuk-hon; Producer: Lo Wei; Action Director Director: Sammo Hung Kam-po. Cast: Ti Lung (Tan Szu-tung), Rosamund Kwan Chi-lam (Noblewoman), Cynthia Yang Li-ching (Nine Catties), Ngai Sing (Siu-chuen), Wong Kam-kong (King Yee), Yip Wing-cho (Nobleman), Lau Shun (Ngo Pai), James Tien Chun (Bandit Leader), Sammo Hung Kam-po (Yu Man-san). 1.85:1. VHS: Tai Seng. Import LD/VCD: Star Entertainment. Import DVD: China Star. 103 minutes.

A weak entry in the period swordplay cycle, **Blade of Fury** boasts a good cast of genre regulars but comes up short in all other departments. The film opens with a group of nationalists called The Black Flag Troop getting killed in a vain attempt to obliterate a troop of Japanese invaders. The story then picks up a few years later, in 1898, with Tan Tzu-tung and his servant, Nine Catties, stopping off to rest in a small town. The place is quickly besieged by bandits out to assassinate a government official, but their plans are thwarted by Tan, Nine, and a blacksmith. The latter turns out to be Wang Wu, the former leader of the Black Flag fighters and the only survivor from that group. Tan enlists Wang to help him with his mission to reform China, and the latter sets up a kung fu school in order to pass on his skills. However, subsequent political turmoil prompts Tan and Wang to try and overthrow The Empress Dowager, a goal that meets with tragedy.

Some proficiently staged action set-pieces are marred by undercranking and silly-looking wirework, and the various dramatic conflicts are not compelling enough to maintain viewer interest (save for the sequence that delineates the fate of Ti Lung's character). Rosamund Kwan is completely wasted in a superfluous supporting role, but Cynthia Yang gives a solid performance in one of the more interesting parts she has been offered to date.

91. Bless This House

(1988; D & B Films Co.) ★: 6/10. *Maang gwai fat tiu cheung* (Cantonese), *Meng gui fo tiao qiang* (Mandarin): "Fierce Ghost Buddha Jumps Wall." Cinematographer: Poon Hang-sang; Art Director: Fong Ying; Music: Richard Yuen Cheuk-fan; Writers: Chim See-yuen, John Ng Chong-chau, Clifton Ko Chi-sum; Producer: Linda Kuk Mei-lai; Action Director: Leung Siu-lung; Director: Ronny Yu Yan-tai. Cast: Bill Tung Biu (Bill Chang), Loletta Lee Lai-chun (Jane), Deborah Dik Bo-lai (Mrs. Chang), Stephen Ho Kai-nam (Burly), Ricky Yee Fan-wai (Ho), Manfred Wong (Bespectacled Exorcist), Victor Hon Kwan (Ghost Father). 1.85:1. VHS: Tai Seng (Poor Subtitles). Import VCD: Mega Star. 82 minutes.

After twenty years of faithful service, architect Bill Chang gets a promotion and the opportunity to move his family from their cramped apartment into a company-owned house. The place turns out to be on "Dog Belly Hill" (ie. the middle of nowhere) and, as the Changs quickly discover, haunted to boot. A bumbling Taoist proves no match for the spirits, and Bill ends up possessed by his ghostly counterpart, a deranged Peking Opera performer. The previous tenants were burned alive by this madman, and it looks increasingly like Bill is destined to subject his loved ones to the same fate.

An uneven mix of family-oriented slapstick and comic fright sequences for most of its running time, **Bless This House** transforms into a flat-out horror thrill ride in its final reel, with berserk camerawork, bleeding walls, exploding mirrors, and the like. There is nothing particularly original here, but the execution is good and the final product is a worthwhile, if fairly tame, addition to the '80s horror cycle. Co-writer Clifton Ko cameos as a TV reporter.

92. Blind Romance

(1996; Jing's Production) ★: 4/10. *Tau tau oi nei* (Cantonese), *Tou tou ai ni* (Mandarin): "Secretly Love You." Cinematographer: Apple Kwan Pak-suen; Art Director: James Cheung Ying-wah; Music: Clarence Hui Yuen; Writer: Unknown (credited with pseudonym "But Sze Lui Yan"); Producer: Wong Jing; Director: Tam Long-cheung. Cast: Chingmy Yau Suk-ching (Yim Tung-tung), Tony Leung Chiu-wai (Wing), Eric Kot Man-fai (Yim Sai-chung), Jay Lau Kam-ling (Chan Dai-di/Chi-sum), Roy Chiao Hung (Tung-tung's Grandfather), Annabelle Lau Hiu-tung (Ching-ha), Manfred Wong (Station Manager), Dennis Chan Kwok-san (Eric). 1.85:1. VHS/LD: World Video. Import LD/VCD/DVD: Mei Ah. 99 minutes.

Typically cast as a vamp, Chingmy Yau tried a change of pace role in this formulaic romantic comedy which owes a large debt to the Hollywood hit **While You Were Sleeping**. She plays Tung-tung, an attractive but terminally mild-mannered girl who holds several jobs at once. She gets yet another one after running into old school friend Dai-di, who is now rock star "Chi-sum." It's love at first sight for Tung-tung when she sees Wing, her new boss' handsome boyfriend. When Wing gets into a car accident that leaves him blind, possibly for good, Tung-tung pretends to be his private nurse. Further complications arise when Wing's heartless brother seizes control of the family company and freezes him out.

Yau tries but is both too pretty and too mannered to be convincing, and the storyline is tiresomely predictable. Even Tony Leung Chiu-wai, widely regarded as one of HK's best actors, cannot breathe any life into this one. Roy Chiao sends up his award-winning role in **Summer Snow** by playing Tung-tung's grandpa, who is stricken with Alzheimer's Disease.

93. The Blonde Fury

(1989; Golden Harvest/Paragon Films) ★: 4/10. *Si je daai saai* (Cantonese), *Shi jie da shai* (Mandarin): "Master Sister Big Sunshine." Cinematographers: Bill Wong Chung-po, Peter Ngor Chi-kwan; Art Director: Tony Au Ding-ping; Music: Chris Babida; Writer: Shum Chi-leung; Producers: Sammo Hung Kam-po, Corey Yuen Kwai; Action Director-Director: Mang Hoi. Cast: Cynthia Rothrock (Cindy), Elizabeth Lee Mei-fung (Judy Yu), Chin Siu-ho (Undercover Officer), Mang Hoi (Shorty), Ronny Yu Yan-tai (Ronny Dak), Roy Chiao Hung (Prosecutor Yu), Keith Kwan Chiu-chung (Keith), Wu Ma (Shorty's Dad), Tai Po (Turbo), Chung Fat (Break-and-Enter Thief), Billy Chow Bei-lee (Billy Chow), Jeff Falcon (Thug), Vincent Lyn (Thug), Melvin Wong Kam-sun (Melvin Wong), James Tien Chun (Assistant Prosecutor), Yip Wing-cho (Judge). 1.85:1. VHS: Tai Seng (No Subtitles). Import LD: Star Entertainment (No Subtitles). 88 minutes. Also known as **Above the Law II: The Blonde Fury** (UK video title), **Lady Reporter** (Tai Seng title).

Awful comedy relief and insipid dialogue detract severely from this otherwise competent showcase for Cynthia Rothrock's fighting skills. She plays an FBI agent sent to HK to bust an evil newspaper editor (a rare acting turn by director Ronny Yu) who is using his company's presses to print counterfeit bills. Teaming up with old friend Judy, crusading reporter Shorty, and another cop masquerading as an insurance agent, Cindy takes on the villain's flunkies (all martial arts experts, naturally) in a series of exhilarating confrontations.

Shooting began in 1987 and then halted midway through, picking up several months later. As a result, continuity errors are evident (watch Rothrock's hairstyle change from scene to scene) and the storyline makes little sense, even for the action genre (top quality counterfeit bills done on newspaper presses?!). Still, there is an exciting fight on bamboo scaffolding and a climactic battle on a giant rope spider web (don't ask). The character names listed above are from the horribly dubbed English version, which will hopefully be supplanted someday by a domestic subtitled edition. In the meantime, if you must watch, keep your remote control handy.

Blood of the Black Dog *see* **An Accident**

94. Bloody Beast

(1994; Giant Film Production Co.) ★: 2/10. *Laang huet yan long* (Cantonese), *Leng xue ren lang* (Mandarin): "Cold-Blooded Wolf Person." Cinematographer: Li Hsin-yeh; Art Director: Andy Tam Tak-shing; Music: Not Original; Writer: Jimmy Leung Chi-ming; Producer: Lau Ying-lung; Action Director: Ridley Tsui Bo-wah; Directors: Andy Tam Tak-shing, Yeung Kuen. Cast: Lawrence Ng Kai-wah (Chen Siu-hsiong), William Ho Kar-kui (Shing), Kenneth Tong Chun-yip (Captain Suen), Lau Siu-ming (Chen's Father). 1.85:1. VHS: Tai Seng. Import LD/VCD: Ocean Shores. 89 minutes.

This dreary Category III thriller slavishly follows the formula set out by **Dr. Lamb** (1992) but adds nothing of value to the subgenre. After sixteen days of torture and several suicide attempts, vicious Mainland serial killer Chen Siu-hsiong decides to confess to his captors. Flashbacks show his troubled youth where, deprived of a mother and forced to take care of his younger sister, he suffered at the hands of his uncouth father. As a boy, Chen was aroused by the sight of a mother breast feeding her child. The woman proceeded to tempt and then slap him, and this humiliation deeply scarred him. Later, as an adult, he murders and then rapes a woman after seeing her nurse her baby in public, and later preys on several other unsuspecting girls in the same fashion.

As with all films of this ilk, the characters and situations are exaggerated to the point of absurdity, making it impossible to sympathize with anyone or care about the outcome (particularly since the opening reel already spells out exactly what will happen). There is also the usual dark humor, though it is particularly insipid in this case.

95. Bloody Brotherhood

(1989; Chun Sing Film Co.) ★: 5/10. *Tung gan sang* (Cantonese), *Tung gen sheng* (Mandarin): "Same Origin Born." Cinematographer: Yu Chik-lim; Art Director: Tsang Siu-kuen; Music: Teddy Robin Kwan, Richard Lo Sai-kit; Writer: Tang Wing-hung; Producer: Yuen Kam-lun; Action Directors: Simon Tam Tung, Hung San-lam; Director: Johnny Wang Lung-wei. Cast: Andy Lau Tak-wah (Cheung Ka-wah), Irene Wan Pik-ha (Kiu), Lam Wai (Wai), Michael Chan Wai-man (Tong Fai), Shum Wai (Ma Guai-hoi), Ku Feng (The Boss), Phillip Ko Fei (Fei), Lung Ming-yan (Killer from Holland), Ken Lo Wai-kwong (Wu Chi-ko), Dick Wei (Killer from Vietnam). 1.85:1. VHS: Tai Seng. 92 minutes.

After struggling to survive by doing menial work, temperamental illegal immigrant Wah joins "good" triad leader Tong Fai's gang. In the process, he angers his boss' competitor, Hoi, who sends a gang to mess up Wah's wedding celebration. When Hoi gets Tong framed for possession, Wah and his new bride flee to Taiwan. Seven years pass and Hoi approaches Wah about going into a partnership with him and some Vietnamese drug smugglers. When Wah refuses, Hoi sends his newest lieutenant, Wai, to kidnap Wah's little girl. In the process, Wai accidentally kills his captive, prompting Wah to return to HK where (in a sequence copied from **A Better Tomorrow**) he discovers Tong reduced to a destitute drug addict. To make matters worse, Wai is actually the brother that Wah was separated from when he and his family escaped China years earlier.

The characters are well drawn for this sort of effort but the plotting is contrived and unadventurous (the film is set in the 1960s but could just as easily have been contemporary, as nothing of interest is done with the time period), never challenging one's expectations.

96. Bloody Brothers

(1994; Student) ★: 3/10. *San daai siu bat leung* (Cantonese), *Xin da xiao bu liang* (Mandarin): "New Master Is Not Kind." Cinematographer: Tsui Tung-heung; Music: Not Original; Writer: Cheung Man-wah; Producer: Tsang Choi-lung; Action Director: Law Cheung-on; Director: To Hoi-sang. Cast: Dicky Cheung Wai-kin (Shiu Chi-hung), Kent Cheng Chuk-see (Uncle), Yvonne Yung Hung (Yue Li-chin), William Ho Kar-kui (Chin Chiu-hwa), Dick Wei (Chang Tung-pin). 1.85:1. VHS/LD: World Video. Running time unknown.

Anachronisms abound in this cheap, cliche-ridden gangster film set in the 1920s. Looking to find fame and fortune in Shanghai, Shiu Chi-hung tries to ingratiate himself with triad boss Tu Wu and ends up with a fistful of cash but no job. Meanwhile, a drug war is heating up, with Tu and his gang soon annihilated by rival gangster Chin Chiu-hwa. With the help of his cousin, dishonest policeman Kang, Shiu becomes a part of Chang Tung-pin's gang. Rising quickly through the ranks, Shiu soon has his own house and substantial status. When Chin's top assassin tries to liquidate him, Shiu gets revenge by eliminating both him and his boss. However, this initiative is not appreciated by Chang, who is worried about the amount of power Shiu now wields and the latter's refusal to reveal how he was able to get the guns used in the killings. The inevitable, bloody confrontation soon results, but Shiu also faces one more potentially lethal threat.

You know you are in trouble in the first few minutes when Yvonne Yung starts "singing" and a scratchy old record is heard on the soundtrack. Aside from some attractive Mainland locations (which do not always match the period in which the film takes place), this proceeds strictly by-the-numbers and offers virtually nothing of interest. Even the gunplay and fight choreography are substandard.

97. A Bloody Fight

(1988; Attraction Film Co.) ★: 4/10. *Lit huet fung wan* (Cantonese), *Lie xue feng yun* (Mandarin): "Violent Blood Turbulence." Cinematographer: Mo Chi-yan; Music: Not Original; Producer: Cheung Wai-yee; Director: Wilson Tong Wai-shing. Cast: Norman Tsui Siu-keung (Chui Kang), Gordon Lau Kar-fai (Fai), Lau Kar-leung (Leung), Chor Yuen (Cho), Fung Hark-on (Fung), Shum Wai (Wai), Tai Po (Cop). 1.85:1. VHS: Tai Seng. Import LD: Golden Cinema City. 92 minutes.

You've heard this one before: A world-weary assassin seeks to retire from "The Club" so that he can be a responsible husband and father. Not surprisingly, his boss isn't about to let him go and orders his termination. The hit fails to kill Tsui, but his family and a sympathetic associate die in the process. Meanwhile, a dedicated cop investigating the grisly result of Tsui's last contract killing comes to realize that the perpetrator is his childhood friend and sparring partner. Worse yet, Tsui falls in love with the cop's sister, resulting in her subsequent rape and murder by Chu's men. Putting their ideological differences aside, the two men join forces to exact suitably bloody revenge.

This heavy-handed effort generally accomplishes its goals in spite of a formulaic plot riddled with contrivance (though most viewers will be too distracted by the habitual bursts of nasty violence to care). Hardly challenging viewing, but the solid cast helps this over some of its rougher spots. Of the Lau brothers, only Kar-leung is given much of a chance to showcase his exemplary martial arts skills.

98. Bloody Friday

(1996; Simpson Performance & Productions Co.) ★: 4/10. *Huet sing FRIDAY* (Cantonese), *Xue xing FRIDAY* (Mandarin): "Bloody Friday." Cinematographer: Keung Kwok-man; Art Director: Ken Chiu Kin-san; Music: Tommy Wai Kai-leung; Writers: Danny Ko Lam-pau, Yeung Kei; Producers: Wong Yiu-tai, Yu Sha-li; Action Director: Lee Chi-kit; Director: Danny Ko Lam-pau. Cast: Simon Yam Tat-wah (Ko Cheuk-hung), Loletta Lee Lai-chun (Maggie), Ada Choi Siu-fan (Ada), Au Kam-tong (Lau Wai-ken), Elvis Tsui Kam-kong (Ko's Superior), Emily Kwan Bo-wai (Cheung Ka-lam), Ivy Leung Si-man (Ping), Bobby Yip King-sang (Pimp). 1.85:1. VHS: Tai Seng. Import LD/VCD: Universe. 94 minutes.

Director Danny Ko followed up his intriguing mystery-thriller **The Crucifixion** with this mediocre potboiler starring HK's reigning king of bad movies, Simon Yam. A black leather-clad killer on a motorcycle is preying on young women walking the streets alone. Dubbed the "Friday Killer" because he always strikes on that day only, the murderer manages to claim an undercover policewoman as his next victim. The woman's boyfriend, a fellow cop named Lau, blames Ko, the officer in charge of the investigation, for her death. After attacking Ko, Lau is given a one month suspension. Shortly thereafter, a flaky prostitute named Maggie is targeted but manages to escape. Ko begins receiving threatening calls from the killer, who boasts that he will kill Maggie and several other girls within thirty days time.

Lee's bright and appealing performance aside, this by-the-numbers exercise has little to recommend it. Some mild suspense is generated along the way as clues about the murderer's identity start to surface, and there is some impressive stunt riding, but the final revelation is less than satisfying and the climax is ludicrous.

99. Bloody Money

(1983) ★: 3/10. *Huet hon gam chin* (Cantonese), *Xie han jin qian* (Mandarin): "Hard-Earned Money." Cinematographer: Cheung Yiu-cho; Music: Not Original; Writer: Alfred Cheung Kin-ting; Producers: Vicky Leung Lee Siu-ha, Hon Chi-kwan; Action Directors: Lau Chin-ho, Chan Tien-lung; Director: Wong Shu-tong. Cast: Chow Yun-fat (Bullet), Chan Man-ngai, Lam Chiao, Chu Tien-ho. 2.35:1. VHS: J & M Chevalier, Arena/Xenon. Import LD: Winson Entertainment. 91 minutes. Also known as **Hong Kong Specialist** (Arena/Xenon title).

Hong Kong films routinely feature amazing stuntwork, and the story behind the men who perform these dangerous feats could make for a fascinating film; this plodding, unfocused drama isn't it. Chow Yun-fat (billed under his little-used English name, Aman Chow) stars as Bullet, the leading light of a movie stunt team. Headed up by his father and brother, the group has been plagued by accidents both on and off the set. Bullet eventually decides to accept a better offer from a Taiwan movie company, leaving the partners to struggle on their own. In need of money and ashamed to be supported by his son, the aged father agrees to do a dangerous stunt and is severely injured in the process, necessitating an expensive operation. Unable to contact the now-successful Bullet to pay for the procedure, the other brother resorts to robbery and holds hostages in order to force the hospital to proceed with the surgery, leading up to a most melodramatic (and unconvincing) finale.

Diehard Chow fans may want to check this out, as it provides a rare chance to catch their favorite star in period garb, but it's hardly worth the trouble, and the final product certainly doesn't fulfil the possibilities offered by its premise. For a much more interesting look at the lives of HK stuntmen, see **Goodbye Hero**.

Bloody Tattoo *see* **The Loot**

100. The Blue Jean Monster

(1991; Golden Harvest/Paragon Films) ★: 5/10. *Jeuk ngau jai foo dik Jung Kwai* (Cantonese), *Zhuo niu zi ku de Zhong Kui* (Mandarin): "Jung Kwai Wearing Blue Jeans" or "Zhong Kui Wearing Blue Jeans." Cinematographer: Chong Chuen Kin-yat (Cantonese name for unknown Japanese technician); Art Director: Andy Lee Yiu-kwong; Music: Tsui Yat-kan; Writer: Ng Chin-hung; Producer: Chow Chan-tung; Director: Ivan Lai Kai-ming. Cast: Shing Fui-on (Tsu Hsiang), Pauline Wong Siu-fung (Chu), Gloria Yip Wan-yee (Gucci), Amy Yip Chi-mei (Death-rays). 1.85:1. VHS: Tai Seng. Import LD: Universe. 94 minutes.

This is one of the most tasteless—yet wacky—horror-comedies you will ever see! Veteran character actor Shing Fui-on gets a rare lead role as Tsu, a dedicated police officer who is killed in the line of duty by bank robbers, only to be reanimated by a combination of cat pee and electricity. Now a zombie with immense strength and a constant need for a re-charge, Tsu tries to stay in one piece so he can apprehend his killers and witness the birth of the baby his very pregnant wife is carrying. Among Tsu's more bizarre attributes: He is now impervious to bullets, can pull undigested food out of a hole in his stomach, and can seal up his wounds with sanitary napkins and cookie dough! If that were not enough, there is also the infamous scene in which he squeezes a prostitute's breasts so hard they burst like water balloons, spraying milk in his face! This is all, of course, played for laughs and usually garners them through sheer shock value. The rest of the comedy (tired sight gags, gay jokes, half-translated insults, etc.) is shrill and annoying, but there is something to be said for any film that can jolt complacent viewers out of their chairs through sheer quirkiness. The whole thing wraps up with this touching eulogy: "He didn't count much among humans but would be great help in Hell." Indeed. The name mentioned in the Chinese title is that of a demon fighter in Chinese mythology.

101. Blue Lightning

(1991; Cinema City Co.) ★: 6/10. *Laam sik pik lik feng* (Cantonese), *Lan se pi li hou* (Mandarin): "Blue Lightning Fire." Cinematographer: Joe Chan Kong-hung; Art Director: Andy Lee Yiu-kwong; Music: Carli Fabio, Lo Tai-yau; Writers: Bryan Cheung Wai-hung, Abe Kwong Man-wai; Producer: Raymond Wong Pak-ming; Action Director: Tony Leung Siu-hung; Director: Raymond Lee Wai-man. Cast: Danny Lee Sau-yin (Lam Sau-yat), Tony Leung Kar-fai (Ching Hay), Olivia Cheng Man-ar (Ellen Fong), Lau Siu-ming (Lai Sai-leung), Wong Kwan-yuen (Lim), Victor Hon Kwan (Mar Sing). 1.85:1. VHS: Tai Seng. Import LD: Golden Cinema City. 93 minutes.

Blue Lightning is a Danny Lee cop actioner with a twist—instead of his usual stalwart detective role, Lee plays an ex-cop turned foul alcoholic. Tony Leung Kar-fai is the detective here, investigating the execution-style murder of a man and woman that was witnessed by the latter's young son. Lee plays the boy's father, whose life changes for the better when he is forced to care for the boy and become responsible once again. Frustrated by Leung's by-the-book tactics, and egged on by the boy, Lee undertakes his own investigation. After the usual friction, the two men settle their differences and start working as a team. However, when the trail of evidence points to an influential political figure, their efforts are hindered by the powers that be.

The script is routine but the cinematography is adept, and it is a pleasure to see Danny Lee do a variation on his usual cinematic persona. However, judging from the film's poor showing at the box office, HK audiences were not ready to accept Lee as a tarnished hero, so he went back to playing his usual stoic everyman officer. While Lee remains the definitive HK movie cop, it is a shame, based upon his persuasive work here, that he rarely gets a chance to try his hand at other parts. Tony Leung Kar-fai, an actor who rarely *ever* plays a policeman, does an admirable job, and Wong Kwan-yuen is also a step above most child actors. The climax is effective, if not entirely logical.

Blue Valentine *see* **Rose (1992)**

102. Boat People

(1982; Bluebird Movie Enterprises) ★: 8/10. *Tau ban no hoi* (Cantonese), *Tou ben nu hai* (Mandarin): "Escaping Anger Through the Sea." Cinematographer: Wong Chung-kei; Art Director: Tony Au Ding-ping; Music: Law Wing-fai; Writer: Yau Tai On-ping; Producer: Ha Mong; Director: Ann Hui On-wah. Cast: George Lam Chi-cheung (Shiomi Akutagawa), Season Ma Si-san (Cam Nuong), Cora Miao Qian-ren (Nguyen's Mistress), Andy Lau Tak-wah (To Minh). Import LD: Star Entertainment (No Subtitles). Import DVD: China Star (No Subtitles). 106 minutes.

Set three years after the Liberation of Danang in 1975, director Ann Hui's provocative, commercially successful look at life in Vietnam remains the film she is best known for in the West. Japanese photo-journalist Shiomi Akutagawa is sympathetic to the plight of the Vietnamese people and has arrived in the country to record its efforts to rebuild. After being shown dozens of happy and healthy children by government officials, he wins permission to travel around alone and take pictures of whatever he pleases. He soon runs across Cam Nuong, a young girl from an exceedingly poor family who regards him with suspicion at first but, gradually, accepts him as a friend. It does not take long for Akutagawa to see that life for the everyday people is far different than the government-sanctioned picture. Soldiers routinely terrorize the populace, while children search the bodies of just-executed prisoners for valuables and sort through stretches of garbage containing live explosives. Then there are the "New Economic Zones," government-run camps in the countryside whose real function is far from what Akutagawa is led to believe.

Boat People was shot primarily in China, which is ironic, as it is an obvious metaphor for the trepidations over Communist rule that many HK citizens were starting to experience around this time. While the events feel somewhat compressed and the presentation veers, perhaps unavoidably, into melodrama at times (particularly the ending), this is a persuasive and involving drama and a worthy companion piece to Hui's **The Story of Woo Viet**. While George Lam is merely adequate, newcomer Season Ma impresses, as does Cora Miao as a world-weary but elegant bar girl who has survived by attaching herself to various military commanders over the years. Andy Lau also appears (in his movie debut) as a young man willing to go to great lengths to escape from the country. The film swept the Hong Kong Film Awards, winning Best Picture, Best Director, Best Screenplay, Best Art Direction, and Best Newcomer (Season Ma).

103. The Bodyguard from Beijing

(1994; Eastern Productions) ★: 4/10. *Chung Nam Hoi bo biu* (Cantonese), *Zhong Nan Hai bao biao* (Mandarin): "The Bodyguard from Chung Nam Hoi" or "The Bodyguard from Zhong Nan Hai." Cinematographer: Tom Lau Moon-tong; Art Director: Jason Mok Siu-kei; Music: William Woo Wai-lap; Writers: Gordon Chan Kar-seung, John Chan Kin-chung; Producer: Jet Li Lianjie; Action Directors: Corey Yuen Kwai, Yuen Tak; Director: Corey Yuen Kwai. Cast: Jet Li Lianjie (Hui Ching-yeung), Christy Chung Lai-tai (Michelle Yeung), Kent Cheng Chuk-see (Leung Kam-po), Ngai Sing (Wong Kin-kwan), Wong Kam-kong (Chiu Kwok-man). 1.85:1. VHS/LD/DVD: World Video (Remastered for the English market). VHS/LD: World Video (Chinese market version). Import LD/VCD: Mei Ah. 93 minutes.

A tiresome knockoff of the equally unbearable Kevin Costner/Whitney Houston hit **The Bodyguard** (1991), this film casts Jet Li and Christy Chung in the lead roles, and they don't have one ounce of chemistry. After she witnesses businessman Chiu Kwok-man committing murder, spoiled rich girl Michelle Yeung finds her life in danger. Her boyfriend hires ace Mainland bodyguard Hui Ching-yeung to protect her, and it is hate at first sight. Hui forbids Michelle from going outside her home but, after numerous complaints, he relents and takes his client on a shopping trip. A squad of killers are waiting, and only quick action by Hui saves Michelle's life. Consequently, Michelle finally realizes just how much danger she is in and begins appreciating the concern Hui is showing for her. Love soon blossoms, but the opposition brings in an ex-Chinese soldier who is Hui's equal when it comes to fighting.

Even those who have not seen the Hollywood model will find the story tediously predictible.

As a result, there is no reason to care about the characters when their fates are so easily deduced. The mall sequence might have been effective at half the length; as is, it drags on and on, and the number of killers popping out of the woodwork is simply laughable. The action in the final reel is up to the standards set by director Corey Yuen (who has a cameo) in his earlier work; if it were not for the sheer energy and bravado on display during the finale, the film would be a complete waste of time. The battle between Jet Li and Ngai Sing in a room filled with poison gas is copied from Yuen Woo-ping's **Tiger Cage**. Jet Li must be fond of that particular bit: It turned up again in another movie of his, 1996s **Black Mask**, which was choreographed by Yuen Woo-ping. Beware of World Video's English market version, which is missing the bottom third of the picture!

104. Bodyguards of the Last Governor

(1996; BOB & Partners Company) ★: 3/10. *Gong duk jui hau yat goh bo biu* (Cantonese), *Gang du zui hou yi ge bao biao* (Mandarin): "The Hong Kong Governor's Last Bodyguard." Cinematographer: Tam Chi-wai; Art Director: Andy Lee Yiu-kwong; Music: Ronald Ng Luk-shing; Writers: Wong Jing, Alfred Cheung Kin-ting; Producer: Manfred Wong; Action Director: Dion Lam Dik-on; Director: Alfred Cheung Kin-ting. Cast: Eric Kot Man-fai (Lugo), Law Kar-ying (Yan Chien-fai), Chingmy Yau Suk-ching (Lugo's Wife), Michael Chow Man-kin (Daikan), Law Koon-lan (Chung Fang An-sin), Spencer Lam Sheung-yee (Bao), Liz Kong Hei-man (Yan's Daughter). 1.85:1. VHS: World Video. Import LD/VCD/DVD: Mei Ah. 94 minutes.

This is an extremely local satire which will mean virtually nothing to those unfamiliar with Hong Kong politics and will not even be very amusing to those who are. In the days leading up to the handover of HK to China, the British remove their current governor (Noel Lester Rands doing a broad impersonation of Chris Patten) and replace him with Chinese cook Yan Chien-fai. Having resided in Britain for years, Yan knows nothing about politics but that ignorance doesn't prevent him from being a target for assassins. Mismatched policemen Lugo and Daikan are assigned to protect him, and their already rocky relationship is further complicated by the fact that Daikan used to date Lugo's wife. The jokes are drearily obvious, but Law Kar-ying manages to squeeze a few laughs out of the material.

105. Bogus Cops

(1993) ★: 1/10. *Jau liu wai lung* (Cantonese), *Zou lao wei long* (Mandarin): "Walking Guy Might of Dragon." Cinematographer: Sung Kong; Art Director: Ring Law Chi-keung; Music: Not Original; Action Directors: Leung Kar-yan, Nam Chim-si, Lo Lai-yin; Producers: Leung Kar-yan, Claudie Chung Chun; Writer-Director: Leung Kar-yan. Cast: Leung Kar-yan (Karl Choi/Choi's Wife), Veronica Yip Yuk-hing (Rose), Eric Tsang Chi-wai (Ching But-cam), Chen Kuan-tai (Officer Wu), Johnny Wang Lung-wei (Hood), Gordon Lau Kar-fai (Hood), Jamie Luk Kim-ming (Hung Pak-lam), William Ho Kar-kui (Hood), Kenneth Tong Chun-yip (Hood), Simon Lui Yu-yeung (Triad with Sunglasses), Cheung Kwok-keung (Keung), Gabriel Wong Yat-san (Car Thief), Paul Chun Pui (Doctor), Shing Fui-on (Karaoke Patron), Lee Hoi-sang (Triad in Bar), Sophia Crawford (Imported Hooker), Melvin Wong Kam-sun (Insurance Cop), Yuen Woo-ping (Sleeping Cop). 1.85:1. VHS: Tai Seng. Import LD/VCD: Ocean Shores. 94 minutes.

This witless cop comedy is almost worth enduring for its cast of old favorites, but goodwill can only be stretched so far and this thoroughly unfunny farce will test the patience of any viewer with a double digit I.Q. Perennial screw-ups Choi and Ching are a disgrace to the Royal HK Police Force, running away from responsibility at every turn. When Choi is misdiagnosed with AIDS, he buys a huge insurance policy and turns into a reckless supercop, hoping to get himself killed in the line of duty (not exactly a fresh premise). He soon has his hands full battling a gang of inept bombers in the employ of Sadam Hussein(!). Ching, meanwhile, is romancing the beautiful but lisping and atonal prostitute Rose, who is actually a martial arts expert.

Writer-director-star Leung Kar-yan and his old movie buddies are clearly having the time of their lives, but absolutely none of it carries over to the audience. No mystery why this languished on the shelf for over a year before getting a five day theatrical run.

106. Bomb Disposal Officer: Baby Bomb

(1994; Universe Film Productions Co./Galaxy Films) ★: 5/10. *Chaak daan juen ga bo booi ja daan* (Cantonese), *Chai dan zhuan jia bao bei zha dan* (Mandarin): "Bomb Disposal Expert: Baby Bomb." Cinematographer: Jimmy Wong Kam-shing; Art Director: Andy Lee Yiu-kwong; Music: Healthy Poon Kin-hong, Cacine Wong Kar-sin; Writers: Law Kam-fai, Leung Hung-wah; Producer: Leung Hung-wah; Director: Jamie Luk Kim-ming. Cast: Anthony Wong Chau-sang (John Wu), Lau Ching-wan (Peter Chan), Esther Kwan Wing-ho (Mary Kwan), Parkman Wong Pak-man (Cop), Jamie Luk Kim-ming (Chow), Alexander Chan Mong-wah, Joseph Cheung Tung-cho. 1.85:1. VHS: Tai Seng. Import LD/VCD: Universe. 94 minutes.

A mad bomber is terrorizing HK, and goofy bomb disposal experts John and Peter must take care of the lethal booby traps he is creating. They must also deal with Mary, a spunky young girl who has been impregnated by one of them following a rowdy night of drinking. Neither one of the men wants to take responsibility, but they eventually reconsider their prospective status as fathers and are soon doting over her. However, the killer nabs Mary and fits her with an explosive device that monitors both her pulse and that of the baby. If either one goes above or below a certain rate, the bomb will detonate. Keeping Mary calm will be a bit of a problem for John and Peter, as she has gone into labor.

Anthony Wong and Lau Ching-wan are an inspired comic team, and their by-play makes this weak comedy more entertaining than it otherwise would have been. While it is possible that a Hollywood film might be constructed around this premise, chances are it would not open with a cute little kid getting blown to smithereens—as this one does. Director Jamie Luk never seems to hit quite the right note: Most of the comic scenes are too broad, while the dramatic sequences seem like something out of an entirely different movie. Regardless, this odd genre hybrid does have some bright moments, and Esther Kwan is quite appealing as the boys' rather daffy girlfriend.

107. Bomb Lover

(1995; Soulmate Entertainment Co.) ★: 6/10. *Cha daan ching yan* (Cantonese), *Zha dan qing ren* (Mandarin): "Bomb Lover." Cinematographer: Wong Po-man; Art Director: Ho Chi-hang; Music: Lai Wan-man; Writers: Takkie Yeung Yat-tak, Yuen Kai-chi; Producer: Ko Kam-tong; Director: Yeung Yat-tak. Cast: Mark Cheng Ho-nam (Tommy Tang), Christine Ng Wing-mei (Anna Ngok), Bonnie Fu Yuk-ching (Ling), Kent Cheng Chuk-see (Inspector Seito), Law Koon-lan (Tommy's Mother). 1.85:1. VHS: World Video. Import LD/VCD: Universe. 95 minutes.

Good performances lend weight to this low-key drama. When her husband Tat-shing is murdered by a mad bomber, Anna Ngok must come to grips with the fact that the evidence points soundly at her friend and former lover, Tommy Tang. Through flashbacks, it is revealed that Tommy developed a fascination with firecrackers at a young age which later turned into a love for explosives. When his mother was accidentally blown up, Tommy found comfort in the arms of Anna. The two swore their eternal love for each other but, when Tommy went to England and did not answer Anna's letters, she married Tat-shing. When Tommy returned and discovered this, he took a flat next to Anna so that he could spy on her. After trying various means to ruin her relationship with Tat-shing, Tommy sent him a package bomb. His current girlfriend, Ling, a real estate agent whose loneliness has caused her to lose all perspective, helps Tommy escape police custody. He attaches a bomb to his chest, captures Anna, binds her hand to his, and takes her to a radio station so that they can be on a call-in show he listens to religiously.

That final sequence at the station verges perilously close to self-parody, but retains a palpable level of suspense, while the remainder of the film is a mature and intelligent examination of romantic obsession and its effect on the human condition.

108. Born to Defence

[*sic*] (1988; Sil-Metropole Organisation) ★: 3/10. *Jung wa ying hung* (Cantonese), *Zhong hua ying xiong* (Mandarin): "Chinese Hero." Cinematographer: Cho Him; Art Director: Huang Jiping; Music: Hou Dejian, Ou Xiaosong; Writers: Shi Yangping, Jie Erge; Producer: Fu Chi; Action Director: Tsui Siu-ming; Director: Jet Li Lianjie. Cast: Jet Li Lianjie, Zhao Erkang, Song Jia, Kurt Roland Pettersson, Paulo H.P. Tocha. 1.85:1. VHS: World Video (Poor Subtitles), SYS/Youngtze. Import LD: Star Entertainment (No Subtitles). 92 minutes.

Jet Li made his only trip behind the camera to date for this contrived action cheapie, which does manage to score a few points for sheer grittiness. Following the end of World War II, hordes of drunken, uncouth American sailors are bullying innocent Chinese citizens, prompting tough young kung fu expert Jet to fight back. After defeating one braggart in a boxing match (of sorts—Jet uses some kung fu to emerge victorious), he gives most of his prize money to the poor and becomes a pedicab driver. When the Americans destroy his rickshaw for no reason, Jet is tricked into allowing himself to be used as a "sparring partner" (i.e. punching bag) for the Americans. The next day, the Navy Captain, a towering hulk that just happens to be proficient in martial arts, stands in for his men. He and Jet have a protracted battle in a downpour (easily the highlight of the film), which turns into a veritable riot. Jet emerges victorious but, in retaliation, the Americans kill two of his friends and pin the murders on him. Escaping from prison, Jet aims to even the score.

A Mainland production, this depicts all of the foreigners as vicious animals, but a subplot in which Jet's old friend manages to reconcile with his prostitute daughter at least gives the Chinese characters a smidgen of realism. However, the film is so redundant (it seems like half of the running time consists of Jet getting repeatedly beaten) and formulaic, it simply grates on one's nerves after a while.

109. Boys?

(1996; Fruit Productions) ★: 2/10. *Ga naam ga nui* (Cantonese), *Jia nan jia nu* (Mandarin): "Fake Man, Fake Woman." Cinematographer: Kwan Chi-chin; Art Director: Tung Yao; Music: Million Music Copyright; Writer: Sui Kwoh; Producer-Director: Jon Hau Wing-choi. Cast: Chan Kwok-bong (Joey), Edmond Leung Hon-man (Edmond), Siu Kwok-wah (Bitchy), Pauline Chan Po-lin (Pauline), Fennie Yuen Kit-ying (Fanny). 1.85:1. VHS: World Video. 91 minutes.

If **He's a Woman, She's a Man** was a half step forward in regards to HK cinema's depiction of homosexuals, then this laughable effort from the consistently deadly hand of director Jon Hau is about ten backwards. Dramatically trite and peopled with tiresome caricatures in place of characters, **Boys?** is easily the worst entry in the mini trend of gay-themed films from the mid '90s. The storyline follows the lives of some gay teens (one a transvestite) and the trials and tribulations they undergo in their love lives: Drag queen Joey has the hots for straight guy Edmond, who doesn't realize that she is a he (yeah, right); Fanny's relationship with her boyfriend crumbles when he takes her little brother to a sauna, which awakens "gay feelings" in the boy; and Peter and Jaffee are on the outs because of the latter's infidelity, but Jaffee's female friend Pauline wants to take their relationship to the next stage.

Thoroughly unconvincing from start to finish, this simple-minded effort is an embarrassment to gay and straight viewers alike. Incidentally, the writer's credit is a pseudonym that means "fruit," though one suspects that there is a more fundamental reason for the person wanting to remain anonymous.

110. Boys Are Easy

(1993; Chang-Hong Channel Film & Video Co./Wong Jing's Workshop) ★: 6/10. *Chu laam chai* (Cantonese), *Zhui nan zai* (Mandarin): "Chasing Boys." Cinematographer: Jingle Ma Cho-shing; Art Director: Andrew Cheuk Man-yiu; Music: Lowell Lo Kwun-ting; Producers: Hui Pui-yung, Wong Jing; Action Director: Lee Chung-chi; Writer-Director: Wong Jing. Cast: Brigitte Lin Ching-hsia (Ching Siu-tung), Tony Leung Kar-fai (Simon Tse Sai), Maggie Cheung Man-yuk (Ching Siu-nam), Jacky Cheung Hok-yau (Wu Ying), Chingmy Yau Suk-ching (Ching Siu-sze), Jimmy Lin Chi-ying (Ching Siu-pei), Dior Cheng Yee-kin (Lee Chi-ko), Richard Ng Yiu-hon (Ching Sing), Sandra Ng Kwan-yu (Chan Chi-sum), Ken Lo Wai-kwong (Wild Dog), Woo Fung (Uncle Zai), Shing Fui-on (Jerk), Wong Yat-fei (Hypnotist), Ronald Wong Pan (Chicken), Yuen King-tan (Bowling Alley Floozy), Helena Law Lan (Mrs. Lee), Ha Ping (Mrs. Wu). 1.85:1. VHS/LD: Tai Seng. Import LD/VCD: Star Entertainment. 97 minutes.

Only Wong Jing could come up with something like this: When they think that their father is dying of testicular cancer(!), sisters Siu-tung (a butch supercop), Siu-nam (a social worker), and Siu-sze (a doctor) try to make him happy by getting boyfriends in time for his birthday party. Siu-tung picks effeminate gigolo Simon Tse Sai, Siu-nam hooks up with crass triad tough guy Wu Ying, and Siu-sze chooses 27-year-old virgin Chi-ko. After various trials and tribulations, the girls find that their temporary choices are actually ideal ones, but the party has two unexpected visitors: dad's fortune-hunting pen pal from overseas and the vicious killer Wild Dog, who is gunning for Siu-tung.

The jokes are predictably scattershot but the cast is game, and their enthusiasm goes a long way in making this a worthwhile diversion. Highlights include Leung's masochistic pursuit of Lin, the former's wicked Bruce Lee imitation, and the Triad Olympics," which features contestants engaging in underworld versions of events like the long jump (they are weighted down with big bags of heroin) and the 4 × 100 Relay (runners are armed with machetes instead of batons). Good fun all around.

111. The Brave Archer

(1977; Shaw Brothers) ★: 6/10. *Se diu ying hung juen* (Cantonese), *She diao ying xiong zhuan* (Mandarin): "Legend of the Eagle Shooting Hero." Cinematographer: Kung Mu-to; Art Director: Johnson Tsao; Music: Not Original; Writers: Jin Yong, Ngai Hong; Producer: Mona Fong Yat-wah; Action Director: Li Chi-hsing; Director: Chang Cheh. Cast: Alexander Fu Sheng (Kuo Ching), Tien Niu (Yung-er), Ku Kuan-chung (Yung-er's Father), Danny Lee Sau-yin (Au Yang Feng), Johnny Wang Lung-wei (Au Yang's Master), Ku Feng (Hung, aka The Nine-Fingered Beggar), Dick Wei (Lao-yi), Kara Hui Ying-hung (Nin-chi), Phillip Kwok Tsui (Cho), Fan Mui-sang (Ling). 2.35:1. No official domestic video release. 127 minutes. Also known as **Kung Fu Warlords** (US Title).

Adapted from Jin Yong's famous novel *The Eagle Shooting Heroes* (also the basis of **Ashes of Time**, **Dong Cheng Xi Jiu**, and numerous TV mini-series), this kung fu epic unfolds in the Sung Dynasty. After his father is murdered, young Kuo Ching is instructed in kung fu by a group of experts until he reaches the age of eighteen. One of Ching's instructors is murdered by an opponent using the "Skeleton Claw" technique, which allows the user to plunge their fingers through an opponent's flesh and bone. In a desperate move, Ching stabs the man in the stomach, inadvertently hitting the killer's one vulnerable point. The lad then befriends a beggar who later reveals herself to be the noblewoman Yung-er, and the pair receive instruction from Hung. Known as The Nine-Fingered Beggar, Hung's incredible kung fu allows him to shatter a tree trunk with only one blow. Armed with this ability, Ching's fighting prowess is significantly increased and further instruction from an eccentric master named Cho gives him even more power. However, if Ching wishes Yung-er's hand in marriage, he will have to undergo three tests, two of which do not involve kung fu (in the traditional sense anyway).

The extremely involved plot certainly plays out like a novel adapted for film, and viewers unfamiliar with the source material will quickly find themselves confused by the steady stream of characters, loyalties, and betrayals. Occasional input from a narrator helps, but many Westerners will still find their initial viewing a rather confounding experience. Still, the quality of the martial arts and the inclusion of some interesting fantasy elements provide good compensation. Ti Lung, Lu Feng, and Jamie Luk Kim-ming are among the familiar faces who also appear. The stock soundtrack includes cues that would later be used in **Dawn of the Dead**. Character names above are from the dubbed version. It was followed by **The Brave Archer Part II** (1978), **The Brave Archer Part III** (1981), and **The Brave Archer and His Mate** (1982).

112. The Bride with White Hair

(1993; Mandarin Films/Yes Pictures) ★: 10/10. *Baak faat moh nui* (Cantonese), *Bai fa mo nu* (Mandarin): "The Evil White-Haired Lady." Cinematographer: Peter Pau Tak-hei; Art Director: Eddie Ma Poon-chiu; Music: Richard Yuen Cheuk-fan; Writers: Ronny Yu Yan-tai, David Wu Tai-wai, Lam Kei-to, Elsa Tang Pik-yin; Producers: Raymond Wong Pak-ming, Wong Hak-hoi; Action Director: Phillip Kwok Tsui; Director: Ronny Yu Yan-tai. Cast: Leslie Cheung Kwok-wing (Cho Yi-hang), Brigitte Lin Ching-hsia (Lien Ni-chang, aka The Wolf Girl), Elaine Lui Siu-ling (Female Chi Wu-shuang), Francis Ng Chun-yu (Male Chi Wu-shuang), Yammie Nam Kit-ying (Ho Lu-hua), Pau Fong (Master Tzu Yang), Law Lok-lam (Pai Yun), Joseph Cheng King-kei (Hsin Cheng), Eddy Ko Hung (General Wu San-kuei). Dolby Stereo. 2.35:1. VHS/LD/DVD: Tai Seng (Remastered for the English market; subtitled or dubbed). Import LD/VCD/DVD: Universe. 89 minutes.

The key HK fantasy of the '90s thus far, **The Bride with White Hair** is one of the most visually resplendent, graceful, and romantic films the genre has produced in some time. Based on the 1950s novel by Leung Yu-sang (first adapted in 1970 by director Chen Hsin-yen as **The White-Haired Devil Lady**, and then corrupted by Pearl Chang Ling's demented **Wolf Devil Woman** [1982; aka **Wolfen Ninja**]), the film takes the key elements of its source and updates them through the inclusion of a morally flawed protagonist, a darker and more sensual tone, and a particularly outrageous villain. Set in the genuine historical period when Manchurians were invading the Chung Yuan province, the story chronicles the campaign waged by the provincial clans against a vicious blood cult led by Chi Wu-shuang, supernaturally-gifted Siamese twins joined at the back. A "Romeo and Juliet" angle enters into the story when top clan warrior Cho Yi-hang becomes infatuated with The Wolf Girl, the blood cult's beautiful and powerful assassin. Abandoned as a baby and raised by a pack of wolves, Wolf Girl has never been allowed to experience compassion and love, but Yi-hang's affection causes these feelings to soon blossom within her. Giving his lover the name "Lien Ni-chang" and promising to never betray her trust, Yi-hang seeks to find a place where they can leave the fighting and horror of battle behind. However, the male half of Chi Wu-shuang has become hopelessly infatuated with Ni-chang and, when she seeks to leave the cult, he makes her walk a gauntlet of death. When Ni-chang survives the punishment and leaves to rejoin her lover, the twins seek vengeance by setting in motion a plan that will devastate Yi-hang's clan and set him against the woman to whom he has pledged his life.

An impeccably designed production from top to bottom, the film comes alive with the sort of imagery that dazzles the eye and arouses the senses—thanks to the efforts of director Yu and cinematographer Peter Pau (*Saviour of the Soul, The Phantom Lover*). Although the tone of the story varies, the visuals are always abundantly colorful, possessing a shading and natural texture that is in keeping with the florid standards of Chinese fantasy while also displaying darker and more contemporary stylistics. The offbeat casting of Leslie Cheung in a role that would usually be played by a martial arts star like Jet Li is one of the director's most astute decisions. In contrast to the classically stolid and moral martial arts hero, Yi-hang has real doubts about his people and the direction his master is herding him, and this greater depth of character requires a more seasoned and diverse actor like Cheung to really pull it off. Cheung excelled at playing a similarly flawed protagonist in **Rouge** (where he also betrayed the female lead), and his performance here mixes the strengths of that portrayal with the complexity of a man uncertain of his allegiances and feelings. As Ni-chang,

Chinese fantasy film queen Brigitte Lin gives one of her most memorable characterizations. Lovingly photographed (with two particularly striking close-ups of her eyes) and clad in dazzling costumes created by noted Japanese designer Emi Wada (**Ran**), Lin cuts an imposing but fascinating figure: a remorseless killer who experiences new feelings (love, joy, sexual ecstasy, etc.) with all the unrestrained delight of a child. Francis Ng and Elaine Lui have a high old time as the villainous twins (a hermaphrodite in the original story), overamping every emotion to the nth degree, and Eddy Ko is memorable in a supporting role as the real-life figure General Wu San-kuei, whose ambitions and failings contrast with those of Yi-hang. A sequel followed a few months later.

113. The Bride with White Hair 2

(1993; Mandarin Films/Yes Pictures) ★: 8/10. *Baak faat moh nui 2* (Cantonese), *Bai fa mo nu 2* (Mandarin): "The Evil White-Haired Lady 2." Cinematographer: Joe Chan Kong-hung; Art Director: Bill Lui Cho-hung; Music: Richard Yuen Cheuk-fan; Writers: Raymond To Kwok-wai, David Wu Tai-wai, Ronny Yu Yan-tai; Producers: Ronny Yu Yan-tai, Clifton Ko Chi-sum; Action Director: Phillip Kwok Tsui; Director: David Wu Tai-wai. Cast: Brigitte Lin Ching-hsia (Lien Ni-chang), Sunny Chan Kam-hung (Fung Chun-kit), Christy Chung Lai-tai (Ling Yuet-yee, aka Moon), Joey Maan Yee-man (Lyre), Ruth Winona Tao Kwun-mei (Chen Yuen-yuen), Leslie Cheung Kwok-wing (Cho Yi-hang), Richard Suen Kwok-ho (Liu Hang), Lily Chung Suk-wai (Ying-wai), Cheung Kwok-leung (Siu Lau), Yeung Tak-ngai (Yee), Ng Chun-fung (Lan Long), Lee Heung-kam (Yip Pak-chow), Helena Law Lan (Wu Tang Clan Elder), Eddy Ko Hung (General Wu San-kuei). 1.85:1. VHS/LD/DVD: Tai Seng (Remastered for the English market; subtitled or dubbed). Import LD/VCD: Mei Ah. 80 minutes. Also known as **The White-Haired Swordswoman II**.

The tragic love story of Lien Ni-chang and Cho Yi-hang continues in this satisfying follow-up, which proceeds along a slightly different path from its acclaimed predecessor. Following the massacre of the Wu Tang clansmen at the climax of Part I, Cho has gone into retreat atop Mount Shin Fung to await the blossoming of the magic flower that can cure his lover. Transformed by her severe anguish into an ashen witch with a long mane of poisonous hair, the spurned Ni-chang establishes an all-female cult and vents her rage against men by vowing to exterminate the remaining members of The Eight Clans of Chung Yuan. The clan elders gather together a group of young warriors from among their dwindled numbers in order to launch a desperate preemptive strike against Ni-chang and her bloodthirsty disciples.

This sequel (which shifts from the romantic fantasy of its predecessor to something more closely aligned with the horror genre) has been criticized for pushing the central plot into the background (reducing Leslie Cheung to a mere eight minutes of screen time in the process), concentrating instead on its cast of newcomers. While their respective tales are not as compelling, they all acquit themselves well (particularly Canadian-born Christy Chung as the chain-smoking tomboy warrior "Moon"), and director David Wu (editor and co-writer of the first film) does a good job of preserving the ambience of the preceding chapter. Although Ni-chang isn't as alluringly mysterious this time around, Lin (looking hauntingly beautiful in the pallid make-up) does a skilful job of rendering her divided nature; it is hard to imagine any other actress handling both the poignant and menacing aspects of the role with the same degree of affecting conviction. The fiery climax, which closes the story in definitive fashion, compares favorably with all the finest moments of the original—not surprising when one learns that it was actually directed by Yu.

114. Broken Oath

(1977; Golden Harvest/Paragon Films) ★: 7/10. *Poh gaai* (Cantonese), *Po jie* (Mandarin): "Broken Buddhist." Cinematographers: Wong Wing-lung, Wong Tik; Music: Frankie Chan Fan-kei; Writer: Shin Kon; Producer: Raymond Chow Man-wai; Action Directors: Yuen Woo-ping, Hsu Hsia; Director: Chang Cheung-wo. Cast: Angela Mao Ying (Lotus Lin), Michael Chan Wai-man (Chou Tsai/Yuan Sing), Dean Shek Tien (To's Man at Brothel), Bruce Leung Siu-hung. 2.35:1. VHS: Tai Seng (No Subtitles). Running time unknown.

This period kung fu thriller is constructed around the usual revenge scenario, but the fighting is excellent and the beautiful Angela Mao is beguiling in a role that is a major change from her usual heroines. Following the brutal murder of her husband, a noblewoman is able to gouge out the eye of one assailant. He turns out to be a captain of the guards, and she is sent to a prison island for life. Before dying, she gives birth to a daughter, and the baby is brought up by some female monks. Given the name Lotus, the girl (who likes to keep deadly scorpions as pets) grows up to be an expert fighter, but her violent nature and all encompassing interest in kung fu soon gets her expelled from the monastery. After learning the details of her mother's plight, Lotus sets out to exact revenge. Working as a pickpocket, she gradually hunts down the men responsible for her mother's death twenty years earlier. After eliminating the first two, she has herself sold to a brothel in order to kill the man who runs it. However, things take an unexpected turn when Lotus is poisoned and needs the aid of the only man with the medical knowledge to save her. The identity of this man is not difficult to deduce, but there is also a military conspiracy at work behind the scenes.

Lotus is an unusual character for Mao because the girl possesses a dark and violent streak even before she knows that revenge is going to be a part of her destiny. The basics of the plot have been lifted from Toshio Fujita's Japanese film **Lady Snowblood** (1974), and while **Broken Oath** is a much more conventional effort, it remains an exciting showcase for Mao's considerable talents. The in-your-face combat almost seems to have been designed with 3-D in mind, as blades, swords, spears, poles, and fire constantly shoot into the camera. Sammo Hung Kam-po, Yuen Yat-chor, and Lam Ching-ying are among the numerous henchmen Mao punches and kicks into a bloody pulp. Born in South Korea, director Chang Cheung-wo is best known for helming the Shaw Brothers film **King Boxer** (1972) which Warner Brothers released in North America to great success in 1973 as **Five Fingers of Death**. Character names listed above are from the dubbed version.

115. Brotherhood

(1987) ★: 5/10. *Yee boon mo yin* (Cantonese), *Yi ben wu yan* (Mandarin): "Chivalry Needs No Words." Cinematographer: Cheung Tak-wai; Art Director: Yank Wong Yan-kwai; Music: Richard Yuen Cheuk-fan; Writer: Wong Ying; Producer: Charles Heung Wah-keung; Action Director: Power Lee King-chu; Director: Billy Chan Wui-ngai. Cast: Ko Chuen-hsiang (Ho Chen-tung), Chow Yun-fat (Hui), Lam Wai (Han), Dick Wei (Mai Chih-chieh), Shum Wai (Wei), Shing Fui-on (Li Piao), Dennis Chan Kwok-san (Chang), Danny Lee Sau-yin (Mai's Superior). 1.85:1. VHS: Tai Seng, Ocean Shores (Dubbed). Import LD: Ocean Shores. 88 minutes. Also known as **Code of Honour** (Ocean Shores LD title), **Triad Savagers** [*sic*], **Triad Savages** (Ocean Shores dubbed VHS title).

Despite his prominent billing, Chow Yun-fat only has a supporting role in this dreary triad thriller. Taiwanese actor Ko Chuen-hsiang plays Ho, an aged ganglord who seeks to conduct his affairs in a civil fashion, a goal made difficult by his brutal underlings. A police inspector, determined to see him behind bars to avenge the crippling of his brother, arrests some of Ho's men and convinces them to testify against him. Han, a Vietnamese refugee who had saved Ho's life years before and has remained friends with him, eliminates the witnesses without obtaining Ho's permission. This forces the courts to dismiss the gangster for lack of evidence, but the police compile evidence that makes it look as if Ho ordered the murders. Chow (who only has about ten minutes of screen time) plays Ho's disillusioned son, who has chosen to live in Australia rather than be a party to his father's ways. Nothing new here. Believe it or not, a sequence in which Shum Wai rapes a defenceless girl was reused by director Billy Chan in his 1994 comedy **Beginner's Luck**! Arena/Xenon's **Hong Kong Corruptor** is a retitled version of **Return Engagement** "supplemented" by footage of Chow Yun-fat lifted from **Brotherhood**.

116. Buddha's Lock

(1987; Shenzhen Film Enterprise/ Highland Films Enterprises) ★: 5/10. *Tin po shan* (Cantonese), *Tian pu sa* (Mandarin): "Heavenly Buddha." Cinematographer: Lu Yue, Wang Xiaolie; Art Director: William Cheung Suk-ping; Music: Zhao Jiping; Writer: Kong Liang; Producers: Zheng Huili, Wang Zanxian; Director: Yim Ho. Cast: John X. Heart (James Wood), Zhang Lutong (Niu Niu), Hu Xiaobao, Yan Bide, Wei Zongwan. 1.85:1. Import LD: Ocean Shores. 96 minutes.

Based on a real incident, this HK-China co-production unfolds in an extremely remote part of the Mainland where slavery was regularly practised until the Red Army put a stop to it in the mid 1950s. In 1945 American soldier James Wood is kidnapped, taken into the Liang Mountains, and sold as a slave to the Shama clan. Treated like one of the village's animals, he tries to escape but quickly discovers that the area is surrounded by high cliffs. Forced to do manual labor, Wood (called "La Tie" by the Shamas) eventually learns the language. As time passes, the clan acquires another slave, a pretty young girl named Niu Niu, and the pair soon fall in love. However, after he is caught fraternizing with the chief's daughter, Wood is sold again and separated from Niu Niu (who wants nothing to do with him anyway, since she perceives the incident as a betrayal). They are reunited when all of the slaves are freed, but Niu Niu is not yet ready to forgive him.

Essentially an up-market version of movies like **A Man Called Horse** and **Man From Deep River** (which, like the latter, possesses sequences that will make animal lovers cringe), **Buddha's Lock** proceeds in much the same fashion but actually does not dwell enough on the clash of cultures for the scenario to be convincing. Heart's no-better-than-adequate performance is a further hindrance (the English language sequences setting up the story are extremely stilted). When all is said and done, the film's primary asset is its magnificent location work and depiction of a segment of Chinese society rarely seen in movies. The title refers to the way the Shama men wear their hair, a style that Heart's character eventually adopts.

117. The Buddhist Fist

(1980; Peace Film Production Co.) ★: 6/10. *Fat jeung lo hon kuen* (Cantonese), *Fo zhang luo han quan* (Mandarin): "Buddha Palm Disciple of Buddha Fist." Cinematographer: Michael Ma Koon-wah; Music: Chan Fan-chi; Writers: Lam Chiming, Wong Jing, Tsui Siu-ming; Producers: Leung Wing-yin, Yuen Woo-ping; Action Direction: The Yuen Clan; Director: Yuen Woo-ping. Cast: Yuen Shun-yee (Shang), Tsui Siu-ming (Si-ming), Simon Yuen Siu-tien (Old Guard at the Temple), Fan Mui-sang (Fat Master), Peter Chan Lung (Yu), Lee Hoi-sang (Chen), David Wu Tai-wai (Police Captain), Yuen Cheung-yan (Leader of Thugs). 2.35:1. VHS: World Video, Arena/Xenon (Dubbed). DVD: Arena/Xenon. 86 minutes.

One of director Yuen Woo-ping's lesser works, **The Buddhist Fist** still features some excellent martial arts and will please most fans of old school genre films. Bumbling barber Shang is fired from his job and sets out across the countryside to visit his father. Upon arriving home, he is unable to find the man but does encounter his childhood friend, Si-ming, who is now a monk. Both men were raised by the same Shaolin master and are martial arts experts. A while back, Si-ming violated his vows by getting drunk and was framed for the rape and murder of a woman. Now he is being forced to commit criminal acts by a mysterious figure who threatens to reveal Si-ming's crimes to the public unless he complies. After assassins try to kill him, Shang learns from a policeman that his father had discovered a plot hatched by foreigners to steal some of China's treasures. The man blackmailing Si-ming is also part of the scheme, and Shang faces a difficult decision when he learns of his friend's involvement.

Neither the story nor the characters are as interesting as their counterparts in Yuen's other work from this period. However, the kung fu is up to standard (particularly an extended duel between Yuen Shun-yee and Lee Hoi-sang), and veterans Simon Yuen and Fan Mui-sang are quite appealing in supporting roles. Character names are from the dubbed version.

118. The Buddhist Spell

(1993) ★: 3/10. *Pooi tai yau gwai* (Cantonese), *Pu ti you gui* (Mandarin): "Mystical Boddhi Ghost." Cinematographer: Seng Hsi-lin; Art Director: Wang Yi-hsiao, Li Bao-lin; Music: Not Original; Writers: Wu Wen-liang, Wang Kai, Cheng Man-wah; Producer: Li Rongfang; Action Director: Wang Yao; Director: Chao Lu-chiang. Cast: Sharla Cheung Man (Miss Shen), Mark Cheng Ho-nam (Feng Yun-tin), Wu Ma (The Fa Da Monk), Lung Fong (Register), Lau Shun (Da Hung Leader). 1.85:1. VHS/LD: World Video. Import LD/VCD: Mei Ah. 91 minutes.

This low-budget Taiwanese period fantasy is good for little beyond a few unintentional laughs, though it does deserve a few points for being earnest. After being raped by the evil Register [*sic*], Miss Shen seeks vengeance but is killed when the Register rams her head into a tree trunk that is being transported by woodsman Feng Yun-tin. This is no ordinary tree, however; it is magical, thousand-year-old sacred wood and now houses the dead girl's soul. Miss Shen asks Yun-tin's help to get revenge, threatening to possess him forever if he refuses. As thanks for his assistance, she stays with Yun-tin while he transforms the wood into a holy statue of Kwanyin which will, unfortunately, have the side effect of dispersing Miss Shen's spirit upon completion. Now in love with the ghostly beauty, Yun-tin is having second thoughts about his assigned task. The malevolent leader of the Da Hung religious cult does not want the idol completed either, as it will prevent him from unleashing the monstrous "Blood Kid" on the world.

While it does offer up a couple of novel ideas and has no shortage of action, **The Buddhist Spell** is far too cheap for its ambitions. A group of vicious birdmen sport spandex tights and dimestore monster masks, the opticals are really cheesy, and the Blood Kid looks like something out of a teenager's backyard Super 8 epic. There is also the (admittedly novel) sight of people being chased and killed by a glowing plastic log! If you must watch this, be sure to avoid the World Video tape and LD, which are derived from a very worn and censored print with Bahasa subtitles floating around the middle of the screen. The soundtrack includes music lifted from **Maniac** and **Mad Max**.

119. Bullet for Hire

(1991; Vediocam Film Productions Co.) ★: 5/10. *Chi daan chut cho* (Cantonese), *Zi dan chu zu* (Mandarin): "Bullet for Hire." Cinematographer: Johnny Koo Kwok-wah; Art Director: Ken Yip Kwok-kin; Music: Mak Ho-lan; Producer: Chan Kin-ting; Action Directors: Wong Kwan, Cheung Long; Writer-Director: Yuen Chun-man. Cast: Jacky Cheung Hok-yau (Shan), Simon Yam Tat-wah (Han), Dick Wei (Dick), Lo Lieh (Ngok), Sheila Chan Sak-lan (Lan). 1.85:1. VHS/LD: World Video. Import LD/VCD: Ocean Shores. Import DVD: Winner's Workshop. 93 minutes.

This downbeat, grungy-looking action-thriller delivers what it promises but has little to offer beyond that. Close friends Han and Ngok are veteran contract killers hired to take care of a foreign dignitary in HK for a conference on how to combat triad gangs. The partners perform the hit, but a female agent (**Angel**'s Elaine Lui) manages to escape them. Their boss insists that they take on the young, inexperienced Vietnamese refugee Shan as a new partner. The rookie then proceeds to botch his first assignment and must be bailed out by Han's prompt intervention. After carrying out a number of jobs, Shan's confidence and proficiency start to grow, and he becomes a worthwhile assistant to Han. However, the police have discovered Ngok's daughter, whom he has kept secret from his employers, and use her to blackmail him into informing for them. During a subsequent assignment, Ngok is "killed" and goes into hiding but is found by Han, who cannot carry out the order to terminate him. When Ngok is fatally wounded by other gunmen, he makes Han promise to take care of his daughter, but she is soon murdered as well. When the leader of the organization begins to suspect Shan's loyalty, he has the man's girlfriend kidnapped, but she is accidentally killed while trying to escape. With nothing left to lose, Han and Shan plot to take out their boss in a suicidal assault on his lavish residence. There is a surplus of gunplay here but no elan, and certainly none of the invigorating sense of excitement that permeated director Yuen's **Forbidden Arsenal** (1990).

120. Bullet in the Head

(1990; John Woo Productions) ★: 9/10. *Dip huet gaai tau* (Cantonese), *Die xie jie tou* (Mandarin): "Bloodshed on the Streets." Cinematographers: Ardy Lam Kwok-wah, Wilson Chan Pui-kai, Somchai Kittikun, Horace Wong Wing-heng. Art Director: James Leung Wah-sang; Music: James Wong Jim, Romeo Diaz; Writers: John Woo Yu-sen, Patrick Leung Pak-kin, Janet Chun Siu-chun; Action Director: Lau Chi-ho; Producer-Director: John Woo Yu-sen. Cast: Tony Leung Chiu-wai (Ben), Jacky Cheung Hok-yau (Frank), Waise Lee Chi-hung (Paul), Simon Yam Tat-wah (Luke), Yolinda Yan Cho-sin (Sally Yen Sau-ching), Fennie Yuen Kit-ying (Jane), Lam Chung (Y.S. Leong), Lau Sek-yin (Fatso), John Woo Yu-sen (Policeman). Dolby Digital (DVD Only). 1.85:1. VHS: Tai Seng. Import LD: Golden Cinema City. Import VCD: Mei Ah. Import DVD: Mega Star. 100/117/119/130 minutes.

John Woo's most emotionally powerful film, **Bullet in the Head** comes so close to being a masterpiece that it is genuinely tragic to see it go off the rails in the final reel. It opens in Hong Kong in 1967 during the period when Communist sympathizers were protesting against British rule by violently clashing with police in the streets. After secretly giving a loanshark the deed to his parents' home in order to pay for his friend Ben's wedding reception, Frank is badly beaten by gangster Ringo and his men, who are out to steal the money. In spite of his serious injuries, Frank manages to escape; later that evening he and Ben exact revenge on Ringo, accidentally killing him in the process. Pursued by both the authorities and the underworld, Ben, Frank, and their buddy Paul decide to smuggle medical supplies and fake Rolexes to Vietnam, figuring that the state of lawlessness caused by the war will allow them to make a quick buck. Almost immediately after their arrival, the goods are blown up during an assassination attempt, they are almost executed by the army, and their passports are confiscated. Spurred on by the increasingly money-hungry Paul, the trio join forces with Eurasian hitman Luke to extort money from Leong, the club owner they were supposed to deliver the supplies to. An arms dealer, Leong is supplying the North Vietnamese with guns and possesses a strongbox filled with stolen US Army gold. The robbers make off with the strongbox and also Sally Yen, a HK singer whom Leong has intentionally gotten addicted to heroin, but she is shot during their escape. The friends plan to take a boat back to HK but are attacked before they can leave. Sally dies, and Ben, Frank, and Paul are taken to a Vietcong POW camp. Accused of being CIA spies, the men are rescued by Luke and the American army, but the increasingly deranged Paul cares only about his gold. Frank is shot saving Paul's life, but the latter, convinced that Frank's cries of pain will give their position away to the VC soldiers nearby, proceeds to shoot him in the head. Unfortunately for Frank, the wound is not fatal, and doctors are unable to extract the slug, leaving him a brain-damaged, heroin-addicted lunatic in constant, agonizing pain. After seeing what has happened to his friend, Ben returns to HK in order to find his wife and confront Paul, now a wealthy and respected businessman.

It would not be the least bit specious to call **Bullet** a tearjerker for men. The film offers the same male bonding and high emotions that characterize Woo's earlier gangster pictures and unfolds amidst a surfeit of bloody but stylish violence. However, the superb, melancholy score by James Wong and Romeo Diaz manipulates one's emotions to a greater degree, and the juxtaposition of physical cruelty, mental anguish, and human debasement in the face of war gives this film a more powerful impact. This is never more true than in the sequence where Tony Leung Chiu-wai desperately tries to communicate with the mentally stricken Jacky Cheung by relating anecdotes from their ten-year friendship. Even after all of the horror and loss Ben has experienced in the time leading up to this moment, he has managed to cling to the hope of returning home with his buddy. With this tragic meeting, that last spark of faith evaporates and it is devastating to watch. Though the influence of **The Deer Hunter** is obvious, Woo's picture grabs you from the very opening (a montage introducing the characters, set to The Monkees' "I'm a Believer," which is also reprised at several other points)—while one could skip the first hour of the Michael Cimino picture and miss virtually nothing of import. Unfortunately, the film takes a wrong turn in the final act, concluding with a redundant car chase-shootout that would fit more comfortably into any triad actioner of the time. After all of the pain and the atrocities depicted during the Vietnam sequences, and the emotional crescendo of the meeting between Ben and Frank, it is simply too much to have to sit through more explosions and gunplay: If there was ever a film that needed to end on a whimper and not a bang, it's **Bullet In the Head**. Ironically, that is precisely how it does end on the VCD version, which features a much more emotionally satisfying climax in the boardroom of Paul's company. Alas, that edition is missing other footage that appears in the longer versions, so it is not entirely successful either. Other editions of the film are in circulation, including one that is whittled down to only 100 minutes; Woo's director's cut clocks in at 136 minutes.

121. Burning Ambition

(1989; Long Shong Pictures) ★: 7/10. *Lung chi chang ang* (Cantonese), *Long zhi zheng ba* (Mandarin): "Dragons Fighting for Supremacy." Cinematographer: Michael Ma Koon-wah; Music: Wong Fuk-ling; Writer: Merit Miracle Writers Group; Producers: Yu Su, Frankie Chan Fan-kei; Action Directors: Fung Hark-on, Austin Wai Tin-chi. Director: Frankie Chan Fan-kei. Cast: Frankie Chan Fan-kei (Chi-shau), Simon Yam Tat-wah (Tat-hwa), Miu Kiu-wai (Wai), Yukari Oshima (Chau Siao-tao), Ko Chuen-hsiang (Chau Hsiong), Kara Hui Ying-hung (Chau Siu-hong), Roy Chiao Hung (Hwa's Father), Eddy Ko Hung (Kau Chen), Austin Wai Tin-chi (Chau Chi-chung), Lau Siu-ming (Uncle Yee), Lau Chi-wing (Superintendent Lau), Jeff Falcon (Caucasian Killer), Robin Shou Wan-bo (Iron Club), Shing Fui-on (Cab Driver), Yam Sai-kwoon (Chen's Man), Fung Hark-on (The Witness). 1.85:1. VHS: Tai Seng. Import LD/VCD: Universe. 97 minutes.

Action and double-crosses dominate this lean and very satisfying triad thriller, which rarely ever stops to take a breath. The murder of a crime family's patriarch is the result of plotting by his brother, Chau Hsiong. He plans to utilize his weak-willed nephew, Wai, to usurp power from the latter's brother, Tat-hwa, but the family matriarch becomes wise to his skullduggery and orders Chau's death. Although he escapes with his life, the man's son and daughter do not, prompting Chau to contact his remaining son, Chi-shau. The latter arrives from Holland with a group of friends to seek revenge, setting the stage for a final, decisive battle for leadership.

More intricately plotted than most films of this type, **Burning Ambition** is also unique in that it offers no one who would qualify as heroic or be easy to empathize with. There is also nothing glamorous about the underworld life that is depicted here, which is another major departure from the norm. Of course, such digressions are nothing more than subtext in a Frankie Chan film; the focus is on action, first and foremost. The stuntwork and fight choreography are first-rate—in particular, an incredible, prolonged battle in a parking garage that features Yukari Oshima swinging a mean baseball bat (ouch) and Kara Hui having to fight in stocking feet on broken glass (double ouch!).

122. Burning Paradise

(1994; Golden Harvest/DLO Film Production/Silver Medal Productions) ★: 7/10. *Foh siu hung lin ji* (Cantonese), *Huo shao hong lian si* (Mandarin): "The Burning of Red Lotus Temple." Music: Mak Chun-hung; Writer: Nam Yin; Producer: Tsui Hark; Action Director: Chris Lee Kin-sang; Director: Ringo Lam Ling-tung. Cast: Willie Chi Tian-sheng (Fong Sai-yuk), Carman Lee Yeuk-tung (Tou-tou), Wong Kam-kong (Elder Kung), Yang Sheng (Hung Hei-kwun), Lam Chuen (Brooke), John Ching Tung (Crimson). 1.85:1. VHS: Tai Seng. Import LD/VCD: Star Entertainment. 104 minutes.

The bleakest martial arts thriller in many a moon, **Burning Paradise** finds legendary Ching Dynasty heroes Fong Sai-yuk and Hung Hei-kwun caught up in the Manchu government's quest to exterminate the students of Shaolin Temple (the premise of several martial arts films produced at Shaw Brothers). Following his capture at the hands of the Manchu general Crimson, Fong is incarcerated with his fellow pupils at Red Lotus Temple, a subterranean netherworld riddled with booby traps. Turning his back on Shaolin, Hung allies himself with the prison commander, Elder Kung, a brutal psychopath who likes to adorn his garish paintings with human blood and seeks new specimens for his collection of mummified women.

Almost unrelentingly dark and misanthropic (aside from some effectively droll moments in the opening reel), **Burning Paradise** can be looked upon as the antithesis of producer Tsui Hark's quixotic **Once Upon a Time in China** series, playing more like a cross between director Ringo Lam's nerve-wracking condemnation of the HK educational system, **School on Fire** (1988), and his fierce, yet decorative gangster thriller, **Full Contact** (1992). Particularly effective is the second act (highlighting the students' attempt to escape the dungeon), which unfolds tautly amidst the most cogent visuals of the director's career. The one stumbling block the film cannot overcome is its lack of a strong central performance, a key component of Lam's best work. When stacked up against a seasoned character actor like Wong Kam-kong, the young cast of newcomers make little impact when they aren't darting around on the lavish, multi-tiered sets. A box-office disaster, this forceful production's reputation should almost certainly improve with time, and it already enjoys a cult following in the West.

123. Burning Sensation

(1989; Golden Harvest/Bo Ho Films/Paragon Films) ★: 5/10. *Feng chuk gwai* (Cantonese), *Huo zhu gui* (Mandarin): "Fire Ghost." Cinematographers: Raymond Lam Fai-tai, Tom Lau Moon-tong; Art Director: Fu Chi-chung; Music: Anders Nelsson; Writers: Yuen Kai-chi, Ng Hong-cheung; Producers: Sammo Hung Kam-po, Chan Pui-wah; Action Directors: Sammo Hung Stuntmen Association, Chow Yuen-mo; Director: Wu Ma. Cast: Kenny Bee (Chien), Carol Cheng Yu-ling (Li Fan-hua), Wu Ma (Ma Hou-pao), James Wong Jim (Blindman), James Tien Chun (The Commissioner), Blackie Ko Shou-liang (Taxi Driver), Yip Wing-cho (Fatty). 1.85:1. VHS: Tai Seng. Import LD: Star Entertainment (No Subtitles). Import VCD: Mega Star (No Subtitles). 90 minutes.

Veteran character actor Wu Ma made one of his occasional trips behind the camera for this derivative and lackadaisical supernatural comedy. Peking Opera performer Li Fan-hua is accidentally burned to death during a live television performance in the 1950s. Thirty years later, fireman Chien rescues her spirit tablet from a burning building; in gratitude, she becomes his benefactor. Fired from his job, Chien moves in with his uncle Ma, a DJ nicknamed "The Ghost Ombudsman," who reads scary stories on the air (giving Wu a chance to sing his signature tune from **A Chinese Ghost Story**). Li inhabits their TV, where she appears on the opera set along with the rest of the cast and can interact with anyone watching (a gag handled with more success in Woody Allen's Buster Keaton homage **The Purple Rose of Cairo**). Li assumes human form to ward off a second female spook with a monstrous tongue (another **Chinese Ghost Story** reference) who seeks to drain Chien's lifeforce. Naturally, she and Chien soon fall in love but must first deal with the persistent ghost and the fact that Fan's allotted time in the human world is running out.

The first hour of **Burning Sensation** makes only occasional use of its supernatural elements, relying instead on a pretty tired catalogue of mistaken identity gags and situations. The final half hour picks up a bit during the subsequent rematch between Cheng and the other female spirit, but there's nothing on display here that hasn't been handled just as well (or better) elsewhere. The climax, which finds Chung joining in the Peking Opera performance in order to save Cheng from her predestined death, is clever but too reminiscent of the wrap-up in Johnny To Kei-fung's megahit **Eighth Happiness** (released the year before) to seem entirely satisfying.

124. Bury Me High

(1991; Golden Harvest/Bo Ho Films/Tsui Siu Ming/Paragon Films) ★: 6/10. *Wai Si-lei ji ba wong se gaap* (Cantonese), *Wei Sili zhi ba wang xie jia* (Mandarin): "Wai Si-lei: Tyrant Strip Armor" or "Wei Sili: Tyrant Strip Armor." Cinematographer: Peter Pau Tak-hei; Art

Director: Daniel Lee Yan-kong; Music: Chris Babida; Writers: Tsui Siu-ming, Cheung Wah-po, Sit Kar-wah; Action Directors: Tsui Siu-ming, Cho Wing; Producer-Director: Tsui Siu-ming. Cast: Moon Lee Choi-fung (Anna Wong), Tsui Siu-ming (Chen Chang-ching), Chin Kar-lok (Wisely), Sibelle Hu Hui-chung (Nguen Van Vong), Yuen Wah (General Nguen), Cho Wing (Van Bao), Kenneth Tsang Kong (The President), Corey Yuen Kwai (Wei Tien-hsien), Paul Chun Pui (Nguen). Dolby Stereo. 1.85:1. VHS: Tai Seng (Poor Subtitles). Import LD: Ocean Shores (Poor Subtitles). 102 minutes.

Inspired by **Raiders of the Lost Ark**, this big budget fantasy adventure concerns a mountain region in Carrinan which possesses such potent *feng shui* that the descendants of those buried in its soil are rewarded with gifts like great knowledge or immense wealth. However, such blessings only last for a period of 24 years unless a special ritual is performed. Americans Anna Wong (whose corporation is facing ruin) and Wisely (who is dying of a brain tumor) travel to the area, accompanied by UCLA professor Chang, seeking to reverse their recent ill-fortune. What they find is a country coming apart at the seams. The power-mad General Nguen has taken over and plans to use the district's magical properties to turn his small country into a world power. Joining forces with a local rebel group, the Americans try to stop the General before he can implement his plan.

Beautifully photographed by Peter Pau (**The Bride with White Hair**) on some spectacular locations, **Bury Me High** features a near-constant series of action sequences, some staged on a scale rarely seen in HK cinema. These factors, combined with some fine martial arts and a unique (if not exactly plausible) storyline, make this well worth catching. The Wisely character is a famous figure in Chinese literature and has also been utilized in such films as **The Seventh Curse**, **The Legend of Wisely** and **The Cat**.

125. Butterfly & Sword

(1993; Chang Hong Channel Film & Video Co.) ★: 8/10. *San lau sing woo dip gim* (Cantonese), *Xin liu xing hu die jian* (Mandarin): "New Comet, Butterfly Sword." Cinematographer: Chen Rong-shu; Art Director: Andy Lee Yiu-kwong; Music: Chris Babida; Writer: John Chong Ching; Producers: Mark Wu Dan, Jessica Hsu Pei-rong; Action Director: Ching Siu-tung; Director: Michael Mak Dong-kit. Cast: Tony Leung Chiu-wai (Sing), Michelle Yeoh Chu-kheng (Sister Ko), Joey Wang Tsu-hsien (Butterfly), Donnie Yen Chi-tan (Yip Cheung), Jimmy Lin Chi-ying (Prince Cha), Elvis Tsui Kam-kong (Master Suen), Tou Chung-wah (Lui), Yeh Chuan-chen (Ho Ching). 1.85:1. VHS: Tai Seng (Subtitled), Youngtze (Dubbed). LD: Tai Seng. Import LD: Golden Cinema City. 87 minutes. Also known as **Butterfly Sword**, **Comet, Butterfly & Sword** (Youngtze video title).

Out of all the entries in the period fantasy craze, this Taiwanese production features the most amazing action scenes. It's a striking ballet of beautifully choreographed bloodshed (courtesy of the great Ching Siu-tung) which belies its middling production values and familiar storyline. An adaptation of Ku Long's novel of the same name (first filmed in the '80s by director Chor Yuen for Shaw Brothers as **Killer Clan**), the film is, reportedly, faithful to its source. The plot is an intricate yarn about a group of childhood friends caught up years later in a tangle of betrayal and court machinations. Sister Ko and her followers in the "Happy Forest" clan do the bidding of the terminally ill Eunuch Tsao. His final mission for Ko is that she steal a valuable scroll and kill Master Suen, the head of "Elite Villa." After an initial attack (led by Yip Cheung), fails, Ko enlists the services of Sing. A proficient killer, Sing is also the object of her affections. However, he only has eyes for his wife-to-be, Butterfly, who is unaware of his activities in the martial world. Sing manages to gain Suen's confidence and infiltrates Elite Villa, encountering his old friend Ho Ching, whom Ko also has working undercover (unbeknownst to Sing). When Ching's cover is blown, she is murdered, leading to an angry confrontation between Sing and Ko, a final showdown with Elite Villa, and the unmasking of a traitor in the ranks.

Even by the standards of Chinese fantasy, the combat is incredibly fluid and wonderfully outrageous: Opponents ricochet off walls, floors, and trees; swordsmen fly through the air using knives as makeshift helicopter blades; and bamboo stalks become weapons as deadly as swords. The wildest martial arts stance on display is undoubtedly "The Flying Arrow," which features Yeoh using her sash to propel the sword-wielding Leung right *through* his enemies! The principals are all fine, but it is Yeoh who walks away with the film, handling both the action and the more earthbound components of the part with her customary skill and finesse. The inclusion of pop singer Jimmy Lin is an unfortunate commercial concession to the teen crowd but, thankfully, he only appears briefly. Chu Yen-ping (who is often erroneously credited with directing this film) later recycled footage, costumes, and sets from this film in his period softcore bore **Slave of the Sword** (1993). The domestic video versions are missing the original ending (found in Taiwan prints), which runs about one minute extra and features two of the main characters leaping off a cliff into the ocean. The viewer is left to decide whether their fall is fatal or not.

126. The Butterfly Murders

(1979; Seasonal Film Corporation) ★: 8/10. *Dip bin* (Cantonese), *Die bian* (Mandarin): "Butterfly Transformation." Cinematographer: Fan Chin-yu; Writer: Lam Fan; Producer: Ng See-yuen; Action Director: Wong Shee-tong; Director: Tsui Hark. Cast: Lau Siu-ming (Fong), Michelle Mai Suet (Green Shadow), Eddy Ko Hung (Kwok, aka "Hell's Fire"), Hsia Guang-li (The Lieutenant), Wong Shee-tong, Chan Kei-kei, Cheung Kwok-chu. 2.35:1. VHS: World Video (Poor Subtitles). Import LD: Far East Music. Import VCD: Mei Ah (Poor Subtitles). 89 minutes.

Tsui Hark's directorial debut is a most unusual effort: Imagine a traditional swordplay adventure restructured like a murder mystery and spiced with horror elements from Alfred Hitchcock's **The Birds** (1963). The storyline tells of a noble family beset by a most unusual threat: clouds of bloodsucking butterflies, which may be the result of a curse. Travelling writer/adventurer Fong and his enthusiastic female assistant, Green Shadow, arrive at the family's castle and must soon take shelter with them in the catacombs when the insects begin their attacks anew. During a period of calm, the master instructs his servants to cover the central building with giant nets, keeping the butterflies out but, just as effectively, sealing the humans inside. In spite of this precaution, the creatures invade the castle through air ducts and kill the master in his study. As per instructions in the man's will, a trio of skilled killers (called "The Thunders") are summoned but their assistance seems dubious, particularly as their arrival coincides with that of an armor-clad assassin who stalks the castle corridors.

Tsui was hired to direct **The Butterfly Murders** on the basis of **The Gold Dagger Romance**, his television miniseries adaptation of Ku Long's celebrated martial arts novel. While the series is lamentably unavailable for viewing on video, one can speculate that it engendered the devices that Tsui utilizes throughout **Butterfly**: quick cuts, shock edits, and layered sound (fairly unremarkable, perhaps, by Western standards but more detailed and intriguing than most HK productions). Beautifully shot and lit, the film's atmosphere is palpable and foreboding even before Fong and Green Shadow arrive at their destination. Lau Siu-ming plays the wandering hero, who records history in his memoirs while also shaping it. He is not, however, a martial artist. Instead, he fulfils the role of detective, making him a unique protagonist in the genre. By contrast, the abilities of Michelle Mai's sprightly Green Shadow provide a preview of the high-flying, wire-enhanced acrobatics that would dominate Tsui's later period fantasies. The story's resolution is as offbeat as the events leading up to it, and highly satisfying. The version previewed did not provide credits for some behind-the-scenes personnel. Lam Fan is the only credited writer on the print, but some sources attribute the screenplay to Lam Chi-ming and Leung Nan-kan. Similarly, there is no onscreen music or art director credit, but Chan Chun-chi and Joseph Koo Kar-fai are sometimes listed as the composers (there are several familiar library cues, regardless), and Chan Ching-san is occasionally acknowledged in the latter category. Incidentally, if you watch the Far East Music LD, don't be surprised when a *commercial* appears midway through the film!

Butterfly Sword *see* **Butterfly & Sword**

127. By Hook or By Crook

(1980) ★: 6/10. *Haam yue faan sang* (Cantonese), *Xian yu fan sheng* (Mandarin): "Salted Fish Turned Over." Cinematographer: Ho Ming; Art Director: Yuen Tai-yung; Music: Not Original; Writer: Raymond Wong Pak-ming; Producer: Karl Maka; Action Direction: Sammo Hung Stuntmen Association; Director: Karl Maka. Cast: Sammo Hung Kam-po (Fatso), Dean Shek Tien (Skinny Gee), Wu Ma (The Flower Kid), Karl Maka (Sheriff Butcher Wing), Chung Fat (Chung Fa-pai, aka "The Golden Killer"), Lam Ching-ying (Gang Leader), Eric Tsang Chi-wai ("The Cold Killer"). 2.35:1. VHS: Tai Seng (Poor Subtitles). Import LD: Golden Cinema City. Import VCD: Mega Star. 92 minutes.

This old-fashioned period kung fu farce is uneven but aficionados are sure to enjoy it for its cast of old favorites, each in their prime. A series of robberies has the countryside up in arms. The single bloom left at the scene of each crime points to the culprit being none other than "The Flower Kid," China's answer to Robin Hood. When he is unable to apprehend the bandit himself, bumbling Sheriff Butcher Wing blackmails local layabout Skinny Gee to help him slap the cuffs on the troublesome fugitive. Skinny discovers that the crimes are actually being committed by Fatso, a corpulent but martially talented young man, who is merely impersonating the fabled thief. Seeking out the Real McCoy, Skinny and Fatso discover that The Flower Kid is now a cowardly old man who certainly does not live up to his reputation. Nonetheless, Fatso is overjoyed to meet his idol and is eager to try and get him back into shape, when a woman jilted by The Flower Kid several years ago hires the ruthless "Golden Killer" to do the old man in. With a little deception and an equal portion of silver, Skinny and Fatso help The Flower Kid to regain his confidence and his abilities.

The humor in the first half misses the mark more often than not (though there are a couple of gags involving anachronisms that are genuinely inspired) but the film remains watchable. The second half is a marked improvement, serving up somewhat sharper writing and a better selection of both comic and serious martial arts. The plot is not unlike that of a western and, fittingly enough, most of the musical cues have been stolen from various spaghetti western soundtracks. If at all possible, try and see the Golden Cinema City laserdisc, which has a beautiful letterboxed transfer (if only all films of this vintage were presented this well!).

128. Cageman

(1992; Filmagica Productions) ★: 8/10. *Lung man* (Cantonese), *Long min* (Mandarin): "Cage People." Cinematographer: Ardy Lam Kwok-wah; Art Directors: Yank Wong Yan-kwai, Chin Yiu-hang; Music: Eugene Pau Yee-ching; Writers: Yank Wong Yan-kwai, Ng Chong-chau, Jacob Cheung Chi-leung; Producer-Director: Jacob Cheung Chi-leung. Cast: Roy Chiao Hung (Koo Yiu-cho), Michael Lee Ming-yeung (7-11), Wong Kar-kui (Mao), Liu Kai-chi (Sam), Teddy Robin Kwan (Tong Sam), Ku Feng (Luk Tung), Victor Wong Chi-keung (Sissy), Lau Shun (The Taoist), Woo Fung (Lam Tsung), Lau Yee-tat (Man Gambling), Joe Junior (Charlie), Dennis Chan Kwok-san (Councillor Tsui), Herman Yau Lai-to (TV Director). Stereo Sound (LD only). 1.85:1. VHS: Tai Seng. Import LD/VCD: Universe. 144 minutes.

So many HK films concentrate on wealth and glamor that this Best Picture award winner comes as a sobering reminder that reality is often much harsher. The titular men are so-called because they live in wire cages (little bigger than those often used to house dogs) clustered together in rundown buildings, with no privacy or other comforts one takes for granted. One such establishment is The Wah Ha Men's Hostel, run by Koo and his retarded son, Sam. When the building's owners announce that they plan to evict everyone in eight weeks time, Koo enlists the aid of two opposing local politicians to try to either stave off the notice or at least increase the amount of compensation being offered. However, the councillors merely regard the problem as a photo opportunity and do nothing substantial to halt the eviction. As the date approaches, it becomes clear that the men are going to be victims of a deceptive bureaucracy that cares only about progress.

Superbly acted by all (especially Michael Lee as a 99-year-old who never leaves his cage, and Teddy Robin Kwan as a shyster pediatrician who sells illegal medicine on the street with his pet monkey), **Cageman** is social commentary with a heart. Its dramatic content is buttressed with ample comic asides that humanize these unfortunate men and make the viewer identify with them and their plight to the point where the film leaves a lasting impression. Liu Kai-chi won the Best Supporting Actor prize for his turn as Sam; while he does a good job, it is the type of role that draws attention to itself and the performer. There are several other performances here that are just as impressive. The film received the Category III rating because of its coarse, realistic language.

129. Call Girl 1988

(1988; Alan and Eric Films Co.) ★. 3/10. *Ying jiu nui long 1988* (Cantonese), *Ying zhao nu lang 1988* (Mandarin): "Call Girl 1988." Cinematographer: Jingle Ma Cho-shing; Art Director: Bill Lui Biu; Music: T and T; Writers: Raymond To Kwok-wai, Joan Lau Woon-kwan, Shum Sai-shing; Producer: Joe Chan Wing-kwong; Director: David Lam Tak-luk. Cast: Maggie Cheung Man-yuk (Jenny Lin), Petrina Fung Bo-bo (Mei-feng, aka Tsui-tsui), Carrie Ng Kar-lai (Shan-shan), Elsie Chan Yik-si (Ling-yu), Stanley Fung Shui-fan (Fang), Kenneth Tong Chun-yip (Actor in TV Show), Lam Chung (Uncle Yen), Lau Siu-ming (Ling-yu's Godfather). 1.85:1. VHS: Tai Seng. 93 minutes. Also known as **Girls Without Tomorrow**.

This laughably overwrought drama chronicles the lives of various women working as prostitutes, including TV actress Jenny (who turns tricks in Thailand, where she hopes not to be recognized), Mei-feng (who goes by the name Tsui-tsui and must pay for her ailing husband's kidney dialysis treatments), and Shan-shan (who is deeply in debt and addicted to pills). Naturally, their pasts come back to haunt them in ways ranging from tragic to outright deadly.

One of the most financially successful entries in the "Hostess" subgenre (which mix softcore sleaze and melodrama, with the emphasis on the latter), **Call Girl 1988** is so heavy-handed and poorly written it eventually descends into outright camp. The fact that the movie consists of nothing more than cliche-ridden vignettes is made especially clear by the desperate manner in which they are linked: Characters constantly bump into each other as a way of providing a lead-in to the next person's story. **Call Girl '92** and **Girls Without Tomorrow 1992** have no direct connection to this film but are both somewhat better examples of the form.

130. Call Girl '92

(1992; Long Shong Pictures/Lui Ming Film Enterprises/Prairie Productions) ★: 6/10. '*92 Ying chiu lui long* (Cantonese), '*92 Ying shao nu lang* (Mandarin): "'92 Call Girl." Cinematographer: William Yim Wai-lun; Art Director: Jon Hau Wing-choi; Music: Johnny Chen; Writers: Andy Chin Wing-keung, Cheung Lai-ling; Producers: Wang Ying-hsiang, Lui Ming; Director: Andy Chin Wing-keung. Cast: Veronica Yip Yuk-hing (Sue), Sharla Cheung Man (Carman), Cecilia Yip Tung (Nancy), Carrie Ng Kar-lai (Liza), Vincent Wan Yeung-ming (Lam), Elaine Wu Chi-li (Lily), Kenneth Chan Kai-tai (Joe), Jamie Luk Kim-ming (Darkie). 1.85:1. VHS: Tai Seng. Import LD/VCD: Ocean Shores. 99 minutes.

A superficial but very watchable drama, this bears no direct relation to **Call Girl '88** (1988) but proceeds along similar lines. After being divorced by her husband, the pretty, reserved Carman figures that the best way to put her life back on track is to become a prostitute(!). She starts working for her old school friend Liza, now a successful madam, who teaches her the basics (and seduces her in the process). The plot examines her experiences, along with the lives of other escorts, their clients, their families, and their search for the perfect (i.e. rich) husband.

As usual with this type of film, the leading ladies provide the main reason to watch, in particular Cecilia Yip, who once again makes the most of a sketchy character. Her story is the most melodramatic (she's an alcoholic with a deeply troubled mother, who falls for a classical musician) but the sincerity and depth of her performance go a long way in giving this conventional material emotional legitimacy. The sync sound recording on the Cantonese version is a welcome plus, aiding the performances and heightening what little verisimilitude there is. It also allows one the rare chance to hear Cheung's real voice. Some of the cast members went on to appear in a similar feature by director Andy Chin, **Love Among the Triad**, the next year.

131. Carry on Pickpocket

(1982; Always Good Film Co.) ★: 6/10. *Tai fong siu sau* (Cantonese), *Di fang xiao shou* (Mandarin): "Guard Against Small Hand." Cinematographer: Ricky Lau Koon-wai; Music: Not Original; Writer: Barry Wong Ping-yiu; Producers: Guy Lai Ying-chau, Frankie Chan Fan-kei; Director: Sammo Hung Kam-po. Cast: Sammo Hung Kam-po (Rice Pot), Frankie Chan Fan-kei (Chimney), Richard Ng Yiu-hon (Wu), Deanie Yip Tak-han (Inspector Ling), Peter Chan Lung (Chou Meng-sheng). 2.35:1. VHS: Tai Seng (Poor Subtitles). Import LD: Golden Cinema City. Import VCD: Mega Star (Poor Subtitles). 96 minutes.

Rice Pot and Chimney are two highly successful pickpockets, making a very comfortable living preying on unsuspecting shoppers. Trouble arises when Rice Pot falls for police Inspector Ling, who is willing to forgive his crimes if he agrees to steal a pouch from mob courier Chou, whom she is investigating. After much trouble, the snatch is actually pulled off by Chimney, who discovers that he has inadvertently stolen millions of dollars worth of diamonds. He and Rice Pot are soon on the run from Chou's minions (including Dick Wei and Jamie Luk Kim-ming), who are out to retrieve the stones at any cost.

This likeable action-comedy goes off base in the final reel by throwing in a disturbingly violent and bloody conclusion that is just too drastic a shift in tone, even for HK cinema. Still, there is much to enjoy here, particularly the physical grace of the two stars during the elaborate pickpocketing gags, and Hung even gets to do a disco variation on a classic Charlie Chaplin bit from **The Gold Rush** (1925)! Richard Ng contributes his usual hairbrained policeman shtick in a largely superfluous supporting role, and there are a number of cameos by the likes of Nat Chan Pak-cheung, James Tien Chun, and Wu Ma, among others. The soundtrack includes a cue lifted from **Phantasm** (1978).

132. Carry on Wise Guy

(1980) ★: 6/10. *Poh gaai daai bye* (Cantonese), *Po jie da shi* (Mandarin): "Breaking Restriction Big Master." Cinematographer: Wong Yu-tai; Music: Not Original; Producer: Peng Cheng; Action Direction: The Lau Family; Director: Lau Kar-wing. Cast: Gordon Lau Kar-fai (Tien Fa), Eric Tsang Chi-wai (Fat Dragon), Lau Kar-wing (Captain Wang), Fung Hark-on (Yuen On), Peter Chan Lung (Collaborator). 2.35:1. VHS: Ocean Shores (Poor Subtitles or Dubbed), Arena/Xenon (Dubbed). 100 minutes. Also known as **Warrior from Shaolin** (Title for Ocean Shores dubbed version and Arena/Xenon tape).

An oddball kung fu comedy of the old school, **Carry on Wise Guy** unfolds during the Japanese occupation of China. The monk Tien Fa has been entrusted to transport a secret map (which shows Japanese troop deployment) across the countryside to a band of resistance fighters. He is accompanied in his travels by Hsiao Ma and Fat Dragon, two less-than-honest boatmen. Always on the lookout for a fast buck, the pair believe that the box carried by Tien is filled with valuables and are just waiting for a chance to swipe it. The trio have a series of adventures (including an encounter with a group of hopping vampires!) and must also evade the traitorous Captain Wang and his gang of turncoat deputies, who know of the map and are eager to get their hands on it.

Inspired moments alternate with tedious stretches, but Gordon Lau's amazing martial arts skills are sufficiently showcased (particularly during a memorable sequence where the monk is tricked into entering a brothel), and Eric Tsang's Bruce Lee imitation is not to be missed!

133. Carry on Yakuza!!

(1989; Silver Bird Films) ★: 7/10. *Hak do fuk sing* (Cantonese), *Hei dao fu xing* (Mandarin): "Wicked Path Lucky Stars." Cinematographer: Michael Ma Koon-wah; Art Director: Fred Chan Chi-chung; Music: Luk Kwan-lun; Writers: Chan Sau-keung, Phillip Chan Yan-kin; Producer: Michael Chan Wai-man; Action Director: Phillip Ko Fei; Director: Phillip Chan Yan-kin. Cast: Michael Chan Wai-man (Charlie Chan), Cheung Kwok-keung (Ricky), Lau Kar-wing (Wong), Deanie Yip Tak-han (Mrs. Wong), Phillip Chan Yan-kin (Willie), Shing Fui-on (Pusher), Maria Cordero (Fong-fong, aka "Twiggy"), Dennis Chan Kwok-san (Wong's Student), Tai Po (Wong's Student), Phillip Ko Fei (Yakuza), Ha Chi-chun (Female Yakuza), Eddie Maher (Narcotics Cop). 1.85:1. VHS: Tai Seng. Import LD: Ocean Shores. 99 minutes. Also known as **Carry on Yakuzas**, **Charlie & the Yakuza** (Tai Seng title).

Veteran tough guy Michael Chan stars in this enjoyable action comedy as Charlie, a boxer in Japan for a bout against a local fighter. When a group of *yakuzas* order Charlie to take a dive during the fight, he refuses and clobbers his Japanese opponent instead. He and his coach must flee for their lives and are saved from death only by the intervention of Yakoda, the *yakuza* boss' superior. In order to impress their savior, the pair pretend to be the leaders of a powerful (non-existent) triad faction called "The Marlboro Gang," a ruse that will come back to haunt them. When Yakoda is murdered by his underling, the late man's wife sends Wakako, their Cantonese-speaking daughter, to HK to keep her from being killed. Charlie and company agree to help the girl but must also put up a convincing front so the family will believe that they are big shot gangsters. When Wakako is kidnapped, Charlie comes to her rescue, and lends his services again when the girl's mother is disfigured in an assassination attempt.

Even though Charlie is not a gangster, he observes all of the triad codes of loyalty, so Michael Chan is essentially just playing a more loveable variation on his trademark role. *Carry on Yakuza!!* is a formulaic but quite satisfying effort which presents its Japanese characters in a more sympathetic light than is the norm for HK cinema.

Carry on Yakuzas *see* **Carry on Yakuza!!**

Cascading Feeling *see* **Midnight Whispers**

134. The Case of the Cold Fish

(1995; Magnum/Uniden Investments) ★: 8/10. *Yuet hak fung go* (Cantonese), *Yue hei feng gao* (Mandarin): "Moon Black, Wind High." Cinematographer: Ko Chiu-lam; Art Director: Raymond Lee King-man; Music: Wong Bong; Writers: Law Kam-fai, Van Lam Wan-hong; Producer: Danny Lee Sau-yin; Director: Jamie Luk Kim-ming. Cast: Michael Wong Man-tak (Michael Cheung Fat-loin), Michael Chow Man-kin (Dick Chow Long-dong), Emily Kwan Bo-wai (Daisy), Ricky Yee Fan-wai (Simon), Valerie Chow Kar-ling (Linda), Shing Fui-on (Keanu Reeves), Eric Kei Kar-fat (Richard), Frankie Chin Chi-leung (Tiny), Danny Lee Sau-yin (Lee). 1.85:1. VHS: Tai Seng. Import LD/VCD: Star Entertainment. 94 minutes.

This offbeat, laidback farce is one of the most endearing HK comedies in some time. The police officers patrolling Tai O village on sleepy Lantau Island are so lacking in work that slovenly chief Dick Chow doesn't even bother putting on his uniform. So when real estate agent Simon turns up dead in the street one evening, the cops are at a loss, especially when drunk Eurasian tourist Michael Cheung blurts out that he had a fight with the dead man earlier that evening. After spending a night in the cooler, Cheung sobers up, identifies himself as a chief inspector, and takes command of the investigation. A former Special Duty Unit trainer, Cheung is horrified by the local law's utter lack of professional standards, but, after a time, he comes to appreciate that there are just some things you cannot rush.

The majority of contemporary HK films celebrate life in the city, with the emphasis on beautiful upper class people or equally well-off gangsters, so it is a pleasure to see the flipside presented here. The characters are all well-drawn, and the culture clash humor is consistently amusing and well-observed. Michael Chow has his best role to date, and even the notoriously stilted Michael Wong isn't bad (viewers who dislike the actor will take much sadistic pleasure in the way the script makes light of his rotten Cantonese). Aside from giving some of the characters dumb, jokey names, the subtitles are above average and the sync sound recording is a nice plus, too. *The Cast of the Cold* Fish is a congenial little sleeper, well worth catching.

135. Casino Raiders

(1989; Win's Movie Production) ★: 8/10. *Ji juen mo seung* (Cantonese), *Zhi zun wu shuang* (Mandarin): "Most Respected, No Superior." Cinematographers: Henry Chan Chun-kit, Lee Chi-wai; Art Director: Jason Mok Siu-kei; Music: James Wong Jim, Romeo Diaz; Producer: Jimmy Heung Wah-sing; Action Directors: Billy Chan Wui-ngai, Chin Yuet-sang, Power Lee King-chu; Writers-Directors: Jimmy Heung Wah-sing, Wong Jing. Cast: Alan Tam Wing-lun (Sam Law), Andy Lau Tak-wah (Crab Chan), Idy Chan Yuk-lin (Tong Koyan), Rosamund Kwan Chi-lam (Bo Bo), Lung Fong (Taro), Charles Heung Wah-keung (Lon), Che-Kirk Wong Chi-keung (Telly), Shum Wai (Club Owner), Eddy Ko Hung (Gold Teeth), Ronald Wong Pan (Informer), Robin Shou Wan-bo (Hitman). 1.85:1. VHS: Tai Seng (Poor Subtitles). Import LD/VCD: ERA Video (Poor Subtitles, 114 minutes). 127 minutes.

Many believe it was **God of Gamblers** which started the whole gambling movie craze in HK but this popular production actually predated it by six months. The inspiration for **Casino Raiders** can probably be traced to **The Shell Game** (*Chin wong ji wong*, which can be translated as "King of a Thousand Kings" or "King of Con Kings"), a 1980 TVB miniseries written by Wong Jing and produced by his father, Wong Tin-lam. It told of the competition (and eventual partnership) between master gamblers Lo Sei-hoi (Patrick Tse Yin), aka "The Mystical Eyes of the South," and Chek Yut-fu (Yeung Kwan), "The Magic Hands of the North." A smash hit, it spawned a sequel (which co-starred a young Chow Yun-fat) whose Chinese title translates as "Meeting of the Con Kings."

In **Casino Raiders** master gamblers Sam Law and Crab Chan are reunited when the latter is released from jail. The pair head to America, where Sam helps a casino manager nail some Japanese sharks who have won over $60 million from the establishment in just two weeks. While there, Sam meets beautiful heiress Tong Koyan and uses a rather elaborate practical joke to help win her favor. Unfortunately, the Japanese hire men to get revenge and, in the process of saving Sam's life, Crab's left hand gets slashed, effectively ending his days as a lightning-fast con artist. After a further attempt on his life, Sam accepts an offer tabled to him by Koyan's father: Sam will receive a job in his company if he agrees to leave his life of crime behind him. Unable to support himself and unwilling to take money from Sam, Crab challenges the Japanese gangsters to a high stakes game, but Sam refuses to go to the match with him. Crab swindles his opponents out of their money, and the Japanese retaliate by kidnapping Koyan, setting the stage for multiple tragedies.

Darker than most of the imitations it spawned, **Casino Raiders** is closer in tone to the gangster films being produced at this time in the way it mixes melodramatic plotting with strong male bonding and acrobatic gunplay. Alan Tam and Andy Lau both deliver solid performances, and the big game finale is enjoyably tense, with a surprising denouement. However, some viewers may be put off by the brutality directed towards women here, something that Wong Jing's work has often been criticized for. Actor/director Che-Kirk Wong gives a typically colorful turn as a crooked cop. The original HK theatrical version reportedly runs 127 minutes, but the ERA laserdisc (which is choppy in spots and has no opening or closing credits) runs only 114 minutes. **Casino Raiders II** and **No Risk, No Gain: Casino Raiders—The Sequel** have no direct connection to this production.

136. Casino Raiders II

(1991; Paka Hill Film Production Co./Win's Movie Production) ★: 6/10. *Ji juen mo seung II wing au tin gwong* (Cantonese), *Zhi zun wu shang II yong ba tian xia* (Mandarin): "Most Respected, No Superior II: Forever Superior." Cinematographer:

Horace Wong Wing-hang; Art Director: Danny Yuen Ching-yeung; Music: William Woo Wai-lap; Writer: Sammy Tsang Kan-cheung; Producer: Jimmy Heung Wah-sing; Action Director: Ching Siu-tung; Director: Johnny To Kei-fung. Cast: Andy Lau Tak-wah (Chicken Feet), Jacqueline Wu Chien-lien (Lin), Wang Chieh (Kit), Monica Chan Fat-yung (Kit's ex), Kelvin Wong Siu (James), Anthony Wong Chau-sang (Pow), Lau Siu-ming (Fan), Lau Kong (King Kong). 1.85:1. VHS: Tai Seng (No Subtitles). Import LD/VCD/DVD: ERA. 87 minutes.

Following the substantial success of **A Moment of Romance** (1990), Paka Hill Film Production Company quickly re-teamed Andy Lau and Jacqueline Wu for this in-name-only follow-up to Win's 1989 blockbuster, **Casino Raiders**, which also starred Lau. Their chemistry, stylish cinematography and an accomplished score gave this melodramatic work more significance than it would otherwise have generated. Lau plays "Chicken Feet," a cardsharp who works for Fan, a wheelchair-bound gambling master who was crippled while escaping from James, a traitorous underling. Both men seek to obtain a pair of jade pieces which, when reunited, allows the bearer to invoke the power of the god of gamblers. When James finally does manage to kill Fan, the master's other pupil, Kit, returns from overseas to attend his funeral. Chicken Feet and his girl, Lin, seek to avenge Fan, but Kit, who has forsaken gambling following a prison sentence, only wants to reunite with the young daughter he left behind. James kidnaps the child to ensure that Kit will not participate in a forthcoming tournament of champions. In order to get his daughter back, Kit cuts off his hand and convinces Chicken Feet and Lin to join him in a legitimate business venture. Seeing that her boyfriend's thirst for vengeance will never be satiated, Lin seeks out and discovers one of the jade pieces, not knowing that she has been followed by James' men. In the ensuing battle, Lin is murdered and Chicken Feet is blinded. In response, Kit and Chicken Feet enter the gambling competition, facing off against James for a prize of 15 million U.S. dollars.

The subplot about the jade pieces is almost entirely superfluous: The conflict between Chicken Feet, Kit and James would have been a sufficient basis for the drama. In fact, Chicken Feet actually throws one of the pieces away, relying on his own skills to defeat James. While invoking the magic of the gods may seem like a dramatic cheat, the fact that this element is introduced without being expanded upon is equally unsatisfying. Still, the quality of the performances and the near-hypnotic effect of To's layered visuals (which lose some of their effectiveness in the current video transfers) help to retain one's involvement, even when the storyline does not. As the lead villain, Kelvin Wong is more subdued than usual, but Anthony Wong (in an early role) gives a characteristic turn as James' flaky second-in-command. Monica Chan's character is not given a name in the English subtitles, which is an inadvertent comment on the fact that she does little more than provide attractive scenery. Veterans Tien Feng and Lau Shun have cameos. Followed by the unrelated **No Risk, No Gain: Casino Raiders—The Sequel.**

137. Casino Tycoon

(1992; Samico Films Production/ Cosmopolitan Film Productions) ★: 5/10. *Do sing daai hang (san goh chuen kei)* (Cantonese), *Du cheng da heng (xin ge chuan qi)* (Mandarin): "Gambling City Magnate (New Older Brother Legend)." Cinematographer: Gigo Lee Chi-hang; Art Directors: Jason Mok Siu-kei, Andrew Cheuk Man-yiu; Music: Lowell Lo Kwun-ting; Action Directors: Yuen Bun, Wong Chi-ming; Writer-Producer-Director: Wong Jing. Cast: Andy Lau Tak-wah (Benny Ho Hsin), Chingmy Yau Suk-ching (Mei), Joey Wang Tsu-hsien (Vivian Cheng Lo-erh), Alex Man Chi-leung (Kuo Ying-nan), Kwan Hoi-shan (Fu Lao-cha), Wilson Lam Chun-yin (Fu Chia-chin), Paul Chun Pui (Wong Chang), Lau Siu-ming (Nieh Ao-tien), Wong Yat-fei (Dentist). 1.85:1. VHS: Tai Seng. Import LD/VCD/DVD: Mei Ah. 133 minutes.

138. Casino Tycoon II

(1992; Samico Films Production/ Cosmopolitan Film Productions Co.) ★: 4/10. *Do sing daai hung II ji ji juen mo dik* (Cantonese), *Du cheng da heng II zhi zhi zun wu di* (Mandarin): "Gambling City Magnate II: Extremely Respected and Invincible." Cinematographer: Gigo Lee Chi-hang; Art Directors: Jason Mok Siu-kei, Andrew Cheuk Man-yiu; Music: Lowell Lo Kwun-ting; Action Director: Wong Chi-ming; Writer-Producer-Director: Wong Jing. Cast: Andy Lau Tak-wah (Benny Ho Hsin), Chingmy Yau Suk-ching (Mei), Michelle Lee Kar-yan (Ti Yun), Lau Siu-ming (Nieh Ao-tien), Alex Man Chi-leung (Kuo Ying-nan), Joey Wang Tsu-hsien (Vivian Cheng Lo-ehr), Sandra Ng Kwan-yu (Chu Lin-lin), John Ching Tung (Niu), Dennis Chan Kwok-san (Feng Shui Master), Yuen King-tan (Hsien). 1.85:1. VHS: Tai Seng. Import LD/VCD/DVD: Mei Ah. 110 minutes.

An uncharacteristically serious project for Wong Jing, the two-part **Casino Tycoon** is an attractive but languid trip through familiar territory. Overcoming a life of poverty, Hsin has risen to the top of his university class, winning a scholastic prize. In the process, he has garnered the ire of Fu Chia-chin, a rich scoundrel who seeks to steal Hsin's girlfriend, Vivian. When the Japanese invade HK in December 1941, Hsin and his uncouth buddy, Nan, travel to Macau and are hired as dock coolies. After coming up with a way for casino boss Fu Lao-cha to defeat some gamblers who were on the verge of bankrupting him, Hsin is brought into the inner circle of Macau's gambling world. Volunteering to go on a boat trip to get badly needed medical supplies, Hsin and Nan are almost killed as part of a trap set up by the unscrupulous dock boss, Wong Chang. Arriving back in Macau with their cargo, the two are made equal partners by Fu, and Hsin wins the hand of Mei, the lovely young daughter of an associate. Arriving for his wedding is none other than Fu Chia-chin, who not only turns out to be the son of Fu Lao-cha, but has also married Vivian in the interim. When Lao-cha is kidnapped by Wong's men, Hsin and Nan are able to save him but, as they cannot prove Wong's involvement, end up being framed for the crime. Hsin, Mei, and Nan are then exiled from Macau for ten years time. During the next decade, Hsin and Nan make their fortunes in the HK real estate business and, with backing from Lao-cha's former associate Nieh, decide to bid for a casino licence in Macau. Driven to the brink of madness, Chia-chin goes gunning for Hsin at Wong's bidding, but attacks and paralyses Mei instead, before taking his own life. Outraged, Hsin offers a $5 million bounty for Wong's head. Overly melodramatic even by genre standards, the storyline piles one tragedy on top of another, but, as we do not really care about or even doubt the fate of any character, the effect is simply wearisome. Andy Lau and Alex Man (the latter giving a typically colorful performance) are both convincing, but the script has neither the depth nor the resonance of the best gangster films. Also at fault are Paul Chun and Wilson Lam's tiresomely one dimensional characters and a ludicrous finale, which is supposed to be darkly humorous but emerges as simply laughable.

In Part II, Ho Hsin falls for beautiful actress Ti Yun and faces increasing pressure from his former partner, Nieh Ao-tien. When his son is murdered, Ho calls in every favor he has to locate the killer. Subsequent events reveal that the mastermind behind the crime has ties to Vivian. Ho must also deal with a group of mathematicians(!) who have won millions at his casino by using an ingenious (and highly implausible) form of Morse Code! While not as overwrought as its forerunner, this chapter is just as listless and trite, and the large-scale mounting just makes these inadequacies all the more glaring. The final reel is particularly weak. As in **Lee Rock II**, Lau is not very convincing as someone in his golden years, and neither are Chingmy Yau or Joey Wang for that matter.

139. The Cat

(1992; Golden Harvest/Paragon Films) ★: 4/10. *Lo maau* (Cantonese), *Lao mao* (Mandarin): "Old Cat." Cinematographer: Mak Hoi-man; Art Director: Ho Kim-seng; Music: Phil Chan Fei-lap; Writers: Chan King-ha, Gordon Chan Kar-seung; Producer: Chua Lam; Action Director: Phillip Kwok Tsui; Director: Nam Nai-choi. Cast: Waise Lee Chi-hung (Wisely), Gloria Yip Wan-yee (Alien Girl), Christine Ng Wing-mei (Pai So), Lau Siu-ming (Errol), Phillip Kwok Tsui (Wang Chieh-mei). 1.85:1. VHS: Tai Seng. Import LD: Mei Ah. 88 minutes.

Nam Nai-choi, the man behind the wonderfully ridiculous horror-actioner **The Seventh Curse**, struck out with this similarly foolish but far less entertaining horror–sci-fi mishmash. Waise Lee plays the horror novelist/adventurer Wisely (portrayed in other films by actors like Chow Yun-fat, Chin Kar-lok, and Sam Hui Koon-kit), who gets involved in a bizarre case involving a pair of aliens and their magical cat. The extraterrestrials require two ancient octagons to destroy a rampaging blob monster which is on the loose in HK. The cat manages to secure the first artifact from a museum, but is interrupted by the creature before the other can be obtained. Unaware of the aliens' benevolent intentions, Wisely not-so-wisely decides that the best way to catch a cat is to use a big, slobbering dog. When the cat tries to take the remaining octagon, there is a prolonged feline vs. canine battle (a mixture of cut-rate stop motion animation, puppets, and genuine animals that would make S.P.C.A. members cringe), with the alien creature emerging victorious but losing its tail in the process. Seeking to retrieve the missing body part, the aliens contact Wisely, but his home is decimated in a **Terminator**-style assault by Wang, a police officer who has been possessed by the creature. Taking on immense proportions, the blob threatens to engulf everything unless the cat and the second octagon can be joined together. Aside from a plethora of gooey but silly-looking special effects, this is sloppy, lethargic fare that is not nearly as much fun as it sounds.

140. Cat vs. Rat

(1982; Shaw Brothers) ★: 8/10. *Yue maau saam hei gaam mo sue* (Cantonese), *Yu mao san xi jin mao shu* (Mandarin): "Imperial Cat Three Shows Beautiful Fur Mouse." Cinematographer: Art Director: Music: Not Original; Writer: Ngai Hong; Producer: Mona Fong Yat-wah; Director: Lau Kar-leung. Cast: Alexander Fu Sheng (Pai Yu-tang, aka Rat), Adam Cheng Siu-chau (Chan Chao, aka Cat), Hsiao Hou (Chiang Ping), Kara Hui Ying-hung (Chan's Sister), Lau Kar-wing (The Master), Gordon Lau Kar-fai (Emperor Yung Hsi). 2.35:1. No official domestic video release. 97 minutes.

The humor in this period kung fu comedy (which appears to have its origins in Peking Opera) may be too Chinese for some Western viewers to grasp, but it has other rewards and is certainly an interesting addition to director Lau Kar-leung's filmography. Mortal enemies "Rat" Pai Yu-tang and "Cat" Chan Chao are engaged in a prolonged battle to determine who is the superior swordsman. After numerous skirmishes, they consult their master, who, much to their dismay, announces that they are both equal in ability. The old man gives Pai his "Nine Ring Sword" which allows him to defeat his opponent. Not one to show favoritism, the master proceeds to give Chan a spear that will counter the sword, and he emerges victorious over Pai in a re-match. Their next bout ends in yet another draw but concludes with the two families beating each other up! Chan and his sister encounter Emperor Yung Hsi when they inadvertently rescue him from thieves out to grab his invaluable jade seal. The emperor (who believes himself to be a kung fu master but cannot even perform the most basic moves) rewards Chan by making him a royal guard. Infuriated, Pai vows to steal the jade seal but is framed by his cohorts and left behind to be captured. Accepting Chan's plea for leniency, Yung gives Chan and Pai one day to find and return the royal insignia.

There are outstanding acrobatics throughout, and the heroes' climactic battle against the traitorous "rats" (including Johnny Wang Lung-wei and Chang Chan-peng)—who attack from under the water, beneath the ground, and through walls—is delightful fun. The entire film flows with the grace and precision of a play that the stars have been performing in for years and their energy and enthusiasm are well communicated to the viewer. Currently available only as a badly cropped bootleg, **Cat vs. Rat** remains sublime entertainment even in less than pristine form.

141. Center Stage

(1992; Golden Harvest/Golden Way Films/Paragon Films) ★: 9/10. *Yuen Ling-yuk* (Cantonese), *Ruan Lingyu* (Mandarin): "Yuen Ling-yuk" (Subject's name in Cantonese) or "Ruan Lingyu" (Subject's name in Mandarin). Cinematographer: Poon Hang-sang; Art Director: Pok Yeuk-muk; Music: Johnny Chen; Writer: Yau Tai On-ping; Producers: Willie Chan Chi-keung, Tsui Siu-ming; Director: Stanley Kwan Kam-pang. Cast: Maggie Cheung Man-yuk (Ruan Ling-yu), Tony Leung Kar-fai (Tsai Chu-sheng), Chin Han (Tang Chi-shan), Carina Lau Kar-ling (Lily Li), Lawrence Ng Kai-wah (Chang Ta-min), Cecilia Yip Tung (Lin Chu-chu), Waise Lee Chi-hung (Li Min-wei). Dolby Digital (DVD only). 1.85:1. VHS: Tai Seng (Long version, Poor Subtitles). Import LD/VCD: Star Entertainment (Short version, No Subtitles). Import VCD/DVD: Mega Star (Short version). 118/147 minutes. Also known as **Actress**.

Maggie Cheung gives a magnificent, award-winning performance in this superb docudrama about Ruan Ling-yu, the most famous Chinese star of the silent screen, who died at the young age of 25. Mixing clips from Ruan's few surviving films (only 6 out of 25) with staged sequences and scattered black and white segments in which the actors, director, and some personalities from the era talk about Ruan, director Stanley Kwan paints a complex and compelling portrait of a remarkable, delicate woman driven to suicide by a hateful and perfidious news media. The film opens in 1929, with Lienhua Studio executives deciding to make Ling-yu one of the studio's new movie queens. Her popularity soars, but success does nothing to improve her troubled marriage to boor Chang Ta-min, who gambles and openly cheats on her. By 1932 the Japanese have begun to bomb Shanghai and soon occupy the city, forcing the Nationalist government to curtail the production of movies with anti-Japanese themes and characters. Ling-yu falls for Lienhua partner Tang Chi-shan and divorces Chang but must provide him with monthly alimony. Ling-yu then moves in with Tang, even though the latter is still married. Her downfall comes when she stars in **New Woman** for socialist filmmaker Tsai Chu-sheng. Harshly critical of reporters (whom it accuses of working with the Japanese), the film draws a hostile reaction from the Shanghai Press Union, which demands that all footage depicting them in a negative light be deleted. Hungry for vengeance, they viciously persecute Ling-yu and are instrumental in getting Chang to file a lawsuit over her adulterous relationship with Tang.

In a role originally to have been undertaken by Anita Mui Yim-fong, Maggie Cheung radiates beauty, sophistication, and despair in a performance that is so ethereal yet commanding that you cannot take your eyes off of her. Appropriately, the film also takes a subtle, measured approach to its subject, and the juxtaposition of the different perspectives, times, and movie segments ("real" and "reel") is both daring and remarkable. Exceptional cinematography and gorgeous production design complete the package. If at all possible, try and see Kwan's cut of the film, which runs about a half hour longer than the standard version and is definitely more in keeping with his vision than Golden Harvest's re-edit.

142. Centipede Horror

(1982) ★: 5/10. *Ng gung jau* (Cantonese), *Wu gong zhou* (Mandarin): "Centipede Curse." Cinematographers: Lee Yip, Philip Ma Kam-cheung; Music: Not Original; Writer: Amy Chan Suet-ming; Producer: Stephen Chan Chu-kwong; Director: Keith Li Pak-ling. Cast: Margaret Lee Tin-long (Yeuk-chee), Miu Kiu-wai (Pak Kai-lum), Stephen Yip Tin-hang, Chan Fuk-choi. 1.85:1. VHS: World Video. LD: Winson Entertainment. 93 minutes.

Effectively gruesome but otherwise undistinguished, this horror thriller tells of female student Pak Kay who travels to South East Asia against the wishes of her mother. While there, she is attacked and poisoned by some centipedes. The girl's condition grows progressively worse and she finally dies, with centipedes burrowing out through her wounds. Her brother, Kai-lum, learns that their grandfather accidentally killed the inhabitants of a village. In order to exact revenge, the local chieftain cursed the Pak family with the powerful "centipede spell" which claimed the life of Kay. Now seeking to murder Kai-lum, the priest puts a spell on the man's girlfriend, Yeuk-chee, and orders her to steal the protective necklace that Kai-lum wears, so that he will fall victim to the army of centipedes the priest has sent to destroy him.

Infamous for a sequence in which one cast member vomits up a horde of live centipedes (no computer generated fakery here, folks!), the film has several other moments that will leave squeamish viewers reeling. Unfortunately, the remainder is only moderately entertaining, lacking the fiendish invention and manic energy of the best horror outings (though the "chickens" conjured up by a benevolent priest to battle the ravenous bugs are pretty memorable). Some will appreciate the director's no-nonsense approach to the material, which is in definite contrast to the majority of HK genre pictures. The soundtrack includes music lifted from **Sorcerer**.

143. A Certain Romance

(1984; Far-Sun Film Co.) ★: 4/10. *Siu nui yat gei* (Cantonese), *Shao nu ri ji* (Mandarin): "Young Girl's Diary." Cinematographer: Daniel Chan Man-fai; Art Director: Yim Chim-lam; Music: Not Original; Writer: Yip Chung-ping; Producer-Director: Yeung Fan. Cast: Ng Mei-chi (Magy), Tang Ho-kwong (Lily), Tsui Hak-ying, Chan Chun-kwok, Sally Yeh Chian-wen (Phys Ed Teacher). 1.85:1. VHS: World Video. Running time unknown.

Professional photographer Yeung Fan made his directorial debut with this formulaic tale of a young girl's coming-of-age. Magy is nearing the end of high school and developing an attraction towards older boys. She is especially captivated by handsome Tong Kar-ming, whom she briefly encountered one day, but her pushy little sister is determined to set her up with Kar-ming's buddy, David. Kar-ming, meanwhile, remembers Magy and has had her in his thoughts ever since. Unfortunately, he has not been able to find the girl and is busy with instructing his ballet class. He is also trying to enliven the spirits of Ur-lang, a girl Magy's age, who is terminally ill. Finally bringing herself to tell David how she really feels about him, Magy unsuccessfully attempts to find Kar-ming, but it does not take much imagination to deduce that she will run across him before the end credits roll.

Glossy and superficial, **A Certain Romance** is the Cantonese cousin of a popular series of 1970s Taiwanese melodramas based on the works of female author Qiong Yao. Like those films, it has all of the elements one expects from this sort of story, supplemented by some heavy-handed tragedy, contrived plotting, and emotions that never really ring true. The director's 1988 film **Last Romance** is essentially more of the same but a bit more successful at achieving its goals.

144. C'est La Vie, Mon Cheri

(1993; Film Unlimited/Newport Entertainment) ★: 8/10. *San bat liu ching* (Cantonese), *Xin bu liao qing* (Mandarin): "New Endless Love." Cinematographers: Tam Chi-wai, Peter Ngor Chi-kwan; Art Director: Hai Chung-man; Music: Chris Babida, William Woo Wai-lap; Producer: Alexander Chan Mong-wah; Writer-Director: Derek Yee Tung-sing. Cast: Anita Yuen Wing-yee (Min), Lau Ching-wan (Kit), Carrie Ng Kar-lai (Yan-ling), Carina Lau Kar-ling (Tracy), Petrina Fung Bo-bo (Min's Mother), Paul Chun Pui (Uncle, aka "Cheung Po-tsai"), Sylvia Chang Ai-chia (Min's Doctor), Lau Yee-tat (Tats), Joe Junior (Cover Singer), Jacob Cheung Chi-leung (Fortune Teller), Jamie Luk Kim-ming (Blacky), Herman Yau Lai-to (Man in Club). 1.85:1. VHS/LD: Tai Seng. Import LD/VCD/DVD: Universe. 98 minutes. Also known as **Endless Love** (Singapore title).

Struggling songwriter Kit has seen better days, especially now that his relationship with star singer Tracy has fallen apart. Broke, he moves into a rundown tenement above Min, an incredibly perky young girl who is determined to get Kit out of his shell and won't take no for an answer. Min's family are street singers and, as Kit soon surmises, the girl has great potential to move beyond this modest existence and into the recording industry. Transformed by his exposure to Min, Kit makes plans with her to start a career, but the unimaginable happens: After over ten years of perfect health, the bone cancer Min experienced as a child has returned. The willpower and zest for living which has helped keep Min alive for this long quickly extinguishes, and it is up to Kit to help her try and regain it.

The sleeper hit of 1993, **C'est La Vie, Mon Cheri** was produced on a small budget with little-known leads but won over HK moviegoers to a phenomenal degree and walked away with the Best Picture, Best Actress (Anita Yuen), Best Director, Best Screenplay, Best Supporting Actor (Paul Chun), and Best Supporting Actress (Petrina Fung) prizes at The HK Film Awards. Any synopsis makes the movie sound like the most hackneyed tearjerker in memory, and the final third does resort to some familiar devices. However, it does not really matter because by that point the audience is fully caught up in the lives of these characters and are ready to stay with the film, no matter what direction the plot takes. Derek Yee's script and direction sidestep most of the pitfalls intrinsic to this sort of material, and there is a wonderfully varied selection of music, covering everything from traditional opera to "In the Mood." A key factor in the movie's popularity can be traced to the fact that it concentrates on common, everyday citizens rather than the rich and glamorous icons who populate many HK features, thus heightening viewer identification. Also, a potent thread of nostalgia envelopes everything from the locations to the old-fashioned storyline, adding to that accessibility. The entire cast gives sensitive, committed performances, but Anita Yuen is simply magical; **C'est La Vie**'s success made her the busiest actress in HK for several years afterwards. In fact, she and Lau Ching-wan were re-teamed for a number of subsequent features, but none of those pairings match the wholly natural and remarkable chemistry they have here.

Challenge of the Ninja *see* **Shaolin Challenges Ninja**

145. The Champions

(1983; Golden Harvest/Peace Film Production Co./Paragon Films) ★: 4/10. *Boh ngau* (Cantonese), *Bo niu* (Mandarin): "Ball Ox." Cinematographers: Michael Ma Koon-wah, Sung Kwong-wah; Art Director: Andy Lee Yiu-kwong; Music: Blue Max Productions; Producer: Raymond Chow Man-wai; Action Directors: The Yuen Brothers; Writer-Director: Brandy Yuen Chun-yeung. Cast: Yuen Biao (Lee Tong), Cheung Kwok-keung (Suen), Dick Wei (King), Moon Lee Choi-fung (Fanny), Eddy Ko Hung (Tong's Uncle). 2.35:1. VHS: Tai Seng (Poor Subtitles). Import VCD: Mega Star (Poor Subtitles). 86 minutes.

Set in the 1960s, this lightweight comedy provides an excellent showcase for the incredible physical skills of Yuen Biao and Dick Wei. Unfortunately, their prowess with a soccer ball far exceeds writer-director Brandy Yuen's ability to come up with anything original or amusing to bridge the game sequences. After he accidentally injures the village chief's son in a competition, Lee Tong leaves his uncle's farm and heads to the city. There he meets Suen, a would-be soccer player who convinces him to try out for the popular Lung Wah team. He is accepted without even so much as a demonstration because King, Lung Wah's star player, wants revenge for an earlier humiliation he suffered at Tong's hands. Demoted to ballboy, Tong experiences one indignity after another but remains resolute in his desire to win a spot in the starting line-up. When King accepts a $100,000 bribe to throw a big game, he feigns an injury and has Tong put in the game, figuring that the ballboy's lack of experience will make the defeat look convincing. Naturally, Tong ends up winning the match and gets beaten up as a result. He then joins the rival Hsin Sang team and wows the fans with his talents, leading up to an inevitable grudge match between the two sports stars. Along the way, just about every sports movie cliche and device comes into play, making this one strictly for diehard fans of its limber stars.

Charlie & the Yakuza *see* **Carry on Yakuza!!**

Chase from Beyond *see* **Demoness from Thousand Years** [*sic*]

146. Cheetah on Fire

(1992; Cheung Yau Production Co.) ★: 5/10. *Lip paau hang dung* (Cantonese), *Lie bao xing dong* (Mandarin): "Hunt Leopard Operation." Cinematographer: Ma Kam-yeung; Art Director: Ruby Ko Pui-yee; Music: Simon Leung Chi-wah, Tony Tam Chan-hung; Writer: Hung Hin-pang; Producer-Action Director: Tsui Fat; Director: Thomas Yip Shing-hong. Cast: Donnie Yen Chi-tan (Ronald), Carrie Ng Kar-lai (Wu Li-yung), Sharla Cheung Man (Peggy), Gordon Lau Kar-fai (Long Hair), Ken Lo Wai-kwong (Long Hair's Man), Eddy Ko Hung (Fok Chi-kien), Shing Fui-on (Tong Yiang), Michael Woods (Black Thug), John Salvitti (White Thug), Mark Houghton (Mak). 1.85:1. VHS: Tai Seng (Subtitled or Dubbed). Import LD: Star Entertainment. 84 minutes.

Produced in tandem with **Crystal Hunt** and featuring much of the same cast, this low budget effort is packed with action, which helps one to forget just how pedestrian the screenplay is. When convict Tong Yiang escapes custody while being transported to the airport for extradition, CIA agent Peggy teams up with the HK police to capture him. Tong has in his possession a computer chip from a top secret weapon that is wanted not only by the CIA but also by two competing groups of criminals. Affluent businessman Fok Chi-kien is the head of one such gang, and he manages to get to Tong first. However, before the chip is turned over to him, Fok is murdered by the forces of his competitor, Long Hair. With the chip in his possession, Long Hair and his men head to Thailand, with the CIA in hot pursuit.

The film proceeds strictly by-the-numbers, and budgetary constraints are in evidence (particularly during the final battle, which is padded out with some real war footage).

147. Cherie

(1984; Shaw Brothers/Brainchild) ★: 3/10. *Suet-yee* (Cantonese), *Xueer* (Mandarin): "Suet-yee" or "Xueer" (the female lead character's name in Chinese). Cinematographer: Bill Wong Chung-bo; Art Director: Chan Kar-ying; Music: Tsui Yat-kan; Writers: Fung Lai-chi, Chan Wan-man, Szeto Cheuk-hon, Patrick Tam Kar-ming; Producer: Selina Chow Leung Suk-yee; Director: Patrick Tam Kar-ming. Cast: Cherie Chung Cho-hung (Cherie Teng), Tony Leung Kar-fai (Hua), Chor Yuen (Chou), Dennis Chan Kwok-san (Po), Michael Lai Siu-tin (Lucy's Cousin). 1.85:1. VHS: World Video. Import LD: Ocean Shores. 92 minutes.

A real comedown for director Patrick Tam after **The Sword** and **Nomad**, this mainstream formula comedy is strictly for fans of Cherie Chung and Tony Leung Kar-fai, both of whom were still pretty new to the business at this point. Middle-aged millionaire Chou flips his lid when he gets a load of beautiful aerobics teacher Cherie Teng. She, however, won't give him the time of day, preferring handsome photographer Hua. Chou goes through all manner of humiliating ploys to try and win Cherie's hand but nothing works. Conceding defeat, Chou offers Hua the opportunity to make his own movie and a blank check—if he agrees to dump Cherie. Hua then pretends to have lung cancer, but this just makes the girl all the more determined to spend every waking minute with him. When Cherie's cousin learns the truth and lets her know, Cherie plots elaborate revenge on both men. Utterly predictable and lacking any genuine laughs, this dismal affair just drags on and on. Watch co-star Chor Yuen's **Diary of a Big Man** instead.

148. Cherry Blossoms

(1988; Golden Harvest) ★: 8/10. *Yuk Dat-foo chuen kei* (Cantonese), *Yu Ta-fu chuan ji* (Mandarin): "The Legend of Yu Ta-fu." Cinematographer: Wilson Chan Pui-kai; Art Director: Lee Chi-ngai; Music: Unknown Japanese Artist; Producer: Stephen Shin Kei-yin, Writer-Director: Eddie Fong Ling-ching. Cast: Chow Yun-fat (Yu Ta-fu as an adult), Fok Tak-wah, Wong Kwok-ling, Muthumi Itakura, Sachiko Nakamura. 1.85:1. VHS: Tai Seng (No Subtitles). LD: Winson Entertainment. Import VCD: Mega Star. 95 minutes.

An engrossing, thoughtful film, **Cherry Blossoms** explores the gulf between the Chinese and Japanese cultures with intelligence and compassion. The handsome, superbly acted drama is the story of Chinese author Yu Ta-fu, who worked as a Japanese interpreter during the final days of World War II. Through flashbacks we are shown his days as a youth in Japan, where he and his brother studied science and technology. While visiting a hot springs one day, Ta-fu met and immediately fell for a pretty young girl. Desperate to become worthy of her, Ta-fu learns Japanese and travels to Nagoya to continue his education. There he boards with a group of similarly disenfranchised Chinese students, and endures the rigors of the military-style schooling. The boy happens upon that same girl one day and, after repeated rejections, finally wins her friendship. He learns that her name is Lung and that she and her father are actually Chinese. The man aided Sun Yat-sen in the revolution and forbids his daughter from revealing their true nationality to anyone for fear of reprisal. The timid Ta-fu soon must compete with his more handsome and confident Japanese friend Isao for Lung's hand. Their motives, however, could not be more different: Ta-fu's pursuit springs from love, while Isao's quest springs from a sense of duty—his way of helping to protect the girl from the Japanese army.

Cherry Blossoms began as a Shaw Brothers production but the company closed down its theatrical production arm not long after the film was completed in 1985. It was later sold to Golden Harvest. Somewhere along the line, more nude scenes were added to increase its commercial potential, prompting director Eddie Fong to disavow the version that eventually did make its way to theaters. Chow Yun-fat fans will be disappointed to learn that he only appears briefly in the opening and closing reels.

149. Chicken a la Queen

(1990; Cinema City Co.) ★: 2/10. *Faai lok dik siu gai* (Cantonese), *Kuai le de xiao ji* (Mandarin): "Happy Little Chickens." Cinematographer: Wong Chi-wai; Art Director: Bill Lui Cho-hung; Music: Violet Lam Man-yee; Writer: Ella Chan Bo-wah; Producer: Clarence Fok Yiu-leung; Action Director: Yuen Tak; Director: Lee Hon-to. Cast: Sarah Lee Lai-yui (Lam Bi-sheng), Loletta Lee Lai-chun (Bi-qi), Roy Cheung Yiu-yeung (Long), Shing Fui-on (Mak). 1.85:1. VHS: Tai Seng. LD: World Video. Import LD: Golden Cinema City. 108 minutes.

Teenage prostitutes Bi-sheng (who is deaf because of beatings she endured as a child) and Bi-qi try to eke out a living on Temple Street in this dreadful drama which tries to mix a little social commentary and characterization into an overly familiar exploitation scenario. After angering their psychotic pimp (to whom Bi-sheng owes $100,000), the pair barely manage to escape with their lives. Soon afterwards, Bi-qi is kidnapped by the pimp and his thugs, but the girl's triad boyfriend, Long, manages to get her back. Bi-sheng develops feelings for Long (who also serves as a procurer for her) but he is actually an undercover cop, and the psychotic pimp wants all three of them dead.

Relentlessly unpleasant (85% of the running time seems to consist of beatings), one can deduce early on that (like its protagonists) **Chicken a la Queen** is not going to amount to much of anything, and, sure enough, it doesn't. The script is puerile, the performances are overwrought (most of the dialogue is screamed), and the film certainly could have done without the sequence where Bi-sheng is repulsed and physically sickened by the fact that she has to service a black client—the sort of racism that is seen far too often in HK cinema. Even the continuity stinks: Bi-sheng is caught cheating in a mahjong parlor and has her hands smashed repeatedly with bricks, yet they look fine shortly thereafter. Incidentally, prostitutes are referred to in Cantonese as *kai*, or "hen," hence the bizarre English and Chinese titles.

150. Chicken and Duck Talk

(1988; Hui's Film Production Co.) ★: 8/10. *Gai tung aap gong* (Cantonese), *Ji tong ya jiang* (Mandarin): "Chicken with Duck Talk." Cinematographer: Derek Wan Man-kit; Art Directors: Hai Chung-man, Ben Lau Man-hung; Music: Richard Yuen Cheuk-fan; Writers: Michael Hui Koon-man, Clifton Ko Chi-sum; Producer: Ronny Yu Yan-tai; Director: Clifton Ko Chi-sum. Cast: Michael Hui Koon-man (Hui), Sylvia Chang Ai-chia (Mrs. Hui), Ricky Hui Koon-ying (Cuttlefish), Yip Wing-cho (Pang), Lowell Lo Kwun-ting (Chim), Lawrence Ng Kai-wah (Danny Poon), Ku Feng (Richard). 1.85:1. Import LD: Mei Ah. 99 minutes.

One of Michael Hui's best outings, **Chicken and Duck Talk** is a witty and thoroughly engaging send-up of both the fast food business and the cutthroat techniques often employed by conglomerates to crush independent competition. Hui plays a like-named everyman who runs an absolutely filthy, hole-in-the-wall restaurant. A notorious skinflint who regularly cheats his staff, he also happens to be a world class chef who makes the most exquisite Cantonese BBQ duck around. However, things are looking grim for Hui: His sarcastic mother-in-law has just moved in, one of the employees wants to steal his secret duck recipe, and multi-millionaire Danny Poon has just opened up one of his ultra-modern fried chicken outlets across the street. Using strict Japanese management techniques, Danny's Chicken is a force to be reckoned with, and, on opening day, Poon is already planning on bankrupting Hui and demolishing his restaurant. Desperate to save his floundering business, Hui tries to modernize his approach by transforming the establishment into the world's first karaoke "B.B.Q. Duck Lounge"(!) and even introduces a homemade store mascot. However, Poon's assistant arranges for the health inspector to show up on Hui's doorstep—just after Poon has infested the building with rats. Facing ruin, Hui swallows his pride and seeks financial aid from his mother-in-law. After extensive renovations, Hui's eatery is a smashing success that has Poon running scared.

The storyline provides the perfect set-up for Hui to work his magic as the struggling little guy who just cannot get ahead, and Chang is charming as his patient wife. Ricky Hui also provides fine support as sadsack waiter Cuttlefish, who is fired by Hui and defects to the enemy, working as their mascot. The sequence in which Ricky (clad in the store's chicken suit) and Michael (wearing his ratty duck costume) get into a street fight is the film's oft-acknowledged highlight. Sam Hui Koon-kit has an amusing cameo as himself, and director Clifton Ko (as one of Hui's new employees), producer Ronny Yu (as a construction worker), and Paula Tsui Siu-fung also appear briefly. Parts of Richard Yuen's score are very reminiscent of tracks from **Beverly Hills Cop** and **Streets of Fire**.

151. China Dolls

(1992; Kong Lung Movie Arts Distribution) ★: 2/10. *Dak kui oi no* (Cantonese), *Te qu ai nu* (Mandarin): "Special Area Love Slave." Cinematographer: Yu Chun; Art Director: Ruby Ko Pui-yee; Music: Sing Kam-wing; Writers: Yuen Chi-kin, Brian Chung Wai-hung; Producer: Law Chi-wing; Action Director: Chan Siu-lung; Director: Yeung Chi-kin. Cast: Amy Yip Chi-mei (May So), Charlie Cho Cha-lei (Charlie), Wu Ma (Lao), Lam Ching-ying (Officer #19174). 1.85:1. VHS/LD: World Video. Import LD/VCD: Ocean Shores. 91 minutes.

Buxom Amy Yip headlines this dreary Category III thriller, an unpalatable mix of drama, softcore pelvic slamming, sexual violence, and gunplay. Mainland girl May So, her husband, and newborn child must flee to HK after an attack on May leaves the would-be rapist dead. Shortly after they escape across the border, May's husband is killed in a shootout with police. Facing deportation, May asks one of the cops to take her baby. A few years pass and May is back in China and looking for a way to return to HK and get back her child. She joins up with a group of girls heading to Macau, but the men transporting them turn out to be criminals running a prostitution ring. The girls are all put through a series of psychological and physical tortures until they agree to become hookers. May eventually accepts her situation and becomes the favorite girl of a rich man from Portugal. In actuality, he is an undercover agent assigned to help bust up the crime ring controlling May. Strictly by-the-numbers and not even erotic, this tiresome effort is solely for the most diehard fans of Ms. Yip, aka "The Queen of Bust" [*sic*].

152. China White

(1989; Fu Ngai Film Production Co.) ★: 5/10 (Both versions). *Gwang tin lung foo wooi* (Cantonese), *Hong tian long hu hui* (Mandarin): "Sky Shattering Meeting Between Dragon and Tiger." Cinematographer: Andrew Lau Wai-keung; Art Director: Raymond Fung Yuen; Music: Bruce Miller, Les Gock; Writers: F.W. Silleroy, Victor Hon Kwan; Producer: Jim Choi Chiming; Action Director: Chris Lee Kin-sang; Director: Ronny Yu Yan-tai. Cast: Russell Wong (Bobby Chow), Steven Vincent Leigh (Danny Chow), Lisa Schrage (Anne Michaels), Billy Drago (Scalia), William Ho Kar-kui (Phong), Victor Hon Kwan (One Hand), Tommy Wong Kwong-leung (Mute), Ku Feng (Uncle Chi), Frank Sheppard (Rasta), Cahit Olmez (Amead), Ricky Ho Pui-tung (Kong), Ronny Yu Yan-tai (Tong Leader). Additional Cast in HK Version: Alex Man Chi-leung (Bobby and Danny's Father), Andy Lau Tak-wah (The Boys' "Adopted Father"), Shing Fui-on (Tuko), Carina Lau Kar-ling (Yen). 1.85:1. Ultra Stereo. VHS: Imperial Entertainment, World Video (HK version). LD: Image. Import LD/VCD: Universe (HK version). 98 minutes/104 minutes (HK version). Also known as **The Deadly Sin** (Title for World and Universe releases).

Predominantly in English, this HK financed action thriller has a certain novelty value and is passable formula entertainment. Young, ambitious triads Bobby and Danny Chow seek to expand their operations beyond Chinatown but meet resistance from their aged boss, Uncle Chi. Not long afterwards, Chi is assassinated by Vietnamese hood Phong and his men, who are in league with Italian mobster Scalia and Turkish kingpin Amead. Bobby avenges Chi's death and uses a cop on his payroll to drive a wedge between the Turks and the Mafia. Deciding that this is the time for he and Danny to make their move, Bobby heads to The Golden Triangle and makes a deal that will guarantee him a steady supply of opium paste. However, Bobby's new girlfriend is an undercover operative whose mission is destined to bring an end to his new empire.

Aside from a few unintentional laughs (Bobby sites *Ross Perot* as one of his heroes!), this boasts above average production values, some good stunts, and nice location work in Holland, Thailand, and Paris. The story follows the usual genre tenets, but director Ronny Yu (who cameos as a cocky gang leader) keeps things slick and interesting enough to put this slightly above the pack. The HK version, entitled **The Deadly Sin**, runs six minutes longer and features extra scenes presented as a ten minute-long flashback to the days when the Chow brothers were children. This footage (shot with sync sound, like the rest of the picture) stops the movie dead in its tracks and adds little of value, though Alex Man makes the most of his brief screen time as the boys' flamboyant father. One bit, where a prostitute is killed in crossfire, features a slightly more explicit take in the HK cut. The Caucasian performers retain their voices, while Russell Wong and Steven Vincent Leigh are dubbed in Cantonese during instances where they are speaking with other Asian performers. William Ho and the other actors playing the Vietnamese speak only Cantonese and English in both versions.

China's Last Eunuch *see* **Lai Shi, China's Last Eunuch**

153. Chinatown Kid

(1977; Shaw Brothers) ★: 6/10. *Tang yan gaai siu ji* (Cantonese), *Tang ren jie xiao zi* (Mandarin): "Chinatown Kid." Cinematographer: Kung Mu-to; Art Director: Johnson Tsao; Music: Chen Yung-yu; Writers: Ngai Hong, James Wong Jim, Chang Cheh; Producer: Mona Fong Yatwah; Action Directors: Li Chia-ting, Tai Chi-hsieh; Director: Chang Cheh. Cast: Alexander Fu Sheng (Tan Tung), Sun Chien (Yang Ching-wen), Johnny Wang Lung-wei (Chu Ho), Phillip Kwok Tsui (White Dragon Boss), Lo Mang (Green Tiger Boss), Ha Ping (Woman Who Hires Tan), Kara Hui Ying-hung (Girl in Whorehouse), Dick Wei (Kung Fu Student), Chiang Sheng (Hood), James Wong Jim (Gambler), Lu Feng (Hood). 2.35:1. VHS: Southgate (Dubbed), Fox Lorber (Dubbed). 115 minutes.

Eager but none-too-swift youth Tan Tung joins up with triad boss Chu Ho, who is impressed by Tung's kung fu skills. When Tan double-crosses Chu by helping one of his prostitutes escape, the gangster has some corrupt cops frame him for possession. Escaping to San Francisco, Tan and Taiwanese college student Yang live and work illegally in a Chinatown restaurant. It doesn't take long for Tan to run afoul of the Green Tiger gang and their egotistical leader. When the rival White Dragon gang hears about how easily Tan defeated the Tigers in a street fight, they quickly engage his services. With their new fighter's help, the Dragons soon obliterate their opposition and Tan quickly moves up in the underworld ranks. Yang, unable to cope, has become a junkie, prompting Tan to begin shutting down his gang's illegal operations. His actions, naturally, don't go over well with the bosses, so they decide to finish him off.

A change from Chang Cheh's usual period yarns, this kung fu actioner has not aged well, particularly in regards to its awful score, hideous '70s fashions, and heavy-handed messages about morality and materialism. The fights, however, are exhilarating, and Alexander Fu is terrific in the title role, displaying the charisma and dexterity that made him a popular performer in the Shaw Brothers' stable. A bit of actual location shooting is another plus. Character names above are from the dubbed version.

154. The Chinese Feast

(1995; Mandarin Films/Film Workshop) ★: 7/10. *Gam yuk moon tong* (Cantonese), *Jin yu man tang* (Mandarin): "Gold Jade Full Hall." Cinematographer: Peter Pau Tak-hei; Art Director: William Cheung Suk-ping; Music: Lowell Lo Kwunting; Writers: Tsui Hark, Ng Man-fai, Phillip Cheng Chung-tai; Producer: Raymond Wong Pak-ming; Action Director: Yuen Bun; Director: Tsui Hark. Cast: Leslie Cheung Kwok-wing (Chiu Kongsun), Anita Yuen Wing-yee (Au Ka-wai), Kenny Bee (Liu Kit), Law Kar-ying (Au Siu-fung), Zhao Wenzhou (Lung Kwunbo), Xiong Xinxin (Wong Wing), Joyce Ngai Suk-kwan (Miss Cheuk), William Ho Kar-kui (Chiu's Boss), Lau Shun (Mr. Kawasaki), Wong Yat-fei (Kitchen Staff Member), Peter Lai Bei-tak (Kitchen Staff Member), Peter Pau Tak-hei (Chef from North West Restaurant). 2.35:1. VHS: Tai Seng. Import LD: Cameron Entertainment. Import VCD. Mei Ah. 103 minutes.

Looking to immigrate, loan shark Chiu Kong-sun decides to ensure his acceptance into Canada by winning a cooking contest that a Toronto hotel has sponsored. He gets disqualified for cheating but, with the assistance of master chef Lung Kwun-bo, manages to get a job at a local restaurant run by the harried Au Siu-fung. Au has an old grudge with Lung, so he proceeds to make Chiu's life hell, not a difficult task as the gangster is a complete disaster in a kitchen. Chiu takes a fancy to Ka-wai, the boss' kooky, punked-out daughter, and this earns him the wrath of his ex-girlfriend. More pressing matters emerge in the form of egotistical master gourmet Wong Wing, director of the massive "Super Group" conglomerate which seeks to corner the HK food industry. He challenges the boss to a cooking competition: If Au wins, he gets $50 million; if he loses, he forfeits his restaurant. When his staff is bribed by the Super Group to quit, Au has a heart attack, prompting Chiu and Ka-wai to enlist the aid of Master Lung. He points them toward the only man who can prepare the incredibly intricate dishes required by the bet: famous Guangzhou chef Liu Kit. Unfortunately, Liu is now a shiftless alcoholic, and it will take more than a little effort to whip him back into shape.

Amiably dumb slapstick humor alternates with intoxicatingly photographed food preparation in this pleasing Lunar New Year's farce. Aside from the fact that the climactic cooking contest is presented like a form of culinary kung fu, there is nothing on display to suggest that Tsui Hark is behind the camera. Regardless, like most holiday features of this type, it is really the performers who have center stage, and top honors here go to Anita Yuen. She is so engagingly daffy as the openly disrespectful Ka-wai, it is a shame when, in the second half, her character loses the red hair, bizarro make-up, and hellraiser attitude. As with **Shogun and Little Kitchen**, make sure to have plenty of your favorite Chinese food on hand to satisfy the hunger you will develop watching the preparation of some incredible traditional dishes.

155. A Chinese Ghost Story

(1987; Cinema City/Golden Princess Film Production/Film Workshop) ★: 8/10. *Sien nui yau wan* (Cantonese), *Qian nu you hun* (Mandarin): "Sien, the Female Ghost." Cinematographers: Poon Hang-sang, Sander Lee Kar-ko, Tom Lau Moon-tong, Horace Wong Wing-hang; Art Director: Hai Chung-man; Music: James Wong Jim, Romeo Diaz; Writer: Yuen Kai-chi; Producer: Tsui Hark; Action Directors: Ching Siu-tung, Phillip Kwok Tsui, Lau Chi-ho, Tsui Chung-san, Woo Chi-lung; Director: Ching Siu-tung. Cast: Leslie Cheung Kwok-wing (Ning Tsai-shen), Joey Wang Tsu-hsien (Nieh Hsiao-tsing), Wu Ma (Yen Che-hsia), Lau Siu-ming (The Tree Devil), Sit Chi-lun (Ching), Lam Wai (Hsia-hou). Dolby Digital (DVD only). 1.85:1. VHS: Tai Seng. Import LD: Golden Cinema City. Import VCD: Mei Ah (No Subtitles). Import DVD: Mega Star. 95 minutes.

Based on a famous story by writer Pu Songling (first adapted in 1960 by director Li Han-hsiang for Shaw Brothers as **The Enchanting Shadow**), Ching Siu-tung's beguiling period fantasy, **A Chinese Ghost Story**, is one of the films that re-ignited Western interest in HK cinema and ranks as one of the most imitated productions in memory. In order to evade a pack of wolves, bumbling tax collector Ning Tsai-shen makes the mistake of spending the night at dilapidated Lan Ro Temple. There he encounters powerful swordsman Yen Che-hsia, who is in the midst of a long-running battle with his enemy, Hsia-hou. The latter encounters the beautiful Nieh Hsiao-tsing (called "Siu-sin" in some versions) and is killed by a mysterious force that sucks all of the life from his body. Shortly thereafter, Ning also meets up with Hsiao-tsing, who is actually a ghost ordered by The Tree Devil to lure wandering travellers to their doom. Touched by Ning's gentleness and humility, Hsiao-tsing decides to spare him, but Ning accidentally intrudes upon the demon's villa and Hsiao-tsing must risk losing her chance to reincarnate in order to save him. After much debate, Yen is able to convince Ning that his love is not of this world, and the pair join together for a literal trip into Hell to save Hsiao-tsing (who is betrothed to the monstrous Lord Black) so that she may escape her servitude and reincarnate.

Some of the horror elements are clearly indebted to Sam Raimi's **The Evil Dead** (in particular, the crumbling wooden temple, the ground level P.O.V. tracking shots that depict the Tree Devil's monstrous tongue approaching victims, and some tree branches that have a life of their own), but the fantasy components are distinctly Chinese: gravity-defying heroes and villains, martial arts-tinged combat, and forbidden love between humans and spirits. The cinematography and art direction are superb, the action is invigorating, and the love story surprisingly touching, making this one of the most captivating and enjoyable fantasies of the post-New Wave period. Joey Wang and Wu Ma would virtually reprise their roles in a number of the film's imitations, and the former would become hopelessly typecast as a result. The soundtrack includes some lovely songs sung by Leslie Cheung and actress/pop star Sally Yeh Chian-wen, and future movie mogul Wong Jing puts in a brief appearance. Two sequels and an animated remake followed.

156. A Chinese Ghost Story II

(1990; Cinema City/Golden Princess Film Production/Film Workshop) ★: 7/10. *Sien nui yau wan II yan gaan do* (Cantonese), *Qian nu you hun II ren jian dao* (Mandarin): "Sien, the Female Ghost II: Human Realm Tao." Cinematographer: Arthur Wong Ngok-Tai; Art Director: William Cheung Suk-ping; Music: James Wong Jim, Romeo Diaz; Writers: Lau Tai-muk, Lam Kei-to, Edward Leung Yiu-ming; Producer: Tsui Hark; Action Directors: Ching Siu-tung, Lau Chi-ho, Woo Chi-lung; Director: Ching Siu-tung. Cast: Leslie Cheung Kwok-wing (Ning), Joey Wang Tsu-hsien (Windy), Michelle Lee Kar-yan (Moon), Jacky Cheung Hok-yau (Autumn), Wu Ma (Yan), Waise Lee Chi-hung (Hu), Lau Siu-ming (Lord Fu), Lau Shun (The High Priest), Ku Feng (Old Man in Cell), To Siu-chun (Rebel). Dolby Digital (DVD only). 1.85:1. VHS: Tai Seng. Import LD: Golden Cinema City. Import VCD: Universe. Import DVD: Mega Star. 103 minutes.

Picking up a few years after the events depicted in its forerunner, **A Chinese Ghost Story II** throws a lot more characters and special FX into the mix and sacrifices some of the charm in the process. However, if judged on its own merits, this action packed fantasy remains above average and quite entertaining. Tax collector Ning and Taoist Yan (called "Yen" last time) have gone their separate ways, and the former is mistakenly arrested by some overzealous bounty hunters. Escaping with the help of his cellmate, Ning encounters rebels who mistake him for the learned writer, Chu. One of the women in the group, Windy, is the spitting image of Ning's lost love which, naturally, causes him to instantly fall in love with her. The girl seeks to rescue her father, Lord Fu (Lau Siu-ming, who plays The Tree Devil in parts I and III), while a troop of royal guardsmen are transporting him to be executed. After taking care of a pesky and quite persistent monster and vanquishing some evil spirits that temporarily take control of Windy, Ning and the group find themselves faced with yet another threat: A demon is impersonating the kingdom's exalted High Priest and threatens the lives of everyone, friend and foe alike. Fortunately, Taoist master Yan is able to lend his services in their fight.

Some of the special FX are pretty clunky this time out, but there are so many of them that this is to be expected and is not a serious problem. Like many HK fantasies, there is so much visual razzle dazzle and dizzying action on display, there is nary an opportunity to be bored. However, the simple but significant pleasures generated by the romance at the heart of the original are absent here, making this entry less satisfying on an emotional level. Acting honors go to Jacky Cheung, who gives a wonderful comic performance as Autumn, a fun loving Taoist swordsman who turns out to be an invaluable asset to Windy and her followers.

157. A Chinese Ghost Story III

(1991; Cinema City/Golden Princess Film Production/Film Workshop) ★: 6/10. *Sin lui yau wan III do do do* (Cantonese), *Qian nu you hun III dao dao dao* (Mandarin): "Sien, the Female Ghost III: The Way, the Way, the Way." Cinematographer: Tom Lau Moon-tong; Art Director: James Leung Wah-sang; Music: James Wong Jim, Romeo Diaz; Writers: Tsui Hark, Roy Szeto Cheuk-hon; Producer: Tsui Hark; Action Directors: Ching Siu-tung, Ma Yuk-shing, Yuen Bun, Cheung

Yiu-sing; Director: Ching Siu-tung. Cast: Joey Wang Tsu-hsien (Lotus), Tony Leung Chiu-wai (Fong), Jacky Cheung Hok-yau (Yin), Nina Li Chi (Butterfly), Lau Siu-ming (The Tree Devil), Lau Shun (Fong's Master). Dolby Digital (DVD only). 1.85:1. VHS: Tai Seng. Import LD: Golden Cinema City. Import VCD: Universe. Import DVD: Mega Star. 108 minutes.

Opening with a montage of highlights from the first film, **A Chinese Ghost Story III** unfolds one hundred years later, skipping over the events depicted in the first sequel. The final entry in Ching Siu-tung's trilogy is largely a remake of the original, bringing Joey Wang back to play yet another benevolent female spirit. Jacky Cheung, Lau Shun, and Lau Siu-ming also return, but as different characters from the ones they essayed in the previous film. While this chapter has its own rewards and makes for engaging viewing, the lack of conceptual inspiration detracts somewhat from the final product. Bumbling monk Fong and his master are transporting a golden Buddha statue across the country to the Imperial Temple. En route, they meet up with Yin, a staunchly materialistic sword-for-hire who accidentally burns down the monks' shelter. While passing through a town, the pair meet up again with Yin (who possesses some rudimentary magical powers, which he uses to make a quick buck now and then) and his clumsiness causes their valuable cargo to be revealed to a group of bandits. Fleeing to the countryside, the monks opt to spend the night in the spooky, dilapidated Orchid Temple. On their heels are the robbers, out to snatch the statue, but they are soon distracted by a lovely female voice which they follow to a handsome villa. Lured inside by the beautiful Lotus, the killers are quickly dispatched and drained of their lifeforce by the girl and her sister, Butterfly, who are under the control of the resurrected Tree Devil. Lotus is sent to seduce and murder Fong but, naturally, the two fall for each other instead. Fong then proceeds to protect Lotus from his demon-hunting master, while she shields him from Butterfly's murderous advances. When the elder monk is captured by the Tree Devil, Fong enlists Yin's services on credit (with the swordsman keeping a running tab on his handy abacus) in order to attack and destroy the creature once and for all.

By following the original plotline so faithfully, **III** relinquishes the novelty of its forerunners, opting instead to be an all-out action/SPFX extravaganza. On that level, it succeeds well enough via some exciting wirework, elementary but effective CGI illusions, and some choice horror elements. In addition to the Tree Devil's ever-popular "giant monster tongue" (which slithers through the forest snagging victims), we also get some amusingly literal shots of the sisters' scaly tongues snaking their way down victims' throats into their stomachs. Best of all, during the climax the previously unseen Mountain Devil finally rears its ugly head, taking the form of a giant temple that uproots itself and sets about trying to crush the protagonists! James Leung's dusty, web-shrouded production design is first rate, and Cheung's lusty materialist is an amusing foil for Tony Leung's resolutely virginal monk to deal with. While it may be best appreciated by those who have not seen the previous entries, **A Chinese Ghost Story III** is preferable to almost all of the series' many imitations and is dependable HK genre fare. Wang and Leung also appeared together in **Fantasy Romance** the same year, which includes a parody of the original **A Chinese Ghost Story**.

158. A Chinese Ghost Story: The Tsui Hark Animation

(1997; Golden Harvest/Film Workshop/Polygram K.K./Win's Entertainment/Cathay Asia Films) ★: 6/10. *Siu-sin* (Cantonese), *Xiaoqian* (Mandarin): "Little Pretty" (the heroine's name in the Chinese versions). Music: Ricky Ho Kwok-kit; Writer-Producer: Tsui Hark; Character Animation Director: Tetsuya Endo; Director: Andrew Chan Wai-man. Voice Cast for Cantonese Version: Jan Lam Hoi-fung (Ning), Anita Yuen Wing-yee (Shine), Eric Kot Man-fai (Ten Miles), James Wong Jim (Red Beard), Raymond Wong Lau-man (White Cloud), Charlie Yeung Choi-nei (Butterfly), Kelly Chan Wai-lam (Madame Trunk), Jordan Chan Siu-chun (Mountain Evil), Tsui Hark (Solid Gold), Vivian Lai Shui-yun (Lan), Ronald Cheng Chung-kei (Fu). Voice Cast for Mandarin Version: Nicky Wu Chi-lung (Ning), Sylvia Chang Ai-chia (Shine), Li Li-chun (Red Beard), Sammo Hung Kam-po (White Cloud), Tommy So Yau-pang (Ten Miles), Liu Cho-ying (Butterfly), Yeung Fan (Madame Trunk), Lo Ta-yu (Mountain Evil), Tsui Hark (Solid Gold), Linda Wong Hing-ping (Lan), Ronald Cheng Chung-kei (Fu). Dolby Digital. 1.85:1. Import LD/VCD/DVD: Carnival. 83 minutes.

This big-budget animated feature offers up a stunning marriage of Japanese-style animation and fluid, computer generated imagery. However, as stimulating as the visuals are, neither the storyline nor the characters are as interesting as those found in its live action counterparts. Dumped by his sweetheart, lowly tax collector Ning wanders the countryside with his loyal dog, Solid Gold. After being saved from some spirits by wizened *sifu* White Cloud and his musclebound pupil, Ten Miles, Ning stumbles into a literal ghost town where he catches sight of Shine (an odd anglicization for Siu-sin/Xiaoqian), a gorgeous young spirit. While Shine is supposed to be collecting Ning's soul in order for it to be fed to her demonic mistress, Madame Trunk, she falls for Ning's naive charm and cannot follow through on her orders. Regardless, Shine's heart belongs to the Mountain Evil, a vain colossus who demands constant worship from his subjects. When Shine accidentally angers the giant, she sees his true nature; with the timely assistance of compassionate Taoist Red Beard, the pair are able to escape the evil. Now resolutely devoted to each other, Ning and Shine try to reach the Reincarnation Gate so they can be together in the next life, but the hardhearted White Cloud and Ten Miles are on their trail, eager to disperse Shine's spirit.

The use of animation allows this to unfold on a scale that would otherwise be financially impossible to attempt, and the depth achieved in some sequences is breathtaking. Unfortunately, the storyline will seem overly familiar to anyone with a grounding in HK fantasy, and the voice casting in the Cantonese version is very weak. Instead of choosing performers who suited the roles, Tsui Hark has instead gone with stars apparently chosen on the basis of their popularity with young audiences. The Mandarin version is better in this regard (the villainous Madame Trunk has a fey male voice—in keeping with the live action interpretations of the character—which is more interesting than pop-star Kelly Chan's rather colorless vocalization), and that language would actually be the more appropriate one for the time period anyway. Tsui incorporates some of his customary political subtext into the proceedings, mainly in regard to the balancing act HK undergoes by remaining true to its Chinese roots while also maintaining its own identity. When all is said and done, though, the merging of animation styles is a joy to behold, and the various components of Chinese fantasy (such as the "void hammers," giant mallets that literally stamp out the memories of those about to be reincarnated) remain fascinating, making this well worth catching, regardless of its shortcomings.

159. A Chinese Legend

(1991; Grand March Movie Production Co.) ★: 8/10. *Chui yat* (Cantonese), *Zhui ri* (Mandarin): "Chase the Sun." Cinematographers: Lau Hung-chuen, Cheung Dik-kei, Yuen Wai-kwok; Music: Richard Lo Sai-kit, Liu Kwok-jim; Writer: Joyce

Mak Shun-ling; Producer: Lo Wei; Action Directors: Lam Moon-wah, Phillip Kwok Tsui; Director: Lau Hung-chuen. Cast: Joey Wang Tsu-hsien (Ku Moon-cher), Jacky Cheung Hok-yau (Kar Yat-long), Sharla Cheung Man (Ching'er), Wu Ma (The Master of Old Sword Mansion), Lau Shun (Yat-long's Master). 2.35:1. Stereo Sound (Laserdisc and DVD only). VHS: Tai Seng (No Subtitles). Import LD/VCD: Star Entertainment (No Subtitles). Import DVD: China Star (No Subtitles). 91 minutes.

While obviously inspired by the **A Chinese Ghost Story** series, and produced on a tight budget, this sombre period fantasy turns out to be an impressive achievement in its own right and one of the finest early '90s fantasies. Haunted by a recurring dream in which he encounters a lovely, veiled maiden and then falls into a bottomless abyss, swordsman Kar Yat-long awakens one evening with part of the woman's bracelet in his hand. While riding one day, he comes across the very same woman (whose name is Ku Moon-cher) about to be sacrificed by some villagers to protect their homes from the malevolent King of Ghosts. While he offers to escort her to safety, she returns for the sake of her people. That evening Yat-long encounters another beautiful girl in a remote part of the forest. Although she provides him with ample opportunity to seduce her, Yat-long does not, for he realizes that the maiden is actually a Fox Goblin which drinks the blood of men that fall into its seductive clutches. Before leaving in the morning, he gives the creature the name Ching'er and earns her unyielding love. Meanwhile, Moon-cher violently rejects the advances of the King, resulting in the destruction of Ku Village and, later, her suicide. Yat-long seeks out and finds Moon-cher's ghost, but she is soon taken by the King, prompting the swordsman and an elderly master to concoct a desperate plan to rescue her soul. Along to aid Yat-long is Ching'er, who is willing to sacrifice herself for him despite the fact that she knows Moon-cher is his true love.

In contrast to its models, **A Chinese Legend** has no comedy relief and is quite downbeat but that actually helps to make it more romantic and affecting. The leads give committed performances, and both the cinematography and the score are quite beautiful and atmospheric, adding greatly to the final product. There are enough positive attributes on hand here for all but the most cynical viewers to forgive some technical shortcomings (like obvious miniatures and flawed rear screen projection). The Taiwanese video release has subtitles but is awkwardly cropped.

160. Chinese Midnight Express

(1997; Cameron Entertainment/The Young Filmmakers) ★: 3/10. *Hak yuk duen cheung goh ji chai sang jue yuk* (Cantonese), *Hei yu duan chang ge zhi qi sheng zhu rou* (Mandarin): "The Broken Gut Song of the Dark Prison: Frame-Up." Cinematographer: Tony Miu Kin-fai; Art Director: Andrew Cheuk Man-yiu; Music: Lincoln Lo Kin; Writers: Candy Cheng, Lee Siu-kei; Producer: Lee Siu-kei; Director: Billy Tang Hin-sing. Cast: Tony Leung Chiu-wai (Chin Ahn), Pinky Cheung Man-chi (Jess Tsai), Ng Man-tat (Plane), Ben Lam Kwok-bun (Ben Cheng, aka Inhuman), Ben Ng Ngai-cheung (Chiang Yiu-joe), Elvis Tsui Kam-kong (David Mak, aka Three-legs), Ng Chi-hung (Brother Dog), Lee Siu-kei (Brother Nan), John Ching Tung (Brother Bill), Law Kar-ying (Guard), Vincent Wan Yeung-ming (Wan Chi-hoe), Peter Lai Bei-tak (Uncle Chien). 1.85:1. VHS: Mecapro. Import LD/VCD/DVD: Mei Ah. 102 minutes.

Aside from being a tamer exploitation exercise than one might expect from the director of **Run and Kill** and **Red to Kill**, this tiresome prison yarn (set in the 1960s) offers no surprises. Investigative reporter Chin Ahn is fired when his reports on police corruption stir up trouble for his editor. The main focus of his articles, officer Chiang Yiu-joe, proceeds to frame him for drug possession, and Chin is sentenced to three years in prison. Inside, he is subjected to beatings, attempted sexual assault, caning, and other indignities, while Chin simply makes his situation worse by challenging the openly corrupt and sadistic warden. Chin's endurance in the face of such brutal adversity wins him the respect of his fellow inmates, and he begins sneaking reports on their plight out of the prison to his old newspaper.

Even if you have only seen one of these prison pictures, you have already seen everything on offer here. It's just the usual cliches enacted by the usual actors giving the usual performances playing the usual characters, with the usual resolution in sight long before the end crawl finally appears. Without any variation to add some interest to this time-worn formula, **Chinese Midnight Express** emerges as a waste of time. Even the superb Tony Leung Chiu-wai simply sleepwalks through it.

161. A Chinese Odyssey Part One—Pandora's Box

(1995; Brilliant Star Development) ★: 7/10. *Sai yau gei dai yat baak ling yat wooi ji yuet gwong bo hap* (Cantonese), *Xi you ji di yi bai ling yi hui zhi yue guang bao he* (Mandarin): "Journey to the West: Moonlight Treasure Box." Cinematographer: Poon Hang-sang; Art Director: James Leung Wah-sang; Music: Chiu Kwai-ping; Writer: Kei On (pseudonym for Jeff Lau Chun-wai); Producer: Yeung Kwok-fai; Action Director: Ching Siu-tung; Director: Jeff Lau Chun-wai. Cast: Stephen Chiau Sing-chi (The Monkey King/Joker), Ng Man-tat (Assistant Master), Law Kar-ying (The Longevity Monk), Yammie Nam Kit-ying (The 30th Madam), Karen Mok Man-wai (Pak Jing-jing), Jeff Lau Chun-wai ("The Grapes"), Athena Chu Yan (Lin Zixia). 1.85:1. VHS: Tai Seng. Import LD/VCD/DVD: Mei Ah. 87 minutes.

162. A Chinese Odyssey Part Two—Cinderella

(1995; Brilliant Star Development) ★: 7/10. *Sai yau gei daai git guk ji sin lei kei yuen* (Cantonese), *Xi you ji da jie ju zhi xian lu qi yuan* (Mandarin): "Journey to the West: Fairy Slipper Magic Encounter." Cinematographer: Poon Hang-sang; Art Director: James Leung Wah-sang; Music: Chiu Kwai-ping; Writer: Kei On (pseudonym for Jeff Lau Chun-wai); Producer: Yeung Kwok-fai; Action Director: Ching Siu-tung; Director: Jeff Lau Chun-wai. Cast: Stephen Chiau Sing-chi (The Monkey King/Joker), Ng Man-tat (Assistant Master), Athena Chu Yan (Lin Zixia), Ada Choi Siu-fan (Lin Qingxia), Law Kar-ying (The Longevity Monk), Yammie Nam Kit-ying (The 30th. Madam), Karen Mok Man-wai (Pak Jing-jing). VHS: Tai Seng. Import LD: Cameron Entertainment. Import VCD/DVD: Mei Ah. 99 minutes.

Jeff Lau directed this opulent, two-part send-up of the classic novel *Xi you ji* (usually translated as "Journey to the West"), a fantasy-filled dramatization of how Buddhism was introduced to China, with comedian Stephen Chiau ideally cast as its hero, Monkey King Sun Houzi (Sun, the Monkey). **Part One** opens with The Goddess of Happiness sentencing The Longevity Monk and his disciples to be reincarnated as mortals. Their banishment from Heaven is retribution for the transgressions of The Monkey King (who sought to eat his master, as consumption of The Monk's flesh engenders immortality). Five centuries later, The Monkey King's new human persona—a bandit chieftain named Joker, who is unaware of his former existence—finds himself caught between two immortal sisters, The 30th Madam and Pak Jing-jing. Once jilted by The Monkey King, Jing-jing falls for Joker, only to be poisoned by her jealous sibling. Seeking to prevent her impending death, Joker uses a magic vessel (the "Pandora's Box" of the English title) to travel back in time but accidentally ends up 500 years in the past. **Part Two** finds the stranded Joker falling for the beautiful Spider Web immortal Lin Zixia, who is actually half of Buddha's lampwick in corporeal form. Now existing prior to the time of The Monkey King's subjugation, Joker sets about rectifying his romantic confusion and changing the past, but must first contend with numerous adversaries, including Zixia's shrewish sister, Lin Qingxia, and the ferocious King Bull, who lords over an army of minions and has his own personal legion of giant fleas!

The cast handles both the comedic and dramatic facets of their roles well, and the script's sentimental passages avoid being overwrought or cloying. But these *are* Stephen Chiau films after all, so poignant moments are soon offset by people getting kicked, punched, or otherwise thwacked in the crotch. Those unfamiliar with Chinese mythology will not be helped by the spectacularly confusing subtitles but can still savor both films' technical merits; in particular, Ching Siu-tung's zero gravity action choreography and the wonderfully baroque and colorful production design. The character make-up is superb, with a barrage of extras transformed into animal-headed warriors, while supporting actors, like frequent Chiau sidekick Ng Man-tat, embody various otherwordly beings (including soul-sucking demons, zombies, and a giant spider). The one serious drawback is the soundtrack, which includes several cues from Frankie Chan and Roel A. Garcia's moody, romantic score for Wong Kar-wai's **Ashes of Time** that are ill-suited to this comparatively lightweight enterprise. There are a number of in-jokes, including the inevitable jest about Lin Qingxia and the like-named fantasy film queen Brigitte *Lin Ching-hsia* (the same name presented in different Mandarin translation forms), and the latter's on and offscreen paramours, Chin Han and Charlie Chin Hsiang-lin.

163. Chinese Torture Chamber Story

(1994; Cameron Entertainment/Wong Jing's Workshop) ★: 4/10. *Moon ching sap dai huk ying* (Cantonese), *Man qing shi da ku xing* (Mandarin): "The Ching Dynasty's Ten Most Cruel Punishments." Cinematographer: Tony Miu Kin-fai; Art Director: Wong Kar-lang; Writer: Cheuk Bing; Producer: Wong Jing; Director: Bosco Lam Hing-lung. Cast: Yvonne Yung Hung (Little Cabbage), Lawrence Ng Kai-wah (Yang Ni-mu), Tommy Wong Kwong-leung (Got Siu-tai), Elvis Tsui Kam-kong (Win Chung-lung), Julie Lee Wah-yuet (Ki Dan-fung), Yuen King-tan (Nanny), Lee Siu-kei (Supreme Court Judge). 1.85:1. VHS: Tai Seng. Import LD: Cameron Entertainment, Mei Ah Gold. Import VCD: Mei Ah. 92 minutes.

One of the most infamous Category III films, **Chinese Torture Chamber Story** pulls the viewer in multiple directions at once, freely mixing stomach churning sadism and over-the-top gore with exuberant softcore sex and comedy ranging from childish to incredibly bizarre. Maiden Little Cabbage is brought before the local magistrate after she is found covered in blood beside the dead body of her husband, Got Siu-tai. The man died after consuming a kind of super aphrodisiac which caused his already immense penis to explode! Flashbacks reveal how Little Cabbage was hired to be a maid in the home of scholar Yang Ni-mu. After accidentally catching her mistress cheating on Ni-mu with the evil Lau Hoi-sing, Little Cabbage was married off to the homely Siu-tai (whose member is so huge that ejaculation could prove fatal to his partners!). When Hoi-sing tries to take advantage of Little Cabbage, he is severely beaten by Siu-tai, setting in motion the events that led to the present court case.

Produced using sets and costumes left over from the Stephen Chiau comedy **Hail the Judge**, this Wong Jing production can be accused of a lot of things—but few would call it boring. Particularly memorable is a send-up of the pottery wheel scene in **Ghost**, accompanied (as in the American film) by "Unchained Melody," played here on Chinese instruments (after witnessing what goes on here, you'll never be able to think of that song again without laughing and/or wincing)! Also unforgettable is a sex scene between C-III regulars Elvis Tsui and Julie Lee. Playing martial arts masters, the two engage in wild, gravity-defying sexual stances like "Invincible Mouth," "Oral Attack," "Invincible Wheel," and "Wonder Screw," with their superhuman pelvic slamming accompanied by video game-style sound FX! Obviously not for all tastes, the film can be marginally enjoyable if approached in the right frame of mind (assuming that is at all possible), but some all-too-serious misogyny, torture, and sexual violence make parts very hard to endure and negatively color the entire experience. Director Bosco Lam went on to write the original story for **Viva Erotica**, and clips from **Torture Chamber** appear in that film during a sequence where Leslie Cheung and Law Kar-ying go to the movies. The unrelated (and far less financially successful) **Chinese Torture Chamber Story II** followed in 1998.

Chinese Untouchables *see* **Tian Di**

164. The Christ of Nanjing

(1995; Golden Harvest/Amuse Group) ★: 9/10. *Laam ging dik gei duk* (Cantonese), *Nan jing de ji du* (Mandarin): "The Christ of Nanjing." Cinematographer: Bill Wong Chung-bo; Art Director: Eddie Ma Poon-chiu; Music: Shigeru Umebayashi; Writer: Joyce Chan Wan-man; Producers: Chua Lam, Akira Morishige; Director: Tony Au Ding-ping. Cast: Tony Leung Kar-fai (Ryuichi Okagawa), Yasuko Tomita (Jin-hua), Tou Chung-wah (Tan Yong-nian), Lau Shun ("Madame"), Chau Ching. Dolby Stereo. 1.85:1. VHS: Tai Seng. Import LD/VCD: Mei Ah. 99 minutes. Also known as **An Affair in Nanjing** (Singapore Title).

A remarkable, courageous performance by Yasuko Tomita is the main strength of this handsome, moving period drama, a HK-Japan co-production. Japanese writer Ryuichi Okagawa has been ill ever since returning from China, where he worked as a reporter. There he met Jin-hua, a spirited young girl with a fervent belief in Jesus Christ. Plagued by severe, congenital headaches, Ryuichi finds his creativity and zest for living reawakened by this uncultured, naive girl, whom he takes to be his bride. However, Jin-hua is shattered when she learns that Ryuichi already has a wife back in Japan. Forced to return home because of a death in the family, Ryuichi leaves the girl behind. Unable to support herself, Jin-hua goes to work in a brothel, where she contracts both a venereal disease and influenza. In a fit of delirium, she imagines a Eurasian customer to be Jesus himself and construes that, by sleeping with him, her ailments will be cured. Racked with guilt, Ryuichi returns sometime later, intending to take Jin-hua back to Japan for treatment, but, as her physical and mental deterioration have become more pronounced, this may no longer be possible.

Based on a Japanese novel of the same name, **The Christ of Nanjing** is filled with the kind of beautiful, natural, and sensual imagery one expects from director Tony Au (**Dream Lovers**), complemented by some interesting asides on faith and Christianity. Apart from the needlessly melodramatic device of having his character plagued by migraines (presumably something carried over from the original source material) that leave him clutching his head in a broad caricature of pain, Tony Leung Kar-fai acquits himself well. However, Yasuko Tomita (who won the Best Actress prize at The Tokyo International Film Festival) is so utterly convincing as Jin-hua, the viewer has no trouble believing for a second that Ruyichi could be so changed by this simple girl. It is a difficult part, filled with nudity and several unflattering moments, but Tomita gives one of the most affecting and natural turns in memory. It is precisely the kind of rare performance that can almost singlehandedly transform a very good film into a great one.

Christmas Romance *see* **It's a Drink, It's a Bomb!**

165. Chungking Express

(1994; Jet Tone Production Co.) ★: 9/10. *Chung Hing sam lam* (Cantonese), *Zong qing sen lin* (Mandarin): "Chungking Forest." Cinematographer: Christopher Doyle; Art Director: William Cheung Suk-ping; Music: Frankie Chan Fan-kei, Roel A. Garcia; Producer: Chan Yee-cheng; Writer-Director: Wong Kar-wai. Cast: Brigitte Lin Ching-hsia (Woman in Blonde Wig), Takeshi Kaneshiro (He Qiwu—Badge #223), Tony Leung Chiu-wai (Badge #663), Faye Wang Jingwen (Faye), Valerie Chow Kar-ling (Air Hostess). 1.85:1. VHS: Miramax (102 minutes), World (98 minutes). LD: Voyager (102 minutes), World (98 minutes). Import LD/VCD/DVD: Ocean Shores.

During a three month break in the editing of his troubled period epic **Ashes of Time** (1994), director Wong Kar-wai crafted this irresistible confection, which is both a contemporary valentine to classic French New Wave cinema and a thoroughly charming celebration of human ardour and the randomness of life in the city. It tells two very different, somewhat interwoven stories, centering on handsome policemen and their encounters with two very different, fascinating women. However, both parts deal equally with Wong's love for and mastery of cinema. Rarely has there been a motion picture (outside of Jean-Luc Godard's filmography) that was so willing to play with the medium's edicts regarding velocity, cadence, image, and texture. He also cares deeply for his lead characters. Like the film itself, they are dynamic, distinctive, and wonderfully quirky. Story #1 centers on Qiwu, aka Badge #223, a hopeless romantic who has just been dumped by his girlfriend, May. He relentlessly muses about fate while consuming can after can of pineapple (May's favourite food)—but only cans that expire on May 1st, his birthday. After a particularly painful evening of soul searching, he crosses paths with the enigmatic "Woman in Blonde Wig" (Lin, as an exquisite incarnation of the classic *noir* heroine), a drug smuggler whose band of East Indian "mules" have absconded with their cargo. After initially passing within inches of each other, they meet again in a bar, get drunk, and end up in bed together ... sort of. Story #2 involves Badge #663, a forlorn cop who has just been dumped by his stewardess girlfriend. He gains a secret admirer in the form of Faye, a flighty young woman who works at The Midnight Express, a fastfood stand that is one of 663's regular haunts. Faye (who is obsessed with The Mamas and the Papas' "California Dreaming," which she plays endlessly at high volume) expresses her affection for 663 in a decidedly original manner: She breaks into and secretly tidies his apartment. Over the course of several visits, she cleans, rearranges furniture, and even switches the labels on tins of food. Slowly but surely, this adds variety and mystery to 663's dreary routine and, in the end, Faye becomes his lover ... sort of.

Better experienced than recounted, **Chungking Express** is gratifyingly clever and worthy of multiple viewings (not a small accomplishment in a decade where 90 percent of the films produced are not worth watching even once). Wong has always twisted narrative conventions, and this effort will be no less disconcerting to those taken aback by his earlier work (there are no introductions, just recapitulations). Despite weak-to-middling box office, his films have already had substantial impact in their home territory, serving as a choice point of reference for critics and comedians alike. Meanwhile, Wong's trademark "Blur-O-Vision" action sequences were picked up on by everyone from Tsui Hark (**The Blade**) to Wong Jing (**Return to a Better Tomorrow**), and became a stylistic requirement of the flourishing *goo wak jai* ("young rascal") crime genre. When all is said and done, **Chungking Express** (which won several prizes at the 1994 HK Film Awards, including Best Picture) will probably be remembered as Wong Kar-wai's signature film. It is laidback and lightning paced, cutting edge and retro, capricious and somber, a mass of incongruous actions, missed opportunities, unguarded sentiment, and unfettered bliss. Just like life ... sort of. There are two domestic video versions of the film to choose from. The film was the first release from Quentin Tarantino's Rolling Thunder Pictures, and he presented Wong's "International Cut" of the film. The World Video tape and disc were derived from the original, shorter HK release. (There is also a HK disc set from Ocean Shores that I haven't seen). Among the differences: The scenes where The Blonde and her mules prepare for the smuggling trip are much shorter in the HK version; the sequence where Qiwu loiters outside his girlfriend's window occurs earlier in the US print; traditional Indian music plays in the background during the smugglers' arrival at the airport in the US print, while the HK version features the title theme; the HK version deletes most of The Blonde's search for the smugglers and all of her subsequent kidnapping of a little Indian girl (in order to extort the whereabouts of the drugs); Faye Wang's rendition of "Dreams" no longer plays in the background of a sequence in the international version but can still be heard later on and during the end credits. The longer version is more satisfying, and I suspect that the HK print may have been shortened for no good reason other than to keep the running time under 100m, thus insuring the requisite five shows a day in theaters.

166. Circus Kids

(1994; Tung Loong Overseas Group) ★: 4/10. *Ma hei siu ji* (Cantonese), *Ma xi xiao zi* (Mandarin): "Circus Kids." Cinematographer: Yeung Ho-cheung; Art Director: Nelson Cheung Hok-yun; Music: Lowell Lo Kwun-ting; Writer: Lee Man-choi; Producer: Martin Lam Yu-sheng; Action Directors: Pan Yun-sang, Yuen Mo, Chow Man-dik; Director: Wu Ma. Cast: Yuen Biao (Lo Yitung), Donnie Yen Chi-tan (Tang Fa), Irene Wan Pik-ha (Lan), Wu Ma (Shen Tinyi), Lam Wai (Chiang Yitien), Lily Li Li-li (May), Ken Lo Wai-kwong (Lung), Bey Logan (Owan). 1.85:1. VHS: World Video. Import LD/VCD: Universe. 94 minutes.

The adventures of a circus troop in 1942 forms the novel focus of this otherwise undistinguished martial arts entry, which is marred by choppy editing and poor production values. The members of Master Shen's Shanfu Circus must flee Shanghai after their tent and equipment are destroyed by Japanese invaders. Relocating to Canton, they are unable to find work and must make a living performing in the streets. Lo Yitung, a talented but impetuous acrobat, constantly finds himself in scrapes with righteous lawman Tang Fa, but escapes punishment thanks to Fa's infatuation with Lo's beautiful co-star, Lan. The performers undergo many hardships trying to make ends meet, even after receiving assistance from Shen's sister. When the men in the group get jobs at a factory that is actually a front for a foreign-run opium operation, tragedy results.

The use of circus performers provides for some interesting acrobatics, but most are so poorly filmed and edited that they amount to very little. Aside from a climactic fight between Yuen Biao and Ken Lo, the martial arts are undistinguished, and the balance is too routine and dull to recommend.

167. City Cop

(1995; Magnum/Uniden Investments) ★: 5/10. *Gung buk II* (Cantonese), *Gong pu II* (Mandarin): "Public Servant II." Cinematographer: Yu Kwok-bing; Art Director: Ho Chi-hang; Music: Mak Chan-hung; Writer: Anna Lee Yee-wah; Producer: Danny Lee Sau-yin; Action Directors: Chin Kar-lok, Yeuk Tin-hung; Director: Herman Yau Lai-to. Cast: Danny Lee Sau-yin (Lee), Michael Chow Man-kin (Michael Chow), Parkman Wong Pak-man (Jackson Wong Chak-shun), Ben Ng Ngai-cheung (Ng Wai-hon), Peter Yung Kam-cheung (Lau Tse-cheong), Tam Suk-mui (Carol). 1.85:1. VHS: Tai Seng. Import LD/VCD: Star Entertainment. 100 minutes.

This police thriller is so intent on adhering to formula that it probably would have worked better as a parody. Fortunately, there is some excellent action along the way to make the ride worthwhile. Ben Ng plays the head of some heavily-armed Mainland thieves plying their murderous trade in HK, while Parkman Wong and Michael Chow are the mismatched cops on his trail. Wong is the seasoned vet trying to stay out of danger for the sake of his wife and kids, while Chow is the Rambo-wannabe, jumping into every situation with no thought for the safety of himself or his men. In between heated discussions on proper procedure, they follow various leads, arrest some likely suspects, and get a few lucky breaks.

After a rather slow first half, there is a genuinely exciting car/foot chase midway and an even better one in the last reel. The climax unfolds inside a movie theater which just happens to be showing Magnum's **The Case of the Cold Fish**. One of Wong's kids mentions how much Chow resembles "Man Bo," the lewd but resourceful detective from the "City Hunter" *manga*, a character that Chow would play the next year in **Mr. Mumble**. In spite of his star billing, Danny Lee only has perhaps fifteen minutes of screen time, while the Chinese title tries to pass this off as a sequel to Lee's 1984 hit **Law With Two Phases**.

168. City Cops

(1989; Joe Siu International) ★: 5/10. *Miu taam seung lung* (Cantonese), *Miao tan shuang long* (Mandarin): "Wonderful Double Dragon Detective." Cinematographer: Joe Chan Kong-hung; Art Director: Jessy Lam Chak-chi; Writer: Barry Wong Ping-yiu; Producer: Joe Siu King-fai; Action Directors: Lau Kar-wing, Ridley Tsui Bo-wah, Hung Cheung-tak; Director: Lau Kar-wing. Cast: Miu Kiu-wai (Ching Shing), Cynthia Rothrock (Cindy), Kenneth Tong Chun-yip (Kent Tong), Suki Kwan Sau-mei (May), Shing Fui-on (Tai Kau), Woo Fung (Wu), Michiko Nishiwaki (Michiko), Mark Houghton (Macquarton), Ken Goodman (Ken). 1.85:1. VHS: Tai Seng. Import LD: Universe. 92 minutes.

Good action alternates with low humor in this predictable outing. Kenneth Tong plays a fugitive in possession of some microfilm wanted by the FBI (represented by Cynthia Rothrock), gangsters *posing* as the FBI (including Mark Houghton and Ken Goodman), and two inept HK cops (Miu Kiu-wai and Shing Fui-on). That is about all the plot there is here (which is surprising, as screenwriter Barry Wong usually delivers intricate, fine-tuned storylines), unless you count Miu's courting of Tong's sister (Kwan), and the love that blossoms between Rothrock and Shing (talk about beauty and the beast!). Michiko Nishiwaki shows up in the final third to provide another opponent for Rothrock, who gets an excellent showcase for her talents in the climactic battle (set in a warehouse, naturally).

The humor (which includes some tasteless gags about AIDS) is pretty feeble, but the fights are well choreographed, save for a few unintended glimpses of Rothrock's male stunt double. Undemanding action fans should find it all to their liking.

169. City Hunter

(1993; Golden Harvest/Paragon Films) ★: 3/10. *Sing si lip yan* (Cantonese), *Cheng shi lie ren* (Mandarin): "City Hunter." Cinematographers: Gigo Lee Chi-hung, Tom Lau Moon-tong, Philip Ma Kam-cheung; Art Director: Hai Chung-man; Music: James Wong Jim, Romeo Diaz; Producer: Chua Lam; Action Directors: Jackie Chan Stuntmen Association, Ching Siu-tung; Writer-Director: Wong Jing. Cast: Jackie Chan (Ryu Saeba), Joey Wang Tsu-hsien (Kaori), Chingmy Yau Suk-ching (Undercover Cop), Kumiko Goto (Kiyoko Imamura), Leon Lai Ming (Kao Ta), Richard Norton (Col. MacDonald), Gary Daniels (Blonde Hulk), Sin Lap-man (Rocky), Eric Kot Man-fai (Singer), Jan Lam Hoi-fung (Singer), Peter Lai Bei-tak (Creep in White Suit), Michael Wong Man-tak (Makimura), Ken Lo Wai-kwong (Chen Ta-wen), Mike Abbott (Mike). Dolby Digital (Mega Star DVD only). 1.85:1. VHS: Tai Seng (Remastered for the English market; subtitled or dubbed). Import LD: Star Entertainment (No Subtitles). Import VCD: Star Entertainment (No Subtitles), Mega Star. Import DVD: China Star (No Subtitles), Mega Star. 94 minutes.

Jackie Chan's movies almost invariably have moments of inspired silliness, and pairing him with director Wong Jing (HK's undisputed king of low comedy) may have been a good idea on paper (Wong's collaborations with Stephen Chiau Sing-chi made a fortune, so why not team him with HK's other box office king?), but it sure doesn't work as a movie. Based on the Japanese *manga* of the same name (also adapted three years later by other parties as **Mr. Mumble**, with Michael Chow Man-kin in the lead), the nonsensical storyline concerns the misadventures of the lazy, sexist, and food obsessed (but undeniably effective) private detective Ryu Saeba. A newspaper magnate hires Saeba to locate his daughter, Kiyoko, who has run away from home and recently been spotted in HK. Saeba finds the girl, but she gives him the slip and boards an ocean liner, with the detective in hot pursuit. Once onboard, his mission is complicated by a team of terrorists (martial arts experts all) who seize the ship and plan to hold the dozens of millionaire passengers hostage for an astronomical ransom.

There are a couple of inventive action setpieces along the way (even the worst Jackie Chan films at least deliver in this respect), but most of the movie is mind-numbingly broad and labored. Inane jokes and sight gags are punctuated with cartoon sound FX, and there is more mugging on display than in a dozen Three Stooges shorts. The oft-cited highlight finds Chan and Gary Daniels transforming into characters from the Streetfighter II video game (Wong Jing would go on to do a feature length parody of that arcade sensation in the same year's **Future Cops**), but even this sequence is bungled, dragging on much too long. Director and star reportedly did not get along so well; Wong would later make **High Risk**, a none-too-subtle send-up of Chan and his persona that, reportedly, infuriated the actor to no end. Ironically, it is the far more successful endeavor.

170. City Kids 1989

(1989; Movie Impact) ★: 4/10. *Yan hoi goo hung* (Cantonese), *Ren hai gu hong* (Mandarin): "Lonely Swan in the Sea of People." Cinematographer: Mark Lee Ping-bing; Art Director: Jessy Lam Chak-chi; Music: Richard Lo Sai-kit; Writers: Clarence Yip Wai-chung, James Yuen Sai-sang, Tsui Tat-cho; Producer: Clarence Yip Wai-chung; Action Director: Blackie Ko Shou-liang; Director: Poon Man-kit. Cast: Max Mok Siu-chung (Third Lam), Andy Lau Tak-wah (Sas), May Lo Mei-mei (May Law), Shing Fui-on (Chuen). 1.85:1. VHS: Tai Seng. Import LD/VCD: Ocean Shores. 90 minutes.

Third Lam and Sas have lived much of their lives on the streets and gotten into various scrapes over the years. In revenge for shortchanging him, a gang boss addicts Third to heroin and, even after finally kicking the drug, the lad has to live with the stigma of once being an addict. After getting teenager May pregnant, Third marries her but, right after the wedding reception, lands back in jail for inadvertently assaulting a police officer. He and Sas are sentenced to six years, do their time, borrow money from a loan shark, and become pimps. In the intervening years, May has become a teacher, and Third makes her acquaintance again. Pressed to repay their debt, Sas and Third are given a choice: help the loan shark steal some money being payed to him as ransom for a child he kidnapped, or get beaten to death. The pair pull off the job but balk when Third realizes that the little girl is one of May's students.

Entirely forgettable from the first frame to the last, **City Kids 1989** is a virtual compendium of triad movie cliches. A couple of decent action sequences and stunts represent the sum total of what it has to offer.

171. City on Fire

(1987; Cinema City) ★: 8/10. *Lung foo fung wan* (Cantonese), *Long hu feng yun* (Mandarin): "Dragon Tiger Turbulence." Cinematographer: Andrew Lau Wai-keung; Art Director: Luk Chi-fung; Music: Teddy Robin Kwan; Writer: Tommy Sham Sai-sang; Producers: Karl Maka, Ringo Lam Ling-tung; Action Director: Chu Kai-sang; Director: Ringo Lam Ling-tung. Cast: Chow Yun-fat (Ko Chow), Danny Lee Sau-yin (Fu), Sun Yueh (Lau Ting-kwong), Roy Cheung Yiu-yeung (John Chan), Lau Kong (Inspector Chow), Carrie Ng Kar-lai (Hung), Maria Cordero (Nightclub Singer), Tommy Wong Kwong-leung (Kwong), Victor Hon Kwan (Bill), Parkman Wong Pak-man (Ah Man), Elvis Tsui Kam-kong (Chan Kam-wah). Dolby Digital (DVD only). 1.85:1. VHS: Tai Seng. Import LD: Golden Cinema City. Import VCD: Mei Ah. Import DVD: Universe. 105 minutes.

The main inspiration for Quentin Tarantino's remarkable **Reservoir Dogs**, this Ringo Lam thriller has many strengths of its own, not the least of which is a bravura performance by Chow Yun-fat. Undercover cop Ko Chow (Chow) has resigned from the force, but his superior, Lau (Taiwanese actor Sun Yueh), convinces him to undertake one last mission: replacing Chan, another undercover man, who was murdered just when he was about to get the goods on a gang of thieves. Against his better judgment, Chow agrees to undertake the assignment, despite the fact he is still suffering from the aftereffects of his last job and that Lau is the only one in the department who knows he is a policeman and not really a criminal. The robbers in question pull off a jewel robbery, which gets out of hand and ends with gang member Fu killing some police officers. Chow is gradually able to gain Fu's confidence and gets invited along on their next job, but in the meantime his life is rapidly falling to pieces. His disenchanted girlfriend, Hung, is about to head off to Canada with another man, and aggressive new officer John Chan is out to usurp Lau's position by making an example of Chow, even if it means getting Lau's man killed.

Chow Yun-fat (who netted the Best Actor prize at The 7th Hong Kong Film Awards) does exemplary work, convincingly handling the varied emotional states his character finds himself in, often in the same scene; Danny Lee (dubbing his own voice for a change) does fine, low-key work as his new friend and partner. There has been much debate over whether Tarantino stole from this film or was merely inspired by it. The latter view seems more plausible (how many films produced these days can label themselves 100% original?), though anyone determined to make a charge of plagiarism does have a case, as **Dogs** does replicate several aspects of the storyline and even some specific moments (e.g. a bit where Danny Lee fires two guns point blank through a police vehicle's windshield, killing the occupants, as Harvey Keitel would do in the American film). The essential difference is that **City** spends far more time on the events leading up to the botched heist, while **Dogs** largely concentrates on its aftermath. Tarantino's dialogue is sharper and the underworld milieu in **Dogs** is a bit more convincing, but **City on Fire** is a tightly directed and involving police thriller that is among the most sustained and intelligent HK filmmakers have offered up to date. As you might expect, the two films make an excellent, thought-provoking double feature. Andrew Lau's stylish cinematography provides a glimpse of the laudable work he would do for Wong Kar-wai and, later, on his own movies (like the **Young and Dangerous** series). Chow and Lee would go on to play essentially the opposite roles two years later in **The Killer**. *City on Fire* was Carrie Ng's film debut.

172. City on Fire

(1993) ★: 1/10. *Dip huet sing si* (Cantonese), *Die xue cheng shi* (Mandarin): "Bloodshed City." Cinematographer: Wong Yung-chung; Music: Not Original; Writers: Chan Siu-ping, Fu Nam-ying; Producer: Chan Kwai-fong; Action Director: Lung Sang; Director: Chow Hung; Cast: Kong Tai-chuen (Chiang), Mark Cheng Ho-nam (Wei-ming), Michiko Nishiwaki (Chia-chi), Wu Ma (Police Chief), Tai Po (Chien). 1.85:1. VHS: World Video. Import LD/VCD: Mei Ah. 88 minutes.

Definitely not to be confused with the Ringo Lam film of the same name starring Chow Yun-fat and Danny Lee, this atrocious actioner is mindnumbingly inept on every conceivable (and inconceivable) level. The main narrative concerns the plight of Chiang, a proud man who turns to alcohol after his beloved is murdered. When he isn't too drunk to stand, Chiang works as a dog trainer for a gangster who stages illegal dog fights. This doesn't sit well with his brother Wei-ming, a police officer, but Chiang receives some behind-the-scenes help from his sibling's girlfriend Chia-chi, despite the fact that she too is a cop. One day, Chiang gains the favor of the boss' daughter when he saves her life after she is attacked by one of the killer canines. However, the man's heart belongs to Ting, a girl with magic powers(!) that come in handy when rival gangsters hire Chien (who also has magical abilities) to sway the outcome of their dogfights. In an equally ridiculous twist, Chiang later turns out to be an undercover officer who has spent the last decade trying to track down and arrest his boss in retribution for the latter's involvement in the murder of Chiang's ladylove.

Michiko Nishiwaki and Mark Cheng have been in more than their share of terrible movies but none worse than this pitiful exercise, which takes a bounding leap over the thin line dividing the enjoyably horrible and the just plain *horrible*. Composer Brad Fiedel would not be pleased to learn that most of the music here is stolen from his soundtrack for **Terminator 2: Judgment Day**!

173. City War

(1988; Cinema City Co.) ★: 7/10. *Sing si jin jaang* (Cantonese), *Cheng shi zhan zheng* (Mandarin): "Loyalty Courage Red Lips." Cinematographer: Li Hsin-yeh; Art Director: Jason Mok Siu-kei, Eric Lam Shi-chin; Music: Michael Lai Siu-tin; Writers: Tung Lo, Leung Wai-ting, Chung Kai-cheong; Producer: Dean Shek Tien; Action Director: Yuen Bun; Director: Sun Chung. Cast: Chow Yun-fat (Dick Lee), Ti Lung (Ken Chow), Norman Tsui Siu-keung (Ted Yiu), Tien Niu (Penny), Lo Lieh (Uncle Kuen), Michael Chow Man-kin (Bobby), Ricky Yee Fan-wai (Wu), Robin Shou Wan-bo (Killer).

Dolby Digital (DVD only). 1.85:1. VHS: Tai Seng. Import LD: Golden Cinema City. Import VCD: Mei Ah. Import DVD: Universe. 96 minutes.

In the wake of **A Better Tomorrow**, it was inevitable that someone would re-team Chow Yun-fat and Ti Lung, and their interplay here elevates a disposable gangster yarn into one well worth catching. Old friends Dick Lee and Ken Chow represent the opposite ends of the scale when it comes to police work: The charismatic Dick is a level-headed negotiator, while Ken is a loose cannon whose outbursts threaten to get him kicked off the force. After spending ten years in jail, triad Ted Yiu is back on the streets and anxious to kill Ken, the man who put him behind bars. Meanwhile, Dick has fallen for Penny, a beautiful girl he met in a bar, not knowing that she is actually Ted's girlfriend. The gangster dispatches two assassins he has smuggled in from the Mainland to eliminate Ken, but they miss their intended target, killing the man's wife and daughter instead. The policemen swear vengeance, but Dick incapacitates Ken to prevent him from throwing his life away, and sets out alone.

Director Sun Chung (best known for his Shaw Brothers kung fu films) does not possess John Woo's lyrical style but presents the grim storyline in an appropriately dark and gritty fashion. The climactic gun battle (set, for a change, in a bus yard instead of a warehouse) also lacks the mesmerizing choreography of Woo's work, but, taken for what it is, **City War** more than fulfils its goals and is exhilarating action fare. Ti and (especially) Chow supply their characters with more resilience than the script calls for, and Norman Tsui is at his intense best as their mortal enemy.

174. City Warriors

(1988; Dragon Ray Motion Pictures) ★: 5/10. *Saat chut Heung Gong* (Cantonese), *Sha chu Xiang Gang* (Mandarin): "Fight Out of Hong Kong." Cinematographers: Yu Chi-lin, Lau Hung-chuen; Music: Not Original; Producer: Tsui Chi-keung; Action Directors: Johnny Wang Lung-wei, Tam Tong, Hung Shin-nan; Director: Johnny Wang Lung-wei. Cast: Dick Wei (Lok Han), Carina Lau Kar-ling (Mak Ying-ying), Ko Chuen-hsiang (Mak), Ken Lo Wai-kwong (Tang Sai-kit), Chor Yuen (Chor Ping), Shum Wai (Old Sister), Phillip Chan Yan-kin (Superintendent Chan). 1.85:1. VHS: Tai Seng. Import LD: Mei Ah. Import VCD: Cameron Entertainment. 91 minutes.

Visiting HK with a tourist group, Mainland soldier Lok Han is making the excursion for the sole purpose of finding his sister, Ling-ling. He is distressed to discover that she has spent the last two years working as a prostitute for her gangster husband, under the false assurance that he will eventually take the girl to America. The police locate Ling-ling on the estate of prominent councilman Chor Ping, who is up for re-election. The leader of a drug and prostitution ring, Chor is faced with disgrace and imprisonment should Ling-ling agree to testify against him. The rest is easy to forecast.

As with other films directed by former Shaw Brothers villain Johnny Wang, there is lots of action and gory violence but not much in the way of elan. Regardless, this remains fairly enjoyable, thanks to a fast tempo, the change-of-pace casting of Dick Wei in a heroic role, and an outrageous turn by veteran character actor Shum Wai as a transvestite "madam" named "Old Sister!" The final voice-over, in which hardened communist Lok Han recognizes the value of a capitalist enclave like HK, is laughably spurious.

175. Clan of the White Lotus

(1980; Shaw Brothers) ★: 8/10. *Hung Man-ding saam por bak lin gaau* (Cantonese), *Hong Wending san po bai lian jiao* (Mandarin): "Hung Man-ding Defeats The White Lotus Clan Three Times" or "Hong Wending Defeats The White Lotus Clan Three Times." Producer: Mona Fong Yat-wah; Director: Lo Lieh. Cast: Lo Lieh (The White Lotus), Gordon Lau Kar-fai (Hong Wen-ting), Kara Hui Ying-hung (Mei-hsiao), Johnny Wang Lung-wei (Kau Tin-chung), Yeung Ching-ching (Ching-ching), Hsiao Hou (White Lotus' Personal Swordsman). 2.35:1. VHS: Vista (Dubbed). 88 minutes. Also known as **Fists of the White Lotus** (US title).

Lo Lieh makes his directorial debut and stars in this excellent period kung fu effort, which is a follow-up of sorts to Lau Kar-leung's **Executioners from Shaolin**. The release of Shaolin students from prison is perceived as a threat to The White Lotus Clan. Their leader, The White Lotus, orders his followers to slaughter the rebels to avenge the death of his classmate, Pai Mei. Some of the Shaolin fighters manage to escape, including Hong Wen-ting, though most die in the ensuing attacks. After spending time working on his Tiger Crane style of kung fu, Wen-ting sets out to challenge The White Lotus but is thoroughly outclassed by the old master. The problem with Wei-ting's technique is not one usually encountered: He is using *too much* force and must learn a more gentle form of combat to counter White Lotus' powers! After much practice, he merges a new effeminate style with the Crane Beak and seeks out White Lotus again. Although most effective, he is unable to locate his opponent's vulnerable spot. Badly injured, he is saved from certain death only by a revolutionist's acupuncture treatment. This inspires Wen-ting to add yet another facet to his martial arts.

Likeable heroes, a wonderful villain, and offbeat kung fu combine to make this a superior Shaw Brothers effort. In contrast to **Executioners from Shaolin**, the tone here is generally lighter, but there is still a fair amount of character development. The various skirmishes are well-staged, and the training sequences are particularly good. On the basis of what he achieves here, it is a genuine shame that Lo has directed so few films. Character names are from the dubbed version.

176. Close Escape

(1989; Y.C. Lai Films Production Co.) ★: 5/10. *Fei yuet aau cheung* (Cantonese), *Fei yue wei qiang* (Mandarin): "Fly Over Dangerous Wall." Cinematographer: Stanley Hung Hin-shing; Art Director: Dominique Lo Kar-yiu; Music: John Wong Sai-cheung; Writers: Bryan Cheung Wai-hung, Wing Chow Chan-wing; Producer: Fan King-kung; Action Director: Phillip Kwok Tsui; Director: Wing Chow Chan-wing. Cast: Max Mok Siu-chung (Lam Wai-leung), Miu Kiu-wai (Lam Wai-tung), Aaron Kwok Fu-shing (Ben Kwok), Yukari Oshima (Migi), Dick Wei (Chiu Ying kau), Charine Chan Kar-ling (Mun/April). 1.85:1. VHS: Tai Seng. Import LD/VCD: Ocean Shores. 92 minutes.

Some well-staged martial arts battles can't do much to make this routine action melodrama any more than passably interesting. Miu Kiu-wai plays a thief who makes off with some valuable diamonds owned by gangster Dick Wei. Trying to extort $1 million from Dick for the stones, Miu falls prey to the hood's minions and is murdered. Still looking for his stones, Dick has his men lean on Miu's brother (played by Max Mok) and, when he does not receive the desired information, has Mok framed for murder. Shot and on the lam, Mok is nursed back to health by Yukari Oshima, playing a Japanese reporter on assignment in HK. However, her intentions may not be as honorable as they seem.

The hand-to-hand battle between Oshima and Dick Wei is certainly worth waiting for (albeit much too short) but this forgettable effort will really only be of interest to completists. In one of his earliest roles, "Heavenly King" Aaron Kwok plays the police inspector handling the case.

177. The Club

(1981; Bang! Bang! Films) ★: 7/10. *Miu teng* (Cantonese), *Wu ting* (Mandarin): "Dance Hall." Cinematographer: Johnny Koo Kwok-wah; Art Director: Shen Chin; Music: Danny Chung Teng-yat, Yung Kar-chi; Writer: Tan Tian-nan; Producer: Yau Tat-sing; Action Directors: Michael Chan Wai-man, Lam Man-wah; Director: Che-Kirk Wong Chi-keung. Cast: Michael Chan Wai-man (Sai), Norman Tsui Siu-keung (Fei), Kent Cheng Chuk-see (Kun), Phillip Ko Fei ("Fingers" Hung). 1.85:1. VHS: Ocean Shores (Subtitled or Dubbed). Import LD: Ocean Shores (No Subtitles). 86 minutes.

The story is slight and the fashions have dated badly, but this triad action thriller still packs a punch and foreshadows the technique that would distinguish director Che-Kirk Wong's later films. Michael Chan plays Sai, a tough mob enforcer whose job is to patrol the dance bar owned by his boss and protect the girls that work there. Ownership of the club is sought by two different parties—one semi-legitimate, the other a rival gang. When the owner is murdered, all hell breaks lose, with Sai and his men under siege from all sides. The film's dark, gritty milieu gives this an almost documentary-like quality, which is also complemented by the long takes and nasty, unstylized violence (particularly the infamous outboard motor execution of Sai's boss).

If you have only seen the "Hero" subgenre spawned by **A Better Tomorrow**, or the wave of triad youth films which followed the success of **Young and Dangerous**, you should make a point of catching **The Club**, which really laid the groundwork for those efforts. The action choreography, while fairly low-key by contemporary standards, includes some terrific knife fights (with the sequence where Chan singlehandedly takes on a dozen opponents in a parking garage being the highlight). Unfortunately, the video transfer on the subtitled cassette is too dark, making the proceedings difficult to discern; the dubbed version and the unsubtitled laserdisc are much better in this regard. British film critic Tony Rayns provided the excellent English subtitles on the original HK prints. The music track differs somewhat between the subtitled and dubbed versions, with the latter using alternate tracks to replace some American rock songs which were used without permission. However, an instrumental version of "Gonna Raise Hell" and the cues lifted from Tangerine Dream's soundtrack for Michael Mann's **Thief** (1981) remain.

Code of Honour *see* **Brotherhood**

178. Combo Cops

(1996; Sam Po Film) ★: 1/10. *Gwok chaan suet gap wai lung* (Cantonese), *Guo chan xue ge wei long* (Mandarin): "Country Made Snow Clam Mighty Dragon." Cinematographer: Philip Ma Kam-cheung; Art Director: Nelson Cheung Hok-yun; Music: Not Original; Writer: Siu Ching-man; Producers: Wong Siu-ming, Chan Choi-yin; Action Directors: Dion Lam Dik-on, Mak Wai-cheung; Directors: Wong Siu-ming, Yiu Man-kei. Cast: Michael Wong Man-tak (James Fok), Yu Rongguang (Hwang Fei), Christine Ng Wing-mei (Mona), Law Kar-ying (Tiger), Yuen King-tan (Chin), Jerry Lam Hiu-fung (Bespectacled SDU Trainee), Manfred Wong (CP). 1.85:1. VHS: Tai Seng. Import LD/VCD: Fitto Mobile. 93 minutes.

Combo Cops is another irredeemable misfire from the fine folks at Sam Po Film. As the Chinese title suggests, this is a spoof along the lines of Stephen Chiau Sing-chi's **From Beijing with Love**; if only it had one tenth as many laughs. Hwang Fei is a supercop sent from China to HK where he is paired with Scotland Yard alumnus James Fok. The two are ordered to whip a bunch of SDU screw-ups into shape, but the men's differing approaches create friction between them—which threatens to turn into outright hostility when Hwang's sister, Mona (who goes to bars dressed like Marilyn Monroe), develops the hots for Fok. When Hwang and Fok fail to prevent a valuable painting from being stolen by a bunch of bumbling criminals, they must get the picture back before a major exhibition begins in order to save face for the department.

The humor here is not so much from another culture as it is from another *planet*. On the other hand, this does feature the ultimate improbable kung fu match-up: skinny and middle-aged Law Kar-ying vs. the sleek and muscular Yu Rongguang!

179. Come Fly the Dragon

(1993; Scholar Films/Han Shing Dissem Ination Co.) ★: 2/10. *Baan dou lut lau* (Cantonese), *Fan dou ma liu* (Mandarin): "Rebel Fights Monkey." Cinematographers: Tom Lau Moon-tong, Ho Yung-ching; Art Directors: Ben Luk Man-wah, Cheung Kwai-ping; Music: Richard Lo Sai-kit; Writer: Yiu Hing-kong; Producers: Chow Hau-yau, Choi Chung-lam; Action Directors: Frankie Chan Fan-kei, Blackie Ko Shou-liang; Director: Eric Tsang Chi-wai. Cast: Andy Lau Tak-wah (Chow Chun-kit), Tony Leung Chiu-wai (Lau Kar-lun), Fennie Yuen Kit-ying (Kuen), Frankie Chan Fan-kei (Li Yan-chak), Shing Fui-on (Chiu), Miu Kiu-wai (Li's Second), Ben Lam Kwok-bun (Leung Wai-man), Norman Tsui Siu-keung (Colonel Ng). 1.85:1. VHS: World Video. Import LD/VCD: Mei Ah. 94 minutes.

This insufferable misfire plays like a juvenile parody/remake of Andy Lau's 1989 vehicle **Proud and Confidence** [*sic*], which was not an especially inspired enterprise to begin with. A group of recruits (including Lau and Tony Leung Chiu-wai) are selected and put through their paces by a tough commander (Tsui) assigned to create an elite strike force that will take on major crime syndicates. When Lau is discharged for getting into a bar fight, the flighty daughter of a vicious triad gang leader develops a crush on him and eventually wins Lau over through sheer persistence. However, his dismissal was merely a set-up: When the soldiers stage a bogus attempt on the gangster's life, Lau "saves" him, thus gaining his trust. The second phase of the plan then comes into play: Lau will convince his new boss to bring him along for a big weapons transaction, allowing his buddies to locate and wipe out all of the major arms suppliers in one fell swoop.

With no genuine wit to be found anywhere in the script, the film relies heavily on Lau and Leung's charms to pass muster, but the material is so grating and obnoxious that there is little they can do to embellish it. *Come Fly the Dragon* is a major disappointment from director Eric Tsang (**Aces Go Places 1** & **2**).

180. Come from China

(1992; Sam Po Film Co.) ★: 5/10. *Po Ging daai gip on* (Cantonese), *Pu Jing da jie an* (Mandarin): "Po Ging Big Theft Case." Cinematographer: Cheung Tak-wai; Art Director: Chow Keung; Music: Not Original; Writer: James Fung Shui-hung; Producers: Lau Chun-fai, Cheung Pan; Action Director: Fung Dik; Director: To Pak-hong. Cast: Chin Siu-ho (Wan), Lam Wai (Li Chun-hsin), Joanna Chan Pui-san (Ling), Kam Hing-yin (Chiang Hau), Ha Chi-chun (Female Robber), Mondi Yau Yuet-ching (Little Macau's Wife), Dick Wei (Tank), To Siu-chun (Thug). 1.85:1. VHS: Tai Seng. 85 minutes.

This low-budget action thriller incorporates so many double-crosses it becomes unintentionally comical at times. Brothers Chun-hsin and Wan would like to raise money to pay for their elderly mother's eye operation but find themselves inadvertently mixed up in a robbery. Two of their associates, Chiang and Little Macau, stole a large sum of cash from a team of thieves who had just pulled off an armoured car job. When corrupt cop Chung extorts much of the haul from Little Macau, Macau tells the original thieves that the policeman and his cohorts were the ones who cleaned them out. When faced with death, Chung, in turn, gives them Chiang's address, and the hoods proceed to bust up his place until they are expelled by Chun-hsin and Wan. The criminals then kidnap the brothers' mom and Chiang's son, setting up the requisite warehouse shootout finale.

Periodic bursts of decently choreographed kung fu and gunplay keep this routine entry moderately diverting, though there is nothing here that one cannot find in several dozen other films of this ilk. The soundtrack includes music swiped from **Escape from New York**.

Comet, Butterfly & Sword *see* **Butterfly & Sword**

Commando Amazon *see* **Golden Queens Commando**

181. Comrades, Almost a Love Story

(1996; Golden Harvest/United Filmmakers Organization/Golden Movies International) ★: 8/10. *Tim mat mat* (Cantonese), *Tian mi mi* (Mandarin): "Honeysweet." Cinematographer: Jingle Ma Cho-shing; Art Director: Hai Chung-man; Music: Chiu Chang-hei; Writer: On Sai; Producer: Raymond Chow Man-wai; Director: Peter Chan Ho-sun. Cast: Leon Lai Ming (Li Xiao-jun), Maggie Cheung Man-yuk (Li Chiao), Kristy Yeung Kung-yu (Xiao-ting), Eric Tsang Chi-wai (Pao), Christopher Doyle (Jeremy). 1.85:1. VHS: Mecapro. Import LD/VCD/DVD: Mei Ah. 116 minutes.

Winner of nine prizes at the 1997 HK Film Awards (including Best Picture, Best Actress, Best Director, and Best Supporting Actor), this is an affecting romantic drama with strong performances by its leads, particularly, Maggie Cheung, making her first appearance in a HK film after a hiatus of almost three years. The story (which covers a decade) begins in 1986 with the arrival in HK of naive Mainlander Li Xiao-jun. While adjusting to this new and confusing place, Xiao-jun meets Li Chiao, another Mainland *emigre*. She has adjusted much more quickly to HK's money-mad lifestyle and works several jobs at once in order to attain her goal of self-sufficiency and eventual wealth. In spite of all this activity, Chiao is just as lonely as Xiao-jun, and they begin to spend more and more time together, soon falling in love. However, when Chiao loses all of her savings in the stock market crash of 1987, she becomes gravely worried about the future and leaves Xiao-jun for Pao, a gentle triad boss. The story resumes in 1990, with Xiao-jun marrying his longtime girlfriend, Xiao-ting, while Chiao remains devoted to Pao. During the ensuing years, Xiao-jun and Chiao retain their feelings for one another but seem destined to remain apart.

Almost from the very start of her career, Maggie Cheung has been one of HK's most fascinating and accomplished performers. She is superb here, as is Leon Lai, shedding his pop idol image and displaying ability rarely evident in his previous work. The screenplay makes excellent use of the Chinese search for identity in the modern world (as Xiao-jun observes, everyone in China wishes to come to HK, while everyone in HK wishes to immigrate) as an undercurrent that influences the characters' outlooks and, in turn, shapes their destinies. The final reel's adherence to genre convention is a bit disappointing, but **Comrades** remains a charming picture with universal appeal. The Chinese title is the name of a song by the late Taiwanese singer Teresa Teng Li-chun, whose works and presence figure prominently. Acclaimed cinematographer Christopher Doyle (**Chungking Express**) has a supporting role.

182. Conduct Zero

(1986; D & B Films Co./Apollo Films) ★: 4/10. *Cho hang ling fan* (Cantonese), *Cao xing ling fen* (Mandarin): "Moral Conduct Zero Points." Cinematographer: Sander Lee Kar-ko; Art Director: Sin Ngai-lung; Music: Winds of Mind; Writer: Fung Lai-chi; Producers: John Sham Kin-fun, John Chan Koon-chung; Director: Simon Yip Wong. Cast: Stephen Ho Kai-nam, Chindy Lau Chin-tai (Celine), Leung Siu-hung, William Tang Chin-fuk, Wong Kam-kong (Cadet Team Leader). 1.85:1. VHS: Tai Seng. 86 minutes. Also known as **Zero Mark.**

Juvenile delinquents Horlick, Meaty, and Nutty Boy are arrested for attempted car theft and sentenced to six months probation. Ordered by the court to deliver gas cylinders, the trio immediately start slacking off and are on the verge of being sent to prison. Their new parole officer, Big Hung, manages to tap into the one passion the youths have: bicycles. Hung convinces them to form a team and participate in the Annual Youth Bicycle Race, but first they will have to get better bikes and the necessary equipment. In order to raise the funds, the boys throw themselves into their work, allowing them to fulfil the obligations of their parole. Most importantly, however, the race will provide them with the chance to defeat the police cadets' bike team, which has gone out of its way to humiliate them in the past. This gets a "7" for effort, a "5" for entertainment, and a zero for originality.

Conjugal Affairs *see* **The New Age of Living Together**

183. The Contract

(1978; Golden Harvest/Paragon Films) ★: 8/10. *Maai san kai* (Cantonese), *Mai shep qi* (Mandarin): "Sold Body Contract." Cinematographer: Tom Lau Moon-tong; Art Director: Chu Sing-hei; Producer: Raymond Chow Man-wai; Writer-Director: Michael Hui Koon-man. Cast: Michael Hui Koon-man (Chih-wen), Sam Hui Koon-kit (Shih-chieh), Ricky Hui Koon-ying (Frog), Yeung Wei. Dolby Digital (DVD only). 2.35:1. VHS: Tai Seng (Poor Subtitles). Import VCD: Mega Star (No Subtitles). Import DVD: Universe. 96 minutes.

With its ratings dropping through the floor, the struggling MTV Network (whose company symbol is a rat in front of a test pattern!) adopts desperate new measures in the form of the ruthless Miss Wang, who has some radical programming ideas. Fired from just about every possible position at the station, bumbling Chih-wen is hired to host a ridiculous, rigged game show (one contestant must choose between the life of her dog or the chance to win $5 million!), which somehow earns him a lucrative contract offer from the rival TVC Network. Unfortunately, he signed an eight year deal with MTV, and Wang will not hear of him leaving. Desperate, Chi-wen enlists the aid of Frog, his wacky inventor brother (whose greatest marvels are a remote-controlled "Laughing Bomb" and "Super Double Strength Glue"), to get his contract out of the company safe. After numerous close calls, the document is in Chih-wen's hands ... but Frog is locked in the safe! Enlisting the aid of struggling magician Shih-chieh, Chih-wen races to free his brother before he suffocates, while at the same time evading Wang's deadly henchmen.

A virtual non-stop barrage of sight gags, slapstick, and frenetic chases, **The Contract** also mixes in a dash of Warner Brothers cartoon dementia for good measure (the latter influence is particularly evident during the climactic demonstration of Frog's "Feel-Surround Television" invention, which subjects the viewer to everything unfolding onscreen). The end result is totally disarming and one of The Hui Brothers' most consistently amusing efforts.

184. Couples, Couples, Couples

(1988; Golden Harvest/Paragon Films) ★: 4/10. *Saam dui yuen yeung yat jeung chong* (Cantonese), *San dui yuan yang yi zhang chuang* (Mandarin): "Three Couples, One Bed." Cinematographer: Raymond Lam

Fai-tai; Music: Lowell Lo Kwun-ting; Writer: Hoi Dik; Producer: Choi Lan; Director: Cheung Chi-kok. Cast: Cherie Chung Cho-hung (Mary Huang), Jacky Cheung Hok-yau (John Chen), Melvin Wong Kam-sun (Dick Szutu), Lowell Lo Kwun-ting (Pao Niu), Lawrence Cheng Tan-shui (John's Friend in Bar), Corey Yuen Kwai (Boy Scout #1), Wu Ma (Boy Scout #2). 1.85:1. VHS: Tai Seng. Import VCD: Mega Star. 90 minutes.

When their friends start fighting, John and Mary end up caring for the couple's baby girl, Snow White (so named because she has seven "dwarf" spots on the bottom of one foot). After a month with the child, they prove to be far better parents than their friends and miss the baby when it comes time for her to go back home. While both John and Mary now want a child of their own, the former resists, not wanting the responsibility or the marriage contract that is part of the deal. Mary presses ahead, however, sabotaging John's condoms and cooking up aphrodisiacs like "Deer's Antler and Spanish Fly" soup. Her plan is a success and she becomes pregnant ... and promptly leaves John, moving into an apartment with her sister (whose marriage has major problems of its own)! Numerous misunderstandings follow.

Lightweight fluff, **Couples, Couples, Couples** is fairly pleasant, thanks to the efforts of its cast, but much too contrived and predictable to work. About the only thing that separates this sort of fare from comparable Western productions is a subplot involving Melvin Wong's character, who thinks that he has contracted AIDS. While a hot topic in HK at the time of the film's production, the juvenile emphasis on it here just seems desperate.

185. The Crazy Companies

(1988; Win's Movie Production) ★: 6/10. *Jui gaai suen yau* (Cantonese), *Zui jia sun you* (Mandarin): "The Best Way to Hurt Your Friend." Cinematographer: Henry Chan Chun-kit; Art Director: Jason Mok Siu-kei; Music: Not Original; Producer: Wallace Cheung Kwok-chong; Writer-Director: Wong Jing. Cast: Andy Lau Tak-wah (Tsui Ting-kwai), Chingmy Yau Suk-ching (Beanny), Stanley Fung Shui-fan (Frank), Nat Chan Pak-cheung (Tam Sad-chiu), Charlie Cho Cha-lei (Kim), Idy Chan Yuk-lin (Joanne), Joan Tong Lai-kau (Happy), Yung Sai-kit (Tsui Ting-fu), Sandra Ng Kwan-yu (Dorlina Lee), Shing Fui-on (Beanny's Brother), James Wong Jim (Priest). 1.85:1. VHS: Tai Seng. Import LD: Ocean Shores. 98 minutes.

This is a typical outing from prolific director Wong Jing (who has a cameo) in that it sets up its premise and then meanders all over the place, doing everything but advancing the storyline. Fortunately, it still has enough in its favor to make it worth the watch. Tsui Ting-kwai stands to inherit half of his late father's $10 billion estate if he can work, without incident, as an office boy for six months at the family company. If he decides to leave before then, he forfeits his share. Determined to snatch all of the money, his evil brother hires three idiots to work alongside Ting-kwai and make him look bad. Instead, the trio become friends with Ting-kwai and help him foil his evil sibling.

Essentially a series of sketches built around old gags like hypnotic suggestion, a false diagnosis of AIDS, feigned blindness, Bruce Lee imitations, and dating two women at the same time without the other one knowing, **The Crazy Companies** lacks the infectious zaniness found in Wong's most successful films but kills time in agreeable fashion. **The Crazy Companies II*** followed the next year.

186. Crazy Hong Kong

(1993; EDKO Classics Films/Golden Flare Films Co./New Arts Pictures) ★: 2/10. *Heung gong wun fung kwong* (Cantonese), *Xiang gang ye feng kuang* (Mandarin): "Hong Kong Is Crazy Too." Cinematographer: Apple Kwan Pak-suen; Art Director: Chan Wing-leung; Music: Lau Yee-tat; Writers: Kong Fei, Lau Kin-chi; Producers: Edwin Kong Chi-man, Leung Po-chi, Peter Shepherd; Director: Wellson Chin Sing-wai. Cast: N!xau (Himself), Carina Lau Kar-ling (Shirley Heung), Cecilia Yip Tung (Winnie), Lau Ching-wan (John), Conrad Janis (Jack), James Pak Chin-shek (Tony Li), Wong Kam-kong (Mike), Michael Chow Man-kin (Truck Driver). 1.85:1. Import LD: Golden Flare. Import VCD: Panorama Entertainment. 95 minutes. Also known as **The Gods Must Be Crazy in Hong Kong, Mr. Africa**.

Preceded by **Crazy Safari**, this is the second of three HK knockoffs of the overrated South African hit **The Gods Must Be Crazy**. All of them actually star N!xau, the bushman made world famous by the original. In Africa to shoot a commercial, Shirley Heung accidentally bops N!xau on the head with a coke bottle. When the bushman tries to return it to her, he is inadvertently knocked unconscious and loaded onto her plane. Arriving in HK, N!xau finds himself adrift in a bizarre, alien world and it becomes Shirley's responsibility to take care of him. This leads to repetitive and seemingly endless fish-out-of-water sequences where N!xau wanders off and tries to comprehend all manner of things like escalators, TVs, cars, etc., before being rescued by Shirley. The flimsy storyline has Shirley trying to keep her American boss (a Texan who runs the Malibu Burger fast food chain) happy by procuring the location for a fortieth outlet in HK. The rest of the proceedings seem to have been improvised on the spot and go nowhere fast.

Unlike **Crazy Safari**, which was able to mix in HK horror and comedy elements to good effect, **Crazy Hong Kong** simply apes its foreign model by utilizing undercranking and other ancient devices to try and breathe life into some very uninspired sight gags. Carina Lau and Cecilia Yip (as Shirley's sexy biker babe friend) emerge unscathed, but Lau Ching-wan is reduced to the level of comic relief stooge (he does seem to be having fun improvising during his scenes with N!xau, however). Although one cannot help but feel he is being exploited once again, N!xau's natural charm and infectious laugh helps to make the film a bit less painful, but few viewers will want to stick this out just to see him. Conrad Janis, from TVs *Mork and Mindy*, plays Lau's boss, and it is even stranger to see *him* (sporting a cowboy hat and ponytail) walking the streets of HK! This was followed by **The Gods Must Be Funny in China** (1994).

187. Crazy Love

(1993; Ko Chi Sum Films Co.) ★: 3/10. *Mat to sing suk si* (Cantonese), *Mi tao cheng shu shi* (Mandarin): "When the Sweet Peach Ripens." Cinematographer: Kin Lee Kin-keung; Art Director: Choi Man-chong; Music: John Wong Sai-cheung; Writers: Vincent Kok Tak-chiu, Roman Cheung Siu-lun; Producer: Clifton Ko Chi-sum; Director: Roman Cheung Siu-lun. Cast: Loletta Lee Lai-chun (Jane), Tom Poon Chan-wai (David), Tommy Wong Kwong-leung (Guy at Airport), Shing Fui-on (Lonely). 1.85:1. VHS: Tai Seng. Import LD/VCD/DVD: Mei Ah. 77 minutes.

Presenting star Loletta Lee nude within the first few seconds, this Category III comedy-drama has little in the way of plot, even for a sex flick. Young exhibitionist Jane is supposed to fly to England but decides to stay and wreak havoc in HK.

**Unavailable for review.*

Upon getting a guy who tried to pick her up in trouble and catching her boyfriend with another girl, Jane goes off into the countryside for some quality time. After fending off an attempted rape, she watches her neighbors having sex and stays with them for a while. Creatively frustrated screenwriter David is her next conquest, and he just may be the man she is looking for.

Most male viewers will be happy just seeing Loletta Lee in the buff—no matter what the pretext—which is fortunate, as the film does not even try to offer anything else. To kill time between the fleshy interludes, portions of Madonna's **Truth or Dare** are re-staged, including a bit where Lee demonstrates fellatio using a Coke bottle. Those infatuated with her will find this worth a rental, though it is, ultimately, more sleep inducing than erotic (especially the easy listening score).

Crazy Love for You *see* **Don't Stop My Crazy Love for You**

188. Crazy Nuts

(1981; Filmway Pictures) ★: 2/10. *Lin waan daai dau faat* (Cantonese), *Lian huan da dou fa* (Mandarin): "Chain of Rings, Big Legal Fight." Cinematographer: Cheung Kuen; Music: Not Original; Producer: Guy Lai Ying-chau; Director: Ban Lam Kuen. Cast: Melvin Wong Kam-sun (Golden Dragon), Liu Wai-hung (Black Lama), Tai Po (Shaw). 1.85:1. VHS: Tai Seng (Poor Subtitles). 87 minutes.

Golden Dragon and Black Lama are both determined to nail jewel thief Tseng Tsao-tai first and so deprive their counterpart of the glory. The pair intentionally get themselves thrown into jail when they learn that an old associate of Tseng is in custody serving a one hundred year sentence. Dragon and Lama bust the old man out of prison and eventually determine that both their target and the valuable diamond he has in his possession will be at a masquerade party.

Lacklustre in every department, this spirited but desperate farce swipes a large portion of its jokes from Western features, including **Airplane!**, which came out only the year before.

189. Crazy Safari

(1991; Win's Movie Production/Samico Films Production) ★: 7/10. *Fei jau woh seung* (Cantonese), *Fei zhou he shang* (Mandarin): "African Buddhist Monk." Cinematographer: Henry Chan Chun-kit; Art Director: Fred Chan Chi-chung; Music: Lowell Lo Kwun-ting; Writer: Barry Wong Ping-yiu; Producers: Charles Heung Wah-keung, Jimmy Heung Wah-sing; Action Director: Power Lee King-chu; Director: Billy Chan Wui-ngai. Cast: Lam Ching-ying (The Priest), N!xau (Himself), Sam Christopher Chan San-ho (The Kid), Peter Chan Lung (The Vampire), Peter Pau Tak-hei (Szeto), Stephen Chiau Sing-chi & Ng Man-tat (Narrators for the Cantonese Version). 1.85:1. VHS: Tai Seng (No Subtitles). Import LD: Star Entertainment (No Subtitles). Import VCD: Mega Star. 96 minutes.

This is the first of three unofficial HK sequels to the amateurish but exceedingly popular South African comedy **The Gods Must Be Crazy**, all of which star N!xau (credited with Chinese characters "Lik So"), the bushman made world famous in the original. HK filmmakers have come up with some bizarre hybrids over the years and this is one of the wackiest, grafting the plot of **Gods** onto a traditional vampire horror-comedy! While transporting the long-dead body of his great grandfather back home, a young man and a taoist master he has hired find themselves stranded in Africa when their plane goes down. Having lost track of the corpse (a vampire, naturally), the pair wander for hours before running into N!xau and his fellow bushmen. They eventually find the vampire and head for civilization, but first they must foil some diamond hunters who have taken N!xau's people hostage. However, the villains have their own secret weapon: a giant native zombie!

Most of the comedy is unimaginative fish-out-of-water material, but there is undeniable enjoyment to be found watching the vampire bouncing around (and over) natives, not to mention the unforgettable sight of Lam Ching-ying trying to stop a charging rhino with spell paper, riding an ostrich, and using his kung fu on some evil tribesmen. The justifiably famous climax has Lam helping N!xau by calling upon the spirit of Bruce Lee to possess him! This was followed by **Crazy Hong Kong** and **The Gods Must Be Funny in China**.

190. Crazy Shaolin Disciples

(1985; Shaw Brothers) ★: 5/10. *Dai ji ya fung kong* (Cantonese), *Di zi ye feng kuang* (Mandarin): "Disciples Are Also Crazy." Cinematographer: Cheung Yuk-wah; Art Director: Chan Lei-wah; Music: So Chun-hau, Sing Kam-wing; Producer: Mona Fong Yat-wah; Action Directors: Lam Moon-wah, Cho Hung-sang, Chan Pang-fei; Director: Yau Kar-hung. Cast: Gordon Lau Kar-fai (Ching), Wong Yue (Fang Chih-yu), Lo Mang (Hung Hsi-kuan), Chin Siu-ho (Hui-chien), Lo Lieh (Chief Chih Lien-chia), Phillip Kwok Tsui (Master Kuai), Lee Hoi-sang (Master Kua). 2.35:1. VHS: World Video (Poor Subtitles), Arena/Xenon (Poor Subtitles). DVD: Arena/Xenon (Poor Subtitles). Import LD: Ocean Shores (Poor Subtitles). 84/93 minutes. Also known as **Enter the 36th Chamber of Shaolin** (Arena/Xenon title).

This minor Shaw Brothers period outing is another story about the famous heroes Fong Sai-yuk and Hung Hei-kwun (identified in the subtitles as Fang Chih-yu and Hung Hsi-kuan, the Mandarin version of the names), this time with a decidedly comic bent. After Hung offends the powerful Ching chief Chih, he and Fang travel to Shaolin Temple to learn kung fu and take sanctuary. They and their fellow newcomers (The South Pupils) get into all manner of trouble lusting after a girl, angering the monks (The North Pupils), disobeying their master, etc. Chih shows up at the temple demanding that the two men be turned over to him, along with a gold medal that Hung has in his possession. The invader is subsequently defeated but the damage is done: The monks decide to eject Hung on the basis that he is not a serious student and merely wants to hide from his enemy. Hung pleads his case and is allowed to stay, but Chih returns looking to even the score.

The martial arts are diverting but there is very little story here and too much of the running time is expended on the practical joke war between the North and South Pupils. It was competent but utterly routine efforts like this that caused Shaw Brothers' period kung fu films to fall out of favor with the public and contributed to the company's decision to stop producing films for a number of years. The soundtrack includes music lifted from **Phantasm**. Beware of Arena/Xenon's legally suspicious version, which is cut to 84 minutes and missing all mention of Shaw Brothers and the film's cast and credits.

191. Crazy Spirit

(1987; Focus Film Co.) ★: 4/10. *Yeung gwai ji* (Cantonese), *Yang gui zi* (Mandarin): "Raise a Ghost." Cinematographer: Cheung Tak-wai; Art Director: Wong Mo-hung; Music: Chow Kai-sang, Tang Siu-lam; Writer: Tang Wing-luk; Producers: William Cheung Kei, Chiu Wing-lam; Action Directors: Wong Wai-tong, Power Lee King-chu; Director: Chin Yuet-sang. Cast: Sibelle Hu Hui-chung (Alice Hwang), Ray Lui Leung-wai (Lei Wei), Peter Chan Lung (Te), Shum Wai (Chau), Phillip Chan Yan-kin (Inspector Chen), Tai Po (Taxi Driver), Lam Wai (Lin Wei), Chen Jing (Robber). 1.85:1. VHS: Tai Seng. Import LD/VCD: Ocean Shores. 82 minutes.

Desperate for an heir, jewellery store owner Chau journeys to Thailand and enlists the services of Taoist Te, a master of Mao Shan magic. After performing a rite that will create a "spirit baby," Te journeys to HK to deliver the charm containing the being to Chau. However, he loses the charm in a cab and it is found by Castle Peak nurse Alice Hwang. Her marriage to cop Lei Wei is on the rocks due their seeming inability to have children. In an effort to retrieve the spirit baby using magic, Te accidentally shatters the case it is sealed in and Alice cuts a finger on the glass, causing a drop of her blood to land on the charm. The result is a mischievous little boy with magical powers. After some initial trepidation, Alice and Wei accept the boy as their own and become much happier together. However, the child does not belong in this world, and the couple face great danger.

Peter Chan has been playing evil Taoists to perfection as far back as **Encounter of the Spooky Kind**, and, while his character eventually strays over to the side of good here, Chan still cuts an effectively malevolent figure. However, aside from an enjoyably berserk climax, most HK horror aficionados will find this family-oriented effort too dull and juvenile to be of any more than passing interest. The soundtrack includes music lifted from Tangerine Dream's score for **Firestarter**.

192. Crime Story

(1993; Golden Harvest/Paragon Films) ★: 8/10. *Chung ngon cho* (Cantonese), *Chong an zu* (Mandarin): "Serious Crime Unit." Cinematographers: Poon Wai-keung, Ardy Lam Kwok-wah, Poon Hang-sang, Andrew Lau Wai-keung; Art Directors: Tony Au Ding-ping, Bill Lui Cho-hung, Luk Chi-fung; Music: James Wong Jim, Mark Lui Chung-tak; Writers: Chan Man-keung, Cheung Lai-ling, Chun Tin-nam, Cheung Chi-sing, Teddy Chan Tak-sam; Producer: Chua Lam; Directors: Che-Kirk Wong Chi-keung, Jackie Chan (uncredited). Cast: Jackie Chan (Inspector Chan), Kent Cheng Chuk-see (Inspector Hung Ting-bong), Law Kar-ying (Wong Yat-fei), Christine Ng Wing-mei (Lara), Chung Fat (Ng Kwok-wan), Ken Lo Wai-kwong (Ng Kwok-yan), Wan Fat (Simon Ting), Blackie Ko Shou-liang (Captain Ko). 1.85:1. VHS/LD: Dimension (Dubbed). Import LD/VCD: Star Entertainment (No Subtitles). Import VCD/DVD: China Star (No Subtitles). 104 minutes.

With **Crime Story**, Jackie Chan took a break from his widescreen action-comedy spectaculars and signed on for this grim, well-paced, and highly involving police procedural, which is based on a true case. There *is* some excellent stuntwork on display but, first and foremost, this is a tough, no-nonsense thriller, completely lacking in the goofy humor that is one of the star's trademarks. When a car bearing the same men is spotted parked outside one of his building sites for several days running, millionaire developer Wong Yat-fei fears that he may be a target for abduction and enlists the aid of the HK police. The job of heading up the assignment is given to Inspector "Jackie Chan" ("Eddie Chan" in the subtitled version). While Chan is able to protect Wong from a riot by some angry workmen, the millionaire and his wife are snatched later on when they are away from police protection. The trail leads to Taiwan, and Chan is sent there, along with fellow HK inspector Hung, who had rescued Wong from a previous abduction. However, unbeknownst to Chan, Hung is actually the mastermind behind the latest crime and is undermining the investigation at every turn.

Chan does not often get a chance to display his dramatic potential, but he makes the most of this opportunity, giving a focused and intense characterization which blends perfectly with the relentless tenacity his characters always possess. Kent Cheng (one of HK's most dependable character actors) is also quite effective, but all of the performances here are undermined by the English version's insipid dubbing. Highlights include a confrontation between the two leads in the hold of a decrepit freighter, and a climactic battle between Chan, Chung Fat, and Ken Lo which ends with an inferno. Production actually began with Jet Li Lianjie in the lead. When he didn't work out, shooting resumed some time later with Chan, who ended up directing much of the film himself but gave sole credit to Che-Kirk Wong (ironically, **Crime Story** is usually cited as the film that got Hollywood interested in Wong). Wong Chat-fai, the real-life millionaire who served as the basis for Law Kar-ying's character, was also the subject of another film from the same year, Ko Sin-ming's **The Kidnap of Wong Chak Fai**, which adheres closer to the facts. In what cannot be a coincidence, the inspector out to save him is played this time by none other than Kent Cheng!

193. Crippled Avengers

(1978; Shaw Brothers) ★: 8/10. *Chaan kuet* (Cantonese), *Can Que* (Mandarin): "Incomplete." Music: Not Original; Writers: Ngai Hong, Chang Cheh; Producer: Run Run Shaw; Director: Chang Cheh. Cast: Chen Kuan-tai (Tu Tin-to), Phillip Kwok Tsui (Chin Sun, the Blind Man), Lo Mang (Wei, the Deaf Mute), Chiang Sheng (Wang Yi, the Idiot), Sun Chien (Kuei, the Legless Man), Lu Feng (Tu To-chang, the Armless Man), Johnny Wang Lung-wei (Wan), Dick Wei (Tinan Tiger), Jamie Luk Kim-ming (Tinan Tiger). 2.35:1. VHS/DVD: Crash Cinema (Dubbed). 107 minutes. Also known as **Mortal Combat** (US theatrical title), **The Return of the Five Deadly Venoms** (Crash Cinema title).

This is a superior Chang Cheh kung fu thriller with a terrific gimmick: Four fighters who are crippled in different ways must use their imagination and remaining skills to overcome their disability and get revenge on the man who ordered their mutilation. When the Tinan Tigers cut off his wife's legs and his son's arms, Tu Tin-to avenges them by slaughtering the culprits. A decade later, Tu's son, Tu To-chang, has perfected the use of metal hands (the fingers serve as deadly darts and the hands can also extend out a foot in front of him) to replace his own, allowing him to become a formidable martial artist. Capturing the now-adult sons of the Tigers, Tu has his son cripple each of them. Driven mad by grief, the elder Tu takes his anger out on those he feels have offended him, disabling them also. Four such men, Chin (blind), Wei (deaf and mute), Kuei (legless), and Wang (brain-damaged), receive special instruction from the latter's master. Kuei is given iron legs, while Chin and Wei are taught to make optimum use of their other senses. Wang is already a kung fu master, and the others tolerate his childish behavior in deference to the loss he suffered on their behalf. He is, however, a definite asset to the team when he sets his mind to helping out. After three years of intense preparation, the men are ready to attack Tu and his legions, but the psychopath has prepared a special line of defence that may prove unbeatable.

As you would expect with this premise, the training sequences are among the most unique in the genre and are made even more fascinating by superb choreography and the exceptional abilities of Chang's "Venoms" team (as they are known to their Western fans). While a tad drawn out at almost two hours, this is still a first-rate production that even inspired a low-budget knockoff called **Crippled Masters**. Going Chang's film one step "better," it stars two men with real disabilities, but it cannot hold a candle to its model. The character names listed above are from the English-dubbed version.

194. Crocodile Hunter

(1989) ★: 6/10. *Juen diu daai ngok* (Cantonese), *Zhuan diao da e* (Mandarin):

"Expert at Fishing for Big Crocodiles." Cinematographer: Gigo Lee Chi-hang; Art Director: Jason Mok Siu-kei; Music: Lowell Lo Kwun-ting; Action Directors: Stephen Tung Wai, Benz Kong To-hoi, Tony Poon Kin-kwan; Writer-Producer-Director: Wong Jing. Cast: Andy Lau Tak-wah (Happy Chiu), Alex Man Chi-leung ("Bad Odor" Chuan), Sandra Ng Kwan-yu (Bitch Ying), Alvina Kong Yan-yin (Lam Chia-hsin), Cheung Kwok-keung ("Stalled Engine" Te), Lung Fong (Fu), Lau Kong (Wei), Ricky Yee Fan-wai (Lin Tien-fu), Shing Fui-on (Chiang), Ronald Wong Pan (Fink Fai), Charlie Cho Cha-lei (Chu Li-yin), Eddie Maher (Shrimp), Frankie Chin Chi-leung (Convulsion), Maria Cordero (Maid). 1.85:1. VHS: Tai Seng. Import LD/VCD/DVD: Mei Ah. Running time unknown.

This typical Wong Jing concoction opens with a hostage-taking in a movie theater that is broken up by supercop Happy Chiu. However, in the process he is shot in the head and doctors are unable to remove the shell. After nine months in bed, Happy recovers but must retire from SDU because any further trauma to his head could prove lethal. Instead, he works for the force in a secondary capacity, teaming up with slovenly cop "Bad Odor" Chuan. The pair strike up a deal with prisoner "Bitch" Ying: If she will aid police in the arrest of wanted killer Fu and his henchmen, the authorities will grant her an early release. Fu is mixed up in a plot to kill a business magnate and rob the priceless antiques from his safe. His collaborator in the scheme is the old man's greedy son, who wants him and his brother out of the way so that he may assume control of his father's company.

The finale bears more than a slight resemblance to **Die Hard** (though not as much as Wong's later film, **High Risk**), but this amiable action-comedy boasts some terrific shootouts and reasonably amusing comic asides. Alex Man's character is forced to parade through the final reel naked and the lengths the filmmakers (not to mention the TV crew covering the crisis in the movie) go to avoid showing him frontally nude provide some of the best laughs here. Rosamund Kwan Chi-lam has an amusing cameo.

195. Crossings

(1994; Riverdrive Productions) ★: 8/10 (103 minute version), 6/10 (92 minute version). *Chor oi* (Cantonese), *Cuo ai* (Mandarin): "Intersecting Love." Cinematographer: Jamie Silverstein; Art Director: William Cheung Suk-ping; Music: Kung Chi-shing; Writers: Joyce Chan Wan-man, Evans Chan Yiu-shing; Producer: Willy Tsao Shing-yuen; Director: Evans Chan Yiu-shing. Cast: Anita Yuen Wing-yee (Mo-yung), Simon Yam Tat-wah (Benny), Lindzay Chan Ling-chi (Rubie), Monica Ha Man-ar (Mabel), Ted Brunetti (Joey), Marian O'Quinn (Julie). 1.85:1. VHS: Riverdrive Productions (103 minutes), Tai Seng (92 minutes). Import LD/VCD: Universe (92 minutes).

Inspired by an interracial murder in a New York City subway station during the mid–1980s, this unique merging of HK cinema and the New York independent film is a worthy follow-up to director Evans Chan's justly celebrated debut, the provocative, politically-charged **To Liv(e)** (1991). Instead of following the wishes of her parents and flying to Toronto, Mo-yung journeys to New York City in the hopes of finding Benny, a mysterious photographer she has become smitten with. There she meets Rubie (Eurasian actress Chan, reprising her character from **To Liv(e)**), a sympathetic clinic worker who becomes friends with Mo-yung and helps her settle down in the city. As Mo-yung's search for Benny continues, Rubie discovers that Benny had previously been indicted on drug charges. An inspection of the tripods which Mo-yung had brought over from HK for him proves her suspicions correct: Benny has used the girl to unknowingly smuggle heroin. Complicating the matter further is the fact that Mo-yung is pregnant with Benny's child and is now an illegal alien with nowhere to go, having since been ostracized by her family. However, before these concerns can be addressed, both women's lives are destined to be shattered by the actions of Joey, a dangerously violent and schizophrenic special ed teacher who has stopped taking his medication and is now stalking Rubie.

As with **To Liv(e)**, the dialogue is vital and smart, expressing the sort of observations and concerns these characters really would share. Chan also takes the opportunity to re-explore the anxieties faced by disparate Hong Kong citizens, as symbolized by several characters here who choose to cross over into new cultures and relationships, in the face of the colony's 1997 reunification with China. The cast is fine all around but it is the two female leads who shine. Yuen is superb, making the most of a rare chance to display the full range of her talents, and Lindzay Chan gives a genuine, touching performance, projecting very real intelligence and compassion. The drama is aided further by Kung Chi-shing's moody and varied soundtrack (available on CD), and there are also well-integrated songs by noted Mainland singer Cui Jian and HK art rocker Anthony Wong Yiu-ming. As was evident in his first feature, Chan is a careful and attentive director when it comes to both his performers and his compositions, and he makes excellent use of the New York locations available to him here. Still, as successful as these respective elements are, one does leave the film wondering why he and co-writer Joyce Chan would expend so much time and effort making the Chinese characters so authentic while leaving the others so one-dimensional, thus undermining the success of the drama. That question is answered once one has the chance to see Chan's original 103 minute cut, which has had selected screenings in North America and is now being offered on tape by the director. The HK distributor, wanting something more straightforward and commercial, re-cut the film for its run there, and it is that version which has been released on domestic tape by Tai Seng and on import laserdisc. Sadly, the editorial thinking apparently consisted of little more than removing every scene featuring caucasian and black actors that was not absolutely essential to the plot, along with an introductory quote (the Chinese saying, "Life, unlike goods, becomes cheap once it leaves home") and one brief instance where Joey verbally abuses a Chinese prostitute. In addition to marring the film's meticulous, abstract structure, these changes leave the Joey character seeming like a walking amalgam of all the evils inherent to this city, leading some to perceive the film as both anti-white and anti-New York. One large deletion in the final reel is especially damaging, robbing the film of a powerful and essential dramatic exchange which finds two disparate characters struggling to reach some common ground in the wake of senseless, shocking tragedy. In the longer cut, Joey's more gradual breakdown, the backstory explaining the reasons behind his obsession with Asian women, and the role his sister has in the narrative make that component of the storyline much more satisfying. The re-edit is worth seeing for the fine performances, affecting drama, and the director's estimable intentions, but it simply does not match the degree of power and satisfaction that **Crossings** yields in its original, undiluted form.

196. The Crucifixion

(1994; Golden Harvest/P.U. Production/Sum Wing International) ★: 7/10. *999 Sui si hung sau* (Cantonese), *999 shei shi xiong shou* (Mandarin): "999 Who's the Murderer?" Cinematographer: Cheung Yiu-cho; Art Director: Sukie Yip Suk-wah; Music: Tommy Wai Kai-leung; Writers: Abe Kwong Man-wai, Chu Kang-kei; Producers: Wellson Chin Sing-wai, Joey Lau Suk-kuen, Shirley Yan Yuk-ngor;

Director: Danny Ko Lam-pau. Cast: Michael Chow Man-kin (Ho Tin-nam), Hilary Tsui Ho-ying (Jacky Wong), Jay Lau Kam-ling (Wah's Wife), Liu Kai-chi (Leung Chi-wah), Miki Ng Miu-yee (Tang Mei-ping), Shing Fui-on (Chan Fu), William Ho Kar-kui (Yau Ting-kin), Helena Law Lan (Jogger), Ha Ping (Yau's Mother). 1.85:1. VHS: Tai Seng. Import LD/VCD: Universe. 92 minutes.

An intriguing mystery-thriller with appealing characters, **The Crucifixion** is the sort of low-key sleeper that motivates one to experiment with lesser known productions. A stray dog leads CID officers Ho Tin-nam and Jacky Wong to a crucified body out in the wilderness. Investigation reveals that the deceased drove a truck and was close friends with fellow drivers Leung, Chan, and Yau. When the remains of the dead man's wife are discovered, all fingers point towards Chan, but he evades capture and later turns up dead. Then the dog that led the detectives to the original victim is killed. The drivers reveal that they hired a Mainland prostitute named Yin-fong to service them whenever they stayed overnight in Shenzhen. However, when she wanted to end this arrangement, the men refused to let her, prompting Yin-fong to kill herself. Now it would appear that the girls's twin sister, Mei-ping, is out for vengeance but this theory loses credence when another victim turns up at a time when Mei-ping couldn't have possibly committed the murder.

There are a few too many false scares, but this remains an intelligent and engrossing thriller centered around two leads who are more quirky and personable than those generally encountered in this genre. The interplay between Michael Chow and Hilary Tsui is entertaining, and both performers endow their seemingly mismatched protagonists with personality and feeling. The developing mystery and its resolution are also quite satisfying. "999" in the Chinese title is the HK equivalent of the "911" emergency number.

197. Crystal Fortune Run

(1994; Super Film Production) ★: 5/10. *Bo fung ngaan* (Cantonese), *Bao feng yan* (Mandarin): "Eye of the Storm." Cinematographer: Ko Chi-yat; Art Director: Sam Kin-yip; Music: Mak Chun-hung; Writer: Candy Cheng; Action Director: Lai Sing-kwong; Producer-Director: Chris Lee Kin-sang. Cast: Anita Yuen Wing-yee (Ko Kit), Simon Yam Tat-wah (Kwong), Sharla Cheung Man (Wind Yip), Che-Kirk Wong Chi-keung (Lung Yu), Chris Lee Kin-sang (Yau Tin-chik). 1.85:1. VHS: World Video. Import LD/VCD: Mei Ah. 84 minutes.

This futuristic actioner attempts to be the live action equivalent of a Japanese *anime* fantasy; but while the visuals and stunts are ambitious, the narrative is too aimless to effectively sell them. Set in an unspecified time and place, the story opens with a group of high tech thieves, led by flaky computer wiz Ko Kit, burglarizing the crooked Tung Tik mega-conglomerate. Little do they know that another robber, Wind Yip, has also broken through the facility's security system and seeks the same prize: the invaluable "Diamond of Emperor Chen." The gem acts as a key that will lead the owner to a prize equivalent to "half of the money in the world." Wind (who has a powerful mechanical hand) and Kit strike up an uneasy alliance, while the alcoholic Special Squad officer Kwong (who has been tracking Wind for the past three years) tries to apprehend them and get the goods on the Tung Tik's chief executive as well.

The production design is quite elaborate for the budget, recalling **Blade Runner** in its marriage of the mundane and the futuristic, though the film lacks the budget necessary to attain the visual heights of that Hollywood classic. However, such attention to detail is undone by unaccountable slip-ups, like having Anita Yuen use a *Canadian* fifty dollar bill to pay for a drink (the film was partially shot in Vancouver, but that is no excuse). Speaking of Yuen, she is allowed to take her bubbly persona to annoying extremes, while Sharla Cheung's characterization goes too far in the opposite direction and Simon Yam's cop is a one-dimensional stereotype the actor can do little to enliven. *Crystal Fortune Run* is an interesting misfire worth catching for its aspirations and novelty value.

198. Crystal Hunt

(1991; Cheung Yau Production Co.) ★: 5/10. *No foh wai lung* (Cantonese), *Nu huo wei long* (Mandarin): "Fury Might of Dragon." Cinematographers: Chan Chuen-lai, Luk Kin-lok; Music: Not Original; Writer: Hung Hin-pang; Producer: Tsui Fat; Action Director: Tsui Fat; Director: Tsui Pak-lam. Cast: Donnie Yen Chi-tan (Chi-liang), Sibelle Hu Hui-chung (Superintendent Wu), Carrie Ng Kar-lai (Lisa Li), Ken Lo Wai-kwong (Chin Kwong), Gordon Lau Kar-fai (Liang), Leung Kar-yan (Man), Michael Woods (Muscular Black Thug), John Salvitti (White Thug), William Ho Kar-kui (Man with Glasses). 1.85:1. VHS: Tai Seng (Dubbed or Unsubtitled Chinese versions). Import LD/VCD: Star Entertainment (No Subtitles). 89 minutes.

There is virtually wall-to-wall action in this efficient B-picture, which looks to have been shot back-to-back in Thailand with **Cheetah on Fire**. Beautiful and affluent Lisa Li mounts an expedition to locate the mythical "Gold Crystal God," which reportedly has the power needed to heal her gravely-ill father. The professor Lisa relies on for information about the crystal is kidnapped by a group of rivals who also want to get their hands on the magical treasure. Lisa and her group proceed with their plan, accompanied (unwillingly) by the professor's daughter, policewoman Wu, and tour guide Chi-liang (a former cop). After much running and shooting, the stone is located in a booby-trapped cavern, and the interested parties fight to the death to determine who will be the ones to bring it back to civilization.

No surprises here, but this is a well-paced and competently executed kick, punch, and shoot 'em-up that has a slight edge on its companion feature. Stay tuned for outtakes under the end credits. The soundtrack includes music lifted from Tangerine Dream's score for **Wavelength**.

199. Cupid One

(1985; Cinema City Co.) ★: 3/10. *Oi san yat ho* (Cantonese), *Ai shen yi hao* (Mandarin): "Love God Number One." Cinematographer: Joe Chan Kong-hung; Art Director: Dominique Lo Kar-yiu; Music: Wong San, Antonio Arevalo Jr.; Writers: Ringo Lam Ling-tung, Wellington Fung Wing; Producers: Dean Shek Tien, Raymond Wong Pak-ming; Director: Ringo Lam Ling-tung. Cast: Sally Yeh Chian-wen (May Yeung Yee-ching), Mark Cheng Ho-nam (Keung), Eric Chan Kar-kei, Cho Yin-lung, Bee Lee-tan. Dolby Digital (DVD only). 1.85:1. VHS: Tai Seng. Import LD: Golden Cinema City. Import VCD/DVD: Mega Star. 95 minutes.

This early effort by Ringo Lam is a strained and formulaic romantic comedy for two thirds of its running time before taking a left turn into psycho thriller territory. It's a tiresome, headache-inducing mess any way you slice it. May is a spoiled girl who has car trouble on the way to her wedding. While trying to flag down a car for help, she accidentally causes Keung (Mark Cheng, in his film debut) and his girlfriend to veer off the road and down a hillside, causing the man to swear that he'd kill her if they ever crossed paths again. Naturally, later that evening, events unfold that will cause just such a reunion. A drunken May passes out aboard the yacht "Cupid One," which Keung just happens to be piloting. Not realizing she is aboard, he weighs anchor and heads for his planned destination: Thailand. When the two discover each other and their situation, they are too far out at sea to turn back. An endless amount of bickering and screaming ensues before, naturally, they start to like each other. Ten days later they finally arrive in Thailand, only to be thrown in the clink (she has no passport and he is suspected of slave trading). When that dilemma is cleared up, another one arises: Keung, not knowing that May is engaged, has fallen for her and won't take no for an answer. When she continues to spurn his advances, he pursues her through the streets with seemingly violent intent.

In interviews Lam has stated his dislike for this sort of material and one feels that this displeasure arises from the fact that he just has no feel for it (not that the script here could have worked for *anyone*). The final reel is more typical of the material, Lam would become known for, and, not coincidentally, it is the most successful portion. However, just what are we to make of this mongrel? Is it a romantic comedy? Is it a thriller about an obsessive psycho-in-the-making who finally pops his cork? Did the screenwriters have any clue as to just how unevenly this mixing of genres would play out? The balancing act just doesn't work, but, amazingly, the film ends precisely the way you expected it would, even before it went off on that detour. The ham-fisted approach and jarring shift in tone would also mar Lam's **The Other Side of the Gentleman** [*sic*], a similarly misguided and ill-advised effort. Both productions are strictly for those determined to sample his entire filmography.

200. Curry and Pepper

(1990; Movie Impact) ★: 6/10. *Ka lei laat jiu* (Cantonese), *Ga li la jiao* (Mandarin): "Curry Hot Pepper." Cinematographer: Andrew Lau Wai-keung; Art Director: Ben Luk Man-wah; Music: Richard Lo Sai-kit; Writer: James Yuen Sai-sang; Producer: Wallace Cheung Kwok-chung; Action Director-Director: Blackie Ko Shou-liang. Cast: Jacky Cheung Hok-yau (Curry), Stephen Chiau Sing-chi (Pepper), Ann Bridgewater (Joey Law), Blackie Ko Shou-liang (Abalone), Eric Tsang Chi-wai (Tenny), Barry Wong Ping-yiu (Chow), Michael Dinga (Ma), John Sham Kin-fun (King). 1.85:1. VHS: Tai Seng. 101 minutes.

Teaming up Stephen Chiau and Jacky Cheung for a buddy cop comedy seems like a stroke of genius, and while this uneven effort does not take full advantage of their talents, it's still good fun. Curry and Pepper are a pair of perfectly matched partners: They're both lazy and insubordinate. They're also the best cops in crime-ridden Tsimshatsui. When their superior is forced to allow TV reporter Joey Law to tag along with the men for a few days, both fall head over heels in love with her. However, when Joey shows a preference for Curry, it all but ruins his friendship with Pepper. Meanwhile, despite the wishes of the department chief, the pair involve themselves in an investigation targeting a group of arms dealers. This makes them the number one target of the criminals' vicious trigger man, Abalone (played by the film's director, ace stuntman Blackie Ko).

From the point where Curry and Pepper's friendship is strained to the moment where Curry realizes that Joey is out of his league, the movie simply spins its wheels and grows quite tedious. Things get back on track for the finale, an extended gun battle onboard a ship that covers just about every inch of the craft. Eric Tsang does a nice supporting turn as a stoolie trying to better himself but unable to shake his devious ways. The following year Cheung teamed up with Stephen Tung Wai for the terrific **Pom Pom and Hot Hot**, which could easily have been a follow-up to this film.

201. Dance of the Drunk Mantis

(1979; Seasonal Film Corporation) ★: 7/10. *Laam bak chui kuen* (Cantonese), *Nan bei zui quan* (Mandarin): "South North Drunk Fist." Cinematographer: Cheung Hon; Music: Not Original; Writer-Producer: Ng See-yuen; Action Directors: Corey Yuen Kwai, Yuen Shun yee, Yuen Chen-wai, Chin Yuet-sang; Director: Yuen Woo-ping. Cast: Simon Yuen Siu-tien (Sam the Seed), Yuen Shun-yee (Sam's Son), Hwang Jang-li (Rubber Legs), Yam Sai-kwoon (Sickness Master), Corey Yuen Kwai (Rubber Legs' Student), Dean Shek Tien (Money Bags). 2.35:1. VHS: World Video (Poor Subtitles). Import LD: Far East Music. Import VCD: Mei Ah (Poor Subtitles). 95 minutes.

Jackie Chan did not return for this **Drunken Master** follow-up, but wily old Simon Yuen did and the result was one of the best kung fu comedies of its era. After a trip across country, slovenly martial arts master Sam the Seed returns home to find that his wife has adopted a son. Much to Sam's chagrin, the boy is a total klutz who cannot even perform the most basic kung fu moves. Although his wife orders him to instruct the boy, Sam torments him instead with meaningless and painful training exercises. Rival kung fu great "Rubber Legs," master of the Northern Drunk Mantis style, soon tracks Sam down, with the intention of killing him in a duel. Although Sam dominates the bout at first, Rubber Legs eventually bests him with his hybrid style. Before he can finish Sam off, the old man's son saves him. While out to get herbs to treat his wounded father, the boy encounters the "Sickness Master," who instructs him in his technique: an unusual variation on the drunken boxing style which can defeat Rubber Legs if properly mastered.

While it follows the usual formula, **Dance of the Drunken Mantis** boasts some outstanding kung fu. The highlight is the initial fight between Hwang and Simon Yuen, which starts off with simple hand movements and gradually progresses to an all out bout. The training sequences are first rate too, with a number of intricate workouts that run the gamut from painful to humorous (Yuen Shun-yee trying to catch squares of tofu without crushing them is the best example of the latter). Like most films of this type, the stock music (which includes a cue lifted from **Sorcerer**) is overbearing, emphasizing the jokes to an unnecessary degree, but the traditional martial arts mastery transcends this annoyance.

202. Dances with the Dragon

(1991; Win's Movie Production) ★: 4/10. *Yue long gung mo* (Cantonese), *Yu long gong wu* (Mandarin): "Dance Together with the Dragon." Cinematographer: Henry Chan Chun-kit; Art Director: Jason Mok Siu-kei; Music: Lowell Lo Kwun-ting; Producer: Jimmy Heung Wah-sing; Action Director: Wong Kwan; Writer-Director: Wong Jing. Cast: Sharla Cheung Man (Moon), Andy Lau Tak-wah (Lone Ka-chun), Alfred Cheung Kin-ting (Martin Kung), Deanie Yip Tak-han (Shi-yi, aka "Baby"), Yvonne Yung Hung (Diana Kung), May Lo Mei-mei (Charmy), Ng Man-tat (Uncle Fly), Sin Lap-man (Shi), Wu Ma (Uncle Prawn), Paul Chu Kong (Chu Chi-keung, aka "Tomato"), Wong Yat-fei (Chung) John Ching Tung (Ng I-kong). 1.85:1. VHS: World Video. Import LD/VCD/DVD: Mei Ah. 108 minutes.

Fans of Sharla Cheung and Andy Lau will want to catch this overly formulaic Wong Jing comedy, but others will find little in this wish fulfilment fluff to hold their attention. It's love at first sight for rich developer Lone Ka-chun when he gets a load of Moon, a spunky career girl from a common background. In order to get back at his mother (who wants him to date a girl he despises), Ka-chun pretends to be an illegal immigrant and gets a job at a store run by Moon's mom on Lantau Island. When Moon needs a date for a high society party, she takes Ka-chun, who secretly uses his wealth to impress her. The two are soon in love, but Ka-chun must first deal with an underhanded competitor who wants to force Moon and her mom off of their land.

Despite the efforts of a good cast, there is not enough worthwhile material here to justify the running time, and the numerous digressions from the main storyline (via con games played by Moon's mother) are tiresome distractions. The humor is pretty desperate but there *are* nice in-joke references to **Lee Rock** and Hitchcock's **Strangers on a Train**.

203. Dangerous Duty

(1996; Star Film Workshop) ★: 1/10. *Aau him yam miu* (Cantonese), *Wei xian ren wu* (Mandarin): "Dangerous Mission." Cinematographer: Cheung King-nin; Art Director: Andy Lee Yiu-kwong; Action Directors: Wilson Tong Wai-shing, Cho Chi; Music-Producer-Director: Wilson Tong Wai-shing. Cast: Diana Pang Dan (Ling Peidan), Max Mok Siu-chung (Chen Chong), Ben Ng Ngai-cheung (Yin Yingming), Peter Yung Kam-cheung (Guo Chenyong), Elvis Tsui Kam-kong (Bald Hitman), Lo Lieh (Luo), Tai Po (Hitman), Bobby Yip King-sang (Beat Cop). 1.85:1. VHS: Tai Seng. 91 minutes.

There is nothing of interest to be found in this exceedingly dull, very poorly staged police actioner. Max Mok, Ben Ng, and Peter Yung play HK cops assigned to P.W.U., a newly established witness protection unit. Their first mission is to guard flaky witness Diana Pang, while a determined hitman (Tsui) seeks to take her out before she can testify. The proceedings move along with all the thrust of molasses in winter, and then stop dead midway so Mok's character can display his hypnotic powers, which come in handy later on (Kreskin has nothing on this guy!). The absolute pits, but you have to give the production credit for being hip enough to include a parody of the lunch counter banter between Faye Wang and Tony Leung Chiu-wai from **Chungking Express**. Pang re-enacts Sharon Stone's interrogation scene from **Basic Instinct**, but don't get your hopes up.

204. Dangerous Encounter—1st Kind

(1980; Fotocine) ★: 6/10. *Dai yat lui ying aau him* (Cantonese), *Di yi lei xing wei xian* (Mandarin): "The First Kind of Danger." Cinematographer: David Chung Chi-man; Art Director: Tony Au Ding-ping; Music: Not Original; Writers: Roy Szeto Cheuk-hon, Chan Fong, Eddie Fong Ling-ching; Producer: Thomas Fung Wing-fat; Action Director: Ching Siu-tung; Director: Tsui Hark. Cast: Lin Ching-chi (Wan-chu), Lo Lieh (Tan), Tse Bo-law, Lung Tin-sang, Au Siu-keung, David Wu Tai-wai (Tour Guide), Ray Lui Leung-wai (Cop), Bruce Baron (Bruce). 2.35:1. Import LD: Mei Ah. 95 minutes. Also known as **Don't Play with Fire** (Title for dubbed version).

One evening three teenage joyriders accidentally run over and kill a pedestrian. The crime is witnessed by teenage sociopath Wan-chu, who spends her spare time gruesomely murdering animals, playing with her police officer brother's gun, constructing bombs out of illegal firecrackers, and making life miserable for anyone unfortunate enough to cross her path. She threatens to turn the boys in unless they join her on a bus-hijacking. Later on, Wan-chu steals a box from a foreigner which is filled with money orders for millions of Japanese yen. She reveals her discovery to the boys, and together they set about trying to turn the notes into HK currency. Unfortunately for them, the money belongs to some ex-CIA agents who will stop at nothing to get their money (and a contract that was also in the box) back.

Like some Italian horror productions from its era, Tsui Hark's third film contains repugnant, entirely real cruelty to animals (a pin being inserted into the head of a mouse and the rodent's subsequent death throes are shown, as well as a cat being thrown from the roof of a building and impaled) that will be beyond the tolerance level of some viewers and almost call into question the entire movie's artistic viability. The rest of the film is not quite as repellant, but it remains an aggressively unpleasant experience. Initially banned by local censors because of its political content, **Dangerous Encounter— 1st Kind** had to be extensively re-worked before finally getting a release, and then proceeded to fail at the box office. Tsui presents a remarkably amoral world peopled by unlikeable and morally irredeemable characters, and the plentiful violence is presented with a casual ruthlessness that makes it doubly disturbing (quite a change from the stylized bloodshed of **The Butterfly Murders** and the cartoonish carnage in **We're Going to Eat You!**). The director's talent shines through via several dynamically staged suspense sequences and some bravura camerawork, but this is such a relentless, one-note film, it is largely just a chore to sit through. Those interested in charting Tsui's progress as an artist will find this of much greater use than casual viewers. Tsui, director Ronny Yu Yan-tai, and John Sham Kin-fun have cameos. The stock soundtrack includes music lifted from **Dawn of the Dead** and **Star Trek: The Motion Picture**.

205. The Daredevils

(1979; Shaw Brothers) ★: 7/10. *Jaap gei mong ming dui* (Cantonese), *Za ji wang ming mui* (Mandarin): "Multi-Talented Fugitive Squad." Cinematographer: Tsao Hui-chi; Art Director: Johnson Tsao; Music: Not Original; Writers: Ngai Hong, Chang Cheh; Producer: Mona Fong Yat-wah; Action Directors: Chiang Sheng, Chen Yu-wen; Director: Chang Cheh. Cast: Phillip Kwok Tsui (Leung), Chiang Sheng (Chin Feng), Lu Feng (Fu), Sun Chien ("Mr. Hsin"), Lo Mang (Yang Tau-ying), Wang Li (General Han), Cho Tat-wah (Leung's Father). 2.35:1. No official domestic video release. 105 minutes. Also known as **Daredevils of Kung Fu** (US title).

When his family is murdered in a military coup by the villainous General Han, Yang Tau-ying joins with his martially skilled friends to exact revenge. However, the realization that their opponents number over ten thousand convinces Yang to go it alone to spare his friends from inevitable death. Still wanting to help, the friends decide to steal some guns from a military outpost. They succeed but are unable to acquire bullets before the base security is on to them. Yang proceeds with his plan and is killed, prompting the others to adopt a different strategy that will allow them to get close to their target. Knowing Han's lust for power, they deceive him into thinking that he will acquire one thousand machine guns from them, thus allowing him to overthrow his political rival.

While a bit on the torpid side, this Chang Cheh/Ngai Hong collaboration is well-plotted and serves up some excellent performance sequences (the men make a living by demonstrating their skills in the streets), with Phillip Kwok and Chiang Sheng coming off particularly well during their acrobatic routines. The climax unfolds in a warehouse and features some terrific relay fighting. Character names are from the English version.

Daredevils of Kung Fu *see* **The Daredevils**

206. Daughter of Darkness

(1993; Mandarin Films) ★: 2/10. *Mit moon chaam on ji yip saai* (Cantonese), *Mie men can an zhi nie sha* (Mandarin): "Destroy Gate Massacre: Evil Killer." Cinematographer: Kin Lee Kin-keung; Art Director: Vincent Lam Wai-sam; Music: Wong Bong; Writers: Kimmy Suen King-on, Ivan Lai Kai-ming; Producer: Kimmy Suen King-on; Director: Ivan Lai Kai-ming. Cast: Lily Chung Suk-wai (Mak Wei-fong), Anthony Wong Chau-sang (Captain Lui), William Ho Kar-kui (Wei-fong's Father), Hugo Ng Toi-yung (Kin), Money Lo Man-yee (Dong Huan). 1.85:1.

VHS: Tai Seng (Poor Subtitles). Import LD/VCD: Ocean Shores (Poor Subtitles). 96 minutes.

This Category III thriller is a decidedly distasteful mixture of low-brow humor and protracted sexual violence. Set in China, it tells of the police investigation into the brutal murder of the Mak family as reported by its only surviving member, Mak Wei-fong. Captain Lui, an uncouth but competent detective, deduces that the crime must have been committed by Wei-fong's boyfriend, Kin, a fellow policeman. With his back against the wall, Kin confesses, only to have Wei-fong insist that she is the true killer. When Kin's account of the murders does not add up, Lui realizes that Wei-fong is indeed the actual culprit. The second half of the film is an extended flashback which documents the horrific sexual abuse Wei-fong suffered at the hands of her psychopathic stepfather and the resulting breakdown that led her to kill him and her other relatives.

The "mystery" is agonizingly transparent, and the process through which Lui comes to his conclusion is dull in the extreme. Things get bogged down even further by Lui's alleged sense of humor, which makes the sexual antics in the *ng fook sing* movies seem like Shakespearean farce in comparison. The rest is simply ugly, made even more unpalatable by the grotesque characters (the father may be the real malefactor but the rest of the Mak family is just as unappetizing). A surprise hit at the box office, this spawned two wholly unnecessary sequels: **Brother of Darkness** and **Daughter of Darkness II**. The former would again pair up Lily Chung and Hugo Ng (who would later become husband and wife off-screen) as the troubled lovers, and tap William Ho to portray yet another seething psycho.

207. The Day That Doesn't Exist

(1995; Golden Harvest/Good Standard International/P.U. Production) ★: 6/10. *Yee yuet saam sap* (Cantonese), *Er yue san shi* (Mandarin): "February 30th." Cinematographers: Cheung Yiu-cho, Jimmy Wong Kam-shing; Art Director: Sukie Yip Suk-wah; Music: Tommy Wai Kai-leung, Chan Chi-hong; Writers: Abe Kwong Man-wai, Matthew Chow Hoi-kwong, Cheung Siu-fong; Producers: Anthony Chow Ting-on, Wellson Chin Sing-wai; Directors: Wellson Chin Sing-wai, Danny Ko Lam-pau. Cast: Dayo Wong Chi-wah (Charles Chan), Sheila Chan Sak-lan (Poon Ka-sze), Kenneth Chan Kai-tai (Lam Wang-tsun), Bowie Lam Bo-yee (Li Man-kit), Anthony Wong Chau-sang (Raymond Shiu Chi-li), Eileen Tung Oi-ling (Jessica), Yuen King-tan (Tang Siu-lin). 1.85:1. VHS: Tai Seng. Import LD/VCD: Mei Ah. 103 minutes.

The Day That Doesn't Exist, by directors Wellson Chin (**The Inspector Wears Skirts**) and Danny Ko (**The Crucifixion**), spins two horror tales (both of which arise from automobile crashes), bridged by the presence of Dayo Wong (**Mr. Sardine**) as a flaky cop investigating the bizarre goings on. The first story recalls the venerable resurrection tale "The Monkey's Paw," and offers comedienne Sheila Chan a dramatic turn as a bride-to-be whose fiance is killed in a car accident while attending a meeting in the Mainland. A month later the man appears on her doorstep alive but sporting huge, stitched-up gashes in his throat and chest. While all initially appears to be well, he soon starts to decompose and requires amniotic fluid to retard the putrefaction. The story's dramatics are effective (with love, rather than bloodlust, motivating the ghoul's actions), and the blackly humorous asides are an effective component. The other story is even better. Bowie Lam plays Li, an impoverished truck driver and good-for-nothing husband who is apparently killed in a highway collision. When he awakens three years later, he finds that his spirit is now trapped inside the body of Raymond (Anthony Wong), who had an accident on the same spot. Unable to resume his former life because his wife doesn't believe him, Li decides to settle into Raymond's upper class existence. Everything is fine until Raymond's wife, Jessica (Eileen Tung), starts to display bizarre, masochistic tendencies. After further observation, it becomes evident to Li that the couple are *cannibals* and the Mrs. cannot fathom hubby's newfound squeamishness.

A good balance between comedy and tension is generated and maintained throughout, with the climax serving up irony, horror, and humor in equally strong portions. The one serious problem with the film, however, is that neither story is ever genuinely scary. Dayo Wong and Yuen King-tan would reprise their characters two years later in **24 Hrs. Ghost Story**.

208. A Day Without Policeman

[*sic*] (1993; Perfect Films Production Co.) ★: 1/10. *Mo ging si fan* (Cantonese), *Mou jing shi fen* (Mandarin): "A Time Without Police." Cinematographer: Chan Tung-chuen; Music: Lau Yee-tat; Writers: Johnny Lee King-kai, Lai Kwong-fai, Koo Ping-kit, Wu Wei-chun; Producers: Steven Siu Yim-kwan, Lam Siu-ming; Action Director: Lam Man-wah; Director: Johnny Lee King-kai. Cast: Simon Yam Tat-wah (Chan Wai), Yu Li (Li Li), Tommy Wong Kwong-leung (Nam). 1.85:1. VHS/LD: Tai Seng. 98 minutes.

98 minutes without entertainment: Simon Yam stars in this dreadful Category III thriller as Chan Wai, an impotent, good-for-nothing cop (modelled somewhat after Harvey Keitel's character in **Bad Lieutenant**) patrolling one of HK's outer islands. One day, while peeping at a woman bathing on a boat, he witnesses a group of thugs board the craft and try to molest her. However, Chan is too stoned to properly intercede and the thugs rape and murder their victim after severely beating her husband. The survivor enlists some of his Vietnamese war buddies to exact revenge but things quickly get out of hand. Armed with AK47s and large hunting knives, the killers proceed to slaughter about half the island's population without finishing off their target, even after they've captured him!

A Day Without Policeman is a painfully drawn out and often repugnant example of the "Idiot Plot," and the spectacularly incoherent subtitles just make matters worse. Yu Li is wasted in a demeaning role as Yam's estranged wife, whose courage and resourcefulness far outweigh his.

209. The Days of Being Dumb

(1992; United Filmmakers Organization) ★: 6/10. *Ah Fei yue Ah Kei* (Cantonese), *Ya Fei yu Ya Ji* (Mandarin): "Ah Fei and Ah Kei." Cinematographers: Andrew Lau Wai-keung, Jingle Ma Cho-shing; Art Directors: Ben Luk Man-wah, James Cheung Ying-wah; Music: Richard Lo Sai-kit; Writers: James Yuen Sai-sang, Cheung Chi-sing, Joe Ma Wai-ho; Producer: Peter Chan Ho-sun; Action Director: Tai Kwai-bo; Director: Blackie Ko Shou-liang. Cast: Jacky Cheung Hok-yau (Keith), Tony Leung Chiu-wai (Fred Tung), Kenneth Tong Chun-yip (Kwan), Anita Yuen Wing-yee (Jane), Eric Tsang Chi-wai (Ball), Glen Chin (The General), Jamie Luk Kim-ming (Darkie), Tania Wong (Lisa). 1.85:1. VHS: Tai Seng. Import LD/VCD/DVD: Mei Ah. 91 minutes.

More likeable than genuinely funny, this mild comedy has nothing to do with Wong Kar-wai's **Days of Being Wild**. Instead, it's a hit-and-miss send-up of triad movies from an action choreographer/director who has worked on his share. Gangster wannabes Fred and Keith are such jinxes that their previous bosses died within days of them joining up. Blacklisted by the gangs, the pair decide to go into the prostitution business by importing a hooker from Singapore. Trouble is, no one told Jane that she was supposed to be a prostitute, and neither Fred nor Keith are ferocious enough to make her walk the streets. Things take an odd turn when the boys are recruited by Kwan, the most vicious gangster in HK, because he believes that their extreme negative influence will inadvertently make him invincible. Known as "The Red and White Jinxes," Fred and Keith enjoy instant fame, but their wave of good fortune ebbs when the pair fall in love with Jane and she proceeds to leave both of them. Things get much worse, however, when the police make it look like the duo are about to betray Kwan in court.

Tony Leung Chiu-wai and Jacky Cheung are both terrific here, and their amiable performances help the film over its rough spots (like the uninspired action climax). Anita Yuen isn't given much of interest to do in her screen debut. The film Keith and Jane go to see is **Curry and Pepper**, a buddy cop comedy from the same director that pairs Jacky Cheung and Stephen Chiau.

210. Days of Being Wild

(1990; In-Gear Film Productions Co.) ★: 7/10. *Ah Fei ching chuen* (Cantonese), *A Fei zheng chuan* (Mandarin): "The True Story of Ah Fei." Cinematographer: Christopher Doyle; Art Director: William Cheung Suk-ping; Music: Chan Ming-to; Producer: Rover Tang Kwong-chow; Action Director: Stephen Tung Wai; Writer-Director: Wong Kar-wai. Cast: Leslie Cheung Kwok-wing (Yuddy), Andy Lau Tak-wah (Tide), Maggie Cheung Man-yuk (Su Lizhen), Carina Lau Karling (Mimi Leung Fung-ying), Jacky Cheung Hok-yau (Zeb), Rebecca Pan Di-hua (Rebecca), Tony Leung Chiu-wai (Man in Final Scene). 1.85:1. VHS/LD: World Video. Import LD/VCD/DVD: Mei Ah. 93 minutes.

Wong Kar-wai's second film is set in 1960 and revolves around Yuddy, a handsome cad who is either incapable or unwilling to treat women with any degree of compassion. After taking up with shy, withdrawn Su Lizhen, he soon moves on to scatterbrained dancing girl Mimi, who is more willing to put up with the sort of games he plays. Yuddy's behaviour can, at least partially, be attributed to his foster mother. A former courtesan turned embittered alcoholic, she refuses to tell Yuddy who his real mother is, forcing him to stay with her by dangling this bit of crucial information just out of reach. Policeman Tide notices Lizhen brooding outside Yuddy's apartment building and, over time, becomes her confidant. Tide's interest eventually turns into unrequited love, a situation that also befalls Yuddy's friend Zeb, who desires Mimi but is soundly rejected by her. Yuddy is finally able to learn the whereabouts of his true mother and heads off to the Philippines in search of her. There he finds both rejection and Tide, who is now a sailor.

If **As Tears Go By** makes a few concessions to commerciality, then **Days of Being Wild** qualifies as the first "true" Wong Kar-wai movie. It's all here: the similarities in approach to Jean-Luc Godard's early output, the underlying theme of unrequited love, measured pacing, skeletal narrative structure, languid takes of beautiful, brooding protagonists, alternating voiceover monologues, and gorgeous compositions complementing some impeccable art direction (finding great beauty in squalor this time). Also, as with the films he is best known for, this is best appreciated through multiple viewings, though the undercurrents here are not as rich or extensive as those found in the director's later work. The performances are all very good, especially Leslie Cheung as the mother-fixated lothario and Carina Lau as Cheung's hopelessly misguided lover, who refuses to accept what is painfully obvious to those around her. Tony Leung Chiu-wai appears in the final minute in a bit designed to set up a sequel. As **Days** was poorly received by audiences, a sequel has yet to be produced, but Wong's **Ashes of Time** is as good a companion piece as any.

211. Days of Tomorrow

(1993; Team Work Production House) ★: 7/10. *Tin cheung dei gau* (Cantonese), *Tian chang di jiu* (Mandarin): "The Length of the Sky, the Duration of the Earth." Cinematographer: Arthur Wong Ngok-tai; Art Director: James Leung Wah-sang; Music: Lowell Lo Kwun-ting; Writer: Kei On (pseudonym for Jeff Lau Chun-wai); Producer: Tsui Wai-kwok; Director: Lau Yu-ming. Cast: Andy Lau Tak-wah (Fong Tak-shing), Jay Lau Kam-ling (Ling), Carrie Ng Kar-lai (Nancy Mei), Yip San (Sheung), Henry Fong Ping (Lui), Hilary Tsui Ho-ying (Yan), Deanie Yip Tak-han (Ling's Mother), Lau Kong (Lam), Chan Kwok-bong (Leung). 1.85:1. VHS: Tai Seng. Import LD/VCD: Universe. 93 minutes.

This intriguing drama concerns teenager Yan, who gets a job on a remake of the 1960s film "Days of Tomorrow," which starred her late father, Fong Tak-shing. By working on this project, she hopes to learn more about her dad, who passed away shortly after she was born. Her mother, still smarting from bad memories of Tak-shing, refuses to tell Ling anything about him, creating a large rift between the two. Through flashbacks, we see Tak-shing go from rebellious "Teddy Boy" to debonair leading man under the tutelage of glamorous movie star Nancy Mei. Regardless, he has never gotten over his old girlfriend, Ling, and it is she who is chosen to star opposite him in "Days of Tomorrow." Aged studio head Lui seeks to have Ling for himself, and when she becomes pregnant with Tak-shing's child, he is determined to keep them apart.

More intelligent and even handed than most of the dramas penned by Jeff Lau, **Days of Tomorrow** is well-acted and beautifully designed, wonderfully evoking an era of HK moviemaking that Westerners rarely ever get to see, warts and all. It was Hilary Tsui's film debut.

212. The Dead and the Deadly

(1983; Golden Harvest) ★: 7/10. *Yan haak yan* (Cantonese), *Ren he ren* (Mandarin): "People Frighten People." Cinematographers: Ricky Lau Koon-wai, Lee Yao-tong; Art Directors: Chin Sum, Mak Wor; Writers: Sammo Hung Kam-po, Barry Wong Ping-yiu; Action Directors: Sammo Hung Kam-po, Yuen Biao, Lam Ching-ying, Billy Chan Wui-ngai; Director: Wu Ma. Cast: Sammo Hung Kam-po (Fatboy), Wu Ma (Ma Lucho), Lam Ching-ying (Uncle), Cherie Chung Cho-hung (Yuen), Chung Fat (Priest). 2.35:1. VHS: Tai Seng (Poor Subtitles). LD: Media Asia. Import VCD: Mega Star (Poor Subtitles). 97 minutes (tape), 99 minutes (LD).

Sammo Hung stars in this period horror-comedy which, while not as rambunctious as some of its type, serves up terrific martial arts and some amusingly base humor amid typically lush Golden Harvest production values. When Ma Lucho is found dead from natural causes, his eternally loyal friend Fatboy is suspicious. He becomes even more skeptical upon discovering that the impotent man's wife is now pregnant. Determined to prove his theory that Lucho was murdered, Fatboy decides to perform his own unauthorized autopsy. The only problem is that Lucho has faked his death in order to sell all of the precious antiques his father has willed to him. This leads to some rather tense moments for the bogus corpse when Fatboy arrives on the scene with his set of cleavers. Before the lad can slice the body open and check the color of his buddy's innards, he is interrupted by a powerful priest and persuaded to give up the plan. However, Lucho's partners in deception discover that the antiques are actually worthless junk, and that Lucho's widow will inherit a genuine fortune once she has given birth to an heir. Realizing he is worth more to them dead than alive, the priest and Lucho's wife have Lucho killed for real this time, only to be confronted by his vengeance-seeking ghost. Unable to overcome the priest's powers, Lucho possesses Fatboy, but the host dies when the lad's disembodied spirit is unable to return to its body before dawn. Determined to save Fatboy's soul, his wizened *sifu* and loyal girlfriend, Yuen, concoct a plan to foil the demons charged with escorting Fatboy's soul down to Hell.

Hung displayed a distinct talent for caricature when he provided an unbelievably good Bruce Lee imitation for the raucous **Return of the Dragon** parody, **Enter the Fat Dragon** (1978). He does an equally good job here as the possessed Fatboy, perfectly mimicking Wu Ma's mannerisms, and his fighting skills are above reproach. The final reels provide a detailed primer in Chinese mythology, much of which is both fascinating and outrageous by Western standards (when Fatboy's soul is temporarily housed inside the body of a beetle, Yuen keeps the insect hidden from the Hell sentinels by putting it inside her sanitary napkin!). A key film of its genre, **The Dead and the Deadly** is required viewing for those interested in the roots of HK horror, and is one of the earlier examples available to English audiences in a comfortably viewable and translated form. The soundtrack includes some early Tangerine Dream.

Dead Heat *see* **Thunderbolt**

213. Deadful [*sic*] Melody

(1994; Film City Distribution/Super Class Production) ★: 7/10. *Luk chi kam moh* (Cantonese), *Liu zhi qin mo* (Mandarin): "The Six-Fingered Strings Demon." Cinematographer: David Chung Chi-man; Art Directors: Kung Kwok-choi, William Cheung Suk-ping; Music: James Wong Jim, Mark Lui Chung-tak; Writers: Johnny Lee King-kai, Lee Man-choi. Producers: Ng Min-kan, Chi Yu; Action Directors: Mang Hoi, Power Lee King-chu; Director: Ng Min-kan. Cast: Brigitte Lin Ching-hsia (Snow), Yuen Biao (Lui Lun), Carina Lau Kar-ling (Tam Yuet-wah), Elvis Tsui Kam-kong (Tung Fong-pak), Wu Ma (Fire Master), Lam Wai (Ghost Master), Peter Chan Lung (Lui Lun's Master), Chung Fat (Hon Suen). 1.85:1. VHS/LD: Tai Seng. Import LD/VCD: Star Entertainment. Import DVD: China Star. 92 minutes. Also known as **Devil Melody, The Six-Fingered Strings Demon.**

As with Benny Chan's Film Workshop production, **The Magic Crane** (1993), this well-crafted period fantasy (adapted from a novel by popular fantasy author Ngai Hong) revolves around the use of sound waves generated by musical instruments (in this case, a lyre) as powerful weapons in the war to decide leadership of the martial world. In the years following the slaughter of her parents by a throng of ghoulish villains, Snow has harnessed the destructive powers of the lyre in order to exact revenge. Her objective faces unexpected complications thanks to the intervention of her long lost brother Lui Lun, his perpetually tardy *sifu*, and a plucky martial arts student.

The film offers nothing innovative plotwise but benefits from some garish special effects and brooding, horror-influenced visuals. Like many recent films of this type, the darker moments are offset by some shrewd satire, invariably at the expense of the power-mad villains (though unlike similar productions from Film Workshop, there is no overt political subtext here). The action scenes are among the liveliest and most bizarre in memory, with numerous flying swordsmen being blasted to atoms by Snow and her lyre. As the avenging "witch" of the piece, Lin offers her imposing screen presence but seems rather hemmed in by this familiar character (who, predictably, spends a great deal of time disguised as a man). In contrast, Carina Lau gives a wonderfully animated performance that is almost matched by veterans Wu Ma and Lam Wai, who obviously relished the chance to play such comical grotesques. The excellent score includes cues heard previously in **The Moon Warriors** and **The Sword Stained with Royal Blood.**

214. Deadly Angels

(1977; Shaw Brothers) ★: 3/10. *Ciu taam neui giu wa* (Cantonese), *Qiao tan nu jiao wa* (Mandarin): "Cute Detectives Female Lovely Cuties." Cinematographers: Kuang Han-le, Li Hsin-yeh; Music: Not Original; Writers: Ngai Hong, Chin Shu-mei; Producer: Mona Fong Yat-wah; Action Directors: Tang Chia, Yuan Tayen; Director: Pao Hsueh-li. Cast: Yen Nan-hsi, Shaw Yin-yin, Dana, Chin Cheng-lan, Evelyne Kraft (Eve), Lee Hoisang (Bald Thug), Fung Hark-on (Thug), Yuen Cheung-yan (Opponent in Simulation). 2.35:1. No official domestic video release. 88 minutes.

The "Charlie's Angels" series was the obvious inspiration for this dull actioner, which certainly does not in any way measure up to the three "official" **Angel** films (starring Moon Lee Choi-fung) that would be produced a decade later. A team of heavily armed jewel thieves are terrorizing HK and then using girls to transport the stones to Japan. Once the smuggling missions are complete, the women are brutally done away with. In response, the HK authorities enlist the aid of some policewomen volunteers, headed by Eve from Scotland Yard (**The Mighty Peking Man**'s Evelyne Kraft), to infiltrate the gang by becoming couriers. Operating out of a nightclub (and led by a knife thrower), the criminals soon find their finely tuned operation running into a few unexpected snags.

The female leads were obviously chosen for looks rather than their fighting or acting abilities, and, aside from occasional bursts of sex and violence, there is nothing here to hold one's attention (and no camp value either). The angels utilize a variety of secret weapons (like a crossbow that fires exploding pellets), but the fine martial arts choreography found in so many of Shaw Brothers period films is rarely in evidence here, and the gunplay is even less impressive.

Deadly China Dolls *see* **Lethal Panther**

Deadly China Hero *see* **Last Hero in China**

215. Deadly Dream Woman

(1992; Carrianna Film Production) ★: 6/10. *Lui hak hap wong au* (Cantonese), *Nu hei xia huang ying* (Mandarin): "Female Black Heroine Nightingale." Cinematographer: Herman Yau Lai-to; Art Director: Ho Chi-hang; Music: Lau Chi-yuen, Lau Yee-tat; Writer: Manfred Wong; Producer: Wong Jing; Action Directors: Yuen Cheung-yan, Tony Leung Siu-hung, Pang Bei-lee; Director: Taylor Wong Tai-loi. Cast: Sharla Cheung Man (Nightingale Wong), Chingmy Yau Suk-ching (Ching), Deanie Yip Tak-han (Witch Woman), Jacky Cheung Hok-yau (Big Nose Fu), Ken Lo Wai-kwong (Jaguar Lui), Kwan Hoi-shan (Yip). 1.85:1. LD: Network Kingdom. Import LD/VCD: Star Entertainment (No Subtitles). Import DVD: China Star (No Subtitles). 89 minutes.

Beating Johnny To Kei-fung's **The Heroic Trio** to theaters, this lower budget superheroine saga goes a slightly different route by having its alluring masked avenger, Nightingale Wong, *aiding* triad gang activities. Dispatched to HK from America to assist Yip (her gangster foster father) in dealing with traitorous gang lieutenant Jaguar Lui, Nightingale gets caught in the crossfire when their meeting is ambushed. The aftermath finds Yip dead and Nightingale with amnesia. She is found and sheltered by a mother and daughter madam team, "Witch Woman" and Ching, who believe her to be a millionaire's missing progeny. Hoping for a reward, the two bide their time by convincing the potential meal ticket that she is really one of their girls. Not surprisingly, Nightingale crosses Jaguar's path at a nightclub, which helps to jog her memory. Teaming up with Ching's former triad hitman boyfriend, "Big Nose" Fu, Nightingale launches a final assault on Jaguar and his boys.

Like most disposable HK pop entertainment, **Deadly Dream Woman** fuses together all manner of commercial elements with reckless abandon, but the resulting hybrid is quite palatable. Sharla Cheung and Chingmy Yau exude playful sexuality, and the shootouts are executed with *panache*, though the mid-section lags somewhat. Fans of Sharla Cheung will note that the film provides a vivid, albeit comic, recollection of her early role as a naive hooker in Joseph Cheung Tung-cho's superior action-melodrama **Bet on Fire** (1988).

216. The Deadly Island

(1994) ★: 1/10. *Mor wik jui hung* (Cantonese), *Mo yu zhui kong* (Mandarin): "Pursuing Terror Into Evil Territory." Cinematographer: Cheung King-nin; Director: Chan Ching-hing. Cast: Mark Cheng Ho-nam (Ray Pang), Austin Wai Tin-chi (Cheung Ming), Lam Wai (Chung), Shum Wai (Wai). 1.85:1. VHS: Tai Seng. 88 minutes.

A group of triad arms smugglers led by Chung get more than they bargained for when they do business on Man-eating Island [*sic*] in this cheap and very poorly directed thriller. The place (just off the Philippines) is inhabited by some decidedly unfriendly natives, and the criminals barely escape with their lives. After staging a fake murder to establish his credentials, undercover cop Cheung Ming goes to Manila and signs on with Chung for a return trip to the island in order to retrieve some weapons that were left behind. After a prolonged skirmish with the inhabitants, Chung and his men are captured and sentenced to death. Meanwhile, their cohort, Ray Pang, has fallen in love with the chief's daughter and wins the old man's favor when he easily defeats a rival in hand-to-hand combat. The criminals manage to get loose but are later trapped inside a cavern, with Cheung (sporting a Mickey Rourke t-shirt, just to show how tough he is) soon caught in the middle of a deadly battle between Chung and his partner. This is a real snoozer, in spite of rib-tickling lines like, "Ching, we have to leave this jungle of death." Watch **Stone Age Warriors** instead.

The Deadly Mantis *see* **Shaolin Mantis**

Deadly Sin, The *see* **China White**

Deception *see* **Web of Deception**

217. Demoness from Thousand Years

[*sic*] (1990; Chan's Film Company) ★: 3/10. *Chin nin lui yiu* (Cantonese), *Qian nian nu yao* (Mandarin): "Thousand Year Female Demon." Cinematographers: Gary Ho Bo-yiu, Lam Chiu; Art Director: Tam Hong-ming; Music: Lau Yee-tat; Writer: Tam Wai-shing; Producers: Lau Chi-wing, Cheng Ting-tung; Action Directors: Hsiao Hou, Yee Fei; Director: Cheng Wing-chiu. Cast: Joey Wang Tsu-hsien (Yun Yu-yi), Jacky Cheung Hok-yau (Fat Mambo), Gloria Yip Wan-yee (Siu-yi), Andy Hui Chi-on (An), Hsiao Hou (The Teacher), Ku Feng (Yu-yi's Master), Gabriel Wong Yat-san (The Retard), Cho Tat-wah. VHS/LD: World Video. Import LD/VCD: Universe. 88 minutes. Also known as **Chase from Beyond**.

This low-budget fantasy-comedy starts off with some promise but disintegrates quickly once the action switches to the present day. When her master is destroyed by a powerful female demon, beautiful fairy Yun Yu-yi steals the "Bead of Hell" and escapes, with the creature in pursuit. The film then switches to 1990 as the two continue their thousand year-old battle in contemporary HK. Yu-yi meets up with cocky cop Fat Mambo(!), who possesses a birthmark on his arm that can repel her opponent. Mambo's buddy initially misconstrues Yu-yi's intentions and asks his Taoist teacher to try and dispel her, but the pair ultimately come to Yu-yi's aid when the creature captures her. One of Mambo's co-workers is tricked into slicing off the birthmark (which is actually The Mark of Buddha), but the priest reveals that the evil can be dispelled when the Bead of Hell is combined with the Heaven's Sun Bead. Unfortunately, the latter now resides inside Mambo and cannot be unleashed unless he is dead.

Cheesy special FX and numerous time-killing digressions involving the supposedly humorous antics of Mambo's colleagues send this one irreparably off track, and the ending is anything but satisfying. Fans of Joey Wang may want to make the effort, but she has played similar roles in at least a dozen other fantasies—all of which have more going for them than this one.

218. Descendant of the Sun

(1983; Shaw Brothers) ★: 7/10. *Yat gip* (Cantonese), *Ri jie* (Mandarin): "Sun Disaster." Cinematographer: Lam Chiu; Music: Sing Kam-wing, So Chun-hau; Writer: Shaw's Writing Team; Producer: Mona Fong Yat-wah; Action Directors: Yuen Bun, Yuen Wah, Wong Po-kei; Director: Chor Yuen. Cast: Derek Yee Tung-sing (Shih-sheng), Cherie Chung Cho-hung (The Princess), Ku Kuan-chung, Yeung Ching-ching (Pao). 2.35:1. VHS: World Video (Poor Subtitles). Import LD: Ocean Shores (Poor Subtitles). 92 minutes.

This Shaw Brothers period fantasy has some amusing parallels to **Superman**, despite an introductory sequence (consisting of clips from earlier SB productions) stating that it is based on a Chinese legend. Current video versions are horribly cropped, rendering the subtitles and action difficult to follow, but the basic scenario is still accessible. After successfully defeating a flying demon, the spirit of priest Hsuan travels to a fortress in the frozen north. A villager discovers a male infant encased in the ice there and brings the baby (whom he names Shih-sheng) home. As the boy grows up, it becomes apparent that he possesses incredible strength, can levitate people and objects, and talk to animals. He can even cause frozen branches to sprout blossoms and fruit. Upon becoming a man, Shih-sheng (who receives his strength from the sun) journeys back to the fortress and encounters the consciousness of his true father, who teaches him how to transform into a super warrior in a flashy gold outfit. After accidentally intruding on the palace grounds, the timid Shih-sheng is able to save himself from execution by displaying his talents to the beautiful Princess. Meanwhile, the kingdom's villainous Regent has been "cleansing" the people by destroying hundreds of infants that he deems to be inferior. Worried that the princess will learn of his activities and put a stop to them, the Regent dispatches assassins to kill her, but they are all foiled by Shih-sheng. As in **Superman**, no one is able to recognize this flying avenger (who cannot be harmed by swords and is now referred to—even in the subtitles—as "Superman"), and Shih-sheng elects to keep his identity a secret. When the Regent tries once again to kill the princess, the gold Superman saves her but the Regent is not defeated yet. He uses his blood to revive the demon previously confined by Hsuan, and it proves to be a formidable opponent for Shih-sheng, particularly when an eclipse robs the latter of his powers.

Aimed at general audiences, the film is a mixture of juvenile fantasy elements and instances of violence one would never find in comparable Western productions (the villains like to rip out the hearts of their adversaries, and Shih-sheng is attacked by flesh-eating zombies at one point). The costumes and rainbow colored set design are gorgeous and possess an East

Indian influence not generally seen in more contemporary HK productions. While it cannot be fully appreciated when cropped to television dimensions, **Descendant of the Sun** remains an eye-popping spectacle filled with magical combat, and is one of the few Chor Yuen fantasies not locked away from view in the SB vaults.

219. The Descendant of Wing Chun

(1978; Sunrise Film Trading Co.) ★: 2/10. *Fut shan Jahn seen san* (Cantonese), *Phu san Jahn sen shun* (Mandarin): "Fut Mountain, Mr. Jahn." Cinematographer: Erh Don-lung; Writer: Pak Fei; Music: Not Original; Producer: Chan Mei-ling; Action Director-Director: Wong Ha. Cast: Norman Tsui Siu-keung (Moneychanger Hua), Melvin Wong Kam-sun (Liang Chen), Fung Hark-on (Hsiao Fei), Lee Hoi-sang (Ma Lung). 2.35:1. VHS/DVD: Tai Seng (Dubbed). 91 minutes.

Some good fighting technique is not enough to salvage this cheap independent production, which will try the patience of all but the most undiscriminating kung fu fans. Pig butcher Fatty Kwei has a big mouth and it is always singing the praises of his kung fu, which is actually no better than average. Due to circumstances not worth relating, Kwei inadvertently triumphs over two opponents who are reputed to be among the best fighters in the region but meets his match in the form of Wing Chun master Liang Chen. Kwei's teacher has a duel with Liang and the two decide to switch students: Kwei will study Liang's techniques, while Moneychanger Hua (already a fine fighter) shall receive instruction from Kwei's hapless master. However, two robbers out to settle an old score with Liang cause trouble for everyone.

Slow paced and thoroughly lacking in surprises and suspense, films like this are the reason that HK cinema used to have such a bad reputation in the West. The insane mix and match soundtrack includes some music by Tangerine Dream and Riz Ortolani's main title theme for the spaghetti western **Days of Wrath**. Character names are from the dubbed version (which identifies "Wing Chun" as "Yong Chuan," the Mandarin form of that name).

220. Destination—9th Heaven

(1997; Mandarin Films) ★: 1/10. *Cheung seung gau chung tin* (Cantonese), *Chong shang jiu chong tian* (Mandarin): "Rush Up Nine Levels of Heaven." Cinematographer: Sander Lee Kar-ko; Art Director: Nelson Cheung Hok-yun; Music: Mak Chun-hung; Writers: Leung Fung-chi, Raymond Wong Pak-ming, Wong Kwong-cham; Producer: Raymond Wong Pak-ming; Director: Wong Chun-man. Cast: Tony Leung Kar-fai (Chiang Shan), Winston Chao Wen-hsuan (Chin Ching), Gigi Lai Chi (Mona Chin), Christine Ng Wing-mei (Joey Yick), Sunny Chan Kam-hung (Raymond). 1.85:1. VHS: Tai Seng. 91 minutes.

Released not long after the handover, this shameless propaganda piece tries to sell the merits of China without so much as a shred of objectivity (or, for that matter, an ounce of entertainment). Taiwanese star Winston Chao (**The Wedding Banquet**) plays an eternally loyal HK businessman who wants to invest in China's rocket program, hoping to launch a satellite to celebrate HK's re-unification with the Mainland. Gigi Lai plays his spoiled daughter, a supposed physics major who at first looks down on China's top rocket scientist (played by Tony Leung Kar-fai). However, as she grows to know him, Lai realizes that this dedicated, non-materialistic communist is to be envied, and she quickly falls for him—despite the fact that he is already married. Chao's dream is soon threatened by "disloyal" concerns (i.e. HK capitalist businessmen out to make a buck), and Leung is diagnosed with stomach cancer. However, he is determined to put the nation's interests first and continues to work until the project is completed and launched on schedule.

Laughable, stereotypical characters (especially the caucasians), stilted dialogue, and melodramatic plotting make this already labored production a real chore to sit through. Fortunately, the film's poor performance in HK guarantees that audiences will not have to suffer through any more simple-minded flag waving for the time being.

221. Devil Fetus

(1983; Lo Wei Films) ★: 5/10. *Moh toi* (Cantonese), *Mo tai* (Mandarin): "Devil Fetus." Music: Not Original; Writers: Yeung Chi, Tsang Man-wah, Lo Ching-yao; Producer: Hsu Li-hwa; Cinematographer-Director: Lau Hung-chuen. Cast: Ngai Dik, Lui Sau-ling, Liu Pui-pui. 2.35:1. VHS/Import VCD: Ocean Shores (Poor Subtitles). 88 minutes.

A silly but amusingly gruesome entry in the early '80s gross-out cycle, this opens with a young woman named Shu-ching purchasing a mysterious looking vase at an auction held during "The Festival of Hungry Ghosts." As she sleeps, a repulsive creature materializes and has sex with her. When her husband walks in on another one of these unnatural trysts, he smashes the vase, which emits a mist that causes his face to melt away. Horrified, he throws himself out a window to his death. Shu-ching is then inexplicably attacked by her cat and falls over a railing to her death. During the subsequent funeral ceremony, the presiding priest uses his powers to see inside the coffin and observes a creature exploding out of her stomach. He has the casket sealed and places magic talismans in the family's home to protect the deceased's relatives from evil spirits. A few years later, the charms are disturbed by a guest, with predictable results: A birthday cake becomes infested with worms, the dog goes berserk, one of the family members becomes possessed and eats the canine's intestines before raping and murdering the maid, etc.

Some of this film's more revolting moments have been truncated by HK censors, but if any of the characters behaved in a remotely logical fashion, the running time would be cut in half. Still, fans of Eastern horror will find much to their liking here. Many of the spfx are too ambitious for the budget but you have to admire the zeal with which they are staged. The pirated music track includes "La Petite Fille de la Mer," a composition from Vangelis' 1973 album, *L'Apocalypse Des Animeaux*, as well as a cue from Ennio Morricone's score for **The Thing** (1982). Director-cinematographer Lau would later go on to helm the estimable period fantasy **A Chinese Legend** (1991). Star Ngai Dik is often credited in English as "Eddie Chan."

222. Devil Hunters

(1989; Jia's Motion Picture Co.) ★: 6/10. *Lip mo kwan ying* (Cantonese), *Lie mo qun ying* (Mandarin): "Group of Heroes Hunting Demons." Cinematographer: Chan Chuen-lai; Music: Not Original; Writer: Chan Man-kuai; Producers: Lo Kar-po, Cheung Chung-lung; Action Director: Tsui Fat; Director: Wong Chun-yeung. Cast: Ray Lui Leung-wai (Chai Yuet), Moon Lee Choi-fung (Bing), Sibelle Hu Hui-chung (Madam Tong), Alex Man Chi-leung (Superintendent Tsang), Francis Ng Chun-yu (Chiu Shing), Michael Chan Wai-man (Yin Fu), Chan Pui-kei (Bing's Sister), Ken Lo Wai-kwong (Thug), Lau Siu-ming (Chai Yan). 1.85:1. VHS: Tai Seng (Dubbed only), World Video (Subtitled only). 90 minutes. Also known as **UltraForce 2**.

In spite of the sentiment conveyed by both the English and Chinese titles, this is not a horror movie. Instead, it's a standard but lively actioner concerning a power struggle between two rival ganglords. On the one side is Hon San, a leader whose hold over his men is far more tenuous than he suspects. On the other side is Chai Yan, who is under the protection of his tough son Yuet. When the enemies stage a clandestine meeting in an amusement park, the police intercede, leading to a pitched gun battle. The two bosses escape but Chai is later murdered by the minions of Chiu Shing, Hon's right hand man, who then frames his boss for the killing as part of his plan to take over the gang. However, Hon's daughter Bing has plans of her own and tricks Madam Tong, a tough female cop, into helping her rescue her father from Chiu's men. Subsequent events prompt Bing and Yuet to join forces in their fight against Chiu.

The action is a bit too undercranked, causing it to look sped up and unnatural, but the choreography is decent and the cast is much better than one usually finds in a modest enterprise like this. As a bonus, we get Francis Ng in one of his earliest villain roles, and one of the most bizarre torture scenes in memory (it involves locusts!). The final shot of the film (Moon Lee, Ray Lui, and Sibelle Hu jumping out of a building as it explodes) takes on extra significance when one learns that the three performers were burned by the blast. Untranslated (in the subtitled version) newspaper reports on the accident run under the credits.

Devil Melody *see* **Deadful** [*sic*] **Melody**

223. Devil's Box

(1994) ★: 3/10. *Gwai jin* (Cantonese), *Gui zhan* (Mandarin): "Ghost War." Cinematographer: Yeung Ping-tong; Art Directors: Yank Wong Yan-kwai, Honny Lam Sai-lok; Music: Not Original; Producer: Ringo Wong Lai-chuen; Writer-Director: Tommy Chin Ming-cheung. Cast: Simon Yam Tat-wah (Tang), Flora Chung Chor-yee (Anna), Newton Lai Hon-chi, Shirley Kwan Suet-lai, Edwin Tsui Yuk-wong. 1.85:1. Import LD/VCD: Ocean Shores. 83 minutes.

This low-budget horror thriller was released on video prior to its April 1994 HK theatrical run and looks to have been made at least a year or two before that date. While director Tang (Simon Yam, looking a bit like Tsui Hark here) is shooting a commercial at a desolate, decaying home, one of his technicians falls from the roof and is severely injured. Not long afterwards, his editor sees something strange in the dailies and then is found strangled and hung from the ceiling by strips of film. A truck driver tries to run Tang off the road but later tells him that he was actually trying to save Tang from a figure perched on the car's roof. Nightmares and inexplicable visions of death and horror follow, with Tang eventually able to deduce that they are somehow related to a mysterious old trunk found at the location. A doctor insists that they are the result of a brain tumor pressing on his nervous system, but the visions persist even after he has surgery. Has Tang gone mad?

Director Tommy Chin makes a concerted attempt to generate atmosphere and unease, but too much of the film is monotonous, ineffectual, and downright silly. A good portion of the music is stolen from the Tangerine Dream album **Logos—Live at the Dominion—London '82**; the cues in question would later be utilized in that group's soundtrack for Michael Mann's WWII horror thriller, **The Keep**. There is also music from John Williams' score for **Raiders of the Lost Ark**. Directors Allen Fong Yuk-ping and Alfred Cheung Kin-ting appear briefly.

Devil's Vendetta *see* **Devil's Vindata** [*sic*]

224. Devil's Vindata

[*sic*] (1991; High Grow Film Distributors/Rising Sun Films Co.) ★: 7/10. *Yiu moh do* (Cantonese), *Yao mo dao* (Mandarin): "Demon Road." Cinematographer: Derek Wan Man-kit; Art Directors: Cheung Hoi-ching, Fred Chan Chi-chung; Music: Jonathan Wong Bong-yin; Writers: James Fung Shui-hung, Shum Chi-leung, Tam Wai-shing, Cheng Man-wah; Action Director: Chin Yuet-sang; Producer-Director: Cheung Hoi-ching. Cast: Sharla Cheung Man (Mandy), Vivian Chow Wei-man (Tracy), Ngai Chun (Liu Chun), Stanley Fung Shui-fan (Principal You Tse-nam), Billy Lau Nam-kwong (Dawn, aka Tan Tin-kong), Mondi Yau Yuet-ching (Twiggy), Tai Po (Servant). 1.85:1. VHS: World Video. Import LD: Golden Flare. 96 minutes. Also known as **Devil's Vendetta**.

This low-budget period fantasy-comedy is bursting with action, comedy, and colorful special FX, which more than compensates for its weak storyline and ridiculous subtitles. Magical fairies Mandy and Tracy are part of an all-female sect called "The Micro-Wave Group"(!) who find themselves without a leader when Mandy's mentor passes away after fighting the powerful demoness, Twiggy(!). Unbeknownst to Tracy, she is Twiggy's daughter and can be used to open "The Door of Evil" if she is not married by a certain time on a certain date. She was betrothed to young Liu Chun, but the boy fled before the ceremony and joined up with the fairies' less-than-honorable male counterparts, "The Truth Division" (who spend all of their time coming up with boneheaded ways to peep on the women). With time running out on the appointed day, Liu and Tracy must quickly make love, while the two sects combine their skills to keep Twiggy at bay.

Among the many highlights: a giant cockroach that transforms into a beautiful woman, hopping kiddie vampires, a flying disembodied hand, Billy Lau transforming himself into a talking bar of soap (complete with glasses!), a "vampire competition," and all manner of spells and supernatural combat. Highly recommended to genre aficionados!

225. Devil's Woman

(1996; Extra Film) ★: 5/10. *Naam yeung dai yat cheh gong* (Cantonese), *Nan yang di yi xie jiang* (Mandarin): "South Seas First Evil Spell." Cinematographer: Paul Yip Pak-ying; Art Director: Ring Law Chi-keung; Music: Not Original; Writers: Philip Cheng Chung-tai, Ring Law Chi-keung; Producers: Eddie Wong Hon-wah, Otto Chan Ah-to; Action Director: Ng Cheung-pang; Director: Otto Chan Ah-to. Cast: Elvis Tsui Kam-kong (Lam Kwok-kong), Marianne Chan Miu-ying (Dr. Mary Fu Wai-lun), Cammy Choi Mei-lan (May), Ben Ng Ngai-cheung (Tsui Kam-lung), Ivy Leung Si-man (Cheung Si-man), Helena Law Lan (Si-man's Grandmother), Chan Kwok-bong (SDU Officer Bong). 1.85:1. VHS: Tai Seng. Import LD/VCD: Universe. 94 minutes.

A follow-up of sorts to **The Eternal Evil of Asia**, this Category III cheapie is not as amusingly demented but still offers plenty of exploitation elements to hold one's attention. Following a disastrous rescue mission (during which a pregnant woman was shot in the back at such close range that her fetus blasted out and hit him), SDU officer Lam begins seeing sexy psychiatrist Dr. Mary Fu in order to deal with the nightmarish visions he has been experiencing. Meanwhile, in a desperate quest for fame, struggling actress May allows herself to become the murderous puppet of an evil sorcerer (Ben Ng, essentially reprising his role from the earlier film) who is able to control her through a weird spider venom potion he introduces into her system. After May gruesomely dispatches a doctor and his nurse, Lam and his assistant, Si-man, are assigned to investigate. Things get hairy when the wizard places a sex curse on Lam, leaving him in a perpetual state of heat and wanting to attack everything female in sight. With information provided by Si-man's spiritually enlightened grandmother, Lam is able to deduce that Mary is the next victim on the killer's list. Her rare birth date of

February 29 corresponds with that of the sorcerer's late wife, and the necromancer plans on introducing her soul into Mary's body.

Along the way we are treated to such sights as death by poisoned fingernails, a rampaging killer cat (which is later stuffed into a microwave with predictably explosive results), flesh-eating zombies pulling victims down into the bowels of Hell, a group of benevolent ghost children (who play with a red ball, shown bouncing down a staircase *á la* Mario Bava's **Kill, Baby ... Kill!**), and a decent serving of softcore eroticism.

226. Devoted to You

(1986; D & B Films Co.) ★: 5/10. *Chi sam dik ngoh* (Cantonese), *Chi xin de wo* (Mandarin): "Infatuated Me." Cinematographer: Bob Thompson; Art Director: Yank Wong Yan-kwai; Music: Nonoy O'Campo; Producer: Linda Kuk Mei-lai; Writer-Director: Clifton Ko Chi-sum. Cast: Jacky Cheung Hok-yau (Jacky), Loletta Lee Lai-chun (Loletta Lee), May Lo Mei-mei (May), Michael Wong Mantak (Mike), Ku Feng (Loletta's Father), Lau Siu-ming (May's Father), Yip Wingcho (School Official), Lam Chung (Cop), Bill Tung Biu (TV Racing Commentator), Clifton Ko Chi-sum (Scared Guy at Beach). 1.85:1. VHS: Tai Seng. Import VCD: Mega Star. 87 minutes.

High school friends Loletta (a bad girl from the wrong side of the tracks) and May (a spoiled rich girl) experience love in this mild teen drama. Loletta falls for biker Mike (a triad who is in trouble with his boss), while May has eyes for Canadian university student Jacky (who will be returning back home to Toronto at the end of his vacation). Neither girl respects her parents, and a lack of guidance causes the pair to make errors in judgment that they must learn from.

Director Clifton Ko graduated from Cinema City's lightweight teen pics like **Happy Ghost I & II** to this more serious effort which, while including some situational comedy, also tackles weightier topics like irresponsible parenting, sex, and murder. The dramatic situations depicted, however, are overly familiar, and Ko brings nothing new to them. It is interesting to see Jacky Cheung and May Lo together; the pair became an item offscreen as well, and later married.

227. The Diary of a Big Man

(1988; Cinema City Co./Film Workshop) ★: 8/10. *Daai jeung foo yat gei* (Cantonese), *Da zhang fu ri zi* (Mandarin): "Big Husband's Diary." Cinematographer: Li Hsin-yeh; Art Director: Fong Ying; Music: James Wong Jim, Romeo Diaz; Writers: Ng Man-fai, Philip Cheng Chung-tai; Producer: Tsui Hark; Director: Chor Yuen. Cast: Chow Yun-fat (Chow Ting-fat), Joey Wang Tsu-hsien (Joey), Sally Yeh Chian-wen (Sally), Waise Lee Chi-hung (Chi-hung), Carrie Ng Kar-lai (Ka-lai), Kent Cheng Chuk-see (Inspector Cheng), David Wu Tai-wai (Cheng's Assistant), Shing Fui-on (Darkie), Tai Po (Piggy). Dolby Digital (DVD only). 1.85:1. VHS: Tai Seng. Import LD: Golden Cinema City. Import VCD: Mei Ah. Import DVD: Universe. 90 minutes.

This engagingly silly effort is reminiscent of the Hollywood screwball comedies from the 1930s, though its main inspiration appears to have been Blake Edwards' 1984 film **Micki and Maude**. Stockbroker Chow Ting-fat has a real problem: He's in love with boutique owner Joey *and* stewardess Sally and he can't marry them both ... or can he? In fact, he does just that, keeping each woman in the dark about the other. Although it is rough going at first, Ting-fat eventually gets his bed-hopping down to a science, with a little help from his loyal buddy, Chi-hung. However, things almost fall apart when both women end up in the same place one day. The arrival of two different women claiming to be Chow Ting-fat's wife arouses the suspicions of humorless Inspector Cheng, who starts snooping around and creating even more troubles for the increasingly harried bigamist. The close calls eventually start happening several times a day, and Ting-fat must go to increasingly desperate (and amusing) lengths to keep up the ruse. Eventually, the two women discover the truth and join forces to get even.

The storyline is incredibly contrived by design and the absurd coincidences add greatly to the fun. A highly animated Chow Yun-fat is at his charismatic best here as the slightly geeky protagonist and he has a great deal of infectious fun with this rather absurd persona. The rest of the cast provides excellent comic support, and there's even a fun music video-style number ("Oh, Very Nice!") that appears out of nowhere! Composer James Wong Jim has a cameo.

228. Die Harder

(1995; Hang Sing Production Co.) ★: 1/10. *Wong Daai Sin woo sue* (Cantonese), *Huang Da Xian wu shu* (Mandarin): "Wong Dai Sin Black Rat" or "Huang Da Xian Black Rat." Cinematographer: Pang Chun-wai; Music: Chow Kam-cheung; Writer: Lee Man-choi; Producers: Eddie Wong Hon-wah, Tong Chien-wah; Action Director: Chow Yun-kin; Art Director-Director: Lam Yee-hung. Cast: Lily Chung Suk-wai (Sonia Chan), Ben Ng Ngai-cheung (Fu Yung-lin), Linda Cheung Lan-ying (Mainland Officer), Cheung Kwok-leung, Wong Wan-choi. 1.85:1. VHS: Tai Seng. Import LD/VCD: Fitto Mobile. 90 minutes.

This cheap, bottom-of-the-barrel actioner concerns Chien and Liang, a couple of small-timers who are framed for murder by the corrupt Officer Fu. After Fu reneges on his promise to give them money and orders men to kill them, Chien and Liang flee to the Mainland. Fu is arrested by ICAC (the HK police department's Internal Affairs division) but is rescued by his cronies and takes great pleasure in personally executing the arresting officers. Sonia Chan, policewoman and wife of one of the slain men, campaigns for the department to allow her to pursue Fu into China. When (for obvious reasons) she is refused, Sonia goes anyway and gets a job as the in-house singer at a Karaoke bar run by Fu. While she plans her revenge, Chien and Liang are devising their own way of dealing with Fu. When Sonia rescues the men following a knife fight, they decide to work together toward their common goal.

Incompetent on every level, this is one of those films that all but dares you to keep watching. In an apparent attempt to reach the magic 90 minute mark, scenes are allowed to drag on endlessly, and the action choreography is the worst in memory (the ICAC officers and Fu's men fire at each other from near point blank range and no one gets hit!). Even taking the poor translation into account, the scripting is beyond bad. Typical example: When Chien reports to Liang that Fu has arrived in China, he asks if his friend still remembers the man. Let's see ... Fu was the one who framed them, tried to have them killed, and forced them to flee their homeland *and* leave their loved ones behind. What do you know? Liang still remembers him. Incidentally, Wong Dai Sin is a district in Hong Kong.

229. Dirty Ho

(1979; Shaw Brothers) ★: 8/10. *Laan tau Ho* (Cantonese), *Lan tou He* (Mandarin): "Rotten Head Ho." Cinematographers: Arthur Wong Ngok-tai, Au Chihchun; Art Director: Johnson Tsao; Music: Not Original; Writer: Ngai Hong; Producer: Mona Fong Yat-wah; Action Director-Director: Lau Kar-leung. Cast: Gordon Lau Far-fai (Wang Ching-chin), Wong Yue (Ho Qi), Lo Lieh (General Liang), Kara Hui Ying-hung (Choi Hung), Johnny Wang Lung-wei (Fan Chin-kong), Hsiao Hou (Hsia Liu), Peter

Chan Lung (Bitter Face). 2.35:1. No authorized domestic video release. 103 minutes.

Wang Ching-chin, a kung fu master and The 11th Prince, amuses himself by constantly foiling hapless conman Ho Chi, while keeping his real identity a secret from his victim. After making it look like Ho has been defeated in combat by a club girl (and poisoned by her to boot), Wang blackmails Ho into becoming his disciple. Aware that someone wants to see him dead, before he can reach the palace, The Prince brings the swindler along with him because he knows that, even though the lad is not an expert fighter, Ho could still save his life someday. Badly injured by an assassin, Wang reveals to Ho that he does not really crave the throne, but that has not stopped murderous plots from being hatched among some of his brothers. In order to fully be able to protect Wang, Ho asks that The Prince help him improve his kung fu so that the two of them will be able to stave off future attackers and arrive at the palace in time for the announcement of the heir.

One of Lau Kar-leung's most entertaining Shaw Brothers productions, **Dirty Ho** boasts martial arts choreography every bit as expert as one would expect from the director. However, it also possesses a wry sense of humor and marvellous characters. Highlights include: Gordon Lau secretly manipulating Kara Hui's actions in order to make her look like a kung fu expert; Lau's two bouts of "clandestine kung fu" (first with Johnny Wang while the pair pretend to taste wine, and later with an antiques collector who is also under orders to kill him); and a terrific scene where Lau and Wong Yue are attacked by archers and spearmen while crossing through the desolate area between a village and the typhoon wall built to shelter the people from the area's intense wind. The sequence involving a gang of fey, masochistic kung fu fighters was a bad idea, however. Character names above are from the dubbed version.

230. Dr. Lamb

(1992; Heroes United Films/Grand River Film) ★: 3/10. *Go yeung yi sang* (Cantonese), *Gao yang yi sheng* (Mandarin): "Lamb Doctor." Cinematographer: Tony Miu Kin-fai; Art Director: Horace Ma Kwong-wing; Music: Jonathan Wong Bong-yin; Writer: Law Kam-fai; Producer-Director: Danny Lee Sau-yin. Cast: Simon Yam Tat-wah (Lam Gor-yu), Danny Lee Sau-yin (Lee), Kent Cheng Chuk-see (Bing), Lau Siu-ming (Lam's Father), Emily Kwan Bo-wai (Female Cop), Parkman Wong Pak-man (Buffalo Hung), Eric Kei Kar-fat (Eric). 1.85:1. VHS: Tai Seng. Import LD/VCD: Star Entertainment (No Subtitles). 88 minutes.

One of the most infamous entries in the early '90s "True Crime" cycle, **Dr. Lamb** established the formula for this subgenre, but it is such a dreary and predictable film that it will hold little interest for viewers who are not merely looking for tawdry sex, violence, and gore. Based on horrors committed by real-life serial killer Lam Guo-wen (whom star Simon Yam had previously played in a TV miniseries), the film opens with the troubled childhood of its subject, Lam Gor-yu, before switching to the present day. When eerie photos of a naked (and seemingly dead) woman are submitted to a photo shop for developing, the manager alerts police. They apprehend Lam, who refuses to talk, in spite of extensive beatings. He confesses only after the police show his family some obscene photos he took of his sister's little girl. The remaining two thirds of the film depict Lam's crimes, committed while he was working nights as a taxi driver.

Put together with some style, and possessing a few effective instances of black humor, **Dr. Lamb** nonetheless emerges as an unpleasantly exploitative and inconsequential film. It does raise an interesting moral dilemma for the viewer, in that the fascistic measures employed by the police (the nominal "heroes" here) to get suspects to talk (which would become a regular facet of Danny Lee's increasingly trashy *oeuvre*) are almost as reprehensible as the villain's crimes. However, like every other film that followed in this cycle, there is no suspense, no genuine insight, and, consequently, no point. Several instances of foul language have been bleeped from the Cantonese soundtrack, and the Star VCD is also missing much of the gore.

231. Doctor Mack

(1995; United Filmmakers Organization) ★: 7/10. *Lau man yi sang* (Cantonese), *Liu mang yi sheng* (Mandarin): "Tramp Doctor." Cinematographer: Bill Wong Chung-bo; Art Director: James Cheung Ying-wah; Music: Pau Yee-ching; Writer-Producer-Director: Lee Chi-ngai. Cast: Tony Leung Chiu-wai (Dr. Lau Mack), Lau Ching-wan (Chiu), Andy Hui Chi-on (Dr. Sam So), Alex To Tak-wai (Dr. Roger Jaw), Christy Chung Lai-tai (Jamie), Eileen Tung Oi-ling (Lok Mei), Gigi Leung Wing-kei (May), Hilary Tsui Ho-ying (Zin), Richard Ng Yiu-hon (Professor Bao), Jerry Lam Hiu-fung (Tong Ching), Farini Cheung Yui-ling (Nurse), Law Kar-ying (Street Preacher), Jordan Chan Siu-chun (The Singer), Wong Hei (Triad), Lawrence Ng Kai-wah (K.T.). 1.85:1. VHS: Tai Seng. Import LD/VCD/DVD: Fitto Mobile. 98 minutes. Also known as **Mack the Knife**.

Dr. Lau Mack is not your average HK physician. In fact, he is a genius, even though his practice is located in the red light district and he got his medical degree in a small African country. Mack's former associate, Dr. Roger Jaw, is considered to be the top surgeon in HK and a candidate for chairman of the board at his hospital. He actually deserves neither honor, being an inferior surgeon to Mack. In fact, he wouldn't even be employed there if Mack had not taken responsibility for a medication mistake Roger made in medical school. His prospects dashed as a result, Mack had to get his degree overseas. When a robber is shot in the head near his modest clinic, Mack provides Roger with advice on a tricky surgery case. The new technique is a success, but Roger takes the credit and acclaim that come his way afterwards. This prompts one of his students, So, to leave the hospital and assist Mack in the clinic. When Mack saves a boy scout, shot during an assassination attempt, Roger takes credit for that too. As a result, the latter's girlfriend, Jamie, begins to take a serious interest in Mack. In concurrent storylines, Mack helps his mentor (who has gotten rather dotty and frail in his old age) get his thesis published; ragged undercover cop Chiu takes an interest in the welfare of beautiful prostitute Lok Mei; and Sam starts a relationship with terminal cancer patient Zin (whose fate reminds Mack of the way in which his wife died).

Based on a Japanese *manga*, the film wraps up all of its story threads just a little too neatly, and there are some racist jokes directed at black people that are jarringly inappropriate. That said, the film remains an appealingly low-key affair (from both a dramatic and comedic standpoint) peopled by performers who manage to make their colorful characters both intriguing and plausible. The one exception is Alex To's Roger; the viewer is never inclined to believe that he could attain the heights he reaches in the profession and get away with the deceptions he perpetrates for as long as the story would have us believe. Director Lee's next film, the excellent **Lost and Found**, is similar in some ways to this effort but manages to be more genuine and poignant. If you like that film, chances are you will respond favorably to this one as well.

232. Doctor Vampire

(1990; Golden Harvest/Paragon Films) ★: 7/10. *Geung see yee saang* (Cantonese), *Jiang shi yi sheng* (Mandarin): "Dr.

Stiff Corpse." Cinematographer: James Yeung Jim; Art Director: Oliver Wong Yui-man; Music: Tsui Yat-kan; Producer: Chua Lam; Action Directors: Yuen Mo, Jamie Luk Kim-ming; Writer-Director: Jamie Luk Kim-ming. Cast: Bowie Lam Bo-yee (Chiang Ta-tsung), Ellen Chan Ar-lun (Alice), Sheila Chan Sak-lan (May Chen), Crystal Kwok Kam-yan (Joy), David Wu Tai-wai (Doctor), Peter Kjaer (Vampire Master), Shing Fui-on (Ta), James Wong Jim (The Assistant Director). 1.85:1. VHS: Tai Seng. Import LD/VCD: Mei Ah. 98 minutes.

In contrast to most HK vampire films, this wonderfully wacky comedy tackles *Western* horror, with a dash of traditional genre tenets and a plethora of sexual gags thrown in for good measure. While on business in the UK, the virginal Dr. Chiang is seduced by a gorgeous Chinese girl named Alice. Upon returning home to HK, Chiang begins to display an aversion to sunlight and food, while taking a fancy to capes and frilly dress shirts. When he starts drooling uncontrollably during operations, the doctor comes to the realization that his condition can no longer be hidden. As the audience already knows, Alice is a vampire and she has been ordered to bring Chiang back so that her caucasian master can gorge himself on the doc's succulent blood. However, she now loves Chiang and divulges that he can be cured as long as he doesn't drink any blood. Unfortunately, Chiang's girlfriend slips him a love potion containing some of her blood, causing him to become a full-fledged bloodsucker. Deciding to make the best of the situation, Chiang soon has big trouble on his hands when the vampire master arrives from England to finish the job himself.

Filled with martial arts-style action and irreverent parody, **Doctor Vampire** presents some amusing variations on standard horror imagery: Bloody cotton balls act as tea bags in a vampiric beverage, an upended wardrobe doubles as a makeshift coffin, an operating theater's overhead light provides a makeshift cross, etc. The climax starts off inside the hospital and finishes at a Peking Opera performance, where the heroes get a little otherworldly assistance from the powerful Chinese god, General Kwan. A definite must-see for students of HK horror-comedy and those looking for a good introduction to the genre. Actor/director David Wu plays one of Chiang's bumbling co-workers.

233. Dr. Wai in the Scripture with No Words

(1996; Win's Entertainment/Eastern Production) ★: 4/10. *Mo him wong* (Cantonese), *Mao xian wang* (Mandarin): "King of Adventurers." Cinematographer: Tom Lau Moon-tong; Art Director: Jason Mok Siu-kei; Music: Frankie Chan Fan-kei; Writers: Sandy Shaw, Roy Szeto Cheuk-hon, Lam Wai-lun; Producers: Charles Heung Wah-keung, Alex Wong Ching-ping; Action Directors: Ching Siu-tung, Ma Yuk-shing; Director: Ching Siu-tung. Cast: Jet Li Lianjie (Chow Si-kit), Rosamund Kwan Chi-lam (Monica Kwan/Cammy), Takeshi Kaneshiro (Shing), Charlie Yeung Choi-nei (Yvonne), Law Kar-ying (Headmaster), Ngai Sing (The Movie Star/Hung Sing), Billy Chow Bei-lee (Chan/Japanese Embassy Guard). Dolby Digital. 2.35:1. VHS/LD: World Video. Import LD/VCD/DVD: Mei Ah. 90 minutes.

An overstuffed and tiresome adventure thriller, this is a major disappointment from director Ching Siu-tung, who is capable of so much better. Nerdy writer Chow Si-kit's problems with his wife Monica are seriously hindering his output. His "King of Adventurers" series (in which he envisions himself as the title character) is set in 1930s China and concerns a fearless, Indiana Jones-style hero who uses his wits and martial arts skills to battle Japanese villains. Desperate to help their boss meet his deadline, Chow's assistants, Shing and Yvonne, decide to concoct a story for him, and it is presented to the viewer with all of the characters played by people in the author's life. The Chinese government enlists Chow the hero to steal a letter from the Japanese embassy, but Chow the author dislikes the fact that Cammy, the heroine of the piece, reminds him of his wife. He re-writes the premise, making Cammy one of the antagonists, but Shing and Yvonne also add their own input. As the story's plot continues to unfold, Chow and Shing search for a magical Pandora's Box (also sought by the Japanese and the malevolent Salt Gang) which can be used to foretell the future. It also can inflict great harm upon those who are foolish enough to open it without the necessary precautions, as Salt Gang leader Hung Sing finds out. At this point, Monica takes over the writing and the story takes yet another new turn, pointing the protagonists toward the location of the magical scripture needed to safely utilize the powers of the box.

Dr. Wai was conceived to be an epic and certainly has the look of one: The production values are lavish, the art direction is detailed and consistently eye-catching, the costumes are superb, and the widescreen cinematography is well-composed. Alas, the action sequences are often sped-up or blandly staged, the ever-evolving storyline incorporates too many characters and conflicts, the humorous asides are weak, and the characters are either obnoxious or completely uninteresting. Thus, one is left with a film that is all surface, making it difficult to care about anything other than the next opulent set or beautiful vista. An alternate cut of the film exists which deletes all of the contemporary sequences and adds additional ones set in the past. That version was not available for preview but sounds like it might be a bit more satisfying.

234. Doctor's Heart

(1990; Golden Harvest/Bo Ho Films/David Lam Films/Paragon Films) ★: 3/10. *Gau ming suen yin* (Cantonese), *Jiu ming xuen yan* (Mandarin): "Save Life Declaration." Cinematographer: Lau Hung-chuen; Art Director: Bill Lui Cho-hung; Music: Lo Tai-yau, Fa Pei-on; Writers: Joe Ma Wai-ho, James Yuen Sai-sang; Producer: Clifton Ko Chi-sum; Director: David Lam Tak-luk. Cast: Mark Cheng Ho-nam (Wong Man-tsun), Simon Yam Tat-wah (Lawrence Chu), Michelle Lee Kar-yan (Anita Yeung), Lowell Lo Kwun-ting (Dr. Ngau, aka Suckling), Amy Yip Chi-mei (May), Bill Tung Biu (Man-tsun's Father), Clifton Ko Chi-sum (Dr. Chan). 1.85:1. VHS: Tai Seng. Import LD/VCD: Universe. 90 minutes.

Dedicated intern Wong Man-tsun is not above rocking the boat at his hospital, an attitude that immediately makes him an enemy of hospital administrator Dr. Chu (cartoonishly overplayed by Simon Yam), who proceeds to flunk him on his medical exam. Not wanting to disappoint his father (who was a physician back when they lived in China), Man-tsun pretends to be a doctor while still working as an intern. He soon falls for beautiful social worker Anita Yeung, not realizing that she is Chu's girlfriend. When a drunken Man-tsun humiliates Chu at a Christmas Party, he is sent down to the morgue, where he manages to revive a man everyone thought was dead. Chu proceeds to take credit for the miracle, prompting Anita to refuse his subsequent marriage proposal. However, she has a brain tumor and requires a complicated, emergency operation and Chu (the only qualified surgeon) refuses to help, setting up the ultimate test of Man-tsun's medical skills.

Produced back in the days when Mark Cheng was cast as something other than a cop, gangster, or psychopath, this inane, by-the-numbers drama strains credibility at every turn and will try the patience of anyone who has ever sat through more than two episodes of **Marcus Welby M.D.** Still, it is hard to completely hate any movie that casts acclaimed martial arts novelist Ngai Hong as a cantankerous, besotted coroner named *Dr. Lam!*

235. Dong Cheng Xi Jiu

(1993; Scholar Films/Jet Tone Productions) ★: 7/10. *Se diu ying hung ji dung sing sai jau* (Cantonese), *She diao ying xiong zhi dong cheng xi jiu* (Mandarin): "The Eagle Shooting Heroes: East Meets West." Cinematographer: Peter Pau Tak-hei; Art Directors: Alfred Yau Wai-ming, William Cheung Suk-ping; Music: James Wong Jim; Producer: Tsai Mui-ho; Action Director: Sammo Hung Kam-po; Writer-Director: Jeff Lau Chun-wai. Cast: Leslie Cheung Kwok-wing (Wang), Tony Leung Chiu-wai (O Yang-fon), Tony Leung Kar-fai (Dwan), Jacky Cheung Hok-yau (Beggar), Brigitte Lin Ching-hsia (The Third Princess), Joey Wang Tsu-hsien (Wang's Cousin), Maggie Cheung Man-yuk (The Imperial Master), Carina Lau Kar-ling (Chou Po-ting), Veronica Yip Yuk-hing (The Queen), Kenny Bee (Wang Chon-yang). 1.85:1. VHS: World Video. Import LD/VCD/DVD: Mei Ah. 113 minutes. Also known as **The Eagle Shooting Heroes**.

In the midst of shooting his troubled period epic **Ashes of Time**, Wong Kar-wai also served as executive producer for this frenzied parody, which is based on the same source novel. It also features much of the same cast and even beat *Ashes* into theaters! The nominal plot revolves around betrayal and intrigue in an ancient kingdom perpetrated by a duo of would-be throne usurpers (Tony Leung Chiu-wai and Veronica Yip), but it's really just an excuse to let the all-star cast run wild. Standouts include Brigitte Lin as an addle-brained princess whose mastery of supernatural kung fu is very much in doubt; Tony Leung Kar-fai as a would-be angel who ends up as a disembodied flying head (a gag recycled from director Jeff Lau's **Operation Pink Squad II**); Carina Lau in drag as a middle-aged man; and Kenny Bee as a venerated *sifu* who suffers the decidedly dishonorable fate of having a shoe become impaled in his head ("It's not a shoe! It's a projectile!"). The comedic highlight is an extended duel between Tony Leung Chiu-wai and Jacky Cheung which pokes fun at the various animal form styles of martial arts, with such ridiculous stances as "Blue Dragon Drinking Water" and "Toad Has a Pee Pee." Newcomers to HK cinema will find the proceedings all but incomprehensible but seasoned viewers will be charmed by both the cast and the endearingly nonsensical goings-on, which feature everything from super accelerated kung fu battles to musical numbers! Some prints run about 20 minutes shorter and feature more coherent subtitles than are found on the HK video versions.

236. Don't Fool Me!

(1991) ★: 3/10. *Chung Waan ying hung* (Cantonese), *Zhong Huan ying xiong* (Mandarin): "Hero of Central" (Central is a district in HK). Cinematographer: Yu Kwok-bing; Art Director: Ho Chi-hang; Music: Shui Ching-mai; Writers: Lam Chiu-wing, Chung Kai-cheung; Action Director: Lam Moon-wah; Producer: Liu Kin-fat; Director: Taylor Wong Tai-loi. Cast: Andy Lau Tak-wah ("Hero" Hwa), Tony Leung Chiu-wai (Chiang Ho-chie), Teresa Mo Shun-kwan (Miss Mui), Fennie Yuen Kit-ying (Fanny), Michael Chan Wai-man (Fanny's Father), Shing Fui-on (Mad Bo), Charine Chan Kar-ling (Margaret), Gabriel Wong Yat-san (Nerd in Bar), Anthony Wong Chau-sang (The Nerd's Brother), Yung Sai-kit (Yung), Tien Feng (Yip Chi-mei), Lee Hoi-sang (Big Mouth). 1.85:1. VHS: Tai Seng. 98 minutes.

Insurance broker Chiang Ho-chie is diagnosed with a brain tumor his doctor cannot remove and told he only has a short time before it bursts and kills him. While mourning his bad fortune, Ho-chie runs into Hwa, an old school buddy turned low-level gangster. Against his better judgment, Ho-chie gets Hwa a job at his company, and the latter manages to stave off a quick dismissal by wooing his spinsterish boss. Looking for excitement, Ho-chie gets mixed up with motorcycle-riding tough girl Fanny, and gradually both he and Hwa settle comfortably into each other's worlds and fall in love. However, potentially fatal trouble arises when Ho-chie decides to leave Fanny before he dies in order to spare her the grief. His gesture is, naturally, misunderstood, prompting the girl's triad boss father to send his men after Ho-chie. There is no shortage of chases and mayhem but precious few laughs to be had in this tiresome, formulaic misfire. What a waste of talent!

237. Don't Give a Damn

(1995; Bojon Films Company/Long Shong Pictures/Rambo Films) ★: 4/10. *Mo min bei* (Cantonese), *Mou mian bei* (Mandarin): "No Face to Give." Cinematographer: Lau Hung-chuen; Music: Frankie Chan Fan-kei; Writers: Roy Szeto Cheuk-hon, Kwok Wai-chung, Brian Chung Wai-hung; Action Directors: Sammo Hung Stuntmen Association, Chin Kar-lok, Yuen Mo, Cho Wing; Producer-Director: Sammo Hung Kam-po. Cast: Sammo Hung Kam-po (Pierre Lau), Yuen Biao (Wong Yuk-man), Eileen Tung Oi-ling (Anna), Takeshi Kaneshiro (Tang Chuen-shek), Kathy Chow Hoi-mei (Yau-ching), Annabelle Lau Hiu-tung (May), Kelvin Wong Siu (Yamamoto), Ngai Sing (Yamamoto's Man), Robert Samuels (Bobby), Blackie Ko Shou-liang (Stupid Robber), Yip Wing-cho (Officer Yip), Nat Chan Pak-cheung (Deranged Cop), Cheung Kwok-keung (Superman), Chin Siu-ho (Spiderman), Billy Lau Nam-kwong (Fainting Cop), Richard Ng Yiu-hon (Old Bluffer on Bus), Wu Ma (Hawker), Melvin Wong Kam-sun (Wong's Superior), Yvonne Yung Hung (Sun Flower), Lau Kar-wing (Statement Cop), Leung Kar-yan (No-Nonsense Cop), Miu Kiu-wai (Cop), Peter Chan Lung (Rapist), Eddie Maher (Thug). 1.85:1. VHS: World Video. Import LD/VCD: Universe. 95 minutes.

For three quarters of its length, this is a pleasing action comedy, but the final portion contains a sequence that is so misguided and offensive it cannot be forgiven. Veteran cop Pierre finds himself teamed up with by-the-book yuppie Tang; and, since this is a formula buddy cop picture, the two have totally opposing views on how to solve cases. Gung ho customs officer Wong Yuk-man causes all kinds of trouble for Pierre but, when thugs employed by Japanese drug dealers bomb the police station, the two finally put their differences aside and join forces with Tang to bring the felons to justice.

Up to this point, **Don't Give a Damn** is a diverting effort that is made even more enjoyable by a barrage of cameos from Sammo Hung's industry buddies. However, the film goes completely off the rails when Yuen Biao and Takeshi Kaneshiro don blackface in order to fool some black criminals ... and succeed! The bit is so appallingly racist, it quickly evaporates all of the good will the film has built up to that point. HK cinema depicts black characters in a negative light far more often than not, but this is one of the worst examples yet—a shame as the big setpiece (criminals disguised as SDU officers break into the police station to steal confiscated narcotics) is impressively staged, and there is some excellent fighting during the finale.

Don't Play with Fire *see* **Dangerous Encounter—1st Kind**

238. Don't Stop My Crazy Love for You

(1993; Golden Power Productions) ★: 2/10. *Dong bat chu dik fung ching* (Cantonese), *Dang bu zhu de feng qing* (Mandarin): "The Crazy Love That Can't Be Blocked." Cinematographer: Peter Ngor Chi-kwan; Art Director: Luk Chi-fung; Music: Mak Chun-hung; Writers: Nam Yin, Wong Wan-choi, Chau Ting; Producers: Nam Yin, Lam Chung-kwok; Director: Hong Wai-tat. Cast: Simon Yam

Tat-wah (Fred Suen), Yvonne Yung Hung (Kitty Wong), Vincent Wan Yeung-ming (Chiu), Michael Wong Man-tak (Charlie Fok), Ha Ping (Miss Ho). 1.85:1. VHS: Tai Seng (Poor Subtitles). Import LD/VCD/DVD: Ocean Shores (Poor Subtitles). 92 minutes. Also known as **Crazy Love for You**.

This leering psycho thriller/rape fantasy offers nothing new and is a weak undertaking, even by the less than stringent standards of Category III fare. Simon Yam gives his usual mannered and twitchy performance as computer programmer Fred Suen, who is dangerously obsessed with popular TV reporter Kitty Wong. He starts off by peeping on her and beating some thugs who heckled Kitty during an interview. He then progresses on to lewd phone calls, illegal entry, and vandalism. The latter action prompts the woman's boyfriend, Charlie, to enlist someone to design an electronic alarm system to protect her. That someone is, of course, Fred, and while his set-up looks impressive, it is merely a front and no impediment to him. When Kitty throws a costume party to announce her engagement to Charlie, Fred attends and uses the opportunity to eliminate the "competition." Fed up, Kitty invites the killer to her home, planning on finishing him herself but he doesn't oblige. With the help of a technician from the station, Kitty is able to deduce the identity of her tormentor and lures him once again. The climax of their eventual meeting is a much too foregone conclusion.

239. Downtown Torpedoes

(1997; Golden Harvest/Paragon Films) ★: 7/10. *San tau dip ying* (Cantonese), *Shen tou die ying* (Mandarin): "Godly Thief Spy Shadow." Cinematographer: Cheung Man-bo; Art Director: Eddie Ma Poon-chiu; Music: Peter Kam Pui-tat; Writer: Poon Yuen-leung; Producer: Chan Shek-hong; Action Director: Stephen Tung Wai; Director: Teddy Chan Tak-sum. Cast: Takeshi Kaneshiro (Jackal), Jordan Chan Siu-chun (Cash), Charlie Yeung Choi-nei (Sam), Ken Wong Hap-hei (Titan), Theresa Lee Yee-hung (Phoenix), Alex Fong Chung-sun (Stanley Wong). Dolby Stereo. 1.85:1. VHS: Mecapro. Import LD/VCD/DVD: Mei Ah. 89 minutes.

The English title is a real head-scratcher, but this high-tech espionage thriller more than makes up for in excitement what it lacks in credibility. Jackal, Cash, Sam, and Titan, leading members of ATM (Available Tactical Mercenaries), are blackmailed by the HK government to perform a high tech raid on MI5 headquarters. Their objective: steal some virtually flawless US currency printing plates which the British agency has taken from a criminal element in Iran and apparently plan to make use of themselves. Hooking up with computer whiz Phoenix, the team pulls off the job without a hitch. However, the briefcase carrying the evidence the government is holding over their heads also houses a bomb, and one of the team is killed in the subsequent blast. The remaining members must determine how they can retrieve the plates in order to clear their names. To reveal more would compromise some enjoyable twists but, suffice to say, the climax unfolds in Budapest, with an exciting chase through some beautiful locales.

This variation on **Mission Impossible** (with a little James Bond thrown in for good measure) quite easily eclipses its tiresome American model. Aside from some shoddy digital FX work, the film is first-rate on a technical level, with tight pacing and well-choreographed and edited action that is never jumbled and confusing (like so many recent Hollywood pictures). The leads do a fine job, though (with the exception of Theresa Lee's super hacker) the characters could have benefitted from some more personality. Regardless, this is first rate escapist entertainment that more than fulfils its goals. **Downtown Torpedoes** earned an unfortunate footnote in HK film history when a crew member was killed by a piece of shrapnel during an on-set explosion. The production company had not received the proper clearance in advance to perform this particular pyrotechnic effect, and subsequent news reports revealed that this type of safety violation was actually commonplace in the industry and could result in far more accidents of this sort. Additionally, this turned out to be the last film for noted art director Eddie Ma (**The Bride with White Hair, The Phantom Lover**), who succumbed to cancer at a young age.

240. Dragon Chronicles: The Maidens of Heavenly Mountain

(1994; Win's Movie Production/Golden Harvest) ★: 7/10. *San tin lung baat biu chi tin saan tung liu* (Cantonese), *Xin tian long ba bu zhi tian shan tong lao* (Mandarin): "New Eight Section Sky Dragon: The Ancient Virgin of Heavenly Mountain." Cinematographer: Poon Hang-sang; Art Director: Oliver Wong Yui-man; Music: Violet Lam Man-yee; Writer: Charcoal Cheung Tan; Producer: Jimmy Heung Wah-sing; Action Director: Tony Poon Kin-kwan; Director: Andy Chin Wing-keung. Cast: Brigitte Lin Ching-hsia (Li Chou-shui/Li Chong-hoi), Gong Li (Mo Han-wen), Sharla Cheung Man (Purple), Frankie Lam Man-lung (Hui-chok), Norman Tsui Siu-keung (Ting Chun-chou), Liu Kai-chi (Sing Hoi), James Pak Chin-shek (Tai Hung). 1.85:1. Dolby Stereo, Dolby Digital (DVD only). VHS: Tai Seng. Import LD/VCD/DVD: Mei Ah. 96 minutes. Also known as **Semi-Gods and Semi-Devils** (Tai Seng title).

Gorgeously designed, hectically paced, and insanely plotted, this fantasy lampoon (loosely based on Jin Yong's classic novel *Demi-Gods and Semi-Devils*) ranks as a genuine treat for the initiated and a bewildering experience for everyone else. The central storyline charts the on-going magical duel between outcast San Sect members Li Chou-shui and Mo Han-wen, with the latter's apparent omnipotence compromised by her lesbian cravings for Chou-shui's twin sister, Chong-hoi. Meanwhile, Sing Suk Sect leader Ting Chun-chou is consolidating his power by annihilating all rivals in anticipation of taking over in the aftermath of Mo and Li's increasingly destructive confrontations. Putting a damper on his plans is Purple, an ambitious underling who has snatched both the scroll containing the all-powerful Yi-ken sutra and a Shaolin monk to decode it for her.

Director Andy Chin gives the satirical screenplay just the right degree of over-the-top velocity, turning this into an appealingly berserk live-action cartoon (with visuals and sound effects to match). The fact that he had three of the top leading ladies in Chinese cinema at his disposal certainly didn't hurt either. Sharla Cheung gets another chance to hone the persona she has utilized in her many previous period efforts: the sly and sexy opportunist whose amoral exterior conceals a soft heart. Mainland icon Gong Li supplies the perpetually crestfallen Mo with equal shares of anger and wounded pride, making her the perfect victim for Chou-shui's petty humiliations and an apt comic foil. As the Li twins, Brigitte Lin gets to pull out all the stops, basking in the immoral excesses of Chou-shui's impenitent evil with a wonderfully hammy performance, and endowing the saintly Chong-hoi with the requisite amount of exaggerated innocence. The cryptic subtitles make the proceedings rather difficult to take in with one viewing, but the satire and wildly colorful special effects are easily appreciated.

241. The Dragon Family

(Movie Impact; 1988) ★: 4/10. *Lung chi fung chuk* (Cantonese), *Long zhi gu zu* (Mandarin): "Dragon Clan." Cinematographers: Au Yang-ying, Yip Yau-han, Kong Sze; Art Director: Wai Kan; Music: Joseph Chan Wing-leung; Writers: Yuen Kai-chi, Chan Shu; Producer: Wallace Cheung

Kwong-chung; Director: Lau Kar-wing. Cast: Kenneth Tong Chun-yip (Yip), Alan Tam Wing-lun (Allan), Andy Lau Tak-wah (Hua), Norman Tsui Siu-keung (Keung), William Ho Kar-kui (Ko), Kent Cheng Chuk-see (Po), Ko Chuen-hsiang (Lung Ying), Ku Feng (Ho E), Miu Kiu-wai (Kar-wai), Max Mok Siu-chung (Chung), Lau Kar-wing (Sik), Stanley Fung Shui-fan (Fung), Shing Fui-on (Bill). 1.85:1. VHS: Tai Seng. Import LD/VCD: Mei Ah. 91 minutes.

An excellent cast slightly elevates this gangster drama, a weak entry in the "hero" genre. Ko Chuen-hsiang plays a Triad headman who seeks to steer the Lung clan away from crime and into legitimate business. His sons and subordinates consist of the usual stereotypes: the cool-as-ice killer who must seek refuge in Taiwan (Tam), the hothead (Miu) and his level-headed counterpart (Lau), the gambling addict destined to bring ruin to the family (Tong), the scholarly young son (Mok), etc. As a result of plotting by two men (Norman Tsui and William Ho) from a rival family, Ko is killed and his family is ambushed at the funeral. Tsui then murders his own boss (Ku Feng) and assumes control of his empire. Ko's two surviving sons, Lau and Mok, team up with Tam to enact revenge.

Shamelessly melodramatic *á la* **A Better Tomorrow** but lacking all of that film's emotional power, **Dragon Family** just goes through the motions in half-hearted fashion. Even the final battle seems mechanical. On the other hand, how often do you get to see *Kent Cheng* doing kung fu? Phillip Ko Fei and Kara Hui Ying-hung put in brief appearances.

242. Dragon Fight

(1989; Grand March Movie Production Co.) ★: 5/10. *Lung joi tin aai* (Cantonese), *Long zai tian ya* (Mandarin): "Dragon at the End of the World." Cinematographer: Abdul M. Rumjahn; Art Director: Ganni Ma Chi-ming; Music: Violet Lam Man-yee; Writer: James Yuen Sai-sang; Producer: Henry Fong Ping; Action Director: Dick Wei; Director: Billy Tang Hin-sing. Cast: Jet Li Lianjie (Lee Kwok-lap), Nina Li Chi (Kuen), Stephen Chiau Sing-chi (Yau), Dick Wei (Wong Wai), Henry Fong Ping (Marco). 1.85:1. VHS: Tai Seng. Import LD/VCD: Star Entertainment (No Subtitles). 97 minutes.

In San Francisco for an exhibition, China's national martial arts team loses member Wong Wai when the aging performer decides to flee from the airport. Star acrobat Lee Kwok-lap pursues him and, in the process, misses the flight home himself. Wong later kills a police officer, and Lee is blamed when the latter's wallet is found near the dead man. Realizing that he will never get a fair trial, Lee escapes police custody and stays with Yau, an enthusiastic fan. Wong, meanwhile, has been moving up the underworld ladder as a bodyguard/hitman for triad boss Marco. When Wong starts getting a little too ambitious for his tastes, Marco tries to set him up by tipping the police off about a drug buy. During the subsequent shootout, a bag of cocaine falls into Yau's hands and he decides to make some money by selling it. However, the drugs are accidentally lost, and Wong, believing that Lee is in league with Yau, decides to kill them both.

Even though this was shot Stateside, the Western actors are as poor as ever, but, in a strange way, this is actually fitting, as **Dragon Fight** plays very much like a shoddy American Grade B actioner (there is even a scene set in a strip bar, a genre requirement in Hollywood films of this nature). However, with Jet Li and Dick Wei (billed here as "C.I. Tu") in the cast, the martial arts are of a much higher standard, and many viewers will tolerate the film's shortcomings just to see them in action. Similarly, fans of Stephen Chiau will also enjoy seeing him in a part almost 180 degrees removed from the persona that would make him a superstar two years later. Director Billy Tang doesn't show nearly the same degree of enthusiasm for this material as would later be apparent in his infamous Category III sleaze thrillers **Run and Kill** and **Red to Kill**.

243. Dragon Fist

(1979; Lo Wei Motion Pictures) ★: 6/10. *Lung kuen* (Cantonese), *Long quan* (Mandarin): "Dragon Fist." Cinematographer: Chen Rong-shu; Music: Frankie Chan Fan-kei; Writer: Wong Chung-ping; Producer: Hsu Li-hwa; Action Director: Jackie Chan; Director: Lo Wei. Cast: Jackie Chan (Tang How-yuen), Nora Miao Ker-hsiu (San-thye's Daughter), James Tien Chun (Fang Kang), Yam Sai-kwoon (Chung Chien-kuen). 2.35:1. VHS: All-Seasons (Dubbed), UAV (Dubbed), Simitar (Dubbed). DVD: Simitar (English and Cantonese tracks). Import LD/VCD: Ocean Shores. 92 minutes.

This early Jackie Chan effort is another entry in the time-honored "You killed my master! You must die!" sub-genre of vintage kung fu thrillers. When his mentor, San-thye, is killed in battle by rival martial arts expert Chung Chien-kuen of The Patience Clan, Tang How-yuen takes the man's wife and daughter along on his quest for vengeance. Upon locating Chung, Tang reluctantly agrees to honor the man's request that their duel be delayed for a period of three days. When the appointed time comes, the trio return to find that Chung has cut off one of his legs in retribution for the murder of San-thye. Although Tang feels cheated out of his vengeance, he must focus his attention on another matter. The evil Wei family has secretly poisoned San-thye's widow and possesses the only remedy that can save her. After providing Tang with the cure, they convince him to stay in the region and aid them in their battle against The Patience Clan. However, when the Wei clan's actions become so dishonourable that he can no longer justify them, Tang finds himself caught in the middle when the two rival forces go to war.

Serious in tone from start to finish, **Dragon Fist** offers up some excellent traditional fight choreography (i.e. long takes and few edits), but the formula-bound plot attenuates the dramatic content. Chan proves himself perfectly capable of playing the grim avenger, but such a role does not allow him to display charm and enthusiasm, his two main assets as an actor. Thus, the film seems rather empty and is less satisfying than it would have been with a more stoic lead like Gordon Lau Kar-fai or Jimmy Wang Yu. Although Frankie Chan is credited with composing the score, there are still several stock music cues, including the theme from **The Sand Pebbles**.

244. The Dragon from Russia

(1990; Cinema City) ★: 6/10. *Gung cheung fei lung* (Cantonese), *Gong chang fei long* (Mandarin): "Red Wall Flying Dragon." Cinematographers: Peter Ngor Chi-kwan, Wong Chi-wai; Art Director: William Szeto Wai-yung; Music: Violet Lam Man-yee; Writer: Ella Chan Po-wah; Producer: Dean Shek Tien; Action Director: Yuen Tak; Director: Clarence Fok Yiu-leung. Cast: Sam Hui Koon-kit (Yao), Maggie Cheung Man-yuk (May Yip), Nina Li Chi (Chimer), Carrie Ng Kar-lai (Huntress), Loletta Lee Lai-chun (Pearl), Yuen Tak (The Master of the Dead), Dean Shek Tien (Snooker), Sarah Lee Lai-yui (Queenie), Lau Shun (Kishudo). 1.85:1. VHS: Tai Seng. Import LD: Golden Cinema City. 96 minutes.

Like **Killer's Romance**, this actioner is loosely based on Kazuo Koike's Japanese *manga Crying Freeman.* Unlike that Phillip Ko film, however, **The Dragon from Russia** suffers from aggressively peculiar and muddled plotting, a common fault of director Clarence Fok's work. A group of powerful assassins called "The Eight Hundred Dragons" ruthlessly hunts down any of their members who leave the organization. One such man, Snooker, has managed to avoid the clan for several years by hiding in Russia. When his whereabouts are revealed, the Dragons' leader, "The Master of the Dead," finds and executes both him and his daughter. The Master also kidnaps Manchurian swordsman Yao, a friend of Snooker, and brainwashes him. After subjecting Yao to rigorous (and often humorous) training, The Master is attacked by one of his traitorous former students, and he orders Yao to be taken to another clan sanctuary. Now known as "Freeman," Yao successfully carries out a series of assassinations under the direction of senior clan member Chimer. During one such mission, Yao slays Kishudo, "The Godfather of Japan," who was under the protection of Huntress, one of The Master's former students. While escaping, Yao is recognized by May, his old girlfriend from Russia, who has not seen him since he was kidnapped. As she is a witness, he is ordered to eliminate her but cannot, even though he has no memory of their love for one another. Yao must then protect May from his fellow killers while also dealing with the vengeful Huntress.

A very handsome production, **Dragon** boasts location work in several countries, and four of the most beautiful leading ladies in HK cinema, all dressed to the hilt in a variety of stunning costumes (many of which incorporate traditional Japanese designs). The action scenes are absolutely spectacular, highlighting some of the most elaborate and thrilling wirework you will ever see. Unfortunately, the storyline is a wearisome mix of hackneyed foundations, jarring mood swings, and haphazard transitions, making for a less than satisfactory whole. The film's Action Director, Yuen Tak, also has a supporting role.

245. Dragon in Jail

(1990; Legend Films Co.) ★: 6/10. *Yuk chung lung* (Cantonese), *Yu zhong long* (Mandarin): "Dragon in Jail." Cinematographer: Abdul M. Rumjahn; Art Director: Eric Lam Sai-kan; Music: Lowell Lo Kwun-ting; Writer: Nam Yin; Producer: Eddy Chan Kar-ho; Action Director: Blackie Ko Shou-liang; Director: Kent Cheng Chuk-see. Cast: Andy Lau Tak-wah (Henry Tse), Kenny Ho Kar-king (Wayne), Gigi Lai Chi (Winnie Sung), William Ho Kar-kui (Charlie Ma), John Ching Tung (Skinny), Lung Fong (C.K. Chong), Melvin Wong Kam-sun (Prison Officer), Victor Hon Kwan (Henry's Father). 1.85:1. VHS: Tai Seng. 97 minutes.

Not the action film the title suggests, this is a fairly compelling drama that benefits from some effective performances and competent direction by character actor Kent Cheng. Wayne is a temperamental rich kid whose unruly behavior lands him a modest prison sentence. While in jail, he befriends Henry, a poor kid from the wrong side of the tracks serving a four year sentence for manslaughter. Upon their release, Wayne travels to Britain to study law, while Henry tries to make ends meet as a teacher. However, his past comes back to haunt him in the form of Charlie, a vicious triad who demands Henry pay him $100,000, as compensation for the killing of his underling. When Charlie's men brutally injure a member of Henry's family, the latter joins the same triad society as a way of diffusing the situation. Naturally, this is the wrong course of action: Henry gets addicted to heroin and becomes a high-ranking criminal. Wayne returns from the UK and helps his buddy get straight; but when Henry is framed for murder, Wayne must defend him in court.

While awkwardly melodramatic at times, **Dragon in Jail** is a sufficiently entertaining effort that mixes and matches genres with customary abandon. The prison sequences are easily the most cheerful you will ever see in a HK production.

246. Dragon Inn

(1992; Seasonal Film Corporation/Film Workshop) ★: 8/10. *San lung moon haak chan* (Cantonese), *Xin long men ke zhan* (Mandarin): "New Dragon Gate Inn." Cinematographers: Tom Lau Moon-tong, Arthur Wong Ngok-tai; Art Directors: William Cheung Suk-ping, Mark Chiu Kwok-san; Music: Phil Chan Fei-lap; Writers: Tsui Hark, Charcoal Cheung Tan, Hiu Wo; Producer: Tsui Hark; Action Directors: Ching Siu-tung, Yuen Bun; Director: Raymond Lee Wai-man. Cast: Brigitte Lin Ching-hsia (Yau Mo-yin), Tony Leung Kar-fai (Chow Wai-on), Maggie Cheung Man-yuk (Jade), Donnie Yen Chi-tan (Eunuch Tsao), Lau Shun (Cha), Lawrence Ng Kai-wah (Siu-chuen), Xiong Xinxin (Ngai), Elvis Tsui Kam-kong (The General), Yam Sai-kwoon (Ho Fu), Yuen Cheung-yan (Iron). 1.85:1. VHS: Tai Seng. Import LD/VCD: Mei Ah. 88 minutes (Theatrical version), 103 minutes (Video versions).

More densely plotted than King Hu Chin-chuan's 1966 original, this remake unfolds in the Ming Dynasty, when the emperor was just a pawn and the eunuchs were the true power brokers. As the film opens, Eunuch Tsao, the psychotic leader of the East Chamber, executes one of his chief rivals in the government. Seeking to capture the official's second-in-command, Chow Wai-on, Tsao orders that the dead man's children be exiled and taken through the desert, in the hope that Chow will try and rescue them. The Eunuch's plan is only half correct, however, as the siblings are saved instead by Chow's lover, Yau Mo-yin. Accompanied by her small troop of fighters, Yau takes the children to Dragon Inn, a desolate establishment run by the sexy, double-dealing Jade. Chow arrives at the Inn and catches Jade's eye, but before he and Yau can get the children to safety, Tsao's three subordinates (Shun, Ng, Xiong) materialize with their troops. Throughout the stormy night and the day that follows, the two sides play an uneasy game of deceit, while Jade profits by selling her services to both parties. However, her deepening affection for Chow soon forces her into choosing sides, just as Tsao and his forces arrive at the Inn for an all-out offensive.

This is a Tsui Hark production and the action directors are Ching Siu-tung and Yuen Bun, so it goes without saying that the martial arts choreography is spectacular. Unlike some of Tsui's other efforts from this period, however, the story is consistently engrossing and effectively builds tension through intrigue and character interaction rather than just the threat of impending violence. Lin is formidable in one of her characteristic roles, and Cheung is amusing as the sly and seductive proprietress (the two have a memorable confrontation early on that is better seen than described). Another strong component is the excellent score by Phil Chan, which makes use of traditional instruments and features a reprise of the original's opening credits theme, one of the most recognized pieces in all of Chinese cinema. On a lesser note, **Dragon Inn** has also gained some notoriety for its cannibalism subplot: Jade has her "barbarian" chef gather up all the bodies that accumulate in the establishment and transform them into meat buns for the unwitting guests (this seems to happen in a lot of HK films from recent years). The chef also earns his stripes on the battlefield, using his impeccable carving skills to flay all the flesh from one opponent's arm and leg before the startled party even feels any pain. Theatrical prints of the film run 88 minutes, while both the Tai Seng tape and the Mei Ah LD and VCD releases contain an extra 15 minutes of footage.

247. Dragon Lord

(1982; Golden Harvest/Paragon Films) ★: 6/10. *Lung siu yau* (Cantonese), *Long shao ye* (Mandarin): "Dragon Little Master." Cinematographers: Chan Ching-chu, Chan Chung-yuen, Chan Chung-shu; Writers: Barry Wong Ping-yiu, Edward Tang King-sang; Producer: Leonard Ho Koon-cheung; Action Directors: Jackie

Chan, Corey Yuen Kwai, Fung Hark-on; Director: Jackie Chan. Cast: Jackie Chan (Dragon), Feng Sing (Cowboy), Michael Chan Wai-man (Tiger, the Lieutenant), Tien Feng (Ho), Whang Ing-sik (The Captain), Fung Hark-on (Killer). Dolby Digital (DVD Only). 2.35:1. VHS: Tai Seng (Poor Subtitles), Cinema Group (Dubbed), Xenon/Arena (Dubbed). LD: Media Asia. Import VCD: Universe (Poor Subtitles). Import DVD: Universe. 95 minutes. Also known as **Young Master in Love** and **Dragon Strike** (Xenon/Arena video title).

Dragon Lord, a follow-up to **The Young Master**, retains the comic approach of the earlier film but with somewhat less success. Regardless, those who prefer Chan's early period efforts will not be disappointed. Chan (who again did double duty behind the camera) plays Dragon, the unruly son of a strict patriarch, who constantly gets into mischief with his buddy, Cowboy. One day, while the two are out making mischief, they stumble across Tiger, who is on the run from a mob of pursuers. Tiger participated in the theft of some of China's national treasures from the Forbidden City but walked out on his partners (former Imperial Guards) when they decided to sell the booty to foreigners. Their leader, The Captain, is also secretly working with Cowboy's father, unbeknownst to the son. When Tiger manages to return and steal some of the pieces, The Captain and his men desperately give chase, as the buyers will back out of their deal if some of the treasures are missing. Unaware of just what is transpiring, Dragon and Cowboy give Tiger shelter, and this leads to grave danger when The Captain arrives on the scene.

The first half of the film is less than focused, leading viewers to wonder just where it is heading and when a genuine storyline will emerge. Things pick up around the midpoint with an exciting shuttle-cock match, which is soon followed by a terrific sequence in which Chan struggles to maintain his balance on a steep rooftop while men inside the building plunge their spears through the ceiling, just missing him. However, the highlight of **Dragon Lord** is indisputably the climactic duel between Chan and Whang Ing-sik which unfolds inside a large barn and utilizes just about every available inch of the two-floor structure. Chan's acrobatics are simply incredible, and the sequence is so meticulously choreographed that it must have taken ages to shoot. Following the example of **The Cannonball Run** (which he had appeared in the year before), Chan ends the film with a series of *ouch*-takes, which would become a standard feature of his work.

Dragon Strike *see* **Dragon Lord**

248. Dragons Forever

(1988; Golden Harvest/Paragon Films) ★: 7/10. *Fei lung maang cheung* (Cantonese), *Fei long meng jiang* (Mandarin): "Flying Dragon Fierce Challenge." Cinematographers: Jimmy Leung Chi-wing, Cheung Yiu-cho; Art Director: Horace Ma Kwong-wing; Music: James Wong Jim; Writer: Roy Szeto Cheuk-hon; Producer: Leonard Ho Koon-cheung; Action Direction: Sammo Hung Stuntmen Association, Jackie Chan Stuntmen Association; Director: Sammo Hung Kam-po. Cast: Jackie Chan (Jackie Lung), Sammo Hung Kam-po (Wong Fei-hung), Yuen Biao (Tung Tak-biao), Yuen Wah (Hua Hsien-wu), Deanie Yip Tak-han (Miss Yip), Pauline Yeung Po-ling (Wen Mei-ling), Roy Chiao Hung (Judge Lo Chung-wai), Crystal Kwok Kam-yan (Jackie's Assistant), Phillip Ko Fei (Unemployed Thug), Dick Wei (Thug), Stanley Fung Shui-fan (Tak's Psychiatrist), Shum Wai (Lawyer), Benny "The Jet" Urquidez (Thug), Lau Kar-wing (Thug), Fung Hark-on (Thug), Chung Fat (Thug), Woo Fung (Man, the Attorney), Lam Wai (Thug), Billy Chow Bei-lee (Thug), Lau Kar-wing (Thug), Tai Po (Head Waiter), Shing Fui-on (Mao Shih-cheng), Lo Lieh (Gangster), Chen Jing (Gun Buyer), Lee Kar-ting (Thug), Peter Chan Lung (Thug). Dolby Digital (DVD Only). 1.85:1. VHS/LD: Tai Seng (Remastered for the English market; subtitled and dubbed). LD: Winson Entertainment. Import LD: Star Entertainment (No Subtitles). Import VCD: Mei Ah. Import DVD: Universe. 93 minutes.

Womanizing lawyer Jackie Lung is hired by mobster Hua Hsien-wu to help him beat a court injunction filed by the affluent Miss Yip. She charges that Hua's chemical factory is polluting the local water supply, but Hua (who is secretly manufacturing drugs) refuses to halt production, preferring to have his lawyer settle the matter through less than ethical means. Jackie enlists his buddies Wong Fei-hung and Tung Tak-biao to help him convince Miss Yip to sell her fish ponds. Fei-hung moves next door to the woman and turns on the charm; Jackie goes after her pretty lawyer, Wen Mei-ling; and the decidedly unhinged Tak gets into all manner of trouble, messing up the works in the process. The ruse, naturally, falls to pieces, but both Jackie and Wong have now really fallen in love, prompting them to do the right thing and put Hua out of business.

The final teaming to date of Jackie Chan, Sammo Hung, and Yuen Biao, **Dragons Forever** serves up martial arts that are just as good as you would expect from this team, and the bad guys are played by just about every single one of Hung and Chan's associates from the time. In a venture like this, the material between the fights is not of primary concern, but writer Roy Szeto does an adequate job of maintaining one's interest and injecting some reasonably amusing humor. The action highlights are Chan's battle with knife-wielding killers aboard a fancy yacht and his climactic confrontation with Benny "The Jet" Urquidez (sporting so much eye make-up, he looks ready to audition for **The Rocky Horror Picture Show**!), a bout that almost equals the excitement and intensity of their encounter in **Wheels on Meals**. Acting honors, this time out, go to Yuen Biao, who is clearly having a wonderful time playing Tak, the most loveable hyper neurotic nutball in memory. Tai Seng's subtitled tape is missing two brief scenes featuring Yuen's character visiting his psychiatrist; the bits appear on their English dubbed tape and as supplementary material on the company's laserdisc.

249. Dreadnaught

(1981; Golden Harvest/Paragon Films) ★: 8/10. *Yung je mo gui* (Cantonese), *Yong zhe wu ju* (Mandarin): "Brave, No Fear." Cinematographer: Michael Ma Koon-wah; Music: Chen Hsun-chi; Producer: Raymond Chow Man-wai; Writer-Action Director-Director: Yuen Woo-ping. Cast: Yuen Biao (Mousey), Leung Kar-yan (Leung Foon), Kwan Tak-hing (Wong Fei-hung), Yuen Shun-yee (White Tiger), Lily Li Li-li (Mousey's Sister), Fan Mui-sang (The Superintendent), Fung Hark-on (The Demon Tailor), Phillip Ko Fei (Master Tam), Tang Ching (Mousey's Girlfriend), Lau Wing (Iron Fingers), Kam Kar-fung (White Tiger's Wife), Chow Yuen-kin (Kwun), Yuen Cheung-yan (Policeman), Chiu Chung-hing (Chee). 2.35:1. VHS: Tai Seng (Remastered for the English market; subtitled or dubbed), Cinema Group (Dubbed). Import LD: Star Entertainment (No Subtitles). Import VCD: Mega Star (Poor Subtitles). 91 minutes.

A terrific old school kung fu thriller filled with superb martial arts, **Dreadnaught** is a fine vehicle for revered veteran Kwan Tak-hing and future star Yuen Biao (in his second lead role). The psychotic killer White Tiger is terrorizing the countryside, violently foiling all attempts to capture him. In order to avoid the authorities, Tiger joins an opera company and hides his very distinctive facial birthmark under malevolent-looking performance make-up. A citizen in the town where the company is performing, the aptly named Mousey is a timid youth who is afraid of his own shadow. His buddy, Foon, decides that the best way for Mousey to overcome his shyness is for him to receive instruction in kung fu from his master, Wong Fei-hung. However, Mousey's continued run-ins with White Tiger may be just the thing to finally awaken a sense of courage in him.

A well-balanced mixture of comedy, drama, and moments of surrealistic horror, **Dreadnaught** remains one of Yuen Woo-ping's paramount accomplishments. Yuen Biao displays fine form throughout, even during the moments when his character is supposed to be a clumsy fool. Kwan Tak-hing (who played Wong Fei-hung more times than any other actor) still moves really well at an age where many people cannot get out of bed without aid, and the lion dance sequences are among the best to be seen in any HK film. **Dreadnaught**'s status as one of Golden Harvest's finest genre films can also be measured by just how many elements from it have turned up in later movies. The memorable sequence in which Yuen Shun-yee attacks Leung Kar-yan while wearing an elaborate, two-headed opera costume (that allows him to deceive his opponent by splitting into two separate fighters) would be reprised by the actor in Stephen Chiau's period farce, **Forbidden City Cop** (and it is also one of the highlights of that film). The scene where Yuen Biao combines his laundry duties and kung fu training together would later be slavishly copied by Chris O'Donnell's "Robin" in **Batman Forever**, and another bit involving Kwan and Fung Hark-on (in which the latter tries to murder the former while pretending to measure him for a new suit) would be restaged by Jet Li and Chingmy Yau in Wong Jing's **New Legend of Shaolin**. As Wong wrote the original story for this film, he can be forgiven for recycling one of his most inspired ideas. The character names above are from the dubbed version.

250. Dream Killer

(1995; Pan Pacific Productions) ★: 7/10. *Yau sing dik haai hau* (Cantonese), *Ye xing de xie hou* (Mandarin): "Acquaintance of the Savages." Cinematographer: Gigo Lee Chi-hang; Art Directors: Bill Lui Cho-hung, Kung Kwok-choi; Music: Tse Chiu-kwong, Rock Head Music Team; Writer: James Yuen Sai-sang; Producer: Wong Jing; Director: Jeffrey Chiang Chia-chun. Cast: Mark Cheng Ho-nam (Chan), Valerie Chow Kar-ling (Michelle Lau), Chan Kwok-bong (Lai Chi-hung), Michael Wong Man-tak (Cheng), Bonnie Fu Yuk-ching (Joyce), Alex Fong Chung-sun (Cheong). 1.85:1. VHS: World Video. 90 minutes.

An interesting screenplay by acclaimed writer James Yuen (**He's a Woman, She's a Man**) and stylish direction elevate this serial killer thriller above the norm. Chan and Lai are police officers assigned to investigate a perpetrator who dispatches his female victims with a single knife wound in their spine. The women were all members of a singles club, and one of the other investigators on the case, Cheng, also belonged to the same club. His association with the group makes him the prime suspect in Lai's eyes, though the detective also has another, private reason for wanting to see Cheng take a fall. Chan, meanwhile, has begun a tentative relationship with Michelle Lau, a blind psychologist who has offered her assistance to help solve the case. Michelle's analysis of the killer proves to be quite accurate and a tremendous aid, but Chan has a terrible secret in his past, and his plans for Michelle will put her life in great danger.

With the relatively small cast of characters, the murderer's identity is not a complete surprise, and some aspects of the storyline do not hold up under close scrutiny. Regardless, the proceedings grab and hold one's attention right up until the final two reels, which are suspenseful and effectively mounted. The denouement is also quite unique and pleasing in its ambiguity. Director Chiang followed this up with **The Killer Has No Return** (1996), in which he slavishly imitated Wong Kar-wai's technique, with dismal results. Michael Wong is dubbed here by another actor who, nonetheless, replicates the actor's trademark Canto/English patter.

251. Dream Lover

(1995; Win's Entertainment/Cheung Man Movie Production Co.) ★: 3/10. *Yat chin ling yat yau chi mung chung yan* (Cantonese), *Yi qian ling yi ye zhi meng zhong ren* (Mandarin): "Dream Person of 1001 Nights." Cinematographer: Horace Wong Wing-hang; Art Director: Jason Mok Siu-kei; Music: Danny Chung Teng-yat; Writers: Leung Wai-ting, Cheuk Bing, Tessa Choi Ting-ting, Wong Ho-wah, Chung Ngoi-fong; Producers: Sharla Cheung Man, Gordon Chan Kar-seung; Director: Bosco Lam Hing-lung. Cast: Tony Leung Kar-fai (Cheung Kar-shing), Jacqueline Wu Chien-lien (Kitty), Nat Chan Pak-cheung (Ah Man), Jack Gao Jie (Kwok Ping-tak), Lau Shun (The Master), Spencer Lam Sheung-yee (TV Commentator), Law Kar-ying (Kitty's Uncle), Lee Siu-kei (Groom). 1.85:1. VHS: Tai Seng. Import LD/VCD: Mei Ah. 91 minutes.

This sappy romantic comedy-drama-fantasy is kept afloat (just barely) by the charismatic and photogenic Jacqueline Wu, but even she can do little to offset the improbable storyline and uninspired jokes. Inventor/illegal road racer Shing has found his dream goddess: the affluent and beautiful Kitty. The two begin to hit if off but a crisis erupts when Kitty's father skips town owing creditors $10 million. Kitty then leaves HK without telling Shing about the situation or where she can be found. Not long afterwards, a Japanese company pays Shing $10 million for a special chip he has invented, but this new-found affluence does little to alleviate his sadness. At a party, he discovers that Kitty is married to rich, corrupt businessman Kwok Ping-tak and, as a result, stumbles into a scheme hatched by Kwok and a spiritual master to relieve Shing of his money.

The story behind this instantly forgettable effort is far more interesting than what managed to make it to the screen. **Dream Lover** was produced by actress Sharla Cheung Man, and she clashed with star Tony Leung Kar-fai following production, saying that his refusal to make himself available for reshoots ruined the film and caused her to lose money. Cheung then proceeded to make the film *again* as **Romantic Dream**, this time playing the female lead role herself. Incredibly, the two films hit HK theaters the same month (**Dream** on June 17 and **Romantic** on June 24), but Cheung had the last laugh: **Romantic** turned out to be better and out-grossed its rival by a margin of more than three to one.

252. Dream Lovers

(1986; D & B Films) ★: 9/10. *Mung chung yan* (Cantonese), *Meng zhong ren* (Mandarin): "Dream People." Cinematographer: Bill Wong Chung-bo; Art Director: William Cheung Suk-ping; Music: Law Wing-fai; Writers: Manfred Wong, Yau Tai On-ping; Producer: Dickson Poon Dik-sun; Director: Tony Au Ding-ping. Cast: Chow Yun-fat (Song Yu), Brigitte Lin Ching-hsia (Cheung Yuet-heung), Cher Yeung Suet-yee (Wah-lei), Kwan San (Hark-nam), Lam Chung (Li Chang). Dolby Digital (DVD only). 1.85:1. VHS: Tai Seng. Import LD: Mei Ah. Import VCD/DVD: Mega Star. 95 minutes.

Production designer-turned-director Tony Au crafted this mature and sentimental allegory about reincarnation, lost love, and inexorable tragedy, which ranks as one of the most melancholy fantasies in memory. It also remains the only film to date to co-star Chow Yun-fat and Brigitte Lin. Chow plays Song Yu, a revered symphony conductor plagued by visions of a beautiful, beckoning maiden in traditional attire and a terracotta statue bearing his likeness. At an exhibition of Qin artifacts, he encounters Cheung Yuet-heung (Lin, sporting the close-cropped male hairstyle she wore in **Peking Opera Blues**), the spitting image of the woman in his dream. She, too, has been experiencing visions, but of a more disconcerting nature (like Yu being strangled by imperial soldiers, and others she's too afraid to impart). With the help of a blind medium, Yu learns that he and Yuet-heung are the reincarnation of these figures, lovers who met a tragic fate 2200 years earlier. Together, the two try to come to grips with their emotions and the question of Yu's devoted girlfriend, Wah-lei, who correctly surmises that there is no place for her in a love spanning twenty two centuries.

Unabashedly emotional and solemn by turns, **Dream Lovers** uses its fantastic premise as a springboard for its narrative—and not vice-versa—making the film somewhat unique when compared to similar ventures. Aside from fine work by Chow and Lin, and Au's artful compositions, the main asset here is Law Wing-fai's award-winning score, which is potent and yet soothing in its subtle approach. Its ever-constant, enveloping presence is a key ingredient in supporting the tenor of each scene (there is no comedy relief—only a few pensive smiles). The story and the conflicts portrayed therein bear some similitude to Au's debut feature, the Paris-lensed **The Last Affair** (1983), which paired Chow with Carol Cheng; but **Dream Lovers** is more compelling and pleasing in both a dramatic and cinematic sense. The ending has been criticized in some quarters but, if viewed in the context of the preceding events and the genre itself, it is credible and fitting.

253. Dreaming the Reality

[*sic*] (1991; T & M International Film Co.) ★: 3/10. *Mung sing huet mei ting* (Cantonese), *Meng xing xue wei ting* (Mandarin): "Dream Awaken, Blood Not Stop." Cinematographers: Wong Kar-fai, Wong Chit; Art Director: Ko Pui-yee; Music: 108 Recording Corporation; Writer: Lee Ho-kwan; Producer: Tsui Fat; Action Directors: Lung Sang, Fan Kin-hung; Director: Wong Chun-yeung. Cast: Sibelle Hu Hui-chung (Si Lan-fa), Moon Lee Choi-fung (Silver Fox), Yukari Oshima (Silver Fox's Sister), Ben Lam Kwok-bun (Rocky), Eddy Ko Hung (Fok). 1.85:1. VHS: Tai Seng. 103 minutes.

From a very young age, Silver Fox and her sister have been raised by their uncle Fok to be ruthless killers, unencumbered by emotion or sentiment. However, when one of their hits accidentally wipes out some young children, Fox begins to develop a conscience. The pair are dispatched to Thailand to steal a computer disc containing evidence that would allow the authorities to convict Fok. While there, the two are almost killed carrying out the assignment and Silver Fox suffers a severe blow to her head. Stricken with amnesia (a favorite HK film concept), she ends up staying with butch boxing manager Si Lan-fa and her rather thick brother, Rocky. Suspecting that Fox has betrayed him, Fok orders that she be found and eliminated.

A slack, ill-conceived film, **Dreaming the Reality** (terrible title) is at least a reel too long for such scant material, padding out its running time with kick-boxing matches and other uninteresting digressions. Sibelle Hu does the best work here, transforming her patented "tough cop" persona into an equally exaggerated, chain-smoking tomboy. It's an amusing turn and one which provides just about all of what little entertainment there is to be had here.

254. Dreams of Glory, A Boxer's Story

(1991; D & B Films Co.) ★: 7/10. *Kuen wong* (Cantonese), *Quan wang* (Mandarin): "Boxing King." Cinematographers: George Chan Lok-yee, Wong Po-man, Apple Kwan Pak-suen; Art Director: Yank Wong Yan-kwai; Music: Rupert Leung Kiu-pak; Writers: Chan Man-keung, Sin Kam-ching; Producer: Stephen Shin Kei-yin; Action Directors: Chan Tak-hing, Lee Kar-ting; Director: Lawrence Ah Mon. Cast: Jackie Lui Chung-yin (Yip Chi-ming), To Siu-chun (Law Yat-tak), Rain Lau Yuk-tsui (Yat-tak's Girlfriend), Lau Kong (Yat-tak's Father), Lam King-kong, Chan Tak-hing. 1.85:1. VHS: Tai Seng. Import LD/VCD: Ocean Shores. 103 minutes.

The world of competitive "freefighting" is profiled in this engrossing film from director Lawrence Ah Mon (**Gangs**). A group of young men, The Flying Eagles, train hard to help their small school regain its past glories. Newcomer Law Yat-tak quickly discovers just how gruelling his coach's training regime is and, while he does show some aptitude, the lad decides to keep his dream of competing a secret from his father. Yip Chi-ming has been with the school for two years and won all four of the matches he has fought. However, he is overpowered in his fifth bout and heads to Thailand (the mecca of kick-boxing in Asia) for vigorous, dusk-till-dawn training. In addition to improving his abilities, Chi-ming also grows as a person and decides to stay beyond the original planned length of eight weeks. Yat-tak, meanwhile, is becoming more and more determined to succeed in the sport and will soon be fighting in his first tournament.

A synopsis makes it sound like any other film of this genre, but **Dreams of Glory** seems comparatively fresh because of the sport (rarely ever documented with any seriousness or accuracy in Western cinema), the locations, and the importance (to both society and the individual) of maintaining this cultural tradition. The latter is particularly reflected in the Thailand sequences (directed by Apple Kwan), where the locals begin training almost from the time they can walk and rely on the income from fighting to support themselves and their family. Aside from an English language sequence that comes off a bit stilted, the performers are natural and engaging (particularly the wonderful Rain Lau, from the director's **Queen of Temple Street**), and the matches are shot in a straight-forward, realistic fashion that is a refreshing change from the flashy and contrived manner Hollywood generally utilizes. An interesting score and sync sound recording are additional strengths.

255. Drugs Fighters

(1995; New Treasurer Films Co.) ★: 2/10. *Chap duk sin fung* (Cantonese), *Qi du xian feng* (Mandarin): "Vanguards Fighting Drugs." Cinematographer: Pang Chun-wai; Art Director: Tsui Chung-san; Music: Not Original; Writer: Tam Wai-shing; Producer: Wu Ming-choi; Director: Yiu Tin-hung. Cast: Ngai Sing (Li Fan), Yukari Oshima (Yi Chian), Yuen Wah (Lin Chia-teng), Lam Wai (Feng Shiu), Ken Lo Wai-kwong (Chang). 1.85:1. VHS: Tai Seng. Import LD/VCD: Universe. 91 minutes.

Location shooting in China gives this formula actioner an extra level of interest, but it is not nearly enough to overcome the mediocre plotting. Ngai Sing receiveds top billing but basically has an extended cameo as a train cop who aids in the capture of a wanted drug lord (Ken Lo). The real stars are Yukari Oshima and Lam Wai, playing officers heading up a task force tracking down a gang of drug runners who smuggle their wares inside statues.

The action sequences are reasonably good, but the central storyline constantly screeches to a halt while the running time is padded out with tired subplots: Ngai and Oshima making goo-goo eyes at each other; Lam fretting over his blind mother's impending eye operation; the travails of another officer whose wife wants him to leave the force; etc. There are literally hundreds of similar entries far more worthy of your attention than this. Yuen Wah is wasted in a supporting role as another villain.

256. Drunken Master

(1978; Seasonal Film Corporation) ★: 8/10. *Jui kuen* (Cantonese), *Zui quan* (Mandarin): "Drunken Fist." Cinematographer: Chang Hai; Art Director: Ting Yuen-tai; Music: Not Original; Writers: Yuen Woo-ping, Hai Wah-on; Producer: Ng See-yuen; Action Directors: Yuen Woo-ping, Hsu Hsia; Director: Yuen Woo-ping. Cast: Jackie Chan (Huang Fei-hong), Simon Yuen Siu-tien (Su Hua-chi), Hwang Jang-li (Yen Tieh-hsin), Dean Shek Tien (Kai-hsien), Yuen Shun-yee (Chen Kuo-wei). 2.35:1. VHS: World Video, Bulldog Entertainment (Dubbed), Madacy (Dubbed). Import LD: Far East Music. Import VCD: Mei Ah (Poor Subtitles). 111 minutes. Also known as **Drunken Monkey in the Tiger's Eyes.**

Following the success of **Snake In the Eagle's Shadow**, Yuen Woo-ping quickly paired his father Simon Yuen and rising star Jackie Chan once again for this wonderful period martial arts comedy. The young Huang Fei-hong is far from the great hero he would later grow up to be: A disrespectful layabout, his actions constantly bring shame to his noble father, Huang Chi-ying. Desperate to put his son back on the right road, he forces him to become a student of the ruthless master Su Hua-chi, whose pupils often end up crippled. Sure enough, Master Su puts Fei-hong through the tortures of Hell with his intensive training techniques. After numerous attempts to escape, Fei-hong finally manages to elude the old man but gets into a fight with the deadly Yen Tieh-hsin, who beats him senseless. Humiliated, Fei-hong returns to Master Su and begins to take his instruction seriously, so that he may exact revenge. Fei-hong's new skills will be put to the test sooner than he expects, as Yen has been hired to murder Chi-ying.

Filled with virtually non-stop kung fu and some outstanding training sequences, **Drunken Master** is the best of Jackie Chan's films from the '70s. The comedy is amusing but rarely overbearing, the dramatics are plausible, and the martial arts are consistently first rate. Yuen and Chan are the ultimate teacher and student team, and every second they share is wonderful; it is a shame that they were not paired again (Yuen died the following year, during the filming of **The Magnificent Butcher**). *Drunken Master* is compulsory viewing for both Chan fans and those whose tastes lean toward traditional martial arts films. A belated but even better sequel followed in 1994.

257. Drunken Master II

(1994; Golden Harvest/Paragon Films) ★: 9/10. *Jui kuen II* (Cantonese), *Zui Quan II* (Mandarin): "Drunken Fist II." Cinematographers: Cheung Yiu-cho, Jingle Ma Cho-shing, Cheung Tung-leung, Nico Wong Wan-man; Art Directors: Eddie Ma Poon-chiu, Cyrus Ho Kim-hung; Music: William Woo Wai-lap; Writers: Tong Man-ming, Yuen Kai-chi, Edward Tang King-sang; Producer: Leonard Ho Koon-cheung; Action Directors: Lau Kar-leung, Jackie Chan Stuntman Association; Director: Lau Kar-leung. Cast: Jackie Chan (Wong Fei-hung), Anita Mui Yim-fong (Mrs. Wong), Ti Lung (Wong Kei-ying), Felix Wong Yat-wah (Tso), Lau Kar-leung (General Fu), Chin Kar-lok (Sang). 2.35:1. VHS: Tai Seng. Import LD/VCD: Mei Ah. 102 minutes.

Still Jackie Chan's best film of the decade thus far, **Drunken Master II** (the late-in-coming follow-up to Yuen Woo-ping's 1978 classic) is a near-perfect blend of comedy, drama, and showstopping martial arts, a welcome throwback to the style and appeal of the star's finest work. Set in 1913, the plot is fairly insignificant: The mischievous Wong Fei-hong (Chan) comes into possession of a valuable jade seal which is sought by a valiant general (Lau Kar-leung, who directed only part of the film but received sole credit), while foreign villains use a steel mill as a front to smuggle China's national treasures out of the country.

Despite its adherence to certain genre conventions, **Drunken Master II** is much better written than most of what Chan has done since, an apparent side effect of his growing connection to Hollywood (at the reported insistence of New Line Cinema, **Mr. Nice Guy** became a virtual remake of the mediocre but popular-in-America **Rumble in the Bronx**). The action setpieces are sprinkled at regular intervals throughout the storyline and never disappoint, mixing different styles and degrees of fervor. Chan's fight with Lau *under* a train is a classic example of "close quarters kung fu," and what kung fu aficionado wouldn't pay to see Chan share the screen with the great Ti (splendid as Fei-hong's ever noble and upright father). Not to be outdone by the men, Anita Mui gives a wonderful comic turn as Fei-hong's feisty stepmom. At forty, Chan was at least 15 years too old for the part (he was a decade older than Mui, and only slightly younger than Ti), but he pulled it off thanks to his ageless enthusiasm and incredible acrobatic skill. His final battle with Korean martial arts champ Ho Sung Pak and *high* kicking Ken Lo Wai-kwong (a frequent co-star, and Chan's bodyguard offscreen) is a knockout and one of the action highlights of the star's filmography. Andy Lau Tak-wah, Bill Tung Biu, and many other familiar faces turn up in cameos. **Drunken Master III** is not connected with this film or the original.

258. Drunken Master III

(1994; Super Film Production) ★: 3/10. *Jui kuen III* (Cantonese), *Zui quan* (Mandarin): "Drunken Fist III." Cinematographer: Peter Ngor Chi-kwan; Art Director: Luk Chi-fung; Music: Mak Chun-hung; Writer: Siu Wing; Producer: Chris Lee Kin-sang; Action Directors: Lau Kar-leung, Lau Kar-yan, Lai Sing-kwong; Director: Lau Kar-leung. Cast: Willie Chi Tian-sheng (Wong Fei-hong), Michelle Lee Kar-yan (Sum Yu), Adam Cheng Siu-chau (Wong Kei-ying), Lau Kar-leung (Uncle Yan), Andy Lau Tak-wah (Yeung Kwun), Simon Yam Tat-wah (Gay Man on Bus), William Ho Kar-kui (Yuan Shi-kai), Gordon Lau Kar-fai (Governor Li). 1.85:1. VHS/LD: World Video. Import LD/VCD/DVD: Mei Ah. 91 minutes.

Don't be fooled by that title—this limp kung fu comedy has nothing to do with the previous two films and cannot hold a candle to either one. Reportedly, after being removed from the helm of **Drunken Master II**, director Lau Kar-leung undertook this project in order to make the "real" **Drunken Master** sequel. Whatever his motivation, the resulting film is a disaster and easily the lowpoint of Lau's directorial career. This time out, Wong Fei-hung and Wong Kei-ying become involved with protecting Manchu Princess Sum Yu, who is the target of both nationalists supporting Dr. Sun Yat-sen and the evil White Lotus Cult (inexplicably run this time by some *white* goons). They receive aid from Uncle Yan, a wine merchant/kung fu expert who teaches Fei-hong various new stances. Eventually, the Manchus collaborate with the Cult and hand the princess over to them for a sacrificial ritual.

There is some good kung fu to be found in this mess but it is soon forgotten when placed in such a slapdash scenario filled with consistently lame humor and ridiculous anachronisms like Frankenstein masks during a Halloween party(?!), Fei-hong skateboarding on an abacus, and Simon Yam as a stereotypically fey villain. What a waste of talent! Die hard martial arts aficionados are advised to proceed with caution and have their remote control at the ready to dispense with all of the nonsense in between the setpieces.

Drunken Monkey in the Tiger's Eyes *see* **Drunken Master**

259. Drunken Tai-Chi

(1984; Dragons Group Film Co.) ★: 6/10. *Siu taai gik* (Cantonese), *Xiao tai ji* (Mandarin): "Laughing Tai Chi." Cinematographer: Chen Jung-shu; Music: Not

Original; Writers: Yuen Woo-ping, Brandy Yuen Cheung-yeung; Producer: Wu Gown, P.C. Chang; Action Direction: The Yuen Clan; Director: Yuen Woo-ping. Cast: Donnie Yen Chi-tan (Chin Dao), Yuen Cheung-yan (The Puppeteer), Yuen Shun-yee (The Killer Bird), Yuen Yat-chor (Ping), Lydia Shum Tin-ha (Fatty). 2.35:1. VHS: Ocean Shores (Dubbed), SYS/ Youngtze (Dubbed). 91 minutes.

Donnie Yen made his film debut in this rollicking period kung fu farce which features some incredible acts of agility. Fun-loving Chin Dao is always getting into trouble. One day, he humiliates the son of a local boss; when the boy tries to take revenge using firecrackers, Chin fights back and accidentally drives his opponent mad. The stricken boy's father hires a mute assassin called "The Killer Bird" to wipe out Chin's family. Dao is not at home when The Bird attacks, and he loses his father and brother as a result. Unsure of what to do with his life, Dao meets up with an eccentric puppeteer and his extra-large wife, who try to teach him a trade. Dao's incompetence soon finds him back on the street, where he inadvertently saves The Bird's son from some kidnappers. In spite of this act of charity, the mute still tries to eliminate Dao, and the latter barely escapes alive. The Puppeteer then agrees to instruct Dao in the "Soft Style" of tai chi, the only successful defense against Bird's great strength.

Some of the low brow humor grates, but this remains a highly enjoyable outing, reminiscent of Yuen's **Drunken Master** in its approach. The training sequences are wonderfully inventive making great use of such unlikely teaching aids as birds and cotton), and Donnie Yen is incredibly graceful and agile. There are a number of anachronistic gags; the best one finds Yen engaging in a little makeshift breakdancing! Only the routine storyline and weak ending keep the film from attaining the same heights as its model. The soundtrack includes music lifted from **Battlestar Galactica**. Character names are from the English dubbed version.

260. Duel to the Death

(1983; Golden Harvest/Paragon Films) ★: 8/10. *Sin sei kuet* (Cantonese), *Xian si jue* (Mandarin): "First to Die Duel." Cinematographers: Lee Yao-tong, Lau Hung-chuen; Music: Michael Lai Siu-tin; Writers: Manfred Wong, David Lai Tai-wai, Kong Lung; Producer: Raymond Chow Man-wai; Action Director-Director: Ching Siu-tung. Cast: Damian Lau Chung-yan (Bo Ching-wen, "The Sword Saint"), Norman Tsui Siu-keung (Lord Hashimoto), Flora Cheung Tien-oi (Sheng Nan), Eddy Ko Hung (Kenji). 2.35:1. VHS/LD: Tai Seng (Remastered for the English market; subtitled or dubbed). Import LD: Star Entertainment (No Subtitles). Import VCD: Mega Star. 86 minutes (Subtitled), 85 minutes (Dubbed).

Many sources credit Tsui Hark's **Zu: Warriors from the Magic Mountain** (1983) as being the film that revolutionized Chinese period martial arts cinema. While it was certainly the first one to consolidate Western techniques, **Duel to the Death** (which hit HK theaters a month before **Zu**) deserves at least as much credit for introducing the sort of kinetic, gravity-defying action that would become the genre's signature during the period fantasy craze in the late '80s/early '90s. The lion's share of that honour must be bestowed upon rookie helmer Ching Siu-tung, who displays precisely the sort of skill and ingenuity that would distinguish his later directorial outings, like the **A Chinese Ghost Story** series and the spectacular **Swordsman II** (1992), as well as those productions that employed him as the martial arts director. **Duel** centers on a contest, held once every decade during the Ming Dynasty, in which China and Japan seek to determine which country rules the martial world. Prior to the time of their arranged combat, the Chinese contestant, Bo, and his Japanese counterpart, Lord Hashimoto, discover that the integrity of this particular match has been tainted by a conspiracy involving officials from both camps. The top martial artists invited to the event have been kidnapped by a band of ninjas under the command of a bogus monk in league with a local master who believes his daughter should rightfully be China's representative in the clash.

If you've seen any of Ching's work in the genre, you know what to expect, and **Duel** delivers all of the acrobatic combat and kinetic bloodshed that fans of HK fantasy could ask for. The inclusion of the ninjas, however, allows Ching to take things even further, with their mystical abilities (never presented to proper effect in those cheesy Cannon and Joseph Lai ninja films) providing ample opportunity for additional, outlandish FX. The most famous sequence has them surprising one opponent from above by flying in on kites, but there are other setpieces just as memorable, and the combination of Chinese and Japanese cultural traditions (the latter presented more respectfully than is the norm in HK film) provides a fascinating backdrop. In addition to recommending this to the converted, the meld also serves to create the perfect film for fans of samurai cinema, should they wish to equate themselves with its Chinese parallel. The inter-country competition premise would later be parodied in Wong Jing's sporadically amusing fantasy-comedy **Holy Weapon** (1993), which finds Damian Lau (as "Heaven's Sword," a variation of his **Duel** character, "The Sword Saint") facing off against Simon Yam Tat-wah's "Super Sword of Japan." It also includes a shabby but inspired send-up of the earlier film's "giant" composite ninja.

The Eagle Shooting Heroes *see* **Dong Cheng Xi Jiu**

Eagle's Shadow *see* **Snake In the Eagle's Shadow**

261. The East Is Red

(1993; Golden Princess/Long Shong Pictures/Film Workshop) ★: 5/10. *Dung Fong Bat Baai: fung wan joi hei* (Cantonese), *Dong Fang Bu Bai: feng yun zai qi* (Mandarin): "Invincible Asia: Turbulence Rises Again." Cinematographer: Tom Lau Moon-tong; Art Director: Eddie Ma Poon-chiu; Music: William Woo Wai-lap; Writers: Tsui Hark, Szeto Wai-cheuk, Charcoal Cheung Tan; Producer: Tsui Hark; Action Directors: Ma Yuk-shing, Dion Lam Dik-on; Directors: Ching Siu-tung, Raymond Lee Wai-man. Cast: Brigitte Lin Ching-hsia (Invincible Asia), Joey Wang Tsu-hsien (Snow), Yu Rong-guang (Koo), Eddy Ko Hung (Chin), Lau Shun (Warden of the Holy Altar), Jean Wang Ching-ying (Dai), Yuen King-tan (Madam). 1.85:1. VHS: Tai Seng. Import LD: Golden Cinema City. 97/110 minutes.

The runaway success of **Swordsman II** was due, in no small part, to Brigitte Lin's marvellous "Invincible Asia" character, so producer Tsui Hark decided to make her the centerpiece of this second sequel. Unfortunately, **The East Is Red** is not nearly as well structured, being overly chaotic, even as these films go. It still has a few pleasures, though, not the least of which are Lin's vivid characterization and a lovely score by William Woo. With Asia believed to now be dead, imitators have emerged, using the powerful warrior's name as a quick means to fame and fortune. When Asia is informed of this by loyal Han officer Koo, she sets out to destroy the imposters. The premiere charlatan is Snow, Asia's former lover and now the leader of the highlanders' Sun Moon Sect, who plans to bring down The Ming Dynasty using arms she has bought from traitorous soldiers. However, Asia's quest to clear her name is soon forgotten as she launches on a path of destruction. Koo tries to introduce some element of humanity and reason into the mounting chaos but this is an increasingly difficult task, especially since he has become smitten with Snow.

The delicious sexual ambiguity of **Swordsman II** gives way to teasing, designer lesbian interludes this time, sacrificing one of the previous film's most intriguing subtexts (though, considering the beautiful participants, it is doubtful that many male viewers will object). The main goal this time out seems to have been to continually defy viewers' expectations, and the movie just ends up being too outlandish for its own good. To wit: a Japanese warship that can transform into a *submarine*, Lin flying through the air on a swordfish and later breaking into song in a camp of prostitutes, a formidable ninja master turns out to be a dwarf in disguise, etc. While certain elements in HK fantasy may seem curious due to cultural differences, this movie goes out of its way to showcase these bits; there is none of the narrative discipline that made the first sequel such a tight and thrilling fable. The gravity-defying action sequences are plentiful and Lin has absolutely spectacular presence here, but **The East Is Red** ends up being little more than a screwball spectacle constantly in danger of crossing the line into outright satire. It is an amusing mess but a mess all the same and one that eventually wears out its welcome. The Golden Cinema City LD set is padded out with additional flashback footage from the first two films, increasing the running time to 110 minutes.

262. Eastern Condors

(1987; Golden Harvest/Bo Ho Films Co.) ★: 8/10. *Dung fong tuk ying* (Cantonese), *Dong fang tu ying* (Mandarin): "Eastern Condors." Cinematographer: Arthur Wong Ngok-tai; Art Director: Raymond Lee King-man; Music: Not Original; Writer: Barry Wong Ping-yiu; Producers: Wu Ma, Jeff Lau Chun-wai, Corey Yuen Kwai; Action Directors: Sammo Hung Kam-po, Yuen Biao, Corey Yuen Kwai, Lam Ching-ying, Yuen Wah. Director: Sammo Hung Kam-po. Cast: Sammo Hung Kam-po (Tung Ming-sun), Yuen Biao ("Rat" Chieh), Joyce Godenzi (Leader of Cambodian Guerillas), Lam Ching-ying (Colonel Lam), Charlie Chin Hsiang-lin (Szeto Chin), Billy Lau Nam-kwong (Ching), Yuen Woo-ping (Grandfather), Corey Yuen Kwai (Judy Vu), Yuen Wah (Vietnamese Commander), Dr. Haing S. Ngor (Rat's Uncle), Cheung Kwok-keung (Ching), Ha Chi-chun (Traitor), Melvin Wong Kam-sun (Colonel Yang), Peter Chan Lung (Ma Puk-kau), Billy Chow Bei-lee, Phillip Ko Fei, Yasuaki Kurota, Dick Wei (Vietnamese Soldiers). Dolby Digital (DVD Only). 2.35:1. VHS/LD: Tai Seng (Remastered for English Market; subtitled or dubbed). Import LD: Star Entertainment (No Subtitles). Import VCD: Mei Ah. Import DVD: Universe. 93 minutes (Subtitled), 94 minutes (Dubbed).

Sammo Hung directed and stars in this terrific actioner which smoothly blends martial arts and Vietnam war action elements together into a very satisfying whole. In 1976 the US government assembles a group of Chinese/Vietnamese prisoners into a **Dirty Dozen**-style combat force whose mission is to parachute back into Vietnam and destroy a hidden arsenal of US Army weapons that was left behind, before it falls into Vietcong hands. While in Vietnam, the troops meet up with three exceedingly tough female Cambodian guerillas who act as their escorts. Later, following a close call with the VC, they also pick up black market goods dealer "Rat" Chieh and his deranged uncle, and Chieh's knowledge of the terrain is a valuable aid in locating the underground complex. Hot on their trail is a psychotic Vietnamese colonel (Yuen Wah, in a positively reptilian performance), who locates and confronts the Condors for a showstopping final duel in the rocketbase (a very elaborate and impressive bit of production design).

The fight choreography is consistently inventive, making ingenious use of the jungle environment (in one memorable instance, Hung transforms *leaves* into deadly projectiles), and Yuen and Hung (the latter looking noticeably thinner than usual) are at the peak of their form. The dubbed version changes most of the characters' names (making all of the soldiers of solely Chinese descent) and deletes a sequence near the beginning (where Lam Ching-ying climbs up a flagpole), as well as two brief instances of violence from the climax.

263. Easy Money

(1987; D & B Films Co.) ★: 6/10. *Tung tin daai do* (Cantonese), *Tong tian da dao* (Mandarin): "Lead to Heaven Big Thief." Cinematographer: Tomato Chan Man-to; Art Director: Lee Chi-ngai; Writers: Yip Kwong-kim, Pang Chai-choi, Wai Kar-fai; Producer: Dickson Poon Dik-sun; Director: Stephen Shin Kei-yin. Cast: Michelle Yeoh Chu-kheng (Michelle Yeung), George Lam Chi-cheung (Lam), Kent Cheng Chuk-see (Ken), Ku Feng (Chan), Chen Jing (San Kai). Dolby Digital (DVD Only). 1.85:1. VHS: Tai Seng. Import VCD: Mega Star. Import DVD: Universe. 92 minutes.

Out of all the films Michelle Yeoh did for D & B Films prior to marrying company president Dickson Poon and briefly retiring, this lightweight caper flick is the least known. It's a mildly diverting entry (with a plot that anticipates John Woo's **Once a Thief** to a certain degree) that her fans will enjoy, if they can accept the comparative lack of action. Yeoh plays a glamorous millionairess who engineers an armored-car heist of $HK33 million in race track receipts simply for the fun of it. An insurance investigator with his own unique style and high tech accoutrements doggedly pursues her throughout Europe, abetted by a tough and resolute HK cop.

In an amusing touch, George Lam uses his computer to determine what entries in his extensive video library most resemble the crime (with **Topkapi**, **48 Hrs.** and **Tightrope** being chosen), and then proceeds to watch the three selections simultaneously, reasoning that most criminals derive their plans from movies. Director Stephen Shin incorporates location work in Britain, skiing in the Swiss alps (which is the closest Yeoh comes to martial arts here), hang-gliding over the French countryside, and a car chase through the streets of Paris (marred, unfortunately, by undercranking), and wraps things up with a climactic twist that is not unexpected but still satisfying.

264. Easy Money

(1991) ★: 5/10. *Lo biu faat chin hon* (Cantonese), *Lao biao fa qian han* (Mandarin): "Cousin Gives Money to the Poor." Cinematographers: Abdul M. Rumjahn, Cheung King-nin; Art Director: Bill Lui Cho-hung; Music: Chow Kai-sang, Writer: Lam Kei-to; Producer: Eddy Chan Kar-ho; Action Director: Benz Kong To-hoi; Director: Ko Sing-pui. Cast: Amy Yip Chi-mei (Susie Yip), Shing Fui-on (Tai), Wan Kwong (Losall), Simon Lui Yu-yeung (Tom), Gabriel Wong Yat-san (Wong Fee-hung). 1.85:1. VHS: Tai Seng. Running time unknown.

This unashamedly lowbrow comedy finds knuckleheads Tai, Losall, and Tom flat broke and desperate for work ... any work. They are hired to keep an eye on visiting heiress Marilyn but end up mistaking the girl for her buxom friend, Susie (a stripper who won't get totally naked, a clever reference to sexbomb Amy Yip's refusal to show all in her movies). The plan is for the trio to obtain compromising photos of Marilyn so that their boss (Gabriel Wong, in a performance that redefines the term "twitchy") can blackmail her, but Tom has fallen for Marilyn and Tai is infatuated with Susie. Losall, however, loves only money, and tries to figure out a way that he can still profit from the situation.

The jokes may not be original or even all that inspired. but this independently produced cheapie is so eager-to-please and energetically staged (particularly the martial arts movie send-ups) that it is hard to resist. The highlight is a parody of **A Chinese Ghost Story**, with Wan and Yip as the lovers, and Shing as The Tree Devil!

265. Easy Money

(1994; Beetles Film Production House) ★: 5/10. *Sin gong mei loi chin* (Cantonese), *Xian guang wei lai qian* (Mandarin): "First to Spend Future Money." Cinematographer: Philip Ma Kam-cheung; Art Director: Chan Kwok-kwong; Music: Tony Tam Chan-hung, Simon Leung Chi-wah, Ritchie Law Chung-leung, Jackson Wong Kam-kong; Writers: Wai Wang, Yee Lam; Producers: Danny Chow Chi-fu, Chan Kwok-kwong; Director: Simon Leung Chi-wah. Cast: Francis Ng Chun-yu (Chan Siu-wan), Athena Chu Yan (Sisi Li), Teresa Mak Kar-kei (Dee), Law Kar-ying (Chiang Chia-cheh), Yuen King-tan (Do Do Chan). 1.85:1. VHS: Tai Seng. Import LD/VCD: Ocean Shores. 93 minutes.

Credit card fraud is the theme of this comedy, which is ultimately too congenial and lightweight for its own good. Chiang and his cronies operate a highly lucrative credit card forgery ring using a department store as their front. They use customers' card numbers to create multiple forged cards and have lackeys travel around making extravagant purchases, which they then return for a refund. One day, they choose the wrong mark to bilk: Sisi, a feisty young bank employee who is not about to let them take her to the cleaners. Enlisting the aid of her perennially broke friends and a feisty debt collector, Sisi strikes a deal with the manager of her bank: They will beat the thieves at their own game and, in exchange, the bank will cover everyone's debts.

Francis Ng did not dub his own voice here, which detracts somewhat from his performance, and the climactic sting doesn't have the complexity or comedic punch found in the best films of this type. It's a pleasant timewaster but nothing more.

266. Ebola Syndrome

(1996; Wong Jing's Workshop) ★: 2/10. *Yi boh laai beng duk* (Cantonese), *Yi bo la bing bu* (Mandarin): "Ebola Virus." Cinematographer: Yu Kwok-bing; Art Director: Ho Chi-hang; Music: Mak Chun-hung; Writer: Candy Cheng; Producer: Wong Jing; Action Director: James Ha Chim-see; Director: Herman Yau Lai-to. Cast: Anthony Wong Chau-sang (Kai), Vincent Wan Yeung-ming (Yeung), Lo Mang (The Boss), Marianne Chan Miu-ying (Har), Shing Fui-on (Annoyed Husband), Bobby Yip King-sang (Short Ugly Triad). 1.85:1. VHS: Tai Seng. Import LD/VCD: Universe. 97 minutes.

Anthony Wong and director Herman Yau re-teamed for this revolting enterprise, a virtual remake of their infamous Category III horror yarn **The Untold Story**. After committing three murders in 1986, unmitigated sleazeball Kai went to South Africa to hide out from authorities. The story picks up ten years later with Kai illegally working for slave wages as a cook in a local Chinese restaurant. While out buying pigs from a native tribe, Kai rapes a woman infected with the ebola virus, becoming a carrier. After the disease begins to manifest itself in his system, Kai decapitates his boss and rapes and murders the man's wife. He then dismembers the corpses and uses the meat to make "African Buns," infecting everyone who eats them. Fleeing to HK, the increasingly demented Kai goes on a rampage, throwing the populace into a panic.

As with **The Untold Story**, there are moments which will shock and/or disgust many viewers, but the film itself is too simple-minded and exploitative to justify such excesses in the guise of black comedy. Anthony Wong deserves some kind of award for committing barbarous acts onscreen that most people wouldn't even want to think about, but he has given better performances in far more preferable films.

267. Edge of Darkness

(1988; D & B Films Co.) ★: 7/10. *Nam jeng bin yuen* (Cantonese), *Xian jing bian yan* (Mandarin): "Edge of the Trap." Cinematographer: Michael Ma Koon-wah; Art Director: Ho Yung-tsai; Music: Noel Quinlan; Writer-Producer: Phillip Chan Yan-kin; Action Directors: Fung Hark-on, Dai Bak-si, Ming Kei; Director: Fung Hark-on. Cast: Chin Siu-ho (Kay), Idy Chan Yuk-lin (Ling), Alex Man Chi-leung (Wong), Lo Lieh (Choi), John Sham Kin-fun (Chu Kar-mann), William Ho Kar-kui (Playboy Wah), Fung Hark-on ("Nut-cracker"), John Ching Tung ("Big Circle" Thug), Chen Jing ("Big Circle" Thug), Ronald Wong Pan (Cop). 1.85:1. VHS: Tai Seng. Import LD/VCD: Ocean Shores. 99 minutes.

A box office flop in HK and all but unknown in the West, this highly efficient police thriller deserves a wider audience and greater acclaim. Kay is an undercover officer who has spent four years in triad gangs; his true identity is known only by his superior, Officer Wong. When Kay reluctantly carries out an execution ordered by his gang boss, he is apprehended by police. That episode is resolved but the strain on Kay's relationship causes him to accidentally reveal his true occupation to both his girlfriend and fellow police officer Chu. A short time before Kay is scheduled to be pulled out of the field, Wong's gambling debts catch up with him. Faced with the choice of being murdered by triads or sent to prison for stealing confiscated drug money, Wong comes up with a different plan: He sells out Kay to the triads for over a million in cash. He then plans to cover his tracks by killing everyone involved in a drug deal the gangsters have arranged with some *Yakuza*.

Very well acted (especially by Alex Man, who is rarely cast in a role that so perfectly suits his smooth but edgy persona) and offering up the sort of twists HK genre films are not noted for, **Edge of Darkness** is a genuine sleeper well worth seeking out. In contrast to the norm, the action scenes are, perhaps, the film's weakest element, being more efficient than showy. The climax is not quite as creative as that which proceeds it, but still packs a punch and is quite satisfying. Among the action directors is one "Dai Bak-si," which means "Great White Shark" in Cantonese!

268. The Eight Diagram Pole Fighter

(1984; Shaw Brothers) ★: 9/10. *Ng-long baat gwa gwan* (Cantonese), *Wulang ba gua gun* (Mandarin): "Ng-long's Eight Diagram Staff" or "Wulang's Eight Diagram Staff." Cinematographer: Cho On-sun; Art Directors: Cheng Ching-shen, Teng Kuang-hsien; Music: So Chun-hou, Sing Kam-wing; Writers: Ngai Hong, Lau Kar-leung; Producer: Mona Fong Yat-wah; Action Directors: Lau Kar-leung, Ching Chu, Hsiao Hou; Director: Lau Kar-leung. Cast: Gordon Lau Kar-fai (Yang No. 5), Kara Hui Ying-hung (Yang No. 8), Alexander Fu Sheng (Yang No. 6), Lily Li Li-li (Yang Matriarch), Ku Ming (Pan Mei), Johnny Wang Lung-wei (Yeh Li-lin), Chu Tieh-hu (Ying Kuei), Phillip Ko Fei (Reverend), Lau Kar-leung (The Hunter), Yeung Ching-ching (Yang No. 9), Wong Yue (Yang No. 1), Mai Te-lo (Yang No. 3), Lau Kar-wing (Yang No. 2), Hsiao Hou (Yang No. 4), Chang Chan-peng (Yang No. 7). 2.35:1. No official domestic video release. 100 minutes. Also known as **The Invincible Pole Fighters** (Title for dubbed version).

When all but two of the men in the Yang family are massacred (the result of a plot orchestrated by Sung Dynasty general Pan Mei and his Mongol allies), only son No. 6 is able to return home to impart the grim news. Unfortunately, he has been driven insane by the horror, while son

No. 5 has become separated from his brother and is wandering the countryside. Narrowly escaping death at the hands of Pan's troops, No. 5 decides to bide his time by becoming a monk at Ching Lang Temple. However, his rage and thirst for vengeance is a violation of fundamental Buddhist teachings, causing the monks to reject him. Undeterred, No. 5 proceeds to shave his head anyway and, refusing to leave, causes the monks much grief. Meanwhile, word has come back to Lady Yang that her fifth son still lives, so she orders her eldest daughter, No. 8, to disguise herself as a man and bring him back home. Pan's spies are everywhere, however, and she is soon captured, forcing No. 5 to come out of hiding and attempt a rescue.

A superb period thriller, **The Eight Diagram Pole Fighter** is exceptional in every department, combining a traditional but exciting storyline (which provides ample opportunity for tragedy and high emotion) with outstanding martial arts (the stick fighting battle between Gordon Lau and Phillip Ko is the standout among several highlights). Co-star Alexander Fu died in a car accident mid-shoot, prompting a re-write that transformed Gordon Lau's character into the protagonist. This tragedy may partially account for the downbeat tone of the film, which is resolutely serious from beginning to end and ranks among the very best of director Lau Kar-leung's productions for Shaw Brothers. The Chinese title is the name of the staff technique that Yeung Ng-long (or Yang Wulang in Mandarin) developed from the Yeung Family Spear Technique. In real life, there are two stories as to why Yeung/Yang became a monk. One has him becoming disgruntled with fighting wars and becoming a monk in order to escape the carnage. The other has him being captured and offered a chance to join up with the enemy. He refuses, stating that he would rather become a monk than join with his rivals, a pledge that the enemy general makes him keep. Character names above are from the dubbed version.

269. The Eight Hilarious Gods

(1993; Crown Film Co.) ★: 3/10. *Siu baat sin* (Cantonese), *Xiao ba xian* (Mandarin): "Eight Laughing Immortals." Cinematographer: Wong Kar-fai; Art Director: Yeung Siu-siu; Music: William Woo Wai-lap; Writer: Siu Lung; Producer: Tommy Leung Yee-kei; Action Director: Alan Lo Kwok-wai; Director: Jeffrey Chiang Chia-chun. Cast: Adam Cheng Siu-chau (Ben), Rosamund Kwan Chi-lam (Lotus), Deric Wan Siu-lun (Smart Han), Ng Man-tat (Lousy Han), Lawrence Cheng Tan-shui (Uncle Cheung), Sandra Ng Kwan-yu (Buddy Wall), Shing Fui-on (Sheriff Lee), Peter Lai Bei-tak (Uncle Tsao), Lau Shun (Lucifer). 1.85:1. VHS: World Video. Import LD/VCD/DVD: Mei Ah. Running time unknown.

Hilarious? More like sporadically amusing at best. To call this period fantasy spoof (lensed in Singapore) lowbrow is an understatement of the first order. Looking to retrieve "The Six Blessed Pearls," immortals Ben and Buddy Wall descend to Earth and end up using their powers to battle the monstrous demon Lucifer. When the creature demands that six of the area's children be sacrificed to him, Ben and Buddy join forces with six fellow warriors who are destined to face off against the evil. Together they must stop Lucifer from eating the blessed pearls or all of mankind will be doomed.

If one were to subtract all of the gags that involve bodily fluids, homosexuality, or slovenly behavior, the joke count would seemingly be in the single digits. Rosamund Kwan does a droll imitation of Maggie Cheung's character from **Dragon Inn**, but the rest of the material here is rarely better than puerile (the outtakes under the end crawl offer more laughs than the entire feature!) and even the fantastic aspects of the plot are lacklustre. **Flying Dagger** and **Holy Weapon** are more successful send-ups of the genre.

270. Eight Taels of Gold

(1989; Golden Harvest/Maverick Films) ★: 7/10. *Baat a gam* (Cantonese), *Ba ya jin* (Mandarin): "Eight Taels of Gold." Cinematographer: Bill Wong Chung-bo; Art Director: Rebecca Lee Lok-si; Music: Lo Tai-yau, Richard Lo Sai-kit; Writers: Alex Law Kai-yui, Mabel Cheung Yuen-ting; Producer: John Sham Kin-fun; Director: Mabel Cheung Yuen-ting. Cast: Sammo Hung Kam-po (Slim Cheng), Sylvia Chang Ai-chia (Jenny, aka Odds-and-Ends), Law Kwok-ping, Ho Tak-hung. 1.85:1. VHS: Tai Seng. Import LD: ERA. 101 minutes.

After an absence of sixteen years, tubby New York City cabbie Slim heads home to China to visit his family. Upon arrival, he discovers that his sister is about to have a second baby, in defiance of the country's law forbidding couples from having more than one child. To evade the authorities, she has moved to the countryside, along with Slim's parents. Hooking up with his rather dimwitted cousin Jenny, Slim's journey is filled with mishaps, thanks to Jenny's inability to tell left from right. After finally reaching his relatives, Slim must deal with his feelings of guilt (he left during The Cultural Revolution and only wrote home once in the ensuing years), his mother's embarrassing attempts at matchmaking, and his burgeoning feelings for Jenny. She, however, is already betrothed and the wedding is imminent.

Sammo Hung is best known in the West for his action films, but he is also a fine actor, as had already been proven in Alex Law's **Painted Faces**. He gives a subtle, touching performance in this bittersweet film which thoroughly wins one over, in spite of its fairly obvious course and structure. Perhaps because she has played so many intelligent, strong-willed women over the years, Sylvia Chang is less convincing as a Mainland country girl, but the scenes she shares with Hung in the final act are quite touching and one's overall impression of her work remains positive. The rural people we meet here are a welcome change from the one-dimensional characters found in so many HK films, as is the seemingly realistic depiction of their life.

271. The 18 Shaolin Golden Boys

(1996; Sam Po Film) ★: 1/10. *Goo wak kei bing ji bing hang him jeuk* (Cantonese), *Gu huo qi bing zhi bing xian zhe* (Mandarin): "Sneaky Soldiers: Dangerous Operation." Cinematographer: Yeung Ke-leung; Art Director: Sek Ping-lun; Music: Wong To; Writer: Law Kei; Producer: To Hoi-sang; Action Directors: Fung Hark-on, Cheung Ping-chan; Director: To Wai-tat. Cast: Willie Chi Tian-sheng (Rocky), Cherie Chan Siu-ha (Maria), Yu Rongguang (Pao), William Ho Kar-kui (Yuen Mo), Billy Chow Bei-lee (Pao's Man), Shing Fui-on (Ahn). 1.85:1. VHS: Tai Seng. Import LD/VCD: Universe. 90 minutes.

You can't get any worse than this awful Mainland martial arts indie, which manages to prevail over the abysmal **Iron Monkey 2** as the indisputable low point to date of the '90s kung fu movie cycle. Dispatched by his dying master, Chinese American kung fu expert Rocky journeys from San Francisco to Shaolin Temple. After proving himself to the abbot (this must be the only film to ever have its hero dodging laser beams as part of a Shaolin Temple martial skills test!), Rocky is allowed to stay. His talents come in handy when a gang of antique smugglers (led by Yu Rongguang, in desperate need of a career boost) try to steal an invaluable Flying Horse statue from the temple. The title characters are a group of obnoxious child monks who perform their kung fu stances (which have names like "Chastity Dynamite") covered in gold spray paint.

A painful (not to mention painfully slow) 90 minutes, this cheapjack affair ruins its few accomplished displays of martial arts prowess by inserting silly wirework. The plotting is sophomoric and the jokes (which run the gamut from inane to the sort of scatological gags that will make most Westerners cringe) are desperate. The film even goes so far as to steal a sequence from the Tom Hanks movie **Big**! HK audiences weren't fooled: This disappeared from local screens after only two days and a total gross of HK$73,955 (about *$9,000* in US funds). *The 18 Shaolin Golden Boys* is yet another unmitigated disaster from the folks at Sam Po Film, HK's worst production company.

272. Eighteen Springs

(1997; Mandarin Films) ★: 6/10. *Boon sang yuen* (Cantonese), *Ban sheng yuan* (Mandarin): "Affair of Half a Lifetime." Cinematographer: Mark Lee Ping-bing; Art Directors: Bruce Yu Kar-on, Yank Wong Yan-kwai; Music: Ye Xiao-gang; Writer: John Chan Kin-chung; Producers: Raymond Wong Pak-ming, Leung Fung-yee; Director: Ann Hui On-wah. Cast: Jacqueline Wu Chien-lien (Gu Manjing), Leon Lai Ming (Shen Shijun), Anita Mui Yim-fong (Gu Manlu), Ge You (Zhu Hongcai), Annie Wu Chen-chun (Shi Cuizhi), Huang Lei (Xu Shuhui), Wang Zhowen (Zhang Yujin). Dolby Digital. 1.85:1. VHS/LD: World Video. Import LD/VCD/DVD: Mei Ah. 126 minutes.

Adapted from an Eileen Chang novel and set in 1930s Shanghai, this attractively made, leisurely paced romantic drama benefits immensely from what female lead Jacqueline Wu is able to bring to her traditional role as the tragic heroine. Co-workers Gu Manjing and Shen Shijun are formally introduced by a mutual friend and the pair gradually fall in love. The Gu family once held a prominent place in society but now ranks far below that of the Shen clan; because of this, there is a certain hesitation by both parties in the relationship, in spite of the fact that the two clearly love each other. Shijun's father falls gravely ill, necessitating that Shijun return to Nanjing and take over the family business. Manjing comes with him but, because of her resemblance to older sister Manlu (a ballroom girl who has entered into a loveless marriage with affluent Zhu Hongcai), the latter's past becomes known to Shijun and he decides that he cannot marry Manjing because of this. The situation grows much worse when Hongcai comes home drunk one night and rapes Manjing, impregnating her. He and Manlu imprison Manjing, and when the girl has the baby, they take it and leave her behind. Shijun still loves Manjing but, because of various acts of fate, the two cannot be together again until it is too late.

The ending is never in doubt and the melodramatic indulgences of the original source cannot be overcome, but **Eighteen Springs** remains palatable, thanks to its elegant images, subtle manner, and, especially, Jacqueline Wu's performance as Manjing. Leon Lai is a handsome blank as Shijun, but Wu gives one of her finest turns, projecting genuine, affecting emotions (director Ann Hui wisely gives her a number of close-ups in which to convey even the subtlest of them), completely winning the viewer's empathy. Anita Mui received the Best Supporting Actress prize at The Hong Kong Film Awards, but her performance pales in comparison to what Wu is able to accomplish with a far less flamboyant persona.

273. The Eighth

(1996; Keen Pearl International) ★: 2/10. *Dai baat jung jui* (Cantonese), *Di ba zong zui* (Mandarin): "The Eighth Ancestral Sin." Cinematographer: Joe Chan Kong-hung; Music: Lai Wan-man; Writer: Cho Po-lan; Action Director: Chin Kar-lok; Producers: Mo Sai-chiu, Tam Yung-chuan, Ho Kin-cheng; Art Director-Director: Jon Hau Wing-choi. Cast: Catherine Hung Yan (Yi), Lam Kar-tung (Jie), Vincent Wan Yeung-ming (Ming), Carrie Ng Kar-lai (Li), Pauline Chan Po-lin (Pauline), Wong Chi-yeung (Lin Jinwen). VHS: World Video. Import LD/VCD: Universe. 89 minutes.

Jon Hau, one of HK's least talented but most prolific filmmakers, strikes again with this plodding drama. The Chinese title makes reference to the 1995 Hollywood hit **Se7en** but, alas, there is no connection. Instead, we are served up the decidedly uninteresting story of "Mad Bull" Jie, an ex-con just released from jail after serving a murder sentence. Earlier in life he killed his father, whom he caught molesting his sister Li (who was left withdrawn and nearly catatonic). Back on the streets, Jie meets Yi, a flighty girl in HK on vacation from America, and the two begin a relationship. Li, meanwhile, is starting to come out of her shell, thanks to all the tender attention she is receiving from Ming, Jie's gangster friend. When Ming's boss orders him to execute mob traitor Lin Jinwen before the latter can testify in court, events ensue that change everyone's lives forever.

As if the pacing weren't glacial enough, a gang fight and a sex scene unfold in interminable slow motion. The ending manages to be as stultifying as it is predictable, which is the only accomplishment this bomb will ever be remembered for.

274. The Eighth Happiness

(1988; Cinema City Co.) ★: 6/10. *Baat sing biu choi* (Cantonese), *Ba xing bao xi* (Mandarin): "Eight Stars Greetings." Cinematographer: Joe Chan Kong-hung; Art Director: Raymond Chan Kam-ho; Music: Antonio Arevalo Jr.; Writers: Raymond Wong Pak-ming, Edward Lee Kui-ming, Philip Cheng Chung-tai, Ng Man-fai; Producer: Raymond Wong Pak-ming; Director: Johnny To Kei-fung. Cast: Chow Yun-fat (Fang Chien-lang), Cherie Chung Cho-hung (Beautiful), Carol Cheng Yu-ling (Do Do Cheng), Petrina Fung Bo-bo (Wu Hsiu-fang), Jacky Cheung Hok-yau (Fang Chien-sang), Raymond Wong Pak-ming (Fang Chien-hui), Fennie Yuen Kit-ying (Ying-ying), Wong Kwan-yuen (Ming-ming), Michael Chow Man-kin (Roy), Charlie Cho Cha-lei (Do Do's Prospective Suitor), Lawrence Cheng Tan-shui (Beautiful's Boyfriend), John Sham Kin-fun (Audience Member), Karl Maka (Audience Member), Ringo Lam Ling-tung (Audience Member), Teddy Robin Kwan (Hsiu-fang's Husband). Dolby Digital (DVD Only). 1.85:1. VHS: Tai Seng. Import LD: Golden Cinema City. Import VCD: Mei Ah. Import DVD: Universe. 91 minutes.

Director Johnny To reportedly abhors this Lunar New Year smash, but it is above average for its type and far more entertaining than actor/producer Raymond Wong's more recent holiday comedies. It also features Chow Yun-fat in one of his wildest roles as an effeminate sissy who is catnip to the ladies! The story (such as it is) centers around the romantic exploits of The Fang Brothers, who have been aided in their quest to snare the women of their dreams by a telephone malfunction (don't ask). Carefree cartoonist Chien-sang has his heart stolen by jogger Ying-ying; incorrigible Chien-lang looks and acts homosexual but is splitting his time between department store clerk Beautiful and stewardess Do Do; eldest brother (and TV cooking show host) Chien-hui is middle-aged and single but has his eye on Cantonese opera star Wu Hsiu-fang, not knowing that she is the woman he has been having a running crank call battle with. As you would expect, things go from bliss to disaster for Chien-lang and Chien-hui, and then, following a round of desperate ploys, back to bliss.

Star power is paramount in this kind of movie and everyone concerned comes off favorably. Chow Yun-fat and Cherie Chung are especially fun to watch as the ultimate pair of obnoxious hedonists and the climax (which has all of the principals participating in an opera performance) cleverly ties up the loose ends.

275. Encounter of the Spooky Kind

(1981; Golden Harvest/Bo Ho Films Co.) ★: 8/10. *Gwai chuk gwai* (Cantonese), *Gui da gui* (Mandarin): "Ghost Strikes Ghost." Cinematographer: Lee Yao-tong; Music: Chan Chun-chi (HK version), Avalon Music (Dubbed version); Writers: Sammo Hung Kam-po, Wong Ying; Producer: Raymond Chow Man-wai; Action Director-Director: Sammo Hung Kam-po. Cast: Sammo Hung Kam-po (Courageous Cheung), Chung Fat (Tsui), Peter Chan Lung (Chin Hoi), Wong Har (Master Tam), Lam Ching-ying (The Inspector), Tai Po (Lau), Wu Ma (Fa Kau), Cheung Ti-hong (Lau), Leung Suet-moi (Cheung's Wife), To Siu-ming (Tao). 2.35:1. VHS: Tai Seng (Remastered for the English market; subtitled or dubbed). Import VCD: Mega Star (Poor Subtitles). 102 minutes (Subtitled version), 98 minutes (Dubbed version). Also known as **Spooky Encounters**.

A bonafide classic of the HK horror-comedy genre, **Encounter of the Spooky Kind** set the standard for the many that followed. Loudmouth braggart "Courageous" Cheung is actually anything but. In fact, he is a blithering coward under the thumb of his shrill, bitchy wife who is having a secret affair with Tam, a powerful politician. When Cheung almost catches the pair in bed together, Tam gets worried about his image being sullied. He decides to have Cheung killed and enlists the aid of the wizard Chin Hoi to do the deed. Setting up a trap, Chin's friend, Fa Kau, bets Cheung that he cannot live up to his nickname and spend the entire night in a haunted temple. Cheung agrees to the wager, but on his way to the temple he is stopped by Tsui, one of Chin's associates. Tsui refuses to allow his sect to participate in such underhanded doings and instructs Cheung on how to spend the night in safety. Come midnight, Chin re-activates a dormant *gyonsi* and it prowls the premises looking for Cheung. Just as the creature is about to finish him off, the sun rises and the monster retreats. While still in a daze after his perilous ordeal, Cheung is tricked into spending *another* night in the temple; Once again he survives thanks to Tsui's help. Tam then decides to take a different approach, framing Cheung for the murder of his wife. Arrested by a resolute inspector and facing execution, Cheung manages to escape prison. Tsui decides to take him as a pupil, instructing him as best he can in the ways of occult self-defense. The climax finds Tsui and Chin facing off in a thrilling magicians' duel, with Cheung, Tam, and Chin's assistant acting as supernaturally controlled surrogate fighters.

In contrast to most of the later entries, the horror sequences are played straight, with an emphasis on gruesomely decomposed corpses and bloody, arcane rituals. The screenplay allows for a number of martial arts sequences which are smoothly integrated and necessary to the plot. The best occurs after Chin puts a curse on Cheung, causing him to lose control of his hand (anticipating a similar sequence in **Evil Dead II**) while trying to fight off a number of attackers. The finale is an intense tour-de-force, highlighted by an ingenious comedic conceit that will be lost on most Western viewers: In order to increase the power of the combatants, the magicians invoke the spirits of various Chinese gods to inhabit their bodies. This leads to a number of broad characterizations, the best being Hung's chattering Monkey King, which allows the actor to present a spectacular display of monkey-style kung fu. Hung also stars in Ricky Lau Koon-wai's **Encounter of the Spooky Kind II** (1991), though the film is a sequel in name only. The mix and match soundtrack on the Cantonese version includes cues lifted from **Horror Express** and **Phantasm**.

276. Encounter of the Spooky Kind II

(1990; Golden Harvest/Bojon Films Co.) ★: 6/10. *Gwai aau gwai* (Cantonese), *Gui yao gui* (Mandarin): "Ghost Bites Ghost." Cinematographer: Tom Lau Moon-tong; Art Director: Ben Lau Man-hung; Music: Lowell Lo Kwun-ting; Writer: Barry Wong Ping-yiu; Producer: Sammo Hung Kam-po; Action Directors: James Tien Chun, Siu Tak-fu, Chow Kam-kong, Sammo Hung Stuntmen Association; Director: Ricky Lau Koon-wai. Cast: Sammo Hung Kam-po (Po), Lam Ching-ying (The Master), Mang Hoi (Hoi), Yip Wing-cho (Chu). 1.85:1. VHS: Tai Seng. Import LD: Mei Ah. 99 minutes.

Bearing no direct connection to the original, this period horror-comedy is a much more routine effort. Poor Po has more than his share of troubles, thanks to his arrogant, would-be father-in-law. In order for Po to marry his betrothed sweetheart, Little Chu, he has to come up with an enormous dowry that is well beyond his meager means. One evening, Po encounters a female spirit named Hung. In return for helping her still-living mother, the ghost agrees to aid Po in his battle against the rich jerk trying to steal Little Chu away. However, the plan goes awry and Po's strict master tries to dispel Hung's spirit. He eventually relents and offers to help Hung, but a rival wizard (under the employ of Po's rival) dispatches two nasty, cockroach-filled(!) zombies to vanquish the understandably shocked man. When that fails, Po's soul is captured and placed in the body of a piglet. Po's master is able to restore him, but the wizard takes control of Chu's father and sends him out to kill Po.

There are a number of amusingly bizarre spells, and Sammo Hung deserves some kind of award for letting dozens of roaches swarm over him at one point. The action choreography is also good, and Lam Ching-ying remains HK cinema's definitive Taoist master. Still, even with all of these assets, the film generally lacks the demented inventiveness of the best films in this subgenre and is a little disappointing, considering the talent involved.

277. End of the Road

(1993; Chang Hong Channel Film Co.) ★: 5/10. *Yi wik ji mei lo yung hung* (Cantonese), *Yi yu zhi wei lu ying xiong* (Mandarin): "Hero at the End of the Road in a Foreign Land." Cinematographer: Chen Rong-shu; Art Director: Wang Tong; Music: Wong Kin-cheung, Lo Tai-yau; Writers: Wu Nian-chen, Yeh Yun-chiao; Producer: Hui Pui-yung; Director: Chu Yen-ping. Cast: Tony Leung Chiu-wai (Fan Long), Tou Chung-wah (Ke Bao-den), Ko Chuen-hsiang (General Hau), Ray Lui Leung-wai (Lo Huei), Ng Man-tat (Chei), Yeh Chuan-chen (The Schoolteacher), Jimmy Lin Chi-ying (Din), Rosamund Kwan Chi-lam (Chei's Wife). 1.85:1. VHS: Tai Seng. Import LD: Golden Cinema City. 87 minutes.

Taiwanese director Chu Yen-ping's follow-up to **A Home Too Far** suffers from the same limitations as its forerunner but is partially salvaged by solid performances. Threatened by the Burmese army, The Nationalists decide to disarm. However, the enemy is not about to let them escape with their lives. Following a raid on their camp, some of the men defect and join a gang of rebels in the mountains. The remaining Nationalists continue to fight against the Min Communists and eventually join up with the Thai armed forces. Their first assignment is to vanquish bandit Lo Huei, whose troops include some of the Nationalist men who had left the ranks some time before. Faced with the prospect of possibly having to kill old friend Fan Long (who had previously saved his life when they were imprisoned together at a Burmese camp), Bao-den decides to visit Fan and warn him of the impending offensive.

As with the first chapter, there are battles galore and much patriotic rhetoric, but, for all of the flag waving, few emotions are stirred, and Chu's attempts to duplicate elements from **Apocalypse Now** fall flat. Amid the cliches, some of the performers manage to stand out, particularly Ng Man-tat as an aged soldier with a weak spot that proves to be his undoing. While definitely a continuation of **A Home Too Far**, there are odd lapses in continuity regarding names and characters, evidently a side effect of the very poor English translation provided here; the introduction and all of the intertitles are left only in Chinese, which will hopelessly confuse those who have not seen the previous installment.

Endless Love *see* **C'est La Vie, Mon Cheri**

278. Enemy Shadow

(1995) ★: 3/10. *Ying chi dik yan* (Cantonese), *Ying zi di ren* (Mandarin): "Shadow Enemy." Cinematographer: Cheung Man-bo; Art Director: Cyrus Ho Kim-hung; Music: Patrick Lui Yau-fai; Writer: Law Kwan-cho; Producer: Lam Siu-ming; Action Director: Dion Lam Dik-on; Directors: Peter Mak Tai-kit, Chan Tung-chuen (uncredited). Cast: Jade Leung Ching (Jade), James Pak Chin-shek (Panther), Kenneth Chan Kai-tai (Officer Choi Chi-ken), Ben Ng Ngai-cheung (Man San), Moses Chan Ho (Tung), Shing Fui-on (Keung), Law Koon-lan (Sister), Peter Chan Lung (Hood). 1.85:1. VHS: Tai Seng. Import LD/VCD: Universe. 92 minutes.

This troubled production (which began with Chan Tung-chuen at the helm and was completed by Peter Mak) presents a familiar storyline in an annoyingly overstylized and superficial manner, tied together with reams of pretentious, laughable narration. Jade is a rookie cop who witnesses her boyfriend's murder at the hands of some masked bank robbers. Too shocked to react, she watches the killers drive away without firing so much as a shot. She then tries her hand at undercover work for the anti-drug squad but becomes too involved with her criminal targets, suffering unbearable guilt upon turning them in. Quitting the force, she becomes acquainted with Panther, a suave criminal who gradually leads her over to the other side of the law. In spite of her resignation, Jade's former superior, Officer Choi, successfully enlists her to spy on Panther. However, Choi and Panther have a relationship that goes beyond cop and criminal, just as Panther's bond with Jade prevents him from killing her, even after he learns the truth.

HK action movies are often criticized for being formulaic, assembly-line efforts with little or no artistic pretensions; if **Enemy Shadow** represents the flipside of this particular coin, then the industry need not bother changing its ways. The film relies so much upon slow motion and empty symbolism to provide atmosphere and meaning to mundane situations and characters, it degenerates into an exercise in ennui that is sparked only by an occasional shootout or gang fight. The second half plays out in a somewhat more satisfying manner (presumably being the work of the other director) but the final reel strains credibility to the breaking point. Aside from Dion Lam's polished action choreography and Ben Ng's amusing supporting performance (as a flamboyantly gay gangster), there is precious little here that clicks. Regardless, Jade Leung's fans may still want to look the film up, as she is lovingly photographed throughout. Her back was burned when a planned, on-set explosion went awry, and, in typical HK fashion, the sequence (which shows Leung running down a hallway and being engulfed in a fireball) remains in the finished product.

Enforcers *see* **Seven Warriors**

279. The Enigma of Love

(1993; Chun Yue Amusement Production) ★: 2/10. *Fei yuet mai ching* (Cantonese), *Fei yue mi qing* (Mandarin): "Fly Over Enigma Love." Cinematographer: Tam Chi-wai; Art Director: Ken Chiu Kin-san; Music: Fung Chiu-seng; Writer: Law Kam-fai; Producer: To Leung-shun; Director: Sherman Wong Ching-wah. Cast: Jacky Cheung Hok-yau (Jacky), Maggie Cheung Man-yuk (Tammy Cheung), Wilson Lam Chun-yin (David Lam), Maria Cordero (Kwai Fa-pon), Parkman Wong Pak-man (Wong). 1.85:1. VHS: World Video. 96 minutes.

There isn't a single fresh idea or genuine emotion to be found in this witless formula comedy, which will strain the patience of even the most forgiving viewers. Jacky Cheung (miscast in a role better suited to Simon Yam Tat-wah) plays Jacky, the king of gigolos and proprietor of the most notorious "gigolo shop" in all of HK. When the police, led by Officer Lam, try to raid the place, Jacky foils them in embarrassing fashion, prompting the department to enlist two female oàcers: kickass tomboy Tammy Cheung (Maggie Cheung, miscast in a role better suited to Sibelle Hu Hui-chung) and the massive Kwai Fa-pon. The pair have more success when they return to the establishment the next evening, but Jacky is nowhere to be found, having gone on a trip with a client. In order to get revenge, Jacky decides to court Tammy by pretending to be a terminally ill artist with only three months to live. He feigns being hit by the woman's car, laying a severe guilt trip on her and prompting the policewoman to take care of him. When Tammy saves Jacky from falling over a cliff, he develops guilt of his own and genuinely falls for her. Naturally, when he tells her the truth, she hates him, but, compared to the dishonorable intentions of the unstable Lam (who has fallen for her as well), Jacky isn't such a bad guy.

The one and only enigma here is why Maggie Cheung (who does not dub her own voice) and Jacky Cheung would agree to appear in such a shabby, mindless enterprise as this, a career low for both. In spite of the composer credit, most of the music consists of familiar library cues.

280. Enjoy Yourself Tonight

(1997; Hang Ngai Films Co.) ★: 2/10. *Nei goh mat ye cheung* (Cantonese), *Ni ge mie ye chang* (Mandarin): "What Kind of Turf Is This?" Cinematographer: Ngai Man-yin; Music: Not Original; Writers: Fong Tin-man, To Hun-kit; Producer: Wong Siu-ming; Director: Hou Shu-pui. Cast: Michael Chow Man-kin (Ming), Francoise Yip Fong-wah (Susan), Teresa Mak Kar-kei (Fei), Mok Ho-yun (Kan), Lo Mang (Fang), Yu Rongguang (Nan). 1.85:1. VHS: Tai Seng. Import LD/VCD: Universe. 85 minutes.

Despite multiple storylines, nothing entertaining occurs in this low-budget mess, which unfolds during the course of one evening at a nightclub. *Mamasan* Susan is dumped by her boyfriend of five years; two of her hostesses (Fei and Kan) are deeply in debt and triad collector Ming is desperate to get back what they owe; one of Susan's girls is a drug addict *and* a minor; and four youths having a bachelor party can't pay their $8000 tab. To make matters worse, one of the patrons drops dead in a corridor, Fei kidnaps Ming's young son and demands a $200,000 ransom, and Ming's vicious boss (a triad/small-time movie producer) orders him to ice one of his competitors.

This all might have made for a mildly amusing comedy of errors if the script had some semblance of wit. Alas, it doesn't and the proceedings actually turn serious in the latter third, a fatal mistake when the characters command no viewer interest or sympathy. Enjoy *yourself* tonight by watching something else. Despite being featured prominently on the poster, Yu Rongguang appears only briefly.

281. Enter the Fat Dragon

(1978; H.K. Fong Ming Film Co.) ★: 6/10. *Fei lung gwoh gong* (Cantonese),

Fei long guo jiang (Mandarin): "Fat Dragon Crossing River." Cinematographer: Ricky Lau Koon-wai; Music: Frankie Chan Fan-kei; Writer: Ngai Hong; Producer: Lee Sun; Action Director-Director: Sammo Hung Kam-po. Cast: Sammo Hung Kam-po (Lung), Roy Chiao Hung (Chiu), Leung Kar-yan (Bearded Fighter), Meg Lam Kin-ming (Pa-chieh), Fung Hark-on (Gene), Eric Tsang Chi-wai (Party Host's Son), Feng Sing, Chung Fat, Mang Hoi, Yuen Biao (Fighters in Opening Credit Sequence). 2.35:1. VHS/DVD: Crash Cinema. 91 minutes.

Forget Bruce Li—the greatest Bruce Lee imitator is ... Sammo Hung! Yes, you read that right: Hung has Lee's moves and gestures down *perfectly*, and that, combined with his tremendous martial arts skills, make him the perfect lead for this raucous spoof of **Return of the Dragon** (1973; aka **Way of the Dragon**). Hung plays Lung, a tubby assistant on a pig farm who is also a Bruce Lee fanatic and spends every waking hour imitating his idol. Sent to the city to help out at a relative's food stall, Lung ends up battling a group of deadbeat hoods (whose ranks include Yuen Biao). The thugs return later on and trash the premises, so Hung finds new employment as a dishwasher. A bizarre antiques collector craves one of the waitresses at the establishment and has his men drug and kidnap her. Coming to his friend's rescue, Lung must face off against the villain's bodyguards, all kung fu experts, naturally.

A lot of the incidental humor falls flat (having Lee Hoi-sang play a Jim Kelly-like villain in blackface and an afro wig anticipates a similarly embarrassing gag at the climax of Hung's 1995 film, **Don't Give a Damn**) but the Lee parodies are so good, you will keep watching anyway. The best sequence finds Lung hired to be a background fighter in a Bruce Lee ripoff feature called "The Death Appointment." Naturally, he thoroughly outclasses the film's cocky star and easily defeats his entourage (look fast for Lam Ching-ying and Mang Hoi). The final battle between Hung and Leung Kar-yan (in a warehouse that just happens to have some traditional weapons on hand) is outstanding.

Enter the 36th Chamber of Shaolin *see* **Crazy Shaolin Disciples**

282. Erotic Ghost Story

(1990; Golden Harvest/Paragon Films) ★: 5/10. *Liu jai yim taam* (Cantonese), *Liao zhai yan tan* (Mandarin): "Dark Tales: Vibrant Tale." Art Director: Lau Sai-wan; Music: Phil Chan Fei-lap; Writer: Chang Kwan; Producer: Chow Chan-tung; Action Director: Phillip Kwok Tsui; Cinematographer-Director: Nam Nai-choi. Cast: Man So (Pai So-so), Amy Yip Chi-mei (Hua-hua), Sin Lap-man (Wu Ming), Lam Chung (Hsuan Kuei), Ha Chi-chun (Mrs. Wang), Manfred Wong (Wang). Dolby Digital (DVD Only). 1.85:1. VHS: Tai Seng (Remastered for the English market; subtitled or dubbed). Import LD: Mei Ah. Import VCD: Mei Ah, Mega Star. Import DVD: Universe. 88 minutes.

Alternating between amusingly cheesy and enticingly erotic, this period Category III film (patterned very closely after **The Witches of Eastwick**) was a box office success and spawned two sequels. Fairy sisters So-so, Fei-fei, and Hua-hua must retain human form for 36 days; once this time has passed, they will become immortal. However, So-so makes the mistake of thinking carnal thoughts about the multi-headed god Wutung while in the deity's temple, and Taoist priest Hsuan Kuei warns her that this may well lead to disaster. One day, she saves handsome scholar Wu Ming from some brigands. Taking a liking to the man, So-so offers to support Wu until he finishes his studies. One by one, Wu seduces each of the sisters and eventually becomes quite brazen in his sexual pursuit of the women. One morning, the sisters find that they have inexplicably started to revert to their animal forms and, upon investigating, discover that Wu is not what he seems.

There are a number of tasteful sexual encounters, some of which are staged amid handsome artificial exterior sets, reminiscent of those found in classic Shaw Brothers films. Unfortunately, the make-up and special FX look like they date from that era as well, making the film's fantastic content something less than plausible. Chances are that most male viewers will not care.

283. Erotic Ghost Story II

(1991; Golden Harvest/Diagonal Pictures/Paragon Films) ★: 6/10. *Liu jai yim taam chuk chap neung tung san* (Cantonese), *Liao zhai yan tan xu ji wu tong shen* (Mandarin): "Dark Tales Vibrant Tale Concluding Episode: Five Powerful Gods." Art Director: Raymond Lee King-man; Music: BMG Melody Bank; Writers: Szeto On, Lam Tai-ho, Choi Suk-yin, Abe Kwong Man-wai, Peter Ngor Chi-kwan; Producer: Casey Chan Lai-ying; Cinematographer-Director: Peter Ngor Chi-kwan. Cast: Charine Chan Kar-ling (Fang Yu-yin), Anthony Wong Chau-sang (Wutung/Chiu-sheng), Chik King-man (Chen), Kwok Yiu-wah (Shan-ken). Dolby Digital (DVD only). 1.85:1. VHS: Tai Seng. Import LD/DVD: Universe. Import VCD: Universe, Mega Star. 97 minutes.

Opening with a recap of the original, this lively sequel then goes on to even more fantastic and deliriously stylized heights than its predecessor. Wutung transposes himself into another demonic satyr, named Chiu-sheng (played this time by Anthony Wong in outrageous make-up that makes him look like a back-up singer for Twisted Sister), and falls for maiden Hsiao-yen, who is determined to try and cleanse him of his evil. The girl is destroyed by two heavenly nuns (cameo appearances by original stars Amy Yip Chi-mei and Man So), but, in an act of compassion, one puts the dead girl's spirit inside a newborn. Several years then pass. Seeking to appease the still-angry Chiu-sheng, one village sacrifices a young virgin to the demon once every year. Fang Yu-yin is chosen for the latest ritual but is saved by brawny fisherman Shan-ken, who mutilates Chiu-sheng with an axe. The demon retreats to the netherworld to lick his wounds (in a manner of speaking) and has one of his minions track Yu-yin down. Not surprisingly, the girl turns out to be the one possessing Hsiao-yen's spirit, making her conquest of supreme importance to the creature.

Charine Chan is a wooden bore as the female lead, but Anthony Wong has a great time as the growling satyr (who has a phallic tail with a life of its own). In addition to offering up more sex, the film mixes in all manner of new elements: dope smoking, mild S & M (dripping candle wax, biting, whipping, and Chiu-sheng accidentally tearing his partners in half during sex!), coupling on all manner of weird contraptions, suggestions of bestiality and necrophilia, etc. The production design in the netherworld sequences is a gorgeously tacky cornucopia of melted plastic, paper mache, dry ice smoke, and red ectoplasmic ooze. Sexploitation fans will definitely get their money's worth here.

284. Erotic Ghost Story III

(1992; Golden Harvest/Paragon Films) ★: 6/10. *Liu jai saam chap chi dang cho wing seung* (Cantonese), *Liao zhai san ji zhi deng cao han shang* (Mandarin); "Dark Tales Third Episode: Light Grass Monk." Cinematographer: Bill Wong Chung-bo; Art Director: Fong Ying; Music: Lau Yee-tat; Writer: San Gap Yuen Yit (Cantonese version of a Japanese name); Producer: Chow Chan-tung; Action Director: Phillip Kwok Tsui; Director: Ivan Lai Kai-ming. Cast: Pauline Chan Po-lin (Yun I-meng), Shing Fui-on (Reverend Wick), Chik King-man (Liu Su-su), William Ho Kar-kui (Chia Yuan), Cheung Ching-wah. Dolby Digital (DVD only). 1.85:1. VHS:

Tai Seng (No Subtitles). Import LD: Star Entertainment (No Subtitles). Import VCD: Star Entertainment (No Subtitles), Mega Star. Import DVD: Universe. 94 minutes.

Set during the Tang Dynasty, this entry is more sedate than its immediate predecessor but certainly not lacking in the elements one expects from these films. While looking for a place to sleep one evening, Chu Chung and his betrothed, Liu Su-su, encounter the bumbling but helpful Reverend Wick, who can shrink himself down to microscopic size. Wandering through a deserted structure, Chu accidentally passes through a painting into another world. There he encounters three beautiful women and makes love to one, the maiden Yun I-meng. However, she is actually a pawn in a scheme to vanquish the benevolent god, Chia Yuan. Chu is led to believe that Chia raped numerous women and kidnapped I-meng, leading him to confront the villain and slay him. He discovers afterward that he has been tricked by the cunning demoness Vixen, who wants Chia's powerful Yang energy, which she can obtain by eating his flesh. An apologetic I-meng helps Chu to escape back to his world, but Su-su ends up on the other side, forcing Chu and Wick to journey there in order to save her.

Attractively designed and peopled by equally beautiful performers (well, not counting character actors Shing Fui-on and William Ho), the film has plenty of kinky comedic asides (like a tiny Wick entering a "cave" that turns out to be just what you might expect) and fantasy-oriented action to complement its reasonably intriguing storyline.

285. Escape from Brothel

[*sic*] (1992; Ocean Shores) ★: 3/10. *Dut gaai kwong ban* (Cantonese), *Hua jie kuang ben* (Mandarin): "Flower Street Wild Run." Cinematographer: Wong Chi-wai; Music: Not Original; Writer: Jamie Luk Kim-ming; Producer: Hung Leung-tak; Action Director: Hung San-lam; Director: Johnny Wang Lung-wei. Cast: Pauline Chan Po-lin (Hung), Alex Fong Chung-sun (Sam Ma), Rena Murakami (Ann), Billy Chow Bei-lee (Billy), William Ho Kar-kui (Inspector Chan), Sophia Crawford (Caucasian Girl). 1.85:1. VHS: Tai Seng. Import LD/VCD/DVD: Ocean Shores. 96 minutes.

While better produced than most Category III sex flicks, this dreary drama has little to offer outside of generous views of its beautiful stars, Pauline Chan and Rena Murakami. Hung is an illegal immigrant from China who must work as a prostitute in order to make ends meet. Sam, her Mainland boyfriend, gets a chance to visit her in HK when he is offered a lucrative business opportunity. Unfortunately, he has been duped and is forced to participate in a "Big Circle" robbery of a jewellery store as part of an insurance scam. When the caper goes awry, Sam soon finds himself on the run from Billy, the gang's ring leader, who wants to silence him. Despite being partially poisoned, Sam eventually manages to make contact with Hung. Under the mistaken impression that Hung is a factory worker, Sam is mortified when he discovers her true profession but, eventually, comes to his senses. When Billy is able to track Sam down via his relationship with Hung, the two are able to elude him, thanks to help from Ann. However, Ann's intervention results in dire consequences for her.

Like a number of HK softcore films, **Escape from Brothel** (*sic*) ends on a downbeat note, which almost seems like a way for the filmmakers to escape possible censure by demonstrating that they are not endorsing the perverse and illegal acts their characters commit. Whatever the case, the film exists solely for its sex scenes, and most viewers will find them satisfactory, though there are instances of sexual violence that will not go over well with some. Sophia Crawford appears briefly as a female con artist/kung fu expert out to extort money from Billy. When her scheme goes awry, she ends up fighting him ... while completely naked! It's just that kind of film.

286. Escape from Coral Cove

(1986; Xeaco Holdings Co./Solarville Co.) ★: 3/10. *Tiu chut saan woo hoi* (Cantonese), *Tao chu shan hu hai* (Mandarin): "Escape from the Coral Sea." Cinematographer: Tony Fan Chuen-kam; Music: Not Original; Writers: Terence Chang Chia-chen, Yiu Man-kei; Producer: Wong Sam; Director: Terence Chang Chia-chen. Cast: Leung Yuen-ching (Irene), Alex Fong Chung-sun (Alex), Woo Fung (Priest), Roy Cheung Yiu-yeung (The Creature). 1.85:1. VHS: Tai Seng (Poor Subtitles). Import LD/VCD: Ocean Shores (Poor Subtitles). 82 minutes.

The only film to date directed by John Woo's partner, Terence Chang, **Escape from Coral Cove** is a dull slog through slasher territory. A group of teens and a young boy on a sailing trip make the mistake of travelling to Coral Cove, which is being terrorized by some kind of humanoid creature that has risen up from the depths. When one of the girls is separated from her friends, she is pulled underwater and torn apart, with only her severed hand later turning up. After killing another of the kids, the monster takes on a more recognizably human form (Roy Cheung, sporting white contact lenses) and continues to stalk the remaining teenagers.

While the locale may be different, the formula is the same and it wore thin long ago. Fans of this sort of fare will not find the minimal sex and gore to be sufficient compensation. The tedium is heightened by the fact that the English subtitles are practically offscreen for most of the Tai Seng transfer, and the Ocean Shores LD is reportedly the same. The Taiwan version might be better in that regard, but this limp, derivative entry is not worth the trouble of acquiring. The pirated soundtrack includes music lifted from **Brainstorm**.

Escape from Hong Kong *see* **Long Arm of the Law III**

287. Espirit D'Amour

(1983; Cinema City) ★: 6/10. *Yam yeung cho* (Cantonese), *Yin yang cuo* (Mandarin): "Dark and Light Are Wrong for Each Other." Cinematographer: Bill Wong Chung-bo; Art Director: Hai Chung-man; Music: Violet Lam Man-yee; Writers: Clifton Ko Chi-sum, Lo Kin, Raymond Fung Sai-hung; Producer: Karl Maka; Director: Ringo Lam Ling-tung. Cast: Alan Tam Wing-lun (Koo Chi-ming), Joyce Ngai Suk-kwan (Chang Siu-yiu), Cecilia Yip Tung (Ivy), Phillip Chan Yan-kin (John Tang), Bill Tung Biu (Chi-ming's Father), Tang Pik-wan (Chi-ming's Mother), Tien Feng (Dr. Han), Billy Lau Nam-kwong (Insurance Agency Worker). Dolby Digital (DVD only). 1.85:1. VHS: Tai Seng. Import LD: Golden Cinema City. Import VCD/DVD: Mega Star. 93 minutes.

Early on in the shooting of this romantic comedy/ghost fantasy, producer Karl Maka, unhappy with the rushes, removed the film's director. He gave the assignment of finishing the picture to Ringo Lam, and the young filmmaker went on to earn his first directorial credit. Insurance agent Koo Chi-ming is not sure about his girlfriend Ivy, who is a domineering, bitchy shrew. Little does Chi-ming know it but he will soon have a second woman in his life: Chang Siu-yiu. Assigned to investigate a claim involving a girl who jumped to her death from a building, Chi-ming discovers that the girl's name is identical to the one that came up when he and his friends were playing with a Ouija board the night before. Siu-yiu died when she accidentally slipped and fell to her death, and when Chi-ming's boss insists that the case be classified as a suicide, she makes a fool out of him on live television. Love blossoms between Chi-ming and the pretty spirit, but, as is the rule in these films, their relationship is doomed: Ivy and his family have hired a Taoist priest to disperse Siu-yiu's spirit.

Pretty standard as these films go, **Espirit D'Amour** possesses a modicum of charm, and, while it bears no resemblance to the kind of work he would become known for, Lam directs the proceedings with confidence and style. Of particular interest is the climax, which juxtaposes shots of the exorcism with a macabre, modern dance performance, creating some effectively eerie imagery. The supernatural action that follows is quite exciting. Cecilia Yip is billed here as "Cecilia Chan," an English name she ended up discarding.

288. The Eternal Evil of Asia

(1995; Wong Jing's Workshop/Art Top Movie Productions) ★: 5/10. *Lam yeung sap dai che sui* (Cantonese), *Nan yang shi da xie shu* (Mandarin): "The Ten Great Evil Arts of the South Seas." Cinematographer: Tony Miu Kin-fai; Art Director: Andrew Cheuk Man-yiu; Music: Marco Wan Ho-kit; Producer: Ma Yin-leung; Action Director: Dion Lam Dik-on; Director: Chin Man-kei. Cast: Ellen Chan Ar-lun (May), Lily Chung Suk-wai (Mei), Chan Kwok-bong (Bon), Elvis Tsui Kam-kong (Kong), Ben Ng Ngai-cheung (Laimi), Julie Lee Wah-yuet (Chusie). 1.85:1. VHS: Tai Seng. Import LD: Cameron Entertainment. Import VCD: Mei Ah. 89 minutes.

A gleefully absurd Category III horror-comedy, **The Eternal Evil of Asia** is certainly not a film that one can recommend with a clear conscience, but it contains images and Chinese horror lore that even the most jaded HK movie completist will find hard to resist. Set (for no discernible reason) in the 21st century, the plot concerns a group of friends who take a pleasure trip to Thailand, where they accidentally kill the sister of a powerful sorcerer. Upon returning home to HK, they are beset by the wizard's curse, which quickly begins to dwindle their numbers. One man chops up his family with a cleaver and then jumps off a building, impaling himself on some fluorescent bulbs(!)—which, naturally, remain lit afterwards. Another is afflicted with the "Hungry Ghost Hex," which turns him into a famished cannibal who takes bites out of restaurant patrons before chowing down on his own arm! May and her boyfriend would seem to be the next targets, but, luckily, her best friend Mei just happens to be a Thai enchantress with her own special gifts.

Busy character actor Elvis Tsui suffers most of the indignities here, being transformed into a literal dickhead (leading to some jawdropping urination and masturbation jokes) and later, a cut-rate version of **Hellraiser**'s "Pinhead" demon (thanks to the wizard's "Pin Hex.") In addition to the weirdness on display in the main feature, director Chin also includes an instructional prologue offering advice on how viewers can protect themselves from the evils of the spirit world (e.g. ghost children love to go to movies, so if a pale-faced kid is in the seat beside you, be nice but *do not* escort him to the bathroom!). Busy adult film star Julie Lee participates in a wild, acrobatic sex scene (a demonstration of the so-called "The Mating Hex") which is a less elaborate recreation of the similarly airborne intercourse she had with Tsui in **Chinese Torture Chamber Story** (1994). Yuen King-tan makes a trademark appearance as a shrill hairdresser, and Shaw Brothers strongman Lo Mang also shows up briefly as an ill-fated Taoist priest. Chin went on to helm the equally nutty **Sex and Zen II**; both are heartily recommended to those who are game for this sort of demented sleaze. **Devil's Woman** is a sequel of sorts, with Ng essentially playing the same role.

EU Strike Force *see* **Big Bullet**

289. Evening Liaison

(1996; Seasonal Film Corporation) ★: 5/10. *Yan yeuk wong fan* (Cantonese), *Ren yue huang han* (Mandarin): "People Meet at Dusk." Cinematographers: Xiao Feng, Zhao Weijian; Art Director: Ting Yuen-tai; Music: Tang Siu-lam, Ye Xiaogang; Writer-Producer: Ng See-yuen; Director: Chen Yifei. Cast: Tony Leung Kar-fai (Xu), Mabel Zhang Jinqiu (The Woman), Xia Tian, Rosary Yang Shu-hua, Lu Di. 1.85:1. VHS: Tai Seng. Import LD/VCD: Mei Ah. 97 minutes.

A HK/China co-production (adapted from Xu Xu's story *Gui Luan*—"Ghost Love"), this handsome but disappointing drama does not live up to its potential and will even have some viewers checking their watches by the halfway point. Set in 1930s Shanghai, it tells of journalist Xu who is bewitched by a woman he encountered one evening. Xu meets with the nameless *femme* (who insists that she is a ghost) on several more occasions, to the point where it almost becomes a ritual for them. However, she will not discuss her past and no more clues are forthcoming through conventional avenues, so Xu seeks out a fortune teller. The man informs him that he can find no trace of her soul in the netherworld; while this just muddies the waters further, it prompts Xu to further intensify his quest. What he finds is a series of revelations that have their roots in a two-year-old homicide case.

The art direction and cinematography here are quite stunning, but looks and atmosphere can only carry a film so far when the characters and storyline are of only marginal interest. The mystery builds too slowly, the machinations involving Mabel Zhang's character are disappointing, and the attempts by the director to generate a degree of suspense invariably fall short. Tony Leung Kar-fai and Zhang (who bears some resemblance to Anita Mui's ghostly heroine in the vastly superior **Rouge**) are adequate leads, but only those interested in the technical aspects of cinema and period production design will derive much satisfaction from this lukewarm endeavor. Leung made headlines by suing Seasonal Film, claiming that they had defaulted on money owed to him for this role, and was temporarily blackballed by the industry as a result.

Everlasting Rhapsody *see* **Goodbye My Love**

290. Evil Black Magic

(1992; Hong Kong Films Co.) ★: 2/10. *Chih lui dik yau gam* (Cantonese), *Chu nu de you huo* (Mandarin): "Seduction of the Virgin." Cinematographer: Lam Kwok-cheung; Art Director: Wong Cheung-sau, Music: Not Original; Producer: Chow Fook-leung; Action Director: Poon Hing; Director: Ho Meng-hua. Cast: Lawrence Ng Kai-wah (Ming), Ruth Winona Tao Kwun-mei (Chun Yin), David Wu Tai-wai (Wong Wai), Eddy Ko Hung (La Pin). 1.85:1. VHS/LD: World Video. 90 minutes.

Director Ho Meng-hua, best known in the West for his gruesome Shaw Brothers thrillers **Black Magic** (1975) and **Black Magic II** (1976; aka **Revenge of the Zombies**), and **The Mighty Peking Man**, directed this laughable yarn which is essentially a cheap, half-assed remake of the first two films. La Pin is an evil Thai sorcerer-for-hire who puts curses on unsuspecting victims, in exchange for a fee. His instrument of death is Fa La-ting, a female zombie he controls via a metal spike he has pounded into her head. After disembowelling her latest victim, Fa is set upon by a gang of horny midget dwarf ghosts under the control of the sorceress Sofia. Meanwhile, third wheel nerd Ming covets the beautiful Chun Yin but can't seem to get the girl away from her handsome boyfriend, Wong Wai. Flying to Nanyang, Ming convinces

La to take him as a student. After learning all of the sorcerer's spells, he invites Yin and Wai to Thailand in order to enslave the former and murder the latter. Ming places a "crazy love curse" on Yin, and Wai must team up with Sofia in order to save his love.

Those hoping for the dollops of gore found in the original films will be disappointed to learn that, outside of a brief bit of centipede chomping, some oozing sores, and a couple of rubbery skin tears, this one is almost entirely dry. Much of the running time is taken up by female clients' "love curses," which provide a convenient excuse for sex scenes (which are cut in several spots). The editing and cinematography are awful (several sequences unfold completely out-of-focus, though the subtitles remain nice and sharp), and most of the soundtrack is stolen from **Wavelength**, **A Nightmare on Elm Street**, and **Sudden Impact** (Lalo Schifrin's theme music plays during two of the numerous softcore interludes!). Tao and Wu are popular MTV Asia veejays who also appear together in **Finale in Blood**, a mediocre exploitation version of **Rouge** that is still head and shoulders above this amateurish fiasco.

291. Evil Cat

(1987; Cinema City/Dennis Yu Film Production Co.) ★: 7/10. *Hung mau* (Cantonese), *Xiong mao* (Mandarin): "Ferocious Cat." Cinematographer: Arthur Wong Ngok-tai; Art Director: Sita Yeung Leng; Music: Law Wing-fai; Writer: Wong Jing; Producer-Director: Dennis Yu Wan-kong. Cast: Lau Kar-leung (Master Cheung), Mark Cheng Ho-nam (Long), Tang Laiying (Cheung Siu-chuen), Wong Jing (Handsome Wu). 1.85:1. VHS: Tai Seng. Import LD: Golden Cinema City. 91 minutes.

This intriguing horror fantasy begins with a group of construction workers accidentally opening a chasm containing the spirit of a cat demon, allowing it to escape confinement. Possessing nine lives (naturally), the creature returns every fifty years, and it has been the responsibility of the Cheung family to contain it over the past four centuries with their *Mao Shan* abilities. Despite being terminally ill with cancer, Master Cheung, the last protector, is determined to deal with the creature before expiring. When it begins to terrorize HK, he receives assistance from his TV reporter daughter and Long, a chauffeur whose employer has been possessed by the monster. After failing to destroy the creature's spirit, Cheung gives Long a crash course in *Mao Shan* techniques, which come in handy when the demon returns inside a new host.

While there are some humorous asides (provided mainly by Wong Jing as a bumbling cop with a crush on Cheung's daughter), the horror sequences are played straight and are, for the most part, quite well handled. Like many HK horror films, numerous set-ups are bathed in an eerie, blue light, but there is also creative use of reds and yellows. A number of the scare sequences unfold in an office building and its adjoining parking garage (the latter will be familiar to anyone who has seen **A Better Tomorrow**), and the contemporary urban setting provides a nice contrast to the traditional spells and charms used by the heroes. In one of his last leading roles to date, martial arts master Lau Kar-leung does a fine job in the sort of part usually essayed by Lam Ching-ying or Wu Ma.

292. Evil Instinct

(1996; My Way Film Company) ★: 3/10. *Gik diy sau sing* (Cantonese), *Ji du shou xing* (Mandarin): "Extreme Animal Instinct." Cinematographer: Joe Chan Kong-hung; Art Director: Jon Hau Wing-choi; Music: Siu San, Siu Cheung; Writers: Chu Wai-kwong, Lu Bing; Producer: Wong Kar-kui; Director: Chu Wai-kwong. Cast: Carrie Ng Kar-lai (Penny Ng), Diana Pang Dan (Wendy Pang), Bowie Lam Bo-yee (Sam Hui), Mak Cheung-cheng, Yung Sai-kit. 1.85:1. VHS: World Video. Import LD/VCD: New City. 95 minutes.

An amusingly dumb Category III variation on Roger Corman's 1959 horror clunker **The Wasp Woman** (which was remade in 1995 by Jim Wynorski, with Corman producing), **Evil Instinct** actually presents its ludicrous premise with straight-faced earnestness. Carrie Ng stars as a high-ranking insurance agent who performs sexual favors for her rich clients, thus motivating them to up their premiums accordingly. However, she suffers from a weird addiction that requires her to inject a serum behind her ear at regular intervals. Bowie Lam is a cop investigating a series of bizarre murders in which the affluent male victims appear to have been poisoned and have traces of snake DNA in their bodies. Could there be a connection? Blame it on some disreputable Russian scientists and their "Snake's Serum Beauty Research Project."

During one instance of venom withdrawal, Ng has nightmares about snakes (and even writhes around like one) but is quite obviously doubled during sex scenes. Meanwhile, Diana Pang (as an ambitious competitor out to bed and steal Ng's clients) continues retired sex queen Amy Yip Chi-mei's fascinatingly frustrating practice of showing her breasts without really showing them, and gets whipped in a wholly gratuitous S & M scene. While one has come to expect this sort of enterprise from her, Ng and Lam are too talented for this junk, which will satisfy only Category III completists.

293. Excuse Me, Please!

(1989; Golden Sun Light Production Co.) ★: 5/10. *Maang gwai saan fan* (Cantonese), *Meng gui shan fen* (Mandarin): "Strong Ghost Mountain Grave." Cinematographer: Hung Tai Cinematography Team; Music: Cheung Siu-lam; Writer: Lee Ping-lun; Producer: Keung Po-lai; Action Director: Hung Cheung-tak; Director: Yee Lui. Cast: Richard Ng Yiu-hon (Cock), Shum Wai (Wai), Lee Ching, Yee Lui, Lee Kwok-lun. 1.85:1. Import LD/VCD: Ocean Shores. 93 minutes.

This minor league production (a rare directorial effort by veteran comedian Yee Lui) starts off like a typical horror-comedy before detouring down a darker path. Richard Ng stars as Cock, a bumbler who agrees to pose as a woman and marry a ghost for money. However, the comic possibilities of this premise are quickly forgotten when some of his buddies rape a young woman named Siu-fah and murder her mother. The girl's stepfather, Taoist Wai, plans on selling her to a loanshark in order to pay off his debt to the gangster. On the advice of some friendly spirits, Siu-fah kills herself and returns as a deadly ghost exactly seven weeks later. As a result, one man goes crazy, murders his wife, and disembowels himself, and another is burned alive. Meanwhile, Cock (who didn't actually participate in the crime) desperately tries to convince Siu-fah of his innocence before it's too late. Luckily for him, she already knows and convinces Cock to help her exact revenge. However, with Wai's considerable mystical abilities, this will be no easy task. There is some effective black comedy along the way (particularly a bit involving a severed ear) but the end result is largely routine as these films go.

294. Executioners

(1993; China Entertainment Film Production/Paka Hill Film Production Co.) ★: 8/10. *Yin doi ho hap juen* (Cantonese), *Xian dai hao xia zhuan* (Mandarin): "Legend of the Modern Day Wonder Heroes." Cinematographer: Poon Hang-sang; Art Director: Bruce Yu Kar-on; Music: Cacine Wong Kar-sin; Writer: Susanne Chan Suk-yin; Producers-Directors: Johnny To Kei-fung, Ching Siu-tung. Cast: Michelle Yeoh Chu-kheng (Number 3), Maggie Cheung Man-yuk (Number 7),

Anita Mui Yim-fong (Tung), Damian Lau Chung-yan (Lau), Anthony Wong Chau-sang (Kim), Lau Ching-wan (Tak), Paul Chun Pui (The Colonel), Takeshi Kaneshiro (Chong Hon), Kwan San (The President). 1.85:1. VHS/LD/DVD: Tai Seng (Remastered for the English market; subtitled or dubbed). Import LD/VCD: Universe. 96 minutes.

The bleak, underrated follow-up to **The Heroic Trio, Executioners** used its future setting to make political analogies that were remarkably stark, considering that the colony's reunification with China was close at hand. Set a few years later, after an unspecified nuclear accident has irradiated the water supply, the film opens with the trio having gone their separate ways: Tung has hung up her mask in order to concentrate on raising her young daughter; Number 7 hijacks water trucks and sells the booty to the highest bidder; Number 3 devotes herself to caring for the needy and protecting shipments of medical supplies from raiders, with the aid of a newly domesticated Number 9. Non-contaminated water is at a premium and under the control of psychotic mutant Kim, inventor of a purification system and chairman of the powerful "Clear Water Corporation." A high-ranking official (Paul Chun, who also appears in the first film as a different character) strikes up an alliance with Kim in order to facilitate a military coup. When the subsequent political machinations and chaos result in Lau's death and Tung's imprisonment, Number 3 works with a government deputy to protect the deposed president's life and free her friend, while Number 7 and cocky soldier Tak (Lau Ching-wan, dubbed by another actor) set out on a desperate quest for a fresh water source.

Unlike its predecessor, the plot of **Executioners** has a basis in reality, taking its cues from two less than stellar moments in recent Chinese history. In 1989 the student occupation of Tiananmen Square in Beijing was violently suppressed by the Mainland government, with countless demonstrators either slaughtered on the scene or imprisoned afterwards. Not long after these events unfolded, China began construction on a nuclear power plant in Dai Ah Bay, about 80 miles from HK. When officials were questioned about the facility's safety and contingency plans in the event of a nuclear meltdown, they offered no sound answers, and HK residents were outraged that their water supply had no real protection from contamination (fortunately, there have been no serious problems at the plant to date). Both occurrences led to large-scale protests in the colony and a growing fear among the residents about what turns their lives might take after reunification. The radiation angle and the Communist government's ruthless methods of control are mirrored here: Some protestors are gassed and shot, others are imprisoned without trial and fed poisoned food, ordinary people's lives are destroyed without a second thought, and the military engineers the assassination of the head demonstrator (Takeshi Kaneshiro, in a role patterned after the Mainland student leaders) to use the subsequent unrest as an excuse to instigate martial law. While the first film is a wonderful fantasy and somewhat better produced, the concluding chapter is a bolder piece of filmmaking that deserves equal respect from those who praised the original but rashly dismissed this movie without stopping to appreciate what it had to say about the importance of individual liberty. The performances are consistently excellent, and, in addition to its brazen politics, the storyline takes a number of narrative risks that are rare in contemporary cinema. **Executioners**' one serious flaw is its intrinsic need to adhere to at least some of the parameters of the action-adventure genre. The inclusion of the customary chases and explosions clashes with the creators' loftier aims, creating a strangely unsatisfying whole. Regardless, this is a film that should be experienced at least once, and, ideally, several times more after that.

295. Executioners from Shaolin

(1977; Shaw Brothers) ★. 8/10. *Hung Hei-kwun* (Cantonese), *Hong Xiguan* (Mandarin): "Hung Hei-kwun" (name in Cantonese) or "Hong Xiguan" (name in Mandarin). Cinematographer: Lo Yun-cheng; Art Director: Tsao Chuang-sheng; Music: Not Original; Writer: Ngai Hong; Producer: Mona Fong Yat-wah; Action Director-Director: Lau Kar-leung. Cast: Chen Kuan-tai (Hong Hsi-guan), Lo Lieh (Pai Mei), Wong Yue (Hong Wen-ding), Lily Li Li-li (Fang Yung-chun), Cheng Kang-yeh (Hsiao Hu), Gordon Lau Kar-fai (Tung Chien-chen), Tien Ching (Wang Yeh), Kong To (Kao Chin-chung), Shen Lao (Yung-chun's Uncle), Lee Hoi-sang (Chi San). 2.35:1. VHS: Vista (Dubbed). 98 minutes. Also known as **Executioners of Death** (US theatrical and television title), **Shaolin Executioners** (US video title).

Following the burning of Shaolin Temple and the death of head monk Chi San at the hands of priest Pai Mei, some of the surviving Shaolin students manage to evade the Manchurians by posing as travelling opera performers. Hero Hong Hsi-guan marries the lovely Fang Yung-chun, a fiery lass who is his equal in kung fu. The couple have a young son, whom they name Wen-ding. As the years pass, Hsi-guan practices his Tiger Style kung fu in preparation for a duel with Pai, while Yeung-chun instructs Wen-ding in the Crane Style. Ten years after the birth of his son, Hsi-guan seeks out Pai but is clearly not his equal and barely escapes alive. After a further seven years of training, Hsi-guan challenges Pai again. This time he knows about the priest's weak point and that Pai's kung fu is at its weakest between 1PM and 3PM. Unfortunately, Pai is now able to move this vulnerable spot to different parts of his body, and Hsi-guan is defeated. However, Wen-ding swears to avenge his father's death and begins training.

A large portion of the story is devoted to Hsi-guan and his family, and this attention to character is one of the film's prime assets. The martial arts are superbly executed and the training sequences are equally stirring. Chen Kuan-tai gives a commendable performance and Lo Lieh is an impressively malevolent adversary. On the strength of his portrayal, Lo would go on to play Pai Mei again in **Abbot of Shaolin** and a very similar classmate of Pai in **Clan of the White Lotus** (which he also directed). Character names are from the English version.

Executioners of Death *see* **Executioners from Shaolin**

296. Exorcist Master

(1993; Bo Hung Movie Distribution Company) ★: 5/10. *Kui mor do jeung* (Cantonese), *Qu mo dao zhang* (Mandarin): "Expel Spirits Taoist Priest." Cinematographers: Ng Kwok-yan, Chun Chong-yin, Tse Tsang-yin; Art Director: Yip Wing-cho; Music: Not Original; Writers: Chiu Yin-hung, Cheung Man-wah; Producer: Lee Yiu-ting; Action Direction: Siu Tak-fu, Sammo Hung Stuntmen Association; Director: Wu Ma. Cast: Lam Ching-ying (Chiou), Wu Ma (Priest Wu), Ngai Sing (Star), Yip Wing-cho (The Mayor). 1.85:1. LD: Network Kingdom. Import LD/VCD: Universe. 91 minutes.

It is Taoism vs. Christianity in this modest period horror-comedy, which is not on par with the best efforts of its veteran stars, Lam Ching-ying and Wu Ma. Years after tragedy struck in a Catholic church (the caucasian parish priest was impaled on a cross by an unseen force), the building is reopened by Priest Wu, who has just arrived from the Vatican. His actions are opposed by Chiou, a Taoist master who is unable to convince the villagers that they are tempting fate. While the two have a very public argument about which faith is superior, one of Wu's helpers is bitten by the revived corpse of the original victim. The resulting bloodsucker is dispatched, but the corrupt mayor is in league with a "vampire shepherd" to smuggle drugs, using lackeys disguised as *gyonsi*. The fake vampires are soon transformed into real ones and Priest Wu must seek the aid of his rival before the white vampire drains the entire village. However (in a plot twist rehashed from Lam's superior 1989 effort, **Vampire vs. Vampire**), the Taoist quickly discovers that his magic will not work against this Western evil.

As these films go, this is pretty routine, though the climactic mix of religious disciplines supplies a satisfying wrap-up. The soundtrack includes music lifted from **Near Dark**.

297. The Extras

(1978; Bang! Bang! Films/Film Force) ★: 5/10. *Ke lei fe* (Cantonese), *Jia li fei* (Mandarin): A HK slang term meaning "Extras." Cinematographer: Johnny Koo Kwok-wah; Music: Lau Pang, Phillip Chan Yan-kin; Writers: Phillip Chan Yan-kin, Yim Ho, Ronny Yu Yan-tai; Producers: Ronny Yu Yan-tai, Phillip Chan Yan-kin; Director: Yim Ho. Cast: Yee Lui (Hakky Ho), Idy Chan Yuk-lin (Siu-fong), Kenneth Tsang Kong (Ting Chung), Melvin Wong Kam-sun (Cop), Lee Hoi-sang (Tiger). 1.85:1. Video Distributor Unknown. 86 minutes.

Yim Ho's directorial debut bears little resemblance to his best known work but is a mildly amusing (if wholly unbelievable) look at the misery extras must go through in the HK film industry. Frustrated, would-be actor Hakky Ho gets work as an all-but-unpaid extra and soon finds that moviemaking is not the glamorous business he dreamed it would be. After getting scared silly by some squibs and forgetting his cue to fall off of a building, he almost drowns, starts a fire, and destroys the director's car. There is one fringe benefit: beautiful bit part player Siu-fong, the only person on the location who treats him with civility. After a period of unemployment, Ho finally manages to get his old job back. His first job: biting the head off of a snake! If that were not depressing enough, he catches Siu-fong at a hotel with narcissistic leading man Ting Chung. When Ho refuses to lie about Ting's whereabouts to the actor's violently jealous wife, Ting and his stuntmen cronies plot to get even.

The contrivances pile up quickly but the satire occasionally hits the mark, and there is an amusing turn by Kenneth Tsang as aging matinee idol Ting, whose ego exceeds his acting ability by a margin of about ten to one.

298. An Eye for an Eye

(1990) ★: 3/10. *Wai ngoh duk juen* (Cantonese), *Wei wo du zun* (Mandarin): "Only I Alone Respect." Cinematographer: Abdul M. Rumjahn; Art Director: Bill Lui Cho-hung; Music: Lowell Lo Kwun-ting; Writer: Chan Chao-ying; Producer: Eddy Chan Kar-ho; Action Directors: Benz Kong To-hoi, Tony Poon Kin-kwan; Director: Ko Sing-pui. Cast: Max Mok Siu-chung (Chung), Joey Wang Tsu-hsien (Wong Fung-yee), Wilson Lam Chun-yin (Lui Kin-tat), Lung Fong (Ho Sai-cheong), John Ching Tung (Fei), Ricky Yee Fan-wai (Waye), Melvin Wong Kam-sun (Lau). 1.85:1. VHS: Tai Seng. Import LD: Mei Ah. 85 minutes.

Riddled with cliches and empty melodrama, this vicious but insipid gangster thriller will be of little interest even to fans of the genre. Joey Wang plays the daughter of an aged triad leader, though she is still good friends with police officers Max Mok and Wilson Lam, the latter also being her boyfriend. One of her father's subordinates rats him out to the police, and Lam is forced to bring the old man and his associates in for questioning. When her father is convicted and imprisoned, Wang is given control of his corporation and decides to close down all of its shady businesses. Naturally, this displeases much of the organization and prompts ambitious underling Lung Fong to begin plotting against her. Meanwhile, Wang's relationship with Lam is quickly unravelling under the strain of him being placed in charge of the department's investigation of her. When Lung rapes Wang and captures the attack on video, he uses it and the threat of violence against her father to blackmail her, effectively giving him control. *An Eye for an Eye* is tediously overwrought and unconvincing.

Eye of the Dragon *see* **Magnificent Bodyguards**

299. Faithfully Yours

(1988; Golden Princess) ★: 3/10. *Jui gaai nui sai* (Cantonese), *Zui jia nu xu* (Mandarin): "Best Son-in-Law." Cinematographer: Lau Hung-chuen; Art Director: Hadd Ng Kwok-hung; Music: 108 Recording Studio; Writer: Cheung Hoi-hung; Producer-Director: Wong Wah-kei. Cast: Jacky Cheung Hok-yau (Happy Chan), Stephen Chiau Sing-chi (Puddin Lai), Max Mok Siu-chung (Ki Ho-yan), Richard Ng Yiu-hon (Ying's Father), Lydia Shum Tin-ha (Ying's Mother), Sharla Cheung Man (Ying), Yip Wing-cho (Barber Shop Customer), Liu Kai-chi (Medical Lab Worker), Woo Fung (Taxi Driver). Dolby Digital (DVD only). 1.85:1. VHS: Tai Seng. Import LD: Golden Cinema City. Import VCD/DVD: Mega Star. 91 minutes.

Happy Chan opens a hair salon next to an old-fashioned barber shop and delights in tormenting his competitor ... until he and buddies, Puddin and Ho-yan, get a load of the old man's beautiful daughter, Ying. After a night of drinking with the girl at her home, the men pass out in Ying's room. Not long afterwards, Ying discovers that she is pregnant, but no one knows who the father is. After much consternation (and threats of violence from Ying's parents), the guys convince her to have the baby and then take a medical test to determine who the real father is. The lucky one in question will get Ying's hand in marriage ... and the responsibility of paying her father's demand of half a million dollars in compensation.

What can you say about a comedy where the creator hires Stephen Chiau and then has someone else dub his voice? In addition to the steals from **Three Men and a Baby**, a pie-throwing sketch from **Monty Python Live at the Hollywood Bowl** is copied verbatim, and the numerous gags depicting the men's bumbling attempts at handling domestic chores are from any number of sources. Desperate.

300. Faithfully Yours

(1995; Yiu Wing Movie Enterprise Co.) ★: 3/10. *Boon yik ching yuen* (Cantonese), *Pan ni qing yuan* (Mandarin): "Rebellious Love." Cinematographer: Nico Wong Man-wan; Art Director: James Cheung Ying-wah; Music: Mak Chun-hung; Writer: Hoi Dik; Producer-Director: Tam Long-cheung. Cast: Cecilia Yip Tung (Kitty), Emil Chow Wah-kin (Pao Wing-cheung), Christy Chung Lai-tai (Miss Tang), Lau Siu-ming (Uncle Tim), Peter Lai Bei-tak, Bonnie Fu Yuk-ching (Kitty's Cousins), Cheung Kwok-keung (Dubber), Yuen King-tan (Lan), Bowie Lam Bo-yee (Wing-cheung's Brother). 1.85:1. VHS/LD: World Video. Running time unknown.

This well-intentioned but shallow drama concerns voice dubbing artist Pao Wing-cheung and the choices he must make for his family as the spectre of the 1997 re-unification looms large on the horizon. His wife Kitty is eager to immigrate to Canada and is pushing Wing-cheung in that direction, much to his chagrin. Meanwhile, Miss Tang, his beautiful new boss, does not want him to leave because it would jeopardize both her position and the company's potential, highly lucrative contract with Walt Disney. Tempted by a major pay raise, Wing-cheung agrees to stay, while Kitty and their daughter head off to British Columbia. He and Miss Tang then begin sleeping together, a dalliance that will cause great distress for Kitty and, finally, open Wing-cheung's eyes to his boss' true motives.

The premise is intriguing and highly relevant to the time, but the plotting is simplistic and the execution is overwrought. As a result, very little here rings true. In an offbeat touch, the film concludes with the performers talking about their characters to the camera, but their explanations do nothing to sway one's opinion of the final product or compensate for its glaring conceptual weaknesses.

301. Fake Emperor

(1995; Mandarin Films) ★: 3/10. *Mou paai wong dai* (Cantonese), *Mao pai huang di* (Mandarin): "Fake Emperor." Cinematographer: Lee Tai-wai; Art Director: Cheung Ah-fong; Music: Ng Kar-kei; Writers: Raymond Wong Pak-ming, Lau Kwok-kuen; Producers: Raymond Wong Pak-ming, Li Ning; Action Director: Chan Hoi-ming; Director: Lau Kwok-kuen. Cast: Francis Ng Chun-yu (Emperor Kuang-hsu/Eunuch Li/Ma Bian/Jacky Cheung/Jackie Chan/Chow Yun-fat), Petrina Fung Bo-bo (The Empress Dowager Tzu Hsi), Catherine Hung Yan (Xiao-hung), Cheung San-yuen, Chan Kar-ming. 1.85:1. VHS: Tai Seng. Import LD/VCD: Mei Ah. 86 minutes.

This listless, largely unfunny period farce casts Francis Ng in five roles but does not give him enough worthwhile material for even one. In 1900 A.D. foreign armies are on the verge of conquering China, and The Empress Dowager is getting more senile by the day. When the British demand that the Emperor apologize for the death of an officer (who had an epileptic attack and fell off his horse), the Empress Dowager orders that barber Ma Bian (who is the spitting image of her cretinous nephew) be sent instead. Unfortunately for all involved, Ma is an obnoxious bumbler who has no intention of showing The Empress (or anyone else in the palace) an ounce of respect.

Ng gives it his best shot (and does a genuinely funny impersonation of Jacky Cheung along the way) but this is a Stephen Chiau part if there ever was one. The film has no sense of comedic pace and the script is so weak that even those with knowledge of the events that unfolded in the Ching Dynasty will find little to laugh about. At least the costumes, production design, and location work are attractive.

302. Fallen Angels

(1995; Jet Tone Production) ★: 8/10. *Doh lok tin si* (Cantonese), *Duo luo tian shi* (Mandarin): "Fallen Angels." Cinematographer: Christopher Doyle; Art Director: William Cheung Suk-ping; Music: Frankie Chan Fan-kei, Roel A. Garcia; Producer: Jeff Lau Chun-wai; Action Director: Tony Poon Kin-kwan; Writer-Director: Wong Kar-wai. Cast: Leon Lai Ming (Ming), Takeshi Kaneshiro (He Qiwu), Charlie Yeung Choi-nei (Charlie Young), Michelle Lee Kar-yan (The Agent), Karen Mok Man-wai (Baby), Chen Wan-lei (Qiwu's Father), Benz Kong To-hoi (Hoi), Chan Fai-hung (Man Forced to Have Hair Washed and Eat Ice Cream), Toru Saito (Sato), Wu Yuk-ho (Man Forced to Have His Clothes Washed). 1.85:1. VHS: World Video, Kino on Video. DVD: Kino on Video. Import LD/VCD/DVD: Ocean Shores. 96 minutes.

Wong Kar-wai's follow-up to **Chungking Express** is very much in the same style and spirit as that film. Reportedly, one of the stories in this film was originally planned for its forerunner and a modicum of the footage here was also left over from that film. Some have accused Wong of simply repeating himself with **Fallen Angels**, but, more accurately, the two movies are interconnected, utilizing the same stylistic approach and recurring motifs (like the resonant use of a pop song).

Love, again, provides the main narrative linchpin, along with the fleeting bonds created by random encounters. Ming, a suave but lazy assassin, receives his orders from The Agent, a beautiful, melancholy, chain-smoking woman dressed in various provocative outfits. She is obsessed with him, but he's never even met her once during the nearly three years they've been working together. The Agent lives in a building owned by the father of He Qiwu. Mute since the age of five (when he ate a can of expired pineapple), Qiwu is a free spirit in the most uninhibited sense. "Re-opening" various stores, in the middle of the night and conducting business with passersby (whether they want to or not), Qiwu exists in his own world, even when spending time with his aged father. After one close call too many, Ming decides to call it quits. After letting The Agent know (in a rather unique, albeit characteristically passive manner), he encounters blonde-wigged "Baby," who hides her loneliness beneath a berserk exterior. While making his rounds, Qiwu continually encounters Charlie, an even more deranged girl who is out to get revenge on someone named "Blondie" for stealing her man. Qiwu develops feelings for Charlie but she is far too single-minded and vacant to notice.

Like **Chungking Express**, the visuals and structure are aggressively offbeat, and the film is filled with a joyous, creative energy (even when the characters are brooding endlessly) that makes almost every set-up seem magical. The action unfolds at every speed and cadence imaginable, the editing and camerawork alternate freely between hyper and comatose, and the image is both over and undersaturated. Grain, glare and distortions are stylistic enhancements. Musical underpinning comes courtesy of Frankie Chan and Roel A. Garcia's *tres chic* score, supplemented by songs from Laurie Anderson, Marianne Faithful, Shirley Kwan Suk-yee, and others. While there are resonant moments, running the gamut from darkly comic (such as one poor man's misfortune to continually be one of Qiwu's "customers," culminating in he and his family being forced to consume gallons of ice cream) to poignant (Qiwu's relationship with his understandably exasperated but loving father), **Fallen Angels** is also filled with some marvellous asides, such as when Ming (who has just performed a hit and is trying to keep a low profile) runs into an obnoxious junior high classmate who won't leave him alone. If it takes a darker view of life and love than the unabashed romanticism of the previous film, **Fallen Angels** still manages to end on an upbeat note, leaving one both smiling and dazzled. The film won the cinematography, music, and Best Supporting Actress (Karen Mok) prizes at the Hong Kong Film Awards.

303. Family Honor

(1990; Oiland Company) ★: 4/10. *Mo ming ga juk* (Cantonese), *Wu ming jia zu* (Mandarin): "Unknown Family." Cinematographer: Michael Ma Koon-wah; Art Director: Lee Kam-lun; Music: Not Original; Writer-Producer: Barry Wong Ping-yiu; Action Director: Tony Leung Siu-hung; Director: Norman Law Man. Cast: Wilson Lam Chun-yin (Fu Sai-hang), Joey Wang Tsu-hsien (Hor-yee), Meg Lam Kin-ming (Ming), Shing Fui-on (Tao), Dick Wei (Wai), Max Mok Siu-chung (Chung), Miu Kiu-wai (Koo), Richard Ng Yiu-hon (Ming's Husband), Lo Lieh (Triad Boss), Ronald Wong Pan (Tao's Man), Ben Ng Ngai-cheung (Leung), Lam Chung (Police Officer), Barry Wong Ping-yiu (Internal Affairs Officer). 1.85:1. VHS: World Video. 98 minutes.

This run-of-the-mill crime thriller concerns the conflicts faced by police officer Fu Sai-hang, whose stepbrother, Tao, is a loan shark. Naturally, he has kept his sibling a secret from his fellow officers, for fear of dismissal from the force. However, Tao is continually being hassled by unethical police officer Koo, and one evening Sai-hang must come to his brother's defense when Koo beats him in the street. When murderous hood Wai escapes from the police station while being watched in an interrogation room by Sai-hang, Koo refuses to believe the latter's version of what happened. Upon investigating Sai-hang's apartment, Koo's men discover $50,000 in cash that Tao had stashed inside the sofa. With Internal Affairs breathing down his neck, Sai-hang will have to reveal his secret to the department. Further troubles await both him and Tao unless Wai is apprehended quickly.

Devoid of style and originality (in addition to the usual influences, the sequence in which Wilson Lam is forced to watch the murder of his best friend is lifted right out of Ridley Scott's **Black Rain**), this proceeds from A to B in mechanical fashion. The one genuinely enjoyable element here is the casting of comedian Richard Ng as a tough guy triad turned meek house husband who is happy for a chance to get back in the thick of the action. The soundtrack includes music lifted from **The Killer**, John Carpenter's **Christine**, and Tangerine Dream's score for **Shy People**.

Fangs of the Tigress *see* **My Young Auntie**

304. Fantasy Mission Force

(1984; The Chang Chiang Film Co./Cheung Ming Film Co.) ★: 5/10. *Mai nei dak gung dui* (Cantonese), *Mi ni te gong dui* (Mandarin): "Mini Special Attack Force." Cinematographer: Liao Ching-song; Art Director: Chang Chi-ping; Music: Not Original; Writer: Wei Hsing; Producer: Shen Hsiao-yin; Action Director: Lin Wan-chang; Director: Chu Yen-ping. Cast: Brigitte Lin Ching-hsia (Lily), Jackie Chan (Sammy), Jimmy Wang Yu (Duan Wen), Pearl Chang Ling (Emily), Sun Yueh (Sun), Adam Cheng Siu-chau (Leader of the Amazons). 2.35:1. VHS: Tai Seng, All Seasons (Dubbed), UAV (Dubbed), Hollywood Select (Dubbed), Madacy (Dubbed). 88 minutes.

While Jackie Chan does appear in this incredibly bizarre action comedy, he is not the star and it is certainly not one of his usual vehicles. It *is*, however, a very typical product from the demented mind of Chu Yen-ping, Taiwan's reigning king of schlock, and very much in the same spirit as the director's **Golden Queens Commando** and **Pink Force Commando**. Set in World War II (but filled with blatant anachronisms), the skeletal storyline finds a group of experts, assembled by Jimmy Wang Yu's tough-as-nails lieutenant, assigned to rescue some Allied generals being held captive by the Japanese. The team includes Brigitte Lin (essentially playing the same character she essayed in the **Commando** movies) as a black leather clad tough girl with a bazooka, Sun Yueh (inexplicably dressed as a hobo), a master escape artist, and two comedians in *kilts*, while Jackie Chan and Pearl Chang show up periodically as a couple of con artists out to take back some money they were swindled out of. The group must battle a tribe of hooded amazons (headed up by a fey Adam Cheng) and some bloodsucking wizards before they learn that the prisoners have been taken from their Japanese captors by a gang of Asian Nazis(?!) who drive around in vehicles left over from **The Road Warrior**.

By any critical yardstick, **Fantasy Mission Force** is a pretty horrendous piece of filmmaking (the editing is particularly incompetent), but it possesses such a flaky, dog-eared charm, one cannot help but enjoy the wacky proceedings. Mixing broad comedy bits dating back to the silent era, Mandarin musical numbers, gun battles, explosions, and a smattering of kung fu, the movie never stops serving up *something*, and its ability to entertain through sheer absurdity should not be underestimated. The soundtrack includes music lifted from **Halloween II**, **Dressed to Kill**, and **Sorcerer**. Character names are from the dubbed version.

305. Fantasy Romance

(1991; H.K. Fong Ming Motion Picture Co.) ★: 4/10. *Moh wah ching* (Cantonese), *Mo hua qing* (Mandarin): "Demon Painting Love." Cinematographer: Herman Yau Lai-to; Art Directors: Raymond Lee King-man, Lau Man-yu; Music: Bobby Chan Dik-hong; Writer: Chan Kiu-ying; Producer: Yeung Kwan; Director: Taylor Wong Tai-loi. Cast: Joey Wang Tsu-hsien (Ching-ching), Tony Leung Chiu-wai (Shing), Deanie Yip Tak-han (Ghost Prostitute), Paul Chun Pui (Li, aka "Lemon Head"), Tien Feng (Taoist Priest). 1.85:1. VHS: Tai Seng. Import LD: Golden Cinema City. Import VCD: Mega Star. 86 minutes.

This weak fantasy comedy-drama is best left to those who just cannot get enough of Joey Wang, the most gorgeous ghost in movies. Tony Leung Chiu-wai plays a struggling comic book artist whose life is turned upside down by the unearthly Wang (who is photographed in a very flattering manner throughout). After a period of adversity, the two, naturally, fall for each other, and she uses her powers to improve his station at work, making him an overnight success. Their happiness is threatened by the ghost of a prostitute (Yip) who discovers that Wang is the King of Hell's wayward daughter-in-law. Hoping to strike a deal so that her ill-fated son can reincarnate in human form, Yip plots to capture Wang and return her to Hades.

There is a brief parody of **A Chinese Ghost Story**, with Leung in the Leslie Cheung part (Leung and Wang would actually appear together in **A Chinese Ghost Story III** that same year), that grabs one's attention, but very little else here clicks. The pair's courtship is unconvincing (after what seems like ages of her getting on his nerves, they are suddenly obsessed with one another), and neither the comedy nor the dramatic angle of the story leaves much of an impression. The climax, which finds Leung entering the world of his drawings (rendered in flowing black and white, sketch-like animation) in order to rescue Wang is intriguing (and, no doubt, saved the production company some money), but it is too little, too late. For a somewhat more effective take on the world of HK comic artists, try the much different **From Zero to Hero** (1994).

306. Farewell China

(1990; Golden Harvest/Paragon Films) ★: 3/10. *Oi joi bit heung dik gwai jit* (Cantonese), *Ai zai bie xiang de ji jie* (Mandarin): "The Season of Love in Another Land." Cinematographer: Jingle Ma Cho-shing; Art Director: Rebecca Lee Lok-si; Music: Jim Shum Sing-tak; Writer: Eddie Fong Ling-ching; Producer: Teddy Robin Kwan; Director: Clara Law Cheuk-yiu. Cast: Tony Leung Kar-fai (Zhao Nansan), Maggie Cheung Man-yuk (Li Hung), Hayley Man Hei-lin, Liu Chin. 1.85:1. VHS: Tai Seng. Import LD: Mei Ah. Import VCD: Mei Ah, Mega Star. 114 minutes.

After several rejections, Mainland woman Li Hung is finally granted a visa to go and study in America. However, within a few weeks, it is clear from her letters that things are not going well. Her husband Nansan insists that she stay there for the good of their baby son. She soon asks for a divorce but he refuses. After a while, she stops writing altogether. Unsure of what to do, Nansan enters New York illegally. With nowhere to go (his one friend refused to let him stay, for fear of losing his job), Nansan inadvertently gets into trouble with a street gang but is befriended by 15-year-old Chinese American hooker Jane. After much searching, Nansan discovers that Hung advertised for a husband in a local newspaper and found a way to divorce him in spite of his refusal. Still determined to find her, Nansan ends up working as Jane's pimp for a spell. When he finally does locate his wife, Nansan barely knows the woman anymore.

This premise could have been the basis for a strong, involving drama, but **Farewell China** is so heavy handed and mired in cliches, one could almost swear that it was actually produced by the Chinese government for use as a tool to convince Mainlanders not to try and defect. The West is not the paradise many people apparently believe it is and the travails depicted here are no doubt real, but this is a film that just never knows when to let up; it's not powerful, just exaggerated and tiresome. Even the performances are off; Maggie Cheung is so overwrought in virtually every scene, her only direction seems to have been something along the lines of "More!" **An Autumn's Tale** and **Comrades: Almost a Love Story** tackle similar storylines with far greater success.

307. Fast Fingers

(1983; Shaw Brothers) ★: 6/10. *Leong seong gwan zi* (Cantonese), *Liang shang jun zi* (Mandarin): "Gentleman on the Bridge." Cinematographers: Ko Muk, Ngor Ko-hei; Music: Lam Mo-tak; Writers: Yip Kai, Kwan Yiu-wing, Chan Chun-wing; Producer: Mona Fong Yat-wah; Action Directors: Hsu Hsia, Cheung Yau, Yuen Fai, Cheung Fan-sun; Director: Hsu Hsia. Cast: Bill Tung Biu (Uncle Piao), Chin Siu-ho (Chi), Lo Mang (Captain Tieh Li-wei), Johnny Wang Lung-wei (The Big Boss), Charlie Cho Cha-lei (Cad in Casino), Tai Po (Richard Lee). 2.35:1. VHS: World Video (Poor Subtitles). Import LD: Ocean Shores (Poor Subtitles). 98 minutes.

Bill Tung (best known on this side of the world for his supporting roles in several of Jackie Chan's pictures) stars in this passable Shaw Brothers comedy which appears to be set in the 1930s but incorporates a number of anachronistic gags. Fresh out of jail, master pickpocket Uncle Piao and his two pupils make life hell for the dedicated but not very bright police captain, Tieh Li-wei. Just when Tieh is finally able to put the grab on his quarry, he has to let them walk because the girl he has a crush on turns out to be Piao's daughter. One day, while making their rounds, Piao's boys unknowingly snatch the wallet of a triad boss and barely escape with their lives. Soon afterwards, Piao plies his trade at a casino card table, not knowing that the establishment is run by the same mobsters. Once again they almost send him and his pupils to an early grave. When the gang tries to assassinate the police commissioner, Piao agrees to help Tieh nail the crooks.

The martial arts are good (particularly the climactic battle, which has Shaw veterans Lo Mang and Johnny Wang squaring off) but the storyline is wafer thin, and some Western viewers may find it all a bit too broad, particularly the overstated score.

308. Fatal Love

(1988; Cinema City Co.) ★: 4/10. *Saat ji luen* (Cantonese), *Sha zhi lian* (Mandarin): "Fatal Love." Cinematographers: Paul Chan Chung-chau, Horace Wong Wing-hang, Poon Hang-sang, Pau Hei-ming; Art Director: Raymond Chan Kam-ho; Music: Violet Lam Man-yee; Writers: Raymond Wong Pak-ming, Lee Hong-wah, Lee Mak, Tong Siu-fan, Lau Tai-chi; Producer: Raymond Wong Pak-ming; Director: Leung Po-chi. Cast: Leslie Cheung Kwok-wing (Chi Ken-wing, aka "Chicken Wing"), Cherie Chung Cho-hung (Cecilia Yau Tai-kam), Ann Bridgewater (Ann), Melvin Wong Kam-sun (Sam Tsao), David Wu Tai-wai (David), Phillip Kwok Tsui (Pow). 1.85:1. VHS: Tai Seng. Import LD: Golden Cinema City. Import VCD: Mei Ah. 92 minutes.

Out driving alone one evening, Wing encounters Cecilia, a beautiful young woman who disappears almost as mysteriously as she appeared. Further investigation by Wing points to the seemingly inexplicable conclusion that Cecilia was, in fact, a ghost. Eventually he is able to determine that his dream girl is, indeed, human and has a very jealous and violent boyfriend named Sam. Cecilia went to the trouble of making it look like she was dead so that Wing would not bother pursuing her, but he persists and is roughed up by Sam's men. Cecilia eventually takes a liking to Wing, and the pair decide to go off together, but Sam has other plans.

The contrivances pile up fast and the stars are unable to make their characters personable or interesting enough to fully compensate for the hackneyed script (it took five people to come up with this scenario?). It is clear that Cinema City added the ghost subplot only to cash in on Leslie Cheung's identification with **A Chinese Ghost Story** (released the year before); it adds nothing to the proceedings and stands out like the proverbial sore thumb. The one saving grace is a sequence in which Wing and Cecilia go to visit the latter's dying grandfather in an old age home. Only this bit has the emotional pull that the remainder of the film aspires to convey. The David Wu listed above is the actor/editor/director, not the like-named Taiwanese actor from **Full Throttle**.

309. Fatal Love

(1993; Suen Woo Film Productions Co.) ★: 1/10. *Ngai ching* (Cantonese), *Wei qing* (Mandarin): "Dangerous Romance." Cinematographer: Joe Chan Kong-hung; Art Director: Woo Lai-ming; Music: Wong Kwing-kai; Producer: Chan Chi-shun; Writer-Director: Lo Kin. Cast: Ellen Chan Ar-lun (Debbie Fung), Michael Wong Man-tak (Law Fuk-tin), Maria Cordero (Debbie's Mother), Wong Chi-yeung (Ma). 1.85:1. VHS: Tai Seng. Import LD/VCD: Star Entertainment. 84 minutes.

Only Ellen Chan fans need bother with this odious, poorly written Category III thriller in which she plays Debbie Fung, an unemployed policewoman who is lured back to the force to serve as an undercover officer. Her assignment: become personally involved with multi-millionaire Law Fuk-tin, whom the police suspect of having committed several grisly murders (one victim was stabbed *138 times*). After spending a great deal of time with Law, Debbie is swayed by his looks and charm, an error in judgment that costs her dearly.

One of those films that would be over in twenty minutes if the protagonist displayed an ounce of sense, **Fatal Love** (not to be confused with the 1988 film of the same name) meanders through its well-worn scenario without an ounce of tension or dramatic credibility. It is also burdened by some repugnant S & M murder sequences which move beyond the amusing excesses of stylish vehicles like **Naked Killer** into outright misogyny.

Fatal Mission *see* **Heart of Dragon** [*sic*]

310. Fatal Obsession

(1994; Full Country Entertainment Development/Golden Power Productions) ★: 3/10. *Yap moh* (Cantonese), *Ru mo* (Mandarin): "Enter Evil Spirit." Cinematographer: Poon Yiu-ming; Art Director: Mark Chiu Kwok-san; Music: Chan Kin-tak; Writer: Erica Lee Man; Producers: Simon Cheng Kwok-fai, Siu Kam-kan; Director: Raymond Lee Wai-man. Cast: Yvonne Yung Hung (Violet Cheung), Vincent Wan Yeung-ming (Frankie), Lily Chung Suk-wai (Clara), Elvis Tsui Kam-kong (Chan Tat-ming), Cheung Kwok-keung (Officer Yip). 1.85:1. VHS: Tai Seng. Import LD/VCD: Universe. 93 minutes.

Too mild to be frightening and too predictable to be interesting, this meandering thriller eventually turns downright ludicrous. Violet, the lead dancer in an avant-garde troupe, is suffering from hallucinations brought about by stress. One evening, while driving with friends, her car goes off the road, coming to a stop near an eerie, dilapidated mortuary. After everyone gets out to investigate, Violet disappears and must be taken to the hospital upon being found. From the moment she is discharged, the girl begins to display macabre behavior, leading her superstitious director to suspect possession (or, as the subtitles say, "obsession") as being the cause. After taking her to a seance, the cause of Violet's troubles is revealed: The spirit of Yumada, a Japanese warlord who raped her grandmother, seeks vengeance because the girl disturbed his body. Soon Violet, brandishing a sword and dressed in a Japanese military uniform, is stalking her friends.

In adherence to one of the prime tenets of bad horror movies, the characters (who are just about the most loyal friends in history) are separated from one another, leading to suspense sequences that almost invariably have no payoff. Only during the climax, with its queasy display of necrophilia, does this well-produced but utterly superficial effort come anywhere near being effective.

311. Fatal Termination

(1990; D & B Films Co./Regent Film) ★: 7/10. *Chik sik daai fung bo* (Cantonese), *Chi se da feng bo* (Mandarin): "Red Big Storm." Cinematographer: Chim Pak-hung; Art Directpr: Raymond Kwok Siu-keung; Music: Not Original; Writers: Lee Man-choi, Pang Chi-ming; Producers: Phillip Ko Fei, Cheung Sek-kui; Action Director: Wong Kwan; Director: Andrew Kam Yeung-wah. Cast: Ray Lui Leung-wai (John), Moon Lee Choi-fung (Moon), Simon Yam Tat-wah (Jimmy Li), Phillip Ko Fei (Ko Mok-fu), Robin Shou Wan-bo (Wai Loong), Miu Kiu-wai (Miu Chun-fan). 1.85:1. VHS: World Video. Import LD: Laser-Video Entertainment. 89 minutes.

Terrific stuntwork highlights this above average action-thriller which is sure to please aficionados. Arab terrorists make a deal with a crooked customs inspector so that their highly illegal cargo will enter HK without a hitch. When the determined Inspector Li uncovers the plot, innocent customs officer Miu is framed and, later, murdered. His brother-in-law, John, decides to investigate the case, putting himself and his family in mortal danger, not only from the terrorists but also an old enemy out for revenge.

Better written and acted than one would expect, **Fatal Termination** does not exceed the boundaries of its genre but takes its conventions to new heights of intensity. Of particular note is a hair-raising sequence in which one of the villains speeds away in a car while holding Moon Lee's young daughter out of the window ... by her *hair*! While this is occurring, Lee (who has caught up with the kidnappers) is hanging onto the hood of the vehicle trying to punch her way through the windshield. Director Andrew Kam co-helmed the excellent crime thriller **The Big Heat**, but his approach there is a sharp contrast to the tone of this film: The earlier movie was almost casual in its depiction of violence, while this one explodes with anger and nihilistic fury. **Fatal Termination** and **Killer's Romance** also proved that producer Phillip Ko was capable of making quality product, but his subsequent work in The Philippines proved to be beyond wretched.

312. Fatal Vacation

(1990; Golden Harvest/Paragon Films) ★: 2/10. *On lok jin cheung* (Cantonese), *An le zhan chang* (Mandarin): "Cozy Battlefield." Cinematographer: Jingle Ma Cho-shing; Art Director: Fong Ying; Music: Violet Lam Man-yee; Writer: Nam Yin; Action Director: Ng Min-kan; Producer-Director: Eric Tsang Chi-wai. Cast: Eric Tsang Chi-wai (Bob), Irene Wan Pik-ha (Candy), Tang Pik-wan (Grandma), Tommy Wong Kwong-leung (Big Eyes), Victor Wong Chi-keung (Grandpa), Emily Kwan Bo-wai (TV Crew Director). 1.85:1. VHS: Tai Seng (No Subtitles). Import LD: Mei Ah. Import VCD: Cameron Entertainment. 94 minutes.

Set in 1985, this dreadful thriller paints a less than flattering portrait of the Philippines (*á la* **Marianna**), but that is nothing compared to the torture it inflicts on the viewer. A group of HK tourists (including some triads) vacationing in that country are taken hostage by Communist guerrillas who hijack their bus. Driven out into the jungle, they are subjected to the expected indignities (rape, Russian Roulette execution, etc.) before getting ahold of weapons and making a break for it, Rambo-style (it's amazing how quickly you can master automatic weapons when the heat is on!).

With its one-dimensional characters, hamfisted direction, formulaic situations, and utter dearth of logic, this is exploitation filmmaking at its most inane. The sole interesting element is the way in which the Filipino communists are clearly meant to imply what HK might be faced with after the 1997 reunification. It's a ludicrous analogy but, coming so close on the heels of the 1989 student crackdown in China, one that reflected the anxiety that was present at the time, which keeps this from being a complete waste of time.

313. Father and Son

(1981; Fenghuang) ★: 7/10. *Foo ji ching* (Cantonese), *Fu zi qing* (Mandarin): "Father Son Love." Cinematographer: Patrick Wong Shan; Music: Yu Lun; Writers: Chan Chu, Lillian Lee Pik-wah, Alfred Cheung Kin-ting; Producer: Wong Kai-chuen; Director: Allen Fong Yuk-ping. Cast: Shek Lui (Law San-muk), Chu Hung (Law's Wife), Yung Wai-man (Law Family Younger Brother), Cheung Yu-ngor (Law Kar-hing), Yun Sin-mei (Law Kar-hei). 1.85:1. VHS: World Video. 97 minutes.

Winner of Best Picture and Best Director at The First HK Film Awards, Allen Fong's directorial debut is based largely on the rocky but ultimately fulfilling relationship he had with his own father. After earning his university degree, Law Ka-hing returns home from America to his family. His father, Law San-muk, passed away not long before Ka-hing's arrival due to a heart attack brought on by the excitement he experienced upon receiving Ka-hing's diploma in the mail. Through flashbacks Ka-hing reflects on his youth and San-muk's single-minded desire to see him succeed academically, even if it meant that the entire family must do without basic needs and comforts. A shy boy with an earring, Ka-hing had to enrol in several different schools and was constantly set upon by bullies. Not interested in studying, he spent most of his spare time thinking about movies and comics. San-muk wants to send his son to an overseas college but is continually passed over for promotion and cannot come up with the money. Regardless, he still leans hard on Ka-hing to succeed in school. While there is eventually a measure of improvement, the lad is still off in another world and even sells all of the family's dictionaries and English books in order to buy film for an 8mm movie camera he borrowed. Things really come to a head when San-muk decides that the problem of Ka-hing's college tuition can be settled by getting his daughter to marry and having her new husband cover the costs.

A revolutionary film in its day, **Father and Son** offers a look at an ordinary, struggling HK family, stressing realism over traditional genre tenets. It is a simple, unpretentious work, well acted by its cast of unknowns and a valuable document of the time. Distributor Fenghuang is now known as Sil-Metropole Organisation.

Trivia: Ka-hing's favorite literary character is the fearless middle-aged freedom fighter "Uncle Choi," who is played by Dean Shek Tien in Ching Siu-tung's **The Raid**.

314. The Fearless Hyena

(1979; Lo Wei Motion Picture Co.) ★: 6/10. *Siu kuen gwaai jiu* (Cantonese), *Xiao quan guai zhao* (Mandarin): "Laugh Fist Strange Call." Cinematographer: Chen Rong-shu; Art Director: Chow Chi-leung; Music: Not Original; Producer: Hsu Li-hwa; Writer-Action Director-Director: Jackie Chan. Cast: Jackie Chan (Shing Lung), Yam Sai-kwoon (Yen), James Tien Chun (Grandpa), Li Kuen (The Master), Chan Hui-lau (The Unicorn), Dean Shek Tien (The Coffin Seller). 2.35:1. VHS: All Seasons (Dubbed), UAV (Dubbed), Simitar (Dubbed). DVD: Simitar (Cantonese and English Tracks). 95 minutes.

Jackie Chan's directorial debut, **The Fearless Hyena** gets off to a weak start and suffers from truly horrendous English dubbing but overcomes these hurdles with inventive choreography and Chan's infectious energy. He plays his stock character: a martially talented but lazy and impetuous youth who just needs the right teacher to help him gain control and confidence. While working as chief instructor at a third-rate martial arts school, Lung's skills attract the attention of various masters who proceed to challenge him. News of his abilities reaches Yen, a ruthless Qing official who is hunting Lung's grandfather (a former rebel) with the intention of killing him. After Lung inadvertently causes his grandfather's demise at Yen's hands, he receives instruction from "The Unicorn" (Chan Hui-lau, playing the "aged but wily" master role that became a genre prerequisite after Simon Yuen Siu-tien's memorable turn in **Drunken Master**), a crippled but still deadly kung fu master. After enduring rigorous training in a bizarre form of martial arts that utilizes the emotions as a secret weapon, Lung is ready to face Yen and his three spear-wielding vassals.

Much of the comedy in the opening third is pretty painful (particularly when it is being related by Australian-accented voice actors) but things get back on track fairly quickly. The training sequences are both impressive and amusing, while the extended climactic fight between Chan and Yam (which suffers badly in the current pan-and-scan video transfers) is fully deserving of all the praise it has received. The final shot of Lung pushing The Unicorn along in a cart is an in-joke reference to the Japanese **Lone Wolf and Cub** movie and TV series, and is even accompanied by a snippet from the TV show's theme song! The soundtrack also includes music lifted from **Superman**! It was followed by an unrelated sequel.

315. Fearless Hyena II

(1983; Lo Wei Motion Picture Co.) ★: 3/10. *Lung tang fu yeuk* (Cantonese), *Long teng hu yue* (Mandarin): "Dragon Jumps, Tiger Leaps." Cinematographer: Yiu Kie; Music: Not Original; Producer: Le Ching-fu; Action Director: Hsu Shao-hung; Director: Chan Chuen. Cast: Jackie Chan (Chan Lung), Austin Wai Tin-chi (Tung), Chan Hui-lau (Chan Chi-pei), James Tien Chun (Old Chan), Yam Sai-kwoon (Heaven and Earth Society Leader), Dean Shek Tien (Jaws Four). 2.35:1. VHS: All Seasons (Dubbed), UAV (Dubbed), Simitar (Dubbed). DVD: Simitar (English and Cantonese tracks). Import LD/VCD: Ocean Shores (Poor Subtitles). 91 minutes.

Pieced together largely from leftover and recycled footage, this in-name-only follow-up was among the first of far too many Jackie Chan rip-off movies. When The Heaven and Earth Society sets out to destroy the Yin Yang clan, old Chan and Lung, his good-for-nothing son, must flee their home. They seek out the boy's uncle, who is also a clan member and on the H & E's death list. When disaster strikes, Lung must motivate his cousin to improve his kung fu so that the two of them can be ready for the inescapable showdown with their adversaries.

The first half consists almost entirely of unrelated and decidedly unfunny comedic vignettes (including anachronistic jokes about "long-haired hippies," "electronic calculators," and "the subway"). When the storyline finally gets back on track, there are only a handful of instances where Chan (who is obviously doubled in several spots) can work his usual magic, and that is little recompense for the lame humor and shoddy, patchwork editing. This is strictly for die-hard Chan fans, and even they are advised to keep the remote control handy. The soundtrack includes music lifted from **Raiders of the Lost Ark** and **Aces Go Places**.

316. Feel 100%

(1996; BOB & Partners Company) ★: 3/10. *Baak fan baak gam gok* (Cantonese), *Bai fen bai gan jue* (Mandarin): "Feeling 100%." Cinematographer: Cheung Man-bo; Art Director: Stanley Cheung Sai-kit; Music: Lincoln Lo Kin; Writers: Joe Ma Wai-ho, Matthew Chow Hoi-kwong; Producers: Manfred Wong, Andrew Lau Wai-keung; Director: Joe Ma Wai-ho. Cast: Dior Cheng Yee-kin (Jerry), Eric Kot Man-fai (Hui Lok), Sammi Cheng Sau-man (Cherrie), Gigi Leung Wing-kei (Fong-fong), Allen Ting Chi-chun (Thomas Li), Christine Ng Wing-mei (Rachel), Law Kar-ying (Robert), Vincent Kok Tak-chiu (Fat Party Guest), Lee Siu-kei (Tung Zhi-chuen), Wyman Wong Wai-man (Mahjong Player), Lan Sai (Mahjong Player), Spencer Lam Sheung-yee (Principal). 1.85:1. VHS: Tai Seng. Import LD/VCD/DVD: Universe. 97 minutes.

Buddies Jerry (the handsome one) and Lok (the goofy comic relief one) share an apartment and have a large group of friends, including Cherrie (the unappreciated female friend). While Lok becomes infatuated with an anonymous older woman who frequently calls on the telephone, Jerry's ever-wandering eye settles on young student Fong-fong (the temptation for the hero) who needs a place to stay and is invited to move into a spare room. Lok is having kinky sex with his deranged phone friend; Jerry is in love with Fong-fong; Cherrie is jealous; and Fong-fong is being tormented by her rich, egomanical ex-boyfriend. The requisite "serious" conflict arises when Fong-fong gets the chance to study in France and must break the news to Jerry that her career is more important to her than staying in HK with him. Will he realize that he really should be directing his affections towards Cherrie? Will she reciprocate? Will they be together by the final fade? Is there even a microbe of doubt?

"100% Artificial" would have been a more appropriate title for this tepid comedy-drama which induces complete apathy, a state that is inadvertently reinforced by the slick cinematography and production values (which were obviously of much greater importance to the filmmakers than the script). The one saving grace is pop star Sammi Cheng, who is relaxed and personable in a thankless role. A follow-up hit theaters only five months later.

317. Feel 100%...Once More

(1996; Golden Harvest/BOB & Partners Company/Everwide) ★: 5/10. *Baak fan baak ngam FEEL* (Cantonese), *Bai fen bai yan FEEL* (Mandarin): "Feeling 100% Right." Cinematographer: Cheung Man-bo; Art Director: Stanley Cheung Sai-kit; Music: Lincoln Lo Kin; Writers: Joe Ma Wai-ho, Matthew Chow Hoi-kwong; Producer: Manfred Wong; Director: Joe Ma Wai-ho. Cast: Dior Cheng Yee-kin (Marco), Sammi Cheng Sau-man (Yen), Gigi Leung Wing-kei (Emma), Eric Kot Man-fai (Monster), Chingmy Yau Suk-ching (Gobby Li), Cheung Tat-ming (Small Man), Law Kar-ying (Director), Andy Hui Chi-on (Alan), Lan Sai (Yen's

Friend), Michael Tse Tin-wah (Galinano). 1.85:1. VHS: World Video. Import LD/VCD/DVD: Universe. 94 minutes.

The same cast portrays different characters in this in-name-only sequel which suffers from the same set of deficiencies that sank the original but manages to be a bit more palatable. Their relationship having lost some of its spark over time, Marco and Yen take a trip to Japan, only to get into an argument and split up. Marco runs into Gobby Li, an actress he met on the airplane, and the pair spend time together. When Yen finds out, she is ready to leave Marco for good. Marco and Gobby eventually move in together, but several coincidental (and one not-so coincidental) meetings with Yen help to slowly rekindle the love between her and Marco. In a superfluous subplot, pretty Emma is dumped by her basketball-loving boyfriend and takes up with the far less handsome but loyal "Small Man." However, the latter's pronounced lack of self-confidence may end up scuttling their relationship.

The plot mechanics are shamelessly contrived, and the way in which the main conflict is resolved is right off page one of the "Bad Screenwriting 101" handbook. That lack of originality is a shame as **Once More** starts off rather well, with the Japanese location work providing a nice backdrop. That section and a handful of bright moments (including a brief parody of **Full Throttle** and a kissing lesson) help to elevate this slightly above its predecessor but still leave one wishing that director Joe Ma would leave fluff like this behind and once again display the promise he showed with **The Golden Girls**.

318. Feeling of Love

(1996; Yen Ping Films Production) ★: 1/10. *Chung hing oi ching gam gok* (Cantonese), *Zhong qing ai qing gan jue* (Mandarin): "Chungking Feeling of Love." Cinematographer: Chen Rong-shu; Music: Fu Lap; Writer: Kwok Jing; Producer: Law Tiu-wai; Director: Chu Yen-ping. Cast: Takeshi Kaneshiro (Simon Hing Dah-li), Athena Chu Yan (Yin), Wong Yat-fei (Simon's Dad), Tommy So Yau-pang, Lam Siu-lau. 1.85:1. VHS: World Video. Import LD/VCD: Mei Ah. 88 minutes.

Simon and his perpetually horny, drooling buddies spend all of their spare time cruising chicks to no avail. When Hing stumbles across his dream girl, Yin, she tells him in no uncertain terms, to hit the road. Simon continues to run into his would-be lover and learns that not only is she his new boss at work but also the daughter of his father's new girlfriend! Yin takes every opportunity to humiliate Simon on the job, but it doesn't matter: He is hopelessly in love and will not be swayed.

One does not approach a Chu Yen-ping film looking for subtle, drawing room humor, but the jokes here are merely inane, derivative, and at times just plain embarrassing. Takeshi Kaneshiro's romantic pursuit of Athena Chu is never believable, and the storyline's arbitrary resolution certainly isn't either. Fantasy sequences, numerous in-joke references to **Chungking Express**, and a Spuds McKenzie-type dog sidekick are no help. Remove the outtakes and this dud would not boast so much as one single laugh. The soundtrack includes music lifted from Brian DePalma's **Dressed to Kill**.

319. Fight Back to School

(1991; Win's Movie Production Co./Samico Films) ★: 6/10. *To hok wai lung* (Cantonese), *Tao xue wei long* (Mandarin): "Escape from School Mighty Dragon." Cinematographer: Cheng Siu-keung; Art Director: Horace Ma Kwong-wing; Music: Wong Bong; Writers: Barry Wong Ping-yiu, Gordon Chan Kar-seung; Producer: Wong Jing; Action Director: Wong Kwan; Director: Gordon Chan Kar-seung. Cast: Stephen Chiau Sing-chi (Star Chow), Sharla Cheung Man (Miss Ho), Ng Man-tat (Tso Tat-wah), Roy Cheung Yiu-yeung (Brother Teddy), Gabriel Wong Yat-san (Turtle Wong), Dennis Chan Kwok-san (Cheng), Paul Chun Pui (Lam), Yuen King-tan (Miss Leung), Barry Wong Ping-yiu (Police Commissioner). 1.85:1. VHS: Tai Seng. Import LD/VCD/DVD: Mei Ah. 100 minutes.

One of Stephen Chiau's biggest hits, this gets off to a slow start but picks up steam as it goes. Star Chow is a cocky police officer who does not understand the concept of teamwork. After a particularly disastrous practice drill, he is assigned to go undercover in a college to try and locate the commissioner's prized gun, which was stolen by a student. After only three days of classes, Chow is on the verge of being expelled but is saved thanks to some tutorial help from the beautiful guidance counsellor Miss Ho. Filled with newfound confidence, Chow becomes the most popular student in the school, but his blossoming relationship with Miss Ho turns sour when she discovers his true identity. Chow is able to retrieve the pistol but also discovers an arsenal of guns belonging to a local triad leader, leading to a showdown back at the school.

Chiau gets a chance to show off his martial arts skills during the action scenes, and the climactic shootout (which takes place inside a giant maze constructed for the school's open house) is nicely staged. The gags run hot and cold, with the most amusing idea actually replicated from **God of Gamblers III: Back to Shanghai** (also 1991): Chiau uses a mobile phone to secretly get test answers from the grumpy commissioner (an amusing turn by co-writer Barry Wong), while Ng Man-tat (whose character is named after fellow comedian Cho Tat-wah) desperately tries to convey the messages to him. It was followed by two superior sequels.

320. Fight Back to School II

(1992; Win's Movie Production Co.) ★: 7/10. *To hok wai lung 2* (Cantonese), *Tao xue wei long 2* (Mandarin): "Escape from School Mighty Dragon 2." Cinematographer: Cheng Siu-keung; Art Director: Horace Ma Kwong-wing; Music: Mahmood Rumjahn; Writers: Gordon Chan Kar-seung, John Chan Kin-chung, Yuen Kai-chi; Producer: Jimmy Heung Wah-sing; Action Director: Chris Lee Kin-sang; Director: Gordon Chan Kar-seung. Cast: Stephen Chiau Sing-chi (Chow Sing-sing), Sharla Cheung Man (Ho Ming), Ng Man-tat (Tat), Athena Chu Yan (Sandy Lai), Gabriel Wong Yat-san (Tortoise), Sarah Lee Lai-yui (Jacky), Deanie Yip Tak-han (Lydia), Michael Chow Man-kin (Mark), James Wong Jim (Minister Wong), Blackie Ko Shou-liang (Belligerent Hood), Michael Dinga (Peter), Spencer Lam Sheung-yee (Judo Teacher). 1.85:1. VHS: Tai Seng. Import LD/VCD/DVD: Mei Ah. 106 minutes.

Opening with a seven minute montage of highlights from the original, this superior follow-up benefits greatly from sync sound recording, making one wish that more of Chiau's films were produced that way. Thanks to a less than impressive first impression with his new superior, Sing (called "Star" in the previous film's subtitles) gets demoted to the post of traffic cop, while Tat receives a promotion. Fed up, Sing quits and decides to secretly help Tat with his undercover investigation at a local school. Demanding the return of their imprisoned leader, a team of terrorists have threatened to blow up a HK school unless their demands are met before Christmas. However, their warning is the least of Sing's worries: Pretty student Sandy Lai has fallen in love with him right on the eve of his marriage to Ming, and he has spent all of the money intended for his wedding on the undercover operation. In a plot turn lifted from the Hollywood bomb **Toy Soldiers**, the villains take over the institution and use the students as hostages, leaving Sing to come to the rescue, with some help from his old S.D.U. buddies.

More consistently amusing than its forerunner, the film still has its share of failed gags, but it mixes and matches genre components quite adeptly (the action finale plays like a warm-up for director Chan's S.D.U. thrillers **The Final Option** and **First Option**). Besides, you haven't lived until you've seen Ng Man-tat as *The Terminator*! Film critic Paul Fonoroff, Mark Houghton, and John Wakefield make brief appearances.

321. Fight Back to School III

(1993; Win's Movie Production) ★: 7/10. *To hok wai lung ji lung gwoh gai nin* (Cantonese), *Tao xue wei long guo ji nian* (Mandarin): "Escape from School Mighty Dragon: Dragon Goes Through the Year of the Chicken." Cinematographer: Gigo Lee Chi-hang; Art Director: Jason Mok Siu-kei; Music: Lowell Lo Kwun-ting; Producer: Stephen Siu Yeuk-yuen; Writer-Director: Wong Jing. Cast: Stephen Chiau Sing-chi (Chow Sing-sing), Anita Mui Yim-fong (Judy Tong), Sharla Cheung Man (Man), Leung Kar-yan (Officer Lai), Anthony Wong Chau-sang (Taior Lam), Nat Chan Pak-cheung (Man's Cousin), Kathy Chow Hoi-mei (Man Ching), Phillip Chan Yan-kin (Chan). 1.85:1. VHS: Tai Seng. Import LD/VCD/DVD: Mei Ah. 89 minutes.

Wong Jing took the helm for this, the third (and last to date) of the **Fight Back to School** series, supplying it with an even wackier tone than its predecessors. Jettisoning the collegiate setting, this is a broad spoof of **Basic Instinct**, with Sing-sing assigned to impersonate Million Wong, the murdered spouse of socialite Judy Tong, in order to sniff out his killer. Having her husband-to-be in such close proximity to a sexually uninhibited woman like Judy makes Sing-sing's wife Man understandably jealous, but the whole situation takes an unexpected turn when *she* becomes the object of Judy's affections! However, there is yet another figure intruding on this triangle, and danger looms for all.

Anita Mui is ideally cast in the Sharon Stone role (yes, there is a spoof of the infamous leg-crossing interrogation scene), and while Nat Chan is a bit of a disappointment as Ng Man-tat's stand-in, Leung Kar-yan gives a rambunctious supporting performance as Sing-sing's nasty superior. The film contains a fair amount of Chiau's difficult to translate *mo lei tau* wordplay, but there are a great number of sight gags as compensation (Chiau performs some pretty amazing feats with a vacuum cleaner) and the star's comic timing is as sharp as ever (particularly during the sequence where he tries to extinguish a fire, with predictably disastrous results). This being a Wong Jing film from the early '90s, there is a wholly gratuitous gambling subplot (allowing for cameo appearances by Paul Chun Pui and John Ching Tung) which is simply an excuse for Chiau to reprise his popular "Knight of Gamblers" character from **All for the Winner** and **God of Gamblers II** and **III**.

322. Fighting Fist

(1992; Gold Harbour) ★: 4/10. *Ba do jung waang* (Cantonese), *Ba dao zong heng* (Mandarin): "Control Everywhere by Force." Cinematographer: Kwan Chi-kan; Art Director: Wong Kam-kong; Music: Tritone; Writers: Casey Chan Lai-ying, Shan Bwoon-yau; Action Director: Ho Wing-cheung; Producers: Chan Hin-fai, Wong Yuk-wah; Director: Casey Chan Lai-ying. Cast: Sibelle Hu Hui-chung (Julia Cheung), Ken Lo Wai-kwong (Chi Wang-cheung), Chin Kar-lok (Teddy Wong), Masashi Ishibashi (Sato's Master), Sonny Chiba (The Superintendent). 1.85:1. VHS/LD: World Video. 91 minutes.

Aside from being a HK/Japan co-production, this crime thriller has little to distinguish it from the rest of the pack. Cops Julia Cheung and Teddy Wong arrive too late to prevent the massacre of some drug dealers by Japanese policeman Sato Mitsuda, who is not exactly going by the book in his attempts to destroy mobster Jimmy Lee's South-East Asian crime syndicate. Although Teddy is able to capture Sato fleeing the scene of the crime, he lets him go because they are old friends. Lee lost his three sons in the attack and blames the two police officers for their murders because one of his men saw Teddy let Sato escape. The gangster's thugs brutally eliminate the cop and most of his family. The one survivor, Teddy's sister Sally, is Sato's lover; refusing to believe that he could be involved in the circle of killings, she flies to Japan to find him. Also headed to Japan is Julia, who thinks that Sato committed the executions. When she learns the truth about what really happened, Julia teams up with Sato to exact revenge.

This combines cliches from both the gangster and kung fu genres (Sato visits his old karate master so that he may learn a method that will counteract the "Dark Fist" style used by Lee's main henchman) into a decidedly dull mix; even the various bouts and shootouts are no better than average. Sonny Chiba appears briefly as Sato's superior (who is the mastermind running the "Death Squad" movement) but does not participate in any of the action setpieces. He does not even share any scenes with Masashi Ishibashi, who fought against him in the first two of Chiba's **Streetfighter** films.

323. Figures from Earth

(1990; Taylor Film and Video Production Centre) ★: 5/10. *Chut si kei bing* (Cantonese), *Chu shi qi bing* (Mandarin): "Go Forth Scholar: Ingenious Military Move." Cinematographer: Cheng Siu-keung; Art Director: Ringo Cheung Sek-wah; Music: Not Original; Producer: Mo Wen-ha; Writer-Director: Chun Wong. Cast: Alex Man Chi-leung (Thunderrod), Liu Kai-chi (The Thin Constable), Chun Wong (The Fat Constable), Stanley Fung Shui-fan (Master Thunderbolt). 1.85:1. VHS: Tai Seng. Import LD/VCD: Ocean Shores. 89 minutes.

This inconsequential horror-comedy starts off well but runs out of ideas around the halfway mark. It opens in the Ming Dynasty, with the beautiful Lady Chu being forced to recruit male victims for an evil witch so that the latter can drain their lifeforce. Two bumbling plainclothes constables team up with the only slightly more competent sorcerer Master Thunderbolt in order to trap and kill the sorceress before she kills again. When the creature cuts off Thunderbolt's secret weapon (a giant, penile appendage patterned after the monster tongue in **A Chinese Ghost Story**), the sorcerer gives the constables two immortality pills, which they quickly swallow. Unfortunately, he forgot to tell them that unless the pills are taken under the proper conditions, they will cause the user to freeze solid for 500 years. Cut to HK in the present day as the pair thaw out and find themselves in a totally alien world. After various "fish-out-of-water" incidents, they join forces with a cute thief and Thunderbolt's descendent to destroy the creature, who is again using Chu to lure unsuspecting police officers to their deaths.

The climax is a real letdown, and much of the humor is shamelessly crude. It does hit the mark occasionally, however, and the send-up of elements from **A Chinese Ghost Story** is genuinely amusing. Top-billed star Alex Man only has about ten minutes of screen time. The soundtrack includes music lifted from **Phantasm**.

324. The Final Judgement

(1993; Triumph Pictures) ★: 5/10. *Ji hap chong si ji gung sam* (Cantonese), *Zhi he cang shi zhi gong shen* (Mandarin): "The Case of the Corpse in the Cardboard Box." Cinematographer: Tony Miu Kin-fai; Art Director: Ring Law Chi-keung; Music: John Wong Sai-cheung; Writers: Tessa Choi Ting-ting, Philip Cheng Chung-tai; Producer: Steven Lo Kit-sing; Director: Otto Chan Ah-to. Cast: Simon Yam Tat-wah (Au Ping-keung), Cecilia Yip Tung

(Cheung Tsui-fung), Bill Tung Biu (Officer Kent Chan), Paul Chun Pui (Stanley Wu Tai-kit), Kenneth Chan Kai-tai (Lee), Esther Kwan Wing-ho (Lee Ching-yee), Law Koon-lan (Prosecutor), Frankie Chin Chi-leung (Musclebound Cop). 1.85:1. VHS: Tai Seng. Import LD/VCD: Star Entertainment. 94 minutes.

A quality cast gives this Category III "True Crime" thriller, set in the 1970s, an extra level of interest, but the end result is an uneasy marriage of graphic exploitation elements and traditional courtroom drama. Doting husband Au Ping-keung is suspected of raping, murdering, and mutilating a teenage girl. Using the newly developed method of forensic evidence to back up their suspicions, the police arrest Au and charge him with the crime. He is then subjected to brutal interrogation torture but refuses to confess. During the subsequent trial, the evidence against Au is overwhelming and he is found guilty. Sentenced to death, he is continually beaten and abused by his fellow inmates, while Au's poverty-stricken wife is taken advantage of by a con man. Thanks to aid from a reporter, however, the woman meets up with lawyer Stanley Wu, who is able to have a new trial ordered.

The murder and mutilation scenes would fit right into fare like **Dr. Lamb** (also starring Simon Yam) and clash with the remainder of the film, which tries to function as a legitimate, mainstream trial drama. Good performances by Cecilia Yip and Paul Chun and a reasonably interesting premise keep it worthwhile, but the various intertitles are presented in Chinese only, making some aspects of the story and its resolution unclear.

325. Final Justice

(1988; Magnum) ★: 7/10. *Pik lik sin fung* (Cantonese), *Pi li xian feng* (Mandarin): "Thunderbolt Vanguard." Cinematographer: Cho Wai-kei; Art Director: Horace Ma Kwong-wing; Music: The Melody Bank; Writer: James Fung Shui-hung; Producer: Danny Lee Sau-yin; Action Director: Yuen Bun; Director: Parkman Wong Pak-man. Cast: Danny Lee Sau-yin (Cheung), Stephen Chiau Sing-chi (Boy), Shing Fui-on (Judge), William Ho Kar-kui (Chicken), Tommy Wong Kwong-leung (Bull), Ricky Yee Fan-wai (Lo), Ken Lo Wai-kwong (Kong). 1.85:1. VHS: Tai Seng. Import LD: Golden Cinema City. Import VCD: Mei Ah. Import DVD: Universe. 98 minutes.

Here's **48 Hrs.** HK-style with Danny Lee Sau-yin in the Nick Nolte cop role and a pre-superstardom Stephen Chiau Sing-chi in the Eddie Murphy thief part. While this set-up makes one expect a rollicking action-comedy, the screenplay plays things straight for the most part. Boy is a thief who steals cars used for getaways by a gang of robbers, headed up by Judge. One night the thieves clean out an illegal gambling outlet, murdering two of the patrons in the process. When District Sergeant Cheung picks up Boy for car theft, his overbearing superior, Inspector Lo, insists that the prisoner be charged with the killings as well. Realizing that Boy is being railroaded, Cheung gets him out of jail on the condition that he aid him in rounding up Judge and his cronies.

Viewers used to seeing Chiau mug his way through his recent string of hit comedy vehicles will be surprised at how well he acquits himself in what is, for all intents and purposes, a straight role (which won him Best Supporting Actor honors at Taiwan's 25th Golden Horse Awards). Still, here and there traces of the insolent, authority-defying persona that would soon win him fame manage to break through, breathing extra life into a very run-of-the-mill script. While the film suffers from the cardboard characters and familiar plot turns often found in Danny Lee's cop actioners, Chiau's fine work makes **Final Justice** of more interest than most and well worth a look. Director Parkman Wong has a cameo as an ambulance attendant in the final scene.

326. Final Justice

(1997; Media Asia Group/Media Asia Films Partners I/Milkyway Image Production) ★: 4/10. *Jui hau poon kuet* (Cantonese), *Zui hou pau jue* (Mandarin): "Last Judgment." Cinematographer: Cheung Tung-leung; Art Director: Cheung Kai-san; Music: Raymond Wong Ying-wah; Writers: John Chan Kin-chung, Lu Bing; Producer: Johnny To Kei-fung; Director: Derek Chiu Sung-kei. Cast: Lau Ching-wan (Li Chi-ho), Eric Tsang Chi-wai (Kim Shun-fat), Carman Lee Yeuk-tung (Koo May), Almen Wong Pui-ha (Donna Cheung), Peter Chan Lung (Chi-lone). 1.85:1. VHS: Tai Seng. Import LD/VCD/DVD: Mei Ah. 105 minutes.

In a momentary lapse of judgment, Catholic priest Li Chi-ho allows himself to be seduced by Donna Cheung, a depressed and confused woman who had just been jilted by her lover. When he refuses to sleep with her a second time, Donna falsely accuses Chi-ho of rape and he is arrested. The priest's childhood friend, Kim Shun-fat (a mob kingpin who always comes to Chi-ho for confession after he has committed murder) hires noted attorney Koo May to defend him.

There are a number of interesting themes here involving guilt, repression, selective interpretation, and desire, and director Derek Chiu imbues the film with some impressive stylistic touches. Unfortunately, the screenplay all but self-destructs in the second half, adopting a movie-of-the-week approach to the material that jettisons all subtlety; the final crawl, delineating the fate of the characters, is painfully ridiculous. With a measure of restraint and a rewrite, this could have been a far more portentous work. Lau Ching-wan and Eric Tsang are so good in their respective roles, they almost make this worth watching anyway.

327. The Final Option

(1994; Golden Harvest/Harvest Crown) ★: 5/10. *Fei foo hung sam* (Cantonese), *Fei hu xiong xin* (Mandarin): "Flying Tiger Great Ambition." Cinematographer: Horace Wong Wing-hang; Art Director: Cyrus Ho Kim-hung; Music: Richard Yuen Cheuk-fan; Producer: Yip Kwong-kim; Action Director: Bruce Law Lai-yin; Writer-Director: Gordon Chan Kar-seung. Cast: Michael Wong Man-tak (Stone Wong), Peter Yung Kam-cheung (Ho Chi-wai), Chan Kwok-bong (Bond), Carman Lee Yeuk-tung (May Lee), Vindy Chan Wai-yee (Windy), Bruce Law Lai-yin (Bruce), Paul Fonoroff (Police Official). 1.85:1. VHS: Tai Seng. Import LD/VCD: Mei Ah. 103 minutes.

A surprise success that spawned a prequel (called, appropriately enough, **First Option**) and several knockoffs, this modestly budgeted action thriller is really no better than routine and suffers from a laughable central performance by the wooden Michael Wong. In response to the increasingly heavy artillery used by criminals to commit robberies, the HK police decide to start having streets observed by members of the S.D.U. (Special Duty Unit, HK's answer to SWAT). Candidates from among the police force are taken to a training camp under the supervision of the ruthless Stone Wong. His job is to subject the men to every possible adversity so that only the cream of the crop will pass. After a series of exercises (which play out like a somewhat more brutal variation on what one always sees in these movies), the field is whittled down to a handful of candidates. These men undergo an additional six months of intensive instruction and are then ready for duty. The chance to test their skills comes in the form of some thieves, but the team's major objective remains to destroy the gang whose ruthless exploits brought about the creation of the unit.

There is more of an emphasis on character development here than in most films of this type, but the protagonists are pretty run-of-the-mill and so are their predicaments. Michael Wong has neither the presence nor the authority to convincingly play a commander, and his inept line readings just make things worse. Disappointingly, the action scenes are more along the lines of American TV shows than what one expects from contemporary HK cinema.

328. Final Run

(1989; Regent Film) ★: 4/10. *Muk jung mo yan* (Cantonese), *Mu zhong wu ren* (Mandarin): "Eye Center, No Human." Cinematographer: Cheung Hoi; Art Director: Leung Kar-ming; Music: Not Original; Producer: Lam Pak-heng; Action Directors: Phillip Ko Stunt Team, Ridley Tsui Bo-wah, Fok Wing-foo, Yiu Chan-lam, Yukari Oshima; Director: Phillip Ko Fei. Cast: Miu Kiu-wai (Ma Chun-fun), Simon Yam Tat-wah (Yan Yu-yiang), Cheung Kwok-keung (Chiang Chi-nan), Francis Ng Chun-yu (Wan Kwok-chuen), Yukari Oshima (Mon Ta Yee-wa), Dick Wei (Bull), Phillip Ko Fei (Sgt. Kau), Ha Ping (Chiang's Mother), Shum Wai (Chu Biao), Lung Ming-yan (General Wu), Ha Chi-chun (Jensy), Leung Kar-yan (Mon's Boss), Ridley Tsui Bo-wah (Thug with Glasses), Mark Houghton (Caucasian Thug). 1.85:1. VHS: Tai Seng (Subtitled or Dubbed). Also known as **Kickfighter** (Title for Tai Seng dubbed version). 87 minutes.

This routine actioner concerns a group of heroin smugglers based in The Golden Triangle who want to get their product into HK. Police Inspector Ma Chun-fun is one of the leaders of the group and needs the cooperation of his old school friend, straight-laced customs official Chiang Chi-nan. When the latter refuses, one of Ma's men has Chiang's family murdered. After failing to exact revenge in HK, Chiang heads for Thailand and takes refuge with a relative. Ma soon learns his whereabouts and eliminates virtually all of Chiang's allies, but when the drug runners murder a partner who was trying to take advantage of them, Chiang gets some unexpected help from the victim's fiancée.

Like most of Phillip Ko's films, the storyline wanders all over the place, incorporating an absurdly large number of characters for such a routine genre programmer. Aside from picturesque Thailand locales and a handful of decent action set-pieces, there is not much of interest here. The soundtrack includes music swiped from **Aliens** and **Escape from New York**.

329. The Final Test

(1987; Golden Harvest/Bo Ho Films/ Paragon Films) ★: 4/10. *Ji hau yat jin* (Cantonese), *Zui hou yi zhan* (Mandarin): "Final Fight." Cinematographer: Raymond Lam Fai-tai; Art Director: Kong Hoi-ming; Music: Violet Lam Man-yee; Writer: Chan Wai; Producer: Sammo Hung Kam-po; Action Directors: Brandy Yuen Chun-yeung, Austin Wai Tin-chi; Director: Lo Kin. Cast: Austin Wai Tin-chi (Sum Ying-mo), Deborah Sims (Jo Jo), Yuen Wah (The Chairman), Blackie Ko Shou-liang (The Foreman), Billy Lau Nam-kwong (Dirty Nose), Eric Tsang Chi-wai (Sum's Contact), Chin Siu-ho (Assassinated Worker). 1.85:1. VHS: Tai Seng. 89 minutes.

A rare foray into HK science fiction, this action thriller is a limp imitation of the Sean Connery film **Outland**, set in an amusingly low-tech 21st century where people sit around playing Space Invaders on computers that date from the mid '80s. Austin Wai plays a martially adept secret agent assigned to infiltrate the Cosmos IV mining operation, which is giving its workers dangerous, addictive drugs to increase productivity. After being hired on as a Security Chief, he allies himself with a sullen doctor (Eurasian actress Deborah Sims), who is being forced to produce the chemical, to put an end to its distribution. When Wai takes care of the villainous foreman and his lackies, the company chairman dispatches his crack troop of killers to liquidate him.

There are a few decent fights and shootouts along the way but nothing one couldn't find in any number of American direct-to-video cheapies, and the storyline is too derivative and unrewarding to maintain interest. Director Jacob Cheung Chi-leung (**Cageman**) has a supporting role.

330. Final Victory

(1987; D & B Films Co.) ★: 4/10. *Chui hau sing lee* (Cantonese), *Zui hou sheng li* (Mandarin): "Final Victory." Cinematographer: Ardy Lam Kwok-wah; Music: Danny Chung Teng-yat; Writer: Wong Kar-wai; Producer: Dickson Poon Dik-sun; Art Director/Director: Patrick Tam Kar-ming. Cast: Eric Tsang Chi-wai (Hung), Loletta Lee Lai-chun (Mimi), Margaret Lee Tin-long (Ping), Tsui Hark (Big Bo), Dennis Chan Kwok-san (Mahjong Club Manager), Chen Jing (Thug). 1.85:1. VHS: Tai Seng. Import LD: Mei Ah. 93 minutes.

A tiresome, ill-conceived comedy-thriller, this is the last film to date from New Wave director Patrick Tam, who never lived up to the promise he showed in his early features. When his hot-tempered brother, Big Bo (played in decidedly over-the-top fashion by director Tsui Hark), is sent off to prison, the eternally put-upon Hung is ordered to look after Bo's two women, Mimi and Ping. The former is somewhere in Japan and the latter owes a huge debt to loan shark Choy. Hung and Ping decide to leave HK until things cool off, and set out to find Mimi. Hung discovers the girl being forced to perform in a live sex show and rescues her, but the porn shop's owners take Mimi hostage, demanding 500,000 yen for her release. Luckily, Hung hits the jackpot at a *Pachinko* parlor and the three head back to HK. However, Choy is waiting for them and there is another, major problem: Mimi has fallen in love with Hung, prompting Bo to announce plans to ice her and Hung upon his release.

Final Victory occupies a strange and uncomfortable niche: It clearly wants to be offbeat, but most of the humor and situations can be found in any number of mainstream comedies, and the characters are not so much quirky as just plain annoying. Wong Kar-wai's fans may want to take a look, if only to see how his writing evolved during the time between this and his own features, especially **Chungking Express**.

331. Finale in Blood

(1993; Golden Harvest/Paragon Films) ★: 5/10. *Daai lau gong cheong lung* (Cantonese), *Da nao guang chang long* (Mandarin): "Disturbance of Fortunate Fate." Cinematographers: David Chung Chi-man, Peter Ngor Chi-kwan; Art Director: Ray Lam Chan-fai; Music: Law Wing-fai; Writer: Chan Hing-ka; Producers: Chua Lam, Tony Au Ding-ping; Director: Fruit Chan Kwoh. Cast: Lawrence Cheng Tan-shui (Cheng Ming-pao), Ruth Winona Tao Kwun-mei (Fang Yin), David Wu Tai-wai (Ma Kuang-shen), Josephine Koo Mei-wah (Lei-sha), Chikako Aoyama (Ma's Mistress), Peter Lai Bei-tak (Chen Chi). 1.85:1. Import LD/VCD: Universe. 94 minutes.

Completed in 1991, this ghost story spent two years on the shelf before garnering a six day theatrical run in November of 1993. After picking up a discarded umbrella one day, radio announcer Cheng Ming-pao finds himself face to face with beautiful ghost Fang Yin. Killed when she was thrown through the window of a building, Yin's soul has become trapped inside the umbrella. Seeking Cheng's help to exact revenge, she convinces him to tell her story on the air and uses her powers to make the broadcast a hit. We learn that she fell in love with police officer Ma Kuang-shen, who proves to be something less than an ideal man, openly cavorting with a voluptuous prostitute. When Ma hears the broadcasts, he realizes that it is his story that is being told and arrests Cheng; but even with Cheng in custody, the program goes on as scheduled. Yin has Cheng exhume her body and, after re-inhabiting the dead shell, goes to confront Ma.

An uneasy combination of **Rouge** and unabashed exploitation, this is moderately successful until the finale, which is such a badly miscalculated mix of drama and slapstick humor, it undermines everything that precedes it. The production design is beautiful (the film unfolds in what appears to be the 1940s, though no date is given) and the cinematography is lush, but some viewers will feel that the production's most notable achievement is how it managed to include so much nudity and still get a Category II rating. Tao and Wu also worked together as veejays on MTV Asia and in **Evil Black Magic**. Tony Leung Kar-fai has a bizarre running cameo. This was the directorial debut for Fruit Chan, whose second film, **Made in Hong Kong**, would turn out to be far more momentous.

332. Fire Dragon

(1994; Regal Films Co.) ★: 6/10. *Foh wan chuen kei* (Cantonese), *Huo yun chuan qi* (Mandarin): "Fire Cloud Legend." Cinematographer: Jingle Ma Cho-shing; Art Director: Ben Lau Man-hung; Music: Lowell Lo Kwun-ting; Writer: Elsa Tang Pik-yin; Producer: Thomas Ng Chun-chuen; Action Director: Yuen Cheung-yan; Director: Yuen Woo-ping. Cast: Brigitte Lin Ching-hsia (Fire Dragon), Max Mok Siu-chung (Yuen Ming), Sin Lap-man (Prince Six), Sandra Ng Kwan-yu (Tang Lyn-yu), Yeh Chuan-chen (Snow). 1.85:1. VHS: Tai Seng. Import LD/VCD: Ocean Shores. 90 minutes. Also known as **The Fiery Dragon Kid** (Tai Seng tape title).

First announced as **The Fiery Romance**, this kinetic action-fantasy seems to have been designed primarily to give director Yuen Woo-ping numerous opportunities to top the pyrotechnic-laden finale of his 1993 cult favorite **Iron Monkey**. Dispatched by the corrupt Prince Six to retrieve a letter revealing his plans to overthrow the emperor, powerful assassin Fire Dragon has her mission thwarted by loyalist swordsman Yuen Ming. Adopting civilian guise, the two infiltrate a performing company and continue their battle in clandestine fashion, much to the bewilderment of the troupe's cretinous leader, Lyn-yu. Through exposure to the actors and their families, Fire Dragon learns the blessings of honor and compassion, which leads her to turn against the prince and her sister assassin, Snow.

Unlike most of the '90s fantasies, **Fire Dragon** sports a plot that is refreshingly straightforward. Unfortunately, clarity comes at the expense of virtually all originality. The storyline has been adapted numerous times before, the most obvious example being **The Killer** (never mind the numerous American and European variations on the theme). Fire Dragon herself is more than a little reminiscent of Lin's supernatural killer, "Lien Ni-chang," from **The Bride with White Hair** but with little of that character's complexity and singular appeal. Lin gives the mundane role more than it deserves, but Fire Dragon is ultimately more interesting when personified by the various stunt performers who shoot flames from their hands and wield various incendiary weapons. Said action scenes are consistently spectacular and go a long way in making up for the film's various shortcomings (like Sandra Ng's shrill comedy relief). Lowell Lo contributes an excellent, driving score that complements the action and dramatic interludes splendidly. Max Mok was either injured or otherwise not available for the final battle, as he is quite obviously doubled throughout.

The First Mission *see* **Heart of Dragon** [*sic*]

333. First Option

(1996; Media Asia Group/Media Asia Films Partners I/People's Production) ★: 6/10. *Fei foo* (Cantonese), *Fei hu* (Mandarin): "Flying Tiger." Cinematographer: Horace Wong Wing-hang; Art Director: Alfred Yau Wai-ming; Music: Chan Kwong-wing; Writer: Chan Hing-ka; Producers: John Chong Ching, Yip Kwong-kim; Action Director: Bruce Law Lai-yin; Director: Gordon Chan Kar-seung. Cast: Michael Wong Man-tak (Don Wong), Gigi Leung Wing-kei (Minnie Kwan), Damian Lau Chung-yan (Inspector Lau), Yip Kwong-kim. Dolby Stereo. 1.85:1. VHS: Tai Seng. Import LD/VCD: Mei Ah. Import DVD: Mei Ah, Mega Star. 90 minutes.

This prequel to (you guessed it) **The Final Option** follows Michael Wong's character (renamed "Don Wong" in the subtitles here) in the days before he became a training officer. After a customs raid goes disastrously wrong, SDU is called in to track the criminals, who are highly proficient with firearms. A large heroin bust reveals that a major drug deal is going down, and Customs and SDU reluctantly pool their resources in an effort to determine the location of the buy. When S.D.U. is ambushed, it becomes clear that there is an informant on the team. Some information leads Wong to surmise that the targets are hiding out on an island, and when his stressed out superior agrees to look the other way, Wong leads his men there to take them out.

The action is more exciting this time (though the final battle is right out of the **Rambo** movie of your choice), but Michael Wong is as ineffectual as ever (try to keep a straight face when he says, "Good heart he had, seduced by the dark side he was"—a line that only Alec Guinness might have gotten away with) and Gigi Leung is miscast in a role better suited to a more versatile and mature actress like Carrie Ng Kar-lai. Passable formula fare but, considering the talent behind the camera, this ultimately ranks as another disappointment from the increasingly uneven Gordon Chan. Kathy Chow Hoi-mei has a cameo. Chan Kwong-wing's stirring theme music would later be used by Media Asia in their DVD promotional spots.

334. First Shot

(1993; David Lam Films) ★: 5/10. *Lim jing dai yat gik* (Cantonese), *Lian zheng di yi ji* (Mandarin): "Honest Administration First Strike." Cinematographers: Wong Po-man, Abdul M. Rumjahn; Art Director: Bill Lui Cho-hung; Music: Lowell Lo Kwun-ting; Writers: So Man-sing, Chan Kiu-ying, Wong Ho-wah; Action Directors: Yuen Tak, Tony Leung Siu-hung; Producer-Director: David Lam Tak-luk. Cast: Ti Lung (Wong Yat-chung, aka Tamerlane), Simon Yam Tat-wah (Sam Mok), Maggie Cheung Man-yuk (Annie Ma), Waise Lee Chi-hung (Luk Tai-chiu, aka Faucet), Andy Hui Chi-on (Lo Kam-shiu, aka Waterloo), Lau Sek-ming (Yip Chun-wan), Jamie Luk Kim-ming (Kung Fu Instructor), Frankie Chin Chi-leung (Muscle), Bobby Yip King-sang (Ugly Assassin), Lee Hoi-sang (Rice Shop Boss). 1.85:1. VHS: Tai Seng. Import LD/VCD: Universe. 100 minutes.

One of several HK knockoffs of Brian DePalma's **The Untouchables**, this weak actioner (which copies some dialogue and camera set-ups from the Hollywood film almost verbatim) goes from point A to point B with very little in the way of excitement or energy and absolutely no originality. Set in 1973, the story concerns the events that led to the formation of the I.C.A.C. (Independent Commission Against Corruption); attempts to stamp out criminal activity among civil servants; and the fight against powerful triad Luk Tai-chiu, the man behind much of the underworld activity in HK. After being shot in the back for refusing to take a bribe, upright cop Wong Yat-chung signs on with the newly formed commission and recruits other officers who share his moral viewpoint. He even enlists the aid of Sam Mok, the man who shot him six months earlier. Members of a squad that doesn't officially exist (and caught between both the police and the mob), Wong and his associates have their work cut out for them.

Ti Lung's commanding, charismatic performance and some decent gunplay go a long way in making this tiresomely predictable effort palatable, but the poor screenplay is a major liability. The low point comes when Wong and the men go undercover in a gay bar to try and nab a prissy triad accountant. Lowell Lo's score sounds very much like a cross between his music for the **God of Gamblers** films and **The Black Panther Warriors**.

335. First Strike

(1996; Golden Harvest/Paragon Films) ★: 6/10 (HK version); 5/10 (US Version). *Ging chaat goo si IV ji gaan daan yam mo* (Cantonese), *Jing cha gu shi IV zhi jian dan ren wu* (Mandarin): "Police Story IV: A Simple Mission." Cinematographer: Jingle Ma Cho-shing; Art Director: Oliver Wong Yui-man; Music: Wong Chung-yin (HK version), J. Peter Robinson (US version); Writers: Stanley Tong Kwai-lai, Nick Tramontane, Greg Mellot, Elliot Tong Ming-kei; Producer: Barbie Tung Wan-sze; Action Directors: Jackie Chan, Stanley Tong Kwai-lai; Director: Stanley Tong Kwai-lai. Cast: Jackie Chan (Jackie), Jackson Liu Hsieu-hsien (Tsui), Annie Wu Chen-chun (Annie), Bill Tung Biu (Uncle Bill), Jouri Petrov (Colonel Gregor Yegorov). Dolby Digital. 2.35:1. 107 minutes (HK version), 84 minutes (US version). VHS: New Line (84 minutes). LD: Image (84 minutes). Import LD/VCD: Mei Ah (107 minutes). Also known as **Jackie Chan's First Strike** (US title), **The Story of CIA—First Strike** [*sic*] (Singapore title).

Jackie Chan's foray into James Bond territory, **First Strike** unfolds in HK, the Ukraine, and Australia. Accepting an invitation to help the CIA track the movements of a woman connected to an international arms smuggler named Tsui, Chan (once again playing a like-named character) soon finds himself in harm's way as escalating events put him right in the middle of the intrigue. Tsui is in possession of a nuclear missile that various parties, specifically the Russian mafia and the American feds, would love to get their hands on. This leads to a snowboard/ski chase right out of the Bond film of your choice, and various small-scale skirmishes, culminating with an underwater fight in a shark-filled tank at an Australian waterpark. The oft-cited highlight of the film finds Chan taking on a gang of stickfighters using a ladder as his only defense, but also unforgettable is the moment where he uses a pair of stilts to kick an opponent who is on the second floor of a building!

Despite its eagerness to please, **First Strike** emphasizes what is wrong with most of Chan's recent films, not the least of which is the attempt to make him seem younger by choosing leading ladies (in this case, cute Taiwanese actress Annie Wu) who are less than half his age, a practice which has precisely the opposite effect. As on his previous collaborations with Chan, the direction by former stuntman Stanley Tong is merely functional, presenting the action setpieces with great aplomb and everything else in a straightforward manner befitting television (it is easy to see why Disney felt Tong was the man to helm a pre-fab action-comedy product like **Mr. Magoo**). Concessions to make the film sellable to Western markets permeate the enterprise, from the generic espionage plotting to the extensive English dialogue, but the biggest problem is actually the most elemental one: **First Strike** lacks the sense of exhilaration and awe that runs throughout Chan's top work from the '80s. It is a fitfully entertaining star vehicle and nothing more. Eleven months after the film's bow in HK, New Line Cinema opened it in America with a new moniker, **Jackie Chan's First Strike**, an entirely different score, a drastically altered structure, and a shameless ad campaign which implied that the action unfolded Stateside. Removing 30 minutes of footage, American editor Michael J. Duthie carved the film down to its bare essentials. The original had no character development to speak of, so the short version does not suffer in that sense. Gone, however, is any sense of grace the production possessed. While the HK cut does lag a bit in spots, the New Line version is accelerated to the point of absurdity. With some of the exposition and most of the transitional scenes snipped, a marginal plot is now a skeletal framework. The events now rocket by, doing nothing but setting up the next action setpiece. Chan dubbed his own voice, but the rest of the re-voicing is awful at best and idiotic at worst (what is the point of Chan having a translator sitting beside him during a meeting with Russian military men when everyone in the room speaks English?). Also, if an 83 minute running time seems ridiculously short for a major theatrical release in the '90s, consider that when you subtract the new opening and closing credit sequences, the time is actually only *76*! Stick with the HK cut, available on import disc.

336. The First Time Is the Last Time

(1989; Seven mm Film Production Co.) ★: 5/10. *Dai yat gaan* (Cantonese), *Di yi jian* (Mandarin): "The First Flower Bulb." Cinematographers: Philip Ma Kam-cheung, Andrew Lau Wai-keung, Paul Chan Chung-chau; Art Director: Chu Lai-kwong; Music: Lowell Lo Kwun-ting; Writer: Yu Fan; Producer: Leung Ming; Action Director: Woo Chi-lung; Director: Raymond Leung Pan-hei. Cast: Carrie Ng Kar-lai (Winnie Wong), Season Ma Si-san (Yuk), Andy Lau Tak-wah (Yung), Meg Lam Kin-ming (Inmate 5354), Kenneth Tsang Kong (Jenny's Father), Lam Chung (Mang), Johnny Wang Lung-wei (Triad Boss). 1.85:1. VHS: Tai Seng. Import LD: Mei Ah. 92 minutes.

Carrie Ng's strong, persuasive performance gives this violent women's prison thriller an extra level of interest, though the final product stays well within the usual boundaries. After taking a drug possession rap for her boyfriend Robert, timid Yuk ends up with a six month jail sentence. Inside, she meets Winnie Wong, a hardened (and seemingly insane) inmate who saves Yuk from being bullied by the vicious "He-Man" and her cronies. Through flashbacks we learn that Winnie was a junkie prostitute and fell in love with undercover cop Yung. The latter was murdered after his triad cohorts learned his true identity, and Winnie was imprisoned for taking bloody revenge on the murderers. Robert, a member of the same gang, wants Yuk to kill Winnie to avenge the death of his friends, but she and Winnie have developed a bond of friendship that cannot be broken.

The women-in-prison genre is consistently dreary and formulaic, and this entry is no exception, though director Raymond Leung imbues it with a fair amount of style. Carrie Ng's intense interpretation makes the simplistic dramatic conflicts seem more substantial and effective than they really are. Winnie is typical of the gritty, atypical roles Ng would routinely take, helping to make her one of the most arresting and multifaceted actresses in HK cinema. On some prints the English subtitles stop nine minutes before the movie ends, though the events that unfold remain fairly easy to follow.

337. A Fishy Story

(1989; Golden Harvest/Bo Ho Films Co./Mobile Film Production/Paragon

Films) ★: 6/10. *Bat tuet mat dik yan* (Cantonese), *Bu tuo wa de ren* (Mandarin): "People Who Always Protect Themselves." Cinematographer: Peter Pau Tak-hei; Art Director: Szeto Wai-yung; Music: Richard Yuen Cheuk-fan; Writers: Lo Wing-keung, Eddie Fong Ling-ching, Anthony Chan Yau; Producer: Chan Pui-wah; Director: Anthony Chan Yau. Cast: Kenny Bee (Kung), Maggie Cheung Man-yuk (Huang), Anthony Chan Yau (Paul Chen), Josephine Koo Mei-wah (Mrs. Ku), Carrie Ng Kar-lai (Actress), Lam Chung (The Director), Gujjar Singh (Indian Tenant), Season Ma Si-san (Communist Demonstrator). 1.85:1. VHS: Tai Seng. Import LD: Star Entertainment (No Subtitles). Import VCD: Mega Star (No Subtitles). 99 minutes.

This formulaic but intermittently charming romantic comedy-drama (which initially looks like it will be HK's answer to **Breakfast at Tiffany's**) is set in the late '60s, during the time of the student riots. When impoverished cab driver Kung (who is reluctantly prostituting himself out to an older, affluent lady to make ends meet) and snooty, would-be actress Huang end up living in the same building, it's hate at first sight. Huang's attitude gets her into trouble on the set of "Taxi Dancers in Paris," but this humiliating experience fails to humble her at all. However, after the two are accidentally caught up in a riot and arrested one evening, the shared experience helps to bring them closer. At no loss for suitors, Huang is eventually offered the chance to go to America and live in luxury as the mistress of a model agency owner. While this is what she has dreamed of, the death of Huang's mother changes her perspective on life, prompting the girl to stay behind and go into business with Kung. Their road to happiness and self-sufficiency is lined with more than a few potholes.

Maggie Cheung (looking quite beautiful in a variety of fashions from the time) and Kenny Bee both give highly appealing performances (even if their characters are not always especially loveable), and their chemistry helps the film through its more predictable stretches. The incorporation of events from the period (the riots, the taxi strike, etc.) at least gives the story a few fresh angles, and the art direction and cinematography are quite captivating.

338. Fist and Guts

(1979) ★: 7/10. *Yat daam ji lik saam gung fu* (Cantonese), *Yi dan er li san gong fu* (Mandarin): "One Guts, Two Strengths, Three Kung Fu." Cinematographer: Arthur Wong Ngok-tai; Music: Not Original; Writer: Wong Hoi-ming; Producer: Ho Sau-har; Action Directors: The Lau Brothers; Director: Lau Kar-wing. Cast: Gordon Lau Kar-fai (The Master), Lau Kar-wing (Yeung), Lo Lieh (The Housekeeper), Lee Hoi-sang (Big Pang). 2.35:1. VHS: Ocean Shores (Dubbed). Import LD: Ocean Shores (No Subtitles). 91 minutes.

This comic period kung fu yarn finds Shaw Brothers favorite Gordon Lau scouring the countryside in search of his housekeeper, a master of disguise who absconded with his employer's inheritance. Teaming up with a pair of bumblers (amusingly played by director Lau Kar-wing and Lee Hoi-sang), Lau is able to catch up with the thief, but he turns out to be the wrong man. After several more false leads (including a near fatal detour to a leper colony), the trio seems no closer to apprehending their target. Meanwhile, the fugitive (Lo Lieh) has ingratiated himself with a sadistic general in order to get his hands on a priceless Jade Buddha in the official's possession. Lau is eventually able to deduce this scheme, but as the story progresses, it becomes clear that neither he nor Lo are what they seem.

As one has come to expect from The Lau Brothers, the martial arts here are sensational (particularly a sequence where Gordon Lau and an opponent battle in silence so as not to alert the armed guards patrolling outside), though all current video versions are so badly cropped, it is not always easy to appreciate the choreography. The best is saved for the final reel, as Lee and the Laus must work their way through a corridor filled with **Raiders of the Lost Ark**-style booby traps in order to reach Lo and take him on. The soundtrack includes music lifted from **Psycho**! Character names listed above are from the dubbed versions.

339. Fist from Shaolin

(1993; Mei Ah Film Production Co.) ★: 5/10. *Wong Fei-hung ji naam yi dong bo gwok* (Cantonese), *Huang Feihong zhi nan er dang bao guo* (Mandarin): "Wong Fei-hung: Man Dedicates His Life to His Country" or "Huang Feihong: Man Dedicates His Life to His Country." Cinematographer: Chan Hoi-yan; Music: Not Original; Producer: Wong Chi-wei; Action Director: Wong Chi-hung; Writer-Director: Lau Kwok-wai. Cast: Sharon Kwok Sau-wan (13th Aunt), Gabriel Wong Yat-san (So), Chi Chuen-hua (Eleven), Wong Kwan, Mak Ha-si. 1.85:1. VHS: World Video. Import LD/VCD: Mei Ah. 94 minutes.

Opening with footage of Jet Li Lian-jie cribbed from the **Shaolin Temple** films Li made in China, this modest period entry doesn't pretend to offer anything new but does a reasonably good job of following genre tenets. The local prefect and some other scoundrels plan to shanghai workers on the behalf of some foreigners, who will pay 50 taels a head for laborers to help build the railroad in America (of course, opium smuggling also figures into their plans). After Wong Fei-hung (identified in the subtitles as Huang Fei-hong, the Mandarin form of the name) witnesses their tactics firsthand, he decides to open a clinic in Foshan so that he can stay and help the townsfolk defend themselves. In the meantime, 13th Aunt arrives from overseas fully westernized and tries to rescue one of the clinic's housemaids from a nearby nunnery, which is actually a brothel in disguise. Master Wong's principles cause him to commit acts that interfere with the prefect's opium and slave smuggling, setting the stage for a final showdown, with Wong and the kidnapped workers joining forces to vanquish their foes.

For once, the lone caucasian character is an honorable man, one who has been misled by his partners and atones for his actions by helping Master Wong. Aside from that, **Fist from Shaolin** adheres pretty closely to formula, but the fight choreography should please those who prefer more traditional combat (the wirework is minimal), and the actor playing Wong offers an effective interpretation that differs just enough from that of Jet Li and Zhao Wenzhou to make a favorable impression on its own terms.

340. Fist of Fury 1991

(1991; Chung Sing Film Co.) ★: 6/10. *San cheng miu moon 1991* (Cantonese), *Xin jing wu men 1991* (Mandarin): "New Jing Wu Society 1991." Cinematographers: Chan Yuen-kai, Jimmy Leung Chi-ming; Art Directors: Chan Wing-bo, James Cheung Ying-wah; Music: Lowell Lo Kwun-ting; Writer: Jeff Lau Chun-wai; Producers: Jeff Lau Chun-wai, Corey Yuen Kwai; Director: Cho Chung-sing. Cast: Stephen Chiau Sing-chi (Lau Ching), Kenny Bee (Brother Smart), Sharla Cheung Man (Mandy), Corey Yuen Kwai (Fok Wan), Vincent Wan Yeung-ming (Cheng Wai), Shing Fui-on (Chiu Tung), Woo Fung (Teacher with Glasses), Chen Jing (Brother Leung), Ha Chi-chun (Flutty Ping), Jeff Lau Chun-wai (Tournament Official). 1.85:1. VHS: World Video. Import LD: Star Entertainment (No Subtitles). Import DVD: China Star (No Subtitles). 100 minutes.

This enjoyable Stephen Chiau farce casts him as Mainland hick Lau Ching, who comes to HK with little more than his powerful right hand punch, which has the force of a truck. He is robbed by petty thief Brother Smart but ends up being friends with him. The pair run across the revered kung fu teacher Fok Wan, and Lau hopes that the master will teach him to properly harness and control his power. In a parody of Bruce Lee's **Fist of Fury** (known in America as **The Chinese Connection**), a group of Japanese masters challenge Fok's students, but Lau saves the day with his super fist. Fok's beautiful daughter Mandy becomes attracted to Lau, much to the consternation of the school's top student, Cheng Wai. Wanting the girl for himself, Cheng makes it look like Lau and Smart tried to rape Mandy, and the two friends are expelled. After receiving instruction from some very unconventional teachers, Lau enters a martial arts tournament that offers a prize of $10 million.

As with many of Chiau's films, much of the humor is obvious but still often induces laughter, thanks to his timing and body language. Highlights include the comedian's wonderful Bruce Lee impersonation and in-joke references to **Rocky** and **A Better Tomorrow**. Ng Man-tat, Nat Chan Pak-cheung, and Josephine Siao Fong-fong (who co-stars with Chiau in the awkwardly titled sequel **Fist of Fury 1991 II**) have cameos.

341. Fist of Fury 1991 II

(1992; Chung Sing Film Co.) ★: 7/10. *Maan ung wai lung* (Cantonese), *Man hua wei long* (Mandarin): "Cartoon Mighty Dragon." Cinematographers: Chan Yuen-kai, Jimmy Leung Chi-ming; Art Directors: Chan Wing-bo, James Cheung Ying-wah; Music: Lowell Lo Kwun-ting; Writers: Ho Tung, Jeff Lau Chun-wai; Producers: Corey Yuen Kwai, Jeff Lau Chun-wai; Action Directors: Corey Yuen Kwai, Yuen Tak; Director: Cho Chung-sing. Cast: Stephen Chiau Sing-chi (Lau Chin), Josephine Siao Fong-fong (Peony, aka "Ngou Chat"), Kenny Bee (Chu Kor-chun, aka "Smartie"), Sharla Cheung Man (Min/Yuen Chuen), Nat Chan Pak-cheung (Ngou Pi), Yuen Wah (Cheng Wan-to), Mui Siu-wai (Chu-chu), Ku Feng (Chu-chu's Father), Woo Fung (Trainer). 1.85:1. VHS: World Video (No Subtitles). Import LD: Star Entertainment (No Subtitles). Import DVD: China Star (No Subtitles). 93 minutes.

In this engagingly silly sequel, Lau Chin (called "Lau Ching" in the previous film's subtitles) is a champion in the ring—but a bankrupt one after his managers lose all of his money. To make matters worse, Min (through a series of events too complicated to relate) thinks he's gay, his landlady wants his head, and he is plagued by Ngou Pi, a hopeless dolt who wants to be his student. To top it all off, Cheng Wan-to, the brother of the opponent Chin last fought, wants to break every bone in his body. After being badly beaten by Cheng's men, Chin and Pi are saved by the intervention of "Ngou Chat," a masked heroine who is actually Pi's martially skilled aunt, Peony. While recuperating at Pi's home in the country, Chin falls head over heels for his host's cousin, Yuen Chuen, who just happens to be a dead ringer for Min (called "Mandy" last time). When Pi and Chuen are kidnapped, Chin must get back into the ring to save them, and only the Ngou family's secret "Electric Fist" technique will allow him to prevail over Cheng.

Teaming up Stephen Chiau and Josephine Siao was an inspired decision, and the two play off each other like old pros (they could just stand around and improvise for 90 minutes and it would still be a joy). Siao (who would work again with Corey Yuen on **Fong Sai Yuk**, **Fong Sai Yuk II**, and **Mahjong Dragon**) is wonderful throughout, and there are a number of amusing jabs at her 1960s films that can still be appreciated even by those who haven't seen them. The silliness gets a little too unbridled during the climax but there is still much to be amused by here, and, as there is little reliance on Chiau's *mo lei tau* wordplay, the jokes are easily discerned by Westerners. Only the Taiwan video release has English subtitles, but it is well worth tracking down.

342. Fist of Legend

(1994; Eastern Productions) ★. 8/10. *Cheng miu ying hung* (Cantonese), *Jing wu ying xiong* (Mandarin): "The Hero of Jing Wu Society." Cinematographer: Derek Wan Man-kit; Art Director: Horace Ma Kwong-wing; Music: Joseph Koo Kar-fai; Producer: Jet Li Lianjie; Action Directors: Yuen Woo-ping, Yuen Cheung-yan, Yuen Shun-yee; Writer-Director: Gordon Chan Kar-seung. Cast: Jet Li Lianjie (Chen Zhen), Shinobu Nakayama (Mitsuko), Chin Siu-ho (Ting-en), Yasuaki Kurota (Funakoshi), Ada Choi Siu-fan (Xian-hong), Billy Chow Bei-lee (General Fujita), Paul Chun Pui (Nong), Jackson Liu Hsiu-hsien (Akutagawa), Yuen Cheung-yan (Captain Jie), Yuen Shun-yee (Ngai). 1.85:1. VHS: Tai Seng. Import LD: Cameron Entertainment, Mei Ah Gold. VCD: Mei Ah. 101 minutes.

Regarded by many kung fu enthusiasts as Bruce Lee's best film, Lo Wei's **The Chinese Connection** (1971; aka **Fist of Fury**) showcased its star at the height of his abilities, with Lee's power and presence ample recompense for the routine narrative and crass dubbing. This accomplished remake cannot fully match that film's raw appeal, but it is a more thoughtful and better-produced work which also delivers a plethora of exciting combat. After learning that his mentor, Master Huo, has been killed in a match against a Japanese fighter, Chen Zhen terminates his studies in Japan and returns home to the Jing Wu martial arts society in Shanghai. He challenges and easily defeats Huo's killer, Master Akutagawa, leading him to suspect foul play. An autopsy reveals that Huo had been poisoned prior to the contest, and the growing animosity between the Jing Wu members and the rival Japanese school reaches its boiling point when Akutagawa is found dead and Chen is framed for the crime. Thanks to the testimony of his devout Japanese girlfriend, Mitsuko, Chen is declared innocent, but subsequent events force him into a final duel with the fanatical Japanese general who orchestrated Huo's murder and now seeks to destroy the reputation and influence of Chinese martial arts.

Bruce Lee's Chen was fiercely patriotic and emotional, with this intense loyalty to his school and culture usually finding him teetering on the brink of violence. However, Lo Wei allowed the actor to display both animalistic fury and, in quieter moments, a fuller range of emotions, making him a better realized character than Jet Li's Chen, who is comparatively stolid and passionless. This is unfortunate, as Li has proven to be both intense and personable in other films, particularly his collaborations with director Corey Yuen Kwai on **Fong Sai Yuk I & II** (both 1993) and **My Father Is a Hero** (1995). However, there is no questioning his considerable fighting skills, which are given full reign here by martial arts director Yuen Woo-ping. The various setpieces contain instances where wirework has been used to enhance force and technique, but the FX trickery does not detract from the performers' natural abilities. While the villains are standard issue, other foreign characters, like Mitsuko (who is initially spurned by Chen's peers because of her heritage) and the greying but formidable Master Funakoshi, are sympathetic and well-delineated, a rarity for Japanese characters in Chinese cinema. A subplot involving the competitive friendship between Chen and his senior colleague and the latter's covert relationship with a compassionate prostitute is less noteworthy but helps define a further parallel between the two men as their relationships with these "undesirable" women are harshly condemned by the school's conservative elder. Trivia note: Composer Joseph Koo also created the original music used in **The Chinese Connection**; on English dubbed prints, he is credited as C.H. Ku, which is short for his Mandarin name, Ku Chia-hui.

Fist of the White Lotus *see* **Clan of the White Lotus**

The Five Deadly Venoms *see* **Five Venoms**

343. Five Element Ninja

(1982; Shaw Brothers) ★: 5/10. *Yan je mo dik* (Cantonese), *Ren zhe wu di* (Mandarin): "Ninja, No Enemy." Music: Not Original; Writers: Chang Cheh, Ngai Hong; Producer: Mona Fong Yat-wah; Director: Chang Cheh. Cast: Michael Chan Wai-man (The Ninja Leader), Lo Mang (Chi Shang), Chien Tien-chi, Chan Pui-san, Lung Tin-cheung. 2.35:1. VHS: Vista (Dubbed). 105 minutes. Also known as **Super Ninjas** (US and Vista video title).

This Chang Cheh period kung fu thriller is one of his best known films here in the West, but one suspects this is due more to its over-the-top violence and gore than anything else. A Chinese martial arts school is challenged by a group of Japanese ninjas called "The Five Elements." As per the name, their fighting styles utilize components of Gold, Wood, Fire, Water, and Earth. Unfamiliar with the concept of ninjitsu, the school dispatches a group of students to face the Japanese, who quickly annihilate them with their decidedly unsportsmanlike techniques. The ninjas then set their sights on the school's headquarters, using one of the women in their group to infiltrate and provide a map of the structure. The Chinese fighters are decimated by the surprise attack, with only one escaping alive. He receives instruction from an old master on how to counter the ninjas' tactics and, joining with three other skilled fighters, challenges the Japanese to a second duel.

Chang's films tend to be quite violent, and this one may just be the nastiest of the lot. However, it is also rather crudely made, and Chang's new group of fighters sorely lack the charisma of their predecessors. This remains worth catching for the exaggerated combat in its final act and the creative methods the Chinese use to defeat their opponents. The English dubbing on Shaw Brothers films is invariably bad, but the revoicing on this one is especially abominable.

344. Five Venoms

(1978; Shaw Brothers) ★: 8/10. *Ng duk* (Cantonese), *Wu du* (Mandarin): "Five Venoms." Cinematographers: Kung Mu-to, Tsao Hui-chi; Art Director: Johnson Tsao; Music: Not Original; Writers: Ngai Hong, Chang Cheh; Producer: Mona Fong Yat-wah; Action Directors: Liang Ting, Tai Chi-hsieh, Chu Lu-feng; Director: Chang Cheh. Cast: Phillip Kwok Tsui (Officer Ho Yun-hsun), Chiang Sheng (Yang Te), Lo Mang (Li Ho), Sun Chien (Captain Ma Tao), Lu Feng (Tang San-kwei), Wei Pai (Hung Wan-tung), Johnny Wang Lung-wei (The Magistrate), Ku Feng (Scholar Yuen), Dick Wei (Yang's Master). 2.35:1. VHS: Steeplechase. VHS: Steeplechase (Dubbed). 102 minutes. Also known as **The Five Deadly Venoms** (US and Steelchase title).

One of the Shaw Brothers' most memorable martial arts films, this intricate period mystery-thriller has developed a substantial cult following in Western fan circles. Young martial arts student Yang Ti is instructed by his dying master to seek out the man's former students. Known respectively as "The Centipede," "The Snake," "The Scorpion," "The Lizard," and "The Toad," the men were top members of The Poison Clan, skilled in the techniques they were named after. However, each always wore a mask to keep their identities secret. The old teacher is worried that his pupils are using their talents for evil and wants Yang (who has learned a bit of each man's style) to locate them and investigate. Journeying to a small town, Yang meets several men whose martial talents suggest Poison Clan training, but he is unable to determine this for certain. Meanwhile, Yuen, an old friend of Yang's master, is accosted by The Centipede and The Snake, who are intent on obtaining some clan money the elderly scholar has hidden away. Unable to find what they came for, the men brutally kill Yuen and his family. With the assistance of Li Ho (who is actually The Toad), the authorities are able to arrest The Centipede, but he is released by a corrupt magistrate. Li is framed for the crime and tortured. Upright police officer Ho (who is actually The Lizard) teams up with Yang to set things right.

Those who dismiss kung fu films as being mindless and plotless have obviously not seen this one, which features a mystery as intricate and intriguing as what one finds in mainstream thrillers. Unlike many efforts of this sort, the story remains consistently interesting and is not simply padding between the fights. The various animal styles on display are wonderful, particularly during the surreal training sequences used to introduce each expert. Familiar Shaw villain Johnny Wang again plays a miscreant here but, interestingly enough, does not perform any martial arts at all! The character names listed above are from the dubbed version.

345. Flag of Iron

(1980; Shaw Brothers) ★: 6/10. Chinese titles unknown. Art Director: Johnson Tsao; Music: Not Original; Writers: Ngai Hong, Chang Cheh; Producer: Mona Fong Yat-wah; Action Directors: Phillip Kwok Tsui, Lu Feng, Chiang Sheng; Director: Chang Cheh. Cast: Phillip Kwok Tsui (Lo Hsien, aka Iron Panther), Chiang Sheng (Yuen Liang, aka Iron Monkey), Lu Feng (Chau Feng, aka Tiger), Wang Li, Lung Tien-sheng. 2.35:1. No official domestic video release. 114 minutes. Also known as **The Spearman of Death** (US title).

When Lo Hsien and Yuen Liang, members of the Iron Flag clan, discover that some of the rival Eagle clan men are running illegal operations, they close them down. The Eagles' master invites the Iron Flag clan to a celebration as a form of peace offering. Ever wary of treachery, Iron Flag clansman Chau Feng enlists the services of notorious assassin Yen Hsiu, better known as The Man in White. Sure enough, the party is a trap and Yen must act to save the unarmed Iron Flag members. While they easily triumph over the Eagles, Iron Flag's leader is attacked from behind by an unseen assailant utilizing an unknown weapon and dies from his injuries. In order to keep the authorities off their backs, Lo decides to take the blame for the deaths and leaves the area. New clan leader Chou pledges to send Lo money but he turns out to be even more corrupt than the Eagles' patriarch. He dismisses Yuen and enlists "The Ten Killers of the Underworld" (who have names like "The Fortune Teller," "The Killer Butcher," "The Book Keeper," and "The Dangerous Kid") to eliminate both men. Lo and Yuen decide to seek revenge against Chou, and The Man in White pledges to help them.

The kung fu setpieces in this simple but effective period offering are not as elaborate as those in some of Chang's films from this period, but the campier elements of the storyline help hold one's attention (The Book Keeper wields a deadly abacus!). At nearly two hours, however, the film is a bit too distended, given the basic plotting. The character names are from the dubbed version.

346. Flaming Brothers

(1987; Golden Harvest/In-Gear Film Production Co.) ★: 7/10. *Gong woo lung foo moon* (Cantonese), *Jiang hu long hu men* (Mandarin): "Underworld Dragon Tiger Gate." Cinematographer: Jingle Ma Cho-shing; Art Director: William Cheung Suk-ping; Music: Violet Lam Man-yee, Cheng Ching-chung, The Melody Bank, Bruton Music; Writer: Wong Kar-wai; Producer: Alan Tang Kwong-wing; Action Directors: Stephen Tung Wai, Benz Kong To-hoi, Tony Poon Kin-kwan; Director:

Joseph Cheung Tung-cho. Cast: Alan Tang Kwong-wing (Alan Chen Wai-lun), Chow Yun-fat (Chang Ho-tien), Pat Ha Man-chik (Ka-hsi), Patrick Tse Yin (Kao), Phillip Chan Yan-kin (Chen), Norman Tsui Siu-keung (Hsu), Ng Hong-ning (Hsu's Man). Dolby Digital (DVD only). 1.85:1. VHS: Tai Seng (No Subtitles). Import LD: Star Entertainment (No Subtitles). Import VCD/DVD: Universe. 99 minutes.

Wong Kar-wai wrote this gangster thriller, one of the better efforts to follow in the wake of **A Better Tomorrow**. Inseparable childhood buddies Ho-tien and Alan rise up from the streets to become top triad bosses. When Ho-tien is kidnapped by rival gangster Hsu, Alan kills the latter, raising the ire of the man's brother, Kao. After initially threatening vengeance, Kao relents and offers to involve Alan in a money-making proposition. Journeying to Thailand, Alan is almost shot (as per Kao's plan) but saves his would-be killer's life, winning his favor. Alan begins romancing singer Jenny while, back home, Tien has taken up with Ka-hsi, who used to bring him food when he and Alan were starving kids. The gentle, Christian woman convinces Ho-tien that he should leave the mob, a thought that infuriates Alan, who regards such an action as betrayal. To make matters worse, Kao backs out on his end of their deal, forcing Alan into a gang war he didn't want. To ensure his brother's safety, Alan tries to sever all ties with him, but Kao's goons use a trap to wipe out many of Alan's men, prompting Ho-tien to pick up his gun once more.

While the plot is routine, Wong does manage to humanize the characters somewhat. Chow (who does a hilarious impersonation of Anita Mui, lip-syncing to her smash single "Why Why, Tell Me Why?") and Tang (an excellent, charismatic actor who deserves to be better known in the West) give engaging performances, and the gunplay is sensational. That English title is an unfortunate choice, particularly as there are a number of instances where characters joke about the possibility of Alan and Ho-tien being gay! The film's memorable ending was later restaged in **A Taste of Killing and Romance**.

Flash Future Kung Fu *see* **Health Warning**

347. Flirting Scholar

(1993; Win's Movie Production) ★: 8/10. *Tong Pak-fu dim Chou-heung* (Cantonese), *Tang Bohu dian Qiuxiang* (Mandarin): "Tong Pak-fu Chooses Chou-heung" or "Tang Bohu Chooses Qiuxiang." Cinematographer: David Chung Chi-man; Art Director: Jason Mok Siu-kei; Music: William Woo Wai-lap; Writers: Vincent Kok Tak-chiu, Lee Lik-chi; Producer: Stephen Siu Yeuk-yuen; Director: Lee Lik-chi. Cast: Stephen Chiau Sing-chi (Tong Pak-fu/Tong Tin-ho), Gong Li (Chou-heung), Nat Chan Pak-cheung (Chuck Chi-shan), Cheng Pei-pei (Madam Wah), James Wong Jim (Mr. Wah), Leung Kar-yan (Mo Chong-yuen), Gordon Lau Kar-fai (The Evil Scholar), Lam Wai (King Ning), Gabriel Wong Yat-san (Wah-man), Vincent Kok Tak-chiu (Tu Chuen-chang), Yuen King-tan (Shek-lau), Mimi Chu Mi-mi (Chussy), Peter Lai Bei-tak (The Teacher), Yammie Nam Kit-ying (Tong's Wife), Francis Ng Chun-yu (Member of "The Four Scholars"). 1.85:1. VHS: World Video. Import LD/VCD/ DVD: Mei Ah. 102 minutes.

In this highly amusing period comedy, Stephen Chiau is Tong Pak-fu, a celebrated painter and poet whose eight wives would rather gamble from dusk to dawn than pay him any attention. His wandering eye soon fixes upon Chou-heung (played by Mainland superstar Gong Li, who is dubbed by another actress in the Cantonese version), the beautiful head maid of Madam Wah. In order to woo his target and circumvent the long-standing hatred that exists between the Tong and Wah families, he sells himself to the latter household as a slave. Tong's verbal and martial skills come in handy when his mistress' palace is invaded by The Evil Scholar, a martial arts master responsible for the death of Tong's father, Tin-ho (played by Chiau in an amusing flashback).

While the humor in a pivotal sequence (where Tong uses his masterful vocabulary to defeat a pompous opponent) is all but lost in the awkwardly translated subtitles, most of the comedic and action setpieces manage to hit home, making this one of Chiau's best efforts to date. Among the highlights: Tong's impromptu use of his weaselly brother (played by Chiau's perennial comic foil, Nat Chan) as a human paintbrush; Madam Wah and The Evil Scholar's bout of "clandestine kung fu" (a sly *homage* to Lau's famous duel with Johnny Wang in **Dirty Ho**); Tong's rapid fire cure when Chou-heung is turned hideously ugly by The Evil Scholar's "Faceless Kick"; and a bravura finale in which the scholar must select his bride-to-be from a mob of gown-clad maidens—without touching or speaking to them. Gong Li more than holds her own in the midst of Chiau's comic maelstrom, coming across as an affable and fetching straightwoman.

348. Flying Dagger

(1993; Chang Hong Channel Film and Video Company) ★: 7/10. *San ging do yue fei tin maau* (Cantonese), *Shen jing dao yu fei tian mao* (Mandarin): "Crazy Dagger and Flying Sky Cat." Cinematographer: Chen Rong-shu; Art Director: Andy Lee Yiu-kwong; Music: Not Original; Writer: Wong Jing; Producer: Mark Wu Dan; Action Director: Ching Siu-tung; Director: Chu Yen-ping. Cast: Tony Leung Kar-fai (Big Dagger), Sharla Cheung Man (Big Bewitchment), Jacky Cheung Hok-yau (Nine Tails Fox), Maggie Cheung Man-yuk (Flying Cat), Jimmy Lin Chi-ying (Little Dagger), Gloria Yip Wan-yee (Little Bewitchment), Ng Man-tat (Leslie Cheung), Yuen King-tan ("Fifth Lady"), Yuen Cheung-yan ("Never Die"), Pauline Chan Po-lin (Evil Lady of Yi-ho). 1.85:1. VHS: Tai Seng, SYS/Youngtze (Dubbed). LD: Tai Seng. Import LD: Golden Cinema City. 85 minutes.

Although **A Home Too Far** (1991) and **End of the Road** (1993) proved him capable of crafting competent dramatic fare, Taiwanese director Chu Yen-ping seems more interested in solidifying his position as one of Asia's most eccentric filmmakers. While this period fantasy-comedy doesn't quite attain the absurd heights previously scaled by Chu's feminist "Eastern Westerns" **Golden Queens Commando** and **Pink Force Commando** (both 1984), it is the director's most entertaining film to date, offering his trademark mix of frenzied action, off-kilter plotting, and broad, scatological comedy. Bounty hunters Big and Little Flying Dagger and their female counterparts, Big and Little Bewitchment, manage to put their professional rivalry aside long enough to pursue the notoriously prehensile criminal, Nine Tails Fox, and his screeching feline of a wife, Flying Cat. The quartet capture their quarry but must eventually side with them when they are challenged by a bizarre array of Chinese and Japanese villains.

Flying Dagger takes the low road all the way, yet jokes about lust-inducing incense and coma-inducing flatulence become strangely endearing when delivered by such a paramount cast. Martial arts director Ching Siu-tung provides the kind of high-flying action setpieces that habitual viewers of Chinese fantasy have come to expect from him, but just as technically impressive is a lascivious severed hand (inspired by "Thing" from **The Addams Family**) that becomes a surprise ally. Good fun. The rousing score consists almost entirely of stock cues, as well as tracks swiped from **A Fish Called Wanda** and Jay Chattaway's soundtrack for **Maniac**.

349. Fong Sai Yuk

(1993; Eastern Productions) ★: 7/10. *Fong Sai-yuk* (Cantonese), *Fang Shiyu*

(Mandarin): "Fong Sai-yuk" (hero's name in Cantonese) or "Fang Shiyu" (hero's name in Mandarin). Cinematographer: Jingle Ma Cho-shing; Art Director: Ben Lau Man-hung; Music: James Wong Jim, Romeo Diaz, Mark Lui Chung-tak; Writers: Kei On (pseudonym for Jeff Lau Chun-wai), John Chan Kin-chung, Choi Hong-wing; Producer: Jet Li Lianjie; Action Directors: Corey Yuen Kwai, Yuen Tak; Director: Corey Yuen Kwai. Cast: Jet Li Lianjie (Fong Sai-yuk), Josephine Siao Fong-fong (Miu Tsui-fa, Sai-yuk's Mother), Michelle Lee Kar-yan (Lui Ting-ting), Sibelle Hu Hui-chung (Lee Siu-wan), Chen Sung-yung (Tiger Lui), Paul Chu Kong (Fong's Father), Zhao Wenzhou (Governor Oryeetor), Peter Chan Lung (Macu), Adam Cheng Siu-chau (Chan Ka-lok). 1.85:1. VHS: Tai Seng. Import LD/VCD/DVD: Universe. 105 minutes. Also known as **The Legend of Fong Sai Yuk** (Title for dubbed version).

Fong Sai Yuk is a broad but largely enjoyable period martial arts entry highlighted by Jet Li's incredible athletics and the comedic skills of popular veteran actress Josephine Siao. Young, exuberant kung fu expert Fong Sai-yuk is always getting into trouble, and invariably must be bailed out by his equally mischievous (not to mention equally lithe) mother. Sai-yuk falls head over heels for the beautiful maiden Lui Ting-ting and jumps at the chance to win her hand in marriage by participating in a martial arts duel against her mother. After a spectacular fight (which carries over into and *on top of* the spectators), Sai-yuk intentionally loses upon discovering that Ting-ting has been replaced as the prize by her homely maid. Determined to defend the family honor, Sai-yuk's mom enters the fray (under the name Fong *Tai*-yuk) and *wins*, resulting in all manner of misunderstandings and romantic chaos. Meanwhile, the ruthless Manchu governor Oryeetor has arrived in Canton as part of his ongoing effort to destroy the rebellious Red Flower Society. His actions are a direct threat to the Fong family, as Sai-yuk's father is one of that Han group's leaders and possesses a rebel name list that Oryeetor wants at any cost.

Hemmed in by the stoic characters he generally plays, Jet Li is allowed to give his all as Sai-yuk and is spirited and charming throughout. The spectacular, gravity-defying kung fu setpieces rely heavily on wire-enhanced feats but are so energetic and fun to watch that only the most ardent martial arts purists will object to the trickery. Less inspired are the aggressively unsubtle, cartoonish physical gags, which are clearly the work of co-writer Jeff Lau. Still, there are some laughs to be had along the way, thanks almost entirely to Josephine Siao's comic timing, and the exciting martial arts battles more than make up for the script's shortcomings. Director Ann Hui On-wah is credited here with "Production Design" but, reportedly, played a much bigger role behind the scenes. The soundtrack includes music recycled from **The Moon Warriors**. Trivia note: Zhao Wenzhou would go on to replace Li as Wong Fei-hung in parts four and five of the **Once Upon a Time in China** series. *Fong Sai Yuk* was followed by a sequel.

350. Fong Sai Yuk II

(1993; Eastern Productions) ★: 6/10. *Fong Sai-yuk juk jaap* (Cantonese), *Fang Shiyu xu ji* (Mandarin): "Fong Sai-yuk Sequel" or "Fang Shiyu Sequel." Cinematographer: Mark Lee Ping-bing; Art Director: James Leung Wah-sang; Music: Lowell Lo Kwun-ting; Writers: Kei On (pseudonym for Jeff Lau Chun-wai), John Chan Kin-chung; Producer: Jet Li Lianjie; Action Directors: Corey Yuen Kwai, Yuen Tak; Director: Corey Yuen Kwai. Cast: Jet Li Lianjie (Fong Sai-yuk), Josephine Siao Fong-fong (Miao Cui-hua, Sai-yuk's Mother), Michelle Lee Kar-yan (Ting-ting), Adam Cheng Siu-chau (Chen Jia-luo), Amy Kwok Oi-ming (Princess Angie, aka Spring Flower), Chi Chuen-hua (Yu), Corey Yuen Kwai (Li Guo-bang), Peter Chan Lung (Magu). 1.85:1. VHS: Tai Seng. Import LD/VCD/DVD: Universe. 96 minutes. Also known as **The Legend of Fong Sai Yuk II** (Title for dubbed version).

Produced in haste (it arrived in theaters only five months after the original), **Fong Sai Yuk II** is ill-conceived but still manages to entertain by virtue of its lightning fast martial arts. Now a member of The Red Flower Society, Sai-yuk earns the wrath of his leader, Master Chen, when he faces off against Yu, a senior member. In spite of this, Sai-yuk is sent on an important mission to steal a box (containing a scroll revealing that Chen is actually a Manchu by birth) from some Japanese samurai. While he fails at this task, he does (once again) make the acquaintance of Princess Angie, who had earlier taunted him while in the guise of a man. Sai-yuk is ordered to court Angie (who now possesses the box), allowing him ample opportunity to steal it from her, but is also now obliged to enter a martial arts competition to win the girl's hand. He is victorious but his actions earn him the wrath of Ting-ting, who has understandable trouble with the idea that her fiancé is planning to marry another woman for the sake of China. Greater trouble looms, though, as Yu proceeds with his scheme to assume control of The Red Flower Society and tries to lure Sai-yuk into a trap by kidnapping the youth's mother.

While the original had a few effectively humorous moments, the comedy here falls almost completely flat, the storyline is perfunctory, and the villain entirely forgettable. Also, the action is not as well choreographed, with stunt doubles more obvious this time out. Regardless, the kung fu remains exhilarating and the climactic fight is mind-boggling in both design and execution: Sai-yuk must battle Yu atop a stack of benches while avoiding causing the death of his mother—who is suspended on the top with a noose around her neck!

351. Forbidden Arsenal

(1991; D & B Films Co.) ★: 6/10. *Dei ha bing gung chong* (Cantonese), *Di xia bing gong chang* (Mandarin): "Underground Munitions Factory." Cinematographer: Ko Chiu-lam; Art Director: Oliver Wong Yui-man; Music: Jonathan Wong Bong-yin; Writer: Leung Hung-wah; Producer: Stephen Shin Kei-yin; Action Directors: Phillip Kwok Tsui, Wong Kwan; Directors: Yuen Chun-man, Cheng Siu-keung. Cast: Cynthia Yang Li-ching (Madam Yeung), Waise Lee Chi-hung (Chen Ao-quan), To Siu-chun (Hua Zhi-yong), Gary Chow King-yeung (Ben), Loletta Lee Lai-chun (Edna), Robin Shou Wan-bo (Paul), Phillip Kwok Tsui (Tam). 1.85:1. VHS: Tai Seng. Import LD/VCD: Universe. 92 minutes.

"The Three Chinas" join forces to battle weapons smugglers in this customarily action-packed D & B Films outing. HK policewoman Madam Yeung, Taiwanese undercover cop Chen Ao-quan, and Mainland officer Hua Zhi-yong pool their talents and resources to take out the gang running a weapons production factory in China. The criminals are smuggling the firearms into HK and then distributing them to crime syndicates in Taiwan and other parts of the globe. While working on the case, Chen starts romancing the decidedly uninterested Yeung, while Hua takes up with university student Edna. This a mistake, however, as Edna's brother is nothing less than the leader of the gang they seek.

Some markets reportedly passed this off as yet another entry in the **In the Line of Duty** series, which is not inappropriate, as it adheres closely to that series' formula. The storyline here is flimsy even by those standards, but the fights and stuntwork are terrific and the characters are amiable. The in-fighting between the different law enforcers is played for laughs (with the expected number of "Mainland Hick" jokes), unlike later, more serious looks at inter-country cooperation like **Asian Connection** and **Rock 'n' Roll Cop**. In **The Big Heat**, Phillip Kwok plays a cop who shoots a hostage in the leg so that he will drop to the ground, giving partner Waise Lee a clear shot at the perpetrator. That bit (later copied in the Hollywood movie **Speed**) is restaged here, with a slight variation.

352. Forbidden City Cop

(1996; Win's Entertainment/Samico Films Production) ★: 8/10. *Daai laap mat taam 008* (Cantonese), *Da nei mi tan 008* (Mandarin): "Big Inside Cop Ling Ling-fat." Cinematographer: Kin Lee Kin-keung; Art Director: Cyrus Ho Kim-hung; Music: Lau Yee-tat; Writers: Stephen Chiau Sing-chi, Vincent Kok Tak-chiu, Lo Man-sang; Producer: Wong Jing; Action Director: Tony Poon Kin-kwan; Directors: Stephen Chiau Sing-chi, Vincent Kok Tak-chiu. Cast: Stephen Chiau Sing-chi (Ling Ling-fat), Carina Lau Kar-ling (Kar-ling), Carman Lee Yeuk-tung (Gum Tso), Law Kar-ying (Fat-yan), Cheung Tat-ming (The Emperor), Yuen Cheung-yan (No Face's Wife), Yuen Shun-yee (Two Face), Lau Yee-tat ("The Ghost"), Wong Yat-fei (Yip Koo-shing), Manfred Wong (Luk Siu-fung), Yuen King-tan (Madam), Alvina Kong Yan-yin (Dizzy Patient), Vincent Kok Tak-chiu (Doctor). 1.85:1. VHS: World Video (Poor Subtitles). LD: World Video (Subtitles?). Import LD/VCD/DVD: Mei Ah. 89 minutes.

A follow-up of sorts to Stephen Chiau's popular James Bond send-up **From Beijing with Love**, this terrific period fantasy-comedy is one of the star's best vehicles to date. Ling Ling-fat is easily the most incompetent member of The Forbidden City Cops, an elite guard unit assigned to protect the emperor and his possessions. Ling-fat works as a gynaecologist in his civilian life, while also cooking up all manner of wacky, Rube Goldberg-type contraptions. When a bizarre creature, dubbed "The Flying Fairy," drops from the heavens in Gum Kingdom, all of China's doctors are ordered to go and dissect its body. However, it is all a ruse set up by the villainous (and literally faceless) "King of No Face" and his demonic family, who want to slaughter all of his enemies' physicians, thus facilitating their planned invasion. Ling-fat manages to save the day and gets a much higher degree of respect in the kingdom but Gum Tso, a gorgeous new prostitute from the enemy kingdom threatens to destroy Ling-fat's blissfully happy marriage.

One of Chiau's most stylish and compact films, **Forbidden City Cop** also finds the comedian giving his most consistently likeable performance to date. While Ling-fat possesses some of the smart-aleck traits Chiau is known for, he is also a loyal and loving husband. The scenes the comedian shares with Carina Lau (delightful as Chiau's eternally devoted wife) are wonderful and seem largely off-the-cuff. The screenplay is also a step up, allowing for numerous genre send-ups as well as a reasonably inventive plot twist involving Carman Lee's mysterious *femme fatale*. Actor/composer Lau Yee-tat gives a hilariously deadpan turn as a zombie-like transvestite, Law Kar-ying is amusingly daft as Ling-fat's put-upon sidekick, and the climax features a great visual reference to one of the most famous moments in **Raiders of the Lost Ark**. As two of the villains, the Yuen brothers have a chance to poke fun at their earlier work in **Dreadnaught** and **The Miracle Fighters**, both of which were directed by their brother, Yuen Woo-ping. Equally recommended to seasoned Chiau fans, those looking for a film to try him out, and those looking to give him another chance.

Force of the Dragon *see* **In the Line of Duty III**

353. The Fortune Code

(1990) ★: 5/10. *Foo gwai bing tuen* (Cantonese), *Fu gui bing tuan* (Mandarin): "Wealthy Military Unit." Cinematographer: Derek Wan Man kit; Art Director: Jessy Lam Chak-chi; Music: Richard Lo Sai-kit; Writers: Barry Wong Ping-yiu, Wong Jing; Action Directors: Austin Wai Tin-chi, Power Lee King-chu, Billy Chan Wui-ngai, Yuen Bun; Producers: Kent Cheng Chuk-see, Wallace Cheung Kwok-chung; Director: Kent Cheng Chuk-see. Cast: Andy Lau Tak-wah (Wah), Alan Tam Wing-lun (Robin), Anita Mui Yim-fong (Jone), Billy Lau Nam-kwong (Donald Duck), Eric Tsang Chi-wai (Runaway), Nat Chan Pak-cheung (Dragon), Miu Kiu-wai (Little Robot), Max Mok Siu-chung (Little Candy), Ben Lam Kwok-bun (Little Dragon Fly), Sammo Hung Kam-po (Brother Hung), Kent Cheng Chuk-see (Chocolate), Wilson Lam Chun-yin (Red Horse), Shing Fui-on (Ugly POW), Austin Wai Tin-chi (Little Tortoise), Lung Fong (Japanese General), Joan Tong Lai-kau (Nurse), Charine Chan Kar-ling (Nurse), Parkman Wong Pak-man (Japanese Soldier), Blackie Ko Shou-liang (Hideki), Ken Lo Wai-kwong (Japanese Soldier), Chung Fat (Japanese Soldier), Charlie Cho Cha-lei (Peter), Che-Kirk Wong Chi-keung (Paul), Chen Kuan-tai (Triad Boss Gambler), Frankie Chan Fan-kei (Commander in White), Gordon Lau Kar-fai (Commander in Blue), Tsang Kwong-chin (Camp Doctor), Ridley Tsui Bo-wah (Japanese Soldier). 1.85:1. VHS: Tai Seng. Import LD: Mei Ah. 85 minutes.

This is one of those lunar New Year movies where the producers figured (correctly) that all they needed was an all-star cast, some action, and an offbeat setting to pull in the crowds. Consequently, unless you're a diehard action fan or an inveterate star watcher, there is not much here that will hold your attention. The film takes place in 1942 at Japanese prisoner-of-war Camp 732, which houses dozens of Chinese POWs. Thanks to a diversion, the dashing Wah is able to escape, but not long after getting out, he is ordered right back *in*. The mission: find "The God of Fortune," the only person who knows the code to a Swiss Bank account containing $500 billion the Chinese government needs for the war effort. When Wah finally locates his target, the man is dead, but he has left a clue, allowing Wah to determine that the Japanese commander's parrot now knows the code. However, time is running out for the prisoners: They will be executed after putting on a variety show for some visiting dignitaries.

As you might expect from the above line-up, most of the budget seems to have been spent on the cast and not the settings (which are awfully chintzy-looking at times), and the jokes are disappointingly routine for a Barry Wong/Wong Jing collaboration. Eric Tsang gets all the best lines as a pint-sized and decidedly unenthusiastic pilot who is more than ready to sell out his stiff companions in exchange for some action with a pretty *geisha*. Incidentally, Camp *731* is the real-life hellhole where the Japanese conducted medical experiments on their Chinese captives.

354. Fox Hunter

(1995; Kingsway Production) ★: 7/10. *Choh tai jui gik jo hap* (Cantonese), *Cuo ti zhui ji zu he* (Mandarin): "Wrong Body Pursues Fleeing Enemy Team." Cinematographer: William Yim Wai-lun; Art Director: Raymond Lam Chi-wai; Music: Mak Chun-hung, Ha Kwun-leung; Writer: New Images Group; Producers: Benz Kong To-hoi, Joseph Cheung Tung-cho; Action Directors: Stephen Tung Wai, Benz Kong To-hoi, Tony Poon Kin-kwan; Director: Stephen Tung Wai. Cast: Jade Leung Ching (Jenny Yeung), Jordan Chan Siu-chun (Chan Hong), Yu Rongguang (Yu), Yim Kwong-ming, Guy Lai Ying-chau. 1.85:1. VHS: World Video. Import LD/VCD: Universe. 96 minutes.

The storyline (credited to several writers calling themselves New Images Group) is generic, but this modestly budgeted thriller delivers exciting action setpieces throughout and is well worth one's time. With the help of cowardly pimp Chan Hong, policewoman Jenny Yeung poses as a prostitute in order to nab vicious criminal Yam Tung. The ruse works and the target is captured, but he later manages to escape. Gaining entrance to Jenny's apartment, Yam forces her to kill her uncle and then sexually assaults the woman before fleeing to China. Jenny and Chan then illegally enter the Mainland (the latter coming along under threat of death) in order to exact revenge. When Chan tries to escape, the pair are arrested but break custody and lure the killer to a motel. From this point on, the film turns into one long (rarely interrupted) battle, with Yam and his cronies pursuing Jenny and Chan throughout the countryside, while the pair try to elude both him and the local authorities. The climax plays out in a crowded shopping mall that the villains have wired with high explosives.

Veteran action coordinator Stephen Tung keeps things perking along with a steady stream of well-choreographed mayhem, and the end result is Jade Leung's best vehicle to date. Jordan Chan delivers enough comic relief to perfectly offset Leung's stern determination, and the Mainland setting adds some novelty to the mix. If the plot had something more to offer, **Fox Hunter** could have become a high water mark in the genre rather than the rousing timewaster it is.

355. Fox Legend

(1991; J & J) ★: 5/10. *Leng woo* (Cantonese), *Ling hu* (Mandarin): "Spirit Fox." Cinematographers: Kwok Mok-sing, Ng Kwok-yan; Music: James Wong Jim; Writer: Chan Kam-cheung; Producer: Wong Tai-wai; Action Director: Siu Tak-fu; Director: Wu Ma. Cast: Joey Wang Tsu-hsien (Snow Lady), Wu Ma (Hunt King), Kelly Yiu Wai (Snow's Mother), Lee Wai-keung, Ling Fung. 1.85:1. VHS: Tai Seng (No Subtitles). Import LD: Star Entertainment (No Subtitles). 91 minutes. Also known as **Foxy Spirits** (Tai Seng tape and Star LD title).

Yet another imitation of **A Chinese Ghost Story**, this low-budget fantasy casts Joey Wang and Wu Ma in virtually the same roles they essayed in the Ching Siu-tung classic. Instead of sexy ghosts leading unsuspecting men to their doom, we have sexy wolf demons: normal looking women who sprout bushy tails when they are about to attack. The Wei family, who have been animal skin traders for six generations, are facing destruction at the hands (paws?) of a powerful wolf demon who seeks the family's magic emblem (which, when stamped on the skinned pelt of a wolf, prevents it from returning as a ghost). The being commands her beautiful daughter, Snow Lady, to bring back the heart of Brother Ten, the Wei family's young master, but she is too kind and compassionate to follow through on her orders, falling in love with the man instead. When Brother Ten is possessed by a wolf spirit and his family's demise seems inevitable, the powerful, enigmatic Hunt King takes it upon himself to vanquish the evil creatures.

The subtitles refer to the creatures as wolves, though they display all of the characteristics of the fox demons found in Chinese literature, right on down to the ability to subdue enemies with potent blasts of rectal gas! Under the direction of Wu Ma, the film moves well and has no shortage of action and dynamic framing. However, in spite of all that unfolds, it is also never more than passably interesting, being too derivative and predictable to really score. The cheap and cheesy special FX don't help matters either. James Wong is credited with the music, but a large percentage of it has simply been swiped from **A Nightmare On Elm Street**. The Taiwan tape version has English subtitles. For a more effective tale about a fox demon, see **A Chinese Legend**.

Foxy Spirits *see* **Fox Legend**

356. Fractured Follies

(1988; Cinema City Co.) ★: 6/10. *Cheung duen geuk ji luen* (Cantonese), *Chang duan jiao zhi lian* (Mandarin): "Love of the Short Legs vs. Love of the Long Legs." Cinematographer: James Chan Sau-ming; Art Director: Louise Kwong Hoi-ming; Music: Antonio Arevalo Jr.; Producer: Dean Shek Tien; Director: Wong Chung. Cast: Chow Yun-fat (Joe Leung), Joey Wang Tsu-hsien (May Yau), James Wong Jim (Yau Kwong-nam), Nina Li Chi (Scarlet), Wong Ching (Sea Leung), Bonnie Law Ming-chu (Cher), Wong Yat-fei (Rival Shop Owner). 1.85:1. VHS: Tai Seng. Import LD: Golden Cinema City. Import VCD: Mei Ah. Import DVD: Universe. 95 minutes.

When Joe Leung runs into May Yau with his cab, it definitely isn't love at first sight, but you just know that will change soon enough in this minor but entertaining comedy. Since he has no insurance and accidentally causes all of the Yau family supermarket staff to quit, Joe tries to make up for the misfortune he has caused by helping out at the market. All of the Yau's money is later stolen, prompting Joe to sell his taxi and invest the capital in the business. May's vehemently vicious feelings towards Joe eventually soften, but the store faces potential ruin, thanks to some new competition across the street.

Although it is burdened by a few too many subplots, **Fractured Follies** (the English title refers both to the injury sustained by May in the accident and some impromptu song-and-dance numbers, while the Chinese title is a reference to the fact that one of May's legs is an inch shorter than the other) is engagingly silly, thanks in no small part to Chow Yun-fat's cartoonishly goofy performance and Nina Li's amusing turn as the Yau's rich but decidedly crazy in-law.

357. Framed

(1989) ★: 5/10. *Cham dai ngok* (Cantonese), *Chen di e* (Mandarin): "Bottom Feeding Crocodile." Cinematographer: Lau Hung-chuen; Music: Tang Siu-lam, Hau Chi-keung; Producer: Cheung Suk-sang; Action Director: Mang Hoi; Director: Alex Cheung Kwok-ming. Cast: Alex Man Chi-leung (Lui Tai-yung, aka Rambo), Simon Yam Tat-wah (Cheung Kai-wah), Ray Lui Leung-wai (Yip), Shum Wai (Shum), Yukari Oshima (Kitty Li), Wong Yue (Ching), Yung Sai-kit (Kit). 1.85:1. Import LD/VCD: Ocean Shores. 90 minutes.

This shopworn action drama opens with former police officer Cheung Kai-wah being released from jail. He is free after serving a ten year sentence for drug possession, a crime for which he was framed by some fellow officers. Cheung begins eliminating those responsible, making one of the killings look like the work of renegade cop Lui Tai-yung. Arrested and beaten during his subsequent interrogation, Lui (who was the cop that arrested Cheung a decade earlier) manages to escape and locates Kitty Li, the woman who witnessed the killing and placed him at the scene. He manages to plant a seed of doubt in her mind, but Lui's superior and several of his co-workers want to see him dead in order to save their own skins. With only his partner and Kitty to back him up, Lui must hunt down Cheung before the police get to him. There is some decent action along the way but nothing that one cannot easily find in a hundred other films of this ilk.

358. From Beijing with Love

(1994; Win's Movie Production) ★: 6/10. *Gwok chaan Ling Ling-chat* (Cantonese), *Guo chan Ling Lingqi* (Mandarin): "Country-Made 007." Cinematographer:

Kin Lee Kin-keung; Art Director: Jason Mok Siu-kei; Music: William Woo Wai-lap; Writers: Stephen Chiau Sing-chi, Roman Cheung Siu-lun, Vincent Kok Tak-chiu, Lee Lik-chi; Producers: Charles Heung Wah-keung, Jimmy Heung Wah-sing; Action Director: Tony Poon Kin-kwan; Directors: Stephen Chiau Sing-chi, Lee Lik-chi. Cast: Stephen Chiau Sing-chi (Ling Ling-chat), Anita Yuen Wing-yee (Siu-kam), Pauline Chan Po-lin (Mystery Woman), Law Kar-ying (Da Mansi), Wong Kam-kong (The Commander/The Man with the Golden Gun), Yu Rong-guang (Mainland Soldier), Cheng Cho (Mystery Woman's Partner). 1.85:1. VHS: Tai Seng. Import LD: Cameron Entertainment, Mei Ah Gold. Import VCD: Mei Ah. 83 minutes.

Disappointed by the choice of Pierce Brosnan as the new 007? Well, how about Stephen Chiau? HK's reigning king of slap*shtick* stars bumbling Mainland pork vendor/superspy Ling Ling-chat (whose name sounds like "007" but literally means "Frozen Frozen Rain") in this violent, chaotic Bond send-up. When the skull of China's only dinosaur fossil is purloined by a renegade calling himself "The Man with the Golden Gun," Ling is dispatched to HK in pursuit, oblivious to the fact that his contact there, an assassin named Siu-kam, has been ordered to liquidate him. Soon realizing that Ling's unbounded luck and unmatched stupidity make him invincible, Siu-kam switches sides, with ensuing events leading the pair back to China for a final clash with Ling's superior who is, in actuality, the armor-clad menace they seek.

Though it makes no attempt to poke fun at the large-scale stunts and chase sequences for which the Bond cycle is noted, a number of other ingredients receive a good skewering. There is the requisite lampoon of the series' fashionable title sequences, and Ling preps for the mission by watching bootleg Bond videos (a clip from **Moonraker** is shown). Comedian Law Kar-ying plays China's answer to "Q," cooking up hopeless inventions like the world's first solar-powered flashlight(!). William Woo's score includes a variation on the Bond theme, while also riffling on Ennio Morricone's score for **The Untouchables** (which works quite well in this context). As for *femmes fatales*, former softcore star Pauline Chan receives prominent billing (but little screen time) as a rival agent with flame-throwers built into her breastplate who is partnered with a "Jaws" lookalike. Anita Yuen is amusingly stoic in a very atypical role, and there is even a brief send-up of her 1993 smash hit **C'est La Vie, Mon Cheri**. In a rather daring move (considering that the 1997 reunification was just around the corner), the Mainland characters here are all dense, corrupt, or just plain psychotic. Although there are a number of universally appreciable moments, the proceedings get awfully bloody for a parody, and the film lacks the visual stimulation of Chiau's period fantasy spoofs from earlier in the decade. Nonetheless, the substantial success of **From Beijing with Love** prompted Chiau to continue poking fun at Western fare in **The Sixty Million Dollar Man** (1995). **Forbidden City Cop** is a follow-up of sorts.

359. From the Same Family

(1995) ★: 3/10. *Jim dung seung fu* (Cantonese), *Jian dong shuang hui* (Mandarin): "Twin Tigers of East Tsimshatsui." Cinematographer: Kong Ting-wing; Art Director: Wong Ching-ching; Music: Barry Cheung Fu-ling, Sam Leung Yiu-san, Oman Mui Siu-kei; Producer: Maybo Chiu Mei-bo; Action Director: Chu Kai-sang; Writer-Director: Johnny Lee King-kai. Cast: Roy Cheung Yiu-yeung (Ling Chun), Hilary Tsui Ho-ying (May), Frankie Lam Man-lung (Li Ying-wai), Michael Tse Tin-wah (Taky). 1.85:1. VHS: World Video. Import LD/VCD: Ocean Shores. 96 minutes.

This feeble triad thriller charts the rise and fall of "Tiger" Ling Chun, top mobster in Tsimshatsui's entertainment circle. Although Ling and his buddy Li Ying-wai are in separate gangs, the pair negotiate a truce between the various bosses, thus forging an alliance. As the pair rise to the top of the underworld, their power and wealth grows, prompting Ling to consider going into legitimate business. However, when one of his cocaine-addicted underlings becomes paranoid and power crazed, it is the beginning of the end for Ling's empire.

No one plays triads better than Roy Cheung, but he cannot breathe any life into the flaccid dramatic situations that make up this lethargic, formula-bound effort (though it is interesting to see him playing a mature and level-headed boss, as opposed to his usual mad wolf lieutenants). Even the street fights are badly staged, and that is the one element that even the weakest films of this type usually present with a degree of competence.

360. From Zero to Hero

(1994; Sunshine Film Production House/Top Ten Development) ★: 4/10. *Luen sai chiu yan* (Cantonese), *Luan shi chao ren* (Mandarin): "Superman in the Messy World." Cinematographer: Ardy Lam Kwok-wah; Art Director: Angelo Bernardo Castilho; Producer: Leung Ching; Action Director: Phillip Kwok Tsui; Music-Writer-Director: David Wu Tai-wai. Cast: Francis Ng Chun-yu (Joe), Anita Lee Yuen-wah (Bella Chung), Cheng Pei-pei (Joe's Mom), Dayo Wong Chi-wah (Liu), Emily Kwan Bo-wai (Miss Wai). 1.85:1. VHS: Tai Seng. Import LD: Universe. 96 minutes.

This superhero parody starts off beautifully but runs out of ideas by the halfway point. Nerdy comic book artist Francis Ng (who still lives with his domineering mom) is the creator of the extremely popular "Superman in the Messy World" comic strip, which is the subject of protests by civic groups because of its extreme sex and violence. Leading the protesters is none other than his mother (well-played by kung fu great Cheng Pei-pei), a school principal who isn't aware of what he is working on. Constantly hounded by his greedy editor (who is always demanding that he draw bigger breasts on the female characters), he fantasizes about being his own Japanese-speaking superhero creation. After getting fired, he stitches together his own black Superman outfit and battles injustice wherever he encounters it. The only problem is that, like his character, he takes advantage of whomever he saves.

The opening reel features a terrific depiction of an archetypal *manga* action sequence, complete with everyone speaking Japanese. However, the film gradually degenerates into a dull love story as Ng falls for Anita Lee's struggling TV reporter, who then betrays his trust by revealing his identity on the air. The climax, which finds the crestfallen Ng having to regain his confidence in order to save a school assembly from some gangsters, is thoroughly uninspired and blandly staged. Writer-director David Wu should not be confused with the Taiwanese star of **Full Throttle**. The soundtrack includes some music recycled from Wu's **The Bride with White Hair 2**, and the opening title montage includes footage lifted from Ron Mann's documentary **Comic Book Confidential**.

361. Front Page

(1990; Topping Time Films) ★: 5/10. *San boon gan baat ah* (Cantonese), *Xin ban jin ba ya* (Mandarin): "New Half Pound Eight Ounces." Cinematographer: Ardy Lam Kwok-wah; Art Director: David Chan Chi-wai; Music: Chow Kai-sang; Writers: Michael Hui Koon-man, Phillip Chan Yan-kin; Producer: Michael Hui Koon-man; Director: Phillip Chan Yan-kin. Cast: Sam Hui Koon-kit ("Mad" Bill Lee), Michael Hui Koon-man (Hui), Ricky Hui Koon-ying (Fly), Catherine

Hung Yan (Cheung San-san), Yip Wing-cho (Kent), Winnie Lau Siu-wai (Pinky), Law Koon-lan (May), Paul Chun Pui (Dr. Pong), Lau Siu-ming (Leader of the Robbers), Yuen Shun-yee (Martial Arts Instructor), Tai Po (Angry Stuntman), Teresa Mo Shun-kwan (Miss Ho), Lee Hoi-sang (Fake Ghost). VHS: World Video. Import LD/VCD: Mei Ah. 92 minutes.

All three of the Hui Brothers star in this lackluster outing, a slightly modified remake of their '70s blockbuster **The Private Eyes** (1976). While it can't hold a candle to that film, **Front Page** remains fairly pleasing if one's expectations are held in check. In this send-up of HK tabloid publishing, Michael plays the editor of Truth Weekly, a floundering rag which lacks the sex and sizzle scandal fanatics crave. Facing financial ruin, he hires Sam, a former martial arts instructor, to help him concoct various schemes to raise circulation. When their harebrained ideas all fail, the boys decide to sully the reputation of a beautiful and saintly young actress (Catherine Hung) by taking photos which suggest she is having a secret affair with Sam. Suffering an uncharacteristic fit of conscience, Sam steals the pictures and negatives on the eve of publication and tries to return them to her at a lavish engagement party. However, he, Michael, and Ricky end up in the soup when a gang of robbers also decide to crash the festivities.

Short on fresh ideas, the screenplay places the comedians in a number of routine predicaments, some of which drag on long after every possible laugh has been milked from them. Still, there are enough genuinely amusing moments here (like when the three are forced at gunpoint to sing a karaoke version of the Anita Mui hit "Why, Why, Tell Me Why?") to make this a passable diversion.

362. The Fruit Is Swelling

(1997; Cameron Entertainment Co.) ★: 6/10. *Mat to sing suk si 1997* (Cantonese), *Mi tao cheng shu shi 1997* (Mandarin): "When the Sweet Peach Ripens 1997." Cinematographer: Lai Yiu-fai; Art Director: Nelson Cheung Hok-yun; Music: Lincoln Lo Kin; Producer-Director: Chin Man-kei. Cast: Jane Chung Chun (Peach Chui), Christine Hung Hiu-wan (Lychee), Stephanie Fong Suen (Baby), Elvis Tsui Kam-kong (Lo Lanto Chui Siu-fung), Jimmy Wong Shu-kei (Danny), Yuen King-tan (Tsang Siu-yue). 1.85:1. VHS: Tai Seng. Import LD/VCD/DVD: Mei Ah. 90 minutes.

Eight-year-old Peach Chui is curious about sex, and that interest is heightened when her parents accidentally leave a porn tape in the VCR one evening. No one will give her a straight answer about the facts of life because of her age, so she and a school friend journey to The Sacred Tree and wish to become adults. The next morning, both girls are ten years older! An innocent in the body of a pretty and mature adult, Peach quickly charms swimming instructor Danny with her looks and sheer naivete. After learning how to kiss from her sister, Peach inches towards having sex with Danny. However, his vengeful ex-girlfriend discovers Peach's true age and decides to fool her into thinking that he does not really love her.

The Chinese title tries to connect this to the Loletta Lee vehicle **Crazy Love**, but **The Fruit Is Swelling** is actually rather sweet ... as Category III sex films go. Regardless, it would never have been made in the West. In addition to the rather obscene sounding premise, the English translation is decidedly on the crude side, resulting in the pre-transformation eight-year-old using terms like "dick" and "pussy." If you can get past that, some lame humor, and the fact that the story is slipshod even by genre standards, this is a light and enjoyable fantasy that is a nice change from the rather mean-spirited and sexually violent C-III films that dominated the mid–90s. Hsu Chi "introduces" the movie in a bikini and appears again at the very end for no real reason other than to give the movie another name star.

363. Full Alert

(1997; Brilliant Idea Group) ★: 8/10. *Go do gaai bei* (Cantonese), *Gao du jie bei* (Mandarin): "High Level Prevention." Cinematographer: Ardy Lam Kwok-wah; Art Directors: Chu Chung-pang, Wong Ching-ching; Music: Peter Kam Pui-tat; Producer: Li Kuo-shing; Action Director: Fok Wing-foo; Writer-Director: Ringo Lam Ling-tung. Cast: Lau Ching-wan (Pao), Francis Ng Chun-yu (Mak Kwan), Chin Kar-lok (Bill), Monica Chan Fat-yung (Pao's Wife), Emily Kwan Bo-wai (Policewoman), Amanda Lee Wai-man (Chung Lai-hung), Peter Yung Kam-cheung (Yung), Jack Gao Jie (The Taiwanese). Dolby Digital. 1.85:1. Import LD/VCD/DVD: Mei Ah. 99 minutes.

Upon completing the Jean-Claude Van Damme thriller **Maximum Risk**, Ringo Lam returned to HK and helmed this grim, highly engrossing crime thriller which is highlighted by deeper characterization than HK genre films are generally known for. When a bloated, decomposing body is discovered in an apartment building's water tank, police officer Pao arrests former construction demolitionist Mak Kwan. After blueprints and bomb-making materials are discovered in his apartment, Mak confesses that he accidentally killed the victim and hid his body but will not admit to anything else. Mak's Taiwanese partners make a desperate attempt to rescue their buddy while he is being transported to court. In the subsequent chaos, one of their men is killed and Pao loses one of his in a car crash. Mak is later able to escape with some inside help, so the police concentrate on his girlfriend. The mounting pressure on Pao causes him to become reckless and, in an attempt to apprehend Mak, he wounds an innocent motorcyclist. The police are eventually able to determine that Mak's target is the safe at the HK Jockey Club. While it seems an impossible task, Mak is an architectural design expert and has determined the one weak spot that will allow access.

Lau Ching-wan and Francis Ng are both excellent as the adversaries compelled to best one another in a competition that is akin to a children's game, with deadly consequences for those around them. Very well shot and scored, the film includes a bravura car chase that seems to encompass half of HK, but action and violence are not the main preoccupations here. While Lam's previous thrillers boast colorful antagonists, Mak Kwan is a far more intelligent and humane individual. The viewer does not condone his actions but one does empathize with him, and this attention to character (which also extends to the various officers under Pao's command) and clever scripting make **Full Alert** one of Lam's most striking and gratifying works to date.

364. Full Contact

(1992; Golden Princess) ★: 7/10. *Haap dou Ko Fei* (Cantonese), *Xia dao Gao Fei* (Mandarin): "Chivalrous Thief Ko Fei" or "Chivalrous Thief Gao Fei." Cinematographers: Lau Hung-chuen, Joe Chan Kong-hung, Peter Ngor Chi-kwan; Art Director: Ray Lam Chan-fai; Music: Teddy Robin Kwan; Writer: Nam Yin; Action Director: Lau Kar-wing; Producer-Director: Ringo Lam Ling-tung. Cast: Chow Yun-fat (Jeff), Simon Yam Tat-wah (Judge), Anthony Wong Chau-sang (Sam), Ann Bridgewater (Mona), Bonnie Fu Yuk-ching (Virgin), Frankie Chin Chi-leung (Deano), Victor Hon Kwan (Kau), Chris Lee Kin-sang (Chung). 1.85:1. VHS: Tai Seng (HK Version). Import LD: Golden Cinema City (HK version). Import DVD: Mei Ah. 96/99 minutes.

Bouncer/thief Jeff (a needless anglicization of the name Ko Fei) saves his debt-ridden buddy Sam when the latter was about to be executed by a loan shark.

Afterwards, the pair and their mutual friend Chung, go on a job with gay psychopath Judge and his two equally sociopathic cronies, nymphomaniac Virgin and her musclebound imbecile of a husband, Deano. Paid off by the loan shark and knowing that Sam is too much of a coward to act against him, Judge betrays Jeff and Chung, leaving the latter dead. Jeff, meanwhile, loses two of his fingers and is presumed to have perished in an explosion. After several months of seclusion (during which time he trains himself to shoot left-handed), Jeff heads to HK and finds that Sam has taken up with his wife, Mona. Unable to bring himself to kill Sam, Jeff decides to work with him to exact revenge.

Tough and stylish, **Full Contact** is high class exploitation, marred somewhat by a routine storyline that is far less interesting than the set-ups in director Ringo Lam's best work. Chow Yun-fat exudes cool, but it is Simon Yam, portraying a politically incorrect nightmare of a character, who gives the most memorable turn here. The violence is raw and brutal, and the gunplay is presented with great aplomb, particularly the bullet P.O.V. shots (a memorable effect director Ringo Lam would use again four years later in the Jean-Claude Van Damme vehicle **Maximum Risk**). The film ran into trouble with HK censors and had to be cut in several spots to avoid a Category III rating. Unfortunately, it is that censored cut that is the most prevalent. The Taiwan video version is more complete and includes an extended version of the car scene featuring Sam and Virgin, for a total of about three extra minutes. The DVD is also uncut.

365. Full Moon in New York

(1990; Shiobu Film Co.) ★: 6/10. *Yan joi nau yeuk* (Cantonese), *Ren zai niu yue* (Mandarin): "People in New York." Cinematographer: Bill Wong Chung-bo; Art Directors: Timmy Yip Kam-tin, Nanxy Purple Tong; Music: Peter Chang Hong-yi; Writer: Yau Tai On-ping; Producer: Henry Fong Ping; Director: Stanley Kwan Kam-pang. Cast: Sylvia Chang Ai-chia (Wang Hsiung-ping), Maggie Cheung Man-yuk (Lee Fung-jiau), Siquin Goawa (Zhaohong), Josephine Koo Mei-wah (Stella). 1.85:1. VHS: World Video (No Subtitles). Import LD: Star Entertainment (No Subtitles). Import VCD: China Star (No Subtitles), Mei Ah. Import DVD: Mei Ah. 88 minutes.

Three very different Chinese women are the focus of this multilingual drama, set and shot in New York City. Wang Hsiung-ping is an actress from Taiwan with a penchant for Western boyfriends; Zhaohong is a very traditional Mainlander married to a "banana" (slang for Westernized Chinese, as in "Yellow on the Outside, White on the Inside"); and Lee Fung-jiau, a businesswoman with no time for a personal life, is originally from HK. The three become close friends, attracted to each other not only by their differences but also by their shared experience as Chinese women adapting to life in the West.

The three leads are very good but the script is uneven and awkward at times, alternating between the plausible and the patently unbelievable (specifically, Zhaohong's husband and his parents, who are not realistically drawn, and the treatment Hsiung-ping receives from a white casting director when she auditions for the part of Lady Macbeth). Still, the basic conflicts are consistently interesting, such as the philosophical differences between Zhaohong and her husband (she wants to bring her mother over from China but he, now almost fully Westernized, rejects the idea of living with one's parents) and the way in which Hsiung-ping simply cannot relate to her father (a dyed-in-the-wool supporter of the Kuomintang who is unable to see what a hypocrite he has become). The dialogue is a mixture of Mandarin, Shanghaiese, Cantonese, and English, and the film unfolds in one of the most attractive and idyllic depictions of New York City in memory.

366. Full Throttle

(1995; Win's Entertainment/Film Unlimited) ★. 5/10. *Lit foh jin che* (Cantonese), *Lie huo zhan che* (Mandarin): "Flaming Chariot." Cinematographers: Jingle Ma Cho-shing, David Chung Chi-man; Art Director: Hai Chung-man; Music: Frankie Chan Fan-kei, Roel A. Garcia; Writers: Derek Yee Tung-sing, Law Chi-leung; Producer: Alexander Chan Mong-wah; Action Director: Bruce Law Lai-yin; Director: Derek Yee Tung-sing. Cast: Andy Lau Tak-wah (Joe), Gigi Leung Wing-kei (Yee), David Wu Tai-wai (David Kwan), Paul Chun Pui (Paul), Chin Kar-lok (Jiale), Elvis Tsui Kam-kong (Bartender), Ha Ping (Jiale's Grandmother). Dolby Digital. 1.85:1. VHS: Tai Seng. Import LD/VCD/DVD: Mei Ah. 108 minutes.

A glitzy but superficial drama, Derek Yee's **Full Throttle** is largely just a big-budget remake of Jacob Cheung's **Goodbye Hero**, which starred Yee and David Wu (who plays a virtually identical role here). While flawed, that film did manage to impart an interesting and seemingly realistic look at the life of movie stuntmen; **Full Throttle** simply adheres to formula, offering nothing one hasn't encountered numerous times before. Aging rebel Joe is an illegal motorcycle racer with a suspended licence, an unhappy father he can't communicate with, and a seven-year relationship with a terminally shy and dour girl who can do nothing to please him. To top it all off, his position as unofficial "King of the Road" is being challenged by David Kwan, a cocky rich kid set for life who hopes to join the racing team run by Joe's father. When his suspension ends, Joe is able to get a new licence but is badly injured in a crash. He recovers but his stay in the hospital has changed him in several respects, not the least of which is his view of both racing and his own self-worth.

The plot is too predictable to be involving and, like **Goodbye Hero**, the writers saw the need to add on one more, dramatically unnecessary tragedy in the second half. To Yee's credit, he has coaxed a subtle, mature performance from Andy Lau, and Elvis Tsui is highly amusing as an ex-racer turned acerbic bartender. However, even their laudable work and some exciting second-unit cinematography is not enough to breathe new life into this vehicle, which looks glossy and appealing at first but quickly proves to be just another old clunker with a new paint job.

367. Fun and Fury

(1992; Movie Impact/Impact Films Production) ★: 4/10. *Chi ching fai sai* (Cantonese), *Chi qing kuai xu* (Mandarin): "Crazy Love Son-in-Law." Cinematographer: Michael Ma Koon-wah; Art Director: Dominique Lo Kar-yiu; Music: Roel A. Garcia; Writers: Barry Wong Ping-yiu, Susan Chan; Producer: Wallace Cheung Kwok-chong; Action Director: Fung Hark-on; Director: Frankie Chan Fan-kei. Cast: Leon Lai Ming (Wei Han), Frankie Chan Fan-kei (Yeung Yee), Kent Cheng Chuk-see (Ma), Vivian Chow Wei-man (Ma Ching-ha), Sharon Kwok Sau-wan (The Thief), Norman Tsui Siu-keung (Smiling Tiger), Kim Maree Penn (Blonde Killer). 1.85:1. VHS: Tai Seng. Import LD/VCD: Universe. 101 minutes.

In spite of what is promised by the English title, there is very little fun to be had in this tedious action-comedy from director/co-star, Frankie Chan. Wei Han, a cop from Singapore, is in HK to see his girlfriend Ma Ching-ha, the daughter of a powerful triad boss. Determined to break up their romance, Mr. Ma hires a beautiful female thief to participate in a set-up that will make it appear that Han is cheating on Ching-ha. The expected misunderstandings and eventual reconciliations follow, with Ching-ha defying her father's orders and sneaking out to spend the night with Han. A rival triad society, The

Tigers, launches an attack on the pair and their friend, but it is actually Mr. Ma (coming to the rescue too late) who is injured in the crossfire. Now the head of the family, Ching-ha agrees to meet with the Tigers to talk truce but is kidnapped after her men are wiped out in an ambush. Han and his friend, martial arts master Yeung Yee, set out to rescue her.

The opening two thirds of **Fun and Fury** is a tiresome rehash of the usual cliches found in HK romantic comedies, and prospective viewers would do well to simply skip the opening hour. From that point on, the emphasis is shifted from comedy to gunplay and hand-to-hand combat. However, since said action is merely passable and generally not up to Frankie Chan's usual standards, the best plan is to skip the film altogether and watch **The Outlaw Brothers** instead.

368. The Fun, the Luck & the Tycoon

(1990; Cinema City Co./Golden Princess) ★: 5/10. *Gat sing gung jiu* (Cantonese), *Ji xing gong zhao* (Mandarin): "Lucky Star Join Hands and Shine." Cinematographer: Horace Wong Wing-hang; Art Director: Ringo Cheung Sek-wah; Music: Lo Tai-yau; Writer: Hoi Dik; Producer: Raymond Wong Pak-ming; Action Director: Ching Siu-tung; Director: Johnny To Kei-fung. Cast: Chow Yun-fat (Lam Bo-sun/Mr. Stink), Sylvia Chang Ai-chia (Hung Leung-yuk), Wong Kwan-yuen (Rocky Ma), Beyond (East, West, North, South), Lawrence Cheng Tan-shui (Jim Hsu), Nina Li Chi (Cindy Chan), Woo Fung (Cheung). Dolby Digital (DVD only). 1.85:1. VHS: Tai Seng. Import LD: Golden Cinema City. Import VCD/DVD: Universe. 90 minutes.

Everything is played just a little too broadly in this forgettable New Year's comedy. Lam Bo-sun, an affable billionaire, is being forced into a marriage with his haughty, money-grubbing cousin. Deciding to see what his life would be like without money, he takes a job as a janitor at a fast food restaurant. He gets along well with his co-workers (played by the pop group Beyond and Wong Kwan-yuen, who co-starred with Chow and Sylvia Chang in **All About Ah-Long**) and soon has his eye on the proprietor's sister, Leung-yuk. She, too, is being herded into marriage (with an affluent jerk) by her brother, who is only interested in the Canadian passport this union will get him. Soon the two spurned partners join forces to mess up Bo-sun and Leung-yuk's increasingly happy relationship, with all-too-predictable results.

While this was never intended to be anything more than good-natured holiday fluff, one cannot help but be a bit disappointed considering the people involved. Even the ever-charismatic Chow (who is smiling from the first frame to the last) cannot do much to make this worthwhile.

369. Future Cops

(1993; Wong Jing's Workshop/Fantasy Productions) ★: 3/10. *Chiu kap hok haau ba wong* (Cantonese), *Chao ji xue xiao ba wang* (Mandarin): "Super School Tyrant." Cinematographer: Andrew Lau Wai-keung; Art Director: Raymond Kwok Siu-keung, Jason Mok Siu-kei; Music: Marco Wan Ho-kit, Anthony Lee Hon-kam; Producer: John Higgins; Action Director: Ching Siu-tung; Writer-Director: Wong Jing. Cast: Andy Lau Tak-wah (Ti-men), Jacky Cheung Hok-yau (Broom-man), Simon Yam Tat-wah (Sing), Dicky Cheung Wai-kin (Tai-hung), Chingmy Yau Suk-ching (Chun-may), Dior Cheng Yee-kin (Kim), Ken Lo Wai-kwong (General), Charlie Yeung Choi-nei (Choi-ney), Winnie Lau Siu-wai (Siu-wai, aka "Crab Angel"), Andy Hui Chi-on (Kei-on), Richard Ng Yiu-hon (Richard), Yuen King-tan (Tai-hung's Mom), Aaron Kwok Fu-shing (Lung), Dennis Chan Kwok-san (Headmaster), Billy Chow Bei-lee (Thai King), Nat Chan Pak-cheung (Announcer). 1.85:1. VHS: World Video. Import LD/VCD/DVD: Universe. 94 minutes.

A much-too-silly send-up of the "Street Fighter II" videogame, **Future Cops** does boast a terrific cast and some fun special effects, so patient viewers may find it worthwhile nonetheless. In the year 2043 the arch-criminal "General" has been captured and is about to be tried by the revered judge Yu Ti-hung. General's lackeys travel back in time to 1993 with the intention of brainwashing the judge so that he will release their boss at the later trial. However, their plans have been intercepted by the authorities who send elite "Future Cops" Ti-men, Broom-man, and Sing back in time to stop them. The focus of the story then switches to Tai-hung, a hopelessly nerdy 28-year-old high school student who is bullied by everyone under the sun, including his baby sister. The three Cops strike a deal with Tai-hung: They will take care of his tormentors if he will help them find Yu Ti-hung before the General's men do. Their task becomes more complicated when General escapes from prison and travels back in time to take care of Yu Ti-hung himself.

Dicky Cheung often comes across in his movies as being a poor man's Stephen Chiau, and that is certainly the case here, especially as so much of the humor is reminiscent of Chiau's **Fight Back to School** series. Unfortunately, it is not half as inspired, though there are fun send-ups of Jean-Jacques Annaud's **The Lover**, **A Terracotta Warrior**, and **Ghost**. The climax finds the rest of the cast transforming into the remaining game characters to defeat General and his cronies, but the farcical battle is much too short to justify all of the unfunny high school sequences one must endure to get to it.

370. Gambling Baron

(1994; Cheung Sing Movie Co.) ★: 2/10. *Dei gwong do wong* (Cantonese), *Di xia du wang* (Mandarin): "Underground Gambling King." Cinematographers: Kam Chik-lim, Chan Chuen-lai; Art Directors: Tse Bo-man, Chow Sai-hung; Music: Not Original; Writer: Jimmy Leung Chi-ming; Producer: Ma Tin-yiu; Action Director: To Moon-wah; Director: Yeung Kuen. Cast: Max Mok Siu-chung (Chen Chun), Jacqueline Ng Suet-man (Meila Lin), Roy Cheung Yiu-yeung (San), Lee Suet-man (Fang), Lung Fong (Bolo Guy), Hugo Ng Toi-yung (Big Crown), Billy Chow Bei-lee (Chau). 1.85:1. VHS: World Video. Import LD/VCD: Fitto Mobile. 89 minutes.

Max Mok and Roy Cheung play a couple of small-time Mainland triads who open their own gambling parlour in this tired, low-budget offering. When Mok kills a rival owner (Hugo Ng) in a gang fight, he flees to Hong Kong and takes up with a heroin-addicted prostitute (Lee Suet-man). He helps her to get straight and the two, naturally, fall in love. When his gambling empire (such as it is) is usurped by a rival (Lung Fong, who seems to play the villain in virtually every gambling film ever produced), and his childhood sweetheart (Jacqueline Ng) is murdered, Mok sneaks back into China to set things right.

From the thoroughly routine plotting to the annoyingly inappropriate stock score, this is precisely the type of uninspired fare that led HK audiences to start skipping local product in favour of Hollywood blockbusters. Mok and Cheung clearly should have been cast in each other's roles, the drama is torpid, and the "action" finale is a joke.

371. The Gambling Ghost

(1991; Golden Leaf Film Production Consultant/Ko Chi Sum Films Co.) ★: 5/10. *Hung fuk chaai tin* (Cantonese), *Hong fu qi tian* (Mandarin): "Vast Fortune as High as the Sky." Cinematographer: Sander Lee Kar-ko; Art Director: Raymond Chan Kam-ho; Music: Richard Yuen Cheuk-fan; Writer: Roman Cheung Siu-lun; Action Director: Mang Hoi;

Producer-Director: Clifton Ko Chi-sum. Cast: Sammo Hung Kam-po (Fatty/ Fatty's Father/Hung Kau), Nina Li Chi (Lily), Mang Hoi (Siu-hoi), James Wong Jim (Brother Dragon), Yip Wing-cho (Kau's Partner), Wu Ma (The Swordsman), Lam Ching-ying (Exorcist), James Tien Chun (Taoist), Richard Ng Yiu-hon (Roadblock Cop), Stanley Fung Shui-fan (Motorcycle Cop), Corey Yuen Kwai (Gambler), Paul Chun Pui (Gambler), Chung Fat (Driver), Billy Chow Bei-lee (Thug), Robert Samuels (Thug). 1.85:1. VHS/LD: Quali-Vision. Import LD: Universe. 93 minutes.

Sammo Hung plays three roles in this action farce, which offers up a few chuckles and some decent fighting but is far from his best work, being too unfocused and commonplace to really score. Fatty is a hopeless gambling addict who never gets the windfall he feels he is owed, being the grandson of the legendary conman Hung Kau (known in his day as "The King of Cheating"). After Fatty becomes an embarrassment to the family name one time too many, Kau returns from the beyond to help him win at gambling. However, when Kau demands that Fatty kill the descendent of the man who murdered him, the grandson hires an exorcist to send the spirit back to the netherworld. When that fails, Fatty learns the true circumstances behind Kau's death and agrees to help him exact revenge.

In-joke references to **God of Gamblers** and **A Chinese Ghost Story** (Wu Ma evens shows up as his character from that film) provide solid laughs, but the numerous jibes about reunification, corrupt Mainland officials, and the Gulf War must have seemed uninspired even back when this was new. Director Clifton Ko can be spotted as a TV studio technician. Note: the Quali-Vision LD is just a repackaged version of the Universe disc.

372. Game Boy Kids

(Team Work Production House; 1992) ★: 2/10. *Gei BOY siu ji ji jan fung wai lung* (Cantonese), *Ji BOY xiao zi zhi zhen jia wei long* (Mandarin): "Game Boy Kids: True or False Mighty Dragon." Cinematographer: Jimmy Leung Chi-ming; Art Director: Horace Ma Kwong-wing; Music: Lowell Lo Kwun-ting; Writers: John Chan Kin-chung, Lam Kei-to, Gordon Chan Kar-seung; Producers: David Lai Tai-wai, Chan Pui-wah; Action Director: Yuen Tak; Director: Gordon Chan Kar-seung. Cast: Andy Lau Tak-wah (Wong Kau-tai), Aaron Kwok Fu-shing (Chung), Rosamund Kwan Chi-lam (Kwan Chi-lam), Ng Man-tat (Uncle Seven), Sandra Ng Kwan-yu (Veronica), Yuen Woo-ping (Master Dragon), Spencer Lam Sheung-yee (Police Captain), Lawrence Cheng Tan-shui (Store Manager). 1.85:1. VHS: Tai Seng. Import LD/VCD: Universe. 95 minutes.

Few viewers with ages in the double digits will have the patience for this incredibly obnoxious and virtually laugh-free action-comedy, which almost makes **The Black Panther Warriors** seem like the work of Zhang Yimou. Andy Lau plays an idiot savant (accent on the idiot) who is mistakenly made the head of a triad society when his dwarf-sized lookalike (also Lau) is arrested by police in India. His subsequent childish antics and obsession with toys befuddles everyone, in particular his bodyguard (Aaron Kwok) and second-in-command (Ng Man-tat). When Lau decides that he wants all the gangs to go straight, one mob boss (actor/director Yuen Woo-ping) has his hitwoman daughter (Rosamund Kwan, looking stunning in black leather) marry the cretin, thus allowing her ample opportunities to ice him.

Lau proves once again that he is better suited to roles in serious triad movies like **As Tears Go By** and **A Moment of Romance**, while Ng Man-tat and Sandra Ng are allowed to rampage through the proceedings at their over-the-top worst. With the exception of some mildly amusing shots at Lau and his fellow Canto-pop kings, only Kwok's restrained cool and the unusual casting of Kwan make this the least bit endurable. Director Gordon Chan (**Fist of Legend**) admitted in interviews that he was forced by triads to direct at least one film he wanted nothing to do with; this must be it!

373. The Game They Called Sex

(1988; Tomson Films Co.) ★: 6/10. *Wong sik goo si* (Cantonese), *Huang se gu shi* (Mandarin): "Yellow Stories." Cinematographers: Cheung Wai-kung, Sung Lap-ping; Art Director: Yeung Ke-lap; Music: Sam Kong-yuen, Tang Siu-lam; Writers: Wong Siu-di, Choi Ming-leung, So Wai-ching; Producers: Hsu Feng, Hsu Bun; Directors: Sylvia Chang Ai-chia, Wong Siu-di, Kim Kok-chiu. Cast: Maggie Cheung Man-yuk (Chiu Hsiao-min), David Wu Tai-wai (The Triad), Emil Chow Wah-kin (Tung Tzu-chi). 1.85:1. VHS: World Video. 99 minutes.

Maggie Cheung was granted her first challenging acting assignment in this Taiwanese production and she displays some of the ability that would soon come to full fruition later on under directors like Wong Kar-wai and Stanley Kwan. The film (divided into three sections, each by a different filmmaker) charts a few years in the life of Chiu Hsiao-min, beginning in her teens as part of a strict, ultra-religious family. Never allowed to go on school trips in the past, Hsiao-min is given permission to attend a graduation outing, where she meets extroverted Yo Chao-chun. He gets her out into the school social circle, and Hsiao-min soon begins to overcome her shyness. Hsiao-min's parents, nevertheless, want her to marry a dull lad who seems as ill-at-ease with the idea as she is. When she does tie the knot with another man a few years later, he is more interested in cars and other high-tech toys than he is in her. One day, Hsiao-min's increasingly uneventful routine is disrupted by an intruder, who forces her to strip and then vanishes. She keeps the incident a secret and soon encounters this youth (a triad who seems to always be running for his life) once more. The two spend some time together but he tries to force himself on her and she drives him away. Hsiao-min's husband learns of what has happened and his refusal to listen to her rationale does irreparable damage to their relationship. Following her divorce, Hsiao-min meets Tung Tzu-chi, a one-legged chef whom she develops genuine affection for, but she still possesses some doubts about getting involved again.

In contrast to the fairly frank English and Chinese titles (the latter, "Yellow Stories," indicates erotic content), this is a subtle character study that makes a few unfortunate missteps that diminish its intentions somewhat. The writing in the mid-section, featuring the young hoodlum character (played by Taiwanese actor David Wu), is like something out of an American direct-to-video softcore movie, and some nightmare segments come across as heavy-handed. However, the film eventually regains its footing and ends up being a satisfying, if unsurprising, look at one woman's budding maturity and resilience. Perhaps most notably, it allowed Cheung to display much the same sort of growth as an actress.

374. Gangs

(1988; Sil-Metropole Organisation) ★: 8/10. *Tung dong* (Cantonese), *Tong dang* (Mandarin): "Child Gang." Cinematographer: Chan Kwan-kin; Art Director: Henry Tang, Wong Hok-sin; Music: Joseph Chow Kung-shing; Writer: Chan Man-keung; Producer: Sit Yun-chung; Action Directors: Donnie Fish; Director: Lawrence Ah Mon. Cast: Ricky Ho Pui-tung (Big K), Ma Hin-ting (Lard Cake), Eleven Leung Sap-yat (Coma), Tse Wai-kit (Little Demon), Tam Shan-shan (Kitty), Wong Chun-chuen (Little K), Yung Yee (Chick), Tam Kin-shing (Conditioner), Lau Chi-tat (Blocker). 1.85:1.

VHS: World Video. Import LD: Star Entertainment (No Subtitles). 98 minutes.

A group of teenage dropouts extort, rob, get into street fights, torture rats, and commit all manner of other disreputable acts as junior members of the Sun Hing triad gang. Brothers Big and Little K face misery at the hands of not only rival gang members but also their own father. A former triad (though hardly a paragon of virtue now), he beats the youths whenever he suspects that they have been engaging in gang activity. When that doesn't dissuade them, he even hires a couple of thugs to do it instead. Following a bloody confrontation with some adversaries, the surviving Sun Hing youths find themselves without a leader and on the run, taking shelter in the crowded home of one member's grandmother. Tempers soon flare and the situation rapidly degenerates, with one gang member arrested, the girls forced into prostitution, and the others in mortal danger.

Produced in a semi-documentary style with a cast of credible unknowns, this looks at HK's youth crime problem in a realistic fashion but still ran into the same censorship problems that plague exploitation productions. In addition to ordering over two dozen deletions, the censors also insisted that some lines of dialogue be redubbed, claiming that the movie encouraged gang membership. Those who accuse mid–90s fare, like the **Young and Dangerous** films, of glamorizing young triads will appreciate what director Lawrence Ah Mon (in his theatrical directorial debut, following a career in television) accomplishes with this effort, which makes being a member of a HK gang look like the last thing anyone would want to do with their lives. While it gets a bit too melodramatic in spots and offers no more answers than the regular films in this genre, **Gangs** remains an effective (and at times chilling) drama that rarely strikes a false note.

375. Ghost Fever

(1989; Grand March Movie Production Co.) ★: 7/10. *Gwai gau yan* (Cantonese), *Gui gou ren* (Mandarin): "Ghost Marries Human." Cinematographer: Li Hsin-yeh; Art Director: Jon Hau Wing-choi; Music: Chow Lai-chi; Writer: Wong Jing; Action Director: Sherman Wong Ching-wah; Producer: Wong Tin-lam; Director: Lau Sze-yu. Cast: Wong Jing (Ling Siu-cheong), Rosamund Kwan Chi-lam (Pinkey), Nat Chan Pak-cheung (Au), Pat Ha Man-chik (Mrs. Ling), Charlie Cho Cha-lei (Brands), Max Mok Siu-chung (Hui Zen), Amy Yip Chi-mei (Nancy), Eddy Ko Hung (Johnny Fan). 1.85:1. VHS: Tai Seng. Import LD: Ocean Shores. 92 minutes.

Wong Jing wrote and stars in this engaging horror comedy (which is not to be confused with the dreadful Western film of the same name) but, for a change, didn't direct, assigning that task to Lau Sze-yu (**My Neighbors Are Phantoms!**) instead. When his wife's pregnancy develops complications that require her to be hospitalized, bespectacled nerd Siu-cheong pledges to remain true, despite pressure from his lecherous pals Au and Brands. However, when he encounters the gorgeous Pinkey, a worker from the same building, he gives in to temptation. After an attack of conscience, Siu-cheong breaks a date with the woman the next evening and is then plagued by horrific dreams and visions. When Siu-cheong and his buddies enlist the aid of a spiritualist, all hell literally breaks loose. Further investigation reveals that Pinkey and her family were murdered five years before in Siu-cheong's home and he is now suffering their vengeance. When Siu-cheong is attacked and orally castrated by Pinkey's sister (an act that, while not shown, still puts a bit of a damper on the humor), his wife seeks a little payback of her own. She enlists two Taoist masters but also gets some unexpected aid in the form of Johnny Fan. The gangster who committed the original murders, Fan has broken out of prison in order to vanquish the spectres with the one weapon that will dispel them forever: the axe he used five years earlier.

More intricately plotted than most HK films of this type, **Ghost Fever** also incorporates references to **Poltergeist** (a diminutive female Taoist inspired by Zelda Rubinstein's exorcist), **Evil Dead II** (a variation on the "swallowed demon eyeball" gag, which would also be reprised four years later in Wong's **Holy Weapon**), **Fear No Evil** (Nat Chan is cursed with breasts at one point), **Amazon Women on the Moon** (Charlie Cho gets sucked inside a TV set and finds himself in **The Fearless Hyena**, a 1979 Jackie Chan film), and even the Japanese horror classic **Kwaidan**. Chan and Cho are the Abbott and Costello of HK horror, performing much the same shtick in films like **Return of the Demon**, **Ghostly Vixen**, **My Neighbors Are Phantoms!**, and **Mr. Possessed**, where they are often paired up with other comics like Billy Lau Nam-kwong, Sandra Ng Kwan-yu, and Woo Fung.

376. The Ghost Informer

(1984) ★: 3/10. *Gwai sin yan* (Cantonese), *Gui xian ren* (Mandarin): "Ghost Informant." Cinematographer: Yu Chik-lim; Art Director: Ng Bo-ling, David Lo Kin-ming; Music: Not Original; Writers: Lai Chun-kit, Lam Chi-ming; Producer: Lo Wei; Director: Lau Hung-chuen. Cast: Tony Leung Kar-fai (Tang), Pang Kuen-sun (Fire Unicorn), Joyce Ngai Suk-kwan (Sally), Tai Po (Tei Po), Lee Hoi-sang (Robber), David Wu Tai-wai (Robber), Charlie Cho Cha-lei (Charles), Billy Lau Nam-kwong (Waiter), Jamie Luk Kim-ming (Guy in Bathroom), Yung Sai-kit (Male Model). 2.35:1. VHS: Ocean Shores (Poor Subtitles). Import LD/VCD: Ocean Shores (Poor Subtitles). 84 minutes.

Looking to make a fast buck, Fire Unicorn (played by Pang Kuen-sun, the poor man's Raymond Wong Pak-ming) becomes a professional informer for police officer Tang. Unfortunately for Unicorn, he botches one of his first jobs and ends up being murdered by robber Tei Po, whom he squealed on. With only 49 days before Unicorn's soul leaves Earth, he helps Tang track down the killer. He also helps Tang score with model Sally, by making the latter's snobbish boyfriend look like a sex maniac. Not long before Unicorn is to depart to the netherworld, Tei escapes from prison and kidnaps Sally, using the girl as bait to lure Tang into a trap.

The premise offers ample opportunities to combine the best aspects of both the cop action and ghost thriller genres, but there are precious few laughs to be found here. We lurch from one scene to another, with the monotony occasionally interrupted by some make-up effects modelled after the work Tom Savini did for **Till Death Do We Scare**. While rather poorly executed, they at least provide a temporary respite from the film's main running gag: onlookers thinking that Tang is crazy for talking to his invisible friend.

377. Ghost Lantern

(1993; Scholar Films/Wong Jing's Workshop) ★: 3/10. *Yan pei dang lung* (Cantonese), *Ren pi deng long* (Mandarin): "Human Skin Lantern." Cinematographer: Cheung Man-bo; Art Director: Ring Law Chi-keung; Music: Jonathan Wong Bong-yin; Producer: Wong Jing; Director: Andrew Lau Wai-keung. Cast: Tony Leung Kar-fai (Tong Fai), Chingmy Yau Suk-ching (Yung), Tommy Wong Kwong-leung (Kwong), Roy Cheung Yiu-yeung (Hung), Ronald Wong Pan (Jerk), Yuen King-tan (Lucy). 1.85:1. VHS/LD: World Video. Import LD/VCD/DVD: Mei Ah. 92 minutes.

This weak variation on **Human Skin Lanterns** (1982) is an odd mix of horror, comedy, and Triad gangster movie elements. The story centers on Tong Fai, a crippled street vendor with exceptionally bad luck. Through a visit to a medium he learns that his problems can be traced back to 1963 when his ancestor fell in love with

Yung, the beautiful assistant of a spoiled actress. The latter was seeing the villainous So Hung but craved the attentions of Fai's father. When the elder Fai accidentally killed the woman and tried to expose So's crimes to the police, he was murdered and Yung committed suicide. So had the man's body buried in unlucky ground, effectively cursing his next ten descendants with bad luck, and skinned Yung, turning the remains into a human skin lantern that houses her spirit. Back in the present day, Yung is able to free herself from the confines of the lantern and comes to the aid of Fai. Switching his father's remains with that of So's father, Fai's fortunes change for the better, allowing him to take on So (now a powerful gang leader). At Fai's side is Kwong, a belligerent cop who owes Fai's ancestor a favor, but who eventually grasps that it is his duty as both a man and a police officer to fight this evil.

The flashbacks are very attractively photographed, and here and there the leads manage to share a touching moment together. However, the comedy is crude, the supernatural elements (including possession and a ghost attack) are silly, and the constant shifts in tone are self-defeating. Also, the film is sloppily edited, appearing to have been structured on the fly (which would explain the lack of a writer's credit). Tommy Wong has some amusing moments (especially when Yung's spirit is manipulating his actions and speech), and Roy Cheung somehow manages to radiate villainy despite spending most of his screen time buried under some really silly looking old age make-up. Producer Wong Jing can be glimpsed in the first of a line of photographs during the gambling house scene. **Ghost Lantern** originally received the adults-only Category III rating but was later toned down in order to get the more lucrative Category II classification. It is the latter version that is on video.

378. Ghost Punting

(1992; Choice Film Productions Co.) ★: 5/10. *Ng fuk sing chong gwai* (Cantonese), *Wu fu xing chuang gui* (Mandarin): "Five Lucky Stars Bump Ghost." Cinematographers: Jimmy Leung Chi-ming, Chan Yuen-kai; Art Director: Leung Kar-yu; Music: Not Original; Writer: Barry Wong Ping-yiu; Producer: Yip Wing-cho; Action Directors: Corey Yuen Kwai, Sammo Hung Stuntmen Association; Directors: Sammo Hung Kam-po, Corey Yuen Kwai, Eric Tsang Chi-wai, Ricky Lau Koon-wai. Cast: Sammo Hung Kam-po (Tse Koo-choy), Eric Tsang Chi-wai (Buddha Fruit), Nat Chan Pak-cheung (The Ghost), Stanley Fung Shui-fan (Rhino Skin), Richard Ng Yiu-hon (Da Shan-di), Charlie Chin Hsiang-lin (U.S. Ginseng), Elaine Lui Siu-ling (Liang Lai-di), Sibelle Hu Hui-chung (Madame Wu), Yip Wing-cho (Card Player), Mondi Yau Yuet-ching (Yau Siu-qiu), Chin Ho (Siu-qiu's Boyfriend), Marianne Chan Miu-ying (Pretty-As-Snow). 1.85:1. LD: Network Kingdom. Import LD/VCD: Mei Ah. 94 minutes.

A typical entry in the Lucky Stars series, this outing finds the "sex lupines" under the gun to get dates for an outing on Lantau Island. After trolling for babes in their usual desperate manner, they end up going *sans* feminine accompaniment. When they run across a female ghost taking unnatural advantage of her equally undead partner, the boys request help from Madam Wu, who sends in a team of policewomen to investigate. In between trying to take advantage of their beautiful guests, they must also deal with the antics of the male spirit, who seeks revenge against the drug dealer who had him killed.

All manner of genre elements are tossed into the mix (supernatural comedy, gambling jokes, impersonation, industry in-jokes, some nicely choreographed kung fu), with moderately entertaining results.

379. Ghost Story of Kam Pin Mui

(1991) ★: 3/10. *Liu jai Kam Ping-mui* (Cantonese), *Liao Zhai Jin Pingmei* (Mandarin): "Ghost Story of Kam Ping-mui" or "Ghost Story of Jin Pingmei." Cinematographer: Ngam Lam-cheng; Art Director: Sung Kwong-wah; Music: Not Original; Writer: Tsui Chan-keung; Producer: Chung Chi-kwai; Action Director: Chow Kong; Director: Lee Pak-hong. Cast: Chan Pui-kei (Chin Lin), Man So (Aunt Chui), Ku Feng (The Monk), Wu Ma (The Priest), Wong Siu-ching. 1.85:1. VHS: Tai Seng. Import LD/VCD: Mei Ah. 101 minutes.

Obviously inspired by **Erotic Ghost Story**, this second tier Category III period sex fantasy looks reasonably handsome, but the action choreography and special effects are strictly amateur night. Upright scholar Chiu Tin-yau is charmed by young maiden Chin Lin, whom he saves from drowning one afternoon. However, their time together is short-lived as the girl's evil stepmother sells her to Spring House brothel, where she suffers at the hands of the sadistic madam, Aunt Chui. After experiencing a nightmarish vision of Lin in peril, the scholar tracks down the girl's whereabouts. He helps her to escape from the bordello, but the pair are intercepted by Chui's men and Tin-yau is beaten to death. Returning from the grave as a vengeful ghost, Tin-yau's supernatural activities soon have Spring House's regulars staying away in droves. Meanwhile, a *caucasian* monk from Persia (who can shoot cross-shaped energy beams from his hands) arrives, claiming he can dispel the evil, but he is far from saintly himself.

Outside of a few amusingly nutty touches (like a pair of ghost lackeys that look like undead punk rockers in period garb), this is far more dull than erotic and simply ends right when a real storyline seems about to finally commence.

380. Ghostly Bus

(1995; You & Me Film Workshop) ★: 3/10. *Gwai ba si* (Cantonese), *Gui ba shi* (Mandarin): "Ghost Bus." Cinematographer: Cheung King-nin; Art Director: Fred Chan Chi-chung; Music: Sam Leung Yiu-sun; Writer-Action Director: Johnny Lee King-kai; Producer-Director: Wilson Tong Wai-shing. Cast: Simon Yam Tat-wah (Michael), Valerie Chow Kar-ling (Ling-ling), Vincent Wan Yeung-ming (Bus Driver), Chin Ho (Brother Yiang), Fung Hark-on (Andy), Tai Po (Leon). 1.85:1. VHS: World Video. Import LD: Universe. 87 minutes.

A tepid blend of the ghost and triad movie genres, **Ghostly Bus** might have been passable had it been played as an out-and-out comedy. As is, it only inspires unintentional snickers amid crushing monotony. Vincent Wan plays a bus driver with magic eyebrows(!) which allow him to see ghosts. This is a handy trait, considering that most of the passengers on his shift are the wandering spirits of unfortunate souls killed in a horrible bus crash. Valerie Chow plays one such apparition, and she enlists his services to find Simon Yam's character, a pickpocket on the run from triads. The two were lovers before he inadvertently caused the aforementioned crash that took her life. Now they wish to reunite to take their marriage vows, but some of the other passengers who were killed (quite understandably) want revenge.

Most of the horror sequences are so lame, they wouldn't scare little children, and the tacky special effects certainly don't help matters any (one of the ghosts even sports Freddy Krueger "finger knives"!). The romantic angle is trite, and the action sequences are routine. So, to sum up, you've seen this all before, though probably not in this particular combination.

381. Ghostly Vixen

(1990; Golden Flare Film Co.) ★: 7/10. *Tin si juk gaan* (Cantonese), *Tian shi zhuo jian* (Mandarin): "Angel Catching Rape." Cinematographer: Jimmy Au Kam-hung; Art Director: Oliver Wong Yui-man; Music: Chow Kam-cheung; Writers: Wong Jing, Lau Jun-wai; Producer: Wong Jing; Director: Wellson Chin Sing-wai. Cast: Nat Chan Pak-cheung (Chin Sau-yan), Sandra Ng Kwan-yu (Lumy), Amy Yip Chi-mei (Piao Hung), Shing Fui-on (Miu), Woo Fung (Li Chum-foon), Charlie Cho Cha-lei (Simon), Wu Ma (Chin's Boss), Tai Po (Tony), Bill Tung Biu (Wizard), Yip Wing-cho (Mahjong Maker), Stanley Fung Shui-fan (Thrill Seeker from HK). 1.85:1. VHS/LD: World Video. Import VCD: Panorama Entertainment. 99 minutes.

This unabashedly crass fantasy-comedy is filled with sexist and homophobic humor that will go far beyond the tolerance level of politically correct Westerners. However, those viewers who can get into the spirit of the enterprise will find it splendidly bizarre. Piao Hung, a voluptuous demon, has been preying on the virgin men of Bangkok who were born at 10:00. By performing oral sex on them, she can suck out their essence, increasing her powers. She needs to drain 100 men to achieve ultimate strength. Just after finishing off #98, Piao is attacked by the bumbling wizard Miu but escapes by hiding inside a mahjong game piece. The set containing the piece is subsequently shipped to HK, where it ends up in the vicinity of Chin Sau-yin, a hopeless loser who cannot get any sex no matter what he tries. Finally, after a disastrous night with a hooker, he is not only still a virgin but ends up gang raped by some gay robbers ("Give me back my virgin ass!")! Naturally, he is a perfect target for Piao, who has reached 99 and is anxious to make Chin #100.

Dated somewhat by numerous jokes about the handover in 1997, **Ghostly Vixen** is still jam packed with bizarre spells and comedic stuntwork, supplemented by a great cast of second string comedians. If you are new to the genre, this is a perfect film to start with. Incidentally, the Chinese title is Cantonese slang meaning to catch one's mate cheating.

382. Ghosts Galore

(1983; Shaw Brothers) ★: 6/10. *Moon tin san fat* (Cantonese), *Man tian shen fo* (Mandarin): "Full Sky Magical Buddhist." Cinematographer: Ko Muk; Music: Sing Kam-wing, So Chun-hau; Writer: Yip Kai; Producer: Mona Fong Yat-wah; Action Directors: Yuen Fai, Yeung Wah, Chu Hak, Hsu Hsia; Director: Hsu Hsia. Cast: Chin Siu-ho, Cheung Kam (Fat Chick), Lo Lieh (Magician Lien), Yeung Ching-ching (Junko), Hwang Jang-li (Japanese Sorcerer). 2.35:1. VHS: World Video (Poor Subtitles). Import LD: Ocean Shores (Poor Subtitles). 100 minutes.

This Shaw Brothers horror-comedy-martial arts extravaganza is filled with spells and supernatural kung fu, but the current video versions are so badly cropped that it is difficult to comprehend any more than the basics of the storyline. Chin Siu-ho and Cheung Kam play a pair of bumblers who run afoul of a female ghost. A wizened magician (Lo Lieh) gives them a magic talisman for protection, with the warning that it can only be used once. When the spirit returns that evening, Cheung resorts to using the amulet. Now with no further means of protection at their disposal, the buddies track Lo down and convince him to take them on as students. One evening, Cheung is murdered by a group of Japanese ninja who are pursuing two of their own. The ninja are able to kill one target, but the other, a swordswoman played by Yeung Ching-ching, manages to survive. Chin nurses Yeung back to health and then must protect her from a series of assailants, some of whom possess greater magical powers than he. Fortunately, Cheung is back from the grave to lend them a hand.

Until a letterboxed presentation becomes available, it will be difficult to fully assess this film's merit. In the meantime, those fond of Chinese horror and fantasy will enjoy the supernatural elements and colorful combat. The highlight is a climactic sorcerer's duel between Lo Lieh and Hwang Jang-li in which the combatants call upon various gods to fight for them.

383. Gift from Heaven

(1989; Clever Mark) ★: 6/10. *Da kung kwong seung kuk* (Cantonese), *Da gong kuang xiang qu* (Mandarin): "Wild Dreams of the Working Class." Cinematographer: Kan Wai-lun; Art Director: Jon Hau Wing-choi; Music: Lau Yee-tat; Writer: Fong Chi-ho; Producer: Fung Wai-chan; Director: Andy Chin Wing-keung. Cast: Carol Cheng Yu-ling (Becky Cheng), Joey Wang Tsu-hsien (Angie), Sandy Lam Yik-lin (Candy Lam), Derek Yee Tung-sing (Albert), Mark Cheng Ho-nam (Mark), Cheung Kwok-keung (Man Lee), Woo Fung (Uncle Hsiu), Lau Siu-ming (The Boss), Helena Law Lan (Wu Tse-tien), Bowie Lam Bo-yee (Bowie), Lam Chung (Manager), Yung Sai-kit (Manager), Ricky Yee Fan-wai (Manager), Lau Yee-tat (Watchman Ta). 1.85:1. VHS: Tai Seng. Import LD/VCD: Mei Ah. 94 minutes.

A HK variation on the Hollywood hit **Nine to Five** (1980), this pleasant comedy concerns downtrodden working girls Becky, Angie, and Candy, who are just trying to survive the daily rat race. While working overtime one evening, they find a bag full of money and fantasize about the good life. Reality eventually sets back in and the trio worry that the money might either be counterfeit or the result of some underworld dealings within their company. A security camera captured an image of three suspects but the picture is too scrambled to make out. While the company computer digitizes and cleans up the image, the frenzied girls desperately try to decide what they should do.

Things are a bit too drawn out for such a slight premise, but the leads are pleasant and Lau Yee-tat's score is engagingly offbeat. Sync sound recording is a nice plus, allowing one to hear Joey Wang's real voice for a change.

384. Gigolo and Whore

(1991; David Lam Films) ★: 4/10. *Gai ap luen* (Cantonese), *Ji ya lian* (Mandarin): "Chicken Duck Love." Cinematographers: Abdul M. Rumjahn, Gigo Lee Chi-hang; Art Director: Bill Lui Cho-hung; Music: Lowell Lo Kwun-ting; Writers: Sandy Shaw, On Lok-man; Producer: David Lam Tak-luk; Director: Terry Tong Kei-ming. Cast: Simon Yam Tat-wah (Sam), Carina Lau Kar-ling (Chung Siu-hung), Alex Fong Chung-sun (Dickson), Angile Leung Wan-yui (Kiki). 1.85:1. VHS: Tai Seng. Import LD/VCD: Universe. 91 minutes.

A dumb but sexy comedy-drama, **Gigolo and Whore** stars Carina Lau as Siu-hung, a country girl from China who comes to HK to stay with her sister Kiki, who has graduated from store clerk to prostitute (or "hen" in Cantonese slang). Upon arrival, the girl's luggage is stolen and her fish-out-of-water appearance and manners make her the butt of jokes (the usual collection of Mainland hick jibes found in dozens of HK films). One day, Siu-hung is saved from embarrassment in a restaurant by Sam, a handsome gigolo (or "duck") who works at the same club as Kiki. After a disastrous attempt at waitressing, Siu-hung decides to emulate the gigolo's glamorous lifestyle by having him train her to become "The King [*sic*] of Whores." After an especially personal lesson from Sam, she proves to be a natural and is soon in demand. Seeking to cure his son's depression following the death of the latter's wife, a millionaire offers Siu-hung $300,000 to become the young man's "personal assistant." This leads to love for them but heartache for Sam who, though professing to keep a "professional distance" from his partners, has fallen for Siu-hung.

Like the Hollywood hit **Pretty Woman** (which one character actually brings up in conversation), the depiction of the whole "sex for sale" lifestyle is awash in glamour, with the substantial downside conspicuous by its absence. If you can accept such a whitewash, then this is a fairly entertaining exercise in wish fulfillment. The film is at its best early on, before Siu-hung actually starts plying her trade and is learning from Sam, who instructs her in moaning by pouring sand down her back and suggests she brush up on her sexual techniques by using a pepper mill(!). In addition to the **Pretty Woman** allusions, Lau also gets to re-stage Meg Ryan's restaurant orgasm scene from **When Harry Met Sally** in a department store. Martial arts regular Sophia Crawford shows up briefly as a psychiatrist(!) into handcuffs and whips. There is some fleeting nudity but nothing tops the fully clothed dance floor seduction that runs under the opening credits. **Gigolo and Whore II** followed the next year.

385. Gigolo and Whore II

(1992; David Lam Films) ★: 2/10. *Miu lam ching mei liu* (Cantonese), *Wu nan qing wei le* (Mandarin): "Dance Man Cannot Love." Cinematographer: William Yim Wai-lun; Art Director: Bill Lui Cho-hung; Writers: Ah Nam, So Man-sing; Producer: David Lam Tak-luk; Director: Andy Chin Wing-keung. Cast: Simon Yam Tat-wah (Jack), Rosamund Kwan Chi-lam (Sherin Chan), Veronica Yip Yuk-hing (Jenny), Alex Fong Chung-sun (Johnson Lee), Jackie Lui Chung-yin (Bill), Jacqueline Ng Suet-man (Ching). 1.85:1. VHS: Tai Seng. Import LD/VCD: Universe. 90 minutes.

Simon Yam and Alex Fong are back, but this foolish, distasteful comedy-drama has no connection to the original **Gigolo and Whore**, save for its glamorized depiction of prostitution. Fong plays Lee, a high-ranking executive whose world is turned upside down by the arrival of Sherin. The boss' obnoxious daughter, Sherin has taken control of the company and plans to boot him out. Lee proceeds to do what anyone in this situation would: He goes to a well-known gigolo bar in order to hire one to seduce Sherin and convince her to sell him a controlling interest! Proprietress Jenny suggests Bill, a novice, to handle the assignment. There is just one small problem: Sherin is a "tomboy" (i.e. lesbian), and she and her "buddies" beat Bill to a pulp. When Lee ups the ante to $10HK million, master seducer Jack decides to tackle the case himself and, naturally, falls for Sherin. Not surprisingly, Lee has developed a fondness for the (now ex) tomboy and tries to ruin things by revealing to Sherin the details of his deal with Jack. Meanwhile, Jenny is pining for Jack and mourning the loss of "The Best Gigolo in Hong Kong."

This gets right down to the business of pushing the limits of the Category II rating by having Veronica Yip naked in the opening scene (and again in the second half). However, whereas the original was simple-minded in an amiable manner, this is just plain asinine. The comedy is extremely weak, the dramatic content is feeble, and the gay characters are all the usual stereotypes found in HK cinema. The sequences in which Jack tries to win Sherin over using the oldest tricks in the book are painful enough, but they are made offensive by the film's credo that lesbians just need a good man to "straighten" them out. The real lowpoint features a trio of mincing gays deciding to teach Sherin a lesson by raping her. Right. Strictly for those turned on by the sight of Rosamund Kwan in a suit, tie, and wire-rims.

386. Girls Unbutton

[*sic*] (1994; Golden Harvest/Paragon Films) ★: 3/10. *Bat kau lau dik lui haai* (Cantonese), *Bu kou niu de nu hai* (Mandarin): "Button Not Turned Girl." Cinematographer: Keung Kwok-man; Music: Simon Leung Chi-wah, Tony Tam Chan-hung, Ritchie Law Chung-leung; Writer: Lam Chiu-wing; Producer: Chua Lam; Director: Taylor Wong Tai-loi. Cast: Loletta Lee Lai-chun (Jenny), Elvis Tsui Kam-kong (Lung Mao), Leung Si-ho, Miki Ng Miu-yee, Siu Chung-hang. 1.85:1. VHS: Tai Seng. Import LD/VCD/DVD: Universe. 89 minutes.

Aside from the visual enticement of seeing Loletta Lee and her attractive co-stars in the buff, this softcore farce is pretty weak and often drifts into dullness. The largely plotless proceedings concern the misadventures of nubile young Jenny, who is having trouble finding a suitable boyfriend. She eventually meets the benevolent (not to mention environmentally conscious) triad boss Lung Mao, who seems to be her ideal man. Although they are able to make love, Lung is murdered soon after in a street fight. Jenny later takes up with political candidate Pong Kwong-yim, but their happiness is constantly being thwarted by the man's crazy wife. Ho, a decidedly unambitious marina worker whom Jenny finds making a half-hearted attempt at suicide, is her next lover and the one she seems most compatible with.

Elvis Tsui's animated performance as the eccentric gangster is the best thing here, but he is gone after the opening third. The rest merely induces yawns.

387. Girls Without Tomorrow 1992

(1992; David Lam Films) ★: 5/10. *Ying chiu lui long 1988 chi yee yin doi ying jiu lui long* (Cantonese), *Ying chao nu lang 1988 zhi er xian dai ying zhao nu lang* (Mandarin): "Call Girl 1988 Part 2: Modern Day Call Girl." Cinematographers: Abdul M. Rumjahn, Wong Po-man; Art Director: Bill Lui Cho-hung; Music: Lowell Lo Kwun-ting; Writers: Wong Chi, So Man-sing; Producer: David Lam Tak-luk; Action Director: Tony Leung Siu-hung; Directors: Wong Chi, David Lam Tak-luk. Cast: Carina Lau Kar-ling (Wa), Petrina Fung Bo-bo (Hung), May Lo Mei-mei (Yuen Ling-yuk), Vivian Chow Wei-man (Fong Siu-ling), Pauline Chan Po-lin (Eva), Waise Lee Chi-hung (Peter), Andy Hui Chi-on (Ling-yuk's New Pimp), Dior Cheng Yee-kin (Onn), John Ching Tung (Big Fly), Shum Wai (Simon), Michael Dinga (Wang), Lau Siu-ming (Li), Yung Sai-kit (Man with Eye Trouble), Ricky Yee Fan-wai (Drunk Actor). 1.85:1. VHS: Tai Seng. Import LD/VCD: Universe. 100 minutes.

An in-name-only sequel to co-director David Lam's **Call Girl 1988** (which also goes by the title **Girls Without Tomorrow**), this superficial but mildly diverting yarn is a glossy, sexy soap opera aimed as much at men as women. The ladies of the title are Wa (a seasoned but still sexy nightclub hostess whose years of on-the-job drinking are threatening her health), Hung (a middle-aged madam whose clientele have dropped off dramatically), Eva (who, because of financial troubles, often ends up with clients who brutalize her), TV star Siu-ling (who is forced to perform sexual favors for the station's president and is ashamed of Hung, who is her mother), and teenage hooker Ling-yuk (who is doing upwards of twenty tricks a day so she can raise enough money to attend school in Australia).

The drama becomes heavy-handed, descending into unintentional camp at times, but the performers (particularly Lau and Fung) are better than the material requires and the film is compulsively watchable. The S & M content during Eva's sessions is mild by adult standards but still not what one expects from a mainstream production. As "Hostess Dramas" go, Joseph Cheung's **Bet on Fire** is still the best of the bunch.

388. Gleam of Hope

(1994; Galaxy Films/Universe Film Production) ★: 5/10. *Yat sin saang gei* (Cantonese), *Yi xian sheng ji* (Mandarin): "A Thread of Living Chance." Cinematographer: Jimmy Wong Kam-shing; Art Director: Andy Lee Yiu-kwong; Music: Healthy Poon Kin-hong, Cacine Wong Kar-sin; Writers: James Fung Shui-hung, Leung Hung-wah; Producer: Leung Hung-wah; Action Director: Alan Lo

Kwok-wai; Director: Jeffrey Chiang Chia-chun. Cast: Anthony Wong Chau-sang (Inspector Kim Kuo-hao), Amy Kwok Oi-ming (Lu Yuen-mei), Yu Rongguang (Pai), John Ching Tung (Ho Chi). 1.85:1. VHS: Tai Seng. Import LD/VCD: Universe. 87 minutes. Also known as **Man on the Run**.

Anthony Wong has the Harrison Ford role, and Yu Rongguang does his version of Tommy Lee Jones' determined marshal in this imitation of **The Fugitive**, which was backed by the Universe Laser and Video company. HK Inspector Kim, in China to acquire evidence against drug smuggler Ho Chi, is framed for the murder of his mistress. Escaping custody while being transported to prison, Kim sneaks back into HK to clear his name. Hot on his trail is Inspector Pai, who soon learns of Kim's prior assignment and also takes up an investigation of Ho. While gathering evidence, Kim ascertains that the murder victim was working for Ho in order to pay for a kidney operation needed by her young son.

In addition to borrowing the plot of **The Fugitive**, entire scenes from that film are re-staged, with only minor variations (the dam confrontation now takes place in a sewer, and instead of a hospital, Wong sneaks into the Internal Affairs building). If you can overlook the dearth of originality, this remains a competently executed thriller, but the final revelation about the murder is too illogical and arbitrary to be satisfying.

389. The God of Cookery

(1996; The Star Overseas) ★: 6/10. *Jeung san* (Cantonese), *Shi shen* (Mandarin): "The Eating God." Cinematographer: Jingle Ma Cho-shing; Art Director: James Leung Wah-sang; Music: Ronald Ng Luk-shing; Writers: Stephen Chiau Sing-chi, Sammy Tsang Kan-cheung, Lo Man-sang; Producer: Yeung Kwok-fai; Action Director: Tony Poon Kin-kwan; Directors: Stephen Chiau Sing-chi, Lee Lik-chi. Cast: Stephen Chiau Sing-chi (Stephen Chow), Karen Mok Man-wai (Turkey), Vincent Kok Tak-chiu (Bull Tong), Ng Man-tat (The Old Man), Lee Siu-kei (Goosehead), Law Kar-ying (Competition MC), Nancy Sit Kar-yin (Herself), Yuen King-tan (Fortune Teller), Lau Yee-tat (Wet Dream), Bobby Yip King-sang (Swaying Triad), Liz Kong Hei-man (Reporter at Competition). Dolby Digital (DVD only). 1.85:1. VHS: Tai Seng. Import LD/VCD/DVD: Universe. 95 minutes.

Ruthless master chef Stephen Chow, aka "The God of Cookery," treats everyone with contempt, even though he has a horrible secret: All of his cooking is actually done by others. Fed up with his abuse, underling Bull Tong collaborates with Chow's partners to humiliate the chef in front of reporters, effectively ruining him in the eyes of the public. After going into seclusion, Chow collaborates with horribly disfigured triad street vendor Turkey on a new delicacy: Explosive Pissing Beef Balls! The food equivalent of superballs, these elastic treats unleash an explosion of flavor in the mouth of anyone who bites them. Having regained his old status, Chow prepares for the next God of Cookery competition through special training … at the Shaolin Monastery kitchen!

The comedy is largely hit-and-miss and the ending is a complete misfire, but the concept is very appealing and the sequences depicting the ecstasy brought on by the consumption of the EPBBs, and Chiau's torturous pre-competition training, are genuinely hilarious. Stephen Chiau does nothing special here (indeed, his trademark egomaniacal jerk act is getting a bit stale), but Karen Mok delivers a wonderful and daring comic performance (sporting hideous make-up and false teeth) that few HK actresses would ever agree to undertake. Christy Chung Lai-tai has a cameo. Plans for a Hollywood remake, directed by Chiau and starring Jim Carrey, were announced in 1998.

390. God of Gamblers

(1989; Win's Movie Production) ★: 6/10. *Dao san* (Cantonese), *Du shen* (Mandarin): "God of Gamblers." Cinematographers: David Chung Chi-man, Peter Pau Tak-hei; Art Director: Jason Mok Siu-kei; Music: Lowell Lo Kwun-ting; Producer: Jimmy Heung Wah-sing; Action Director: Wong Kwan; Writer-Director: Wong Jing. Cast: Chow Yun-fat (Ko Chun), Andy Lau Tak-wah (Knife), Joey Wang Tsu-hsien (Jane), Sharla Cheung Man (Janet), Charles Heung Wah-keung (Dragon), Lung Fong (Yee), Pau Hon-lam (Chan Kam-shing), Shing Fui-on (Big Mouth), Ng Man-tat (Brother Shing), Ronald Wong Pan (Crawl), Michiko Nishiwaki (Miss Chi), Michael Chow Man-kin (Casino Manager), Wong Jing (John in Bordello), Dennis Chan Kwok-san (Doctor). 1.85:1. VHS: Tai Seng (Edited version with poor subtitles). Import LD/VCD/DVD: Mei Ah (Edited version with poor subtitles). 124 minutes.

Following the success of **Casino Raiders**, writer-director Wong Jing concocted this equally successful vehicle which features one of Chow Yun-fat's most popular characters. Master gambler Ko Chun is known among his peers as the only unbeatable player to be found in the world. At the behest of a Japanese competitor, Chun agrees to face off against the villainous Chan Kam-shing, who is wanted by so many countries, he can only compete in international waters. Before this match can take place, Chun has an accident and bashes his head. Taken in by small-time conman Knife and his girlfriend Jane, Chun now suffers from amnesia and has the mentality of a child. He has not, however, lost his impeccable gambling skills, as Knife soon discovers. However, when one of the latter's schemes goes awry, a not-totally-functioning Chun must be enlisted to save him. Meanwhile, Chun's less than ethical underling Yee has decided to move in on his absent boss' woman and wealth. Unless Chun returns to normal quickly, he will lose everything.

As one can surmise from the synopsis, this is essentially **Rain Man** embellished with some terrific gunplay. Much of the film is only mildly amusing at best, but Chow Yun-fat commands the screen no matter what he is doing, giving the proceedings a major boost. The climactic card game is beautifully mounted and concludes with the sort of ingenious twist that helped make this genre so popular with HK audiences. The Tai Seng and Mei Ah versions are missing approximately ten minutes of footage from the original release, which can be found in the British and Taiwanese video editions. It was followed by a sequel (**God of Gamblers' Return**), a prequel (**God of Gamblers 3: The Early Stage**), some vaguely related follow-ups (see below), and a multitude of imitations.

391. God of Gamblers II

(1990; Win's Movie Production) ★: 7/10. *Do hap* (Cantonese), *Du xia* (Mandarin): "Knight of Gamblers." Cinematographer: David Chung Chi-man; Art Director: Jason Mok Siu-kei; Music: Lowell Lo Kwun-ting; Producer: Jimmy Heung Wah-sing; Action Director: Wong Kwan; Writer-Director: Wong Jing. Cast: Stephen Chiau Sing-chi (Sing), Andy Lau Tak-wah (Michael Chan, aka Little Knife), Charles Heung Wah-keung (Loong Ng), Sharla Cheung Man (Dream Lo), Ng Man-tat (Tat), Monica Chan Fat-yung (Loong Kau), Sin Lap-man (Hussein), John Ching Tung (Tai-kun), Shing Fui-on (Kau), Blackie Ko Shou-liang (Leader of Hitmen), Ronald Wong Pan (Michael's Buddy), Pau Hon-lam (Chan Kam-sing), Che-Kirk Wong Chi-keung (CN Tai), Ng Hong-ning (Big Guy in Bar), Wong Jing (Son of a Bitch). 1.85:1. VHS: Tai Seng. Import LD/VCD: Mei Ah. 100 minutes.

Following the surprise success of **All for the Winner**, Stephen Chiau and Ng Man-tat were quickly recruited to appear in this similar outing with **God of Gamblers**' stars Andy Lau and Charles Heung, who reprise their characters from that film. Michael Chan, the God of Gamblers' associate, has mastered almost all of his mentor's skills, earning himself the title "Knight of Gamblers." Amateur conmen Sing and Tat seek a meeting with the God of Gamblers in order to show him the former's ability to change cards, see through solid objects, and alter people's perceptions. Michael wants nothing to do with them, but when some hitmen attack, the three end up fleeing together. Out to avenge his foster father, Chan Kam-sing ("The Beast of Gamblers," who got fleeced in the first **God of Gamblers**), criminal Hussein begins impersonating the Knight of Gamblers in order to bilk unsuspecting millionaires who believe they are gambling for charity. Stacking the deck in his favor, Hussein has his casino wired with sophisticated electronic equipment, making cheating all but impossible, and has even recruited his own supernaturally gifted player, just in case.

The mix of the two different films' elements works very well for the most part, though the climactic match lacks the suspense of its counterpart in **God of Gamblers** and the clever twist resolution from **All for the Winner**. This was the first of several collaborations between Chiau and Wong, and, unlike most of their later films, the storyline is not put on the back burner for long stretches at a time. In addition to Chiau's shtick and some energetically rendered gunplay, there are great send ups of **Swordsman** and **A Terracotta Warrior**, and another of the comedian's dead-on Bruce Lee impersonations. **God of Gamblers III: Back to Shanghai** (a direct sequel to this one) followed next.

392. God of Gamblers III: Back to Shanghai

(1991; Win's Movie Production/Samico Films Production Co.) ★: 8/10. *Do hap II seung hoi taam do sing* (Cantonese), *Du xia II shang hai tan du sheng* (Mandarin): "Knight of Gamblers II: The Gambling Saint of Shanghai Beach." Cinematographer: Peter Pau Tak-hei; Art Director: Eddie Ma Poon-chiu; Music: Lowell Lo Kwun-ting; Producer: Jimmy Heung Wah-sing; Action Directors: Yuen Cheung-yan, Yuen Shun-yee, Kuk Hin-cho; Writer-Director: Wong Jing. Cast: Stephen Chiau Sing-chi (Chow Sing-cho), Gong Li (Yu-san/Yu-mong), Ng Man-tat (Tat/Chow Tai-fook), Ray Lui Leung-wai (Ding Lik), Sandra Ng Kwan-yu (Spring), Charles Heung Wah-keung (Brother Five), Wong Wan-si (The Japanese VIP), John Ching Tung (Tai-kun), Lung Fong (Wong Kam-kwai), Tien Feng (The Mayor), Barry Wong Ping-yiu (Commissioner Wong, aka Scissors Legs), Yeung Ching-ching (Ding's Female Bodyguard), Peter Chan Lung (Tiger Lui), Lau Shun (Eunuch Wei), Billy Chow Bei-lee (Japanese Soldier), Wong Jing (Fat Cop). 1.85:1. VHS: Tai Seng. Import LD/VCD/DVD: Mei Ah. 116 minutes.

A wonderful send-up of both **Back to the Future** and the classic **Shanghai Beach** TV series (which made stars out of Chow Yun-fat and Ray Lui Leung-wai; the latter reprises his role here), this remains one of Stephen Chiau's best outings to date. Following his humiliating defeat in the previous film, Mainland gambling master Tai-kun and his men try to murder Sing and Tat. They fail but, after Sing engages in a psychic duel with Tai-kun, the pair disappear in a burst of energy and Sing finds himself in 1937 Shanghai. There he meets Tat's effeminate grandfather, Chow Tai-fook, and Ding Lik, the powerful crimelord and confederate of the late Hui Man-keung. Sing accidentally kills Tiger Lui (the gangster who had murdered Hui the night before), earning him the favor of Ding, who is being challenged by another competitor, Wong Kam-kwai. Sing falls head over heels for beautiful socialite Yu-san, but it is actually her twin sister, Yu-mong (who has the IQ of a five-year-old) that he ends up dating. Wong allies himself with a Japanese VIP in a plot to seize Ding's casino using their secret weapon: Tai-kun. Sing is able to save the day, but a re match is announced and the opposition produces a weapon that even Sing may not be able to counter: the *French* God of Gamblers.

Shanghai Beach (or **The Bund** as it is officially known in English) is quite difficult to see these days and not available with English subtitles, so most Western viewers will not be able to appreciate most of the references to it here. Regardless, much of the humor is readily accessible, and the production design and costumes are gorgeous, making the silly goings-on all the more enjoyable. The twins subplot is overly contrived, but it is great fun watching Mainland art movie star Gong Li romping through the scenery as the dim-witted but ever-smiling, Yu-mong (she would appear again opposite Chiau two years later in **Flirting Scholar**). Writer-director Wong Jing adheres well enough to the doctrines of time travel movies, incorporating some wonderful anachronisms (Sing has a cell phone with him and can call people in the present, and there is a terrific musical parody of McDonald's restaurants), and the ending delivers the sort of twist that makes the best of these gambling films so satisfying. Writer/actor Barry Wong appears briefly in a hilarious reprise of his cement-headed cop character from the **Fight Back to School** films. Sharla Cheung Man also has a fitting cameo.

393. God of Gamblers 3: The Early Stage

(1996; Golden Harvest/BOB & Partners Company/Golden Movies International) ★: 8/10. *Do san 3 chi siu nin do san* (Cantonese), *Du shen 3 zhi shao nian du shen* (Mandarin): "God of Gamblers 3: The Young God of Gamblers." Cinematographer: Arthur Wong Ngok-tai; Art Director: Ringo Fung Kai-fai; Music: Peter Kam Pui-tat, Lau Cho-tak, Lam Chi-yeung; Action Directors: Dion Lam Dik-on, Ma Yuk-shing; Writer-Producer-Director: Wong Jing. Cast: Leon Lai Ming (Ko Chun), Anita Yuen Wing-yee (Sister Seven), Jordan Chan Siu-chun (Lone Ng), Gigi Leung Wing-kei (Hing), Francis Ng Chun-yu (Ko Ngo), Chung King-fai (Kent), Cheung Tat-ming (So), Elvis Tsui Kam-kong (Tai-chin), Ng Chi-hung (Mo Kau), Ngai Sing (Wolf), Moses Chan Ho (Soto). 1.85:1. VHS: World Video. Import LD/VCD/DVD: Universe. 102 minutes. Also known as **Legend of the God of Gamblers** (Title for dubbed version).

On paper, this does not sound like a promising project: Leon Lai, a handsome but not especially charismatic actor/singer playing the legendary Ko Chun in the years prior to the time depicted in the original **God of Gamblers**. However, give credit to both Lai and writer-director Wong Jing: The resulting film is surprisingly good, and while he may not be Chow Yun-fat, Lai makes for a perfectly acceptable substitute. The film opens in 1969 with the young Chun being purchased by master gambler Kent. The story then switches to 1986 as Chun's future bodyguard, Lone Ng, proves his mettle by single-handedly dispatching eleven attackers. Impressed by his abilities, cocky Sister Seven (who once encountered Chun as a child but hasn't seen him since) hires Lone, and the pair meet up with Chun at a card game one night. A "God of Gamblers" competition is going to be held to find the individual qualified to run South East Asia's casinos, and Kent chooses Chun over his other two experts, Hing, and Ngo, to represent him. Chun is deeply in love with Hing and Ngo openly resents him for it. During the tournament finals, Chun is betrayed and this sets the stage for the sort of classic, high stakes finale these films are famous for.

Along the way, we see how Chun acquired his jade pinkie ring, why he loves chocolate so much, and why he gels his hair before a match. The requisite twists and turns are satisfying, as is the outcome, which features one of the series' best resolutions. As mentioned, Lai does well by the role, but it is Jordan Chan (exuding controlled rage and strength) who walks away with this entry. He's sensational and imbues the part with more physicality than Charles Heung, using martial arts skills and not just guns to take out the enemy. There is one major problem, though: The way Lai and Chan's characters meet here completely contradicts their first encounter in the original film!

394. God of Gamblers' Return

(1994; Win's Movie Production) ★: 7/10. *Dao san 2* (Cantonese), *Du shen 2* (Mandarin): "God of Gamblers 2." Cinematographer: Horace Wong Wing-hang; Art Director: Cyrus Ho Kim-hung; Music: Lowell Lo Kwun-ting; Producers: Charles Heung Wah-keung, Jimmy Heung Wah-sing; Action Directors: Yuen Bun, Ma Yuk-shing; Writer-Director: Wong Jing. Cast: Chow Yun-fat (Ko Chun), Tony Leung Kar-fai ("Little Trumpet"), Jacqueline Wu Chien-lien ("Little Guitar"), Chingmy Yau Suk-ching (Hoi Tong), Elvis Tsui Kam-kong (Kok Ching-chung), Wu Hsin-kuo (Chau), Charles Heung Wah-keung (Lung Wu), Xie Miao (Tong Siu-yuen), Pau Hon-lam (Chan Kam-shing), Blackie Ko Shou-liang (Hoi On), Sharla Cheung Man (Yau), Wong Kam-kong (Cheung Po-sing), Ken Lo Wai-kwong (Hoi's Man). Dolby Stereo. 1.85:1. VHS: Tai Seng. Import LD/VCD/DVD: Mei Ah. 124 minutes. Also known as **Battle of Champions**.

Not so much a director as a "packager of entertainment," Wong Jing represents the flipside of directors like John Woo and Wong Kar-wai. Absurdly prolific, he often has several productions going at once and is known to commute from location to location, setting up shots and then leaving the rest to his A.D.s. Consequently, films bearing his name are all over the map stylistically, combining conflicting approaches and wildly contrary swings in mood and tone. However, for all his shortcomings as an artist, Wong has a very keen sense of what HK movie patrons want to see, and he gives it to them in grand fashion: big stars, big action, high melodrama, and low comedy. His films can be very entertaining if you like the performers and approach the experience with the proper mindset. **God of Gamblers' Return**, the *official* sequel to his 1989 blockbuster, is one of Wong's best efforts to date, delivering all the essentials in a slick, robust and disarming manner. Following his substantial triumph at the end of the first feature, Ko Chun (Chow Yun-fat, looking a little on the pudgy side) and his pregnant wife Yau (Sharla Cheung, who played a different character last time out) are living a life of luxury in the South of France. Their idyllic paradise is invaded by the forces of psychopathic Taiwanese gambler Chau (Wu Hsin-kuo, appropriately speaking all of his lines in Mandarin), who seeks to challenge the now-retired Ko to a match. Finding only Yau at home, Chau kills her unborn baby, leaving Yau mortally wounded. In her dying words to Ko, she makes him vow not to reveal his identity or gamble for one year (a ridiculous plot contrivance, typical of Wong's films). Eleven and a half months later, a vacationing Ko befriends Hoi On, the head of a powerful Taiwan triad faction. When hitmen employed by Chau kill Hoi, Ko escapes to the Mainland with the gangster's young son (**The New Legend of Shaolin**'s Xie Miao) in tow. Eluding the local security forces, the pair hook up with brother-and-sister scam artists "Little Trumpet" and "Little Guitar" and manage to secure passage to Taiwan. There they meet Hoi's daughter Tong, setting the stage for a decisive match between Ko and Chau. The stakes: $16 *billion*! Some behind-the-scenes skullduggery and a paranormal villain figure in the outcome.

Like many of Wong's movies, the storyline's primary goal is to facilitate the inclusion of as many famous cast members as possible, with their relevance to the plot being of secondary concern (a major component in the first half, Xie Miao's character simply disappears about halfway through). Regardless, **God of Gamblers' Return** is terrific HK pop entertainment and essentially critic proof; delighted audiences made it the top-grossing HK film of 1994. How much you will tolerate its foolish aspects is in direct correlation to your knowledge of, and affection for, the players. This is hardly a challenging assignment for Chow but it provides him with ample opportunities to display his charm and that trademark grin. That's all he needs and it's all we need. Tony Leung Kar-fai manages to wring solid laughs out of some genuinely silly material, and Jacqueline Wu handles both the comedic and sombre aspects of her role wonderfully well (she and Chow first appeared together in a TV commercial and they make a very photogenic couple). There is less gunplay than last time but it is well-choreographed, and, in addition to the more obvious jests, there's also a great joke at the expense of actor/former triad enforcer Michael Chan Wai-man. Bonnie Fu Yuk-ching ("Virgin" in **Full Contact**) and Law Kar-ying have cameos, and co-producer Charles Heung Wah-keung reprises his role as Lung, Ko's stoic Vietnamese protector.

God of Guns *see* **Hard Boiled**

The God of Killers *see* **Story of Woo Viet**

The Gods Must Be Crazy in Hong Kong *see* **Crazy Hong Kong**

395. The Golden Girls

(1995; Win's Entertainment) ★: 8/10. *Saan shui yau seung fung* (Cantonese), *Shan shui you xiang feng* (Mandarin): "Mountain and Water Eventually Meet." Cinematographer: Apple Kwan Pak-suen; Art Director: Ben Luk Man-wah; Music: Clarence Hui Yuen; Writers: Joe Ma Wai-ho, Cheung Chi-sing; Producer: Cheung Chi-sing; Director: Joe Ma Wai-ho. Cast: Lau Ching-wan (Chun Wei), Anita Yuen Wing-yee (Mei-ball), Ada Choi Siu-fan (Lulu Shum), Francis Ng Chun-yu (Wong Siu-yi), Paulyn Suen Kai-kwun (May Chu), Cheung Tat-ming (Cousin JP), Wong Yat-fei (Lo Kim-choi), Manfred Wong (Director of "Cleopatra"), Michael Tse Tin-wah (Fey Leading Man), Vincent Kok Tak-chiu (Kent). 1.85:1. VHS/LD: World Video. Import LD/VCD: Mei Ah. 94 minutes.

This wonderfully appealing romantic comedy is an affectionate valentine to HK cinema from a more innocent age. In 1965 budding actresses Mei-ball, Lulu, and May struggle to reach the top. Of the three, Mei-ball is clearly the most talented, but it is Lulu who ends up becoming a star. Screenwriter Chun Wei falls hopelessly in love with Mei-ball, who is stuck playing nameless extras because she won't give in to her directors' lecherous advances. Tired of her situation, Mei-ball heads to Borneo. When she comes back a few months later, she finds that Lulu and Wei are living together. Wei still loves her, however, and, when given a chance to direct, he casts Mei-ball as the *male* lead of "The Butterfly Lovers" (a Chinese fable, adapted by Tsui Hark in 1994 as **The Lovers**). The film is a smash, making Mei-ball an overnight star, eclipsing Lulu and threatening their friendship. However, it is Wei's unflagging attraction to Mei-ball that is the real hurdle.

Even if you cannot catch all of the in-jokes (Mei-ball's success at playing male leads is a reference to actress Yam Kin-fai, who became a household name thanks to her numerous cross-dressing roles), it is easy to become swept up in this extremely amiable film. Yuen and Lau re-ignite their chemistry from **C'est La Vie, Mon Cheri**, and Francis Ng has a hilarious cameo as an egomaniacal leading man who tries to turn

"The Butterfly Lovers" into an action movie. The production design, costumes, make-up, and hair-styles look spot-on perfect, as do the recreations of old movies.

396. Golden Queens Commando

(1984; IFD Films & Arts) ★: 5/10. Chinese titles unknown. Cinematographer: Lam Man-kam; Art Director: Ching Kong; Music: Not Original; Writer: Benny Ho; Producer: Joseph Lai; Director: Chu Yen-ping. Cast: Brigitte Lin Ching-hsia (Black Fox), Sally Yeh Chian-wen (Dynamite), Elsa Yeung Wai-san (Black Cat), Silvia Pang Suet-man (Quick Silver), Hilda Lau Hou-yee (Brandy), Sophia Ching (Sugar), Teresa Tsui (Amazon). 2.35:1. VHS: Boomerang Films (Dubbed). 89 minutes. Also known as **Commando Amazon** (Boomerang title), **Jackie Chan's Crime Force** (Arena/Xenon title).

This utterly insane Taiwanese production is seemingly set in World War II but looks more like some parallel universe where every decade from the 20th century has merged together into a bizarre melting pot of cultural influences. It's all in service of the old **Seven Samurai/Dirty Dozen** formula, with martial arts acrobatics, copious gunplay, and odd spaghetti western elements providing the action. Government undercover agent Black Fox (who sports an eyepatch) gets herself arrested so that she may recruit six of her fellow female prisoners (all of whom are sentenced to death and each an expert of some kind) for a secret mission to destroy an enemy chemical lab. They successfully break out of the prison camp and head towards the objective, but several obstacles must be surmounted first.

What the film lacks in originality it makes up for in unabashed absurdity (would you believe a story that incorporates an alcoholic samurai, a jungle girl in a leopard skin outfit, a cardsharp with a gun hidden in her bible, a chainsmoking explosives expert in tight shorts, and a Chinese Southern belle?!) and sheer exuberance, boasting a prison break, a food fight, battles on horseback, booby traps, graverobbers masquerading as ghosts, and combat with many different styles of weapons. No less frenzied is the soundtrack, which steals music from **The Good, the Bad and the Ugly, Battlestar Galactica, Dressed to Kill, Maniac, Tron,** and **My Name Is Nobody**, among others. The English dubbing is awful but fits the cartoonish goings-on and adds to the fun. Incidentally, Arena/Xenon's attempt to hoodwink unsuspecting viewers into believing this to be a Jackie Chan movie is consumer fraud at its height. The company has simply included a Jackie Chan/Sally Yeh music video on the tape as justification for their retitling. This was followed by the equally wacky **Pink Force Commando**.

397. Golden Swallow

(1987; Alan and Eric Films) ★: 7/10. *Gam yin chi* (Cantonese), *Jin yan zi* (Mandarin): "Golden Swallow." Cinematographer: Henry Chan Chun-kit; Art Director: Hai Chung-man; Music: Law Wing-fai; Producer: Eric Tsang Chi-wai; Action Directors: Phillip Kwok Tsui, Yuen Bun; Director: Ko Sing-pui. Cast: Cherie Chung Cho-hung (Hsiao-hseuh/Lu Hsiao-ping), Anthony Wong Yiu-ming (Lo Chih-chiu), Richard Ng Yiu-hon (Hsiang Yu), Eric Tsang Chi-wai (Hsiang Tso), Norman Tsui Siu-keung (Feng Ching-tien), Nat Chan Pak-cheung (Boatman), Chen Jing (Bandit Leader). 1.85:1. VHS: Tai Seng. Import LD/VCD: Ocean Shores. 96 minutes.

One of the first imitations of **A Chinese Ghost Story** to hit theaters, **Golden Swallow** follows that Ching Siu-tung hit closely but has rewards of its own. While travelling across the countryside, scholar Lo Chih-chiu saves a golden sparrow from some children. Unbeknownst to Chih-chiu, the bird transforms into Hsiao Hsueh, a beautiful spirit who is forced to acquire victims for a powerful, soul-draining demon. Hsueh and Chih-chiu fall in love, but the demon discovers their affair and tries to kill the scholar. Hsueh saves Chih-chiu's life and the demon agrees to let him live on the condition that he never reveals anything about the spirit world to anyone. Some time later, Chih-chiu encounters Lu Hsiao-ping, a young woman who, unbeknownst to him, is actually Hsiao-hsueh. The pair gradually fall in love and marry, with a daughter following soon after. Their happiness is shattered one day when Chih-chiu accidentally breaks his vow of silence, prompting the demon to take Hsiao-hsueh and his child away. His only hope to save them from eternal damnation lies in the hands of the powerful swordsman Feng Ching-tien, who fought the creature years before.

As beautifully designed as its model (both the work of celebrated art director Hai Chung-man), **Golden Swallow** is consistently dazzling from a visual standpoint, and its plotting corresponds more to the sort of old-school storytelling one associates with the classics of Chinese literature. The costumes, locations, and special effects are also first rate. The one area where it falls short is the central romance. While attractive, Cherie Chung and Anthony Wong Yiu-ming just do not have the same chemistry that Leslie Cheung and Joey Wang have in **A Chinese Ghost Story**, so the main dramatic conflict of the narrative does not generate the intended anxiety. In an unusual bit of casting, Eric Tsang and Richard Ng provide amusing comic relief as rival Taoist swordsmen who are forever arguing over who has the superior abilities. Memorable line: "There's only one type of man ... the edible ones." Talented composer Law Wing-fai (**Dream Lovers**) is credited with the music but there are also cues lifted from the Hollywood films **No Way Out** and **Near Dark**.

Goliathon *see* **The Mighty Peking Man**

398. The Good, the Bad and the Beauty

(1988) ★: 6/10. *Gwai ma bo biu chaak mei yan* (Cantonese), *Gui ma bao biao zei mei ren* (Mandarin): "Zany Bodyguard, Beautiful Thief." Cinematographer: Yu Chik-lim; Art Director: Liu Kin-ming; Music: Wong Fuk-ling; Action Director: Wong Kwan; Writer-Producer-Director: Frankie Chan Fan-kei. Cast: Frankie Chan Fan-kei (Inspector Ho Chun-sun), Cherie Chung Cho-hung (Ko Sau-ping), Kent Cheng Chuk-see (Inspector Kent Tang Tai-kit), Bill Tung Biu (Uncle Mark), Anthony Chan Yau (Chan), Maria Cordero (Fence). 1.85:1. VHS: Tai Seng. Import VCD: Mega Star. 97 minutes.

As is often the case with Frankie Chan's films, this action-comedy is all over the map, alternating between goofy humor, overwrought drama, and brain-splattering violence. The end result is jarring (to say the least) but it's never dull. Chan and Kent Cheng play mismatched police officers (who are also less-than-compatible roommates) assigned to protect witness Cherie Chung from a mob death warrant. In order to protect herself, Chung (who was forced to smuggle diamonds while working as a stewardess) pretends to be slightly out of her head, which leads rotund bachelor Cheng to fall in love with her. Abetted by Chan's petulant father, the three dodge one hit squad after another while protecting the one remaining (and invaluable) diamond in her possession.

There is no shortage of action and the stuntwork is first rate, but some sequences are staged in such a frantic manner it is not always easy to tell who is doing what to whom. The climax (which features speedboats, gasoline, and dynamite) makes no sense at all, but does offer up a genuine display of showmanship. An uncharacteristically restrained Dicky Cheung Wai-kin co-stars as one of Chan and Cheng's fellow officers.

399. Goodbye Hero

(1990; Filmagica Productions) ★: 5/10. *Waan meng seung hung* (Cantonese), *Wan ming shuang xiong* (Mandarin): "Two Heroes Who Risk Their Lives." Cinematographer: Kin Lee Kin-keung; Art Directors: Sin Ngai-lung, Yank Wong Yan-kwai; Music: Joseph Chan Wing-leung; Writer: Lee Chi-ngai; Action Directors: Tang Wing-yiu, Cheng Tai-kim; Producer-Director: Jacob Cheung Chi-leung. Cast: Derek Yee Tung-sing (Tony), David Wu Tai-wai (Jerome), Vivian Chow Wei-man (Tony's Sister), Chin Siu-ho (Panzer), Loletta Lee Lai-chun (Panzer's Wife), Lam Ching-ying (Frank), Ching Siu-tung (The Director), Petrina Fung Bo-bo (Tony's Friend), Cora Miao Qian-ren (Tony's Wife). 1.85:1. Ultra Stereo. VHS: World Video. Import LD: Star Entertainment (No Subtitles). Running time unknown.

A routine drama, **Goodbye Hero** nonetheless provides an interesting look at the life of HK stuntmen. Tony is an industry veteran/motorcycle champ who is carrying a lot on his shoulders: He is not getting any younger, his wife has left him and moved to Canada, and he accidentally crippled one of his fellow stuntmen while doing a car stunt. Cocky young up-and-comer Jerome starts hounding Tony to teach him all the tricks of the trade, and after some initial discord, the two gradually develop a brotherly relationship. They pool their respective talents and provide some spectacular stunts for the picture being made by Jerome's uncle, but tragedy strikes and Tony must make a crucial decision about his future.

Neither the dramatic conflicts nor their resolutions are up to director Jacob Cheung's usual standards (though the final result is still a step up from both **Ah Kam** and **Bloody Money**, which cover similar subject matter), and the storyline offers no real surprises. Teen idols David Wu and Vivian Chow (the latter cast as a grease monkey in an unsuccessful attempt to change her girl-next-door image) are their usual plastic selves, but Derek Yee gives a fine character performance in the lead and there is a rare in-front-of-the-camera role for master stuntman/director Ching Siu-tung (as the director of the movie-within-the-movie). Interesting side note: Five years after starring in this film, Yee went on to direct the popular Andy Lau/Gigi Leung vehicle **Full Throttle**. That film concerns an aging motorcycle racing champ with myriad personal problems and a young up-and-comer out to challenge him for his top spot ... played by David Wu! Coincidence?

400. Goodbye, My Friend

(1988; Chien Hua Film Company) ★: 2/10. *Joi gin ying hung* (Cantonese), *Zai jian ying xiong* (Mandarin): "Goodbye Hero." Cinematographer: Sung Kwong-wah; Music: Not Original; Action Director: Yip Wai-keung; Directors: Ho Lin-chow, Jass S. Cast: Chow Yun-fat (Hung), Kenneth Tsang Kong (Lung), Cheng Tai-lun, Wong Wai-leung, Yu Chi-wai. 2.35:1. VHS: World Video (Poor Subtitles?), Arena/Xenon. 81 minutes. Also known as **Shanghai Killer** (Arena/Xenon title).

This exceedingly tedious thriller was produced in Thailand in the early '80s and later spiced up with new footage. It was then released in HK in 1988 in order to cash in on Chow Yun-fat's subsequent fame. Fortunately, local audiences knew a scam when they saw one and stayed away, causing it to close after only a week. Unfolding during the second World War, the film opens with a meeting of a triad group, led by Master Lung (this superfluous footage sets up what follows and is the extra material mentioned above). We then segue into the main story involving Chow's character. When his parents are killed, Hung returns from Shanghai to avenge their murder, which has been attributed to a group of fanatics called "The Blood Sect." More murders follow, while Hung is forced to act without the cooperation of the local authorities. Eventually he does join forces with the police in an all-out offensive against the cult which unfolds inside their booby trap-laden lair.

Unfortunately, said events unfold with no style or urgency, and after a reel or two, most viewers will have stopped caring. The Thailand locations and accoutrements are novel at least, but certainly not enough to justify a rental or the waste of 81 minutes. The soundtrack includes music pilfered from **Re-Animator** and **The Terminator**. The running time listed above refers to the Taiwan version released on the New Ship label, which has cropped subtitles that occasionally drop offscreen.

401. Goodbye My Love

(1986; Cinema City Co.) ★: 2/10. *Ok naam* (Cantonese), *E nan* (Mandarin): "Evil Man." Cinematographer: Michael Ma Koon-wah; Art Director: Chung Yau; Music: Phil Chan Fei-lap; Writers: Frankie Chan Fan-kei, Wong Kar-wai; Action Director: Wong Kwan; Producer-Director: Frankie Chan Fan-kei. Cast: Joan Chen Chong (Ling Ti), Frankie Chan Fan-kei (Chung Wu-erh), Lau Chi-wing (Officer Lau), Wong Wan-si (Aunt May), Woo Fung (Alan Teng Li-chun), Shum Wai (Wei), Ken Boyle (Diamond Seller), Anders Nelsson (Dr. A. Nelson), Wong Ching (Man with Watches), Shih Kien (Man in Picture). 1.85:1. VHS: Tai Seng. Import LD: Golden Cinema City. Import VCD: Mega Star. 105 minutes. Also known as **Everlasting Rhapsody** (Tai Seng title).

Frankie Chan is a man of many talents but he has absolutely no aptitude for drama, as proven once again by this tiresome drivel, which must not rank high on co-writer Wong Kar-wai's list of credits. Diagnosed with terminal cancer and given only six months to live, Wu Ling-ti must locate someone to look after her young brother and sister, now that their father has died. After finding a rich, middle-aged man, Ling-ti makes arrangements for her siblings' future but is terribly unhappy about leaving them behind. The answer to her dilemma may just lie with flat mate/smuggler Chung Wu-erh, who is always just one small step ahead of the law.

Goodbye My Love starts off as a sophomoric comedy with a few extraneous action scenes and then becomes a sappy melodrama with an entirely unnecessary climactic shootout. The one consistent factor is the sheer, heavy-handed stupidity of it all. This was Mainland-born actress Joan Chen's HK film debut, and it gives one a new appreciation for the mostly awful Hollywood movies she did later on.

The Great Adventurer *see* **The Adventurers**

402. The Great Conqueror's Concubine

(1994; Great Dragon Films Company) ★: 7/10. *Sai choh ba wong* (Cantonese), *Xi chu ba wang* (Mandarin): "The West Zhu Tyrant Emperor." Cinematographer: Cheng Siu-keung; Art Director: Horace Ma Kwong-wing; Music: James Wong Jim, Romeo Diaz; Writers: Stephen Shin Kei-yin, Hiu Wo, Shi Yanping; Producer: Zhang Yimou; Action Director: Benz Kong To-hoi; Director: Stephen Shin Kei-yin. Cast: Ray Lui Leung-wai (Xiang Yu), Zhang Fengyi (Liu Bang), Gong Li (Lu Zhi), Rosamund Kwan Chi-lam (Lady Yu Miao-ge), Lau Shun (Fan Zeng), Wu Hsin-kuo (Zi Qi), Elvis Tsui Kam-kong (Zhong Li-mei), Chen Sung-yung (Fan Kuai), Yeh Chuan-chen (Courtesan). 2.35:1. VHS: Tai Seng. Import LD/VCD: Star Entertainment. Import DVD: China Star. 87 minutes.

403. The Great Conqueror's Concubine II

(1994; Great Dragon Films Company) ★: 7/10. *Sai choh ba wong* (Cantonese),

Xi chu ba wang (Mandarin): "The West Zhu Tyrant Emperor." Same cast and crew, credits as Part One. 2.35:1. VHS: Tai Seng. Import LD/VCD: Star Entertainment. Import DVD: China Star. 94 minutes.

Released theatrically and on video in two parts, this lavish HK-China co-production is reminiscent of the "Cast of Thousands" epics by directors Akira Kurosawa and Anthony Mann, offering the sort of spectacle that has become all but cost-prohibitive for Western filmmakers. Set primarily in 206 B.C., Part One charts the uneasy alliance undertaken by the respective forces of military officers Xiang Yu and Liu Bang in their bid to topple the oppressive Qin Dynasty. Not long after this goal has been attained, Liu's ambitious wife, Lu Zhi, convinces her husband to turn against Xiang in a bid for absolute power. Guided more by emotional impulse and love for his concubine, Lady Yu, than the voice of experience offered by his chief advisor, Xiang makes numerous logistical errors which eventually prove devastating. Part II charts his decline as he falls victim to the machinations of Lu Zhi, who uses the naive Lady Yu's hold over her lover to turn the tide in Liu Bang's favor.

As is usually the case with HK prints, the English subtitles have been translated much too literally from the original Chinese, resulting not only in garbled sentences but also little in the way of historical background. The latter is hardly surprising as the events depicted here are more-or-less common knowledge for the target audience. Fortunately, the main narrative is easily appreciated, as it parallels the plotting in several classics of Western literature, most notably via the character of Lu Zhi (clearly cut from the same deceitful cloth as Lady Macbeth). Blessed with this most colorful role, Mainland star Gong Li turns in a memorably wicked performance, while her HK counterpart, Rosamund Kwan, is left with little to do other than look radiant and/or pensive (reportedly, the two were originally cast in each other's roles but switched at the behest of producer Zhang Yimou). Mainland actor Zhang Fengyi does a fine job as the urbane and duplicitous Liu Bang, while HK star Ray Lui is heroic and authoritative in a role that is the antithesis of the triad kingpins he specializes in playing. After years at the helm of far more modest endeavors, director Stephen Shin makes a creditable transition here, handling the quieter, character-driven moments adeptly while still keeping the story moving along. The battle scenes often impress by their sheer magnitude, and cinematographer Cheng Siu-keung deserves much credit; the sequences depicting the fiery destruction of the opulent Qin palace and the mass, premature burial of 200,000 enemy soldiers are truly striking. Veteran character actor Kwan Hoi-shan has a bizarre supporting role in the first part as a gay servant.

Great Hero of China *see* **Martial Art Master Wong Fai Hung** [*sic*]

404. The Greatest Lover

(1988; Golden Harvest/Johnny Mak Productions) ★: 5/10. *Gung chi doh ching* (Cantonese), *Gong zi duo qing* (Mandarin): "Susceptible High Official." Cinematographer: Peter Pau Tak-hei; Music: Joseph Chan Wing-leung; Writers: Johnny Mak Dong-hung, Stephen Siu Yeuk-yuen; Producer: Stephen Siu Yeuk-yuen; Director: Clarence Fok Yiu-leung. Cast: Chow Yun-fat (Locomotive), Anita Mui Yim-fong (Anita), Elizabeth Lee Mei-fung (Fiona), Nina Li Chi (Lychee), Pauline Wong Siu-fung (Fong), Eric Tsang Chi-wai (Skyscraper), Shing Fui-on (Chicken Noodles), Wong Ching (See), Wong Jing (Tung), Sandra Ng Kwan-yu (Miss Hong Kong Wannabe), Yuen Wah (Mainland Fink). Dolby Digital (DVD only). 1.85:1. VHS: Tai Seng (No Subtitles). Import LD: Star Entertainment (No Subtitles). Import VCD: Universe (No Subtitles). Import DVD: Universe. 115 minutes.

Up until recently, this broad comedy was difficult to find with translation (the Universe VCD is supposed to have subtitles, but does not) but is still fairly entertaining even without any English. Locomotive, Skyscraper, and Chicken Noodles are three Mainland bumblers who swim to HK to commit a "Big Circle" bank robbery. They become separated, and Locomotive ends up at a high society function, where he sees "Headman" See humiliated by the glamorous beauty Lychee and her partner in snobbery, Fong. Seeking revenge, See hires the dowdy Locomotive and has him receive lessons in gentility from Anita (Mui, modelling every glamorous outfit the production could acquire), a decidedly unconventional teacher who sports a riding crop. See's plan is to have Locomotive dazzle and then disgrace Lychee. Transformed into "Nelson Chow from America," Loco is an immediate hit, winning over both Lychee *and* Fong. He subsequently leaves them both at the altar and starts courting another affluent beauty, Fiona, whom See also wants to embarrass. Loco, however, refuses to follow through on the deal, and See exposes him as a fraud in front of Fiona and her wealthy friends. Although Fiona is still willing to marry him, Loco finally realizes that there is only one true love in his heart: (you guessed it) Anita.

The denouement is just as corny as it sounds (and might actually be harder to bear *with* translation), but Chow has ample opportunities to display his charm, and a good percentage of the humor is universal and easily appreciated. The character names listed above come from the English synopsis on the VCD cover.

405. Green Hat

(1995) ★: 3/10. *Daai luk miu dik lui yan* (Cantonese), *Dai lu mao de nu ren* (Mandarin): "Woman Wearing a Green Hat." Cinematographer: Tam Chi-wai; Art Directors: Bill Lui Cho-hung, Raymond Lam Chi-wai; Music: Richard Lo Sai-kit; Writer-Producer-Director: Alfred Cheung Kin-ting. Cast: Alfred Cheung Kin-ting (John/Sean), Jade Leung Ching (Pearl/Joyce), Farini Cheung Yui-ling, Dick Cho Kin-nam, Kong Man-seng. 1.85:1. VHS: World Video. Import LD/VCD: Fitto Mobile. 89 minutes.

This forgettable relationship comedy is of interest only for its casting of action star Jade Leung in a comic role as Pearl, the nerdy wife of John (director Cheung), an equally unexciting doctor. After five years together their marriage is sour, so the two accept the advice of friends and go out on the prowl in disguise. When John (as an artist named "Sean") unknowingly hits on the now-sexy Pearl (as "Joyce") one night at a bar, she decides to go along with the ruse and arranges a follow-up date. Predictably, "Sean" makes a complete ass of himself, and Pearl decides to continue seeing him in this guise in order to see just how far he will go.

While pleasant, the proceedings are never genuinely funny or credible (John cannot recognize his wife because she is wearing contact lenses, make-up, and a different hairstyle?), and the pacing is leaden. Leung is the best thing here, giving a committed and convincing performance in the sort of role that Carol Cheng Yu-ling built her career on. She deserves another opportunity to showcase this previously hidden talent; hopefully, she will get that chance in a better vehicle than this one. The Chinese title is an expression meaning a woman who is being unfaithful to her husband.

406. The Green Hornet

(1994; Sil-Metropole Organisation) ★: 1/10. *Cheng fung hap* (Cantonese), *Qing feng xia* (Mandarin): "Green Hornet Hero." Cinematographer: Ricky Lau Koon-wai; Art Director: Chen Zizhong; Music: Not Original; Writer: Zhu Weiguang; Action Director: Chen Wendi; Producer-Director: Lam Ching-ying. Cast: Chin Kar-lok

(Dong/The Green Hornet), Yu Rongguang (Police Captain), Esther Kwan Wing-ho (Tom), Lam Ching-ying (Uncle). VHS: World Video. Import LD/VCD: Fitto Mobile. 88 minutes.

In spite of what is implied by the title, the famous comic book hero is nowhere to be found here. Instead, Chin Kar-lok plays The Green Hornet's *partner* Kato in this depressingly poor action-comedy directed by the great character actor Lam Ching-ying (who also has a supporting role). Paced like molasses in winter and apparently made on a budget lower than one episode from the 1960s TV series, this Mainland production is precisely the sort of effort that cynics expected to be the norm once HK reverted back to China. When he is not fighting crime on the docks, the masked hero is really a country boy named Dong who lives with his two uncles and their large collection of pigeons. Tom, a crusading girl reporter from HK, is rescued by the Hornet one day and falls in love with him. Trying to get pictures and a story on the mystery man, she constantly needs to be rescued from the villainous "Rat" and his band of slavers. However, a gang of caucasian terrorists called "The Black Sun" are about to put the Hornet to his greatest test ever.

Taking amusing liberties with the comic book's premise, the film states that there have been Green Hornets dating back at least as far as *The Qin Dynasty*, all of whom were undone because they broke "the rule" and fraternized with women! The previous Hornet, Dong's teacher, was none other than Bruce Lee himself(!), whose "death by natural causes" was actually a penalty for breaking "the rule" (you guessed it: *women*). Chin and Yu Rongguang are superior martial artists but a good portion of the kung fu here is undercranked to the point of looking absurd. The remainder of the choreography is just plain inept and poorly edited to boot. As for the screenplay, if you can't say something nice...

407. Green Snake

(1993; Seasonal Film Corporation/ Film Workshop) ★: 9/10. *Ching se* (Cantonese), *Qing she* (Mandarin): "Green Snake." Cinematographer: Ko Chiu-lam; Art Director: Bill Lui Cho-hung; Music: James Wong Jim, Mark Lui Chung-tak; Writer-Producer-Director: Tsui Hark. Cast: Maggie Cheung Man-yuk (Green), Joey Wang Tsu-hsien (White), Zhao Wenzhou (Fa-hai), Wu Hsin-kuo (Hsui-xien), Tien Feng (Spider). 2.35:1. VHS/LD: Tai Seng (Poor Subtitles). Import LD/VCD: Mei Ah. 98 minutes.

A classic Chinese folktale about two snake sisters, White (*Bok*) and Green (*Ching*), their experiences living alongside humans, and White's doomed love affair with a naive scholar, forms the basis for this dazzling period fantasy, one of director Tsui Hark's grandest endeavors in the genre to date. The fable is one of the "Four Great Tales of China," so it is fitting that each of "The Three Chinas" has contributed an adaptation. In 1976 Mainland director Sha Dan created a Peking Opera musical version called ***Duan qiao*** ("Broken Bridge"), with Du Jinfang and Shan Timing as the sisters and Ye Shenglan as the male lead. In 1978 Taiwanese directors Si Ma Ke and Chen Chi-hua produced another Mandarin version, **Love of the White Snake** (*Xin bai she zhuan*—"The New White Snake Story"), with Brigitte Lin Ching-hsia as White, Chin Chi-min as Green, and Charlie Chin Hsiang-lin as the object of White's affections. Tsui's HK rendition is set in the Sung Dynasty, and while the recreation of the period seems perfect (from the structures to the costumes), his use of color effects throughout (which harken back to the work of the great Italian director Mario Bava) heralds the close proximity of supernatural beings and forces. White (who is never actually addressed by a name this time, and is played here by Joey Wang) and Green (actually called *Siu-ching*/"Little Green" this time, and played by Maggie Cheung) are able to assume human form after hundreds of years of training. White, the older and more mature of the pair, seeks to experience love and sets her sights on Hsui-xien (**Temptation of a Monk**'s Wu Hsin-kuo), a timid and repressed scholar. The two sisters hold humans in the highest regard, using their powers to heal the sick and divert raging flood waters, with the tacit approval of the powerful monk Fa-hai, who has devoted his life to hunting down and vanquishing demons that roam the Earth in human guise. Green's immaturity and inability to maintain her human body for extended periods soon begins to threaten both the sisters' safety and White's relationship. When Hsui-xien accidentally sees Green in her true form, he dies of fright, prompting White and Green to steal a precious herb needed to bring him back from the dead. Their actions put them in conflict with Fa-hai, who decides, in lieu of punishment, to have Green try and seduce him as a test of his will power. When he succumbs to human lust, he seeks revenge on the sisters, with his subsequent actions having tragic consequences not only for the snakes, but for the entire countryside.

While **Green Snake** shares some plot components with the **A Chinese Ghost Story** series (in particular, a sage and his disciples try to expose the non-humans' masquerade, and a naive scholar as male protagonist), the extensive application of Buddhist ideology makes this seem very fresh and imaginative when compared to the majority of films produced during the period fantasy craze. Sexuality has never played much of a role in Tsui's films, presumably by design but possibly due to the restrictions HK censors place on the Category II rating, being much more tolerant of violence than eroticism. However, sex is right in the forefront here, from White's desire to experience it and Green's jealous yearning to share in anything her sister undergoes, to Fai-hai's desperate efforts to suppress his base human urges. Oddly, despite all of these salacious undercurrents, **Green Snake** has occasionally been faulted for being emotionally aloof, though it clearly also displays the same sort of playful romanticism found in Tsui's **The Lovers**, which also deals with forbidden love and ends on an equally sombre note. Cheung is thoroughly engaging in one of her most playful and provocative characterizations to date, and Wang gives an amusingly exaggerated caricature of the traditionally obsequious Chinese wife, precisely the sort of "more human than human" overcompensation you would expect from a creature craving to *be* human. Zhao (who took over the Wong Fei-hung role from Jet Li in Tsui's **Once Upon a Time in China** series) gives an appropriately severe performance, effectively capturing Fa-hai's rigid adherence to his Buddhist doctrines and also the character's near complete failure to empathize with the creatures he has coldly pledged to destroy. The moral transformation he undergoes at the climax is a nice, contemporary spin on the traditional infallibility of religious characters in this genre. Taiwanese star Wu Hsin-kuo (whose name is curiously mistranslated in the English credits as "Wu Kuo Chiu") is cast against type here, and while competent, he never seems to settle comfortably into his part, being better suited to the sort of intense, character-driven roles that originally brought him fame. The score by James Wong and Mark Lui (available on CD) is a wonderful amalgam of traditional instrumentation, contemporary ambience, and South East Asian influences, and complements both the visuals and the drama in highly satisfying fashion. The film was rushed through post-production in order to make its release date and, as a result, some of the digital and blue screen work is not up to par. However, Tsui's artistry is not significantly compromised, and most of the FX are so ambitious that either a gargantuan budget or top of the line technology would have been required to present them with complete verisimilitude. In spite of this shortcoming, there are moments here (particularly the early sequence in which where Fa-hai is tempted by his desires, which personify themselves as grotesque, naked humanoids that dance around and taunt him) which rank among the most piquantly visual that Tsui has ever staged, and serve to reconfirm his status as the preeminent filmmaker working in the genre today. As is often the case with HK features, Taiwan prints run a bit longer; in this case, approximately 4 minutes.

The Guerillas *see* **Killer Army**

408. Gun Is Law

(*sic*) (1983; Seasonal Film Corporation) ★: 5/10. *Tui yau taam cheung* (Cantonese), *Tui xiu tan chang* (Mandarin): "Retired Chief Detective." Cinematographer: Sung Kwong-wah; Art Director: Ting Yuen-tai; Music: Not Original; Writers: Ng See-yuen, Norman Law Man, Yip Ka, Lai Yung; Producer: Ng See-yuen; Director: Norman Law Man. Cast: Phillip Chan Yan-kin (Chan Shing-fung), John Sham Kin-fun (Liu King), Melvin Wong Kam-sun (Inspector Wong), Wong Wan-si (Sergeant). 1.85:1. VHS: World Video. Import VCD: Mei Ah (Poor Subtitles). 101 minutes.

Former real-life police officer Phillip Chan plays yet another tough guy cop with an attitude in this standard issue thriller. Chief Chan Shing-fung gets the job done but in his own, admittedly unorthodox, way. Placed under the command of a superior trained in the UK, Chan immediately clashes with the man's illogical and inappropriate methods. When Chan's brutal apprehension of a suspect winds up on the front page of an English daily, he is demoted and resigns from the force. To make matters worse, the brother of a man Chan killed during a bank robbery is out to kill him and his young son.

Surprise ending aside, this one proceeds strictly by the numbers and is best left to completists. In the only novel idea to be found here, the villain is able to smuggle a gun into HK by having it concealed inside an E.T. doll! The World Video version has new, video generated subtitles, but they are harder to read than the regular theatrical ones! The soundtrack includes music lifted from **Dawn of the Dead** and **Star Trek II: The Wrath of Khan**.

409. Gun n' Rose

(1992; In-Gear Film Production Co.) ★: 5/10. *Lung tang sei hoi* (Cantonese), *Long teng si hai* (Mandarin): "Dragon Rises Four Seas." Cinematographer: Wong Chi-wai; Art Director: Ganni Ma Chi-ming; Music: Lowell Lo Kwun-ting; Writer: Wai Kar-fai; Producer: Rover Tang Kwong-chow; Action Director: Lau Hok-fung; Director: Clarence Fok Yiu-leung. Cast: Alan Tang Kwong-wing (Alan Lung), Andy Lau Tak-wah (Andy), Leon Lai Ming (Leon), Carrie Ng Kar-lai (Carrie), Simon Yam Tat-wah (Simon Lung), Loletta Lee Lai-chun (Loletta), Monica Chan Fat-yung (Monica Shum), Bowie Lam Bo-yee (Bowie Lung), John Ching Tung (Bee), Michael Chan Wai-man (Chicken), Tien Feng (Lung Yat-fu). 1.85:1. VHS/LD: World Video (Poor Subtitles). Import LD/VCD: Mei Ah. 99 minutes.

A stylish but muddled triad thriller, this starts off with a bang and rarely lets up. Unfortunately, in its quest to become the cinematic equivalent of a Japanese *manga* (minus the sex), it merely seems slapdash, forgetting that the comics generally sport intriguing storylines, thus giving their exploitation elements greater impact. When his father is nearly killed by a gunman, triad boss Alan Lung blames his brother Bowie. This sets off a chain of events which finds Bowie taking revenge by leaking information to the police. When his ailing father discovers this betrayal, he orders son Simon to kill his traitorous brother. Simon, however, is jealous of the way his father has lavished his love on Alan, who is adopted. On Alan's wedding day, a squad of Simon's men bust in. During the subsequent gunplay, Alan's bride, Monica, is shot and paralyzed. The pair flee the underworld, with Alan making a meager living as a delivery man. Circumstances later bring Alan together with flaky gang leader Andy, an alliance that eventually leads to the pair taking on Simon and his men.

Like the majority of Clarence Fok's films, **Gun n' Rose** can charitably be described as a mess. The cinematography is stunning and the action choreography is wildly acrobatic and highly enjoyable, but the nonsensical storyline and "colorful" (i.e. ridiculous) characters are tiresome. Every so often, the sheer sweeping entertainment value of Fok's work can justify his indulgences (like with **Naked Killer**, still his best film to date), and he just barely gets away with it here. **The Black Panther Warriors**, Fok's next collaboration with Alan Tang, suffers from exactly the same problems and is not as fortunate.

410. Gunmen

(1988; Cinema City Co./Film Workshop) ★: 8/10. *Tin law dei mong* (Cantonese), *Tian lun di wang* (Mandarin): "Dragnet." Cinematographers: Ardy Lam Kwok-wah, Andrew Lau Wai-keung; Art Directors: Andy Lee Yiu-kwong, Eddie Ma Poon-chiu; Music: Danny Chung Teng-yat; Writers: Law Kam-fai, Lip Wan-fung; Producer: Tsui Hark; Action Director: Fung Hark-on; Director: Che-Kirk Wong Chi-keung. Cast: Tony Leung Kar-fai (Ding Chun-bee), Waise Lee Chi-hung (Ching), Mark Cheng Ho-nam (Kwong), David Wu Tai-wai (Fan), Adam Cheng Siu-chau (Haye), Elizabeth Lee Mei-fung (Mona Fong), Carrie Ng Kar-lai (Chu-chiao), Elvis Tsui Kam-kong (The Superintendent), Wong Kam-kong (Haye's Man). 1.85:1. VHS: Tai Seng. Import LD: Golden Cinema City. Import VCD: Mega Star. 87 minutes.

Easily the standout among several HK imitations of Brian DePalma's **The Untouchables**, **Gunmen** is set in the late 1920s, a time when the Shanghai police department was riddled with corruption. Ding Chun-bee is a noble recruit determined to play by the rules but also to make a dent in the wave of crime that permeates the streets and the station house. When Ding's superior is murdered by Haye, an old war enemy, a tough new superintendent is put in charge by the French. Determined to exact revenge for his friend's death, Ding drafts some of his old war buddies into the force, and together they make great headway battling the local opium dealers. However, in their zeal to nail Haye they seize a shipment of what turns out to be medical supplies, causing Haye's seriously ill confederate to expire before the penicillin can reach him. Haye's men seek vengeance, leading to an all-out gun war.

The storyline would be fairly easy to predict even without the Hollywood connection, Tony Leung Kar-fai is distractingly dubbed by another actor, and the female roles are weakly written. Regardless, **Gunmen** is shot and edited with such invigorating style and rhythm, it confirms Che-Kirk Wong's place as one of HK cinema's preeminent technicians, more so than any other title in his filmography. The period detail is excellent, the action is bloody and intense, and the stuntwork (which includes some elaborate fire "gags") is outstanding. Most of the score is original but there are also tracks lifted from **The Hidden**.

411. Guns of Dragon

(*sic*) (1993; Mandarin Films/Great & Bright) ★: 4/10. *Foo yuet tiu lung chi gwang tin haam cheng* (Cantonese), *Hu xue tu long zhi hong tian xian jing* (Mandarin): "Tiger's Den Slaughter Dragon: Explode Sky Trap." Cinematographer: Sander Lee Kar-ko; Art

Art Director: Eric Lam Sai-kan; Music: John Wong Sai-cheung; Writer: James Yuen Sai-sang; Producers: Chan Chiu-mo, Raymond Wong Pak-ming; Director: Tony Leung Siu-hung. Cast: Ray Lui Leung-wai (Lam Kwok-ching), Yvonne Yung Hung (Kitty), Mark Cheng Ho-nam (Prince), Alex Fong Chung-sun (Alex), John Sham Kin-fun (Yip), Jackson Liu Hsiu-hsien (Tai Fei). 1.85:1. VHS: Tai Seng. Import LD/VCD: Mei Ah. 91 minutes. Also known as **American Dragon** (UK video title).

Location shooting in New York City and Puerto Rico, and sync sound recording give this standard Ray Lui actioner an extra level of interest, though it is not enough to surmount the pedestrian, implausible storyline. Lui plays Lam, a former HK cop who travels to The Big Apple to meet up with his wife (Yung) and young son, with the trio then planning to settle in Toronto. Before they can leave, Lam is attacked by Prince, a thug he locked horns with in HK, who is now operating stateside. When Prince kidnaps his wife, Lam joins forces with the FBI, tracking him to Puerto Rico where a big counterfeiting scheme is taking shape.

Some of the action (including the **Terminator**-style annihilation of a NYC police station) is well-staged, but much of it is not and the climax is particularly weak. John Sham provides some welcome comic relief in the first half and is sorely missed thereafter.

412. Hail the Judge

(1994; Win's Movie Production) ★: 7/10. *Gau ban chi lut goon baak min Pau Ching-tin* (Cantonese), *Jiu pin zhi ma guan bai mian Bao Qingtian* (Mandarin): "9th Ranked Sesame Officer: White-Faced Pao Ching-tian." Cinematographer: David Chung Chi-man; Art Director: Andrew Cheuk Man-yiu; Music: William Woo Wai-lap; Producers: Charles Heung Wah-keung, Jimmy Heung Wah-sing; Writer-Director: Wong Jing. Cast: Stephen Chiau Sing-chi (Pao Lung-sing), Ng Man-tat (Yau Wai), Sharla Cheung Man (Chi Siu-lin), Elvis Tsui Kam-kong (Panther), Christy Chung Lai-tai (Stone Mansion), Ada Choi Siu-fan (Yu Yin), Ngai Sing (Shang Wai), Lawrence Ng Kai-wah ("Mirror" Fong Tong-kan), Lau Shun (Eunuch Li Lin-ying), Gabriel Wong Yat-san (The Emperor), Wong Yat-fei (Magistrate Chan Pak-cheung), Yuen King-tan (Madam), Ku Feng (Navy Commander Shang Kwan), John Ching Tung (Lui Fook). 1.85:1. VHS/LD: Tai Seng. Import LD/VCD/DVD: Mei Ah. 106 minutes.

Although the untranslated trailer suggested that it might be a second sequel to Wong Jing's popular period fantasy-comedy **Royal Tramp** (1992), this amusing Stephen Chiau outing (also directed by Wong) is actually a follow-up (of sorts) to the comedian's *other* 1992 blockbuster, **Justice, My Foot!** Chiau plays Pao Lung-sing, a young magistrate who hopes to strike it rich by accepting bribes but lacks the smarts to succeed even at being corrupt. He soon changes his ways when a case he is presiding over, involving the murder of a family by a politically connected psychopath, results in the sole survivor being framed for the crime. Pao's quest for justice results in a cross-country trek to appeal his case to The Emperor, which culminates in a heated courtroom battle with crooked lawyer "Mirror" Fong and the diabolical Eunuch Li.

While some of the verbal humor is lost in translation, this scattershot comedy works for the most part, thanks mainly to Chiau's enjoyably obnoxious comic persona. Co-star Elvis Tsui gives him a run for the money in the laughs department as Panther, the kung fu master whose bark is literally worse than his bite. As with all of Wong Jing's comedies, the cast is first rate, and although Chiau regular Nat Chan Pak-cheung is conspicuously absent, one of the film's slimiest characters is named after him. The costumes and sets were re-used that same year for the nasty Category III drama **Chinese Torture Chamber Story**, which also featured Lawrence Ng.

413. Half a Loaf of Kung Fu!

(1978; Lo Wei Motion Pictures Co.) ★: 5/10. *Dim ji gung foo gaam gaan daan* (Cantonese), *Dian zhi gong ku gan jian dan* (Mandarin): "Not Just Kung Fu That Simple." Cinematographer: Chen Chin-kui; Music: Frankie Chan Fan-kei; Writer: Tang Min-ji; Producer: Hsu Li-hwa; Action Director: Jackie Chan; Director: Chen Chi-hua. Cast: Jackie Chan (Jiang Tao), James Tien Chun (Mao), Dean Shek Tien (Beggar), Wu Ma (Man with Scythe). 2.35:1. VHS: All-Seasons (Dubbed), UAV (Dubbed), Simitar (Dubbed). DVD: Simitar (English and Cantonese tracks). Import VCD: Ocean Shores (Poor Subtitles). 96 minutes.

Those who have little patience for the humor in Jackie Chan's pictures won't make it through the first reel of this shamelessly lowbrow kung fu comedy, which spent two years on the shelf upon completion. However, those who can tolerate the uninspired storyline, juvenile gags, and non-stop mugging will be rewarded with some enjoyable kung fu. Chan plays young Jiang Tao, who wishes to be a martial arts master but lacks the discipline to even hold a job. While travelling through the countryside one day, he witnesses a battle between a notorious criminal and the legendary "Whip Hero." As a result of his interference, The Whip Hero is killed but not before mortally wounding his opponent. When he discovers that the fugitive has a bounty of 500 silver pieces on his head, Jiang impersonates the fallen Hero and claims the reward. He continues to play the Hero but, naturally, his impersonation falls to pieces whenever anyone challenges him to combat (which happens a lot). Desperate to learn kung fu, Jiang persuades a beggar to instruct him and (through a series of loosely connected events not worth relating) ends up as one of the men guarding the priceless antidote "Evergreen Jade" and the life-restoring "Soul Pills," both of which are sought by The Poison Clan (who else?).

The disjointed, meandering plot and sloppy editing, coupled with all of that insipid comedy tends to get the enigmatically titled **Half a Loaf of Kung Fu!** cited as Chan's worst effort. While it is far from his best, the film does have a certain shaggy dog appeal to it, growing more interesting and accessible as it goes. It also deserves credit for anticipating the many kung fu comedies that would follow in its wake. The final battle, while much too long, contains some inspired choreography, though even the most forgiving viewer will wonder just how Jiang could go from fool to martial arts master in such a short period of time. Frankie Chan is credited with the score but one gets the feeling that he only chose the cues, since not one single note sounds original.

414. Handsome Siblings

(1992; Win's Movie Production) ★: 6/10. *Jueh doi shuen giu* (Cantonese), *Jue dai shuang jiao* (Mandarin): "The Two Beauties That End All Dynasties." Cinematographer: Jingle Ma Cho-shing; Art Director: Jason Mok Siu-kei; Music: Lowell Lo Kwun-ting; Writer: Cheuk Hon; Producer: Stephen Siu Yeuk-yuen; Action Director: Phillip Kwok Tsui; Director: Eric Tsang Chi-wai. Cast: Andy Lau Tak-wah (Fishy), Brigitte Lin Ching-hsia (Eva More), Sharla Cheung Man (Eva), Ng Man-tat ("Big Mouth" Lee), Deanie Yip Tak-han (Sissy To), Francis Ng Chun-yu (Kong Yuk-long), Cheung Kwok-chu (Kong Pi-hawk), Fung Hark-on (Monk Blackie), Miu Kiu-wai (Yin Nam-tin), Anita Yuen Wing-yee (Madam Ti), Richard Ng Yiu-hon, Wong Ching (The Supremes), Josephine Koo Mei-wah (Black Widow), Shing Fui-on (Ko Chi-sum). 1.85:1. VHS: Tai Seng. Import LD/VCD/DVD: Mei Ah. 102 minutes.

An all-star cast and beautiful production design bolster this big-budget period fantasy, which suffers somewhat from a surplus of broad comedy (pretty much a given for any movie with Ng Man-tat, Deanie Yip, and Richard Ng in the cast). The storyline (derived from a Ku Long novel) revolves around Fishy and his bumbling compatriots, "The Ten Untouchable Villains," whose last crime resulted in the deaths of *470,440* people, raising the understandable ire of Eva, Supreme Ruler of the Martial World. In the eighteen years following her first attempt to bring the Villains to justice, Eva has raised her adopted daughter, Eva More (Brigitte Lin, looking luminous throughout), to succeed her as chief adjudicator, with the post to be officially determined by a royal contest. Matters grow thorny thanks to a blossoming love affair between Fishy and Eva More, and the murderous agenda of tournament competitor Kong Yuk-long, who recognizes this as the perfect chance to seize power over the domain.

Under the direction of veteran comedian Eric Tsang, **Handsome Siblings** presents all of the genre's prerequisite ingredients (palace intrigue, supernaturally enhanced martial arts battles, winsome female leads successfully impersonating men simply by donning male garb) with the expected aplomb of Tsang's earlier projects, but the proceedings never quite overcome the miscasting of Lau in a role better suited to the comedic sensibilities of Stephen Chiau. Still, there is much on display to occupy viewers (including the sight of 37-year-old Brigitte Lin almost successfully playing the 18 year old adopted daughter of the twenty-something Sharla Cheung). The subtitles are mediocre at best, but the storyline becomes clear on second viewing, and most period fantasy fans will want to give this one another look anyway. Phillip Kwok's action choreography is top-notch, but suspension cables are almost constantly visible throughout (blame for which rests at least partially on the shoulders of the cinematographer). Composer Lowell Lo contributes another excellent soundtrack (performed largely on traditional instruments), and there are some truly lovely costumes on display. Incidentally, the English translation of the Chinese title is an obvious reference to Lin and Lau. *Jueh doi*, or "End Dynasty," is a term used by the ancient Chinese to describe those possessing great beauty. The person or persons are so stunning that future dynasties will never see their like. So this is one of those rare occasions where the English export title is actually fairly close to the original.

415. Happy Din Don

[*sic*] (1986; Golden Harvest/Hui's Film Production/Paragon Films) ★: 4/10. *Foon lok ding dong* (Cantonese), *Huan le ding dong* (Mandarin): "Happy Ding Dong." Cinematographer: Ardy Lam Kwok-wah; Art Director: Carman Wan Siu-wai; Music: Michael Lai Siu-tin, Producer: Raymond Chow Man-wai; Action Directors: Yuen Shun-yee, Cheung Wai-ching; Writer-Director: Michael Hui Koon-man. Cast: Michael Hui Koon-man (Fat), Cherie Chung Cho-hung (Din-din), Michael Lai Siu-tin (Tat), Bill Tung Biu (Ma Masa, The Crocodile King), Wong Wan-si (Ms. Lee), Yuen Cheung-yan (Ironhand), Wong Ching (One Eye), Ricky Hui Koon-ying (Man in Bed), Anita Mui Yim-fong (Singer in Club), Shum Wai (Club Owner), Cho Tat-wah (Captain Chan), Tai Po (Blindman). 1.85:1. VHS: Tai Seng. 94 minutes.

Far below Michael Hui's usual standards, this knockoff of **Some Like It Hot** (which goes so far as to include the exact same ending) is rarely amusing and poorly paced. Buddies Fat and Tat are up to their ears in debt and always in trouble. One evening, Fat witnesses drug dealers (under the command of their semi-bionic boss "Ironhand") murdering some rivals but manages to escape. Through a series of bizarre incidents, Fat is blamed for the killings and disguises himself as a girl so he can hide out. He joins an all-female band aboard a cruise ship but must spend the trip evading one of Ironhand's killers and the shrewish band director (who threatens to turn him in unless he obeys *all* of her commands), while also romancing gorgeous singer Din-din.

The humor is pretty desperate, being of the sort where one can finish punch lines and predict sight gags with near 100% accuracy. The only genuinely creative bit finds Hui and Wong Ching in an extended martial arts battle that perfectly mirrors the movie playing on a television set behind them.

416. The Happy Ghost

(1984; Cinema City Co.) ★: 4/10. *Hoi sam gwai* (Cantonese), *Kai xin gui* (Mandarin): "Happy Ghost." Cinematographer: Bob Thompson; Art Directors: Hai Chung-man, Jessy Lam Chak-chi; Music: Mahmood Rumjahn; Writers: Raymond Wong Pak-ming, Clifton Ko Chi-sum; Producers: Karl Maka, Dean Shek Tien, Raymond Wong Pak-ming; Director: Clifton Ko Chi-sum. Cast: Raymond Wong Pak-ming (Stewart Pik, the Happy Ghost), Bonnie Law Ming-chu (Bonnie Lam), Loletta Lee Lai-chun (Juliet), Sandy Lam San-san (Venus), Teresa Carpio (Sister Lee), Clifton Ko Chi-sum (Judge). 1.85:1. VHS: Tai Seng. Import LD: Golden Cinema City. Import VCD: Mega Star. 96 minutes.

The first in a series of teen-oriented fantasy-comedies, this one established the formula and remains one of the better entries in the series. While on a camping trip to "Haunted Beach," some teenage girls and boys take refuge from a storm in a decrepit temple. Bonnie Lam brings back a piece of rope which houses the spirit of Ching Dynasty scholar Stewart Pik, who committed suicide using that particular rope. After initially scaring Bonnie half to death, the two become friends and Stewart uses his powers to help her team win an athletics competition and tease their teachers. After numerous bizarre instances, the staff nuns take action.

The humor is pretty inane (though it is not everyday that one gets to see Raymond Wong dressed as Boy George!), and adult viewers will probably only find this interesting as an example of just how different teen movies from other cultures can be. There are some rather uncomfortable sexual undercurrents in Stewart's friendship with these underage girls, and one of them even gets pregnant and is then abandoned by her boyfriend, elements that you certainly would not find in Western productions of this ilk. It was the film debut for Loletta Lee and Bonnie Law. Four sequels followed.

417. Happy Ghost II

(1985; Cinema City Co.) ★: 2/10. *Hoi sam gwai fong sue ga* (Cantonese), *Kai xin gui fang shu jia* (Mandarin): "The Happy Ghost Takes a Summer Vacation." Cinematographer: Bob Thompson; Art Director: Ben Lau Man-hung; Music: Mahmood Rumjahn; Writers: Clifton Ko Chi-sum, Raymond Wong Pak-ming; Producers: Karl Maka, Dean Shek Tien, Raymond Wong Pak-ming; Director: Clifton Ko Chi-sum. Cast: Raymond Wong Pak-ming (Sam Hong), Fennie Yuen Kit-ying ("The Chairman"), May Lo Mei-mei (May Kan), Charine Chan Kar-ling (King Yiu), Melvin Wong Kam-sun (Rival Coach), Clifton Ko Chi-sum (Judge). 1.85:1. VHS: Tai Seng. Import LD: Golden Cinema City. Import VCD: Mega Star. 96 minutes.

At the conclusion of the previous film, the Happy Ghost was reincarnated, and this sequel finds him all grownup and a teacher named Sam Hong (which would make it about the year 2015, but no matter). Working at "Saint Holy" school, he finds that his new class is controlled by "The Meanies Club," a group of misbehaving girls led by "The Chairman." As in the previous film, he uses his powers to help the girls win a sports competition but remains the object of their practical jokes. Wishing to be a normal human being, Sam is stripped of his powers but, of course, eventually grows to miss them, particularly with the girls' need of his abilities to help them win the volleyball championship. Unfunny from start to finish, the witless proceedings are made all but intolerable by an especially sophomoric musical score. Notable only as the film debut of Fennie Yuen, May Lo, and Charine Chan.

418. Happy Ghost III

(1986; Cinema City Co.) ★: 5/10. *Hoi sam gwai chong gwai* (Cantonese), *Kai xin gui chuang gui* (Mandarin): "Happy Ghost Bumps Ghost." Cinematographer: Bob Thompson; Art Directors: Dominique Lo Kar-yiu, Raymond Chan Kam-ho; Music: Joseph Koo Kar-fai; Writer-Producer: Raymond Wong Pak-ming; Action Director: Ching Siu-tung; Director: Johnny To Kei-fung. Cast: Raymond Wong Pak-ming (Hoi Sam-kwai), Maggie Cheung Man-yuk (Tsui Pan-han), Fennie Yuen Kit-ying ("The Prefect"), Charine Chan Kar-ling (Yiu King), Wong Ching (Pimp), Tsui Hark (Reincarnation Director), Charlie Cho Cha-lei (Rock Hudson). VHS: Tai Seng. Import LD: Golden Cinema City. Import VCD: Mega Star. 89 minutes.

The best entry in this weak series, **Happy Ghost III** benefits from some behind-the-scenes personnel changes and the presence of charming Maggie Cheung. This time out, Hoi Sam-kwai (called "Sam Hong" last time) accidentally messes up the reincarnation of cute spirit Tsui Pan-han, who then proceeds to make his life hell by playing various tricks and possessing the body of a student. When The Happy Ghost is unable to help him, Sam-kwai tries a different strategy and romances Pan-han instead. This works but, thanks to some triads, Pan-han may end up missing her last chance at reincarnation.

There is the obligatory sports match (with Sam-kwai trying to help the soccer team this time but getting foiled by Pan-han) and other familiar series elements, but this sequel still seems fresher than its forerunners and displays a bit more ambition. While less than convincing, the special FX are fun, particularly during the climax, which starts as a conventional car chase and ends with the vehicle driving *across* buildings and down a manhole!

419. Happy Ghost IV

(1990; Pak Ming Films/Ko Chi Sum Films Co.) ★: 4/10. *Hoi sam gwai gau hoi sam gwai* (Cantonese), *Kai xin gui jiu kai xin gui* (Mandarin): "Happy Ghost Rescues Happy Ghost." Cinematographer: Sander Lee Kar-ko; Art Director: Raymond Chan Kam-ho; Music: Beyond; Writers: Joe Ma Wai-ho, Ng Man-fai, Philip Cheng Chung-tai; Action Director: Tony Leung Siu-hung; Producer-Director: Clifton Ko Chi-sum. Cast: Raymond Wong Pak-ming (Hong Sum-kwai), Pauline Yeung Po-ling (Annie), Beyond (Man, Mo, Ying, Kit), Woo Fung (Annie's Father), Charlie Cho Cha-lei (Chiu), Tommy Wong Kwong-leung (Crazy Bill), Lau Shun ("Crazy" Kwan Yeung), James Wong Jim (Judge), Clifton Ko Chi-sum (Man in Washroom). 1.85:1. VHS: Tai Seng. Import LD/VCD: Ocean Shores. 88 minutes.

With the **Happy Ghost** formula really starting to show its age, Raymond Wong switched from girls to boys, adding the teen rock group Beyond (Wong Kar-kui, Wong Kar-keung, Wong Koon-chung, Yip Sai-wing) to the mix, in an attempt to reverse declining box office returns. The final result is pretty much the same, however, and did nothing to reverse the downward trend at the box office. The Beyond boys (called "Behind" here) discover an ancient suit of armor that houses the spirit of the villainous "Crazy" Kwan Yeung, who proceeds to possess the teens. While the boys perform malicious deeds under Kwan's control, the evil ghost pursues Hong's girlfriend, who is the spitting image of the woman who killed him centuries before.

The most ambitious film of the batch, **Happy Ghost IV** delivers some reasonably good optical FX and even a little animation. There are also some mildly amusing horror gags, but all of them have been done just as well or better in other movies. Jokes are also lifted from the American hit **Weekend at Bernie's** (assassin Tommy Wong desperately tries to ice Raymond Wong and is perplexed by his ability to survive), and there are a couple of visual steals from **A Nightmare on Elm Street**. In a supporting role, Charlie Cho is far more obnoxious than funny as Annie's sleazy cousin and gets far too much screen time. Former series stars Loletta Lee Lai-chun, Fennie Yuen Kit-ying, May Lo Mei-mei, and Charine Chan Kar-ling put in brief appearances, and one wishes that they had been retained as the lead players here. Postscript: Beyond's lead singer, Wong Kar-kui, would be killed in a freak accident in 1993 during the taping of a Japanese game show. Kar-kui's brother, Kar-keung, took over as lead singer and the band continued on with only three members.

420. Happy Ghost 5

(1991; Mandarin Films) ★: 2/10. *Hoi sam gwai seung cho san* (Cantonese), *Kai xin gui shang cuo shen* (Mandarin): "Happy Ghost Enters the Wrong Body." Cinematographer: Wong Po-man; Art Director: Fong Ying; Music: Danny Chung Teng-yat; Writer-Producer: Raymond Wong Pak-ming; Action Director: Tony Leung Siu-hung; Directors: Norman Chan Hok-yan, Raymond Wong Pak-ming. Cast: Raymond Wong Pak-ming (The Happy Ghost/Magic as a Human Being), Kris Aquino (Kathy), Roger Kwok Chun-on (Jack), Tommy Wong Kwong-leung (Bank Robber), Vincent Kok Tak-chiu (George). 1.85:1. VHS: Tai Seng. Import LD: Citimax. 91 minutes.

The final entry to date in Raymond Wong's teen comedy series does not have one single fresh idea to help it along, save for the unique casting of former Philippines president Corazon Aquino's daughter as the female lead. Kathy is the contented owner of a large dog named Magic, who monopolizes her affections, much to the annoyance of her thoughtless boyfriend Jack. When he puts out a fire in a temple, Magic is greeted by The Happy Ghost, who promises to grant him any wish he desires. The dog chooses to become a human being and the ghost grants his wish, with the warning that he cannot reveal his transformation and will revert to being a canine after 49 days. The ghost then helps Magic become accustomed to life as a human by getting him a job in a grocery store. While stocking the shelves, he meets up with Kathy. While she does not recognize him as her former pet, Kathy takes a liking to Magic and gives him a better position in a pet store (leading to a multitude of painful talking animal gags). When Jack once again tries to make some moves on Kathy, Magic intercedes and seemingly puts an end to their relationship once and for all. Unfortunately, he is falling for her himself, which leads to major complications. Everything is resolved in 91 minutes, but it seems more like a dog's age.

421. Happy Hour

(1995; Entertainment Today/United Filmmakers Organization) ★: 5/10. *Foon lok shut gwong* (Cantonese), *Huan le shi guang* (Mandarin): "Happy Times." Cinematographer: Apple Kwan Pak-suen; Art Director: Angelo Bernardo Castilho; Music: Clarence Hui Yuen, Wong Wai-nin; Writer: Susanne Chan Suk-yin; Producer: Peter Chan Ho-sun; Director: Benny Chan Muk-sing. Cast: Jordan Chan Siu-chun (David Wong), Andy Hui Chi-on (Hung Hui-sing), Julian Cheung Chi-lam (Cheung Pak-sheung), Lau Ching-wan (Chong Tsang), Ng Siu-wai (Angel Yu), Yeung Wing-nam (Mandy), Moses Chan Ho (Sing's Roommate), Jerry Lam Hiu-fung (Bespectacled Car Thief), Meg Lam Kin-ming (TV Reporter), Vincent Kok Tak-chiu (Director). 1.85:1. VHS: Tai Seng. Import LD/VCD: Fitto Mobile. 101 minutes.

Buddies David, Sing, and Pak-sheung go for a night on the town and end up leaving a singles' bar with luscious Angel Yu. She seduces all three of the men but later falls from the apartment balcony and is gravely injured. After some hesitation, the men call the police but find that the authorities are not so ready to believe their account of what happened. To make matters worse, Angel lies, saying that the men raped her. The friends manage to make bail, but the press hounds them relentlessly and their flaky lawyer, Chong Tsang, does not exactly inspire a great deal of confidence. To make matters even worse, the judge presiding over the case is Chong's ornery father-in-law. During the subsequent trial, Sing and Pak-sheung lie about what happened, hoping to save their skins, leaving only David as the one determined to tell the truth.

While the synopsis may make this sound like an intense courtroom drama, there are a number of humorous asides. Far too many, in fact. While many of these sequences show off Jordan Chan and Lau Ching-wan at their best, they work against the film as a whole, causing a serious loss in credibility. More detail and less frivolity (for guys facing severe prison sentences and the destruction of their lives, they sure are chipper!) would have made this a much more effective undertaking. As it stands, the opening reel is so good that it leaves one expecting a far more interesting film than what materializes.

422. Happy Together

(1997; Block 2 Pictures/Prenom H Co./Seowoo Film Co./Jet-Tone Production) ★: 8/10. *Chun gwong ja sit* (Cantonese), *Chun guang zha xie* (Mandarin): "A Sudden Leak of Spring Light." Cinematographer: Christopher Doyle. Art Director: William Cheung Suk-ping; Music: Danny Chung Teng-yat; Writer-Producer-Director: Wong Kar-wai. Cast: Tony Leung Chiu-wai (Lai Yiu-fai), Leslie Cheung Kwok-wing (Ho Po-wing), Chang Chen (Chang). 1.85:1. Dolby Stereo. VHS: Kino on Video, World Video. DVD: Kino on Video. Import LD/VCD/DVD: Mei Ah. 97 minutes.

Wong Kar-wai won the Best Director prize at Cannes for this estimable work which, while more readily accessible than some of his earlier projects, still beautifully conveys the director's characteristic themes. Ho Po-wing and Lai Yiu-fai are a gay couple living in Buenos Aires whose relationship is winding down. The pair soon split up, with Yiu-fai supporting himself by working as a nightclub doorman, while Po-wing sells himself on the streets. Yiu-fai does his best to avoid Po-wing but takes him back into his life when the hustler is badly beaten one evening. Shamelessly manipulative but also utterly dependent, Po-wing seeks to restart the sexual element of their relationship but Yiu-fai resists. Eventually, the two begin arguing once again, prompting Yiu-fai to leave and switch jobs. He meets Chang, a Taiwanese tourist who has run out of money and works to support himself, and the two strike up a platonic friendship that eventually helps Yiu-fai see where he wants to go with his life. Racked with boredom, Po-wing returns to hustling, and the two men seem to have finally parted company. Still, no matter how much he seemingly wants to extricate himself from Po-wing, Yiu-fai keeps the man's passport, making it impossible for them to ever be totally apart.

Like the director's earlier films, the predominant topics here are loneliness, the longing for love, and the waiting one must undergo for affection to be reciprocated. Cinematographer Christopher Doyle gives **Happy Together** an even more varied and unique look than that found in his other collaborations with Wong, juxtaposing stark black and white and hazy, high contrast color. Time is manipulated through the use of slow motion, random freeze frames, time lapse, jump cuts, and flash frames, and everything unfolds to an eclectic selection of music that ranges from local standards to Frank Zappa. While it lacks the narrative density of **Ashes of Time** and the playful restlessness of **Chungking Express** and **Fallen Angels**, this is an engrossing, deceptively simple character study, buoyed by three superb performances. The production gained some notoriety prior to release when Tony Leung Chiu-wai revealed to the press that he had agreed to do the film on the basis of what turned out to be a fake script. Only once he was in Argentina did Leung see the real pages, and he was none too happy about the gay sex scene he had to do with Leslie Cheung (it occurs in the opening moments and was also the first scene to be shot). His discomfort seems discernible at times but in no way hinders his interpretation of the character or the quality of his work.

423. Happy Together

(1997; Times Production) ★: 1/10. *Hei hei bak yan* (Cantonese), *Xi qi bi ren* (Mandarin): "Happy Mood Compels People." Cinematographer: Wong Kar-fai; Art Director: Nelson Cheung Hok-yun; Music: Chow Kam-wing; Writer: Times Production; Producer: Fu Pui-yu; Director: Sherman Wong Ching-wah. Cast: Lydia Shum Tin-ha (Lam Siu-fa), Ng Man-tat (Siu-fa's Boss), Max Mok Siu-ching (Eric Chow Lik-ping), Christine Ng Wing-mei (King King), Linda Wong Hing-ping (Mei), Ronald Wong Pan (Eric's Friend). 1.85:1. VHS: Tai Seng. Import LD/VCD/DVD: Mei Ah. 88 minutes.

Not to be confused with the like-named Wong Kar-wai movie (which opened in HK theaters four months earlier), this is a laughless comedy about a group of Mainland tourists visiting HK to see the re-unification festivities. Thanks to a reservation mix-up, they have nowhere to stay and end up in a house belonging to the boss of bumbling housekeeper Lam Siu-fa. Pretty tour guide King King falls for Siu-fa's handsome actor son, Eric, much to the consternation of the trip's inept organizer. The group runs into more problems, but Eric is able to use his influence and connections to set everything right, though misunderstandings and practical jokes still follow as the organizer makes numerous pathetic attempts to win King King's approval.

Unless you are in the mood for endless travelogue footage, you can safely pass by this awful farce. While not quite as excruciating as the same production team's **Top Borrower**, most viewers will agree that it is certainly close enough.

424. Hard Boiled

(1992; Golden Princess/Milestone) ★: 9/10. *Lat sau san taam* (Cantonese), *La shou shen tan* (Mandarin): "Hot-Handed God of Cops." Cinematographer: Horace Wong Wing-hang; Art Directors: James Leung Wah-sang, Joel Chong Kwok-wing; Music: Michael Gibbs; Writer: Barry Wong Ping-yiu; Producers: Linda Kuk Mei-lai, Terence Chang Chia-chen; Action Director: Phillip Kwok Tsui; Director: John Woo Yu-sen. Cast: Chow Yun-fat (Tequila), Tony Leung Chiu-wai (Tony), Teresa Mo Shun-kwan (Theresa Chang), Phillip Chan Yan-kin (Pang), Phillip Kwok Tsui (Mad Dog), Anthony Wong Chau-sang (Johnny Wong), Kwan Hoi-shan (Hui), Bowie Lam Bo-yee (Lung), Stephen Tung Wai (Foxy), Bobby Au Yeung Chun-wah (Lionheart), Lau Kong (Hospital Director), John Woo Yu-sen (Woo), Ng Shui-ting (Chung), Lo Mang (Lonny), Michael Dinga (Victim in Library), Lai Hoi-shan (Librarian). 1.85:1. VHS: Tai Seng (Censored 123 minute version), Fox-Lorber (Subtitled or Dubbed; 127 minutes). LD/DVD: Criterion (Subtitled and Dubbed; 127 minutes). Import LD: Golden Cinema City (Censored 123 minute version). Also known as **God of Guns** (Taiwan title).

John Woo's last HK film before heading Stateside, **Hard Boiled** is a highly entertaining collection of spectacular action setpieces, bridged by charismatic performances from leads Chow Yun-fat and Tony Leung Chiu-wai, and Woo's trademark directorial touches. When his partner is brutally killed during a raid on some gun runners, dedicated cop Tequila relentlessly tracks down the men behind the ring. Unfortunately, Tequila is inadvertently endangering the work of undercover cop Tony, who has managed to gain the confidence of ganglord Hui and is now about to ingratiate himself with Hui's deranged competitor, Johnny Wong. Tequila launches a sneak attack on Wong and single-handedly wipes out almost all of his men. He also almost kills Tony in the process but, at the moment of truth, his gun jams. Although he could put a bullet through his opponent's head, Tony spares Tequila's life, confirming the latter's suspicions that his boss has been keeping him in the dark about the investigation. The two cops decide to work together to bring down Wong and learn from a snitch that the triad has come up with an ingenious hiding place for his gun cache: the basement of a hospital.

Hard Boiled lacks the involving, high drama of Woo's best works, but it was clearly never intended to be in the same vein as **A Better Tomorrow** or **The Killer**: This is a tailor-made showcase for Woo's proficiency as a technician. The gunplay is incredibly kinetic, particularly the final half hour stand-off in the hospital (which includes a now legendary bit where Chow and Leung do battle with a small army of attackers in a 2 minute and 42 second sequence that contains only a single, almost undetectable edit). Woo does incorporate his familiar themes of honor and male comradery, but some aspects of the storyline are best not examined too closely (writer Barry Wong passed away before finishing the screenplay and the last minute patchwork is evident at times), and Anthony Wong is a surprisingly lacklustre villain here (his distinctive voice accounts for a large part of his strength as an actor and he has been dubbed by someone else). Fortunately, Chow and Leung are magnetic heroes, and that, combined with the sheer razzle-dazzle of the action choreography and Woo's command of the medium, is enough to overcome any weaknesses.

Hard Boiled 2: The Last Blood *see* **The Last Blood**

Hard Boiled Killers *see* **Modern Heroes**

425. The Haunted Cop Shop II

(1988; In-Gear Film Production Co.) ★: 7/10. *Maang gwai hok tong* (Cantonese), *Meng gui xue tang* (Mandarin): "Fierce Ghost in the School Halls." Cinematographer: Johnny Koo Kwok-wah; Art Director: Raymond Lee King-man; Music: Phil Chan Fei-lap, Chow Kam-cheung; Writers: Barry Wong Ping-yiu, Jeff Lau Chun-wai, Laurence Lau Chun-wah; Producer: Alan Tang Kwong-wing; Director: Jeff Lau Chun-wai. Cast: Jacky Cheung Hok-yau (Kam Mark-k), Ricky Hui Koon-ying (Man-chill), Sandy Lam Yik-lin (Miss Bad Luck), Billy Lau Nam-kwong (Lazy-bone), Charlie Cho Cha-lei (Near-Sighted Vampire), Woo Fung (Superintendent), Yee Lui (Romeo), Barry Wong Ping-yiu (Senior Inspector), Wong Kar-wai (Wong), Jeff Lau Chun-wai (Cop), Helena Law Lan (Woman at Police Station). 1.85:1. VHS: World Video. 92 minutes.

The original **Haunted Cop Shop** is difficult to obtain in subtitled form (the Taiwan version is reportedly translated), but this sequel is easily found and offers plenty of fun. A vampire is loose in Sha Tau Kok police headquarters, and bumbling cops Kam and Man-chill are ordered to find and destroy it. The objective is achieved but Man-chill is bitten, though the creature only managed to sink one fang into his neck. Since he was not entirely vampirized, Man-chill is doomed whenever the full moon appears to transform into a one-fanged creature that is half vampire and half werewolf! Not surprisingly, he keeps his condition a secret from everyone, including Kam. As a "reward" for their bravery, Man-chill and Kam are ordered to establish a special division dedicated to the eradication of ghosts and vampires (called, not surprisingly, "The Ghostbuster Team"). Consisting entirely of third-rate police men and women, the team journeys to an old army base to train, unaware that the place is infested with bloodsuckers and zombies.

The film starts off like gangbusters with gags and vampire attacks seemingly every few seconds. The pace slows down a tad once the action shifts to the army camp, but director Jeff Lau keeps things interesting via some effectively staged horror sequences (bathed in blue light—a HK horror tradition) which, while never actually scary, are certainly atmospheric. Billy Lau's climactic method of dispatching the main vampire is already the stuff of legend among HK horror fans and something you will *never* see in a Western horror-comedy. Those who only know Wong Kar-wai for his art movies will be amused to see him in a cameo as a goofy cop; he also co-wrote the original film. Important vampire busting tip: A female vampire can be subdued if you fondle her breasts!

426. He Ain't Heavy, He's My Father

(1993; United Filmmakers Organization) ★: 7/10. *San naam hing naan dai* (Cantonese), *Xin nan xiong nan di* (Mandarin): "New Two of a Kind." Cinematographers: Andrew Lau Wai-keung, Tony Miu Kin-fai; Art Directors: Suzy Cheung Kai-san, Ben Luk Man-wah; Music: Richard Lo Sai-kit; Writer: Lee Chi-ngai; Producers: Peter Chan Ho-sun, Claudie Chung Chun; Directors: Peter Chan Ho-sun, Lee Chi-ngai. Cast: Tony Leung Kar-fai (Feng), Tony Leung Chiu-wai (Yuen), Anita Yuen Wing-yee (Yee/Lynn), Carina Lau Kar-ling (Laura Watt), Anita Lee Yuen-wah (Kan), Chor Yuen (Lord Watsons), Lawrence Cheng Tan-shui (Lone/Chuen), Lawrence Ng Kai-wah (Loanshark Fung), Waise Lee Chi-hung (Lee Kar-shing), Michael Chow Man-kin (Cheung), Valerie Chow Kar-ling (Dr. Jenny Chung). 1.85:1. VHS: Tai Seng. Import LD/VCD/DVD: Mei Ah. 97 minutes.

Ignore the terrible English title—this is a winning romantic comedy-time travel fantasy inspired by **Back to the Future**. Real estate agent Yuen has never gotten along with his father, Feng, who is generous to a fault, giving away practically everything he has to anyone who is down on his luck. When the old man is injured by a robber, Yuen visits a wishing well he remembers from childhood and wishes that he could see how his parents were back in the old days. Before he knows it, Yuen is back in time thirty years and not believing his eyes: Feng is dashing and his portly mom is a knockout babe! Trouble quickly brews, however, and Yuen tries to use his knowledge of the future to improve things for everyone. Along the way, he falls in love with Lynn, a dead ringer for his old girlfriend, Yee, and tries to come up with a way to help pay off a huge debt that has been forced upon her. Through his various experiences, Yuen comes to realize just how wonderful his father and Yee really are.

The time travel paradoxes are not as cleverly resolved here as in the Hollywood film, but the cast and material are very likeable and the sentimental aspects of the story are effective without being heavy handed. Buried under a ton of prosthetic old age make-up, Tony Leung Kar-fai and Carina Lau are barely recognizable in the contemporary scenes.

427. He and She

(1994; Moreart Productions) ★: 6/10. *Ji mooi ching sam* (Cantonese), *Jie mei qing shen* (Mandarin): "Sisters' Deep Love." Cinematographer: Horace Wong Wing-hang; Art Director: Ben Luk Man-wah; Music: Tang Siu-lam; Writers: Lawrence Cheng Tan-shui, Leung Chi-wai; Producer:

Yip Kwong-kim; Director: Lawrence Cheng Tan-shui. Cast: Anita Yuen Wing-yee (Tai Lok-yee), Tony Leung Kar-fai (Lai Chi-kai), Lawrence Cheng Tan-shui (Martin Cheng Sai-kit), Christine Ng Wing-mei (Kwok Wai-wai), Annabelle Lau Hiu-tung (Chan Pai-wah), Law Kar-ying (The Magistrate), Alex Fong Chung-sun (Chi-kai's Brother), Sheila Chan Sak-lan (Chi-kai's Sister-in-Law), Yuen King-tan (Woman in Waiting Room). 1.85:1. VHS: Tai Seng. Import LD/VCD/DVD: Ocean Shores. 97 minutes.

A talented cast manages to keep this predictable comedy-drama afloat. Naive Tai Lok-yee accidentally gets pregnant, but, even after being abandoned by her partner, she decides to keep the child. Her kind, gay friend Chi-kai offers to act as the child's father and the two enter in a marriage of convenience. While Lok-yee tries to earn a better living for herself and her new daughter, Chi-kai stays at home and raises the child. The pair gradually begin to fall for one another. but the cad who got Lok-yee in trouble returns and she decides to go to Australia with him. This leads to a court battle in which Chi-kai must try to prove that he is both a better father for the child and a better mate for Lok-yee.

The jokes are predictable and the outcome is never in doubt, so one's opinion of the leads is paramount here. Anita Yuen is her usual bubbly self, but this role does not place many demands on her, leaving Tony Leung Kar-fai as the film's most interesting performer. Leung is an excellent actor, but his character is precisely the sort of unprogressive gay stereotype that dominates HK cinema (Kai's homosexuality is due, in large part, to the fact that he was dumped by a girl at the prom, and the film hints that all a gay man needs is a good woman); it is a credit to Leung's talent that the viewer can put that aside and enjoy his extremely appealing performance all the same. The supporting players are all fine, in particular Christine Ng and Annabelle Lau as Chi-kai's flaky roommates. Sync sound recording is an extra plus.

428. He Comes from Planet K

(1997; Cameron Entertainment/Brilliant Idea Group) ★: 2/10. *Gung sing sin sang* (Cantonese), *Gang xing xian sheng* (Mandarin): "The Man from the Dorky Planet." Cinematographer: Jingle Ma Cho-shing; Art Director: Ben Luk Man-wah; Music: Wallace Kwok Kai-wah; Writers: Joe Ma Wai-ho, Lam Kei-to, Matt Chow Hoi-kwong; Action Director: Ridley Tsui Bo-wah; Producer-Director: Joe Ma Wai-ho. Cast: Eric Kot Man-fai (PK), Anita Yuen Wing-yee (Moon), Nicola Cheung Sun-yuet (Carol), Cheung Tat-ming (Won-hoi), Wyman Wong Wai-man (Bold Cheung), Lan Sai (Nancy), Bobby Yip King-sang (Chiu Chou-tung), Helena Law Lan (Granny Lone). 1.85:1. VHS: Mecapro. Import LD/VCD/DVD: Mei Ah. 95 minutes.

Hong Kong science fiction movies are so few and far between that one is always inclined to watch them, no matter how derivative or uninspired the premise might be. A vehicle for broad comedian Eric Kot, this feeble comedy boasts such a low jokes-to-footage ratio, one can almost be forgiven for forgetting it is supposed to be funny. Kot plays PK (short for *poo kai*, a derogatory Cantonese expression usually translated in English subtitles as "Asshole!" or "Go to Hell!"), the bizarre result of his human mother being abducted and impregnated by aliens. While largely humanoid in appearance, PK also sports Spock ears, antennae (which he uses to blast cockroaches), and extra long middle fingers. After accidentally ending up as a member of a SDU unit and rescuing wanted gangster Chiu Chou-tung (a prolonged sequence with virtually no comic payoff), PK is discovered by Moon, the alien-obsessed chairwoman of the HK UFO Association. She and her group have a great time teaching PK Earth customs, but the authorities eventually catch up with the extraterrestrial and dissect him. Moon and her friends must try and get the creature back into one piece so that he can meet his "father" at an appointed rendezvous and go home.

In spite of references to **E.T.**, **Close Encounters of the Third Kind**, and **Men in Black**, there is precious little to laugh at here, and the film's mawkish dramatic asides are painful to behold. PK go home ... please!

429. He Lives by Night

(1982; Cinema City Co.) ★: 6/10. *Ye ging wan* (Cantonese), *Ye jing hun* (Mandarin): "Night Thriller." Cinematographer: Arthur Wong Ngok-tai; Art Director: Oliver Wong Yui-man; Music: Violet Lam Man-yee; Writer: Lo Kin; Producers: Karl Maka, Dean Shek Tien; Director: Leung Po-chi. Cast: Sylvia Chang Ai-chia (Sissy), Kent Cheng Chuk-see (Dragon), Simon Yam Tat-wah ("Lousy" Wong), Eddie Chan (Eddie Wong), Eric Tsang Chi-wai (Convenience Store Robber), Billy Lau Nam-kwong (Cashier). 1.85:1. VHS: Tai Seng. Import LD: Golden Cinema City. Import VCD: Mega Star. 90 minutes.

Opening with a murder patterned after a famous sequence in Dario Argento's **Tenebrae**, and incorporating references to **Psycho** and Mario Bava's **Kill, Baby ... Kill!** (among others), this diverting thriller is marred by a few too many humorous asides but generally hits the mark. A transvestite killer (Ngai Dik, billed under his English name, Eddie Chan) is slashing and strangling women he comes across wearing a garter belt and white fishnet stockings. Late night DJ Sissy has been receiving death threats from a man claiming to be the murderer and seeks protection from bumbling cops Dragon and Wong. The former is hopelessly infatuated with Sissy and she uses this to get a closer look at the department's clues and murder scene photos. When her deductions aid the investigation, Dragon uses Sissy as a decoy to lure out the killer. Tracing a phone call to the radio station, the police nab their suspect but he/she turns out to be the wrong one, leaving the disc jockey alone and at the real psychopath's mercy.

Too much time is spent on lovesick nerd Kent Cheng's feeble pursuit of Sylvia Chang's character, and there are some hoary cliches, but the scare sequences are fairly tense. The film's goal to be nothing more than a lightweight thrill ride can be summed up by the comic outtakes under the end credits, which culminate in a final image that pokes fun at the overabundance of horror sequels. Chang is very good in a role that is quite different from the kind of part that most Westerners know her for.

430. The Head Hunter

(1982; New Century Film Productions H.K.) ★: 6/10. *Lip tau* (Cantonese), *Lie tou* (Mandarin): "Hunt Head." Music: Not Original; Writer: Roy Szeto Cheuk-hon; Producer: Hung Kuen-hoi; Action Director: Wong Cheung; Director: Lau Shing-hon. Cast: Chow Yun-fat (Nguyen Dich), Rosamund Kwan Chi-lam (Vicky Lee), Phillip Chan Yan-kin (Kim Tai-yung), Ko Chuen-hsiang (Lee Hung-fat), Melvin Wong Kam-sun (Inspector Lau). 1.85:1. VHS: Tai Seng (Subtitled and Unsubtitled versions). 98 minutes.

A year after his superb performance as a Vietnamese refugee in Ann Hui's **The Story of Woo Viet**, Chow Yun-fat signed on for a similar role in this low-budget exploitation thriller. He plays Nguyen, an immigrant from Vietnam who works as a movie special effects technician while also committing contract killings for the "Eagles." The one thing that keeps him going is his dream of bringing the rest of his family over to HK. While investigating a series of murders and an apparent gas attack on an elementary school, TV reporter Vicky Lee discovers that the homicide victims were killed by Sarin and Somin gas, which were used in the

Vietnam War. After exploring a series of factories, she narrows her search down to the film company Nguyen works for. He and Vicky develop a rocky relationship that soon turns into genuine love. Upon learning that his family has died while trying to escape Vietnam, Nguyen reveals to Vicky that his employer is manufacturing chemical weapons for the Americans to use in retaliation for Russia's use of Agent Orange. When Vicky's father turns up dead, Nguyen realizes that he was the one who pulled the trigger. Complicating matters further is Kim Taiyung, a soldier that Nguyen left behind during the war after he fell into a Vietcong trap. Driven psychotic by his ordeal and now employed by the Russians, Kim is stalking his former friend, hungry for vengeance.

While the plotting is a bit too convenient and the finale overly melodramatic, **The Head Hunter** still manages to push some buttons in regards to the Vietnam conflict and its lasting scars. The idea that the "Eagles" and "Bears" (as they are referred to throughout) simply moved the battleground *underground* (making the unsuspecting citizens of major population centers potential "casualties of war") also provides for a more layered and engrossing premise than is usually found in the Vietnam exploitation cycle. Chow is quite convincing, and Phillip Chan (a former real-life police officer who is almost always cast as a cop) has a *very* atypical part that he attacks with relish. The stock score includes music lifted from **Sorcerer** and **Dawn of the Dead**. Tai Seng has apparently released both subtitled and unsubtitled versions of the film; the former is now no longer available.

431. Health Warning

(1983; Bang! Bang! Films/Verdull) ★: 6/10. *Dai lui toi* (Cantonese), *Da lei tai* (Mandarin): "Fighting for the Top Spot." Cinematographers: Henry Chan Chun-kit, Abdul M. Rumjahn, Larry Siu Yuen-chi, Peter Ngor Chi-kwan, Arthur Wong Ngok-tai; Music: Jim Shum Sing-tak; Writer: Jerry Liu Wing-leung; Producer: Kimmy Suen King-on; Action Director: Shum Mo-keung; Director: Che-Kirk Wong Chi-keung. Cast: Johnny Wang Lung-wei (Killer), Eddy Ko Hung (The Master), Ray Lui Leung-wai (Gei), Elvis Tsui Kam-kong (Tall Skinhead Fighter). 1.85:1. VHS: Ocean Shores (Dubbed). Import LD: Ocean Shores (No Subtitles). Import VCD: Film City (No Subtitles). 78 minutes. Also known as **Flash Future Kung Fu** (Title given to aforementioned video releases).

Imagine an '80s dance movie directed by Shinya Tsukamoto (**Tetsuo**, **Tokyo Fist**) and you will get some idea of the look and feel of this ambitious low-budget sci-fi thriller. In the 21st century major technological breakthroughs are made, but instead of improving things, the advancements only destroy the work ethic and spawn social unrest. As a result of the growing animosity among the working class, a group of Chinese neo-Nazis called "The X Gang" rises to prominence in HK. Clinging to the old ways, a kung fu school master tries to steer his students away from the drugs and mindless violence that now consume the era's young people. Fighters Gei and Killer get mixed up with two of the female fascists and the latter nearly dies as a result. A gang of Nazi skinheads proceed to trash the martial arts school, and their leader announces a plan to lobotomize the masses as a way of ensuring total obedience to the party. Killer and the master invade the X Gang's headquarters and, along with one of the women (who has repented her ways in light of the fact that her three-year-old daughter will soon be surgically altered), try to put a stop to them.

While derivative of **Blade Runner** and **The Road Warrior**, the film's look is quite accomplished, considering the meager finances director Che-Kirk Wong had to work with. Bleak and crumbling interiors, fanciful lighting, smoke, neon, fuzzy TV screens, and bizarre electronic music are combined with sado-masochistic elements and homosexual imagery to create a fascinating milieu. That, combined with the clever transmuting of the traditional kung fu movie plot (martial arts students take revenge on the evil government responsible for the destruction of their school) help to compensate for some dated components and an overabundance of dull boxing sequences. Character names above are from the dubbed version.

432. Heart Against Hearts

(1992; D & B Films Co.) ★: 4/10. *Saam yan jo sai gaai* (Cantonese), *San ren-zuo shi jie* (Mandarin): "Three Person Made World." Cinematographer: Chan Ying-kit; Art Director: Danny Yuen Ching-yeung; Music: Danny Chung Teng-yat, George Lam Chi-cheung; Writers: Stephen Shin Kei-yin, Lee Man-choi, Ng Wai-shek, Lau Miu-yuet; Producer-Director: Stephen Shin Kei-yin. Cast: George Lam Chi-cheung (Alex Lui), Carol Cheng Yu-ling (Judy), Vivian Chow Wei-man (Vivian), Paul Chun Pui (Edmond Tang), Elaine Kam Yin-ling (Judy's Friend), Suki Kwan Sau-mei (Suki Wong), Phillip Chan Yan-kin (Phillip), Manfred Wong (Ah Man), Yip Wing-cho (Vivian's Uncle), Dennis Chan Kwok-san (Dennis), Chen Jing (Little Beard). Dolby Stereo. 1.85:1. VHS: Tai Seng. 98 minutes.

This formula-bound romantic comedy stars George Lam and Carol Cheng as newlyweds who find out on their honeymoon that they have lost every cent of their savings, forcing Lam to close down his company. When creditors seize their car, flat, and all of their other possessions, Cheng's daughter (played by Vivian Chow) finds a new place for the family but neglects to tell her that it is owned by Cheng's ex-husband. To make matters worse, unemployment is robbing Lam of all his dignity, and Cheng's slimy boss plans on using her as a patsy when his corrupt business dealings finally catch up with him.

The cast is filled with talented performers, but the script gives them very little of interest to do and is sorely lacking in wit and invention. Sync sound recording is a minor plus. This was the last of three films pairing Lam and Cheng; Rosamund Kwan Chi-lam and Maggie Cheung Man-yuk appear here in flashback sequences lifted from those earlier entries, **Heart to Hearts** (1988) and **Heart into Hearts** (1990).

433. Heart of Dragon

[*sic*] (1985; Golden Harvest/Bo Ho Films Co./Paragon Films) ★: 6/10. *Lung dik sam* (Cantonese), *Long de xin* (Mandarin): "Dragon's Heart." Cinematographer: Arthur Wong Ngok-tai; Art Directors: Cheung Yun-keung, Sin Ngai-lung; Writer: Barry Wong Ping-yiu; Producer: Leonard Ho Koon-cheung; Action Direction: Sammo Hung's Stuntman Association; Director: Sammo Hung Kam-po. Cast: Jackie Chan (Tat), Sammo Hung Kam-po (Do-do), Emily Chu Bo-yee (Jenny), James Tien Chun (Kim), Mang Hoi (Yan), Melvin Wong Kam-sun (Inspector Wong), Tai Po (Keung), Wu Ma (Restaurant Owner), Dennis Chan Kwok-san (Waiter), Lam Ching-ying (SWAT Commander), Yip Wing-cho (Maitre d'), Anthony Chan Yau (Fung), Woo Fung (Principal Pang). Dolby Digital (DVD only). 1.85:1. VHS/LD: Tai Seng (Remastered for the English market; subtitled or dubbed). Import LD: Star Entertainment (No Subtitles). Import VCD: Mei Ah. Import DVD: Universe. 89 minutes. Also known as **The First Mission** (Dubbed version).

Weary of the skimpy, formulaic plotting in Jackie Chan's recent features? Try this earlier effort, a tearjerker spiced with action, directed by and starring his old Peking Opera schoolmate and "Big Brother," Sammo Hung. Chan plays Tat, a HK cop recently transferred from a tour with the colony's SWAT unit who must keep a watchful eye on his retarded older brother Do-do (Hung, sporting a toddler's wardrobe and Moe Howard's haircut). Do-do's gullibility frequently gets him into trouble, and Tat soon realizes that he must sacrifice his dream of sailing around the world in order to take care of him and pacify his marriage-minded girlfriend (**A Better Tomorrow**'s Emily Chu). One day Do-do comes into possession of a satchel containing a cache of jewels from a recent heist. The criminals (led by '70s kung fu star James Tien) take Do-do hostage, forcing Chan and his old SWAT buddies to take matters into their own hands and launch a rescue attempt.

Certain aspects of **Heart of Dragon** may be too melodramatic for some Western viewers, and on the whole, the film is more bittersweet than a Hollywood adaptation of such material would be. However, Chan and Hung handle the emotional aspects of their roles very well, and the martial arts are presented with the sort of spectacular choreography one has come to expect from the two stars. A closing montage, revealing the fates of the characters, is a nice directorial touch and provides a very satisfying wrap-up to the storyline. The supporting cast is a veritable "Who's Who" of Chan and Hung's action movie associates from the time, including Chin Kar-lok, Dick Wei, Yuen Wah, Peter Chan Lung, Phillip Ko Fei, Blackie Ko Shou-liang, Fung Hark-on, Lee Hoi-sang, and Ben Lam Kwok-bun. Japanese video and theatrical prints include two additional action scenes which were directed by Jackie Chan and are unique to that version. The first occurs in the opening reel, with Chan taking on a group of thugs at a hospital. The other unfolds in the second reel and finds Chan and his fellow off-duty officers having a comical fight against some thugs who bullied Jenny.

434. Heart of Killer

[*sic*] (1995; Quicken Development/Sinocean International Holdings/Fortune Stars Films Co.) ★: 4/10. *Yin ching naam jui gik* (Cantonese), *Ran qing nan ju ji* (Mandarin): "Male Sniper Who Loves Passionately." Cinematographer: Chim Pak-hung; Art Directors: Ray Lam Chan-fai, Angelo Bernardo Castilho; Music: Oman Mui Siu-kei, Sam Leung Yiu-san, Barry Cheung Fu-ling; Writers: Wing Chow Chan-wing, Philip Kwok Wai-chung, Andrew Kam Yeung-wah; Producers: Lee Kin-hing, Andrew Kam Yeung-wah; Action Directors: Wong Wing-kwan, Chan Tat-kwong; Director: Andrew Kam Yeung-wah. Cast: Yu Rongguang (Ko Lap), Max Mok Siu-chung (Kung Kwan), Eileen Tung Oi-ling (Bin Yee), Jiang Rong, Wong Ting. 1.85:1. VHS: Tai Seng. Import LD/VCD: Fitto Mobile. 92 minutes.

A HK/China co-production, this forgettable actioner concerns hitmen Ko Lap and Kung Kwan, who operate in the Mainland. One day Lap murders an old man who turns out to be the father of pretty Bin Yee, whom Kwan is attracted to. When Yee meets Lap, she recognizes him from somewhere but does not make the connection. As time passes, Yee and Kwan fall deeply in love, while Lap, too, finds a woman and decides that he wants to live a normal life. However, the man who originally hired Lap to murder Yee's father now also wants her dead as well. Lap saves both her and Kwan from a pair of assassins but, in doing so, inadvertently jogs the girl's memory, creating a new problem.

The script tries to develop the characters by devoting a good amount of time to each killer's lovelife, but as the protagonists are not very interesting (the one distinguishing characteristic of Yu's character is that he always guzzles distilled water while performing his hits), this just slows the movie down to a crawl. The various action sequences are passably staged but not exciting enough to justify slogging through everything else.

435. Heartbeat 100

(1987; Cinema City Co.) ★: 5/10. *Sam tiu yat baak* (Cantonese), *Xin tao yi bai* (Mandarin): "Heart Beats One Hundred." Cinematographer: James Chan Hau-ming; Art Director: Andy Lee Yiu-kwong; Music: Not Original; Writers: Raymond Wong Pak-ming, Philip Cheng Chung-tai, Ng Man-fai; Producer: Raymond Wong Pak-ming; Action Director: Lau Kar-wing; Directors: Kent Cheng Chuk-see, Lo Kin. Cast: Maggie Cheung Man-yuk (Maggie Cheung), Lui Fong (Wat, aka Weeny Eyes), Bonnie Law Ming-chu (Chu-chu), Mark Cheng Ho-nam (Toa Nam), Woo Fung (Uncle Yam), Wong Ching (Pink Panther), Shing Fui-on (See Tai-hoi), Kent Cheng Chuk-see (Sergeant Chu). 1.85:1. VHS: Tai Seng. Import LD: Golden Cinema City. Import VCD: Mega Star. 93 minutes.

A fairly silly mystery-thriller, **Heartbeat 100** shuttles uneasily between teen movie conventions and graphic exploitation elements. Not long after a brutal double murder has occurred in HK, teenagers Maggie, Chu-chu, and Wat travel to peaceful On Lok Village for an outing. Along the way they encounter police inspector Toa Nam, who is travelling to On Lok because the two victims of the aforementioned homicides originally hailed from the village. Maggie is working on a mystery script and hopes that she will discover the killer as a means of acquiring creative inspiration. The kids rent a run-down house in the village and soon encounter "Pink Panther," a local retarded man who likes to play with snakes. When Maggie witnesses a murder, the police are unable to find any evidence of a crime but the threat soon becomes very real.

Aside from one or two effectively creepy moments, thrills are pretty scarce, with the proceedings playing out much like an American slasher film with heightened humor. Recommended mainly to fans of Maggie Cheung, who is ostensibly playing herself here!

436. A Hearty Response

(1986; Golden Harvest/The Wing Scope Film Production) ★: 5/10. *Yee gui wan tin* (Cantonese), *Yi gai yun tian* (Mandarin): "Chivalry Overshadows Clouds and Sky." Cinematographer: Sung Kwong-wah; Art Director: Jon Hau Wing-choi; Music: Danny Chung Teng-yat, Chow Kam-cheung; Writer: Lai Man-cheuk; Producer: Rover Tang Kwong-chow; Action Directors: Tony Leung Siu-hung, Luk Chuen, Benz Kong To-hoi; Director: Norman Law Man. Cast: Chow Yun-fat (Ho Ting-bon), Joey Wang Tsu-hsien (Kwong Sun), Lui Fong (Cheong Yan), Shum Wai (Snake Man), Paul Chun Pui (Lui Tak), Wong Wan-si (Wan), Kent Cheng Chuk-see (Beat Cop). Dolby Digital (DVD only). 1.85:1. VHS: Tai Seng. Import VCD: Mei Ah (No Subtitles). Import DVD: Universe. 89 minutes.

HK films are known for their dramatic shifts in tone, and **A Hearty Response** is a primary example, going from a breezy, romantic comedy to an exceptionally nasty revenge thriller in its final third. Kwong Sun is an illegal immigrant from China who is unable to contact her relatives in HK. Having no money, she is caught shoplifting one day by undercover cop Cheong Yan. He and his partner, Ho Ting-bon, are camped out in the supermarket, waiting to capture a drug dealer who uses the place to make drop-offs and pick-ups. The felon just happens to show up right when Yan is apprehending Sun, and in the skirmish that follows, the girl is injured. Feigning amnesia so that she won't be deported, Sun insists on treating Ting-bon like he is her husband, a charade that goes over great with the cop's mother and disastrously with his girlfriend. Ting-bon eventually discovers the truth, but after a period of anger, he decides to let Sun stay with him. At this point the film switches gears as Kwong-sun is kidnapped by a lowlife who had previously tried to rape her.

The first two-thirds is formulaic (it even includes the "montage set to a pop tune" break) but enjoyable, thanks to Chow's charisma and Wang's convincing turn. However, the final reel is so violent and unpleasant (and, in terms of its resolution, so ludicrous) that it leaves a sour taste in one's mouth.

Heaven and Earth *see* Tian Di

437. Heaven Can Help

(1984; Cinema City Co.) ★: 6/10. *Seung tin gau ming* (Cantonese), *Shang tian jiu ming* (Mandarin): "Heaven Save Life." Cinematographers: Au Chih-chun, Tom Lau Moon-tong; Art Director: Lam Sai-cheung; Music: Chung Wah-fung; Producers: Dean Shek Tien, Karl Maka; Director: David Chiang Da-wei. Cast: Eric Tsang Chi-wai (Don Hugh Mak, aka "Downhill"), Cherie Chung Cho-hung (Cathy), Charlie Chin Hsiang-lin (Killer), Wong Wan-si (Mak's Sister), Richard Ng Yiu-hon (Chan Siu-ming), Paul Chun Pui (Shek), Woo Fung (Mak's Boss). 1.85:1. VHS: Tai Seng. Import LD: Golden Cinema City. Import VCD: Mega Star. 90 minutes.

This enjoyable fantasy-comedy-thriller stars Eric Tsang (HK's answer to Lou Costello) as a hapless loser named Don Hugh Mak ("Downhill" to his friends) whose luck is so bad, he can singlehandedly sink the most successful business and kill pets just by touching them. Mak's luck finally runs completely out when he is accidentally killed while on a drinking binge. He arrives in a Purgatory-type netherworld called "The Time Tunnel," manned by animal-headed guardians (like several Chinese fantasy comedies, including Tsang's 1993 effort **Shyly Spirit**, entering Heaven or Hell is akin to going through Customs). Not surprisingly, a mistake has been made and Mak is allowed to return to Earth. However, the sentinels warn that he will truly die and go to Hell unless he can prevent three forthcoming murders. Upon arriving home, Mak almost trips over the body of the first person on the list, a millionaire named Wong. "Super Detective" Chan Siu-ming (Richard Ng doing his best Inspector Clouseau imitation) is soon on the case but turns out to be an even bigger dimwit than Mak. Meanwhile, the second victim, an actress named Ms. Pao, gets offed while taking a shower. Her sleazy producer, Shek, is next in line and is almost killed in an auto wrecking yard by a mysterious assailant. While trying to protect Shek, Mak meets up with the man's sister, Cathy, and runs afoul of Chan, who accuses him of the crimes and places him under arrest. With Mak behind bars, Shek is easy prey for the killer, who now sets his sights on Cathy. It turns out that Pao, Shek, and the psycho kidnapped Wong and murdered him, even though their ransom demands were met. The latter then decided that he didn't feel like splitting up the loot. With all three of the people he was supposed to protect now dead, Mak figures he's got nothing to lose and this lack of concern inadvertently gives him the fortitude he needs to take on the murderer.

One of the horror farces produced by the fledgling Cinema City company during the early '80s, **Heaven Can Help** is a lively and enjoyable diversion. Some viewers may be put off by the way things go from the light farce of the first two thirds to the nasty, slasher-inspired action of the final reel but such radical shifts in tone are par for the course when it comes to HK cinema. One of the movie's most engaging components is the oddball pairing up of Tsang with the beautiful Chung. The two would re-team a few years later for a **Fatal Attraction**-style parody in the best segment of Jeff Lau Chun-wai's scattershot farce, **Carry On Hotel** (1988). Director David Chiang appears briefly as a speed-crazed cabbie.

438. Heaven Can't Wait

(1995; Entertainment Today/United Filmmakers Organization) ★: 5/10. *Gau sai san gwan* (Cantonese), *Jiu shi shen gun* (Mandarin): "World Saving Holy Stick." Cinematographer: Bill Wong Chung-bo; Art Director: James Cheung Ying-wah; Writers: Lee Chi-ngai, James Yuen Sai-sang, Peter Chan Ho-sun; Lam Ngoi-wah; Producer/Director: Lee Chi-ngai. Cast: Tony Leung Chiu-wai (Wong Tai-fung), Jordan Chan Siu-chun (Chan Chun), Bowie Lam Bo-yee (Calvin Ng Che), Karen Mok Man-wai (Joan), Jerry Lam Hiu-fung (Lo), Alex To Tak-wai (Pao), Kent Cheng Chuk-see (Tsui), Lawrence Cheng Tan-shui (On), Dennis Chan Kwok-san (Uncle Lam), Richard Ng Yiu-hon (Taoist), Meg Lam Kin-ming (Reporter), Ha Ping (Chun's Grandmother), Anita Yuen Wing-yee (The Moon Lady), Law Kar-ying (Ng Kong). 1.85:1. VHS: Tai Seng. Import LD/VCD: Fitto Mobile. 107 minutes.

Tai-fung has worked in the religious con game since he was a child. When his latest partner, Calvin, decides to dump him and go out on his own, Tai-fung declares that he can find a replacement within 24 hours. It ends up taking three months but his new meal ticket, goofy would-be actor Chan Chun, just may be his ultimate student. Re-christened "Master Da Da," a self-proclaimed expert in "digital healing," Chun becomes an instant celebrity by reviving "comatose" pop star Pao. The new media darling, Chun is now worth a lot of money to Tai-fung, who will not even consider an offer of $10 million from Calvin and his new partner to take the kid off his hands. In the meantime, seemingly against all odds, the dim-witted Chun keeps coming up with the right answers, predicting an earthquake and the crash of the Tokyo Stock Market, prompting another offer from Calvin. When Tai-fung once again declines, an assassin is dispatched to take him out but the bullet winds up in Chun's skull instead. Pronounced dead on the operating room table, Chun miraculously sits up a few minutes later, claiming to have visited Heaven and now taking his duties with the utmost seriousness. Convinced that he must die for HK's sins, Chun agrees to participate in a massive religious variety show that will climax with him going up in flames ... for real.

The subject is a ripe one for satire but the targets here are largely obvious and the humor is neither witty nor black enough to really hit home; the climax literally fizzles. Tony Leung Chiu-wai and Jordan Chan do good work but not enough attention is paid to the mechanics of their cons; everything falls into place much too conveniently. Karen Mok (as a TV reporter hot to make a buck off Da Da's newfound fame) commands the screen but even her character is not exploited properly and is all but forgotten by the time the credits roll. The term "Holy Stick" in the Chinese title is slang for a religious conman.

439. Her Fatal Ways

(1990; Golden Harvest/Bo Ho Films Co./Mobile Film Production/Paragon Films) ★: 5/10. *Biu je, nei ho ye!* (Cantonese), *Biao jie, ni hao ye!* (Mandarin): "Sister, You're Great!" Cinematographer: William Yim Wai-lun; Art Director: Oliver Wong Yui-man; Music: Violet Lam Man-yee; Writers: Alfred Cheung Kin-ting, Wong Wang-kei; Producer: Chan Pui-wah; Action Director: Chin Kar-lok; Director: Alfred Cheung Kin-ting. Cast: Carol Cheng Yu-ling (Cheng Shih-nan), Tony Leung Kar-fai (Wu Wei-kuo), Alfred Cheung Kin-ting (Hsiao-sheng), Lam Kau (Wu Tien-tzu), Michael Chow Man-kin (Niu), Sheila Chan Sak-lan (Hsuen Pi), Cho Tat-wah (Old Soldier), Lam Chung (Inspector Mo). 1.85:1. VHS: Tai Seng (No Subtitles). Import LD: Universe. 100 minutes.

The Three Chinas are at odds in this farce, which scored with HK audiences but will probably not go over as well with most Western viewers. Dedicated communist

Sister Cheng is dispatched to HK with the task of turning over felon Niu to the local authorities. The transfer is successfully completed but Niu manages to escape custody, necessitating a joint mission be undertaken by Cheng and HK cop Wu Wei-kuo. A by-the-book socialist, Cheng causes all manner of troubles for Wu, especially when she and her assistant are forced to stay with the policeman's father, a rabid supporter of Taiwan.

Most of the culture clash/fish-out-of-water humor is thuddingly obvious and the Mainland stereotypes are no less subtle. An occasional joke hits the mark (Sister Cheng sees **The Terminator** playing on TV and interprets it to be a battle between Marxist Leninists and Capitalism!) but **Her Fatal Ways** has not aged well. With 1997 having come and gone, with few changes resulting from the handover, the film's underlying message about how HK and China will be working together does not really hold water and the formulaic storyline barely holds one's interest. Carol Cheng *is* ideally cast, though, and the film would be far less palatable without her. Sync sound recording (several years before that became common) is another asset. Followed by three sequels (the first two currently difficult to locate in subtitled form) and an imitation called **His Fatal Way**.

440. Here Comes a Vampire

(1990) ★: 5/10. *Maang gwai daai ha II* (Cantonese), *Meng gui da sha II* (Mandarin): "Fierce Ghost Large Mansion II." Cinematographer: Jimmy Leung Chi-ming; Art Director: Chan Wing-bo; Music: Not Original; Writer: Lau Jun-wai; Producer: Chan Wai-chi; Action Directors: Yuen Shun-yee, Poon Cheung, Ko Man-dik; Director: Yuen Cheung-yan. Cast: Sandra Ng Kwan-yu (Sister Nine), Billy Lau Nam-kwong (Yung), Joanna Chan Pui-san (San), Woo Fung (Wu), Sin Lap-man (Long), Charlie Cho Cha-lei (Charlie), Andy Hui Chi-on (Myths), Sze Ma-yin (Sze Ma-yin), Lau Yuk-ting (May), Meg Lam Kin-ming (Scimkovaca), Cho Tat-wah (Chan), Yuen King-tan (The Ghost). 1.85:1. VHS: World Video. Import LD/VCD: Mei Ah. 93 minutes.

Another entry in the "Police Academy Meets the Monsters" horror/comedy cycle, a combination unique to HK cinema. The plot this time concerns an attempt by the police force to cut corners by intentionally abusing a group of male and female officers to the point where they will resign, saving the head office the trouble of firing them. While clowning around one evening, the cops in question accidentally conjure up a vicious female ghost, who proceeds to possess one of the men. The spirit is eventually expelled but enters policewoman May, who proceeds to kill some SWAT team members and one of the commanders.

The first half of this nominal sequel to **Operation Pink Squad II** is standard **Inspector Wears Skirts**-style farce with the supernatural elements not really kicking in until later on. The film picks up considerably at that point but remains a lesser entry in this short-lived trend, lacking the manic energy and imaginative special effects found in the best ones. The soundtrack includes music swiped from **Phantasm** and **A Nightmare on Elm Street Part 2: Freddy's Revenge**.

441. Hero

(1997; Shaw Brothers) ★: 3/10. *Ma Wing-jing* (Cantonese), *Ma Yongzhen* (Mandarin): "Ma Wing-jing" (the protagonist's name in Cantonese) or "Ma Yongzhen" (the protagonist's name in Mandarin). Cinematographer: Tom Lau Moon-tong; Art Director: Ben Lau Man-hung; Music: William Woo Wai-lap, Raymond Wong Ying-wah, Lincoln Lo Kin; Writer: Kei On (pseudonym for Jeff Lau Chun-wai); Producer: Mona Fong Yat-wah; Action Directors: Corey Yuen Kwai, Yuen Tak; Director: Corey Yuen Kwai. Cast: Takeshi Kaneshiro (Ma Wing-jing), Yuen Biao (Tam See), Jessica Hester (Kim Ling-tze), Valerie Chow Kar-ling (Yam Yeung-tien), Yuen Wah (Ma Tai-cheung), Yuen Tak (Yang Shuang), Corey Yuen Kwai (Uncle Po). 1.85:1. VHS/LD: Mecapro. Import LD/VCD: Universe. 96 minutes (Censored HK version).

In 1898, many refugees from Shantung fled to British-controlled Shanghai. Brothers Ma Wing-jing and Ma Tai-cheung are among those seeking a new life in the luxurious but crime-ridden city. They discover that Shanghai is controlled by two rival gangsters, Tam See (in league with the British) and Yang Shuang (who has the backing of the police). The former takes a liking to Wing-jing, recognizing that his brash nature and martial arts abilities could be of use to him in the future. While Wing-jing resists Tam's financial rewards (even after saving the gangster's life during an ambush), he remains on friendly terms with him. Wing-jing strikes out on his own, acquiring several territories and many followers but his judgement is swayed by the beautiful club owner, Yam Yeung-tien, who is secretly working for Yang. When she betrays Wing-jing, both he and Tam suffer harsh consequences.

A remake of Chang Cheh's **Boxer from Shantung** (1972), this is the first Shaw Brothers period martial arts film in over a decade. Unfortunately, it bears little resemblance to the company's classic productions, most of which benefitted from compelling storylines concocted by the great Ngai Hong (who co-wrote **Boxer** with Chang). **Hero** suffers from the unmistakably heavy hand of Jeff Lau, a writer/director best known for his aggressively silly comedies. Unfortunately, most of his dramatic ventures are forged with all the subtlety of a pie in the face and this one is no exception. Cliches abound and the humorous asides are often painfully inane. While devilishly handsome, Kaneshiro is unable to muster the authority befitting his rank, both as the central protagonist and as a fearsome triad. Yuen Biao, on the other hand, is engaging in one of the best parts he's had in a dog's age. Still looking quite youthful, Yuen would have been quite convincing as the nominal hero of the piece but even his best efforts could not have been enough to keep this bomb afloat. The HK version is heavily cut, making the Taiwan release preferable.

442. Hero Beyond the Boundary of Time

(1993; Movie Impact/Impact Films Investment) ★: 3/10. *Wai Siu-bo ji fung ji kau nui* (Cantonese), *Wei Xiaobao zhi feng zhi gou nu* (Mandarin): "Wai Siu-bo—Wooing Women on Imperial Orders" or "Wei Xiaobao—Wooing Women on Imperial Orders." Cinematographer: Andrew Lau Wai-keung; Art Directors: Ben Luk Man-wah, Ringo Cheung Sek-wah; Music: Richard Lo Sai-kit; Writers: Matthew Chow Hoi-kwong, Joe Ma Wai-ho, Clarence Yip Wai-chung; Producer: Clarence Yip Wai-chung; Action Directors: Blackie Ko Shou-liang, Cheung Tai-wor, Siu Bo, Tsui Chung-san; Director: Blackie Ko Shou-liang. Cast: Tony Leung Chiu-wai (Wai Siu-bo), Veronica Yip Yuk-hing (Tsang Yau), Dicky Cheung Wai-kin (Chiu), Jacqueline Ng Suet-man (Siu-ha), Jamie Luk Kim-ming (Hung), Kenneth Tong Chun-yip (His Majesty). 1.85:1. VHS: Tai Seng (No Subtitles). Import LD/VCD: Star Entertainment (No Subtitles). Import DVD: China Star (No Subtitles). 94 minutes.

Tony Leung Chiu-wai became a star playing "Wai Siu-bo" in a 1985 TV miniseries adaptation of Jin Yong's novel, "The Duke of Mount Deer." Following the success of **Royal Tramp** (which starred Stephen Chiau Sing-chi as Wai), Leung was enlisted to reprise the part in this ill-conceived time travel farce. The film opens in the 17th. century, with Wai ordered to be the guinea pig for a test run of "The Time Adventure Wheel." The teapot-shaped device is supposed to send its occupant 300 years into the future but has, on all earlier tests, merely blown up. Wai's mission: find a new, virginal wife for The Emperor. Miraculously, the time machine works and Wai finds himself in present day HK, where he is instantly arrested as an illegal immigrant. Aided by lame-brained police officer Chiu (who is secretly selling Wai's possessions, all of them now valuable antiques), Wai travels to Tsimshatsui to begin his search, though he already has his eye on pretty country girl, Siu-ha. However, one of Wai's enemies in the past has dispatched two assassins to 1993 to liquidate him. If that weren't enough, some of Wai's eight wives come back, too.

The premise offers ample opportunity for imaginative fish-out-of-water gags but most of the humor is the sort of broad slapstick and limp sexual jibes one can find in any third-rate comedy. The film eventually wraps up with a high flying, fantasy-oriented battle in an amusement park that comes right out of left field but is, at least, a welcome relief from the lame jokes. Watch the two **Royal Tramp** films instead. Much of the soundtrack consists of music lifted from **Aliens** and **Cape Fear**. The Taiwan video release has English subtitles but is heavily censored.

443. Hero Dream

(1992; Super Power Motion Picture Co.) ★: 2/10. *Yam yiu ho ching* (Cantonese), *Yin yao hao qing* (Mandarin): "Seductive Passions." Music: Not Original; Producer: Lau Siu-kwan; Director: Lau Keung-fu. Cast: Chin Siu-ho (Li Chi-hao), Chin Kar-lok (Lok), Carrie Ng Kar-lai (Kiki), Michiko Nishiwaki (Yi), Sophia Crawford (Blonde). 1.85:1. VHS: Tai Seng (Poor Subtitles). 92 minutes.

This sleazy, decidedly unappetizing Category III action/sex film stars real-life brothers Chin Siu-ho and Chin Kar-lok, talented actors and terrific martial artists, who deserve to be in far better material than this. Police officer Hao takes his newly pregnant wife Kiki to Thailand as an anniversary present. Shortly after their arrival, the woman is kidnapped by some local hoods, who mistakenly think that Hao has some of their drugs in his possession. Hao launches a rescue attempt (how and where he managed to get such heavy artillery in such a short time is one of many things here that make no sense) but Kiki is mortally wounded in the process. The cop spends the rest of the film caught in the middle of a violent war between rival gangs of drug runners, eventually teaming up with a disgraced member of one outfit to exterminate the lowlifes who killed Kiki (they are certainly easy to spot: every single one wears jeans and a black tee shirt).

Tedious, ineptly staged shootouts and numerous softcore sex scenes (most featuring transsexuals, some of whom are still hermaphrodites) certainly do nothing to make this dubious affair any more palatable.

444. Hero of Tomorrow

(1988; Movie Impact) ★: 5/10. *Gong woo jip baan yan* (Cantonese), *Jiang hu jie ban ren* (Mandarin): "Triad Successor." Cinematographer: Mark Lee Ping-bing; Art Director: Jessy Lam Chak-chi; Music: Lo Kit; Writer: Clarence Yip Sai-chung; Producer: Wallace Cheung Kwok-chong; Action Director: Wong Shu-tong; Director: Poon Man-kit. Cast: Max Mok Siu-chung (Crow Yeung Tin-shun), Miu Kiu-wai (Lee Sam), William Ho Kar-kui (Billy), Cheung Wing-ching (Little Shan-tung), Joan Tong Lai-kau (Naive Ng), Kam Siu-mui (Yeung Lai-ling), Lung Ming-yan (Lung), Ku Feng (Uncle Chung), Blackie Ko Shou-liang (Peter), James Tien Chun (Officer Tso), Chen Sung-yung (Big Ma), Phillip Kwok Tsui (Big B), Tommy Wong Kwong-leung (Ng Kong), Chen Jing (Hood With Moustache), Phillip Chan Yan-kin (Crow's Target). 1.85:1. VHS: Tai Seng. Import LD/VCD: Ocean Shores. 86 minutes.

Another imitation of **A Better Tomorrow**, this violent triad thriller covers the genre bases competently, emphasizing the theme of honor among thieves from the vastly superior John Woo film. Upon his release from jail, gangster Lee Sam gets revenge on the men who put him there and then flees to Taiwan. There, he hooks up with gang boss Billy, a dishonorable and hair-triggered thug if there ever was one. While trying to diplomatically repair one of Billy's outbursts against a rival leader, Lee is saved from death at the last minute by Crow Yeung, a new and enthusiastic recruit. Lee then decides to leave "the life," while Yeung quickly rises through the ranks. When Billy inadvertently chooses Yeung's girl as his rape *du jour*, the stage is set for several tragedies and Lee to join with his old friend to seek vengeance. Aside from having most of the action unfold outside of HK, there is nothing new here. Many character actors turn up in bit parts.

445. Heroes Among Heroes

(1993; Art Sea Films Company) ★: 5/10. *So hat yi* (Cantonese), *Su qi er* (Mandarin): "So, the Beggar" or "Su, the Beggar." Cinematographers: Michael Ma Koon-wah, Poon Tak-yip; Music: William Woo Wai-lap; Writers: Lau Tai-muk, Tsui Tat-cho; Action Direction: The Yuen Clan; Producers/Directors: Yuen Woo-ping, Chan Chin-chung. Cast: Donnie Yen Chi-tan (So Chan), Fennie Yuen Kit-ying (Princess Yi Teh-tai), Xiong Xinxin (Prince Barac), Wong Yuk (Wong Fei-hung), Ng Man-tat (Yin), Sheila Chan Sak-lan (Aunt Jean), Kwan Hoi-shan (Beggar So), Pau Fong (Officer Lam Che-chu). 1.85:1. VHS/LD: World Video. 91 minutes. Also known as **Beggar Su**.

This thoroughly routine entry in the early 90s Wong Fei-hung sweepstakes finds the socially conscious hero leading a movement to rid China of opium and, more specifically, opium dealers. The foreigners distributing the drug ally themselves with the corrupt Prince Barac, who reasons that the best way to get rid of a Canton Tiger like Wong is to pit him against his own Tiger: So Chan (Yen, in the role essayed the year before by Stephen Chiau Sing-chi in **King of Beggars**). An impetuous and undisciplined youth, Chan spends most of his time acting as referee for his bickering Aunt Jean (Chan, at her shrillest) and his good-for-nothing father (Ng, in his familiar put-upon slob role). He also excels at martial arts, thanks to his training from the legendary drunken master, Beggar So (Kwan, in the part immortalized by Simon Yuen Siu-tien in **Drunken Master**). In order to facilitate his plans, Barac gets Chan addicted to opium and joins with the fanatical Fire Lotus Gang in a cowardly and devastating attack on Beggar So and his followers. After nursing Chan through his withdrawal pains, Fei-hung joins forces with him in a final assault on Barac and his allies.

The aura of **Once Upon a Time In China** hangs heavily over this exercise, which plays like a road company version of Tsui Hark's popular series. The action scenes are plentiful and adequately presented but could have benefitted from that extra element of excitement and finesse that Ching Siu-tung always brings to the films he choreographs. Chan finally adopts the drunken stance in the concluding battle but there is nothing on display that comes close to matching the final 15 minutes of **Drunken Master II** (or even **Drunken Master I** for that matter). Yen displays his impressive physical prowess once again but this role seems like a demotion for him after his fine work as Wong Kei-ying in **Iron Monkey**. Wong Yuk catches one's attention during the fight scenes but isn't particularly memorable or charismatic. Adequate fare for fight fans who don't mind periodically leaning on their fast forward buttons to escape the deadly comedy relief; others need not apply.

446. Heroes of the East

(1978; Shaw Brothers) ★: 8/10. *Chung wah cheung fu* (Cantonese), *Zhong hua zhangfu* (Mandarin): "Chinese Husband." Music: Not Original; Writer: Ngai Hong; Producer: Mona Fong Yat-wah; Action Director-Director: Lau Kar-leung. Cast: Gordon Lau Kar-fai (Ho Tao), Yasuaki Kurota (Sanzo), Yuko Mizuno (Kuda), Simon Yuen Siu-tien (Tao's Teacher), Norman Tsui Siu-keung (Chang), Lau Kar-leung (Drunken Master), Lee Hoi-sang (Bald Pupil). 2.35:1. VHS: Vista (Dubbed). 101 minutes. Also known as **Challenge of the Ninja** and **Shaolin Challenges Ninja** (Vista title).

An arranged marriage between a Chinese man and a Japanese woman forms the basis of this excellent Shaw Brothers production from director Lau Kar-leung. Tao and Kuda are a happy couple, but a cultural clash soon arises when she proceeds to demolish half of the house with her destructive Japanese martial arts. When Tao defeats her using Chinese forms and weapons, she refuses to learn the more demure style of Chinese kung fu and returns home to Japan. A ruse by Tao to try and get Kuda to return backfires and results in seven skilled Japanese fighters journeying to China with the intention of defending the honor of their martial arts techniques. Desperate to get out of this fix, while also preserving the honor of his fellow Chinese fighters, Tao utilizes various facets of his training in order to triumph against his diverse opponents.

The portion of the film devoted to the marital conflict is simplistic and tiresome (a flaw heightened by especially insipid dubbing in the English version), but the presentation of cultural differences in both life and martial arts is an excellent premise. In addition to being a welcome change from the usual genre conventions (not one single person dies!), the film is an excellent showcase for Gordon Lau's incredible skills, which seem to encompass every fighting discipline. The final bout, pitting Lau against Yasuaki Kurota's ninjitsu tricks, is a particular pleasure to behold and a far more reverent depiction of that Japanese art than one regularly finds in American movies. The character names listed above are from the dubbed version.

447. Heroes Shed No Tears

(1986; Golden Harvest/Paragon Films) ★: 4/10. *Ying hung mo lui* (Cantonese), *Ying xiong wu lei* (Mandarin): "Heroes—No Tears." Cinematographer: Kenichi Naragawa; Art Director: Raymond Fung Yuen; Music: Tang Siu-lam; Producer: Leonard Ho Koon-cheung; Action Director: Chin Yuet-sang; Writer-Director: John Woo Yu-sen. Cast: Eddy Ko Hung (Chan Chung), Lam Ching-ying (Vietnamese Colonel), Lau Chau-sang (Chau-sang), Cecile Le Baily (French Girl), Chin Yuet-sang. 1.85:1. VHS/LD: Tai Seng (Remastered for the English market; subtitled or dubbed). Import VCD: Mega Star. 81 minutes. Also known as **The Sunset Warrior**.

John Woo has disowned this war actioner, which was taken out of his hands by Golden Harvest and spiced up with sex and violence inserts (which Woo speculates may have been done in an attempt to obtain a European video deal). Even after these changes, the company remained dissatisfied with the final product and consigned it to the shelf. The film finally opened in the fall of 1986 after the phenomenal success of **A Better Tomorrow** increased its exploitation value, but still managed only a week in theaters. Aside from its ferocious violence and Woo's familiar theme of the strong bond and intense loyalty between friends, there is little to distinguish this from any number of other jungle combat thrillers that followed in the wake of **Rambo: First Blood Part II** (1985). In a rare heroic role, Eddy Ko plays the leader of some Chinese soldiers of fortune sent into the Golden Triangle to smash a heroin operation. Upon accomplishing their mission, they take the druglord hostage and are pursued by his remaining forces. They soon have more to worry about after preventing some Vietnamese border guards from raping a young French girl. In the subsequent skirmish, the Vietnamese commander (Lam Ching-ying, also cast against type) has one of his eyes shot out, which launches him on a single-minded quest for vengeance.

With virtually no plot and few sympathetic characters, the dramatic scenes have little effect and the action displays none of the finesse that would characterize Woo's later work, consisting largely of soldiers simply mowing each other down. The relationship between Ko's character and his resourceful young son intentionally mirrors the Japanese **Lone Wolf and Cub** samurai series; Woo even restages a key scene from **Lone Wolf and Cub: Baby Cart in Peril** (1972) in which the swordsman's boy covers himself in mud to escape a raging fire. However, the father and son team here are not nearly as richly drawn, and neither is the storytelling.

448. The Heroic Trio

(1993; China Entertainment Film Production/Paka Hill Film Production) ★: 8/10. *Dung fong saam hap* (Cantonese), *Dongfang san xia* (Mandarin): "The Three Asian Heroines." Cinematographers: Poon Hang-sang, Tom Lau Moon-tong; Art Director: Bruce Yu Kar-on; Music: William Woo Wai-lap; Writer: Sandy Shaw; Producer-Action Director: Ching Siu-tung; Director: Johnny To Kei-fung. Cast: Michelle Yeoh Chu-kheng (Number 3), Maggie Cheung Man-yuk (Number 7), Anita Mui Yim-fong (Tung), Damian Lau Chung-yan (Inspector Lau), Anthony Wong Chau-sang (Number 9), James Pak Chin-shek (The Doctor), Paul Chun Pui (Commander), Yam Sai-kwoon (The Demon), Wong Yat-fei (Car Thief), Lee Siu-kei (Leader of Robbers at Chemical Factory). 1.85:1. VHS/LD/DVD: Tai Seng (Remastered for the English market; subtitled or dubbed). Import LD/VCD/DVD: Universe. 87 minutes.

Greeted with relative indifference by HK audiences, this wonderful futuristic action fantasy has developed a significant cult following in Western countries thanks to its wild action, appealing stars, and inventive visual design, which blends elements from Chinese fantasy, Japanese *manga*, and **Blade Runner**. It opens with HK plagued by a rash of baby kidnappings perpetrated by an invisible assailant. The children are taken below ground to the lair of an ancient demon (veteran kung fu movie villain Yam, dubbed with a female voice) who plans to choose one to become the new emperor of China as the opening act in his bid for world domination. Aiding the monster in this goal is Number 3/"Invisible Girl," who is actually the phantom abductor, thanks to a robe of invisibility created by a dying scientist (**Big Trouble in Little China**'s Pak) who is unaware that his invention is being used for evil. Hot on her trail is Tung, who moonlights as a silver-masked crime fighter nicknamed "Wonder Woman" (unbeknownst to her husband Inspector Lau), and Number 7/"Thief Catcher," a cavalier bounty hunter who had previously been under the demon's spell. Discovering that Number 3 is her long lost friend from childhood, Tung successfully appeals to her veiled humanity, and soon the three women join forces to combat the creature and his henchmen, led by the mindless brute Number 9.

The specifics of the plot don't really hold up well under scrutiny (e.g. Number 7 causes the death of a baby but receives little more than a slap on the wrist), and some more backstory would have been beneficial, but the film perfectly fuses the tried-and-true HK action formula (rousing choreography, colorful characters, unyielding comradery, fluid cinematography, humor and melodrama in equal portions) to Eastern and Western fantasy elements, creating an irresistible piece of entertainment. It was followed by the much grimmer **Executioners**.

449. He's a Woman, She's a Man

(1994; United Filmmakers Organization) ★: 8/10. *Gam chi yuk sip* (Cantonese), *Jin qi yu she* (Mandarin): "Golden Branch, Jade Leaf." Cinematographer: Henry Chan Chun-kit; Art Director: Hai Chung-man; Music: Clarence Hui Yuen; Writer: James Yuen Sai-sang; Producer-Director: Peter Chan Ho-sun. Cast: Anita Yuen Wing-yee (Lam Gee-wing), Leslie Cheung Kwok-wing (Sam), Carina Lau Kar-ling (Rose), Jordan Chan Siu-chun (Fish), Eric Tsang Chi-wai ("Auntie"), Jerry Lam Hiu-fung (Sam's Assistant), Law Kar-ying (Joseph). 1.85:1. VHS: Tai Seng. Import LD/VCD/DVD: Fitto Mobile. 106 minutes.

In short order, the United Filmmakers Organization became one of HK's premiere production companies, and **He's a Woman, She's a Man** (a hip redo of Blake Edwards' **Victor/Victoria**) emerged as one of their most honored and successful projects. Obsessed with pop music diva Rose, incorrigible tomboy Lam Gee-wing disguises herself as a guy to meet her idol at an audition for male singers which is being staged by Rose's producer-boyfriend Sam. However, "pop's perfect couple" are at a crossroads in their relationship, and Sam signs the talentless "boy" to a recording contract just to spite his temperamental girlfriend. Moving into their lives (and soon their home), Gee-wing cheerfully provides the veneration, pampering, and support both Sam and Rose desperately crave, and soon they rekindle their love—for *her*!

This comedy-drama of errors is sincerely performed by a proficient cast that consistently hits the right notes, even down to some of the rather broad supporting players, such as Sam's unabashedly gay image consultant "Auntie" (Tsang, in a performance that stops just short of being an unmannerly caricature). However, the film's ace-in-the-hole is Yuen; her unbridled energy and convincingly male persona make the gimmick work and netted her "Best Actress" at the 1995 HK Film Awards. However, one needs to be somewhat familiar with the HK entertainment industry to appreciate the considerable humor in Sam's attempt to come to grips with his sexual confusion, which derives its laughs from the casting of Cheung (an actor/pop star on the level of Elvis, whose sexual preferences are a gossip staple in tabloids) as well as the script's witty takes on both the music industry (where capability takes a back seat to marketability) and fan culture (a world of monomaniacal devotion with no parallel in the West). A sequel, **Who's the Woman, Who's the Man?**, followed in 1996.

450. High Risk

(1995; Upland Film Corporate/ Wong Jing's Workshop) ★: 6/10. *Sue daam lung wei* (Cantonese), *Shu dan long wei* (Mandarin): "Mouse Courage, Dragon Might." Cinematographer: Tom Lau Moon-tong; Art Director: Jason Mok Siu-kei; Music: Richard Yuen Cheuk-fan; Producer: Yang Teng-kuei; Action Director: Corey Yuen Kwai; Writer-Director: Wong Jing. Cast: Jet Li Lianjie ("Bold" Li Kit), Jacky Cheung Hok-yau (Frankie Lone), Chingmy Yau Suk-ching (Reporter), Valerie Chow Kar-ling (Fai-fai), Kelvin Wong Siu (The Doctor), Charlie Yeung Choi-nei (Joyce), Yang Chung-hsien (Joyce's boyfriend), Wu Ma (Frankie's father), Charlie Cho Cha-lei (Charlie), Ben Lam Kwok-bun (Killer with Sunglasses), Billy Chow Bei-lee (Bond), Suki Kwan Sau-mei (Li's wife), Vincent Kok Tak-chiu (Cameraman), Bobby Yip King-sang (Ugly Stuntman). Dolby Stereo. 1.85:1. VHS: Tai Seng. Import LD/VCD/DVD: Universe. 101 minutes.

In 1993 Wong Jing helmed the Jackie Chan action-comedy **City Hunter**, and the two reportedly had a less-than-congenial working relationship. Now Wong has struck back by injecting a rather caustic send-up of Chan into this spirited **Die Hard** knockoff (the Chinese title for that Bruce Willis film is "Tiger Courage, Dragon Might"). Popular movie star Frankie Lone (Jacky Cheung, sporting Chan's old Beatles mop-top hairstyle) is revered by his fans because he does all his own stunts. In reality he is a bumbling fool whose most dangerous feats are actually performed by his bodyguard, Li Kit. One evening Frankie and his entourage attend a party at a skyscraper where a priceless collection of Russian gems is on display. A group of thieves, led by "The Doctor," seize the building, sending Li on a one-man search-and-destroy mission to rescue the hostages and avenge his wife and son, who were killed in a bomb blast triggered two years earlier by the same ringleader.

As is increasingly the case, Jet Li is saddled with a role that does not allow him much emotional range. While his martial skills are above reproach and he possesses an increasingly confident, genial screen presence, it would be nice to see him undertake the sort of part he had in his early films, like the **Shaolin Temple** trilogy. Jacky Cheung can also be a very versatile and winning leading man, but the material calls for him to do little but mug, squandering the more measured comic aptitude he has displayed in films like **Pom Pom and Hot Hot** and **The Days of Being Dumb** (both 1992). He does acquit himself well in the humorous martial arts scenes (which also poke fun at Bruce Lee's movies), but the film's poor performance in both HK and Taiwan would indicate that the devotion of Chan's fans is not easily swayed. However, **High Risk** follows the dependable Wong Jing formula, mixing brisk action, silly comedy, and an attractive all-star cast into a consistently enjoyable package. Wu Ma has one of his best roles in recent years as a respectful emulation of Jackie Chan's father, while Charlie Cho serves up a swishy caricature of the star's manager, Willie Chan Chi-keung (no relation).

451. Highway Man

(1995) ★: 5/10. *Ma lo ying hung II fei fat choi che* (Cantonese), *Ma lu ying xiong II fei fa sai che* (Mandarin): "Road Heroes II: Illegal Car Racing." Cinematographer: Herman Yau Lai-to; Art Director: Ho Chi-hang; Music: Henry Lai Wan-man; Producer: Yip Wing-cho; Action Director: Chu Kai-sang; Writer-Director: Lau Sui-hung. Cast: Julian Cheung Chi-lam (Chung), Loletta Lee Lai-chun (Carmen Lee), Anthony Wong Chau-sang ("Doctor"), Christine Ng Wing-mei (Mandy), Marco Ngai Chun-kit (Officer Wu), Tommy Wong Kwong-leung (Lo Yi). 1.85:1. VHS: World Video. Import LD/VCD: Star Entertainment. Import DVD: China Star. 92 minutes.

A follow-up of sorts to **Off Track**, this also features Loletta Lee but has no direct connection. Illegal racing is again the theme, and car magazine writer Chung is one of the best on the road. His main opponent is Lion King, a deranged triad car thief who isn't above running other competitors off the road. Chung's reckless behavior in the past caused an accident that led his wife Carmen to divorce him, but his feelings for her remain strong. She, however, still remains unsure about whether she can handle Chung's driving, particularly as he gets behind the wheel while inebriated. The authorities, meanwhile, are launching a crackdown on the racers, and after several close calls at roadblocks, it is only a matter of time before one of their confrontations with the youths will lead to fatalities on both sides.

The racing sequences are not as well staged as those in **Off Track,** but they still remain fairly exciting. However, with the exception of Anthony Wong's fatherly mechanic, none of the characters are especially interesting, and the dramatic situations are facile.

452. His Fatal Way

(1991; D & B Films Co.) ★: 4/10. *Lo biu nei ho ye!* (Cantonese), *Lao biao ni hao ye!* (Mandarin): "Cousin, You're Great!" Cinematographer: Chan Ying-kit; Art Director: Danny Yuen Ching-yeung; Music: Wong Bong; Writers: Wong Wang-kei, Alexander Chan Mong-wah, Leung Hung-wah; Producer: Stephen Shin Kei-ying; Action Director: Cho Wing; Director: Alexander Chan Mong-wah. Cast: Alfred Cheung Kin-ting (Cheung Po-shing), Teresa Mo Shun-kwan (Ming's Sister), Suki Kwan Sau-mei (Suki), Lam Kau (Hung Kam-hoi), To Siu-chun (Ming), Waise Lee Chi-hung (Hung), Cho Wing (Xiang Dong, "Facing East"). 1.85:1. VHS: Tai Seng. 93 minutes.

This tepid imitation of **Her Fatal Ways** finds Alfred Cheung essentially reprising his character from that film, but he and Teresa Mo do not have much comic chemistry and the writing here is decidedly uninspired. When a pair of robbers (about to set out on a "big circle" caper) manage to elude his men, dedicated Mainland cop Cheung Po-shing heads to HK to find them, figuring that a one in three million chance is reasonable odds. His partner for this venture is local police officer Ming, who (mistakenly) allows Po-shing to move in with him, his TV reporter girlfriend, and butch sister. Following various leads, Po-shing is able to locate the duo's middle man, as a means to learning their whereabouts. After he and Ming attempt to apprehend the fugitives and fail, Po-shing is ordered back to China, but a lucky break allows him one more chance to fulfil his mission and return home a hero.

The plot is just a flimsy set-up for the obligatory fish-out-of-water bits and instances where Po-shing uses his Mainland know-how to resolve various crises. The jokes and situations are consistently stale, and while Alfred Cheung occasionally manages to hit the right comic note with his portrayal, the end result is still tedious and forgettable. The one genuinely funny bit is a brief send-up of **A Better Tomorrow** featuring Waise Lee. As with **Her Fatal Ways,** sync sound recording is a welcome plus.

453. Hocus Pocus

(1984; Golden Harvest/Bo Ho Films Co.) ★: 6/10. *Yan haak gwai* (Cantonese), *Ren xia gui* (Mandarin): "People Frighten Ghost." Music: Not Original; Writer: Au Bing-nam; Producer: Sammo Hung Kam-po; Action Direction: Sammo Hung Stunt Team; Director: Chin Yuet-sang. Cast: Stephen Tung Wai (Kuei), Lam Ching-ying (Sheng), Peter Chan Lung (Piao), Chin Yuet-sang (The Ghost), Wu Ma (Old Man). 2.35:1. VHS: Tai Seng (Poor Subtitles). 93 minutes. Also known as **Hogus Pogus** [*sic*] (Tai Seng title).

This Sammo Hung production pales in comparison to **Encounter of the Spooky Kind** and **The Dead and the Deadly,** but it is not without merit. Trouble befalls a Peking Opera troop when one of their number urinates on a grave. As a result, the company soon finds their performances disrupted by a clumsy and fairly harmless phantom (director Chin in shoddy make-up). Some of the performers and the spectre take turns scaring the daylights out of Chia, a conceited lead actor. The ghost then takes the process one step further by possessing Chia and wreaking destructive havoc. This prompts the actors to stage a special performance to trick the spook into revealing why it is haunting the theater. They learn that its bones are buried beneath the stage and must be properly interred in order for the ghost to reincarnate. After that is accomplished, all appears to be well but the original, offended spirit comes to earth and raises hell during a banquet celebration, killing many of the guests.

Much of the film is routine, but the opera performances offer up some excellent acrobatics, and the finale consists of a fervently staged, action-packed exorcism that will please devotees of the genre. The soundtrack includes music lifted from **Suspiria.**

Hogus Pogus [*sic*] *see* **Hocus Pocus**

454. Holy Flame of the Martial World

(1983; Shaw Brothers) ★: 8/10. *Mou lam sing foh gam* (Cantonese), *Wu lin sheng huo jin* (Mandarin): "Present Holy Flame of the Martial World." Cinematographer: Philip Ma Kam-cheung; Music: So Chun-hau, Sing Kam-wing; Writers: Lu Chin-ku, Cheung Kwok-yuen; Producer: Mona Fong Yat-wah; Action Directors: Yuen Tak, Phillip Kwok Tsui; Director: Lu Chun-ku. Cast: Max Mok Siu-chung (Yin Tien-chu), Lau Suet-wah (Tu Chuan-erh), Yeung Ching-ching (Yin Tan-feng), Phillip Kwok Tsui (The Yama Elder), Lau Siu-kwan (Tuan). 2.35:1. VHS/LD: World Video (Poor Subtitles). Import LD: Ocean Shores (Poor Subtitles). 91 minutes.

Shaw Brothers' answer to Golden Harvest's big budget epic **Zu: Warriors from the Magic Mountain, Holy Flame of the Martial World** is a wildly colorful, action-packed fantasy that belies its comparatively modest origins and delivers as much excitement and spectacle as its model. A group of power-crazed martial arts masters (including Elvis Tsui Kam-kong and Lam Wai) seek to learn the whereabouts of the magical Yin and Yang swords from a young husband and wife, whom they subsequently murder when the information is not forthcoming. Before they can also dispose of the couple's twin babies, the powerful Yama Elder appears and subdues the killers with his hurricane-strength "Ghost Cries." He then takes the male infant, promising that the child, Yin Tien-chu, will return to seek vengeance in 18 years. Deciding that they need a worthy opponent to protect them, the villains' female leader takes the girl child, Yin Tan-feng, with the intention of passing on her fighting skills. The story picks up 18 years later, with Tien-chu now a skilled fighter on a mission to retrieve his family's Yang Sword from inside a danger-filled cave. After braving several trials, he succeeds in securing the weapon and, with fellow swordsman Tuan at his side, proceeds to rescue maiden Tu Chuan-erh from a cult about to sacrifice her. Tien-chu and Chuan-erh later encounter Tan-feng during their travels, but no one realizes the familial link between the two warriors. However, Tan-feng's evil mistress possesses the Yin Sword, which she has kept hidden for the day that the male child will return to seek revenge. Giving the weapon to Tan-feng, she tells the girl that it was the Elder who slaughtered her parents, leading to an inevitable encounter between the two unwitting siblings and the uniting of the Yin and Yang Swords.

Director Lu Chun-ku (**Killer Angels**) invests the proceedings with incredible energy and a rainbow of colors, helping to make this one of the most winning period fantasies to be found in the genre. There are spots where budgetary constraints are in evidence (some of the cult's minions are clearly wearing Don Post-style monster masks), but the film is so congenial and eager to please that such faults are entirely forgivable. The wildly acrobatic, lightning-paced kung fu and swordplay (a clear precursor to the sort of no-holds-barred wirework found in '90s productions like **Butterfly & Sword, Deadful** [*sic*] **Melody,** and **Fire Dragon**) are executed with admirable skill, and the narrative manages to incorporate a few surprises while also adhering to genre requirements. Highlights include an acid-filled lake inhabited by flying animated demons, a wonderful sequence in which Tien-chu must literally battle the Chinese characters that make up a riddle he needs to solve, an *English-speaking* ghoul ("Diamond! I like it! I like it!"), and a benevolent snake girl whose pet serpent/weapon endows Chuan-ehr with magical powers. Now, if only a letterboxed version was available...

455. The Holy Virgin vs. the Evil Dead

(1991; Cheung Yau Films) ★: 5/10. *Moh sun gip* (Cantonese), *Mo chun jie* (Mandarin): "Evil Lips Robber." Cinematographer: Wong Kit; Music: Not Original; Writer: Lee Ho-chun; Producer: Leung Ching. Action Director: Tsui Fat; Director: Wong Chun-yeung. Cast: Donnie Yen Chi-tan (Shiang Chin-fei), Pauline Yeung Po-ling (Princess White), Ben Lam Kwok-bun (Sgt. Chen Yu), Kathy Chow Hoi-mei (Chor Yi-yin), Ken Lo Wai-kwong (The Moon Monster), Sibelle Hu Hui-chung (Sgt. Hu). 1.85:1. VHS/LD: Quali-vision. Import LD/VCD: Mei Ah. 92 minutes.

No film could possibly live up to a title like **The Holy Virgin vs. the Evil Dead** (or **Evil Lips Robber** for that matter), but this low-budget production has its moments and is pretty irresistible on a trash level. After his female students are raped and murdered on a school outing, teacher Shiang Chin-fei has a hard time convincing the police that he is not the one responsible. The real culprit is actually "The Moon Monster" (played by Jackie Chan's former bodyguard and frequent co-star, Ken Lo), a vampiric superman with glowing green eyes who is on a murderous rampage. The creature (which hails from Cambodia and worships a goddess with a male head and female body) is prowling around HK in order to find the perfect mate for a ritual that will make him invincible. When the authorities can no longer dispute his story, Shiang joins up with police officer Chen, the latter's girlfriend, and a reporter to travel to Cambodia. Shortly after their arrival, they encounter White, a magical, flying princess from the High Wind Tribe who vows to help them destroy the evil being.

Serving up a steady quota of undercranked action (gunplay and high-flying kung fu) and lots of cheap (but energetically applied) special FX, this is rigorous, no-brainer fun. It also boasts a much better cast than most Category III efforts, though one suspects that the performers signed on only for the free vacation. At least one version in circulation is missing all of the abundant nudity.

456. Holy Weapon

(1993; Regal Films Co.) ★: 5/10. *Mo hap chat gung jue* (Cantonese), *Wu xia qi gong zhu* (Mandarin): "The Seven Martial Arts Princesses." Cinematographer: Gigo Lee Chi-hang; Art Director: Andrew Cheuk Man-yiu; Music: Danny Chung Teng-yat; Writer: Lam Wai-lun; Producer: Ng Yun-chuen; Action Director: Ching Siu-tung; Director: Wong Jing. Cast: Michelle Yeoh Chu-kheng (Mon Ching-sze), Damian Lau Chung-yan (Mo Kake), Dicky Cheung Wai-kin (Ng Tung), Sharla Cheung Man (Spider), Maggie Cheung Man-yuk (Princess Tin Heung), Carol Cheng Yu-ling (Doll), Simon Yam Tat-wah (Liu Sang), Ng Man-tat (Ghost Doctor), Sandra Ng Kwan-yu (Lam Kin-fai), Charine Chan Kar-ling (Butterfly). 1.85:1. VHS/LD: World Video (Poor Subtitles). Import LD/VCD: Universe. 98 minutes.

Wong Jing has emerged as one of HK's most successful directors, and this outlandish period fantasy-comedy (set in the Ming Dynasty) showcases both the positive and negative aspects of his work. Liu Sang, "The Super Sword of Japan," is a seemingly invincible warrior rampaging his way through China with his birdman lackeys. Riding to the rescue is "Heaven's Sword" Mo Kake who wins their duel, prompting Super Sword to demand a rematch in three years time. He returns unprepared for Mo's new secret weapon: a team of virgins skilled in the "Yuen Tin Sword Position," which merges them into a giant composite fighter (providing one of the most bizarre images you will ever see). With the aid of his pupils, Heaven's Sword must subjugate the interloper and rescue the princess super sword has taken hostage.

Holy Weapon opens and closes with battle sequences which are truly offbeat, even by the inventive standards of HK fantasy cinema. Unfortunately, the mid-section is burdened by too much emphasis on lame sexual and scatological gags, typical of the director's scattershot "something-for-everybody" approach (though a possession sequence, which purloins the "swallowed eyeball" gag from Sam Raimi's **Evil Dead II**, is amusing). Two moments stand out: a haunting shot of Yam standing atop a giant wooden cross surveying the bodies of numerous dead soldiers while his minions soar overhead; and a disquieting sequence (inspired by the *anime* **The Wicked City**) wherein Sharla Cheung transforms into a seductive spider woman whose giant web glistens in the darkness with the blood of her victims. If Wong had spent more time on imagery of this sort and less on the low-brow antics of Sandra Ng (HK cinema's reigning queen of termagants), this could have been more than just a likeable diversion. Reportedly, a good portion of the film was actually directed by Dennis Chan Kwok-san without credit.

457. A Home Too Far

(1990; Movie Impact/Yen Ping Film Co.) ★: 5/10. *Yi wik* (Cantonese), *Yi yu* (Mandarin): "Foreign Land." Cinematographer: Chen Rong-shu; Art Director: Chang Chi-ping; Music: Ricky Ho; Writer: Hsiao Yun-chiao; Producers: Wallace Cheung Kwok-chong, Charles Heung Wah-keung; Director: Chu Yen-ping. Cast: Tou Chung-wah (Ke-pao), Andy Lau Tak-wah (Tu), Ko Chuen-hsiang (General Li Kuo-hui), Jean Wang Ching-ying (The Schoolteacher), Ku Feng (General Li Mi), Lung Si-hung (Old Cheng), Siquin Gaowa. 1.85:1. VHS: Tai Seng. Import LD/VCD: Ocean Shores. 100 minutes.

Chu Yen-ping, Taiwan's reigning king of schlock, directed this war drama with a more serious approach than usual, but that does not help much to convince one of its objectivity. Opening in 1950, it charts the defeat suffered by a division of the Nationalist Army in China and the survivors' awful trek through the mountains to the Yuan River. Soon after reaching their destination, the troops are besieged by Communist soldiers and suffer heavy losses. Upon meeting up with another unit, commanded by General Li Kuo-hui, the men and their families are then forced to flee again into the jungle, where they spend a month with virtually no food. Finally reaching the border of Burma, they set up a camp, allowing the refugees some measure of peace. However, the Burmese government refuses to allow them to stay, resulting in another battle. When the smoke clears, the 1000+ squad of Nationalists has triumphed over the entire Burmese National Army, prompting command to order the troops back into China for an ill-advised counterattack. Things take an even darker turn when the Burmese (backed up by Indonesian forces) step up their efforts to eliminate the Nationalists.

There is more attention to artistry here than is usually found in Chu's work, particularly the sequence depicting the slaughter at the Yuan River: The camera assumes the perspective of a wounded or dead person lying in the water, with the massacre at the top of the screen while turbulent, blood red water fills the lower portion. Unfortunately, no attempt is made to present a balanced view of the conflict. Not only are there no Communist lead characters, one can barely even make out their faces. That, compounded with all of the war movie cliches and heavy handed approach, significantly dilutes the film's impact. Andy Lau has a supporting role as a guerilla fighter but is apparently just along to provide marquee value. The story continues in **End of the Road**.

458. Homecoming

(1984; Bluebird Movie Enterprises/Target Film Company) ★: 8/10. *Chi sui lau nin* (Cantonese), *Si shui liu nian* (Mandarin): "The Years Flow by Like Water." Cinematographer: Poon Hang-sang; Art Director: William Cheung Suk-ping; Music: Kitaro; Writer: Kong Liang; Producer: Xia Meng; Director: Yim Ho. Cast: Josephine Koo Mei-wah (Coral Zhang), Siquin Gaowa (Pearl), Xie Weixiang, Zhou Yun, Zhang Jugao. 1.85:1. Video Distributor Unknown. 96 minutes.

This Yim Ho film is a HK/China co-production, which is entirely fitting, as the storyline looks at how different and yet how similar life can be for Hong Kongers and their Mainland counterparts. Travelling to China to visit the grave of her recently deceased grandmother, Coral Zhang returns to her ancestral home in the countryside for the first time in twenty years. Meeting up with her old friends Pearl and Tsong (who are now married to one another and have a daughter), Coral re-experiences the simple life she left behind at a young age. Life in HK has been less than satisfying; Coral's magazine has failed and she and her sister are engaged in a legal battle over a piece of land that made up their late father's estate. Never married, she has had two abortions. The longer she stays, however, the more Coral notices that something is missing from Pearl's life, too. When Coral arranges for the children from Pearl's school to go to Guangzhou (a major city), tensions that were bubbling beneath the surface finally come to the fore.

A sensitive, beautifully scored drama, **Homecoming** perceptively examines the inevitable clash of cultures that reunification would bring on and, via the region's picturesque landscapes, contrasts the tranquillity of the simple agrarian life still the norm in Southern China with the bustling cityscape that is HK and, possibly soon, a good portion of the Mainland. The film swept The HK Film Awards, winning Best Picture, Best Actress (Siqin Gaowa), Best New Performer (Josephine Koo), Best Art Direction, and Best Screenplay.

459. Hong Kong Adam's [*sic*] Family

(1994; Supreme Film Production Co.) ★: 1/10. *Gaan yan sai ga* (Cantonese), *Jian ren shi jia* (Mandarin): "Evil People, Noble Family." Cinematographer: Wong Kar-fai; Art Director: Raymond Kwok Siu-keung; Music: Tang Chen-hung, Simon Leung Chi-wah; Producer: Lung Fong; Action Directors: Hung Shin-nan, Yiu Man-chi; Director: Bosco Lam Hing-lung. Cast: Shih Kien (Kan San), Michael Chan Wai-man (Kan Saint), Shing Fui-on (Kan Kui), Wong Chi-yeung (Kan Sin), Woo Fung (Kan Fei), Lung Fong (Ko Yee), Maria Cordero (Fatty Ha), Shum Wai (Sum Kung-ching), Wong Yat-fei (God of Gamblers), William Ho Kar-kui (Cop). 1.85:1. VHS/LD: World Video. 90 minutes.

This thoroughly unfunny comedy has no direct connection to the American **Addams Family** TV series and movies (though Vic Mizzy's famous theme song does pop up a couple of times on the soundtrack). The Kan family is the most notorious bunch of criminal vermin in HK—and proud of it. On the day of their patriarch's 80th birthday, they learn that one of their clan has died and left them a $10 billion inheritance. However, there is one major catch: They can only collect if they perform good deeds for an entire month. The five brothers proceed to help the elderly, try to adopt some orphans, and setup a benefit concert to aid villagers whose homes were destroyed. Meanwhile, their relative Kan Fei (who will get the money if the Kan brothers fail to meet the conditions of the will) allies himself with gangster Ko Yee to undermine their attempts to go straight.

The comedy is agonizingly lame, relying on gimmicks like fast motion and sound effects from cartoons to punch up jokes that date back to the beginning of cinema; the storyline is of about the same vintage. Upon completion in 1992, the film understandably languished on the shelf until it finally received a token five day theatrical run in March of 1994.

Hong Kong Corruptor *see* **Return Engagement**

460. Hong Kong Graffiti

(1995; Mandarin Films/Tedpoly Films) ★: 3/10. *Heung Gong fa yuet ye* (Cantonese), *Xiang Jiang hua yue yu* (Mandarin): "Hong Kong Hot Nights." Cinematographer: Cheung Tung-leung; Art Director: Danny Yuen Ching-yeung; Music: Teddy Robin Kwan; Writers: Erica Lee Man, Chan Kam-cheung, Ng Man-fai; Action Directors: Stephen Tung Wai, Benz Kong To-hoi; Producer-Director: Teddy Robin Kwan. Cast: Teddy Robin Kwan (Johnny K), Kevin Cheng Kar-wing (Kelvin), Raymond Tso Wing-lim (Chee), Zoe Chan Ngai-ming (Jane), Dennis Chan Kwok-san (Leung Ping), Kent Cheng Chuk-see (Seven), Yuen King-tan (Mrs. Seven), Alfred Cheung Kin-ting (Mahjong Player), Chor Yuen (Small Lee), Vincent Kok Tak-chiu (Jing), Helena Law Lan (Auntie Lone), Shing Fui-on (Mad Dog), Jacob Cheung Chi-leung (Cheung), Linda Wong Hing-ping (Singer Doing Teresa Teng Song), Amanda Lee Wai-man (Anita Li), Wong Kam-kong (Big Lee), Joe Junior (Philip), Pak Kar-sin (Debbie), Manfred Wong (Tommy). Dolby Digital. 1.85:1. VHS: Tai Seng. Import LD/VCD: Fitto Mobile. 108 minutes.

Hong Kong 1967: The pop music scene is ruled by diminutive singer Johnny K, who specializes in English language songs. Six years later, Johnny is a washed-up alcoholic, and the latest trend is Mandarin songs. Spurred on by two young, enthusiastic fans and nightclub owner Leung Ping, Johnny agrees to start performing again. As time passes, Cantonese songs finally become the rage, and Teddy's young proteges, Kelvin and Chee, hone their skills over time to the point where they could become the next big thing ... if Johnny can just convince a record label to sign them. Called "The Marbles," the pair finally manage to hit the big time, but Chee quickly seems to forget just who it was that guided them to their success. Taking Kelvin under his wing, Johnny sets out to make him a solo star.

Producer-director-lead actor Teddy Robin Kwan used to be a singing sensation himself and one expects something better from him than this meandering embarrassment, which is not so much an attempt at nostalgia as just plain wishful thinking. Trite, peopled solely with one-dimensional characters, and leadenly unfunny, **Hong Kong Graffiti** seems to drag on for much longer than its running time. Even the music is forgettable, though Linda Wong and Amanda Lee come off well during their respective numbers.

461. Hong Kong Grafitti

[*sic*] (1985) ★: 2/10. *Nui yan fung chung wa* (Cantonese), *Nu ren feng qing hua* (Mandarin): "Flirtatious Female Talk." Cinematographer: Derek Wan Man-kit; Art Directors: Dominique Lo Kar-yiu, Andy Lee Yiu-kwong; Music: Alvin Kwok Siu-lam; Writer: Lee Mak; Producer: Lo Wei; Director: Terry Tong Kei-ming. Cast: Olivia Cheng Man-ar (Susan Yang), Joyce Ngai Suk-kwan (Fang), Yeung Kwan (Kelly Chan), Polly Chan Yuen-lai (Lu Ping-ting), Victor Hon Kwan (Molester in Airport). 1.85:1. VHS: Ocean Shores. Import LD/VCD: Ocean Shores. 94 minutes.

The meaning of the English title is as elusive as the point of this meandering drama about the lives of four young women trying to make a living in HK. Baby products employee Susan Yang has her hands full when sister-in-law Lu Ping-ting arrives from the Mainland to stay with her. Susan's flat is also occupied by her roommate Belinda, a flaky stewardess. At the same time, Fang, the daughter of

Susan's middle-aged boyfriend, Kelly, comes to HK and she moves in as well. After some initial friction, Susan gets Fang a job at her firm and they become close friends. Anxious to get ahead in this capitalist mecca, Ping-ting (who has adopted the English name "Plenty") develops an interest in Kelly and they begin sleeping together. Unhappy with the way her life is going, Susan decides to sell the flat and switch to a rival firm, but a tragic event changes everything for both her and her roommates. *Hong Kong Grafitti* is formulaic in every respect and deadly dull to boot. Polly Chan won the Best Newcomer Award for her performance.

462. Hong Kong 1941

(1984; D & B Films Co./Bo Ho Films Co.) ★: 7/10. *Dang doi lai ming* (Cantonese), *Deng dai li ming* (Mandarin): "Waiting for Dawn." Cinematographers: Brian Lai Shui-ming, David Chung Chi-man; Art Director: Hai Chung-man; Music: Violet Lam Man-yee; Writer: John Chan Koon-chung; Producer: John Sham Kin-fun; Action Direction: Sammo Hung Stuntmen Association, Lam Ching-ying; Director: Leung Po-chi. Cast: Chow Yun-fat (Yip Kim-fay), Cecilia Yip Tung (Ha Yuk-nam), Alex Man Chi-leung (Wong Hak-keung), Paul Chun Pui (Fa Wing), Ku Feng (Shui), Shih Kien (Ha Chung-sun), Wu Ma (Chairman Liu Yan-mau), Billy Lau Nam-kwong (Factory Foreman), Yung Sai-kit (General Kanezawa). Dolby Digital (DVD only). 1.85:1. VHS: Tai Seng (Remastered for the English market; subtitled or dubbed). LD: Media Asia. Import VCD: Mega Star. Import DVD: Universe. 100 minutes.

Chow Yun-fat and Cecilia Yip give excellent performances in this award-winning drama which opens just prior to the Japanese occupation of HK in World War II. After a run-in with the law, rice factory laborers Yip Kim-fay and Wong Hak-keung decide to head for China, with the latter's girlfriend, Ha Yuk-nam, in tow. Unfortunately, the morning they choose to leave turns out to be the day that the Japanese break through the Allies' defenses. The friends decide to stay, but the evening before the occupation army arrives, bands of looters break into Yuk-nam's home and she is raped. Hak-keung asks the girl's father for her hand in marriage and he accepts, but it is Kim-fay that Yuk-nam truly loves. Becoming a collaborator, Kim-fay uses his station to supply the couple with food and medical supplies, but it is increasingly obvious that Yuk-nam favors him, a situation that comes to a head when the commander of the Japanese forces decides to take her as his wife.

Some aspects of the film seem a bit rushed, particularly the final act, which would have been more satisfying had it unfolded at a more measured tempo. Regardless, this remains a compelling and intelligent contrast to exploitation fare like the **Man Behind the Sun** series and **1941 Hong Kong on Fire**, which are content to merely catalogue atrocities and not bother with the human aspect of the war in Asia. In films like **A Better Tomorrow** and **City on Fire**, Chow Yun-fat is granted one or two of those show stopping "movie star moments" that really cement his character, but the drama here is more subtle and so is Chow's performance. He does an excellent job conveying both Kim-fay's guarded feelings and his resolve to not come between his friends. One of the finest actresses in Chinese cinema, Cecilia Yip does predictably laudable work, perfectly projecting Yuk-nam's emotional travails and the increased maturity she gains through her experiences. One of the project's strongest components is the compelling score by Violet Lam (one of HK's most innovative composers), which beautifully accentuates both the subtleties and the horrors by fusing delicate, traditional influences with more progressive electronic elements. It is one of the most distinctive and effective musical accompaniments to be heard in a HK production from this period.

463. Hong Kong Playboy

(1983; Shaw Brothers) ★: 2/10. *Fa sam daai siu* (Cantonese), *Hua xin da shao* (Mandarin): "Flower Heart Big Little." Cinematographer: Li Hsin-yeh; Music: Cheng Ching-chung, So Chun-hau; Producer: Run Run Shaw; Action Director: Yuen Bun; Writer-Director: Wong Jing. Cast: Alexander Fu Sheng (Romantic Sheng), Cherie Chung Cho-hung (Mei), Nat Chan Pak-cheung (Lolanto), Shih Kien (Wu). 1.85:1. VHS: World Video. Import LD: Ocean Shores. 99 minutes.

This irritating comedy concerns the troubled love life of Romantic Sheng, HK's most spirited playboy. Sheng's style is severely cramped when his mother shows up out of the blue, accompanied by her humorless nurse Mei. When Sheng's mom states that she will not leave until he has married a woman of her choosing, he agrees to go along with her plan and pretends to be blind in order to woo a TV actress. When that relationship falls apart, Sheng finds himself competing with Valentine [*sic*], a suave, middle-aged lothario, for the hand of another beauty. However, there is one major obstacle that must be dealt with first: the woman's man-hating guardian, a task they assign to Lolanto, a bumbling would-be stud. Of course, while all of this nonsense is going on, Sheng's ideal woman is right under his nose.

Martial arts star Alexander Fu Sheng proved with this frivolous comedy that he was quite capable of carrying more than just period kung fu thrillers. Unfortunately, his death in a car crash the same year that **Hong Kong Playboy** was released cut short a stellar career that had not yet even peaked. His performance is the only reason to endure this insipid farce, which plays like an episode of **Love, American Style** stretched out to four times its normal length. Wong Jing is not known as a master of comedic invention, but when even he is desperate enough to introduce itching powder into the scenario, it is time to find something else to watch.

464. Hong Kong Show Girl

(1996; Fortune Star Films Co.) ★: 3/10. *Din ma nui long ji yat ye ching* (Cantonese), *Dian ma nu lang zhi yi ye qing* (Mandarin): "Mad Horse Lady: One Night Love." Cinematographer: Tony Fan Chuen-kam; Art Director: Angelo Bernardo Castilho; Music: Sam Leung Yiu-sang, Onam Mui Siu-kei, Barry Cheung Fu-ling; Writers: Lee Ping-kwong, Lee Ping-leung, Wong Yuk-ting, Wing Chow Chan-wing; Producer: Lee Kin-hing; Action Directors: Lee Kin-hing, Huang Hsin-chun; Director: Wing Chow Chan-wing. Cast: Betty Chan Yee-ming (Grace), Suen Hing (Dicky), Elvis Tsui Kam-kong (Tai-hing), Mahalion Mendez, Ronald Gan, Kris Aguilar. 1.85:1. VHS: World Video. Import LD/VCD: Mei Ah. 97 minutes.

Not to be confused with the family-oriented **Hong Kong Show Girls** (see below), and bearing absolutely no relation to Paul Verhoeven's infamous **Showgirls**, this tedious Category III yarn centers instead on some criminals led by psychotic gang boss Tai-hing. Dividing his time between his jealous wife Danna and top revue dancer Grace, the triad has more than his share of woman problems. Grace's beauty catches the eye of Chan, a local councillor, and Tai-hing is quick to notice. He teaches Chan a lesson, and this initiates several instances of tit for tat violence, as goons from either side repeatedly pummel and slice each other up. Chan is eventually disposed of, but Dicky, one of Tai-hing's closest confidants, has now taken up with Grace and is doing far more than just looking. Tai-hing catches the two together and takes revenge but makes the mistake of letting Dicky live (don't they always?).

While somewhat better produced than many C-III endeavors, this remains one of those movies which would run all of about 20 minutes with the extraneous footage removed. Aside from an above average score and some fairly exciting action in the closing reel, this is too dreary, humorless, and mechanical to be entertaining, even for those on the lookout for mindless schlock.

465. Hong Kong Show Girls

(1996; Kin Pui International) ★: 1/10. *Gwai gek yuen ji ging ching yim nui long* (Cantonese), *Gui ju yuan zhi jing qing yan nu lang* (Mandarin): "Ghost Theater: Scared Sexy Ladies." Cinematographer: Joe Chan Kong-hung; Art Director: Tung Yao; Music: M.O.M.; Writer: Wilson Yip Wai-san; Producers: Chan Chi-shun, Jon Hau Wing-choi; Director: Jon Hau Wing-choi. Cast: Veronica Yip Yuk-hing (Yip Hing-heung), Diana Pang Dan (Tai-dan), Pauline Chan Po-lin (The Ghost), Woo Fung (Woo), Ha Ping (Mary), Cammy Choi Mei-lan (Dancer), Wong Yat-fei (Fai). 1.85:1. VHS: Tai Seng. Import LD/VCD: Universe. 90 minutes.

What a ripoff! The title and ad campaign promise a sexy HK version of Paul Verhoeven's infamous adults-only epic, but we end up with a family-oriented ghost movie...and a downright awful one at that. Luckily, local audiences were not so easily fooled and this disappeared from screens after only three days. A struggling theatrical troupe needs a venue in which to rehearse, so they use an old porno theater. When strange events begin to occur, it eventually becomes clear that the venue is haunted by the spirit of a dancer killed there in a blaze decades earlier.

Seemingly improvised on the spot, the virtually non-existent story plods along, padded with endless amounts of dull chatter and laughable rehearsals (out of the leads, the only one even close to being convincing as a dancer is Diana Pang ... who really *is* a dancer). The horror sequences are a joke, and those who stick around long enough to see how the story resolves itself will be shaking their heads in disbelief. This is another hour and a half of utter swill from HK's worst director, the hapless Jon Hau. Not to be confused with **Hong Kong Show Girl** (see above), which *is* a Category III sex film but is just as hard to sit through.

Hong Kong Specialist *see* **Bloody Money**

466. Horrible High Heels

(1996; Yes Films Co.) ★: 1/10. *Yan pei go jang haai* (Cantonese), *Ren pi guo zheng xie* (Mandarin): "Human Skin High Heels." Cinematographer: Wong Wing-chung; Music: Chik Yuk-lung; Writer: Chow Cheung; Producer: Lau Chi-wing; Directors: Chan Wai-on, Chow Cheung, Mo Keung-bong. Cast: Dick Wei (Police Captain), Shing Fui-on (Kuen), Billy Chow Bei-lee (Teddy Bear), Suen Tung-tung, Chow Yuk-ling. 1.85:1. VHS: Tai Seng. Import LD/VCD/DVD: New City. 95 minutes.

This amateurish Category III horror yarn concerns a scar-faced killer who sells the skin from his victims to a shoe factory, claiming that the nice, soft material is "deer skin from Africa!" The new product line is an instant success, so the killer (who dreams of opening his own shoe store) keeps up his grisly work. Employee Sherry has him murder two people in exchange for sex, but balks when it comes time to live up to her side of the bargain. When two other workers find the decaying carcass of the owner, they try and blackmail Sherry, but the police are already on the case.

The fact that it took three directors to piece this mess together is certainly telling. Plot is all but dispensed with in favor of scenes that barely have any correlation to one another and drag on with no apparent point. Every once in a while we get some softcore sex, a catfight, or another murder, and the unabashed misogyny apparent in the latter scenes is pretty revolting. While they may be reprehensible, films like **Dr. Lamb** and **The Untold Story** do have some merit; this one makes virtually no sense and is bereft of one single worthwhile moment or element. Shing Fui-on and Billy Chow have very little screen time, and their footage bears only a tenuous relationship to the main storyline, suggesting that the movie may have been assembled from two (or maybe even three) incomplete or otherwise unreleased features. The soundtrack includes music swiped from **Near Dark, Phantasm, Phantasm II**, and **Hard Target**, among others.

467. How Deep Is Your Love

(1994; Golden Harvest/Good Standard International/Prairie Productions Co./Paragon Films) ★: 5/10. *Ngai hung gwong goon go go gwa ji nui gung yue* (Cantonese), *Ni hong guang guan gao gao gua zhi nu zi gong yu* (Mandarin): "Raise the Neon Light: Female Apartments." Cinematographer: Poon Hang-sang; Art Director: Jon Hau Wing-choi; Writer: Charcoal Cheung Tan; Producers: Barbie Tung Wan-sze, Jon Hau Wing-choi; Director: Andy Chin Wing-keung. Cast: Charlie Yeung Choi-nei (Ken), Max Mok Siu-chung (Joe), Jacqueline Wu Chien-lien (Siu-fu), Vincent Wan Yeung-ming ("King of Curry"), Yuen King-tan (Nurse), Kenneth Chan Kai-tai (Leon). 1.85:1. VHS: Tai Seng. Import LD/VCD: Mei Ah. 87 minutes.

This minor slice-of-life drama stars Charlie Yeung as a medical student from Los Angeles who travels to Tsimshatsui to put her late brother's affairs in order. She meets Max Mok, the brother's gay landlord, and the pair develop a love that eventually progresses beyond the platonic. There is the usual collection of colorful characters, including Jacqueline Wu as a Taiwanese singer/songwriter, a pair of cocaine-addled lesbians (one of whom Yeung must save after an overdose), a transplanted Mainland woman with a child who is half Chinese and half Indian, an older friend of Mok who finds that the man he lusts after has a family, etc. Yeung eventually learns that her brother and Mok were lovers, which leads to the inevitable question of whether he only likes her because she reminds him of her sibling.

In spite of good performances all around, the film really offers nothing fresh or particularly innovative. In fact, it may be most noteworthy for having its characters actually live among some of the thousands of East Indians who dwell in HK but are only ever seen in local movies playing doormen, criminals, and the like. Sync sound recording provides a nice mix of languages. The Chinese title is a play on Zhang Yimou's **Raise the Red Lantern** (1991), which is "Big Red Lantern High High Hang" [*sic*]. Derek Yee Tung-sing has a cameo.

468. How to Meet the Lucky Stars

(1996; Grand March Movie Production Co.) ★: 4/10. *Wan choi ng fuk sing* (Cantonese), *Yun cai wu fu xing* (Mandarin): "Fortune Five Lucky Stars." Cinematographer: Sung Kong; Art Director: Kwan Mei-bo; Music: Roel A. Garcia; Writers: Ivy Lee Mo-king, Lee Ping-kwong, Lee Chi-wai; Producer: Eric Tsang Chi-wai; Action Directors: Feng Sing, Yuen Cheung-yan; Director: Frankie Chan Fan-kei. Cast: Eric Tsang Chi-wai (Lo Han-kuo), Stanley Fung Shui-fan (Pee), Richard Ng Yiu-hon (Dee), Miu Kiu-wai (Ginseng), Francoise Yip Fong-wah (Francoise), Kong Suet-fa (Sheung Kun Fai-fa, aka Gambling Flower), Diana Pang Dan (Nurse), Cheng Pei-pei (Gambling Teacher), Cho Tat-wah (Walter Tso), Nat Chan Pak-cheung (The King of Swindlers), Sammo Hung Kam-po (Chi Koo-choi/Tau), Chen Kuan-tai (Lui Tin, aka The King of Gamblers), Shing Fui-on (Brother Saur), Lowell Lo Kwun-ting (Waiter), Kim Maree Penn (Blonde Henchwoman), Mark Houghton (Blonde

Henchman), Feng Sing, Yuen Cheung-yan (Mahjong Players), Tai Po, Yuen King-tan, Yip Wing-cho, Ricky Yee Fan-wai, Lung Fong (Card Players), Gabriel Wong Yat-san (Man in Green Suit), Benny Lai Wai (Henchman). 1.85:1. VHS/LD: World Video. Import LD/VCD: Mei Ah. 112 minutes.

The Lucky Stars boys got together one more time for this charity feature, which relies heavily on their talents and audience good will to stay afloat. When the evil "Gambling Flower" Sheung Kun Fai-fa cheats the "King of Gambling" Lui Tin out of all his money, the latter commits suicide. In order to get revenge, Lui's daughter collaborates with Uncle Tso and the Lucky Stars in a plan to make Gambling Flower suffer the same fate. However, they must first come up with ten million dollars—with only a week left before the competition. They manage to scam the cash, only to lose it all to the aptly named "King of Swindlers."

In order to accommodate his stars and the many performers appearing in cameos, director Frankie Chan lets scenes drag on far too long (the running time exceeds the number of inspired gags by a factor of ten), and the episodic nature of the story is wearisome. By the time the big game finally rolls around, the film feels like it should be over, and the match itself lacks the inspired ploys and elaborate deceptions found in Wong Jing's gambling movies. Even the action pales in comparison to most of the preceding entries. Eric Tsang sings the theme song.

469. Hu-Du-Men

(1996; Golden Harvest/Ko Chi Sum Films Co./Golden Movies International) ★: 5/10. *Fu do moon* (Cantonese), *Hu du men* (Mandarin): "Entrance from the Platform Side." Cinematographer: Bill Wong Chung-po; Art Director: Bill Lui Cho-hung; Music: Yoshihide Otomo; Writer: Raymond To Kwok-wai; Producer: Clifton Ko Chi-sum; Director: Shu Kei. Cast: Josephine Siao Fong-fong (Lang Kim-sum), Anita Yuen Wing-yee (Yip Yuk-sheung), Daniel Chan Hiu-tung (Wong Man-chun), Chung King-fai (Chan Yiu-cho), Waise Lee Chi-hung (Lung), David Wu Tai-wai (Lam), Lee Heung-kam (Piano). 1.85:1. VHS: Mecapro. Import LD/VCD: Mei Ah. 98 minutes. Also known as **Stagedoor**.

Forty-year-old Peking Opera superstar Lang Kim-sum (who specializes in playing male roles) is about to retire and emigrate to Australia, but it is a destination that she hardly even played a part in choosing. Consumed by her career and love of contests, Kim-sum places less of an emphasis on the more mundane aspects of life than her husband, Yiu-cho. Convinced their teenage daughter Mimi is becoming a lesbian, Yiu-cho has turned into a tyrant and all but alienated the girl. Meanwhile, Kim-sum is asked to instruct Yuk-sheung, a young opera star from Singapore whose father wants her to become known in HK. The man, however, does not approve of Yuk-sheung's boyfriend, Man-chun, and beats his daughter because of her refusal to break off with him. As it turns out, Man-chun is well known to Kim-sum, and his presence creates problems for her. Further anxieties include a performer who becomes pregnant, the troupe's young director ruffling the feathers of the veteran performers, and some unexpected financial worries.

Director Shu Kei helped Raymond To adapt his own play, and this was clearly a mistake, as they could not distance themselves enough from the material to edit it down sufficiently. Consequently, the film tries to pack in far too much, and with several unresolved plot threads and numerous extraneous characters, it is overstuffed and unsatisfying. Especially vexing is the fact that the story hardly explores the irony found in the fact that Kim-sum plays roles in drag, while Mimi is in love with a boyish girl. Josephine Siao, however, is wonderful; as with **Summer Snow** and **Mahjong Dragon**, it is her impeccable comedic and dramatic talents that keep this third-rate material bearable and, on occasion, genuinely entertaining. Incidentally, "Hu-Du-Men" is the imaginary line that separates backstage (or real world) from the stage.

470. Human Lanterns

(1982; Shaw Brothers) ★: 7/10. *Yun pei dung lung* (Cantonese), *Ren pi deng long* (Mandarin): "Human Skin Lanterns." Cinematographers: Siu Feng, Ma Chung-yiu; Music: Sing Kam-wing, So Chun-hau; Writers: Ngai Hong, Sun Chung; Producer: Mona Fong Yat-wah; Action Directors: Tang Chia, Wong Po-kei; Director: Sun Chung. Cast: Lau Wing (Lung Shu-ai), Lo Lieh (Chao Chun-fang), Chen Kuan-tai (Tan Fu), Sun Chien (Constable Pan), Tin Lei (Lung's Wife), Lo Mang (Kuei Szu-yi), Ha Ping (Brothel Madam). 2.35:1. No official domestic video release. 95 minutes.

Desperate to best rival Tan Fu in the annual lantern contest, impudent nobleman Lung Shu-ai offers luxury and riches to mysterious craftsman Chao Chun-fang in exchange for a prize-winning entry. The misanthropic Chao accepts, provided that Lung agrees never to visit him until the lantern is completed. Lung and Chao met in battle some years before, and their contest ended with Lung deeply scarring Chao's face. The latter, now seeking revenge, preys upon a woman Lung desires, skinning her alive. With the police suspecting Lung, Chao proceeds to kidnap Tan's sister, Chung-hua, effectively setting Tan and Lung at each other's throats. While the two of them point fingers, Chao continues to claim more human raw materials for his work.

This arresting period film unfolds largely amidst the usual gorgeous Shaw Brothers studio settings, giving the proceedings a gloss that is a nice contrast to the atmospheric sequences in and around the ghoulish lair where Chao performs his bloody deeds. Lo Lieh is wonderfully malevolent in a role similar to the one he essayed in the studio's 1976 production **Black Magic Part II** (released stateside by World Northal as **Revenge of the Zombies**), and the mixture of horror and kung fu is reminiscent of a Shaw co-production with Britain's Hammer Studios, **Legend of the Seven Golden Vampires** (1973; aka **The Seven Brothers Meet Dracula**). If not quite in the same league as that film, **Human Lanterns** is still an effective hybrid of screenwriter Ngai Hong's signature martial arts mystery and the kind of gruesome horror that began to appear in HK theaters during the mid '70s. Although this does not seem to have been included among the Shaw Brothers films issued domestically by World Video, it was released by the Taiwanese New Ship Film Enterprise label in a heavily cropped (the English subtitles are severely compromised) and censored edition (all nudity is excised, and apparently so is some of the carnage). The above running time reflects that version. The soundtrack includes music lifted from the first film in the Japanese **Majin** trilogy and, in the final moments, **Phantasm**.

471. Husband & Wife

(1995) ★: 1/10. *Waan si gok dak nei jui ho* (Cantonese), *Hai shi jue de ni zui hao* (Mandarin): "Still Feel You Are the Best." Cinematographer: Ko Chi-wah; Music: Sam Leung Yiu-sang; Writer: Siu Sun; Producer: Simon Cheng Kwok-fai; Director: Hugo Ng Toi-yung. Cast: Hugo Ng Toi-yung (George Chun), Lily Chung Suk-wai (Judy), Anthony Wong Chau-sang (Wah Tino), Wong Hei (Keith), Farini Cheung Yui-ling (Tse Yuet-ling). 1.85:1. VHS/LD: Tai Seng. Import LD/VCD: Ocean Shores. Running Time Unknown. Also known as **Husbands & Wives**.

The '90s saw an explosion of relationship comedies appearing in HK cinemas, and this dreadful no-budget exercise is easily the worst of them. Real-life couple Hugo Ng and Lily Chung play George and Judy, two of the least appealing people you would ever want to spend five minutes with (let alone the rest of your life). He is a jealous, hyper-sensitive hypochondriac, and she is an absent-minded, motor-mouthed simpleton. George's perpetual misery is compounded one morning by two events: the arrival of Wah Tino, an obnoxious rival from his school days who still carries a torch for Judy, and an overheard phone conversation which convinces him that he only has a month to live. The usual misunderstandings, unmotivated suspicions, and desperate lies follow.

The script does not offer a single intelligent observation about relationships, and the pathetic attempts at humor (including scatological jokes and *a talking dog*) are "augmented" by the use of sound FX from cartoons. Absolutely unbearable!

Husbands & Wives *see* **Husband & Wife**

I Am Green *see* **The Wild Ones**

472. I Am Sorry

(1989; Golden Harvest/Golden Way Films/Paragon Films) ★: 6/10. *Suet fong dik nui yan* (Cantonese), *Shuo huang de nu ren* (Mandarin): "Lying Woman." Cinematographer: Christopher Doyle; Art Director: William Cheung Suk-ping; Music: Anthony Lun Wing-leung; Writer: Yau Tai On-ping; Producers: Willie Chan Chi-keung, Vicky Leung Lee Siu-ha; Director: Tony Au Ding-ping. Cast: Carina Lau Kar-ling (Carole Chang), Pat Ha Man-chik (Sheng Wen-yueh), May Lo Mei-mei (Cindy), Lawrence Ng Kai-wah (Edgar), Elaine Kam Yin-ling (Sabrina), Kenneth Tsang Kong (Edward Sung), Rosamund Kwan Chi-lam (Alice), Ken Lo Wai-kwong (Man at Table), Frankie Chin Chi-leung (Man at Table), Manfred Wong (Lo). 1.85:1. VHS: Tai Seng (No Subtitles). Import LD: Star Entertainment (No Subtitles). Import VCD: Mega Star. 96 minutes.

Neighbors Carole and Wen-yuen are a study in contrasts: The former is a flighty kept woman, while the latter is successful, independent, and level-headed. While out for dinner one evening, Carole intervenes in a fight between Edgar, Alice, and the latter's Japanese companion. Regretting her actions afterwards, Carole tries to apologize to Edgar but ends up getting even more angry with the man and humiliates him at work. In between spending time with Wen-yuen (who is seeing several men) and her other female friends (known as "The Gang of Four"), Carole intentionally undermines her relationship with middle-aged beau Edward, and sees Edgar once again. This time the two respond more favorably to one another, with her energy and spontaneity offsetting his timid hesitancy. The pair move in together but begin to experience second thoughts, largely due to the feelings Edgar still harbors for Alice. Edward, meanwhile, has started seeing Wen-yuen, prompting Carole to leave the city and her friends behind for a few weeks so that she can make up her mind about just what it is that she wants out of life.

Attractively designed and peopled with talented performers, **I Am Sorry** is a welcome change of pace from the usual HK romantic comedies, which adhere so closely to convention, one can almost finish the characters' sentences. Carole's brazen eccentricities and Edward's gentle, pliable nature mark them as fresh subjects for this genre, though one suspects that the characters in the film are far more tolerant of Carole's antics than real people would be. The writing runs hot and cold and the ending is too easy to forecast, but this remains a moderately entertaining endeavor highlighted by Carina Lau's tour-de-force performance.

473. I Have a Date with Spring

(1994; Media Asia Films/Ko Chi Sum Films Co.) ★: 6/10. *Ngoh woh chun tin yau goh yeuk wooi* (Cantonese), *Wo he chun tian you ge yue hui* (Mandarin): "I Have a Date with Spring." Cinematographer: Sander Lee Kar-ko; Art Director: Choi Yee-hang; Music: Chung Chi-wing, Anthony Lee Hon-kam, Marco Wan Ho-kit; Writer: Raymond To Kwok-wai; Producers: Clifton Ko Chi-sum, Koo Tin-lung, Raymond To Kwok-wai; Action Director: Chung Chi-wing; Director: Clifton Ko Chi-sum. Cast: Alice Lau Ar-lai (Butterfly Yiu), Law Koon-lan (Lulu Gold), David Wu Tai-wai (Karl Sum), Fung Wai-hung (Eagle), So Yuk-wah (Nancy), Yip Wing-cho (Po), James Wong Jim (Triad), Teresa Mo Shun-kwan (Woman at Concert Hall), Raymond Wong Pak-ming (Maitre'd), Anita Lee Yuen-wah (Bar Girl), Petrina Fung Bo-bo (Concert M.C.). 1.85:1. VHS: Tai Seng. Import LD/VCD/DVD: Universe. 86 minutes.

One of the sleeper hits of 1994, **I Have a Date with Spring** was produced on a modest budget and features a cast of virtual unknowns but managed to win over audiences with its nostalgic look at a bygone era. The setting is a reunion concert, with the story (which takes place in the late '60s) presented in flashbacks. It tells of some female singers, known as "The 4 Big Nuts," and their efforts to make a living at their craft while HK is in the midst of turmoil caused by the student riots. Fung-ping is saddled with a no-account gambler for a boyfriend, Eagle squanders her talent singing in sailor bars, Lulu is a loyal friend to all, and Butterfly gets her big break when the main act does not appear at the club one evening. The main focus is on Butterfly and her on-again, off-again relationship with handsome sax player Karl, which ends when he goes off to New York. Trouble arises back in the present when Butterfly discovers that Karl has been invited to the concert. Time has not healed her wounds and she has no desire to see him ... at least that is her initial reaction.

The performers are engaging and the story has the kind of built-in happy ending that will appeal to some viewers. However, the film settles for the obvious too often, and that, coupled with some directorial shortcomings (like presenting both the present *and* the past sequences in filtered soft focus, a look that quickly grows tiresome), prevents it from being anything more than a congenial diversion.

474. I Love Maria

(1988; Golden Princess/Film Workshop) ★: 8/10. *Tit gaap miu dik ma lee a* (Cantonese), *Tie jia wu di ma li ya* (Mandarin): "Invincible Maria's Iron Armour." Cinematographer: Lo Wan-shing; Art Director: James Leung Wah-sang; Music: Romeo Diaz, James Wong Jim; Writer: Yuen Kai-chi; Producers: Tsui Hark, John Sham Kin-fun; Action Director: Ching Siu-tung; Director: David Chung Chi-man. Cast: Sally Yeh Chian-wen (Maria/The Robot), John Sham Kin-fun (Curly), Tsui Hark (Whisky), Tony Leung Chiu-wai (T.Q. Zhuang), Lam Ching-ying (Whisky's Mentor), Ben Lam Kwok-bun (Saviour), Paul Chun Pui (Police Captain), Dennis Chan Kwok-san (Curly's Boss), Che-Kirk Wong Chi-keung (Bartender). Dolby Digital (DVD only). 1.85:1. VHS: Tai Seng. Import LD: Golden Cinema City. Import DVD: Universe. 100 minutes. Also known as **Roboforce** (Dubbed version).

A highly enjoyable sci-fi action romp from Tsui Hark's Film Workshop company, this ambitious production even features Tsui in a supporting role. A group of high-tech thugs who call themselves "The Hero Gang" have been pulling a series of major robberies with the aid of a giant, seemingly invincible robot called Pioneer I. Their leader, Saviour, has a second, human-sized robot constructed to look exactly like his ruthless underling/lover Maria. One evening, discredited inventor Curly meets and befriends "Whisky," a Hero gang member whose drinking has him on the outs with his fellow criminals. The bumbling alcoholic is suspected of treason, so the robot Maria is dispatched to eliminate him. After several close calls, Curly is able to reprogram her, just in time to save them from being killed by the rampaging Pioneer I. Armed with Curly's "Electro-sonic Cannon" and joined by fearless reporter T.Q. Zhuang, these unlikely heroes decide to invade Saviour's headquarters in order to put him and his mechanical henchman out of commission.

Some of the comedy is a bit too repetitive, but the visuals are often stunning and there are a number of ambitious, well-realized special FX. Tsui gives a fine, comic performance, and Sally Yeh does an excellent job as the mechanical Maria but is less convincing as her human model. Terrific fun, the film, alas, bombed in HK, disappearing from theaters after only six days. Most of the music is swiped from the Chuck Norris actioner **Invasion USA**, supplemented with a few cues from Tangerine Dream's **Wavelength** soundtrack; the robot sound FX come from **Aliens** and **Robocop**. The English dubbed version reportedly has a different score. Watch carefully during the end credits for John Woo (hanging the medal around Paul Chun Pui's neck).

475. I Wanna Be Your Man

(1994; Mandarin Film Production/Scholar Film Co.) ★: 6/10. *San taam moh luk* (Cantonese), *Shen tan mo lu* (Mandarin): "Mythical Detective Moh Luk." Cinematographer: Apple Kwan Pak-suen; Art Director: Gemma To Ching-ching; Music: Veronica Lee Tuen-han, Arion; Producers: Raymond Wong Pak-ming, Tsai Mui-ho; Writer-Director: Cheung Chi-sing. Cast: Lau Ching-wan (Lu Che-mo), Christy Chung Lai-tai (Ron), Christine Ng Wing-mei (Susan Wong Suet-san), Francis Ng Chun-yu (The Barrister), Bobby Yip King-sang (Sam). 1.85:1. VHS: Tai Seng. Import LD: Cameron Entertainment. Import VCD/DVD: Mei Ah. 96 minutes.

Flaky detective Lu Che-mo is on the verge of getting canned from his job, until he accidentally discovers that his female superior, Susan Wong, is gay. Since he keeps his mouth shut, she cuts him a break and he is able to stay on the force. Che-mo begins a friendship with Susan that contains some overt but comical flirting on his part. However, Che-mo also gets to know his boss' beautiful lover, Ron, who is annoyed that Susan is spending so much time with him. Susan soon catches Ron with a man, and both women end up seeking solace from poor Che-mo, whose natural urges are becoming overwhelming. Meanwhile, Che-mo's old barrister friend is venting his frustration with the legal system by murdering criminals who have managed to evade prosecution. When Susan's investigation begins to point towards him, she receives an anonymous threat stating that if she doesn't back off, her relationship with Ron will be revealed to the department head.

The vigilante subplot never meshes well with the main storyline, and the film would have been better off just focusing on the three-way relationship at its core, unbelievable as it may be. Lau Ching-wan and Christine Ng are both engaging, and while not entirely successful, the script at least tries to make relevant observations about love and relationships between those of the same sex instead of just going for cheap laughs like most HK films concerning homosexuals.

476. I Want to Go On Living

(1995; Mandarin Films) ★: 6/10. *Ngoh yiu wood ha hui* (Cantonese), *Wo yao huo xia qu* (Mandarin): "I Must Live On." Cinematographer: Jingle Ma Cho-shing; Art Director: Chong Chi-leung; Music: Chan Kin-tak, Ng Kwok-yan; Writers: Raymond Wong Pak-ming, Sylvia Chang Ai-chia; Producer: Raymond Wong Pak-ming; Director: Raymond Lee Wai-man. Cast: Sylvia Chang Ai-chia (Pui Yan), Anita Yuen Wing-yee (Yip Fan), Emil Chow Wah-kin (Man Chi-yeung), Winston Chao Wen-hsuan (Ko Chun), Alvina Kong Yan-yin (Fei-fei). 1.85:1. VHS: Tai Seng. Import LD/VCD: Fitto Mobile. 98 minutes.

Adapted from a novel by Liang Fengyi, this earnest drama suffers from the flaw inherent in many such endeavors—namely, the condensation of multiple storylines into a single, average-length film. Characters change and events rush by much too quickly, without a proper build-up to lend credence. Pui Yan is a single woman in China who marries an older man, the owner of a restaurant in England. By doing this Yan hopes that she can bring her grandmother over to her new home so that the ailing woman can receive the medical treatment she desperately needs. Yan's hopes of a better life evaporate the first day she arrives in the UK: Her husband is a vicious, impotent man with a crippled daughter who has not gone outside in years. The girl, Yip Fan, was injured in a car accident caused by her father's negligence. An aspiring dancer, she not only lost the use of her right leg but also her mother, who died from injuries sustained in the wreck. Although her marriage cannot be salvaged, Yan develops great affection for Fan and resolves to help the girl put her life back together. When her husband loses the restaurant to a loan shark and disappears, Yan journeys to HK in search of relatives that can help her. This innocent quest for help gets her involved in a legal battle and another unhappy marriage of convenience. Fan, meanwhile, comes to HK and begins to receive treatment from Yan's childhood sweetheart, Man Chi-yeung, and their subsequent relationship proves difficult for Yan to accept.

Awfully soapy by Western standards, the film still offers a stellar turn by the eternally youthful Sylvia Chang and pleasing, effective performances from Anita Yuen and Winston Chao (the latter's character, while largely peripheral, is the least predictable). Their work, coupled with attractive locations and photography, help to keep this worthwhile.

477. I Will Finally Knock You Down, Dad!

(1984; Shaw Brothers) ★: 5/10. *Mong ji sing chung* (Cantonese), *Wang zi cheng chong* (Mandarin): "Ambitious Son Becomes a Pest." Cinematographer: Wong Chit; Art Director: Ng Bo-ling; Music: Sing Kam-wing, So Chun-hau; Writers: Yip Fai, Kwan Hung-wing, Kwan Chun-wing; Producer: Mona Fong Yat-wah; Action Directors: Hsu Hsia, Yuen Fai, Cheung Siu, Cheng Fan-sang; Director: Hsu Hsia. Cast: Chin Siu-ho (Chen Chung), Bill Tung Biu (The Monk), Chen Kuan-tai (Iron Fingered Chen), Lo Lieh (Father of the Bride), Lily Li Li-li (Chung's Mother), Phillip Ko Fei (Lung), Charlie Cho Cha-lei (Bird Fight Referee). 1.85:1. VHS: World Video (Poor Subtitles). Import LD: Ocean Shores (Poor Subtitles). 92 minutes.

This period yarn revolves around Chen Chung, a martially talented but undisciplined lad who is constantly getting into trouble, much to the chagrin of his esteemed father. One day Chung and his servants cause trouble in a dye mill, prompting the establishment's owner, Lung, to visit the Chen household. When Lung easily bests Chung in combat, his father cancels the boy's wedding and all but disowns him for shaming the family, prompting Chung to leave home. He hooks up with a wandering Shaolin monk who, following much cajoling, agrees to help him improve his kung fu. After challenging his father to a test of skills, Chung learns the hard way that his instructor is nothing but a conman. Now armed with the determination he needs, Chung sets out to get himself into top condition in order to prove himself to his father.

Chin Siu-ho is a personable lead and the martial arts are good, but the story has a tedious inevitability to it and the comedy (which includes anachronistic gags like breakdancing) never really clicks. The speed with which Chung's kung fu improves is also questionable, suggesting that an extra jolt of self-confidence was all he really needed to succeed. When one considers the major defeats he suffers earlier in the proceedings, that notion just doesn't wash.

478. I Will Wait for You

(1994; Mandarin Films) ★: 4/10. *Nin nin yau gam yat* (Cantonese), *Nian nian you jin ri* (Mandarin): "Every Year Like Today." Cinematographer: Sander Lee Kar-ko; Music: Violet Lam Man-yee; Writer: Szeto Wai-kin; Producer: Raymond Wong Pak-ming; Director: Clifton Ko Chi-sum. Cast: Tony Leung Kar-fai (So Yau-shing), Anita Yuen Wing-yee (Cheung Wai-sum), Sandra Ng Kwan-yu (Mei-lan), James Wong Jim (Thief), Francis Ng Chun-yu (Lam Wai-man), Clifton Ko Chi-sum (Poultry Merchant). 1.85:1. VHS: Tai Seng. Import LD/VCD: Mei Ah. 100 minutes.

An imitation of the 1978 Alan Alda-Ellen Burstyn vehicle **Same Time, Next Year**, this disappointing farce unfolds just like a play, utilizing only a handful of sets and a tiny cast. Opening in 1964 (and in black-and-white), the film finds strangers So Yau-shing and Cheung Wai-sum spending the night together in a rented house to avoid a bad storm. Despite the fact that he is married and she is about to be, they share the same bed and pledge to meet in the same place on the same day the next year. We visit the pair again in 1973 (when their solitude is invaded by a hapless thief), 1978 (when Wai-sum turns up pregnant and, predictably, goes into labor), 1984 (with Yau-shing's wife making a surprise appearance), 1987 (with the plunging stock market threatening to wipe out Wai-sum's savings, and with her marriage on the rocks), and, finally, in 1994 (as Wai-sum must make an important decision).

Leung and Yuen are both in fine form here, but most of the jokes are telegraphed well in advance and the dramatic content is routine, resulting in tedium. By the time Leung is running around with a giant plastic turkey stuck on his head, all hope is lost.

479. The Iceman Cometh

(1989; Golden Harvest/Johnny Mak Production) ★: 6/10. *Gap dung gei hap* (Cantonese), *Ji dong ji xia* (Mandarin): "Deep Freeze Strange Knight." Cinematographers: Poon Hang-sang, Wong Chi-wai, Peter Pau Tak-hei, Johnny Koo Kwok-wah, Jingle Ma Cho-shing, Ardy Lam Kwok-wah; Art Director: Fong Ying; Music: Joseph Chan Wing-leung; Writers: Stephen Siu Yeuk-yuen, Johnny Mak Dong-hung; Producer: Stephen Siu Yeuk-yuen; Action Directors: Yuen Biao's Stunt Group, Yuen Wah, Yuen Tak, Chin Kar-lok; Director: Clarence Fok Yiu-leung. Cast: Yuen Biao (Fong Sau-ching), Maggie Cheung Man-yuk (Polla), Yuen Wah (Fung San), Tai Po (Pimp), Elvis Tsui Kam-kong (Scientist), Alvina Kong Yan-yin (Hooker), Sarah Lee Lai-yui (Hooker), Chen Jing (Arms Dealer), Wong Jing (Crane Operator), Corey Yuen Kwai (Bum), Sin Lap-man (Robber), Liu Wai-hung (Angel), Stanley Fung Shui-fan (Santa Claus). Dolby Digital (DVD only). 1.85:1. VHS: Tai Seng. LD: Media Asia. Import LD: Star Entertainment (No Subtitles). Import DVD: Universe. 114 minutes. Also known as **Time Warriors**.

This Johnny Mak Dong-hung production is a hybrid of **Time After Time** and **Iceman**, with some additional similarities to the latter's low-budget knockoff, **Sword Kill** (aka **Ghost Warrior**) and scattered visual echoes of **Highlander**. In the Ming Dynasty, royal swordsman Fong Sau ching is ordered to pursue and capture rapist/murderer Fung San. Just as Fong finally locates his quarry, Fung activates a magical "Time Wheel" which propels him and his adversary 350 years forward into the present day. Landing in a snowy mountain region, the two resume their fight and, at the height of combat, plunge off a cliff to their apparent deaths. A scientific expedition discovers their frozen bodies and takes them to HK for study, but the pair are accidentally thawed out by some thieves. Fong is given shelter by Polla, a cocky prostitute who tricks the warrior into becoming her servant/bodyguard. Fung, meanwhile, adapts more quickly to modern-day life and continues his string of deadly sexual assaults, while also pulling smash and grab robberies on the side. When the men's paths inevitably cross, Fung threatens to kill Polla unless Fong drinks a poison that will destroy his martial arts abilities. He complies and Polla is freed. However, Fong refuses to abandon his vow of allegiance to his king and trains incessantly until he has recovered his abilities. Fung, meanwhile, learns that the Time Wheel will soon be on display at an exhibition of Buddhist artifacts. On a certain day and at a certain hour, the wheel's powers can be accessed, and Fung plans to use this opportunity to return to the 17th century with a cache of 20th century weapons in tow.

Like many films by director Clarence Fok Yiu-leung (**Naked Killer, The Black Panther Warriors**), **The Iceman Cometh** is all over the place, dauntlessly mixing wild action, juvenile humor, and archaic melodrama. The final blend is lumpy but entertaining, thanks primarily to Yuen Biao and Maggie Cheung. Yuen is characteristically charming and quite convincing, handling the fish-out-of-water gags with restrained comedic skill, the emotional aspects with dignity, and the physical elements with panache. Cheung is wonderfully expressive and steals almost every scene she graces. While far too beautiful to really be convincing as a low-class street urchin, she is still a joy to watch. Unfortunately, she has been dubbed here by another actress, which is quite distracting for those familiar with her voice. Yuen Wah is a superb martial artist but his one-dimensional role gives him little to do but grimace. He also disappears from the storyline for too great a time, only to be artificially injected back in when the time for more action arises. Johnny Mak's productions always boast healthy production values and this one is no exception, serving up several large scale setpieces. The Time Wheel is an impressive, full-scale prop that resembles a metallic Venus fly trap from some pre-mechanized age, and the Ming sequences are lushly designed and photographed along the lines of the **A Chinese Ghost Story** series.

480. I'm Your Birthday Cake!

(1995; Jing's Production/Wong Jing's Workshop) ★: 5/10. *Bat do dak dik lai mat* (Cantonese), *Bu dao de de li wu* (Mandarin): "Immoral Gift." Cinematographer: Andrew Lau Wai-keung; Art Director: Silver Cheung Sai-wang; Music: Marco Productions; Writer: But Sze Lui Yan; Producer: Wong Jing; Director: Yip Wai-man. Cast: Chingmy Yau Suk-ching (Cher Lo), Dior Cheng Yee-kin (Water Lam), Michael Wong Man-tak (Honey Chan), Kong Wah (Mountain Lam), Amanda Lee Wai-man (Sorry). 1.85:1. VHS/LD: World Video. Import LD/VCD/DVD: Mei Ah. 94 minutes.

This typical Wong Jing concoction is leeringly juvenile and exists in some alternate universe that has little in common with the way people act and behave in this one. That said, it does (like many of Wong's films) have moments and makes for adequate, mindless escapism. After being unceremoniously dumped by her boyfriend, the conservative but beautiful Cher Lo is approached with a most unusual offer: she will be paid $HK30 million to be a human birthday present. After saving his brother, Water, from an accident,

Mountain Lam became impotent and got an erection for the first time in five years after catching a glimpse of Cher (in a recreation of Marilyn Monroe's famous billowing skirt scene from **The Seven Year Itch**). Water wants Cher to make love with his brother on the latter's birthday and is willing to pay her that monumental sum to do it. In order to save her father's failing company, Cher agrees to the deal and begins three weeks of instruction on how to be sexy, under the tutelage of limp-wristed playboy Honey Chan. However as the big day approaches, Water develops his own attraction to Cher.

No surprises here, outside of the fact that Michael Wong's outrageously stereotypical performance as the gay instructor is, oddly enough, more effective and endearing than his attempts at straight drama in other films! Singer Amanda Lee provides brassy comic relief as Cher's obnoxious friend. Incidentally, the writer's credit is a pseudonym meaning "Not a Woman," which is also used on another Wong Jing/Chingmy Yau collaboration, **Blind Romance** (1996).

481. The Imp

(1981; Century Motion Picture & Distribution Co.) ★: 5/10. *Hung bong* (Cantonese), *Xiong bang* (Mandarin): "Evil List." Cinematographer: Bob Thompson; Art Director: Kam Kam-ming; Music: Not Original; Writers: Kam Ping-hing, Lee Dun, Cheung Kam-moon; Producer: Lau Jun-wai; Director: Dennis Yu Wan-kong. Cast: Charlie Chin Hsiang-lin (Keung), Kent Cheng Chuk-see (Fatty), Wong Ching ("Mr. Hong Kong"), Ngok Wah. 1.85:1. VHS: Tai Seng. Import VCD: Mei Ah. 95 minutes.

After being fired from numerous jobs, the perpetually unlucky Keung (whose wife is due to have a baby in the near future) is hired to be a night security guard at an office building. A week after he starts work, all manner of mysterious things happen: An elevator goes berserk and starts filling with water, a fellow employee chokes on a bone and then springs back to life on the operating table, and the head guard is killed in his home by unknown forces. Keung learns that, prior to the construction of the building, the site was occupied by a gang of child kidnappers who often murdered their victims. A geomancer comes to his aid and, after various tests, determines that a restless spirit seeks to reincarnate by possessing Keung's unborn son. Keung's only hope is to destroy the ghost's hiding place before dawn; otherwise, he, his wife, and his son are doomed. Some intriguing visuals and a couple of decent shock sequences follow.

A not entirely successful effort from Dennis Yu (director of **The Beasts** and **Evil Cat**), this thriller is a bit too familiar to completely hit the mark. The ending is worth sticking around for, though.

482. The Imp

(1996; Golden Harvest/Paragon Films) ★: 3/10. *Che saat* (Cantonese), *Xie sha* (Mandarin): "Evil Killer." Cinematographers: Cheung Yiu-cho, Sung Kong; Art Director: James Cheung Ying-wah; Music: Golden Harvest Music Studio; Writer: Sam Leung Tak-sam; Action Director: Lai Keung-kuen; Producer: Lau Jun-wai; Director: Ivan Lai Kai-ming. Cast: Diana Pang Dan (Ching Kwok-shan/Fun-fun), Mark Cheng Ho-nam (Mark), Emiko Ishizuka (Angie), William Ho Kar-kui (Uncle Tao), Dick Lau Dik-chi (King Kong). 1.85:1. VHS: Tai Seng. 96 minutes.

This silly Category III horror yarn has dollops of nudity and sex but is still an utter bore for two thirds of its running time, coming to life only during its extended climax. A HK TV crew travels to a remote part of China to shoot the "Rite of Sacrifice," a ritual performed once a year by some aborigines. They are joined by Kwok-shan, who has come looking for her twin sister, Fun-fun. Afflicted by fainting spells and weird visions of her sibling, Kwok-shan seeks the assistance of a blind shaman, who warns her to leave the area immediately. It quickly becomes apparent (to the audience, anyway) that there is something seriously wrong with the nymphomaniac running the local inn (with a mute hunchback assistant, no less) everyone is staying at, but the crew goes off to shoot the ritual anyway. Kwok-shan has another of her weird spells and interferes with the ceremony, prompting a predictable response from the natives. Meanwhile, an unseen woman is making mincemeat of the guests.

The final reel does offer a surprise or two and some disturbingly perverse content but not enough to make it worth enduring the silliness and stupidity that proceeds it.

In Between *see* **The New Age of Living Together**

483. In the Heat of Summer

(1994; Flying Colours Film Productions Company/Flying Colours Productions & Agency Company) ★: 7/10. *Dim ji bing bing ji ching nin gon taam* (Cantonese), *Dian zhi bing bing zhi qing nian gan tan* (Mandarin): "Finger Soldiers: Young Detectives." Cinematographer: Apple Kwan Pak-suen; Art Director: Ben Luk Man-wah; Music: Chung Chi-wing; Writer: James Yuen Sai-sang; Action Directors: Chin Kar-lok, Yee Tin-hung, Bruce Law Lai-yin; Producer-Director: Teddy Chan Tak-sum. Cast: Jordan Chan Siu-chun (Leung Siu-ming, aka Monk), Chan Kwok-bong (Daddy), Marco Ngai Chun-kit (Tak), Moses Chan Ho (Sam Hui), Jack Gao Jie (Chan Wei-cheng), Christine Ng Wing-mei (Maggie), Mark Houghton (David Morris). 1.85:1. VHS: Tai Seng. Import LD/VCD: Fitto Mobile. 98 minutes.

When his friend is killed (thanks to the incompetence of his British superior), soldier Chan Wei-cheng tries to have the man brought up on charges. Four years and several lawsuits later, Chan is no closer to achieving justice and goes berserk. Imprisoned, dismissed from the service, and abandoned by his wife, Chan escapes from jail and kidnaps his little girl. He then begins to extort money from the authorities by planting bombs all over HK. A team of young police officers are on the case and they must juggle the strain of their job with the pressures in their privates lives (children, gambling debts, etc.). The police put Chan's wife and child under protective custody, prompting him to retaliate by placing a bomb inside the station house.

Peopled by interesting characters and constructed around plausible situations, this is an above average police procedural. Taiwanese actor Jack Gao gives a reserved but tense performance, while Jordan Chan and Chan Kwok-bong are very good as the two most colorful of the young policemen. Only the predictable nature of the central plot prevents this from attaining a higher grade. Directors Gordon Chan Kar-seung, Jacob Cheung Chi-leung, and Lee Chi-ngai have cameos.

484. In the Lap of God

(1991; Cinema Capital Entertainment) ★: 6/10. *Maan fong dik tung wa* (Cantonese), *Mau huang de tong hua* (Mandarin): "Fairy Tale from the Savage Wilderness." Cinematographer: Tony Fan Chuen-kam; Art Director: Louise Kwong Hoi-ming; Music: Violet Lam Man-yee; Writers: Wellington Fung Wing, Lo Kin, Edward Leung Yiu-ming; Producers: Richard Cheung Kuen, Wellington Fung Wing; Action Director: Ridley Tsui Bo-wah; Director: Lo Kin. Cast: Roy Cheung Yiu-yeung (Roy), Irene Wan Pik-ha (May Tse), Francis Ng Chun-yu (Alex Ng), Leung Si-ho, Man So. 1.85:1. VHS: Tai Seng. Import LD: Golden Cinema City. 88 minutes.

This romantic comedy-adventure is fashioned after **Romancing the Stone** (even replicating a handful of shots and situations from that film verbatim) but remains a uniquely HK enterprise in terms of execution. When her boyfriend Alex is arrested in Rangoon and sentenced to death, office worker May Tse must come up with US$200,000 in bribe money to win his freedom. She is able to, thanks to a small fortune in diamonds that were dropped into her purse during a robbery. However, the underworld parties involved learn that May has acquired the stones and sent them to Burma, so crooked cop Roy is ordered to accompany her there to retrieve them. The two end up right in the middle of the country's civil war and quickly run afoul of corrupt government soldiers. After being pursued across miles of jungle, they meet up with some rebels who lead a raid on the local army stronghold where Alex is being held.

Typecast as a villain, Roy Cheung gets to be the nominal good guy here and displays a rugged charm that fulfils the requirements of the role perfectly. The various car, motorcycle, jeep, and foot chases are merely adequate and the humor is decidedly hit and miss, but everything moves along well and the exotic locales (actually Thailand) add an extra level of interest. In order to avoid the Category III rating, a sequence featuring a group of natives bathing in a river has been optically fogged, to hide the lower frontal nudity.

In the Line of Duty *see* **Royal Warriors**

In the Line of Duty 2 *see* **In the Line of Duty 5**

485. In the Line of Duty III

(1988; D & B Films Co.) ★: 5/10. *Wong ga si je ji III chi hung daai do* (Cantonese), *Huang jia shi jie zhi III ci xiong da dao* (Mandarin): "Royal Hong Kong Policewoman III: A Couple of Big Thieves." Cinematographers: Jimmy Au Kam-hung, Wong Po-man; Art Directors: Sita Yeung Leng, Eric Lam Sai-kan; Music: Phil Chan Fei-lap; Writers: Chan Kui-ying, Law Tai-man; Producer: Stephen Shin Kei-yin; Action Directors: Chris Lee Kin-sang, Tony Leung Siu-hung, Brandy Yuen Chun-yeung, Yuen Cheung-yan, Yuen Yat-chor; Directors: Arthur Wong Ngok-tai, Brandy Yuen Chun-yeung. Cast: Cynthia Yang Li-ching (Rachel Yeung), Michiko Nishiwaki (Michiko Nishiwaki), Hiroshi Fujioka (Hiroshi Fujioka), Yung Sai-kit (Nakamura Genji), Paul Chun Pui (Inspector Cameron Chuen), Dick Wei (Diamond Fence), Sandra Ng Kwan-yu (Cop), Melvin Wong Kam-sun (Michael Wong), Chris Lee Kin-sang (Ken), Richard Ng Yiu-hon (Neddy the Ninja), Eric Tsang Chi-wai (Neddy's Friend), Stanley Fung Shui-fan (Airport Security Officer), Robin Shou Wan-bo (Bodyguard), Season Ma Si-san (Waitress). Dolby Digital (DVD only). 1.85:1. VHS: Tai Seng. Import VCD: Mega Star. Import DVD: Universe. 84 minutes. Also known as **Force of the Dragon**.

Cynthia Yang's first outing in the D & B series, this lesser entry still finds her to be a worthy replacement for Michelle Yeoh. In Japan, Red Army terrorists Nakamura and Michiko Nishiwaki (played by the actress of that name) pull off a major robbery that appears to be part of an insurance fraud scheme. Having lost his partner while trying to apprehend the criminals, local cop Hiroshi Fujioka (played by the like-named actor) follows the two to HK, eager to exact revenge. HK policewoman Rachel Yeung is ordered to simply shadow Fujioka and keep him out of trouble, but when the latter stumbles upon his targets, he loses control and a number of innocent people die. The HK police allow Fujioka to stay in the country (one of several implausibilities in the storyline), and he continues to track the two killers. When Rachel kills Nakamura, Nishiwaki swears vengeance.

The plotting is simplistic, even for these films, but the action is entertaining, though the final showdown between Nishiwaki and Yang is disappointingly short. An alternate version of the film exists which is missing some of the violence and Michiko Nishiwaki's nude scene. The character names and running time listed above are from the English-dubbed version released on Japanese video.

486. In the Line of Duty 4

(1989; D & B Films Co.) ★: 7/10. *Wong ga si je ji IV jik gik jing yan* (Cantonese), *Huang jia shi jie zhi IV zhi ji zheng ren* (Mandarin): "Royal Hong Kong Policewoman IV: Attacking the Witness Head-on." Cinematographers: Michael Ma Koon-wah, Jimmy Au Kam-hung; Art Director: Lee Chi-ngai; Music: Richard Yuen Cheuk-fan; Writers: Anthony Wong Wing-fai, Cheung Chi-sing; Producer: Stephen Shin Kei-yin; Action Directors: Yuen Shun-yee, Wong Kwan, Cho Wing; Director: Yuen Woo-ping. Cast: Cynthia Yang Li-ching (Madam Yeung), Donnie Yen Chi-tan (Donny), Yuen Yat-chor (Luk Wan-ting), Michael Wong Man-tak (Michael Wong), Liu Kai-chi (Ming), Yuen Shun-yee (Hood with Moustache), Eddie Maher (Loan Shark), Michael Woods (Black Killer), John Salvitti (Caucasian Killer on Motorcycle), Cho Wing (Triad/Bespectacled CIA Fighter). Dolby Digital (DVD only). 1.85:1. VHS: Tai Seng. Import LD: Ocean Shores. Import VCD: Mega Star. Import DVD: Universe. 94 minutes. Also known as **The Witness**.

One of the best entries in this loosely connected series, part **IV** serves up a remarkable amount of action. Honest Seattle dock worker Luk Wan-ting accidentally gets himself involved in America's drug wars when he stumbles into a shootout and is erroneously blamed for the death of a DEA operative. He flees to HK, with Inspector Yeung and officers Donny and Michael in pursuit. They apprehend Luk and plan to extradite him to America, but he is shot en route and must be hospitalized. While the criminals make further attempts on his life, Madam Yeung and Donny become increasingly suspicious of Michael, whose actions suggest that he is undermining their efforts. This is confirmed when Michael admits to being a CIA agent. He is part of an unauthorized operation to raise money by selling drugs, with the cash going to anti-government rebels in an unnamed Latin American country.

Essentially one long, exciting chase, this entry features some spectacular fights, with Yen at his limber best throughout. Highlights include Yang battling an opponent on top of a speeding ambulance, and Yen engaging big Michael Woods in an extended shovel and sledge hammer battle on motorcycles. The plot provides an adequate framework for the skirmishes and that is all that's really required in this genre. Richard Yuen's score is derivative of the music John Carpenter created for his sci-fi actioner **Escape from New York**.

487. In the Line of Duty 5

(1990; D & B Films Co.) ★: 6/10. *Wong ga si je ji jung gaan yan* (Cantonese), *Huang jia shi jie zhi zhong jian ren* (Mandarin): "Royal Hong Kong Policewoman: Middle Man." Cinematographer: Cheng Siu-keung; Art Director: Ben Luk Man-wah; Music: Phil Chan Fei-lap; Writers: Leung Hung-wah, Patrick Yuen Yau-kwong; Producer: Stephen Shin Kei-yin; Action Director: Chris Lee Kin-sang; Director: Cha Chuen-yee. Cast: Cynthia Yang Li-ching (Yang Lei-ching), David Wu Tai-wai (David Ng), Alvina Kong Yan-yin (May), Chris Lee Kin-sang (Killer in Shades), Billy Chow Bei-lee (Scarfaced Killer), Lo Lieh (Alan's Godfather), Lau Kong (Officer Wong), Kim Maree Penn (Blonde). Dolby Digital (DVD only). 1.85:1. VHS: Tai Seng. Import LD: Ocean Shores. Import VCD: Mega Star. Import DVD: Universe. 94 minutes. Also known as **In the Line of Duty 2** (Taiwan title), **Middle Man** (Tai Seng title).

A routine but moderately enjoyable entry in the series, part 5 tells of a criminal organization operating out of South Korea that is selling stolen American military secrets to the Russians. Innocent Marine David Ng is framed for the actions of his (now) dead buddy, who was a member of the gang and under investigation by the CIA. David manages to escape from his captors and, after initially refusing it, enlists the aid of Madam Yang to prove his innocence. The key to his case is teenager May, the only witness who can speak on David's behalf. The climax takes place in Korea as our heroes confront the villains on their home turf.

There is as much action as one would expect, but it is not always as well choreographed as in previous entries (though Yang and Kim Maree Penn have a terrific fight during the climax), and Taiwanese actor David Wu is a lacklustre leading man. Comedienne Alvina Kong is wasted as the secondary female lead, a part that gives her nothing of interest to do and no opportunities for humor.

488. The Incorruptible

(1993; Mandarin Films) ★: 6/10. *Lee Lok-fu kei on* (Cantonese), *Li Luofu qi an* (Mandarin): "The Strange Case of Lee Lok-fu" or "The Strange Case of Li Luofu." Cinematographer: Wong Chi-wai; Art Director: Bill Lui Cho-hung; Music: Richard Yuen Cheuk-fan; Writers: Ng Man-fai, Yip Kai; Producer: Ronny Yu Yan-tai; Director: Anthony Lee Ying-lok. Cast: Ray Lui Leung-wai (Charles Lee), Simon Yam Tat-wah (Cheng Wah), Waise Lee Chi-hung (Lee Choi-fat), Tommy Wong Kwong-leung (Lee Ping), Anita Yuen Wing-yee (Joss Lee), Carrie Ng Kar-lai (Siu-tsui), Lau Siu-ming (Mainland Boss). 1.85:1. VHS: Tai Seng. Import LD: Universe. 81 minutes.

Another HK imitation of **The Untouchables**, this one is set in the 1950s and concerns the formation of a special branch of the police to deal with the triad gang problem. Inspector Charles Lee is given command of the Anti-Triad Squad, and he assembles his own team of men, including disgraced, alcoholic cop Wah. The team experiences a humiliating defeat when a rat tips off some hoods about an upcoming raid, but Lee comes up with a new system to preserve the element of surprise. Threatened by the squad's successful raids on his gambling sites, mobster Lee Choi-fat tries to buy Lee off, but the cop pulls some strings and has him deported to Taiwan. Lee is not so easily beaten, however, and makes his way back to HK for revenge.

The period detail is very nice, the performances are good, the direction is competent and Richard Yuen delivers another fine score. Unfortunately, everything else is too familiar for this to be anything more than lively escapism.

489. The Innocent Interloper

(1986; Always Good Film Co.) ★: 5/10. *Lau man ying hung* (Cantonese), *Liu mang ying xiong* (Mandarin): "Hoodlum Hero." Cinematographer: Nico Wong Man-wan; Art Director: Richard Cheung Yee-fung; Music: Phil Chan Fei-lap; Writer: Wong Ying; Producer: Guy Lai Ying-chau; Director: Johnny Wang Lung-wei. Cast: Lawrence Ng Kai-wah (Shee), Elaine Lui Siu-ling (Lan Hung), Shum Wai (Uncle Shee), Shing Fui-on (Wicked Brain), Hwang Jang-li (Paleface), Chan Cheuk-fai (Chuen). 1.85:1. VHS: Tai Seng. Import LD: Golden Cinema City. 97 minutes.

Johnny Wang Lung-wei, the memorable villain of many Shaw Brothers kung fu films, directed this routine but reasonably entertaining action-comedy. After stealing a valuable counterfeiting plate from his boss, the traitorous mobster Paleface manages to stash it in a library book before being captured and tortured by his gang. After an unsuccessful attempt by the criminals to retrieve the book, it comes into the possession of perennial bookworm Shee, who is soon under siege from various parties trying to steal it back. During one such episode, Shee (who does not have a clue what these people want) is rescued by Lan Hung, a beautiful brothel bodyguard, and the two become fast friends. When Shee's layabout father stumbles across the plates, the trio concoct a scheme to exchange them with the gangsters for a cool $20 million.

The action scenes are largely undistinguished (Lui's male stunt double is much too obvious) and Shum's comedy relief is grating, but Hwang gets an excellent chance to showcase his skills during the climactic fight and the plot moves along well enough to hold one's interest most of the time. Lots of cameos here, including Bill Tung Biu (as himself), Wong Jing (as a cardsharp), Danny Lee Sau-yin (as, surprise, "Inspector Lee"), Charlie Cho Cha-lei, Tai Po, Felix Wong Yat-wah, and, most memorably, Michael Chan Wai-man, as an ill-fated cat burglar named "Flying Mouse!"

490. Insanity

(1993; Mandarin Films) ★: 2/10. *Chuk muk geng sam* (Cantonese), *Chu mu jing xin* (Mandarin): "Touch Eye, Surprise Heart." Cinematographer: Paul Chan Chung-chau; Art Director: Wong Pui-yee; Music: Jonathan Wong Bong-yin; Writer-Producer: Raymond Wong Pak-ming; Action Director-Director: Tony Leung Siu-hung. Cast: Simon Yam Tat-wah (Tang Sau), Kathy Chow Hoi-mei (Mrs. Wong), Raymond Wong Pak-ming (John Wong). Dolby Stereo. 1.85:1. VHS: Tai Seng. Import LD/VCD: Ocean Shores. 77 minutes.

One of the tamest Category III films in memory, this laughable effort starts off like a supernatural thriller and then transforms into a slasher movie. However, frequent doses of intentional, dark humor can do little to mask the creative bankruptcy here. Raymond Wong and Kathy Chow play a couple who decide to move into a new housing development. A good luck idol provided by Chow's mother seems to have a malevolent life of its own, causing various strange accidents and weird hallucinations. At about midway point, a mysterious cloaked figure with a very large knife murders Wong and the couple's poodle, and begins to stalk Chow. Simon Yam turns up as a helpful police officer but quickly begins to display demented behaviour. Catching a TV news report, Chow learns that Yam murdered his wife, and the schizophrenic soon begins to see her as the deceased woman, making him want to kill her all over again.

Director Tony Leung Siu-hung (not to be confused with the two actors using "Tony Leung" as their English name) trots out every suspense film trick in the book (the prowling camera, shadowy figures, loud noises, shock cuts, etc.), but nothing works (in the current video versions, much of the film is too dark to see anyway). In fact, the only positive thing about **Insanity** (aside from some attractive poster art) is that it is one of the shortest films in memory. The soundtrack includes a cue lifted from John Carpenter's **Christine**.

The Inside Story *see* **Triads: The Inside Story**

491. Inspector Chocolate

(1986; Golden Harvest/Paragon Films) ★: 7/10. *San taam ju goo lik* (Cantonese), *Shen tan zhu gu li* (Mandarin): "Godly Inspector Chocolate." Cinematographers: Poon Hang-sang, Michael Ma Koon-wah; Art Director: Carman Wan Siu-wai; Music: Law Dik; Writers: Michael Hui Koon-man, Phillip Chan Yan-kin; Producer: Raymond Chow Man-wai; Action Director: Michael Chan Wai-man; Director: Michael Hui Koon-man. Cast: Michael Hui Koon-man (Chocolate), Anita Mui Yim-fong (Chiao-chiao), Ricky Hui Koon-ying (Egg-tart), Sibelle Hu

Hui-chung (Mrs. Lin), Roy Chiao Hung (Chiao), Michael Chow Man-kin (Liang), Michael Chan Wai-man (Kidnapper), Fung Hark-on (Chen Lung), Tai Po (Jesus). 2.35:1. VHS: Tai Seng (Poor Subtitles). Import VCD: Mega Star. 101 minutes.

This is one of Michael Hui's most enjoyable comedies and serves as a fine introduction to the brand of humor that made him HK's top comedian of the '70s and '80s. He plays a chocolate-addicted cop nicknamed Chu Ku-lik (Cantonese for "chocolate") who hasn't been promoted in a dog's age and must endure the taunts of his slick co-worker Liang. After one foul-up too many, the chief demotes Chocolate to the "Missing Persons" desk and further insists that the harried inspector keep an eye on Chiao-chiao, a rookie policewoman *and* Miss HK contestant who also happens to be the chief's daughter. Mrs. Lin, a TV cooking show hostess, has had one of her twin boys kidnapped, and Chocolate is assigned the task of recovering the missing child. After bungling an initial arrest, Chocolate, his partner Egg-tart, and Chiao-chiao manage to apprehend their suspect, but he turns out to be an opportunist who just wanted to cash in on the situation. Further investigation and a vital tip from an unlikely source leads Chocolate into a potentially fatal confrontation with the real perpetrator.

Anita Mui gets to poke fun at her pop glamour image, and the script incorporates ample opportunities for Hui to launch into both his "slow-burn" and "humbled sycophant" styles of comedy. However, the funniest sequence occurs during a stakeout when Chocolate attempts to pass himself off as a female dwarf and gets caught in a compromising position when he has to go into the ladies room! The film's use of sync sound recording (very rare on productions from its era) is a major plus, as Hui's fine-tuned timing and delivery remain spontaneous and natural. Two comedic bits (a cockroach loose in a bakery kitchen and Hui dressed up in a giant dog suit) would be reprised and expanded upon for the comedian's fast-food send-up **Chicken and Duck Talk** (1988). Elvis Tsui Kam-kong, Maria Cordero, and Dennis Chan Kwok-san appear briefly.

492. Inspector Pink Dragon

(1991; Golden Harvest/Paragon Films) ★: 3/10. *San taam Ma Yue-lung* (Cantonese), *Shen tan Ma Rulong* (Mandarin): "Mythical Detective Ma Yue-lung" or "Mythical Detective Ma Rulong." Cinematographer: Cheng Siu-keung; Art Director: Horace Ma Kwong-wing; Music: Blue Max, Mahmood Rumjahn; Writer: John Chan Kin-chung; Producers: Chua Lam, Lawrence Cheng Tan-shui; Action Directors: Tony Leung Siu-leung, Dion Lam Dik-on; Director: Gordon Chan Kar-seung. Cast: Lawrence Cheng Tan-shui (Ma Ju-lung), Rosamund Kwan Chi-lam (Julia), Waise Lee Chi-hung (Shih Ching), Tony Leung Kar-fai (Ma Yu-yu), Damian Lau Chung-yan (Teng Kuo-chiao), Nina Li Chi (Tan Lan-ching), Kenneth Tsang Kong (Pao), Yuen King-tan ("Emmanuelle"), Lily Lee Li-li (Shih's Assistant). 1.85:1. VHS: Tai Seng. Import LD: Universe. 94 minutes.

An exceedingly mild and not especially funny vehicle for comedian Lawrence Cheng, this comedy fails largely because the protagonist is obnoxious—but not in an endearing fashion—so the viewer finds him just as annoying as the characters onscreen do. Inspector Ma Ju-lung is the jinx of the police force and constantly on the verge of losing his job. His old classmate Ma Yu-yu gets him mixed up with corrupt developer Teng, who seeks to block the construction of a road through his properties. Yu-yu passes the bumbling cop off as his superior, so Teng decides to deal with Ju-lung instead, instructing his men to bump off Yu-yu. Another old schoolmate, Julia (Yu-yu's partner in the scam), teams up with Ju-lung in the hopes of sharing in his bribe money. Meanwhile, Lan-ching, Ma's jealous cousin/fiancée from the Mainland, sees him with this beautiful woman and naturally suspects him of cheating. Sync sound recording is a plus, but this has no energy and is sorely lacking in comic invention.

493. The Inspector Wears Skirts

(1988; Golden Harvest/Golden Way Films/Paragon Films) ★: 6/10. *Ba wong fa* (Cantonese), *Ba wang hua* (Mandarin): "Beautiful Bullies." Cinematographers: Andrew Lau Wai-keung, Jimmy Au Kam-hung; Art Director: Andy Lee Yiu-kwong; Music: New Note Music Production; Writer: Cheng Kam-fu; Producer: Jackie Chan; Action Direction: Jackie Chan Stuntmen Association; Director: Wellson Chin Sing-wai. Cast: Sibelle Hu Hui-chung (Madam Hu), Kara Hui Ying-hung (May), Ann Bridgewater (Karen), Sandra Ng Kwan-yu (Amy), Ellen Chan Ar-lun (Jean), Regina Kent (Ailene), Stanley Fung Shui-fan (Chien), Billy Lau Nam-kwong (Bespectacled Tiger Squad Member), Cynthia Rothrock (Madam Lo), Alex To Tak-wai (Wen), Jeff Falcon (Robber), Shing Fui-on (Robber), Michael Chow Man-kin (Peter), Bill Tung Biu (Commissioner Tung), Ricky Hui Koon-ying (Cook), Ken Lo Wai-kwong (Tiger Squad Member), Feng Sing (Tiger Squad Member), Dennis Chan Kwok-san (Club Manager). Dolby Digital (DVD only). 1.85:1. VHS: Tai Seng (No Subtitles). Import LD: Star Entertainment (No Subtitles). Import VCD: Mega Star. Import DVD: Universe. 95 minutes. Also known as **Top Squad** (Dubbed version).

The first and best entry in Golden Harvest's answer to the American **Police Academy** series, this lowbrow but likeable action comedy (also apparently inspired by the success of Sammo Hung's *ng fuk sing* series) concerns an attempt by the HK police to establish an all-female commando unit. Prospective candidates are sent to a training camp under the command of the humorless Madam Hu and Madam Lo. While being put through their paces on the various obstacle courses, the girls are romanced by their male counterparts from the neighboring Tiger Squad (aka SDU) camp. Naturally, the two squads are eventually paired up to stand guard at a fashion show where expensive jewellery is on display. When a group of robbers crash the festivities, the female commandos get the chance to show what they are made of.

The comedy is sophomoric but the various bouts of hand-to-hand combat are terrific, and there is also a wild, impromptu roller derby-style battle at a roller rink. In addition to having several members of Jackie Chan's stunt team in supporting roles, the film also showcases just about every single one of Golden Harvest's contract players of the period. A smash hit that played for over three months in HK theaters, this spawned three inferior sequels.

494. The Inspector Wears Skirts II

(1989; Golden Harvest/Golden Way Films/Paragon Films) ★: 4/10. *San yung fei foo ba wong fa* (Cantonese), *Shen yong fei hu ba wang hua* (Mandarin): "Mythical Courageous Elite Beautiful Bullies." Cinematographer: Cheung Yiu-cho; Art Director: Oliver Wong Yui-man; Music: Noel Quinlan; Writers: Abe Kwong Man-wai, Lee Man-choi; Producer: Jackie Chan; Action Direction: Jackie Chan Stunt Team; Director: Wellson Chin Sing-wai. Cast: Sibelle Hu Hui-chung, Sandra Ng Kwan-yu, Kara Hui Ying-hung, May Lo Mei-mei, Angile Leung Wan-yui, Joanna Chan Pui-san, Amy Yip Chi-mei, Regina Kent, Bill Tung Biu, Stanley Fung Shui-fan, Billy Lau Nam-kwong, Melvin Wong Kam-sun, Jeff Falcon, Ken Lo Wai-kwong, Feng Sing, Ricky Hui Koon-ying. 1.85:1. VHS: Tai Seng (No Subtitles). Import LD: Star Entertainment (No Subtitles). 96 minutes.

Difficult to locate in subtitled form, this action comedy is still pretty easy to follow without English translation. This time out, the female commandos receive some new members (including Angile Leung, Amy Yip, and May Lo), which results in a major rivalry brewing. Amid much in-fighting and low practical jokes, there are the usual training exercises, indignities inflicted upon hapless Sandra Ng and Billy Lau, and leering, juvenile sex gags. Conflict finally arises in the form of some terrorists who take Melvin Wong's commander hostage.

Unfortunately, the action sequences here are much shorter than those in the previous film and are not as well staged, leaving the comedy as the main component. For most viewers, that will not be enough. Ricky Hui reprises his cameo as the squad cook from the original.

The Inspector Wears Skirts III *see* **Raid on Royal Casino Marine**

495. The Inspector Wears Skirts IV

(1992; Golden Harvest/Paragon Films) ★: 4/10. *Ba wong fa: chung chut gong woo* (Cantonese), *Ba wang hua: chong chu jiang hu* (Mandarin): "Return of the Beautiful Bullies." Cinematographer: Cheung Yiu-cho; Art Director: Ring Law Chi-keung; Music: Lui Pui-yin; Writers: Lau Jun-wai, Abe Kwong Man-wai; Action Director: Tsui Chung-san; Producer-Director: Wellson Chin Sing-wai. Cast: Cynthia Yang Li-ching (Madam Yang), Moon Lee Choi-fung (Madam Lee), Sandra Ng Kwan-yu (Amy), Kara Hui Ying-hung (May), Billy Lau Nam-kwong (Lou Nan-pin), Sheila Chan Sak-lan (Lou), Woo Fung (Hu), Paul Fonoroff (The Commander), Peter Chan Lung (Fat Thug), Yip Wing-cho (The Commissioner), James Tien Chun (Big Brother). 1.85:1. VHS: Tai Seng (No Subtitles). Import LD: Star Entertainment (No Subtitles). Import VCD: Mega Star. 93 minutes.

The final entry to date in Golden Harvest's female-kung fu-**Police Academy** series chugs along with the usual mix of sophomoric humor and reasonably good action scenes. After a particularly gruelling mission, the regular members of The Female Commando Unit are either mental or physical wrecks recovering in asylums, convents, or seclusion. Commanding officer Madam Lee is a blithering coward who is constantly at odds with her superior, the by-the-book Madam Yang, who boasts an arsenal of high-tech devices (including boots that allow her to fly). The negligible plot has the squad taking on a gang of killers who like to make their victims swallow miniature time bombs—when they aren't just shooting them.

Much of the humor is pretty embarrassing, but there are two enjoyable jabs at the original **Police Story** which parody the bus chase and the shopping mall finale. Also present is the usual barrage of scatological gags which will horrify unprepared *gweilo* viewers (imagine a row of very young school kids dropping their pants and defecating on a sidewalk). Cynthia Yang is relegated to the role of straight woman but she acquits herself well—as a contrast to Sandra Ng and (especially) Sheila Chan's mugging. Fans of Moon Lee can relish her comedic talents but will be disappointed by the fact that her character can't fight and is just there to get bashed around. Former Shaw Brothers star Kara Hui easily steals the show as the brilliant, talented, and thoroughly crazy May. Her sanity hearing, presided over by a group of equally loony doctors, is the comedic high point here.

Instructors of Death *see* **The Martial Club**

496. The Intellectual Trio

(1985; Always Good Film Co.) ★: 5/10. *Lung fung ji doh sing* (Cantonese), *Long feng zhi duo xing* (Mandarin): "Dragon, Phoenix, Wiseguy." Cinematographers: Paul Chan Chung-chau, Chan Kwok-keung; Art Director: Dominique Lo Kar-yiu; Music: Not Original; Writers: Wong Kar-wai, Barry Wong Ping-yiu; Producer: Frankie Chan Fan-kei; Director: Guy Lai Ying-chau. Cast: Leslie Cheung Kwok-wing (Chan), Billy Lau Nam-kwong (Simon Tang), Joyce Ngai Suk-kwan (Pretty Eyes), Sandy Lam Yik-lin (Slant Eyes), Charlie Cho Cha-lei (Smarty), Stanley Fung Shui-fan (Chan's Superior). 1.85:1. VHS: Tai Seng (Poor Subtitles). Import LD: Golden Cinema City. Import VCD: Mega Star. 89 minutes.

Sibling pickpockets Pretty Eyes and Slant Eyes (that's the name given in the subtitles) get themselves in deep trouble when they target a professional killer who has just completed a hit. Pretty manages to elude him by letting herself get arrested. Upon release, she accepts a ride from bumbling but persistent Taiwanese Interpol agent Simon Tang. After Pretty gives him the slip, the assassin breaks into Tang's apartment and tries to kill him. Tang and HK cop Chan become friends with the sisters, but the killer appears again, with tragic results.

The story takes a couple of unexpected turns (though it is not at all like the sort of fare co-writer Wong Kar-wai would later become famous for), but the climax will not surprise anyone who has seen the Hollywood production **Nighthawks**. The film is mainly of interest for the chance to see pop superstar Sandy Lam in one of her few film roles. The soundtrack includes music lifted from **Escape from New York**.

497. Intimates

(1997; Golden Harvest/United Filmmakers Organization/Golden Movies International) ★: 6/10. *Ji soh* (Cantonese), *Zi shu* (Mandarin): "Self Combed." Cinematographers: Yang Lun, Ardy Lam Kwok-wah; Art Director: Fok Tat-wah; Music: He Chongzhi; Writer: Siu Tong; Producer-Director: Jacob Cheung Chi-leung. Cast: Carina Lau Kar-ling (Wan), Charlie Yeung Choi-nei (Foon), Theresa Lee Yee-hung (Wai), Gui Yalei (Wan as an Old Woman), Stephen Tung Wai (Chan Yiu-chung), Winston Chao Wen-hsuan (Wai's Boyfriend), Chin Kar-lok (Shing), Cher Yeung Suet-yee (*Ji Soh* Woman). 1.85:1. VHS: Mecapro. Import LD/VCD/DVD: Mei Ah. 112 minutes.

The *ji soh* (or "self-combed") of the Chinese title were a group of women who swore to lead a life of strict celibacy and faced a punishment of death if they broke their vow. In the 1930s young Foon decides to escape an arranged marriage by joining these women. When the groom's relatives try to take her away, she is saved by the affluent Wan, who pays them off. Foon (who works at a factory run by Wan's husband, which employs a number of *ji soh* women) becomes friends with her benefactor and is taken along by Wan as a companion on trips. However, when Wan's husband uses her as a bargaining chip for a business deal, she leaves him (and his seven other wives), joining Foon and the other women. Wan begins to show romantic feelings for Foon, but the latter is disturbed by her advances and has actually already had sex with Shing, a childhood friend. Unfortunately, this dalliance has left Foon pregnant and, in a desperate act, she aborts the baby herself. Wan spends the rest of her money saving Foon's life, and that act of generosity makes the two inseparable.

Intimates was cut by Golden Harvest to the tune of about 50 minutes, and the deletions cause scenes to end too early; just as the mood and effect of a moment begin to take hold, we are off somewhere else, usually with a different group of characters. Carina Lau and Charlie Yeung are both very good, but their relationship is not explored in enough detail here and the male characters are all one-dimensional stereotypes. The film is further burdened by having its 1930s sequences presented as flashbacks in service of a framing story (featuring Gui Yalei, Theresa Lee, and Winston Chao) that adds nothing worthwhile. Consequently, in spite of some fine qualities (which also include beautiful cinematography and art direction), the film ends up seeming rather empty and cursory. Director Jacob Cheung's original version has received some limited exposure and is reportedly more satisfying; those interested might be better off waiting for an opportunity to see that edition, though additional footage will only partially remedy some of the movie's faults.

498. Into the Fire

(1989; Bojon Films Company) ★: 4/10. *Lit foh gaai tau* (Cantonese), *Lie huo jie tou* (Mandarin): "Raging Fire Street Corner." Cinematographer: Raymond Lam Fai-tai; Art Director: Kong Hoi-ming; Music: Lowell Lo Kwun-ting; Producer: Sammo Hung Kam-po; Action Directors: Lau Chau-sang, Hau Chi-chung, Sammo Hung Stunt Team; Writer-Director: Lo Kin. Cast: Ngai Sing (Chou Hsiao-lung), Chin Siu-ho (Lu Chia-le, aka Spitfire), Chan Wing-chi (Anna), Yip Wing-cho (Superintendent Yeh), Woo Fung (Hsiao-lung's Father), Tai Po (Fattie Ming), Frankie Chin Chi-leung (Musclebound Triad), Billy Chow Bei-lee (Triad), Wong Yat-fei (Spitfire's Father). 1.85:1. VHS: Tai Seng. Import LD: Mei Ah. Import VCD: Cameron Entertainment. 92 minutes.

Ngai Sing and Chin Siu-ho are cast against type in this violent Category III thriller which proceeds along conventional lines. Clean cut Chou Hsiao-lung and hateful triad Spitfire are both arrested on the same evening for misdemeanors. The next morning, while leaving the police station, the two get into a fight and are handcuffed together. At that moment, an assassin bursts into the station and executes a number of officers. In the confusion, the authorities deem Chou and Spitfire to be accessories and give chase. With Spitfire's prostitute girlfriend Anna in tow, the fugitives try to flee Hong Kong, only to be betrayed by their "friends" at every turn. To make matters worse, the officer heading up the case, Superintendent Yeh (who wears an outrageous yellow suit, like the corrupt cop in **Blue Velvet**), is out to get Chou for seducing his daughter. The Internal Affairs division launches an investigation of Yeh's illegal activities, and it becomes a question of whether he will be able to catch and kill Chou and Spitfire before the government gathers enough evidence to remove him from his post. There is some decent action along the way, but Chin's relentlessly over-the-top performance is tiresome, and the ending is absurd.

499. Intruder

(1997; China Star Entertainment Group/Win's Entertainment/Milkyway Image) ★: 7/10. *Hung bo gai* (Cantonese), *Kong bu ji* (Mandarin): "Horrifying Chicken." Cinematographer: Cheng Siu-keung; Art Director: Silver Cheung Sai-wang; Music: Cacine Wong Kar-sin; Producers: Johnny To Kei-fung, Wai Kar-fai; Action Director: Yuen Bun; Writer-Director: Sammy Tsang Kan-cheung. Cast: Jacqueline Wu Chien-lien (Yieh Siu-yan), Lai Yiu-cheung (Chen Chi-min), Moses Chan Ho (Kwan Fai), Bonnie Wong Man-wai, Yuen Bun. 1.85:1. VHS: Tai Seng. Import LD/VCD: China Star. 86 minutes.

This dark and humorless Category III thriller opens with psychotic fugitive Yieh Siu-yan strangling a Shenzhen prostitute and assuming her identity. She then successfully crosses over the border into HK and picks up taxi driver Chen Chi-min, who is out cruising for hookers. After the pair spend the night together, Siu-yan follows Chen the next evening and runs him over with a car. She then takes the crippled man prisoner in his own home, with the intention of having her Mainland boyfriend Fai assume their captive's identity. The plan takes an unexpected turn when Fai's arrival is delayed by a typhoon, meaning that Chen's mother and young daughter must also be taken care of.

The directorial debut of veteran screenwriter Sammy Tsang (**Royal Warriors**, **Magnificent Warriors**), **Intruder** fashions elements of the Stephen King yarn **Misery** into a suspenseful thriller that is blessed with some fiendishly macabre twists. While there is some intense violence and gore, such sequences are not as prolonged or unrelenting as that found in films like **The Untold Story**. However, **Intruder** is just as disturbing in its own way, particularly during the scenes shared by Jacqueline Wu (who is quite effective in a role that most HK actresses would avoid like the plague) and the little girl. In an American movie there would be very little doubt over whether she would kill the child, as it is practically a taboo and almost certainly guarantees problems with the ratings board; in HK the killing of children onscreen happens with far greater frequency, so the suspense here borders on agonizing. One can read into the scenario an underlying theme of HK citizens losing their identities in the face of the colony's reunification with China, but the film is equally effective if simply taken at face value. It is definitely not for the squeamish, however. In regards to the rather odd Chinese title, *kai* (or "hen/chicken") is Cantonese slang for hooker. Hence, another translation for the title could be "Horrifying Hooker."

500. Invincible

(1992; Win's Movie Production/Samico Films Production Co.) ★: 4/10. *Chin lung joi yau* (Cantonese), *Zhan long zai ye* (Mandarin): "War Dragons in the Wild." Cinematographers: Joe Chan Kong-hung, Wong Po-man, Lee Tak-wai; Art Director: Jason Mok Siu-kei; Music: Richard Lo Sai-kit; Writers: Nam Yin, Chan Man-keung; Producer: Stephen Siu Yeuk-yuen; Action Directors: Blackie Ko Shou-liang, Wong Kwan; Director: Blackie Ko Shou-liang. Cast: Wong Kit (Wong Yan-kit), Sharla Cheung Man (Mandy Wong), Blackie Ko Shou-liang (Cheung Hark), Leung Kar-yan (Long), Billy Blanks (Billy), Stefanos Miltsakakis (The Commander), Lung Fong (Kwong), Danny Lee Sau-yin (Brother Fire). 1.85:1. VHS: Tai Seng. Import LD: Star Entertainment. 94 minutes.

Stuntman extraordinaire Blackie Ko directed and co-stars in this violent action thriller set during The Gulf War. After murdering a triad who was molesting his friend Mandy, Yan-kit flees with the woman to France. They find life extremely difficult, prompting Yan-kit to enlist in the Foreign Legion, despite the fact that he is hardly cut out for it. Somehow managing to survive the torturous training regimen (thanks, in no small part, to his friendship with seasoned tough guy Cheung Hark), Yan-kit joins his squad on a mission to rescue the royal family in Kuwait. Surviving the incursion into enemy territory, he returns to HK to take revenge on the gangsters who have made his life hell. In response, the triads hire some ex-Legionnaires to level the playing field.

A near-complete collection of genre cliches, **Invincible** is further crippled by an inadequate lead performance. Wong Kit's spineless character is an unappealing protagonist, and his inevitable transformation from coward to hero (this is one of those movies where one reaches "manhood" by cutting off a snake's head and drinking its blood) is not the least bit believable. Some good action setpieces and an exciting climax help to keep the film watchable, but they are not impressive enough to overcome the conceptual weaknesses. American martial artist Billy Blanks has been in a lot of bad movies, but his role here as a gay rapist (presumably the reason that this received a Category III rating) is definitely something he should leave off of his resume.

The Invincible Pole Fighters *see* **The Eight Diagram Pole Fighter**
Iron Angels *see* **Angel**
Iron Angels II *see* **Angel II**
Iron Angels III *see* **Angel III**

501. The Iron Monkey

(1977; Ching Hua) ★: 6/10. *Tit ma lau* (Cantonese), *Tie ma liu* (Mandarin):

"Iron Monkey." Cinematographer: Chan Ching-kui; Music: Not Original; Writer: Ngai Hong; Producer: Lam Wing-fong; Action Directors: Chan Sau-chung, Chan Muk-chuen; Director: Chen Kuan-tai. Cast: Chen Kuan-tai (Iron Monkey), Chi Kuan-chun (Fung Kong), Leung Kar-yan (Captain Ti), Wilson Tong Wai-shing (Ho Yin). 2.35:1. VHS: Tai Seng (Poor Subtitles), Arena/Xenon (Dubbed). DVD: Arena/Xenon (Dubbed). 95 minutes.

After his family is massacred by Manchurian troops, layabout gambler "Iron" seeks to reform himself by receiving martial arts instruction at Shaolin Temple. The Abbott grants his request and he is admitted, despite the fact that he will not divulge his identity. Iron proves to be an extremely adept pupil and is given the name "Iron Monkey." Deemed ready to learn the powerful "Shaolin Monkey Fist" style, he undergoes several years of training to master the skill. He then leaves the temple and joins the Manchurian troops, where his superb fighting skills cause him to quickly advance through the ranks. Iron Monkey's plan is to get close enough to the Manchu commander to kill him, but when the Manchurians declare war on the Shaolin students, Iron must act sooner than he expected.

A very handsome independent production, **The Iron Monkey** is routinely plotted, and the training sequences are disappointingly short and staged without much flair. The kung fu is good, though, and Chen's direction is confident, so fans of old school martial arts films will find this more than satisfactory. Chen broke his contract with Shaw Brothers to make this film but was forced to return to the studio when he lost a subsequent lawsuit. Wu Ma has a cameo as the man who dresses Chen down in the gambling den sequence. The character names listed above are from the dubbed version.

502. Iron Monkey

(1993; Golden Harvest/Long Shong Pictures/Film Workshop/Paragon Films) ★: 8/10. *Siu nin Wong Fei-hung ji tit ma lau* (Cantonese), *Shao nian Huang Feihong zhi tie ma liu* (Mandarin): "The Young Wong Fei-hung: Iron Monkey" or "The Young Huang Feihong: Iron Monkey." Cinematographers: Arthur Wong Ngok-tai, Tam Chi-wai; Art Director: Ringo Cheung Sek-wah; Music: William Woo Wai-lap, Johnny Yeung Kei-cheung; Writers: Tsui Hark, Elsa Tang Pik-yin, Lau Tai-muk; Producer: Tsui Hark; Action Directors: Yuen Cheung-yan, Yuen Shun-yee, Kuk Hin-chu; Director: Yuen Woo-ping. Cast: Yu Rongguang (Dr. Yang/Iron Monkey), Donnie Yen Chi-tan (Wong Kei-ying), Jean Wang Ching-ying (Orchid Ho), Tsang Sze-man (Wong Fei-hung), Yam Sai-kwoon (Hin Hung), James Wong Jim (Governor Cheng), Yuen Shun-yee (Master Fox), Li Fai (The Witch), Hsiao Hou (Disfigured Swordsman). Dolby Digital (DVD only). 1.85:1. VHS: Tai Seng (Remastered for the English market; subtitled or dubbed). Import LD/VCD: Mei Ah. Import DVD: Mega Star. 89 minutes.

Arguably the most entertaining picture in the early '90s crop of period kung fu adventures, **Iron Monkey** is a charming, super-kinetic pleasure. The title character is a masked Ching Dynasty Robin Hood, robbing from corrupt officials and giving to the commoners, who are suffering the aftereffects of a devastating flood. In reality, the gentleman bandit is kindly Dr. Yang, who gives free medical treatment to those who cannot afford it. When he learns that the Legate Officer is due to arrive soon, the unscrupulous Governor Cheng has his men arrest many innocent people in order to lure the Monkey out into the open. The plan works but the target manages to escape after a protracted battle with venerated kung fu master Wong Kei-ying. Recognizing that this man represents his best chance to get the Monkey, Cheng blackmails Kei-ying by imprisoning his young son Fei-hung. He gives Kei-ying one week to apprehend the fugitive or the boy will face the consequences. The Monkey impersonates the Legate Officer and fleeces Cheng once again, but the genuine article soon arrives in the form of Hin Hung, a powerful but treacherous monk who was responsible for the burning of Shaolin Temple. While Cheng is nothing but a sadistic fool, it will take the kung fu mastery of both the Monkey and Kei-ying to vanquish this new foe.

Purists will be put off by the amount of wirework and other behind-the-scenes manipulation on display here, but the martial arts remain tremendously enjoyable. The climactic battle, which takes place on burning Shaolin poles, is a wonder of choreography, it remains fantastic no matter how many times one views it (it would later be copied closely in the American made-for-video feature **Young Hercules**). In contrast to producer Tsui Hark's **Once Upon a Time in China** series, Wong Fei-hung (played by Tsang Sze-man, a young *girl!*) is just a child here but is already a tremendous fighter. It is a shame that the film did weak business (Golden Harvest waited so long to release it, bootlegs of the Taiwanese video were already widely circulating in HK), as it would have almost certainly led to more lead roles for Yu Rongguang, who makes for a very personable hero. Beware of the abominable **Iron Monkey 2**, which has no connection to this film.

503. Iron Monkey 2

(1996; Jin Teng Film Co.) ★: 1/10. *Gaai tau saat sau* (Cantonese), *Jie tou sha shou* (Mandarin): "Street Assassin." Cinematographer: Tong Yu-tai; Music: Not Original; Writer: Lee Man-choi; Producers: Woo Fuk-wan, Lo Hoi-chung; Action Director: Yuen Woo-ping; Director: Cho Lo-kong. Cast: Donnie Yen Chi-tan (Iron Monkey), Wu Ma (Jin Dah-fon), Billy Chow Bei-lei (Shang-xiong). 1.85:1. VHS/LD: World Video. 92 minutes.

Bearing absolutely no connection to either the 1977 or the 1993 films, this astoundingly inept enterprise will tax the patience of even the most devoted martial arts fan. Set during World War II, the film casts Donnie Yen as the Iron Monkey, though his disguise has much more in common with "The Monkey King" than his cinematic predecessors. His target is "The Jade-Faced Tiger" (mistranslated in the especially idiotic subtitles as "Yu-Face Tiger"), a vicious smuggler in league with the Japanese and two equally nasty Westerners. The remainder of the running time is given over to a pair of young scam artists who cheat a martial artist looking to find his father. The man in question is an old friend of the Iron Monkey, and he joins up with the mysterious vigilante to put an end to The Tiger and his minions.

The direction, editing, production design, and stock music are the absolute pits and even Yuen Woo-ping's choreography is not up to snuff, though Donnie Yen somehow manages to escape with his dignity intact. Unwatchable.

504. The Iron-Fisted Monk

(1977; Golden Harvest) ★: 6/10. *Saam Dak woh seung yue Chung Mai-luk* (Cantonese), *San De huo shang yu Chong Miliu* (Mandarin): "Monk Sam Tak and Chung Mai-luk" or "Monk San De and Chong Miliu." Cinematographer: Lee Yao-tong; Music: Chen Shen-chi; Writers: Huang Feng, Sammo Hung Kam-po; Producer: Raymond Chow Man-wai; Action Director-Director: Sammo Hung Kam-po. Cast: Sammo Hung Kam-po (Husker), Chen Sing (Tak), James Tien Chun (Husker's Master), Fung Hark-on (The Official), Dean Shek Tien (Goofy Manchu), Wu Ma (Boatman in Brothel), Yam Sai-kwoon (Manchu Thug), Eric Tsang Chi-wai (Shu-liu Worker), Chung Fat (Shu-liu Worker), Feng Sing (Shu-liu Worker), Lam Ching-ying (Shu-liu Worker), Peter Chan Lung (Manchu Thug). 2.35:1. VHS: Tai Seng (Poor Subtitles). Import VCD: Mega Star. 93 minutes.

Sammo Hung made his directorial bow with this period kung fu yarn that, while not on the level of his later Golden

Harvest efforts, remains above average. When he is humiliated by some Manchu brutes, tubby Husker decides to take the advice of monk Tak (who came to his rescue) and join Shaolin Temple. After spending several years perfecting his martial skills, Husker escapes from the Temple with the intention of seeking revenge. A group of Manchus, led by a particularly sadistic official who likes to sexually assault young maidens, are terrorizing the village and earn the ire of dye worker Liang, who also seeks vengeance. Liang's impulsive murder of one scoundrel has the unintentional effect of making Husker appear to be guilty of the crime. When the official's men are made fools of by Husker, they choose a new approach that will bankrupt Liang's boss, thus eliminating one of their key enemies. When that fails also, the Manchus then adopt a more direct and violent method, prompting Husker and Tak to intercede on behalf of their friends.

The Iron-Fisted Monk differs from Hung's subsequent works by including two rape scenes (the first rather prolonged and fairly explicit) and further gratuitous nudity at a brothel. There is also a bit less in the way of martial arts here, and the choreography (supervised by Hung, under the name "Chu Yuan-lung") is not quite as impressive (undercranking is plainly evident at times). The storyline is a traditional Han vs. Manchu revenge tale, but the star is able to keep one entertained on the strength of his personality, and Chen Sing's monk is an interesting variation on the norm for this sort of character (he will eat the occasional helping of dog meat and enter a brothel in disguise but remains essentially true to Buddha's teachings).

505. The Island

(1985; D & B Films Co.) ★: 6/10. *Saang sei sin* (Cantonese), *Sheng si xian* (Mandarin): "The Line Between Life and Death." Cinematographer: Poon Hang-sang; Art Director: Hai Chung-man; Music: Law Dik; Producer: Sammo Hung Kam-po; Action Directors: Yuen Wah, Ng Min-kan; Director: Leung Po-chi. Cast: John Sham Kin-fun (Mr. Cheung), Peter Chan Lung (Tai-fat), Chen Jing (Yee-fat), Ronald Wong Pan (Ronald), Tse Ching-yuen. 1.85:1. VHS: Tai Seng. Import VCD: Mega Star. 92 minutes.

Reminiscent of Dennis Yu Wan-kong's **The Beasts** and American films like **The Hills Have Eyes**, this grim thriller stars John Sham as a teacher who takes six of his teenage students to remote Tung Ping Chau island for a two day outing. Unbeknownst to everyone, the place is inhabited by three homicidal lunatic brothers, and it doesn't take long before the group encounters them. For a while, the two parties have a friendly, if uneasy relationship, but things quickly turn ugly when the men decide to take one of the girls for breeding purposes. With no way to escape and their boat not due for another day, the outsiders barricade themselves inside a dilapidated house and suffer through a night-long siege.

The Island is quite effective in spots, thanks to Poon Hang-sang's atmospheric camerawork (which won the Best Cinematography prize at the HK Film Awards), an effectively malevolent performance by kung fu veteran Peter Chan (as the leader of the psychos), and the beautiful yet foreboding island locales. Unfortunately, this is yet another one of those horror films where the characters behave stupidly throughout, lessening the overall impact.

506. Island of Fire

(1990; Golden Harvest/Blaine & Blake) ★: 5/10. *Foh siu do* (Cantonese), *Huo shao dao* (Mandarin): "Burning Fire Island." Cinematographer: Chen Rong-shu; Art Director: Chang Chi-ping; Music: Not Original; Writers: Fu Li, Yeh Yun-chiao; Producer: Ko Chuen-hsiang; Action Director: Lin Wan-chang; Director: Chu Yen-ping. Cast: Tony Leung Kar fai (Huang Wei), Sammo Hung Kam-po (Liu Hsi-chia), Jackie Chan (Lung), Jimmy Wang Yu (Kui), Andy Lau Tak-wah (Triad), Ko Chuen-hsiang (Warden), Yeh Chuan-chen (Fong). 1.85:1. VHS: Tai Seng. Import LD/VCD: Universe. 92 minutes.

As a favor to martial arts legend Jimmy Wang Yu, Jackie Chan took a supporting role in this gritty Taiwanese actioner set in an almost comically corrupt prison. Unfortunately, Chan's presence in the cast led to the belief that he is the star of the film, which is certainly not the case. Tony Leung Kar-fai plays a police officer who goes undercover in the pen, hoping to determine how the fingerprints of a recently killed felon could belong to a con who had been executed two years before. While inside, he goes through the tortures of hell after getting involved in matters that were better left alone (much like the character he played three years earlier in Ringo Lam's **Prison on Fire**). His fellow prisoners include Chan (in for accidentally killing a card player while trying to raise money to pay for an operation to save his girlfriend's life), Andy Lau (as the brother of the dead man who has himself thrown in jail to exact revenge), Wang (as one of the leaders of the prisoners), and Sammo Hung (as a compassionate but pathetic inmate who frequently escapes to visit his young son). When Leung kills a guard and is sentenced to a firing squad, the film goes off in a whole new direction, revealing that "deceased" cons are actually being used by the evil warden (Ko Chuen-hsiang) as hitmen to assassinate untouchable criminals!

Brute Force this ain't, but the off-kilter plotting (a Chu Yen-ping trademark) certainly provides a respite from all the prison movie cliches in the first two-thirds, and there is some well-staged action, so undiscriminating viewers should find this entertaining enough. Like most of Chan's films, outtakes run under the end credits, a rather off-putting conclusion to such an unrelentingly grim enterprise. The composite musical track includes cues lifted from the American films **Wavelength** (1983) and **Body Double** (1984), as well as library music heard in dozens of low budget Taiwanese and HK films. The Taiwanese tape version (from Long Shong Video) serves up a considerably different film than the HK cut. It runs about 35 minutes longer and features much more in the way of character development, with the Taiwanese actors like Wang and minor players like Yip Wing-cho given considerably more screen time.

507. Island of Greed

(1997; China Star Entertainment Group/Win's Entertainment/Johnny Mak Production) ★: 6/10. *Hak gam* (Cantonese), *Hei jin* (Mandarin): "Black Gold." Cinematographers: Jingle Ma Cho-shing, Cheung Tung-leung; Art Director: Raymond Lee King-man; Music: Landy Wei Lan-dak; Writer-Producer: Johnny Mak Dong-hung; Action Director: Yuen Bun; Director: Michael Mak Dong-kit. Cast: Andy Lau Tak-wah (Fong Kuo-fai), Tony Leung Kar-fai (Chao Chiu-sen), Paulyn Suen Kai-kwun (Miu-heung), Annie Wu Chen-chun (Ling Fai), Winston Chao Wen-hsuan (The Commissioner). Dolby Digital. 2.35:1. VHS: Tai Seng. Import LD/VCD/DVD: Mei Ah. 124 minutes.

Another bloated but impressively staged gangster epic from Johnny and Michael Mak, **Island of Greed** often overwhelms the viewer through sheer bravado but lacks the kind of cogent screenplay that imparts a sense of order and exigency to all of its pageantry. Powerful Taiwanese triad Chao Chiu-sen seeks to protect himself from prosecution by running for The Nationalist Party and winning a seat on The Legislative Council. Opposing him is investigator Fong Kuo-fei, the righteous head of a high tech task force that seeks to discredit or bring down Chao before the election takes place. Fong is able to get one of Chao's cronies to secretly tape a meeting detailing the gangster's plan to rig government building contracts, prompting the latter's boss to put an end to his election campaign. However, the scope of his opposition's power becomes clear to Fong when his tape is suppressed and he is suspended. Working independent of the department, Fong is able to collect enough videotaped evidence of Chao's activities to convince the top man in the department to let him proceed with further surveillance. Meanwhile, Chao defies his bosses by running in the election as an independent candidate, and through various publicity-generating tactics and the murder of his closest rival, he emerges victorious.

Started by Clarence Fok but finished by Michael Mak (with only the latter receiving credit), the film's strength is its sense of spectacle, a Mak Brothers trademark. Highlights include Fong and his team racing through a field on motorcycles, desperately trying to save one of Chao's victims, who is being dragged behind a jeep pursued by an army of German Shepherds out to tear him limb from limb; hundreds of taxi drivers bringing Taipei to a standstill via a bloody riot in the streets; a squad of killers trying to liquidate Fong and his partners in a crowded outdoor market; and the finale which features Fong and his men trying to escape from Taipei while being targeted by missile-laden helicopters. The production values are among the most spectacular to be seen in a HK production; the affluent world of the triads is presented with seemingly complete verisimilitude. Unfortunately, while the theme is the very real problem of underworld infiltration of Taiwan politics, the narrative is both simplistic and muddled. While one can too easily surmise some aspects of the storyline, it is not always clear just who all of the supporting characters are (seemingly not a fault of the English translation, as some Chinese reviewers also found fault with the film in this regard). By the finale, Fong's team is utilizing peel-off make-up right out of the old **Mission Impossible** TV series, and all credibility is lost. Leung does not project enough menace or charisma to be completely convincing in the sort of role Ray Lui Leung-wai essayed in the Maks' **To Be Number One** and **Lord of East China Sea**, while Andy Lau merely walks through the sort of part he clearly has played on too many occasions. More impressive are Paulyn Suen as Leung's fiercely loyal wife, and Annie Wu as a TV reporter who uses her media influence to help Lau obtain his goal.

508. The Isle of Fantasy

(1985; Cinema City Co.) ★: 3/10. *Hoi sam lok yuen* (Cantonese), *Kai xin le yuan* (Mandarin): "Happy Paradise." Cinematographer: Johnny Koo Kwok-wah; Art Director: Dominique Lo Kar-yiu; Music: Mahmood Rumjahn; Writer: Raymond Wong Pak-ming; Producers: Raymond Wong Pak-ming, Karl Maka, Dean Shek Tien; Director: Michael Mak Dong-kit. Cast: Raymond Wong Pak-ming (Cannon Wong), Fennie Yuen Kit-ying (Fanny), Loletta Lee Lai-chun (Jane), Ann Bridgewater (Ann), May Lo Mei-mei (May), Bonnie Law Ming-chu (Bonnie), Charine Chan Kar-ling (Charine), Teresa Carpio (Guide Leader), Mark Cheng Ho-nam (David). 1.85:1. VHS: Tai Seng. Import LD: Cinema City. 86 minutes.

Strictly for the kiddies, this feeble effort (lensed in Thailand) is yet another would-be comedy featuring middle-aged nerd Raymond Wong getting mixed up with a batch of cute teenage girls (some of whom were also appearing in his **Happy Ghost** series). Door-to-door salesman Cannon Wong and a band of girl guides end up on a deserted tropical island when their plane crashes. The repressed guide leader takes an instant dislike to Cannon, but a couple of the girls help the bumbling misfit keep from freezing and/or starving to death. A big gorilla, a hungry crocodile, and a man-eating plant keep everyone on their toes, and (in a bit you would never see in a Western movie of this type) one of the girls unknowingly uses wild hemp for tea leaves, getting all of the castaways stoned! The ape turns out to be the friendly pet of an old man who has been calling this lonely tropical paradise home for over 40 years. When a gang of pirates/drug smugglers briefly show up on the far side of the island, the girls decide to set a series of traps to foil them the next time they appear.

As with the **Happy Ghost** films, only those interested in seeing where future stars Fennie Yuen, Loletta Lee, May Lo, and Charine Chan got their start need bother watching. Director Michael Mak would later helm **Sex and Zen**!

509. It's a Drink, It's a Bomb!

(1985; D & B Films Co.) ★: 4/10. *Sing daan kei yue git leung yuen* (Cantonese), *Sheng dan qi yu ji liang yuan* (Mandarin): "Christmas Adventure: Connect Fine Destiny." Art Director: James Leung Wah-sang; Music: Lowell Lo Kwun-ting; Writer: Sammy Tsang Kan-cheung; Producer: Sammo Hung Kam-po; Action Director: Blackie Ko Shou-liang; Cinematographer-Director: David Chung Chi-man. Cast: George Lam Chi-cheung (Bobo Lam), John Sham Kin-fun (Stewart Pik, aka Lion Head), Maggie Cheung Man-yuk (Cat), Eddy Ko Hung (Bearded Killer), Elvis Tsui Kam-kong (Big Killer), Lau Kong (B.D.O. Wong), Liu Kai-chi (Ronnie), Paul Chun Pui (Befuddled Cop), Michael Lee Ming-yeung (Cat's Grandfather), Lowell Lo Kwun-ting (Contest Host), Wu Ma (Gas Station Attendant), Dennis Chan Kwok-san (Loony in Police Station). 1.85:1. VHS: Tai Seng. Import LD: Mei Ah. Import VCD: Mega Star. 95 minutes.

It's a bomb, alright, but how often do you get to see a HK Christmas movie, let alone one with sci-fi overtones? A pair of Japanese killers are after a small but powerful explosive device that an unscrupulous scientist has created and stashed inside a can of Sarsae pop (as you might expect, about a million cans of the stuff are prominently placed throughout the movie, and the brand name is mentioned as many times as possible). Cab driver Stewart, cyclist Cat, and scientist Bobo soon find themselves pursued by the assassins, who think that the trio know the whereabouts of the explosive soda can. Numerous chases follow, accompanied by all kinds of frenetic behavior and some decent action, but there are few laughs and far too many time killing exchanges that lead nowhere. John Sham does make for an amusing Santa Claus, though.

510. It's a Wonderful Life

(1994; Mandarin Films) ★: 4/10. *Daai foo ji ga* (Cantonese), *Da fu zhi jia* (Mandarin): "Big Rich Family." Cinematographer: Sander Lee Kar-ko; Art Director: Fong Ying; Music: John Wong Sai-cheung; Writer: Raymond To Kwok-wai; Producer: Raymond Wong Pak-ming; Director: Clifton Ko Chi-sum. Cast: Leslie Cheung Kwok-wing (Roberto), Tony Leung Kar-fai (Yam Kau-kwai), Teresa Mo Shun-kwan (Yam Kau-ann), Lau Ching-wan (Hou Chung), Anita Yuen Wing-yee (Sau-kit), Raymond Wong Pak-ming (Yam Kau-fu), Carol Cheng Yu-ling (Miss Ho, aka "Plain Coffee"), Petrina Fung Bo-bo (Yuet-yung), Kwan Tak-hing (Grandpa), Cho Tat-wah (Foon), James Wong Jim (George). VHS: Tai Seng. Import LD/VCD/DVD: Mei Ah. 94 minutes.

Bearing no connection to the James Stewart classic of the same name, this is another one of those Raymond Wong Lunar New Year comedies which waste the talents of an all-star cast by saddling them with fourth-rate material. Adhering to the **All's Well, Ends Well** formula, it finds the Yam family on the verge of destroying itself: Kau-fu and his wife have split up because of the former's drinking; stuttering comic book artist Kau-kwai is so immersed in his work he never leaves his room; and daughter Kau-ann comes back home from France with hippie Roberto, much to the chagrin of her parents and lovelorn cousin, Chung. Desperate to avoid hurting Chung's feelings by turning down his marriage proposal, Kau-ann looks to Roberto for help, but he just makes things worse by saying that he already has proposed to her. Kau-kwai, meanwhile, has found his Juliet in the form of primary school teacher Sau-kit, but faces a formidable obstacle: the girl's spinsterish sister, "Plain Coffee."

As one has come to expect from these films, comic invention is virtually nonexistent. Even the more imaginative concepts (like a musical parody of period costume films *and* **Jurassic Park**) fall flat, and that goes double for a subplot swiped from **Mrs. Doubtfire** (Kau-fu pretends to be a female maid so that he can spend time with his young daughter). Any film with *this* cast has to have moments of interest, and this one does (particularly the bits showing Cho Tat-wah still playing second fiddle to Kwan Tak-hing, decades after their onscreen partnership in the Wong Fei-hung films)—but not enough to justify a viewing.

511. It's Now or Never

(1992; Wui Fung Film Production) ★: 7/10. *Fei nui jing juen* (Cantonese), *Fei nu zheng zhuan* (Mandarin): "Wild Girl True Story." Cinematographer: Gigo Lee Chi-hang; Art Director: Jon Hau Wing-choi; Music: Danny Chung Teng-yat; Writer: Stephen Siu Yeuk-yuen; Producers: Jimmy Heung Wah-sing, Stephen Siu Yeuk-yuen; Action Directors: Cho Wing, Kong Chuen; Director: Chan Kwok-hei. Cast: Sharla Cheung Man (Ying, aka Crazy Chicken), Alfred Cheung Kin-ting (Shing), Cynthia Yang Li-ching (Moon, aka Little-bun, aka Bitchy-bun), Ng Man-tat (Tat, aka Lady-killer), Rain Lau Yuk-tsui (Tracy Wong), Bowie Lam Bo-yee (Peter), Pauline Chan Po-lin (Chewing-gum), Dennis Chan Kwok-san (Judge Hsu). 1.85:1. Import LD/VCD: Mei Ah. 107 minutes.

An engaging juvenile delinquent drama-triad thriller set in the 1960s, **It's Now or Never** is one of the more offbeat HK films of the '90s and is well worth catching, despite some problems in its final third. Tattooed Teddy Girl Ying and her no-good sister and father practically have their own cell reserved at the local police station. One of the female cops there has a particular grudge against Ying and her gang, resulting in numerous acts of petty revenge by both parties. Rather than end up as a hooker or club girl, Ying plans on snaring some rich dupe and living off him for the rest of her days. Consequently, when nerdy, poverty-stricken cop Shing comes repeatedly calling for her, she nonetoo-subtlely tells him to take a hike. When Shing rescues one of her friends from a brothel and saves her sister from some triads, Ying begins to form a different opinion of him. However, trouble arises in the form of some vicious triads out to kill her father.

As sexy bad girl Ying, Sharla Cheung is ideally cast; the scene in which she seduces the virginal Alfred Cheung is slyly written and splendidly performed by both. Ng Man-tat is also amusingly sleazy as Ying's low-life father, the most unkempt gigolo in HK. The costumes, cinematography, and production design are gorgeous, and action star Cynthia Yang has a great change-of-pace role as a cowardly gang member who brags that she knows kung fu, only to have the stuffing constantly knocked out of her. The only real weakness here is the dark and violent turn the story takes. The change in tone is more gradual than in some HK films but remains rather jarring and self-defeating. The wrap-up is quite satisfying, though the end title cards revealing the fates of the main characters are presented only in Chinese.

512. I've Got You, Babe!

(1994; United Filmmakers Organization) ★: 5/10. *Boh jung ching yan* (Cantonese), *Bo zhong qing ren* (Mandarin): "Sowing Seed Lovers." Cinematographer: Apple Kwan Pak-suen; Art Director: Danny Yuen Ching-yuen; Music: Violet Lam Man-yee; Producers: Jacob Cheung Chi-leung, Claudie Chung Chun; Writer-Director: Cheung Chi-sing. Cast: Anita Yuen Wing-yee (Ron), Lau Ching-wan (Charcoal), Dayo Wong Chi-wah (Richard), Kitty Lai Mei-han (Ada Ho), Annabelle Lau Hiu-tung (Joyce). 1.85:1. VHS: Tai Seng. Import LD/VCD/DVD: Mei Ah. 92 minutes.

A pleasant but stale and formulaic romantic comedy-drama, this UFO production stars everyone's favorite HK movie couple, Anita Yuen and Lau Ching-wan. Ron and Charcoal meet through their friends and begin a courtship that gradually progresses through the usual stages of dating, cohabitation, and, inevitably, marriage. Ron wants to take the next step and have a child, much to Charcoal's chagrin. However, he eventually comes around to her way of thinking, and the two begin the preparations for parenthood. However, Ron has a miscarriage and Charcoal's ex-girlfriend, Joyce, arrives back in HK, apparently wanting to start seeing him again. Ron is able to get pregnant again but both she and Charcoal still have lingering doubts about the future.

Aside from providing one or two perceptive observations about the pressures and responsibilities involved in both a relationship and raising a family, the screenplay is content to fall back on familiar dramatic situations and parallels (the protagonist's lives are contrasted with those of their friends, who split up after the woman became pregnant). Thus, the film relies heavily on the talent and appeal of its stars to entertain. They can only carry the ball so far, however, making this an atypically ordinary effort from the customarily creative UFO team. Yuen's character watches **The Days of Being Dumb** on TV at one point, which just so happens to be the film in which she made her debut.

Jackie Chan Versus Wang Yu *see* **The Killer Meteors**

Jackie Chan's Crime Force *see* **Golden Queens Commando**

Jackie Chan's First Strike *see* **First Strike**

Jackie Chan's Police Force *see* **Police Story**

513. Jail House Eros

(Golden Harvest/Paragon Films; 1990) ★: 6/10. *Gaam yuk bat chit fong* (Cantonese), *Jian yu bu she fang* (Mandarin): "Jail Undefended." Cinematographer: Philip Ma Kam-cheung; Art Director: Ho Kim-seng; Music: The Melody Bank, Alastair Monteith-Hodge; Writers: Cheng Man-wah, Yu Hon-wing, Cheng Yau-hing; Producer: Chow Chan-tung; Action Director: Yuen Bun; Director: Ha Sau-hin. Cast: Loletta Lee Lai-chun (Jane), Joanna Chan Pui-san (Blackie), Amy Yip Chi-mei (Chesty), Stanley Fung Shui-fan (Feng), Maria Cordero (Big Sister), Ha Chi-chun (The Ghost). 1.85:1. VHS: Tai Seng. Import LD/VCD: Mei Ah. 84 minutes.

Irresistible on a trash level, **Jail House Eros** is the incredibly wacky "You Asked for It" merger of the HK ghost movie with that exploitation perennial, the women-in-prison film. Jane is the ghost of a former inmate who perished while trying to escape several years earlier. As she died while still incarcerated, a Taoist traps her soul for fifteen years, forcing Jane to serve out her sentence in death. She cannot reincarnate until after that time has elapsed and a mortal has transported her soul outside of the prison walls. After finally being released from the spell, she befriends a girl named Blackie, who is just as anxious to escape as she was. Jane uses her powers to try and assist the girl, in the hope that Blackie will take her spirit to freedom as well. When the plan is foiled by a jealous inmate, Jane possesses the double-crosser and has her run riot, quickly leading to talk of ghosts. Both the inmates and the staff are understandably upset at the prospect of a haunted prison, so three Taoist "priests" are enlisted to dispel the spirits. Trouble is, they are just a trio of hired workmen who see this as a chance to score with their favorite inmates. Their mock ceremony accidentally releases the spirit of the sadistic captain of the guards, which puts everyone's lives in danger.

The film concludes with a wild supernatural battle in the best knockabout HK tradition. In addition to all of this, **Jail House Eros** also serves up the requisite showers, hosedowns, food fights, and frock tearing one expects from the genre. What more could you ask for from a junk movie? The subtitles are pretty entertaining, too ("Who's that in outlandish clothes?").

514. The Jail of No Return

(1994; Wah Sze Film Production) ★: 1/10. *Sei mong gaam yuk* (Cantonese), *Si wang jian yu* (Mandarin): "Death Jail." Cinematographer: Ko Chi-ho; Art Director: Mok Siu-chung; Music: Sam Leung Yiu-san, Onam Mui Siu-kei; Writer: Jimmy Leung Chi-ming; Producers: Tam Wah-hung, Chu Yin-tung; Director: Hugo Ng Toi-yung. Cast: Wong Chi-yeung (Dumb Dog), Ku Feng (Wrinkly Dog), Richard Grosse (The Warden), Bobby Yip King-sang (Square Dog). 1.85:1. VHS: Tai Seng. 96 minutes.

Actor Hugo Ng (**Daughter of Darkness**) directed this predictably nasty and numbingly insipid thriller set on a remote island that serves as the titular institution. The prisoners (who have all been named after dogs by the psychotic Caucasian warden) may only be released when (or, more likely, if) they reach the age of 60. There is no plot to speak of, just the prisoners violating various rules and being tortured in the manner usually seen in these films. Prisoner Dog Shit collaborates with the warden and is not only released but is even given a job as a guard. The final third deals with the horribly abused inmates' attempts to exact revenge.

Sync sound recording gives this a slight push towards realism, but it still consists of the usual tired cliches and is not the least bit interesting or entertaining. As the stereotypical *gweilo* villain, Grosse's performance can be charitably described as wretched, but, thankfully, veteran character actor Ku Feng lends some desperately needed class as the island's oldest inmate (who is ten days away from being released, so you know what that means). If there was ever a genre that needed to be retired, it is this one.

515. Journey to Beijing

(1997; Riverdrive Productions) ★: 8/10. *Buk jing* (Cantonese), *Bei zheng* (Mandarin): "The Northern March." Cinematographers: Wong Ping-hung, Wang Jie, Philip Gerrard, Garret Sokoloff; Music: Milos Raickovich, Yoshihide Otomo, Anthony Wong Yiu-ming, Carolyn Goor Hutchinson, Luc Tai; Writer-Director: Evans Chan Yiu-shing. Interviewers: Evans Chan Yiu-shing, Lindzay Chan Ling-chi. Interview Subjects/Speakers: Rocco Lam, David Cheung, S.C. Tam, Paul Leader, Yu Yat-tung, Christine Loh, Lew Young, Peter Humphrey, Charles Shu, Jon Resnick, Circle Yuen, Mark Lam, Stanley Kwan Kam-pang, Julian Chan, Ken Yeung, K.K. Ling, Elaine Chim, Lo Fu, Ronald Fung, Yuen Po, Lao Siguang, Helen Lai, Micon Chan, Joanna Chan, Lee Yee, Chan Yuen-han, Szeto Wah, Swana Luk, Philip Bowring, Martin Lee, Xu Yongguang, Meijo Law, Sammy, Lei Jeqiong, Jody Hirsh, Ye Wei, Lau San-ching, Yan Li. Unidentified Stereo Process. 1.33:1. VHS: Riverdrive Productions. 110 minutes.

This ambitious, absorbing documentary (shot on video and transferred to 35mm) intermingles coverage of both a four-month philanthropic walk from Hong Kong to Beijing (to aid underprivileged children in China) which unfolded between February 16 and June 15, 1997, and the countdown to the July 1 handover of HK to China. Director Evans Chan and actress Lindzay Chan (star of Chan's **To Liv(e)** and **Crossings**) interview various participants and onlookers, with their subjects' input providing a multi-faceted look at this historic time in history. Every aspect of the transition is covered, from the political, environmental, and human components to the inevitably ridiculous illustrations of capitalism at its worst (one would-be entrepreneur sells "canned colonial air"). Out of all the figures sharing their thoughts, the most unforgettable is a former aviator who fought against the Japanese in WWII (in a genuinely affecting moment, he unsuccessfully tries to mask his sadness when remembering his war buddies who never came home) and once piloted a plane carrying Deng Xiaoping. Through speakers like him the viewer is afforded all manner of different perspectives as the changeover gradually draws nearer.

Perhaps **Journey to Beijing**'s most noteworthy accomplishment is that it provides a wholly unique, unbiased perspective. Shunning the political agendas of both the Eastern and Western media, Chan delivers a clear and unbiased record of this key moment in Chinese history, imbuing the pomp, pageantry, and pretension with the sort of human outlook that would otherwise be forgotten as the years pass and memories fade. Ironically, the journey itself ends up mirroring the handover by being both a triumph (China's stance on how the change reunites the HK people with their own) and a defeat (the West's view on the presumed loss of freedoms and human rights): The walkers raise over $US2 million, but the image-obsessed Mainland government spends so much on hospitality, police escorts, celebrations, and the like, they inadvertently compromise the whole point of this charitable gesture by squandering money that should be put towards the betterment of its people. A segment dedicated to Post Colonial Sexuality includes an excerpt from Stanley Kwan Kam-pang's excellent British Film Institute documentary **Yin + Yang: Gender in Chinese Cinema—A Film to Celebrate 100 Years of Cinema. Journey to Beijing** is available in two different versions: English subtitled or with English narration and no subtitles.

516. July 13th

(1996; Media Asia Group/P.U. Production/Media Asia Films Partners I) ★: 3/10. *Chat yuet sap saam ji lung poh* (Cantonese), *Qi yue shi san zhi long po* (Mandarin): "July 13th: Dragon Granny." Cinematographer: Jimmy Wong Kam-shing; Art Director: Sukie Yip Suk-wah; Music: Tommy Wai Kai-leung; Writers: Abe Kwong Man-wai, Matthew Chow Hoi-kwong, Taures Chow Yin-han; Producers: Wellson Chin Sing-wai, Abe Kwong Man-wai; Action Director: Lee Chi-kit; Director: Wellson Chin Sing-wai. Cast: David Wu Tai-wai (Alan Kwok Ka-lun), Michelle Lee Kar-yan (Laura), Dayo Wong Chi-wah (Pierre Kwan Tak-ying), Helena Law Lan (Aunt Lung), Lee Suet-man (Shuet), Money Lo Man-yee (Cardin), Manfred Wong (Officer Ko), Yuen King-tan (Castle Peak Nurse). 1.85:1. VHS: Tai Seng. Import LD/VCD: Universe. 95 minutes.

The suspicious suicide of a teenage girl sends police officers Alan and Laura on an odd investigation that leads them to incarcerated mental patient Pierre Kwan. A former cop himself, Pierre, as deranged and incoherent as he is, seems to be the only one who can help the partners find Aunt Lung, a ghostly old woman who has appeared at the scene of two deaths. After leading Alan and Laura on more than a few wild goose chases, Pierre finally disappears. While tracking him down, the partners discover Aunt Lung, who claims that it is her job to lead those who no longer value life to their deaths.

This tedious horror-comedy takes forever to get going, with the first half bogged down almost entirely by Dayo Wong's unfunny ramblings. When the plot finally inches toward a conflict and resolution in the second half, neither is interesting enough to compensate for the boredom that precedes them. A particularly bad English translation does not help matters.

517. Just Heroes

(1989; Magnum) ★: 7/10. *Yee daam kwan ying* (Cantonese), *Yi dan qun ying* (Mandarin): "A Righteous Group of Heroes." Cinematographers: Cho Wai-kei, Derek Yee Tung-sing; Art Directors: Ringo Cheung Sek-wah, Andy Lee Yiu-kwong; Music: Romeo Diaz, James Wong Jim; Writers: Ngai Hong, Tommy Hau Chi-keung; Producer: Tsui Hark; Action Directors: Lau Kar-wing, Yuen Bun; Directors: John Woo Yu-sen, Wu Ma. Cast: Danny Lee Sau-yin (Sou), David Chiang Da-wei (Wai), Wu Ma (Ma), Stephen Chiau Sing-chi (Jacky), Chen Kuan-tai (Tai), James Wong Kim (Solicitor Wong), Ti Lung (Loon), Tien Niu (Annie), Shing Fui-on (Wah), Phillip Ko Fei (Thug), Bill Tung Biu (Gwai), Paul Chun Pui (Tai), Ku Feng (Tsou's Man), Lau Kar-wing (Tsou's Man), Parkman Wong Pak-man (Lee), Lo Lieh (Law), Fung Hark-on (Informant), Yuen Woo-ping (Triad), Ricky Yee Fan-wai (Triad). 1.85:1. VHS: Tai Seng. Import LD: Golden Cinema City. 97 minutes.

Produced as a benefit film for veteran martial arts director Chang Cheh, this gangster thriller is filled with actors who had worked for Chang over the years. This also holds true for the two directors, John Woo and Wu Ma. If stacked up against Woo's **A Better Tomorrow** or **The Killer**, **Just Heroes** is a rather shallow and lacklustre effort bolstered by a terrific cast. However, if you can forget its pedigree and judge it merely as another HK gangster film, **Just Heroes** is an entertaining and engrossing effort that is well above the norm. When their leader, Tsou, is assassinated, a group of his followers try to come to grips with his death. The dead man's will names Wai to replace him as leader of "the company," but the man has gone straight and rejects his boss' wishes. Instead, the gang members are told that Tsou has selected Sou to be his successor. Senior member Tai (who seemed like the sure candidate for the position) receives a phone call from a man claiming to be Tsou's killer, who tells him that the murder was committed on Sou's orders. This prompts Jacky, Tai's righthand man, to seek vengeance against Sou, first by critically injuring the man's pregnant wife. However, Sou mistakenly believes rival gangster Wah to be responsible and kills him, leading to a bloody and ruinous cycle of murder and betrayal.

Despite the formidable assembly of talent, the characters are just not flamboyant or original enough to engender the same level of interest and viewer empathy as their counterparts in Woo's genre classics. Regardless, the double crosses and behind-the-scenes machinations remain intriguing, even though the story surrounding them is pretty tired. Aside from the male bonding and loyalty angles, Woo's influence can be seen primarily in the slow motion montages and, of course, the intermittent gunplay (the final shootout is suitably spectacular). Wai's simple-minded friend also emulates Chow Yun-fat's "Mark" character from **A Better Tomorrow** and, during the finale, even "seeds the flower pots" with guns *à la* the Taiwan rubout sequence in the earlier film. It is interesting to see comedy superstar Stephen Chiau in an early, serious role (the year after he won an award for his dramatic work in **Final Justice**), but his voice has been dubbed by someone else this time.

518. Just Like Weather

(1986; Sil-Metropole Organisation) ★: 7/10. *Mei gwok sum* (Cantonese), *Mei guo xin* (Mandarin): "American Heart." Cinematographers: George Chan Lok-yee, Michael Chan Ping-lam; Art Director: Wong Sau-ping; Music: Law Wing-fai; Writer: John Ng Chong-chau; Producer: Cheung Chi-sing; Director: Allen Fong Yuk-ping. Cast: Christine Lee Yuk-kuen (Christine), Chan Hung-nin (Chan Hung), Lee Chi-keung (Himself), Lam Ying-wah (Herself), Che-Kirk Wong Chi-keung (Repo Boss). 1.85:1. VHS: World Video. 95 minutes.

Allen Fong directs and appears as himself in this neo-realist film which follows the lives of Hung and Christine, a young HK couple. The pair are travelling across America by van from San Francisco to New York to visit the former's mother. Through flashbacks we learn more about their lives leading up to the trip. Already struggling to make ends meet, the couple's problems increase when Christine discovers that she is pregnant. With Hung not expressing an opinion one way or the other, Christine gets an abortion. Hung wants to immigrate to America (not necessarily in legal fashion) because his prospects in HK are likely to remain poor; Christine balks because she has no relatives there and does not want to leave her family. The pair split up and get back together on two occasions, and Christine seems reluctant to reconcile, as she fears that the pattern will just continue. Meanwhile, Hung's job at a shady repo operation is causing trouble, and his boss (played by director Che-Kirk Wong, uncredited here but the only one of the leads to continue appearing in films) now wants him to join his HK/Japan smuggling operation. Fong appears on-camera periodically to talk to the leads about various topics, with the discussions providing a lead-in to the next flashback sequence. We are also shown the problems the production experienced, having to deal with changing weather patterns (the English title mirrors the state of Christine and Hung's relationship), icy winter roads, etc., and the way the cast and crew spent their time during down periods.

Just Like Weather does an effective job of presenting those moments in life, be they mundane, spontaneous, or germane, that rarely appear in mainstream cinema, and the principals are natural and convincing. While not as moving as Fong's debut, **Father and Son**, it is a worthy and interesting production of the sort rarely found in HK cinema. The film picked up the Best Director, Best Editing, and Best New Performer (Christine Lee) prizes at The Hong Kong Film Awards.

519. Justice, My Foot!

(1992; Cosmopolitan Film Productions Co./Shaw Brothers) ★: 7/10. *Sam sei goon* (Cantonese), *Shen si guan* (Mandarin): "Interrogate to Death Official." Cinematographer: Peter Pau Tak-hei; Art Director: Ben Lau Man-hung; Music: William Woo Wai-lap; Writer: Sandy Shaw; Producer: Mona Fong Yat-wah; Action Director: Ching Siu-tung; Director: Johnny To Kei-fung. Cast: Stephen Chiau Sing-chi (Sung Shih-chieh), Anita Mui Yim-fong (Madam Sung), Ng Man-tat (Lord Ho Yu-ta), Carrie Ng Kar-lai (Yang Hsiu-chen), Paul Chun Pui (The Inspector General), Leung Kar-yan (Lord Tien, Chief Secretary of Shansi), Eddy Ko Hung (Yang Ching), Mimi Chu Mi-mi (Maid), Yuen King-tan (Mrs. Yao), Wong Yat-fei (Fu), Cho Wing (The Inspector General's Man). 1.85:1. VHS: Tai Seng. Import LD/VCD/DVD: Universe. 103 minutes.

One of Stephen Chiau's most popular vehicles, **Justice, My Foot!** is a somewhat frustrating experience for English-speaking viewers. It relies heavily on the comedian's *mo lei tau* nonsense humor, some of which simply cannot be translated. That leaves one knowing that the Canto wordplay is probably funnier than what is being relayed by the subtitles. Fortunately, a good portion of the jokes are still accessible and the film has other pleasures as well. During the years when he practised law, silver-tongued Sung Shih-chieh was the top attorney in the area. Against the wishes of his wife, Sung reconsiders his retirement when offered a mountain of gold by a potential client. The riches will be his, provided he can successfully get an affluent man's son off the hook for murder. Sung accepts and wins the case, even though he knew the defendant was obviously guilty of the charges. His baby son dies in an accident soon after, convincing Sung that the Heavens are making him pay for his lapse of ethics. He then decides to retire once and forever, but Madame Sung convinces him to break that vow so that he may defend a helpless maiden framed for murder. Sung agrees, but the guilty party's family has plenty of bribe money to spread around and a bureaucratic conspiracy also exists, making this case the toughest in the solicitor's career.

Stephen Chiau and Anita Mui have wonderful chemistry in this period comedy, and it is particularly amusing to watch Chiau trying to evade the wrath of his stronger (and taller) wife. The final trial unfolds at a breakneck pace, making the particulars somewhat confusing, but the sight gags are universal (there is even a visual reference to **The Silence of the Lambs**) and many of the verbal jests still come across. There is also Mui's wonderful, high flying kung fu moves (which provide a glimpse of the feats her characters would later perform in **The Heroic Trio** and **Drunken Master II**), courtesy of master choreographer Ching Siu-tung. The marginally related **Hail the Judge** and **Lawyer Lawyer** followed.

The Justice Women *see* **Midnight Angel**

Karate Exterminator *see* **Killer Constable**

Karate Ghostbuster *see* **Spiritual Kung Fu**

Kawashima Yoshiko *see* **The Last Princess of Manchuria**

520. Kickboxer

(1993; Regal Films/Yuen Biao Films Company) ★: 6/10. *Wong Fei-hung chi gwai geuk chat* (Cantonese), *Huang Feihong zhi gui jiao qi* (Mandarin): "Wong Fei-hung's Ghost Foot Seven." Cinematographer: Bill Wong Chung-bo; Art Director: Wong Yui-keung; Music: Tang Siu-lam, John Wong Sai-cheung; Writer: Lee Man-choi; Producer-Action Director: Yuen Biao; Director: Wu Ma. Cast: Yuen Biao (Lau Zhai), Lui Sau-ling (King Siu-ling), Wu Ma (So), Yuen Wah (Chairman Wah), Yam Sai-kwoon (Gold Panther), Sheila Chan Sak-lan (Jane), Tai Po (Ming). 1.85:1. VHS: World Video, SYS/Youngtze (Dubbed). LD: World Video. Import LD/VCD: Star Entertainment (No Subtitles). Import DVD: China Star (No Subtitles). 93 minutes.

Here's an imitation of the **Once Upon a Time in China** series ... but Wong Fei-hung is nowhere to be found! Instead, the hero is Lau Zhai, a would-be student of Master Wong, who is brought to Po Chi Lam clinic under the sponsorship of So (director Wu Ma, essaying the "Bucktooth So" role). Lau's impetuous nature constantly gets him into trouble, causing law enforcement officials to eye him with suspicion. When a large quantity of illegal opium is found on the grounds of Po Chi Lam, Gold Panther, the leader of the local constabulary, has no doubt that Lau is the man responsible for it being there. However, Panther (who fights wearing his solid gold "Wonder Shoes") is ordered by his superior, Chairman Wah, to let Lau go, and the evidence is subsequently burned. In order to restore his reputation, Lau leaves the clinic and takes a job working for Wah, the mastermind behind the local drug trade. Unbeknownst to his old friends at the clinic, Lau is secretly working with Panther to put Wah out of business. However, Wah is aware of Lau's duplicity and has plans of his own.

The martial arts sequences (which include a game of kung fu chess!) are plentiful and generally well-staged (though there is a lot more wirework than one would expect from a project featuring Yuen Biao and Yuen Wah). Fans of period films will certainly approve, but **Kickboxer** (a typically generic English title) would have been more interesting had it strived to be more than just a modest imitation of the Tsui Hark spectacles. Regardless, Yuen gives a spirited performance, and it is nice to see veteran villain Yam (**The Fearless Hyena, Iron Monkey**) on the right side of the law for a change.

521. Kickboxer's Tears

(1992; Jia's Motion Picture Co.) ★: 3/10. *San lung chang fu dau* (Cantonese), *Xin long zheng hu dou* (Mandarin): "New Dragon Strive Tiger Fight." Music: Not Original. Producer: Lee Yuk-hing; Action Director: Siu Tak-fu; Writer-Director: Shum Tat-wai. Cast: Moon Lee Choi-fung (Feng), Wilson Lam Chun-yin (Yin), Mark Cheng Ho-nam (Nan), Lung Fong (Wang), Gabriel Wong Yat-san (Quy), Yukari Oshima (Wang's wife), Billy Chow Bei-lee (Billy Chow), Ken Lo Wai-kwong (Li Lung), Shum Wai (Cook). 1.85:1. VHS: Tai Seng (Subtitled or Dubbed). Import LD: Star Entertainment (No Subtitles). 90 minutes.

The cliches fly faster than the fists in this slow-moving cheapie that will only pass muster with the hardiest of Moon Lee's fans. She plays Feng, a kickboxer (naturally) whose brother is killed in the ring by fighter Billy Chow, who has coated his gloves with "irritating oil." She challenges Chow to an underground match and paralyzes him, prompting the man's cousin (Oshima) to demand a rematch. When Lee refuses, her associate Nan is kidnapped, forcing her to accept the challenge. She wins the fight but discovers that Nan has been murdered anyway, leading to a final battle with the criminals.

Some of the action is well-choreographed, but this pedestrian effort has little to recommend it. Lee is personable, but Oshima is wasted in what amounts to an extended cameo, and Wilson Lam and Gabriel Wong compete to see who can provide the most annoying comedy relief (it's a draw). Kickboxing aficionados will enjoy seeing real-life champions Ken Lo and Billy Chow in the ring together, though their match is blandly photographed and edited without any sense of pace or style. Then again, those same charges can be directed toward the entire film.

Kickfighter *see* **Final Run**

522. A Kid from Tibet

(1991; Yuen Biao Productions) ★: 5/10. *Sai jong siu ji* (Cantonese), *Xi zang xiao zi* (Mandarin): "The Tibetan Kid." Cinematographers: Arthur Wong Ngok-tai, Chan Tung-chuen; Art Directors: Raymond Lee King-man, Lau Man-yu; Music: Violet Lam Man-yee; Writers: Shum Chi-leung, Barry Wong Ping-yiu, Chan Kam-cheung; Producer-Action Director-Director: Yuen Biao. Cast: Yuen Biao (Wong La), Michelle Lee Kar-yan (Chiu Seng-neng), Yuen Wah (Black Section Sorcerer), Nina Li Chi (The Sorcerer's Sister), Roy Chiao Hung (Robinson), Michael Dinga (Michael), Wu Ma (Wong's Master), Billy Lau Nam-kwong (Airport Security Guard). 2.35:1. VHS: World Video, SYS/Youngtze (Dubbed). LD: World Video. Import LD/VCD: Universe. Import DVD: Winner's Workshop. 97 minutes.

Yuen Biao's first and only stint behind the camera to date, **A Kid from Tibet** combines elements of **The Peacock King** and Jackie Chan's **Armour of God** films into a fairly diverting package. The film opens with Robinson, a crippled lawyer, journeying through the mountains of Tibet in search of Potala Palace. His client has instructed him to contact the lamas there so that he can return a magical bauble called the "Babu Gold Bottle," which the holy men had previously used to defeat the villainous "Black Section" many years before. When the bottle is reunited with its cap, the vessel's powers can be reactivated. Upon arriving at the palace, Robinson is greeted by the young lama Wong La who uses his magic to heal the lawyer's disabled leg. The youth is then dispatched to the village of Lhasa where he meets up with Robinson's assistant, Seng-neng. Saving her from a gang of killers (led by a dwarf in a suit), the two journey to HK in order to retrieve the vessel, but a sinister brother and sister team are out to terminate them so that they can use the vessel's magic to avenge the defeat of The Black Section.

The action scenes are fairly well-staged, but Yuen's lack of directorial experience is occasionally betrayed by his choice of camera angles, which tend to reveal suspension wires and Nina Li's male double. Apart from the scenes in the mountains and the village, **Kid** lacks the sense of spectacle that permeates the **Armour of God** films, the standard bearers for this subgenre. The characters are also quite one-dimensional, even for this sort of escapist fare (Li and Yuen Wah's characters are not even given names). In an interview for *Eastern Heroes Video Magazine* #1, Yuen actually cited this forgettable trifle as his best film! Jackie Chan makes an eyeblink cameo during the airport sequence as a passerby who bumps into Seng-neng.

523. The Kid with the Golden Arm

(1978; Shaw Brothers) ★: 7/10. *Gam bei tung* (Cantonese), *Jin bi tong* (Mandarin): "Golden Arm Kid." Cinematographer: Tsao Hui-chi; Music: Not Original; Writers: Ngai Hong, Chang Cheh; Producer: Mona Fong Yat-wah; Action Directors: Chiang Sheng, Lu Feng, Tai Chi-hsieh; Director: Chang Cheh. Cast: Phillip Kwok Tsui (The Drunk), Sun Chien (Yang Yu-hang), Chiang Sheng (Short Axe), Lo Mang (Golden Arm), Wei Pai (Li Chin-ming), Lu Feng (Silver Spear), Johnny Wang Lung-wei (Iron Robe), Jamie Luk Kim-ming (Chi Sah fighter). 2.35:1. No official domestic video release. 86 minutes.

This period kung fu outing centers on a shipment of gold meant to aid victims of a famine. The head official, Yang Yu-hang, learns that the villainous Chi Sah gang (led by the seemingly invincible Golden Arm, who fights without weapons) will attempt to steal it *en route* to its destination, but they surprise everyone by snatching the gold even before it is transported. However, the gang's wagon loses a wheel and one of their top fighters is murdered by Hai To, a mysterious drunk with incredible fighting abilities who is actually a government agent. With the gold retrieved, Yang continues on the planned route, but Chi Sah booby traps kill several of his soldiers and a powerful, unaffiliated killer named Iron Feet poses an even greater threat to him and his mission than the Chi Sah.

The narrative does not offer as many twists and betrayals as the best of Chang Cheh and Ngai Hong's collaborations, but it still remains of interest. The decision to have Phillip Kwok's character perform best when he is inebriated was no doubt inspired by the runaway success of Jackie Chan's **Drunken Master**, but the character also serves as an effective contrast to Wei Pai's stoic swordsman who would rather die a hero than live as a common man. The kung fu is of the high standard ones expects from Chang's films, but the pacing is a bit slack at times and the stock music is sometimes at odds with the emotions being expressed in a given scene. The character names listed above are from the English dubbed version.

524. The Kidnap of Wong Chak Fai

(1993; Win's Music & Video Enterprises) ★: 3/10. *Bong ga Wong Chat-fai* (Cantonese), *Bang jia Huang Qihui* (Mandarin): "Kidnap Wong Chat-fai" or "Kidnap Huang Qihui." Cinematographer: Eric Chu Kwok-fai; Art Director: Leung Chi-hung; Music: Sing Kam-wing; Writers: Jimmy Heung Wah-sing, Wong Jing, Lee Sai-hung; Producer: Lee Siu-wah; Action Director: Fung Hark-on; Director: Ko Sin-ming. Cast: Kent Cheng Chuk-see (Chung), Paul Chun Pui (Wong Chat-fai), Francis Ng Chun-yu (Cheung Sing), Jacqueline Law Wai-kuen (May), Cheng Pei-pei (Kung Tse-sam). 1.85:1. VHS: World Video. Import LD/VCD: Mei Ah. 90 minutes.

In June of 1993 Jackie Chan's **Crime Story** hit HK theaters and presented a fictionalized account of an infamous kidnapping case from a decade earlier involving millionaire Wong Chat-fai. Two months after that film opened, this one appeared, offering another depiction of the same incident. Kent Cheng (who played the villain in the Chan film) plays Chung, a veteran detective on the verge of retirement who rescues Wong from some Taiwanese kidnappers. Hoping to obtain a favor in exchange, Chung prompts Wong to go into a construction partnership with his son Ming, who is new to the world of business. Wong agrees and proceeds to take unfair advantage, leaving Ming bankrupt and targeted for death by a triad loan shark. When Wong continually refuses to pay what he owes, Ming attempts suicide, prompting Chung to formulate a new plan: He will kidnap Wong himself and demand a ransom of $US30 million! Unfortunately, Chung's old underling is onto him.

A good premise is badly undermined by the screenplay, which turns the Wong character into a ridiculously exaggerated caricature (Ebenezer Scrooge is a philanthropist in comparison) and makes plausible events seem absurd. There is even an implied oral sex scene which was apparently included for the sole purpose of getting the film a Category III rating. Kent Cheng and Francis Ng are both dubbed by other actors, leaving Cheng Pei-pei to give the best performance as Wong's ever-faithful wife.

525. The Killer

(1989; Cinema City/Golden Princess/ Magnum/Film Workshop) ★: 10/10. *Dip huet seung hung* (Cantonese), *Die xie shuang xiong* (Mandarin): "A Pair of Blood-Splattering Heroes." Cinematographers: Horace Wong Wing-hang, Peter Pau Tak-hei; Art Director: Ben Luk Man-wah; Music: Lowell Lo Kwun-ting; Producer: Tsui Hark; Action Directors: Ching Siu-tung, Lau Chi-ho; Writer-Director: John Woo Yu-sen. Cast: Chow Yun-fat (John), Danny Lee Sau-yin (Li), Sally Yeh Chian-wen (Jenny), Paul Chu Kong (Sidney), Kenneth Tsang Kong (Chang), Shing Fui-on (Johnny Weng), Ricky Yee Fan-wai (Killer in Sunglasses), Yip Wing-cho (Tony Weng), Barry Wong Ping-yiu (Li's Superior), Tommy Wong Kwong-leung (Eddie Hung), Parkman Wong Pak-man (Cop), Lam Chung (John's First Victim). Dolby Digital (Import DVDs only). 1.85:1. VHS: Fox Lorber (Subtitled or Dubbed). LD/DVD: Criterion. Import LD: Golden Cinema City. Import VCD: Mei Ah. Import DVD: Mega Star, Universe. 111/136 minutes.

While performing a contract job in a nightclub, suave professional assassin John (called "Jeff" in some versions) accidentally injures singer Jenny, who is in the wrong place at the wrong time. Plagued by guilt, he makes it his duty to look after the all-but-blind woman but stops short of revealing to her just who he is. Fed up with the business, John wants to quit, but he decides to pull one more hit for triad boss Johnny Weng before taking Jenny abroad for a cornea transplant. However, upon performing the killing, John is betrayed by his middleman, Sidney, under orders from Weng. While he has every reason to kill Sidney, John spares him out of friendship. Inspector Li (one of the cops assigned to protect the man John just murdered) gets onto the killer's trail quickly and gains significant ground by befriending Jenny without disclosing his identity or intentions to her. After an initial confrontation results in John's escape, Li manages to catch John and Jenny together, but before he can take them into custody, a small army of assassins appear and the trio barely escape with their lives. The incident cements a growing mutual respect between the killer and the policeman that blossoms into intense camaraderie when the two men lose their best friends to Weng's gunmen and must fight for their lives against wave after wave of heavily armed opponents.

Inspired by Jean-Pierre Melville's 1967 classic ***Le Samourai*** (released in America in a dubbed and truncated version called **The Godson**), and possessing roots in the classic Chinese swordplay dramas of director John Woo's mentor, Chang Cheh, **The Killer** is a rapturous mixture of ripe melodrama, elegant introspection, vivid characterizations, intoxicating style, and incredible, over-the-top gunplay, all framed by Woo's distinctive views of honor and male bonding. Moving, exciting, tragic, noble, and wonderfully unselfconscious, this is the archetypal gangster tragedy kinetically reinvented by a master filmmaker and anchored by one of Chow Yun-fat's most iconic performances. Lowell Lo contributes a fine score, but cues lifted from the Hollywood films **Red Heat** and **Hero and the Terror** (both 1988) can still be detected by perceptive viewers. Taiwanese prints run an extra 25 minutes, fleshing out the characters but compromising the pacing. However, if you are deeply impressed with the HK cut, this version is still well worth seeing, if only to reveal how Woo tightened and improved this, his finest achievement to date.

526. Killer Angels

(1989; Jia's Motion Picture Co. H.K.) ★: 6/10. *Saat sau tin si* (Cantonese), *Sha shou tian shi* (Mandarin): "Killer Angels." Cinematographer: Wong Chit; Music: Not Original; Writers: Szeto On, Tsang Tiu-hon; Action Director: Tsui Fat; Producers: Law Kar-fu, Cheung Chung-ling; Director: Lu Chin-ku. Cast: Moon Lee Choi-fung (Yau Li), Gordon Lau Kar-fai (Michael), Leung Kar-yan (Chu Chung-seng), Ng Man-tat (Tat), Chan Pui-kei (Blue Angels Team Leader), Mark Houghton (Oto), Shing Fui-on (Hood). 1.85:1. VHS: Tai Seng (Dubbed only), World Video (Subtitled only). Import LD: Star Entertainment (No Subtitles). 91 minutes. Also known as **Ultra Force** (Alternate title for dubbed version).

If you're looking for unabashed girls-with-guns action, you could do far worse than this energetic low-budgeter which stars the extraordinary Moon Lee. Yau Li and Lo Sa, two members of the "Blue Angels" female anti-crime group, are hired to protect Jacky Chen(!), an American triad from the "Shadow Gangsters" who has a list of names that could seriously compromise the organization. With Chen's help, the Angels set their sights on nightclub tycoon Chu Chung-seng, who is running a slavery ring that supplies young girls to Middle East clients. Assigned to work undercover at one of Chu's clubs, Li gets a job as a singer and befriends Michael, Chu's top hitman, who has a secret connection to her. Li's investigation is compromised by Chu's daughter, who discovers the ruse and tries to kill Li one evening. When that fails, she sets a trap for the girl, but Li is saved by the last minute intervention of Michael. Chu then orders Michael to kill Li, but the assassin is torn between his love for the girl and his loyalty to the organization. Chen (who was only lying about the list) is executed by his employers, so the Angels load up some major firepower to finish Chu's slave trading business once and for all.

The action scenes have been shot with a slightly undercranked camera, but unlike many second-tier productions, they never look silly. Rather, the slight acceleration gives the fights and shootouts a supercharged look that makes them all the more exhilarating. There are a couple of subplots involving a traitorous hood (Ng Man-tat, looking odd without his moustache) and another Angel (who seeks to kill Jacky in order to avenge the murder of her son) which tend to slow things down a bit. However, the film serves up an incredible amount of gunplay and no shortage of kung fu, covering all the genre bases quite satisfactorily. First and foremost, **Killer Angels** is a terrific showcase for Lee, the world's cutest martial arts star. In addition to her physical abilities, she has a terrific song and dance number while clad in a black leather outfit that is to die for.

527. Killer Army

(1983; Shaw Brothers) ★: 5/10. Chinese Titles Unknown. Cinematographer: Tsao Hui-chi; Art Director: Johnson Tsao; Music: Not Original; Writers: Ngai Hong, Chang Cheh; Producer: Runme Shaw; Action Directors: Phillip Kwok Tsui, Lu Feng, Chiang Sheng; Director: Chang Cheh. Cast: Phillip Kwok Tsui (Wong), Chiang Sheng (Yu), Lo Mang (Chen Chin-ping), Lu Feng (Chen), Sun Chien (Teng), Chin Siu-ho (Spearman). 2.35:1. No official domestic video release. 99 minutes. Also known as **The Guerillas**.

Fleeing from murderous soldiers and weakened by starvation, a group of martially skilled refugees are offered jobs by employers impressed by their abilities. These young men (all from the same province) become blood brothers but soon find themselves caught in the turmoil of the time when they are framed for a political assassination. They receive help from the head of a martial arts school but are betrayed and decide to join a group of southern rebels. However, before they can escape, the men are betrayed again and must fight their way to freedom.

First rate kung fu keeps this lesser period martial arts entry moderately enjoyable. The narrative proceeds strictly by the numbers, lacking the twists and turns found in the best of Chang Cheh's collaborations with writer Ngai Hong, but the "Venoms" team is in excellent form, so fans will be satisfied. Character names above are from the English dubbed version.

528. Killer Constable

(1980; Shaw Brothers) ★: 8/10. *Maan yan gan* (Cantonese), *Wan ren jin* (Mandarin): "Beheader of 10,000 Persons." Cinematographer: Li Hsin-yeh; Art Director: Johnson Tsao; Music: Not Original; Writer: Szeto On; Producer: Mona Fong Yat-wah; Action Directors: Ito Shikamura, Huang Pei-chih; Director: Kuei Chih-hung. Cast: Chen Kuan-tai (Leng Tian-ying), Ku Feng (Fang Feng-jia), Jason Pai Piao (Fan Jin-diao), Cho Tat-wah (Liu Jing-tian), Yu Tsui-ling (Fong Lan-gu), Dick Wei (Suen-heng), Ha Ping (Woman with Baby). 2.35:1. Video distributor unknown. 98 minutes. Also known as **Karate Exterminator, Lightning Kung Fu** (US video title).

After two million taels worth of gold bars are stolen from the royal treasury, ruthless Manchu chief constable Leng Tian-ying is dispatched to apprehend the five thieves responsible. Commanding a small company of men, Leng journeys into the countryside and discovers some clues near an abandoned temple. However, he also starts losing his men to adversaries who attack in the dark of night, and also faces competition from fellow lawman Fan Jin-diao, who lacks Leng's dedication to duty and is merely interested in grabbing the gold for himself. The bandits' leader, Fang Feng-jia, may prove to be Leng's match, but even if the constable does prevail over him, another, seemingly inconceivable, obstacle is in his path.

A very interesting and exciting contrast to the kind of period kung fu fare being produced by Chang Cheh and Lau Kar-leung for Shaw Brothers during this period, **Killer Constable** is fashioned more along the lines of a horror movie. Director

Kuei Chih-hung (**Bamboo House of Dolls**) stages some of the swordfights in semi-darkness, and most of the action unfolds in ruined, smoky locales and black, gnarled forests. The tone is also much grimmer, and the swordplay (co-directed by a Japanese action choreographer) is less stylish and more savage than the norm. The atmosphere is thick with impending death; Leng spends half of the film on the verge of dying from his wounds, and even the weather is against him. A scene in which Leng and Fang must pretend to be old friends so that the latter's blind, delicate daughter will not know what is really transpiring must have been the inspiration for a similar sequence in John Woo's **The Killer**. Character names above are from the dubbed version. Note: The tape released by Master Arts Video, under the title **Lightning Kung Fu**, is a different film.

529. The Killer Has No Return

(1996; Canaan Film Production) ★: 3/10. *Sai sau sam fan boon chung* (Cantonese), *Sha shou san fen ban zhong* (Mandarin): "Assassin: Three and a Half Minutes." Cinematographer: Wong Kar-fai; Art Director: Kwok Man-kam; Music: Tang Siu-lam; Writers: Lau Wing-kin, Leung Hung-wah; Producer: Leung Hung-wah, Action Directors: Alan Lo Kwok-wai, So Hon-san; Director: Jeffrey Chiang Chia-chun. Cast: Wong Hei (Wong Hei), Carol Lee Siu-mei (Jenny Ho), Ng Man-tat (Uncle Tat), Yu Rongguang (Killer), John Ching Tung (Shek Fu-an). 1.85:1. VHS: Tai Seng. Import LD/VCD: Ocean Shores. 89 minutes.

Director Jeffrey Chiang followed up his stylish thriller **Dream Killer** (1995) with this meandering drama, which has all the style of that film but none of its tension. The main problem, however, is that Chiang is so intent on aping the technique of Wong Kar-wai (**Fallen Angels**) that nothing here seems fresh or even interesting. Wong Hei plays a like-named assassin (with an affinity for hot chocolate) who specializes in taking out other killers. After a successful job in China, he travels to Malaysia for his next target: a wealthy business magnate named Shek. After spending several days in the country, biding his time, the day for him to kill Shek finally arrives. However, the millionaire is not at the social function he was supposed to attend, and another, more proficient assassin (Yu Rongguang) has also appeared on the scene—with Wong on his death list.

Wong's quiet, ultra-cool killer reminds one of Leon Lai Ming's sullen hitman in **Fallen Angels** (1995); the use of "Blur-O-Vision" during action scenes and the preponderance of voiceover narration are also reminiscent of that film. Carol Lee (as an ultra-perky bar girl who takes a liking to Wong for no reason one can fathom) even breaks into the killer's hotel room and rearranges his things á *la* Faye Wang in another Wong Kar-wai entry, **Chungking Express** (1994). Those two films were able to utilize such stylistic devices and quirky digressions to heighten their atmosphere. Here they just seem laboured, and inadvertently emphasize what a shallow and empty film they are propping up. The ending is especially unsatisfactory.

530. The Killer Meteors

(1977; Lo Wei Motion Picture Co.) ★: 4/10. *Fung yu seung lau sing* (Cantonese), *Feng yu shuang liu xing* (Mandarin): "Turbulent Meteors." Art Director: Chow Chi-leung; Music: Not Original; Writer: Ku Long; Producer: Hsu Li-hwa; Action Director: Chan Shun-yat; Director: Lo Wei. Cast: Jimmy Wang Yu (Mi Wei, The Killer Meteor), Jackie Chan (Wa Wu-bin), Yu Ling-ling, Nam Yu-li, Li Sisi. 2.35:1. VHS: Simitar (Dubbed). DVD: Simitar (English and Mandarin tracks). Import VCD: Ocean Shores (Poor Subtitles). 104 minutes. Also known as **Jackie Chan versus Wang Yu**.

An involved period martial arts thriller, this Taiwanese production is included because it features Jackie Chan in a rare villainous role. The star is actually Jimmy Wang Yu, who plays Mi Wei (aka "The Killer Meteor"), a proficient assassin with a formidable reputation. One day, a man approaches Mi with news that he has been invited to appear before Wa Wu-bin, who is reported to have mystical powers. Wa hires Mi to do two things: murder his wife, Madame Tempest, and secure an antidote to the poison she has given him. Said cure is guarded night and day by four deadly masters who possess amazing supernatural powers. While these instructions seem straightforward enough, the path ahead contains many twists and turns that Mi must negotiate to fulfill his mission and stay alive.

While some aspects of the storyline are a bit convoluted, the developing mystery remains engrossing, right up to the less-than-lucid ending. However, the kung fu is disappointing, the English-dubbed dialogue is even more laughable than usual (if you are genuinely interested in catching this, try to locate the VCD edition instead), and Wang's secret weapon is something less than impressive. Chan makes an adequate antagonist, though this is mainly due to the sheer novelty of seeing him in such a part.

531. A Killer's Blues

(1990; Cinema City Co.) ★: 7/10. *Bim yuen sui yuet* (Cantonese), *Bian yuan sui yue* (Mandarin): "Borderline Years." Cinematographer: Joe Chan Kong-hung; Art Director: Eddie Ma Poon-chiu; Music: Lo Tai-yau, Richard Lo Sai-kit; Writer: Nam Yin; Producer: Raymond Wong Pak-ming; Action Director: Tony Leung Siu-hung; Director: Raymond Lee Wai-man. Cast: Ti Lung (Wai Yi-ming), Olivia Cheng Man-ar (Wai), Fennie Yuen Kit-ying (Tse Ming-shuet), Roy Cheung Yiu-yeung (Chung), Mark Cheng Ho-nam (Kit), Lo Lieh (Tai). 1.85:1. VHS: Tai Seng. Import LD: Golden Cinema City. 92 minutes.

Nam Yin, the brother of director Ringo Lam, wrote this engrossing drama which benefits immensely from Ti Lung's fine performance as a compassionate triad hitman trying to atone for his mistakes. In 1975 Wai Yi-ming executes a mob traitor, only to discover that the victim's little girl witnessed the murder. Rather than kill her, he adopts the child, Tse Ming-shuet, and puts her in the care of his girlfriend Wai while he goes to America on "business." While reading a newspaper one morning, Wai discovers that Yi-ming has been arrested and sentenced to 14 years in an American jail. She then spends the intervening years raising Ming-shuet until Yiming returns to HK in 1990, a free man. The gang Yi-ming left behind is engaged in a power struggle that is certain to spell defeat and death for its leader, a close friend of Yi-ming who once saved his life. When the dissension quickly escalates into brutality and murder, Yi-ming promises Ming-shuet that he will go straight, but Yi-ming's sense of loyalty is divided between his family and his boss.

While the ending is more or less a foregone conclusion, **A Killer's Blues** remains effective and fits in nicely with Nam Yin's other crime dramas, which are often built around honorable protagonists whose gangland dealings invariably lead them into seemingly hopeless dilemmas. As mentioned above, Ti anchors the film with one of his customarily quiet yet commanding portrayals, while Fennie Yuen is also effective as Ming-shuet, whose lack of a father figure in her formative years has left her confused and emotionally vulnerable. Gunplay fans will be happy to learn that the film also includes intermittent doses of action, including a climactic shootout with a clever twist.

532. The Killer's Love

(1993; Far East Film Co.) ★: 3/10. *Leung seung ching yuen* (Cantonese), *Liang xiang qing yuan* (Mandarin): "Mutual Consent." Cinematographer: Wong

Po-man; Art Director: Bill Lui Cho-hung; Music: Simon Leung Chi-wah, Tony Tam Chan-hung; Producer: David Lam Tak-luk; Action Directors: Jamie Luk Kim-ming, James Ha Chim-see; Writer-Director: Jamie Luk Kim-ming. Cast: Simon Yam Tat-wah (Cheung Wai-lum), Carol Cheng Yu-ling (Lee Tai-ho), Wong Chi-yeung (Alex), Angile Leung Wan-yui (Lam Kar-kar), Jamie Luk Kim-ming (Shum Fu-kwei), David Wu Tai-wai (Lee Tai-shui), James Ha Chim-see (Card Cheater), Benny Lai Wai (Shum's Goon). 1.85:1. VHS: Tai Seng. Import LD/VCD: Universe. 87 minutes.

Prudish Shui Tau village teacher Lee Tai-ho has her regimented routine turned upside down by the arrival of Cheung Wai-lum. A contract killer, Wai-lum needs a place to lay low while staking out his next victim (a former colleague). Pretending to be a gigolo, Wai-lum amuses himself by teasing the repressed Tai-ho, but he will actually develop feelings for her, thanks in part to the arrival of psychotic comrade Alex. In addition to murdering Wai-lum's assistant, Alex ruthlessly executes both Wai-lum's target and the man's baby son. When Wai-lum objects to his methods, Alex turns his sights on him, meaning that Wai-lum must now protect both himself and Tai-ho.

Simon Yam has fun with a role that allows him to indulge in both his tough guy and gigolo personas, but little else in **The Killer's Love** is memorable. While it has served her well elsewhere, Carol Cheng's spinster act quickly wears thin here, and the humor inherent in the premise is limited. On top of that, the mixture of sophomoric, formulaic comedy and bloody shootouts is far more tedious than entertaining. As if the film were not derivative and unfocused enough already, there is even an attempt to cash in on the success of **Fight Back to School** by having Yam act as a substitute teacher.

533. Killer's Romance

(1990; Regent Films) ★: 6/10. *Long man sa sau ji yau yan* (Cantonese), *Long man sha shou tze yo ren* (Mandarin): "Romantic Killer Freeman." Cinematographer: Philip Ma Kam-cheung; Art Director: Raymond Kwok Siu-keung; Music: Wong Chi-hung; Writers: Tam, Phillip Ko Fei; Action Directors: Luk Chuen, Pau Wah, Yasuyoshi Shikamura; Producer-Director: Phillip Ko Fei. Cast: Simon Yam Tat-wah (Nidaime), Joey Wang Tsu-hsien (Jenny), Phillip Ko Fei (Chan Ben), Lau Siu-ming (Uncle Pa), Carman Lee Yeuk-tung (Carmen). 1.85:1. VHS: World Video (Subtitled only), Tai Seng (Dubbed Only). DVD: Tai Seng (Dubbed). Import LD: Mei Ah. 93 minutes.

Like **The Dragon from Russia** (also 1990), this is a loose adaptation of the popular Japanese *manga* "Crying Freeman." In contrast to the humorous and wildly uneven **Dragon, Killer's Romance** is a more straightforward and routine effort, though viewers enamoured of the incredible shootouts HK cinema is famous for will not be disappointed. Nidaime, the adopted son of a Japanese mob boss, travels to England in order to kill the Chinese gangsters who murdered his father. Two of his hits are witnessed by young student Jenny, who also manages to take his picture. Nidaime is ready to silence Jenny but falls for her instead, saving the girl's life when they are attacked by the forces of Chan Ben, the last of his father's killers. Through his assistant Eko, Nidaime learns that it was actually his cohort Yoshikawa who had his father killed, over the latter's refusal to deal in drugs. Chan Ben and Yoshikawa struck a deal to eliminate their respective bosses, and then enter into a partnership which would give them sole control over the drug trade in London Chinatown. Nidaime sets out to kill both men, but faces unforeseen complications when the Japanese ganglord kidnaps Jenny. The spectacularly bloody closing reel offers a rousing one-two combination of gunplay and Japanese swordplay.

Simon Yam's role gives him few chances to convey emotion, but he successfully projects the pain and disillusionment Nidaime is suffering and is absolutely convincing in the physical aspects of the part. While the film avoids the needless narrative confusion that plagued **Dragon**, the screenplay here proceeds from A to B in a frustratingly linear fashion, offering nothing innovative, save for its London locations (some of the same cast and crew would also work there on **Phantom War**). While only slightly above the norm, **Killer's Romance** is still worth seeking out, and it is a near masterpiece compared to director-star Phillip Ko's later productions in the Philippines. This was Carman Lee's film debut.

534. Killing Me Hardly

[*sic*] (1997; Times Production) ★: 1/10. *Yuen chuen chui fa sau chaat* (Cantonese), *Wan quan cui hua shou ce* (Mandarin): "Handbook to Completely Destroy Flowers." Cinematographer: Wong Kar-fai; Art Director: Nelson Cheung Hok-yun; Music: Tang Siu-lam; Writer: Times Production; Producer: Benny Fu Ching-wai; Action Director: Sherman Wong Sa-man; Director: Fu Pui-yu. Cast: Jade Leung Ching (Sunny), Christine Ng Wing-mei (Moony), Paulyn Suen Kai-kwun (Starry), Michael Chow Man-kin (Bob), Lam Wai (Li). 1.85:1. VHS: Tai Seng. Import LD/VCD: Panorama Entertainment. 90 minutes.

Every bit as awful as its English title, this low-budget **Charlie's Angels** knockoff is so hard-up for ideas, it even features a lead character named Charlie who is heard but never seen! Presented with neither style nor urgency, the film follows beautiful freelance crime fighters Sunny, Moony, and Starry (oh brother), who are pursued and abetted by bumbling, bespectacled reporter Bob. Apart from numerous tedious subplots in which the angels try to deal with their personal problems, the main story concerns the threat posed to them by Andy (everyone is on a first name basis in this film), a psychotic arms dealer who seeks revenge against Charlie for killing his wife during an FBI raid. Since Charlie is not easily found, Andy takes his murderous anger out on the man's friends and associates, leading him, naturally, to the angels.

Given the large number of **Angel** pictures released in the last decade and the sheer simplicity of the set-up, it would seem pretty hard for this one to strike out, but strike out it does. The cardboard characters have no dimension at all (e.g. Starry's distinguishing characteristic is that she is addicted to Coca Cola); there isn't enough story for a 20 minute short, let alone a feature; the action sequences are far from special; and if you can't guess how this movie will end, you need to find a new form of recreation. Hopeless.

535. Killing Me Tenderly

(1997; Brilliant Idea Group) ★: 5/10. *Oi nei oi do saat sei nei* (Cantonese), *Ai nin ai dao sha si nin* (Mandarin): "Love You to Kill You." Cinematographer: Joe Chan Kong-hung; Art Director: Ko Chan-wai; Music: Ha Sum-mei, Arion Ah Lei-si; Producer: Joe Ma Wai-ho; Writer-Director: Lee Lik-chi. Cast: Sammi Cheng Sau-man (Cindy), Leon Lai Ming (Lai Su-kan), Wyman Wong Wai-man (Foster Mother), Sandra Ng Kwun-yu (Siu), Vincent Kok Tak-chiu (Aunt), Cheng Cho (Auntie), Ruby Wong Cheuk-ling (Ada), Ha Ping (Su-kan's Mother), Spencer Lam Sheung-yee (Su-kan's Superior), Bobby Yip King-sang (Ugly Guy Selling Pirate CDs). 1.85:1. VHS: Mecapro. Import LD/VCD/DVD: Mei Ah. 102 minutes.

Jet Li's **The Bodyguard from Beijing** was a less than wonderful action-oriented knockoff of the Kevin Costner/Whitney Houston hit **The Bodyguard**. HK filmmakers took another shot at the concept and had a bit more success with this romantic comedy-thriller. When Cantopop superstar Cindy has a box full of live tarantulas tossed on her at a record signing, it becomes clear that she needs someone other than her staff to protect her. Actually, Cindy is in even more serious need of protection than she knows: A psychotic admirer has sent several threatening letters, but they were intercepted before she could read them. Looking for a new challenge, rural cop Lai Su-kan transfers to the city in search of a dangerous assignment and gets one: He is assigned to be Cindy's new bodyguard. Correction, he is to be Cindy's new *gay* bodyguard, as she only hires homosexual men, *and* she is not to know that he is a bodyguard. The former chief of his village, Su-kan is not used to serving women, and the pair get off to a decidedly rocky start. Su-kan proves his worth to Cindy, however, and the two become attracted to one another. However, an unstable fan is becoming more overt in his advances towards Cindy and is a serious threat to her life.

No surprises here, but real-life singing stars Sammi Cheng and Leon Lai give relaxed, likeable performances and the script manages to incorporate some genuinely amusing situations. The dramatic aspects of the story, however, are less inspired and knock the film down a notch.

536. King of Beggars

(1992; Win's Movie Production) ★: 7/10. *Mo jong yuen: So hat yi* (Cantonese), *Wu zhuang yuan: Su qi er* (Mandarin): "Top Martial Scholar: Beggar Su" (or "Beggar So" in Cantonese). Cinematographer: David Chung Chi-man; Art Director: Horace Ma Kwong-wing; Music: Joseph Koo Kar-fai; Writer: John Chan Kin-chung; Producers: Charles Heung Wah-keung, Jimmy Heung Wah-sing; Action Director: Yuen Cheung-yan; Director: Gordon Chan Kar-seung. Cast: Stephen Chiau Sing-chi (So Chan), Sharla Cheung Man (Yu-shang), Ng Man-tat (The General of Canton), Norman Tsui Siu-keung (Chiu), Lam Wai (Seng Ko Lin-chin), Nat Chan Pak-cheung (The Secretary for Justice), Lawrence Cheng Tan-shui (The Professor), Yuen King-tan (Madam Pimp), Yuen Woo-ping (Hung Yat-san), Peter Lai Bei-tak (Uncle Cheng). Dolby Stereo, Dolby Digital (DVDs only). 1.85:1. VHS: Tai Seng. Import LD/VCD: Mei Ah. Import DVD: Mei Ah, Mega Star. 100 minutes.

A beautifully designed, big-budget period fantasy-comedy, **King of Beggars** casts Stephen Chiau as So Chan (a character also portrayed by Donnie Yen Chi-tan in **Heroes Among Heroes**), a wealthy layabout who becomes enamoured of beautiful prostitute Yu-shang (who is actually an undercover rebel trying to assassinate the power-hungry martial arts master/sorcerer Chiu). To impress his would-be bride, So enters the "Kung Fu Scholar" competition, only to be cheated out of his subsequent victory. Chiu's pull with the emperor gets So and his father tossed out of luxury's lap and into the streets, forcing them to live as beggars. A later encounter with Chiu leaves So severely injured, but upon recovering, he finds himself elected the unlikely head of "The Beggars Association," which he leads in a fight to bring down their common enemy.

Although the action setpieces do not approach the level of a Tsui Hark/Ching Siu-tung collaboration, this slick offering (which reunites Chiau with his **Fight Back to School** director, Gordon Chan) boasts attractive Mainland exteriors (including footage taken at The Great Wall) and excellent cinematography by David Chung (**The Lovers**); unfortunately, the wirework isn't as undetectable as it should be. So is finally able to triumph over his opponent by using the "Sleeping Fist" technique, an inspired variation on the kind of comic kung fu popularized by Jackie Chan in the late '70s. The film's sentimental moments come across with reasonable success, but it is Chiau's timing and body language that really embellish the proceedings and sell the jokes.

537. King of Chess

(1992; Golden Princess/Film Workshop) ★: 8/10. *Kei wong* (Cantonese), *Qi wang* (Mandarin): "Chess King." Cinematographers: Poon Hang-sang, Lo Wan-shing; Yeung Wai-hon; Art Directors: David Chan Chi-wai, James Leung Wah-sang; Music: Lo Tai-yau; Writers: Yim Ho, Tony Leung Kar-fai; Producer: Tsui Hark; Directors: Yim Ho, Tsui Hark (uncredited). Cast: Tony Leung Kar-fai (Wong Yat-sun), John Sham Kin-fun (Ching), King Shih-chien ("Lanky" Ngai), Yim Ho (Chung). 1.85:1. VHS: Tai Seng. Import LD: Golden Cinema City. Import VCD: Mega Star. 110 minutes.

This troubled production was started by director Yim Ho (**Red Dust**) but finished by producer Tsui Hark, who took over the film mid-shoot. It tells two stories, both revolving around chess players from different countries and very different times who, nonetheless, possess several distinct affinities. Hong Kong advertising man Ching journeys to Taipei to help make a ratings winner out of a show called "Whiz Kids World." A possible contestant for the program is a young genius known as "The Chess King," who, as it turns out, does not know how to play the game in its traditional sense. This does not phase Ching, however, because he has discovered that the child possesses amazing extrasensory powers that will allow him to triumph over a conceited chess champion Ching has engaged to play against the boy on a live national television broadcast. All of the talk about chess reminds Ching of Wong Yat-sun, a man he met while in China during The Cultural Revolution. Flashbacks are interspersed throughout the narrative, detailing what happened to Wong (a chess master of phenomenal skill), who was persecuted by party zealots because of an innocent error on his part.

A central theme in both segments is how a human life can become trivial, either through capitalist commerce (the program's hostess is revered one minute and then on the verge of being fired almost overnight because of declining ratings) or politics (the monstrous suppression and misery brought on by The Cultural Revolution), and the depths individuals can sink to in order to save themselves from ruin. While Yim has more or less disowned the film, **King of Chess** remains a compelling, well-acted allegory, and the behind-the-scenes discord is not at all evident. The final reel (which juxtaposes the televised match with a game Wong played against eight other masters simultaneously) is an exciting and inspiring bit of cinema. Noted Taiwanese director Hou Hsiao-hsien served as associate producer.

538. The King of Robbery

(1996; Wing Fat Film Production) ★: 5/10. *Hon fei* (Cantonese), *Han fei* (Mandarin): "Armed Robber." Cinematographer: Wong Po-man; Writer: Lau Wing-kin; Producer: Chan Chi-ming; Action Director: Chin Kar-lok; Director: Chung Siu-hung. Cast: Simon Yam Tat-wah (Chan Sing), Roy Cheung Yiu-yeung (He), Anita Lee Yuen-wah (Fan), Chin Kar-lok (Zhong), Bowie Lam Bo-yee (Lee). 1.85:1. VHS: World Video. Import LD/VCD/DVD: Universe. 82 minutes.

One of Simon Yam's better recent starring vehicles, this action thriller kills time agreeably, but it could have been so much more engrossing had it been content to do more than just follow the usual course. Yam plays a psychotic thief (whose speciality is robbing goldsmiths) who manages to break out of confinement at an asylum. Rejoining his gang, the men buy some heavy artillery (including an AK-47) and pull five daring daylight robberies in one fell swoop. Going out of his way to challenge the police, Yam becomes a media sensation, prompting a record reward of $HK1 million. However, with his grip on reality becoming even more tenuous than before, his cronies rightfully start to worry about their safety.

There is some invigorating action (courtesy of Chin Kar-lok, who co-stars as an undercover cop in Yam's gang) and slick cinematography, but no interesting characters and no fresh concepts. Like far too many HK films, this ends with a still frame and a Chinese-only message about the fate of the characters, which is not much help for English-speaking viewers. Talented Anita Lee is wasted in a superfluous role as a dippy waitress who takes a liking to Yam and tags along with the gang. Memorable line: "Don't think that you can afford to bully a vegetarian!"

539. Kitchen

(1997; Golden Harvest/Amuse/Pineast Pictures/Harvest Crown) ★: 7/10. *Ngoh oi chue fong* (Cantonese), *Wo ai chu fang* (Mandarin): "I Love Kitchen." Cinematographer: Poon Hang-sang; Art Directors: James Leung Wah-sang, Jason Mok Siu-kei; Music: Yoshihide Otomo, Kazuhisa Uchihashi; Producers: Yim Ho, Akira Morishige; Action Director: Stephen Tung Wai; Writer-Director: Yim Ho. Cast: Jordan Chan Siu-chun (Louie), Yasuko Tomita (Aggie), Law Kar-ying (Emma), Karen Mok Man-wai (Jenny), Law Koon-lan (Chika), Lau Siu-ming (Chiu). 1.85:1. Import LD/VCD/DVD: Mei Ah. 112 minutes.

Based on Banana Yoshimoto's best seller of the same name (previously adapted in 1990 by Japanese director Yoshimitsu Morita), **Kitchen** tells the story of Aggie, a beautiful young girl who has just lost her grandmother. With her building about to be torn down, she moves in with hairdresser Louie (who looks gay but is straight) and his transsexual mother. Deeply depressed and catatonic, Aggie spends her time staring off into space, and sleeps straight through three days and nights. After that hibernation period, she begins to come out of her shell and starts doing all of the cooking for her hosts. Louie's relationship with flighty girlfriend Jenny comes to an end and he quickly becomes deeply captivated by Aggie, but while she treasures his company, the girl is not interested in having a conventional relationship with him. Desiring solitude again, Aggie moves out, but a tragic event in Louie's life generates in him the same need for support that Aggie once had.

A quiet and contemplative film filled with lovely images, **Kitchen** boasts a premise that, one would think, could only play out as a black comedy. However, director Yim Ho (**Red Dust**) treats the material in a serious, even-handed manner that works surprisingly well. There are a few stylistic indulgences on his part that either fall flat or are at odds with the mood of a particular scene, but Yasuko Tomita (who is granted many flattering close-ups) and Jordan Chan are both highly effective, and the film's simple message about the importance of hopes, dreams, and living life to the fullest comes across nicely. David Cronenberg's version of **The Fly** can be seen playing on a television in one scene.

540. Knockabout

(1979; Golden Harvest/Paragon Films) ★: 8/10. *Jaap ga siu ji* (Cantonese), *Za jia xiao zi* (Mandarin): (roughly) "Jack-of-All-Trades Kid." Cinematographer: Ricky Lau Koon-wai; Music: Chan Chun-chi; Writer: Huang Chik-chin; Producer: Raymond Chow Man-wai; Action Director-Director: Sammo Hung Kam-po. Cast: Yuen Biao (Zippo), Leung Kar-yan (Harpo), Lau Kar-wing (Koo Wu-tai, aka "The Fox"), Sammo Hung Kam-po (The Beggar), Karl Maka (Police Captain), Lee Hoi-sang (Danno), Feng Sing (The Tiger), Peter Chan Lung (Broker), Chung Fat (Monty). 2.35:1. VHS: Tai Seng (No Subtitles). Import VCD: Mei Ah. 92 minutes (Dubbed version).

Yuen Biao made his debut as a leading man in this excellent period kung fu comedy, which follows the popular "student-learning-from-slovenly-master" formula to the letter. Zippo and Harpo are a pair of bumbling conmen who can never seem to get ahead. After unsuccessfully trying to bilk old man Koo out of his bag, the pair are then beaten to a pulp by him. They beg Koo to teach them his martial arts techniques and, after much flattery, he agrees. The pair's kung fu improves remarkably under Koo's instruction, and he has them defeat a couple of his old enemies. However, when Zippo sees Koo kill a policeman, the truth about his master becomes clear: He's really "The Fox," a murderous bandit who has simply been using his two pupils. The Fox then murders Harpo, but Zippo manages to escape. Receiving additional instruction from a martially adept beggar (including the "Garbage Style," an amalgam of several different techniques), Zippo seeks out Koo for a final clash.

The formula may be old hat, but the acrobatics on display are absolutely superb. Yuen is astoundingly good, both in combat and in the involved training sequences, doing multiple somersaults with the sort of grace and ease the rest of us can only dream of. While Hung reserves the spotlight for his old school buddy, he also gives himself a colorful supporting role as the skilful beggar (who has more than a few tricks up his sleeve). During the final duel, he and Yuen face off together against Lau Kar-wing, utilizing the monkey style, and it is a remarkable display of comedy and dexterity. Look fast for Lam Ching-ying as one of the gambling den henchmen. The above character names are from the English dubbed version released in Japan by Pony Video.

541. Kung Fu Cult Master

(1993; Win's Movie Production) ★: 6/10. *Yi tin to lung gei ji moh gaau gaau jue* (Cantonese), *Yi tian tu long ji zhi mo jiao jiao zhu* (Mandarin): "Heaven Slaughter Dragon Story: The Evil School Master." Cinematographer: Bill Wong Chung-bo; Art Director: Jason Mok Siu-kei; Music: Joseph Koo Kar-fai; Producer: Jet Li Lianjie; Action Director: Sammo Hung Kam-po; Writer-Director: Wong Jing. Cast: Jet Li Lianjie (Chang Mo-kei), Chingmy Yau Suk-ching (Siu Chiu), Sharla Cheung Man (Yan So-so/Chao Min), Sammo Hung Kam-po (Chang San-fung), Ngai Sing (Sung Ching-su), Gigi Lai Chi (Chow Chi-yu), Richard Ng Yiu-hon (Wai Yat-siu, The King of Green Bat), Francis Ng Chun-yu (Chang Tsui-san), Leung Kar-yan (Deer Jinx), Cho Wing (Shaolin Monk). 1.85:1. VHS: World Video, Arena/Xenon. LD: World Video. Import LD/VCD/DVD: Mei Ah. 103 minutes. Also known as **Lord of the Wu-tang** (Arena/Xenon title).

In contrast to its wonderfully absurd English title, this lush period fantasy aims high but hits the mark only thanks to the concerted efforts of its excellent cast, who struggle gamely with a screenplay that redefines the term "cluttered." Various martial arts clans are at war over possession of the magical To Lung sword, resulting in the deaths of numerous innocent people. During a clash with two rival clansmen, Chang Tsui-san and his wife Yan So-so are gravely injured and commit suicide. The villains leave their young son Mo-kei alive but greatly debilitated. As he grows into adulthood, Mo-kei is kept alive only by periodic energy transference from his 100 year old *sifu*. Mo-kei is finally able to regain his dignity after he hooks up with the wily handmaiden Siu Chiu (who seeks the equally powerful Yee Tin Sword), and tricks a clan rival into teaching him the "Great Solar Stance." During the course of their adventures, they battle various evil sects and must escape from a booby-trapped tomb. Mo-kei then duels with a Shaolin monk and wins the allegiance of the bloodsucking King of Green Bat, while also uniting the dissenting clans and dealing with the sinister deeds perpetrated by Chao Min, a mysterious Yuen princess who is the spitting image of his late mother.

Attempting to grasp **Kung Fu Cult Master** on the basis of a one paragraph synopsis is not unlike trying to absorb the intricacies of "War and Peace" by reading Cliff Notes. From the opening narration to the final battle, the screen is awash in so many characters, expository passages, magical kung fu stances, betrayals, and stylized duels that the open ending will leave most viewers with equal portions of relief and dread. By comparison, director Wong Jing and star Jet Li's other collaborations—**Last Hero in China** (also 1993) and **The New Legend of Shaolin** (1994)—were able to accomplish similar goals in far less confounding fashion (the fractured English subtitles are only part of the problem here). Yet there are some very appealing performances, to be found amidst the narrative chaos, particularly Chingmy Yau's impishly cute martial maiden (who sports a hair style that is a cross between Princess Leia and Minnie Mouse) and Sharla Cheung Man's mischievous princess. As with all of Wong's fantasies, the production values are superior, but the action scenes suffer from some jumbled, berserk editing which reduces Sammo Hung's action choreography to a confusing barrage of soaring combatants and severed body parts. This remains well worth seeing, but be prepared to watch it twice if you care at all about following the storyline. The Arena/Xenon version has been ineptly shortened by several minutes.

542. Kung Fu Scholar

(1993; In-Gear Film Production) ★: 4/10. *Lun Man-chui lo dim Lau Sin-hoi* (Cantonese), *Lun Wenxu lao dian Liu Xiankai* (Mandarin): "Lun Man-chui old dot Lau Sin-hoi" or "Lun Wenxu old dot Liu Xiankai." Cinematographer: Lau Hung-chuen; Art Director: Chan Kwok-fai; Music: Henry Lai Wan-man; Writers: Lai Man-cheuk, Yip Kai; Producer: Rover Tang Kwong-chow; Action Directors: Benz Kong To-hoi, Tony Poon Kin-kwan, Stephen Tung Wai; Director: Norman Law Man. Cast: Aaron Kwok Fu-shing (Liu Sin-hoi), Dicky Cheung Wai-kin (Lun Man-chui), Vivian Chow Wei-man (Ching-ching), Ng Man-tat (The Headmaster), Leung Kar-yan (Lee Tai-chun), Gordon Lau Kar-fai (His Excellency), Michael Chow Man-kin (Bully), Lee Hoi-sang (Copper Head), Yuen King-tan (Lun's Mother), Kent Cheng Chuk-see (Fat Cat), Gabriel Wong Yat-san (Quiz Contestant). 1.85:1. VHS: Tai Seng. Import LD/VCD: Star Entertainment. 92 minutes.

This mild period fantasy spoof relies heavily on the sort of nonsense wordplay that made Stephen Chiau a star. While much of Chiau's *mo lei tau* shtick does not translate well into English, his films usually have other components that will appeal to Western viewers. However, **Kung Fu Scholar** lacks both Chiau and the inspired zaniness of comparable efforts like **Flying Dagger** and **Holy Weapon**, leaving little of value for English speakers outside of some high flying action. Lun Man-chui, a master of insults and deception, is coerced by his family to become the first Cantonese scholar. Facing off against him for that honor is handsome kung fu master Liu Sin-hoi, who is Lun's equal when it comes to verbal dexterity. The pair put their differences aside to help their teacher, Lee Man-lung, who is actually an undercover agent fleeing from the villainous East Chamber, which seeks to find and murder his master. While the three battle the renegades, their school engages in a quiz competition which will determine scholastic superiority.

As mentioned, there is a good amount of fantasy-oriented martial arts fighting (fans of vintage kung fu will particularly enjoy seeing Shaw Brothers veterans Gordon Lau and Leung Kar-yan going at it), but the inaccessibility of so many of the jokes makes for frustrating viewing. The Chinese title means "Lun Man-chui Fooled Lau Sin-hoi."

Kung Fu Vampire Buster *see* **New Mr. Vampire**

543. Kung Fu vs. Acrobatic

[*sic*] (1990; Win's Movie Production) ★: 6/10. *Moh dang yue loi san jeung* (Cantonese), *Ma deng ru lai shen zhang* (Mandarin): "Modern Buddha Magic Palm." Cinematographer: David Chung Chi-man; Art Director: Jason Mok Siu-kei; Music: Lowell Lo Kwun-ting; Writer: Wong Jing; Producer: Jimmy Heung Wah-sing; Action Director: Yuen Wah; Director: Taylor Wong Tai-loi. Cast: Andy Lau Tak-wah (Charles), Joey Wang Tsu-hsien (Princess Wendy), Nat Chan Pak-cheung (Chi), Mui Siu-wai (Mandy), Yuen Wah (Tin), Cho Tat-wah (Master Koo), Lau Shun (Yim Chun), Lau Chi-wing (Cop with Megaphone), Chen Jing (Lecherous Comrade), Shing Fui-on (Motorcycle Cop). 1.85:1. VHS: World Video. Import LD/VCD: Universe. 98 minutes. Also known as **Kung Fu vs. Acrobats** (UK video title), **Thunderbolt '91**.

Opening with a montage of black and white clips from vintage swordplay fantasies, this pleasant comedy finds bumbling ad men Fai and Chi sent by their boss to a remote area of China. Their mission: locate artifacts to be used in the company's new hair tonic commercial. The pair stumble across a subterranean cavern and inadvertently release the beautiful Princess Wendy and her servant Mandy, who have been in suspended animation since the Yuen Dynasty. The pair take the women to HK, followed closely by Tin, a powerful villain who was also revived when the men trespassed. Fai and Chi (who now have 50 years worth of magical energy in their bodies thanks to a pill they found and ate) use their newfound abilities to foil some loan sharks and fly around without wires in a "Hero Hamburger" commercial. However, even their combined energy is no match for Tin, who has arrived in HK to proclaim his love for Wendy and won't take no for an answer. Fortunately, the monk Yim Chun, who is equally powerful, has also arrived on the scene.

Several sequences are poorly edited but this remains an inspired venture, mixing many traditional spells and practices with some clever fish-out-of-water gags and the usual knockabout slapstick. In a nice touch, Cho Tat-wah (who used to star in this sort of film) puts in an appearance, and the numerous optical effects are presented along the same lines as those seen in the vintage classics. Yuen Wah is a scream as the limber and deadly but decidedly confused villain who believes everything he sees in TV advertisements.

Kung Fu Warlords *see* **The Brave Archer**

544. Kung Fu Zombie

(1982; The Eternal Film H.K. Co.) ★: 3/10. *Wu lung tin si jiu jik gwi* (Cantonese), *Hu long tian shi zhao ji gui* (Mandarin): "Cocky Master Wu Lung." Art Directors: Kwok Wu-lun, Lui Kwun; Music: Not Original; Writer: Bao Kwok-lan; Producer: Pal Ming; Action Director-Director: Hwa I-hung. Cast: Billy Chong Chuen-lee (Pang Fong), Chan Lau, Kong To, Cheng Kar-ying. 2.35:1. VHS: Ocean Shores (Dubbed). 81 minutes.

The title is the best thing about this obnoxious period horror comedy, which is done in by too much lowbrow humor and headache-inducing dubbing. Local ex-con Lu Dai hires a bumbling Mao Shan magician to help him take revenge on Pang Fong, the young man who got him thrown in jail five years earlier. Their plot goes awry, and it is the con who ends up dead. His spirit seeks a new home and forces the priest to find him one: scarfaced killer Lung Yee, who was just killed in battle by Pang. Unfortunately, the soul transformation fails, inadvertently making Lung an invincible, undead killer. Lu's consciousness is instead moved into the body of Pang's father but the ritual is interrupted at its height, leaving him in a state halfway between life and death. The two zombies then join forces to exact revenge on Pang.

The slapstick sequences are sped up to make them look like the silent classics but that doesn't make them funny, and the kung fu battles are so over-edited, they are a pain to watch. Watch **Mr. Vampire** or any of its follow-ups instead. The Cantonese version released on Japanese video runs about 20 minutes longer than this English edition.

Lady Hunter *see* **Madam City Hunter**

545. Lady in Black

(1987; Cinema City Co.) ★: 5/10. *Duet meng gai yan* (Cantonese), *Duo ming jia ren* (Mandarin): "Beautiful Lady Killer." Cinematographer: Henry Chan Chun-kit; Art Director: Kong Chuen; Music: Not Original; Writers: Siu Wai-hung, Law Kam-fai, Edward Leung Yiu-ming; Producer: Dean Shek Tien; Action Director: Phillip Kwok Tsui; Director: Sun Chung. Cast: Brigitte Lin Ching-hsia (Leung May-fung), Tony Leung Kar-fai (Chan Kin-sang), Shih Kien (Grandpa), Phillip Kwok Tsui (Kern), Kwan San (Sang's Boss), Lam Chung (Lam), Wong Kam-kong (Shanghai Wong). 1.85:1. VHS: Tai Seng. Import LD: Golden Cinema City. Import VCD: Mega Star. 92 minutes.

While its unabashedly melodramatic storyline often threatens to descend into outright camp, this overwrought thriller remains compelling, thanks to a superb performance by its star, Brigitte Lin. She plays Leung May-fung, who is convinced by her husband Chan Kin-sang to secretly withdraw $500,000 from her company's bank account. Kin-sang claims that he can turn the money over quickly, thanks to an investment tip, so that May-fung can put it back before anyone is the wiser. In actuality, he uses the cash to pay off his huge gambling debts. His plan to get replacement money from a relative in Thailand fails, and, despondent, he is ready to take his life by jumping off the back of a boat. However, in trying to stop him, it is May-fung who falls overboard. While he could easily save her, Kin-sang lets go of her hand and leaves his wife to drown. The HK police believe his story, and since May's crime has now come to their attention, they rule her death a suicide. However, May-fung has survived, though she is now badly disfigured and cannot speak. Making her way back to HK, she discovers that Kin-sang has now risen through the ranks of his company and become the powerful man he had always dreamed of being. With the help of two close friends, May-fung seeks to put her life back together, but further tragedy ensues.

Filled with overwrought stock music and boasting scenes that would fit right into a second rate horror film, **Lady in Black** amplifies every emotional clash to the nth degree. When the situation calls for it, Lin is able to inject some subtle touches into her performance, helping to increase this less-than-worthy vehicle's artistic validity and, on rare occasions, even making it genuinely gripping.

Lady Reporter *see* **The Blonde Fury**

546. Lady Super Cop

(1993; Perfect Films Production) ★: 4/10. *Lui ngai dong chi geung* (Cantonese), *Nu er dang zi jiang* (Mandarin): "A Woman Should Be Self-Sufficient." Cinematographer: Eric Chu Kwok-fai; Art Director: Daniel Lee Yan-kong; Music: Teddy Robin Kwan; Writers: Ng Siu-ping, Wong Man-yu; Producer: Maybo Chiu Mei-bo; Action Directors: Lam Man-wah, Alan Lo Kwok-wai; Director: Chung Siu-hung. Cast: Carina Lau Kar-ling (Wenine Chang Mi-hua), Teresa Mo Shun-kwan (Lo), May Lo Mei-mei (May), Chin Ho (The Killer), Waise Lee Chi-hung (Edmond), Michael Chan Wai-man (Mechanic), Eric Tsang Chi-wai (Sandworm), Gabriel Wong Yat-san (Nerd in Bar), Henry Fong Ping (Tzeng). 1.85:1. VHS/LD: World Video. 85 minutes.

Carina Lau is miscast in the title role of this dull action thriller (not to be confused with **Super Lady Cop**), which is done in by a hackneyed, threadbare storyline and some jarringly nasty violence. Wenine Chang is a determined policewoman out to nab a brazenly psychotic arms dealer. Along the way, a number of people are horribly killed, including a small-time operator who is tortured to death in a scene that goes far beyond the infamous tooth drilling sequence from **Marathon Man**. When Wenine needlessly puts an informer's life in jeopardy, the girl is tracked down and killed, setting the stage for an inevitable showdown between Wenine and her quarry.

There is really very little else to the scenario, which reaches feature length through the inclusion of Teresa Mo as Lau's ultra-cheap cousin/partner who keeps a running tab on everything imaginable while pulling any scam she can to make a buck. The quality cast, competent action, and Teddy Robin Kwan's score (which includes a cue or two recycled from his **Full Contact** soundtrack) engender some interest but also inadvertently emphasize just how superficial and mechanical the proceedings are. The Chinese title is a play on the local name for **Once Upon a Time in China 2**.

547. Lai Shi, China's Last Eunuch

(1988; Golden Harvest/Bo Ho Films/ Paragon Films) ★: 6/10. *Jung gwok jui hau yat goh taai gaam* (Cantonese), *Zhong guo zui hou yi ge tai jian* (Mandarin): "China's Last Eunuch." Cinematographer: Lau Hung-chuen; Art Director: Eric Lam Sai-kan; Music: Joseph Chan Wing-leung; Writer: Eddie Fong Ling-ching; Producer: Sammo Hung Kam-po; Director: Jacob Cheung Chi-leung. Cast: Max Mok Siu-chung (Liu Lai-shi), Wu Ma (Lord Ting), Irene Wan Pik-ha (Tsou-ti), Sammo Hung Kam-po (Opera Boss), Andy Lau Tak-wah (Han-ming), Lam Ching-ying (Chiang Fu), Pauline Wong Siu-fong (Soo, aka One Stroke), Manfred Wong (Lee), James Tien Chun (General Lei), Anthony Chan Yau (Interpreter for the Japanese), Alfred Cheung Kin-ting (Man on Horse). 1.85:1. VHS: Tai Seng. Import DVD: Universe. 90 minutes. Also known as **China's Last Eunuch** (Tai Seng title).

With the Ching Dynasty approaching an inglorious end at the beginning of the 20th century, poverty-stricken boy Lai-shi admires a parade of eunuchs passing through his village. He reasons that if he becomes a eunuch himself, his family will always have food, and then manages to convince his father to perform the requisite castration. Unfortunately, this occurs right when the Emperor loses his throne, seriously cheapening the role of a eunuch in society. In the intervening ten years, Lai-shi works as a Peking Opera performer but must flee when a general becomes smitten and wants to "marry" him. Lai-shi wants to flee with Tsou-ti, a girl from his village who now works as a prostitute, but she rejects him upon learning about his unusual state. Left with little in the way of alternatives, Lai-shi journeys to the Imperial Palace. Re-christened Chun Lu, he quickly gains the favor of his master, Lord Ting, by showing the sort of loyalty and devotion that has all but vanished. Shortly thereafter, the eunuchs are all ejected from the palace, prompting Lai-shi to find Tsou-ti once again, and the pair start a business together. With the woman's child (fathered by rebel Han-ming, whom Lai-shi believes to be dead), the pair can now be a family; but before their marriage can take place, Han-ming returns home very much alive.

While it is well-acted by all (particularly by Max Mok and Sammo Hung), the film suffers from the sort of deadening inevitability that often plagues historical adaptations, an obstacle that director Jacob Cheung is not able to surmount. More effective than the dramatics is the dark humor that arises from the plight of poor Lai-shi and his fellow outcasts. The sequence in which Lai-shi's less-than-swift father (nicely played by Lam Ching-ying) castrates him goes from casually absurd (with the boy literally begging for him to do it) to frighteningly vivid. Also, like all eunuchs, he must keep his "thing," for unless it is buried with him after death, he will not be complete in the next life. Mok and Irene Wan would go on to appear in a similar film, **Twilight of the Forbidden City**, which suffers from much the same problems as this one.

548. Lam Ah Chun

(1978) ★: 4/10. *Lam A-Jun* (Cantonese), *Lin Yazhen* (Mandarin): "Lam Ah Chun" or "Lin Yazhen." Cinematographer: David Chung Chi-man; Music: Wong Kui-yan; Writers: Ricky Chan Kar-suen, Josephine Siao Fong-fong; Producer: Josephine Siao Fong-fong; Director: Ricky Chan Kar-suen. Cast: Josephine Siao Fong-fong (Lam Ah-chun), Yee Lui (Master Ting), Pau Hon-lam (Elder Ting), David Wu Tai-wai (Barber), Alan Tang Kwong-wing (Handsome Guy). 1.85:1. VHS: Tai Seng. 94 minutes.

This broad comedy (spun off from a TV program) strives for zaniness at every turn but ends up merely being tiresome. Josephine Siao plays the titular character, a tomboyish bookworm whose bumbling causes misery for everyone she encounters. Looking for a job, Ah-chun is sent off into the countryside to a seemingly haunted mansion. After being scared half out of her wits, she learns that it is all a plot by the young master of the household. Previously, he had been cheated by a woman who looked like Ah-chun and now goes around tormenting any girl unfortunate enough to have the same appearance. Ting's father hires Ah-chun to stay around the house and do odd jobs, hoping this will placate his increasingly crazy son. While in the park one day, she stumbles across a dying man and inadvertently becomes involved with gangsters who want a dried duck that is in Ah-chun's possession (there is secret writing on it).

Siao displays some fine physical comedy skills (particularly during an extended chase on roller skates) but this is very uninspired material, unworthy of both her talents and the viewer's time. It was followed by **Lam Ah Chun Blunders Again** and **Plain Jane to the Rescue**, the latter directed by John Woo.

549. Lantern

(1994; Great Man Film Production) ★: 5/10. *Dang lung* (Cantonese), *Deng long* (Mandarin): "Blue Lantern." Cinematographer: Poon Yiu-ming; Music: Patrick Lui Yau-fai; Writer: Brian Chung Wai-hung; Producers; Lau Kar-yung, Lau Yuk-king; Action Director-Director: Lau Kar-yung. Cast: Max Mok Siu-chung (Cheung Fung), Ng Man-tat (Yung), Athena Chu Yan (Fong), Law Koon-lan (Han), Lawrence Ng Kai-wah (Fai), John Ching Tung (Shek). 1.85:1. VHS: Tai Seng. Import LD/VCD: Ocean Shores. 91 minutes.

HK censors have certain restrictions on coarse language and will also not allow certain triad terminology to be used in movies; it is not uncommon to hear such words or phrases loudly bleeped on Cantonese soundtracks. There is so much of this bleeping in **Lantern** that it becomes the cinematic equivalent of a traffic jam and an irritating film to sit through (during censored sequences, the English and Chinese subtitles still sometimes appear; evidently, these lines are alternate dialogue). Various gang hand gestures are even covered with black circles! The Mandarin dubbed version is, presumably, free of these irritants.

As for the film itself, **Lantern** is a standard young rascals drama with a lot of flashy visuals and a thin, uninvolving storyline. Ng Man-tat delivers a fine dramatic performance as a former triad-turned-restaurant owner who hires only ex-cons, with just-released gangster Max Mok being his latest employee. When Ng's son joins a gang and gets into a scrape with a particularly vicious boss, Mok saves his life, and the boy's mother negotiates a settlement for him. However, the lad's inability to stay out of trouble creates discord in his family and soon spells disaster for everyone. Nothing new here.

550. The Last Affair

(1983; The Pearl City Films) ★: 6/10. *Fa sing* (Cantonese), *Hua cheng* (Mandarin): "Flower City." Cinematographer: Bill Wong Chung-bo; Art Director: William Cheung Suk-ping; Music: Law Wing-fai; Writer: Fung Mo; Producer: Vicky Leung Lee Siu-ha; Director: Tony Au Ding-ping. Cast: Carol Cheng Yu-ling (Rebecca Leung Ha-ching), Chow Yun-fat (Kwong-ping), Pat Ha Man-chik (Bing), Season Ma Si-san (Mei-lan). 1.85:1. VHS: Tai Seng. LD: Winson Entertainment. 89 minutes.

The directorial debut of Tony Au Ding-ping, this stylish, aloof drama was shot entirely in Paris and makes excellent use of the local color and scenery. Travelling to France, Ha-ching plans on a month-long visit with her old high school friend Bing, who will be getting married shortly. One evening, while in the subway, she encounters handsome busker Kwong-ping and meets him again soon after at a party for Bing's fiancé. The two begin a relationship that finds Ha-ching infatuated with Kwong-ping but seriously distracted by his flirtatious manner and barely concealed womanizing. When Ha-ching's insensitive husband arrives from HK for a conference, she must decide whether to leave him and stay in France, but the decision is complicated when she catches Kwong-ping and Bing in bed together.

The Last Affair is interesting mainly for the glimpse it provides of Chinese people trying to make a living, often as artists, in this foreign land. As drama, it is less successful, held together mainly by the strong performance of Carol Cheng (who would later make her mark in HK cinema playing a variety of obnoxious and materialistic women in formula comedies) and the director's occasional allusions to Bergman and Fellini. The Chinese title "Flower City" is what Paris is called in that language. Au and Chow Yun-fat would team-up again three years later for the mesmerizing **Dream Lovers**.

551. The Last Blood

(1991; Movie Impact) ★: 7/10. *Ging tin sap yi siu si* (Cantonese), *Jing tian shi er xiao shi* (Mandarin): "12 Hours of Fear." Cinematographer: Jingle Ma Cho-shing; Art Director: Fong Ying; Music: Lau Yee-tat; Producer: Wallace Cheung Kwok-chong; Action Director: Blackie Ko Shou-liang; Director: Wong Jing. Cast: Alan Tam Wing-lun (Lui Tai), Andy Lau Tak-wah (Brother Bee), Eric Tsang Chi-wai (Fatty), Leung Kar-yan (Stone), Chin Ho (Terrorist Leader), May Lo Mei-mei (Ling), Nat Chan Pak-cheung (Ferrai), Jackson Liu Hsiu-hsien (Saporo). 1.85:1. VHS: Tai Seng. Import LD/VCD: Ocean Shores (Poor Subtitles). Also known as **Hard Boiled 2: The Last Blood** (UK video title). 96 minutes.

Lensed in Singapore, this Wong Jing outing has plenty of action and dopey comedy, held together by a remarkably thin plot. It's pleasing if you don't fret about the details (good advice when approaching any Wong Jing picture, for that matter). Interpol agent Lui Tai is part of the team assigned to protect the *Daka* Lama (no point risking a lawsuit over a picture like this, is there?) during his visit to Singapore. Upon his landing in the country, the lama is attacked by "Order of the Death" (*sic*), a faction of Japanese Red Army terrorists disguised as flight attendants(!). He is wounded, along with Ling, the girlfriend of triad leader Brother Bee. Both victims possess the same rare blood type "P," so the

Red Army killers set about murdering the three people in the country who could provide a transfusion. After two of them are dispatched, the remaining prospective donor, Fatty, is sought by both Lui and Bee. When they finally manage to catch up with him, they embark on one very long and very dangerous trip across town to the hospital.

The action choreography is not quite top drawer, but once the shooting starts, it rarely lets up; and it's fun watching Singapore's perennially crime (and chewing gum) free streets, beaches, and shopping plazas get blown to smithereens by machine gun-wielding loonies. While not as exciting, the climactic battle in the hospital anticipates the climax of **Hard Boiled**, which led to this film being passed off as a sequel to the John Woo film in England. As is often the case with HK films, the English subtitles are more amusing than the intentional humor (one cop sells out his buddies to the Japanese because they offered to pay him "ten thousand million U.S."). This is solid no-brainer entertainment from a director who certainly has the formula down pat.

552. Last Hero in China

(1993; Win's Movie Production) ★: 7/10. *Wong Fei-hung chi tit gai dau neung gung* (Cantonese), *Huang Feihong zhi tie ji dou wu gong* (Mandarin): "Wong Fei-hung: Iron Rooster vs. the Centipede." Cinematographer: Jingle Ma Cho-shing; Art Director: Jason Mok Siu-kei; Music: James Wong Jim; Producer: Jet Li Lianjie; Action Director: Yuen Woo-ping; Writer-Director: Wong Jing. Cast: Jet Li Lianjie (Wong Fei-hung), Sharla Cheung Man (Ti Yin-er), Dicky Cheung Wai-kin (So), Leung Kar-yan (Leung Fu), Anita Yuen Wing-yee (Miss Nine), Nat Chan Pak-cheung (Mass Tar Wong), Gordon Lau Kar-fai (Master Liu Hung), Yuen King-tan (Madam), Chung Fat (Thug Using "Monkey Style"). 1.85:1. VHS: World Video, Arena/Xenon. LD: World Video. Import LD/VCD/DVD: Universe. 106 minutes. Also known as **Deadly China Hero** (Arena/Xenon title).

After a falling out with Golden Harvest, Jet Li left the **Once Upon a Time in China** series and brought his trademark "Wong Fei-hung" character over to Win's for this entertaining kung fu comedy. Forced to move Po Chi Lam clinic due to rapidly escalating rental fees, Wong inadvertently relocates next to a brothel run by the like-named pimp "Mass Tar Wong" (a gag that doesn't really survive translation). The great hero is soon at odds with Lui Yat-siu, Canton's openly corrupt police chief, who is a member of the illegal Boxer's Association and in league with a group of evil monks. Operating out of Nun-yan Temple, the monks kidnap young girls and transport them to clients in South Asia. Looking for her missing sister, swordswoman Ti Yin-er sneaks into Nun-yan one evening but is badly injured by Lui. Fei-hung's bumbling pupils, Fu and So, attempt to rescue the captured girls but must be aided by their master. When Lui tries to frame Fei-hung for the havoc in the temple, the magistrate is pressured by local businessmen to let him go. However, one of Lui's confederates poisons Fei-hung, causing him to go deaf.

The climax features one of the wildest kung fu battles you will ever see. At a Lion Dance competition, Lui and his men participate using a giant, flame-shooting metal centipede contraption! Deducing that nature provides the best answer to this situation, Fei-hung adopts the guise of a rooster, complete with a comb, a beak, and metal spurs on his feet! The sight of him flying, kicking, scratching, and clucking is not easily forgotten. Almost all of the martial arts are presented with extensive wire trickery, so those looking for traditional athletics need not bother with this one. However, the action is consistently entertaining and still takes good advantage of Li's talents. In spite of all the silliness surrounding him, Li plays his signature role straight, providing an effective contrast to the broad antics of Dicky Cheung and Nat Chan. While not in the same league as the opening two chapters in the **Once Upon a Time...** series, **Last Hero in China** ranks above the remaining sequels and is diverting period fare. Li and director Wong Jing re-teamed soon after for **Kung Fu Cult Master**.

553. Last Hurrah for Chivalry

(1978; Golden Harvest) ★: 9/10. *Hui hap* (Cantonese), *Hao xia* (Mandarin): "Chivalrous Knights." Cinematographers: Cheung Yiu-cho, Yu Ching; Music: Frankie Chan Fan-kei; Producer: Raymond Chow Man-wai; Action Director: Fung Hark-on; Writer-Director: John Woo Yu-sen. Cast: Damian Lau Chung-yan (Tsing Yi), Wei Pai (Chang), Lau Kong (Kao Pun), Lee Hoi-sang (Pak Chun-tong), Fung Hark-on (Pray). 2.35:1. VHS/LD: Tai Seng (Remastered for the English market; subtitled or dubbed). 107 minutes (Subtitled version), 101 minutes (Dubbed version).

The last of four martial arts films directed to date by John Woo, this is a superior effort which contains elements foreshadowing Woo's later work while also exhibiting the influence of his mentor, the great Shaw Brothers director Chang Cheh. Woo proved himself to be a good pupil: **Last Hurrah for Chivalry** is in the same league as Chang's greatest works and is one of the very best kung fu movies of the '70s. The film opens with the wedding celebration of Master Kao Pun being disrupted by the forces of Pak Chung-tong (Lee, who played the villain in about half of the kung fu movies produced during the '70s), who seeks to retake the villa Kao's father seized from him three years earlier. After most of his guests are murdered, Kao manages to escape and plans to avenge himself by engaging the services of the skilled fighter, "Magnificent Sword" Chang (Wei from **The Five Deadly Venoms**). When his offer is rebuked, Kao hires Pray (Fung, who also served as Martial Arts Director), a swaggering assassin, to goad Chang into a duel. After vanquishing his opponent (in a superbly choreographed clash), Chang develops a fast friendship with alcoholic loner Tsing Yi (Damian Lau in a highly personable performance), who is Chang's equal with a sword. Kao, meanwhile, has deceived Chang into becoming friends with him. After a bogus suicide attempt by Kao, Chang pledges to avenge him by killing Pak. Accompanied by Tsing, Chang must surmount numerous traps and attackers before he and his friend can face off against their target in a chamber lit by hundreds of candles (a justifiably famous confrontation).

Last Hurrah proffers some of the ingredients found in Woo's later work (strong male bonding, the juxtaposition of violence and conversation between different parties in different locations, the mesmerizing use of slow motion during action sequences, etc.), all of which work just as effectively in a period setting. For a picture of this sort, the editing is quite innovative, particularly in the use of transitional left-to-right wipes. The exciting martial arts setpieces are filmed at the standard 24 frames-per-second (instead of 21 f.p.s., as is common on newer films), with minimal wirework and long takes to showcase the performers' abilities. The structure of Woo's screenplay is impeccable, as the proceedings alternate smoothly between tragedy, comedy, and romance, always remaining focused. On a lesser note, the main female characters fall squarely into the "treacherous whore or angelic saviour" stereotypes, something else that Woo inherited from his mentor and has only sought to change in his most recent American films—notably, the preposterous but wonderful **Face/Off** (1997). Ironically, **Last Hurrah** turned out to be prophetically titled: it was one of the last of its breed, supplanted by the New Wave efforts of directors like Tsui Hark and Ching Siu-tung, which opted for flashier technique and a more contemporary take on plot and character. Norman Law Man sings the memorable song that plays under the opening titles.

554. The Last Princess of Manchuria

(1990; Golden Harvest/Paragon Films) ★: 8/10. *Chuen do fong ji* (Cantonese), *Chuan dao fang ji* (Mandarin): "Kawashima Yoshiko." Cinematographer: Jingle Ma Cho-shing; Art Directors: Mok Kwan-kit, Fong Ying; Music: Jim Shum Sing-tak; Writer: Lillian Lee Pik-wah; Producer: Teddy Robin Kwan; Action Director: Fung Hark-on; Director: Eddie Fong Ling-ching. Cast: Anita Mui Yim-fong (Yoshiko Kawashima, aka Kam Bik-fai), Andy Lau Tak-wah (Fook), Derek Yee Tung-sing (Amakasu), Lawrence Ng Kai-wah (Lam), Ken Lo Wai-kwong (Tanaka's Assistant). 1.85:1. VHS: Tai Seng. Import LD: Mei Ah. Import VCD: Mei Ah, Mega Star. 96 minutes. Also known as **Kawashima Yoshiko** (Tai Seng title).

This engrossing, methodically paced drama tells of Yoshiko Kawashima, the 14th princess of Manchuria, whose troubled life paralleled that of Mata Hari in some ways. After spending three years in an arranged marriage to a Mongolian prince, Yoshiko leaves her powerless husband and becomes a willing puppet for the Japanese in order to fulfil her dream of rebuilding the Manchu dynasty. Her murderous persecution of anti-Japanese protesters leads to numerous attempts on her life and her eventual downfall at the end of World War II, when she is tried in Chinese court as a traitor.

Intelligently scripted by novelist Lillian Lee and soberly directed, the film offers a plumb role for Anita Mui that almost seems based on her pop star persona, alternating as it does between male and female. Mui is utterly convincing, as is Andy Lau as a Peking Opera performer/rebel that Kawashima harbors great affection for. Utilizing battered and tinted newsreel footage as authentic establishing shots, the production also makes excellent use of regal locations in Beijing, Chang-chun, Harbin, Shanghai, Tianjin, Japan, and Macau. Two different endings are in circulation. In one, Kawashima is executed; in the other, the execution is performed using blanks and she escapes overseas. The latter version includes a song by Mui that is heard during these sequences. Oddly, the Mei Ah laserdisc includes the Chinese lyrics for the song onscreen but it is not heard on the Cantonese soundtrack, and the disc concludes with the abbreviated ending.

555. Last Romance

(1988; Far-Sun Film Co.) ★: 6/10. *Lau gam sui yuet* (Cantonese), *Liu jin sui yue* (Mandarin): "Flow Golden Years." Cinematographer: Jingle Ma Cho-shing; Art Director: Yim Chim-lan; Music: Danny Chung Teng-yat; Producer: Lam Tsui; Writer-Director: Yeung Fan. Cast: Cherie Chung Cho-hung (Chu So-so), Maggie Cheung Man-yuk (Nancy Cheung), Tang Ho-kwong (Sung Chia-ming), Kenneth Tsang Kong (Li Chih-cheng), Lau Siu-ming (Nancy's Father), Michael Lai Siu-tin (Tseng), Yung Sai-kit (Philip Hsieh). 1.85:1. VHS: Tai Seng. Import LD: Mei Ah. 105 minutes.

First meeting in school, Chu So-so and Nancy quickly become inseparable friends who spend all of their time together. One day they encounter Sung Chia-ming, a writer of Chinese and Japanese descent, who tags along with them and plans to use the girls in a story. As they grow older, Nancy and So-so take different paths in life: Nancy goes off to university while So-so becomes a nightclub hostess. The latter fulfils her dream of security, while Nancy meets up with Chia-ming, who has been out of contact for several years but now works in HK as a reporter. It is clear to Nancy that Chia-ming harbors great affection for So-so but she intentionally keeps the two apart, due to her own growing love for the man. However, with So-so about to enter into a loveless marriage, Nancy has a change of heart and brings the two back together. Regardless, So-so goes ahead with the wedding and Chia-ming moves to Japan. When her relationship disintegrates, So-so tracks down Chia-ming, while Nancy finds herself increasingly jealous and unhappy with her lot in life.

Coming from a background in professional photography, it is not surprising that director Yeung Fan has a keen eye for detail and compositions. He has cinematographer Jingle Ma give the proceedings a misty, soft-focus look that differs from the style customarily adopted by glossy soap operas. At its core, the film is quite reminiscent of the 1970s Taiwanese melodramas adapted from the works of popular female romantic novelist Qiong Yao (Brigitte Lin, Chin Han, and Charlie Chin are among those who regularly starred in these films). With its beautiful backdrops and lovely leads helping to take one's mind off the various narrative weaknesses, **Last Romance** is very much in the same spirit and is a moderately successful HK counterpart. Acting honors go to Kenneth Tsang, who is quite good in an atypical role as a middle-aged admirer of So-so who looks out for her best interests, even though he knows they will never be together.

556. Last Song in Paris

(1986; Rical Film Production Co.) ★: 4/10. *Ngau jin* (Cantonese), *Ou ran* (Mandarin): "Accidentally." Cinematographer: Li Hsin-yeh; Art Director: Eric Lam Yau-sang; Music: Tsui Yat-kan; Writer-Director: Chor Yuen. Cast: Leslie Cheung Kwok-wing (Louie), Anita Mui Yim-fong (Anita Chou), Cecilia Yip Tung (Yuan Yu-shih), Joey Wang Tsu-hsien (Julia), Paul Chu Kong (Kent), Tin Cheng (Hsu), Charlie Cho Cha-lei (Charles). 1.85:1. VHS: J & M Chevalier (Poor Subtitles). 86 minutes.

This far-fetched, heavy-handed drama teams up Leslie Cheung and Anita Mui, two of the most popular singers in the history of Cantopop. Spoiled singing sensation Louie sleeps with dancer Anita one evening and learns of her dream to be a singer. During his next concert, he brings the girl up on stage and has her do a number. Anita is an instant smash, but it is love at first sight for Louie when he gets an eyeful of the beautiful Julia. There is one major problem, however: Julia is dating Louie's father! Disgusted by the situation, Louie cancels all of his concert dates and flees to Paris. After drinking away his money, a sickly Louie is saved one evening by French-speaking Vietnamese immigrant Yuan Yu-shih. Pretending to be a refugee, Louie gets a job as a cook at the girl's restaurant. The pair fall in love and Yu-shih becomes pregnant, but an old wound she sustained during the war threatens her health. The situation takes on a new wrinkle when Anita appears on the scene, still carrying a torch for Louie.

There is enough corny melodrama here for ten movies, but veteran director Chor Yuen and the leads manage to keep this hackneyed material marginally entertaining, and the plethora of beautiful location footage certainly doesn't hurt either. Still, this is definitely a case where less would have been more. Fans of Cheung and Mui will definitely want to track this down, as it includes a great deal of concert footage and provides English translations for the song lyrics.

557. Laughing Times

(1981; Cinema City Co.) ★: 2/10. *Waat kai si doi* (Cantonese), *Hua ji shi dai* (Mandarin): "Comic Times." Cinematographer: Ho Ming; Art Director: Yuen Tai-yung; Music: Frankie Chan Fan-kei; Producer: Karl Maka; Writer-Director: John Woo Yu-sen. Cast: Dean Shek Tien (The Tramp), Karl Maka (Master Ting), Wu Ma (The Drunk), Lee Hoi-sang (Thug), Wong Yat-fei (Man Whose Hair Gets Sheered), Raymond Wong Pak-ming (Man Eating Bananas). 1.85:1. VHS: Tai Seng. Import VCD: Mega Star. 101 minutes.

This early John Woo film is a showcase for Dean Shek and his Charlie Chaplin imitation. Shek's Little Tramp (who wheezes like Lou Costello when excited) goes through all the familiar paces: stealing food, falling for a pretty, equally underprivileged girl, evading the police, taking up with a child sidekick (modelled after Jackie Coogan in **The Kid**), wreaking havoc on a series of menial jobs, trying to scam welfare, etc. Eventually, a plot emerges when the child and the girl are snatched by the evil Master Ting, who plans on selling them into slavery.

This was Woo's first film for Cinema City but he made it while still under contract to Golden Harvest. Hence, he is credited here with the Chinese pseudonym "Wu Shang-fei." Shek has all of Chaplin's mannerisms down to a tee, and Woo even resorts to undercranking the camera at times in order to replicate the fast, jerky look silent films have when they are projected at the wrong speed. While he and Shek may be able to duplicate the mood and a couple of the gags, **Laughing Times** has none of the heart that distinguished Chaplin's work from most of his contemporaries; Shek's attempts at pathos fail miserably. Completely devoid of laughs, the film's inherent curiosity value vanishes after just a few minutes, making this strictly for Woo completists. The soundtrack includes music lifted from John Williams' score for **1941**. The onscreen English title is simply **Laughing Time**.

558. The Law Enforcer

(1986; Always Good Film Co.) ★: 5/10. *Wong ga fan* (Cantonese), *Huang jia fan* (Mandarin): "Royal Rice." Cinematographer: Rudolf Chiu Wai-kei; Art Director: Cheung Yan-keung; Music: Phil Chan Fei-lap; Producer: Frankie Chan Fan-kei; Action Director: Law Hau-keung; Writer-Director: Danny Lee Sau-yin. Cast: Danny Lee Sau-yin (Chen), Mak Tsui-han (Anna Yeh), Parkman Wong Pak-man (Wen), Lung Ming-yan (Kent), Ricky Yee Fan-wai (Tiger), Shing Fui-on (Bad Brain). 1.85:1. VHS: Tai Seng. Import LD: Golden Cinema City. Import DVD: Universe. 97 minutes.

This thoroughly routine Danny Lee police thriller concerns Kent, a dedicated officer who turns vigilante after a diagnosis of epilepsy requires him to hand in his gun. Interrupting an attempted robbery/rape, Kent saves Anna Yeh from her attackers, and when police ask for a description of her benefactor, the grateful woman pretends that she cannot identify him. When Kent later saves a taxi driver from a beating at the hands of mob enforcer "Bad Brain," he is spotted by another cop and identified. When the gangster tries to take revenge, Kent escapes injury but Anna is shot and one of Kent's fellow officers is killed. Kent relentlessly tracks Bad Brain, discovering that he and his cohorts are pulling a series of armoured car robberies.

The final reel offers a good amount of action and suspense, but there is little else of note here. Ben Lam Kwok-bun and Ken Lo Wai-kwong have supporting roles.

559. Law on the Brink

(1994; Universe Film Productions Co.) ★: 2/10. *Lau man lut si* (Cantonese), *Liu mang lu shi* (Mandarin): "Gangster Lawyer." Cinematographer: Law Tat-shing; Music: John Wong Sai-cheung; Writers: Johnny Lee King-kai, Lee Man-choi, Chan Tung-chuen; Producer: Maybo Chiu Mei-bo; Action Director-Director: Chan Tung-chuen. Cast: Ray Lui Leung-wai (Shen Hwa-min), Veronica Yip Yuk-hing (Tieh-pin), Lam Wai (Wu Bin-chin), Elvis Tsui Kam-kong (Hitman). 1.85:1. VHS: Tai Seng. Import LD/VCD: Universe. 89 minutes.

There is a good premise at the heart of this Ray Lui vehicle, but it is undone by poor writing and goofy humor. When his little brother is accused of murder, slick HK barrister Shen Hwa-min travels to China to clear him. While trying to find his sibling (who is still on the run from the police), Shen must dodge female undercover agent Tieh-pin and a hitman employed by the victim's father. In the meantime, rumpled but dedicated Mainland defense lawyer Wu Bin-chin searches for the girl who witnessed the incident in order to convince her to testify.

Instead of a courtroom drama emphasizing the differences between HK and communist law, the first two-thirds is a virtually non-stop barrage of chase scenes, none of which are particularly exciting or well done. The film finally gets back on track in the last half hour, but the race against time to find the murder weapon is handled in such a lackadaisical fashion that it is no more engrossing than that which preceded it. The climax is particularly weak. While Veronica Yip is a talented actress who can play a variety of characters, she is not convincing as a Mainland cop.

560. Law with Two Phases

(1984; Always Good Film Co.) ★: 7/10. *Gung buk* (Cantonese), *Gong pu* (Mandarin): "Public Servant." Cinematographer: Chan Siu-ming; Art Director: Wong Chui-man; Music: Wai Lam; Producer: Frankie Chan Fan-kei; Action Director: Wong Siu-man; Writer-Director: Danny Lee Sau-yin. Cast: Danny Lee Sau-yin (B), Eddie Chan (Yip Che-kit), Parkman Wong Pak-man (Blacky), Tai Po (Druggy Shing). 1.85:1. VHS: Tai Seng. Import VCD: Mega Star. Import DVD: Universe. 95 minutes.

Danny Lee captured Best Actor honors for his performance in this popular police drama. Dedicated cop "B" is respected by both his coworkers and the various gang members and informants he deals with. Breaking in Yip Che-kit, his new and rather green partner, B cracks a case involving some potential gas station robbers, thanks to a tip from his informant. However, while pursuing triad drug dealer Blacky, who is suspected of murder, B accidentally shoots and kills a little boy. His only hope is that he and Yip can apprehend Blacky, whose testimony would prove that B was indeed firing at him and not the child.

While some aspects of the story seem overly familiar now, this remains an efficient and consistently interesting production. Lee gives a solid performance, and it is interesting to see the actor settling into the persona that would serve him so well over the next decade. The film is also noteworthy for establishing the moral stance those future police thrillers would routinely adopt (for example: Yip becomes a "better" cop when, like B, he starts bending the rules by beating suspects and framing them). Co-star "Eddie Chan" is more commonly known as Ngai Dik. The Chinese title of 1995's **City Cop** tries to pass it off as a sequel to this film.

561. Lawyer Lawyer

(1997; Brilliant Idea Group) ★: 6/10. *Suen sei cho* (Cantonese), *Suan si cao* (Mandarin): "Calculate Death Grass." Cinematographer: Cheung Man-bo; Art Director: Jason Mok Siu-kei; Music: Lincoln Lo Kin; Writers: Joe Ma Wai-ho, Wong Ho-wah; Producer: Li Kuo-hsing; Director: Joe Ma Wai-ho. Cast: Stephen Chiau Sing-chi (Chan Mon-gut), Eric Kot Man-fai (Ho Foon), Bowie Lam Bo-yee (Ho), Karen Mok Man-wai (Wu-man), Chingmy Yau Suk-ching (Lotus Shui), Paul Fonoroff (The Judge), Vincent Kok Tak-chiu (Li), Simon Lui Yu-yeung (Restaurant Owner), Cheung Tat-ming (Restaurant Owner), Law Kar-ying (Fong Tong-ken), Spencer Lam Sheung-yee (Priest), Bobby Yip King-sang (Juror). 1.85:1. VHS/LD: Tai Seng. Import LD/VCD/DVD: Mei Ah. 85 minutes.

Carrying on the tradition of Stephen Chiau's **Justice, My Foot** and **Hail the Judge**, this period comedy (set in 1899) casts him as Chan, a brilliant lawyer and practical joke expert known as the "King of

Brain-trusters." The butt of his jokes is inevitably Foon, his dopey but hopelessly loyal assistant. One day, after decades of abuse, Foon decides to strike out on his own and heads for HK (which has just been taken over by the British). When he is framed for a murder, Chan agrees to help him, but it will not be easy to get away with his unorthodox methods in a British court of law. When Chan is inevitably charged with contempt of court, his wife, Wu-man, must take over Foon's defense.

Chiau is up to his usual form and Karen Mok does an excellent job as straightwoman (there is a genuinely touching scene in which her lonely character tells Chiau that the English phrase "I Love You" means something else, so that he will express his affections to her more often), but there are too many limp scatological gags even by Chiau's standards and the loophole Chan uses to win the trial is disappointingly obvious. Also, Eric Kot's limitations as a comedian become glaringly obvious any time that he and Chiau share a scene. Law Kar-ying has an amusing cameo as Fong Tong-ken, the conniving lawyer played by Lawrence Ng Kai-wah in **Hail the Judge**. The subtitle translation here is better than most Chiau movies, but when the prosecutor mentions in court that he has been reading the famous sex novel *Yuk Po Tuen*, the English subs say "A Tale of Two Cities," which isn't close to being the same thing! The English title is a clever reference to Jim Carrey's **Liar Liar**, while the Chinese title is a euphemism meaning someone who is very stingy.

562. Lee Rock

(1991; Win's Movie Production) ★: 7/10. *Ng yi taam jeung Lui Lok juen* (Cantonese), *Wu yi tan zhang Lei Luo zhuan* (Mandarin): "The Five Million Dollar Detective: The Story of Chief Lui Lok." Cinematographers: Gigo Lee Chi-hang, Andrew Lau Wai-keung; Art Director: Jason Mok Siu-kei; Music: Joseph Chow Kung-shing; Writer: Chan Man-keung; Producers: Jimmy Heung Wah-sing, Wong Jing; Action Directors: Corey Yuen Kwai, Wong Kwan; Director: Lawrence Ah Mon. Cast: Andy Lau Tak-wah (Lee Rock), Sharla Cheung Man (Pak Yu-shun), Kwan Hoi-shan (Uncle), Paul Chun Pui (Ngan), Ng Man-tat (Piggy), Chingmy Yau Suk-ching (Lee's Girlfriend), Lung Fong (Master Snake), Michael Chan Wai-man (King Crab), James Tien Chun (Pak), Wong Yat-fei (The Father of Lee's Girlfriend), Eddy Ko Hung (Police Instructor), William Ho Kar-kui (Triad), Jamie Luk Kim-ming (Ma). 1.85:1. VHS: Tai Seng. Import LD/VCD/DVD: Mei Ah. 125 minutes.

Beginning in 1949 and spanning two decades, this lushly produced, two part drama covers the life of celebrated real-life police officer Lui Lok (anglicized to "Lee Rock" in the subtitles). Andy Lau plays Lee who, upon joining the force, refuses the payoffs regularly taken by his fellow officers. He becomes friends with Uncle, a crusty old inspector who believes it is right to accept bribes because, "If you don't take the money, then someone else will." Lee hopes to marry his sweetheart, but her low-class father demands a dowry of $50,000. Desperate for money, Lee gets into a scrape with Snake, a gangster running an illegal betting parlor, when the cop forcibly tries to sell him Uncle's revolver. A fight ensues and Lee is badly beaten. On the basis of this incident, the young officer's attitude changes: He begins accepting kickbacks, reasoning that no one will ever respect him without money. At a birthday celebration for Uncle, Lee insults the swaggering but powerful Officer Ngan, who has his men burn down the young cop's house in retribution. Lee soon meets and falls for tough girl Pak Yu-shun, the daughter of a powerful triad leader; after a whirlwind courtship, the two decide to marry. Following another confrontation with Ngan, Uncle leaves the force and Lee gets transferred out into the sticks, but the latter is soon able to get back to the city, thanks to the influence of his new father-in-law. When Snake takes Uncle hostage over a gambling debt owed by the son of the old man's employer, Lee is able to save his life and humiliate Ngan in the process. The British officers running the force are in the process of selecting a new Chief Detective for the district, with both Ngan and Lee in the running for the position. Ngan strikes a deal with some of the local triad leaders to secure the post, knowing what a windfall it will be for him to control the pier (and its steady flow of narcotics). However, Lee has some tricks up his sleeve that just may turn the tide in his favor.

Beautifully photographed on picturesque locations and filled with authentic period detail, **Lee Rock** covers familiar territory but does so with such elegance and style that it remains engrossing all the same. Paul Chun has a field day in the film's most colorful role (which he would essentially reprise a year later in **Arrest the Restless**), and Andy Lau is able to hold his own with his more experienced co-stars. Unfortunately, the English translation is very poor, muddling the plot, ignoring the transitional intertitles, and not even bothering to assign names to some of the major characters. Consequently, only the most patient of Western viewers will derive much pleasure from the storyline and characterizations, though it is certainly worth the effort of trying. The ending is left open for **Lee Rock II**, which was shot back-to-back and opened in theaters on the heels of this entry.

563. Lee Rock II

(1991; Win's Movie Production) ★: 5/10. *Ng yi taam jeung Lui Lok juen ji yi* (Cantonese), *Wu yi tan zhang Lei Luo zhuan zhi er* (Mandarin): "The Five Million Dollar Detective: The Story of Chief Lui Lok Two." Cinematographers: Gigo Lee Chi-hang, Andrew Lau Wai-keung; Art Director: Jason Mok Siu-kei; Music: Joseph Chow Kung-shing; Writer: Chan Man-keung; Producer: Jimmy Heung Wah-sing, Wong Jing; Action Directors: Corey Yuen Kwai, Kong Chi-leung; Director: Lawrence Ah Mon. Cast: Andy Lau Tak-wah (Lee Rock), Sharla Cheung Man (Hsiun), Aaron Kwok Fu-shing (Bill Lee Chun-hsien), Chingmy Yau Suk-ching (Har), Ng Man-tat (Lio), Paul Chun Pui (Ngan Tung), James Tien Chun (Pak), Michael Chan Wai-man (King Crab), Charles Heung Wah-keung (Lam Kung), Peter Chan Lung (Fire Dragon). 1.85:1. VHS: Tai Seng. Import LD/VCD: Mei Ah (Subtitles?). Import DVD: Mei Ah (No Subtitles). 120 minutes.

Lee Rock concluded with the arrival of Lee's old girlfriend, Har (who was not given a name in the first film), from China. As **Lee Rock II** opens, she reveals that he is the father of her little boy but soon flees with the child, feeling that her return will destroy Lee's marriage to Hsiun (called "Shun" last time out). Ngan is able to secure the post of Chief Detective for the district but Lee outsmarts him again by having a new, higher ranking post created for himself. When Ngan conspires with the druglord King Crab to have his nemesis murdered, the plan fails when Hsiun takes the bullet in Lee's place. As the 1970s roll around, Lee's highly profitable empire of corruption is threatened by a new British superior, the creation of the I.C.A.C. (Internal Committee Against Corruption) unit, and an entirely new structure of command. Sensing that his time is up, Lee announces his retirement, but Ngan is not finished with him yet.

No one would call the original film high art, but the sequel proceeds along such predictable lines that you just know it will take a shootout to tie up all of the loose ends (unfortunately, it's not even a well-staged shootout). In addition to the lack of creativity, the screenplay asks one to believe that Lee and Har's child would turn out to be a senior officer in the anti-corruption investigation of his father. While quite good the last time out, Andy Lau is just not convincing as Lee in his later years. With silver tinted hair that changes in practically every other scene and a limited repertoire of grimaces and smirks, Lau comes perilously close to self-parody; the film would have been better served had an older actor taken up the part for the last decade or so of the story. The subtitle translation is slightly improved here, but some of the returning characters now have different names, and the various intertitles are still presented in Chinese only. The following year's **Arrest the Restless**, from much of the same team, is a prequel to **Lee Rock II** and concentrates on Charles Heung Wah-keung's "Lam Kung" character, another real-life HK cop.

564. Legacy of Rage

(1986; D & B Films Co.) ★: 6/10. *Lung joi gong woo* (Cantonese), *Long zai jiang hu* (Mandarin): "Dragon All Over the Country." Cinematographer: Jimmy Chan Hau-ming; Art Director: Tony Au Ding-ping; Music: Richard Yuen Cheuk-fan; Writers: Clifton Ko Chi-sum, Raymond Fung Sai-hung; Producers: John Sham Kin-fun, Linda Kuk Mei-lai; Action Director: Mang Hoi; Director: Ronny Yu Yan-tai. Cast: Brandon Lee (Brandon Ma), Michael Wong Man-tak (Michael), Regina Kent (May), Michael Chan Wai-man (Yee), Mang Hoi (Hoi), Ku Feng (Prison Guard), Bolo Yeung (Thug), Lam Chung (Sharky Kau), Shing Fui-on (Fool), Che-Kirk Wong Chi-keung (Inspector Lau), Ng Man-tat (Captain of the Guards), Yip Wing-cho (Brandon's Boss). Dolby Digital (DVD Only). 1.85:1. VHS/LD: Tai Seng (Remastered for the English market; subtitled or dubbed). Import LD: Mei Ah. Import VCD: Mega Star. Import DVD: Universe. 87 minutes.

Fans of Brandon Lee should make a point of seeing this D & B Films actioner, the late actor's only HK film. Lee (whose real voice is not heard in any version) plays an honest but somewhat slow-witted young man whose gangster "friend" (Michael Wong) frames him for the murder of a corrupt, blackmailing narcotics officer. While serving an eight year prison sentence, he befriends a wily gunrunner (Mang Hoi), who joins forces with him upon their release for a final assault on the villain's estate.

Legacy of Rage proceeds much along the same lines as Lee's later Hollywood efforts, **Showdown in Little Tokyo** (1991) and **Rapid Fire** (1992), with the formula plot periodically allowing its star to engage in methodically staged action setpieces (the most memorable being an early hand-to-hand skirmish with Bolo Yeung, who appeared with Lee's father in **Enter the Dragon**). The requisite stock characters are all present and accounted for: the doomed girlfriend (Kan Wai-ling, billed under her English name, Regina Kent), the benevolent prison guard (Shaw Brothers veteran Ku Feng), the fatherly boss, the young son he didn't know he had, etc. Lee does well enough with this hackneyed material but, sadly, it wouldn't be until his final performance in **The Crow** (1994) that he really exhibited the talent and presence to be more than just another action hero. Similarly, genre conventions also bind director Ronny Yu, giving him few chances to display the proficiency that would be so evident throughout **The Bride with White Hair**. Apparently influenced by John Woo's **A Better Tomorrow** (released in August of 1986, four months before **Legacy**), Yu stages the bullet-riddled finale along much the same lines, as did every other HK gangster flick until the cycle finally ran its course in the early '90s.

565. Legal Innocence

(1993) ★: 6/10. *Yung si kei on* (Cantonese), *Rong shi qi an* (Mandarin): "Dissolve Corpse Strange Case." Cinematographer: Sung Kong; Art Director: Eric Lam Yau-sang; Music: Chow Kam-wing; Writers: Chung Kai-cheung, Eric Lam Kei-to, Chung Ngoi-fung; Producers: Cha Chuen-yee, Chung Kai-cheung; Director: Cha Chuen-yee. Cast: Francis Ng Chun-yu (Patrick Wong), Cecilia Yip Tung (Shirley Cheng), Anthony Wong Chau-sang (Lau), Ivy Leung Si-man (Kitty Yuen), Paul Chun Pui (Prosecutor). VHS: Tai Seng (Poor Subtitles). Import LD/VCD: Ocean Shores (Poor Subtitles). 95 minutes.

Based on a real-life murder case, this Category III drama takes a somewhat more sober approach than **Remains of a Woman**, another adaptation of the same incident which hit theaters four months later. Troubled social worker Shirley seeks to cure the severe depression of Kitty, a client in jail for murder. Kitty tried to commit suicide when her lover, Patrick (who is also incarcerated), did not reply to her letters. Shirley (who is vulnerable because of a bad relationship) visits Patrick on death row and immediately falls under his spell. Through flashbacks, we learn that Patrick was also openly seeing a second woman named Brenda, whom the police later find dismembered and partially dissolved in a trunk filled with acid. Patrick claims to have found religion and, after several more visits, Shirley agrees to marry him. When a retrial of the case is called, Patrick is found innocent, but thanks to a police detective who worked on the original case, the viewer is left feeling otherwise.

Cecilia Yip and Francis Ng are both very good here, and it is the quality of their work that helps the film over some awkward, melodramatic stretches, misjudged comic relief, and one thoroughly unforgivable lapse in logic (we are supposed to believe that a videotape, featuring Patrick and the two women, was not checked by police simply because it was labelled "L.A. Law"). Well directed by the talented but uneven Cha Chuen-yee (**Once Upon a Time in a Triad Society 1 & 2**) and atmospherically scored, **Legal Innocence** makes for compelling, but not entirely satisfying, viewing.

566. Legend of a Fighter

(1982; Seasonal Film Corporation) ★: 8/10. *Fok Yuen-gap* (Cantonese), *Huo Yuanjia* (Mandarin): "Fok Yuen-gap" (character's name in Cantonese) or "Huo Yuanjia" (character's name in Mandarin). Cinematographer: Michael Ma Koon-wah; Art Director: Ting Yuen-tai; Music: Chow Fook-leung; Writer: Peace Writing Team; Producer: Ng See-yuen; Action Director: Yuen Brothers; Director: Yuen Woo-ping. Cast: Leung Kar-yan (Huo Yuen-chia as a Man), Yasuaki Kurota (Chiang Ho-shan), Phillip Ko Fei (Master Fok), Yuen Yat-chor (Huo Yuen-chia as a Youth), Yuen Cheung-yan (Kung Fu Master on Ship), Fung Hark-on (White Man's Lackey). 2.35:1. VHS: World Video (Poor Subtitles?). Import LD: Far East Music. Import VCD: Mei Ah (Poor Subtitles?). 95 minutes.

His revered father having branded him a weakling and forbidden him from learning the family's secret martial arts style, Huo Yuen-chia seems doomed to suffer beatings and humiliation for the rest of his days. To make matters worse, the lad's new teacher, Chiang Ho-shan, turns out to be another in a long line of spies out to steal the Huo technique...or is he? While he constantly sneaks a peak at Master Huo's secret training sessions, he also agrees to teach Yuen-chia kung fu. Chiang (a Japanese master in China to learn more about the local styles) eventually heads home but leaves Yuen-chia with an instruction manual that will teach him everything else he needs to know. As the years pass, Yuen-chia's technique improves dramatically and he even ends up saving his father's life one day. His reputation leads to many challenges, including one from a Japanese fighter. The outcome of this match leads Yuen-chia to encounter Chiang once more, this time under very different circumstances from their last meeting.

Another terrific kung fu film from Yuen Woo-ping, **Legend of a Fighter** incorporates many of the narrative devices and character types found throughout this genre, but thanks to a stately presentation, they transcend stereotype, making this an "old school" film in the best sense of the term. The fight sequences and training techniques are up to the Yuen clan's usual high standards, and excellent work by both Leung Kar-yan and Yasuaki Kurota helps to keep the jingoism of the storyline from overwhelming the emotional conflicts.

The Legend of Fong Sai Yuk *see* **Fong Sai-yuk**
The Legend of Fong Sai Yuk II *see* **Fong Sai-yuk II**

567. Legend of the Dragon

(1991; Magnum) ★: 7/10. *Lung dik chuen yan* (Cantonese), *Long de chuan ren* (Mandarin): "Descendent of the Dragon." Cinematographer: Abdul M. Rumjahn; Art Director: Horace Ma Kwong-wing; Music: Phil Chan Fei-lap; Writer: Law Kam-fai; Action Directors: Corey Yuen Kwai, Yuen Wah; Producer-Director: Danny Lee Sau-yin. Cast: Stephen Chiau Sing-chi (Chow Siu-lung), Leung Kar-yan (Yun), Teresa Mo Shun-kwan (Mo), Yuen Wah (Master Chow Fei-hung), Lung Fong (Loan Shark), Shing Fui on (Hood with Glasses), Amy Yip Chi-mei (Boutique Owner), Jimmy White (Himself), Corey Yuen Kwai (Cop), Lee Hoi-sang (Blindman), Ricky Yee Fan-wai (Hood). 1.85:1. VHS: Tai Seng. Import LD: Golden Cinema City. Import VCD/DVD: Universe. 96 minutes.

In **All for the Winner**, Stephen Chiau hit it big as a Mainlander with powers that made him a master at cards. Here he plays Lung, a peasant from Tai O (an island about ninety minutes from HK by ferry) who is an ace at snooker. Lung is the lazy but likeable son of the esteemed kung fu master Chow Fei-hung, the proud owner of a large tract of land on Tai O. Despite numerous lucrative offers, Fei-hung refuses to sell out to developers, as the property has been in the Chow family for centuries. Yun, an old friend of the master who owes a million dollars to a loan shark, turns up on the island with the intention of staying until the coast is clear back home. After scamming $5000 from Fei-hung, he agrees to take Lung on his first trip to HK. While there, Lung's mastery of billiards saves Yun from a potentially ugly situation, so the conman enters the naive boy in numerous matches. Lung wins them all, prompting Yun's loan shark to come up with a plan: Yun will convince Fei-hung to put up the deed to his land as collateral in a match pitting Lung against world champion Jimmy White. Viewing the contest as a way for the Chinese people to prove their mastery over foreigners, Chow's father agrees. When Lung loses the match, the gangsters move in, forcing everyone from their homes. After much despair, it is decided that the remainder of the island's properties will be risked in an all or nothing rematch.

The film successfully follows the dependable *do sing* (Saint of Gamblers) formula to the letter, even casting Lung Fong (the villain in practically every gambling film of the period) as the heavy. Chiau's comedic skills are sharp, and he handles himself quite impressively during the martial arts sequences. Yuen Wah is an inspired choice to play his stern dad (who is really a marshmallow on the inside), and Teresa Mo is amusing in a less-than-flattering role as Master Chow's powerful but timid female student who has a major crush on Lung. *Legend of the Dragon* is heartily recommended to both general audiences and seasoned Stephen Chiau fans.

568. Legend of the Drunken Tiger

(1992; Chi Film Production Co./ Filmswell International) ★: 3/10. *Jui hap hang* (Cantonese), *Zui xia xing* (Mandarin): "Actions of the Drunken Hero." Cinematographer: Tommy Tong; Music: Wilson Chow; Writer: Cindy Lee; Producer: Richard Chi; Director: Robert Tai. Cast: Kara Hui Ying-hung (Leela), Ku Feng (Rong Lu), Chan Sze-man, Wang Chen-chao. 1.85:1. VHS/DVD: Tai Seng (Dubbed). 93 minutes.

This low budget Taiwanese yarn looks to have time-warped in from the '70s and may appeal to fans who prefer old-style martial arts fare, but even they will have to be willing to cut it a lot of slack. At the end of the 19th century, the Ching Dynasty's forces are ruthlessly cracking down on any and all rebellious factions instead of using their resources to effectively combat foreign invaders. San, a master of drunken style kung fu, is the rebels' greatest asset, though in his perpetually inebriated state, he is not exactly reliable or easily managed. With his betrothed bride Leela (also an excellent fighter) at his side, San battles both the Chings and the Caucasian plunderers.

The comedy is very broad and the storyline jumps around with little rhyme, reason, or continuity, suggesting that big chunks of the film have been edited out. Still, it is good to see Shaw Brothers favorite Kara Hui back in a period effort rather than wasting her talents in yet another gangster actioner. Attractive locales and nice production design are also assets, but the lack of funds results in a number of unintentional laughs (many of the invaders from countries like Russia and America are played by Chinese extras in Harpo Marx-style wigs, while the few caucasians look more like hardware store clerks than soldiers), and the wire-enhanced stunts are ineptly executed. Character names above are from the dubbed version.

Legend of the God of Gamblers *see* **God of Gamblers 3: The Early Stage**
The Legend of the Golden Pearl *see* **The Legend of Wisely**

569. Legend of the Liquid Sword

(1993; Wong Jing's Workshop) ★: 5/10. *Siu hap Cho Lau-heung* (Cantonese), *Xiao xia Chu Liuxiang* (Mandarin): "Comic Hero Cho Lau-heung" or "Comic Hero Chu Liuxiang." Cinematographer: Ko Chiu-lam; Art Director: Andrew Cheuk Man-yiu; Music: James Wong Jim; Writers: Wong Jing, Lam Wai-lun; Producer: Wong Jing; Action Director: Lau Shung-fung; Directors: Wong Jing, Yeung Wai-yip. Cast: Aaron Kwok Fu-shing (Fragrant Chu), Gloria Yip Wan-yee (Ron), Winnie Lau Siu-wai (Sweetie), Anita Yuen Wing-yee (Red), Deric Wan Siu-lun (Hu, aka Metal Flower), Wong Wan-si (Sea Weed), Chingmy Yau Suk-ching (Flowerless/ Night Bloom), Fennie Yuen Kit-ying (Chung Yuan), Loletta Lee Lai-chun (Batman's Lover), Julian Cheung Chi-lam (The Prince), Norman Tsui Siu-keung (Lonely), Gordon Lau Kar-fai (The Monk), Sharla Cheung Man (Jelly Fish). VHS: World Video, Arena/Xenon. Import LD/VCD/ DVD: Mei Ah. 82 minutes.

A companion piece to Wong Jing's **Holy Weapon** and Chu Yen-ping's **Flying Dagger** (both 1993), this aggressively wacky period fantasy spoof is not as successful, despite an excellent cast and virtually non-stop action. The convoluted plot concerns the adventures of swordsman Fragrant Chu, his three sisters, and bumbling hero "Metal Flower" Hu. In order to prove his prowess as a skilled fighter, Chu seeks to challenge Buddhist kung fu master Flowerless at a tournament. The two end up having a friendly test of their skills even before they arrive at the competition, and the outcome is a draw. Chu becomes involved with Flowerless' sister, Night Bloom, sullen swordswoman Chung Yuan, and a flying, bloodsucking villain called Batman(!), who kills Chu's master and strips the lad of his kung fu. The only hope Chu has of recovery is to enlist the aid of the enigmatic Jelly Fish, who has the power to heal him and destroy Batman.

The English subtitles are more than a little muddled, making this an exercise in sheer bewilderment the first time one views it. While it boasts eye-catching visuals, some inspired comic ideas (particularly a cameo by "Jesus"), and some of the most frenzied combat to be found in the genre, **Legend of the Liquid Sword** ends up being as wearisome as it is entertaining.

570. Legend of the Wolf

(1997; My Way Film Company/Silver Bullet Film Productions) ★: 4/10. *Jin long chuen suet* (Cantonese), *Zhan lang chuan shuo* (Mandarin): "War Wolf Legend." Cinematographer: Wong Kar-fai; Art Director: Nelson Cheung Hok-yun; Music: Tommy Wai Kai-leung, Kwok Chi-han; Writers: Chin Keung-han, Donnie Yen Chi-tan, Lai Te-wai; Producers: Cheung Chi-ping, Wong Kar-chu; Action Directors: Ho Sai-chou, Wong Kar-chu; Director: Donnie Yen Chi-tan. Cast: Donnie Yen Chi-tan (Fung Man-hin), Carman Lee Yeuk-tung (Wai-yee), Dayo Wong Chi-wah (Wai), Ben Lam Kwok-bun (Bandit Leader), Edmond Leung Hon-man (Ben Chan). 1.85:1. VHS: Tai Seng. Import LD/VCD/DVD: Jumbo Plain. 95 minutes. Also known as **New Big Boss** (UK video title).

After being stuck in several clinkers (notably, the unwatchable **Iron Monkey** 2), Donnie Yen took matters into his own hands for this project, filling in both behind and in front of the camera in order to craft the sort of action film *he* wanted to make. Alas, while ambitious, the end result is really not much of an improvement, suffering from an entirely different set of problems. Most of the film takes place at an undisclosed time after World War II. One day a mysterious stranger enters a remote village. Despite suffering from amnesia, he remembers a temple and pays Wai, a tough young fighter, to accompany him there. On the way, the stranger fights off a small army of attackers in dazzling fashion, single-handedly wiping them out. Not long after reaching his destination, the man is attacked again and, this time, badly injured. He is nursed back to health by Wai-yee, who turns out to be his old lover, and she tells him that his name is Fung Man-hin. It is revealed that Fung was a soldier and lost his memory after being shot by the Japanese; he has been missing for four years. However, Fung is being pursued by a gang of bandits who want his head and are ready to slaughter anyone who stands in their way.

While fleetingly impressive, the action is so undercranked, over-edited, and tightly framed (particularly in the cropped video versions), it is more exhausting than exhilarating. There is so much artifice in these setpieces that they often do not require a proficient martial artist; even Dayo Wong—a comedian—looks impressive! This, combined with a fatuous, self-important script, visuals that ape **Peace Hotel**, and combat inspired by (but inferior to) **The Blade**, results in a production that seems stale while also sagging under the weight of its overly lofty goals. Yen would have been better off shooting for the sort of unpretentious thrills offered by such Yuen Woo-ping collaborations as **Tiger Cage**, **Tiger Cage 2**, and **Iron Monkey**.

571. The Legend of Wisely

(1987; Cinema City Co.) ★: 8/10. *Wai Si-lei chuen kei* (Cantonese), *Wei Sili chuan ji* (Mandarin): "The Legend of Wai Si-lei" or "The Legend of Wei Sili." Cinematographer: Peter Pau Tak-hei; Art Director: Hai Chung-man; Music: Lo Tai-yau; Writers: Gerald Liu Kin-wai, Poon Yuen-leung, Philip Cheng Chung-tai; Producer: Sam Hui Koon-kit; Action Director: Blackie Ko Shou-liang; Director: Teddy Robin Kwan. Cast: Sam Hui Koon-kit (Wisely), Teddy Robin Kwan (David Ko), Ti Lung (Pak Kei-wei), Joey Wang Tsu-hsien (Sue Pak), Blackie Ko Shou-liang ("The Two Headed Snake"), Bruce Baron (Howard Hope), Heidi Makinen (Hope's Assistant). 2.35:1. VHS: Tai Seng (Poor Subtitles). Import LD: Golden Cinema City. Import VCD: Universe. 80/88 minutes. Also known as **The Legend of the Golden Pearl** (UK video title).

While obviously influenced by the Indiana Jones films, this large-scale epic is rousing entertainment that deserves to be better known in this hemisphere. Working in Nepal, science fiction writer/adventurer Wisely (or Wai Si-lei, the hero of several novels written by the prolific Ngai Hong) is enlisted by enigmatic billionaire Howard Hope to locate the former's childhood friend, David Ko. The diminutive David steals an oversized golden "Dragon Pearl" from a group of Buddhist monks, who regard it as a religious artifact. Wisely ends up helping to pull off the heist, despite having journeyed to the distant temple only in the hopes of finding David. The pair escape by plane but it inexplicably loses power and Wisely must bail out. Thinking that David perished in the subsequent crash, Wisely wanders away from the wreckage. Later, he is met by the leader of the monks. Although he is just a five-year-old boy, the monk possesses strong extra sensory abilities, and Wisely agrees to help get back the pearl for him. Jetting back to HK, he finds David with gangster Pak Kei-wei, who seeks to harness the artifact's power. With the help of Pak's sister, Wisely convinces David to return the pearl, and the trio escape from the triad's heavily guarded mansion. However, Pak is not about to give up that easily and neither is Hope, who also desperately wants the prize, but for a wholly different reason.

A grand adventure, **The Legend of Wisely** packs a lot into its fairly short running time. In addition to the expected martial arts and motor vehicle chases, our heroes are pursued by armed brigands on camels, stumble into quicksand, discover underground chambers, and land in several other classic cliffhanger situations. The narrative takes an unexpected but pleasing turn in the final reel, successfully introducing science fiction elements into the mix. Lavish production design and beautiful location photography in The Himalayas, Kathmandu, and Egypt (courtesy of the great Peter Pau, who would later shoot **Saviour of the Soul** and **The Bride with White Hair**) make this one of the most visually stunning productions of its era. The dubbed version, released in the UK, runs eight minutes shorter.

572. Legendary Couple

(1995; Mandarin Films/Nam Yin Production Co.) ★: 1/10. *Ngoh si yat goh chaak* (Cantonese), *Wo shi yi ge zei* (Mandarin): "I am a Thief." Cinematographer: Kwong Ting-ho; Art Director: James Cheung Ying-wah; Writers: Nam Yin, Candy Cheng; Producers: Raymond Wong Pak-ming, Tong Yen-hou, Hui Siu-ti; Action Director: Ridley Tsui Bo-wah; Director: Peter Ngor Chi-kwan. Cast: Simon Yam Tat-wah (Ko Tin-lap), Chingmy Yau Suk-ching (Lui Chi-lan), Vincent Wan Yeung-ming (Chan Sam), Yuen King-tan (Nurse). 1.85:1. VHS: Tai Seng. Import LD/VCD: Fitto Mobile. 82 minutes.

This agonizingly awful action thriller strives to be a hip, darkly comic spoof of the genre *á la* **Raising Arizona** and **Natural Born Killers** but is a miserable failure on every level. Simon Yam plays an innocent man mistakenly blamed for a robbery of $5 million in cash, which he was helping transport to a bank. While the police subject him to a vicious five hour interrogation, his pregnant wife goes into premature labor while waiting for him. The woman dies but the baby survives. Convinced he had a hand in the theft, Yam's boss terminates him and refuses to pay his pension. Seeking to force the man to pay, Yam kidnaps the boss' bratty daughter (played by Chingmy Yau), who eventually sides with him after her father goes back on his word and has the police raid the money drop. With Yam's baby in tow, the pair go on a crime spree, becoming HK's answer to Bonnie and Clyde.

It is hard to believe that such a witless, ill-conceived mess could possibly be the work of Nam Yin (brother of Ringo Lam and author of some of his best films), yet his name is all over it. With virtually nothing to back them up, the cast overact with wild abandon, coming across like drowning rats going down with the sinking ship. While this may not be the worst HK film of the '90s, most viewers will agree that it is close enough. Great poster, though.

573. Legendary Weapons of China

(1982; Shaw Brothers) ★: 9/10. *Sap baat boon saam ngai* (Cantonese), *Shi ba ban san yi* (Mandarin): "Eighteen Ways, Three Skills." Music: Not Original; Writers: Lau Kar-leung, Li Tai-hang; Producer: Mona Fong Yat-wah; Action Directors: Lau Kar-leung, Ching Chu, Hsiao Hou; Director: Lau Kar-leung. Cast: Lau Kar-leung (Lei Kung), Lau Kar-wing (Lei Ying), Gordon Lau Kar-fai (Ti Tan), Hsiao Hou (Tieh Hon), Kara Hui Ying-hung (Fang Shao-ching), Alexander Fu Sheng (Wu). 2.35:1. No authorized domestic video release. 109 minutes. Also known as **Legendary Weapons of Kung Fu** (US title).

A serious problem plagues the Yi Ho Society: Three years after he was sent to Yunnan to set up a new branch of the society, pugilism expert Lei Kung has instead dissolved the group. Master Li Lien-ying orders Lei's death, and three assassins are chosen to carry out the deed: Mao Shan clansman Lei Ying (whose talents include magic), professional killer Tieh Hon, and master pugilist Ti Tan. Each is sent out separately and is unaware of the others. In Guangdong, Tieh Hon encounters aged firewood salesman Yu, and the old man's strength and agility convince him that he may actually be the target. In order to lure Lei Kung out into the open, Lei Ying hires bumbling conman Wu to impersonate the pugilism master, but when a complete cache of the legendary "18 Weapons" is discovered in Yu's home, his ruse is compromised. However, Yi Ho clanswoman Fang Shao-ching (who donned a male disguise and secretly searched for Lei) supports the former leader's ideals and helps him to regain his martial abilities in time for the inevitable challenges he will face.

A superb blend of intricate plotting and stunning fight choreography, this is rightfully regarded as one of the Shaw Brothers' best latter day productions, and even those who only consider themselves to be casual fans of the genre should go out of their way to acquire it. Compared to more recent HK films, the martial arts on display here are presented with a minimum of FX trickery, and the results are most impressive. Although he only has a secondary role, Alexander Fu is a standout, displaying his martial and comedic abilities to excellent effect. The most impressive bit of fighting comes at the climax, providing an outstanding showcase for the considerable talents of brothers Lau Kar-leung and Lau Kar-wing. About the only real weakness here is the stock score (taken from the DeWolfe music library, and including cues some viewers will remember from **Monty Python and the Holy Grail**), which does not always provide an adequate accompaniment for the visuals on display. One could also say that it's unlikely the beautiful Kara Hui could pass herself off as a man, but we'll let that one go. The character names listed above are from the English dubbed version.

Legendary Weapons of Kung Fu *see* **Legendary Weapons of China**

Lethal Lady *see* **She Shoots Straight**

574. Lethal Panther

(1991; Filmswell International) ★: 5/10. *Ging tin lung foo paau* (Cantonese), *Jing tian long hu bao* (Mandarin): "Scare Heaven Dragon Tiger Panther." Cinematographer: Michael Lau Wah; Art Director: Manny Espolon; Music: Not Original; Writers: Charles Ng Chi, Simon Fong Sai-yin; Producers: Bennie Chan, Godfrey Ho Chi-keung; Action Directors: Wayne Mak Wai, Simon Tam Tung, Frank Shum Feng-san; Director: Godfrey Ho Chi-keung. Cast: Maria Jo (Eileen), Yoko Miyamoto (Amy), Sibelle Hu Hui-chung (Betty Lee), Lawrence Ng Kai-wah (Albert), Alex Fong Chung-sun (Tanaka), Ken Lo Wai-kwong (Kent), Lam Chung (Charles Wong), Sylvia Sanches (Sylvia), William Ho Kar-kui (Long). 1.85:1. VHS: World Video (Subtitled only), Tai Seng (Dubbed only). Import LD/VCD: Ocean Shores. 90 minutes. Also known as **Deadly China Dolls** (UK video title).

Shot predominantly in The Philippines, this Taiwanese production is a competent but unremarkable addition to the girls-with-guns subgenre. Competing contract killers Eileen and Amy end up taking on the same target: ganglord Charles Wong. The man behind the assassination is Wong's nephew, Albert, who is counterfeiting American currency, making him the target of CIA agent Betty Lee. Wanting to tie up all loose ends, Albert pays to have the two female killers silenced, so each is assigned to exterminate the other. After nearly finishing each other off, the two women are saved by a prostitute and become friends. Meanwhile, Eileen's brother has been enlisted to knock off one of Albert's enemies and also Eileen, complicating her plans to take revenge on Albert.

Although they rely too much on slow motion and are staged with an emphasis on quantity over quality, the various shootouts are fairly exciting, and Maria Jo is an enticing anti-heroine. The plot, however, is far from extraordinary, and while some attempt is made to develop the characters, periodic Vietnam flashbacks simply add some more cliches to a film that already has more than its share. In addition to some familiar library cues, the soundtrack includes music lifted from **Maniac Cop** and one of the **Halloween** movies. The above character names and running time apply to the English dubbed version released on Japanese video; the Chinese video releases reportedly run a few minutes longer. This film has no connection to **Lethal Panther 2**, a Philippines production starring Yukari Oshima that has been released on UK video as...**Lethal Panther**!

575. Licence to Steal

(1990; Golden Harvest/Bojon Films Co./Paragon Films) ★: 7/10. *Lung fung chaak juk chaak* (Cantonese), *Long feng zei zhuo zei* (Mandarin): "Dragon Phoenix: Thief Arrests Thief." Cinematographer: Chan Tung-chuen; Art Director: Fred Chan Chi-chung; Music: Richard Yuen Cheuk-fan; Writer: Johnny Lee King-kai; Producer: Sammo Hung Kam-po; Action Director: Power Lee King-chu; Director: Billy Chan Wui-ngai. Cast: Joyce Godenzi (Hung), Agnes Aurelio (Ngan), Yuen Biao ("The Swordsman"), Richard Ng Yiu-hon (Ta Hsiang-ken, aka "No. 1"), Ngai Sing (Yang Chuan-kuang), Alvina Kong Yan-yin (Hsiao-yen), Billy Chow Bei-lee (Billy), Lau Shun (Uncle Ting), Corey Yuen Kwai (Patrolman), Peter Chan Lung (Patrolman), Gabriel Wong Yat-san (Gunman). 1.85:1. VHS: Tai Seng. Import LD/VCD: Universe. 91 minutes.

The elder siblings in a family of thieves spanning several generations, sisters Hung and Ngan are bitter rivals. When their uncle decides that Hung should be the one entrusted with a disc containing secret information about the clan's future activities, this "treachery" is the final straw for Ngan: She cripples the uncle and betrays her sister to the police during their next burglary together. Upon her release from prison three years later, Hung is framed for another break-in by Ngan, but is cleared when police officers Ta and Yang verify her whereabouts at the time of the crime. Hung then decides to cooperate with the authorities and arranges a diversion, which allows her to access the disc and discover Ngan's next target: The Mask of Napolean. Foiling Ngan's plan to steal the prize while it is *en route* to a museum, Hung forces her rival into a final face off in the establishment's storage vault.

Terrific martial arts once again prop up a screenplay riddled with inconsistencies (the most glaring example: How could the computer disc possibly contain the locations and dates for robberies that would not be taking place for several *years*), but the storyline sets up the action setpieces efficiently, which is probably all that was ever really expected of it. Joyce Godenzi is a very believable heroine, and it is a shame that her career was cut short by a string of flops (including this one). Yuen Biao is amusing as an eccentric swordsman wannabe, living by a code that went out of fashion hundreds of years ago. The way he appears and disappears throughout the narrative is far more convenient than credible, but the character is a true original and provides Yuen with myriad chances to work his magic and engage in some pleasing mock heroics. The comic relief antics of Richard Ng and Ngai Sing are less inspired, but Ngai gets an excellent showcase for his athletic abilities, particularly during a prolonged battle in a dilapidated parking garage. Producer Sammo Hung has an eyeblink cameo in the final scene.

576. Lifeline

(1997; Cosmopolitan Films Productions/Shaw Brothers) ★: 4/10. *Sap maan feng gap* (Cantonese), *Shi wan huo ji* (Mandarin): "Ten Thousand Fire Urgent." Cinematographer: Cheng Siu-keung; Music: Raymond Wong Ying-wah; Writer: Yau Nai-hoi; Producer: Mona Fong Yat-wah; Action Director: Yuen Bun; Director: Johnny To Kei-fung. Cast: Lau Ching-wan (Yau-shui), Alex Fong Chung-sun (Raymond Cheung Man-kit), Carman Lee Yeuk-tung (Annie), Damian Lau Chung-yan (Cheung Fu-shing), Ruby Wong Cheuk-ling (Lo Ka-wai), Annabelle Lau Hiu-tung (Factory Worker), Kenneth Chan Kai-tai (Annie's Boyfriend). Dolby Digital (Remastered DVD Only). 1.85:1. VHS: Tai Seng. Import LD/VCD/DVD: Universe (2 DVD versions). 109 minutes.

While this firefighter thriller is an amazing technical achievement, the script and dramatics are a heavy-handed embarrassment. Veteran fireman Yau-shui has his already stressful job complicated by the arrival of Cheung, a humorless, by-the-book commander who is said to have driven one of his former underlings to commit suicide. In between domestic problems, the team is involved in various rescue efforts, culminating in a spectacular blaze at a weaving factory that leaves several firemen trapped underground with no conceivable means of escape.

The fire sequences are thrilling, with the lead actors often right in the thick of the flames (no computer fakery here!), but the dramatic conflicts surrounding them are the stuff of bad soap opera: Yau-shui's on-again/off-again relationship with troubled doctor Annie (who falls for him after he talks her out of jumping off a building); Cheung's problems with his estranged, terminally-ill wife (who wants him to take their English-speaking daughter); female team member Lo Ka-wai's husband is pressuring her to get pregnant, even though she signed papers saying she would not have a child until reaching a certain stage in the department; etc. Those who love the spectacular stunts and innovative action in HK movies should definitely have a look, but even they are advised to lean on the fast forward button until some flames pop up. The Chinese title is a fireman's term used in HK.

Lightning Kung Fu *see* **Killer Constable**

577. Liu Jai (Home for the Intimate Ghosts)

(1991; Onwinsee Development) ★: 3/10. *Liu jai tat lung yuet* (Cantonese), *Liao zhai hua nong yue* (Mandarin): "Dark Tales: The Flower Toys with the Moon." Cinematographer: Cheung Tak-wai; Art Director: Andrew Cheuk Man-yiu; Music: Sherman Chow Ching-hung; Writer: Lee Man-choi; Producer: Law Kwok-keung; Action Directors: Lee Chi-kit, Chow Yuen-mo; Director: Lam Yee-hung. Cast: Lam Man-yuen, Elsie Chan Yik-see, Ko Mei-lan, Charlie Cho Cha-lei (Taoist Priest), Chung Fat (High Priest). 1.85:1. VHS: Tai Seng. Import LD: Winson. 93 minutes.

This low-budget Category III sex fantasy was fashioned quickly to cash in on the period softcore subgenre spawned (sorry!) by the success of **Sex and Zen** and **Erotic Ghost Story**. With a wooden and less attractive cast, shoddy production values, and poor direction, it fell well short of those Golden Harvest releases, but managed to turn a healthy profit anyway. The nominal plot tells of a put-upon husband who, tired of his domineering wife, finds solace in the arms (and bed) of a willing servant girl. Subsequent events reveal that both the husband and wife are demons, and the female can become human again once she experiences a certain number of orgasms. Seeking to augment his pleasure, the husband buys a virgin from the local brothel and tries to sneak her into the household by disguising the girl as a servant *boy*. However, a bumbling (but persistent) Taoist priest-in-training is determined to put a stop to all of this unholy carnality.

Too drab to provide much pleasure, **Liu Jai** has occasional moments of demented inspiration (one sex scene is set to music that sounds suspiciously like Vic Mizzy's theme from **The Addams Family**!), and martial arts movie veteran Chung Fat shows up in the final few minutes as a Taoist ghostbuster, but there are far more accomplished films of this type that one should seek out instead. Historical footnote: "Liu Jai" became synonymous with ghost stories as a result of it being the title of a ghost story collection by writer Fu Chung-ling published during the Ching Dynasty.

578. Live Hard

(1989; D & B Films Co.) ★: 3/10. *Tit daam hung fung* (Cantonese), *Tie dan xiong fen* (Mandarin): "Iron Courage Mighty Wind." Cinematographer: Michael Ma Koon-wah; Art Director: Cheung Yuk-yu; Music: Not Original; Writer: Joseph Chan; Producers: Chung Kam-kwai, Lau Cheung-chu; Action Direction: The Ko Stunt Team; Director: Yuen Cheung-yan. Cast: Simon Yam Tat-wah (Hui Tat-ming), Lau Ching-wan (Fai, aka Chief), Elaine Lui Siu-ling (Female Operative), Sarah Lee Lai-yui (Stella), Eddy Ko Hung (Ironman), Hwang Jang-li (Chief Inspector Terry Chiu), Lam Chung (Officer Li), Yung Sai-kit (Stuart), Kim Maree Penn (Kitty). 1.85:1. VHS: Tai Seng. Import DVD: Widesight. 88 minutes.

About as inspired as its title and even less original, this action thriller is tediously predictable from beginning to end. When the son of an American official is blown up by terrorists, police sergeant Hui finds his investigation intentionally thwarted by his superiors. This is because, unbeknownst to Hui, a team of undercover operatives is on the case and eager to take the killers out before they can murder a US politician who is due soon in HK. When operative "Ironman" tries to buy some explosives, he is captured by Hui, and the latter is slapped with a suspension. Undaunted, Hui continues with his investigation, working from leads provided by a Chinese-speaking, Caucasian reporter. She, however, is one of the killers and is simply setting him up.

Neither of the parallel storylines are interesting and the attempts at character development fall flat, as hardly anyone here is any more than a requisite stereotype. Even the action is routine. The only novelty is the chance to see veteran villains Hwang Jang-li, Eddy Ko, and Lam Chung on the right side of the law for a change.

579. The Log

(1996; Entertainment Power) ★: 6/10. *3 goh sau seung dik ging chaat* (Cantonese), *3 go shou shang de jing cha* (Mandarin): "3 Injured Policemen." Cinematographer: Cheung Tung-leung; Art Director: Suzy Cheung Kai-san; Music: Lau Yee-tat; Writers: John Chan Kin-chung, Lu Bing, Teddy Chan Tak-sum; Producer: Tommy Wong Kwong-leung; Action Director: Woo Chi-lung; Director: Derek Chiu Sung-kei. Cast: Kent Cheng Chuk-see (Gump), Michael Wong Man-tak (Dixon), Jerry Lam Hiu-fung (Jerry), Cher Yeung Suet-yee (Gump's Wife), Guy Lai Ying-chau (Uncle Big Mouth). Dolby Digital. 1.85:1. VHS: World Video. Import LD/VCD/DVD: Panorama Entertainment. 95 minutes.

Heavy-handed symbolism aside, this is a well-crafted police drama, highlighted by Kent Cheng's award-winning turn as a veteran officer at the end of his rope. The film takes place entirely on December 31, 1996 and follows the lives of three policemen in the same squad. By-the-book officer Dixon is involved in a stand-off which ends with him accidentally killing one of the criminal's hostages. Charged with manslaughter, Dixon is interrogated and put in lock-up. Deeply in debt to loan sharks (whom he hangs around with during his off-duty hours), patrolman Jerry shoots and kills a triad youth who was actually surrendering to him. There are no witnesses, so he is branded a hero, but his conscience is not easily placated. Slovenly officer Gump's deteriorating marriage finally falls apart, due to the fact that he is never home spending time with his family. Having just lost a colleague (who dropped dead six months after he retired), Gump cracks from the strain of learning that his wife has been seeing his superintendent, whom he has dutifully served for years. Busting into a New Year's Eve celebration for high-ranking officers, Gump holds his boss and the other partygoers at gunpoint.

As mentioned, the symbolic aspects of the film are too overt, from the time period (the end of the last full year before the handover) to the visual metaphors (one of the very first images is a framed portrait of Queen Elizabeth II falling and smashing on the ground), and Michael Wong gives his usual cardboard characterization, all but deflating his segment. Fortunately, Jerry Lam does solid work as the troubled young cop, and there is an offbeat soundtrack by Lau Yee-tat. However, the real draw is Cheng (whose head is partially shaved in order to make him look older), who is at his intense best, adding resonance to what would otherwise be a routine climax.

580. The Long and Winding Road

(1994; Win's Movie Production) ★: 3/10. *Gam sau chin ching* (Cantonese), *Jin xiu qian cheng* (Mandarin): "Bright Future." Cinematographer: Derek Wan Man-kit; Art Director: Horace Ma Kwong-wing; Music: Richard Yuen Cheuk-fan; Writers: Gordon Chan Kar-seung, Chan Hing-ka; Producers: Charles Heung Wah-keung, Jimmy Heung Wah-sing; Director: Gordon Chan Kar-seung. Cast: Leslie Cheung Kwok-wing (Lam Chiu-wing), Tony Leung Kar-fai (James), Rosamund Kwan Chi-lam (Winnie Tsang), Dayo Wong Chi-wah (Sing), Kenneth Tsang Kong (Bosco Chow). 1.85:1. VHS: Tai Seng. Import LD: Cameron Entertainment. Import VCD: Mei Ah. 104 minutes.

This shallow comedy-drama sets out to show how money and success invariably comes at the expense of one's principles, not exactly an original or challenging premise. Lam Chiu-wing is a slick low-life who loses his job and his girlfriend on the same day. He proceeds to take advantage of his friends (in particular, hapless musician/rest home worker James), making them miserable in the process. When James catches a glimpse of beautiful businesswoman Winnie Tsang, it's love at first sight, but Lam undermines James' plans to date her in order to score with Winnie himself. In the process, he manages to finagle a job at her firm and impresses the boss with his ability to lie and not show the slightest trace of guilt. Eventually, however, an event transpires that forces the now-successful Lam to finally evaluate what he has done to his friends and what he has become.

With no genuinely likeable characters, no bonafide wit, and no real insight, this is a very long and winding road indeed; only those infatuated with the leads need bother apply. Michael Wong Man-tak appears in a supporting role, which includes an in-joke reference to his part in director Chan's SDU thriller **The Final Option**.

581. Long Arm of the Law

(1984; Golden Harvest/Johnny Mak Production/Bo Ho Films Co.) ★: 8/10. *Saang gong kei bing* (Cantonese), *Sheng gang qi bing* (Mandarin): "Hong Kong Flag Soldier." Cinematographer: Johnny Koo Kwok-wah; Art Directors: Cheung King-hung, Fung Yuen-chi, Wong Siu-hung; Music: Lam Mo-tak; Writer: Phillip Chan Yan-kin; Producers: Sammo Hung Kam-po, Johnny Mak Dong-hung; Action Director: Billy Chan Wui-ngai; Director: Johnny Mak Dong-hung. Cast: Lam Wai (Tung), Huang Jian (Chubby), Jiang Lung (Chung), Chen Jing (Rooster), Shum Wai (Tai). Dolby Digital (DVD only). 1.85:1. VHS: Tai Seng. Import LD: Star Entertainment (No Subtitles). Import VCD: Universe. Import DVD: Mega Star. 99 minutes.

A groundbreaking crime film (the first and only movie directed, to date, by producer Johnny Mak), **Long Arm of the Law** was shot in a semi-documentary fashion and peopled largely with first-time performers, which helped to create an air of authenticity rarely matched in the genre. It tells of a group of Mainland criminals (all former Red Guards) who plot to pull a "Big Circle" caper (sneak into HK, rob a jewellery store, and flee back across the border to evade capture). The plan gets off to a disastrous start as one of their number is killed by guard dogs while trying to scale a fence at the border. The caper itself is over before it even has a chance to begin: The scene is already swarming with police investigating *another* robbery, and they soon spot and pursue the suspicious looking Mainlanders, suspecting that they were accomplices. In the resulting melee, a policeman is shot and killed. The gang then bides their time, enjoying the capitalist diversions of HK—from junk food (they even make an offering of pizza, a McDonald's burger, and french fries to their dead comrade!) to bar girls. When things have cooled down, they go ahead with the heist, unaware that their middle man, Tai, has made a deal with the authorities to capture them at their rendezvous.

The plot culminates in what is still one of the most suspenseful and well-mounted shootouts in HK cinema. Ben Lam Kwok-bun and Tommy Wong Kwong-leung have small roles as cops on the case. The critical and box office success of the film spawned three unrelated sequels, which play out in less innovative fashion, though **Long Arm of the Law Part 3** is well worth catching.

582. Long Arm of the Law II

(1987; Golden Harvest/Johnny Mak Production) ★: 5/10. *Saang gong kei bing II* (Cantonese), *Sheng gang qi bing II* (Mandarin): "Hong Kong Flag Solider II." Cinematographer: Johnny Koo Kwok-wah; Art Director: Dominique Lo Kar-yiu; Music: Kong Wai-hung; Writer: Phillip Chan Yan-kin; Producer: Johnny Mak Dong-hung; Action Director: Chin Yuet-sang;

Director: Michael Mak Dong-kit. Cast: Elvis Tsui Kam-kong (Li Heung-tung), Ben Lam Kwok-bun (King San), Yuen Yat-chor (Hok Kwan), Alex Man Chi-leung (Biggy), Pauline Wong Siu-fung (Diana), Che-Kirk Wong Chi-keung (Siu Hing), Shing Fui-on (Kwong Ming), Chen Jing (Kwong's Brother). Dolby Digital (DVD only). 1.85:1. VHS: Tai Seng. Import LD: Star Entertainment (No Subtitles). Import DVD: Mega Star. 88 minutes.

The second entry in this series is a much more routine effort that, while not without its good points, emerges as a disappointment. Unable to effectively combat the wave of "Big Circle" robberies plaguing HK (illustrated by a montage of clips from the original), the authorities decide to draft some Mainlanders to infiltrate the gangs. Li Heung-tung, Hok Kwan, and King San are chosen and offered permanent residence in HK if they agree to assist the police for a period of two years. Working under the supervision of a flaky inspector who goes by the name "Biggy," their first assignment is to publicly humiliate blowhard gangster Siu Hung as a way of becoming known in the underworld. Once that is accomplished, the men crack various cases for the government; but the latest one is a problem for King: The mastermind is an old friend who saved his life during the Vietnam War. Matters are complicated further by Hok, who steals $350,000, intending to escape to Hawaii with a club girl. After falling victim to the girl's deception, he loses the money while fleeing from police. The lost currency was part of some evidence that must be returned within two days, and the men's relationship with the officer supervising the undercover work is already on very shaky ground.

Featuring a good premise compromised by so-so scripting, the film still offers solid characterizations by Elvis Tsui and Alex Man, and a well-staged climax. Regardless, it has little of what made its forerunner so notable.

583. Long Arm of the Law Part 3

(1989; Johnny Mak Production/ Movie Impact) ★: 7/10. *Saang gong kei bing dai saam chap* (Cantonese), *Sheng gang qi bing di san ji* (Mandarin): "Hong Kong Flag Soldier III." Cinematographer: Derek Wan Man-kit; Art Director: Fong Ying; Music: Joseph Chan Wing-leung; Writers: Stephen Siu Yeuk-yuen, Johnny Mak Dong-hung; Producers: Johnny Mak Dong-hung, Wallace Cheung Kwok-chong; Action Director: Tony Leung Siu-hung; Director: Michael Mak Dong-kit. Cast: Andy Lau Tak-wah (Li Cheung-kong), Elizabeth Lee Mei-fung (Sheung Mun), Max Mok Siu-chung (Chicken Heart), Elvis Tsui Kam-kong (Mao Heung-yeung), Che-Kirk Wong Chi-keung (Leung), Robin Shou Wan-bo (966). 1.85:1. VHS: World Video. Import LD: Mei Ah. Import VCD: Cameron Entertainment. 107 minutes. Also known as **Escape from Hong Kong**.

Falsely implicated in a robbery, Li Cheung-kong is found guilty and sentenced to death but manages to escape from his firing squad. While trying to cross over the border into HK, his life is saved by Sheung Mun, a pretty girl who is also trying to escape from China. Upon establishing himself in HK, Li learns that Mun has been sold into prostitution and makes an unsuccessful attempt to rescue her. Li then agrees to accompany Mun's captor on a jewellery store heist, thus securing her release in exchange for his participation. After being briefly reunited with his love, Li is told that he will be killed unless he agrees to spend another year with the gang. Making matters worse is the fact that Mao, the persistent Mainland policeman who arrested Li, has journeyed to HK and is systematically tracking him down.

The action scenes are as exciting as one has come to expect from this production team, and the final shootout in a dilapidated apartment building is especially good. Special credit must be given to Andy Lau, who performs some very impressive stunts and more than holds his own during the hand-to-hand combat. The storyline is old hat and, at 107 minutes, too drawn out, but the proceedings remain engrossing, though the ignorant Mainland stereotypes are an embarrassment, even for the time. Actor/director Che-Kirk Wong makes an impressively duplicitous and slimy villain; the interrogation scene he shares with Elvis Tsui (whose character is a none-too-subtle symbol of Communist ruthlessness, from his name on down) is a gem.

Long Arm of the Law IV *see* **Underground Express**

584. Look Out, Officer!

(1990; Cosmopolitan Film Productions) ★: 6/10. *Si hing jong gwai* (Cantonese), *Shi xiong zhuang gui* (Mandarin): "Master Brother Bumps Ghost." Cinematographer: Nico Wong Man-wan; Art Director: Fred Chan Chi-chung; Music: Chow Kam-cheung; Writer: Tsui Ching-hong; Producer: Lau Tin-chi; Action Directors: Benz Kong To-hoi, Tony Poon Kin-kwan; Director: Lau Sze-yu. Cast: Stephen Chiau Sing-chi (Hsing), Bill Tung Biu (Chang Piao), Stanley Fung Shui-fan (Chin), Vivian Chan Tak-yung (Yu), Mui Siu-wai (Beautiful), Amy Yip Chi-mei (Chin's Superior). 1.85:1. VHS: World Video. Import LD/VCD/DVD: Mei Ah. Running time unknown.

One of several low-budget comedies Stephen Chiau made prior to hitting the big time with **All for the Winner**, **Look Out, Officer!** is a fairly amusing, old fashioned horror farce, apparently inspired by **Magic Cop**. While checking out an illegal drug manufacturing warehouse, police officer Piao is shot dead. Arriving in the netherworld for judgment, he bribes the local magistrate with "ghost money" to let him return to earth and solve his own murder. According to the official's instructions, he is to be aided in his investigation by Hsing, a bumbling rookie cop. The two make an agreement: Hsing will help Piao if the ghost helps him win the hand of his superior's beautiful daughter. Piao's old partner, Chin, just happens to be a Taoist priest on the side, which is fortunate, as the villain has a sorcerer of his own to back him up.

The humor is pretty standard (scatological gags, love hexes, Amy Yip breast fetish jokes), and the special FX are amusingly low tech, consisting mainly of photographic and editing tricks that date back to the beginning of cinema. However, Chiau's charisma and a spirited climactic gunfight/magical duel make this worthwhile, if not required, viewing.

585. The Loot

(1980; Lo Wei Films Co.) ★: 5/10. *Chaak jong* (Cantonese), *Zei zang* (Mandarin): "Thief Booty." Cinematographer: Chan Siu-on; Art Director: Chow Chi-leung; Music: Not Original; Writer: Wong Ying; Producer: Hsu Li-hua; Action Directors: Sui Kwai, Ho Sai-bo, Ho Chi-wai; Director: Eric Tsang Chi-wai. Cast: Norman Tsui Siu-keung (Fang Tsung), David Chiang Da-wei (Robert Yang Wei), Lily Li Li-li (Chiang Fei-hsia), Phillip Ko Fei (Kao Yu-cheng), Eric Tsang Chi-wai (Junior Police Officer). 2.35:1. VHS: Ocean Shores (Dubbed or Poor Subtitles). Import VCD: Ocean Shores (Poor Subtitles). 93 minutes. Also known as **Bloody Tattoo** (Title for Ocean Shores dubbed tape).

This lightweight period kung fu comedy-mystery shows some promise early on but ends up being run-of-the-mill. Sarcastic police officer Robert Yang has his hands full trying to apprehend Fang Tsung (a stealthy thief invading the countryside's homes), but he soon has even more to deal with. Several affluent (but disreputable) citizens have been receiving death notices from a ruthless killer called The Spider, prompting them to hire Yang to be their bodyguard. Regardless, the murders continue and appear to be connected to the twenty year old robbery of a jewellery store run by Fang's father. Putting their differences aside, Yang and Fang team up to get to the stashed stones before The Spider and his cronies. Before they can do that, the pair must locate the map which points the way to the lair...and is tattooed on a maiden's back!

The kung fu is routinely staged and most of the comedy is strained (Chiang is more obnoxious than endearing in a part better suited to the likes of Alexander Fu Sheng), but the developing mystery is fairly engrossing, making this an adequate time killer for devotees of old-school martial arts movies. One year prior to this feature, comedian Eric Tsang directed David Chiang and Norman Tsui in another film, **The Challenger**.

586. Lord of East China Sea

(1993; Golden Harvest/Johnny Mak Production) ★: 7/10. *Seung hoi wong dai ji sui yuet fung wan* (Cantonese), *Shang hai huang di zhi sui yue feng yun* (Mandarin): "Shanghai Emperor: The Turbulent Years." Cinematographer: Horace Wong Wing-hang; Art Director: Ho Kim-seng; Music: Lo Tai-yau; Writers: Johnny Mak Dong-hung, Stephen Siu Yeuk-yuen; Producers: Johnny Mak Dong-hung, Raymond Chow Man-wai; Director: Poon Man-kit. Cast: Ray Lui Leung-wai (Luk Yu-san), Kent Cheng Chuk-see (Chief Wong), Elvis Tsui Kam-kong (Yuen Siu-kwan), Carina Lau Kar-ling (Ms. Liu), Cecilia Yip Tung (Donna Mang), Lam Wai (Hau Fei), Kenneth Tong Chun-yip (Shan), Miu Kiu-wai (General Ku Yu), William Ho Kar-kui (Pei Su-ching), Kelvin Wong Siu (Ng Keung). Dolby Digital (Mega Star DVD only). 2.35:1. VHS: Tai Seng. Import LD/VCD: Universe. Import DVD: Universe, Mega Star. 148 minutes.

587. Lord of East China Sea II

(1993; Golden Harvest/Johnny Mak Production) ★: 5/10. *Seung hoi wong dai ji hung ba tin ha* (Cantonese), *Shang hai huang di zhi xiong ba tian xia* (Mandarin): "Shanghai Emperor: Powerful Overlord Rule." Cinematographer: Horace Wong Wing-hang; Art Director: Ho Kim-seng; Music: Lo Tai-yau; Writers: Johnny Mak Dong-hung, Stephen Siu Yeuk-yuen; Producers: Johnny Mak Dong-hung, Raymond Chow Man-wai; Director: Poon Man-kit. Cast: Ray Lui Leung-wai (Luk Yu-san), Kent Cheng Chuk-see (Chief Wong), Elvis Tsui Kam-kong (Yuen Siu-kwan), Cecilia Yip Tung (Donna), Carina Lau Kar-ling (Ms. Liu), Lam Wai (Hau Fei), Kenneth Tong Chun-yip (Shan), Miu Kiu-wai (General Ku Yu), Kelvin Wong Siu (Ng Keung), Isabella Chow Wang (Wong's Mistress). Dolby Digital (Mega Star DVD only). 2.35:1. VHS: Tai Seng. Import LD/VCD: Universe. Import DVD: Universe, Mega Star. 103 minutes.

Released theatrically and on video in two parts, this Mak Brothers epic charts the rise of Luk Yu-san from pear vendor to the ganglord emperor of Shanghai. Opening in 1913, part one tells of how Luk uses his cunning to gain employment at a casino run by the corrupt police chief Wong, who supervises the opium trade for the French government. However, Luk's new lifestyle alienates him from Donna, an opera singer, who deserts him. Rising in influence and importance, Luk decides to broker a deal between his boss and the notorious thief and killer, Yuen Siu-kwan, who has been purloining the opium shipments. The resulting partnership proves highly lucrative and the men are soon known as "The Three Tycoons of Shanghai." Luk falls for Ms. Liu, a prostitute-turned-madam, but his affections for Donna are re-ignited when he encounters her at a theatrical performance. Trouble arises when Wong unknowingly insults the son of a high-ranking military officer; in order to save him from execution, Luk must offer Liu to Officer Pei, an opera-loving sadist. In addition, the three are forced to take Pei and his associate on as partners in their opium dealings. The tycoons also become embroiled in the war between the communists and the Kuomintang nationalists, siding with the latter. However, the men are betrayed by the K.M.T. leaders and framed for the massacre of left wing unionists and their supporters. Shortly after discovering that he has contracted asthma, Luk is wounded in an assassination attempt engineered by his old enemy, Hau Fei.

Part Two opens in the 1930s, with Luk aiming to go into legitimate business by opening a bank. When none of the existing financial institutions will give him face, Luk conspires with his K.M.T. ally General Ku to force them into accepting him as a board member. He also tries to better himself by learning to read and write, and to curtail his increasingly detrimental addiction to opium. He also devotes himself to the war effort, but when the Japanese invade Shanghai in 1937, he and Donna flee to Hong Kong, while Wong and Yuen stay behind. Desperate for capital, Luk gets back into the opium business, while Wong puts up a brave front and Yuen collaborates with the Japanese. Following the war, Luk (his health starting to fail) returns to Shanghai, only to find a very different oligarchy in power.

Like Poon's **To Be Number One** and **Shanghai Grand**, the films ultimately work best as pageantry, offering up lavish production design, multitudes of extras, and a genuinely authentic feel. On that level, they are basic but intoxicating entertainment: modest soap opera played out on a Wagnerian stage by pleasing performers. As one has come to expect from the Mak Brothers, the miscreants are figures of honor, while the politicians are the real villains, collaborating when need be and then throwing the gangsters to the dogs afterwards. Despite a combined running time of over four hours, events still seem condensed (Luk has a wife, three mistresses, and six sons, though, aside from two of the concubines, hardly any are given attention) and Poon's direction of Part II is distressingly ham-fisted. During the invasion of Shanghai, one shot features a Japanese soldier raping a Chinese woman in the foreground while the silhouette of a baby impaled on a bayonet looms behind, and the Japanese attempt to kidnap Luk turns into an unintentionally comic *homage* to the "Odessa Steps" sequence from **Battleship Potemkin**. Worst of all is the bit where Luk is saved from death by his well-trained dog, which thoughtfully removes a bundle of lit dynamite that was about to obliterate him! The extended finale also comes perilously close to outright camp. As Luk, Ray Lui is adequate, but veteran character actors Kent Cheng and Elvis Tsui easily overshadow him. In fact, the most memorable turn is by Kenneth Tong as Shan, an alcoholic assassin whose incontinence is merely a ruse. Tong barely strings together a hundred words over the course of two films and yet Shan is the one you are most happy to see, even if he is just sleeping it off in his usual corner.

Lord of the Wu-tang *see* **Kung Fu Cult Master**

588. Lost and Found

(1996; Golden Harvest/United Filmmakers Organization/Golden Movies International) ★: 9/10. *Tin aai hoi gok* (Cantonese), *Tian ya hai jiao* (Mandarin): "Edge of the World." Cinematographer: Bill Wong Chung-bo; Art Director: James Cheung Ying-wah; Music: Mark Lui Chung-tak; Writer-Producer-Director: Lee Chi-ngai. Cast: Kelly Chan Wai-lam (Kelly Chai Lam), Takeshi Kaneshiro ("That Worm"), Michael Wong Man-tak (Ted), Hilary Tsui Ho-ying (Wai), Josie Ho Chiu-yee (Yee), Jordan Chan Siu-chun (Chu), Cheung Tat-ming (Ming),

Henry Fong Ping (Chai Ming), Maria Cordero (Jane's Mom), Moses Chan Ho (Lone), Teddy Chan Tak-sum (Teddy). Dolby Stereo. 1.85:1. VHS: Tai Seng. Import LD/VCD/DVD: Mei Ah. 109 minutes.

A life-affirming and genuinely heartwarming drama, **Lost and Found** has the kind of storyline that one hesitates to relate to friends for fear they will dismiss the movie out of turn, particularly as it sounds like an imitation of **C'est La Vie, Mon Cheri**. It is definitely more than that and ranks among the United Filmmakers Organization's best productions to date. 23-year-old woman Chai Lam has been diagnosed with leukemia and is given only a thirty percent chance of recovery. One day she sees a man fishing a wallet out of a garbage can. He turns out to be a Mongolia-born "lost and found" expert whose name translates into Cantonese as "That Worm." A gregarious sort, Worm (who knows nothing about Lam's condition) tackles the woman's request that he find Eurasian sailor Ted, whom she last saw four days ago. She has become interested in Ted and his home, the Scottish island of St. Kilda which consists mostly of graveyards. When her rather cold and distant father refuses to allow her to continue working, Lam throws away her medication and decides that she would like to visit the island, which is known as "The Edge of the World." She and Worm are eventually able to track Ted down just as he is about to fly back home and take over running the family inn. Before she accepts Ted's invitation to visit him on St. Kilda, Lam helps Worm try and grant the wish of a young girl, whose mother is in the hospital and on the verge of death.

Lam's terminal illness can be interpreted as a metaphor for the countdown to the July 1, 1997 reunification, with all of the uncertainty that date posed for HK's citizens, and **Lost and Found** is primarily about life, love, and identity. While the film has its share of quirky moments, writer-producer-director Lee Chi-ngai displays a steady hand when it comes to sentimentality, keeping things from going too far in any direction, thus readily allowing the viewer to be drawn in and moved by the characters, their observations, and the imagery. The Scottish locations are predictably beautiful, and effective use is made of different musical styles (particularly Leonard Cohen's "Dance Me to the End of Love," which is heard several times). The performances are all on target; even the usually hapless Michael Wong does good work, though one is hard-pressed to believe that he has a drop of Scottish blood in him. Depending on how receptive you have been to everything preceding it, the final sequence just might reduce you to tears, but it is a good cry in both senses of the term.

589. Lost Boys in Wonderland

(1995; Petrvs Production) ★: 8/10. *Waai haai ji kui lok bo* (Cantonese), *Huai hai zi ju le bu* (Mandarin): "Bad Boys Club." Cinematographer: Jacky Tang Hon-bong; Art Director: Ben Luk Man-wah; Music: Alvin Kwok Siu-lam; Writers: Samson Chiu Leung-chun, James Ha Chim-see; Producer: Steven Lo Kit-sing; Action Director: James Ha Chim-see; Director: Samson Chiu Leung-chun. Cast: Darrin Lam Ming-lun, Chan Hau-ngok, Samuel Leung Foh-moon, Lois Kwok Ching (Lois), Shirley Wong Sa-lei, James Ha Chim-see (Head Guard). 1.85:1. VHS: World Video. Import LD/VCD: Ocean Shores. 94 minutes.

When his buddy Chan Hou-man is thrown into prison, Chi intentionally gets himself arrested by committing a pointless act of arson. Not exactly the brightest guy around, Chi soon finds out just what he has gotten himself into when he earns the disfavor of the head guard. Worst of all, he discovers that Hou-man got into a fight and isn't even at that facility anymore! After getting off to a rough start with his fellow cellmates, Chi begins to adapt and wins their respect. Most importantly, though, Chi finds a goal to strive for: if he can keep his buddies out of trouble for one week's time, the warden will consider his request that the prisoners receive music instruction as part of their special interest time.

Shot with sync sound, and cast almost entirely with unknowns, this is certainly one of the most realistic depictions of prison life to be found in HK cinema, generally avoiding sensationalism and concentrating on plausible situations that these boys would have to face every day. Candy is the currency of choice, some are ready to kill for a cigarette (only adult prisoners are allowed to smoke), while others will take whatever kind of chemical they can inhale. The cast is uniformly good and cinematographer Jacky Tang is able to endow the proceedings with more interesting visuals than one usually finds in this genre. This would make an excellent double bill with Lawrence Ah Mon's **Gangs**, a similarly realistic look at troubled HK youth.

590. Love Among the Triad

(1993; Long Shong Pictures/Lui Ming International Film Enterprises/ Prairie Productions Co./Flying Color Film Productions Co.) ★: 5/10. *Oi joi hak se wooi dik yat ji* (Cantonese), *Ai zai hei she hui de ri zi* (Mandarin): "Love in the Underworld Days." Cinematographer: William Yim Wai-lun; Art Director: Jon Hau Wing-choi; Music: Johnny Chen; Writers: Andy Chin Wing-keung, Joey Cheung Cho-ngai, Elizabeth Lau Sin-man; Producer: Jon Hau Wing-choi; Action Director: Stephen Tung Wai; Director: Andy Chin Wing-keung. Cast: Simon Yam Tat-wah (Ching Kit), Rosamund Kwan Chi-lam (Kwok Hoi-lam), Cecilia Yip Tung (Cecilia Lee), Veronica Yip Yuk-hing (Sue), Pauline Wong Siu-fung (Ma Man-fung), Vincent Wan Yeung-ming (Tong Chun), James Pak Chin-shek (Pak-shek), Jamie Luk Kim-ming (Qun). 1.85:1. VHS: Tai Seng. Import LD/VCD: Ocean Shores. 90 minutes.

A textbook example of how star power can prop up weak material, this minor drama is the polar opposite of most triad thrillers. Instead of concentrating on the gang wars and shakedowns, we spend almost all of our time with the handsome, rich bosses and their equally beautiful wives. They plot alliances, party in nightclubs, cheat on their partners, negotiate with Portuguese gangsters for control over casinos in Macau, and watch their love lives get torn apart by duplicity and jealousy.

More like a couple of episodes from a TVB miniseries than a feature film, this never really amounts to much of anything, though the stars manage to retain one's interest (sync sound recording helps). By the same token, when you consider the calibre of talent involved, one has the right to expect more than just this mildly engrossing time-waster.

Love and Death in Saigon *see* **A Better Tomorrow III**

591. Love and Sex Among the Ruins

(1996; Media Asia Films Partners I/Film-Seed Communications) ★: 8/10. *Yan gan sik seung* (Cantonese), *Ren jian se xiang* (Mandarin): "Humans' Many Faces of Sex" or "Humans' Many Perverted Looks." Cinematographer: Apple Kwan Pak-suen; Art Director: Gemma To Ching-ching; Music: Danny Wong Dan-yee; Producer: John Chong Ching; Writer-Director: Cheung Chi-sing. Cast: Dayo Wong Chi-wah (Man Cheung); Cheung Tat-ming (Tung), Ada Choi Siu-fan (Billie), Liz Kong Hei-man (Wu Wan Kei-man), Paulyn Suen Kai-kwan (Madam Ron), Vincent Kok Tak-chiu (Psychiatrist). 1.85:1. VHS: Tai Seng. Import LD/VCD/ DVD: Universe. 101 minutes.

Not to be confused with Denys Arcand's Canadian feature **Love and**

Human Remains (1993), **Love and Sex Among the Ruins** is a witty, poignant, and sexy comedy-drama geared toward a twentysomething audience. It also provides a fitting vehicle to showcase the talents of its two male leads, stand-up comedians Dayo Wong and Cheung Tat-ming. Wong plays Man Cheung, a taxi driver who is quietly obsessed with one of his regular fares, Mainland *emigre* Wu Wan Kei-man (whose name means "Happiness"). She works as a Wanchai club girl in order to pay back a loan required to get her flaky artist husband (Cheung, doing riffs on the "Mainland rube" stereotype) out of China. After a comically disastrous one night stand leaves him impotent, Cheung takes a vacation to a neighboring island on the advice of his doctor (a goofy cameo by actor/director Vincent Kok). Securing employment at a local watering hole, Cheung sees his chance to strike up a relationship with Kei-man, who is also a resident of the island. That fantasy is quickly dashed by the arrival of her husband but Cheung discovers that it was the bar's slinky, bisexual owner, Billie, who loaned Kei-man the money she needed, as a pretext to seduce her. One of Billie and Kei-man's sexual encounters is observed by both Cheung and Kei-man's husband, prompting the latter to push his Marxian ideal of a "People's Community" with its credo of "share and share alike" (especially when it comes to sharing the *women*). Magnifying Cheung's sexual depression even further is his deepening attraction to yet another woman, Madam Ron (Paulyn Suen, a former Miss Singapore), a fetching policewoman determined to be the one to cure his affliction (a surprisingly sweet subplot).

Love and Sex Among the Ruins arrived on the scene at a time when HK filmmakers had taken the relationship film in all manner of unexpected directions, spurred on by the critical and financial success of Peter Chan Ho-sun's **He's a Woman, She's a Man** and other hip, upscale productions from the United Filmmakers Organization. Even if it had nothing else to offer, **Love and Sex** would be notable simply for presenting a scenario in which heterosexuality and homosexuality coexist on equal, natural planes, a radical concept for HK cinema, which always depicts gay characters (male and female alike) in exceedingly broad strokes. Dayo Wong has developed something of a name for himself playing eccentric, obnoxious cretins, but his performance here is more tempered and realistic, allowing the viewer to both empathize with Man Cheung and be amused by his predicament. Of the actresses, Kong and Suen are both splendid, but it is Choi who really dazzles, giving a bold, risky performance that's a dramatic departure from her usual assignments as a *fa jun* (Cantonese for "flower vase," a term Chinese actresses use to describe decorative roles that give them nothing to do). Some of the script's sharper asides are deflated by the awkwardly translated subtitles but, overall, the film survives this minor irritation without significant harm.

592. Love and the City

(1994; Citimagic) ★: 3/10. *Do si qing yuen* (Cantonese), *Du shi qing yuan* (Mandarin): "City Love." Cinematographer: Arthur Wong Ngok-tai; Art Director: James Leung Wah-sang; Music: Lowell Lo Kwun-ting; Writer: Kei On (pseudonym for Jeff Lau Chun-wai); Producer: Jacky Pang Yee-wah; Action Director: Wong Kwan-hong; Director: Jeff Lau Chun-wai. Cast: Leon Lai Ming (Wu), Jacqueline Wu Chien-lien (Jo Jo), Ng Man-tat (Chung), Liz Kong Hei-man (Sue). 1.85:1. VHS: Tai Seng. Import LD/VCD/DVD: Ocean Shores. 97 minutes.

If classified using Western moviegoer terminology, this contrived and heavy-handed drama would definitely fall under the heading of "Chick Flick." Perpetual loser Wu has just been released from jail, a place where he has spent more than a few years of his life. One day he spots and is instantly in love with the beautiful Jo Jo, the fiancée of an affluent businessman. Although Jo Jo's boyfriend has thugs beat Wu up, the handsome but shiftless young man cannot stay away from the girl and she eventually agrees to a date. Love seems to be blossoming between the two, but Wu becomes wrongly implicated in a murder and becomes a fugitive after escaping from police. Wu and Jo Jo get in touch via their pagers and plan a rendezvous, but the authorities are alerted by the pager company and capture him before she arrives. Sentenced to two years in jail, Wu does his time and, in the process, reconciles with his father (whom he has hated since childhood), but will Jo Jo come back to him? Is there really even a microbe of doubt?

Utilizing the same hamfisted approach he uses on comedies, writer-director Jeff Lau drains any and all possible subtlety out of this tired premise. The situations are so contrived and the secondary characters are so exaggerated (in particular, an evil policeman out to make Wu's life hell), the film loses credibility almost from the get go. Neither Leon Lai nor Jacqueline Wu can do much to make us care about their one dimensional characters, but Ng Man-tat gives a fine dramatic performance as Lai's troubled father, who loves his son but cannot understand him.

593. Love, Guns & Glass

(1995; Bold Team Films Co.) ★: 3/10. *Boh lee cheung dik oi* (Cantonese), *Bo li qiang de ai* (Mandarin): "Glass Gun's Love." Cinematographer: Johnny Koo Kwok-wah; Art Director: Nelson Cheung Hok-yun; Music: Henry Lai Wan-man; Writers: Candy Cheng, Lai Kai-keung; Producer: Paul Lau Hoi-wing; Action Director: Phillip Kwok Tsui; Director: Lai Kai-keung. Cast: Simon Yam Tat-wah (Yung Siu-wing), Cecilia Yip Tung (Lau Yuk-ching), Chin Ho (Blackie Yiu), Roy Cheung Yiu-yeung (Fai), Farini Cheung Yui-ling (Yung's Wife). 1.85:1. VHS: World Video. Import LD/VCD: Universe. 105 minutes.

This foolish, poorly written thriller is kept afloat (barely) by two strong central performances. Yung Siu-wing, a kind-hearted triad boss, is sent to prison after he is betrayed by an undercover cop. After serving his ten year sentence for drug trafficking, Yung returns home to find that his slutty wife has gambled away everything, and his young daughter has turned into a delinquent. One evening a pretty woman named Lau Yuk-ching approaches one of Yung's underworld associates about a loan. It is love at first sight for Yung, who proceeds to shield Yuk-ching from her many creditors. When the woman's long-time lover unceremoniously cheats on her, Yung asks for and wins Yuk-ching's hand in marriage. However, in a painfully ridiculous moment, the priest makes Yung promise to go straight before he will pronounce them man and wife. Naturally, Yung agrees, and the couple struggle to start their own business. However, psychopath Blackie Yiu (played in an insufferably over-the-top manner by Chin Ho), whom Yung had previously disfigured, wants revenge at all costs.

Cecilia Yip is excellent as always, and Simon Yam delivers one of his best characterizations to date; the scenes they share together before the wedding are very romantic, and their love for each other (born of both betrayal and circumstance) seems entirely believable. Unfortunately, such fine work is for naught when placed in such a senseless, hackneyed scenario. The final sequence, in which Yung brings Yuk-ching back from the dead through sheer force of love (or something), takes camp to a new level. Cheung Kwok-keung, Shing Fui-on, and Mark Houghton also appear.

594. Love in a Fallen City

(1984; Shaw Brothers) ★: 6/10. *King sing ji luen* (Cantonese), *Qing cheng zhi lian* (Mandarin): "Love in a Fallen City." Cinematographer: Anthony Ho Tung-lei;

Art Director: Tony Au Ding-ping; Music: Violet Lam Man-yee; Writer: Fung Suk-yin; Producer: Mona Fong Yat-wah; Director: Ann Hui On-wah. Cast: Chow Yun-fat (Fan Liu-yuan), Cora Miao Qian-ren (Pai Liu-so), Chung King-fai (Hsu), Keung Chung-ping, Chiu Kao, Kam Chuen. 1.85:1. No official domestic video release. 96 minutes.

Ann Hui followed her critically and financially successful **Boat People** with this expensive and unsuccessful love story which unfolds during the early 1940s. Shanghai divorcee Pai Liu-so is ostracized by her relatives (who irrationally blame her for their poor financial state) and unsure of her future. A concerned friend takes Liu-so to HK and introduces her to the affluent, handsome, and charming Fan Liu-yuan who is just back from overseas. Liu-so considers herself to be a country bumpkin with old fashioned values, but that is one of the reasons that the Westernized Liu-yuan quickly becomes attracted to her. However, while his affections are genuine, she politely resists his gentlemanly advances. Liu-yuan remains determined and rents a flat for Liu-so so that she may stay in HK during a time that he will be away from the area. A Japanese attack forces Liu-yuan's ship to turn back, and both he and Liu-so must continue their lives amid the Japanese occupation of HK, a shared struggle that brings them closer together.

Exquisitely photographed and employing the sort of attention to composition and period detail that truly transports the viewer to another place and era, **Love in a Fallen City** still emerges as a disappointing affair. Adapted from an Eileen Chang novel, the screenplay is staid and the character's emotions are usually held in check. Consequently, while it avoids the melodramatic pitfalls inherent in the premise, the film is never especially involving, save for its visual attractions. Fine performances by Cora Miao and Chow Yun-fat help, as does Violet Lam's score (which won a Hong Kong Film Award).

595. Love in the Time of Twilight

(1995; Golden Harvest/ERA International/Film Workshop/Paragon Films) ★: 6/10. *Fa yuet gaai kei* (Cantonese), *Hua yue jia qi* (Mandarin): "Flower Moon Wedding Day." Cinematographer: Peter Pau Tak-hei; Art Directors: William Cheung Suk-ping; Music: William Woo Wai-lap, Raymond Wong Ying-wah; Writers: Tsui Hark, Szeto Wai-cheuk, Sharun Hui Salong; Action Director: Yuen Bun; Producer-Director: Tsui Hark. Cast: Charlie Yeung Choi-nei (Yan-yan), Nicky Wu Chi-lung (Kong), Eric Kot Man-fai (Little Shrimp), William Ho Kar-kui (The Devil King), Lau Shun (Yan-yan's Father), Cheung Ting (Cheung Siu-ying), Peter Lai Bei-tak (Magician), Wong Yat-fei (Theater Manager). 1.85:1. VHS: Tai Seng. Import LD/VCD: Mei Ah. 103 minutes.

Following the success of **The Lovers**, Tsui Hark quickly re-teamed Charlie Yeung and Nicky Wu for this ambitious, but not entirely successful, science fiction-fantasy. Unappreciated Peking Opera performer Yan-yan and bank clerk Kong bump into each other one day, an accident that leads to several acts of petty revenge on the part of both teenagers. Kong is tricked into aiding some robbers and is choked to death for his trouble. His ghost appears to Yan-yan and explains that his spirit is trapped in the electric wires used to strangle him; when she turned on a light in the theater, he was released. Kong enlists Yan-yan's aid on a most unusual mission: Using his powers, he "splits" her into a second being and the two travel back in time. As a spirit, he cannot get too close to his "real" body, so he needs Yan-yan's help to change the circumstances that led to his murder. It's an ingenious plan, but everything that can go wrong does and the pair find themselves going in circles trying to alter destiny. In the meantime, "Devil King," the gangster who killed Kong, is himself murdered and dies next to the same utility poll. Subsequently, he too is split into two entities, making the task even more difficult.

Reminiscent of **Back to the Future**, the narrative twists and turns on itself in pleasing fashion, and ambitious computer animation is used to create several amusing effects (particularly instances where Yan-yan's fellow performers become hopelessly confused by the way she seems to change clothes and manner from one second to the next) and an amazing, surreal world that exists between this one and the next. However, a large portion of the proceedings are much more routine, relying too heavily on poor-to-middling comic interludes to advance the narrative. Some of the FX are also less than convincing, and when one of Devil King's halves is hit in the face by a bullet, the result is on the level of a Don Post monster mask. Another debit is Eric Kot's obnoxious and tediously unfunny performance in a supporting role that could have been dispensed with entirely. Tsui's customary political undertones provide some subtextural distraction (the film takes place around the time of The Cultural Revolution, and one can read into the splitting of the individual and the attempt to bring order to chaos by going back to the past as a parallel to what was done in the years after the upheaval).

596. Love Is a Fairytale

(1993; Golbal Investment) ★: 3/10. *Fung yat ching mei liu* (Cantonese), *Jia ri qing wei le* (Mandarin): "Summer Sun: Love Cannot Understand." Cinematographers: Kevin Chu Kar-wang, Hau Ching-keung; Art Director: Danny Yuen Ching-yeung; Music: Romeo Diaz; Writers: Kevin Chu Kar-wang, Law Kam-fai; Producer: Danny Lee Sau-yin; Director: Kevin Chu Kar-wang. Cast: Aaron Kwok Fu-shing (Hung), Rosamund Kwan Chi-lam (Michelle), Gabriel Wong Yat-san (Dee), Peter Lai Bei-tak (Hung's Boss), Miu Kiu-wai (John Hui). 1.85:1. VHS/LD: World Video. Import LD/VCD: Mei Ah. 94 minutes.

A spurious wish fulfilment fantasy for teenagers, this offers generous views of its two photogenic stars (plus a multitude of designer clothes and expensive vehicles) but is sorely lacking in substance. Canto pop "Heavenly King" Aaron Kwok plays Hung, a college student working as a Clearwater Bay boat boy during summer break. He spends most of his day staring at a billboard picture of Michelle, HK's top model. When Michelle turns up in the flesh, Hung loses all control and sets about trying to win the favor of this older woman. Stuck in a relationship with an abusive boyfriend, Michelle starts spending more and more time with Hung, not realizing just how serious he is.

Numerous montages and "Hit Single" breaks pad out the running time, and only fans of the leads will care enough to see this all the way through to the absolutely predictable conclusion.

597. Love on Delivery

(1994; Cosmopolitan Film Productions Co./Shaw Brothers) ★: 7/10. *Poh waai ji wong* (Cantonese), *Po huai zhi wang* (Mandarin): "Destroyer King." Cinematographer: David Chung Chi-man; Art Director: Luk Chi-fung; Music: William Woo Wai-lap; Writer: Vincent Kok Tak-chiu; Producer: Mona Fong Yat-wah; Action Director: Ching Siu-tung; Director: Lee Lik-chi. Cast: Stephen Chiau Sing-chi (Ho Kam-an), Christy Chung Lai-tai (Lily), Ng Man-tat (Tat, aka Devil Killer), Ben Lam Kwok-bun (Tuen Shui-lau), Paul Chun Pui (Chan), Phillip Chan Yan-kin (TV Commercial Pitchman), Peter Lai Bei-tak (Guy with a Fly in His Soup), Vincent Kok Tak-chiu (Niu), Cheng Cho (Master Blackbear), Gabriel Wong Yat-san (Turtle), Wong Yat-fei (Ho's Boss), Billy Chow Bei-lee

(Taekwando Master). 1.85:1. VHS: Tai Seng. Import LD/VCD/DVD: Mei Ah. 100 minutes.

One of Stephen Chiau's more subdued vehicles (subdued being a relative term when describing his filmography), **Love on Delivery** casts him as put-upon delivery boy Ho Kam-an. The sort of timid schlub women will not give the time of day to, Ho's world changes in an instant when he is kissed by gorgeous judo student Lily. She, however, is not so smitten with him, and Ho decides that the only way he can win her heart is to become a kung fu master. He signs up for lessons from "Devil Killer," who claims to be an expert but is merely a conman. Bogus or not, the training exercises imbue Ho with a new sense of confidence. When Lily's arrogant judo teacher tries to molest her, Ho (who hides his identity behind a hilarious-looking Garfield mask) comes to the rescue and actually manages to defeat him. Lily now yearns for her mysterious benefactor, but as Ho has no way to prove it was really him, she believes the masked hero to be evil Japanese karate instructor Tuen Shui-lau. This leaves Ho with only one choice: He must challenge Tuen in the ring and defeat him.

Instead of the *mo lei tau*-spouting smart guy found in most of his earlier work, **Love on Delivery** serves up a kinder, gentler Stephen Chiau as the sort of loveable underdog character any audience can identify with. Some of the humor is a bit too obvious to work but much of it does and there are amusing send-ups of **The Terminator** and **Ultraman**. The exaggerated combat sequences are well-staged by veteran choreographer/director Ching Siu-tung, and Jacky Cheung Hok-yau has a terrific cameo that is one of the highlights here.

598. Love Recipe

(1994; Film-maker's Co-op) ★: 2/10. *Oi ching sike heung mei* (Cantonese), *Ai qing se xiang wei* (Mandarin): "Love Color Smell Taste." Cinematographers: Eric Chu Kwok-fai, Sander Lee Kar-ko, Tony Chan Tak-wah; Art Director: Raymond Fung Yuen; Music: Jibson Yeung Siu-hung, James Yeung Jim, Peter Woo Chun-kit; Writer: Gladys Pang Mei-fung; Producer: Wong Tso-chi; Director: Leonard Heung Lap-hang. Cast: Kathy Chow Hoi-mei (Ann), Alex Fong Chung-sun (James), Linda Cheung Lan-ying (Porsche), Thomas Lam Cho-fai, Sam Tsang Hong-sang. 1.85:1. VHS: World Video. Running time unknown.

In this awful romantic comedy-drama, Kathy Chow plays a woman who decides to leave her dentist husband after their sex life becomes nonexistent. Travelling to Thailand for the opening of a friend's restaurant, she spends the night with a transvestite who dresses like a woman out of guilt for the way that he mistreated women in the past (wait, it gets worse). She is then courted by Alex Fong's suave waiter, only to have hubby show up and profess his love. The plot occasionally detours to cover the romantic travails of her friends, including a womanizer, a homosexual, and a big-breasted bubble-head (Linda Cheung).

With its banal characters and trite observations about love, this is merely a recipe for boredom, and the final reel is too ludicrous for words. At least the Thailand locales are nice to look at.

599. Love Soldier of Fortune

(1988) ★: 5/10. *Oi dik to bing* (Cantonese), *Ai de tao bing* (Mandarin): "Love's Evading Soldier." Cinematographer: Wilson Chan Pui-kai; Art Director: Jessy Lam Chak-chi; Music: Lau Yee-tat; Writers: Stanley Fung Shui-fan, Barry Wong Ping-yiu, Clarence Yip Wai-chung; Producer: Wallace Cheung Kwok-chong; Director: Stanley Fung Shui-fan. Cast: Alan Tam Wing-lun (Antonio Go Ha-chai), Maggie Cheung Man-yuk (So See-dai), Miu Kiu-wai (Lam Shu-fu), Stanley Fung Shui-fan (Go San-liu), Sandra Ng Kwan-yu (Candy Ho), Nat Chan Pak-cheung (Saridon), Wong Jing (Wong). 1.85:1. VHS: Tai Seng. Import LD: Mei Ah. Import VCD: Mega Star. 95 minutes. Also known as **Soldier of Love**.

Timid piano tuner Antonio Go is secretly in love with radio DJ So See-dai and never misses her show. One day, while working at the home of egotistical singer Lam Shu-fu, he is able to meet his dream girl and makes something of a good impression. When his mother leaves HK, Antonio is forced to move into his relatives' spooky old home, which is haunted by the spirit of his grand uncle, Go San-liu. See-dai invites Antonio to be a guest on the program, and even though he makes a fool of himself, she is intrigued by this eccentric but well-meaning fellow. Meanwhile, Uncle San decides to help Antonio make his fortune by composing some songs for the lad to sell. The buyer is none other than Lam, who pays peanuts and makes a fortune off the subsequent hits. When See-dai figures out what is going on, she decides to help Antonio embark on his own career. He is an instant success, but fame changes him for the worse and this alienates See-dai. To complicate matters further, Uncle San has decided to leave for Canada to find his lost ghostly love, leaving Antonio on his own with nothing but his natural talents to help him get by.

A likeable cast and the supernatural angle keep this formula-bound romantic comedy afloat, but, ultimately, it is neither funny nor interesting enough to really hit the mark. It still makes for pleasant viewing, however. Actor/composer Michael Lai Siu-tin has a cameo.

600. The Love That Is Wrong

(1993; Sam Po Film) ★: 2/10. *Naam yue nui* (Cantonese), *Nan yu nu* (Mandarin): "Boys and Girls." Cinematographer: Mok Chat-yun; Art Director: Ray Lam Chan-fai; Music: Not Original; Writer: Tam Wai-shing; Producers: Lau Chun-fai, Chan Choi-yin; Director: Ho Shu-pau. Cast: Ellen Chan Ar-lun (Ann Shioko Kawashima), Michael To Tai-yu (Wang Yin-yu), Lam Wai (Li), Charlie Cho Cha-lei (Voyeur). 1.85:1. VHS: Tai Seng. Import LD/VCD: Universe. 89 minutes.

Lesbian lovers Ann and Amy decide they want to have a child in this puerile Category III offering. Amy seduces their coworker Wang Yin-yu, with the intention of dumping him after she becomes pregnant. However, when Amy starts to succumb to Wang's affections, Ann gives her an ultimatum: him or me. The distraught Amy commits suicide, driving Ann over the edge from grief. She begins to seek out men who will come on to her, with the intention of killing them in brutal ways. However, she makes the mistake of developing feelings for the goofy detective investigating the crimes.

The erotic content isn't bad; the rest is too dumb to be offensive and is mildly enjoyable if approached on the level of camp. What is rather objectionable is the fact that the character of Ann is made Japanese for no reason other than that she is the villain. Her name is even a reference to the notorious war traitor Yoshiko Kawashima, played by Anita Mui in **The Last Princess of Manchuria**.

601. Love to Kill

(1993; Uniden Film Distribution) ★: 2/10. *Yeuk ji luen* (Cantonese), *Nu zhi lian* (Mandarin): "Cruel Love." Cinematographers: Gigo Lee Chi-hang, Joe Chan Kong-hung; Art Director: Jon Hau Wing-choi; Music: Chow Kai-sang; Writers: Law Kam-fai, Lau Wing-kin; Producers: Danny Lee Sau-yin, Yang Teng-kuei; Director: Chung Siu-hung. Cast: Anthony Wong Chau-sang (Sam Wong Wai-sum), Danny Lee Sau-yin ("Fire Ball" Lee), Elizabeth Lee Mei-fung (Jade), Julie Lee Wah-yuet (Jenny), Eric Kei Far-fat (Kay). 1.85:1. VHS: Tai Seng. Import LD: Golden Cinema City. 87 minutes.

Despite being heavily cut by HK censors, this Category III thriller remains one of the most repugnant in memory. Sam Wong is a psychotic businessman who periodically abuses his wife Jade in horrifying ways. One evening, after sadistically raping her, he is beaten and arrested by police officer "Fire Ball" Lee. However, Wong is able to leave the station a free man when Jade, fearing for her life, refuses to press charges. Concerned for her safety, Lee has the woman and her young son move into his apartment. When Sam threatens to murder her invalid mother unless she complies, Jade returns to her home, where Sam promptly assaults her and leaves her chained to a wall. He then goes to Lee's apartment and rapes his girlfriend, leaving her brain damaged and in a coma. Jade then decides that she must avenge herself for the cruelty she has endured.

A pointless wallow in sadism and misogyny, topped off with leering, juvenile humor, **Love to Kill** is strictly for those interested in exploring the extremes of HK cinema. Anthony Wong, Danny Lee, and Julie Lee already went this route in **The Untold Story**, but what is Elizabeth Lee (**Gunmen**) doing in this garbage?

602. Love Unto Waste

(1986; D & B Films Co./Pearl City) ★: 8/10. *Dei ha ching* (Cantonese), *Di xia qing* (Mandarin): "Underground Love." Cinematographer: Johnny Koo Kwok-wah; Art Director: William Cheung Suk-ping; Music: Violet Lam Man-yee; Writers: Lai Kit, Yau Tai On-ping; Producer: Vicky Leung Lee Siu-ha; Director: Stanley Kwan Kam-pang. Cast: Tony Leung Chiu-wai (Tony Cheung), Elaine Kam Yin-ling (Liu Yuk-ping), Chow Yun-fat (Detective Lan), Irene Wan Pik-ha (Billie Yuen Bui-yee), Tsai Chin (Chiu Suk-ling). 1.85:1. VHS: Tai Seng. Import LD: Mei Ah. Import VCD: Mega Star. 96 minutes.

Tony, Billie, and Yuk-ping find their lives turned upside down when mutual friend Suk-ling is brutally murdered one evening in what looks to be a robbery gone wrong. Lan, the detective assigned to the case, instigates a circuitous line of questioning and has a highly eccentric method of digging for the truth (he correctly likens himself to Peter Falk's "Columbo" character at one point). An autopsy reveals that the victim had recently undergone an abortion, and Lan begins showing up at the oddest times, with seemingly no real motivation, just to talk. While his intrusions are greeted merely with patient courtesy at first, the friends grow to like him and learn that he is lonely and suffering from the regret of mistakenly divorcing his wife. In the aftermath of the tragedy, Tony's relationship with Billie weakens, while his attraction to Yuk-ping grows, with ironic results. The situation comes to a head when Tony, Billie, and Yuk-ping take Suk-ling's ashes back to her relatives in Taiwan.

The mystery is a secondary aspect of this measured, engrossing character study about life, love, and wasted youth. The performances are estimable (particularly Chow, in an offbeat role), the observations and conclusions are heartfelt, and director Stanley Kwan (**Rouge**) incorporates some simple, lovely imagery (a shower of rice being the most indelible). The film won the Best Screenplay and Best Supporting Actress (Elaine Kam) prizes at The Hong Kong Film Awards.

603. Lover of the Last Empress

(1995; Win's Entertainment) ★: 6/10. *Chi Hei bei mat sang woot* (Cantonese), *Ci Xi mi mi sheng huo* (Mandarin): "Chi Hei's Secret Life" or "Ci Xi's Secret Life." Art Director: Jason Mok Siu-kei; Music: William Woo Wai-lap; Producer: Wong Jing; Cinematographer-Director: Andrew Lau Wai-keung. Cast: Chingmy Yau Suk-ching (Hui Yu-lan), Tony Leung Kar-fai (Prince Kung), Yu Rongguang (Hsien-feng), Ku Feng (Su Shun), Valerie Chow Kar-ling (The Queen), Chan Kwok-bong (Xiao-an), Yuen King-tan (Da-niu), Lau Shun (Courtier), Yvonne Yung Hung (Lady Li), Ha Ping (Yu-lan's Mother). 2.35:1. VHS: Tai Seng. Import LD/VCD/DVD: Mei Ah. 100 minutes.

If graphic Category III fare like **Chinese Torture Chamber Story** and **Sex and the Emperor** are not your cup of tea, here is a more upscale (though still C-III) version of the same thing. **Lover of the Last Empress** tells of how lowly concubine Hui Yu-lan climbed the social ranks to eventually become the most powerful woman in The Ching Dynasty. From the very second she arrives at the palace, Yu-lan catches the eye of His Majesty, Hsien-feng, but her first night with him is a disaster. When one of the other concubines cooks her pet cat, Yu-lan goes berserk and brutally murders the woman but is saved from arrest by Prince Kung. Infatuated with Yu-lan (whom he had previously saved from some bandits), Kung covers up the killing. Receiving sexual instruction from some seasoned prostitutes (a silly but undeniably erotic scene), Yu-lan proceeds to win over Hsien-feng and bears his child. When the King dies at a young age, Yu-lan becomes the Empress Dowager and equal in power to the queen, thus paving the way for her to assume control of the entire country, with Kung at her side.

Definitely not to be taken as an accurate historical account (it is amazing how, in Wong Jing productions, sex always plays such a major role in shaping history), this remains a well-mounted, if predictable, drama. While not entirely convincing, Chingmy Yau is better than expected, and the production values are conspicuously higher than normal for this sort of sexploitation fare.

604. Lover of the Swindler

(1993; Regal Films Co./Image Film & Entertainment) ★: 6/10. *Chin wong ching yan* (Cantonese), *Qian wang qing ren* (Mandarin): "Lover of the Swindler King." Cinematographer: William Yim Wai-lun; Art Director: James Cheung Ying-wah; Music: Richard Lo Sai-kit; Writer: Si Woo; Producers: Steven Lo Kit-sing, Lau On; Action Director: Yuen Cheung-yan; Director: Jacky Pang Yee-wah. Cast: Tony Leung Kar-fai (Michael Chan Chun), Carina Lau Kar-ling (Ling), Vincent Wan Yeung-ming (Michael and Doctor Wong's Partner), Kenneth Tsang Kong (Doctor Wong), Anita Lee Yuen-wah (Candy), Pauline Wong Siu-fung (Wong Chi-san), Isabella Chow Wang (Siu-tung), Charine Chan Kar-ling (Chi-san's Assistant). 1.85:1. VHS: Tai Seng. Import LD/VCD: Universe. 91 minutes.

This marginal production benefits from its charismatic leads and some stylish staging. Upwardly mobile club girl Ling goes to pay off a debt owed by a friend to loan shark Michael by a friend, but ends up helping the master gambler with a high stakes card game. Sparks fly between the two and Michael starts trusting her enough to share some of the secrets behind his con games. However, one set-up goes wrong, Ling accidentally kills a policeman, and the money Michael borrowed from some loan sharks for the scam gets lost in the chaos. To save her friend from almost certain death, Ling cleans out her bank account and gives it to Michael ... then doesn't hear from him again. By sheer luck, Ling deduces that one of her coworkers is involved in the swindle and follows her to a warehouse. Inside, she discovers that Michael was indeed in on a plot to rob her but now wants to wash his hands of the affair and refuses to take any of the money. His partners decide to eliminate him, an act that temporarily brings the pair back together, but the road ahead still has a few twists and turns.

For most of its running time, this is a fast and intriguing romantic thriller (with an offbeat, Vangelis-style score), but credibility gets stretched a bit too thin in the final reel. Leung and Lau make a sexy, highly appealing couple, and Isabella

Chow (**Sex and Zen**) is fun as a ditzy hostess whose mangled Cantonese drives everyone batty.

605. Lover's Tear

(1992) ★: 8/10. *Sai bat mong ching* (Cantonese), *Shi bu wang qing* (Mandarin): "Swear Not to Forget Love." Cinematographer: Ardy Lam Kwok-wah; Art Director: Suzy Cheung Kai-san; Music: John Sands; Writers: Jerry Liu Wing-leung, Lee Chi-ngai, Jacob Cheung Chi-leung; Producer: Sammo Hung Kam-po; Action Director: Lam Ching-ying; Director: Jacob Cheung Chi-leung. Cast: Nina Li Chi (Fang I-ling), Ngai Sing (Chung Ao), Sammo Hung Kam-po (Commissioner Kung), Lam Ching-ying (Cheng Ying), Wu Ma (Ling's Father), Ku Feng (Mai Cheng-chun), Elvis Tsui Kam-kong (Lin Wei), Yukari Oshima (Su Ehr). 1.85:1. VHS: World Video. Import LD: Mei Ah. 97 minutes.

Known primarily as a sexpot, Nina Li was given a rare opportunity to essay a straight dramatic role in this offbeat, absorbing drama from gifted director Jacob Cheung (**Cageman**). In Shenzhen on a joint HK/China anti-smuggling investigation, HK cops Chung Ao and Mai Cheng-chun find themselves wanted by the Public Security forces when Mai's connection to fugitive Lin Wei is revealed. While struggling with Lin, Mai accidentally shoots a policewoman, an accident that the local authorities blame on Chung. While being transported to prison, Chung manages to escape with Lin's deaf mistress, Ling. The two travel to Ling's home in the country, where her father reveals that the girl's aunt tried to force her into prostitution. Ling was saved by Lin, a triad who taught her to communicate and took care of her. After spending so much time looking out for each other, Chung and Ling fall in love, but the girl's sense of loyalty to Lin remains strong.

The premise offers ample opportunities for this to degenerate into a silly, melodramatic mess, but the dialogue is carefully composed and the characters have far greater depth than one expects from this sort of enterprise. Beautifully photographed and atmospherically scored, the film draws the viewer in with its elegance and tempered approach, and this restraint also helps to make the brief instances of violence seem especially potent and jarring. Li and Ngai are fine as the star-crossed lovers, and they are backed up by commendable supporting performances. Worthy of special note are Elvis Tsui (who is rarely given a part of this gravity) and Lam Ching-ying (as a brooding gunman who also possesses great affection for Ling). Too slow and introspective for the average HK moviegoer, **Lover's Tear** lasted only a week in theaters, but it is a minor treasure worth locating on video.

606. Lover's Tears

(1996; Powerful Entertainment) ★: 5/10. *Ching yan dik ngaan lui* (Cantonese), *Qing ren de yan lei* (Mandarin): "Lover's Tears." Cinematographer: Gigo Lee Chi-hang; Art Director: Daniel Lee Yan-kong; Music: Henry Lai Wan-man; Writer: Ella Chan Bo-wah; Producers: David Chiang Da-wei, Tang Yat-ming; Director: Lee Kwok-lap. Cast: Carman Lee Yeuk-tung (Lau Heung-ching), Derek Yee Tung-sing (Kam Ming-sang), Tou Chung-wah (Lam Long), Paulyn Suen Kai-kwun (Kam Hing), Bobby Yip King-sang (Suspicious Ugly Guy). 1.85:1. VHS: World Video. Import LD/VCD/DVD: New City. 91 minutes.

When architect Kam Ming-sang is accidentally shot in the head as a result of bad judgment by his police officer friend Lam Long, he survives but lapses into a deep coma. Ming-sang's newly pregnant wife Heung-ching is left with the burden of caring for their children, in addition to spending time with him at the hospital and dealing with her grief. While everyone is of the opinion that Ming-sang will probably never wake up, Heung-ching refuses to accept that possibility. As a result, stress and poverty soon overtake her and the children. In the meantime, a guilt-ridden Long quits the police force and seeks to help, but Heung-ching vehemently refuses to accept anything from him.

Too routine to be entirely effectual, this remains marginally interesting, thanks to competent performances by the leads and, particularly, a bubbly supporting turn by Paulyn Suen. Screenwriter James Yuen Sai-sang has a small role, and co-producer Henry Fong Ping can be spotted as a wheelchair athlete during a basketball game sequence.

607. The Lovers

(1994; Golden Harvest/Film Workshop/Paragon Films) ★: 9/10. *Leung Chuk* (Cantonese), *Liang Zhu* (Mandarin): "Leung Chuk" (the main characters' surnames in Cantonese) or "Liang Zhu" (the main characters surnames in Mandarin). Cinematographer: David Chung Chi-man; Art Director: Joel Chong Kwok-wing; Music: Joseph Koo Kar-fai, James Wong Jim, Mark Lui Chung-tak, William Woo Wai-lap; Writers: Tsui Hark, Sharun Hui Sa-long; Producer-Director: Tsui Hark. Cast: Charlie Yeung Choi-nei (Chuk Ying-toi), Nicky Wu Chi-lung (Leung Shan-pak), Carrie Ng Kar-lai (Ying-toi's mother), Elvis Tsui Kam-kong (Ying-toi's father), Lau Shun (Cheung-kwai). 2.35:1. VHS: Tai Seng. Import LD/VCD/DVD: Universe. 107 minutes.

Tsui Hark's charming adaptation of a revered Chinese folk tale (sometimes translated into English as "The Story of a Tragic Love") ranks among the director's warmest and most rewarding films to date. Set in the first century, the storyline revolves around Chuk Ying-toi, a clumsy teenage girl from an affluent background who disguises herself as a boy to get an education. Sharing her class and accommodations is Leung Shan-pak, a poor but handsome and idealistic fellow student. Ying-toi soon falls for her newfound companion and is at pains to conceal her infatuation, while Shan-pak is perplexed by the new and baffling sensations he feels for his "buddy." When Ying-toi finally abandons her ruse, the two decide to marry, but their plans are curtailed by the girl's class-consumed parents, who are determined to marry their daughter off to a suitor from an influential family. The father has Shan-pak severely beaten, and Ying-toi confined to a room on the family estate, but otherworldly forces ultimately intervene to bring the lovers together.

For this, his second go at adapting one of the "Four Great Tales of China" (following the previous year's **Green Snake**), Tsui has crafted a sentimental but compelling love story which skirts melodramatic excess, remaining on an even keel throughout. Aside from the addition of some peripheral characters, the screenplay remains largely faithful to the fable, echoing its criticism of the period's repressive feudal society, while slightly updating the final act. Tsui presents the material in a manner befitting its source: relaxed and introspective, free of the manic editing and soaring camerawork on display in his other work from the time (like the **Once Upon a Time in China** series). Even by the customarily florid standards of Chinese fantasy, this is a gorgeous film, rivalling the pastoral majesty of **Green Snake** (but with a more realistic, less fantasy-oriented approach) and providing the perfect tableaux for such a warmly regarded parable. The pairing of Canto pop singer Charlie Yeung and Taiwanese singing star Nicky Wu turned out to be a felicitous bit of casting. Under Tsui's direction, the two effectively belie their limited acting experience, embodying the iconic roles in a charming and unaffected manner (Tsui quickly re-teamed the two for **Love in the Time of Twilight**). In contrast to Anita Yuen Wing-yee's "Best Actress"-winning turn in the delightful **He's a Woman, She's a Man** (1994), Yeung does not make for a very convincing male. However, such impersonations rarely seem persuasive (from a Western point of view) in films of this type, and it doesn't hinder one's affection for the character or the certainty of Tsui's presentation in the least.

608. Loving You

(1995; Cosmopolitan Film Productions Co./Shaw Brothers) ★: 6/10. *Mo mei san taam* (Cantonese), *Wu wei shen tan* (Mandarin): "The Tasteless Detective." Cinematographer: Cheng Siu-keung; Art Director: JM; Music: Chung Chi-wing; Writer: Ah Hoi; Producer: Mona Fong Yat-wah; Action Director: Yuen Bun; Director: Johnny To Kei-fung. Cast: Lau Ching-wan (Lau), Carman Lee Yeuk-tung (Lau's Wife), Tou Chung-wah (Drug Dealer), Yip Chun-mei, Wong Chun-fai. 1.85:1. VHS: Tai Seng. Import LD/VCD: Mei Ah. 84 minutes.

Lau is a good cop but a lousy human being, treating his wife poorly on the occasions that he even bothers to come home. Shortly after announcing that she is pregnant with someone else's child and is leaving him, Lau gets drunk and wanders into a trap laid by a drug dealer out for revenge. He is subsequently shot in the head but still somehow manages to apprehend the criminal. Thanks to a miracle, there is no brain damage, but Lau's sense of smell and taste are gone forever (hence the clever Chinese title). With his wife vacillating on what she wants to do, Lau faces more problems: He is suffering from operation side effects that cause dizziness, and the killer has escaped custody.

Clearly inspired by the awful **Regarding Henry** (see also **Murder** for another HK variation on that Harrison Ford film), **Loving You** benefits immensely from strong, convincing performances by Lau Ching-wan and Carman Lee, and some sharp direction from Johnny To. The opening reel confrontation and thrilling climax are HK action cinema at its best, but the screenplay's central notion (that Lau has emerged from his near death experience a better person) is communicated only slightly more convincingly here than it was in the American movie; and Tou Chung-wah exudes so little menace as the killer, they might as well have used a cardboard cutout of him.

609. Lucky Stars Go Places

(1986; Golden Harvest/Bo Ho Films/Paragon Films) ★: 5/10. *Jui gaai fuk sing* (Cantonese), *Zui jia fu xing* (Mandarin): "Best Lucky Stars." Cinematographers: Cheung Shing-tung, Lam Lai-hing; Art Directors: Raymond Lee King-man, Raymond Fung Yuen; Music: Violet Lam Man-yee; Writer: Barry Wong Ping-yiu; Producer: Sammo Hung Kam-po; Action Director: Sammo Hung Stunt Team; Director: Eric Tsang Chi-wai. Cast: Sammo Hung Kam-po (Eric Kidstuff), Alan Tam Wing-lun (Top Dog), Kent Cheng Chuk-see (Fat Cat), Andy Lau Tak-wah (Lambo), Anthony Chan Yau (Long Legs), Billy Lau Nam-kwong (Libbogen), Maria Tung Ling (Yum Yum), Cho Tat-wah (Walter Tsao), Wong Ching (Inspector Wong), Karl Maka (Albert), Sylvia Chang Ai-chia (Quito), Stanley Fung Shui-fan (Rawhide), Eric Tsang Chi-wai (Roundhead), Richard Ng Yiu-hon (Sandy), Wong Jing (Tiny), Pauline Wong Siu-fung (Tiny's Wife), James Tien Chun (Lambo's Commander), Norman Tsui Siu-keung (Sum), Fung Hark-on (Thug), Alfred Cheung Kin-ting (Translator), Lau Kar-wing (Cop), Bolo Yeung (Movie Patron). 1.85:1. VHS: Tai Seng (No Subtitles). Import VCD: Mei Ah. Import DVD: Universe. 95 minutes.

The *fuk sing* series carries on with a predominantly new cast, plus a brief visit from the old crew and Karl Maka and Sylvia Chang of Cinema City's rival **Aces Go Places** series. This time out, Tsao enlists Kidstuff's help in bringing down a Japanese arms dealer. After selecting the police force's least desirable officers, Kidstuff turns them over to specialist Yum Yum(!) for training, but (in typical *fuk sing* fashion) she spends most of her time staving off their crude sexual advances. Disguised as Arab sheiks, the group sets up a weapons buy as a front to rob the villain's safe, thus putting him out of business. After they manage to get themselves locked inside, Kidstuff tries to convince Cho to send help, but the commander (afraid of a possible scandal) has him committed to an asylum instead!

The series started to show its age with this entry, which is even more distasteful and sexist than usual. That would be fine if it were reasonably amusing, but it's not and the new crew lack the distinctive personalities of their predecessors. The film only really comes to life when veterans Hung and Maka share the screen, but that only accounts for about a fifth of the running time. Still, the action choreography is good and there are a few isolated moments that stand out (in particular, Kent Cheng's "Chiuchow Missile" and Hung's novel way to win at Russian Roulette). Irene Wan Pik-ha and Miu Kiu-wai also put in appearances.

610. The Lunatics

(1986; D & B Films Co.) ★: 6/10. *Din lo jing juen* (Cantonese), *Dian lao zheng zhuan* (Mandarin): "Lunatics: True Story." Cinematographer: Wilson Chan Pui-kai; Art Director: Yank Wong Yan-kwai; Music: Phil Chan Fei-lap; Producer: Dickson Poon Dik-sun; Writer-Director: Derek Yee Tung-sing. Cast: Stanley Fung Shui-fan (Tsui), Deanie Yip Tak-han (Tina Lau), Paul Chun Pui (Tsuen), Tony Leung Chiu-wai (Doggie), Chow Yun-fat (Chung), Dennis Chan Kwok-san (Ming), Season Ma Si-san (Teacher), John Sham Kin-fun (Dr. Shum). 1.85:1. VHS: Tai Seng. Import LD: Mei Ah. Import VCD: Mega Star. 87 minutes.

This early directorial effort by Derek Yee is a frank, dramatic commentary on the brazen mistreatment and deplorable living conditions endured by homeless mental patients on the streets of Hong Kong. It follows the life of dedicated social worker Tsui, who is accompanied on his rounds for a time by reporter Tina Lau. She becomes interested in Tsui and his work after witnessing him convince a cleaver-wielding mental patient in a market to surrender without violence. Tsui's regulars range from the needle-obsessed "Dr." Shum to paranoid derelict Chung, who buried his son alive after the boy contracted hepatitis. His one success story is Tsuen, a recovered and seemingly well-adjusted man who undergoes a calamitous relapse when his ex-wife takes legal action to prevent him from seeing their young son. Tsuen is soon spending his days breaking the necks of chickens supplied by his mother, who is desperately trying to conceal her son's demented behavior from their neighbors. When Tina captures Tsuen's actions on film and runs the story in her paper, he snaps completely, causing his fellow tenants to try and lynch him. This launches the man on a bloody rampage, which climaxes at his son's school, where he holds the kindergarten teacher and her class at knifepoint.

The Lunatics could have proven to be more consequential had there been greater emphasis on insight and less on blood and thunder dramatics. The mechanics of each situation are presented in a terse manner, in keeping with the film's assertion that the whole issue has become an unresolvable dilemma. However, with few surprises, a climactic standoff that would fit perfectly into a slasher thriller, and a denouement that piles on one tragedy too many, it soon becomes difficult to take the high-minded first half too seriously. With the exception of Chow Yun-fat (who is just too handsome, even when grunged up, to be convincing as a crusty vagrant), the performances are excellent all around. Paul Chun won the year's Best Supporting Actor award for his vivid and frightening characterization.

611. Lung Fung Restaurant

(1990) ★: 4/10. *Lung Fung cha lau* (Cantonese), *Long Feng cha lou* (Mandarin): "Lung Fung Tea House" or "Long Feng Tea House." Cinematographer: Chan Ying-kit; Art Director: Jon Hau Wing-choi; Music: Lowell Lo Kwun-ting; Writers: Clarence Yip Wai-chung, Hau Chi-keung; Producer: Clarence Yip Wai- chung; Action Director: Blackie Ko Shou-liang; Director: Poon Man-kit. Cast: Max Mok Siu-chung (Dragon Ching), Ellen Chan Ar-lun (Gigi), Stephen Chiau Sing-chi (Rubbish Pool), Charine Chan Kar-ling (June Lok Ka-kei), Ng Man-tat (Kent), Parkman Wong Pak-man (Triad Boss), Henry Fong Ping (Chan). 1.85:1. VHS: Tai Seng. Import LD/VCD/DVD: Universe. 88 minutes.

This entirely run-of-the-mill effort stars Max Mok as a low level triad who is back on the streets following a stint in Stanley Prison. After getting a job as a waiter at the titular establishment, Mok picks up where he left off and becomes involved with beautiful bar girl Ellen Chan. He is instantly smitten, but it takes quite awhile for her to develop the same feelings for him. The pair eventually plan to marry and leave their pasts behind, but circumstances force Mok to intercede in a gang fight in order to protect his old boss. One thing leads to another and he is soon out to kill a rival triad leader, an act that drives his love away from him.

Slow paced and unoriginal, the film does try to flesh out its characters, but they remain largely uninteresting nonetheless. An additional problem is the subtitles, which suffer from an especially bad English translation, making one even less inclined to bother following the story. Stephen Chiau fans will enjoy seeing the comedian in a pre-stardom turn as a cocky Chiuchow gangster named "Rubbish Pool."

612. Lust for Love of a Chinese Courtesan

(1984; Shaw Brothers) ★: 6/10. *Oi nou san chun* (Cantonese), *Ai nu xin chuan* (Mandarin): "Beloved Servant New Story." Cinematographer: Lam Chiu; Art Director: Wong Kam-kong; Music: Joseph Chan Wing-leung; Producer: Mona Fong Yat-wah; Action Directors: Yuen Wah, Yuen Bun; Director: Chor Yuen. Cast: Candice Yu On-on (Chun), Woo Koon-chan, Cheung Kwok-chu, Alex Man Chi-leung (Ling Yun), Cho Tat-wah (Old Man in House), Lee Hoi-sang (Bald Swordsman), Yuen Wah (Swordsman). 1.85:1. VHS: World Video. Import LD: Ocean Shores. 92 minutes.

Candice Yu (former wife of Chow Yun-fat) stars in this stylish softcore period drama. Respected upper class woman Chun indulges in all manner of immoral acts, ranging from acting as a go-between for assassinations to using abducted girls for her brothel. One of her newest workers is feisty young Ai-nu, who manages to escape after being gang raped, only to be recaptured shortly thereafter. When Ai-nu murders one of her customers, Chun feels sorry for her and covers up the crime. However, straight arrow constable Ling Yun (who once gave Ai-nu some food when he found her cold and starving one night) smells a rat and begins his own investigation, in spite of being rebuked by the district's corrupt magistrate. By now, Chun has developed more than a proprietary interest in her beautiful underling, and the pair eventually begin sleeping with each other. Ai-nu starts showing an interest in Yun, however, enraging Chun, who orders her male lover, swordsman Hsiao Yeh, to murder the lawman. Yeh is attracted to Ai-nu himself and is finding that his bloodlust has started to fade. Chun and Ai-nu are changing, too, with each now assuming the other's disposition and outlook.

A tasteful erotic outing with peek-a-boo nudity, the film is distinguished by its elegant visuals and cinematography, plus a better-than-usual storyline which comments on the loss of humanity that can accompany the accumulation of wealth and power. The ending is easily deduced, but veteran director Chor Yuen frames the proceedings and, particularly, his performers so seductively, one is easily drawn in for the duration.

Mack the Knife *see* **Doctor Mack**

613. Mad Mad Ghost

(1992; Huge Yield Films Manufacturing) ★: 3/10. *Wong gam do si* (Cantonese), *Huang jin dao shi* (Mandarin): "Golden Taoist." Cinematographer: Chan Tung-chuen; Art Director: Fung Lok-ban; Music: Not Original; Writer: Johnny Lee King-kai; Producer: Chan Kui-yuen; Action Director: Ko Man-dik; Director: Billy Chan Wui-ngai. Cast: Lam Ching-ying (Ying), Jacqueline Law Wai-kuen (Kuen), Peter Chan Lung (Priest), Mark Houghton (Mark), Shum Wai (Realtor), Billy Lau Nam-kwong (Landlord). 1.85:1. VHS/LD: World Video. Import LD/VCD: Mei Ah. 91 minutes.

One of the last (and least) of the late '80s/early '90s horror-comedy cycle, **Mad Mad Ghost** has little going for it outside of Lam Ching-ying, HK cinema's answer to Peter Cushing. He plays Uncle Ying, aka "The Guide of Six Gods," a part-time janitor and full-time Taoist priest/fortune teller. When his floundering business causes him and his students to be expelled from their building for non-payment of rent, Ying moves them into a vacant house. Their new abode just happens to be haunted by the ghosts of Kuen and her wife-beating husband. After dispelling the male spirit, Ying enlists Kuen to help the students with their "ghostbuster" training. Two thugs, posing as Christian ministers, rent a room in the house, with the intention of uncovering a cache of gold which is hidden somewhere on the grounds. When they are caught and dispelled by Kuen, they hire a rival Taoist priest to vanquish her.

There are a number of quaint but amusing special FX, allowing the ghosts to extend their arms, fold up their bodies, and detach their heads, and Law does an amusing imitation of Madonna. However, most of the film consists of broad slapstick that few viewers will have the patience for, and the male ghost's misogynistic outbursts (which are apparently intended to be funny) cross the line from politically incorrect to downright disturbing. The soundtrack includes cues lifted from Lucio Fulci's Italian horror film **The Gates of Hell** (1983).

Mad Mission: Diamondfinger *see* **Aces Go Places**

Mad Mission Part 2: Aces Go Places *see* **Aces Go Places II**

Mad Mission Part III: Our Man from Bond Street *see* **Aces Go Places III: Our Man from Bond Street**

Mad Mission 4: You Never Die Twice *see* **Aces Go Places IV**

614. Mad Monkey Kung Fu

(1979; Shaw Brothers) ★: 7/10. *Fung hau* (Cantonese), *Feng hou* (Mandarin): "Mad Monkey." Music: Not Original; Writer: Ngai Hong; Producer: Mona Fong Yat-wah; Action Director-Director: Lau Kar-leung. Cast: Lau Kar-leung (Chen), Hsiao Hou (Monkey), Lo Lieh (Tuan), Kara Hui Ying-hung (Miss Chen). 2.35:1. No official domestic video release. 116 minutes.

Peking Opera performers Chen and his sister are invited to dine with the affluent Mr. Tuan. However, it's a trap: When Chen gets drunk and passes out, Tuan's wife falsely accuses him of raping her. In lieu of having Chen executed, his sister offers to become Tuan's concubine. Tuan accepts but still orders his men to smash Chen's hands. During the next five years, Chen tries to eke out a living as a street performer, with trained monkey Ah Mo as his main attraction. One day he is attacked by some extortionists and the animal is killed. After bemoaning his fate, Chen comes to the realization that his limber, hyperactive friend "Monkey" could be the perfect substitute for Ah Mo. The two create a successful act but are again robbed by the gangsters. In response, Monkey sets out to exact revenge but ends up badly beaten. Chen decides to teach the boy kung fu, and the pair spend the next few months in the mountains practising monkey style combat. Deciding that he is ready to head back to the city, Monkey returns and beats up the graft artists. They turn out to be employees of Tuan, and Monkey is no match for the man's kung fu. Although he barely escapes with his life, Monkey manages to learn how Tuan deceived Chen. After more intensive training under Chen's instruction, master and pupil are ready to return to Tuan's home for revenge.

An outstanding acrobat and one of the most talented performers in Lau Kar-leung's stable, Hsiao Hou receives an excellent showcase here. Bouncing around the various sets and exteriors (unlike most Shaw Brothers films, this has some footage shot outside the studio) like a somersaulting superball, Hsiao is amazing to watch, and it is a shame that he didn't receive more lead roles. The training sequences are amusingly offbeat, and Lau (taking the starring role himself) proves to be an ideal onscreen teacher. The stock score (which consists mainly of overstated "comic" cues and themes that would be more at home in a blaxploitation thriller) is a liability, but the film's strengths still shine through. Character names are from the dubbed version.

615. Mad Stylist

(1997; Tin Tin Company/Smileland Productions) ★: 1/10. *Ji gik saat yan faan* (Cantonese), *Zhi ji sha ren fan* (Mandarin): "Most Extreme Murderer." Cinematographer: Daniel Chan Man-fai; Art Director: Angelo Bernardo Castilho; Music: Simon Leung Chi-wah; Writer: Roman Cheung Siu-lun; Producer: Annie Koo Mei-ying; Action Director: Billy Chan Wui-ngai; Director: Stephen Yip Tin-hang. Cast: Wong Hei (Dee), Hilary Tsui Ho-ying (May), Annie Man Chung-han (Cheung Siu-fa), Michael Wong Man-tak (Ho Yau-fung), Kent Cheng Chuk-see (Luk Sing), Ricky Yee Fan-wai (Cheung), Peter Chan Lung (Ping). 1.85:1. Import LD/VCD: Universe. 98 minutes.

This nasty Category III thriller proves conclusively that black comedies are an art form that is simply beyond the ken of some writers and filmmakers. Serial killers Dee (a former hair stylist) and May lure victims up to their soundproof apartment, dismember them, do their hair up in strange ways, and then dump the pieces. While disposing of some body parts in a river, Dee is seen by Cheung Siu-fa, a young retarded girl from a local institution. May orders Dee to murder Siu-fa, but the girl ends up saving his life when Dee himself is almost killed by the establishment's transvestite principal (a ridiculous sequence that pretty much sums up the entire film). Dee decides to take Siu-fa home and demand a ransom but starts becoming much too attached to the girl, which drives a wedge into his relationship with May. Meanwhile, mismatched detectives Ho and Luk try to figure things out.

A desperate attempt to emulate the mood and dark humor of **Natural Born Killers** (a poster for which can be glimpsed at one point), this even goes so far as to ape **Pulp Fiction** in its choice of music! The director intercuts the action with random clips from Japanese *anime* and *manga*, as well as Western adult movies and "When Animals Attack"-style footage of various animals fighting, and this labored, pseudo-hip "symbolism" wears out its welcome quickly. While not as inept as say, **Horrible High Heels**, **Mad Stylist** is equally cynical and every bit as unappealing. Animal lovers will find it doubly so. Watch **Intruder** instead.

616. Madam City Hunter

(1993; Art Sea Films Co.) ★: 4/10. *Sing si lui lip yan* (Cantonese), *Cheng shi nu lie ren* (Mandarin): "Lady City Hunter." Cinematographer: Kwan Chi-kan; Art Director: Ring Law Chi-keung; Music: Not Original; Writer: Art Seas Writer's Group; Producer: Yuen Woo-ping; Action Director: Yuen Cheung-yan; Director: Kong Yeuk-shing. Cast: Cynthia Yang Li-ching (Yang Ching), Anthony Wong Chau-sang (Charlie Chan), Tommy Wong Kwong-leung (Kwong), Kara Hui Ying-hung (Siu-hung), Sheila Chan Sak-lan (Blackie), Woo Fung (Mr. Yang). 1.85:1. VHS: World Video (Subtitled only), Tai Seng (Dubbed Only). LD: World Video. Import LD/VCD: Universe. 88 minutes. Also known as **Lady Hunter** (Title for Tai Seng version).

Bearing absolutely no connection to Jackie Chan's **City Hunter** or the original *manga*, this low-budget action-comedy has a few interesting fights and a good cast but little else to offer. Inspector Yang finds herself on the hit list of a gang called "The Five Fingers" after she leads police on a raid of their hideout and kills one of their number. After The Fingers frame her for the murder of some glue-sniffing teenage delinquents, Ching joins forces with her boyfriend/superior and shabby private detective Charlie Chan(!) to nab the gang. However, as if she didn't already have enough problems, Ching's widower father has shacked up with Siu-hung, a beauty half his age, whose rich husbands have a habit of dropping dead.

The martial arts choreography is competent but uncharacteristically routine by the Yuen Brothers' standards, and the storyline is less than compelling. It's a hoot to see the usually villainous Anthony Wong and Tommy Wong cast as comic oafs, though both are dubbed by other actors here. Far less endearing is the perpetually obnoxious Sheila Chan as Wong's screechy partner.

Madam the Great *see* **Way of the Lady Boxers**

617. Made in Heaven

(1997; Skylark International Film Production) ★: 1/10. *Goo waak tin tong* (Cantonese), *Gu huo tian tang* (Mandarin): "Wise Heaven." Cinematographer: Wong Po-man; Art Director: Chiu Chin-yan; Music: Tse Chiu-kwong; Writers: Chan Ching-cheung, Alex Cheung Kwok-ming, Ho Tai-te; Producer: Henry Fong Ping; Action Director: Wong Wai-fai; Director: Alex Cheung Kwok-ming. Cast: Ada Choi Siu-fan (Mak Ah-chat/Lily Wong), Michael Tong Man-lung (Fung-wen), Diana Pang Dan (Sheila), Law Kar-ying (Dr. Law), Bobby Yip King-sang (North). 1.85:1. VHS: World Video. 91 minutes.

For crimes committed in his past life, male thief Mak Ah-chat is sentenced by a heavenly tribunal to be reincarnated as a beautiful woman. While this is not so bad in itself, the descendant (named Lily) will never be able to experience love without something disastrous occurring. She also has the power to sense when others are about to experience grave misfortune. After losing her parents, Lily becomes a hopelessly shy and withdrawn girl who is spurned by almost everyone. She gets work as an insurance agent and sells policies to people she senses are about to die. Naturally, her company is soon bankrupt, but Lily is taken on by a triad leader who wants to use her abilities as an advance warning of future tragedy. However, her influence causes him to see the error of his ways which, naturally, does not sit well with his underlings.

An absolutely hopeless mixture of unfunny humor and gauche melodrama, this is one of the most ill-conceived projects in memory. The only real sense of precognition here belongs to sexpot actress Diana Pang, who signs on for films that invariably turn out to be the worst of their particular years. **Made in Heaven** finds her still batting a thousand; if only her fellow cast members and the filmmakers could have sensed what they were about to inflict on the public.

618. Made in Hong Kong

(1997; Nicetop Independent/Teamwork Production House) ★: 9/10. *Heung Gong jai jo* (Cantonese), *Xiang Gang zhi zao* (Mandarin): "Made in Hong Kong." Cinematographers: Ko Sing-pui, Lam Wah-chuen; Art Director: Ma Kar-kwan; Music: Lam Wah-chuen; Producers: Andy Lau Tak-wah, Doris Yang Chi-ming, Shu Kei; Writer-Director: Fruit Chan Kwoh. Cast: Sam Lee Chan-sam (Autumn Moon), Neiky Yim Hui-chi (Lam Yuk-ping), Wenbers Lee Tung-chuen (Sylvester), Siu Chung (Miss Lee). 1.85:1. Import VCD: Shu Kei's Creative Workshop. 108 minutes.

The Cinderella story of the decade: When his arranged financing fell through, writer-director Fruit Chan convinced Andy Lau's Teamwork production company to give him 40,000 feet of leftover filmstock. Armed with that, a cast who had never acted before, a five man crew, and a great deal of raw determination, Chan turned out this excellent, gritty drama for virtually nothing, and ended up with not only the 1997 Best Picture prize but the Best Director award as well. High school dropout Autumn Moon does what many HK teenagers in the housing projects with no prospects end up doing: He becomes a triad. One day his retarded buddy witnesses a girl committing suicide and takes the two bloody letters he finds lying beside her body. Moon begins to fantasize about the dead girl in his dreams, becoming sexually aroused, even though he has never even seen her face. While collecting a debt, he meets Lam Yuk-ping a girl with a terminal kidney disease. The two develop a friendship, in spite of the open hostility displayed by the girl's mother towards Moon. When his own mother deserts him, Moon decides to do the honorable thing and help Yuk-ping but fate intervenes.

Shot on real locations, **Made in Hong Kong** is a strong, uncompromising film of the sort rarely produced by HK's commercially driven industry. Unlike the glossy **Young and Dangerous** films and their ilk, everything here looks and feels one hundred percent real, particularly the emotions. In spite of its financial limitations, the picture is laudable on a technical level; The editing is dynamic, and a sequence in which Moon sets out to gun down two targets is simply dazzling in its use of imagery. The director has stated in interviews that he added narration by Sam Lee's character during scenes where the performances were not up to par; be that as it may, the cast is fine, and both Lee and Yim are very good (the former, an electrician, won the Best Newcomer statue and has since gone on to appear in numerous other projects). The film is downbeat, perverse, and pessimistic in the extreme. Regardless, it is consistently fascinating and features an ending that is one of the most stirring in memory because Chan clearly cares about these misfit youths and, by extension, their real-life counterparts. *Made in Hong Kong* is a remarkable achievement that reinforces one's faith in the HK film industry at a time when its fortunes have hit an all-time low.

619. Magic Cop

(1990; Movie Impact) ★: 8/10. *Kui moh ging chaat* (Cantonese), *Qu mo jing cha* (Mandarin): "Cop Who Can Drive Away Spirits." Cinematographers: To Fai-tai, Kwan Chi-kan; Art Directors: Cyrus Ho Kim-hung, Leung Ping-kwan; Music: BMG Melody Bank; Writers: Sammy Tsang Kan-cheung, Shum Chi-leung; Producer: Lam Ching-ying; Action Directors: Lam Ching-ying, Lee Chi-kit, Hau Yiu-chung, Chow Kam-kong, Chan Man-chin; Director: Stephen Tung Wai. Cast: Lam Ching-ying (Fung Zee), Wilson Lam Chun-yin (Lam), Miu Kiu-wai (Sergeant No. 2237), Wong Mei-wah (Lin), Michiko Nishiwaki (The Woman), Wu Ma (Ma), Frankie Chin Chi-leung (Eddie), Billy Chow Bei-lee (Servant). 1.85:1. VHS: Tai Seng. Import LD: Mei Ah. Import VCD: Cameron Entertainment. 87 minutes.

An immensely enjoyable blend of the horror and cop action genres, this imaginative effort is the perfect vehicle for its star, the underrated Lam Ching-ying. He plays Fung Zee, a tough-as-nails policeman who is also a Taoist master. His expertise is required when the police must kill a drug trafficker who refused to surrender and behaved like a zombie. Fung's examination of the corpse leads him to a health club in Tsimshatsui, and to Eddie, a musclebound courier who works for a mysterious Japanese woman. When Fung determines the woman's location, he quickly discovers that she is just as skilled in the supernatural as he is, setting the stage for a magical duel of grand proportions.

Almost entirely unpredictable and filled with wild, intricate spells that will amaze most Western viewers, **Magic Cop** is one of the best entries in the horror-comedy craze that was fuelled by the success of **Mr. Vampire** (1985). While obviously produced using the most basic means, the special effects are still terrific, effectively conveying the required illusions no matter how intricate or otherworldly they may be. The magical combat is perfectly staged by veteran stuntman/director Stephen Tung; the climax is paced like lightning, rarely allowing one to catch a breath. A likeable cast and genuinely amusing comic asides are icing on the cake.

620. The Magic Crane

(1993; Long Shong Pictures/Film Workshop) ★: 7/10. *Sin hok san jam* (Camtonese), *Xian he shen zhen* (Mandarin): "Immortal Crane Magical Treasure." Cinematographers: Tom Lau Moon-tong, Ko Chiu-lam, Tony Miu Kin-fai; Art Director: Ringo Cheung Sek-wah; Music: Wong Bong; Writers: Tsui Hark, Tsui Tat-cho; Producer: Tsui Hark; Action Director: Lau Chi-ho; Director: Benny Chan Muk-sing. Cast: Tony Leung Chiu-wai (Ma Kwun-mo), Anita Mui Yim-fong (Pak Wan-fai), Rosamund Kwan Chi-lam (Butterfly Lam), Damian Lau Chung-yan (Yat Yeung-tze), Lawrence Ng Kai-wah (So Pang-hoi), Norman Tsui Siu-keung (Lam Hoi-ping), Jay Lau Kam-ling (Lady Jade Flute), Vindy Chan Wai-yee (Butterfly's Servant), Lau Shun (Reverend of Tai Kok Temple). 1.85:1. VHS/LD: World Video. Import LD/VCD: Universe. 93 minutes.

A flawed but commendably ambitious fantasy, **The Magic Crane** improves upon repeat viewings, as one can more effortlessly comprehend both the complicated plot and frenzied, high-flying action. While on his way to a meeting of the district's kung fu schools, Ma Kwun-mo is saved from riding off a cliff by the beautiful Pak Wan-fai and her giant crane, Yuen Yuk. In return for her gesture, Wan-fai asks that Ma not reveal her identity to anyone. The meeting itself is filled with turmoil, thanks to So Pang-hoi, the evil head of the powerful Tien Lung Tribe. Seeking to dominate, So dispatches a flock of poisonous bats to wipe out the other schools, but most of the pupils are saved in time by Yuen Yuk. While seeking a remedy for those stricken by the bat toxins, Wan-fai encounters Butterfly Lam. The latter was abandoned by her father during an enemy invasion 25 years ago so that he could save the emperor's daughter. Unbeknownst to Wan-fai, she is that royal offspring and her master is Butterfly's father. Embittered by the way fate has treated her, Butterfly seeks to destroy Wan-fai, and the two battle using lethal "sound wave stances" generated by their music instruments/weapons. Meanwhile, So and another power-hungry leader make their play to rule the martial world.

As is occasionally the case with Tsui Hark's productions, the film tries to accomplish too much, packing in enough characters, intrigue, and dramatic conflict to fuel an entire TV miniseries. Similarly, the special FX are not always up to par (the crane looks convincing only in long shots, and a giant turtle is less believable than its counterpart in the Japanese **Gamera** movies), but they generally provide adequate visual equivalents of the various otherworldly powers on display.

621. Magic Crystal

(1986; Movie Impact) ★: 4/10. *Moh fei chui* (Cantonese), *Mo fei cui* (Mandarin): "Evil Jade Crystal." Cinematography: Ai Lung Cinematography Group; Art Director: Jessy Lam Chak-chi; Music: Ai Lung Music Group; Producer: Wallace Cheung Kwok-chong; Action Director: Tony Leung Siu-hung; Writer-Director: Wong Jing. Cast: Andy Lau Tak-wah (Andy Lo), Sharla Cheung Man (Winnie Shen), Wong Jing (Pancho), Siu Bin-bin (Pin-pin), Nat Chan Pak-cheung (Lau Ta), Max Mok Siu-chung (Interpol Agent), Cynthia Rothrock (Cindy Morgan), Richard Norton (Karov), Shih Kien (Sgt. Shi), Shum Wai (Gangster), Phillip Ko Fei (Shen), Chung Fat (Thug), Eddie Maher (Thug), Wong Wan-si (Maureen Yu), Shing Fui-on (Prisoner). 1.85:1. VHS: Tai Seng (Poor Subtitles). 95 minutes.

In order to make contact with old friend Shen, Andy (HK's Number 1 Investigator) and his buddies Pin-pin and Pancho fly to Greece. Not long after their arrival, the trio discover that Shen is being pursued by both the KGB and Interpol. The agents are after a mysterious gemstone that Shen discovered during an archaeological dig, but because of a mix-up, it ends up back in HK with Andy. The slab of jade turns out to be a benevolent alien (rendered with dimestore special FX) wanted by Karov, an evil kung fu master seeking to exploit the being's magical powers. The creature develops an inseparable friendship with young Pin-pin, prompting the child to take the rock back to Greece so that it may be reunited with its spaceship, which resides inside a booby trap-laden cavern.

While the thought of Wong Jing helming a combination knockoff of **E.T.** and **Raiders of the Lost Ark** may sound irresistibly nutty, this amalgam of action and kiddie-oriented comedy wears out its welcome early on. Some well-staged fights and adept stuntwork save it from being a complete waste of time. Character names above are from the dubbed version (which features no credits, save for the inexplicable listing of Richard Norton and Jacques Risi as the directors); the subtitles on Tai Seng's tape are offscreen for about three-quarters of the running time.

622. The Magic Touch

(1992; Hui's Film Production Co./ Topping Time Films) ★: 6/10. *San suen* (Cantonese), *Shen suan* (Mandarin): "Godly Plan." Cinematographer: Herman Yau Lai-to; Art Directors: Peter Mak Tai-kit, Raymond Chan Kam-ho; Writers: Michael Hui Koon-man, Dayo Wong Chi-wah; Producer-Director: Michael Hui Koon-man. Cast: Michael Hui Koon-man ("Feel Bone" Hui), Leon Lai Ming (Yau Ho-kay), Ricky Hui Koon-ying (Fat), Dayo Wong Chi-wah (William), Phillip Chan Yan-kin (The Commissioner), Michael Dinga (Lam Kwok-hung). 1.85:1. VHS: Tai Seng. Import LD/VCD/DVD: Ocean Shores. 100 minutes.

This Michael Hui comedy runs hot and cold, lacking the comic invention of his best works from the '70s but remaining genuinely hilarious in spots. Leon Lai plays a goldbricking revenue agent whose boss orders him to get the goods on Michael Hui's fraudulent fortune teller. When Hui foils a mugging (a terrific sequence), he gets knocked on the head, and the scrambling of his brain cells awakens dormant powers of telepathy. The two strike a deal: Lai will let Hui off the hook if the latter uses his new powers to locate the financial records of a big-time drug smuggler. After numerous bungled attempts to get the ledgers, the pair finally manage to endear themselves to the gangster, but their association just may get them killed.

Lai acquits himself surprisingly well in a role that finds him alternating between straight man and clown, and Hui remains a master of deadpan farce. There are a large number of gay jokes but, unlike in most HK comedies, some are genuinely funny (Hui has to feel the mobster's hand in order to "read" him, leading to a very amusing string of gags in a health spa). The best bit finds Hui trying to explain how he could have so many assets while paying so little tax. His explanation: He's a pimp, his brother Ricky is a gigolo, and his daughter is a part-time prostitute! There is even a brief send-up of the Hollywood hit **Ghost**. Co-writer Dayo Wong and actress/singer Winnie Lau Siu-wai have supporting roles, and Jamie Luk Kim-ming appears briefly as a henchman.

623. Magnificent Bodyguards

(1978; Lo Wei Films Co.) ★: 6/10. *Fei do guen wan saan* (Cantonese), *Fei du juan yun shan* (Mandarin): "Flying Cross Rolled Up Cloud Mountain." Cinematographer: Chen Rong-shu; Music: Not Original; Writer: Ku Lung; Producer: Hsu Li-hwa; Action Directors: Jackie Chan, Luk Chuen; Director: Lo Wei. Cast: Jackie Chan (Lord Ting Chung), James Tien Chun (Chang Wu-yi), Leung Siu-lung, Wang Ping. 2.35:1. VHS: Arena/Xenon. 101 minutes. Also known as **Eye of the Dragon** (Japanese title).

This Jackie Chan period kung fu thriller was originally filmed in 3-D, which explains why swords, staffs, spears, darts, and everything else not nailed down is constantly hurtling towards the camera. Martial arts master Ting Chung is summoned by a princess to escort her and her gravely ill brother through the bandit-laden "Stormy Hills" so that the ailing man can receive treatment from a noted physician. Accompanied by two of Ting's associates, the party faces danger at every turn as they encounter numerous groups of killers (including fake monks in a booby-trapped temple). As the trek continues and the perils mount, Ting discovers that his employer has not been entirely truthful.

When viewed flat, the 3-D FX look awfully silly, but the storyline offers up some good twists (particularly during the climax) and the martial arts are good, though the fact that much of the music has been stolen from **Star Wars**(!) is more than a little distracting. James Tien steals the show as a smooth but vicious assassin who likes to skin his victims. The character names are from the English-dubbed version. The Japanese laserdisc (entitled **Eye of the Dragon**) is apparently the only video version to offer the film in 3-D. It presents the movie dubbed in Japanese, with no subtitles, and comes with two pairs of 3-D glasses.

624. The Magnificent Butcher

(1979; Golden Harvest) ★: 8/10. *Lam Sai-wing (yan je mo dik)* (Cantonese), *Lin Shirong (ren zhe wu di)* (Mandarin): "Lam Sai-wing (Benevolent, No Enemies)" or "Lin Shirong (Benevolent, No Enemies)." Cinematographer: Michael Ma Koon-wah; Writers: Wong Jing, Edward Tang King-sang; Producer: Raymond Chow Man-wai; Martial Arts Directors: Yuen Woo-ping, Sammo Hung Kam-po; Director: Yuen Woo-ping. Cast: Sammo Hung Kam-po (Butcher Wing), Fan Mui-sang (Beggar), Fung Hark-on (Ko Tai-hoi), Lee Hoi-sang (Master Ko), Yuen Biao (Chat), Wei Pai (Foon), Kwan Tak-hing (Wong Fei-hong), Chung Fat (Cat), Lam Ching-ying (Killer with Fan). 2.35:1. VHS: Tai Seng (Remastered for the English Market; subtitled or dubbed). 108 minutes.

Outstanding martial arts choreography highlights this terrific Golden Harvest period entry, which offers an invigorating blend of humor and melodrama. Butcher Wing is the most unruly of Master Wong Fei-hong's students but possesses a good heart, which helps to offset his incredible knack for getting into trouble. One day he intercedes in what appears to be a robbery and beats the suspected felon. This leads to a misunderstanding between Master Wong and the powerful Master Ko, culminating in a bout of "calligraphy kung fu" between the two. After being separated from his brother for a decade, Butcher's sibling, Lam Sai-kwong, arrives in town with his bride, Yuet Mei. Ko's no-good son, Tai-hoi, uses an imposter to hoodwink Sai-kwong into believing that Butcher owes him a great deal of money. When Sai-kwong refuses to pay, Tai-hoi seizes Yuet Mei as compensation and has her husband beaten. Ready to commit suicide, Sai-kwong is saved by the intervention of a slovenly, alcoholic beggar who also happens to be a kung fu master of the first order. When the beggar confronts Tai-hoi about his skulduggery, he deceives the old drunkard into thinking that Butcher has the girl, leading to an impeccably staged duel between Butcher and the beggar. When the truth is finally known, Butcher and the old man trick their way into the Ko estate and rescue Yuet Mei, but Butcher also takes along Master Ko's goddaughter, Lan Hsing, thinking that she was being held against her will. Tai-hoi then murders Lan Hsing and frames Butcher for the crime, leading Master Ko and his men to attack Po Chi Lam clinic in retribution. When Tai-hoi's killing spree extends to Sai-kwong, Butcher faces off against both him and his father.

Sammo Hung is in peak form, and the scenes he shares with Fan Mui-sang have the same light-hearted appeal as those between Jackie Chan and Simon Yuen Siu-tien in **Drunken Master** (1978). In fact, it was Yuen who initially played the beggar role here, but he passed away during shooting and his scenes had to be reshot (Fan was probably chosen as a replacement based on his excellent turn in a similar part for director Chan Wah's **The Mysterious Footworks of Kung Fu**, released the previous year). While the film follows genre conventions to a large extent, it is executed with considerable skill; and the fight sequences, while involved, never drag on to the point of tedium. In an early role, Yuen Biao is given a chance to shine as one of Butcher's fellow students. His duel with Lam Ching-ying's fan-wielding villain is a standout. The Butcher Wing character (Cantonese name: Lam Sai-wing) appeared in several films over the years and would later be played by Kent Cheng Chuk-see in **Once Upon a Time in China** parts I & V.

Magnificent Kung Fu Warriors *see* **Magnificent Wanderers**

625. The Magnificent Scoundrels

(1991; Cinema City Enterprises/ Magnum Films) ★: 8/10. *Ching sing* (Cantonese), *Qing sheng* (Mandarin): "Love Saint." Cinematographer: Abdul M. Rumjahn; Art Director: Danny Yuen Ching-yeung; Music: Richard Lo Sai-kit; Writers: Lee Lik-chi, Edward Leung Yiu-ming; Producer: Wellington Fung Wing; Action Director: Corey Yuen Kwai. Director: Lee Lik-chi. Cast: Stephen Chiau Sing-chi (Valentino), Teresa Mo Shun-kwan (Valentino's Partner), Tien Niu (Ping), Amy Yip Chi-mei (Apple), Wu Ma (Chow Yun-fatt), Roy Cheung Yiu-yeung (Tai-te), Yuen Wah (Ng), Karl Maka (Valentino's Master), Sandra Ng Kwan-yu (Jenny), Gabriel Wong Yat-san (Driver). 1.85:1. VHS: Tai Seng. Import LD: Golden Cinema City. Import VCD: Universe (No Subtitles). Import DVD: Universe. 97 minutes.

Stephen Chiau stars in this terrific ensemble comedy as a bumbling conman who takes on the equally inept Teresa Mo as his student. When a gang of triads, headed up by Roy Cheung, threaten to chop them in half unless Mo repays a debt, the pair try various schemes to get rich quick. When those all fail, Chiau lucks into a fool-proof situation: The owners of a fabulous house mistake Chiau for a guest from America and let him move in. The only problem is that these people (Wu Ma, Tien Niu, and Amy Yip) are all con artists themselves (under the employ of Cheung) and, naturally, they seek to bilk Chiau. After the rogues unsuccessfully try to cheat each other with hare-brained blackmail schemes, they decide to pool their talents to nab the big fish: Cheung.

The sight gags are well-staged (one bit involving an ice cream cone is genuinely hysterical) and most of the wordplay survives translation, making this one of Chiau's best efforts for Western audiences, though all of the leads come off equally well. This was the first of the star's several collaborations with director Lee, and they came up with what could well be the most *hilariously gross* moment in HK cinema: A drunken Amy Yip vomiting down Chiau's throat during a French kiss!

626. Magnificent Wanderers

(1977; Shaw Brothers) ★: 5/10. *Gong woo hon chi* (Cantonese), *Jiang hu han zi* (Mandarin): "Wandering Man." Cinematographer: Kung Mu to; Art Director: Ku I; Music: Chen Yung-yu; Writers: Ngai Hong, Chang Cheh; Producer: Run Run Shaw; Action Directors: Hsieh Hsing, Chen Hsin-I; Director: Chang Cheh. Cast: David Chiang Da-wei (Chu Te-sa), Alexander Fu Sheng (Lin Sai-yu), Chi Kuan-chun (Si Tai-yung), Phillip Kwok Tsui (Wrestler), Jamie Luk Kim-ming (Archer). 2.35:1. No official domestic video release. 101 minutes. Also known as **Magnificent Kung Fu Warriors** (US title).

This period kung fu yarn is played strictly for laughs, but garners only a few. When a stammering Manchurian prince sends troops to arrest him, the affluent fighter Chu Te-sa escapes with the aid of wandering conmen Lin Sai-yu, Si Tai-yung, and Kuan Fei. Chu is so rich he fires gold pellets at his enemies (a very effective way to divert their attention!), but hasn't as much money as is believed, having given most of it to rebels and the less fortunate. The remainder of his fortune is hidden in the houses of various "friends," who have conveniently forgotten about the arrangement and have no intention of turning the gold over to him. Upon recovering part of his valuables, Chu convinces his footloose comrades to steal the remainder of the treasures before they can be delivered to the prince. Their mission is a success, but in order to reach safety, the men are forced to participate in a martial arts competition at a Manchurian army base that may spell their doom.

This is a passable diversion, but the humor tends to be quite broad (a flaw accentuated by the terrible, overstated score) and some jokes are reprised well after all of the potential humor has already been mined. While not quite up to director Chang Cheh's usual standards, the martial arts are lively and keep the proceedings worthwhile. The character names listed above are from the dubbed version.

627. Magnificent Warriors

(1987; D & B Films Co.) ★: 6/10. *Jung wah jin si* (Cantonese), *Zhong hua zhan shi* (Mandarin): "Chinese Warrior." Cinematographers: Ma Chan-wah, Lo Wan-shing; Art Director: Oliver Wong Yui-man; Music: Joseph Chan Wing-leung; Writer: Sammy Tsang Kan-cheung; Producer: Stephen Shin Kei-yin; Action Directors: Stephen Tung Wai, Benz Kong To-hoi, Fung Hark-on; Director: David Chung Chi-man. Cast: Michelle Yeoh Chu-kheng (Fok Ming-ming), Derek Yee Tung-sing (Wong), Richard Ng Yiu-hon (Conman Wong), Lowell Lo Kwun-ting (Youda), Tetsuya Matsui (General Toga), Chindy Lau Ping-tai (Chin-chin), Fung Hark-on (Japanese Thug), Ku Feng (Ming's Grandfather), Hwang Jang-li (Japanese Soldier), Lo Mang (Collaborator), Chen Jing (Gun Runner). Dolby

Digital (DVD only). 2.35:1. VHS: Tai Seng (Remastered for the English market; subtitled or dubbed). Import LD: Mei Ah. Import VCD: Megastar (Poor Subtitles). Import DVD: Universe. 91 minutes.

Michelle Yeoh as Indiana Jones? This enjoyable D & B Films imitation of the Steven Spielberg series serves up the next best thing, and even gives the actress a bullwhip and brown leather jacket for good measure. Set during WWII, it is centered on a plot concocted by the Chinese army to stop Japanese invaders from building a poison gas factory in the walled city of Puttan Kaal. Airplane pilot/spy Fok Ming-ming is dispatched to the area and ordered to make contact with Wong, aka "Secret Agent No. 1." Thanks to a mix-up, she inadvertently helps a conman out of a fix before finally encountering her real contact. Ming-ming's objective is to rescue Prince Youda, Puttan Kaal's cowardly ruler, while No. 1 is to assassinate the leader of the occupation, General Toga. After a botched attempt to steal fuel for Ming-ming's airplane, the pair are captured. They are saved just seconds prior to execution when the populace rises up and expels the Japanese troops. In a nod to **The Seven Samurai**, Ming-ming and Wong must then help the city's woefully ill-equipped denizens defend themselves when their enemy returns with superior firepower.

The action choreography is terrific and the walled city setting is an excellent, atypical backdrop for a D & B film. However, Yeoh plays her character in such a cocky fashion, Ming-ming never seems to feel that she is in much danger, making it difficult for the audience to believe she risks sustaining more than a scratch or two. Another debit is Joseph Chan's overbearing score, which consists of a handful of mock heroic themes repeated over and over throughout the picture. Of the cast, comedian Richard Ng does the best work, going from seedy swindler to committed rebel in creditable fashion. His conman also provides a nice throwback to the sort of comic relief secondary characters found in Hollywood fare from the '30s and '40s, an era of filmmaking that **Magnificent Warriors** is indebted to in more ways than one.

628. Mahjong Dragon

(1997; CineMagic) ★: 4/10. *Lut cheuk fei lung* (Cantonese), *Ma qiao fei long* (Mandarin): "Mahjong Flying Dragon." Cinematographer: William Yim Wai-lun; Art Director: Ben Lau Man-hung; Music: Lowell Lo Kwun-ting; Writer: Kei On (pseudonym for Jeff Lau Chun-wai); Producer: Kristy Leung Kam Choi-man; Action Director: Yuen Tak; Directors: Corey Yuen Kwai, David Lai Tai-wai. Cast: Josephine Siao Fong-fong (Fan Sau-tin), Zhao Wenzhou (Quick-hands), Blackie Ko Shou-liang (Blackie), Desiree Lam Kee-wan (Kwan), Ken Lo Wai-kwong (Tin-lone). 1.85:1. VHS: Tai Seng. Import LD/VCD/DVD: Mei Ah. 97 minutes.

Much too intent on pleasing everyone, **Mahjong Dragon** blends together more genres than a Wong Jing film festival but lacks the sense of rudimentary enjoyment that his work usually provides. Josephine Siao is cast here in the unlikely role of Fan Sau-tin, a middle-aged motorcycle cop/gambling addict who flees to China after her debts get way out of hand. Seeking to find a husband, Sau-tin is introduced to Quick-hands, a master gambler who wants to immigrate so that he can evade a triad boss out to exploit his skills. This marriage of convenience isn't really convenient for either of them: Sau-tin's longtime admirer, Blackie (who also happens to be the one in charge of collecting the debt), won't leave her alone, and Quick-hands only has eyes for cute young Kwan, who longs to visit Paris but only has a short time before she succumbs to brain cancer.

Siao and Zhao are both good, and there is some well-staged action, but the drama is trite and embarrassing, providing further proof, in the wake of **Love and the City**, that Jeff Lau should stick to comedy. Overall, the film's most impressive component is the fine score by Lowell Lo, which combines tranquil charm with action passages reminiscent of his work for **God of Gamblers' Return**. Sandra Ng Kwan-yu has an unfunny cameo.

Man on the Run *see* **Gleam of Hope**

629. Man Wanted

(1995; Sam Po Film Co.) ★: 3/10. *Mong kok dik tin hung* (Cantonese), *Mang jiao de tian kong* (Mandarin): "Mongkok's Sky." Cinematographer: Chim Pak-hung; Art Director: Angelo Bernardo Castilho; Music: Wong Bong; Writer: Chak Ming; Producers: Wong Siu-ming, Chan Choi-yin; Action Director: Ma Yuk-shing; Director: Benny Chan Muk-sing. Cast: Simon Yam Tat-wah (Lok Man-hwa), Yu Rongguang (Lu Chan-feng), Christy Chung Lai-tai (Yung), Eileen Tung Oi-ling (June), Law Kar-ying (Bald Yin), Cherie Chan Siu-ha (Mindy), Kenneth Chan Kai-tai (Tai), Parkman Wong Pak-man (Sgt. Wong). 1.85:1. VHS/LD/DVD: Tai Seng (Remastered for the English market; subtitled or dubbed). Import LD: Fitto Mobile. 92 minutes.

The sort of disposable action film director Benny Chan routinely produced before getting back on track with **Big Bullet**, **Man Wanted** has plenty of noise and explosions but precious little else. Lok Man-hwa is an undercover cop who has cozied up to big-time pusher Lu Chan-feng but gotten a little too close to the man in the process. When the police ambush a clandestine drug buy, Man-hwa hesitates when it comes time to hand his friend over. Chan-feng manages to escape, but his car explodes, apparently sealing his fate. In the aftermath, Man-hwa strikes up a relationship with Yung, Feng's ex, forsaking his righteous girlfriend June. Unfortunately for Man-hwa, Chan-feng has survived and involves him in a kidnap/extortion plot that puts his career in jeopardy and his life on the line.

While logic can be tenuous in Grade B cop actioners, the plotting here is just plain sloppy (biggest lapse in logic: Why would the police be so quick to declare Chan-feng dead when no trace of his body was found in the vehicle?), and the action setpieces are not interesting enough for one to forgive such poor writing. Yam and Chung have no chemistry, and the idea that they would even fall in love in the first place is never communicated in a believable fashion. **Man Wanted** proved to be yet another bad career move for Yam, who (with the exception of **Crossings**) has squandered his talent and besmirched his reputation by starring in one awful movie after another over the last few years. The presence of his name in a cast listing has, sadly, become a warning and not an enticement. The Chinese title for Lau Hung-chuen's **Those Were the Days** (1996) tries to pass that film off as a sequel to this. In 1997 20th Century–Fox bought the US remake rights to **Man Wanted**; why they chose this film out of so many more imaginative and entertaining HK productions is anyone's guess.

630. Marianna

(1982; Century Motion Picture & Distribution Co.) ★: 5/10. *Ban mooi* (Cantonese), *Bin mei* (Mandarin): "Filipino Girl." Cinematographer: Jimmy Leung Chi-ming; Art Directors: Ramon S. Nicdao, Alex Ho; Music: Not Original; Writers: Lee Tan, Siu Kin-wing, Ng Wai-wing; Producers: Dennis Yu Wan-kong, Lau Jun-wai; Director: Cheuk Pak-tong. Cast: Sally Yeh Chian-wen (Nancy Yu), Chin Han (Peter Yu), Anna Malai (Marianna), Steve Palao, Mario Escudero. VHS: Tai Seng (Poor Subtitles). Import VCD: Mei Ah. 88 minutes.

One of the exploitation thrillers produced by Dennis Yu Wan-kong's short-lived

Century Motion Picture company, this grim enterprise opens with deodorant salesman Peter Yu taking time off from a business trip in The Philippines to visit his wife's uncle in the countryside area of Luzon. Peter quickly becomes embroiled in trouble when he helps local girl Marianna evade hoods who are trying to force her to marry a thug from a rival tribe. Returning home to HK, Peter goes about his business, only to have Marianna turn up, asking for his help. Shortly thereafter, his wife Nancy (Sally Yeh in her film debut) catches him in bed with the girl and leaves HK to stay with that very same uncle. Peter follows and his presence causes the tribesmen to believe that he has come after Marianna (who has returned home after being told her parents would be killed if she didn't comply). While driving through the countryside, Peter and Nancy get lost and end up in the jungle, where they are attacked by primitives who look and act like zombies. Separated from their car, they run smack dab into the very natives they most wanted to avoid.

While rarely plausible, **Marianna** does possess a certain raw power and is moderately suspenseful. The main storyline offers nothing fresh, but unlike many low budget HK exploitation films (which have everyone speaking nothing but Cantonese), the dialogue here is a realistic mix of Cantonese, English, and Tagalog. With its spear and machete-wielding savages, ample nudity, footage of a cockfight, the slaughter of a pig, bamboo spike booby traps, and uncivilized antagonists (HK cinema tends to depict Filipinos and Vietnamese as being either subservient or subhuman, with little or no grey area between those extremes), **Marianna** can be considered (along with **We're Going to Eat You**) HK's contribution to the "Third World Horror" cycle initiated by Italian pictures like **The Man from Deep River** (1972) and **Jungle Holocaust** (1976), though it is not as graphic as its European counterparts. A good portion of the music is lifted from Tangerine Dream's 1975 album **Ricochet** and their soundtrack for **Thief**. Eric Tsang's **Fatal Vacation** carried on the "See the Philippines and Die" tradition eight years later.

631. Martial Art Master Wong Fai Hung

[*sic*] (1992; Great Audience Film & Television Production) ★: 5/10. *Wong Feihung hai lit ji yat doi si* (Cantonese), *Huang Feihong xi lie zhi yi dai shi* (Mandarin): "Wong Fei-hung Series: One Generation Teacher" or "Huang Feihong Series: One Generation Teacher." Cinematographer: Yang Ke-liang; Music: Cheng Chin-rong; Writers: Wang Chi-chi, Szeto On, Li Chao; Producer: Chang Shan-gong; Action Directors: Hau Yiu-chung, Wu Nian-chen; Director: Lee Chiu. Cast: Chin Kar-lok (Wang Fei-hung), Lam Ching-ying (Jiubinku Kyoto), Jacqueline Ng Suet-man (Miss Sakura), Kwan Hoi-shan (The Mayor), Sun Guo-ming, Chen Hsiao-peng. 1.85:1. VHS: Tai Seng, York (Dubbed). Import LD/VCD: Universe. 93 minutes. Also known as **Great Hero of China** (York title).

A low-budget Taiwanese attempt to cash in on Tsui Hark's Wong Fei-hung series, this minor period effort has some quality martial arts but no originality or excitement. Chin Kar-lok plays the legendary hero (identified in the subtitles as both "Wang Fei-hung" and "Hwang Fei-hung"), this time out, as an undisciplined young layabout who is always driving his aged father, Wong Kei-ying, to distraction. A few days after the elder Wong finally passes away, his old enemy, Japanese fighter Jiubinku Kyoto, returns to challenge Kei-ying as part of his methodical plan to defeat all of China's top masters. Furious that he has been denied another chance to battle Kei-ying, Jiubinku smashes the dead man's spirit tablet and murders one of Po Chi Lam clinic's senior students. Seeking to exploit the Chinese further, British representatives (in league with the disreputable Master Ha Tieh) open an opium den in the town, earning the instant disfavor of Fei-hung, who proceeds to demolish the place. In spite of his honorable intentions, Fei-hung is ordered by the mayor to apologize to the British, a veritable death sentence, but finds an unexpected ally in the form of Jiubinku. The Japanese master's motives are simple: He does not want anyone to kill Fei-hung until he has had a chance to defeat him in combat.

Chin Kar-lok and Lam Ching-ying display some good form, and the action is choreographed with a fair amount of *chutzpah*, but the staging is comparatively primitive (vaseline is put on the lens at times, in order to hide the wires), and the story enveloping the action is pedestrian. The director and some of the leads worked together again on **Shaolin Avengers**.

632. The Martial Club

(1981; Shaw Brothers) ★: 6/10. *Miu goon* (Cantonese), *Wu guan* (Mandarin): "Martial Art Hall." Cinematographer: Ho Chin-chun; Art Director: Johnson Tsao; Music: Not Original; Writer: Ngai Hong; Producer: Mona Fong Yat-wah; Action Directors: Lau Kar-leung, Ching Chu, Hsiao Hou; Director: Lau Kar-leung. Cast: Gordon Lau Kar-fai (Huang Fei-hong), Mai Te-lo (Yin-lin), Kara Hui Ying-hung (Chu-ying), Johnny Wang Lung-wei (Master Shan), Ku Feng (Huang Chi-ying), Hsiao Hou (Student). 2.35:1. No official domestic video release. 101 minutes. Also known as **Instructors of Death** (US title).

Gordon Lau plays Wong Fei-hung (referred to here in Mandarin form as Huang Fei-hong) in this period effort which features one of popular villain Johnny Wang's most memorable performances but is one of director Lau Kar-leung's lesser Shaw Brothers efforts. Feuding martial arts clans create havoc for Master Huang Chi-ying, while son Fei-hung and his friend Yin-lin spend their time unsuccessfully trying to pass themselves off as kung fu experts. Even after being humiliated by a real martial arts instructor, the pair continue to try and best one another in public by hiring opponents that will take a dive. Thanks to a misunderstanding, Yin-lin is seriously injured by Shan, a kung fu man from the Jing Wu school in the north. When Yin-lin has his leg broken by thugs, this is just the start of an ongoing plot to besmirch the reputation of both his and Fei-hong's schools.

While it sidesteps the usual tired revenge theme, the storyline manages to be both contrived and predictable. Fortunately, as one has come to expect from Lau Kar-leung's work, the kung fu is beautifully choreographed, with Gordon Lau and Kara Hui coming off particularly well. In addition to displaying fine technique, Johnny Wang gives a wonderful performance as the guileless but principled Master Shan, a character quite far removed from his usual ruthless, single-minded Manchu villains. His climactic duel with Gordon Lau (which starts off in a "clandestine" manner, *á la* **Dirty Ho**, before ending with some prolonged, close quarters fighting) is cleverly conceived and executed. Names above are from the dubbed version.

633. Mary from Beijing

(1992; Golden Harvest/Paragon Films) ★: 7/10. *Mung seng shut fan* (Cantonese), *Meng xing shi fan* (Mandarin): "Awaken from Dream Time." Cinematographer: Christopher Doyle; Art Director: William Cheung Suk-ping; Music: The Music Factory; Producer: Hon Pui-chu; Writer-Director: Sylvia Chang Ai-chia. Cast: Gong Li (Ma Lei), Kenny Bee (Wong Kwok-wai), Wilson Lam Chun-yin (Peter Ng), David Chiang Da-wei (Yip), Jan Lam Hoi-fung (Messenger), Lawrence Ah Mon (Immigration Officer), Pau Fong (Speaker at Dedication), Melvin Wong Kam-sun (Stanley), Yuen King-tan

(Mahjong Player). 1.85:1. VHS: Tai Seng. Import LD/VCD: Universe. 96 minutes. Also known as **Awakening**.

Beautiful, Mandarin-speaking Ma Lei (or "Mary" as she is called by some) is having all manner of trouble convincing HK authorities that, even though she grew up in China, she was actually born in HK. She also receives virtually no attention from Peter, her work-obsessed boyfriend, who is worried about what his stern father will think of Lei. Meanwhile, toilet paper salesman Wong Kwok-wai is going through a divorce over his decision to leave England and return to HK, with the goal of eventually opening a factory in China. Lei and Kwok-wai are the perfect answer to the other's problems: Lei wants to work but cannot without an I.D., and Kwok-wai needs an assistant fluent in Mandarin to facilitate his business dealings. Peter refuses to give her permission to work but it doesn't matter: A mutual attraction has developed between Lei and Kwok-wai. However, the pair still must extricate themselves from their current situations.

A slight but quite satisfying romantic comedy-drama, **Mary from Beijing** garners most of its charm from leads Kenny Bee and Gong Li and some nice location work in China. As one can deduce from the synopsis, the plot reflects on the forthcoming 1997 handover via its themes of Kwok-wai returning from an overseas country out of a sense of dedication to his homeland, and the lovers (Cantonese speaking Kwok-wai and Mandarin speaking Lei) personify the reunification of HK and China. While this does date the film somewhat, the subtext remains fairly relevant, and writer-director Sylvia Chang keeps the proceedings both affable and engagingly old fashioned while preventing the predictable storyline from becoming overtly corny. Jan Lam has an amusing running cameo as a messenger boy who is careening up the corporate ladder in record time, and celebrated Mainland director Zhang Yimou (who was seeing Gong at this time) served as the executive in charge of production.

634. Masked Avengers

(1981; Shaw Brothers) ★: 6/10. *Cha sau* (Cantonese), *Cha shou* (Mandarin): "Pronged Hands." Cinematographer: Tsao Hui-chi; Art Director: Johnson Tsao; Music: Not Original; Writers: Ngai Hong, Chang Cheh; Producer: Mona Fong Yatwah; Action Directors: Phillip Kwok Tsui, Lu Feng, Chiang Sheng, Chu Ko; Director: Chang Cheh. Cast: Phillip Kwok Tsui (Kau Yao, The Cook), Chin Siu-ho (Cheng Chuen), Chiang Sheng (Tze Sanyuen), Lu Feng (Master Lin Yen-chi), Wang Li (Fong Siu-kwong). 2.35:1. No official domestic video release. 93 minutes.

A group of ruthless contract killers, who are masters of the trident and hide their identities behind gold masks, slaughter all 29 members of one family. Seeking to avenge the murders, some martial artists set up a meeting at a local inn with the affluent Master Lin. When one of their number sneak into Lin's home, he is fatally wounded by thugs, under the command of one of The Masks, who then attack the inn, killing another man. Two of the assassins are vanquished, thanks to top fighter Cheng Chuen and Kau, the establishment's mysterious cook, who then denies having helped Cheng. When more men turn up dead, Kau is the chief suspect, but Cheng steadfastly defends him, knowing that Kau is not a loyal member of the gang but merely an infiltrator. A man with knowledge of the killers and his own personal reasons for wanting to see them destroyed, Kau manages to win over the trust of the other fighters and helps them attack The Masks' headquarters.

Similar to director Chang Cheh's **Five Venoms**, this kung fu mystery is easier to deduce but still engaging, though Lo Mang and Sun Chien are missing from the "Venoms" line-up this time out. There are several good, gory (even by Chang's standards) battles, but the best is saved for last: Our heroes must use their skills to not only fight against expert foes but also to evade the deadly booby-traps spread throughout the villains' lair. In addition to the usual stock cues from the DeWolfe music library, the soundtrack includes music heard in the original **Mad Max**. Names listed above are from the dubbed version.

635. The Master

(1992; Golden Harvest/Vast Art Film/Film Workshop/Paragon Films) ★: 3/10. *Lung hang tin ha* (Cantonese), *Long xing tian xia* (Mandarin): "Dragon Travels in the Land Under Heaven." Cinematographer: Henry Chan Chun-kit; Music: Not Original; Writers: Lam Kei-to, Lau Tai-muk, Tsui Hark; Producers: Anthony Chow Ting-ou, Michael Lai Siutin, Tsui Hark; Action Directors: Yuen Wah, Brandy Yuen Chun-yeung; Director: Tsui Hark. Cast: Jet Li Lianjie (Jet), Yuen Wah (Chan Hou-tak), Crystal Kwok Kam-yan (May), Jerry Trimble (Johnny), George Kee Cheung (Paul Lee), Billy Blanks (Black Thug). Dolby Digital (DVD only). 1.85:1. VHS: Tai Seng (No Subtitles). Import LD: Star Entertainment (No Subtitles). Import VCD: Star Entertainment (No Subtitles), Mega Star. Import DVD: Universe. 93 minutes. Also known as **Wong Fei-hung '92**.

This dismal action-comedy-thriller spent a good deal of time on the shelf, not reaching theaters until after Jet Li became a superstar, courtesy of **Once Upon a Time in China**. He plays Jet (natch), a martial arts expert (double natch) who journeys to San Francisco in search of his master, Uncle Tak. He discovers that the old man's herbal shop (named Po Chi Lam, no less) has been ransacked and that he has not been heard from for two weeks. The reason is Johnny, a brutish kung fu school owner who is challenging all of the local martial arts experts. His goons confronted Tak one evening and are responsible for the destruction. Eventually able to locate his ailing teacher, Jet himself is soon targeted by Johnny, who will not be happy until he has beaten this incredibly limber and talented youth.

The fight scenes deliver (how can they not, with Jet Li and Yuen Wah in the cast) but nothing else does, making this the low point in Tsui Hark's career to date (well, unless you count **Knock Off**). The story is ludicrous, the dialogue incredibly insipid, and all of the non-Asian characters are really embarrassing and/or offensive stereotypes. This is strictly for Li fans who are willing to sit through anything to see their hero.

Master Killer *see* **The 36th Chamber of Shaolin**
Master of Disaster (Arena/Xenon Video) *see* **New Kids in Town**
Master of Disaster (US theatrical release) *see* **The Treasure Hunters**

636. Master of Zen

(1994; Brandy Film Production Co.) ★: 7/10. *Daat lut jo si* (Cantonese), *Da mo zu shi* (Mandarin): "The Founder of Zen." Cinematographer: Poon Tak-yip; Art Director: Ben Luk Man-wah; Music: Lowell Lo Kwun-ting; Writer: Sam Shum Yeung; Action Directors: Brandy Yuen Chun-yeung, Yuen Mo; Producer-Director: Brandy Yuen Chun-yeung. Cast: Derek Yee Tung-sing (Puti Dharma), Fan Siu-wong (Son Kwong/Wei Ho), Chen Sung-yung (Master Prajna Tara), Wu Ma (Son Kwong's Master), Fan Mui-sang (Fat Monk), Austin Wai Tin-chi (Prince), Eddy Ko Hung (His Majesty). 1.85:1. VHS: World Video. Import LD: Star Entertainment. 89 minutes.

This offbeat feature is a flawed but well-intentioned and interesting look at the life of Bodhidharma (or Puti Dharma, as he is called in the subtitles here), the Indian master who is credited with the creation of Chinese kung fu. Following the death of his father, young prince Puti Tara decides to become a monk and studies under the learned Prajna Tara. Sixty-seven years after Prajna's death, he changes his name to Dharma and journeys to China in order to spread Zen philosophy. Dharma's arrival comes at a time when both the king (who believes that his immense offerings will buy him praise in the eyes of Buddha) and the people are beginning to forget the true meaning of Buddhism. Over the next several decades, Dharma spreads Buddhist philosophy, and spends nine years meditating without eating or drinking, a feat that brings him great recognition and wins many new converts.

As some writers have pointed out, it is ironic that a film which purports to show the creation of martial arts would rely so heavily on wirework to depict them. It is also difficult to gage the historical accuracy of what unfolds, though it is safe to say that the writers have embellished certain events. Regardless, Derek Yee is quite convincing in the title role and imparts Buddhist teachings in a pleasingly celestial fashion (though the actor's refusal to shave his head results in him sporting a phony-looking bald cap throughout). The location footage is quite beautiful, and the film manages the difficult task of educating without being preachy. Recommended to both general audiences and kung fu aficionados; the latter can learn a bit about the ideology that permeates so many of the great period epics they love.

637. Master Wong vs. Master Wong

(1992; Mandarin Films/Ko Chi Sum Films Co.) ★: 5/10. *Wong Fei-hung dui Wong Fei-hung* (Cantonese), *Huang Feihong dui Huang Feihong* (Mandarin): "Wong Fei-hung vs. Wong Fei-hung." Cinematographer: Kin Lee Kin-keung; Art Director: Raymond Chan Kam-ho; Music: James Wong Jim, Mark Lui Chung-tak; Writers: Vincent Kok Tak-chiu, Lee Lik-chi; Producers: Ronny Yu Yan-tai, Clifton Ko Chi-sum; Action Director: Yuen Cheung-yan; Director: Lee Lik-chi. Cast: Alan Tam Wing-lun (Wong Fei-hung), Carol Cheng Yu-ling (Shang Fan-tung), Teresa Mo Shun-kwan (Aunt Yee), Ng Man-tat (So), Eric Tsang Chi-wai (Porky Wing), Anthony Wong Chau-sang (Tse Yin-kwan), Gabriel Wong Yat-san (Rickshaw Man), Vincent Kok Tak-chiu (Master Chin), Wong Yat-fei (Master of the Village). 1.85:1. VHS: Tai Seng. Import LD/VCD/DVD: Ocean Shores. 88 minutes.

This sequel to **Once Upon a Time a Hero in China** (*sic*) finds the bumbling Wong Fei-hung tired of maintaining the facade of a hero. He accepts an invitation to Canton in order to open a new branch of Po Chi Lam clinic, but orders Porky Wing to impersonate him so that he can enjoy a little rest and relaxation. Pretending to be his student, Leung (played last time by Simon Yam Tat-wah), Fei-hung encounters Shang Fan-tung, a powerful female kung fu master who wants to meet her idol: Wong Fei-hung. This leads to all manner of confusion when Fei-hung, So, and Wing all must pretend to be the real master. While drunk, Wing signs an agreement with the villainous Tse that causes numerous people to be cheated. To prove that the document is invalid, Master Wong admits his real identity but must prove it in court when Tse produces his own Wong Fei-hung. The judge decides to let the two Wongs fight it out, leading to the title contest.

While just as broad, part two lacks the comic momentum of its predecessor but remains fairly entertaining, thanks in no small part to the formidable cast of comics. It is especially fun to see Carol Cheng (who usually plays cruel and obnoxious upper class women) getting down and dirty as a kung fu master with a heart of gold. In addition to doing riffs on classic kung fu movies themes, composers Mark Lui and James Wong also include a rollicking send-up of Jackie Chan's signature tune from the **Police Story** films! Yuen Cheung-yan has a cameo.

638. Mean Street Story

(1995; Jing's Production/Wong Jing's Workshop) ★: 4/10. *Miu gai goo si* (Cantonese), *Miao jie gu shi* (Mandarin): "Temple Street Story." Art Director: Cyrus Ho Kim-hung; Music: Marco Wan Ho-kit, Anthony Lee Hon-kam; Writer-Producer: Wong Jing; Action Director: Dion Lam Dik-on; Cinematographer-Director: Andrew Lau Wai-keung. Cast: Dior Cheng Yee-kin (Melvin Wong), Jacqueline Wu Chien-lien (Sue), Eric Kot Man-fai (Crab), Annabelle Lau Hiu-tung (Suzi), Tommy Wong Kwong-leung (Kwong), Lo Mang (Echinus), Mimi Chu Mi-mi (Melvin's Mother). 1.85:1. VHS: World Video. 100 minutes.

While shooting off firecrackers in Shenzhen, Temple Street kid Melvin Wong gets involved in a scuffle defending Sue, a beautiful girl he met only a few minutes beforehand, and accidentally kills one of his opponents. After serving four years on a manslaughter charge, he returns home to HK to find his mother working as a prostitute and his stepfather an embittered alcoholic. Reuniting with his old triad buddy Crab, he discovers that Sue is now the host of a popular radio show. Wanting to pay Melvin back, Sue gets him a job at her father's company. The two fall in love, much to the consternation of Sue's respectable father, who has one of his flunkies frame Melvin for fraud. If he will leave Sue, Melvin is off the hook; if not, he must come up with $400,000 within 24 hours.

Seasoned HK film fans know not to expect much in the way of verisimilitude from one of Wong Jing's screenplays, but there is nary a single moment here that rings true. The hyperactive, **NYPD Blue**-style camerawork, combined with Eric Kot and Annabelle Lau's over-the-top comic relief, will send most viewers to their medicine cabinets in search of Dramamine. Director Andrew Lau and star Dior Cheng had much better luck the following year with **Young and Dangerous**.

639. Mermaid Got Married

(1994; Wishing Well Film Co.) ★: 4/10. *Yan yue chuen suet* (Cantonese), *Ren yu chuan shui* (Mandarin): "Mermaid Legend." Cinematographer: Lau Hung-chuen; Art Director: Danny Yuen Ching-yeung; Music: Tommy Wai Kai-leung; Writer: Cheung Cho-yee; Producer: Clarence Fok Yiu-leung; Director: Norman Law Man. Cast: Christy Chung Lai-tai (The Mermaid/Wong Siu-may), Dior Cheng Yee-kin (Chi), Teresa Mak Kar-kei (Princess), Takeshi Kaneshiro (Kenji), Dennis Chan Kwok-san (Officer Chan), Kent Cheng Chuk-see (The Principal), Yuen King-tan (Miss Yuen), Lau Siu-ming (Uncle Lau). 1.85:1. VHS/LD: World Video. Import LD/VCD: Mei Ah. 92 minutes.

A local imitation of Ron Howard's **Splash**, this uninspired but fairly painless farce also owes a debt to the high school comedy subgenre spawned by Stephen Chiau's **Fight Back to School** series. After she saves drowning teacher Chi by feeding him her magical pearl, a mermaid finds she can no longer get her fish tail to reappear. She follows Chi back to HK in order to retrieve the pearl, and ends up as a student in his school. Mistaken for a girl named Wong Siu-may, she blends in well and begins to fall for Chi. However, her secret is discovered by a gang of fortune-hunters, who capture her and plan on auctioning their oddity off to the highest bidder.

Most of the jokes are obvious (even the proverbial "fish-out-of-water" gags are uninspired), and the underwater sequences were obviously shot in a tiny swimming pool. Still, Christy Chung has such a bubbly, playful presence, she almost single-handedly keeps this assembly-line flotsam afloat.

Middle Man *see* **In the Line of Duty 5**

640. Midnight Angel

(1990; New Treasurer Films Co.) ★: 5/10. *Ng ye tin si* (Cantonese), *Wu ye tian shi* (Mandarin): "Midnight Angel." Cinematographer: Yau Kei; Art Director: Ringo Cheung Sek-wah; Music: Not Original; Writer: Abe Kwong Man-wai; Producer: Ng Ming-toi; Action Director: Tsui Chung-san; Director: Chik Kei-yee. Cast: Yukari Oshima (Ying), May Lo Mei-mei (Rabbit), Angile Leung Wan-yui (Cherry), Miu Kiu-wai (Chief Yau), Mark Cheng Ho-nam (Tak), Melvin Wong Kam-sun (Bull), Shih Kien (Grandpa), Ng Man-tat (Police Commissioner), Cho Tat-wah (Inspector Chao), Tai Po (Gum-Chewing Creep), Lily Chung Suk-wai (Delivery Girl), Kim Maree Penn (Blonde). 1.85:1. VHS: Tai Seng. Import LD: Star Entertainment (No Subtitles). 90 minutes. Also known as **The Justice Women** (Tai Seng title).

This low-budget actioner anticipates **The Heroic Trio** but that is where the similarities end. Tired of the injustice that surrounds her, athletic teenage girl Rabbit transforms herself into "The Cotton Flower" (a low-rent imitation of "Black Rose," the heroine played by Chan Po-chu in Chor Yuen's 1965 film of that name, which is satirized in **92 Legendary La Rose Noire**), a black-clad heroine who aids those in distress. Cotton Flower first appeared thirty years earlier, and Rabbit follows the path of righteousness she blazed by aiding the police in capturing Bull, a notorious drug dealer/murderer. The authorities (led by Inspector Yau), meanwhile, incorrectly suspect that Ying, Rabbit's martial arts expert sister, is the masked crimefighter. When Bull's forces launch a murderous assault on Rabbit's family, Ying and her other sister, Cherry, adopt catwomen outfits of their own and join the fight for justice. Sloppy execution and poor scripting make this of only marginal interest, but it passes the time adequately.

641. Midnight Caller

(1995; Mandarin Films) ★: 2/10. *Long man ye ging wan* (Cantonese), *Lang wen ye jing hun* (Mandarin): "Wolf Kiss Night Thriller." Cinematographer: Cheung Tung-leung; Art Director: Lee Wai-ming; Music: Henry Lai Wan-man; Writer-Producer: Raymond Wong Pak-ming; Action Directors: Wong Pai-chi, Chan Kwok-chuen, Chan Siu-wah; Directors: Alex Cheung Kwok-ming, Raymond Wong Pak-ming. Cast: Diana Pang Dan (Chow Mei-si), Michael Wong Man-tak (Wong Chi-ming), Joyce Ngai Suk-kwan (Wan Siu-yau). 1.85:1. VHS: Tai Seng. Import LD/VCD: Mei Ah. 91 minutes.

This shamelessly idiotic comedy-thriller was designed as a vehicle for Diana Pang, a former dancer and HK's answer to Jayne Mansfield. She plays Mei-si, the hostess of "The Silent Night," a talk radio program. One of her regular callers is a bomber who identifies himself only as "Hungry Wolf" and uses his calls to announce future targets. After he sets off explosives in a hospital and a kindergarten, Mei-si is able to convince slovenly police officer Wong Chi-ming that she can help him trap the killer. The two take an instant, violent dislike to each other, though, naturally, that is not about to stop them from falling in love. After the police trace one of Hungry Wolf's calls, the madman blames Mei-si and threatens to kill her, necessitating 'round-the-clock protection from Wong and his tomboy associate Siu-yau.

Too predictable to be thrilling and too insipid to be funny, this mechanical exercise plods along with nary a single original idea. Fans of bad dance choreography will want to check out Pang's big production number: a cut-rate ripoff of CATS, which would be sent up to good effect the next year by comedienne Alvina Kong Yan-yin in **Banana Club**. Producer Raymond Wong has a cameo as himself.

642. Midnight Express in Orient

[*sic*] (1996; Sam Po Film) ★: 2/10. *Dung fong faai che* (Cantonese), *Dong fang kuai che* (Mandarin): "Eastern Express Train." Cinematographer: Wong Po-man; Art Director: Angelo Bernardo Castilho; Writers: Chung Siu-hung, Ching Si; Producer: Lau Jun-fai; Director: Chung Siu-hung. Cast: Yu Rongguang (Chen Chin-hau), Vincent Wan Yeung-ming (David Chiang), Marianne Chan Miu-ying (Yin), Diana Pang Dan (David's Wife), Jay Lau Kam-ling (Chin-hau's Wife). 1.85:1. Import LD/VCD: Universe. 90 minutes.

This tiresome drama stars Yu Rongguang as a tough trucker who takes his girlfriend for granted, and Vincent Wan as his timid buddy, who is being mistreated by his sexbomb wife (Diana Pang). While the two are out for a night of fun in Shenzhen, Wan picks up a prostitute who is running a blackmail scam with a male partner. When the man threatens Wan with violence, Yu intercedes, accidentally killing both him and the woman. The two hightail it out of the city and decide to hide in Vietnam, so Yu arranges to meet with his wife in order to get some money. On the way to their rendezvous, they pick up a young woman (Chan) who is on the run from a loan shark. However, the gangster follows them and steals the money, thinking it belongs to the girl. This inspires David to rob a restaurant, and the two become increasingly more desperate in their actions.

As one can deduce from the synopsis, this has nothing to do with Alan Parker's **Midnight Express** (1978), which is too bad, as it would almost certainly have been more interesting than the plot that is served up instead. Limply directed and predictable at every turn, this displays none of the visual style and visceral thrills that distinguished director Chung's **The Assassin**, and will have even the most forgiving viewer bailing out before the final fade.

643. Midnight Whispers

(1988; Golden Harvest/Paragon Films) ★: 1/10. *Jun so sam jung ching* (Cantonese), *Jin su xin zhong qing* (Mandarin): "Pouring Out Every Feeling from My Heart." Cinematographer: Cheung Tak-wai; Art Directors: Andy Lee Yiu-kwong, Lam Yau-sheng; Music: Joseph Chan Wing-leung; Producer: Raymond Chow Man-wai; Writers-Directors: Michael Mak Dong-kit, David Lai Tai-wai. Cast: Josephine Koo Mei-wah (Ms. Koo), Moon Lee Choi-fung (Lee Siu-hong), Pak Yun-kam (Yip), Chen Jing (Freeloader). 1.85:1. VHS: Tai Seng (No Subtitles). Import LD: Mei Ah. Import VCD: Mega Star. 96 minutes. Also known as **Cascading Feeling** (Tai Seng title).

Moon Lee received a rare non-action role in this maudlin and tiresome drama (completed in 1987 and shelved for over a year) that is strictly for her most devoted fans. She plays Siu-hong, a Mainland girl who runs off to HK and becomes a prostitute. Her mother (played by Josephine Koo) searches the red-light districts, and through flashbacks we learn about the girl's troubled upbringing. Born into an unhappy family, with a good-for-nothing father and an illiterate, uncouth grandmother, Siu-hong's clan is broken up by a custody suit filed by her mother. The woman wins the case but Siu-hong's grandmother kidnaps the girl and takes her to China. After years of searching, mother and daughter are reunited, but only after the former gives in to the advances of her slovenly boss. However, Siu-hong does badly in school and soon deserts her mom.

Lee and Koo try their best, but the characters are all broad stereotypes (particularly the Mainlanders), the dramatic situations are simplistic, and the resulting film is amateurish and all but unendurable.

644. Midnight Zone

(1997; Media Asia Films Partners I) ★: 4/10. *Wooi juen sau si* (Cantonese), *Hui zhuan shou shi* (Mandarin): "Return of the Old Corpse." Cinematographer: Joe Chan Kong-hung; Art Director: Stanley Cheung Sai-kit; Music: Tommy Wai Kai-leung; Writers: Philip Kwok Wai-chung, Brian Chung Wai-hung, Wilson Yip Wai-san; Producer: John Chong Ching; Director: Wilson Yip Wai-san. Cast: Anthony Wong Chau-sang (Shing), Elvis Tsui Kam-kong (Yan), Liz Kong Hei-man (Yan's Wife), Jerry Lam Hiu-fung (Officer #23481), Yuen King-tan (Qiao), Helena Law Lan (Shing's Mother), Spencer Lam Sheung-yee (Uncle Seven). 1.85:1. VHS: Tai Seng. Import LD/VCD/DVD: Mega Star. 92 minutes.

This tepid horror trilogy boasts some atmospheric cinematography but absolutely no scares and several feeble attempts at humor. "Headless Soul" stars Jerry Lam as a bumbling policeman assigned to guard the creepy scene of a brutal murder after all of the other officers have left. The victim's head was never found and the place seems to be full of mischievous spirits, but, naturally, when Lam radios for help, every strange occurrence is dismissed by a rational explanation. The reason behind the murder is mildly humorous, but the ending is very weak. In fact, there is barely even an ending. "Hit & Run," the weakest of the batch, stars Liz Kong and Elvis Tsui as a dimwitted couple who run down a pedestrian and flee, only to be tormented by their now-undead victim, who has moved in next door. The only endearing bit finds the couple battling the ghost by using their karaoke machine to sing prayers. The final tale, "Midnight Dinner," stars Anthony Wong and Yuen King-tan as a bickering husband and wife who fear the supernatural wrath of the former's mother (Helena Law, who plays creepy old ladies in just about all of the local horror films produced in the mid-to-late '90s), whom they had cremated against her expressed wishes. While she initially appears to have sinister motives, it becomes clear that the grandmother really only wants to see this fragmented, dysfunctional family happy once more before she heads off to the netherworld. Law is very effective here, generating both menace and sympathy, and the story ends up being rather touching. Still, one of out three is too low of a score to make this worth watching, even for her segment.

Midnite Angel *see* **Angel**

645. The Mighty Peking Man

(1977; Shaw Brothers) ★: 2/10. *Sing sing wong* (Cantonese), *Xing xing wang* (Mandarin): "King Orangutan." Cinematographers: Tsao Hui-chi, Wu Cho-hua; Art Directors: Johnson Tsao, Chen Ching-shen; Music: Not Original; Writer: Ngai Hong; Producer: Runme Shaw; Director: Ho Meng-hua. Cast: Danny Lee Sau-yin (Johnny Feng), Evelyne Kraft (Samantha), Ku Feng (Lu Tien), Hsiao Yao (Huang Tsui-hua), Cheng Ping (Lucy), Norman Tsui Siu-keung (Lu's Man). 2.35:1. VHS: Miramax (Dubbed). 90 minutes (Dubbed version). Also known as **Goliathon** (US title for original World Northal release).

The Shaw Brothers' disastrous attempt to cash in on the anticipated success of Dino DeLaurentiis' big budget remake of **King Kong, The Mighty Peking Man** is unintentionally hilarious from start to finish and a must for bad movie addicts. When a giant ape starts crushing villagers in the Himalayas, shifty conman Lu Tien decides to capture the creature and put it on display in HK. He is able to convince adventurer Johnny Feng to head up an expedition through the Indian jungle, where they must fend off stock footage of charging elephants and a tiger that looks more interested in wrestling than mauling. Having lost all of his porters, Lu abandons Johnny, but the latter is saved by Samantha, a beautiful blonde jungle girl in a fashionable animal skin bikini. It just so happens that her "pet," Utom, is the gargantuan ape that has been wreaking havoc in the area. The two fall in love (Johnny and Samantha, that is) and she agrees to let Utom be brought to HK. The ape is put on display to record crowds but breaks out of captivity when he (somehow) manages to see Lu trying to rape Samantha. After stepping on his human opponent for Samantha's affections, Utom proceeds to go ape in the streets.

A major production by Shaw standards, this made a quick exit from HK theaters and reportedly did no better in other territories. The special FX (by a Japanese company) are comically bad, from the $2.98 ape suit right on down to the tinker toy-type miniatures; the rear screen projection work manages to be even worse than that seen in the DeLaurentiis film. The rotten dubbing adds another level of enjoyment, but there is nothing quite so amusing as the sight of Kraft walking the streets of HK in her animal skin bikini and attracting *no attention whatsoever*! The film was first issued in America by World Northal as **Goliathon**, while Quentin Tarantino's Rolling Thunder Pictures reissued it in 1999 under the original export title.

646. Millionaire Cop

(1993; Wong Jing's Workshop) ★: 5/10. *Chin min tin wong* (Cantonese), *Qian mian tian wang* (Mandarin): "Sky King of a Thousand Faces." Cinematographer: Henry Chan Chun-kit; Art Directors: Cheung Chi-ming, Wong Tin-ho; Music: Danny Chung Teng-yat; Writer: Dennis Chan Kwok-san; Producers: Wong Jing, Chan Tai-lei; Action Director: Yuen Tak; Director: Cheung Kon-man. Cast: Aaron Kwok Fu-shing (Lam Gu-won, aka Ball), Maggie Cheung Man-yuk (Jacky Chuck), Chingmy Yau Suk-ching (Shun), Ng Man-tat (Fish), Deric Wan Siu-lun (Jessy Lee), Yuen King-tan (Sze), Xiong Xinxin (Long Hair), Dennis Chan Kwok-san (Lee Car-shing), Chor Yuen (Sergeant Lai). 1.85:1. VHS: World Video. Import LD/VCD: Mei Ah. 91 minutes.

A typical Wong Jing production, **Millionaire Cop** stars Ng Man-tat and pop singer Aaron Kwok as mismatched cops named Fish and Ball(!) on the trail of some vicious robbers who chopped off Fish's hand. While that investigation is in progress, the pair also pull undercover duty for a millionaire who is worried about the safety of his son, Jessy. While impersonating Jessy, Ball falls for his girlfriend, Jacky, while also trying not to alienate his old flame, Shun, who manages to appear at the worst possible times.

In addition to the usual sight gags and scatological bits, there are a few inspired ideas (Maggie Cheung's uptight character becomes voraciously horny whenever she sees anything that is round!) and terrific action sequences (including a kung fu fight on ice skates!), courtesy of veteran choreographer Yuen Tak. The in-jokes include Kwok reprising his "Silver Fox" character from **Saviour of the Soul** during the climactic battle, and Chor impersonating the masked heroine of his 1965 classic **Black Rose**. Ng Man-tat and Yuen King-tan also engage in a fun send-up of the food tasting scene from **9 1/2 Weeks. Millionaire Cop** is passable entertainment for a slow evening.

647. Millionaires' Express

(1986; Golden Harvest/Bo Ho Films Co./Paragon Films) ★: 8/10. *Foo gwai lit che* (Cantonese), *Fu gui lie che* (Mandarin): "Millionaires' Express." Cinematographers: Arthur Wong Ngok-tai, Peter Ngor Chi-kwan; Art Directors: Raymond Lee King-man, Tony Au Ding-ping; Music: Sing Kam-wing; Writers: Barry Wong Ping-yiu, Alfred Cheung Kin-ting; Producer: Leonard Ho Koon-cheung; Action Director-Director: Sammo Hung Kam-po. Cast: Sammo Hung Kam-po (Chin Fong-tin), Yuen Biao (Captain Tsao Cheuk-kin), Olivia Cheng Man-ar (Siu-hon), Kenny Bee (Loi Fook), Eric Tsang Chi-wai (Security Chief Jook Bo), Rosamund

Kwan Chi-lam (Chi), Emily Chu Bo-yee (Bo), Richard Ng Yiu-hon (Han), Lydia Shum Tin-ha (Han's Wife), James Tien Chun (Yun Shiyu), Yukari Oshima, Yasuaki Kurota, Hwang Jang-li (The Japanese), Jimmy Wang Yu (Master Wong), Shih Kien (Master Sek), Billy Lau Nam-kwong (Train Captain), Dick Wei (Bandit Leader), Lau Kar-wing (Kang), Woo Fung (Mayor Yi), Cynthia Rothrock (Female Bandit), Richard Norton (Caucasian Bandit). Dolby Digital (DVD only). 2.35:1. VHS/LD: Tai Seng (Remastered for the English market; subtitled or dubbed). Import LD: Star Entertainment (No Subtitles). Import VCD: Mei Ah. Import DVD: Universe. 92/97 minutes.

HK's answer to **It's a Mad, Mad, Mad, Mad World**, this slight but highly entertaining opus (set in 1920s China but shot mostly in Canada) drops just about every Golden Harvest comedian, leading lady, and martial arts star into a zany storyline that allows for plenty of action and hair-raising stunts. Resourceful conman Chin Fong-tin decides to make amends for his past wrongdoings by reviving the fortunes of his dying home town, Hanshui. Diverting the "Millionaires' Express" and its trainload of rich passengers, Chin plans to use them and their ready cash to revitalize the local economy. Complicating things are a pair of determined lawmen who want Chin behind bars, and a gang of bumbling robbers who were plotting to rob the train. Things take a turn for the worst when a large gang of vicious "mountain bandits" ride in and take the entire town hostage. Chin then unites both his allies and enemies in a desperate bid to drive the miscreants out.

Even by local standards, the stuntwork is incredible. Yuen Biao is at his athletic best throughout, whether jumping off a two-story building and landing on his feet (no double and no editing here, folks) or engaging director-star Sammo Hung in no-holds-barred hand-to-hand combat. The comedy is generally quite broad, and even cartoonish at times, but it is infectiously silly more often than not. Notables among the huge cast include Yukari Oshima (making a terrific impression in a small role), Yasuaki Kurota, and Hwang Jang-li as a trio of Japanese samurai in possession of a valuable map, Olivia Cheng Man-ar (as Chin's devoted lady love), and Cynthia Rothrock (who has a memorable duel with Hung). While newcomers may not derive the same degree of pleasure from the impeccable cast of familiar faces, **Millionaires' Express** is wonderful pop entertainment that should appeal to anyone who has an interest in HK cinema.

648. Miracles

(1989; Golden Harvest/Golden Way Films/Paragon Films) ★: 9/10. *Gei jik* (Cantonese), *Qi ji* (Mandarin): "Miracles." Cinematographer: Arthur Wong Ngok-tai; Art Director: Eddie Ma Poon-chiu; Music: Chow Chi-sang; Writers: Edward Tang Kin-sang, Jackie Chan; Producer: Leonard Ho Koon-cheung; Action Direction: Jackie Chan, Jackie Chan Stuntmen Association; Director: Jackie Chan. Cast: Jackie Chan (Kuo Cheng-wah), Anita Mui Yim-fong (Yang Lu-ming), Bill Tung Biu (Conman Tung), Richard Ng Yiu-hon (Chief Detective Ho), Wu Ma (Uncle Hai), Gloria Yip Wan-yee (Belle), Gui Yalei (Madam Kao), Ray Lui Leung-wai (Lu), Lo Lieh (Fei), Billy Lau Nam-kwong (Tong), Ko Chuen-hsiang (Tiger), Ngai Hong (Mr. Ku's Friend), James Wong Jim (Mr. Ku's Friend), Tien Feng (Ku Hsin-chuan), Billy Chow Bei-lee (Thug), Lui Fong (Snake Ming), Shum Wai (Tiger's Man), Michael Chow Man-kin (Tung), Tai Po (Thug), Lee Hoi-sang (Thug), Feng Sing (Policeman), Woo Fung (Hotel Manager), Lau Siu-ming (Ho's Boss), Ricky Hui Koon-ying (Man), Kenny Bee (Reporter #1), Anthony Chan Yau (Reporter #2), Lawrence Cheng Tan-shui (Reporter #3), John Sham Kin-fun (Reporter #4), Jacky Cheung Hok-yau (Bespectacled Clerk), Yuen Biao (Beggar), Ken Lo Wai-kwong (Thug), Fung Hark-on (Thug), Benny Lai Wai (Man), Amy Yip Chi-mei (Party Guest), Chen Jing (Party Guest), Alvina Kong Yan-yin (Foxy), Chor Yuen (Dignitary), Michael Lai Siu-tin (Felon in Police Station), Simon Yam Tat-wah (Policeman), Melvin Wong Kam-sun (King's Councillor), Louis Roth (Dignitary), Anders Nelsson (Dignitary) ... and many more! Dolby Digital (DVD only). 2.35:1. VHS: Tai Seng (No Subtitles). Import LD: Star Entertainment (No Subtitles). Import VCD: Universe. Import DVD: Mega Star. 106/127 minutes. Also known as **Miracles: The Canton Godfather** (UK video title), **Mr. Canton and Lady Rose** (Alternate English export title and VCD title).

This is Jackie Chan's lavish, all-star remake of Frank Capra's **Lady for a Day** (which Capra himself remade as **A Pocketful of Miracles**), and it is engaging fun from start to finish. Set in the 1930s, the film opens with naive Kuo Cheng-wah learning the hard way not to trust just anyone in HK. Fleeced out of all of his money, Kuo somehow manages to end up in the middle of a shootout between two rival gangs. Just before dying, the leader of one group seemingly appoints him as his successor. Averse to continuing the gang's criminal activities, Kuo decides to transform one of their properties into a ritzy nightclub instead. The venture turns out to be a major success and Kuo feels that he owes much of his good fortune to Madam Kao, a flower vendor he purchases roses from frequently. Tiger, the leader of a rival Shantung gang, wants half of the club and poses a continuing threat to Kuo's welfare. If that were not enough, Kuo cooks up an insane scheme to help the impoverished Madam Kao trick her daughter, who is coming home from Shanghai with her fiancé and his affluent parents. The girl believes her mother to be a member of high society, and with Kuo's help (and money) she will be, if only for a night. Unfortunately, Tiger's gang and a bumbling police chief threaten to ruin the ruse, so Kuo must run himself ragged trying to keep everything proceeding along smoothly.

A delightful mix of wish fulfilment comedy and Chan's customary acrobatics, **Miracles** also benefits from uniformly fine work by a once-in-a-lifetime cast, beautiful cinematography, and absolutely gorgeous period sets and costumes. While not original (there really should have been some acknowledgement of **Lady for a Day** screenwriter Robert Riskin and playwright Damon Runyon), the story here is far more interesting and involving than what one has come to expect from a Chan picture. While relatively few in number, the fight sequences are sensational throughout, with the climactic action in a rope factory (which finds Chan fighting Billy Chow and various other goons in the rafters) the highlight. Taiwan prints reportedly run a few minutes longer.

Miracles: The Canton Godfather *see* **Miracles**

649. Mirage

(1987; Golden Principal Film/Sil-Metropole Organisation) ★: 7/10. *Hoi si jan lau* (Cantonese), *Hai shi shen lou* (Mandarin): "Mirage." Cinematographers: Lee Man-kit, Lee Yao-tong; Art Director: Lok Tak-hou; Music: Joseph Koo Kar-fai, Kwan Pak-chung; Producers: Hon Pui-chu, Lee Chi-man; Writer-Action Director-Director: Tsui Siu-ming. Cast: Yu Rongguang (Tong Ting-hsin), Tsui Siu-ming (Mao), Mak Fung, Fan Tung-yu, Fung Hon, Cho Wing (Bandit). 2.35:1. VHS: World Video (Poor Subtitles). 94 minutes.

In 1930, following The October Revolution, scores of defeated Russians streamed across the border into China and began preying on those travelling The Silk Road. After one such bandit attack, a giant mirage of a woman on horseback briefly appears to the survivors. Photographer Tong Ting-hsin manages to get a picture of the apparition and enlists his old buddy Mao to go on a fantastic quest to find this mysterious woman, wherever she may be. After a trek through the desert and some R & R at a friendly village, Tong is captured by a gang of thieves. In order to escape death at the hands of his captors, he must fight against their chief...the woman from the mirage! Named Gaza Nova, she is a bandit queen and far from the benevolent goddess he imagined. Rescued by Mao, Tong becomes separated from his friend and is pursued across the sands by Gaza, who manages to finally capture him, with both on the verge of death. Tong refuses her advances, however, and Mao (who has recruited an army consisting of the villagers they stayed with earlier) returns with the intention of saving his friend once more and taking out Gaza's forces once and for all.

This large scale action-adventure is an epic of the old school, with a horde of extras, a grand orchestral score, lavish period re-creations, exotic locales, bone-crushing stunts, and some terrific martial arts. Yu Rongguang is a personable and dynamic hero; seeing him here and in **Iron Monkey**, one wonders why he is now seemingly typecast in villainous parts. One of the great unsung personalities of HK cinema, Tsui Siu-ming is reminiscent of Sammo Hung in both body dimensions and fighting ability, and performs an incredible fire stunt here that even Jackie Chan would say is insane. The film drags a bit during the middle third and is dramatically overwrought in spots, but it gets back on track again for the climactic battle, which mixes kung fu, hand-to-hand combat, and gun battles in very satisfying fashion. If at all possible, try and see a version other than the one issued by World Video. Not only are the Panavision image and English subtitles badly cropped, but the source print is so ragged and censored, many portions of the action sequences are missing. Horse lovers be warned: The animals are treated here in a manner that would not please the ASPCA.

650. The Missed Date

(1986; Molesworth) ★: 5/10. *Choh yat sap ng* (Cantonese), *Chu yi shi wu* (Mandarin): "The First and the Fifteenth of the Month." Cinematographer: James Yeung Jim; Art Director: Jon Hau Wing-choi; Music: Tsui Yat-kan; Producer: Jamie Luk Kim-ming; Writer-Director: Teresa Woo San. Cast: Chow Yun-fat (Peter), Olivia Cheng Man-ar (May), Melvin Wong Kam-sun (Ben), Pauline Wong Siu-fung (Ling), Jamie Luk Kim-ming (King Kong). 1.85:1. VHS: World Video. 92 minutes.

Here is a HK entry in the ever-popular "swapping partners" subgenre. Tired of her executive husband pulling long hours and never spending any time with her, housewife May decides she would like to adopt the arrangement that her friends Ben and Ling have: On the first and fifteenth of every month, they see whomever they like. Her husband Philip is all too happy to agree, though he probably would not have been nearly as anxious if he knew May was being aggressively courted by Peter, a handsome tennis instructor. However, just when their relationship is starting to get serious, Philip begins treating May well again, leading her to break off with Peter. However, when Philip goes out with some Japanese clients one evening to seal a deal instead of picking up May's parents at the airport, their relationship goes to pieces.

A handful of moments ring true but the presentation is too heavy-handed (particularly the score), transforming this potentially affecting story into a melodramatic trifle, in spite of some effective performances.

651. Mission of Justice

(1992; J.S. Production/Joe Siu International Film) ★: 2/10. *Gam saam gok gwan ying wooi* (Cantonese), *Jin san jiao qun ying hui* (Mandarin): "Golden Triangle Gathering of Heroes." Cinematographer: Wong Kit; Music: Not Original; Producers: Yeung Yen-shan, Ma On; Action Director: Yuen Po; Writer-Director: Wong Chun-yeung. Cast: Moon Lee Choi-fung (Moon), Yukari Oshima (Bullet), Tommy Wong Kwong-leung (Chiang Tai-su, aka Somi), Carrie Ng Kar-lai (Colonel Carry), Mark Houghton (Blonde Gunman), Sophia Crawford (Cop). 1.85:1. VHS: Tai Seng. Import LD/VCD: Universe. 87 minutes.

One of the most distended films in memory, this plot-barren actioner may be of interest to fans of the female leads but has little to offer casual viewers. Moon and Bullet are HK agents sent to Thailand in order to nab a drug runner/kidnapper and her cohorts operating out of the Golden Triangle. Fortunately for the law enforcers, the shaky alliance struck between this criminal organization and another for a drug deal falls apart, leading the villains to wipe out many of their own people before the remainder fall prey to Colonel Carry (a suitably butch Carrie Ng), Moon, and Bullet's commander and the leader of the back-up troops.

Some of the action is good but most of it isn't, and the proceedings are too cheap and sluggish to hold one's attention. There are also far too many time-killing shots of the criminals hiking/riding/floating across the countryside (if all of the fat were trimmed, this might make an acceptable 45 minute television program). As partial compensation, the Thai scenery is picturesque, particularly some spectacular underground caves. British martial artist Gary Daniels takes on Moon Lee in a superfluous prologue included to pad out the running time even further. The soundtrack consists of music from **Wavelength** mixed with cues heard in many of the **Angel** films.

652. Mistaken Identity

(1988) ★: 6/10. *Woo lung chaak tai san* (Cantonese), *Wu long zei ti shen* (Mandarin): "Mixed-Up Thief Substitute." Cinematographer: Chim Pak-hung; Art Director: Yim Chi-lam; Music: Chris Babida; Producer-Action Director-Director: Tsui Siu-ming. Cast: Richard Ng Yiu-hon (Cheung Kan-sing), Simon Yam Tat-wah (Chow Tak-kan/Chow Man-heng), Nancy Cheung Mei-chi (Nancy Wong), Phillip Ko Fei (Ai B), Carrie Ng Kar-lai (Jenny), Cho Wing (Wing), Wong Yat-fei (Yan Yen-cho), Woo Fung ("The Foreign Expert"), Charlie Cho Cha-lei (Motorcycle Cop), Cho Tat-wah (Tso). 1.85:1. VHS: Tai Seng. Import LD: Ocean Shores. Running time unknown.

This enjoyable action comedy stars Simon Yam as two very different men named Chow: Tak-kan, a nerdy epileptic with buck teeth, and Man-heng, a slick and dangerous thief. While the latter is off pulling a robbery, he is pursued by police and gets into a car accident with the other Chow. Tak-kan is killed and his identity is obscured when his body is buried by a load of hot tar. Man-heng survives, but his fingerprints are burned off and he requires plastic surgery. Following the operation, the patient wakes up and finds himself accused of crimes he didn't perpetrate. Thanks to an error, it was actually Tak-kan who survived, but the police now believe him to be Man-heng and commit him to a mental hospital. Tak-kan's cohorts want the loot that Man-heng made off with, while Inspector Cheung wants to put him behind bars for a long time.

Aside from a great bit where Richard Ng and Phillip Ko battle to retrieve the former's gun which has fallen into a toilet, there is nothing exceptional here; but a likeable cast and some fine stuntwork keep things perking along. Director Tsui Siu-ming cameos in the final scene as a cop.

Mr. Africa *see* **Crazy Hong Kong**

653. Mr. Boo Meets Pom Pom

(1985; D & B Films Co.) ★: 5/10. *Ji yung saam bo* (Cantonese), *Zhi yong san bao*

(Mandarin): "Wisdom Courage Three Treasures." Cinematographers: Arthur Wong Ngok-tai, Wong Choi-keung; Art Director: Wong Yun-tat; Music: Joseph Chan Wing-leung; Writer: Jo Chan Wai-yee; Producer: Sammo Hung Kam-po; Director: Wu Ma. Cast: Michael Hui Koon-man (Mr. Boo), Richard Ng Yiu-hon (Chau), John Sham Kin-fun (Beethoven), Phillip Chan Yan-kin (Inspector Chan), Deanie Yip Tak-han (Beethoven's wife). 1.85:1. Import VCD: Mega Star. 92 minutes.

Teaming up John Sham and Richard Ng with Michael Hui's "Mr. Boo" character for the third **Pom Pom** outing was a stroke of comedic genius, and fans of the three stars will enjoy their interplay. Casual viewers, however, will find the plotless proceedings decidedly hit-and-miss. Ng and Sham play bumbling but oddly efficient cops who team up with Hui's scientifically-inclined inspector when thieves figure out a way to smash the "unbreakable" glass display cases in a jewellery store. The establishment's owner is an unscrupulous millionaire with designs on Hui's wife, who gladly cheats on her milquetoast husband. The rest of the film follows Hui's desperate attempts to win her back and publicly humiliate his rival. This includes a sidetrip to Japan (increasing the film's marketability in that region, where "Mr. Boo" is hugely popular) and the best-known scene (in which Hui takes on a sumo wrestler, using any and all weapons at his disposal). The funniest sequences remain the ones where the hopelessly henpecked Hui desperately tries to rationalize his wife's indisputable infidelity.

Lots of familiar faces put in brief appearances, including director Wu Ma, Peter Chan Lung, Nat Chan Pak-cheung, Yip Wing-cho, Dennis Chan Kwok-san, and Ben Lam Kwok-bun. The soundtrack includes a great deal of music lifted from Brian May's soundtrack for **Mad Max**, which is distractingly out-of-place here. It was followed by **Pom Pom Strikes Back**.

Mr. Canton and Lady Rose *see* **Miracles**

654. Mr. Coconut

(1989; Topping Time Films) ★: 6/10. *Gap ga foon* (Cantonese), *He jia huan* (Mandarin): "Joyful United Family." Cinematographer: Sander Lee Kar-ko; Art Director: Jason Mok Siu-kei; Music: Richard Yuen Cheuk-fan; Writers: Michael Hui Koon-man, Raymond Wong Pak-ming, Clifton Ko Chi-sum; Action Director: Tony Leung Siu-hung; Producer-Director: Clifton Ko Chi-sum. Cast: Michael Hui Koon-man (Ngan Kwai-nam), Raymond Wong Pak-ming (Wong Ka-fan), Olivia Cheng Man-ar (Ping), Ricky Hui Koon-ying (Lime), Joey Wang Tsu-hsien (Ling), Simon Yam Tat-wah (Timothy Hui), Maria Cordero (Miss Ma), Clifton Ko Chi-sum (TV Show Host). 1.85:1. Import LD: Mei Ah. 100 minutes.

This Michael Hui comedy is a one-joke affair (patterned somewhat after the Australian hit **Crocodile Dundee**) that manages to be fairly entertaining in spite of its flimsy premise. Hui plays Nam, a slovenly but good-hearted Mainland hick who moves in with his sister's family in their crowded HK apartment. His presence and complete lack of decorum drives his brother-in-law, Fan, around the bend, particularly when they both start working at the same establishment. Just when the family is ready to string Nam up for ruining their lives, he wins the "Chinese Superman" competition and its Grand Prize of a trip to London. Not long after his departure, Nam's relatives are horrified to hear that his plane has been shot down. However, unknown to them, Nam missed his connection and is now stranded in Africa! Prior to his departure, Nam bought life insurance and his death means a payday of $HK4 million dollars if his body is not found within thirty days. Fan books a trip and puts a down payment on a new house, only to have his bubble burst when Nam shows up in one piece.

The premise leaves little room for the comic invention found in Hui's best work, and the sequence in Africa has some embarrassingly demeaning humor directed towards black people. Still, this remains a likeable, if entirely forgettable, effort. Fennie Yuen Kit-ying, Yip Wing-cho, Lowell Lo Kwun-ting, Tony Leung Kar-fai, and Loletta Lee Lai-chun put in brief appearances.

655. Mr. Mumble

(1996; EMC Motion Pictures) ★: 5/10. *Man Bo* (Cantonese), *Meng Bo* (Mandarin): "Man Bo" or "Meng Bo." Cinematographer: Poon Yiu-ming; Art Director: Bill Lui Cho-hung; Music: Simon Lui Yu-yeung, Kok Chi-yin; Writers: Law Kam-fai, Michael Chow Man-kin; Producer: Eric Kei Kar-fat; Action Directors: Chin Kar-lok, Chan Kai-wing, Lam Yuk-ying. Director: Yuen Chun-man (billed in the English credits as "G-Man"). Cast: Michael Chow Man-kin (Mr. Mumble), Paulyn Suen Kai-kwan (Sheron), Francoise Yip Fong-wah (Yachi), Eric Kei Kar-fat (Chi), Simon Lui Yu-yeung (Simon Chan), Jessica Hester (Wai-heung), Ng Hong-ning (Monster), Ricky Yee Fan-wai (The Assassin), Jamie Luk Kim-ming (Shek Chung), Eddie Maher (Eddie), Money Lo Man-yee (MC). 1.85:1. Dolby Stereo. VHS: World Video. Import LD/VCD/DVD: Panorama Entertainment. 100 minutes.

Like Jackie Chan's **City Hunter**, this is a live action adaptation of the popular Japanese comic book which chronicles the exploits of offbeat hero Ryu Saeba, known in Cantonese as Man Bo (anglicized in the subtitles as "Mumble"). Unfortunately, like the Chan film, some good action and concepts are all but ploughed under by an avalanche of juvenile comedy, though this approach is, admittedly, in keeping with the source. After being fired from SDU because of his goldbricking, Mumble is hired to protect Sheron, the spoiled daughter of a triad boss. Although attempts are made on the girl's life, Mumble foils them and the pair fall in love. However, Mumble's old boss has allied himself with the enemy of Sheron's father, who plans on forcing the girl to sign over her family's tremendous wealth.

The jokes and sight gags are less than inspired, but Michael Chow and Paulyn Suen are congenial leads and the film makes for passable light entertainment, being more effective on its modest level than the overblown Chan misfire. Large character actor Ng Hong-ning gets one of his best roles to date as Mumble's big, bald sidekick, Monster.

656. Mr. Nice Guy

(1997; Golden Harvest/Paragon Films) ★: 6/10 (Both versions). *Yat goh ho yan* (Cantonese), *Yi ge hao ren* (Mandarin): "A Good Person." Cinematographer: Raymond Lam Fai-tai; Art Director: Horace Ma Kwong-wing; Music: Peter Kam Pui-tat (HK version), J. Peter Robinson (US version), Writers: Edward Tang King-sang, Fibe Ma Mei-ping; Producer: Chua Lam; Action Direction: Jackie Chan Stuntmen Association, Cho Wing; Director: Sammo Hung Kam-po. Cast: Jackie Chan (Jackie), Miki Lee Ching-yee (Miki), Richard Norton (Giancarlo), Gabrielle Fitzpatrick (Diana), Karen McLymont (Lakeisha), Barry Otto (Baggio), Vince Poletto (Romeo), Peter Houghton (Richard). Dolby Stereo, DTS Stereo (US version only), Sony Dynamic Digital Sound (US version only). 2.35:1. VHS/DVD: New Line (US version). LD: Image (US version). Import LD/VCD/DVD: Mei Ah. 88 minutes (US version)/94 minutes (HK version).

Following **First Strike**, Jackie Chan headed back to Australia for this enjoyable effort, which has more than enough action and stunts to prop up its flimsy, blithely illogical plot. Jackie is (of course) "Jackie," the assistant chef on a popular TV cooking program. He manages to get himself into a quandary involving investigative reporter Diana and some gangsters, whom the woman videotaped in the midst of a drug deal. Meanwhile, "The Demons," the other buyers caught in the act, are also after the tape, meaning even more thugs on Jackie's heels. The rest of the film is basically one long series of chases, with Jackie pursued through a shopping mall (a sequence almost on par with the climax of the original **Police Story**), outracing the villains on a horse and buggy through the streets of Melbourne, and (most memorably) making ingenious use of equipment and tools on a construction site as weapons.

The domestic success of **Rumble in the Bronx** was clearly an influence here; the plot is virtually identical and the film is almost entirely in English (surprisingly enough, the handful of Cantonese and Mandarin exchanges are retained and subtitled in the American version). **Rumble**'s finale is even reprised, with a giant earth mover destroying a mansion instead of a hovercraft trashing cars on the streets of Vancouver. Even allowing for the lack of creativity, the writing is very weak (a TV crew shooting an important exposé on a *consumer VHS* tape?), and the proceedings stop dead whenever even the most nominal exposition is required. The important factor, of course, is the action quotient. Fortunately, there is plenty and it is very well staged, though the various setpieces would have worked just as well without quite so much jazzed-up, Wong Kar-wai-style slow motion. Director Sammo Hung has a great cameo as a put-upon bike messenger, Emil Chow Wah-kin reprises his ice-cream man character from **Rumble**, and Joyce Godenzi (Hung's wife) can be glimpsed during the mall cooking demonstration.

Unlike the other Chan films that have been altered for American release, New Line's edition of **Mr. Nice Guy** is a perfectly workable variation on the original. A few instances of unnecessary violence against women have been toned down or eliminated altogether, and the movie is better off without them. J. Peter Robinson's new score is adequate, and only a handful of the supporting actors have been re-voiced. The American version is shorter but adds a brief, superfluous dinner table sequence, deleted from the HK cut, featuring Jackie, Barry Otto, and other performers. The outtakes are presented before the end crawl instead of under it. The HK video versions are dubbed entirely in Cantonese or Mandarin.

657. Mr. Possessed

(1988; Cosmopolitan Film Productions) ★: 6/10. *Jong che sin sang* (Cantonese), *Chuang xie xian sheng* (Mandarin): "Mr. Bump Evil." Cinematographer: Li Hsin-yeh; Art Director: Jon Hau Wing-choi; Writers: Wong Jing, Ho Lai-chuen; Producer: Lai Tin-chi; Director: Wong Jing. Cast: Carol Cheng Yu-ling (Tseng Hsiao-yu), Kenny Bee (Riley), Tang Pik-wan (Mrs. Li), Alex Man Chi-leung (Vegetarian Shen Tzu-han), Nat Chan Pak-cheung (Handsome Wang), Chingmy Yau Suk-ching (Baby), Francis Ng Chun-yu (Yu-lung), Lau Kar-wing (Li). 1.85:1. VHS: Tai Seng (Poor Subtitles). 93 minutes.

This passable horror comedy goes off track too often to be a complete success but still makes for enjoyable viewing. Aerobics teacher Hsiao-yu has the worst luck with men, but her travails are nothing compared to those of her male counterpart, Riley. Suffering from a severe jinx, Riley turns into a violent beast whenever he touches (or gets too close to) a woman! The two fall in love and, thanks to Hsiao-yu's unusually high level of yin energy, she and Riley are able to enjoy a fairly normal relationship. When Riley's disagreeable mother takes an instant disliking to Hsiao-yu, her actions threaten Riley's happiness. Furthermore, she reveals that her son suffers not from a jinx, but a bonafide *curse*, which was meant to put an end to the Li family bloodline.

The final battle against the ghost who perpetrated the hex is not as interesting or as well done as most films in this subgenre. There are, however, a few inspired touches (when a grotesque "spirit-taker" arrives from Hell to snatch Riley's soul, the humans try to distract it with such earthly delights as cigarettes, a sex flick, food, and mahjong!), and perennial movie gangster Alex Man enjoys one of his most unusual roles ever: a vegetarian Buddhist priest! Director Wong Jing has a supporting role.

658. Mr. Sardine

(1994; Simpson Communication) ★: 5/10. *Sa din yue saat yan si boon* (Cantonese), *Sha dian yu sha ren shi ban* (Mandarin): "Sardine Murder Business Companion." Cinematographer: Kai Shek; Art Director: Fok Tat-wah; Music: Lau Yee-tat; Writer: Chan Kam-cheung; Producer: Jacob Cheung Chi-leung; Director: Derek Chiu Sung-kei. Cast: Dayo Wong Chi-wah (Sardine), Irene Wan Pik-ha (Anna), Liu Kai-chi (Mong), Poon Fong-fong. Import LD/VCD: Universe. 104 minutes.

This is one of four low budget movies (shot on 16mm filmstock and produced for the US equivalent of $300,000) produced by Jacob Cheung in 1994 as an attempt to make topical, non-commercial cinema outside of the HK studio system. Sardine is a timid, eccentric grocery store employee who lives in an apartment stacked with canned goods. One day his landlady announces that she is going to evict him so that her daughter Anna can move in, and Sardine sees his well-organized world start to unravel. When the woman dies from an accidental overdose of booze and Panadol, Sardine mistakenly believes that he is responsible and tries (unsuccessfully) to dispose of the body. More trouble arises as Anna discovers her mom's body in his apartment and Sardine keeps running into the disreputable Officer Mong, who believes that the extremely suspicious clerk is trying to get him fired from his job.

Dayo Wong is effective in an atypical role as the put-upon nerd, and some of the twists and turns the story takes are amusing. However, as black comedies go, this is not pointed or macabre enough to really click.

659. Mr. Vampire

(1985; Golden Harvest/Bo Ho Films Co./Paragon Films) ★: 7/10. *Geung si sin saang* (Cantonese), *Jiang shi xian sheng* (Mandarin): "Mr. Stiff Corpse." Cinematographer: Peter Ngor Chi-kwan; Art Director: Lam Sai-wing; Writers: Barry Wong Ping-yiu, Roy Szeto Cheuk-hon; Producer: Leonard Ho Koon-cheung; Action Directors: Lam Ching-ying, Yuen Wah; Director: Ricky Lau Koon-wai. Cast: Ricky Hui Koon-ying (Man Choi), Chin Siu-ho (Chou), Lam Ching-ying (Kau), Moon Lee Choi-fung (Ting-ting), Billy Lau Nam-kwong (Wai), Pauline Wong Siu-fong (Jade), Anthony Chan Yau (Taoist Priest), Wu Ma (Rice Seller), Yuen Wah (Vampire). Dolby Digital (DVD only). 1.85:1. VHS: Tai Seng (Remastered for the English Market; subtitled or dubbed). Import LD: Star Entertainment (No Subtitles). Import VCD/DVD: Mega Star. 97 minutes.

The film that started the *gyonsi* horror-comedy craze, **Mr. Vampire** mixes low humor with wildly acrobatic slapstick and atmospheric horror setpieces. Taoist priest Kau and his bumbling assistants Man Choi and Chou seek to end a streak of bad luck that is plaguing the Yam family. Kau deduces that a previous *feng shui* master sought to take revenge on the family by providing the wrong burial instructions for the clan's patriarch. Before everything can be set right, the family's grandfather comes back from the dead and kills his son, who also soon returns from the grave himself. After a comical battle, Kau is able to exterminate the son, but the elderly *gyonsi* remains on the loose. In the meantime, Man Choi has been injured by the creature and Chou has been bitten by a comely female ghost. Both will transform into vampires themselves unless Kau can save them.

Still one of the best HK films of its type, **Mr. Vampire** establishes all the conventions of the genre in exciting fashion. While some of the humor is overly broad by Western standards, this is definitely recommended to both students of Eastern horror mythology and casual viewers alike. Lam Ching-ying is so effective as the erudite *sifu*, he would become typecast in the role right up until his death. In fact, in later films, the screenwriters would simply have him playing himself!

660. Mr. Vampire II

(1986; Golden Harvest/Bo Ho Films Co./Paragon Films) ★: 5/10. *Geung si sin saang juk jaap* (Cantonese), *Jiang shi xian sheng xu ji* (Mandarin): "Mr. Stiff Corpse Sequel." Cinematographers: Andrew Lau Wai-keung, Peter Ngor Chi-kwan, Arthur Wong Ngok-tai; Art Director: Lam Sai-wing; Music: The Melody Bank; Writer: Barry Wong Ping-yiu; Producer: Sammo Hung Kam-po; Action Direction: Sammo Hung Stuntmen Association; Director: Ricky Lau Koon-wai. Cast: Yuen Biao (Jen), Moon Lee Choi-fung (Gigi), Lam Ching-ying (Lin), Chung Fat (The Professor), Billy Lau Nam-kwong ("Chicken"), Woo Fung (Hu), James Tien Chun (Tien). 1.85:1. VHS: Tai Seng. Import LD: Star Entertainment (No Subtitles). Import VCD: Mega Star. 91 minutes.

The first sequel to Ricky Lau's surprise hit is a bit of a disappointment, though it is not without charm. Aimed primarily at children, the film brings back Lam Ching-ying, Billy Lau, and Moon Lee, but relocates the action to the present day. Chung Fat plays a professor who finds three perfectly preserved vampires (a wife, her husband, and their young son) on an expedition. His plan to sell the three corpses is disrupted when the youngest one escapes. The vampire child then meets up with a little girl and her brother, with the proceedings suddenly transforming into a tiresome ripoff of **E.T.**, as the children conceal the boy from their father (Woo), while the creature uses its powers to entertain them. Just when most adult viewers will be ready to raise the white flag, Lam (playing himself!), Yuen Biao, and Lee appear, and things pick up considerably. Yuen accidentally releases the adult creatures, leading to lots of acrobatic kung fu (including one prolonged bout in comical "slow motion") and some well-staged wirework. After being temporarily subdued, the parents escape, prowling the city for their wayward child. Lam and police chief James Tien join together Taoist method and modern hardware to put an end to the creatures once and for all. Stanley Fung Shui-fan and Wu Ma make brief appearances.

661. Mr. Vampire III

(1987; Golden Harvest/Bo Ho Films Co./Paragon Films) ★: 6/10. *Ling waan sin saang* (Cantonese), *Ling huan xian sheng* (Mandarin): "Mr. Unreal Corpse." Cinematographer: Andrew Lau Wai-keung; Art Director: Ho Kim-seng; Music: Not Original; Writers: Roy Szeto Cheuk-hon, LoWing-keung; Producer: Sammo Hung Kam-po; Action Direction: Lam Ching-ying, Stephen Tung Wai, Sammo Hung Stuntmen Association; Director: Ricky Lau Koon-wai. Cast: Richard Ng Yiu-hon (Mao Ming), Lui Fong (Ta Pao), Lam Ching-ying (The Master), Billy Lau Nam-kwong (Chiang), Yip Wing-cho (Party Guest), Corey Yuen Kwai (Party Guest), Wu Ma (Party Guest), Sammo Hung Kam-po (Hung). 1.85:1. VHS: Tai Seng (No Subtitles). Import LD: Star Entertainment (No Subtitles). Import VCD: Mega Star. 88 minutes.

Darker and gorier than its predecessors, this entry brings comedian Richard Ng into the fold as bumbling conman Uncle Ming. Impersonating a Taoist and pretending to vanquish ghosts from haunted homes, he actually scams clients, with the help of his own friendly ghost assistants, Ta Pao and Hsi Pao. A gang of supernatural horse thieves is terrorizing the surrounding area, and their female leader steals Ta Pao away from Ming. Transforming the meek ghost into a monster, she sends it to attack Ming, as a diversion, while she rescues her comrades that were captured in a previous raid. Fortunately, Lam Ching-ying's wizened *sifu* is a resident of the village and ready to lend his extraordinary abilities in the fight against evil. However, once the thieves are dealt with, they come back as vengeance-seeking ghosts.

There are some amusingly demented special effects to bolster the wonderful magic spells and otherworldly martial arts that fans of the series have come to know and love. A much more effective mixture of comedy and terror than Part II, this entry is also overly long, given the slim material, and a bit repetitive.

662. Mr. Vampire 4

(1988; Golden Harvest/Bo Ho Films Co./Paragon Films) ★: 5/10. *Geung si suk suk* (Cantonese), *Jiang shi shu shu* (Mandarin): "Uncle Stiff Corpse." Cinematographers: Tom Lau Moon-tong, Bill Wong Chung-bo, Abdul M. Rumjahn; Art Director: Raymond Lee King-man; Writer: Lo Wing-keung; Producer: Leonard Ho Koon-cheung; Action Direction: Sammo Hung Stuntmen Association, Yuen Wah; Director: Ricky Lau Koon-wai. Cast: Wu Ma (The Buddhist Priest), Anthony Chan Yau (The Four-Eyed Taoist), Loletta Lee Lai-chun (Ching-ching), Chin Kar-lok (Chia-le), Yuen Wah (Effeminate Servant), Chung Fat (The Taoist Crane). 1.85:1. VHS: Tai Seng (No Subtitles). Import LD: Star Entertainment (No Subtitles). Import VCD: Mega Star. 96 minutes. Also known as **Mr. Vampire Saga 4**.

The last official entry in the **Mr. Vampire** series suffers from a flimsy plot, an overabundance of tired slapstick, and the absence of Lam Ching-ying. A Buddhist priest and his neighbor, a Taoist, are longtime enemies who frequently quarrel and place spells on each other. They must put their differences aside and combine their attributes when the Taoist's brother, The Taoist Crane, falls victim to a powerful *gyonsi* which escapes from his control during a violent storm.

The first half is tedious, but things pick up considerably at the midpoint, with the introduction of the seemingly indestructible vampire and his legion of undead victims. This leads to some energetic action sequences, which often make the most of Chin Kar-lok's impressive acrobatic abilities. However, with virtually no storyline to contain them, even these sequences grow tedious after a time and the film lacks the deliciously ghoulish inventiveness that characterized the original, **Magic Cop**, and **The Ultimate Vampire**. Chan (essentially reprising his character from the first film) and Wu attack their roles with relish, but neither can muster the authority and authenticity that Lam always brings to this sort of part. Yuen Wah has his strangest role ever as a gay attendant who is transformed into an equally swishy bloodsucker!

663. Mr. Vampire 1992

(1992; Grand March Movie Production Co.) ★: 6/10. *San geung si sin saang* (Cantonese), *Xin jiang shi xian sheng* (Mandarin): "New Mr. Stiff Corpse." Cinematographer: Raymond Lam Fai-tai; Art Directors: Leung Kar-yu, Fred Chan Chi-chung; Music: Anders Nelsson, Simon Leung Chi-wah; Writer: Lo Wing-keung; Producer: Yip Wing-cho; Action Director: Siu Tak-fu; Director: Ricky Lau Koon-wai. Cast: Ricky Hui Koon-ying (Man Choi), Chin Siu-ho (Chiu Sang), Lam Ching-ying (Lam), Sandra Ng Kwan-yu (Birdie), Billy Lau Nam-kwong (The

General), Suki Kwan Sau-mei (Lin), Yip Wing-cho (Chef). 1.85:1. VHS: World Video. Import LD/VCD: Star Entertainment (No Subtitles). Import DVD: China Star (No Subtitles). Running time unknown.

Featuring performers and personnel from the original film, this unsuccessful attempt to revive the **Mr. Vampire** series turns out to be one of its better sequels. This time out, Master Lam and his bumbling assistants Man Choi and Chiu Sang must take on the malevolent spirit of a dead child which has entered the body of an innocent woman. The demon secretly affects the unborn child of a noblewoman, while Lam and company try to cure her husband, a vampirized general. After destroying the general's undead father, Man Choi and Chiu Sang are dispatched to obtain "vampire tooth powder" (as in ground-up teeth, not toothpaste) and must impersonate *gyonsi* to do so (the film's funniest sequence). When that is finally accomplished, the trio turns their attention towards saving the General's wife and baby. When the creature proves too powerful for him to handle on his own, Lam reluctantly enlists the aid of Birdie, his obnoxious female counterpart who has a crush on him.

Despite being produced independently, the production values are quite good, about on par with the Golden Harvest entries. In addition to the usual scatological jokes, there are some surprisingly perverse elements, like S & M gags and a blood drinking sequence with lesbian overtones. The climax, which features our vampire-hunting heroes battling the demon child *and* an army of vampires, isn't novel, but it is energetically staged and good fun.

Mr. Vampire Saga 4 *see* **Mr. Vampire 4**

664. Modern Heroes

(1980; Cheeter Film Co.) ★: 1/10. *Keung wu tang on* (Cantonese), *Jiang hu dang an* (Mandarin): "Charlatan Files." Cinematographer: Ho Ko-wai; Music: Not Original; Producer: Tse Kit-yok; Writer-Director: Wong Fung. Cast: Chow Yun-fat (Chu Ka-wah). 2.35:1. VHS: Arena/Xenon. 83 minutes. Also known as **Hard Boiled Killers** (Arena/Xenon title), **Police Sir** [*sic*].

Here is another early Chow Yun-fat film that is strictly for his most devoted fans. He plays Chu, a recent graduate from the police academy whose by-the-book deportment constantly lands his colleagues in hot water. When he accidentally gets his British superior busted for illegal gambling, the disgraced official hires thugs to beat Chu up. Chu's buddies try various means to help him out (including a trip to a local wizard), while various dirty cops and a local triad leader try to bring about his ruin. *Modern Heroes* has no fresh ideas, no sense of pacing, and, worst of all, not one genuine laugh. Unless you absolutely must see Chow imitating The Monkey King, avoid this one like the plague.

665. The Modern Love

(1994; David Lam Films) ★: 5/10. *San laam foon nui oi* (Cantonese), *Xin nan huan nu ai* (Mandarin): "New Male Joyful Female Love." Cinematographer: Abdul M. Rumjahn; Art Director: Raymond Lam Chi-wai; Music: Wong Bong; Writers: Wong Ho-wah, David Lam Tak-luk; Producers: David Lam Tak-luk, Lee Yiu-ting; Director: David Lam Tak-luk. Cast: Chingmy Yau Suk-ching (Bo Bo Chung), Anita Lee Yuen-wah (Cola), Lily Chung Suk-wai (Yuen Siu-la), Mark Cheng Ho-nam (Cheung Kit), Lawrence Cheng Tan-shui (Fong Suk-ping), Sunny Chan Kam-hung (Wong), Bobby Yip King-sang (Guy with Pompadour), Frankie Chin Chi-leung (Long Hair). 1.85:1. VHS: Tai Seng. Import LD/VCD: Ocean Shores. 96 minutes.

Rated Category III for no discernible reason, this minor romantic farce is too formulaic to be anything more than an inoffensive time waster. Family planning clinic worker Bo Bo and her roommates, Siu-la (a dimwitted hooker) and Cola (who only believes in one-night stands) meet up with men who just may be the ones to change their futures. Bo Bo falls for nice guy triad Kit; Siu-la enters into a bizarre, adversarial relationship with cranky nerd Fong; and Cola is won over by handsome businessman Wong. Bo Bo must decide if she will stay true to her boyfriend (due back from France in the near future), and Cola begins to feel pangs of jealousy over Wong's open womanizing. Siu-la, on the other hand, helps bring Fong out of his shell, and the two appear destined to walk down the aisle together.

Highly unlikely and instantly forgettable, this remains quite watchable, thanks in no small part to Lily Chung's enjoyably flaky performance, though she doesn't deserve full points as her voice has been dubbed by someone else.

666. Modern Romance

(1994; Upland Film Corporate/Wong Jing's Workshop) ★: 5/10. *Luen oi dik tin hung* (Cantonese), *Lian ai de tian kong* (Mandarin): "Love Affair of Heaven." Cinematographer: Cheung Man-bo; Art Director: Ring Law Chi-keung; Music: Wong Bong; Writers: Lee Lik-chi, Andrew Lau Wai-keung, Wong Jing, Szeto Wai-cheuk; Producer: Wong Jing; Directors: Lee Lik-chi, Lam Wai-lun, Andrew Lau Wai-keung, Wong Jing. Cast: Chingmy Yau Suk-ching (Chanel), Carrie Ng Kar-lai (Liza), Christy Chung Lai-tai (Ady), Sandra Ng Kwan-yu (Frankie Chan Bo-chu), Michael Chow Man-kin (Five Elements), Michael Wong Man-tak (Dino), Roy Cheung Yiu-yeung (Roy), Chan Kwok-bong (Bond), Nat Chan Pak-cheung (Liza's Ex), Bowie Lam Bo-yee (Dr. Alan Tam), Esther Kwan Wing-ho (Pauline), Yuen King-tan (Tam's Nurse), Helena Law Lan (Nancy), Ha Ping (Bartender), Vincent Kok Tak-chiu (Taxi Driver Who Looks Like Buddha). 1.85:1. VHS: Tai Seng. Import LD: Cameron Entertainment. Import VCD: Mei Ah. 95 minutes.

Modern Romance consists of four different love stories about four different female friends from four different directors. Lee Lik-chi's *Mi shun dik lui yan* ("Superstitious Woman") tells of Ady, an ultra-superstitious girl who believes that she will marry her twentieth boyfriend. He will arrive on her birthday and his name will include the five elements. On the predestined day, no less than a "Mr. Five Elements" appears, but boyfriend No. 19, the petty and demented Dr. Alan Tam, is determined to mess up Ady's spiritually inviolate destiny. Lam Wai-lun's *Taam suk dik lui yan* ("Greedy Woman") concerns Liza and her three secret lovers who, naturally, encounter each other under adverse circumstances…not once but twice. Lesbian Frankie Chan is at the center of Andrew Lau Wai-keung's *But si lui yan dik lui yan* ("The Woman Who Is Not a Woman"), fighting tooth and nail with male competitor Bond for the love of singer Pauline, who is out to fleece them both. Naturally, things don't work out as planned and Bond sets his sights on Frankie instead. In Wong Jing's *Kau cheung dik lui yan* ("The Woman Who Relies on Barging"), TV commercial director Chanel falls for handsome Dino, but the guy is so perfect, she is soon going out of her mind from jealousy.

None of the stories are especially memorable, though the first three are pleasant enough and the linking material is effective. Andrew Lau's segment is the most entertaining, thanks to amusing turns by Sandra Ng and Chan Kwok-bong. Wong Jing's concluding chapter is definitely the weakest, emerging as mean-spirited and almost entirely unfunny. The above story titles are literal translations of the Chinese; no English equivalents are provided in the film.

667. A Moment of Romance

(1990; Paka Hill Film Production/ Movie Impact) ★: 7/10. *Tin yeuk yau ching* (Cantonese), *Tian ruo you qing* (Mandarin): "If Heaven Has Love." Cinematographers: Horace Wong Wing-hang, Joe Chan Kong-hung; Art Director: Ringo Cheung Sek-wah; Music: Lo Tai-yau, Fabio Carli; Writer: James Yuen Sai-sang; Producer: Johnny To Kei-fung; Action Director: Yuen Bun; Director: Benny Chan Muk-sing. Cast: Andy Lau Tak-wah (Wah Dee), Jacqueline Wu Chien-lien (Jo Jo Huen), Ng Man-tat (Rambo), Tommy Wong Kwong-leung (Trumpet), Lau Kong (Kong), Lam Chung (John Chan). Dolby Digital (DVD only). 1.85:1. VHS: Tai Seng. Import LD: Mei Ah. Import VCD: Mei Ah, Mega Star. DVD: Mega Star. 87 minutes.

Just about everything clicks in this stylish and involving triad actioner/romantic drama, which remains a high water mark among the youth-oriented films of this nature. Coerced into driving the getaway car for a robbery conducted by members of his gang, low-level mobster Wah Dee takes rich teenager Jo Jo hostage in order to effect his escape. Not only does he not kill the girl, Dee even drops her off at her home. When the police find Jo Jo and bring her in for questioning, she returns the favor by not picking Dee or his cohorts out of a police line-up. In spite of this, Dee's superior, Trumpet, still wants her dead, and Dee must intercede when Trumpet's men try to carry out his wishes. Although he dissuades Jo Jo at first, Dee eventually relents and falls for her, but neither Jo Jo's parents nor fate will let them stay together for long.

The writing is weak but the film is intelligently mounted and unabashedly romantic. Andy Lau gives a most persuasive performance in what would become one of his signature roles, and Ng Man-tat copped a Best Supporting Actor statue for his colorful turn as a destitute low-life who is one of Dee's few loyal friends. In her film debut, Taiwanese actress Jacqueline Wu is charming and handles the emotional facets of the part well, but, as her Cantonese was too limited at this point, she has been dubbed by someone else here. Director Benny Chan juggles genres well here, and the shifts in tone are aided by an excellent soundtrack (though dropping a couple of the pop song interludes wouldn't have hurt) and some accomplished cinematography. *A Moment of Romance* was followed by two in-name-only sequels, the second of which reunites Wu and Lau.

668. A Moment of Romance II

(1993; China Entertainment/Paka Hill Film Production Co.) ★: 4/10. *1993 Tin yeuk yau ching II ji tin cheung dei gau* (Cantonese), *1993 Tian ruo you qing II zhi tian chang di jiu* (Mandarin): "1993 If Heaven Has Love II: Enduring Loyalty." Cinematographer: Ardy Lam Kwok-wah; Art Director: James Leung Wah-sang; Music: William Woo Wai-lap; Writer: Susanne Chan Suk-yin; Producer: Johnny To Kei-fung; Action Directors: Ma Yuk-shing, Dion Lam Dik-on; Director: Benny Chan Muk-sing. Cast: Aaron Kwok Fu-shing (Frank), Jacqueline Wu Chien-lien (Celia), Roger Kwok Chun-on (Jack), Kwan Hoi-shan (Bill), Anthony Wong Chau-sang (Dino), Paul Chun Pui (Frank's Father), William Ho Kar-kui (Gang Boss). 1.85:1. VHS: Tai Seng. Import LD/DVD: Universe. Import VCD: Universe, Mega Star. 87 minutes.

Only Jacqueline Wu returned for this in-name-only follow-up which starts off well but falls apart during the final reel. Mainland girl Celia is working as a hooker in HK in order to help get her brother (who was arrested for his anti-government writings) out of jail. When a gang boss is murdered by one of his subordinates, Celia is blamed but is saved by passing motorcyclist Frank. He lets her move into his apartment; and, in gratitude, she fixes up the decrepit place and even helps his estranged father to assuage his anger and reunite with his son. Deciding that she has been too much of a burden on Frank, Celia decides to turn herself over to the triads.

Beautifully scored by distinguished composer William Woo, the film does get rather schmaltzy—but agreeably so (like many HK dramas of this sort). However, the finale needlessly splits up Frank and Celia in order to throw in an extra climax involving the former's crippled friend. This results in an anti-climactic and poorly-staged motorcycle race that ends the film on a far less satisfying note. Jacqueline Wu does wonders with her stereotypical role, and character actor Kwan Hoi-shan is also quite good as a disgraced cop out to arrest Celia in order to restore his reputation and save her from being murdered.

669. A Moment of Romance III

(1996; Win's Entertainment/Sanqueen) ★: 5/10. *Tin yeuk yau ching III fung foh gaai yan* (Cantonese), *Tian ruo you qing III feng huo jia ren* (Mandarin): "If Heaven Has Love III: Flames of War Beauty." Cinematographer: Poon Hang-sang; Art Director: Bruce Yu Kar-on; Music: William Woo Wai-lap, Raymond Wong Ying-wah; Writers: Sandy Shaw, Yau Nai-hoi; Producer-Director: Johnny To Kei-fung. Cast: Andy Lau Tak-wah (Lau Tin-wai), Jacqueline Wu Chien-lien (Ting Siu-wo), Alex Fong Chung-sun (The Captain). Dolby Digital. 2.35:1. VHS/LD: World Video. Import LD/VCD/DVD: Mei Ah. 95 minutes.

Jacqueline Wu's original onscreen partner, Andy Lau, returns for this third entry, which unfolds during World War II. Chinese Air Force pilot Lau Tin-wai is shot down by the Japanese near Double Mountain Village in rural China. Local girl Ting Siu-wo is charged with caring for him. While helping the handsome stranger get back on his feet, she falls in love with him. When worms threaten the farmers' crops, Tin-wai dismantles his bombs and uses the sulphur inside to kill the insects. In spite of his aid, the village headman is angered by Tin-wai's presence, as Siu-wo's parents promised her hand in marriage to his son. When Tin-wai is able to obtain fuel for his plane, he leaves the girl a note to say goodbye, not realizing that Siu-wo is illiterate. When she finally learns the contents of the message, Siu-wo sets out to find Tin-wai in Wu-han. With the Japanese forces approaching, the government orders everyone to leave for Chungking, but Tin-wai has volunteered for a highly dangerous bombing mission and tries to hurt Siu-wo's feelings so that she will go back to her village and forget him.

While more satisfying than the second film, this lacks the edge of the original and is retrograde to the point where it barely holds one's interest. Lau and, especially, Wu do good work, the production design is beautifully detailed, and Poon Hang-sang's widescreen photography (carefully designed to give the proceedings a nostalgic quality) is striking, providing partial compensation.

670. Mongkok Story

(1996; Hang Ngai Films Co.) ★: 7/10. *Wong gok fung wan* (Cantonese), *Wang jiao feng yun* (Mandarin): "Mongkok Turbulence." Cinematographer: Chiu Fu-keung; Art Director: Angelo Bernardo Castilho; Music: Tommy Wai Kai-leung; Writer: Philip Kwok Wai-chung; Producers: Wu Chi, Wong Siu-ming; Director: Wilson Yip Wai-san. Cast: Edmond Leung Hon-man (Leung-ping), Anthony Wong Chau-sang (Lui Lone), Roy Cheung Yiu-yeung (Ching), Michael Chan Wai-man (Fook). 1.85:1. VHS: Tai Seng. Import LD/VCD: Universe. 94 minutes.

The critical and financial success of Andrew Lau's **Young and Dangerous** trilogy spawned a whole new wave of HK gangster thrillers, reviving a genre that petered out at the beginning of the decade. In contrast to those "hero films" (the name comes from "The Essence of a Hero," the Chinese title for **A Better Tomorrow**), which stressed honor and tradition, the '90s *goo wak jai* ("young rascals") cycle plays with the conventions, adding humor, quirky but genuine characters, and a much fresher perspective to the mix. One of the finest examples of this new trend is Wilson Yip's **Mongkok Story**, a consistently inventive thriller which emphasizes character and droll happenstance to excellent effect. Edmond Leung stars as Leung-ping, a bored busboy who is fascinated by the local triad youths who patronize his restaurant. Sensing his eagerness to join their ranks, they introduce him to mid-level boss, Brother Ching (Cheung), whose knife-fighting exploits have become so grossly exaggerated in the telling, he can reduce rivals to snivelling, grovelling clowns simply by walking into a room. Ching takes the youth under his wing but soon must act on the behalf of his men when they offend Brother Lui Lone (Wong, in an adroit, highly amusing performance), a blithely psychotic boss, who is grooming himself to be an action movie star (we get to see an excerpt from his latest opus, a hilariously awful ripoff of **Desperado**). Although Ching is able to smooth things out, Lui is not so easily bought off, and, through a series of escalating, darkly comic episodes, Leung-ping quickly starts to learn the downside of his chosen profession.

The clever casting of '80s *ging fei pin* icons Cheung (one of Ringo Lam Ling-tung's favorite heavies) and Michael Chan Wai-man (whose exploits as a triad enforcer are supposedly what got him into movies in the first place) lends weight to the script's notion that the glamour and respect their generation purported to enjoy has slipped away in the face of changing times (instead of the usual illicit operations like gun running, racketeering, prostitution, or drugs, the gangs here deal in the high yield/low risk commodity of the '90s: pirate Video CDs). The principals' fates are far closer to reality than the noble, blood-stained deaths usually seen, and the ending is pleasingly ambiguous.

671. The Moon Warriors

(1992; Scholar Films) ★: 7/10. *Chin san chuen suet* (Cantonese), *Zhan shen chuan shui* (Mandarin): "Legend of the War Gods." Cinematographer: Arthur Wong Ngok-tai; Art Director: James Leung Wah-sang; Music: James Wong Jim, Mark Lui Chung-tak; Writer: Alex Law Kai-yui; Producer: Chan Pui-wah; Action Directors: Ching Siu-tung, Corey Yuen Kwai; Director: Sammo Hung Kam-po. Cast: Andy Lau Tak-wah (Philip), Anita Mui Yim-fong (Moony), Kenny Bee (Yin), Maggie Cheung Man-yuk (Merlin), Kelvin Wong Siu (The 14th Prince), Chang Yi (Lan Ning-kwan). 1.85:1. VHS: Tai Seng. Import LD/VCD/DVD: Universe. 90 minutes.

With Sammo Hung Kam-po behind the camera, and Ching Siu-tung and Corey Yuen Kwai choreographing the action, this HK period fantasy promises stirring battles and delivers in spades. That said, this is still a comparatively low-key effort that expends time exploring its characters and their emotions between the expected eruptions of ferocious combat. As the film opens, Yin Sap-sam (Bee), the 13th Prince and ruler of the empire, must flee on horseback from his kingdom (along with a small group of loyalists) when the palace is invaded by enemy troops. At the head of these rebellious forces is his brother, Yin Sap-sei, the 14th Prince (Wong), who seeks to ascend the throne rather prematurely. When Sap-sam stumbles into a trap, he is saved from death by Fei (Lau), a guileless fisherman with tremendous martial abilities and one very unique pet: a domesticated killer whale named Hoi-wai. With Fei in tow, Sap-sam and his troops journey across country where they meet up with Lan Ning-kwan (veteran Taiwanese kung fu movie star Chang), the Emperor of Lan Ning, and his daughter, Princess Yuet Ah-yee (Mui). In the aftermath of a surprise attack, Fei escorts the bratty princess (who has been promised in marriage to Sap-sam) to safety and, after some initial friction, the two fall in love. It is soon revealed that Sap-sam's prime confederate, Hsien (Cheung), is secretly in league with his brother but cannot carry out the traitor's assassination order because she has fallen for the deposed monarch. When Sap-sei discovers that the fugitives are hiding near Fei's village, he orders his troops to massacre the population, the lead-in to a final confrontation between the two brothers.

Cinematographer Arthur Wong (**Iron Monkey**) isn't entirely successful at disguising the fact that footage featuring the whale was shot entirely in an Ocean Park tank. In all other respects, though, this is a slick and well-produced adventure, on par with what one would expect from its creators. Lau gives a conventional performance but Cheung and Mui are well cast in precisely the opposite sort of roles they usually play, and Wong is a sneering, spirited villain. There is also a splendid score by Wong and Lui, which mixes a driving, spaghetti western-influenced theme and stark battle passages performed on traditional instruments with calm, reflective transitions that compliment the dramatic mood very nicely. The tape and disc differ somewhat from the version shown in domestic Chinatown theaters. Those prints had better subtitles (in addition to the bad syntax, the characters here were saddled with anachronistic English monikers like "Philip," "Merlin," "Moony," and "Sea-Wayne," as listed at the top) but lacked the five minutes of post-credits footage found on the tape and disc, which shows Lau training with the whale. Tai Seng and Universe's source print apparently hails from Taiwan, as there are several instances where subtitles appear onscreen when no one is speaking in the Cantonese dub, while the voices in question can be heard in the Mandarin version. Backing this assumption up is the fact that the subtitle font actually changes during the final few minutes, suggesting that two sources were composited (the whale is referred to correctly as "Hoi-wai," not "Sea-Wayne").

Mortal Combat *see* **Crippled Avengers**

672. The Most Wanted

(1994) ★: 3/10. *Lung foo san fung wan tau ho tung chap faan* (Cantonese), *Long hu xin feng yun tou hao tong ji fan* (Mandarin): "Dragon Tiger New Turbulence Head of Wanted Criminals." Music: Gigo Lee Chi-hang; Writers: Clarence Yip Wai-chung, Susanne Chan Suk-yin, Taures Chow Yin-han; Producer: Clarence Yip Wai-chung; Action Director: Cheung Lui; Director: Wong Kam-tin. Cast: Lau Ching-wan (Ho Chi yung, aka Cat), Kent Cheng Chuk see (Cheng Ming-fen), Bowie Lam Bo-yee (Sap), Eileen Tung Oi-ling (Lily Ching), Robin Shou Wan-bo (Gang Leader). 1.85:1. VHS: Tai Seng. Import LD: Cameron Entertainment. Import VCD: Mei Ah. 91 minutes.

A cop thriller modelled after Ringo Lam's **City on Fire**, **The Most Wanted** is too familiar and too poorly mounted to be of much interest. Lau Ching-wan plays an undercover officer whose gambling addiction has got him nearly $HK1 million in debt. After being chosen as the driver for a jewellery store robbery, he is forced to participate in the job and gets shot by police. His picture is captured by a surveillance camera and he soon finds himself a wanted criminal. When his superiors refuse to intercede on his behalf, Lau realizes that he is running out of time and options.

Both Lau and Kent Cheng do good work under the circumstances, and Eileen Tung is fine in her debut role as a sympathetic but street smart Mainland girl trying to forge a living. The rest of this production is an unfortunate cross between the numbingly predictable and the tediously inept. The subtitling is also quite bad here, leaving random lines untranslated.

The Movie Story *see* **The Story of Movie** [*sic*]

673. Murder

(1993; Joe Siu International/People's Productions) ★: 3/10. *Wong fung mei hau jam* (Cantonese), *Huang feng wei hou zhen* (Mandarin): "The Bee's Behind the Tail Sting." Cinematographer: Cheng Siu-keung; Art Director: Fong Ying; Music: Phil Chan Fei-lap; Writers: Yip Kwong-kim, Lawrence Cheng Tan-shui, Wong Man-yu; Producer: Joe Siu King-kai; Director: Lawrence Cheng Tan-shui. Cast: Carol Cheng Yu-ling (Jessica Lau), Damian Lau Chung-yan (Yau Lung), Lawrence Cheng Tan-shui (Chu Chung-hong), Deanie Yip Tak-han (Ma Mei-chun), Wong Kam-kong (Detective), Spencer Lam Sheung-yee (Jessica's Boss). 1.85:1. VHS: Tai Seng. Import LD/VCD: Universe. 98 minutes.

This foolish, tiresome thriller is a limp variation on the Hollywood hit **Regarding Henry** (1991), peopled with ludicrously unpleasant main characters. Jessica, a ruthless lawyer, is representing nurse Mei-chun in a lawsuit involving an act of criminal negligence. Accepting a bribe, Jessica "loses" a key piece of evidence, sabotaging the case and causing Mei-chun to lose her job and face a stiff financial penalty. Jessica's husband Lung launders money on the side, and this interest in accumulating as much wealth as possible is about the only thing the couple has in common. Angry at Lung's philandering, Jessica hides $10 million that her husband owes to a client. In the heat of their subsequent argument, Lung shoots Jessica in the head and decides to blame the crime on a former employee, whom he subsequently murders. However, Jessica has survived the wound and goes into therapy under the supervision of (surprise!) Mei-chun, who takes the opportunity to exact revenge. Having lost her memory, Jessica must begin her life anew, and Mei-chun is the only nurse who is able to control her childish outbursts. In the meantime, Lung's partner (played by director Lawrence Cheng) is pressuring him to locate the money so that they can reimburse their increasingly angry associate. Lung tries everything to jog Jessica's memory, and when the past does start to reassert itself, Jessica (who has subsequently changed into a much more compassionate person) must decide how to extricate herself from this dilemma. The Chinese title refers to the element of surprise, something that is sorely missing in this contrived and tacky melodrama.

674. The Musical Vampire

(1990) ★: 5/10. *Yam lok geung si* (Cantonese), *Yin yue jiang shi* (Mandarin): "Musical Stiff Corpse." Cinematographer: Mok Chat-yun; Writer: Sit Chung-kin; Action Directors: Wilson Tong Wai-shing, Fung Hark-on; Producer/Director: Wilson Tong Wai-shing. Cast: Lam Ching-ying (Uncle Master), Stanley Fung Shui-fan (The Master), Loletta Lee Lai-chun (Chu-chu), Lee Kar-sing (Hoo), Xiong Xinxin (Keung), Charlie Cho Cha-lei (Captain Tsao), Tai Po (Little Three). 1.85:1. VHS: World Video. Import LD: Mei Ah. Import VCD: World Trade. Running time unknown.

A lesser entry in the hopping vampire cycle, **The Musical Vampire** tries to add a couple of fresh angles to an increasingly tired formula but still comes across as routine. While transporting one of his master's vampires across the countryside, bumbling acolyte Hoo is attacked and the creature is taken by a Caucasian scientist who proceeds to inject it with experimental chemicals. The result is a super vampire that can no longer be subdued through traditional means. The monster does have one very unique weakness: The song "London Bridge Is Falling Down" renders it as gentle as a kitten! With the creature decimating the population of Yam's Village, and the local army captain demanding results (or death), Hoo's master tries every trick in the book to destroy the bloodsucker but fails. The one last hope for success lies in the hands of Uncle Master, a rival *sifu* with greater powers.

The various spells and action sequences are not on the level of their counterparts in Golden Harvest's vampire comedies, and too much time is wasted padding the thin premise out with throwaway gags. A solid performance by Lam Ching-ying and an entertaining climax keep the film worthwhile.

675. Muto Bontie

(1996; Art Concept International) ★: 4/10. *Moh dang pooi ne tai* (Cantonese), *Mo deng pu ni ti* (Mandarin): "Modern Buddha." Cinematographer: Poon Yiu-ming; Art Director: Leung Siu-tong; Writer: Jessy Lam Chak-chi; Producer: Chow Ta-wah; Music/Director: Chan Kin-tak. Cast: Lau Ching-wan (Lam Chak-chi/Chi), Alice Lau Ar-lai (Alice), Yip Wing-cho (Inspector Tsoi), Cheung Suet-ling, Annie Man Chung-han. 1.85:1. VHS: Tai Seng. Import LD/VCD: Mei Ah. 88 minutes.

It is not uncommon for HK features to borrow stories or ideas from Hollywood movies, but this production takes a bounding leap over the line dividing imitation and outright plagiarism. It is not just a local version of the Jim Abrahams, David Zucker, and Jerry Zucker farce **Ruthless People**, *it's the exact same movie*, reprising many of the jokes verbatim. The only real difference here is that Lau Ching-wan plays both the Danny DeVito and Judge Reinhold parts. For those unfamiliar with the original, the plot concerns a pair of inept husband and wife kidnappers who make off with the fat, obnoxious spouse of a conniving millionaire. This sits great with the latter, as he was looking for a way to get rid of the shrew, so he refuses to pay the ransom. While the criminals desperately lower their demands, the captive asserts herself and gets back into shape. When it becomes painfully clear that the ransom will never be paid, the spurned spouse joins with her kind-hearted captors to exact revenge.

If you find the premise of interest, you might as well just watch the original, as this version adds no new wrinkles and is not as well mounted or performed. Writer Lam Chak-chi even names the villain after himself; does this person have *no imagination at all*?

676. My Dad Is a Jerk

(1997; Win's Entertainment/Film Unlimited Production) ★: 4/10. *Dui bat hei, doh je nei* (Cantonese), *Dui bu qi, duo xie ni* (Mandarin): "Sorry, Thank You." Cinematographer: Tom Lau Moon-tong; Art Director: Gemma To Ching-ching; Music: Peter Kam Pui-tat, Ronald Ng Luk-shing; Writer: Raymond To Kwok-wai; Producer: Derek Yee Tung-sing; Director: Joseph Cheung Tung-cho. Cast: Lau Ching-wan (Li Lap-cheong), Hsu Chi (Angela), Cecilia Yip Tung (Yip Ting), Terence Lam Bo-lun (Jason), Annabelle Lau Hiu-tung (Club Girl), Dayo Wong Chi-wah (Guy in Street), Chin Kar-lok (Furious Race Car Driver), Bobby Yip King-sang (Ugly Guy Flagging Taxi), Dennis Chan Kwok-san (Kwong), Jamie Luk Kim-ming (Cheong's Boss). 1.85:1. VHS/LD/VCD: Tai Seng. Import LD/VCD: Carnival. 107 minutes.

Parking attendant Cheong is a big kid who never grew up, living life with no responsibilities or goals. One day his ex-wife appears from Canada with their young son Jason. She has filed papers to have Cheong's visitation rights revoked but is willing to give him one more chance: If he can look after Jason on his own for two weeks and do a good job, she will consider dropping the legal action. Having spent almost all of his life overseas, the child turns out to be fully Westernized, speaking far more English than Cheong. He also hates traditional food and is so used to be being coddled by his mother, he drives Cheong crazy. Naturally, the two get along like oil and water, but Cheong's perky girlfriend, prostitute Angela, helps calm the waves, and genuine affection develops.

Appealing performances by Lau Ching-wan, Hsu Chi, and child actor Terence Lam go a long way in making this unabashedly formulaic enterprise palatable and, at times, genuinely entertaining. However, the film makes a major misstep by introducing an incredibly contrived medical emergency in the final third—at the precise spot the end credits should have rolled. The Chinese title refers to the two expressions Cheong finally learns to say, thanks to Jason. Directors Bosco Lam Hing-lung, Guy Lai Ying-chau, Jacob Cheung Chi-leung, and stunt coordinator Benz Kong To-hoi put in appearances.

677. My Darling, My Goddess

(1982; Reel Films) ★: 6/10. *Oi yan nui san* (Cantonese), *Ai ren nu shen* (Mandarin): "Sweetheart Goddess." Art Director: Raymond Lee King-man; Music: Anders Nelsson; Writer: Lee Tung; Producer: Dennis Yu Wan-kong; Cinematographer-Director: Anthony Ho Tung-lei. Cast: Alan Tam Wing-lun (Kok), Michael Chan Wai-lun (Robin/Chopper), Kelly Yiu Wai (Slack Alice, aka Susie), Nat Chan Pak-cheung (Lek), Bill Tung Biu (Don Phew), James Wong Jim (Randy Jim), Charlie Cho Chalei (Gay Man at Nightclub). 1.85:1. VHS: Tai Seng. 85 minutes.

Bored parking lot attendant Kok spends his evenings fantasizing about girls, in particular, a beauty pictured on the wall calendar. One evening gang boss Don Phew suffers a fatal heart attack in the brothel run by Kok's mother. Desperate to dispose of the body before the dead man's thugs return, she has it put in a trunk and hidden under Kok's lot. When the hoods start making threats, Kok's mom tells him to dump the trunk in the harbor, and the trouble really begins.

A breezy, offbeat trifle, this boasts some creative direction, appealing characters, and even an impromptu song and dance number, though it all eventually wears a little thin. Fans of Michael Chan will enjoy watching him play both a police officer and his lookalike, a vicious triad enforcer. The English subtitles are well translated but amusingly anglocentric, utilizing terms like "wanker," "bloody," and "Hey, Squire."

678. My Father Is a Hero

(1995; Win's Entertainment) ★: 7/10. *Kap ba ba dik sun* (Cantonese), *Gei ba ba de xin* (Mandarin): "A Letter to Father." Cinematographer: Tom Lau Moon-tong; Art Director: Ben Lau Man-hung; Music: James Wong Jim, Mark Lui Chung-tak; Writers: Sandy Shaw, Brian Chung Wai-hung; Producers: Wong Jing, Tiffany Chan Lan; Action Directors: Yuen Tak, Corey Yuen Kwai; Director: Corey Yuen Kwai. Cast: Jet Li Lianjie (Kung Wei), Anita Mui Yim-fong (Inspector Fong Yat-wah), Xie Miao (Kung Ku), Blackie Ko Shou-liang (Darkie), Yu Rongguang (Po Kwong), Damian Lau Chung-yan (Yat-wah's Boss), Ngai Sing (Thug), Ken Lo Wai-kwong (Thug), Henry Fong Ping (Auction Bidder), Corey Yuen Kwai (Bartender). Dolby Digital (DVD only). 1.85:1. VHS: Tai Seng. Import LD/VCD/DVD: Mei Ah. 105 minutes.

This entertaining Jet Li vehicle casts him as Mainland policeman Kung Wei, whose undercover work is so secret, even his son and ailing wife do not know about it. He is still a loving father, going so far as to drag a freshly apprehended criminal along with him (in a potato sack!) to his son's kung fu competition. Kung is ordered to infiltrate a gang run by the quite deranged crimelord Po Kwong, and does so by helping inmate Darkie escape from prison. A member of Po's gang, Darkie takes Kung to HK and introduces him to his boss, who takes the newcomer along on an exchange that will net him some undetectable liquid explosives. A shootout ensues and Kung takes policewoman Fong Yat-wah hostage. When he saves the woman from falling to her death, she suspects that he is something other than a common criminal and journeys to China to question his wife and son. While there, Fong is able to deduce that her suspicions were correct, but danger arises for Kung when his son accidentally blurts the cop's name out loud and is overheard by one of Po's men. Tipped off that there is a traitor among his men, Po puts two and two together and comes up with Kung.

Jet Li and Xie Miao (who were also father and son in the previous year's **New Legend of Shaolin**) play off each other perfectly, and Anita Mui's offbeat casting proves to be an asset. However, Yu Rongguang's unbelievably mannered performance as the villain is ludicrous, and the ridiculously large number of chances his character gives Kung to change sides further impedes a movie that is already weak on the credibility front. The action scenes are consistently exciting, though the climax (which finds Kung using his son as a human yoyo!) relies a bit too much on wirework.

679. My Flying Wife

(1991; Silver Medal Productions) ★: 6/10. *Maang gwai yap cham hak sau kooi* (Cantonese), *Meng gui ru qin hei she hui* (Mandarin): "Fierce Ghost Invades the Underworld." Cinematographer: Herman Yau Lai-to; Art Director: Horace Ma Kwong-wing; Music: Lau Yee-tat; Writers: Nam Yin, Candy Cheng; Producer: Nam Yin; Action Director: Chris Lee Kin-sang; Director: Ko Sing-pui. Cast: Sammo Hung Kam-po (Chan Yu-qun), Yu Li (Siu-hung), Fok Shu-wah (Chiu), Roy Cheung Yiu-yeung (Mr. Smartie), Fennie Yuen Kit-ying (Helen Lo), Tommy Wong Kwong-leung (Fatt), Shing Fui-on (The Officer of Reincarnation), William Ho Kar-kui (Qun's Boss). 1.85:1. VHS: World Video. Import LD: Universe. Running time unknown.

Here's an entertaining combination: a triad ghost comedy! Sammo Hung plays Qun, the leader of a triad gang that has gone semi-legitimate. While trying to collect on a debt owed by a suicidal young lady named Helen, gang member Chiu saves the girl from jumping to her death off a building. His actions inadvertently upset the plans of the lovely female ghost Siu-hung. Having lost the chance for her son to acquire Helen's "reincarnation pearl" (a force that can be extracted from the human body after death and is needed for reincarnation to take place), Siu-hung tries to kill Chiu out of vengeance. In response, Qun enlists the aid of Fatt, a blind Taoist priest, but his rites are largely ineffectual. Siu-hung continues with her quest to kill Chiu, but when Qun learns that he is the reincarnation of her lover, he decides to help Siu-hung and his "son" any way he can.

Nam Yin (brother of director Ringo Lam) has written a number of gangster thrillers over the years, and he incorporates familiar genre characters and situations into the scenario here. Of particular interest is his depiction of the netherworld, which is filled with bribery and corruption (and the negotiations between the mortals and the spirits are conducted in the manner of triad meetings!). As the nominal villain, Roy Cheung (arguably the most famous HK movie gangster) essentially plays a somewhat more benevolent (albeit ghostly) variation of his stock character from films like Lam's **School on Fire** and **Wild Search**. The make-up and special FX are cheesy but they get the job done, and this is not the sort of production where technical polish is all that important. Students of HK crime films will note that this is yet another instance where triads are depicted as nice, honorable guys who happen to engage in an "alternative" lifestyle.

680. My Heart Is That Eternal Rose

(1989; Maverick Films) ★: 7/10. *Saat sau woo dip mung* (Cantonese), *Sha shou hu die meng* (Mandarin): "Butterfly Dreams of the Hitman." Cinematographers: Christopher Doyle, David Chung Chi-man; Art

Directors: Patrick Tam Kar-ming, Mok Kwan-kit; Music: Danny Chung Teng-yat; Writers: John Chan Koon-chung, Sammy Tsang Kan-cheung; Producer: John Sham Kin-fun; Action Directors: Tony Leung Siu-hung, Tang Tak-cheung; Director: Patrick Tam Kar-ming. Cast: Kenny Bee (Rick Ma), Joey Wang Tsu-hsien (Lap), Tony Leung Chiu-wai (Cheung), Michael Chan Wai-man (Shen), Gordon Lau Kar-fai (Lai Liu), Kwan Hoi-shan (Uncle Cheung), Ng Man-tat (Tang), Cheung Tat-ming (Rich Man's Son). 1.85:1. VHS: Tai Seng. Import LD/VCD: Ocean Shores. 90 minutes.

As a favor to the father of Lap, the girl he loves, Rick agrees to serve as the driver on an underworld assignment. However, complications ensue, thanks to the greedy meddling of a corrupt policeman, and guns are drawn. In the resulting battle, Rick fatally shoots the cop. Desperate to save her father from being killed as punishment for bungling the mission, Lap goes to rival triad leader Shen. He agrees to help if she willingly becomes his woman. Unaware of Lap's deal with Shen, Rick boards a ship and flees to The Philippines. The film then picks up six years later, with Rick's return to HK as a killer employed by Shen to murder a turncoat in his organization. While fleeing the scene of the hit, Rick encounters Lap and she fills him in on what has transpired. The two make plans to escape together, but one of Shen's goons catches Lap before she can leave. Faced with death, she is saved only by the intervention of Cheung, a minor figure in the organization who has been assigned to protect Lap but has also fallen in love with her. Naturally, Shen is not about to let these betrayals go unavenged.

Beautifully photographed, impeccably designed, and full of clever stylistic touches, **My Heart Is That Eternal Rose** has a fairly run-of-the-mill narrative, but every other aspect of the production is above average compared to most other triad pictures. Sublimely romantic and punctuated with bloody, high impact violence, the film is much like John Woo's gangster hits in the way that it is able to retain its balance and successfully walk that thin line that exists between quality melodrama and puerile trash. The excellent cast is highlighted by Tony Leung Chiu-wai (giving a nicely understated performance that netted him a Best Supporting Actor prize) and former kung fu star Michael Chan (suavely evil as the main heavy). Unfortunately, the film's commercial failure effectively put an end to Patrick Tam's directorial career, and he has only worked as an editor in the intervening years. In regards to the Chinese title, "Butterfly Dreams" is a famous dramatic opera written by Kwan Han-ching which has become synonymous with high drama.

681. My Hero

(1990; Chun Sing Film Co.) ★: 5/10. *Yat boon maan wa chong tin ngaai* (Cantonese), *Yi ben man hua chuang tian ya* (Mandarin): "Once Comic Book: Dash Heaven Earth." Cinematographer: Nico Wong Man-wan; Art Director: Lui Kwok-fu; Music: Chai Tai, Wong Man-ching; Writers: Ho Tung, Leung Kar-yan, Cho Chung-sing; Producer: Yuen Kam-lun; Action Directors: Leung Kar-yan, James Ha Chim-see; Director: Leung Kar-yan. Cast: Stephen Chiau Sing-chi (Sing), Wilson Lam Chun-yin (Chun), Ann Bridgewater (Ann), Shing Fui-on (Bill), Leung Kar-yan (Hung Yi), Yeung Kwan (Wai), Yuen Woo-ping (Master Yi), Lung Ming-yan (Vietnamese Boss), Ng Hong-ning (Wai's Bodyguard). 1.85:1. VHS: World Video. Import LD/VCD: Ocean Shores. 92 minutes.

This adequate production tries to be both a straightforward gangster thriller *and* a parody of the genre at the same time, with predictably disjointed results. It stars Stephen Chiau as Sing, a clumsy waiter who accidentally saves the life of triad leader Wai. As a reward, the aged boss lets him join his ranks. Teaming up with Wai's top gun, Chun, the pair trick and eradicate the gang's top rival. As a result, Sing starts to move up quickly in the ranks and is sent, along with Chun and the hot-headed Bill, to facilitate a drug deal. When things are about to turn fatal, Sing's impulsive bravery saves the day. However, Wai's forthcoming retirement results in unexpected consequences for his three most respected lieutenants.

As with Chiau's later James Bond spoof **From Beijing with Love** (1994), this is just as violent as the films it purports to parody and takes a less-than-critical view of triad life. Still, if viewed simply as the mindless entertainment it was intended to be, it succeeds more often than not and is a passable diversion. **My Hero 2*** followed in 1993, with Dicky Cheung replacing Chiau in the lead.

682. My Lucky Stars

(1985; Golden Harvest/Paragon Films) ★: 6/10. *Fuk sing go jiu* (Cantonese), *Fu xing gao zhao* (Mandarin): "Lucky Stars Shine Highest and Brightest." Cinematographers: Peter Ngor Chi-kwan, Arthur Wong Ngok-tai; Art Directors: Eddie Ma Poon-chiu, Fung Yuen-chi; Music: Michael Lai Siu-tin; Writer: Barry Wong Ping-yiu; Producer: Leonard Ho Koon-cheung; Action Directors: Sammo Hung Kam-po, Yuen Biao, Lam Ching-ying, Yuen Wah, Billy Chan Wui-ngai; Director: Sammo Hung Kam-po. Cast: Sammo Hung Kam-po (Kidstuff), Sibelle Hu Hui-chung (Miss Woo), Richard Ng Yiu-hon (Sandy), Eric Tsang Chi-wai (Roundhead), Charlie Chin Hsiang-lin (Herb), Stanley Fung Shui-fan (Rawhide), Jackie Chan (Muscles), Yuen Biao (Ricky), Cho Tat-wah (Superintendent Walter Tsao), Michiko Nishiwaki (Japanese fighter). Dolby Digital (DVD only). 1.85:1. VHS: Tai Seng (Remastered for the English Market; subtitled or dubbed), Cinema Group (Dubbed), Xenon/Arena (Dubbed). LD: Media Asia. Import VCD: Mei Ah. Import DVD: Universe. 96 minutes (subtitled), 84 minutes (dubbed).

Although often promoted as the star, Jackie Chan only has a supporting part in this hugely successful action-comedy, the second entry in the *ng fuk sing* (Five Lucky Stars) series. Following the style of its forerunner, **Winners and Sinners** (1983), the film opens with HK police officers Muscles and Ricky in hot pursuit of a crooked cop (Lam Ching-ying), with the chase taking them to Japan. While tracking their quarry through a crowded amusement park, Ricky is captured by a band of ninjas, and Muscles, knowing his cover has been blown, goes into hiding. Needing men the enemy is not familiar with, Superintendent Tsao enlists the help of Muscles' disreputable buddies from childhood: "criminal genius" Kidstuff, smash-and-grab expert Herb, incompetent mentalist Sandy, petty opportunist Rawhide, and pint-sized simpleton Roundhead. More concerned with molesting their beautiful police supervisor, Miss Woo, the boys finally make contact with the Japanese gang (who mistakenly believe them to be bank robbers with a huge amount of money on their persons). When the criminals hold them for a ransom, Kidstuff is able to contact Muscles, who moves in to lend his fighting expertise.

The comedy is shamelessly lowbrow but works intermittently, thanks to the personalities of the performers. Those who tire of the jokes (which include some dialect humor that the subtitles cannot convey) will find a fair amount of action to hold their attention, though it mostly occurs in the opening and closing reels. The standout sequence has Chan fighting his way through a haunted house exhibit, which has killers popping out of hidden panels in the walls and trap doors in the

**Unavailable for review.*

floor and ceiling. Sibelle Hu also has a memorable tussle with Michiko Nishiwaki (looking ultra-buff in her first HK film) that is excerpted in **The Deadliest Art: The Best of the Martial Arts Films** and concludes with what is probably the film's funniest moment. James Tien Chun, Lau Kar-wing, Dick Wei, and Bolo Yeung make brief appearances. **Twinkle, Twinkle Lucky Stars** came next.

683. My Neighbours Are Phantoms!

(1990; Grand March Movie Production Co.) ★: 6/10. *Wa gwai jue jing gaak lei* (Cantonese), *Hua gui zhu zheng ge li* (Mandarin): "Noisy Ghosts Live Directly Isolated." Cinematographer: Nico Wong Man-wan; Art Director: Fred Chan Chi-chung; Music: Chow Lap-kei; Writer: Wong Jing; Producer: Wong Tin-lam; Action Directors: Tony Poon Kin-kwan, Benz Kong To-hoi; Director: Lau Sze-yu. Cast: Nat Chan Pak-cheung (Dragon Chan Pak-loong), Sharla Cheung Man (Siu-sin), Mondi Yau Yuet-ching (Siu-hung), Chung Fat (George Chan Kau), Mui Siu-wai (Yummy), Amy Yip Chi-mei (Biggie Tsang), Chingmy Yau Suk-ching (Sandy), Charlie Cho Cha-lei (Charlie Cheung). 1.85:1. VHS: Tai Seng. Import LD: Mei Ah. 96 minutes.

This passable horror-comedy concerns the mischief created by a "family" of ghosts who have managed to escape confinement after being trapped inside a photograph for sixty years by a Taoist priest. As if bumbling cop Dragon Chan didn't already have enough problems, he now must also deal with these energy-sucking spectres, who have taken over the home next door. Chan even falls for one, the beautiful Siu-sin, who objects to her relatives' murderous ways. After using her powers to help Chan nab some criminals, she is ordered by the patriarch to finish him off or he will scatter her ashes, thus preventing reincarnation. Luckily, Chan's associate at work, Chan Kau, is a Taiwanese Taoist who has mastered many different ghost fighting techniques. While Chan Kau's methods work, he gets bashed on the head and becomes a babbling fool, leaving Dragon and his friends to dispel the evil on their own.

While it has less of the wonderfully bizarre and acrobatic supernatural action found in the best efforts of this type, there are some new, amusing ghost fighting techniques, and Nat Chan does a surprisingly good Bruce Lee imitation.

684. My Wife's Lover

(1992; Ting Sau) ★: 5/10. *Tai tai dik ching yan* (Cantonese), *Tai tai de qing ren* (Mandarin): "Wife's Lover." Art Director: Chan Chi-ming; Music: Ben Cheung Siu-hung; Writer: Chau Lan; Action Directors: Bruce Law Lai-yin, James Ha Chim-see; Cinematographer-Producer-Director: Kevin Chu Kar-wang. Cast: Chik King-man (Joanne), Maria Tung Ling (Terry), Vincent Lam Wai, Ching Siu-yuet. 1.85:1. VHS: Tai Seng. Import LD/VCD: Universe. 87 minutes.

Much slicker than the usual Category III fare, this sexploitation yarn uses music video stylistics to enhance a standard genre premise. Weary of her irresponsible, philandering husband Alan, businesswoman Joanne begins to appreciate the attention shown her by Terry, a Eurasian lesbian from her French class. Joanne decides to enlist Terry's professional services as a photographer for a company project but ends up being seduced by the woman. While initially upset, she finds that her subsequent sexual encounter with Alan is much more pleasurable, and that helps to overcome her initial reservations and guilt. However, Alan has also taken an interest in Terry and, upon promising her that he only wants a one-night stand, she agrees to sleep with him. Although he has had more than his share of flings in the past, Alan finds that he cannot do without Terry, and she begins to feel the same way, leaving Joanne out in the cold.

Steering clear of the juvenile humor and sexual violence often found in HK adult films (save for one typical bit where a partner resists a come-on at first and then succumbs), **My Wife's Lover** is moderately erotic and better acted than the usual adult fare. The Lam Wai credited above is not the like-named star of **Long Arm of the Law** and **Project A II**.

685. My Young Auntie

(1981; Shaw Brothers) ★: 8/10. *Cheung booi* (Cantonese), *Chang bei* (Mandarin): "The Elder." Cinematographer: Peter Ngor Chi-kwan; Art Director: Johnson Tsao; Music: Not Original; Writers: Lau Kar-leung, Li Tai-hung; Producer: Mona Fong Yat-wah; Action Directors: Lau Kar-leung, Ching Chu, Hsiao Hou; Director: Lau Kar-leung. Cast: Lau Kar-leung (Yu Ching-chuen), Kara Hui Ying-hung (Cheng Tai-nan), Hsiao Hou (Charlie Yu Tao), Johnny Wang Lung-wei (Yu Yung-sheng), Gordon Lau Kar-fai (James), Mai Te-lo (Robert), Cho Tat-wah (Ching Fu, aka "The Iron Man of Canton"). 2.35:1. No official domestic video release. 121 minutes. Also known as **Fangs of the Tigress** (US title).

If you are only familiar with Lau Kar-leung's stoic and heroic kung fu epics, this comic yarn will come as an enjoyable surprise. Dispatched to Canton to find relative Yu Ching-chuen, martial arts expert Cheng Tai-nan carries with her the will of her recently deceased husband. To keep his assets safely away from his cruel and greedy brother, Yu Yung-sheng, Tai-nan's husband decided to leave them to Ching-chuen, who is still a good fighter despite being middle-aged. Tai-nan's arrival into the Yu household creates a classic case of culture clash when she meets up with Ching-chuen's Westernized son, who prefers to be called "Charlie." Much to his chagrin, Charlie must show respect towards Tai-nan because of her position as a family elder, in spite of her resolutely old fashioned beliefs. The lad does his best to bring Tai-nan up to date by inviting her to a costume ball, where they cut a rug together in impressive fashion. Meanwhile, Yung-sheng's men use the opportunity to break into the Yu home and steal the title deeds belonging to Tai-nan's late spouse. The only way to get them back is by force, but Tai-nan and Charlie are the only ones in the immediate family whose kung fu is good enough.

One of Lau Kar-leung's most offbeat period films, **My Young Auntie** suffers from the studio's use of overstated DeWolfe library music as accompaniment but is an otherwise delightful affair. The energetic slapstick is as wonderfully choreographed as the kung fu, and Kara Hui (winner of the year's Best Actress prize) is the perfect heroine *and* comedienne in what is still her best role to date. The traditional Chinese notions of family are turned upside down. Tai-nan is much younger than Ching-chuen (hence the English title) and the same age as Charlie, resulting in much hierarchal confusion. The manner in which both Tai-nan and Ching-chuen react to Charlie's Western slang and tastes (which were just starting to appear in HK at this point in history, thanks to the British lease on the colony) also adds to the amusement. Character names above are from the English-dubbed version.

686. The Mysterious Footworks of Kung Fu

(1978) ★: 5/10. *Ma Jat* (Cantonese), *Ma Za* (Mandarin): "Ma Chat." Cinematographers: Ho Sin-wai, Michael Ma Koon-wah; Art Director: Ting Yuen-tai; Music: Not Original; Writer: Ng See-yuen; Producer: Jimmy Heung Wah-sing; Action Director: Ming Jai; Director: Chan Wah. Cast: Charles Heung Wah-keung (Three-Eyed Liu), Michael Chan Wai-man (Leng Ching-shan), Fan Mui-sang (Beggar Su), Kong To (Pao Fang). 2.35:1. VHS: Ocean Shores. 99 minutes.

Future movie mogul Charles Heung stars in this period kung fu thriller as Three-Eyed Liu (so named for the prominent scar in the middle of his forehead), a hot-tempered coolie from Chiuchow looking to make a living using his martial abilities. The simple-minded youth befriends crafty Beggar Su, who constantly takes advantage of his naivety but still seems to value his companionship. Liu attracts the attention of respected citizen Shang Hsien, who is impressed by his snake style kung fu and wants to utilize it. However, others are out to hire Liu too, and when he is charged with protecting a cargo of opium from a masked bandit, he discovers that the thief is none other than Shang! Before Shang can explain the reason for his actions, he is murdered by ruthless professional assassin Leng Ching-shan, who is in the employ of the opium dealers. Swearing vengeance, Liu sets out to take on the gang's leaders, but first he will need some instruction from an old master to counter the villains' shrimp and crab style.

This is a very traditional effort with some fairly good kung fu but little in the way of innovation or excitement. The script includes a couple of odd touches: Michael Chan's killer is needlessly depicted as being a homosexual, and the two main villains go from fierce to prissy whenever they get dirty! Fan Mui-sang's ebullient performance is the main reason to watch.

687. Mystery Files

(1996; Canaan Film Production) ★: 5/10. *Kei yi dong on* (Cantonese), *Qi yi dang an* (Mandarin): "Strange Files." Cinematographer: Wong Kar-fai; Art Directors: Ken Chiu Kin-san, Adeline Lo Chiu-yee; Music: Mak Chun-hung; Writer: Kam Tin-yat; Producer: Leung Hung-wah; Directors: Leung Hung-wah, Jeffrey Chiang Chia-chun, Sherman Wong Ching-wah. Cast: Andy Hui Chi-on (Yat), Vivian Lai Shui-yun (Suet), Ada Choi Siu-fan (Mandy Fu), Edmond Leung Hon-man (Ming-chi). 1.85:1. VHS: World Video. Import LD/VCD: Panorama Entertainment. 82 minutes

This modest mystery-thriller is built around three cases investigated by young genius Yat. A HK native, he travels to China to assist the local authorities in solving crimes, accompanied by his cowardly sister Suet. The first story revolves around a victim who was found bludgeoned to death. A wife abuser, the man's actions drove his beautiful spouse into the arms of a labourer, whom the police believe to be the killer. In the second tale, the near simultaneous murder of a man and woman, in different locations, appears to be related to a multiple murder committed sixty years earlier. Are ghosts of the victims responsible or is someone just taking advantage of the villagers' superstitions? The final yarn unfolds on an ocean liner. Yat becomes fascinated with Mandy Fu, a gorgeous, bisexual model whose lovers have a habit of turning up dead.

The mysteries are reasonably interesting and Andy Hui does a good job as the astute amateur detective, but the proceedings are never as suspenseful or original as one would hope. Even the solution to the third story (easily the most bizarre of the set) is too easily deduced. The epilogue does offer up a nice twist, however.

688. Naked Killer

(1992; Golden Harvest/Wong Jing's Workshop) ★: 8/10. *Chik loh go yeung* (Cantonese), *Chi luo gao yang* (Mandarin): "Naked Lamb." Cinematographer: William Yim Wai-lun; Art Director: Fong Ying; Music: Lowell Lo Kwun-ting; Writer-Producer: Wong Jing; Action Director: Lau Shung-fung; Director: Clarence Fok Yiu-leung. Cast: Chingmy Yau Suk-ching (Kitty), Simon Yam Tat-wah (Tinam), Carrie Ng Kar-lai (Princess), Kelly Yiu Wai (Sister Cindy), Madoka Sugawara (Baby), Ken Lo Wai-kwong (Bee). Dolby Digital (Mega Star DVD only). 1.85:1. VHS: World Video, Tai Seng (Remastered for the English Market; subtitled or dubbed). Import LD/VCD: Mei Ah. Import DVD: Mei Ah, Mega Star. 88 minutes.

A deliciously stylish and exploitative reworking of **La Femme Nikita** and **Basic Instinct**, along the lines of a Japanese *manga*, this Wong Jing Category III production has developed a substantial cult following in Western fan circles for reasons that are pretty easy to surmise. Beautiful young hellion Kitty is due for an extended stay behind bars after going on a shooting rampage to avenge the death of her father. However, before she can be apprehended by the police, the girl is recruited by the mysterious Sister Cindy, who trains her to be a ruthless assassin. Romancing unstable, impotent cop Tinam on the side, Kitty settles into her new identity effortlessly, but danger emerges in the lithe form of psychotic lesbian killer Princess (Carrie Ng, in the performance that both made her career and typecast her forever). One of Cindy's former students, Princess (who has been displaying her utter disregard for the male species by leaving a string of castrated corpses all over Hong Kong) wants her teacher's beautiful young protege for herself, and it would seem that Kitty has no say in the matter.

One of the rare occasions where director Clarence Fok's eye for style and near-total disregard for narrative discipline somehow results in a satisfying whole, this is a male adolescent's wet dream transposed to celluloid: deadly but supremely desirable women clad in (and out) of designer fashions, thrillingly brutal violence, lightning paced action, grossout humor (a dimwitted homicide cop investigating one of Princess' hits accidentally devours the victim's severed penis!), and a politically incorrect approach to just about everything and everybody (one of Cindy's "training sessions" consists of locking Kitty in the cellar with a drooling rapist, and Princess and her accommodating sextoy, Baby, make love in a swimming pool stained red with the blood of their latest victim). Attractively photographed by William Yim (with several sequences bathed in blue, the favorite hue of HK cinematographers) and adeptly scored by Lowell Lo in a variety of musical styles, **Naked Killer** is illogical, superficial, morally untenable (women are by far the stronger gender here but still never stray beyond the stereotypical roles favored by the overwhelmingly male target audience for Wong Jing product), and an utterly enthralling guilty pleasure from beginning to end. The memorable trailer (footage from which is used in the title sequence) was photographed by ace cinematographer Peter Pau (**The Bride with White Hair**).

Naked Killer 2 *see* **Raped by an Angel**

689. Naughty Boys

(1986; Golden Harvest/Golden Way Films) ★: 6/10. *Nau gai jaap paai gwan* (Cantonese), *Nui ji za pai jun* (Mandarin): "Turn Gauge Mixed Cards Army." Cinematographer: Cheung Yiu-cho; Art Director: Cheung Yun-keung; Music: Michael Lai Siu-tin; Writers: Edward Tang King-sang, Chung Kwok-fong; Producer: Jackie Chan; Action Direction: Jackie Chan Stuntmen Association; Director: Wellson Chin Sing-wai. Cast: Carina Lau Kar-ling (Bonnie), Feng Sing (Sheng), Kara Hui Ying-hung (Chuan), Clarence Fok Yiu-leung (Liang), Phillip Ko Fei (Ma Hui), Lo Mang (Huo Chiang), Tai Po (Piao), Billy Lau Nam-kwong (Kuang Fu). 1.85:1. VHS: Tai Seng. Import VCD: Mega Star. 95 minutes.

Director Wellson Chin and producer Jackie Chan (who has a cameo) teamed up for this mild action-comedy, which predates their successful **The Inspector Wears Skirts** series. A group of four convicts, due to be released from prison, plot to recover the cache of diamonds they hid before being caught. When Sheng gets out before the others, he goes to retrieve the stones, only to find that someone has substituted them with literal rocks. His partners, naturally, believe that he has absconded with the loot and chase him all over HK. Sheng's sister Chuan and travel agent/conman Liang (Clarence Fok, who would go on to greater fame behind the camera by directing films like **Naked Killer**) lend him assistance. Meanwhile, Bonnie (a beautiful investigator hired by the company that insured the diamonds) cozies up to Sheng in order to keep an eye on him.

In terms of cast and storyline, **Naughty Boys** is no different than a thousand other films of this ilk. The one distinction is that, with Chan producing, the action scenes are more entertaining and elaborately staged (particularly the wildly acrobatic final battle in a huge warehouse) than those found in comparable independent productions. As with most of Chan's films, a selection of *ouch*takes runs under the end credits. If that isn't enough incentive to watch, how often do you get to see perennial second banana Feng Sing (or "Mars," as he is always billed in English) as the male lead? Stanley Fung Shui-fan, Ricky Hui Koon-ying, Charlie Cho Cha-lei, Lui Fong, and Dennis Chan Kwok-san put in brief appearances.

690. Naughty Couple

(1994; Mandarin Films) ★: 6/10. *Jong baan fung lau* (Cantonese), *Zhuang ban feng liu* (Mandarin): "Hitting Board Flirtations" (an expression meaning "to always mess up"). Music: Not Original; Writer: Szeto Wai-kin; Producer: Raymond Wong Pak-ming; Director: Clifford Choi Kai-kwong. Cast: Francis Ng Chun-yu (Ma Kam-hang), Anita Lee Yuen-wah (Ivy), Sunny Chan Kam-hung (Henry), Chan Suk-yee, Pang Hang-ying. 1.85:1. VHS: Tai Seng. 100 minutes.

Despite being adapted from a stage play, this comedy of errors plays a lot like a vintage episode of **Love, American Style**. Ma Kam-hang is a hopelessly nerdy childrens' book publisher lucky enough to be married to the gorgeous (and much more outgoing) Ivy. On the day of his seventh anniversary, Kam-hang agrees to let his lecherous buddy Henry use the house for a tryst. Since Kam-hang and Ivy will be out for dinner and a movie, the plan should go off without a hitch. However, Ivy has unknowingly made the same promise to her friend Linda, who just happens to be Henry's wife. To top it all off, the maid and handyman also plan on using the house for a little quality time of their own. A misplaced love letter, various overheard and misconstrued conversations, and a bunch of unexpected guests (including a famous author who could save Kam-hang's struggling company) lead to a night of juggled identities and desperate improvisation.

Francis Ng and Anita Lee (who were a real life couple at this time) give choice comic performances which help to make the shopworn material palatable and, on occasion, genuinely amusing.

The Nepal Affair *see* **The Witch from Nepal**

691. The New Age of Living Together

(1994; Unique Films) ★: 6/10. *San tung gui si doi* (Cantonese), *Xin tong ju shi dai* (Mandarin): "The New Age of Living Together." Cinematographer: Jacky Tang Hon-bong; Art Director: Ma Man-ming; Music: Alvin Kwok Siu-lam; Producers: Yeung Fan, Tsui Lap-kung; Writer-Directors: Samson Chiu Leung-chun, Yeung Fan, Sylvia Chang Ai-chia. Cast: Jacqueline Wu Chien-lien (Icy), Jan Lam Hoi-fung (Eddie), Sylvia Chang Ai-chia (Anna Lau), Nicky Wu Chi-lung (Steven Chan), Maggie Cheung Man-yuk (Co Co Lau), Winston Chao Wen-hsuan (Wong Man-fai), Eric Kot Man-fai (Keung), Melvin Wong Kam-sun (Joseph Lau). 1.85:1. VHS: Tai Seng. Import LD/VCD/DVD: Ocean Shores. 105 minutes. Also known as **Conjugal Affairs, In Between.**

This triptych about relationships in the '90s concerns the romantic travails of three friends (two men and a woman) who share a house together. The first story tells of hair stylist Eddie and his infatuation with "Icy," who moves in with him for a while. However, Icy eventually disappears, and when she finally gets in touch again, she is on the verge of getting married. She seems reluctant to go through with the ceremony, but Eddie does not seem willing or able to profess his love. Story #2 finds young stock broker Steven trying out a telephone dating service after getting chewed out by his girlfriend. He ends up with Anna, a sexy older woman who is the unhappy wife of his boss. The two begin a platonic relationship, meeting every Friday to talk. The final, longest story concerns Co Co, whose six year relationship with Man-fai has hit a rough patch. One day at work she is swept off her feet by a Russian playboy and spends the night with him. The next day he heads back home but leaves her with something to remember him by: a baby. Co Co must then decide whether she wants to keep the child and, if so, just what she will say to Man-fai if "their" baby has Caucasian traits.

The film benefits greatly from likeable performances (with the notable exception of Eric Kot, whose gay stereotype in the last third is a tiresomely one-note characterization) and some knowing observations about love and commitment. However, none of the stories really rise enough above the ordinary for this to be anything more than a pleasant diversion. Clips from **Saviour of the Soul** and **The Moon Warriors** appear in the second story.

New Big Boss *see* **Legend of the Wolf**

692. New Kids in Town

(1990; Lau's Film Production Company) ★: 5/10. *Choh do gwai ging* (Cantonese), *Chu dao gui jing* (Mandarin): "Beginning at Expensive Borders." Cinematographer: Chim Pak-hung; Art Director: Shum Shuk-man; Music: Sing Kam-wing; Writers: Lau Kar-yung, To Lai-chi; Action Directors: Lau Kar-leung, Lau Kar-yung; Producer-Director: Lau Kar-yung. Cast: Lau Kar-leung (Uncle), Chin Siu-ho (Chi-ho), Moon Lee Choi-fung (Siu-fung), Lee Kar-sing (Chi-shing), Wong Chi-yeung (Yeung), Eddie Maher (Eddie), Sophia Crawford (Miss So). 1.85:1. VHS: Tai Seng, Arena/Xenon (Dubbed). Import LD: Star Entertainment (No Subtitles). 88 minutes. Also known as **New Killers in Town** (UK video title), **Master of Disaster** (Arena/Xenon title).

This modest actioner revolves around Chi-ho and Chi-shing, two expert martial artists who travel from China to HK in order to visit their uncle. While out for a night on the town with their cute cousin, Siu-fung, they are harassed by some triads. The hoods' plan is to injure Siu-fung's friend Mimi so that she will not be able to participate in a special roller derby match against their own female contestant. When Mimi's arm is injured, Siu-fung stands in for her at the competition and easily bests her opponent. The gang then seeks revenge by kidnapping Mimi, but she is accidentally killed while in their custody. They snatch Siu-fung and Chi-shing instead, but the latter manages to escape. When the brothers try to exchange one of the hoods for Siu-fung, tragedy strikes and their uncle must join in the fight to save her.

The storyline is even thinner and less inspiring than what one usually finds in the genre, doing nothing more than setting up the various action sequences. Said battles are fairly well-staged, if not quite up to the

Lau Brothers' usual standards. Moon Lee, Chin Siu-ho, and Lau Kar-leung in the same film is a pretty unbeatable combination, though the latter has no more than about 15 minutes of screen time, in spite of his star billing. Note: Arena/Xenon's version is a composite mishmash that incorporates footage of Moon Lee and Jackie Chan lifted from **The Protector**.

New Killers in Town *see* **New Kids in Town**

693. The New Legend of Shaolin

(1994; Upland Film Corporate) ★: 6/10. *Hung Hei-kwun ji siu lam ng jo* (Cantonese), *Hong Xiguan zhi shao lin wu zu* (Mandarin): "Hung Hei-kwun: The Five Founders of Shaolin" or "Hong Xiguan: The Five Founders of Shaolin." Cinematographer: Tom Lau Moon-tong; Art Director: Raymond Lee King-man; Music: Wong Bong; Producer: Pui Cheung-chuen; Action Director: Corey Yuen Kwai; Writer-Director: Wong Jing. Cast: Jet Li Lianjie (Hung Hey-kwun), Chingmy Yau Suk-ching (Red Bean), Xie Miao (Hung Man-ting), Deanie Yip Tak-han (Red Bean's Mother), Johnny Wang Lung-wei (Commander), Chen Sung-yung (Ma Kai-sin), Chi Chuen-hua (Ma Ling-yee), Damian Lau Chung-yan (Chan Kan-nam). 1.85:1. VHS: Tai Seng, SYS/Youngtze (Dubbed). Import LD/VCD: Star Entertainment. 94 minutes.

This Jet Li-Wong Jing collaboration is very much along the same lines of **Last Hero in China** and **Kung Fu Cult Master**, offering up an exciting mix of kung fu action and lowbrow humor. Martial arts master Hung Hey-kwun and his equally adept seven-year-old son Hung Man-ting fight for the rebellious Heaven and Earth Society in their battle against the tyrannical government. Hung is charged with protecting five young Shaolin students, who have portions of a treasure map tattooed on their backs. When the map is assembled, it reveals the location of a great cache of gold, which H & E needs to finance their efforts. While working as a bodyguard for a rather thick rich man, Hung and son must contend with "The Notorious Mother and Daughter," conniving thieves who use their wiles and kung fu skills to fleece unsuspecting men. However, their greatest threat is Hey-kwun's old enemy, Ma Ling-yee, now a mutated and seemingly invincible madman who rides around in a silver, beetle-shaped "car"!

In addition to the usual genre components, Wong Jing cribs a famous scene from the Japanese **Lone Wolf and Cub** series when Hung offers his baby boy the chance to choose between a rocking horse (which means that he wishes to join his mother in Heaven) or a sword (which means he wants to fight at his father's side). There is also an uninspired reprisal of the famous "embroidery kung fu" bout between Kwan Tak-hing and Fung Hark-on from **Dreadnaught**. Jet Li's character is stoic in the extreme but he plays the role very well, and Xie Miao (who would play Li's son again in **My Father Is a Hero**) is equally impressive. The script's excesses are a bit much (and not only in regards to the Ma Ying-lee character), but if you approach the film with that in mind, chances are you will be sufficiently entertained by the high flying, fantasy-oriented kung fu and amiable presentation. Damian Lau reprises his Chan Kan-nam character from Wong's **Royal Tramp** films, and the director himself makes an unlikely but amusing cameo in the final moments. The soundtrack includes some music recycled from **Last Hero in China**.

694. New Mr. Vampire

(1986) ★: 5/10. *Geung si faan saang* (Cantonese), *Jiang shi fan sheng* (Mandarin): "Stiff Corpse Comes to Life." Cinematographer: Johnny Koo Kwok-wah; Art Director: Ho Kim-seng; Music: Michael Lai Siu-tin; Writer: Wong Ying; Producer: William Chang; Action Directors: Chin Yuet-sang, Power Lee King-chu; Director: Billy Chan Wui-ngai. Cast: Chung Fat (Master Chin), Chin Siu-ho (Wang Choi), Lui Fong (Tai-fa), Pauline Wong Siu-fung (Hsi-wan), Ku Feng (Criminal Boss), Shum Wai (The Marshal), Tai Po (Adjutant), Wu Ma (Hotel Clerk). 1.85:1. VHS: Ocean Shores (Two versions: dubbed or in Chinese with no subtitles). Import LD/VCD: Ocean Shores (No Subtitles). 89 minutes. Also known as **Kung Fu Vampire Buster** (Title for Ocean Shores dubbed tape version)

One of the first **Mr. Vampire** knockoffs, this features more slapstick than martial arts or supernatural content but remains moderately enjoyable. Feuding siblings Master Chin and Priest Wu compete to get the task of burying the brother of a local mob leader. When Chin wins the job, Wu sets out to sabotage things by bringing the corpse back to life as a vampire. While Chin and his pupil, Tai-fa, are trying to deal with this mess, grave robber Wang Choi appears on the scene. While looting a crypt, Wang accidentally breathes into the mouth of the female body inside. The subsequent mixture of Yin and Yang leaves the woman in a half-living/half-dead state which causes her to mimic every one of his actions (a gag that is milked for all it is worth). The zombie turns out to be Hsi-wan, the nineth concubine of a drunken general who is out to nab the culprit that plundered his beloved's tomb. Things go from bad to worse when Wu enhances the vampire's strength, causing it to attack everyone in sight.

The pace lags in spots and the final battle against the vampire is too drawn out, making this one of the weaker entries in the cycle. New addition to the HK vampire mythos: If you crouch down, you can evade a vampire because it can't smell anything under its nose. The soundtrack includes music lifted from **Escape from New York**. The character names above are from the dubbed version. It was followed by **New Mr. Vampire II**.*

695. New Tenant

(1995; Universe Film Productions Co./Galaxy Films) ★: 5/10. *San fong haak* (Cantonese), *Xin fang ke* (Mandarin): "New Neighbor." Cinematographer: Tsang Chun-chung; Art Director: Danny Yuen Ching-chung; Music: Raymond Wong Ying-wah; Writers: Lau Wing-kin, Leung Hung-wah, Anthony Wong Chau-sang; Producer: Leung Hung-wah; Director: Anthony Wong Chau-sang. Cast: Anthony Wong Chau-sang (Alan Tam), Dolphin Chan Hoi-hang (Dolphin), Lawrence Ng Kai-wah (Wong Yu-yan), Dayo Wong Chi-wah (Alan's Doctor), Parkman Wong Pak-man (Officer Lee), Yip Wing-cho (Dolphin's Father), Lau Ching-wan (Joe), Herman Yau Lai-to (Barber), Bobby Yip King-sang (Rapist). 1.85:1. VHS: World Video. Import LD/VCD: Universe. 99 minutes.

Popular character actor Anthony Wong's directorial debut is a strange and uncommercial horror yarn in which he also plays the lead role. After being released from a sanatorium, writer Alan Tam (who is unable to remember why he was there) moves into a building that is scheduled to be demolished in three months time. He begins to experience weird hallucinations and sees what are, apparently, the ghosts of former tenants. Alan soon discovers that one of the "ghosts," a young girl named Dolphin, whose family lived in the building ten years earlier, can hear but not see him. After a while, Dolphin can see Alan and needs his help when her sister disappears, possibly having become a victim of the creepy lecturer downstairs.

Films of this sort are almost never produced in HK, and Wong had a great deal of trouble getting it shown theatrically

**Unavailable for review.*

(when it finally did play, the film ended up being one of the lowest grossers of the decade). There are some effectively creepy and atmospheric moments, but a good portion of the film seems aimless, and the final reel is pretty disappointing. Even though Wong is not quite able to pull it off, **New Tenant** remains an interesting experiment that is worth seeing for its ambitions and novelty value.

696. Night Caller

(1985; D & B Films Co./Pyramid Films) ★: 7/10. *Ping on ye* (Cantonese), *Ping an ye* (Mandarin): "Safe Night." Cinematographer: David Choi Wah-sheung; Art Director: Robert Loh Shu-yuen; Music: Not Original; Producer: Melvin Wong Kam-sun; Action Director: Billy Chan Wui-ngai; Writer-Director: Phillip Chan Yan-kin. Cast: Melvin Wong Kam-sun (James Wong), Phillip Chan Yan-kin (Steve Chan), Pat Ha Man-chik (Porky), Pauline Wong Siu-fung (Bobby), Dick Wei (Allan Lee), Yip Wing-cho (Station Manager). 1.85:1. VHS: Tai Seng. Import LD/VCD: Ocean Shores. 98 minutes.

Here is a unique effort that starts off in the style of Italian horror films from the period before transforming into a police procedural with some clever twists. A model is brutally slain by an unseen assailant named Bobby, who is dressed in the standard *giallo* killer wardrobe: trench-coat, wide-brimmed hat, and gloves—all black, of course. The only witness is the victim's very young daughter, and the shock of the incident has left her catatonic. Officers Wong and Chan (the latter sporting a violent streak that has held him back from promotion in the department) investigate, aided and abetted by tomboy rookie Porky. When the head of the modelling agency is murdered, Chan learns from the company files that his friend Bobby is one of the women employed there. While Chan seeks Bobby out to warn her, Wong discovers that the murder has been recorded on a tape player in the little girl's doll. While hunting for Bobby, Wong is abducted and tortured.

It would be impossible to reveal more without ruining the enjoyment of potential viewers. The aforementioned surprises transpire in what is actually a fairly standard police thriller storyline, peopled by such familiar genre stereotypes as the tough hero, his belligerent boss, the colorful coroner (who eats on the job and uses a human jaw bone for an ash tray), the enthusiastic rookie, and so on. We never learn anything substantial about Bobby, save for the fact that she is a) a lesbian and b) Vietnamese, characteristics in HK cinema that almost invariably indicate a criminal or, at the very least, a misfit. That said, **Night Caller** remains a fresh and interesting entry that more than succeeds as the diverting bit of entertainment it was designed to be. In spite of the mid–1980s production date, the subtitles sport amusing, disco-era phrases like "You jive turkey!" and when one character mentions Anita Mui Yim-fong, the subs substitute Mae West!

697. Night Life Hero

(1992; Videocam Film Co.) ★: 5/10. *Yau jim siu ye* (Cantonese), *You jian shao ye* (Mandarin): "Yau Tsim Young Master." Cinematographer: Yu Kwok-bing; Art Director: Kwan Kin-hing; Music: Mak Ho-lan; Writers: Yuen Chun-man, Lam Koon-ko; Producers: Chan Kin-ting, Tam Lap-fai; Action Directors: Tam Lap-fai, Wong Kar-leung; Director: Yuen Chun-man. Cast: Max Mok Siu-chung (Chung), Fennie Yuen Kit-ying (Baby), Chin Kar-lok (Peter), Shing Fui-on (Chiu), Woo Fung (Uncle James), Yung Sai-kit ("Eleven"), Stephen Tung Wai (Duped Driver), Ridley Tsui Bo-wah (Hwa). 1.85:1. VHS: World Video. Import LD: Mei Ah. 96 minutes.

This mild action-comedy opens with buddies Chung and Peter eliminating the latter's debt with local loan shark Chiu by framing the gangster for car theft. Chung falls for Baby, a beautiful but decidedly spoiled rich girl posing as a club hostess. He saves her from some triad thugs and the pair are soon in love. After a time, Chung even manages to win the approval of the girl's doubting father. When Chiu gets out of prison, he and his men beat up Peter and then kidnap him and Baby, leading to a final showdown with Chung.

There is a steady supply of adeptly choreographed fighting, but this remains a formula effort (complete with a hit single montage) that all but vanishes from memory as soon as the end credits roll. Watch for an inspired send-up of the car park sequence from **A Better Tomorrow**.

698. The Night Rider

(1992; Golbal Investments) ★: 3/10. *Che san* (Cantonese), *Che shen* (Mandarin): "God of Cars." Cinematographers: Kevin Chu Kar-wang, Mok Kim-fai; Art Director: Horace Ma Kwong-wing; Music: Phil Chan Fei-lap; Writer: Van Lam Wan-hong; Producer: Danny Lee Sau-yin; Action Directors: Wong Kai-man, Wong Kar-leung, James Ha Chim-see; Director: Jamie Luk Kim-ming. Cast: Simon Yam Tat-wah (Tommy), Carina Lau Kar-ling (Laura), Ng Man-tat (Uncle Harley), Danny Lee Sau-yin (Lee), Shing Fui-on (Deano), Eric Kei Kar-fat (Kei). 1.85:1. VHS/LD: World Video. Import LD/VCD: Mei Ah. 95 minutes.

A terrific rock score by Phil Chan and some well photographed motorcycle races are about all there is to recommend in this thoroughly mediocre action drama, which is yet another black mark on Simon Yam's filmography. He plays Tommy, king of the illegal road racers, who has been targeted by the police (led, of course, by Danny Lee's "Inspector Lee") after a rival was killed in a gang fight. Tommy and his pregnant girlfriend Laura go into hiding, supplementing their income by stealing cars. When vicious "banana" (as in yellow on the outside, white on the inside) cop Kei crosses the line and beats Tommy's father, the racer retaliates by detonating a huge firecracker bomb outside police headquarters. By following Tommy's father, the police are able to locate his hideout. During the subsequent chase, Laura goes into labour, forcing Tommy to leave her behind at a hospital. Disguised as a doctor, Tommy is able to avoid the guard put on Laura and proceeds to spirit her, and his newborn son, away. When Tommy and his gang swipe a shipment of stolen cars belonging to old rival Deano, the subsequent battle helps the police to zero in on both men.

Devoid of excitement and originality, this dull concoction cruises along with all the speed and conviction of a senior citizen out for a Sunday drive. The comic asides are especially deadly. Kenneth Tsang Kong has a supporting role as Lee's exasperated superior.

699. The Nine Demons

(1983; Hong Kong Chang He Motion Picture Co.) ★: 2/10. *Gau ji tin mor* (Cantonese), *Jiu zi tian mo* (Mandarin): "Nine Sky Demons." Cinematographer: Ng Kwok-yun; Art Director: Koo Sui-yuen; Music: Not Original; Writer: Ngai Hong; Action Directors: Ting Wah-pong, Lee Chung-yat, Chiang Sheng, Lau Yuek-yau; Producer-Director: Chang Cheh. Cast: Chiang Sheng (Master Fu), Lu Feng (Master Law). 2.35:1. VHS: Ocean Shores (Dubbed). Import LD: Ocean Shores (Mandarin and English tracks). 95 minutes.

Following his departure from Shaw Brothers, Chang Cheh helmed this laughable period martial arts horror thriller, which is sunk by unbelievably tacky special effects and some of the worst English dubbing in memory. Joey and Gary(!) are two undisciplined youths always getting into street fights. One day their fathers are assassinated, and after a prolonged battle, Joey barely escapes with his life. While fleeing, the youth falls down a hole into the netherworld, where The Black Prince of Hell makes him an offer: He will give him the power to save Gary (who is about to be executed) if Joey agrees to allow The Nine Demons (a teenage girl and a bunch of obnoxious, back-flipping children) into his body. Anxious to save his friend, Joey agrees and returns to Earth with new powers and abilities. Gary is rescued but Joey needs blood to feed the demons, so innocent victims must perish on a daily basis (which leads to hilarious shots of plastic skulls flying around biting people). After eliminating those responsible for his father's murder, Joey the Demon (as those onscreen call him) helps Gary regain his family estate, arousing the suspicions of a local nobleman, whose men proceed to kill Gary. Joey and his bloodsucking minions take revenge, but can the youth get his soul back from The Black Prince?

While undoubtedly more successful in its original language, **The Nine Demons** is so ill-conceived and ineptly executed it would garner laughter nonetheless. The abominable dubbing and dime store special effects provide a veritable feast for bad movie addicts, but for those who admire Chang's Shaw productions, this is a depressing hour and a half indeed. Only some creatively executed kung fu during the climax saves this from being a total disaster. The soundtrack includes music originally composed for **Blade Runner**!

700. 1941 Hong Kong on Fire

(1994; Wong Jing's Workshop/The Young Filmmakers). ★: 2/10. *Heung gong lun haam* (Cantonese), *Xiang gang lun xian* (Mandarin): "Hong Kong Occupied." Cinematographer: Cho Man-keung; Art Director: Ring Law Chi-keung; Writer: Chan Hing-ka; Producer: Andrew Lau Wai-keung; Director: Chin Man-kei. Cast: Chingmy Yau Suk-ching (Mong Dai), Veronica Yip Yuk-hing (Sun Dai), Law Kar-ying (Hoi), Tou Chung-wah (Sam Fong), Elvis Tsui Kam-kong (Chui), Julie Lee Wah-yuet (Hoi's Wife), Cherie Chan Siu-ha (Oi Dai, aka Rosie), Chan Kwok-bong (Collaborator), Bobby Yip King-sang (Queue Jumper), Ku Feng (Store Keeper). 1.85:1. VHS: World Video. Import LD: Cameron Entertainment. Import VCD: Mei Ah. 91 minutes.

One of the most explicit films to ever receive the Category II rating, this dreadful thriller is an upscale version of the notorious **Man Behind the Sun**, a revoltingly explicit dramatization of the war crimes Japanese soldiers and scientists perpetrated on their Chinese captives. Both films claim to be based on real events, but, like its forerunner, this "mainstream" version is questionable as a historical document and is a failure, even on the low level of sordid entertainment. In a stab at legitimacy, it opens with testimonials from actors who really lived during the period (including the great Shih Kien) before segueing into its story. Mong Dai and Sun Dai are sisters working as movie extras when the Japanese overrun the British and invade Hong Kong. Mong Dai then acts as a volunteer assistant for overworked doctor Sam Fong; he loves her, but Sun Dai loves him. HK is soon officially occupied and citizens are raped and/or slaughtered, with the survivors clambering to get by any way they can. In the face of unbearable poverty, the girls' parents sell out to the Japanese, and Sun Dai is forced to sleep with one of the enemy generals in exchange for food. When the father murders the general for having sex with his wife and trying to rape Mong Dai, the family's life turns into sheer hell on earth.

A risible mix of laughable melodrama, bloody mayhem, and unfunny (not to mention inappropriately placed) comedy, this bomb was actually released to HK theaters during the Christmas Holiday season! While generally one of HK's most appealing performers, Law Kar-ying is so astoundingly over-the-top here, his performance borders on the surreal, which makes it a fitting personification of the artless screenplay.

701. 97 Aces Go Places

(1997; Mandarin Films) ★: 1/10. *Jui gaai paak dong ji jui gaai paak dong* (Cantonese), *Zui jia pai dang zhi zui jie pai dang* (Mandarin): "Best Partners: Drunk Street Partners." Cinematographer: Herman Yau Lai-to; Art Director: Nelson Cheung Hok-yun; Music: Mak Chun-hung; Action Director: Chin Kar-lok; Writer-Producer: Raymond Wong Pak-ming; Director: Chin Kar-lok. Cast: Alan Tam Wing-lun (Ho Sik/Ho's Father), Tony Leung Chiu-wai (Drunk Shooter), Christy Chung Lai-tai (Li Lai-shen), Francis Ng Chun-yu (Lui Yue-yeung), Donna Chu Kit-yee (Mandy), Simon Lui Yu-yeung (Chung Yue), Ben Lam Kwok-bun (Lung), Maria Cordero (Ho's Mother), Billy Chow Bei-lee (Thug), Moses Chan Ho (Thug), Emily Kwan Bo-wai (Driving Teacher). 1.85:1. VHS: Tai Seng. Import LD/VCD: Universe. 92 minutes.

The **Aces Go Places** series is back after an eight year hiatus, and most viewers will agree that this tediously unfunny mess proves conclusively that it should never have been revived. Alan Tam plays the bumbling young heir to his gangster father's fortune who must fulfill the man's dying request before he will see any cash: kill thief Li Lai-shen. To that end, his family hires an alcoholic marksman (Tony Leung Chiu-wai) to help Tam pull off the hit. However, since Lai-shen is played by the gorgeous Christy Chung, Tam can't bring himself to pull the trigger. In fact, Chung and her retarded sister end up going on the run with Tam and Leung, but the former's dream of having a relationship with Chung goes up in smoke when she learns who his father was.

In a film filled with obnoxious characterizations, Alan Tam comes off the worst, mugging like a child in the back row of a grade school play. As the sole appealing character, Chung escapes unscathed and handles herself quite well in the fight sequences. As with Mandarin's **All's Well End's Well '97**, there is a laughably overt Pepsi plug: A stack of Pepsi cans sits in the middle of an office building lobby(!) for no reason than to have someone crash through them. This was an extremely inauspicious directorial debut for veteran actor/action coordinator Chin Kar-lok (whose brother, Chin Siu-ho, has a cameo), who shows no flair for comedy whatsoever. Granted, while Raymond Wong's script is so impossibly bad no one could have pulled it off, letting the performers exaggerate to the nth degree just makes the sheer witlessness all the more painful. Several familiar faces pop up in cameos but will remain unidentified here, to save them further shame.

702. 92 Legendary La Rose Noire

(1992; Hoventin Films Production Co.) ★: 4/10. *92 Hak mooi gwai dui hak mooi gwai* (Cantonese), *92 Hei mei gui dui hei mei gui* (Mandarin): "92: Black Rose vs. Black Rose." Cinematographer: Chan Yuen-kai; Art Director: Joseph Chan Sin-chi; Music: Lowell Lo Kwun-ting; Writer: Kei On (pseudonym for Jeff Lau Chun-wai); Producer: Laura Fau Lok-lin; Action Director: Tony Leung Siu-hung; Director: Jeff Lau Chun-wai. Cast: Maggie Siu Mei-kei (Butterfly Wong), Tony Leung Kar-fai (Keith Lui), Teresa Mo Shun-kwan (Chow Wai-kuen), Petrina Fung Bo-bo (Piu-hung), Wong Wan-si (Yim-fan), Cheung Kwok-leung (Leung), Yip Wing-cho (Insurance Agency Boss), Lawrence Ah Mon (Interviewer). 1.85:1. VHS/LD: World Video. Import LD/VCD: Star Entertainment (No Subtitles). Import DVD: China Star (No Subtitles). 95 minutes.

This rollicking comedy is a frustrating experience for English speaking viewers because it is largely a send-up of TV programs and movies from the 1960s, virtually none of which are readily available for viewing. Consequently, it's not unlike showing **The Brady Bunch Movie** to a

Mainland Chinese audience: You know you should be laughing, but without the proper reference points you are simply baffled. Put-upon Butterfly and her flaky friend Wai-kuen witness a mob rubout and decide to leave a note attributing the responsibility to film heroine "Black Rose" (featured in the like-named 1965 movie about the escapades of a female Robin Hood). When the police find Wai-kuen's fingerprints on the scene, they believe her to be Black Rose. Little does anyone know it but there really *is* a Black Rose, though she has gotten decidedly senile over the years. She imprisons Butterfly and the oddball officer Lui (who has been romantically pursuing Butterfly), demanding to know why the name of Black Rose has been dragged into this criminal case.

Filled with decidedly unsubtle slapstick (particularly the bits where Petrina Fung sends up her child star days), impromptu music numbers, and occasional action sequences, **La Rose** has its moments but, more often than not, barely rates a smile. The best work is done by Tony Leung Kar-fai, doing an amusingly over-the-top parody of the rather effeminate '60s screen idol Lui Kei. It was followed by the semi-related **Rose, Rose, I Love You!** and **Black Rose II**.

703. Ninja in the Deadly Trap

(1983) ★: 6/10. Chinese Titles Unknown. Cinematographer: Yu Kam-chun; Art Director: Le Fu-lin; Music: Not Original; Writer: Shum Sai-shing; Producer: Mark Wu Dan; Action Director-Director: Phillip Kwok Tsui. Cast: Ti Lung (General Chi Chi-kwong), Phillip Kwok Tsui (Mao Tin-yeung), Chiang Sheng (Chau), Lu Feng (Tung Yen), Yasuaki Kurota (Shi Ping-wei, the Ninja Leader). 2.35:1. VHS: Goodtimes (Dubbed), Ocean Shores (Dubbed). 97 minutes.

When Shaw Brothers decided to stop producing kung fu movies, Phillip Kwok arranged financing from Taiwanese producer Mark Wu Dan and got some of director Chang Cheh's regular stars together for this period thriller, which compares favorably to their previous HK productions. The story unfolds during The Ming Dynasty, as Japanese pirates wreak havoc along the Chinese coast, laying waste to entire towns. The situation becomes even more desperate when bands of ninjas start appearing and target the Chinese military commander, General Chi. The Master of the Three Arts (who possesses a book illustrating various ninjitsu techniques) is the only one who can combat this new enemy, so he pledges that his students Chau, Mao, and Tung, will join Chi's army in their fight to wipe out the killers. Meanwhile, the ninja leader has dispatched assassins to eliminate the General, with two having managed to infiltrate his palace.

In contrast to the Shaw films, a large portion of the action here takes place outside rather than in the studio, giving this a very different look and feel right off the top. Kwok largely dispenses with Chang's familiar theme of male bonding, concentrating on action instead. The plot is routine, recycling components from **Five Venoms** and **Five Element Ninja**, and strongman Lo Mang is missed, but there are some effective setpieces and the end result is solid, if unremarkable, genre fare. Character names listed above are from the English version.

704. Ninth of September, the Cursed Day

(1996; Super Power Motion Picture Co.) ★: 2/10. *Gau yuet choh gau san neung taam* (Cantonese), *Jiu yue chu jiu xin niang tan* (Mandarin): "September 9th: The Bridal Beach." Cinematographers: Cheng Man-keung, Philip Ma Kam-cheung; Music: Ng Kin-bo; Producer: Lau Keung-fu; Writer-Director: Chan Siu-cheung. Cast: Michael To Tai-yu (Li Chie/Chiu Yin-lin), Eileen Tung Oi-ling (Florence/Yin-ying), Lau Siu-kwan (Jeff), Hilary Tsui Ho-ying (Florence's Sister). 1.85:1. VHS: Tai Seng. Import LD/VCD: New City. 89 minutes.

When her true love, Yin-lin, is murdered, young bride-to-be Yin-ying drowns herself in a lake. The film then jumps ahead six decades to the present day, as the police try to figure out why people are turning up dead every six months in the area near the lake (now known as "Brides Pool"). Singer Florence (who is the spitting image of Yin-ying) is desired by cop Jeff (the spitting image of the man Yin-ying was being forced to marry), who suspects the killer to be fugitive Li Chie (the spitting image of Yin-lin ... see where this one is going?). As Florence learns more and more about Yin-ying, she becomes convinced that Li couldn't possibly be the killer, but Jeff is intent on forcing her to marry him and history seems destined to repeat itself.

An equal mix of boredom and unintentional laughs, this cheap misfire (which features some of the worst computer animation ever and is sorely lacking in originality and suspense) will impress no one. It's just more irredeemable junk from the folks at Super Power.

705. No More Love, No More Death

(1993; Carrianna Film Production) ★: 2/10. *Taai Ji chuen suet* (Cantonese), *Tai Zi chuan shuo* (Mandarin): "The Legend of Prince." Cinematographer: Herman Yau Lai-to; Art Director: Ho Chi-hang; Music: Wong Yiu-kwong; Writer: Candy Cheng; Producer: Taylor Wong Tai-loi; Action Directors: Yuen Cheung-yan, Lam Moon-wah; Directors: Herman Yau Lai-to, Taylor Wong Tai-loi. Cast: Jacky Cheung Hok-yau (Prince), Rosamund Kwan Chi-lam (Tracy Chan), Carina Lau Kar-ling (Ching-ching), Michael Chan Wai-man (Green Dragon), Chin Ho (Mute). 1.85:1. VHS/LD: World Video. Import LD/VCD: Star Entertainment (No Subtitles). Import DVD: China Star (No Subtitles). 89 minutes.

This prequel to **With or Without You** introduces the characters of Prince and Tracy (known as "Joey" in the original film's subtitles), though it is pretty much one and the same, relying on music video stylistics and attractive stars to sell its simple-minded, formula-bound storyline. After Prince performs a hit in a courtroom (a sequence that will strain the credulity of even the most forgiving viewer), we are shown flashbacks of his father, Tiger Pak, teaching him to be ruthless and presenting him with the beautiful Ching-ching as a "birthday present." Back in the present day, Prince and Ching-ching (his loyal assistant in murder) set out to eliminate rival Green Dragon (who is actually Prince's natural father, though neither man is aware of it). While he fails to ice his target, Prince encounters dancer Tracy, the literal "Girl of His Dreams," and spares her life, despite the fact that she has seen his face. The two start a relationship and, as a result, Prince starts to develop a conscience. When Pak sends a mute hitman to kill Tracy, she is saved by Prince, but Ching-ching has been ordered to finish the job her associate failed to do.

This is an exceedingly tiresome exercise lacking so much as an ounce of wit and originality (unless you consider the police dressing like disco club regulars and driving VW bugs to be innovation); even the gunplay is poorly choreographed.

706. No Regret, No Return

(1993; Hing Fat Film Production Co.) ★: 5/10. *Jau seung bat gwai lo* (Cantonese), *Zou shang bu gui lu* (Mandarin): "Walking the Road of No Return." Cinematographer: Cheung King-nin; Art Director: Ray Lam Chan-fai; Music: Eddie Cheung Wing-hang; Producer: Vicky Bowie Kwong Po-yiu; Action Director-Director: Ridley Tsui Bo-wah. Cast: Max Mok Siu-chung (Victor), Vivian Chow Wei-man (Sylvia Fong), Ridley Tsui Bo-wah (Ho Siu-po), Kenneth Tsang Kong (Lau Sin), Wong Chi-yeung (Bill), Lau Kar-wing

(Inspector Lam), Tommy Wong Kwong-leung (Cheung Ho). 1.85:1. VHS/LD: World Video. 94 minutes.

As is too often the case with HK action films, terrific stuntwork and skilled choreography must once again prop up a weak screenplay, making this thriller a moderately entertaining but shallow and instantly forgettable 94 minutes. After he assassinates a wanted criminal who was about to make a deal with police, hitman Victor's motorcycle is hit by a car (an incredible stunt). Victor forces the driver, Ho Siu-po, to take him to a local hospital, where he plans on rescuing his ailing wife. The plan fails when reporter Sylvia Fong (unconvincingly played by pop star Vivian Chow) alerts security, and Victor is forced to flee, with Siu-po still in tow. Although he initially plans to murder Sylvia, Victor ends up taking her along too when his employer (corrupt politician Lau Sin) sends men to terminate him. Realizing that he needs the hitman alive to prove that he had no part in Victor's various shootouts with police, Siu-po starts cooperating with him. When Lau has Victor's wife murdered, he confronts the politician at a political rally (an ending modelled after the finale of the Tony Leung Kar-fai/Danny Lee actioner **Blue Lightning**). Stick around for some painful looking out-takes during the end credits, particularly the bit where one stuntman gets pinned against a concrete wall by a car!

707. No Risk, No Gain: Casino Raiders the Sequel

(1990; Win's Movie Production) ★: 5/10. *Ji juen gai jong yuen choi* (Cantonese), *Zhi zun ji zhuang yuan cai* (Mandarin): "The Best Plan, the Best People." Cinematographer: David Chung Chi-man; Art Director: Jason Mok Siu-kei; Music: Lowell Lo Kwun-ting; Action Director: Wong Kwan; Writer-Producer: Wong Jing; Directors: Jimmy Heung Wah-sing, Taylor Wong Tai-loi. Cast: Alan Tam Wing-lun (Ray), Andy Lau Tak-wah (Big Dee), Nat Chan Pak-cheung (Mao, aka Leslie), Chen Sung-yung (Cheung Shan-ho), Michelle Lee Kar-yan (Winnie), May Lo Mei-mei (Miss Tsang), Anthony Wong Chau-sang (Yeung Sing), Christine Ng Wing-mei (Maureen), Shing Fui-on (Big Fool), Tien Feng (Yeung Chun), Mui Siu-wai (Sexy). 1.85:1. VHS: Tai Seng (No Subtitles). Import LD/VCD/DVD: Mei Ah. 107 minutes.

Casino Raiders stars Alan Tam and Andy Lau were reunited for this film, which bears no connection to that Wong Jing hit, or to **Casino Raiders II** for that matter. Master card player Ray (aka "The King of Gambling") is coerced into facing off against Taiwanese gambler Cheung Shan-ho in a high stakes game to be played in Macau. On his way there, conmen Big Dee and Mao swipe his suitcase, which contains millions in cash and a gold VIP card issued to Ray by Cheung. The pair use the card to try and crash the contest, but when Ray catches up with them, he decides to encourage this deception rather than quash it. This is a wise plan, as the stepson of their Macau host does not take kindly to these Hong Kong cardsharps and attempts to put them out of commission before the match.

One of the lesser entries in the gambling film craze, **No Risk, No Gain** moves rather slowly, and the humor is decidedly hit and miss (though there is a sequence involving Nat Chan and a gun that is genuinely hilarious). Fortunately, the star-laden cast helps retain interest (particularly Anthony Wong at his sneering, sarcastic best), and the gunplay is reasonably creative. The big game finale is not all that exciting but does end with a nice twist.

708. Nobody's Hero

(1989; Jun Kong Films) ★: 6/10. *Ching yi ngoh sam ji* (Cantonese), *Qing yi wo xin zhi* (Mandarin): "Affection My Heart Knows." Cinematographer: Chim Pak-hung; Art Director: Ringo Cheung Sek-wah; Writer: Sammy Tsang Kan-cheung; Producer: Wu Tai-yan; Action Directors: Tony Poon Kin-kwan, Benz Kong To-hoi; Director: Kuk Kau-leung. Cast: Liu Wai-hung (Leung Gun), Kathy Chow Hoi-mei (Jane), Chen Jing (Chicken), Fong Kong, Lok Ying-kwan. 1.85:1. VHS: World Video. Import LD: Star Entertainment (No Subtitles). 83 minutes.

In a way, this violent action-thriller is HK's answer to **Taxi Driver**, with a plot parallel to **The Killer**. Leung Gun, a homely Mainland immigrant working as a cabbie, is depressed and angered by the social decay that surrounds him in HK. He decides to become a cop, but is rejected when a routine test reveals that he is color blind. To make matters worse, his girlfriend is cheating on him and has her friends humiliate him at a party. Trying to fulfill his need to "make a difference," Leung gets a job as a mall security guard. He also starts to develop a relationship with Jane, a beautiful blind girl who lives in his building. One evening at work, Leung overhears a conversation and learns that the girl's uncle is a drug trafficker. Caught trying to spirit Jane away, Leung is severely beaten. The triads force Jane to courier drugs for them, but Leung is able to intercept her and destroy the shipment. In the hospital for an injury she sustained, Jane is told that she can now have an operation to restore her sight. Needing to make a down payment for the procedure, Leung decides to blackmail the leader of the gang, using a security camera videotape of the man executing one of his underlings. When the plan goes awry, his friend is murdered and Jane's life is put in danger. Leung calls in a favor, gets a gun, and sets out for vengeance.

While short on surprises, the film does work as a gritty melodrama, with Liu's fine performance helping to make the viewer care about the fate of such an atypical protagonist. Liu became a HK TV star in 1979, portraying bumbling Mainland immigrant "Cheung Can" on the comedy series *The Good, the Bad and the Ugly* (*Mong jung yun*—"Man in the Net"). The character became so much a part of local pop culture that HK citizens began referring to transplanted Mainlanders as "Ah Can."

709. The Nocturnal Demon

(1990; Gold Double Productions/Lau Kun Wai Productions) ★: 6/10. *Ye gwai sin sang* (Cantonese), *Ye gui xian sheng* (Mandarin): "Night Ghost Gentleman." Cinematographers: Paul Chan Chung-chau, Raymond Lam Fai-tai; Art Directors: Ben Lau Man-hung, Tam Hong-ming; Music: Lowell Lo Kwun-ting; Writers: Lo Wing-keung, Joyce Cheung Lai-ling; Producers: Yeung Ping-chung, Ricky Lau Koon-wai; Action Director: Cho Wing; Director: Ricky Lau Koon-wai. Cast: Alfred Cheung Kin-ting (Chau Wai-tin), Moon Lee Choi-fung (Wawa Chai), Lam Kau (Wawa's Uncle), Cho Wing (The Killer), Isabella Chow Wang (Yee-tee), Yip Wing-cho (Yip), Anthony Chan Yau (Officer Chan), Billy Lau Nam-kwong (Master Snake), Yuen Wah (Leader of Robbers), Corey Yuen Kwai (Yuen), Tsui Siu-ming (Robbery Cop), Chin Siu-ho (Cop), Richard Ng Yiu-hon (Cab Driver), Barry Wong Ping-yiu (Chef), James Tien Chun (Superintendent), Woo Fung (Painter), Mang Hoi (Paint Victim). 1.85:1. VHS/LD: World Video. 93 minutes.

A film which could only come from HK, this wild horror-comedy opens with a deranged cab driver brutally murdering his female fare. After this disturbing sequence, it switches to goofy comedy, via the arrival of Wawa, a naive Mainland girl who is in HK to visit her cousin Wai-tin. The latter bears a distinct resemblance to the killer, and that gets him in deep trouble when a witness identifies him on the scene of the next murder. Going on the run with Wawa, Wai-tin desperately tries to find the real psychopath in order to clear his name.

Just about every form of humor rears its head here: tasteless gags involving

Wawa's blind uncle (who uses chloroform to quiet down the kids he babysits!), Mainland hick jokes, broad physical slapstick, cross dressing, and even embarrassingly racist blackface gags. There are more misses than hits, but enough genuinely inspired moments transpire (particularly a sequence in which the uncle somehow manages to bungle his way into the police station and steal some files, and a terrific bit where Moon Lee uses her kung fu on a jewel thief...while wearing roller skates!) to keep things interesting. A multitude of familiar faces turn up in cameos, and the final battle is pretty spectacular in its own demented way. Few viewers would call this a good movie, but it certainly isn't a boring one!

710. Nomad

(1982; Century Motion Picture Co.) ★: 7/10. *Lit foh ching chun* (Cantonese), *Lie huo qing chun* (Mandarin): "Flaming Youth." Cinematographer: Bill Wong Chung-bo; Art Director: William Cheung Suk-ping, Jon Hau Wing-choi; Music: Violet Lam Man-yee; Writers: Yau Kong-kin, John Chan Koon-chung, Joyce Chan Wan-man, Eddie Fong Ling-ching; Producer: Dennis Yu Wan-kong; Director: Patrick Tam Kar-ming. Cast: Leslie Cheung Kwok-wing (Louis), Cecilia Yip Tung (Tomato), Pat Ha Man-chik (Kathy), Kenneth Tong Chun-yip (Pong), Yung Sai-kit (Shinsuke Takeda). 1.85:1. VHS: Tai Seng. 93 minutes.

Patrick Tam's study of disaffected HK youth, **Nomad** is often cited as one of the key New Wave films. The central figure is Louis, a well-adjusted boy from an affluent family, who is given to some unwise experimentation, like sniffing gasoline. One evening he helps Tomato, a troubled girl who has just been dumped by her uncouth boyfriend. The two spend the night together and begin seeing each other. Like many HK teens of the time, Louis' sister, Kathy, is obsessed with Japanese culture and has befriended Shinsuke Takeda, a Red Army member whom she has encouraged to desert his fellow terrorists. Her boyfriend Pong (whom Kathy likes because he's physical, meaning that she doesn't "have to waste so much energy on thought") takes an instant dislike to Takeda, but Kathy is fascinated with both men because of the extreme contrast. The teens plan on sailing the family yacht to Arabia, but Takeda's colleagues are in HK, intent on forcing him to commit *seppuku.*

Alternately pensive, erotic, humorous, and disturbing, **Nomad** examines the lives of HK youth with a degree of verisimilitude quite rare for its time. Even during the lighter moments (like Kathy and Pong's desperate quest for a little privacy so that they can make out), the film rings true and is supported by one of Violet Lam's loveliest scores. Alas, the studio-dictated ending remains jarring and unsatisfying no matter how many times one sees the film. It was remade in 1998 by writer/director James Yuen Sai-sang as **Rumble Ages** (which has the same Chinese title as this).

711. Now You See Love ... Now You Don't!

(1992; Golden Princess Film Production/Milestone Pictures Production) ★: 8/10. *Ngoh oi Nau Man-chai (lau man yue do bing)* (Cantonese), *Wo ai Chou Wenchai (liu mang yu dao bing)* (Mandarin): "I Love Nau Man-chai (Rogue Meets Warrior)" or "I Love Chou Wenchai (Rogue Meets Warrior)." Cinematographer: Poon Hang-sang; Art Director: Chong Chi-leung; Music: Anthony Lun Wing-leung; Writer: Mabel Cheung Yuen-ting; Producers: Linda Kuk Mei-lai, Terence Chang Chia-chun; Director: Alex Law Kai-yui. Cast: Chow Yun-fat (Wu Shan-shui), Carol Cheng Yu-ling (Firefly Kwok), Teresa Mo Shun-kwan (Dotty), Carina Lau Kar-ling (Susan Chong), Anthony Wong Chau-sang (Dunno), Lowell Lo Kwun-ting (Piano Player), Paul Fonoroff (Surveyor). 1.85:1. VHS: Tai Seng. Import LD: Golden Cinema City. 95 minutes.

The husband and wife team of Alex Law and Mabel Cheung, the creative force behind such fine motion pictures as **An Autumn's Tale**, **Eight Tales of Gold** and **Painted Faces**, struck gold again with this wonderful, old-fashioned romantic comedy. Wu Shan-shui, the chief of a village in the New Territories, is awaiting the day when his childhood sweetheart, Firefly, returns home from England after a three year stay. The Firefly who returns certainly isn't the one who left: Punked out, and with an attitude to match, she looks to Shan-shui like an alien duplicate, and the two are soon at each other's throats. On the advice of her friend Dotty, Firefly moves to the city and finds a job as a singing waitress. Crestfallen, Shan-shui decides that it is time to "improve" himself. Dragging his buddy "Dunno" along, he heads for the city and opens a shop ... which just happens to be right across the street from where his ex is living. After both endure the horrors of dating other people (and a near-death experience), it finally becomes clear just who is their perfect match.

Hong Kong cranks out more formula-bound movies than just about any other movie-producing territory; that must at least partially be the reason why when one works, it works beautifully. Aside from a few surprise appearances, there is not a single novel idea here, and yet **Now You See Love ... Now You Don't!** remains utterly charming. This is wish fulfillment cinema at its best. Chow Yun-fat and Carol Cheng are both a study in contrasts and yet utterly in sync as the quarrelling lovers, and Anthony Wong has one of his best roles as Shan-shui's loveable blockhead sidekick. Teresa Mo, forever typecast as the "brassy broad" in comedies, reprises that persona here but is also allowed a remarkable dramatic moment during an encounter group session when she is overcome by the accumulated sadness of being dumped by her boyfriend. It is both a sad and amusingly genuine observation about the power of love and the frailty of the human spirit. Well-translated subtitles and sync sound recording are also welcome assets. There are lots of cameos here, including Dennis Chan Kwok-san, Richard Ng Yiu-hon, and producer Terence Chang. In the film's Chinese title, "Nau Man-chai" is not one of the characters but an expression that literally means "Swirl-Marked Log" or a spoiled, stubborn person. Incidentally, Chow and Cheng had previously appeared together in the TV series *The Man in the Net*, which is where Cheng's nickname, "Do Do," comes from.

Nutty Kickbox Cops *see* **Skinny Tiger and Fatty Dragon**

712. 01:00 A.M.

(1995; Newscope Productions) ★: 4/10. *Yau boon yat dim chung* (Cantonese), *Ye ban yi dian zhong* (Mandarin). "Midnight 1:00." Cinematographer: Tam Chi-wai; Art Director: Stanley Cheung Sai-kit; Music: Tommy Wai Kai-leung; Writers: Philip Kwok Wai-chung, So Man-sing; Producer: Andy Chin Wing-keung; Director: Wilson Yip Wai-san. Cast: Veronica Yip Yuk-hing (Nurse), Anthony Wong Yiu-ming (Sunny Wong), Anita Yuen Wing-yee (Fong Siu-yin), Jordan Chan Siu-chun (Officer #36257), Elvis Tsui Kam-kong (Officer #663). 1.85:1. VHS: Tai Seng. Import LD/VCD/DVD: Ocean Shores. 86 minutes.

Ghost stories are a mainstay of HK cinema, and **01:00 A.M.**, by director Wilson Yip (**Mongkok Story**), offers three comical tales aimed at family viewers. In contrast to most horror anthologies, the opening segment here is clearly the best. "Coma Patient" stars Veronica Yip Yuk-hing as a night duty nurse assigned to care for comatose pop star Sunny Wong (played by real-life pop star Anthony Wong Yiu-ming, who found fame with Lau Yee-tat as "The Tat Ming Pair"). One night she sees the singer's spirit being led through the hospital corridors by a young, adoring female ghost. Overhearing their conversation, she learns that the girl is an obsessed fan who died at one of Sonny's concerts and won't allow him to return to his body. Yip (who graduated from Category III softcore films to become a respected dramatic actress) gives a relaxed and appealing performance, and the script takes amusing jabs at prominent HK celebrities. "The Girl with a Queue" was a Mainland girl who stowed away aboard a train destined for HK in order to enter a beauty contest, but died in a freak accident. A plucky college student (Anita Yuen) decides to stake out the area she is reputed to haunt, in order to interview the spectre as part of a class project. Yuen is one of the colony's most engaging performers, but the material gives her little of interest to do and the narrative is slight and predictable. The same problem dogs the closing story, "Snapshot," which features Jordan Chan and Elvis Tsui as bumbling traffic cops assigned to a remote photo radar station who encounter an elderly female ghost. The two play off each other well, but, again, the plot never really amounts to much and is low on both humor and suspense. A surprise success at the box office, the film spawned two follow-ups (called, naturally, **02:00 A.M.** and **03:00 A.M.**) and a trend of equally limp horror anthologies.

713. 02:00 A.M.

(1997; Golden Harvest/Golden Movies International) ★: 3/10. *Ye boon yi dim jung* (Cantonese), *Ye ban er dian zhong* (Mandarin): "Midnight 2:00." Cinematographer: William Yim Wai-lun; Art Directors: Jon Hau Wing-choi, Cindy Mok Kar-wai; Music: Peter Kam Pui-tat; Writers: Andy Chin Wing-keung, Joyce Cheung Lai-ling, Lo Kam-chuen, Tsui Kei-yan, Yu Yiu-lung; Producer: Jessinta Liu Fung-ping; Director: Andy Chin Wing-keung. Cast: Hilary Tsui Ho-ying (Siu-wai), Wyman Wong Wai-man (Siu-fung), Law Koon-lan (Kuen), Helena Law Lan (Chi), Pauline Chan Po-lin (Eva), Michael Chow Man-kin (Michael Wong Fun), Elvis Tsui Kam-kong (Lung), Jordan Chan Siu-chun (Lung's Partner), Lee Siu-kei (Kei). 1.85:1. VHS: Tai Seng. Import LD/VCD/DVD: New City. 92 minutes.

This in-name-only sequel serves up three more horror tales, and, once again, there is not a single scare to be found in any of them. The first stars Law Koon-lan as a veteran make-up artist whose young assistants (Wyman Wong and Hilary Tsui) inadvertently use a mold taken from the face of Eva, an actress who died in a studio fire many years ago. Sure enough, Eva's spirit is soon wandering the premises and driving the cowardly pair crazy with fear. The ending of this one is so lame, you can hardly believe the segment is finished. In story number two, a trio of female back-up singers decide to spy on conceited singer Michael (Michael Chow) after a tabloid story makes it look like the girls are his latest conquests. They follow him to a crematorium and spot a ghost who can remove her head. Is Michael aware of this phantasm or is the spirit actually his lover? This segment is no better than the first but does have one genuinely funny image: The scared girls trying to run while clad in mermaid costumes! The final story reunites Jordan Chan and Elvis Tsui from **01:00 A.M.**, where they played cowardly police officers. This time they play bumbling assistant directors in the employ of a foreigner making a commercial. A ghostly little boy keeps appearing on the location and seems intent on killing his little brother, who has been hired to appear in the ad. This portion (which takes place entirely during the daylight hours) offers up a reasonably inventive twist but certainly not one clever enough to warrant sitting through the rest of this dull misfire.

714. 03:00 A.M.

(1997; Evergood Productions) ★: 3/10. *Ye boon saam dim jung* (Cantonese), *Ye ban san dian zhong* (Mandarin): "Midnight 3:00." Cinematographer: Wong Kar-fai; Art Director: Cindy Mok Kar-wai; Music: C.A.M. Production; Writer: Wong Ho-wah; Producer: Benny Fu Ching-wai; Director: Andy Chin Wing-keung. Cast: Theresa Lee Yee-hung (The Reporter), Jordan Chan Siu-chun (Acne), Cheung Tat-ming (Banana), Spencer Lam Sheung-yee (Dr. Tso), Lee Kin-yan (Shing), Jamie Luk Kim-ming (Card Player). 1.85:1. VHS: Tai Seng. 90 minutes.

This is yet another tepid trio of ghost tales, all of which climax at the titular time. Story number one stars Theresa Lee as a TV reporter who encounters a man claiming that he is possessed each evening by the ghost of a little girl, who committed suicide after being wrongly accused of theft. Lee enlists the aid of professional sceptic Spencer Lam to debunk the claim and the pair spend a seemingly fruitless evening waiting for the spirit to arrive. The resolution is so limp, we are into the next story before one even realizes it. Number two is even more underwhelming. Four teenage girls go on a pleasure trip to Cheung Chau island and are obliged, due to a lack of available accommodations, to stay in a supposedly haunted house. After much carousing and a few odd occurrences, they are forced by a pair of ghosts to...play mahjong. The only segment of any value at all, number three casts Jordan Chan and Cheung Tat-ming as cowardly maintenance men who find a gold chain and decide to keep it. However, the now-dead owner of the trinket wants it back and proceeds to terrorize the pair while they are pulling the late shift on a deserted work site. Chan and Cheung seem to be improvising a good part of the time, and their enthusiasm for the material helps to sell it. Even so, the segment remains mediocre at best, and that description also perfectly sums up the rest of this yawner.

715. The Occupant

(1984; Cinema City Co.) ★: 5/10. *Lung hei bik yan* (Cantonese), *Ling qi bi ren* (Mandarin): "Spirit Compels People." Cinematographer: Ricardo Coll; Art Director: Tony Au Ding-ping; Music: Danny Chung Teng-yat; Writer: Edward Lee Kui-ming; Producers: Karl Maka, Dean Shek Tien, Raymond Wong Pak-ming; Director: Ronny Yu Yan-tai. Cast: Chow Yun-fat (Valentino Chow), Sally Yeh Chian-wen (Angie), Raymond Wong Pak-ming (Hansom Wong), Lo Lieh (Chan), Melvin Wong Kam-sun (Robert). Dolby Digital (DVD only). 1.85:1. VHS: Tai Seng. Import LD: Golden Cinema City. Import VCD/DVD: Universe. 96 minutes.

The people in front of the camera and behind the scenes raise one's expectations for this horror-comedy, but it never quite clicks. Angie is a Canadian university student visiting HK to write a paper on Chinese superstitions. She gets some unexpected first hand experience when she rents a seemingly haunted apartment from nerdy car salesman "Hansom" Wong. A persistent pest, Hansom refuses to leave Angie alone, finding all manner of excuses to get into her place. One evening he is tossed out the window by the ghost of the former tenant, a female singer who committed suicide after accidentally shooting her lover. Teaming up with Valentino (a suave cop who keeps crossing paths with Angie), Hansom and Angie investigate the circumstances behind the incident. When Angie is briefly possessed by the singer's spirit, the men take her to a house in the country, but the cycle of death seems destined to repeat.

The comedy is weak, with the more serious elements (like the initial exorcism of the ghost) coming off more successfully. However, the main problem is Wong's character: His pursuit of Angie in the first half seems uncomfortably close to *stalking* but is meant to evoke laughs. In spite of Danny Chung's composer credit, the soundtrack includes music lifted from Tangerine Dream's **Sorcerer** soundtrack.

716. Odd Couple

(1979; Gar Bo Motion Picture Company) ★: 8/10. *Bok ming dan dou duet ming cheung* (Cantonese), *Bo ming dao duo ming qiang* (Mandarin): "Desperate Sabre vs. Fatal Spear." Cinematographer: Ho Ming; Writers: Lai Wai-man, Raymond Wong Pak-ming; Producer: Karl Maka; Director: Lau Kar-wing. Cast: Sammo Hung Kam-po (The Sword Master/Yao, the Spear Master's Pupil), Lau Kar-wing (The Spear Master/The Sword Master's Pupil), Leung Kar-yan (Hsiao Pa-tien), Feng Sing (Potato), Lee Hoi-sang (Bald Thug with Knives), Dean Shek Tien (Mr. Rocking), Karl Maka (Challenger), Peter Chan Lung (Chuang), Chung Fat (Ti), Lam Ching-ying (Hsia). 2.35:1. Video Label Unknown. 96 minutes.

Period kung fu farces do not come much better than this terrific independent production, which serves up lively, infectious humor amid outstanding martial arts. A master of the spear and a master of the sword have a duel every ten years to determine whose technique is superior. Their bouts have all ended in draws, and now that they are getting on in years, the men decide to recruit pupils to carry on the tradition for them. The swordmaster drafts a foul-tempered lad who spends half of his time trying to kill him, while the spear-master enlists rotund boatman Yao to be his successor. After extensive training, the pair finally have their fight, but midway through they are kidnapped! The perpetrator is Hsiao Pa-tien, an old enemy who was disfigured during skirmishes with the two old masters and is using their new pupils to lure the men into a trap.

Sammo Hung and Lau Kar-wing are at the top of their form here, and they are given ample opportunities to display their skills because, in a great twist, Hung's pupil in the film is played by Lau and vice versa! The premise simply provides a loose framework for numerous kung fu setpieces as the pupils test their newly acquired skills against every ruffian and buffoon that crosses their path. Hung participates in a showstopping Peking Opera parody, and there is even a little anachronistic humor, courtesy of Dean Shek as the lecherous "Mr. Rocking," whose every appearance is accompanied by a drum solo!

717. The Odd One Dies

(1997; Milkyway Image) ★: 8/10. *Leung goh ji nang woot yat goh* (Cantonese), *Liang ge zhi neng huo yi ge* (Mandarin): "Only One Between the Two Can Live." Cinematographer: Cheng Siu-keung; Art Director: Silver Cheung Sai-wang; Music: Raymond Wong Ying-wah; Writer: Wai Kar-fai; Producers: Johnny To Kei-fung, Wai Kar-fai; Action Director: Yuen Bun; Director: Patrick Yau Tat-chi. Cast: Takeshi Kaneshiro (Mo), Carman Lee Yeuk-tung (The Girl), Byun Woo Nin, Kenneth Choi Fung-wah, Tin Man-chuk. 1.85:1. VHS: Tai Seng. Import LD/VCD/DVD: Mei Ah. 90 minutes.

If one were pressed to describe **The Odd One Dies** in only a few words, one could say with some certainty that it mixes the look and style of a Wong Kar-wai opus with the atmosphere and cadence prevalent in the gangster films of "Beat" Takeshi Kitano. This effort has few of the undercurrents that distinguish those films, but as a follow-up of sorts from the production team behind **Too Many Ways to Be No. 1**, it is a beautifully realized exercise in style, jet black humor, and unconventional storytelling. Takeshi Kaneshiro plays an unkempt and seemingly dimwitted lad with an apparent death wish, who looks to hire an assassin to pull off a hit. Carman Lee is the would-be killer, an equally strange and dishevelled woman who seems to take great pleasure running Kaneshiro through all manner of absurd and dangerous situations. He, meanwhile, keeps having run-ins with his boss, who is not exactly holding him in high regard, having had his fingers sliced off by Kaneshiro.

Beautifully photographed and effectively scored with a mixture of styles, the film has minimal dialogue, relying more on the characters' looks, dispositions, elongated pauses, and dreamy, reflective drags on cigarettes to communicate its musings on life, love, and death. Alternately violent, romantic, dreary, and dazzling, **The Odd One Dies** is one of several gutsy, atypical efforts that have surfaced in the wake of the commercial devastation that has plagued HK cinema as of late. It shows that the industry's seemingly dormant spirit of creativity is still alive and kicking; it only needs a willing audience to support and nourish it.

718. Off Track

(1990; Rich Film Productions) ★: 5/10. *Ma lo ying hung* (Cantonese), *Ma lu ying xiong* (Mandarin): "Road Hero." Cinematographer: Michael Ma Koon-wah; Art Director: Sin Ngai-lung; Music: Lowell Lo Kwun-ting; Writer: Cheung Kai-cheung; Producers: Willie Chan Chi-keung, Chan Chi-shun; Action Directors: Lee Kin-hung, Blackie Ko Shou-liang; Director: Cha Chuen-yee. Cast: Jacky Cheung Hok-yau, Max Mok Siu-chung, Loletta Lee Lai-chun, Ellen Chan Ar-lun, Wu Ma, Wong Chi-yeung, Lung Fong, Hung Chi-ming. 1.85:1. VHS: World Video (No Subtitles). Import LD: Star Entertainment (No Subtitles). 95 minutes.

English subtitled video copies of this illegal road racing movie do not seem to be available, but it merits inclusion here nonetheless. Jacky Cheung and Wong Chi-yeung play triads with a love for hot cars and harassing the police. Their main rival is Max Mok, and a race between the two one evening ends up with both being caught by police. Cheung's boss wants Mok's head, and much to his consternation, his sister (played by Loletta Lee) has struck up a relationship with Mok. When his father (Wu Ma) dies in an accident, trying to stop him from continuing with this dead end life of crime, Cheung begins to have doubts about his future.

The plot is simple and predictable enough that Western viewers should be able to follow it without too much difficulty, though the lack of translation leaves the action sequences as the primary attraction. Ace stunt driver Blackie Ko choreographed the races, and they are indeed the main reason to watch this; the sequence in which Cheung and Mok race down the yellow line of a two lane tunnel is edge-of-your-seat exciting. **Highway Man** is a semi-sequel.

719. Oh! My Three Guys

(1994; Regal Films) ★: 3/10. *Saam goh seung oi dik siu nin* (Cantonese), *San ge xiang ai de shao nian* (Mandarin): "Three Loving Youngsters." Cinematographer: Tam Chi-wai; Art Director: Nelson Cheung Hok-yun; Music: Lau Yee-tat; Writer: Raymond To Kwok-wai; Producer: Steven Lo Kit-sing; Director: Derek Chiu Sung-kei. Cast: Lau Ching-wan (Ching Yu-hoi), Eric Kot Man-fai (Kau), Dayo Wong Chi-wah (Fa), Jacqueline Wu Chien-lien (Fok May), Simon Lui Yu-yeung (Donald), Charine Chan Kar-ling ("The Bitchy Air Hostess"), Wong Yat-fei (Chan Yiu-cho), Chik King-man (Nancy), Kenneth Chan Kai-tai (Mike), Manfred Wong (Head Writer), Anthony Wong Chau-sang (Best Actor Winner). 1.85:1. VHS: Tai Seng. 94 minutes.

One of a handful of entries in the short-lived "gay film" fad, this one stars Lau Ching-wan, Eric Kot, and Dayo Wong as three homosexual friends sharing a flat together. Yu-hoi and Fa have trouble in their love lives, while the swishy and uninhibited Kau lives for the moment and is the happiest person they know. When he doesn't respond to her advances, Yu-hoi's new female co-worker, Fok May, thinks he is just being aloof. Yu-hoi encourages this mistaken impression, as he is afraid of being teased at work. When she does finally learn the truth, May sets out to win him anyway, sensing that he is not happy with his current lifestyle and needs a change. AIDS enters into the picture, forcing the friends to reassess their priorities.

While the film's heart is in the right place, it is far too simplistic and cliche-ridden to be effective for either straight or gay viewers. The latter will also be rightfully offended by the not-so-subtle implication that it just takes a good woman to straighten a gay man out.

720. On Fire

(1996; Mandarin Films/Martini Film Company) ★: 1/10. *Wan feng* (Cantonese), *Wan huo* (Mandarin): "Playing with Fire." Cinematographer: Fung Yuen-man; Art Director: Vincent Lam Wai-sam; Music: Lincoln Lo Kin; Writer: Cheung Cho-yee; Producer: Kimmy Suen King-on; Director: Clarence Fok Yiu-leung. Cast: Francoise Yip Fong-wah (Herself), Louis Koo Tin-lok (Michael), Chu Kin-kwan (Sam), Ng Man-tat (Micky), Annabelle Lau Hiu-tong (Nancy). 1.85:1. VHS: World Video. Import LD/VCD: Fitto Mobile. 91 minutes.

While **He's a Woman, She's a Man** poked fun at fan adulation of HK singers, this witless, mean-spirited effort tries to do the same for film stars, by way of Martin Scorsese's **The King of Comedy**. Michael and Sam are a couple of teen losers hopelessly obsessed with the beautiful Francoise Yip Fong-wah (playing herself). They buy supposedly illicit CD-Roms of her, show up at all of her personal appearances, and, finally, get a job as extras on one of her films. When Yip invites them out for dinner and then, apparently, enlists some thugs to beat them up, the pair retaliate by kidnapping her and her assistant Nancy. In a ridiculous plot twist, Yip decides that, since they did not rape her, they must be better than her agent, who is blackmailing her with a sex tape that is in his possession. Consequently, she convinces the boys to capture the man and coerce him into revealing the whereabouts of the video.

Ng Man-tat is absolutely unbearable as a retarded fan who gets involved in the ruse, while Yip and Liu are smacked around and verbally abused so much, the proceedings plunge into outright misogyny. During the climax, Yip ties up and beats her agent with a riding crop, while Ng sodomizes him with a baseball bat (are you laughing yet?). One can only hope that the actress' real-life agent met this same fate as retribution for getting his client involved in such a pathetic, offensive enterprise. This is strictly for those interested in gauging the sometimes immense gulf between Eastern and Western humor.

721. On the Run

(1988; Golden Harvest/Bo Ho Films Co./Mobile Film Production/Paragon Films) ★: 8/10. *Mong ming yuen yeung* (Cantonese), *Wang ming yuan yang* (Mandarin): "Fleeing Couple." Cinematographer: Peter Ngor Chi-kwan; Art Directors: Hai Chung-man, Dominique Lo Kar-yiu; Music: Violet Lam Man-yee; Writers: Alfred Cheung Kin-ting, Wong Wang-kei; Producer: Sammo Hung Kam-po; Action Direction: Sammo Hung Stunt Team, Yuen Wah; Director: Alfred Cheung Kin-ting. Cast: Yuen Biao (Hsiang Ming), Pat Ha Man-chik (Miss Pai), Charlie Chin Hsiang-lin (Lu), Bowie Lam Bo-yee (Johnny), Lo Lieh (Hsi), Idy Chan Yuk-lin (Lo Huan), Yuen Wah (Lu's Man), Phillip Ko Fei (Lu's Man). 1.85:1. VHS: Tai Seng. Import LD: Star Entertainment (No Subtitles). Import VCD: Mega Star. 88 minutes.

When his narcotics inspector girlfriend learns of his underworld dealings, police officer Lu hires female assassin Pai to dispatch her. After the deed is done, the killer's partner discovers that the target was a policewoman and demands more money, prompting Lu to try and have him killed. The dead woman's estranged husband, Hsiang Ming (who is also a cop), manages to capture the woman, but when he phones Lu to send back-up, two killers show up instead. Realizing that Lu is the one who set up the killing, Hsiang tries to flee, but his mother is murdered by one of Lu's men. With the situation now twisted to make it look like he is responsible, Hsiang decides to take his little girl and join with Pai in her flight to The Golden Triangle. However, they are betrayed at every turn and decide to confront their nemesis instead.

Tough, stylish, and succinct, **On the Run** serves up a fine dramatic performance from Yuen Biao and a highly effective one from Pat Ha as the icy assassin whose humanity is gradually awakened through her association with Hsiang and his young daughter. Add above average scripting (both Yuen Biao and Charlie Chin's characters are deeply concerned about the forthcoming reunification with China, and it is what drives the latter to his desperate measures) and you have a highly satisfying thriller that is easily Alfred Cheung's best directorial effort to date.

Once a Cop *see* **Project S**

722. Once a Thief

(1991; Cinema City Co./Golden Princess/Milestone Pictures) ★: 8/10. *Jung waang sei hoi* (Cantonese), *Zong heng si hai* (Mandarin): "Free-Spirited Travels Across Four Seas." Cinematographer: Poon Hang-sang; Art Director: James Leung Wah-sang; Music: Violet Lam Man-yee; Writers: John Woo Yu-sen, Clifton Ko Chi-sum, Janet Chun Siu-chun; Producers: Linda Kuk Mei-lai, Terence Chang Chia-chen; Action Director: Phillip Kwok Tsui; Director: John Woo Yu-sen. Cast: Chow Yun-fat (Joe), Leslie Cheung Kwok-wing (James), Cherie Chung Cho-hung (Cherie), Paul Chu Kong (Chu), Kenneth Tsang Kong (Chow), Woo Fung (Stanley Wu), David Wu Tai-wai (Auctioneer). Dolby Digital (DVD only). 1.85:1. VHS: Tai Seng. Import LD: Golden Cinema City. Import VCD: Mei Ah. Import DVD: Mega Star. 108 minutes.

In the wake of the intense **Bullet in the Head**, John Woo shifted gears and tackled this breezy Lunar New Year's adventure farce, his valentine to the European caper films of the sixties. Professional thieves Joe, Cherie, and James earn a very comfortable living, with their latest job netting them a cool half million. The three were trained, from a very young age, in the craft by their sadistic foster father, Mr. Chow. Ironically, it was policeman Chu who showered the children with the love and care that Chow refused to impart. To this day, the officer stills holds the trio in high regard, despite their ideological differences. The robbers' next assignment is no walk in the park: they must snatch a "cursed" painting from a security-laden castle in Nice. Joe and James pull off the heist but the former is apparently blown up when the pair is pursued by another set of crooks out to take the painting for themselves. Two years then pass. Thinking that their partner is dead, Cherie and James get married and start planning for a family. Joe, however, is still alive, though he is now confined to a wheelchair. No longer an asset to him, Chow severs all ties with Joe, but the latter secretly helps James with his new orders to re-steal the same piece of art they swiped two years before. Tired of Chow's cruelty, the men decide to foil him at his own game.

Beautifully photographed on location, **Once a Thief** is HK pop filmmaking at its most engagingly capricious. The violence may be toned down for a family audience (by HK standards, that is) but the action sequences are every bit as acrobatic and deliciously creative as one would expect from a John Woo project. Chow Yun-fat is dashing and silly in turns, while Leslie Cheung is both appealing and plausible in the kind of action-oriented part that does not often come his way. Cherie Chung, meanwhile, is given little of interest to do, which is par for the course when it comes to the director's work. The reckless mixture of sophomoric humor and traditional thriller elements is a bit too jarring for some Western audiences (particularly the final sequence, which the film would really be better off without), but for a New Year's picture (which is meant to appeal to every audience segment), this approach is quite understandable, and seasoned HK movie fans will not find it a detriment at all. There are several instances of throw-away verbal humor meant for the target audience that the English subtitles do not even attempt to relay, though viewers with a rudimentary grasp of Cantonese will catch a couple of the gags (at one point, Joe mentions Brigitte Lin Ching-hsia's name, while the subs supply a more local substitute: Brigitte Bardot!). In 1996 Woo travelled to Toronto to direct a staggeringly awful made-for-TV remake, which spawned a thankfully short-lived series.

723. Once Upon a Time a Hero in China

(*sic*) (1992; Regal Films/Ko Chi Sum Films Co.) ★: 6/10. *Wong Fei-hung siu chuen* (Cantonese), *Huang Feihong xiao zhuan* (Mandarin): "The Comic Legend of Wong Fei-hong." Cinematographer: Kin Lee Kin-keung; Art Director: Raymond Chan Kam-ho; Music: Mark Lui Chung-tak; Writers: Vincent Kok Tak-chiu, Lee Lik-chi; Producers: Clifton Ko Chi-sum, Ronny Yu Yan-tai; Action Director: Tony Leung Siu-hung; Director: Lee Lik-chi. Cast: Alan Tam Wing-lun (Wong Fei-hung), Tony Leung Kar-fai ("Bad Egg" Ken Shek), Simon Yam Tat-wah (Leung Foon), Eric Tsang Chi-wai (Porky Wing), Ng Man-tat (So), Teresa Mo Shun-kwan (Aunt Yee Siu-dim), Charine Chan Kar-ling (Yu-fa), Paul Fonoroff (Indiana Jones). 1.85:1. VHS: Tai Seng. Import LD/VCD: Star Entertainment (No Subtitles). 93 minutes.

As the English title suggests, this broad farce was inspired by Tsui Hark's popular **Once Upon a Time in China** films. In contrast to Jet Li's learned martial arts master, the Wong Fei-hung depicted here is a bumbling fool who is incapable of healing anyone or performing even the simplest kung fu. In fact, outside of cooking, he is completely useless. However, the common people are unaware of this, thanks to the diligent efforts of his assistants, So, Leung Foon, and Porky Wing. Wong's prime adversary, "Bad Egg" Ken Shek, enters into an alliance with evil businessman Indiana Jones(!), who supplies him with a powerful form of opium. Meanwhile, Aunt Yee arrives at Po Chi Lam clinic with the intention of marrying Fei-hung in order to use his wealth to help out her debt-ridden family. When Shek challenges him to a public duel, Fei-hung must rely on his other skills, in order to prevail.

The comedy consists largely of mugging, pratfalls, and all manner of other physical and scatological gags, so subtlety and invention are in very short supply (would you believe an *AIDS* joke?); but those who are familiar with the subjects and characters being skewered should find the proceedings entertaining. The production values are first rate (better, in fact, than some of the serious kung fu films of that year), and the film has an infectious energy that helps to make up for the gags that fall flat. Besides, how often do you get to see Simon Yam in a period film or Eric Tsang playing a kung fu master? Composer Mark Lui has fun updating and rearranging "The General's Orders" and the other familiar themes heard in the classics of the genre. Co-writer Vincent Kok and veteran kung fu star Shih Kien have cameos. A sequel, **Master Wong vs. Master Wong**, followed the next year.

724. Once Upon a Time in a Triad Society

(1996; Concept Link Productions/ Uni Film Production Co.) ★: 8/10. *Wong kok cha FIT yan* (Cantonese), *Wang jiao zha FIT ren* (Mandarin): "Mongkok's Man in Charge." Cinematographer: Peter Ngor Chi-kwan; Art Director: Vincent Lam Wai-sam; Music: Johnny Njo; Writer: Chung Kai-cheung; Producers: Cha Chuen-yee, Chung Kai-cheung, William Wu Shing; Action Director: Ridley Tsui Bo-wah; Director: Cha Chuen-yee. Cast: Francis Ng Chun-yu (Kwan), Loletta Lee Lai-chun ("Restaurant"/"Cart Noodle"), Spencer Lam Sheung-yee (Sheung-yee), Michael Chan Wai-man (Lone), Jamie Luk Kim-ming (Officer Lam), Pauline Chan Po-lin (Nurse), Farini Cheung Yui-ling (Tailor's Daughter). 1.85:1. VHS/LD: World Video. Import LD/VCD: Mei Ah. 95 minutes.

One of the first **Young and Dangerous** ripoffs, this is a smart, atypical effort anchored by Francis Ng's assured and amusing performance as Kwan, one of the most evil (yet likeable) gangsters in HK movie history. After falling victim to an assassin's bullet, Kwan lies dying in a hospital, with no one in any hurry to save him. Before passing on to the great hereafter, he narrates a journey through his life, beginning in childhood when he was recruited by junkie boss Sheung-yee. After being sold out by Sheung-yee to the police, Kwan switches his allegiance to rival boss Brother Lone, only to be betrayed again. Relocating to Japan, Kwan puts his nose to the grindstone, opens a food stall, and marries his dream girl, only to have his past catch up with him. His wife's subsequent murder prompts Kwan to swear that he will be the most ruthless triad who ever walked the earth.

The above synopsis actually represents only a small portion of the events presented; to reveal any more would undermine one of the film's cleverest narrative devices. Stylish and hip but not oppressively so, **Once Upon a Time** plays with the conventions of the *goo wak jai* genre in an exceedingly clever way, delivering all that is required while also inverting audience sympathies and expectations. The use of *cha* with the English word "FIT" in the Chinese title is Cantonese slang for "being in charge," though such a statement is generally used only in a gangster context. As is often the case with this type of production, some dialogue (coarse language and triad slang) has been bleeped by HK censors. The unrelated **Once Upon a Time in a Triad Society 2** (which reunites Ng and director Cha Chuen-yee) appeared in theaters almost immediately after this one.

725. Once Upon a Time in a Triad Society 2

(1996; Mandarin Films/Concept Link Productions) ★: 8/10. *Hui ba! Ja FIT yan bing tuen* (Cantonese), *Qu ba! zha FIT ren bing tuan* (Mandarin): "Let's Go! Man in Charge Brigade." Cinematographer: Ko Chiu-lam; Art Director: Vincent Lam Wai-sam; Music: Johnny Yeung Kei-cheung; Writer: Chung Kai-cheung; Producers: Cha Chuen-yee, Chung Kai-cheung; Action Director: Ridley Tsui Bo-wah; Director: Cha Chuen-yee. Cast: Francis Ng Chun-yu (Dagger), Roy Cheung Yiu-yeung (Dinosaur), Cheung Tat-ming (Dummy), Ivy Leung Si man (JJ), Ada Choi Siu-fan (Deda), Angie Cheung Wai-yee (Crystal). VHS: Tai Seng. Import LD/VCD: Fitto Mobile. 91 minutes.

While it bears no direct connection to the original, this serio-comic *goo wak jai* entry is every bit as interesting and a welcome change of pace. A big meeting between two rival gangs and the threat of possible bloodletting form the basis of the story, which is presented from the point of view of three characters: Dagger, a low-rent pimp who is much too nice to succeed at his chosen profession; Dinosaur, a swaggering (but sensitive) ganglord wanna-be with an inexperienced crew, who is desperate to get into a rumble...*any rumble*; and Dummy, a harried anti-triad officer who is just trying to do his job without completely alienating his better half. Although negotiations between the gangs avert a battle, the cowardly Dagger accidentally starts a fight which escalates into a full scale riot.

The aftermath of this violence is presented with a refreshing and disturbing realism that goes against the very grain of these films, and that is but one element that distinguishes this entry. The characters are amusingly quirky, the performances are right on target (with Ng doing an especially amusing inversion of his characters from both the original and **Young and Dangerous**), and the sheer invention and experimentation on display (in a genre that was not even a year old) is a joy to behold, making both this and its predecessor more interesting and entertaining than any of the entries in the higher profile **Young and Dangerous** series. Unfortunately, as of this writing, nothing else in Cha Chuen-yee's filmography comes close to the aptitude he displays on **Triad Society 1** & 2, both as a writer and as a director.

726. Once Upon a Time in China

(1991; Golden Harvest/Film Workshop/Paragon Films) ★: 7/10. *Wong Fei-hung* (Cantonese), *Huang Feihong* (Mandarin): "Wong Fei-hung" or "Huang Feihong." Cinematographers: David Chung Chi-man, Bill Wong Chung-bo, Arthur Wong Ngok-tai, Ardy Lam Kwok-wah, Chan Tung-chuen, Wilson Chan Pui-kai; Art Director: Hai Chung-man; Music: James Wong Jim; Writers: Tsui Hark, Yuen Kai-chi, Edward Leung Yiu-ming, Elsa Tang Pik-yin; Action Directors: Yuen Cheung-yan, Yuen Shun-yee, Lau Kar-wing; Producer-Director: Tsui Hark. Cast: Jet Li Lianjie (Wong Fei-hung), Rosamund Kwan Chi-lam (Aunt Yee), Yuen Biao (Leung Foon), Kent Cheng Chuk-see (Porky Wing), Jacky Cheung Hok-yau (Buck Teeth So), Yuen Kam-fai (Kai), Yam Sai-kwoon (Yim), Wong Chi-yeung (Commander Man), Jonathan James Isgar (Jackson), Lau Shun (Naval Commander), Wu Ma (Old Man), Yuen Cheung-yan (Yim's Opponent), Yuen Shun-yee (Honorable Manchu Soldier). Stereo Sound (LD & China Star DVD only), Dolby Digital (Mega Star DVD only). 2.35:1. VHS: Tai Seng (No Subtitles). Import LD/VCD: Star Entertainment (No Subtitles). Import VCD: Mega Star. Import DVD: China Star (No Subtitles), Mega Star. 112/134 minutes.

The premiere entry in Tsui Hark's popular and influential period kung fu series finds China on the verge of being overrun by foreigners out to make their fortune. When extortionists from Shaho make trouble for local businesses, Wong Fei-hung's city militia is blamed for the damage they cause while battling the criminals. As a result, the militia is taken into custody, prompting Fei-hung to begin his own campaign against the undesirable elements (local and foreign) taking advantage of the people. The Shaho brigands proceed to burn down Po Chi Lam clinic, but the act is witnessed by a Jesuit Priest who offers to testify on Fei-hung's behalf when Manchu official Commander Man deems the blaze to be the result of triad warfare instigated by Fei-hung and his followers (who include Rosamund Kwan as "Aunt Yee," Jacky Cheung as "Buck Teeth So," Yuen Kam-fai as "Kai," and Kent Cheng as Lam Sai-wing, aka "Butcher Wing"). Unfortunately, the priest is murdered by a man working for Jackson, an American scoundrel in league with the Shaho men. After much frustration and death, Fei-hung comes to realize that, like it or not, he and China will have to adapt in order to fight back successfully. In the meantime, another threat arises in the form of penniless kung fu master "Iron Vest" Yim, who decides that the quickest way to prosperity is to challenge and defeat the region's best fighter: Fei-hung.

The opening third takes too long to focus, and all but one of the foreign characters are ridiculous caricatures scarcely more believable than the yellowface performers in the Hollywood movies of the '30s and '40s (their dialogue consists mostly of gems like, "Who is this Wong Fei-hung?! The Devil?"). Fortunately, Tsui and his six (count 'em, *six*) cinematographers are able to inject a great deal of picturesque beauty into the proceedings, and the subtle, character-driven moments go a long way in making the story (with its potentially confusing army of supporting characters and villains) more involving. The major attraction, of course, is Jet Li and the spectacular martial arts setpieces. The highlight is unquestionably the climactic battle between Fei-hung and Yim in a storage facility, which finds the combatants using ladders to battle around and above just about every inch of the place and its contents. The one disappointment, performance-wise, is Yuen Biao, who is not able to do all that much with his secondary, largely comic role of bumbling opera performer Leung Foon, who seeks to follow Master Wong but mistakenly takes up with Yim instead (apparently not thrilled by the prospect of playing second fiddle again to Jet Li, Yuen passed on reprising the role and was replaced in the subsequent sequels and TV miniseries by Max Mok Siu-chung). Most HK prints run 112 minutes, but the Taiwan edition and the Mega Star DVD offer the longer cut.

727. Once Upon a Time in China II

(1992; Golden Harvest/Film Workshop/Paragon Films) ★: 8/10. *Wong Fei-hung ji yi naam yi dong ji keung* (Cantonese), *Huang Feihong zhi er nan er dang zi qiang* (Mandarin): "Wong Fei-hung II: A Man Should Be Self-Sufficient." Cinematographer: Arthur Wong Ngok-tai; Art Director: Eddie Ma Poon-chiu; Music: Richard Yuen Cheuk-fan, Johnny Njo; Writers: Tsui Hark, Chan Tin-suen, Charcoal Cheung Tan; Producers: Tsui Hark, Ng See-yuen; Action Director: Yuen Woo-ping; Director: Tsui Hark. Cast: Jet Li Lianjie (Wong Fei-hung), Rosamund Kwan Chi-lam (Siu-qun, aka Aunt Yee), Max Mok Siu-chung (Leung Foon), Donnie Yen Chi-tan (Lan), David Chiang Da-wei (Luke), Xiong Xinxin (Priest Kung), Yam Sai-kwoon (The Governor), William Ho Kar-kui (Mak), Paul Fonoroff (British Consul). Stereo Sound (Laserdisc only), Dolby Digital (DVD only). 2.35:1. VHS: Tai Seng (No Subtitles). Import LD/VCD: Star Entertainment (No Subtitles). Import VCD/DVD: Mega Star. 112 minutes.

Arguably the best of the series, **Once Upon a Time in China II** finds a group of xenophobic fanatics called The White Lotus Cult viciously attacking and murdering all of the foreigners in Canton. Catching a glimpse of Aunt Yee and her Western attire, they try to burn her alive, but Fei-hung successfully intervenes. His actions, however, place him at the top of the cult's enemy list. The Manchurian authorities are battling the sect (in order to appease their British allies) while also tracking down Sun Yat-sen and his followers, including Luke, who is the group's money man. When the Manchu Commander Lan discovers that Luke has taken refuge in the British Embassy (along with Fei-hung, his friends, and some children displaced by the cult), he demands that the rebel be turned over. When the British consul refuses to permit him entry, Lan allows the cult to invade the building and slaughter most of the inhabitants. Deciding that the best way to destroy The White Lotus is from the inside, Fei-hung and Luke pretend to join up with them, allowing the former to battle High Priest Kung. However, a final duel with kung fu master Lan also awaits Fei-hung.

The last reel is virtually non-stop martial arts combat, and Li's individual battles with Xiong Xinxin (who would go on to appear in part **III** as a different character) and Donnie Yen are exciting displays of both natural physical prowess and wire-enhanced dexterity. Like its forerunner, **II** features scenes of idyllic beauty, but here they are juxtaposed with images of horror and death, creating an effective contrast. However, too much time is spent on the developing love between Fei-hung and Yee, a subplot that never goes anywhere (even in later entries) and adds nothing to the development of either character. Taiwan prints open with a 7 minute recap of the original's climax (which must have confused audiences, because Yam Sai-kwoon turns up in this film as a different character) and run 125 minutes.

728. Once Upon a Time in China III

(1993; Golden Harvest/Film Workshop/Paragon Films) ★: 5/10. *Wong Fei-hung ji saam si wong jaang ba* (Cantonese), *Huang Feihong zhi san shi wang zheng ba* (Mandarin): "Wong Fei-hung III: The Lion King Struggles for Supremacy." Cinematographer: Andrew Lau Wai-keung; Art Director: Timmy Yip Kam-tin; Music: William Woo Wai-lap, Tsui Hark; Writers: Tsui Hark, Charcoal Cheung Tan; Producers: Tsui Hark, Ng See-yuen; Action Director: Yuen Tak; Director: Tsui Hark. Cast: Jet Li Lianjie (Wong Fei-hung), Rosamund Kwan Chi-lam (Peony, aka Aunt Yee), Max Mok Siu-chung (Leung Foon), Lau Shun (Wong Kei-ying), Xiong Xinxin (Club Foot), John Wakefield (Tomansky). Dolby Stereo, Dolby Digital (DVD only). 2.35:1. VHS: Tai Seng. Import LD/VCD: Mei Ah. Import VCD/DVD: Mega Star. 111 minutes.

The series began to decline with **Once Upon a Time in China III**, which suffers from an uninspired storyline and slack pacing but does introduce a memorable new regular to the fold. The story this time revolves around a large scale "Lion King Competition" which inadvertently results in all manner of violence between the competing martial arts schools, even before the match gets under way. Fei-hung faces a formidable new adversary in the form of master kicker Club Foot, whose boss is determined to win the contest at whatever cost.

If you are a fan of lion dance exhibitions, this is the movie for you! While this Chinese art can be quite exciting and impressive onscreen (see **Dreadnaught**, for example), there is so much of it here (and so many *lions*), it soon grows redundant and dull. Another problem is that the most memorable fight (a wild skirmish which finds Fei-hung battling hatchet-throwing and sword-wielding opponents while sliding around on an oil-slicked floor) comes in the middle third, and the lack of a strong principal villain merely adds to the torpor of the final act. A good portion of the running time is devoted to the jealousy Fei-hung feels towards a Russian nobleman (part of a secret plot to assassinate the Chinese president, as the lead-in to a foreign takeover of China) who is an old acquaintance of Yee and obviously has deep feelings for her. Li and Kwan just don't click as a screen couple, and while Tsui does his best to kindle sparks between them, their cutesy romantic asides border on the embarrassing this time. The best thing about the film is Xiong Xinxin, who gives a preview of the Tasmanian Devil-like whirlwind he would play later on in Tsui's **The Blade**, and possesses far more vigour on his own than this film does as a whole. Jet Li left the series after this entry because of a salary dispute. Defecting from Golden Harvest over to Win's Entertainment, he would instead play Wong Fei-hung in Wong Jing's **Last Hero in China**. Zhao Wenzhou would take his place for the next two **Once Upon a Time** films, with Li returning to the fold for 1997's **Once Upon a Time in China and America**.

729. Once Upon a Time in China IV

(1993; Golden Harvest/Film Workshop/Paragon Films) ★: 4/10. *Wong Fei-hung ji IV wong je ji fung* (Cantonese), *Huang Feihong zhi IV wang zhe zhi feng* (Mandarin): "Wong Fei-hung IV: Royal Demeanor." Cinematographers: Ko Chiu-lam, Arthur Wong Ngok-tai; Art Director: Raymond Lee King-man; Music: William Woo Wai-lap; Writers: Tsui Hark, Elsa Tang Pik-yin; Producers: Tsui Hark, Ng See-yuen; Action Directors: Xiong Xinxin, Cheung Ping-chuen; Director: Yuen Bun. Cast: Zhao Wenzhou (Wong Fei-hung), Jean Wang Ching-ying (Aunt May), Max Mok Siu-chung (Leong Fu), Xiong Xinxin (Clubfoot), Lau Shun (Wong Kei-ying), Chin Kar-lok (Lui), Billy Chow Bei-lee (Lui's Man), Louis Roth (Priest). 2.35:1. VHS: Tai Seng (No Subtitles). Import LD/VCD: Star Entertainment (No Subtitles). Import DVD: China Star. 101 minutes.

Entry number four in the series serves up a new Wong Fei-hung (Zhao Wenzhou, replacing Jet Li), a new female lead (Jean Wang, replacing Rosamund Kwan), and a new director (veteran action coordinator Yuen Bun, replacing Tsui Hark). The result is dull, graceless, and easily the weakest chapter to date. This time out, eight countries (including America and Germany) challenge China to a lion dance competition, utilizing elaborate animal contraptions of their own. While saving some foreigners from the xenophobic Red Lantern cult, Fei-hung is mistakenly arrested and sentenced to death. Aided by a compassionate priest, he is able to escape but must survive an elaborate series of Red Lantern combat trials in order to save his father and friends. Arriving late to the competition, Fei-hung is unable to aid his confederates and challenges the international teams to a second, decisive match that will allow him to properly defend his country's honor.

As with the last entry, the lion dance competitions grow wearisome through repetition (the animals may be different but the combat is essentially unchanged), and the martial arts sequences are so over-edited it is difficult to appreciate anyone's abilities. The Red Lantern faction (who are little different from The White Lotus Cult in part **II**) and the various Caucasian armies are dull, one-note adversaries, and Yuen's direction is equally unimaginative. Zhao Wenzhou makes for an adequate Fei-hung, though he does not seem entirely comfortable in the role. As Aunt Yee's equally Westernized sister, May, Jean Wang is given virtually nothing to do, other than look lovely and concerned.

730. Once Upon a Time in China V

(1994; Golden Harvest/Film Workshop/Paragon Films) ★: 6/10. *Wong Fei-hung chi neung lung shing chim ang* (Cantonese), *Huang Feihong zhi wu long cheng jian ba* (Mandarin): "Wong Fei-hung V: Dragon City's Murderous Tyrant." Cinematographers: Ko Chiu-lam, Tom Lau Moon-tong, Peter Pau Tak-hei, Derek Wan Man-kit; Art Director: Bill Lui Cho-hung; Writers: Tsui Hark, Lau Tai-muk, Lam Kei-to; Action Director: Yuen Bun; Music-Producer-Director: Tsui Hark. Cast: Zhao Wenzhou (Wong Fei-hung), Rosamund Kwan Chi-lam (Aunt Yee), Max Mok Siu-chung (Fu), Kent Cheng Chuk-see (Butcher Wing), Xiong Xinxin (Clubfoot), Jean Wang Ching-ying (May), Roger Kwok Chun-on (Bucktooth), Elaine Lui Siu-ling (Ying). 2.35:1. VHS: Tai Seng. Import LD/VCD: Universe. 101 minutes.

Tsui Hark returned to the director's chair for this fifth chapter, which is a decided improvement over its immediate predecessor but not in the same league as the opening two chapters. This time out, Wong Fei-hung and his followers (including Kent Cheng's "Butcher Wing," not seen since the original film) come to the aid of some rice farmers who are being terrorized by a brigade of pirates.

The action scenes are rousing and the production design is eye-popping, with the pirates' treasure-laden headquarters looking particularly impressive. The addition of gunplay is an inspired idea, allowing the film to take on an offbeat, spaghetti western-style aura. Fei-hung's romantic travails with Yee and May are brought more into focus here but, naturally, are left up in the air at the conclusion. The regulars all do good work, and newcomer Elaine Lui (**Angel**) is a standout as Ying, the one-eyed pirate queen, duelling with Fei-hung one on one but receiving relatively little screen time overall. While certainly worth seeing, this entry still seems a bit mechanical and half-hearted, and its poor box office take caused the series to move to television for a miniseries featuring several of the same cast members. The theatrical series resumed in 1997 with **Once Upon a Time in China and America**, which found Jet Li Lianjie back in the role of Fei-hung.

731. Once Upon a Time in China and America

(1997; Win's Entertainment) ★: 5/10. *Wong Fei-hung chi sai wik hung shut* (Cantonese), *Huang Feihong zhi xi yu xiong shi* (Mandarin): "Wong Fei-hung: West Territory Mighty Lion." Cinematographer: Walter Gregg; Art Director: Horace Ma Kwong-wing; Music: Lowell Lo Kwunting; Writers: Sharun Hui Sa-long, Sze Mei-yee, Roy Szeto Cheuk-hon, So Mansing, Philip Kwok Wai-chong; Producer: Tsui Hark; Action Director-Director: Sammo Hung Kam-po. Cast: Jet Li Lianjie (Wong Fei-hung), Rosamund Kwan Chi-lam (Aunt Yee), Xiong Xinxin (Seven), Chan Kwok-bong (Sol), Jeff Wolfe (Billy), Richard Ng Yiu-hon (Han). 2.35:1. VHS/LD: Tai Seng. Import LD/VCD/DVD: Carnival. 99 minutes.

After sitting out the fourth and fifth instalments, Jet Li returned to his signature role of martial arts master "Wong Fei-hung" for this kung fu western lensed mostly in Texas. Visiting America to inspect the new branch of Po Chi Lam clinic established by Sol, the wagon train carrying Fei-hung, Yee, and Seven (known in previous entries as "Clubfoot") is attacked by Indians. Fleeing from the carnage, the three are swept down a raging river, with Fei-hung suffering a blow to his head. Separated from his friends and rescued by a tribe of Indians, Fei-hung discovers that he has lost his memory but not his tremendous fighting skills. After Seven is finally able to jog his master's memory (thanks to a pitched recreation of Fei-hung's greatest duel), the Chinese community of workers finds itself with a serious problem: They have been framed for a bank robbery by the racist mayor and his bandit cohorts (their leader certainly knows a lot of kung fu for a 19th century cowboy!). Unless seven of them confess and agree to be hanged, all of them will be put to death.

A project designed to score in both Eastern and Western markets (a key role was reportedly intended for *Quentin Tarantino*!), the film did very well in HK but failed to find a distributor in Hollywood. That can partially be attributed to both political correctness (the majority of the Indians are obviously played by white performers, and their dialogue and mannerisms are right out of an old Randolph Scott movie) and sub-Hollywood production values (the Western town set looks like the corner of a theme park). There is also the larger question of perspective: For aficionados, this is a chance to see old favorites going through their paces in a novel setting; for the uninitiated, this is a sloppy and cliched oater from a bizarre, parallel universe. Aside from Jeff Wolfe (as a young upstart gunslinger who remains loyal to Fei-hung after the latter saves his life), the Caucasian actors are embarrassingly bad and certainly no better than the ones who regularly turn up in HK productions. More enjoyable as an oddity (it is not everyday that one can see *cowboy fu*, undercranked gunfights, and Jet Li sporting braids and warpaint!) than as a continuation of the original story and characters, **Once Upon a Time in China and America** is entertaining as far as it goes but still emerges as another step in the wrong direction for the series.

The One Eyebrow Priest *see* **Vampire vs. Vampire**

732. 100 Ways to Murder Your Wife

(1986; Golden Harvest/Go Go Film Productions Co.) ★: 5/10. *Saai chai yee yan cho* (Cantonese), *Sha qi er ren zu* (Mandarin): "Two-Person Wife-Murdering Group." Cinematographer: Jimmy Leung Chi-ming; Art Director: William Szeto Wai-yung; Writer: Alex Law Kar-yui; Producer: Mona Fong Yat-wah; Music-Director: Kenny Bee. Cast: Chow Yun-fat (Fa), Joey Wang Tsu-hsien (Wang Hsiao-hsien), Kenny Bee (Roberto), Anita Mui Yim-fong (Anita), Wong Jing (Wang), Wu Ma (Bathroom Attendant), Anthony Chan Yau (Chen Chih-tao), Shing Fui-on (Soccer Player). 1.85:1. VHS: Tai Seng. Import VCD: Universe. 91 minutes.

Unabashedly sexist in a 1960s sort of way, this intermittently amusing comedy concerns the travails of miserable soccer players Football Fa and Roberto. Fa is convinced that his wife Hsiao-hsien is cheating on him, while Roberto is tired of the relentless nagging from his wife Anita. One evening, while drinking, the men promise to murder each others' spouses, *á la* Hitchcock's **Strangers on a Train**. When Fa is too drunk to murder Anita, he passes out and she disappears. Assuming that she is dead, Roberto feels honor-bound to complete his end of the bargain but can't bring himself to kill Hsiao-hsien. Thanks to further miscommunication, Fa thinks Roberto has seduced Hsiao-hsien, and Anita thinks that Roberto is cheating on her. When Anita returns home, Roberto thinks she's a ghost come back to torment him but presses on with his promise to do in Hsiao-hsien, collaborating with Fa on some outrageous booby traps involving piranhas, "ice darts," and a hidden blade.

Too formula-bound to be more than passably interesting, this minor farce benefits greatly from Chow Yun-fat's amusingly over-the-top performance. His enthusiasm is infectious and helps one to temporarily forget just how hackneyed the material is. The film was produced by Shaw Brothers but was sold to Golden Harvest as part of a package deal.

733. One Husband Too Many

(1988; Golden Harvest/Paragon Films) ★: 4/10. *Yat chai leung foo* (Cantonese), *Yi qi liang fu* (Mandarin): "One Wife, Two Husbands." Cinematographer: Peter Ngor Chi-kwan; Art Director: William Szeto Wai-yung; Music: Richard Yuen Cheuk-fan; Writers: Alex Law Kai-yui, Alfred Cheung Kin-ting; Producer: Sammo Hung Kam-po; Director: Anthony Chan Yau. Cast: Kenny Bee (Hui Anhua), Cherie Chung Cho-hung (Frances), Anthony Chan Yau (Hsia Chih-hsin), Pat Ha Man-chik (Wellcome), Anita Mui Yim-fong (Park), Michael Chan Wai-man (Elephant), Bolo Yeung (Muscleman). 1.85:1. VHS: Tai Seng (No Subtitles). Import VCD: Mega Star. 87 minutes.

A good cast struggles in vain to keep this strained romantic comedy afloat. Chih-hsin is an inept amateur actor whose love of the theater and lack of success finally proves too much for his wife Park, who leaves him and his debts behind. Needing a place to stay, he looks up with his old pal An-hua, but arrives to find that *his* wife (who used to be married to Chih-hsin) is walking out on *him*. In a series of tired vignettes, the two now-single men wail and complain endlessly, but soon become infatuated with the same girl: Frances, the beautiful make-up artist of Chih-hsin's theater troupe. After getting drunk, Chih-hsin and Frances end up in bed together, but she really only has eyes for An-hua, leading Chih-hsin to try and sabotage their relationship.

There are a couple of amusing bits of physical humor, but this is awfully trite material, unworthy of these performers' talents. The screenplay does deserve credit for serving up an ending that one does not usually encounter with this sort of fare, but it is really not any more satisfying than a conventional wrap-up. The title on the Mega Star VCD packaging is **One Husband Two Many** (*sic*).

734. 1/3 Lover

(1993; Champion Chart Film Production) ★: 4/10. *1/3 ching yan* (Cantonese), *1/3 qing ren* (Mandarin): "1/3

Lover." Cinematographer: Wong Chit; Art Director: Law Siu-ping; Music: Gun Tung Dung Jut (Cantonese name of Japanese artist); Producer: Yukari Oshima; Director: Wong Chun-yeung. Cast: Rena Murakami (Mona Hsia), Yukari Oshima (Lin), Wu Ma (Chen), Mark Cheng Ho-nam (Doctor), Lily Lee Li-li (Lily), Yung Sai-kit (Man in Opening Scene). 1.85:1. VHS: Tai Seng. Import LD/VCD: Ocean Shores. 85 minutes.

Japanese porn star Rena Murakami (**Sex and Zen, Escape from Brothel** [*sic*]) toplines this trashy Category III yarn as the scheming young Mona, who apparently plans on sending her elderly husband Hwang Fei-hung(!), to his grave by repeatedly turning him on until his ticker finally gives out. Mona is actually under the thumb of a corrupt policeman who knows that she murdered a loan shark) and orders her to supply him with a steady stream of hubby's cash or face prosecution. The girl has other plans, however, and when the old man finally kicks the bucket, the now-rich Mona decides to flee from HK with Fei-hung's handsome young godson. Naturally, fate intercedes.

Aside from some unpleasant sexual violence, the erotic content isn't bad, but even as these films go, the story is threadbare nonsense, and a couple of the main performances are outrageously bad. In a novel bit of casting, the film's producer, Yukari Oshima (best known for her tough girl martial arts roles in movies like **Angel**), plays a homely, comic-relief maid named *Lin Ching-hsia*!

735. Only Fools Fall in Love

(1995; Win's Entertainment) ★: 6/10. *Ngoi lo baai sau* (Cantonese), *Dai lao bai shou* (Mandarin): "Dumb Guys Greets Birthday." Cinematographer: Poon Hang-sang; Art Director: Bruce Yu Kar-on; Music: Healthy Poon Kin-hong, Cacine Wong Kar-sin; Writers: Erica Lee Man, Vincent Kok Tak-chiu; Producer: Johnny To Kei-fung; Director: Vincent Kok Tak-chiu. Cast: Lau Ching-wan (Chiu Ford), Jacqueline Wu Chien-lien (Mong Dee), Yuen Wah (Dee's Father), Dayo Wong Chi-wah (Chiu Jack), Jerry Lam Hiu-fung (Ford's Servant), Billy Lau Nam-kwong (Sha Sam), Roy Chiao Hung (Great Uncle), Vincent Kok Tak-chiu (Announcer in White), Wong Yat-fei (Wedding Official). 1.85:1. VHS/LD: Tai Seng. Import LD/VCD/DVD: Mei Ah. 102 minutes.

A pleasant romantic comedy-drama, this period film benefits immensely from the chemistry between Lau Ching-wan and Jacqueline Wu. Conceited genius Chiu Ford holds sway over the locals with his wealth and trickery. When his mother decides it is time for him to marry, Ford's opium-addicted brother, Jack, plots with conwoman Mong Dee to scam his sibling. On top of that, Jack also engineers an "accident" that causes Ford to receive a bad blow to the head which leaves him a babbling idiot. When Dee shows him some kindness, Ford (who is now a scraggly beggar, after being thrown out of the house by Jack) starts following her and won't leave the girl alone. After numerous attempts to get rid of him, Jack earns a place in the household by saving Dee's dad from a snake and becomes a great help with the family business. Naturally, Dee's affection for him grows, but Jack learns that Ford is still alive and sets about to change that, to ensure that he is officially named the head of the family.

While the plot offers no surprises, there are a number of solid laughs along the way and the leads are perfectly cast. Yuen Wah gives a wonderful comic turn as Dee's bumbling father and, after all these years, he is still a tremendous acrobat. All in all, *Only Fools Fall in Love* is a pleasurable film to be sure, though the gags about anachronisms would have been funnier if there weren't so many of them!

Operation Condor *see* **Armour of God II: Operation Condor**

Operation Condor 2: The Armour of the Gods *see* **The Armour of God**

736. Operation Pink Squad

(1988; Golden Flare Films) ★: 4/10. *Ba wong nui fuk sing* (Cantonese), *Ba wang nu fu xing* (Mandarin): "Tyrant King Female Lucky Stars." Cinematographer: Johnny Koo Kwok-wah; Art Director: Chan Wing-bo; Music: Danny Chung Teng-yat; Producer: Wong Hoi; Action Director: Yuen Cheung-yan; Writer-Director: Jeff Lau Chun-wai. Cast: Sandra Ng Kwan-yu (Ng Siu-mui), Ann Bridgewater (Plastic Flower), Sin Lap-man (Piu), Woo Fung (Wu), Elsie Chan Yik-si (Shy Grass), Suki Kwan Sau-mei (Dumb Female Cop), Lowell Lo Kwun-ting (Lovesick Cop), Billy Lau Nam-kwong (Big Nose), Yuen Cheung-yan (Tired-Out Triad), Helena Law Lan (Mrs. Wong), Ng Man-tat (Uncle Wong), Lam Chung (Kei), Charlie Cho Cha-lei (Cop Who Gets Transferred), Yee Lui (Thief at Airport), Ricky Hui Koon-ying (Dumb Ying), Melanie Barter (Diana), Jeff Lau Chun-wai (Airport Cop), Jeff Falcon (Caucasian Killer), Anna Strike (Superintendent's Wife). 1.85:1. VHS/LD: World Video. Import LD: Golden Flare. Import VCD: Panorama Entertainment. 92 minutes.

This uneven action-comedy starts off like gangbusters and then slows down considerably. Out to ruin a group of female detectives who have been constantly embarrassing him, Inspector Wu assigns them to watch over a suspect named Piu. Blind after being taken hostage and injured in a car accident, Piu is regarded as an accomplice by the police, even though they do not have any evidence with which to convict him. Ng Siu-mui, the nominal leader of the women, falls head-over-heels for Piu and pretends to also be blind so that she can gain his trust. Piu, however, knows it is all a ruse, but the razor-wielding female robber who kidnapped him isn't fooling around: She believes Piu has some diamonds that belong to her and threatens to kill him if they are not turned over post haste.

A slapdash blend of gunplay, kung fu, **Police Academy**-style humor, and conventional police thriller ingredients, **Operation Pink Squad** might have been passable had it stuck with just one genre. HK films often perform this sort of juggling act with amusing adroitness but the balls do not remain airborne for long here. The main storyline is predictable and uninteresting and the ping-ponging from jokes to drama and back again is akin to what one might experience during an evening of channel surfing. In regards to the comedy, only Suki Kwan (as a dimwitted cop whose mangled Cantonese drives everyone crazy) garners any real laughs and the best jokes in her scenes barely come across in the English translation. This was followed by an unrelated sequel.

737. Operation Pink Squad II

(1989; Golden Flare Films Co./First Distributors) ★: 7/10. *Maang gwai daai ha* (Cantonese), *Meng gui da sha* (Mandarin): "Fierce Ghost Large Mansion." Cinematographer: Johnny Koo Kwok-wah; Art Director: Raymond Lee King-man; Music: Danny Chung Teng-yat; Producer: Wong Hoi; Action Director: Yuen Cheung-yan; Writer-Director: Jeff Lau Chun-wai. Cast: Billy Lau Nam-kwong (Fat Cop), Sandra Ng Kwan-yu (Fat Cop's Wife), Sharla Cheung Man (Min), Ann Bridgewater (Anna), Suki Kwan Sau-mei (Dumb Policewoman), Woo Fung (Shin), Shing Fui-on (Maddy), Yuen Cheung-yan (The Monk), Helena Law Lan (The Old Woman), Charlie Cho Cha-lei (Man Beaten by Fat Cop), Cho Tat-wah (Buddhist God). 1.85:1. VHS/LD: World Video. Import LD: Golden Flare. Import VCD: Panorama Entertainment. 89 minutes.

Bearing no real connection to the original, save for the same director and some cast members, this is an amusing and energetically mounted horror comedy that is definitely the better of the two films. Four policewoman out to nail a gangster working for some Japanese counterfeiters have more than criminals to worry about: Their apartment building is located above one of the doorways to Hell! A monk manages to capture several dozen of the structure's ghosts and seals them inside the door, but one particularly vicious female spirit manages to evade him. The spectre proceeds to terrorize the women, two bumbling male cops, and their triad target for the rest of the evening. At one point, the spooked officers manage to decapitate the ghost with an axe...and then face attack from both the body *and* the severed head (which can fly around on its own)! Eventually, the police come up with the perfect weapon to take care of the head: a fleet of remote control helicopters armed with tiny missiles! The target is destroyed but more trouble awaits as the spirit unleashes a form of supernatural revenge that attracts all of the region's spooks to the building.

There is the usual plethora of sexual gags, and ample use is made of the blue-tinted lighting found in just about all HK horror films. However, every component here is presented with just a bit more ingenuity than usual, from the horror-oriented sight gags to a terrific spoof of **A Better Tomorrow**'s "gun planting" sequence. The result is one of the best entries to be found in the "Police Academy Meets the Monsters" subgenre inaugurated by director Jeff Lau's **Haunted Cop Shop** films. Lau also makes a brief cameo appearance. A nominal sequel (**Here Comes a Vampire**) and several similar features followed.

738. Operation Scorpio

(1992; Golden Harvest/Bo Ho Films Co./Paragon Films) ★: 7/10. *Kit ji jin si* (Cantonese), *Jie zi zhan shi* (Mandarin): "Deer Skin Soldier." Cinematographers: Wong Po-man, Tsang Chi-chung; Art Director: David Chan Chi-wai; Music: Violet Lam Man-yee; Writers: David Chan Chi-wai, Barry Wong Ping-yiu, Lui Sau-fung; Producer: Chan Pui-wah; Action Director: Yuen Tak; Director: David Lai Tai-wai. Cast: Chin Kar-lok (Fei Yu-shu), Lau Kar-leung (Uncle Yi), May Lo Mei-mei (Hsiao-ju), Yuen Jeung (Sunny), Woo Fung (Uncle Chai), Victor Hon Kwan (Wang), Frankie Chin Chi-leung (Jean Pol), Yuen Shun-yee (Inspector Hua). 1.85:1. VHS: Tai Seng (No Subtitles). Import LD: Star Entertainment (No Subtitles). 99 minutes.

An enjoyable period kung fu thriller, **Operation Scorpio** is set in 1920 and concerns the adventures of daydreaming student Fei Yu-shu. A talented comic book artist bored by school, Fei is constantly in trouble and on the verge of being expelled. One evening he rescues timid maid Hsiao-ju from being sold into prostitution by Wang, her evil, flesh merchant master. Fei's father sends the youth to live with his Uncle Yi and work in the latter's noodle shop. In between his sessions in the kitchen, Fei also receives instruction in strength and power from the musclebound health guru Jean Pol and (after Wang's goons trash the restaurant) martial arts training from Yi. This leaves him ready to put an end to Wang's criminal operations, with a little help from his two mentors.

The portion of the story devoted to Jean Pol and his non-stop flexing is unintentionally amusing (not to mention anachronistic), and when all is said and done, the film is really only a slight variation on the shopworn "eager but undisciplined student trained by wizened master" formula. Regardless, the kung fu is terrific, and Korean martial arts champ Yuen Jeung is outstanding as Wang's equally villainous son. Unbelievably agile, he practices a wild scorpion style of combat, using his left leg as the "stinger," that is amazing to behold. The opportunity to see him and the great Lau Kar-leung in battle more than compensates for many of the film's weaker aspects. The Taiwanese video release has subtitles.

739. Option Zero

(1997; Media Asia Films/People's Productions) ★: 3/10. *G4 dak gung* (Cantonese), *G4 te gong* (Mandarin): "G4 Special Agents." Cinematographer: Horace Wong Wing-hang; Art Director: Alfred Yau Wai-ming; Music: Shigeru Umebayashi; Writer: Chan Hing-ka; Producers: Gordon Chan Kar-seung, John Chong Ching; Action Director: Chin Kar-lok; Director: Dante Lam Chiu-yin. Cast: Julian Cheung Chi-lam (Ben), Carman Lee Yeuk-tung (Kelly), Monica Chan Fat-yung (Monica Leung), Anthony Wong Chau-sang (Sing), Farini Cheung Yui-ling (Grace), Lan Sai (Nancy), Michael Wong Man-tak (G4 Trainer). Dolby Digital. 1.85:1. VHS: Tai Seng. Import LD/VCD/DVD: Mega Star. 109 minutes.

Set one month before the handover, this extremely disappointing entry is another of producer Gordon Chan's high-tech police thrillers, but it's a big step down from its predecessors, **The Final Option** and **First Option**. Even at its most involved, **Option Zero** never comes close to stirring one's emotions or challenging expectations. After a while, it even has trouble maintaining viewer interest. The main plotline concerns Special Branch operatives' investigation of a Korean gang that has been building up a large arsenal of weapons. When one of the team is killed in the line of duty, S.B. is dissolved and the former members apply to be in G4, a sort of elite bodyguard service. Naturally, those very same arms dealers later attempt to assassinate a client under the protection of G4.

The various action sequences are undistinguished, and the characters and their dramatic conflicts (strained relationships brought on by work-related stress, and a possible love triangle between protagonist Ben, his girlfriend, and Ben's female co-worker) are far from gripping. The climax is so ineptly blocked and berserkly edited, it is all but incomprehensible.

740. Organized Crime and Triad Bureau

(1994; Magnum) ★: 7/10. *Chung ngon sat luk O gei* (Cantonese), *Chong an shi lu O ji* (Mandarin): "True Record of Important Case: Department O." Cinematographers: Joe Chan Kong-hung, Horace Wong Wing-hang; Art Director: Jon Hau Wing-choi; Music: Wong Bong; Writer: Lu Bing; Producers: Che-Kirk Wong Chi-keung, Danny Lee Sau-yin; Action Director: James Ha Chim-see; Director: Che-Kirk Wong Chi-keung. Cast: Danny Lee Sau-yin (Lee), Cecilia Yip Tung (Cindy), Anthony Wong Chau-sang (Tung), Elizabeth Lee Mei-fung (Anna), Roy Cheung Yiu-yeung (Chiu), Ricky Yee Fan-wai (Lam), Parkman Wong Pak-man ("Moustache"), Fan Siu-wong (Tak), Li Fai (Female Cop), Eric Kei Kar-fat (Lin). 1.85:1. VHS/LD/DVD: Tai Seng (Remastered for the English market; subtitled or dubbed). 91 minutes.

Although it doesn't quite possess the bracing intensity of director Che-Kirk Wong's two other police procedurals from the period, **Crime Story** (1993) and **Rock 'n Roll Cop** (1994), this is a well-mounted, often exciting actioner which benefits from solid performances by its three leads, embodying their stock characters with laudable conviction. Obsessed with the capture of violent fugitive Tung and his mistress Cindy, O.C.T.B. leader Inspector Lee leads his team on a lengthy pursuit through Hong Kong to a small coastal island. Angered by the noise and police interference in their lives, the residents drive Lee's men off the island, allowing Tung and Cindy to escape. Complicating matters further are a turncoat cop, who is providing Tung with information by blackmailing Lee's debt-ridden girlfriend, and an overzealous Internal Affairs officer with a serious grudge against the bureau and its quasi-illegal procedures. The chase resumes in Wanchai, with the climactic shootout unfolding tautly amidst a huge traffic gridlock.

Those opposed to police brutality will be put off by the interrogation scenes (though they are not nearly as explicit as their counterparts in **The Untold Story** and **Twist**, two other Danny Lee productions), but Wong has a gritty, engaging style that draws one in, and Wong Bong's superior score gives the film added stature. Anthony Wong strayed over to the right side of the law the next year for the director's **Rock 'n Roll Cop**.

741. The Other 1/2 & the Other 1/2

(1988; D & B Films Co./Alan and Eric Films Co.) ★: 5/10. *Ngoh oi taai hung yan* (Cantonese), *Wo ai tai kong ren* (Mandarin): "I Love Astronaut." Cinematographer: Jingle Ma Cho-shing; Art Director: Fong Ying; Music: T and T; Writer: Eddie Fong Ling-ching; Producer: Teddy Robin Kwan; Director: Clara Law Cheuk-yiu. Cast: Tien Niu (June Lee), Kam Kwok-leung (Sam Cheung), Cora Miao Qian-ren (Connie), Eric Tsang Chi-wai (Tak), Law Ka, Fong Lai-chi. 1.85:1. VHS: Tai Seng. Import LD: Ocean Shores. Import VCD: Mega Star. 93 minutes.

With their mates on the other side of the world in Toronto, thirty something professionals June Lee and Sam Cheung share living accommodations back in HK. They both experience incredible problems at their jobs, and Sam finally blows his top and quits. Living together in such close proximity and separated from their better halves, the pair become more and more accustomed to one another and soon begin having trouble fighting off those natural urges. They finally succumb and sleep together, and when their respective spouses show up out of the blue, they run themselves ragged trying to keep everything a secret.

The storyline is based on a situation common to the time: One partner moved overseas in order to meet immigration requirements, while the other remained in HK to work. In order to save money, some did not see each other face-to-face literally for years on end and spoke only briefly over the phone. Tien Niu and Kam Kwok-leung both give very likeable performances and the occasional moment or gag rings true, but the majority of the film does not provoke a reaction one way or the other. It's consistently watchable but fails to take full advantage of the inherent comic and dramatic possibilities. The "astronaut" in the Chinese title was a term used to describe those who flew frequently between HK and Canada, the US, or Australia during the big immigration period (late '80s/early '90s). Nowadays, it is more common for a man to leave his family in HK and travel to China to make money.

742. The Other Side of Gentleman

[*sic*] (1984; Always Good Film Co.) ★: 2/10. *Gwan zi hou kau* (Cantonese), *Jun zi hao qiu* (Mandarin): "Gentleman Who Wants to Marry." Cinematographers: Raymond Lam Fai-tai, Joe Chan Kong-hung, Cheung Chi-keung, Yu Chun; Art Director: Dominique Lo Kar-yiu; Music: Phil Chan Fei-lap; Writers: Wong Ping-fai, Joyce Cheung Lai-ling; Producers: Frankie Chan Fan-kei, Guy Lai Ying-chau; Director: Ringo Lam Ling-tung. Cast: Alan Tam Wing-lun (Alan Ng), Brigitte Lin Ching-hsia (Jo Jo), Barry Wong Ping-yiu (Father Tam), Stephen Tung Wai (Oxy), Jamie Luk Kim-ming (Tough Guy in Parking Garage). Dolby Digital (DVD only). 1.85:1. VHS: Tai Seng (Poor Subtitles). Import LD: Golden Cinema City. Import VCD/DVD: Mega Star. 93 minutes.

The darker side of dating is the subject of this offbeat but muddled and unfocused drama. After being chosen to play the key role in a sociological experiment being conducted by her college instructor/lover, the beautiful Jo Jo is asked to start courting Alan Ng, an irresponsible bar hopper who has no luck picking up girls. Naturally, when this dream girl starts showing him affection, Alan is in seventh heaven, but he eventually catches on to what is happening, causing his behavior to become increasingly hostile and deranged. Determined to convince Jo Jo that their "love" is genuine, he starts stalking the girl and even goes so far as to disrupt her wedding ceremony.

In addition to being badly dated (those hideous New Wave fashions!), this is an unappetizing mixture of lame comedy, hit single interludes for pop star Tam, and overwrought, unconvincing melodrama. Neither the performances nor the scattershot screenplay give us any reason to care about these characters, and the climax is simply ludicrous.

743. The Other Side of the Sea

(1994; Long Shong Pictures/Filmax Production Co.) ★: 3/10. *Hoi gok ngai ching* (Cantonese), *Hai jiao wei qing* (Mandarin): "The Cape of Perilous Love." Cinematographer: Poon Yiu-ming; Art Director: Mark Chiu Kwok-san; Music: Chan Kin-tak, Ng Kwok-yan; Writer: Bryan Cheung Wai-hung; Producer: Yu Shu; Action Director: Lau Chi-ho; Director: Raymond Lee Wai-man. Cast: Michelle Lee Kar-yan (Yip Man-sau), Ma King-to (Ken), Vincent Wan Yeung-ming (Sau's boyfriend), Xiong Xinxin (Bald Killer), Lam Wai (Head of the Organization), Lau Siu-ming (Ford). 1.85:1. VHS: World Video. Import LD/VCD: Fitto Mobile. 90 minutes.

Too pedestrian to be exciting, and too languid to be interesting, this minor league thriller doesn't even kill time efficiently. Similar to **The Black Morning Glory** (1993), the film casts Michelle Lee as an illegal immigrant from Vietnam who works in HK as a professional assassin. After one hit too many, she decides to get out of "the business" and live a quiet life. Taking refuge on the island of Tai O, Lee meets and soon falls in love with the handsome owner of a local store. However, Lee's employers have decided that she knows too much about their activities and order her to be liquidated. Her boyfriend in the city turns out to be one of their hitmen, and several other killers also make attempts on her life. After being wounded and captured by the police, she is hospitalized, but the organization discovers her whereabouts and sends more men to take her out. Escaping with the help of a friend, Sau decides to cooperate with the police, but before she can meet with them, the gunmen strike again. Returning to the island, Lee and her new love must fight their way to freedom after they are surrounded on all sides. *The Other Side of the Sea* is for Michelle Lee fans only.

744. Our Neighbour Detective

(1995, Golden Harvest/Try Ease/ Concept Link Productions/Paragon Films) ★: 5/10. *Gaai fong cha yan* (Cantonese), *Jie fang chai ren* (Mandarin): "Neighborhood Cop." Cinematographer: Sung Kong; Art Director: James Cheung Ying-wah; Music: Not Original; Writers: Chung Kai-cheung, Lam Kei-to; Producers: Chua Lam, Cha Chuen-yee; Director: Cha Chuen-yee. Cast: Anthony Wong Chau-sang (Lau), Yu Li (Lo), Ivy Leung Si-man (Tina), Lawrence Ng Kai-wah (Cheng Kam-fu), Maria Cordero (Cop). 1.85:1. VHS: Tai Seng. Import LD/VCD: Universe. 90 minutes.

Anthony Wong trots out his patented "flaky cop" persona once again, and his enjoyable performance makes this middling mystery more entertaining than it should be, considering the dull, obscure storyline. After managing to lose his gun, slovenly cop Lau is assigned to a missing persons case that turns out to be much more involved than anyone could have guessed. The decidedly suspicious Cheung Kam-fu reports that his wife has gone missing, but only after waiting an entire week to do so. Lau stakes out Cheung's mistress, Lo, all the while ignoring his coroner girlfriend, who becomes increasingly angered by his poor treatment of her. It becomes evident that Lo is a woman with a great many problems, and they seem to relate to the flirtatious Tina and her troubled daughter Milky, a parrot, an instance of non-consensual incest, and a murder that occurred a decade earlier.

The juxtaposition of Lau's surveillance work, the developing mystery, and his increasingly troubled relationship is awkwardly handled, and this lack of focus also extends to the story. The various strands of plot come together adequately at the end, but the writers have a difficult time retaining viewer interest while mapping out the narrative. As good an actor as he is, even Wong cannot always command center stage, though his character has been given a number of eccentricities for the actor to play off of. This received the Category III rating for the aforementioned sexual assault and a dismemberment, neither of which really fit the mood and style of the film.

745. Out of the Dark

(1995; Shaw Brothers/Cosmopolitan Film Productions Co.) ★: 3/10. *Wooi wan ye* (Cantonese), *Hui hun ye* (Mandarin): "The Night of the Spirit's Return." Cinematographer: Wong Chi-wai; Art Director: Andrew Cheuk Man-yiu; Music: William Woo Wai-lap; Writer: Kei On (pseudonym for Jeff Lau Chun-wai); Producer: Mona Fong Yat-wah; Action Director: Tony Poon Kin-kwan; Director: Jeff Lau Chun-wai. Cast: Stephen Chiau Sing-chi (Leon), Karen Mok Man-wai (Kwan), Wong Yat-fei (Bold), Leung Kar-yan (Wu). 1.85:1. VHS: Tai Seng. Import LD/VCD: Mei Ah. 86 minutes.

One of Stephen Chiau's shoddiest and least appealing efforts, this cheesy horror-comedy looks to have been slapped together over the course of a long weekend. That in itself wouldn't be so bad if the film displayed the sort of comic inspiration and giddy fun commonly found in the comedian's work. He plays Leon, an escaped mental patient/bumbling ghost hunter who tries to help out the denizens of an apartment building menaced by a particularly malevolent ghost. Unfortunately, he makes the situation worse by accidentally killing the two murderers who perpetrated the crime for which the spirit sought revenge. Before they die, the female killer promises that she and her husband will return from Hell to make Leon and company pay. Giving the building's incompetent security crew a crash course in spirit-fighting techniques, Leon prepares for a night of Hell on earth that will commence as soon as the clock strikes twelve.

After a promising and amusingly frenetic opening reel, this runs out of ideas in record time. By the halfway point, Chiau is wearing Jerry Lewis novelty teeth and all hope is lost. Parodies of **The Professional**, **Highlander**, and **The Texas Chainsaw Massacre** do little to help. Check out Chiau's earlier supernatural farce **Look Out Officer!** (1990) or just about any horror satires from the period instead.

746. The Outlaw Brothers

(1990; Movie Impact) ★: 8/10. *Jui gaai chaak paak dong* (Cantonese), *Zui jia zei pai dang* (Mandarin): "The Best Thief Partners." Cinematographer: Michael Ma Koon-wah; Art Director: Tan Kwai-chi; Music: Roel A. Garcia; Writer: Barry Wong Ping-yiu; Producer: Wallace Cheung Kwok-chong; Action Directors: Fung Hark-on, Yuen Shun-yee, Cheng Chi-ho; Director: Frankie Chan Fan-kei. Cast: Frankie Chan Fan-kei (James), Max Mok Siu-chung (Bond), Yukari Oshima (Tequila), Miu Kiu-wai (Tai Ching-kwong), Sharon Kwok Sau-wan (Wan), Michiko Nishiwaki (Miego), Sheila Chan Sak-lan (Lan), Ricky Yee Fan-wai (Tall Sum), Jeff Falcon (Thug), Mark Houghton (Thug), Fung Hark-on (Parking Garage Security Chief). 1.85:1. VHS: Tai Seng. Import LD: Mei Ah. 95 minutes.

Terrific martial arts and first-rate stunts elevate this fast-paced outing into the "Must See" category. Brothers James and Bond are HK's top car thieves, specializing in Porsches and Ferraris. However, there's a new sheriff in town and *her* name is Tequila, a ball-busting supercop out to nail them. Just when Tequila is on the verge of arresting James, she is won over by his suave charm and the two begin a relationship (or is it just a ruse?). One evening James swipes the wrong Porsche, ending up with a stash of cash and cocaine belonging to the beautiful Japanese drug runner Michiko (whose name is misspelled as "Miego" in the subtitles). After a dangerous chase, James manages to give her henchmen the slip, but he is destined to cross paths with Michiko once again.

Yukari Oshima burst onto the HK film scene with her memorable turn as the villain of **Angel**, but she gets an even better showcase for her exceptional abilities here, and gives a wonderful comic performance to boot. There are back-breaking stunts throughout, but the climax (which finds Oshima and Chan single-handedly taking on a dozen Caucasian fighters) is the real jaw-dropper and one of the most spectacularly choreographed battles you will ever see. That, coupled with delightful characters, droll comedic asides, and terrific automobile stunts with expensive cars (unlike most HK actioners, which utilize old junkers obtained from the local wrecking yard for $50), makes **The Outlaw Brothers** one of the best HK action-comedies around. It is a real shame that none of Frankie Chan's other vehicles come close to measuring up to this one.

747. Over the Rainbow, Under the Skirt

(1994; United Filmmakers Organization) ★: 6/10. *Gei dak...heung jiu sing suk si II: choh luen ching yan* (Cantonese), *Ji de...xiang jiao cheng shu shi II: chu lian qing ren* (Mandarin): "Remember...Banana Ripening Time II: First Love Sweetheart." Cinematographer: Apple Kwan Pak-suen; Art Director: James Leung Wah-sang; Music: Clarence Hui Yuen, Danny Wong Dan-yee; Producer: Claudie Chung Chun; Writer-Director: Joe Ma Wai-ho. Cast: John Tang Yat-kwan (Bobby Yeung), Eileen Tung Oi-ling (Sharron), Ellen Lo Oi-lun (Ting-ting), Eric Tsang Chi-wai (Bobby's Father), Law Koon-lan (Bobby's Mother), Leslie Cheung Kwok-wing (Himself), Clifton Ko Chi-sum (Himself), Lau Ching-wan (Narrator). 1.85:1. VHS: Tai Seng. 100 minutes.

This sequel to **Yesteryou, Yesterme, Yesterday** finds our teenage protagonist (called "Bobby" this time in the subtitles) separated from Ting-ting when the girl transfers to a different school. When Bobby takes an advance peek inside Hong Kong University, he sees beautiful 19-year-old Sharron and it's lust at first sight. Desperate to impress her, he feigns an interest in Japanese art movies and other forms of culture, and Sharron grows to like him for his down-to-earth qualities. In response, he starts ignoring Ting-ting and finds out himself what it is like to have one's feelings hurt.

This makes some sage observations about the trials of youth and the pain that is part of growing up. However, like its forerunner, the film never quite reaches its full potential, due largely to the fact that Bobby and Sharron do not make a convincing couple, and the device of having Lau Ching-wan narrate the film (as Bobby in his later years) wears thin. It still remains a pleasant exercise, and the cast is uniformly good. There is a clever gag about Leslie Cheung and **A Better Tomorrow** that fans will get a real kick out of. It was followed by **Yesterday You, Yesterday Me** (1997).

748. The Owl vs. Bumbo

(1984; D & B Films Co.) ★: 5/10. *Maau tau ying yue siu fei jeung* (Cantonese),

Mao tou ying yu xiao fei xiang (Mandarin): "Owl and the Little Flying Elephant." Cinematographer: Arthur Wong Ngok-tai; Art Director: Fong Yuen-hei; Music: Chris Babida; Writer: D & B Creative Group; Action Directors: Lam Ching-ying, Yuen Wah; Producer-Director: Sammo Hung Kam-po. Cast: Sammo Hung Kam-po (First Day Chan, aka Bumbo), George Lam Chi-cheung (Yan Fu-wong, aka Owl), Deanie Yip Tak-han (Joyce Leung), Stanley Fung Shui-fan (Inspector Fung), Season Ma Si-san (Bonnie Leung), James Tien Chun (Au Gan), Michelle Yeoh Chu-kheng (Miss Yeung), Ronald Wong Pan (Chan Chee-ming), Wu Ma (Snack Bar Attendant), Phillip Chan Yan-kin (Cop), Phillip Ko Fei (Thug), Dick Wei (Thug), Tai Po (Thug in Yellow Suit), Yip Wing-cho (Maitre'd), Charlie Cho Cha-lei (Bank Manager). 1.85:1. VHS: J & M Chevalier. Import VCD: Mega Star. Import DVD: Universe. 99 minutes.

Master thieves Owl and Bumbo are being blackmailed by someone who claims to have enough knowledge of their past criminal activities to put them behind bars forever. If the pair follow his orders to the letter, he will keep silent. First, they must become social workers at the Kong To Youth Probation Centre and deal with the rowdy, aimless kids there. Then, they are ordered to attend an auction and drive up the price for a plot of land, foiling an attempt by Owl's old nemesis, gangster Au Gan, to buy it. They botch the latter task, but eventually the Kong To kids begin to learn that discipline and hard work are necessary for one to succeed. However, Au is not through with them yet and uses the teens to lure Owl into a trap.

While it is quite common for HK films to blend together a number of different elements, this mixture of comedy, drama, kung fu, and social commentary is lumpier than usual. The one saving grace is Sammo Hung. Whether engaging in an impromptu tap dance routine or chasing a cherry around the table (in *homage* to a classic silent comedy bit), he is charming and a joy to watch. Michelle Yeoh makes her film debut here, and it is the sort of "flower vase" part she would never do again. The soundtrack is credited to Chris Babida but most of the music is lifted from **Escape from New York** and **Phantasm**.

749. Painted Faces

(1988; Shaw Brothers/Golden Harvest) ★: 9/10. *Chat siu fuk* (Cantonese), *Qi xiao fu* (Mandarin): "Seven Little Fortunes." Cinematographer: David Chung Chi-man; Art Director: Yank Wong Yan-kwai; Music: Lowell Lo Kwun-ting; Writers: Alex Law Kai-yui, Mabel Cheung Yuen-ting; Producers: Leonard Ho Koon-cheung, Mona Fong Yat-wah; Action Direction: Yuen Wah, Sammo Hung Stunt Team; Director: Alex Law Kai-yui. Cast: Sammo Hung Kam-po (Yu Jim-yuan), Cheng Pei-pei (Ching), Lam Ching-ying (Wah), John Sham Kin-fun (Stagehand), Wu Ma (Film Director). 1.85:1. VHS: Tai Seng. Import LD: Ocean Shores. 112 minutes.

A rare Shaw Brothers/Golden Harvest co-production, this sombre, well-acted drama looks at the decline and subsequent extinction of Peking Opera Schools in Hong Kong during the 1960s. From a Western viewpoint, such institutions constituted a form of legalized slavery. Parents would indenture their child to a school for an agreed number of years, during which time he would be trained in all the facets of Peking Opera. The master ruled his charges' lives with absolute authority. All income generated from performances was his property, and he was free to discipline the children as he saw fit. If a student was beaten to death, the master was free of legal responsibility. **Painted Faces** is based on the lives of students who were members of the "Seven Little Fortunes" troupe, one of the last schools to exist in the colony. Some of its alumni, who would go on to become some of the biggest stars in HK cinema, are depicted here, specifically, the characters *Dai bei*/"Big Nose," Biao, and Sam-mo, who are patterned after Jackie Chan, Yuen Biao, and Sammo Hung Kam-po respectively. The latter actually stars in the film, playing Master Yu Jim-yuan (based on his real life teacher of the same name), a staunch traditionalist presenting the opera classics to increasingly diminutive crowds. When the school's contract is terminated by its theatre, Yu finds work for "Big Nose," Biao, and Sam-mo as stunt doubles in Shaw Brothers movies. However, the school's fate is finally sealed when the government condemns its headquarters, forcing Yu and his pupils to seek other means of support.

A remarkable directorial debut for Alex Law Kai-yui (**Now You See Love, Now You Don't**), **Painted Faces** showcases a venerable Chinese tradition (also depicted in Chen Kaige's **Farewell My Concubine** (*Bawang bie ji*, 1993) that finally succumbed to the barrage of Western enticements lavished on HK citizens by British colonization (in a series of amusing scenes, Yu's students are far more interested in platform shoes, bell bottoms, and The Beatles than in local traditions). Largely forgotten now, the schools seem unlikely to emerge again, particularly in the wake of changing attitudes about the exploitation of children. Law imparts his story (co-written with his frequent collaborator Mabel Cheung Yuen-ting) by way of a first rate cast. Usually cast as a comic figure in martial arts actioners, Hung gives an exceptional dramatic performance as the master who is as outmoded as the art he is trying to preserve. The emotion on his face during the scene in which he tells the students his plans for the future is strikingly genuine. He is equalled by the great Cheng Pei-pei, ideally cast as the proprietress of a Cantonese school, who can see the writing on the wall and adapt to change. Lam Ching-ying (best known to Western audiences for his outings as the demon fighting "One-Eyebrow Priest" in numerous *gyonsi* horror comedies) is also noteworthy as a compatriot of Yu's whose life is destroyed when he badly injures his head while performing a stunt on the set of a period kung fu movie. Deservedly well-received, the film garnered the Best Actor (Hung) and Best Cinematography statues at the eighth Hong Kong Film Awards, and also claimed the Best Picture, Best Director, Best Original Script, Best Cinematography, Best Original Music, and Best Editing prizes at the twenty-fifth Taiwan Golden Horse Awards. Sammo Hung and Jackie Chan have announced their intention to remake **Painted Faces**, but since every aspect of this production is handled so well, there is really no reason to tell the story again, unless they plan to take it in a substantially different direction. Some prints include an epilogue which shows Sammo Hung, Jackie Chan, Yuen Biao, Corey Yuen Kwai, and other members of the original troupe appearing at a party for Master Yu (who passed away in 1997 at the age of 95).

750. Painted Skin

(1992; New Treasurer Films Co.) ★: 4/10. *Wa pei ji yam yeung faat wong* (Cantonese), *Hua pi zhi yin yang fa wang* (Mandarin): "Painted Skin: The Yin Yang Method King." Cinematographer: Poon Tak-yip; Art Directors: James Leung Wah-sang, Wang Jixian; Music: Ng Tai-kong; Writers: King Hu Chin-chuan, Chung Ah-sing; Producer: Ng Choi-ming; Action Director: Tsui Chung-san; Director: King Hu Chin-chuan. Cast: Adam Cheng Siu-chau (Wang Hsi-tzu), Joey Wang Tsu-hsien (You Feng), Sammo Hung Kam-po (The High Monk), Lau Shun (Zhang Daoling), Wu Ma (Zhang's Apprentice), Lam Ching-ying (The Purple Taoist). VHS: Tai Seng. Import LD/VCD: Universe. 93 minutes.

You Feng is a beautiful spirit trapped between Heaven and Hell, wandering the Earth in human form. She enters the household of lazy scholar Wang Hsi-tzu, who seeks to make her a concubine in order to bolster his dull marriage. You's unearthly origins are soon discovered, prompting Wang to enlist the services of Taoist priest Zhang Daoling and his apprentice. They discover that her spirit is under the control of the Yin Yang King, who subsequently possesses the scholar, thus allowing the entity to wreak havoc on earth. Unable to muster the power necessary to take on such a formidable demon, Zhang seeks the aid of the reclusive High Monk, who would rather spend the rest of his earthly tenure tending his peach farm.

Following his early dismissal as director of Film Workshop's period fantasy epic **Swordsman** (1991), acclaimed veteran director King Hu helmed this modest production, which is presumably more in keeping with what he had originally envisioned for the other film. With his "Inn Trilogy" of **Come Drink with Me** (*Ta tsui hsia*—"Big Drunk Hero," 1965), **Dragon Inn** (*Long men ke zhan*—"Dragon Gate Inn," 1966), and **A Touch of Zen** (*Hsia nu*—"Chivalrous Woman," 1969), Hu laid much of the groundwork for the genre, but this remake of Pao Feng's 1966 original compares poorly to those works and will most likely find favor only with viewers who harbor a fondness for the traditional and less technically-driven efforts from a more innocent age of Chinese fantasy cinema. In spite of fine performances and some interesting visuals (the locales are stunning), **Painted Skin** is a film that one is much more inclined to respect than relish. Those who developed a yen for HK fantasy cinema via entries like **A Chinese Ghost Story** and **Swordsman II** will be quick to dismiss this as an archaic bore, while viewers familiar with Hu's output will experience the same sense of dissatisfaction one gets while viewing Akira Kurosawa's final few efforts. *Painted Skin* is a noble failure but a failure nonetheless.

751. Pantyhose Hero

(1990; Bojon Films Company) ★: 4/10. *Ji fan seung hung* (Cantonese), *Zhi fen shuang xiong* (Mandarin): "Cosmetics Twin Powers." Cinematographer: Jimmy Leung Chi-ming; Art Director: Hai Chung-man; Music: Lowell Lo Kwun-ting; Writers: Barry Wong Ping-yiu, Roy Szeto Cheuk-hon; Action Direction: Sammo Hung Stunt Team, Yuen Chan-cheung, Siu Tak-fu; Producer-Director: Sammo Hung Kam-po. Cast: Sammo Hung Kam-po (Jeff Lau), Alan Tam Wing-lun (Alan), Joan Tong Lai-kau (Chen-chen), Paul Chun Pui (Inspector), Wu Ma (Police Commissioner), James Tien Chun (Tsen), Yip Wing-cho (Building Superintendent), Phillip Chan Yan-kin (Cop Raiding Club), Tai Po (Construction Site Victim), Chung Fat (Thug). 1.85:1. VHS: Tai Seng. Import LD: Mei Ah. 99 minutes.

Just about the most politically incorrect film in memory, this remake of the Ryan O'Neal/John Hurt bomb **Partners** (1982) will entertain some with its sheer shock value. However, beyond that, little here hits the mark, and the script's idea of humor is often just plain embarrassing. When a series of homosexuals are found brutally murdered, smart-aleck cops Sammo Hung and Alan Tam go undercover as lovers in order to crack the case. After doing the bar scene, the pair come up with some leads, but Hung falls in love with the beautiful Joan Tong. This makes it even more difficult to maintain the charade, particularly after Alan and Joan accidentally down some spiked champagne and end up in bed together.

Limp-wristed stereotypes abound, but laughs are in far shorter supply. Luckily, there is some terrific action to keep this from being a complete loss, particularly one amazing stunt where Hung gets hit by a car and somehow manages not to break every single bone in his body.

752. Paper Marriage

(1986; Golden Harvest/Bo Ho Films Co. [Alberta]) ★: 6/10. *Gwoh fau san long* (Cantonese), *Guo bu xin lang* (Mandarin): "Pass Pier Bridegroom." Cinematographer: Jimmy Leung Chi-ming; Art Director: David Hiscox; Music: Joseph Koo Kar-fai; Writers: Alfred Cheung Kin-ting, Wong Wang-kei; Producer: Raymond Chow Man-wai; Action Directors: Lam Ching-ying, Yuen Wah; Director: Alfred Cheung Kin-ting. Cast: Sammo Hung Kam-po (Chien Pao), Maggie Cheung Man-yuk (Jade Li), Joyce Godenzi (Pao's ex-wife), Alfred Cheung Kin-ting (Peter), Billy Chow Bei-lee (Thai Boxer), Phillip Ko Fei (Crazy Eyes). 1.85:1. VHS: Tai Seng (No Subtitles). Import LD: Star Entertainment (No Subtitles). Import VCD: Mega Star. Import DVD: Universe. 87 minutes.

Ex-boxer Chien Pao is an unemployed, woman-hating wreck desperate to pay off a debt owed to a loan shark. He agrees to a marriage of convenience which would allow Jade Li to come to Canada and be with her fiancé Peter. However, after Jade and Pao are wed, Peter skips town with her money, leaving Jade at the mercy of the furious Pao. After several hours of fuming, Pao agrees to let Jade stay with him. The two try various schemes to make a living, including acting as human guinea pigs for a research experiment testing human endurance. After that humiliating ordeal (Jade outlasted him, proving women are stronger than men), Pao decides to go back into the ring for an illegal bout. After winning the match, he is offered the chance to eradicate his debt if he agrees to fight a vicious Thai boxer. Reluctant at first, Pao changes his mind when he discovers that the man is living with his ex-wife. While Pao is emerging victorious once again in the ring, Jade is getting the stuffing knocked out of her trying to make it as a mud wrestler. Fed up, she decides to head back to HK but changes her mind when she discovers a bag filled with money. After they deposit the loot in a joint bank account, Pao and Jade are attacked by the gangsters who lost the money. After they take Jade hostage, Pao sets up an exchange in a large shopping mall. Chaos ensues when Jade grabs the money and refuses to turn it over!

Set in America but obviously shot in Alberta (the finale even takes place at the world famous West Edmonton Mall!), **Paper Marriage** was completed in 1986 but did not open in HK until two years later. Skimpily plotted and formulaic in the extreme, the film still manages to entertain, thanks to its charismatic leads and some deft fight choreography. The stolen money subplot comes right out of left field and serves only as an excuse for even more action. However, considering that said scenes feature the work of Hung, Dick Wei, and Billy Chow, this is only a minor gripe. The same premise would be given serious treatment a few years later in Sylvia Chang Ai-chia's **Siao Yu** (1995), with Rene Lau Yeuk-ying and Daniel J. Travanti as the leads.

753. Parking Service

(1985; Always Good Film Co.) ★: 3/10. *Doi haak bok che* (Cantonese), *Dai ke bo che* (Mandarin): "For Customer Park Car." Cinematographer: James Chan Hau-ming; Art Director: Cho Yue; Music: Phil Chan Fei-lap; Writer: Manfred Wong; Producer: Guy Lai Ying-chau; Director: Angela Mak Leng-chi. Cast: Danny Lee Sau-yin (Lee Ho-sau), Parkman Wong Pak-man (Wong Park-man), Terry Hu Yin-meng (Stella), Ku Feng (Kao), Shing Fui-on (Dummy), Keith Kwan Chiu-chung (Officer Lau). 1.85:1. VHS: Tai Seng. Import LD: Golden Cinema City. Import VCD: Mega Star. Running time unknown.

Although it was released in the mid '80s, this forgettable production seems like a leftover from the '70s; Danny Lee and Parkman Wong look like they just graduated from college! Lee plays a gregarious pig farm assistant who comes to the city and gets a job as a parking valet. He quickly becomes best friends with Parkman Wong, his partner at work, who likes to steal expensive cars for fun. Shing Fui-on plays a rival attendant at an adjacent restaurant who invites Lee to take a client's Mercedes Benz for a little joyride—after making off with the stereo system. Lee hopes the car will impress a local hooker but finds it filled with millions in counterfeit American currency. Lee and Wong concoct an intricate plan to get both the criminal and Shing pinched by the authorities. The naive Wong, meanwhile, falls for the depressed mistress of a heartless millionaire, a relationship that is doomed to failure...or is it? Danny Lee fans may want to take a look, but no one else need bother with this tedious fluff.

754. Passion

(1986; D & B Films Co.) ★: 6/10. *Jui oi* (Cantonese), *Zui ai* (Mandarin): "Most Love." Cinematographer: Jingle Ma Choshing; Art Director: William Cheung Suk-ping; Music: Lowell Lo Kwun-ting; Producer: John Sham Kin-fun; Writer-Director: Sylvia Chang Ai-chia. Cast: Sylvia Chang Ai-chia (Wendy Pai), Cora Miao Qian-ren (Ming), George Lam Chichung (John Lam), Chung King-fai (Dr. King), Pau Hon-lam (John's Father), Yung Sai-kit (Jack), Michael Dinga (Charlie), Loletta Lee Lai-chun (Lina), May Lo Mei mei (Gabriel). Dolby Digital (DVD only). 1.85:1. VHS: Tai Seng. Import LD: Mei Ah. Import VCD/DVD: Mega Star. 90 minutes.

Two middle-aged women reflect on their past over a bottle of wine in this low-key drama directed by its star, Sylvia Chang. Best friends Wendy and Ming are inseparable, but there is one problem: Both are in love with lawyer John. Wendy keeps her love for John a secret from her friend, so he marries Ming, even though his heart tells him it is the wrong decision. In response, Wendy marries the much older Dr. King, a union that ultimately engenders more respect than love. John and Wendy see each other on the side, a dalliance which Ming ultimately becomes aware of. As the day wears onward, the women continue to rehash the past, and, gradually, a secret is revealed that perhaps should have remained buried.

Well acted across the board, **Passion**, however, could use a little more, well, *passion*. Chang directs with skill and restraint, but the characters and their problems never involve the viewer to the extent that they should because everyone stays behind the emotional facades they have constructed for themselves. Thus, after a long buildup, one leaves the film feeling largely indifferent rather than entertained or enlightened.

Passion in the Dream *see* **Passionate Killing in the Dream**

755. Passion 1995

(1995; Wishing Well Film Co.) ★: 3/10. *Mo him yau fai* (Cantonese), *Mao xian you xi* (Mandarin): "Thrill Seeking Game." Cinematographer: Lau Hung-chuen; Art Director: Stanley Cheung Sai-kit; Music: Tommy Wai Kai-leung; Writer: Cheung Cho-yee; Producer: Yuen Ching-lin; Action Director: Lau Chung-fung; Director: Clarence Fok Yiu-leung. Cast: Simon Yam Tat-wah (Dick Wong), Christy Chung Lai-tai (Tina), David Wu Tai-wai (Siu-wei), Teresa Mak Kar-kei (Gucci), Yuen King-tan (Sally, aka Old Eagle), Wong Hei (Lung), Ben Ng Ngai-cheung (Ba), Bobby Yip King-sang (Shing), Melvin Wong Kam-sun (Ha), Victor Hon Kwan (Street Car Driver), Law Kar-ying (Johnny, Man in Photograph). 1.85:1. VHS: World Video. Import LD/VCD: Ocean Shores. 90 minutes.

Another senseless enterprise from director Clarence Fok (**Naked Killer**), this action-comedy-musical hybrid does not know what it wants to be but certainly succeeds at being an insufferable mess. Tina is the leader of some punked-out juvenile delinquents who spend most of their time fried on cough syrup; San Franciscan Dick is in HK looking for his old girlfriend; Gucci is a bored hooker whose schizophrenic mom, Sally, wanders the streets screaming for her lost love; Siu-wei is a lonely, dimwitted beat cop looking for companionship over the phone; Lung is Tina's sleazoid boyfriend who smuggles drugs inside Ultraman toys; and Ba is Lung's sadistic, homosexual partner. All of these characters co-exist in an oddball narrative that incorporates spontaneous dance numbers, rampant music video stylizing, and standard gang movie violence, all of which unfold amid a kaleidoscope of colors.

With the aforementioned elements and its attractive young cast, **Passion 1995** could be called an Eastern punk variation on **Streets of Fire**. There is one essential difference: The American film had a simple but coherent storyline, while this one seems to have been thrown together on the fly. Christy Chung looks spectacular, dolled up in outlandish make-up and a series of florid outfits and wigs, but viewers expecting anything more than eye candy from this folly will come away sorely disappointed.

756. Passion Unbounded

(1995; Jon Hau Productions Co.) ★: 3/10. *Sei kap yan kong* (Cantonese), *Si ji sha ren kuang* (Mandarin): "Category IV Murdering Maniac." Cinematographer: Joe Chan Kong-hung; Art Directors: Jon Hau Wing-choi, Chan Mei-wai, Lo Wai-san; Writer: Cheung Cho-yee; Music-Producer-Director: Jon Hau Wing-choi. Cast: Carrie Ng Kar-lai (Miss Tong), David Wu Tai-wai (Shek Dai-hung), Hilary Tsui Ho-ying (Tong Siu-gei), Christine Ng Wing-mei (Pak Yu-seung), Chin Ho (Martin), Lily Lee Li-li (Hooker), Jamie Luk Kim-ming (Bartender with Moustache). 1.85:1. Import LD/VCD/DVD: Ocean Shores. 95 minutes.

Yet another lemon from director Jon Hau, this Category III thriller is patterned after **Naked Killer**, from the look right on down to having one of its stars (Carrie Ng), but still manages to be a listless bore. Women are being raped and murdered, and the police, led by officer Shek (played by Taiwanese actor David Wu), have not been able to come up with a single lead. We are introduced to Miss Tong, a chic but ice cold woman who picks up a man in a bar, has sex with him in a bathroom stall, and then stabs him to death with one of her high heels. The long-vacant house down the street from her is now occupied by Martin, a mysterious epileptic who becomes a partner in murder with Miss Tong when they drown an unsuspecting teenage girl. The next time Tong dispatches another male victim, she is observed in the act by her sister, Siu-gei, who is understandably upset but unable to solicit help from Shek for fear of what will happen to her sister.

There is nothing worse than a film that builds and builds to a climax and then delivers nothing. The second half of **Passion Unbounded** is nothing more than a series of murder setpieces, as Tong and Martin seek out increasingly bizarre victims (a lesbian, a hooker, a transsexual, etc.). There is no mystery, no suspense, no revelations, and no shocks, just a lot of empty style, designer fashions, sparsely furnished rooms, and glossy photography. The end result is unsatisfying, to say the least, but remains one of Hau's more accomplished productions to date. Christine Ng gives a wildly eccentric performance as a local crazy woman. The Chinese title spuriously claims that this movie is "Category IV," or more explicit than the standard C-III adults-only fare.

757. Passionate Killing in the Dream

(1992) ★: 3/10. *92 Wan yue dai luk gam* (Cantonese), *92 Yun yu di liu gan* (Mandarin): "Love-Making Sixth Feeling." Cinematographer: Tsui Tung-hing; Art Director: Lau Chi-wah; Writer: Lau Chi-wah;

Producers: Tai Pang-ling, Hung Fung; Action Directors: Lee Hin, Ah Wai; Director: Wong Kwok-chu. Cast: Michiko Nishiwaki (Sha-sha), Gordon Lau Kar-fai (Chit-chit), Lam Wai (Hsin Qian, aka Big Buffalo), Lam Pan-kwun, Wong Man-yu. 1.85:1. VHS: Tai Seng. Import LD/VCD: Mei Ah. 87 minutes. Also known as **Passion in the Dream**.

This Category III thriller is more stylish than most adult fare and even includes some martial arts sequences as a diversion. The end result is still pretty forgettable, however, as the plot adheres strictly to the conventions of the psycho killer genre. Photographer Sha-sha has the ability to "see" in her dreams murders committed by a psychopath but is unable to convince the police that she is not just some lunatic. After one such attack, she draws a detailed sketch of the murderer, and her psychologist boyfriend is able to convince a friend on the force of its validity. The picture is run on a TV news broadcast and seen by the madman, who then fools a dimwitted cop into revealing the identity of the "witness."

Michiko Nishiwaki is fine in a rare lead role, but the film alternates between the routine and uneventful, making it difficult to care about the outcome.

758. Passionate Nights

(1997; Italconcepts Fashion/Congrad Company) ★: 1/10. *Ngoh yau ngoh fung kong* (Cantonese), *Wo you wo feng kuang* (Mandarin): "I Have My Craziness." Cinematographer: Kwan Chi-kan; Art Director: Tung Yiu; Writer: Joyce Cheung Lai-ling; Producer-Director: Jon Hau Wing-choi. Cast: Pauline Chan Po-lin (Liu Siu-suen), Kong Suet-fa (Miss Chin), Fennie Yuen Kit-ying (Cha Suk-yin), Ada Choi Siu-fan (Margaret), Suki Kwan Sau-mei (Joe-fai's Sister), Edmond Leung Hon-man (Jet Li), Bowie Lam Bo-yee (Tony), Ha Chi-chun (Sister Cheuk), Spencer Lam Sheung-yee (Head of Security Agency), Ha Ping (Joe-fai's mother), Bobby Yip King-sang (Ugly Triad). 1.85:1. VHS: World Video. Import LD/VCD: Universe. 86 minutes.

When her husband inexplicably drives his car into the harbor, his young, bitchy wife Siu-suen, inherits the man's $30 million estate. He also left a $10 million insurance policy, and claim investigator Cha Suk-yin is ordered by her company to find some proof (*any* proof) that Siu-suen somehow contributed to her husband's death, thus saving the company from having to shell out so much as a dime. Someone begins making attempts on Siu-suen's life, but as just about everyone in Asia has a motive, she is at a loss as to the identity of the would-be assassin. She hires a bodyguard (named *Jet Li* no less) to protect her, but the assailant proves persistent.

This had the makings of an enjoyable trashy mystery, but in the hands of notorious hack director Jon Hau, it is merely a miserable exercise in tedium. The inept lead performances by Pauline Chan and Kong Suet-fa (who is so pale and made-up, she looks like Elvira, Mistress of the Dark) would sink just about any other movie, but bad acting is just the tip of the iceberg here. Dreadful.

759. Peace Hotel

(1995; Golden Princess/Cassia Hill Production Co.) ★: 6/10. *Wing ping fan dim* (Cantonese), *Han ping fan dian* (Mandarin): "Peace Hotel." Cinematographer: Horace Wong Wing-hang; Art Directors: Hai Chung-man, Alfred Yau Wai-ming; Music: Cacine Wong Kar-sin, Healthy Poon Kin-hong; Producer: John Woo Yu-sen; Action Director: Yuen Bun; Writer-Director: Wai Kar-fai. Cast: Chow Yun-fat ("The Killer"), Cecilia Yip Tung (Shau Siu-man), Chin Ho (Ting Moon), Lau Shun (Blindman), Annabelle Lau Hiu-tong (Skinny). 1.85:1. VHS: Tai Seng. Import LD/VCD/DVD: Fitto Mobile. 88 minutes (theatrical version), 90 minutes (video version).

Stuck in Hollywood "Development Hell" following the completion of his American debut feature, **Hard Target** (1993), John Woo journeyed back overseas to produce this offbeat actioner. Set in the early part of the century, it opens with a stark, B&W prologue. A bald, machete-wielding killer has single-handedly exterminated a gang of thieves at an outlying hotel. Setting his sights upon the only remaining survivor, a teenage boy, he slices off his victim's ear but suddenly experiences a change of heart. Haunted by the events of that day, the man, known only as "The Killer," transformed the establishment into "Peace Hotel," a sanctuary for those with a price on their heads. He marked the entrance of the grounds with a sword, and because of his savage reputation, it's a line that no one has yet dared to cross. Ten years after these events unfolded, Shau Siu-man, a beautiful woman in a red *cheongsam*, arrives at Peace Hotel claiming to be the proprietor's wife. An inveterate liar, she soon has the tenants enthralled by stories of her tragic life, but her subterfuge is exposed by the return of first The Killer and then a gang of bandits on horseback. Wanted for the murder of their leader and the theft of his gold, she admits to having stabbed the man once, but neglects to mention the seven bullet holes he also has in his chest. The outlaws' new leader has his men surround the hotel and decides to play a waiting game with the occupants. He also has a personal score to settle with The Killer, and the latter must decide whether to violate his steadfast rule of unquestioned asylum in order to preserve the safety of his other charges.

Something of a Chinese Western, from the look right on down to the Ennio Morricone-style score, **Peace Hotel** is an interesting concept that doesn't quite come off. Writer-director Wai Kar-fai (co-editor of **Hard Boiled**) certainly has a good visual sense, and the production design is consistently impressive, right down to the smallest detail. However, none of his characters are particularly sympathetic or well-drawn, and the two leads must consistently strive to make up for the deficiencies in the script. Chow can do these iconic parts in his sleep, and it's a credit to his talent that we remain interested in him throughout, since the storyline doesn't really give us a good reason to be. Cecilia Yip takes center stage here, giving a strong interpretation of a thoroughly unlikeable character. The fact that she pulls it off without completely alienating the audience can, like Chow, be attributed mainly to her talent. The action sequences are so over-stylized as to be unbelievable in all but a fantastic sense, and character motivation is not entirely clear (the subtitles are not totally at fault in this regard). Definitely a case of style over substance, but a fitfully entertaining and engaging one, **Peace Hotel** has enough in its favor to recommend but falls short of its true potential. Jacqueline Wu Chien-lien puts in a brief but significant appearance. The video versions include a two minute sequence not found in theatrical prints in which Chow uses a machine gun to shoot down some of the bandits.

760. Peacock King

(1989; Golden Harvest/Paragon Films) ★: 7/10. *Hung jeuk wong* (Cantonese), *Kong qiao wang* (Mandarin): "Peacock King." Cinematographers: Ardy Lam Kwok-wah, Kwan Chi-kan; Art Directors: Eddie Ma Poon-chiu, Unknown Japanese Technician; Music: Yoshino Maki; Writers: Edward Tang King-sang, Kong Heung-sang, Shirley Woo Suet-lai; Producer: Chua Lam; Action Directors: Stephen Tung Wai, Phillip Kwok Tsui; Director: Nam Nai-choi. Cast: Yuen Biao (Peacock), Gloria Yip Wan-yee (Ashura), Pauline Wong Siu-fung (Raga), Hiroshi Mikami (Lucky Fruit), Narumi Yasuda (Miss Okada), Eddy Ko Hung (Ku Fong), Gordon Lau Kar-fai (Kubira). Dolby Digital (DVD only). 1.85:1. VHS: Tai Seng. Import LD: Star Entertainment (No Subtitles). Import VCD: Mega Star. Import DVD: Universe. 84 minutes.

A HK/Japan co-production, this ambitious fantasy is adapted from a popular *manga* that has also been produced in animated form. Life on Earth is threatened with extinction when the evil female demon Raga awakens the young Hell Virgin, Ashura, and opens the four gateways to Hell. Young Tibetan monk Peacock is dispatched to Tokyo by his master to locate the gateways, while his Japanese counterpart, Lucky Fruit, also heads towards that city for the very same purpose. Together they use their powers to close one opening located beneath a department store's dinosaur exhibition. They then travel to HK, where Peacock is able to locate Ashura at Ocean World Amusement Park. A series of desiccated corpses reveals the location of another hole, inside of which the monks find Raga and barely escape with their lives when she transforms into a vicious reptilian monster. They take Ashura (who is actually just an innocent pawn in Raga's scheme) to Lama Temple in Tibet, where Peacock's master reveals that the monks are actually twin brothers whose destiny is to save mankind from the giant Hell King, whose rebirth is imminent. First, however, they must defeat the powerful warrior Kubira and his minions, who have been dispatched to eliminate them.

There is all manner of martial arts action (of both the supernatural and the earthbound variety) on display, along with lavish production design, some stunning visuals, and a number of intriguing creatures (some inspired by H.R. Giger's designs for **Alien**). The humorous asides are overly juvenile at times, but the storyline is intriguing and, after a mediocre opening third, the film delivers on its promise of epic fantasy in highly satisfying fashion. Kara Hui Ying-hung and Phillip Kwok Tsui have eyeblink cameos as the monks' parents. It was followed by **Saga of the Phoenix**.

Pedalling Into Fury *see* **Pedicab Driver**

761. Pedicab Driver

(1986; Golden Harvest/Bojon Films/ Paragon Films) ★: 8/10. *Kwan lung hei fung* (Cantonese), *Qun long xia feng* (Mandarin): "A Group of Dragons Playing Phoenix." Cinematographers: Jimmy Leung Chi-ming, Tom Lau Moon-tong, Poon Tak-yip; Art Directors: William Cheung Suk-ping, Chin Yiu-hang; Music: Lowell Lo Kwun-ting; Writers: Barry Wong Ping-yiu, Yuen Kai-chi; Producer: Chan Pui-wah; Action Direction: Brandy Yuen Chun-yeung, Mang Hoi, Sammo Hung Stuntmen Association; Director: Sammo Hung Kam-po. Cast: Sammo Hung Kam-po (Lo Tung), Nina Li Chi (Ping), Sun Yueh (Fang), Max Mok Siu-chung (Mai Chien-tang, aka Malted Candy), Fennie Yuen Kit-ying (Hsiao-tsui), Lowell Lo Kwun-ting (Shan Cha Cake), Mang Hoi (Rice Pudding), John Sham Kin-fun (Master 5), Lau Kar-leung (Boss of Gambling House), Corey Yuen Kwai (Coolie), Billy Lau Nam-kwong (Tan), Billy Chow Bei-lee (Master 5's Man), Alfred Cheung Kin-ting (Jewellery Store Owner), Lam Ching-ying (Sheng), Manfred Wong (Man Selling Pork Buns), Peter Chan Lung (Coolie), Dick Wei (Wei), Chung Fat (Thug), Maria Cordero (Auntie), Eric Tsang Chi-wai (Man with Cleaver), Eddie Maher (Thug). 1.85:1. VHS: Tai Seng. Import LD: Mei Ah. 94 minutes. Also known as **Pedalling Into Fury**.

Sensational martial arts highlight this superior action-comedy-drama, which ranks among director-star Sammo Hung's best works. Rotund pedicab driver Lo Tung has his eye on buxom bakery employee Ping and sets about courting her. Unfortunately, he has two major obstacles in the way: his impeccable ability to get into trouble and Master Fang, his bumbling old boss who also seeks Ping's affections. Ping's beauty has caught the attentions of the evil Master 5, and Tung is barely able to rescue the girl when Master 5 sends his thugs out to snatch her. When the criminals viciously murder two of his friends, Tung and one of his fellow drivers invade Master 5's mansion and seek revenge.

A subplot involving the relationship one driver has, with a girl forced by Master 5 to work as a prostitute is overly melodramatic (though still marginally effective, thanks to Fennie Yuen and Max Mok's sincere work) and John Sham's shrill, cartoonish villain is tiresome. That said, this remains a terrific film, filled with some truly incredible acrobatics. Sammo Hung has a show-stopping stick battle with the great Lau Kar-leung and the final battle finds Hung displaying equally superb form fighting the limber Billy Chow. There is also some amusing comedy, particularly during the comic combat in the opening sequence, which even includes a nod to **Star Wars**!

762. The Peeping Tom

(1997; Golden Harvest/Pan Asia Films Production Co.) ★: 3/10. *Chik juk ging wan* (Cantonese), *Chi zu jing hun* (Mandarin): "Naked Leg Scary Spirit." Cinematographer: Cheung Man-bo; Art Director: James Cheung Ying-wah; Music: Sam Leung Yiu-san; Writer: Sam Leung Tak-sum; Action Director: Ridley Tsui Bo-wah; Producer-Director: Ivan Lai Kai-ming. Cast: Jade Leung Ching (Cheng Hsuen), Mark Cheng Ho-nam (Roy Chen Chih-lai), Miho Nomoto (Kelly), Michael Tse Tin-wah (Ken Chang), Rachel Tucker (Blonde). 1.85:1. Import LD/VCD/DVD: Universe. 96 minutes.

This is another nasty Category III thriller from director Ivan Lai (**Daughter of Darkness**), who has made more than his share. Psychopath Roy Chen Chih-lai is abducting women, raping them, and slicing off their legs. He then wraps the severed limbs in plastic and hangs the trophies from his ceiling. After witnessing policewoman Cheng Hsuen battling armed killers, Chen starts stalking her and even begins secretly living in the woman's apartment. After brazenly announcing his presence, he kidnaps and rapes Hsuen's sister, Kelly, and uses the girl to lure Hsuen into a trap. Hsuen is able to escape but falls into another trap and accidentally kills her boyfriend. Suspended from the force, Hsuen seeks vengeance, as Chen's insane acts even extend to mutilating her fiancé's corpse and threatening her aged mother.

Mark Cheng is exceptionally creepy here, the score is quite effective, and there are several instances of genuine suspense. Unfortunately, the majority of the proceedings are too predictable, illogical, and misogynistic for this to qualify as anything other than trash. The sexual violence so rife in this subgenre is supplemented here with bondage, sado-masochism, and other unpleasantness. The fact that HK censors had no problem with this content, or shots which imply that Kelly is enjoying the forced intercourse, but cut non-explicit footage of the performers thrusting their bodies during sex (something that is often deleted from HK films) is a good example of how standards can really differ between Eastern and Western cultures.

763. Peking Opera Blues

(1986; Cinema City Co./Film Workshop) ★: 9/10. *Do ma daan* (Cantonese), *Dao ma dan* (Mandarin): "Knife, Horse, Dawn" (the name of a Peking Opera character). Cinematographer: Poon Hang-sang; Art Directors: Vincent Wai Kai-sun, Ho Kim-seng, Leung Chi-hing; Music: Music: James Wong Jim; Writer: Raymond To Kwok-wai; Action Director: Ching Siu-tung; Producer-Director: Tsui Hark. Cast: Brigitte Lin Ching-hsia (Tsao Wan), Sally Yeh Chian-wen (Pat Neil), Cherie Chung Cho-hung (Sheung Hung), Mark Cheng Ho-nam (Ling Pak-hoi), Cheung Kwok-keung (Tung Man), Ku Feng (Commander Liu), Kenneth Tsang Kong (General Tsao), Wu Ma (Wong), Paul Chun Pui (Fa), Lee

Hoi-sang (Soldier with Moustache). Dolby Digital (DVD only). 1.85:1. VHS: Tai Seng. Import LD: Golden Cinema City. Import VCD: Mei Ah. Import DVD: Mega Star. 105 minutes.

One of the films that reignited Western interest in HK cinema, **Peking Opera Blues** is a superbly crafted production from the time when director Tsui Hark and his Film Workshop company were vigorously expanding the creative possibilities of HK cinema. Set in 1913, the story opens with the ruthless General Tsao taking control of Beijing, after his rival, General Tun, flees from his own rebelling troops. Tsao's daughter, Wan, is always by his side but is actually plotting against her father, who seeks to purge all democratic opposition. While secretly striving to undermine her father's efforts, Wan (who sports close-cropped hair and dresses like a man) becomes involved with ditzy musician Sheung Hung (who is trying to recover a box of jewellery belonging to Tun's wives that she stole), Pat Neil (the put-upon daughter of the local Peking Opera company manager who dreams of a career onstage even though women are forbidden from performing), stoic revolutionary fighter Ling Pak-hoi, and the bumbling but amiable rebel Tung Man. Together the friends get into all manner of adventures, dodging both Tsao's soldiers and the gunmen serving the unrepentantly corrupt secret police commander, Captain Liu. When Wan helps the rebels steal a secret letter from her father, the General's power is fatally compromised, leading to his death and the return of General Tun. Wan is then arrested and tortured by Liu, prompting a desperate rescue attempt by Pat and Hung.

A beguiling, perfectly paced mixture of adventure, drama, comedy, and romance, **Peking Opera Blues** also benefits from winning performances by its three leads. Brigitte Lin is at her most photogenic in one of the earliest androgynous roles the actress would essay in her career (the most famous being the all-powerful "Invincible Asia" in **Swordsman II** and **The East Is Red**) and effectively conveys the conflicting emotions of Wan's dilemma, caught as she is between aiding the rebels and still caring for her misguided father. While Lin is allowed to display a light touch in the second half, most of the comedic duties are handled quite engagingly by Sally Yeh and Cherie Chung. Cinematographer Poon Hang-sang captures all of the action and intrigue adeptly, and the rainbow of colors found in the opera house and traditional performance costumes is quite intoxicating. Ching Siu-tung's action choreography splendidly incorporates Peking Opera stylistics, as well as a few brief instances of the high-flying escapism that features throughout his period fantasies. Tsui's original cut of the film ran an additional 20 minutes (footage of Sally Yeh scuffling with some policemen can be seen under the end crawl but does not appear in the film itself), and, hopefully, that version will be unveiled someday. James Wong Jim's original music is excellent, but there are also a few 1970s library cues in the mix, and the climax is scored with music swiped from John Carpenter's **Escape from New York** and another, similar electronic soundtrack.

764. People's Hero

(1987; Loong Hsiang Film Co./Maverick Films) ★: 8/10. *Yan man ying hung* (Cantonese), *Ren min ying xiong* (Mandarin): "People's Hero." Cinematographer: Wilson Chan Pui-kai; Art Director: Yank Wong Yan-kwai; Music: Lowell Lo Kwun-ting; Writers: Derek Yee Tung-sing, Lee Pak-ling, Kwan Yiu-wing; Producer: John Sham Kin-fun; Director: Derek Yee Tung-sing. Cast: Ti Lung (Sunny Koo), Tony Leung Chiu-wai (Sai), Tony Leung Kar-fai (Capt. Chan), Paul Chun Pui (Capt. Cheung), Ronald Wong Pan (William Wong, aka Boney), Bowie Lam Bo-yee (Bank Employee), Yip Wing-cho (Fat Customer). 1.85:1. VHS: Tai Seng. Import LD: Star Entertainment (No Subtitles). 82 minutes.

Excellent performances by Ti Lung and Tony Leung Chiu-wai highlight this tense thriller. Amateur robbers Sai and Boney try to hold up a bank and thoroughly botch the job, resulting in a hostage situation. One of their captives turns out to be vicious criminal Sunny Koo, who was there to knock off the institution himself! Disarming the other bandits, Koo takes control of the standoff, ordering the police to provide him with a van. While he has a fearsome reputation, Koo treats his captives with civility, even saving one after he suffers a heart attack. Koo's demeanor begins to take violent swings in the other direction, however, when the police refuse to release his girlfriend from prison. When the authorities finally give in to this demand, the woman refuses to go with Koo, putting the safety of the hostages into question.

Intelligently scripted, well scored, and tightly paced, the film contains several wonderfully suspenseful scenes (particularly one in which the hostages are forced to play an elimination game to determine which two will be killed by Koo). Ti is alternately charismatic and frightening, always commanding the screen. Tony Leung Chiu-wai does equally solid work in a more subdued turn as Sai, who goes from desperate and impulsive to rational and resigned over the course of several tense hours. Ti later sent up his role here in **Run Don't Walk**.

Perfect Exchange *see* **The Sting II**

765. Perfect Girls

(1990; Cosmopolitan Film Productions) ★: 5/10. *Leung juk 100 fan* (Cantonese), *Jing zu 100 fen* (Mandarin): "Beauty Hits 100 Points." Cinematographer: Li Hsin-yeh; Art Director: Jon Hau Wing-choi; Music: Chow Kam-cheung; Producer: Lau Tin-chi; Writer-Director: Wong Jing. Cast: Wilson Lam Chun-yin (Tien-chi), Nina Li Chi (Feng Mu-jen), Michelle Lee Kar-yan (Lo Hsiao-hsiao), Monica Chan Fat-yung (Mu Lan-hua), Keith Kwan Chiu-chung (Robert), Mui Siu-wai (Tsing-tsing), Wong Jing (Litterbox), Shing Fui-on (Leslie Lo Chia-cheng). 1.85:1. VHS: World Video. Import LD/DVD: Mei Ah. Import VCD: Cameron Entertainment. Running time unknown.

This Wong Jing knockoff of the Dudley Moore hit **Arthur** (1981) stars Wilson Lam as 30 year-old virgin Tien-chi, who has to get married within one month's time or lose out on a $300 million inheritance. He hooks up first with the outgoing Hsiao-hsiao, but she proves to be far too extroverted and falls out of favor with Tien-chi's mom. Next, mother and son audition a selection of candidates, most of whom don't fit the bill. The one promising applicant is fearless supercop Lan-hua, who foils a robbery single-handedly, right before Tien-chi's eyes. Regardless, he craves Mu-jen, a stunning model who, unbeknownst to everyone, has been hired by Tien-chi's shifty American cousin to lure him to the altar right before the deadline and then turn him down, thus leaving the cousin in line for the money. Hsiao-hsiao keeps reappearing in Tien-chi's life, however, and she is not about to let him go.

Predictable from the word go, this is still a fairly pleasing effort, though most male viewers will stick with it only to see the seemingly endless assortment of beautiful women who are paraded through. Mui Siu-wai provides her trademark brand of ear-splitting comic relief, while Nat Chan Pak-cheung (sporting Wayne Newton's hair!) has an amusing cameo as a wacky plastic surgeon with a thing for needles.

766. Perfect Match

(1989; Win's Movie Production) ★: 5/10. *Jui gaai naam pang yau* (Cantonese), *Zui jia nan peng you* (Mandarin): "Best

Boyfriend." Cinematographer: Gigo Lee Chi-hang; Art Director: Fong Ying; Music: Joseph Chan Wing-leung; Writer-Producer: Wong Jing; Director: Dennis Chan Kwok-san. Cast: George Lam Chi-cheung (Peter Lai), Carol Cheng Yu-ling (Lok Ka-kay), Andy Lau Tak-wah (Lok Ka-sing), Ellen Chan Ar-lun (Salina), David Wu Tai-wai (David Shek), Shing Fui-on (Joseph), Manfred Wong (Ko-way), Dennis Chan Kwok-san (Dr. Kwong), Chingmy Yau Suk-ching (Doctor), Wong Jing, Nat Chan Pak-cheung, Charlie Cho Cha-lei (Security Guards), Frankie Chin Chi-leung (Giant Triad). 1.85:1. VHS: Tai Seng. Import LD/VCD: Ocean Shores. 92 minutes.

There is not one ounce of reality in this typical Win's production, but it remains reasonably entertaining, thanks in no small part to its congenial cast. Chilly female toy magnate Lok Ka-kay bets her curt underling, Peter Lai, that she can best him in a design competition. If Peter wins, he gets promoted; if Ka-kay wins, Peter will resign. While this is unfolding, Ka-kay's playboy brother, Ka-sing, has taken to romancing Peter's beautiful girlfriend. Ka-sing is anxious to see his sibling get married, as once Ka-kay has a husband, she can no longer control his share of the family business. In order to get Peter out of the way, he makes Ka-kay think that her opponent is actually trying to win her hand. Of course, once the initial hostility subsides, the two really do fall in love, until an employee and Peter's jealous ex-wife set about sabotaging things.

The plot resolution is forced and unconvincing, even for this type of wish fulfilment fluff, and only Wong Jing would feel the need to include gags about mechanical tarantulas, foul-mouthed toys, and chest hair growth formulas in a romantic comedy. If you like the stars, proceed—but with caution. A handful of scenes unfold without subtitles.

767. The Phantom Lover

(1995; Mandarin Films) ★: 9/10. *Ye boon goh sing* (Cantonese), *Ye ban ge sheng* (Mandarin): "Midnight Song." Cinematographer: Peter Pau Tak-hei; Art Director: Eddie Ma Poon-chiu; Music: Chris Babida; Writers: Szeto Wai-cheuk, Raymond Wong Pak-ming, Ronny Yu Yan-tai; Producers: Raymond Wong Pak-ming, Wong Ko-hoi; Director: Ronny Yu Yan-tai. Cast: Leslie Cheung Kwok-wing (Song Danping), Jacqueline Wu Chien-lien (Du Yuyan), Huang Lei (Wei Qing), Pau Fong (Zhao). 2.35:1. DTS Stereo. VHS: Tai Seng (Tiny Subtitles). Import LD/VCD/DVD: Fitto Mobile (Tiny Subtitles). 102 minutes.

Several key personnel from **The Bride with White Hair**—including star Leslie Cheung, director Ronny Yu, cinematographer Peter Pau, production designer Eddie Ma, and editor David Wu—were reunited for this resplendent HK/Singapore co-production lensed in Beijing. A remake of *Ye ban ge sheng*, first produced in the 1930s and then again in 1961 by Shaw Brothers, **The Phantom Lover** is a variation on **Phantom of the Opera**, inserting the primary elements from Gaston Leroux's creation into the framework of an archetypal Chinese romantic tragedy. In execution, it engenders both intoxicating grandeur and poignant emotion: a near-perfect merger of classical narrative and state-of-the-art production techniques. In 1936 an impoverished theatre troupe sets itself up in the burned-out remains of a once opulent opera house to stage their new production. The young lead singer, Wei Qing (Huang Lei, from Chen Kaige's **Life on a String**), learns that the site had previously been the toast of the 1920s dramatic circuit, thanks to the magnetism of its architect and star, Song Danping, who had accrued tremendous fame performing the lead in a Mandarin musical adaptation of *Romeo and Juliet*. Danping fell deeply in love with Du Yuyan, the daughter of an industrialist, who had already promised her hand in marriage to the wealthy Zhao family in order to build a factory. When Yuyan rebelled against her parents' wishes and tried to elope with Danping, her father had his servants disfigure him with acid and set the theatre ablaze. With Danping presumed dead, Yuyan was then forced to wed Zhao's sadistic son, a punishment which eventually drove her insane. During every full moon, she returns to the crumbling auditorium to hear Danping perform the love song that he had composed especially for her. While investigating the theatre's rickety catwalks, Qing discovers that Danping survived the conflagration, and his hooded spectre is soon giving the lad vocal coaching so that he can perform the part of Romeo. However, Danping's motives are not wholly altruistic: He utilizes the youth as his substitute in order to placate the deluded Yuyan by comforting her anguish while also shielding her from his grotesque visage. When the Zhao family becomes aware of the phantom's presence, they set about to eliminate both him and Yuyan once and for all.

Although **Bride** proved him an adept technician, director Ronny Yu never allowed the project's action and special effects to overshadow his star-crossed protagonists. He has successfully repeated this approach here and is aided, as before, by strong central performances. Leslie Cheung makes an ideal Danping, narcissistic but compassionate enough during his romantic interludes with Yuyan to retain viewer sympathy. While a suitably menacing phantom, Cheung is less psychotic than his cinematic predecessors, threatening but never intentionally killing anyone (no chandelier sequence here), and the actor is let down somewhat by a substandard make-up job. Considering Cheung's much-praised turn as the troubled, female-playing vocalist in **Farewell, My Concubine** (1993), it would have been a real innovation to stage the musical drama as a traditional Peking Opera, but his singing here is very good. Since her debut in **A Moment of Romance** (1990), Jacqueline Wu has often played women whose idealistic outlooks on love and humanity are out of touch with the worlds they inhabit, invariably contributing to their ruin. Her ability to inhabit such roles without falling victim to their inherent melodramatic pitfalls engenders audience empathy, and that quality (further accentuated by her delicate beauty) makes Wu the perfect leading lady for this sort of romantic tragedy. The pair make an affecting couple, and if their destiny is not entirely satisfying in a logical sense, it is an emotionally pleasing one. The 1936 sequences (about 70 percent of the running time) were shot on color stock but printed down to near monochrome and tinted in sepia. Intermittent applications of color appear, ranging from a lantern's subtle, incandescent glow to the pale red of lipstick, growing more plentiful and pronounced as the film progresses. In a simple but impressive take on the norm, the *flashbacks* unfold in full, lustrous hues, and the effect is stunning, particularly the deep scarlet of Yuyan's bridal chamber, the myriad fabrics and floral bouquets on display in the opera house, and the crimson glow that heralds the towers of orange flame engulfing the theatre. The film is also noteworthy as the first Chinese production to be mixed in the DTS Stereo process. **The Phantom Lover** was shot with sync sound, with the performers delivering their lines in Mandarin, and that is certainly the best version to see.

768. Phantom War

(1991; D & B Films Co./Regent Film) ★: 2/10. *Ying lun yuet jin* (Cantonese), *Ying lun yue zhan* (Mandarin): "English Vietnamese Relations Fighting." Cinematographer: Philip Ma Kam-cheung; Art Director: Raymond Kwok Siu-keung; Music: Not Original; Producer: Phillip Ko Fei; Action Directors: Yasuyoshi Shikamara, Pao Wah; Directors: Cindy Chow Fung, Simon Yeung Siu-kwong. Cast: Ben Ng Ngai-cheung (Cheng Ho-nan),

Yammie Nam Kit-ying (Yin), Alex Man Chi-leung (Liang), Lau Siu-ming (Lau Min), Phillip Ko Fei (Yuen Tai-fei). 1.85:1. VHS: Tai Seng (Subtitled or Dubbed). Import LD/VCD: Mei Ah. 88 minutes.

Credibility is sorely lacking in this shoddy production which fluctuates between the far-fetched and the thoroughly ridiculous. Ben Ng and Yammie Nam play husband-and-wife Vietnamese resistance fighters who survive the war and come to England to find peace and prosperity. While there, Ng saves the life of a Chinatown boss (Lau Siu-ming), who loans the couple enough money to open a small take-out restaurant. After a second attempt is made on Lau's life, Ng decides to accept the gangster's offer of employment, much to the anger of Nam, who decides to leave him. Everyone's life is endangered by Phillip Ko, playing a fellow Vietnam vet working with Lau's power hungry son (Alex Man) to usurp Lau's position, and who has an old score to settle with Ng.

There is a surplus of mayhem but very little of it is staged well, so action completists will come away unsatisfied; and the characters and storyline are vapid enough to negate the whole enterprise on their own, so there is little here for anyone else. Yammie Nam's effective portrayal and the location shooting in England are about all that keep this one from being a complete write-off. Some of the same cast and crew members also worked on **Killer's Romance**.

Physical Weapon *see* **The Underground Banker**

769. Picture of a Nymph

(1988; Golden Harvest/Bo Ho Films/Paragon Films) ★: 7/10. *Wa jung sin* (Cantonese), *Hua zhong xian* (Mandarin): "The Immortal in the Painting." Cinematographers: Tom Lau Moon-tong, Raymond Lam Fai-tai, Abdul M. Rumjahn; Art Directors: Hai Chung-man, Leung Bo-chan; Music: James Wong Jim; Writers: Wu Ma, Chan Kam-cheung; Producer: Sammo Hung Kam-po; Action Direction: Sammo Hung Stunt Team; Director: Wu Ma. Cast: Yuen Biao (Shih Erh), Joey Wang Tsu-hsien (Mo Chiu), Wu Ma (Wu Men-chu), Lawrence Ng Kai-wah (Tsui Hung-chien), Elizabeth Lee Mei-fung (King Ghost), Sit Chi-lun (Suang), Yuen Wah (Demonic Old Man), Lam Wai (Swordsman in Prologue). 1.85:1. VHS: Tai Seng (No Subtitles). Import LD: Star Entertainment (No Subtitles). 97 minutes. Also known as **Portrait of a Nymph**.

An above average imitation of **A Chinese Ghost Story**, this Golden Harvest production even goes so far as to cast Wu Ma (who also directed), Joey Wang, Sit Chi-lun, and Lam Wai in virtually the same roles they essayed in the earlier film. One evening, wandering ghost catcher Shih Erh saves timid scholar Tsui Hung-chien from a demon disguised as a frail old man. In the process, however, the scholar's house goes up in flames. The pair hit the road together, eventually meeting up with Erh's humorless master, Taoist swordsman Wu Men-chu. Hung-chien falls for the beautiful Mo Chiu, whom he sees one day, and paints a lovely portrait of her. Little does he know it but she is actually the ghost of a maiden who died on the day of her wedding. In order to escape both the evil "King" Ghost (played by the very feminine Elizabeth Lee) and Men-chu, Chiu hides inside Hung-chien's painting. Although he is angered by both the scholar and Erh's refusal to vanquish Chiu, Men-chu rediscovers his humanity in time to help the two men battle King Ghost.

While the artistic inspiration is obvious, the production design and cinematography remain quite beautiful and go a long way in selling the fantasy elements. Yuen Biao is as appealing as always, bringing a very tangible energy to the proceedings, but Lawrence Ng proves why he is much better suited to villainous roles, lacking the looks and charisma to be a convincing hero. While the film rarely strays from convention, its storyline goes even further than its model in the way it emphasizes the power of love and how it can conquer both otherworldly evil and human detachment. Although they are not quite as exciting as those found in the Ching Siu-tung series, the special FX here are colorful and introduce some interesting new elements (like magical little paper cranes that act almost like carrier pigeons). The Taiwan video version has English subtitles.

770. Pink Bomb

(1993) ★: 6/10. *Yan sang dak yi sui jun foon* (Cantonese), *Ren sheng de yi shua jin huan* (Mandarin): "Life Complacent Decline Exhausted Joy." Cinematographers: Yuen Kwok-wai, Wong Kar-fai; Art Director: Chan Yu-kwong; Music: Wong Yiu-kwong; Writer: Dayo Wong Chi-wah; Producer: Chow Wah-yu; Action Director: Cheung Kwok-leung; Director: Derek Chiu Sung-kei. Cast: Waise Lee Chi-hung (Graham), Cynthia Yang Li-ching (Liang Chi-chun), Fennie Yuen Kit-ying (Yeh Yu-shin), Loletta Lee Lai-chun (Li Sin-yi), Gloria Yip Wan-yee (Ann), Lau Ching-wan (Daniel), Dayo Wong Chi-wah (Wang San-ha), Cheung Kwok-leung (Fake Cop), Fung Hark-on (Brother Black). 1.85:1. VHS/LD: World Video. Import LD/VCD: Mei Ah. 95 minutes.

A decidedly offbeat action-comedy, **Pink Bomb** tells of a HK tour group's adventures while vacationing in Thailand. Upon their arrival, the men are propositioned by cute (and seemingly underage) hooker Ann, whom the women later save from being raped by a john. What they don't know is that Ann's trick is a mobster and Ann has stolen the $3 million in counterfeit bills he was carrying. This puts the girl's ex-partner and a horde of local gangsters on their tail. To make matters worse, Graham, their devoutly Christian guide, has been exchanging an awfully large amount of money with shady-looking characters along the way.

While uneven, the film benefits from writer-co-star Dayo Wong's singular brand of humor (his Russian Roulette dream sequence is a real gem), which keeps the scenario intriguingly unpredictable. Martial arts star Cynthia Yang gets several opportunities to display her prowess, and Lau Ching-wan is especially amusing in an offbeat turn as a crazy cabbie (patterned after Robert DeNiro's **Taxi Driver**) who is just aching to try out his gun. *Pink Bomb* is a nice little sleeper that is worth checking out.

771. Pink Force Commando

(1984; IFD Films & Arts) ★: 5/10. Chinese Titles Unknown. Cinematographer: Wu Kam-yung; Music: Not Original; Writer: Benny Ho; Producer: Joseph Lai; Action Director: Philip Lee; Director: Chu Yen-ping. Cast: Brigitte Lin Ching-hsia (Jackal), Sally Yeh Chian-wen (Dynamite Susie), Elsa Yeung Wai-san (Cat), Silvia Pang Suet-man (Rebel Angel), Hilda Lau Hou-yee (Ninja Leader), Teresa Tsui (Woman in White), Sophia Ching (Gang Member), Blackie Ko Shou-liang (Thug in Black Leather Jacket). 2.35:1. VHS: Video Link (Dubbed). 90 minutes.

While not directly related to **Golden Queens Commando**, this loopy Taiwanese production is very much in the same spirit and shares some performers, footage, and behind-the-scenes personnel with its forerunner. Surrounded and facing almost certain death, a gang of female robbers, led by Jackal, decide to fight their way out or die. Jackal and cohort Cat will take the loot, with the plan being that the group will meet again in one year's time to split it up. However, it is all a set-up and Jackal absconds with the gold, thanks to the help of male accomplice "The Pink Commander." The pair then use the booty to build a small town-amusement park called Sin

City. Cat tracks down the remaining gang members and recruits another, Dynamite Susie, with plans to exact revenge. However, they end up joining forces with Jackal (who cuts off one of her arms as penance) and the commander to steal a priceless, magical diamond called "The Oriental Star." That caper results in another act of treachery which leaves Jackal on the verge of death. Her savior arrives in the form of "The Heartbroken Man," a mysterious figure on horseback, who nurses her back to health and provides Jackal with a mini gatling gun to strap onto her stump(!).

Only in a Chu Yen-ping film could you have cowgirls, ninjas, shaolin monks, gamblers, bikers, bounty hunters, and a woman in a superheroine costume all sharing the screen! Less tongue-in-cheek than its forerunner, **Pink Force Commando** is still just as nonsensically bizarre, and if it is far from being a good movie, it is certainly not a dull one. Blackie Ko (a veteran action choreographer/director who is also Taiwan's answer to Evel Knievel) has a supporting role (under the name "Simon Hor") and gets to do a motorcycle leap across a decimated bridge. The soundtrack includes music swiped from **Dressed to Kill, Conan the Barbarian**, and several spaghetti westerns. Character names are from the dubbed version, which credits direction to "Lawrence Full."

772. Plain Jane to the Rescue

(1982; Golden Harvest/Hi-Pitch Co./Paragon Films) ★: 5/10. *Baat choi Lam A-jun* (Cantonese), *Ba ca Lin Yazhen* (Mandarin): "Multi-Talented Lam Ah-chun" or "Multi-Talented Lin Yazhen." Cinematographer: Lau Hung-chuen; Art Director: Alex Ma Yiu-ping; Music: Not Original; Writers: John Woo Yu-sen, Lau Chan-wah; Producer: Raymond Chow Man-wai; Action Direction: Hong Kong Action Stunt; Director: John Woo Yu-sen. Cast: Josephine Siao Fong-fong (Jenny), Ricky Hui Koon-ying (Fang), Michael Lee Ming-yeung (Sand), Charlie Cho Cha-lei (Sand's Son), Woo Fung (Fake Santa), David Wu Tai-wai (TV Director), Chen Sing (Chen), Norman Law Man (Himself), John Woo Yu-sen (Himself), Ng Hong-ning (Muscleman). 2.35:1. VHS: Tai Seng (Poor Subtitles). Import VCD: Mega Star. 90 minutes.

The third of Josephine Siao's "Lam Ah-chun" films, this scattershot comedy tries just about anything for a laugh and manages to garner a few. Ah-chun (renamed "Jenny" in the English subtitles) goes through a series of jobs (including road crew, classical musician, and stunt double) with her customary ineptitude. Hired as a cleaning woman at a high-tech factory, Ah-chun meets up with her old, equally nerdy friend Fang and all but causes an atomic disaster. She is then engaged by the evil Zada Corporation (which is sometimes called "Sanda" in the confusing subs) to perform a most unusual task: teach manners to Sha, an undisciplined old coot who is the father of the chairman. Ah-chun befriends the old man and improves his disposition, but the chairman plans on disposing of his father now that the latter's will has been signed. After numerous screw-ups, Ah-chun and Fang manage to rescue Sha from certain death, but it is a race against time to get the old man to sign a new copy of his will before his evil son takes complete control of the company.

Woo invests the proceedings with a cartoonish energy that helps one get through the weaker material. As mentioned above, the film is all over the map comedically, even incorporating in-joke references to **Lady and the Tramp, Spartacus**, '60s spy movies, and old-style kung fu films. While hardly memorable, **Plain Jane to the Rescue** is a modestly enjoyable footnote in the career of a master filmmaker destined for better things.

773. Point of No Return

(1990; Y.C. Lai Film Production Co.) ★: 6/10. *Do si saat sing* (Cantonese), *Du shi sha xing* (Mandarin): "Big City Evil Spirit Star." Cinematographer: Stanley Hung Hin-shing; Art Director: Lui Kwok-fu; Music: John Wong Sai-cheung; Writers: John Chong Ching, Wing Chow Chan-wing; Action Directors: Hung Cheung-tak, Kwok Ah-cheung, Yip Wing-kin; Producer-Director: Guy Lai Ying-chau. Cast: Jacky Cheung Hok-yau (Dee), Joey Wang Tsu-hsien (Julie), Patrick Tam Yiu-man (KK), Kenneth Tsang Kong (Min), Ken Lo Wai-kwong (Puma), Cherrie Tsui Lap-ngai (Joe Joe), Ricky Yee Fan-wai (Michael), Pau Fong (Kao Wen-pin), Mark Houghton (Blonde Thug), Fung Hark-on (Nightclub Patron). 1.85:1. VHS: Tai Seng. Import LD/VCD: Ocean Shores. 94 minutes.

This routine thriller stars Jacky Cheung as hitman Dee (code name: Eagle), one of the top guns in a secret society of killers. His best friend, KK (the son of Min, his mentor), wants to emulate Dee's lifestyle and profession, to the point of secretly following him on a job in Thailand. This particular hit comes back to haunt Dee in a very dangerous way: The victim's brother, a rival killer named Puma, is out to terminate Dee but does not know what Dee he looks like. Dee enters into a relationship with Julie (or "Joy," as she is initially called in the subtitles), a beautiful insurance salesperson/DJ(!), not knowing that KK has accepted an assignment to murder her father. KK carries out the hit, but Puma, having been tipped off, is also on the scene and tries to kill KK, thinking him to be Dee. When Puma leaves evidence identifying Dee at the site of a murder and the newspapers report it, Dee, Min, and KK are forced into a corner and must face off against the leader of the organization on his own turf.

Good action (including some typically flamboyant gunplay) and some nice opening reel location work in Thailand help make this worthwhile, if overly familiar, entertainment. Irritatingly, this is yet another film that ends with an untranslated crawl revealing the fates of the characters.

Police Assassin *see* **Royal Warriors**
Police Assassin 2 *see* **Yes, Madam**

774. Police Confidential

(1995; Sky Point Film Investment Co./Kingfisher Films) ★: 6/10. *Jan ham sing chau man* (Cantonese), *Zhen han xing chou wen* (Mandarin): "Shocking Sex Scandal." Cinematographer: Ko Chiu-lam; Art Directors: Chiu Chung-pang, Wong Ching-ching; Music: Danny Chung Teng-yat; Writer: Lu Bing; Producer: Che-Kirk Wong Chi-keung; Director: Raymond Lee Wai-man. Cast: Simon Yam Tat-wah (Lui Chun-ying), Zhang Fengyi (Alex Chiang Wai-kei), Linda Wong Hing-ping (Daisy Ma), Carrie Ng Kar lai (Councillor Lau). 1.85:1. VHS: World Video. Import LD/VCD: Universe. 90 minutes.

An excellent score by Danny Chung and some mesmerizing visuals highlight this offbeat but not entirely satisfying thriller. Lui Chun-ying is a cop with a destructive weakness: He is a voyeur. One night he sees a couple engaging in S & M, with the woman appearing to be on the verge of death. When Lui makes his presence known, the masked male flees the scene. Lui's past indiscretions have already set him on thin ice with his superiors, a problem that is quickly exacerbated when he accidentally bungles a stakeout by the ICAC (Independent Commission Against Corruption) division. The ICAC commander, Alex Chiang, sets out to destroy Lui by framing him for taking $200,000 in bribes from pimps. With the help of sympathetic ICAC officer Daisy Ma, Lui discovers that Chiang is out to ruin a councilman that is running against Chiang's mistress in an election. When Daisy reports this information, Chiang is fired, setting the stage for a Legislative Council hearing that will ultimately determine who is really guilty.

The above synopsis relates the storyline in a straightforward fashion, though the film often presents it in non-linear snatches, with tinting designating the moments when we are travelling backward or forward in time. The approach is intriguing, but an overabundance of voiceover narration from Simon Yam's character and some nagging implausibilities (namely, the manner in which the Lui and Daisy characters originally hook up and the manner in which she is able to match the voice pattern on a telephone recording) prevent the film from fully succeeding. Despite being dubbed by another actor in the Cantonese version, Mainland star Zhang Fengyi has tremendous presence and makes for a formidable villain, outclassing Yam right off the screen. Producer Che-Kirk Wong has an eyeblink cameo.

Police Sir [*sic*] *see* **Modern Heroes**

775. Police Story

(1985; Golden Harvest/Golden Way Films/Paragon Films) ★: 8/10. *Ging chaat goo si* (Cantonese), *Jing cha gu shi* (Mandarin): "Police Story." Cinematographer: Cheung Yiu-cho; Art Director: Oliver Wong Yui-man; Music: Michael Lai Siu-tin (HK version), Kevin Bassinson (English export version), J. Peter Robinson (New Line version); Writers: Jackie Chan, Edward Tang King-sang; Producer: Leonard Ho Koon-cheung; Action Direction: Jackie Chan's Stuntmen Association; Director: Jackie Chan. Cast: Jackie Chan (Chan Ka-kui), Maggie Cheung Man-yuk (May), Brigitte Lin Ching-hsia (Salina Fong), Chor Yuen (Chu Tu), Bill Tung Biu (Uncle Bill Chang), Lam Kwok-hung (Raymond, the Superintendent), Feng Sing (Kim), Kenneth Tong Chun-yip (Tom), Kam Hing-yin (Inspector Man), Charlie Cho Cha-lei (John Ko), Lau Chi-wing (Cheung, the Lawyer), Fung Hark-on (Danny Ko), Tai Po (Lee), Wan Fat (Mad Wing), Woo Fung (Sha Tau Kok Station Commander), Money Lo Man-yee (TV Interviewer), Michael Lai Siu-tin (Man Trying to Park Car), Ben Lam Kwok-bun (Thug). Dolby Digital (DVD only). 2.35:1. VHS: Cinema Group (Dubbed, 87 minutes), New Line (Revamped Dubbed Version, 89 minutes), Tai Seng (Poor Subtitles). LD: New Line/Image (Revamped Dubbed Version, 89 minutes). Import LD: Star Entertainment (No Subtitles). Import VCD: Mei Ah. Import DVD: Mega Star (95 minutes). Also known as **Jackie Chan's Police Force** (Cinema Group title).

Winner of the Best Picture and Best Action Choreography prizes at the Fifth HK Film Awards, this terrific Jackie Chan police thriller is a rousing mix of humor and back-breaking stunts that ranks among the star's best works to date. In spite of a raid that goes awry and causes the destruction of a hillside squatter settlement, the HK police department is able to nab criminal boss Chu Tu. Officer Chan Kar-kui apprehended the target practically single-handed and, as a result, is ordered to protect Chu's secretary, Salina Fong, who is being forced to testify against him. Salina's presence sends Ka-kui's girlfriend, May, into a huff but that is the least of Ka-kui's problems: Chu's lawyer manages to get him out of jail and the criminal orders a cop on his pay roll to ice both Ka-kui and Salina. The pair manage to escape and Salina makes copies of Chu's computer files, leading to a decisive showdown between Ka-kui and Chu's men in a crowded shopping mall.

Aside from an overlong courtroom sequence (which has a weak comic payoff), **Police Story** is a nonstop action thrill ride which wholly deserves that overused tag line. The stuntwork is exceptionally good (in particular, an incredibly painful looking bit where Fung Hark-on's henchman character goes bouncing down a moving escalator, and Chan's slide down a very long and very high pole that is covered with electric lights), and the climactic confrontation in the mall (which finds Chan fending off baseball bat wielding attackers) is fantastic, no matter how many times you view it. New Line's dubbed version features different voice and music tracks from Golden Harvest's original export edition. The Japanese laserdisc (which runs 105 minutes) contains footage unique to that version, including an opening reel surprise birthday party prank played on Feng Sing's character. Three sequels followed.

776. Police Story II

(1988; Golden Harvest/Golden Way Films/Paragon Films) ★: 8/10. *Ging chaat goo si juk jaap* (Cantonese), *Jing cha gu shi xu ji* (Mandarin): "Police Story Sequel." Cinematographer: Cheung Yiu-cho; Art Director: Oliver Wong Yui-man; Music: Michael Lai Siu-tin, Michael Lai Siu-tin (HK version), J. Peter Robinson (New Line Version); Writers: Jackie Chan, Edward Tang King-sang; Producer: Leonard Ho Koon-cheung; Action Direction: Jackie Chan Stuntman's Association; Director: Jackie Chan. Cast: Jackie Chan (Chan Ka-kui), Maggie Cheung Man-yuk (May), Lam Kwok-hung (Raymond, the Superintendent), Charlie Cho Cha-lei (John Ko), Bill Tung Biu (Uncle Bill Chang), Chor Yuen (Chu Tao), Crystal Kwok Kam-yan (Policewoman), Angile Leung Wan-yui (Policewoman), Kenny Ho Kar-king (PC12674), Feng Sing (Kim), Wu Ma (Mall Security Guard), Benny Lai Wai (Deaf Criminal), Ben Lam Kwok-bun (Tall Criminal), Kwan San (President Fung), Lau Ching-wan (CID Man #1), Michael Chow Man-kin (CID Man #2), Alvina Kong Yan-yin (Stewardess), Lau Siu-ming (Senior Police Official), Ken Lo Wai-kwong (Fireman), Billy Lau Nam-kwong (Insolent Truck Driver), Dennis Chan Kwok-san (Flustered Merchant), Yip Wing-cho (Board Member). Dolby Digital (DVD only). 2.35:1. VHS: New Line (Dubbed), Tai Seng (No Subtitles). Import LD: Star Entertainment (No Subtitles). Import VCD: Universe. Import DVD: Mega Star. 101 minutes (HK version), 98 minutes (New Line Version).

Although he saved the day in the first film, Chan Ka-kui cost the government so much money in damages he is denied a promotion and reassigned to traffic patrol. To make matters worse, crimelord Chu is certified as being terminally ill and wins a release from prison, instructing his men to exact revenge before he dies. On top of that, Chan must nab a gang who use high explosives to extort millions of dollars out of major corporations. The criminals kidnap May and wire Chan with explosives, forcing him to pick up the money for them.

The subplot involving Chu and his men could have been left out, as it really only serves as an excuse for a couple more action sequences (though no harm in that, when it's a Jackie Chan film). The climactic battle rivals that seen in the original, particularly during the bits where Chan fights Benny Lai Wai, who is one of the most amazing and agile kickers that the star has faced. Chan's original cut reportedly ran about 20 minutes longer but was nixed by Golden Harvest; the star is reportedly dissatisfied with the abbreviated version the company did release, but his cut is, alas, not available for comparison. Poor Maggie Cheung was badly injured when she was conked on the head by a heavy steel rack; it and a lot of other painful looking gaffes are included (as always) in the end crawl.

777. Police Story III: Supercop

(1992; Golden Harvest/Paragon Films) ★: 8/10. *Ging chat goo si III chiu kap ging chat* (Cantonese), *Jing cha gu shi III chao ji jing cha* (Mandarin): "Police Story III: Supercop." Cinematographer: Ardy Lam Kwok-wah; Art Director: Oliver Wong Yui-man; Music: Lee Chung-shing (original version), Joel McNeely (US version); Writers: Edward Tang King-sang, Fibe Ma Mei-ping, Lee Wai-yee; Producers: Edward Tang King-sang, Willie Chan Chi-keung; Action Directors: Stanley Tong Kwai-lai, Tang Tak-wing, Sit Chun-wai, Chan Man-ching, Sam Wong Ming-sing; Director: Stanley Tong Kwai-lai. Cast:

Jackie Chan (Kevin), Michelle Yeoh Chu-kheng (Chief of Security Yang), Maggie Cheung Man-yuk (May), Kenneth Tsang Kong (Chaibat), Yuen Wah (Panther), Bill Tung Biu (Uncle Bill), Josephine Koo Mei-wah (Chaibat's Wife), Kelvin Wong Siu (Peter), Lo Lieh (The General), Ken Lo Wai-kwong (Chaibat's Man), Feng Sing (Panther's Man), Kim Maree Penn (Blonde Gunwoman). 2.35:1. Dolby Digital (US version and Mega Star DVD only). Unidentified Stereo Process (Star LD and China Star DVD only). VHS/DVD: Dimension (US version). LD: Voyager (US version). Import LD/VCD: Star Entertainment (No Subtitles). Import DVD: China Star (No Subtitles), Mega Star. 91/95 minutes. Also known as **Supercop** (US theatrical and video title).

This rousing sequel ingeniously pairs Jackie Chan with his female counterpart, the equally fearless Michelle Yeoh (billed in some versions as "Michelle Khan"). Chan's dauntless HK cop is partnered with Yeoh's no-nonsense Mainland security officer for a mission to bring down a powerful drug lord who seeks to take over Asia's heroin trade. Chan is able to gain the criminal's confidence by rescuing the man's brother (Yuen) from a harsh prison camp. Passing Yeoh off as his sister, the two infiltrate the gang and work to dismantle it from the inside. The plots in Chan's films are always secondary to the action, and what action! Purists have quibbled over the fact that the film features little martial arts *per se*, but that is hardly upsetting when the alternative is sights like Chan dangling hundreds of feet in the air from a helicopter ladder, and nimbly maintaining his balance while fighting atop a moving train. Yeoh is no slouch either, jumping a motorbike onto said train, and hanging on to an armoured car that is careening through the streets of Kuala Lumpur. The ending is weak and much too abrupt, but all is forgiven in light of such showstopping athletics, courtesy of the two most eager-to-please stars in the business. Yeoh reprises her character in **Project S**, a semi-sequel.

Four years after its bow in Asia, **Police Story III: Supercop** was newly dubbed into English and received a major theatrical release in America (through the Miramax offshoot, Dimension Films) as, simply, **Supercop**. In contrast to New Line Cinema's gutting of **Rumble in the Bronx** and **First Strike**, the alterations made here are not too severe. Approximately six minutes of footage was trimmed, but the deletions did not seriously harm the storyline or the character development. With the exception of Chan and Yeoh (who did their own voices), the English dubbing is not substantially improved over the old chop sockies. Some Chinese performers (including martial arts star Conan Lee Yuen-ba) are listed among the voice artists, but the articulation rarely seems natural, and poor Maggie Cheung comes off like a screeching Val Girl bubblehead. The dubbing also tends to make some of the comedy rather laboured, particularly when Chan's superior pretends to be his mother, a bit which was not all that funny to begin with. The new score by Joel McNeeley is reasonably good, if generic and unadventurous, but the opening title sequence (a hyper collage of solarized clips and MTV-style garbage animation) is pretty embarrassing. On the plus side, the Dolby mix is super, giving the action sequences real vigour, abetted by significantly improved foley FX. Still, the American track is quite sloppy at times (when Tsang's character is playing the video game Tetris, sound FX from a martial arts game have been put in!), and the modest scale of some sequences clashes with the grandiose accompaniment. The major irritant, however, is the addition of contemporary pop songs in order to generate a soundtrack album. Having *gangsta* rap tunes in the background is bad enough, but putting a Tom Jones(!) cover of the dreadful '70s novelty tune "Kung Fu Fighting" over the outtakes is unforgivable. The Dimension edition is better than nothing, but if you have access to it, the Hong Kong version is more satisfying and much closer to the original spirit of the enterprise. Character names listed above are derived from Dimension's dubbed version.

778. Pom Pom

(1984; Golden Harvest/Bo Ho Films Co./Paragon Films) ★: 7/10. *San kan seung heung paau* (Cantonese), *Shen yong shuang xiang pao* (Mandarin): "Brave Courageous Double Bang Pow." Cinematographer: Ricky Lau Koon-wai; Art Directors: Cheung King-hung, Wong Yun-tat; Music: Joseph Chan Wing-leung, Mahmood Rumjahn; Writer: Bo Ho Writing Team; Producer: Sammo Hung Kam-po; Director: Joseph Cheung Tung-cho. Cast: Richard Ng Yiu-hon (Chiu, aka "Walker"), John Sham Kin-fun (Beethoven, aka "Johnny"), Deanie Yip Tak-han (Anna), Phillip Chan Yan-kin (Chen), Peter Chan Lung (Sha), Tai Po (Chou the Pimp), Dick Wei (Scarman), Chung Fat (Columbo), James Tien Chun (Chief Inspector). 1.85:1. Video distributor unknown. 100 minutes.

If you are looking for the films that set the standard for the HK "buddy cop" genre, this enjoyable mix of low comedy and terrific stunts is certainly one of them. Richard Ng and John Sham play two supremely bumbling lawmen who, nonetheless, manage to get the job done in spite of themselves. Looking for a way to bust drug smuggler Sha, the pair try to roust leads from their double-dealing pimp stoolie while protecting their jobs from the Chief Inspector, who is out to can them. The best sequence finds Ng desperately trying to hide a drunk hooker from his loving girlfriend, though some will also love the sheer political incorrectness of the interrogation scene in which Ng and Shum mistake a woman for a rape victim. There are lots of familiar faces in bit parts, including Jackie Chan (as a motorcycle cop and also in a clip from **Winners and Sinners**), Wu Ma, Dennis Chan Kwok-san, producer Sammo Hung Kam-po, Charlie Chin Hsiang-lin, Yuen Biao, Stanley Fung Shui-fan, Lam Ching-ying, and Feng Sing.

A box office smash, the film spawned three sequels with Sham and Ng: **The Return of Pom Pom** (also 1984), **Mr. Boo Meets Pom Pom** (1985), and **Pom Pom Strikes Back** (1986). Director Joseph Cheung went on to make **Rosa** (1986), with Yuen Biao and Lowell Lo Kwun-ting taking over as the leads, and **Pom Pom and Hot Hot** (1992), which bears no official connection to the original films but follows the same formula with excellent results. Incidentally, the name **Pom Pom** does not refer to anything. The English title was supposed to be "Pow Pow," but someone accidentally flipped the "w" in each word!

779. Pom Pom and Hot Hot

(1992; New Prima Film Production) ★: 7/10. *San cheung sau yue ka lei gai* (Cantonese), *Shen qiang shou yu ga li ji* (Mandarin): "Top Marksman and Curry Chicken." Cinematographers: Jingle Ma Choshing, Chan Chun-kau, Tom Lau Moontong, Peter Ngor Chi-kwan; Art Director: Bill Lui Cho-hung; Writer-Producer-Director: Joseph Cheung Tung-cho. Cast: Jacky Cheung Hok-yau (Shin Chin-chian), Stephen Tung Wai (Chiang Li-chi), Lam Ching-ying (Shooter Yin), Alfred Cheung Kin-ting (Cha Chiang), Loletta Lee Lai-chun (Cha Shi), Bonnie Fu Yuk-ching (Nancy Ton Yue-lan), Austin Wai Tin-chi (Wu Yuen-shin), Cheung Kwok-leung (Lau Tin-hau), John Ching Tung (Shing), Guy Lai Ying-chau (Chau). 1.85:1. VHS: Tai Seng. Import LD/VCD: Ocean Shores. 93 minutes.

While it bears no official connection to the previous **Pom Pom** films, this terrific buddy cop comedy is certainly in the same spirit and features some of the most amazingly acrobatic gunplay you will ever see! Fun loving partners Shin and Chiang are assigned to investigate a triad drug ring. The task is complicated by the arrival of Shin's Mainland cousins, the tyrannical Cha Chiang and his beautiful, put-upon sister Cha Shi. The pair have come to HK for a visit and Chiang insists on tagging along with the partners while they try and do their jobs. Shin proceeds to put the moves on Shi, and Chiang runs into Nancy, his old flame. The latter witnessed a murder committed by crack shot Wu Yuen-shin at her nightclub and is convinced (in a less-than-honest manner) to testify against the man's boss, prompting him to send Wu after her.

The plot is virtually nonexistent, and there is a long mahjong sequence in which the humor will mean virtually nothing to most Western viewers. Regardless, the film is fast and likeable, and the wild climactic shootout will dazzle even the most jaded action aficionados. Mixing the grace of martial arts duels and the flamboyant staging that modern-day HK actioners are world famous for, it is truly a marvel to see.

780. Pom Pom Strikes Back

(1986; D & B Films Co.) ★: 5/10. *Seung lung to ju* (Cantonese), *Shuang long tu zhu* (Mandarin): "Twin Dragons Local Pearls." Cinematographer: Derek Yee Tung-sing; Art Director: Yank Wong Yan-kwai; Music: Danny Chung Teng-yat; Writer: Jo Chan Wai-yee; Producer: John Sham Kin-fun; Action Directors: Stephen Tung Wai, Benz Kong To-hoi; Director: Yip Wing-cho. Cast: Richard Ng Yiu-hon (Chow), John Sham Kin-fun (Beethoven), Deanie Yip Tak-han (Anna), May Lo Mei-mei (May Lo), Michael Chan Wai-man (Killer), Phillip Chan Yan-kin (Chan). 1.85:1. VHS: Tai Seng. 85 minutes.

The fourth and final of the Richard Ng-John Sham **Pom Pom** films finds the boys assigned to protect a witness (May Lo) from being murdered by a determined triad hitman (Michael Chan) before she can testify against his boss. Unfortunately, that only makes up a small portion of the running time, with the main gags revolving around one of the oldest devices in comedy history: the incorrect diagnosis. Thanks to a computer error, Chow is deemed to have terminal cancer, and Beethoven sets out to make his partner's "final months" as comfortable as possible by buying him a cemetery plot and a trip to Hawaii.

The interplay between the stars remains enjoyable but, without fresh material and spectacular stunt work supporting them, the finished product is only fitfully entertaining. The funniest sequence actually runs under the opening credits, with Chow and Beethoven leading a commando assault on a group of terrorists that ends up as a parody of **Raiders of the Lost Ark**! In addition to his accomplishments as a comedian, thanks to this film, Richard Ng can now also go down in history as the world's worst mariachi singer! Director Yip Wing-cho, Wu Ma, Dennis Chan Kwok-san, and Stanley Fung Shui-fan appear briefly.

781. Porky's Meatballs

(1987; D & B Films Co.) ★: 5/10. *Gwai ma haau yuen* (Cantonese), *Gui ma jiao yuan* (Mandarin): "Zany Campus." Cinematographer: Ardy Lam Kwok-wah; Art Director: Jason Mok Siu-kei; Music: Richard Yuen Cheuk-fan; Writers: Clifton Ko Chi-sum, Joe Ma Wai-ho; Producer: Linda Kuk Mei-lai; Director: Clifton Ko Chi-sum. Cast: Loletta Lee Lai-chun (Jane Li), Nadia Chan Chung-ling (Pak Yat-moon), Russell Wong (Mr. Wong, the Phys Ed Teacher), Yip Wing-cho (Wu Yiu-pong), Ku Feng (Li Pen-fai), Lam Chung (Kan Yan-kin). 1.85:1. VHS: Tai Seng. Import VCD: Mega Star. 93 minutes.

Great title, eh? In contrast to those Western gross-out hits, this teen comedy is a tame affair, though it covers much of the same ground. Cute Jane Li is lusted after by just about every boy in her school and she knows it. One of her admirers from the South Pacific transfers to the school just to be near Jane, but she only has eyes for Mr. Wong, her limber phys ed teacher. On the other hand, the more reserved Yat-moon has fallen for a boy she sees every morning while waiting for the bus. Deciding to take the next step, she goes up to his apartment, only to find that "he" is actually a mannequin. As luck would have it, the new transfer student looks exactly like Yat-moon's "Mr. Right." When a practical joke war between the boys and the girls gets out of hand, the hapless Principal Wu is replaced by ruthless West Point graduate Li Pen-fai, who transforms the school into a veritable prisoner of war camp. Though fairly painless viewing, there is little here that will be of interest to those who are no longer part of the target audience.

Portrait of a Nymph *see* **Picture of a Nymph**

782. Possessed

(1984; Johnny Mak Production) ★: 5/10. *Maang gwai chut lung* (Cantonese), *Meng gui chu long* (Mandarin): "Fierce Ghost Appears." Cinematographer: Bob Thompson; Music: Chan Ti-kwan; Writer: John Au Wah-hon; Producer: Johnny Mak Dong-hung; Director: David Lai Tai-wai. Cast: Gary Siu Yuk-lung (Hsiao), Lau Siu-ming (Kung Hsiao-ming), Irene Wan Pik-ha (Hsiao's Sister), Wong Yat-fei (Master Chen). 1.85:1. VHS: Tai Seng. 84 minutes.

Shortly before his retirement, veteran cop Kung Hsiao-ming stumbles out of a party and into a confrontation with the supernatural in this average horror thriller. While trying to save a woman from her knife-wielding husband, Kung shoots the attacker, only to find that the bullets barely slow him down. After emptying six shells into him, the man finally goes down, but not before briefly transforming into some kind of bizarre apparition. A few days later, Kung and his partner Hsiao are called to the scene of a would-be suicide. The jumper turns out to be a hideous monster, which plummets to the pavement, almost crushing Hsiao. Investigation reveals that the victim was a triad associate of Wang Tsu-yi, the man that Kung had killed earlier. When Hsiao's girlfriend is raped by an invisible being and his sister is murdered, he and Kung enlist the help of Chen, a blind occult master. He reveals that the men's problems arise from acts committed years earlier by Hsiao's now-insane father, who has been institutionalized for over a decade.

The opening confrontation is staged quite effectively, which makes the film's subsequent descent into derivative silliness all the more disappointing. Two sequences are copied directly from **Poltergeist** (a haunted closet and a man peeling his face off while looking in the bathroom mirror), and the blind master's female superior is more than a little reminiscent of Zelda Rubinstein's diminutive exorcist from the Hollywood production. Also, the otherworldly molestation was obviously inspired by **The Entity**, though it lacks the sophisticated special FX found in its model. The finale offers up a lively supernatural battle as partial compensation. It was followed by the unrelated **Possessed II**.

783. Possessed II

(1984; Johnny Mak Production) ★: 6/10. *Yim gwai faat kwong* (Cantonese), *Yan gui fa kuang* (Mandarin): "Pretty Ghost Goes Crazy." Cinematographers: Gary Ho Bo-yiu, Raymond Lam Fai-tai; Art Director: Jessy Lam Chak-chi; Music: Lam Mo-tak; Writer: John Au Wah-hon; Producer: Johnny Mak Dong-hung; Director: David Lai Tai-wai. Cast: Gary Siu Yuk-lung (Inspector Siu), Kong Mei-bo (Macy Ho), Pauline Wong Siu-fung (Michelle), Jayson Case (Hare Krishna). 1.85:1. VHS: Tai Seng (Poor Subtitles). 93 minutes.

Bearing no connection to its forerunner, this follows along similar lines but is the more enjoyable effort. Inspector Siu and his pregnant wife Macy make the mistake of moving into a haunted apartment and soon suffer the consequences. Macy is pushed down the stairs by a ghost and loses her baby. The next day she and their young daughter are possessed by one of the spirits that dwell in the building. While the little girl uses her powers to beat up a school bully, Macy transforms into a werewolf-like creature and chows down on an extra meaty butcher. Realizing that something is definitely afoot, Siu enlists the aid of a fellow cop who is also a Taoist priest. Although he makes a desperate effort to improve the apartment's *feng shui*, the ghosts prove too powerful to combat. With the help of some Hare Krishnas(!), Siu learns that his wife has been taken over by the spirit of Lucy, a prostitute who committed suicide after being impregnated and abandoned by a Caucasian sailor.

While unintentionally amusing in spots, the film's horror elements (including primitive but effective bladder FX copied from **The Howling**, a face being torn off, and a corpse dissolved with acid) are staged with great gusto and highly entertaining. The wild climactic supernatural battle (which finds the Krishnas combining computer technology with more traditional methods to battle the evil) is almost indescribably bizarre. *Possessed II* is a must for fans of Eastern horror.

A Postman Fights Back *see* **Postman Strikes Back**

The Postman Fights Back *see* **Postman Strikes Back**

784. Postman Strikes Back

(1982; Golden Harvest/Peace Film Production) ★: 6/10. *Chun sing ma* (Cantonese), *Xun cheng ma* (Mandarin): "City Patrol Horse." Cinematographers: Brian Lai Shui-ming, Cheung Yiu-cho; Art Director: Tony Au Ding-ping; Music: Not Original; Writers: Ronny Yu Yan-tai, Koo Siu-fung, Chan Chow-ying; Producer: Raymond Chow Man-wai; Action Director: Yuen Cheung-yan; Director: Ronny Yu Yan-tai. Cast: Leung Kar-yan (Ma), Chow Yun-fat (Fu Jun), Yuen Yat-chor (Yao Jie), Fan Mui-sang (Bu), Cherie Chung Cho-hung (Guihua), Eddy Ko Hung (Hu). Dolby Digital (DVD only). 2.35:1. VHS: Tai Seng (Poor Subtitles). Import LD: Star Entertainment (No Subtitles). Import VCD: Mei Ah. Import DVD: Universe. 87 minutes. Also known as **A Postman Fights Back** (VCD title) and **The Postman Fights Back**.

Chow Yun-fat in a period kung fu film? He is indeed a prominent cast member of this early effort from director Ronny Yu (**The Bride with White Hair**) but does not really perform much in the way of martial arts. Lensed in South Korea, the story revolves around four men who have been hired to transport a mysterious case across the frontier within seven days. Ma is an honest postman on the lam after being caught in the company of Yao, a pickpocket, who is also along for the trip. The other two members of the party are Fu, a shifty conman with a price on his head, and Bu, a slovenly explosives expert who likes to play chicken using lit sticks of dynamite. Accompanying them is Guihua, a young girl travelling across country to buy back her sister (who was sold by their destitute father), and Ms. Li, a woman the men rescue from bandits *en route*. Subsequent events reveal Li to be a member of Sun Yat-sen's forces, and she informs the men that the case contains a tribute for Sun's enemy, the warlord Yu Sai-hoi. In a bizarre (but not wholly unexpected) twist, Hu, the man who set up the mission, turns out to be a Japanese ninja in league with Yu. Following delivery of the case, most of the party is murdered after discovering that they have inadvertently delivered a powerful machine gun into the warlord's hands. One of the survivors then sets out for revenge, armed with an army of rats and a whole lot of dynamite.

While routine in most respects, **Postman Strikes Back** serves up enough offbeat touches to make it worth catching (while crossing a frozen lake, the party is attacked by spear-wielding killers on ice skates!), and the Korean locales (which range from deserted forests to wintry mountain regions) provide a fresh backdrop. Some of the tricks utilized by Eddy Ko's ninja anticipate similar moves he would make the next year in Ching Siu-tung's **Duel to the Death**; though, on the whole, the martial arts on display here are nothing special. Chow is not given much to do, but with his cool demeanor and singular good looks, he makes the most of the role.

785. Powerful Four

(1991; David Lam Films) ★: 6/10. *Sei daai taam jeung* (Cantonese), *Si da tan zhang* (Mandarin): "Four Great Senior Detectives." Cinematographer: Wong Po-man; Art Director: Bill Lui Cho-hung; Music: Lowell Lo Kwun-ting; Writer: Wong Chi; Action Director: Yuen Tak; Producer-Director: David Lam Tak-luk. Cast: Danny Lee Sau-yin (Luk Kong, aka "No-head"), Simon Yam Tat-wah (Lui Kit), Waise Lee Chi-hung (Yiu Hung), Kent Cheng Chuk-see (Ho Sum, aka "Fatty B"), Yolinda Yan Cho-sin (Lee Yim-ping), Vincent Wan Yeung-ming (Sam), Frankie Chin Chi-leung (Muscle-bound Suspect "Laichee"). 1.85:1. VHS: Tai Seng. Import LD/VCD: Universe. 108 minutes.

Clearly inspired by the Heung Brothers' big-budget hit **Lee Rock**, this passable cop thriller also concerns the exploits of HK police officers during the 1960s, a period when bribery and corruption thrived unchecked. Luk, Lui, Yiu, and Ho, four sergeant majors from different districts, band together as both friends and colleagues, climb the ladder of success, and get rich from triad kickbacks. Although they are able to deal with their British superiors, they run into trouble from a group of heroin dealers. One hood in particular, Sam, proves to be a serious obstacle, even going so far as to have his men mutilate Luk's girlfriend, nightclub singer Yim-ping. Power crazed, Sam plots to take over the organization by eliminating the competition and acquiring the formula to manufacture heroin, an action that inadvertently aids the four cops in their plan to finish him off and avenge his attack on Yim-ping.

The four stars are fine (Yam, in particular, is at his charismatic best) and there is some good gunplay, but the storyline follows all-too-familiar patterns and the circumstances leading up to the climax are just a little too convenient.

786. Pretty Woman

(1991) ★: 3/10. *Hing boon gaai yin* (Cantonese), *Qing ben jia ren* (Mandarin): "Darling Basis Pretty Human." Cinematographer: Ho Ming; Art Director: Ruby Ko Pui-yee; Music: Not Original; Writers: Yeung Chi-kin, Brian Chung Wai-hung; Producer: Lau Chi-wing; Action Director: Chan Siu-lung; Director: Yeung Chi-kin. Cast: Veronica Yip Yuk-hing (Lo Yin-hsin/Mimin), Mondi Yau Yuet-ching (Miss Ode), Alex Fong Chung-sun (Lin Cha-sin), Kenneth Tong Chun-yip (George), Wu Ma (Mr. Lin), Charlie Cho Cha-lei (Charlie Chau). 1.85:1. VHS: World Video. Import LD/VCD/DVD: Ocean Shores. 93 minutes.

One of the softcore films Veronica Yip did on her way to the mainstream, this foolish drama opens with frustrated office worker George attacking and raping fellow employee Lo Hsin-yin while the latter is working alone one night. During the struggle, he accidentally kills the woman and must dispose of her body. Desperate to hide his crime, George hires prostitute Mimin, a dead ringer for Hsin-yin, to take her place for one day. Mimin will go to work and resign, thus creating a plausible explanation for Hsin-yin's disappearance. Mimin, however, decides to stay on the job when she discovers that the company's vice-president is handsome Lin Cha-sin, who had saved her from being gang-raped the night before. George is understandably perturbed and sets about to change her mind, one way or another.

Naturally, the majority of the movie is given over to various softcore couplings, but the screen only comes alive when Yip is one of the participants (she has a bath-tub masturbation fantasy sequence which takes up almost a tenth of the running time on its own). Yes, there are some token parallels to the Richard Gere/Julia Roberts film of the same name, but the less said about them and the rest of the lamebrained storyline (which also incorporates various kung fu bouts, an office orgy, an attempted diamond heist, and a kidnapping/shootout in Macau!) the better. The Chinese title does not translate well literally but is a proverb that essentially means the same as the English handle.

787. Prince of Portland Street

(1993; Sam Po Films Co.) ★: 2/10. *Boot laan gaai daai siu* (Cantonese), *Bo lan jie da shao* (Mandarin): "Portland Street's Head Prince." Cinematographer: Ma Chak-yan; Art Director: Wai Lam; Music: Cheng Ching-chung; Writer: Yip Kong-yam; Producers: Lau Chun-fai, Lam Siu-ming; Martial Arts Director: Lo Chiang; Director: Cheung Kon-man. Cast: Simon Yam Tat-wah (Pao), Dicky Cheung Wai-kin (Kao Chao), Anita Yuen Wing-yee (Yao-yao), Sarah Lee Lai-yui (Cooky), Tommy Wong Kwong-leung (Chi). 1.85:1. VHS: Tai Seng. Import LD/VCD: Universe. 92 minutes.

One part triad melodrama and one part romantic comedy, this slapdash effort will please no one. Simon Yam plays a slick pimp who turns into a simpleton after being bashed on the head (a concept that would be recycled for Yam's 1996 film **Scarred Memory**). His cowardly underling, played by Dicky Cheung, takes advantage of the situation by switching places with Yam, making *him* the flunky. The pair hook up with club girls Anita Yuen and Sarah Lee, who move in with them after the pair anger vindictive triad boss Tommy Wong. In an unlikely development, Yuen begins to develop feelings for Yam, and when Wong's men arrive looking for revenge, Yam saves her. He is gravely injured in the process, receiving a heavy blow to his head which (naturally) reverses his condition. Cheung and Lee plan to wed, but Yam cannot give up his irresponsible ways and commit to Yuen.

The dramatic twists are highly unbelievable and the finale is painfully ridiculous. This is strictly for the heartiest Anita Yuen fans or those who just have to see Dicky Cheung running through the streets wearing only an Ultraman mask. An annoyingly large number of lines are bleeped in the Cantonese version.

788. Prince of the Sun

(1990; Golden Flare Films Co.) ★: 5/10. *Tai yeung ji ji* (Cantonese), *Tai yang zhi zi* (Mandarin): "Son of the Sun." Cinematographer: Cheung Yiu-cho; Art Director: Leung Ping-kwan; Music: Wong Bong; Writers: Lau Jun-wai, Abe Kwong Man-wai; Producer: Cheung Siu-ping; Action Director: Yuen Tak; Director: Wellson Chin Sing-wai. Cast: Conan Lee Yuen-ba (Tiger), Lam Ching-ying (Khenlun), Sheila Chan Sak-lan (Wan May-ngor), Cynthia Rothrock (Bencheuk), Lau Shun (Khentse), Gabriel Wong Yat-san (Wang San), Woo Fung (Uncle Bach, the Principal), Jeff Falcon (Caucasian Lama), Tai Po (Fu). 1.85:1. VHS: World Video, York (Dubbed). Import LD: Golden Flare. Import VCD: Panorama Entertainment. 93 minutes.

Your tolerance for shrill and silly comedy may be tested by this otherwise enjoyable martial arts fantasy. Benevolent monk Khenlun is framed for murder and the theft of the magical "Holy Stonebead." Fleeing from his temple with the Little Chieftain, a child who is the living embodiment of Buddha, he manages to get the boy to safety in HK but is killed shortly thereafter. His spirit lives on, however, and orders pupil Bencheuk to find the Chieftain and return him to China. The boy hooks up with dimwitted illegal immigrant Tiger and his obnoxious relative May, who is up to her ears in debt to loansharks. The villainous Khentse has dispatched four of his lamas to snatch the Chieftain, leaving only Bencheuk and the spirit of Khenlun to protect the boy. Khentse (who has now transformed into The King of Hell and looks like a giant bat) needs to destroy the child before he can transform into "The Son of the Sun" and reach the height of his powers.

Comedienne Sheila Chan is at her most unrestrained here, and that will probably be more than a lot of viewers can handle. On the other hand, some of the comedy is *so* over-the-top, it successfully evokes laughs, and few would accuse this mishmash of kung fu, ghosts, demons, and magic of being entirely without merit.

789. Princess Fragrance

(1987; Sil-Metropole Organisation /Yeung Tse Kong Movie Enterprises) ★: 7/10. *Heung heung gung jue* (Cantonese), *Xiang xiang gong zhu* (Mandarin): "Fragrant Princess." Cinematographer: Bill Wong Chung-bo; Art Directors: James Leung Wah-sang, Pok Yeuk-muk, Zhao Min, Hu Juantong; Music: Law Wing-fai, Ge Jie; Writer: Chun Sai-sam; Producers: Guo Fengqi, Shen Minhui; Action Director: Hu Jianqiang; Director: Ann Hui On-wah. Cast: Zhang Duofu (Chen Jalo), Liu Jia (Huo Chingtong), Chang Dashi (Emperor Qian Long), Ai Yinuo (Princess Fragrance), Ha Chier (Mu Cherlun). 1.85:1. VHS: World Video. Import LD: Star Entertainment. 94 minutes.

The second half of Ann Hui's period martial arts epic has much the same strengths and weaknesses as its forerunner but emerges as the more successful of the two. Following the events depicted in **The Romance of Book and Sword**, Chen Jalo and Qian Long have joined together to overthrow The Ching Dynasty and set their sights on destroying The Imperial Army and its leader, Prince Shao Wei. Chen travels into the desert to seek the assistance of Mu Cherlun, with Shao and his army soon arriving on the scene to wage war with Mu's people. Following the battle, Chen becomes separated from the main forces, along with Mu's daughters, Chingtong and Hesili. Together they discover a lost city and are barely able to find their way back to the tribe. Although he has fallen in love with Hesili, Chen still leaves her and the Wei tribe behind so that he may re-unite with his brother and Red Flower Society kinsmen. Upon arriving at his brother's home, however, he discovers none other than Hesili. The girl is the only survivor of a devastating attack by Manchu forces, an assault that was ordered by Qian, who desires Hesili. He gives Chen an ultimatum: leave her or lose his help.

The film suffers somewhat from the usual pitfalls that occur when literary works are condensed down to their bare essentials. In particular, the plot lurches forward at times, leaving one temporarily disoriented, in spite of the excellent English subtitles. While the main performers are still not quite able to make their characters three dimensional, **Princess Fragrance** possesses great visual majesty: The battles and intrigue play out amidst gorgeous desert sandscapes and immense, maze-like rock formations, giving the film an intoxicating natural beauty rarely equalled in the genre. That is enough to make it worth seeing, though one still wishes that Hui could have invested the proceedings with a bit more vitality.

790. Princess Madam

(1989; Grandwell Film Production) ★: 5/10. *Gam paai si je* (Cantonese), *Jin pai shi jie* (Mandarin): "Gold Medal Policewoman." Cinematographer: Philip Ma Kam-cheung; Art Director: Richard Leung; Music: Stephen Tsang; Writer: Simon Fong Sai-yin; Producer: George Lai Hing-lun; Action Director: Cheung Chuen; Director: Godfrey Ho Chi-keung. Cast: Sharon Yeung Pan-pan (Lisa Cheung), Moon Lee Choi-fung (Mona), Michiko Nishiwaki (Lily), Kenneth Tsang Kong (Cheung), Liu Kai-chi (Roger), Mark Houghton (Blonde Thug), James Ha Chim-see (Lily's Husband). 1.85:1. VHS: Tai Seng (No Subtitles). Import LD/VCD: Star Entertainment (No Subtitles). 79 minutes (Dubbed version). Also known as **Under Police Protection** (Title for English dubbed version).

Policewomen Lisa and Mona are assigned to protect Jo Jo, the secretary of notorious mobster Lung Siu-tin, who is going to testify against her boss in court. An attack by Uzi-wielding female bikers results in the death of several police officers, but Lisa, Mona, and Jo Jo miraculously emerge unscathed. Becoming increasingly desperate, Lung brings ex-cop Cheung over from Canada to eliminate the pesky witness. The latter faces just as much trouble if Jo Jo talks, but is also burdened by the fact that Lisa is his daughter and unaware of his underworld dealings. Meanwhile, Mona's husband has been seduced by Lily, the vengeful leader of the cyclists, whose husband was killed by the police woman.

Formulaic in the extreme, the film still moves along well and delivers a steady stream of action (Sharon Yeung is in particularly fine form), making it one of veteran hack Godfrey Ho's better efforts. Liu Kai-chi provides lame comic relief as a bumbling cop who has the hots for Lisa. The character names listed above are from the dubbed version.

791. Prison on Fire

(1987; Cinema City Co.) ★: 7/10. *Gaam yuk fung wan* (Cantonese), *Jian yu feng yun* (Mandarin): "Prison Turbulence." Cinematographer: Cinema City Photography Collective; Art Director: Luk Chi-fung; Music: Lowell Lo Kwun-ting; Writer: Nam Yin; Producer: Karl Maka; Action Directors: Lau Kar-wing, Chu Kai-sang; Director: Ringo Lam Ling-tung. Cast: Chow Yun-fat (Chung Tin-ching, aka 41671), Tony Leung Kar-fai (Lo Ka-yiu, aka 51910), Roy Cheung Yiu-yeung (Hung, aka Scarface), William Ho Kar-kui (Micky), Tommy Wong Kwong-leung (Bill), Victor Hon Kwan (Chiu Chow Man), Ng Chi-hung (Blind Snake), Shing Fui-on (Madly). Dolby Digital (DVD only). 1.85:1. VHS: Tai Seng. Import LD: Golden Cinema City. Import VCD: Mei Ah. Import DVD: Universe. 98 minutes.

Chow Yun-fat gives one of his most charismatic performances in this gritty thriller written by Nam Yin, brother of the film's director, Ringo Lam. Meek Lo Ka-yiu, serving a three year sentence for manslaughter, is clearly not cut out for prison life. The one person who might help him survive his stay is Chung, a happy-go-lucky con who can charm the pants off every prison official, with the exception of security chief Hung, aka "Scarface." Disfigured by some triads, Scarface has a psychopathic dislike of the prisoners and frequently uses excessive force on them. When Lo rats on triad leader Micky, the latter conspires with Scarface and frames him, causing fellow "Big Brother" Bill to start bullying Lo as well. When Chung informs the warden about Scarface's activities, Micky is transferred to another institution and things are quiet for the next year. However, Micky is eventually sent back, and Lo makes things worse by complaining to a prison inspector. Embarrassed in front of a superior and feeling his authority threatened, Scarface and Micky finger Chung as the man who initiated a prison-wide fast. Even though he only has two months left in his sentence, Chung is pushed beyond his limits and openly seeks revenge.

The naivete (stupidity?) displayed by Tony Leung Kar-fai's character detracts from the realism, but, otherwise, Nam's script presents a plausible depiction of life behind bars, with its hierarchies and rampant treachery. Prison movies have limited possibilities when it comes to narrative, and this one rarely strays from convention. However, the direction and performances are above average, and the climax is quite powerful; Roy Cheung's steely resolve vs. Chow's crazed fury makes for quite a finale. It was followed by a sequel.

792. Prison on Fire II

(1991; Golden Princess Film Production Co./Cinema City Enterprises) ★: 6/10. *To faan gaam yuk fung wan juk jaap* (Cantonese), *Tao fan jian yu feng yun xu ji* (Mandarin): "Escaped Criminals: Prison Turbulence Sequel." Cinematographer: Tony Fan Chuen-kam; Art Director: William Yam Wai-leung; Music: Lowell Lo Kwun-ting; Writer: Nam Yin; Producer: Karl Maka; Action Director: Lam Moon-wah; Director: Ringo Lam Ling-tung. Cast: Chow Yun-fat (Chung Tin-ching, aka 41671), Chen Sung-yung (Pong Fai-long, aka Dragon), Yu Li (Miss Wong), Tommy Wong Kwong-leung (Bill), Elvis Tsui Kam-kong (Zau), Victor Hon Kwan (Chiu Chow Man), Vincent Wan Yeung-ming (Fai Chi), Ng Chi-hung (Blind Snake). Dolby Digital (DVD only). 1.85:1. VHS: Tai Seng. Import LD: Golden Cinema City. Import VCD/DVD: Universe. 113 minutes.

Following the events that unfolded previously, Stanley Prison is divided along territorial lines, with the Hongkies lashing out at the Mainlanders. Chung befriends Brother Dragon, the nominal leader of the Mainland inmates, which allows him to receive kinder treatment than his fellow Cantonese prisoners. When Chung's mother dies, he is forced to commit his young son to an orphanage. Zau, the new captain of the guards, refuses to grant Chung leave to see the boy, prompting the latter to escape. Chung later surrenders himself to the superintendent but still gets a beating upon his return. When Dragon is incorrectly blamed for a murder and escapes, the real killer tells his Mainland counterparts that Chung betrayed their leader to the authorities. Chung makes a desperate attempt to escape and succeeds, meeting up with Dragon on the outside. The two plan to leave HK, but when Chung tries to take his son from the orphanage, the police arrive. Taken back to Stanley, Chung faces certain death unless he can figure a way out of his predicament.

More time is spent developing Chow Yun-fat's character this time out (through a flashback, we see the crime that originally put him behind bars), and there are several effective, intense moments. However, on the whole, this outing is more routinely written, and the various dramatic conflicts are wrapped up just a little too neatly. Chow and Taiwanese character actor Chen Sung-yung (**Asian Connection**) both do fine work and make a great team. Roy Cheung Yiu-yeung has an amusing cameo.

793. The Private Eye Blues

(1994; Tedpoly Films) ★: 3/10. *Fai seung ching taam* (Cantonese), *Fei chang zhen tan* (Mandarin): "Paranormal Detective." Cinematographer: Jingle Ma Cho-shing; Art Director: Lee Wai-ming; Music: Michael Au Ting-yuk, John Lau Hak-don, Teddy Robin Kwan; Producer: Teddy Robin Kwan; Action Directors: Dion Lam Dik-on, Pang Bei-lee; Writer-Director: Eddie Fong Ling-ching. Cast: Jacky Cheung Hok-yau (The Detective), Kathy Chow Hoi-mei (The Detective's Wife), Mavis Fan Hiu-huen (The Girl), Chin Ho (Shenzhen Mad Dog), Wong Tin-lam (Fat Comrade), Bobby Yip King-sang (Ugly Triad), Frankie Chin Chi-leung (Bodyguard). 1.85:1. Dolby Stereo. VHS: Tai Seng. Import LD/VCD: Fitto Mobile. 95 minutes.

An insufferable comedy spiced with elements of fantasy, **The Private Eye Blues** has been praised by some for its offbeat approach, though many viewers will not be so charitable. A dishevelled, beer guzzling private eye is hired to find and turn over an *obnoxious* teenage girl who is wanted by the Mainland government because she is the "Key Research Object of the State," possessing great paranormal and healing powers. Pretty soon everyone else wants her too: the HK authorities, British agents, the triads (in particular, a cackling loony called Shenzhen Mad Dog), and even the dick's estranged TV reporter wife, who smells a big scoop. With the handover looming, the political sensitivity of the issue just makes everyone involved even more desperate and paranoid, particularly the Chinese government. Their prize subject previously used her abilities to prolong the life of their ailing leader; advance knowledge of when the old man will kick the bucket could prove to be very lucrative to certain parties.

Much too pleased with itself, the film plods from one scene to the next, substituting screeching and screaming for wit, blithely eccentric characters for charm, and style for any real substance. *The Private Eye Blues* is a major disappointment from talented writer-director Eddie Fong (**The Last Princess of Manchuria**). Co-star Wong Tin-lam is the father of prolific producer-director Wong Jing and producer of many classic TVB martial arts miniseries.

794. The Prodigal Son

(1982; Golden Harvest/Paragon Films) ★: 9/10. *Bai ga jai* (Cantonese), *Bai jia zi* (Mandarin): "Son Ruining the Family." Cinematographer: Ricky Lau Koon-wai; Music: Frankie Chan Fan-kei, Phil Chan Fei-lap; Writers: Sammo Hung Kam-po, Barry Wong Ping-yiu; Producer: Raymond Chow Man-wai; Action Directors: Sammo Hung Kam-po, Lam Ching-ying, Yuen Biao, Billy Chan Wui-ngai, Guy Lai Ying-chau; Director: Sammo Hung Kam-po. Cast: Yuen Biao (Leung Chang), Lam Ching-ying (Leung Yee-tai), Frankie Chan Fan-kei (Ngai Fai), Sammo Hung Kam-po (Wong Wa-po), Wei Pai (Au Ru-kwai), Peter Chan Lung (Yee Tong-choi), Dick Wei, Chung Fat (Ngai's Servants), Wu Ma (Iron Palm), James Tien Chun (Ngai's Street Opponent), Lee Hoi-sang (Teacher). Dolby Digital (DVD only). 2.35:1. VHS: Tai Seng (Remastered for the English market; subtitled or dubbed). Import LD: Star Entertainment (No Subtitles). Import DVD: Universe. 100 minutes. Also known as **Pull No Punches**.

Praised by practitioners of Wing Chun as the feature that most accurately depicts that martial art, this Sammo Hung Kam-po film remains one of Golden Harvest's greatest kung fu films. Leung Chang has carved himself a formidable reputation as "The Street Brawler," who can make short work of any opponent and is undefeated after 200 fights. Unbeknownst to Leung, his affluent father has ordered his son's servant to bribe all of the opponents to ensure Chang's safety. The boy gets a harsh taste of reality when he foolishly challenges Peking Opera performer/martial arts master Leung Yee-tai to a duel. One of the opera company's performances is attended by Master Ngai Fai, a martial artist looking for a worthy competitor. He deems Yee-tai to be just that man and goads him into a fight, which comes to a premature end when the actor suffers a serious asthma attack. Just as Leung Chang's father sought to protect him, Ngai's father has ordered two servants to kill anyone who may possess skills superior to those of his son. Taking their order to bloody extremes, the attendants direct a squad of killers to murder the opera company in their beds. Yee-tai awakens in time to save his own life but is crippled by another dose of asthma. The master is saved by Chang, and the two seek refuge at the farm of Wong Wa-po, Yee-tai's brother and a Wing Chun master, whose occasional bouts of clumsiness belie his incredible abilities. Chang uses the brothers' age-old feud to his advantage, appealing to their pride and receiving instruction from both men. When tragedy strikes, Chang challenges Ngai to a final, decisive battle.

Considering the always potent combo of Yuen Biao and Sammo Hung, it is rather surprising to see the film stolen by Lam Ching-ying. His numerous "One Eyebrow Priest" horror comedies required a measure of martial talent, but nothing like the sort of dexterity he is required to display on numerous occasions here. The late character actor also displays the measured timing and droll reactions of a seasoned comedian. While Hung's endearingly broad persona and incredible acrobatics tend to dominate the second half, one leaves the film remembering Lam's character, who is a far cry from the typical wizened *sifu*. Dubbed with a high female voice while in his performance make-up, he is able to have fun with the persona while still maintaining the character's dignity. Frankie Chan is also intriguing in a role that is a departure from his more recent work. While Ngai is seemingly the villain of the piece, he is really just an ethical but misguided young man who needs to be taught a good lesson, something Yuen sees to with customary panache in the final reel.

795. Profiles of Pleasure

(1988; Golden Harvest/Paragon Films) ★: 4/10. *Kwan aau luen miu* (Cantonese), *Qun ying luan wu* (Mandarin): "The Nightingales' Frenzied Dance." Cinematographer: Bill Wong Chung-bo; Music: Law Wing-fai; Writer: Manfred Wong; Producers: Jessinta Liu Fung-ping, Choi Lan; Art Director-Director: Tony Au Ding-ping. Cast: Rosamund Kwan Chi-lam (Luk Chin-chin), Nina Li Chi (Fa Yim-hung), Carina Lau Kar-ling (Lily), Pauline Wong Siu-fung (Sek-ki), Adam Cheng Siu-chau (Cheng Lup-pang), Paul Chun Pui (Chu), Lawrence Cheng Tan-shui (Tall Kao), Lam Chung (Sgt. Chan), Wong Jing (Wong), Ngai Hong (Affluent Client). 1.85:1. VHS: Tai Seng (No Subtitles). Import VCD: Mega Star. 83 minutes.

In the wake of **The Last Affair** (1983) and **Dream Lovers** (1986), this lightweight comedy (set in 1935) came as a real change of pace for director Tony Au (once again serving as his own art director). Unfortunately, he chose to give this new material the same measured pacing, which has the effect of making it seem dull and drawn out. When the British government seeks to ban prostitution in HK, London-born Commissioner Cheng Lup-pang is ordered to investigate the situation first hand. Naturally, local madam Sek-ki has her most beautiful girls attend to him, and he soon falls for both Yim-hung (who has had three husbands die in bed with her) and the elegant Shanghai native Chin-chin. A rivalry quickly develops between the two hookers but fades when Yim-hung discovers that Lup-pang is actually the boy she was bequeathed to as a child. Meanwhile, Lily, Lup-pang's heretofore liberal fiancée, is having second thoughts about granting him so much freedom.

The production design and costumes are stunning, and the players are equally handsome, but the final product never quite clicks. Famous author Ngai Hong appears briefly.

796. Project A

(1983; Golden Harvest/Paragon Films) ★: 8/10. *A gai waak* (Cantonese), *A ji hua* (Mandarin): "Project A." Cinematographer: Cheung Yiu-cho; Art Directors: Poon Yuen-wo, Chim Fuk-sing, So Lok-ting; Music: Michael Lai Siu-tin; Writers: Jackie Chan, Edward Tang King-sang; Producer: Leonard Ho Koon-cheung; Action Direction: Jackie Chan Stuntmen Association; Director: Jackie Chan. Cast: Jackie Chan (Sgt. Dragon Ma), Sammo Hung Kam-po (Fei), Yuen Biao (Inspector Tzu), Dick Wei (Lo San), Tai Po (Tai), Kwan Hoi-shan (Captain Chi), Feng Sing (Big

Mouth), Lee Hoi-sang (Li), Wu Ma (Mahjong Player). Dolby Digital (DVD only). 2.35:1. VHS: Tai Seng (Poor Subtitles). Import LD: Star Entertainment (No Subtitles). Import VCD: Mei Ah (No Subtitles). Import DVD: Mega Star. 105 minutes.

Hong Kong, early 20th century: Pirates are terrorizing the surrounding seas, and the Water Police are unable to stop them. In response, the British transfer all of the officers to the regular police unit, which is under the command of the humorless Captain Chi and his equally strict son, Inspector Tzu. When martially talented Sgt. Dragon Ma apprehends some wanted fugitives by bending the rules, he quits the force rather than acquiesce to Chi (who is afraid to risk angering his superiors). Teaming up with old friend Fei (now a thief, but an honorable one), Dragon sets out to foil the men providing pirate leader Lo with stolen arms. The first step is to determine who in the department is leaking information to the scoundrels, and then get the Water Police division re-established.

A wonderful, old-fashioned adventure with contemporary kung fu and stunts, **Project A** is also Jackie Chan's *homage* to the incredible feats of dexterity performed by silent film stars like Buster Keaton and Harold Lloyd (including a fall from a clock tower that probably should have broken his back). On top of that, there is an incredible bike chase, a barroom brawl, the destruction of a ritzy club, and the final, remarkable battle against Lo (well-played by a heavily tattooed Dick Wei) and his goons on the pirates' secret island. Sammo Hung and Yuen Biao provide fine athletic and comedic support in this box office smash, which spawned an even better 1987 sequel.

797. Project A II

(1987; Golden Harvest/Golden Way Films/Paragon Films) ★: 10/10. *A gai waak juk jaap* (Cantonese), *A ji hua xu ji* (Mandarin): "Project A Sequel." Cinematographer: Cheung Yiu-cho; Art Director: Eddie Ma Poon-chiu; Music: Michael Lai Siu-tin; Writers: Jackie Chan, Edward Tang King-sang; Producer: Leonard Ho Koon-cheung; Action Direction: Jackie Chan Stuntmen Association; Director: Jackie Chan. Cast: Jackie Chan (Dragon Ma), Maggie Cheung Man-yuk (Maggie), Rosamund Kwan Chi-lam (Miss Pak), Carina Lau Kar-ling (Carina), Lam Wai (Chun, aka "Three Wans" Chun), Bill Tung Biu (Police Chief Bill Tung), Ray Lui Leung-wai (Mr. Man), Lau Siu-ming (The Prince), Kenny Ho Kar-king (Kenny Ho), Kwan Hoi-shan (Chi), Michael Chan Wai-man (Tiger Au), Feng Sing (Mars), Tai Po (Tai, aka Mr. B), Bozidar Smiljanic (The Police Commissioner), Johnny Wang Lung-wei (Bravo Wong), Ricky Hui Koon-ying (Homely Cop), Regina Kent (Regina), Lee Hoi-sang (Choy), Ben Lam Kwok-bun (Chun's Man), Ken Lo Wai-kwong (Chun's Man), Fan Mui-sang (Fat Triad), Benny Lai Wai (Pirate), Lui Fong (Man with Bread), Kenny Bee (Cop), Anthony Chan Yau (Cop), Michael Lai Siu-tin (The Maestro). Dolby Digital (DVD only). 2.35:1. VHS: Tai Seng (Remastered for the English market; subtitled or dubbed). Import LD: Star Entertainment (No Subtitles). Import VCD: Mei Ah. Import DVD: Mega Star. 106 minutes.

In this outstanding sequel, Dragon Ma is assigned to keep an eye on Chun, a high-ranking shore policeman who is obviously staging arrests in order to advance his career. Promoted to superintendent and given his own district, Dragon sets out to clean up crime and corruption, beginning with local triad kingpin Tiger Au. That accomplished, he is next ordered to provide protection for the guests at a posh party thrown by the daughter of the police commissioner. Unbeknownst to Dragon, Chun (anxious to make his competitor look bad) has hired some rebels to commit a robbery at the gathering. In the process, they frame Dragon for the crime, but that is not his only worry: The remaining pirates from Lo San's crew are out to avenge their boss by chopping Dragon into small pieces. However, some surprise assistance comes in the form of the rebels, who realize that they have framed an honest man and enlist Dragon's help in foiling some Ching assassins sent to eliminate them.

Jackie Chan is always a joy to watch when he is in motion, but he performs so many incredible moves in this film that it is almost exhausting; why walk or climb when you can jump, slide, somersault, or otherwise careen from one place to another? The highlights just keep on coming here: a spectacular, prolonged fight against Tiger Au and his men (including Shaw Brothers veteran Johnny Wang Lung-wei and Fan Mui-sang); a wild sequence in which Chan is handcuffed to Lam Wai (who wants to kill him), with the pair being chased by the pirates, who want to kill them *both*; an elaborate comic sequence (in which a variety of policemen and thugs all try to hide in Maggie Cheung's apartment at the same time) that is worthy of the best 1930s screwball comedies; and the final, breathtaking fight, which finds Chan foiling all of the remaining villains and recreating Buster Keaton's most famous stunt from **Steamboat Bill, Jr.** Add Eddie Ma's beautiful period art direction and some lovely costumes, and you have an absolute delight from start to finish!

798. Project S

(1993; Golden Harvest/Paragon Films) ★: 7/10. *Chiu kap gai waak* (Cantonese), *Chao ji ji hua* (Mandarin): "Super Plan." Cinematographer: Ardy Lam Kwok-wah; Art Director: Horace Ma Kwong-wing; Music: Richard Lo Sai-kit; Writers: Stanley Tong Kwai-lai, Sandy Shaw; Producers: Siu Hau-leung, Barbie Tung Wan-sze; Director: Stanley Tong Kwai-lai. Cast: Michelle Yeoh Chu-kheng (Yang Chien-hua), Yu Rongguang (Cheng Feng), Emil Chow Wah-kin (Li Kuang-ming), Athena Chu Yan (May), Fan Siu-wong (Kuo Shao-lung), Dick Wei (Chuan), Alain Guernier (Roger Davidson), Bill Tung Biu (Uncle Bill), Yukari Oshima (Red Army Terrorist). 1.85:1. VHS: Tai Seng. Import LD/VCD: Star Entertainment (No Subtitles). Import DVD: China Star (No Subtitles). 102 minutes. Also known as **Once a Cop, Supercop 2: Super Plan** (Taiwan Title).

Michelle Yeoh reprises her **Police Story III: Supercop** character in this entertaining actioner which re-teams her with that film's director, Stanley Tong. After China's Finance Minister is kidnapped by some Red Army terrorists, Security Chief Yang Chien-hua is able to effect a rescue, with the assistance of her boyfriend, Captain Cheng Feng. Yang and Cheng are quite happy together, but Cheng won't propose to her until he feels more financially secure. To that end, he and some other soldiers he served with in Vietnam plan to go to Hong Kong and pull off a major heist. For their first job, they steal security information pertaining to the facility they plan to rob. When the theft results in several fatalities, China sends Yang to HK to lend her expertise. Joining with local policemen Li and Kuo, Yang sets about trying to guess the gang's next move, not realizing that her lover is masterminding everything.

While the action is a bit sparse compared to most HK police thrillers, it is very well staged, making **Project S** a slick and superior outing, in spite of its routine script. Michelle Yeoh gives a convincing dramatic turn and handles the stunt sequences with her usual grace and agility. Yu Rongguang has one of his best roles to date as the misguided criminal boss; his charisma and athleticism help compensate for Emil Chow's bland hero and French actor Alain Guernier's dreadful performance as the *British* criminal with whom Cheng is involved (for a native Brit, his English is awfully mangled). In a bizarre and completely extraneous sequence, one that would have been better left on the cutting room floor, Jackie Chan (also reprising his **Supercop** role) and Eric Tsang Chi-wai have cameos…in drag! Chan's old compatriot, Feng Sing, can also be glimpsed as a jewellery store patron. Richard Lo's score is exhilarating and well-suited to the action, though one track sounds distinctively like a cue heard in **Aliens**.

799. The Protector

(1985; Warner Brothers/Golden Harvest/Eurasia Investments) ★: 5/10 (US version), ★: 6/10 (HK Version). *Wai lung maang taam* (Cantonese), *Wei long meng tan* (Mandarin): "Mighty Dragon Fierce Detective." Cinematographers: Mark Irwin (US version), Cheung Yiu-cho, Ardy Lam Kwok-wah, Johnny Koo Kwok-wah, Jimmy Leung Chi-ming, Gary Ho Bo-yiu (Additional material for HK version); Art Director: Oliver Wong Yui-man; Music: Ken Thorne; Producer: David Chan; Action Direction: Alan Gibbs, Jackie Chan Stuntmen Association; Writer: James Glickenhaus (US version), Edward Tang King-sang (Additional material for HK version); Directors: James Glickenhaus (US version), Jackie Chan (Additional material for HK version). Cast: Jackie Chan (Billy Wong), Danny Aiello (Danny Garoni), Roy Chiao Hung (Harold Ko), Bill Wallace (Benny Garucci), Saun Ellis (Laura Shapiro), Moon Lee Choi-fung (Soo-ling), Yeung Kwan (Lee Hing), Shum Wai (Massage Parlor Manager), Richard Clarke (Superintendent Whitehead), Kim Bass (Stan Jones), Tse Hung (Fortune Teller), Trey Wilson (Truck Driver). Additional Cast for HK Version: Sally Yeh Chian-wen (Sally Ho May-fong), Lee Hoi-sang (Wing). Dolby Stereo (US version only), Dolby Digital (DVD only). 1.85:1. VHS: Warner (US version), Tai Seng (HK version). LD: Warner (US version). Import VCD: Mega Star (HK version, No Subtitles). Import DVD: Universe (HK version). 91 minutes (HK version), 95 minutes (US version).

While this is technically a Hollywood production, it warrants inclusion here, as the HK release differs in a number of ways and features material shot by star Jackie Chan that is unique to that version. When socialite Laura Shapiro (daughter of a local mob boss) is kidnapped and evidence points to the involvement of Asian crimelord Harold Ko, New York cops Billy Wong and slovenly Danny Garoni are sent to HK to see what they can dig up. With the help of some local contacts, Billy is able to confirm Ko's involvement, and he and Danny are soon set upon by a variety of assassins. Ko and Shapiro are actually old partners in the drug business who have had a temporary falling out and are ready to put their differences aside. However, Billy and Danny have discovered the location of Ko's drug processing factory and plan to put a fiery end to the operation.

You know something is wrong early on when it becomes obvious that Danny Aiello is here primarily to provide comic relief, while Chan is expected to play his role almost entirely straight! Director James Glickenhaus (**The Exterminator**) was determined to try and sell the lively HK star to Western audiences as a sullen, Clint Eastwood-style figure, and it just does not work. The film itself is packed to the brim with action and stunts but rarely attains the heights one expects of a Jackie Chan picture. The story and dialogue are mediocre at best, leaving the final product seeming little better than mundane direct-to-video fare. Chan was understandably dissatisfied with this version and made a number of changes for the HK edition (which is dubbed entirely in Cantonese). In addition to eliminating some gratuitous nudity and speeding up the pace, Chan expanded and improved the final fight sequence and added two others (one in a gymnasium and another on a dock, featuring Lee Hoi-sang). There is also some new footage with Sally Yeh as a woman who helps Billy with his investigation, and the characters played by Roy Chiao, Yeung Kwan, Bill Wallace, Shum Wai, and Moon Lee now receive more screen time. Ultimately, the film still falls a little below Chan's usual standards but is definitely more satisfying in this incarnation. Besides, you haven't lived until you've seen Aiello speaking dubbed Cantonese!

800. Proud and Confidence

[*sic*] (1989) ★: 5/10. *Fong hei hung ying* (Cantonese), *Fang qi xiong ying* (Mandarin): "Arrogant Mighty Eagle." Cinematographer: Chan Tung-chuen; Art Director: Wong Ming-Fai; Music: Lowell Lo Kwun-ting; Writer: Johnny Lee King-kai; Producers: Charles Heung Wah-keung, Billy Chan Wui-ngai; Action Directors: Chin Yuet-sang, Power Lee King-chu, Wong Wai-tong; Director: Power Lee King-chu. Cast: Andy Lau Tak-wah (Wah), Rosamund Kwan Chi-lam (Miss Tang), Miu Kiu-wai (Wai), Dick Wei (Popeye), Lam Wai (Chiu), Francis Ng Chun-yu (He-Man), Eddie Maher (I.B.S. Terrorist), Peter Chan Lung (Psycho at Gas Station). 1.85:1. VHS: Tai Seng. Import LD: Ocean Shores (Poor Subtitles). 90 minutes.

This middling actioner starts out like Hong Kong's answer to **Top Gun** (with Andy Lau and Rosamund Kwan in the Tom Cruise and Kelly McGillis roles) before going off in other directions. When a psycho holds a group of children hostage at a gas station, cocky cop Wah is able to save the day with his expert marksmanship. Against the advice of his immediate superiors, Wah is assigned to "Project B.O.B." (Best of the Best), a new division of supercops created to battle terrorists. While in training with the other recruits, Wah strikes up a relationship with one of his instructors, the beautiful Miss Tang. On their first mission, the B.O.B. team saves a group of hostages being held by I.B.S., a team of vicious terrorists made up of ex-Vietnamese soldiers. When Wah's buddy Wai is killed in action by an I.B.S. hitman, he loses all of his confidence and feels he is unable to be of use to the team anymore. When a B.O.B. raid on an I.B.S. stronghold is ambushed, Wah regains his self-assurance and gets the chance to display courage under fire.

There is some well-choreographed action, marred only by some cheesy, optically created bullet hits (objects like tables and poles are supposedly being hit by gunfire, but the shells do not leave a mark of any kind), but this is very routine fare, recommended mainly to Andy Lau fans.

Pull No Punches *see* **The Prodigal Son**

801. Queen of Gamble

[*sic*] (1990) ★: 6/10. *Biu je nei woon ye (do hau)* (Cantonese), *Biao jie ni wan ye (du hou)* (Mandarin): "Cousin, You Play Stuff (Gambling Queen)." Cinematographer: Cheung Tak-wai; Art Director: Raymond Kwok Siu-keung; Music: Chiu Man-hoi; Writers: Siu Sang, Mo Kong; Producer: Chan Muk-chuen; Action Director: Fung Dik; Director: Siu Sang. Cast: Carol Cheng Yu-ling (Nan), Sibelle Hu Hui-chung (Frances Li), Simon Yam Tat-wah (Fu Hon-hwa), Alex Man Chi-leung (Li), Aaron Kwok Fu-shing (Po), Ng Man-tat (Fu Hon-san), Gigi Lai Chi (Linda). VHS: Tai Seng. Import LD/VCD: Mei Ah. Import DVD: Winner's Workshop. 94 minutes.

Not content to simply cash in on the gambling movie craze, this middling comedy also exploits the success of Carol Cheng's **Her Fatal Ways** by casting her as another Mainlander exposed to the capitalist decadence of HK. After running afoul of a Public Security officer, conwoman Sister Nan leaves China and travels to visit her relative in HK. While running a "Three Card Monte" scam, her talents are noticed by handsome playboy

Hon-hwa, who hires her to work at his casino. Hon-hwa's brother, Hon-san, makes a deal with the beautiful cardsharp Francis Li to scam him out of his holdings, leaving him penniless. When Hon-san orders his men to kill Francis rather than give her the agreed-upon percentage of Hon-hwa's holdings, she has a change of heart and seeks to repay her victim. Hon-hwa comes up with an alternate plan: They will work together with Nan to win back all of his lost assets by cheating Hon-san at his own game.

This is passable formula entertainment with the usual quota of gunplay, homosexual jokes, and scatological gags (Alex Man's character is tricked into eating horse dung as a way to determine which animal will be a winner in the next day's race!).

802. Queen of Temple Street

(1990; Sil-Metropole Organisation/ Filmways Production) ★: 8/10. *Miu gaai wong hau* (Cantonese), *Miao jie huang hou* (Mandarin): "Queen of Temple Street." Cinematographer: Chan Ying-kit; Art Director: Yank Wong Yan-kwai; Music: Lau Yee-tat; Writer: Chan Man-keung; Producers: William Tam Tak-cheung, Wong Yat-ping; Director: Lawrence Ah Mon. Cast: Sylvia Chang Ai-chia ("Big Sis" Wah), Rain Lau Yuk-tsui (Yan), Lo Lieh (Elvis), Ha Ping (Older Woman), Josephine Koo Mei-wah (Venus), Yuen King-tan (Candy), Kwan Hoi-shan (Luke), Alice Lau Ar-lai (Swallow), Law Koon-lan (Streetwalker). 1.85:1. VHS: World Video (No Subtitles). Import LD: Star Entertainment (No Subtitles). 109 minutes.

Every day, Temple Street madam "Big Sis" Wah must deal with the trials and tribulations caused by her girls, her two young sons, and her wayward teenage daughter Yan. Discovering that the latter is now working as a hostess, Wah attempts to steer her away before she becomes too firmly entrenched and can do nothing else. Yan will not hear of this, as she is making a very nice living and has no intention of coming back home. In spite of this defiance, Wah agrees to help her recover some nude pictures she posed for, before they are published in a porn magazine. However, when the girl goes from working at a nightclub to becoming a prostitute, Wah realizes that the time has come for her to put anger aside and be straight and honest with Yan before she loses her for good.

A balanced, intelligent look at life in one of HK's most infamous red light districts, **Queen of Temple Street** is much like director Lawrence Ah Mon's **Gangs** in the way that it concentrates on both the characters and their everyday routines (their children, their irresponsible husbands and boyfriends, fending off loansharks, etc.) while shunning the usual exploitation tenets. Sylvia Chang displays her diversity once again with a gritty, persuasive performance in a very atypical part, and Rain Lau (who won the Best Newcomer prize at The Hong Kong Film Awards) is a saucy delight as Yan. The Taiwan video release from Scholar Films has English subtitles.

803. Queen's High

(1991; Rising Fortune Films Co.) ★: 6/10. *Gung fan chi chuen* (Cantonese), *Gong fen zhi zun* (Mandarin): "Red Pink Ultimate Respect." Cinematographer: Lau Hung-chuen; Art Director: Chu Lai-kwong; Music: Richard Lo Sai-kit; Writers: Kong Heung-sang, Shum Wai; Producer: Wong Yung; Action Directors: Chris Lee Kin-sang, Lee Kin-hung, Lee Chung-chi, Poon Cheung; Director: Chris Lee Kin-sang. Cast: Cynthia Yang Li-ching (Kwanny), Simon Yam Tat-wah (Chung), Kenneth Tsang Kong (Fan Yau-tim), Shum Wai (Chau), Billy Chow Bei-lee (Thug). 1.85:1. VHS/LD: World Video. 85 minutes.

A good vehicle for the lovely Cynthia Yang (or "Cynthia Khan," as she is sometimes known), **Queen's High** offers nothing new plotwise but manages to hold viewer interest, thanks to some expertly choreographed action and the appealing presence of its star. Yang plays Kwanny, the soon-to-be-wed daughter of a prominent gang boss. When her father is murdered by rival leader Chau, Kwanny's brother, Chung, avenges his death by plugging Chau at point blank range, right in the middle of an auction. Chau's men then attack Kwanny's wedding procession, killing both Chung and Kwanny's husband-to-be, Peter. Forced to assume control of her father's shipping interests, Kwanny soon discovers that her foster brother (who is secretly trafficking in drugs) engineered the attack at the church and now wants to wrest control of the family business away from her.

The plot lags at times and characterizations are rudimentary at best. However, the film more than delivers on its level (particularly during the climax), and the sight of Yang furiously blasting away with an Uzi while clad in her wedding gown is one of the most indelible HK action images of the decade. Director Lee and his fellow filmmaker Cha Chuen-yee have supporting parts, and martial artist Kim Maree Penn also appears for a show stopping confrontation with Yang. The meaning of the English title (and the Chinese title, for that matter) is anyone's guess.

804. The Raid

(1991; Cinema City Co./Film Workshop) ★: 6/10. *Choy suk ji wong so chin gwan* (Cantonese), *Cai shu zhi huang sao qian jun* (Mandarin): "Uncle Choy: Yellow Rapid Attack Army." Cinematographer: Tom Lau Moon-tong; Art Director: Chung Yee-fung; Music: James Wong Jim; Writers: Tsui Hark, Yuen Kai-chi; Producer: Tsui Hark; Action Directors: Ching Siu-tung, Ma Yuk-shing; Directors: Ching Siu-tung, Tsui Hark. Cast: Dean Shek Tien (Dr. Choy), Tony Leung Kar-fai (Masa), Jacky Cheung Hok-yau (Bobo Bear), Corey Yuen Kwai (Brother Big Nose), Paul Chu Kong (Lieutenant Mang Tai-hoi), Fennie Yuen Kit-ying (Tina, aka WO-1), Joyce Godenzi (Yoshiko Kawashima, aka Kim Pik-fai), Lau Siu-ming (Dying Colonel). 1.85:1. VHS: Tai Seng. Import LD: Golden Cinema City. 100 minutes.

An ambitious attempt to craft a comic adventure along the lines of the old Hollywood serials, this Tsui Hark production is set in the 1930s when Emperor Puyi collaborated with the Japanese, in an attempt to conquer China. Despite being passed over by the army, the aged but crafty Dr. Choy insists on lending his fighting and medical skills to aid the revolution, and with the hapless Lieutenant Mang commanding, the resistance fighters need all of the help they can get. After making contact with operative WO-1 and barely escaping with their lives, the forces seek to destroy a poison gas factory that lies deep behind enemy lines, under the command of the sadistic Masa and the beautiful spy Yoshiko Kawashima.

Based on a series of popular "Uncle Choy" picture books from the 1930s, **The Raid** is even presented in that style, with illustrated, comic book-style bridges that iris in and out between scenes. The customary Tsui Hark pacing is in evidence, with numerous thrills coming fast and furious amid some nice period production design. It all makes for an enjoyable confection, if one is willing to overlook some technical lapses (particularly the sound mixing, which is quite shoddy at times) and the overstuffed narrative, which could stand to lose several of the peripheral characters.

805. Raid on Royal Casino Marine

(1990; Samico Films Production) ★: 5/10. *Wong ga do suen* (Cantonese), *Huang jia du chuan* (Mandarin): "Royal Gambling Ship." Cinematographer: Jimmy

Au Kam-hung; Art Director: Fred Chan Chi-chung; Music: Yeung Chan; Writer: Lee Man-choi; Producer: Billy Chan Wui-ngai; Action Director: Lau Chau-sang; Director: Wellson Chin Sing-wai. Cast: Sibelle Hu Hui-chung (Madam Wu), Stanley Fung Shui-fan (Kan), Sandra Ng Kwan-yu (Amy), Amy Yip Chi-mei (Susanna Yip), Kara Hui Ying-hung (May), Billy Lau Nam-kwong (Nam), Shing Fui-on (Richard), Michael Chow Man-kin (The Captain), Woo Fung (Wu), Manfred Wong (Short Hood), Peter Chan Lung (Bald Gambler), Barry Wong Ping-yiu (King of Gambling). 1.85:1. VHS: Tai Seng. Import LD: Mei Ah. 96 minutes. Also known as **The Inspector Wears Skirts III**.

The third entry in the **Inspector Wears Skirts** series follows the usual formula while throwing in a nod to the gambling movie craze. When the HK police decide to investigate a gambling ship, the dismantled female commando unit is put back into service. After the usual training and lame sexual hijinks, the squad goes undercover on the Royal Casino Marine to get the goods on an illegal triad gambling competition. When their master player is accidentally tossed overboard, one of the gangs bribes Amy to stand in, for a possible payout of $40 million.

In a wise change from its immediate forerunner, this entry dispenses with the drills quickly and gets down to the main storyline by the halfway point. There are amusing parodies of **A Chinese Ghost Story**, as well as the **Friday the 13th** and **A Nightmare on Elm Street** series, but most of the humor is too weak and obvious to be genuinely funny. However, this remains a relatively painless timewaster.

806. The Rape After

(1984) ★: 7/10. *Yin chung* (Cantonese), *Yin zhong* (Mandarin): "Licentious Seed." Art Director: Wong Ko-chen; Music: Not Original; Producer: Tsang Mang-wah; Action Director: Benz Kong To-hoi; Cinematographer-Writer-Director: Tom Lau Moon-tong. Cast: Melvin Wong Kam-sun (Mo Hsien-sheng), Tsang Ching-yuk, Chin Wei-man. 1.85:1. VHS: Ocean Shores (Poor Subtitles). 92 minutes.

One of the best HK horror films, **The Rape After** approaches its subject matter with a straight face, leaving out the comic asides that tend to dominate local genre fare. While on a commercial shoot, womanizing photographer Mo Hsien-sheng steals an unsightly looking statue from a dilapidated temple. After getting drunk with his model, Shu Ya, the pair have sex and then pass out. During the night, a monster emerges from the statue and rapes the girl, though she does not remember the attack in the morning. When Shu Ya later discovers that she is pregnant, Mo (who has since fallen for another woman whom he plans to marry) takes her to an underground clinic for an abortion. However, before the operation can be performed, the doctor and nurse are killed by the creature. A few months later, when Shu Ya is on her way to the hospital to give birth, she is killed in a car crash. When doctors try to perform an autopsy on her charred remains, a monstrous fetus explodes from the corpse and escapes. Mo discovers that the stolen statue houses the ashes of a baby that was killed by his new father-in-law a number of years ago as part of an unsuccessful ritual designed to cure his asthma. The photographer destroys the statue and scatters the ashes, but the family is afflicted by a string of casualties, prompting Mo to enlist the aid of some monks to dispel the evil.

While a few familiar Eastern horror trappings are included (one patient being treated by the monks vomits up green bile-covered toads and even has one extracted from his brain!), **The Rape After** also incorporates a number of elements more commonly found in Western genre efforts (zombies, animal attacks, monstrous babies, etc.), and the mix is quite effective. Well directed by veteran cinematographer Tom Lau (who was also director of photography here and wrote the screenplay) and very atmospherically lit (though the poor transfer on the Ocean Shores tape leaves it looking too dark), the film's no-nonsense approach and gruesome make-up add greatly to its impact. As is generally the case with these films, the characters do not behave all that rationally, and the screenplay goes a bit overboard (Shu Ya is given a horribly disfigured brother, in an institution, and an insane mother; neither one is really integral to the main story, though both receive a good deal of screen time), but those interested in the serious side of HK horror should definitely make a point of locating this increasingly rare release. The pirate soundtrack includes cues lifted from **Sorcerer**, **Star Trek II: The Wrath of Khan**, and **Blade Runner**.

807. Raped by an Angel

(1993; Wong Jing's Workshop) ★: 3/10. *Heung Gong kei on ji keung gaan* (Cantonese), *Xiang Gang qi an zhi qiang jian* (Mandarin): "Hong Kong Strange Case: Powerful Illicit Sexual Relations." Cinematographer: Cheung Man-bo; Art Director: Cheung Toi; Music: Jonathan Wong Bong-yin; Writer-Producer: Wong Jing; Director: Andrew Lau Wai-keung. Cast: Chingmy Yau Suk-ching (Yau Yuk-nam), Mark Cheng Ho-nam (Chuck Chi-sing), Simon Yam Tat-wah (Tat), Jacqueline Ng Suet-man (Chu Kit-man), Yuen King-tan (Turkey), Dennis Chan Kwok-san (The Professor), Linda Cheung Lan-ying (Girl in Opening Sequence). 1.85:1. VHS/LD: Tai Seng. Import LD/VCD: Star Entertainment. Import DVD: China Star. 95 minutes. Also known as **Naked Killer 2**.

Sometimes passed off as a sequel to **Naked Killer**, this Category III thriller has some of the same cast and crew but none of the style and excitement of its predecessor. The premise is fairly promising (suave lawyer/rapist uses his knowledge of the law to escape punishment) but the execution leaves a decidedly sour taste and the narrative is absurdly contrived. After seeing model Yau Yuk-nam in a TV milk commercial, the sadistic Chuck Chi-sing becomes determined to have her. When Yuk-nam rebukes his advances, Chuck moves into her building and brutally rapes the girl's friend, Kit-man. However, he is able to escape prosecution and assaults the girl once more, accidentally killing her this time. The death of Kit-man prompts Yuk-nam to prepare a series of elaborate (and thoroughly implausible) traps to finish the slimy predator once and for all.

The inclusion of an AIDS victim might seem like a daring stance for an adult film, but **Raped by an Angel** uses the individual merely as a *weapon*: Sexual sadist Chuck is tricked into raping her, which the screenplay deems the ultimate penalty for such a monster. The film had significant problems with HK censors, resulting in some very noticeable cuts during sex scenes, leaving little for the target audience save for a few glimpses of nudity, tease footage of Yau in various stages of undress, and some brief but unsavoury violence. Simon Yam appears in a ridiculous but entertaining subplot as a nice triad boss who takes a liking to Yuk-nam. The unrelated **Raped By An Angel 2: The Uniform Fan** and **Raped by an Angel III: Sexual Fantasy of the Chief Executive** followed in 1998, and **Raped by an Angel 4: The Rapist's Union** hit theaters in 1999.

808. Rebel from China

(1990; Silver Medal Productions) ★: 6/10. *Yung chong tin ha* (Cantonese), *Yong chuang tian xia* (Mandarin): "Brave Dash Over Lands Under Heaven." Cinematographer: Joe Chan Kong-hung; Art Director: Lam Sai-fan; Music: Lo Tai-yau; Writers: Nam Yin, Candy Cheng; Producer: Tony Chow Kwok-chung; Action Director: Tony Leung Siu-hung; Director: Raymond Lee Wai-man. Cast: Vincent Wan Yeung-ming (Ming), Cecilia Yip

Tung (Yip Mei-ling), Tommy Wong Kwong-leung (Kuen), John Woo Yu-sen (Kwong), Patrick Tse Yin (Or), Victor Hon Kwan (Shing), Lau Siu-ming (Chan Ting-yu). 1.85:1. VHS: Tai Seng. Import LD: Mei Ah. 94 minutes.

Notable mainly because it features John Woo in a supporting role, this triad actioner is the otherwise conventional tale of Ming, who escapes the horror of The Cultural Revolution by fleeing to HK with his older brother Kwong. The pair become legal citizens and seek to make a living. Trouble arises in the form of Kuen, a brutal loan shark who wants back the $30,000 Ming borrowed from him, and Or, an unscrupulous developer who wants the flat belonging to the grandmother of Ming's girlfriend. Seeking to bail himself out of both messes, Ming concocts a wild scheme whereby he and Kuen will smuggle TV sets to the Mainland, using money that Ming has convinced Or to advance him as a commission for getting the grandmother to agree to sell her home. The plan is a success, prompting Ming and Kuen to try and extort as much money as they can from Or for the deal. The pair become wealthy beyond their wildest dreams, but Or is not through with them yet.

Some well-executed and suspenseful action scenes distinguish this thriller, which also benefits from solid work by Wan and underrated character actor Tommy Wong. Woo does a decent job in a rare acting turn, though a good portion of his screen time merely consists of him getting beaten up.

The Rebel Intruders *see* **Killer Army**

809. Red and Black

(1991; Hatract Films) ★: 5/10. *Gwai gon bo* (Cantonese), *Gui gan bu* (Mandarin): "Ghost Cadre." Cinematographer: Yan Pak-hung; Art Director: Raymond Fung Yuen; Music: Law Wing-fai; Writer: Lillian Lee Pik-wah; Producer: Kam Cheung-kuen; Action Directors: Wan Fat, Siu Tak-fu; Director: Andrew Kam Yeung-wah. Cast: Tony Leung Kar-fai (Liang Kwo-tung), Joey Wang Tsu-hsien (Li Yu-ping), Lam Ching-ying (Lin Chiang), Wu Ma (Ma), Lau Kong (Liang Chosan), Kwan San (Sub-chief Lu, aka Li Fu-min), Ridley Tsui Bo-wah (Red Guard). Stereo Sound (Laserdisc only). 1.85:1. VHS: Tai Seng. Import LD: Star Entertainment (No Subtitles). 93 minutes.

China 1941: When his friend becomes possessed by an unearthly force called the "Blood Evil," villager Liang Chosan neutralizes him and seals the man's body inside a remote cavern. The film then picks up in the late 1960s, during The Cultural Revolution. Villagers sentenced to be re-educated accidentally open the tomb and the evil escapes, entering into the body of Sub-chief Lu (Kwan San, who bears a resemblance to Chairman Mao). Previously condemned for his superstitious beliefs, doctor Lin Chiang is actually the only one who can sense just what is happening, and he is determined to destroy the Blood Evil before it can use the influence this high-ranking official has to cause great harm.

The idea of mixing supernatural horror with the appalling injustices committed during The Cultural Revolution is a natural, but the execution is ham-fisted and the laudable ideas in novelist Lillian Lee's script are almost undone by the schlockier aspects of the production. Still, it remains an intriguing failure.

810. Red Dust

(1990; Tomson Films Co./Pineast Pictures) ★: 8/10. *Gwan gwan hung chan* (Cantonese), *Gun gun hong chen* (Mandarin): "Swirling Red Dust." Cinematographer: Poon Hang-sang; Art Director: Edith Cheung Sai-mei, Jessinta Liu Fung-ping; Music: Shih Jei-yong; Writers: Echo Chen De Quero, Yim Ho; Producer: Hsu Feng; Director: Yim Ho. Cast: Brigitte Lin Ching-hsia (Shen Shao-hua), Chin Han (Chang Neng-tsai), Maggie Cheung Man-yuk (Yueh-feng), Richard Ng Yiu-hon (Yu), Josephine Koo Mei-wah (Shao-hua's Editor), Yim Ho (Yueh-feng's Boyfriend). 1.85:1. VHS: Tai Seng. Import LD/VCD: Ocean Shores. 94 minutes.

While melodrama is viewed with disdain in most cinematic circles, it is often embraced by Chinese directors, who seem to have a much greater capacity for pulling it off. The best of their films are glorious, deeply moving experiences, like this HK/Taiwan co-production which was shot in the Mainland. The story opens in 1938, during the Japanese occupation of China. Imprisoned in the attic by her disturbed father, young Shen Shao-hua is perched on the verge of suicide. When the man eventually dies, Shao-hua is released from her prison and locks herself away in an apartment, using this voluntary solitude to build a career as a successful writer. Chang Neng-tsai is a handsome admirer of Shao-hua's work who makes her acquaintance, and the pair proceed to share their love and knowledge of literature. Neng-tsai is also a collaborator, however, and his work for the Japanese alienates Shao-hua's close friend, Yueh-feng, who is a member of the resistance. When the war draws to a close, Neng-tsai's association with the enemy forces him to flee, and Shao-hua is persecuted by her neighbors, who no longer fear reprisal. Heading out into the countryside, she discovers her lover but leaves when she feels that Neng-tsai has been unfaithful to her. However, in 1949, with the Communists on the verge of overrunning the Nationalist forces and taking over China, fate brings the pair together once again.

Based largely on the life of famous Shanghai-born novelist Eileen Chang, **Red Dust** is blessed with one of Brigitte Lin's most delicate and poignant performances, beautiful location work, and a sense of spectacle that lends weight to the smaller human tragedy at the story's core (the climactic sequence, depicting a frenzied mob trying to get on the last boat from Shanghai, is truly thrilling). Co-writer San Mao (billed in the English credits as Echo Chen De Quero) was herself a famous novelist who, reportedly, shared some of the self-destructive qualities shown by Shao-hua. Not long after **Red Dust** opened, San committed suicide. The film won eight of nine prizes it was nominated for at the Taiwan Golden Horse Awards, including Best Picture, Best Actress (Brigitte Lin), and Best Director. The one it did not attain, Best Screenplay, was the category for which San was nominated, and that may have been the reason behind her actions, though no one seems to be sure.

811. The Red Panther

(1983; H.K. Fong Ming Motion Picture Co.) ★: 5/10. *Hoi si chut sai* (Cantonese), *Hai shi chu shi* (Mandarin): "Born in Evil Times." Cinematographer: Yu Chun; Music: Not Original; Writers: Double Phoenix Golden Script Team; Director: Kong Lung. Cast: Yee Lui (Lai), Lee Tin-long, Lee Tin-hing, Lawrence Cheng Tan-shui (Kiang), Phillip Chan Yan-kin (Lai's Superior). 1.85:1. VHS: Tai Seng. Import LD: Golden Cinema City. Import VCD: Mega Star. 88 minutes.

This decidedly offbeat horror thriller concerns a series of murders committed by a psychopath, who anaesthetizes his victims and then mutilates them. Goofy mama's boy cop Lai (who seems more concerned about sex and his hemorrhoids than police work) is assigned to investigate but makes little progress, spending most of his time being ordered around by his domineering mother. The finger of guilt points at two men: the unhappy Dr. Chu (who wants to immigrate to England but cannot, due to his poor English) and oddball ex-medical student Kiang. Both men were in contact with the latest victim, a prostitute suffering from breast cancer, who was attacked and sliced up in a bar. Lai raids Chu's house and finds jars filled with severed organs, something the latter is hard pressed to explain, but another attack occurs while he is under police observation. Kiang, meanwhile, is caught snooping around the morgue right before a number of bodies are found mutilated.

The mystery is adequately conceived, and there are a couple of interesting visual touches seemingly inspired by the Italian *giallo* thrillers of the time (we see one murder only through the reflection in a monkey's eye). The comedy relief is jarring, however, and tends to short-circuit any credibility the story has, particularly when juxtaposed with some fairly nasty murder sequences. Overall, *The Red Panther* is not a very good film but one certainly worth considering for its curiosity value ... and don't miss the ending!

812. Red Rose White Rose

(1994; First Film Organisation/Golden Entertainment Co./Golden Flare Films Co./Warner Brothers) ★: 7/10. *Hung mooi gwai baak mooi gwai* (Cantonese), *Hong mei gui bai mei gui* (Mandarin): "Red Rose White Rose." Cinematographer: Christopher Doyle; Art Director: Pok Yeuk-muk; Music: Johnny Chen; Writer: Edward Lam Chik-wah; Producers: Hoi Wong, Wu Kao-hsiung; Director: Stanley Kwan Kam-pang. Cast: Winston Chao Wen-hsuan (Tung Zhen-bao), Joan Chen Chong (Wang Jiao-rui), Veronica Yip Yuk-hing (Meng Yen-li), Lin Yanyu (Wu Ma). Dolby Digital. 1.85:1. Import LD: Golden Flare. Import VCD: Panorama Entertainment. 111 minutes.

Based on a novel by Eileen Chang, this Stanley Kwan film (which opens in 1920s Shanghai) is similar in look and tone to the director's best works but is flawed and a bit disappointing all the same. Handsome playboy Tung Zhen-bao seeks to control every aspect of his life and this extends to the women he courts. Jiao-rui is the Westernized wife of a friend, who is already cheating with someone else but soon begins to sleep with Zhen-bao, who finds her irresistibly seductive. Jiao-rui (whose outspokenness and carefree attitude reminds Zhen-bao of his first love, a girl named Rose he met in England) is more than happy to carry on the affair, but when she asks her husband for a divorce, Zhen-bao proceeds to leave her. Now once again "a decent, respectable man," Zhen-bao courts and marries Meng Yan-li, who could not be any more different than Jiao-rui. However, it is soon clear that life with this traditional, stiflingly conservative woman will hardly bring him happiness.

Kwan relies heavily on narration and intertitles (presumably taken directly from the original source) to advance the story and characters; if the intention was for the film to be the book in literal visual form, he has not quite succeeded. Still, Christopher Doyle's customarily exquisite cinematography and some impeccable production design are definite attractions, as are the performances (particularly Joan Chen and Veronica Yip, the latter in a role well-removed from the adult fare she found fame in) and the ironic humor found in Zhen-bao's plight. In reference to the title, "Red Rose" is the name Zhen-bao gives to his mistress, Jiao-rui, while his virtuous wife, Yen-li, is "White Rose."

813. Red Shield

(1991; Magnum) ★: 6/10. *Lui ting so yuet* (Cantonese), *Lei ting sao xue* (Mandarin): "Thunderbolt Clears Out Hideouts." Cinematographer: Tony Miu Kin-fai; Art Director: Horace Ma Kwong-wing; Music: Phil Chan Fei-lap; Writers: Law Kam-fai, James Fung Shui-hung; Producer: Danny Lee Sau-yin; Action Director: Stephen Tung Wai; Director: Parkman Wong Pak-man. Cast: Danny Lee Sau-yin (Lui Te-ken), Leung Kar-yan (Wong Tin-tang), Teresa Mo Shun-kwan (Suk-han), Yip San (Terry), Yuen Wah (Panther), Shing Fui-on (Shing Bill), Ben Lam Kwok-bun (Dragon Ho), Cheung Kwok-keung (Kent), Jackson Liu Hsiu-hsien (Assassin), Michael Dinga (William), Jamie Luk Kim-ming (Mainland Commander), Eric Kei Kar-fat (Cop). Stereo Sound (Laserdisc only). 1.85:1. VHS: Tai Seng. Import LD: Golden Cinema City. Import VCD: Mega Star. Import DVD: Universe. 92 minutes.

This efficient Danny Lee actioner casts the veteran star as Lui, a Special Duty Unit Chief Inspector who is on the trail of some arms smugglers. After the gang launches a devastating raid on a HK pier, the police assign Senior Inspector Wong to assist Lui in his investigation. After the usual period of adversity that partners always go through in these movies, the pair start working together towards their mutual goal.

The plotting is routine and the direction (by frequent Lee co-star Parkman Wong) is, outside of one sequence described below, undistinguished. However, **Red Shield** stands out from most of Lee's action thrillers in a couple of ways. In contrast to the norm, the British cops all speak English and their Chinese counterparts answer with same. There is also a fair amount of character development involving Lui and Wong's relationships with their spouses, though the latter sequences are awkwardly handled and don't really add much to the final product. Yuen Wah has a co-starring role as a Vietnamese villain, and the most suspenseful sequence finds Lui and Wong trying to spirit him from a government-run refugee camp before the inhabitants can overpower and kill them (with the refugee problem in HK grabbing headlines, such one-dimensional depictions of Vietnamese characters were a standard element in HK cinema at the time). Big Taiwanese actor Jackson Liu is done up to resemble Arnold Schwarzenegger in **The Terminator**, complete with similar hair style, black leather jacket, and heavy artillery!

814. Red to Kill

(1994; Martini Film Company) ★: 3/10. *Yeuk saat* (Cantonese), *Ruo sha* (Mandarin): "Feeble Killer." Cinematographer: Tony Miu Kin-fai; Art Director: Kwan Mei-bo; Music: Wong Bong; Writer: Wong Ho-wah; Producer: Kimmy Suen King-on; Director: Billy Tang Hin-sing. Cast: Lily Chung Suk-wai (Kong Yuk-ming), Ben Ng Ngai-cheung (Chan Chi-wai), Money Lo Man-yee (Cheung Ka-lok), Bobby Yip King-sang (Ugly Mental Patient). 1.85:1. VHS: Tai Seng. Import LD/VCD/DVD: Ocean Shores. 91 minutes.

Even those who love HK cinema for its immoderation may get more than they bargained for out of this Category III thriller from Billy Tang (director of the none-too-subtle **Run and Kill**), which attains new heights of tastelessness. A vicious rapist/murderer is preying upon women in an apartment building that also houses a government-run hostel for retarded adults. The perverted killer is none other than Chan Chi-wai, one of the facility's social workers, whose deviant behavior is set off by red dresses. One evening, he molests pretty Kong Yuk-ming, an aspiring dancer who is 21 but has the I.Q. of a ten-year-old. Chan is brought up on charges but is acquitted when the court decides that Yuk-ming is mentally unfit to testify. When Chan continues to torment the girl, social worker Cheung Ka-lok devises a plan to stop him by using herself as bait.

A reprehensible film, **Red to Kill** still deserves some sparse praise. Lily Chung is quite convincing as the feeble-minded heroine; the score by Wong Bong (who has worked on several films of this nature, including **Daughter of Darkness** and **The Untold Story**) is effective; and there is even sync sound recording, a real rarity for adults-only fare. Several scenes are quite stylish, and Ben Ng's performance as the killer is really something to see (it is not what one would classify as good acting, but he captures the character's dementia very effectively). However, the violence (both sexual and physical) perpetrated upon the female characters is nauseatingly prolonged and gratuitous, and both the courtroom sequence and the plot's dramatic elements are ludicrous.

815. Red Zone

(1995; Golden Harvest/Golden Way Films/Good Standard International/ Paragon Films) ★: 5/10. *Baau ja ling* (Cantonese), *Bao zha ling* (Mandarin): "Explosive Decree." Cinematographer: Herman Yau Lai-to; Art Directors: Lee Yuet-lei, Ken Chiu Kin-san; Music: Mak Chun-hung; Writers: Fibe Ma Mei-ping, Lee Wai-yee, Edward Tang King-sang; Producer: Anthony Chow Ting-on; Action Director: Lee Chung-chi; Director: Edward Tang King-sang. Cast: Kenny Ho Kar-king (King), Yu Rongguang ("Pekingman"), Ken Lo Wai-kwong (Kwong), Valerie Chow Kar-ling (Ivy Lau), Waise Lee Chi-hung (Wong Wai-hung), Mark King (Harrison), Feng Sing (Cop with Food). 1.85:1. VHS: Tai Seng. Import LD: Cameron Entertainment. Import VCD: Mei Ah. 97 minutes.

Edward Tang, who wrote the screenplays for several of Jackie Chan's best (and worst) movies, made his directorial debut with this routine police thriller, which is almost done in by its dull, badly structured plot. When crime boss Wong Wai-hung is arrested for possession, his girlfriend (Valerie Chow, now working in America under the name "Rachel Shane") attempts to bribe the trial judge to grant Wong bail. When the magistrate refuses, he is killed in a car bombing. Meanwhile, Wong's underlings are not about to wait for his release and plot to take over his empire, planting remote-controlled bombs and creating other threats for the police officers assigned to the case (including Kenny Ho, Yu Rongguang, and Ken Lo).

After figuring prominently in the first two reels, Waise Lee's character is all but forgotten, and the increasingly flimsy plot is left to lurch along between action scenes. These setpieces, however, are handled quite nicely, particularly the sequence in which Ho, riding a bicycle, is chased down a winding road by a killer in a jeep; and novel use is made of a toy helicopter to dispose of a bomb. It is also refreshing to see Ken Lo (best known as Jackie Chan's chief adversary in **Drunken Master II**) cast as a charismatic Thai undercover officer instead of his usual standard issue villain. It makes for a passable 97 minutes, if you make creative use of speed search and be sure to start rewinding before the absurd epilogue (in which Kenny Ho equates the balance between criminals and the law to a cab ride through Italy!).

816. The Red-Wolf

(1995; Sunton Films Production/ Sharp Productions) ★: 6/10. *Foo maang wai lung* (Cantonese), *Hu meng wei long* (Mandarin): "Fierce Tiger, Mighty Dragon." Cinematographer: Philip Ma Kam-cheung; Art Director: Ho Chi-hang; Music: Not Original; Writer: Ricky Ng Kwok-shing; Producers: Victor Yeung Kar-on, Robin Yeung Kar-wah; Action Directors: Yuen Woo-ping, Cho Wing, Yuen Cheung-yan; Director: Yuen Woo-ping. Cast: Kenny Ho Kar-king (Dragon), Christy Chung Lai-tai (Lai), Ngai Sing (Vice Captain), Elaine Lui Siu-ling (Elaine), Woo Fung (Wu), Cho Wing (Terrorist), Robert Samuels (Bobby), Yuen Cheung-yan (Passenger). 1.85:1. VHS/LD: World Video. Import LD/VCD: Fitto Mobile. 92 minutes.

A cheerfully unabashed ripoff of **Die Hard** and **Under Siege**, this efficient low-budget action thriller kills time in an amiable fashion. New Year's Eve 1994: The cruise liner "White Whale" is highjacked by a gang of multinational terrorists. Their goal: the uranium stolen by the ship's crooked captain, which is stashed in the vessel's safe. Fortunately, security staff member Dragon figures out what is happening and sets about foiling their plans, with the help of spunky waitress Lai.

As far as Yuen Woo-ping's films go, this is not one of his better efforts: The stock musical score is weak, the real name of the ship being used ("Fairy Princess") is visible on a couple of occasions, and the climactic action is more than a little contrived. On the plus side, Kenny Ho and Christy Chung are very likeable leads, the hand-to-hand combat is terrific (once the fighting starts, it rarely ever stops), and the stunts are equally impressive. *The Red-Wolf* is good lightweight fun.

817. Reincarnation

(1987) ★: 5/10. *Tin goon chi fuk* (Cantonese), *Tian guan ci fu* (Mandarin): "Heaven Bestows Good Fortune." Cinematographer: James Yeung Jim; Art Director: Jon Hau Wing-choi; Music: Violet Lam Man-yee; Producers: William Cheung Kei, Tse Loi-wor; Writer-Action Director-Director: Jamie Luk Kim-ming. Cast: Kenny Bee (Li Hsi/Peter Wu), Cecilia Yip Tung (Liu Ah-yu), Julia Nickson (Julia), Tai Po (Hsiao Liao), Yung Sai-kit (David), Kwan Hoi-shan (Peter's Father), Woo Fung (Richard), Charlie Cho Cha-lei (Brown Noser at Office). 1.85:1. VHS: Tai Seng. Import LD/VCD: Ocean Shores. 92 minutes.

Shortly after their wedding, Li Hsi and Liu Ah-yu are killed in a car crash. However, because of a screw-up by the sentinels assigned to escort them to the netherworld, the pair are given a second chance. If they can find new bodies to inhabit within 49 days, they can remain on Earth as human beings. After a night of checking out suitable candidates in the fatality ward of a hospital, the pair finally find the perfect match: a healthy couple who attempted suicide and are on the verge of death. Unfortunately, while the man dies, the woman does not, leaving Hsi's spirit inside this new body, while Ah-yu has no one to inhabit. Hsi's new host is Peter Wu, the none-too-bright son of an affluent man whose eldest son, David, is conspiring to steal the family fortune. David is in league with the beautiful Julia, the woman who was brought into the hospital with Peter that evening. Ah-yu wants Hsi to kill Julia so she can take her body, while David and Julia are trying to kill Peter/Hsi! In the meantime, Peter's father has noticed his son's strange behavior and hired an exorcist.

The script does not fully mine all of the dark humor inherent in the premise, but this supernatural farce (which possesses the action quotient expected from a Jamie Luk project) remains fairly enjoyable and the ending is clever. Singapore-born Julia Nickson (who went by the name Julia Nickson-Soul when she was married to actor David Soul) made her film debut in **Rambo: First Blood Part II** and went on to appear in a number of American movies and TV programs.

818. The Reincarnation of Golden Lotus

(1989; Golden Harvest/Friend Cheers/ Paragon Films) ★: 4/10. *Poon Gam-lien ji chin sai gam sang* (Cantonese), *Pan Jinlian zhi qian shi jin sheng* (Mandarin): "Poon Kam-lien's Past World, This Life." Cinematographer: Jingle Ma Cho-shing; Art Directors: Raymond Lee King-man; Danny Yuen Ching-yeung; Music: Richard Lo Sai-kit, Wai Pang; Writer: Lillian Lee Pik-wah; Producer: Teddy Robin Kwan; Action Director: Tony Leung Siu-hung; Director: Clara Law Cheuk-yiu. Cast: Joey Wang Tsu-hsien (Lotus), Eric Tsang Chi-wai (Wu Ta), Wilson Lam Chun-yin (Wu Lung), Sin Lap-man (Simon Hsiao), Ku Feng (The Principal). 1.85:1. VHS: Indigo Media, Tai Seng. Import LD: Mei Ah. 94 minutes. Also known as **This Day, Last Life**.

An ambitious but tiresome film, director Clara Law's fantasy-tinged drama (written by novelist Lillian Lee) follows the outline of the classic Chinese story *Poon Kam-lien/Pan Jinlian* (or "The Story of Golden Lotus" as it is generally known in English) but is not a literal adaptation. Rather, it opens in the past but quickly switches to modern times. Beheaded for adultery, Lotus finds herself in a strange netherworld which exists on the pathway to reincarnation. While there, Lotus refuses to have her mind cleansed, so that she may remember the crimes inflicted upon her and take revenge in the next life. She is reborn in China around the time of the Cultural Revolution, and it quickly becomes clear that she is doomed to suffer the same indignities as her forerunner. While a teenager, she is raped by the principal of her dance academy, who then accuses the girl of being a counter-revolutionary. She spends the next years of her life tormented by neighbors who believe her to be a "slut," but hope for change appears in the diminutive form of rich HK businessman Wu Ta. Entranced by her beauty, the simple-minded Wu proposes marriage and Lotus accepts, if only because it provides a way for her to escape China. Life in HK initially seems like paradise, especially since her husband's chauffeur turns out to be Wu Lung, a handsome athlete who did nothing to help Lotus when she was wrongly accused of theft by zealous revolutionaries. As her past self begins to dominate, Lotus becomes more reckless and decadent, sleeping with drug-addled designer Simon Hsiao, a dalliance that sets the stage for disaster.

By that point, however, the viewer has become convinced that Lotus' actions are dictated not so much by fate as by the precepts of bad melodrama. Regardless of whether Lee's script adheres faithfully to the structure of its source or not, merely restaging the events of the past in the present without some sort of embellishment does not make for an interesting storyline, particularly when the tale in question is so easily construed. The film was a commercial success, but one suspects that was almost entirely due to the presence of Joey Wang, who was then at the height of her popularity. Wang is very handsomely photographed throughout but, as utilized here, she is ultimately just another lovely prop in a film that registers far more greatly on an aesthetic rather than intellectual or emotional level.

819. Remains of a Woman

(1993; Wishing Well Film Co.) ★: 6/10. *Long sam yue tit* (Cantonese), *Lang xin ru tie* (Mandarin): "A Heart Like Iron." Cinematographer: Gigo Lee Chi-hang; Art Director: Ganni Ma Chi-ming; Music: Lowell Lo Kwun-ting; Writers: Poon Yuen-leung, Dennis Chan Kwok-san; Producers: Dennis Chan Kwok-san, Melvin Wong Kam-sun; Action Director: Chan Chung-tai; Director: Clarence Fok Yiu-leung. Cast: Carrie Ng Kar-lai (Judy Yu), James Pak Chin-shek (Billy Chan), Loletta Lee Lai-chun (Annie Cheung), Jacqueline Law Wai-kuen (Lisa Wong), Melvin Wong Kam-sun (Mel Wong), Dennis Chan Kwok-san (Wong's Associate), Kenneth Tsang Kong (Angry Cop), Money Lo Man-yee (TV Reporter in Green). 1.85:1. VHS: Tai Seng. Import LD/VCD: Mei Ah. 85 minutes.

Based on the same true case depicted in **Legal Innocence** (also 1993), this flawed but interesting Category III thriller also shifts between different time periods in its depiction of the events leading up to the case and the subsequent trials. Slick deviant Billy Chan hooks up with race track cashier Judy Yu, and the latter is soon stealing money to support Billy's cocaine habit. At the same time, Billy is also seeing stewardess Lisa Wong, and this triangle eventually leads to the latter's murder. Behind bars and sentenced to death, Billy and Judy are visited by Annie, a naive church volunteer who soon falls for the former, who is now pretending to have found God, as a means of getting off of death row. With a retrial looming and Annie having accepted Billy's proposal of marriage, Judy decides to tell her side of what happened to the man who served as prosecutor on the first case. However, during the second trial, Judy confesses to the crime and states that Billy did not participate, but the audience learns otherwise.

Carrie Ng is excellent as a woman whose broken marriage and desperate loneliness leads her to perform unconscionable acts, and the frenzied, drug-fuelled orgy of violence, dementia, and paranoia during the climax is very effectively staged. On the downside, Loletta Lee is not at all convincing in a crucial role, and Pak is not charismatic or attractive enough to fully convince one that he could have this sort of hold over these women. The film did weak business in HK but was a surprise hit in Taiwan, with Ng going on to win the Best Actress statuette in that country's Golden Horse Awards.

820. Remember M, Remember E

(1995; Regal Films Co.) ★: 5/10. *Na yau yat tin bat seung nei* (Cantonese), *Na you yi tian bu xiang ni* (Mandarin): "Not a Day Without Thinking of You." Cinematographer: Tam Chi-wai; Art Director: Bill Lui Cho-hung; Music: Mark Lui Chung-tak; Writer: Raymond To Kwok-wai; Producer: Charine Chan Kar-ling; Director: Cheuk Lei. Cast: Chu Kin-kwan (Chu Ah-chai), Nicky Wu Chi-lung (Ricky), Athena Chu Yan (Ching), Lau Shun (Chu), Ko Chuen-hsiang (Ah-chai's Father), Bonnie Fu Yuk-ching (Ah-chai's Stepmother). 1.85:1. VHS: World Video. Import LD/VCD: Ocean Shores. 90 minutes.

School buddies Ricky and Ah-chai are not exactly ideal students and constantly earn the wrath of their humorless teacher, "Stone Fish." One day at the beach they meet a lovely girl and have a great afternoon with her. She turns out to be Ching, Stone Fish's daughter no less, but that does nothing to ease the serious crush the two boys have on her. Ching only likes "mature men," however, and is more concerned about breaking away from her strict mother and travelling to foreign countries. As it turns out, both Ching and Ricky end up running away from home: she to Japan and he away from his domineering father and alcoholic stepmother. Left all by himself, Ah-chai goes through a string of dead-end jobs, while the paths chosen by Ricky and Ching also fail to bring them happiness. However, events beyond their control will change their lives for the better.

A mild comedy-drama aimed at teens, this makes for pleasant but instantly forgettable viewing, coasting along on viewer goodwill instead of coming up with some creative notions. We know from the outset what happens to Ah-chai, as the film is mostly one big flashback, so the dramatic aspects of this wish fulfilment fantasy hold little weight. Director Cheuk Lei is credited simply as "Charlie" in the English credits.

Remember Me *see* **Remember M, Remember E**

821. Retribution Sight Unseen

(1993; Golden Harvest/Mobile Film Production/Master Strength) ★: 4/10. *Maang nui 72 siu si* (Cantonese), *Mang nu 72 xiao shi* (Mandarin): "Blind Woman: 72 Hours." Cinematographer: Tam Chi-wai; Art Director: Suzy Cheung Kai-san; Music: Johnny Yeung Kei-cheung; Writer: So Man-sing; Producer: Alfred Cheung Kin-ting; Director: Chan Wing-chiu. Cast: Veronica Yip Yuk-hing (Mrs. Ng), Anthony Wong Chau-sang (Sam Chu), Anthony Chan Yau (Jack Ng), Jamie Luk Kim-ming (Cop), Alfred Cheung Kin-ting (Dr. Wong). 1.85:1. VHS: Tai Seng. Import LD/VCD: Universe. 88 minutes. Also known as **Three Days of a Blind Girl**.

A film that aspires to provide Category III-style sex and violence but doesn't really deliver because it also wants to be seen as a legitimate thriller, **Retribution Sight Unseen** succeeds only at being a waste of time. Unable to see following an eye operation, Mrs. Ng (who is never referred to by a first name in the subtitles) is assured by her doctor that she will regain her sight within 48 to 72 hours. However, hubby Jack has to go to a medical conference in Macau, leaving her alone with only their maid to keep her company. Not long after the latter steps out, Ng is visited by the jovial but rather odd Sam Chu, who says that he is a childhood friend of her husband. He stays for a while and then returns in the evening with a decided change in disposition. As Chu's behavior gets more and more peculiar, Ng begins to fear for her safety. She has a very good reason to be afraid: Chu has been tracking her movements for over a year and has waited for just this sort of opportunity to arise. He knows that Jack had an affair with his wife and also blames him for her subsequent death. Chu plans to torment and abuse the doctor's wife as a form of twisted tit for tat.

Veronica Yip and Anthony Wong both do good work, and the quality of their performances helps to perk one's interest on occasion. Regardless, this would-be thriller is just too contrived (those darn cell phone batteries run out at the worst times!), illogical, and predictable to succeed.

822. Return Engagement

(1990; In-Gear Productions) ★: 5/10. *Joi chin gong woo* (Cantonese), *Zai zhan jiang hu* (Mandarin): "Battling Again in a Dangerous World." Cinematographers: Jimmy Leung Chi-ming, Tom Lau Moon-tong, Christopher Doyle, Andrew Lau Wai-keung; Art Director: Jon Hau Wing-choi; Music: Violet Lam Man-yee; Producer: Rover Tang Kwong-chow; Action Director: Benz Kong To-hoi; Writer-Director: Joseph Cheung Tung-cho. Cast: Alan Tang Kwong-wing (Lung Ho-tin), Elizabeth Lee Mei-fung (Tsin Siu-fung), May Lo Mei-mei (Siu-lung), Simon Yam Tat-wah (Pang), Andy Lau Tak-wah (Wah), David Wu Tai-wai (David), Carrie Ng Kar-lai (Lung's Wife), Melvin Wong Kam-sun (Wong), Ku Feng (Uncle Hung), Stephen Tung Wai (Cheung Yat-lui), Dennis Chan Kwok-san (Hotel Clerk), Chen Jing (Tung), Chang Yi (Repairman). VHS: World Video, Arena/Xenon (Dubbed). Import LD/VCD: Mei Ah. 108 minutes. Also known as **Hong Kong Corruptor** (Arena/Xenon title).

Vancouver 1973: After his wife is murdered by Mafia assassins, triad leader Lung Ho-tin launches a successful counterattack on his enemies. He is subsequently arrested and given a sixteen year prison sentence. Upon his release, Lung returns to HK in search of his missing daughter, Gaga. He meets up with club owner Tsin Siu-fung, who introduces him to Siu-lung, a juvenile delinquent who claims to know where to find Gaga. After many lies and much running about town, Siu-lung begins to regard Lung as the father figure she sorely needs and reveals the truth about his daughter. Meanwhile, Uncle Hung, Lung's old triad associate, is having his authority questioned by his ambitious underling Pang. When Siu-lung interferes with one of Pang's deals, he orders her death. After an attack by Pang's killers, Siu-fung is kidnapped and Siu-lung is badly injured. Calling in an old favor, Lung enlists several gunmen of his own and sets out to liquidate his nemesis.

Alan Tang is a smooth and handsome actor who can play this sort of hackneyed part with ease, endowing Lung with a convincing amount of both compassion and languor. His stature and screen presence go a long way in selling both the character and the film. This is fortunate because **Return Engagement** has some major problems. The melodramatic first half drags badly and could lose an entire reel without harming the storyline. In addition to the usual post-Woo gangster cliches, there is even a re-creation of the famous "Choose the sword and come with me or choose the ball and join your mother" scene from the popular Japanese samurai movie **Lone Wolf and Cub: Sword of Vengeance** (1972), utilizing a gun and a stuffed animal. Typically, the Caucasian actors are dubbed with hilarious voices, which adds extra chuckles to foolish lines like "What is this guy? Some kind of Hong Kong Rambo?" Indeed he is, but while the bullet-ridden finale is characteristically excessive, it is also surprisingly dull. Arena/Xenon's **Hong Kong Corruptor** is a dubbed version of this film with extra, completely extraneous footage of Chow Yun-fat from **Brotherhood**.

823. The Return of Pom Pom

(1984; D & B Films Co.) ★: 5/10. *Seung lung chut hoi* (Cantonese), *Shuang long chu hai* (Mandarin): "Double Dragons Come from the Sea." Cinematographer: Ricky Lau Koon-wai; Music: Joseph Chan Wing-leung; Writer: Jo Chan Wai-yee; Producer: Dickson Poon Dik-sun; Action Director: Lam Ching-ying; Director: Phillip Chan Yan-kin. Cast: Richard Ng Yiu-hon (Chou), John Sham Kin-fun (Beethoven), Deanie Yip Tak-han (Anna), Kara Hui Ying-hung (Yuen Hung, aka Mimi), Lam Ching-ying (Lo Kin, aka "Flying Spider"), James Tien Chun (Tin), Chung Fat (Sherlock Holmes). 1.85:1. Import VCD: Mega Star. 83 minutes.

The first sequel to **Pom Pom** finds Richard Ng and John Sham transferred to the unit of their nemesis, the fearsome Chief Inspector (James Tien). When their former boss (Phillip Chan, who also directed) is framed for the theft of department funds, he realizes that the true thief is a nimble cat burglar (Lam Ching-ying) who was crippled while the officer was trying to apprehend him twenty years ago. His daughter (Kara Hui), who assisted him with the crime, works as a movie stunt performer, and when Sham catches sight of her, he is smitten for life, making Ng's apprehension of her father more than a little difficult.

While there are some amusing bits (the best finds Ng desperately trying to prove that Lam is not really crippled by tickling his feet), overall, the comedy is less inspired and the action quotient is low. Melvin Wong Kam-sun, Ben Lam Kwok-bun, Lau Kar-wing, Yip Wing-cho, and Anthony Chan Yau appear briefly. It was followed by **Mr. Boo Meets Pom Pom**.

824. Return of the Demon

(1987; Eagle Film Production Co. ★: 7/10. *Moh go yat cheung* (Cantonese), *Mo gao yi zhuang* (Mandarin): "Demon Overhead." Cinematographer: Chan Tung-chuen; Art Director: Fred Chan Chi-chung; Music: Anders Nelsson; Writers: Wong Ying, Johnny Lee King-kai; Producers: Charles Heung Wah-keung, Wong Ying; Action Directors: Cheung Wing-hon, Hon Nin-sang, Yeung Sai-kwan; Writer-Director: Wong Ying. Cast: Charlie Cho Cha-lei (Kin), Shing Fui-on (Fierce), Dick Wei (The Monster), Emily Chu Bo-yee (Tayona), Nat Chan Pak-cheung (Wai), Tsui Sau-lai (Panther), Wu Ma (Kao). 1.85:1. VHS: Tai Seng. Import LD: Golden Cinema City. 96 minutes.

In their quest for treasure, a gang of robbers accidentally unleash an ancient evil in this outlandish horror comedy filled with back-breaking slapstick and spirited gore FX. The thieves team up with Kin, a learned but decidedly eccentric Taoist, to track down and destroy the murderous creature. In order to help find the quarry, Kin performs a spell that gives him the instincts of a tracking dog…as well as a few less-than-desirable canine attributes. The hunt is impeded by Wai, a cheerfully sadistic police captain who subjects the gang to some of his favorite tortures, but the prisoners are able to escape when a full moon transforms Kin into a vicious "were-dog!" Further trouble looms in the form of Tayona, a beautiful ghost who is looking for a virgin willing to die for her so that she can reincarnate. Despite having lived for 280 years, Kin has never been with a woman. He has reached that age by not eating eggs; according to his discipline, each egg you consume shortens your life by four days. In the film's highlight, Tayona decides to finish him off by trapping Kin in a room filled with hundreds of eggs and several banana peels!

Some of the comic sequences and the climactic battle (where the heroes fight the creature and his spike-headed zombie minions) would have been more effective had they been tightened up a bit. That caveat aside, **Return of the Demon** enthusiastically serves up every ingredient that makes HK horror comedies both models of the form and distinctively unique. The soundtrack includes a mixture of new music and library cues.

825. Return of the Evil Fox

(1991; Artview Investment Co.) ★: 3/10. *Maang gwai woo lei jing* (Cantonese), *Meng gui hu li jing* (Mandarin): "Fierce Ghost Fox Spirit." Cinematographer: Ho Ming; Art Director: Cheung Yuk-chu; Music: Not Original; Writers: On Yi, Wu Kong; Producer: Chan Yam-chuen; Action Director: Tam Chan-tung; Director: Leung Cho-chi. Cast: Sandra Ng Kwan-yu (Yu), Charine Chan Kar-ling (Chiang Su-su/Yi), Woo Fung (Chiang Wu), Shing Fui-on (Big Rope), Charlie Cho Cha-lei (Manager), Yuen King-tan (Hung), Gabriel Wong Yat-san (Su-su's Brother), Chor Yuen (Wang). 1.85:1. VHS/LD: Quali-vision. Import LD: Ocean Shores. 91 minutes.

One of the cheapest and cheesiest horror comedies of its period, **Return of the Evil Fox** utilizes special FX that date back to the earliest days of cinema; the plot is about of the same vintage. The Chiang family have practised the Maosan arts for thousands of years. In the 14th century, they used their powers to subdue a female fox demon that was on the loose. Now, in the present day, the creature has escaped its eternal prison and is wreaking havoc in a shopping mall. Once it has drained the souls of 108 men, the she-devil will transform into a "fox elf" and become all-but-invincible. The demon's arrival releases Chiang Su-su, who possesses her current descendent, Yi, and, with the aid of a llama and Yi's Mainland cousin, prepares to destroy the monster before it can transmute.

Shing Fui-on garners a few chuckles as a triad thug who has found God; the shopping mall is a novel setting for the genre; and the climactic combination of three different religious disciplines is intriguing. Regardless, this is a torpid, witless affair that is far from the best of its type and recommended only to completists.

The Return of the Five Deadly Venoms *see* **Crippled Avengers**

Return of the Iron Angels *see* **Angel III**

826. Return of the Lucky Stars

(1989; Children's Town) ★: 2/10. *Fuk sing chong gong wu* (Cantonese), *Fu xing cang jiang hu* (Mandarin): "Lucky Stars Triad Society." Cinematographer: Tsui Wah-bo; Art Director: Jessy Lam Chak-chi; Writers: Wong Jing, Stanley Fung Shui-fan; Producer: Wallace Cheung Kwok-chong; Action Director: Lau Kar-wing; Director: Stanley Fung Shui-fan. Cast: Eric Tsang Chi-wai (Lo-han), Richard Ng Yiu-hon (Tai-shan), Stanley Fung Shui-fan (Rhino), Miu Kiu-wai (Cone), Carina Lau Kar-ling (Banana), Wong Ching (Mao), Cho Tat-wah (Inspector Tso), Kenneth Tsang Kong (Kin), Kent Cheng Chuk-see (Cheng), Wong Jing (Wong), Nat Chan Pak-cheung (Chan), Elsie Chan Yik-si (Bride-to-be), Ng Chi-hung, Chen Jing (Inmates). 1.85:1. VHS: Tai Seng. Import LD: Ocean Shores. Import VCD: Mega Star. 95 minutes.

This tedious entry in the Lucky Stars series finds the gang trying to go legitimate by opening a wedding photography shop. However, they make the mistake of hitting on a gangster's girl and get their business trashed as a result. They then establish a detective agency but are more concerned with attempting to molest their pretty but clumsy secretary, Banana, than trying to get clients. Inspector Tso soon blackmails them into helping the force nab notorious triad boss Mao. The Stars go undercover in prison to befriend Mao's former boss, Dai, and after breaking him out of jail, they join his quest for vengeance.

There is nary a laugh to be found here and, unlike the earlier films, no good action scenes to provide some recompense. The script adheres strictly to formula, rehashing bits from earlier entries, and brief parodies of **Prison on Fire** and **A Better Tomorrow** (with Kenneth Tsang reprising his character) fall just as flat as every other attempt at humor. Even die hard fans of the series need not bother wasting their time with this one.

Return of the Master Killer *see* **Return to the 36th Chamber**

827. Return to a Better Tomorrow

(1994; Good Standard International) ★: 4/10. *San ying hung boon sik* (Cantonese), *Xin ying xiong ben se* (Mandarin): "New Essence of a Hero." Cinematographer: Cheng Siu-keung; Art Directors: Wong Kar-lung, Raymond Kwok Siu-keung; Music: Marco Wan Ho-kit, Lee Hon-chuen; Action Directors: Tony Poon Kin-kwan, Dion Lam Dik-on; Writer-Producer-Director: Wong Jing. Cast: Dior Cheng Yee-kin (Tong Chun), Lau Ching-wan (Boston Lobster), Chingmy Yau Suk-ching (Chili), Michael Wong Man-tak (Duke Simon), Ben Lam Kwok-bun (Lui Wei), John Ching Tung (Chiu), James Wong Jim (Wong Tai-man), Ngai Sing (Holland Boy), Paul Chun Pui (Fred Simon), Parkman Wong Pak-man (But), Lo Mang (Black Ox). 2.35:1. VHS: Tai Seng. Import LD: Cameron Entertainment. Import VCD: Mei Ah. 103 minutes.

Bearing absolutely no connection to any of the **A Better Tomorrow** films, this simple-minded gangster thriller is an overwrought collection of stereotypical characters and cliched concepts. It might have worked as a spoof but is pretty deadly as is. Medium level triad Tong Chun manages to eliminate his rival, Black Ox, but is faced with the possibility of retaliation from Ox's men. However, he should have been watching his back, instead: Tong's superior, Lui Wei, frames him for drug smuggling and sets the young gangster up to be killed. Although his right hand is destroyed by an assassin's bullet, Tong is able to escape to Vietnam. At this point, the film picks up two years later and goes from reasonably plausible to utterly absurd. Tong makes his way back to HK and poses as an illegal immigrant worker, only to discover that he now has nose cancer. His old associate, Boston Lobster, has risen dramatically in the ranks and is now a boss with three thousand men to do his bidding. When Tong convinces Lobster that Lui is simply using him and will betray him sooner or later, the pair declare war on their common enemy, but Lui's trickery will bring tragic results to all.

In stark contrast to its namesake, this has none of the stirring emotions and grandly theatrical drama of the best HK crime thrillers. Instead, the film simply piles on melodramatic subplots: the mistreatment inflicted upon Lobster's little girl by his heartless wife, the suffering Tong's girlfriend undergoes during the years they are apart, Tong's cancer, etc. Some decent shootouts and a colorful turn by Lau Ching-wan as the uneducated but eternally loyal Lobster are the only worthwhile components in this derivative mess. Aficionados of bad acting will not want to miss Michael Wong's hilariously inept performance. The sequence in which he loses his temper and does an Incredible Hulk imitation will leave even the most jaded viewer in stitches.

828. Return to the 36th Chamber

(1980; Shaw Brothers) ★: 7/10. *Siu lam daap paang daai si* (Cantonese), *Shao lin da peng da shi* (Mandarin): "The Shaolin Monk Who Constructs Frames." Music: Not Original; Writer: Ngai Hong; Producer: Mona Fong Yat-wah; Action Director-Director: Lau Kar-leung. Cast: Gordon Lau Kar-fai (Chou Chen-chi), Johnny Wang Lung-wei (Boss Wang), Kara Hui Ying-hung (Hung), Wei Pai (Sun), Hsiao Hou (Chau), Yeung Ching-ching (Hsiao-ching). 2.35:1. No official domestic video release. 104 minutes. Also known as **Return of the Master Killer** (US title).

More of a send-up than a sequel, this lightweight period entry casts Gordon Lau as a conman hired to *impersonate* the Shaolin master he played in the original film. Bossed around by Manchu thugs and denied a proper wage for their work, the employees of the Tai Ching Dye Mill enlist the services of rogue Chi. Passing himself off as San Te (with a little behind-the-scenes help to enhance his non-existent kung fu abilities), Chi tries to scare the Manchus into restoring the workers' salaries. However, the charade comes to an abrupt end when he is forced to face off against evil Boss Wang, a martial arts master. Humiliated by his defeat, Chi tries to get into Shaolin Temple so that he may actually learn some kung fu. He is even less successful at fooling the monks, but the real San Te, taking pity on him, allows Chi to stay on and work. While repairing the walls of the 36th chamber, Chi observes the students practising and comes up with his own equivalent training, using construction materials. In the process, he learns the skills he needs to take on and defeat the Manchus.

Gordon Lau gets to display both his kung fu and comedic skills here and does a terrific job in both areas. Also, the "training sequences" here are amusingly creative variations on those found in the original, making this an above average entry in the subgenre of kung fu comedies. Character names are from the dubbed version.

829. The Returning

(1994; United Filmmakers Organization/Treasure City Distribution Co.) ★: 5/10. *Dang chuek lei wooi loi* (Cantonese), *Deng zhe ni hui lai* (Mandarin): "Waiting for You to Come Back." Cinematographer: Arthur Wong Ngok-tai; Art Director: Ben Lau Man-hung; Music: Violet Lam Man-yee; Writers: Lee Chi-ngai, Jacob Cheung Chi-leung, Raymond To Kwok-wai; Producers: Lee Chi-ngai, Claudie Chung Chun; Director: Jacob Cheung Chi-leung. Cast: Tony Leung Chiu-wai (Lee Yick-chung), Jacqueline Wu Chien-lien (Elaine/Siu Lau), Sandra Ng Kwan-yu (Julia). 1.85:1. VHS: Tai Seng. Import LD: Cameron Entertainment. Import VCD/DVD: Mei Ah. 98 minutes.

In interviews with HK publications, director Jacob Cheung stated that **The Returning** is his tribute to the golden age of suggestive Chinese horror thrillers. Unfortunately, it has neither the passion nor the shocks to succeed at this laudable ambition. Lee is a literary editor obsessed with the writings of female author Siu Lau, who committed suicide in 1949. Seeking to find the right atmosphere to create a compilation of her work, he and long-time girlfriend Elaine move into Siu's last place of residence. Elaine is soon plagued by all manner of inexplicable happenings, which culminate in her possession by Siu's spirit. When Lee's preoccupation with his subject becomes all-encompassing, both his and Elaine's identities begin to slowly ebb away.

The storyline respectfully proceeds through the ghost-house paces, presenting all manner of creaky cupboards, phantom footprints, and self-operating phonographs while a spectral chorus swells periodically on the soundtrack. An effective moment is managed here and there, but, by and large, this decorous production limps along to little or no effect, a victim of its creator's single-minded nostalgia and intemperate notions on how to generate atmosphere and suspense. Leung and Wu, however, offer well-rounded portrayals, and the development of their characters' increasing romantic friction (heightened by the successfully offbeat casting of comedienne Sandra Ng as the couple's third-wheel friend who can no longer mask her attraction to Lee) is effective and inkeeping with Cheung's more thoughtful work.

830. The Revenge of Angel

(1990; Luckfilm Productions) ★: 5/10. *Sui ling lung* (Cantonese), *Shui ling long* (Mandarin): "Crystal-Like Delicate Beauty." Cinematographer: Lee Yao-tong; Art Director: Daniel Lee Yan-kong; Music: Man Chow-bo; Action Directors: Tsui Siu-ming, Kuk Hin-chiu; Producer: Tsui Siu-ming; Director: Yeung Kuen. Cast: Moon Lee Choi-fung (Angel Sui), Liu Chi-wei (Siu-man), Wu Ma (Ma), Alvina Kong Yan-yin (Siu Yin-hung), Chung Fat (Chan Ping), Cho Wing (Ghost). 1.85:1. Import LD/VCD: Ocean Shores. 91 minutes.

Moon Lee plays a character named "Angel" here but this is not in any way related to the three official films from that series. Rather, it is a slight but reasonably interesting supernatural story that provides numerous chances for Lee to display her abilities. Twenty years after she was killed in a fire started by the minions of hoodlum Chan Ping, Peking Opera performer Angel Sui returns from the dead as a ghost. She uses her skills to help fledgling performer Siu-man stand in successfully for an arrogant leading man. The boy then joins with Angel and her old mentor, Ma, to take revenge on Chan. Although she has the chance to kill him, Angel only inflicts a few injuries and leaves him on the verge of death. This act of benevolence earns her the right to reincarnate, but when Siu-man saves the life of a drowning girl right at the moment of Angel's appointed time, he inadvertently spoils her opportunity to begin life anew. She now faces the prospect of spending eternity as a slave in the "Tartarous" (evidently a form of purgatory). To make matters worse, Chan's son hires a Taoist to avenge his wounded father and disperse Angel's spirit.

Released during the period fantasy craze initiated by the success of **A Chinese Ghost Story**, **The Revenge of Angel** is quite old-fashioned in comparison, and this difference in approach will intrigue some viewers while turning off others. Those who fall into the former category will enjoy the juxtaposition of traditional opera and magic, not to mention the quaint special FX and uniquely Chinese belief about the role ladies' underwear can play when battling the supernatural! Lee's fans will enjoy seeing the actress in this atypical part, which is a nice departure from her usual girls-with-guns roles. This is recommended more to seasoned viewers than those just starting to explore HK horror and fantasy.

831. Rich and Famous

(1987; Johnny Mak Production/Win's Movie Production) ★: 6/10. *Gong woo ching* (Cantonese), *Jiang hu qing* (Mandarin): "Underworld Love." Cinematographers: Abdul M. Rumjahn, Johnny Koo Kwok-wah; Art Director: Jessy Lam Chak-chi; Music: Joseph Chan Wing-leung; Writers: Stephen Siu Yeuk-yuen, Manfred Wong; Producer: Johnny Mak Dong-hung; Action Director: Leung Siu-lung; Director: Taylor Wong Tai-loi. Cast: Chow Yun-fat (Li Ah-chai), Alex Man Chi-leung (Tang Kat-yung), Andy Lau Tak-wah (Kwok), Alan Tam Wing-lun (Mak Ying-hung), Carina Lau Kar-ling (Lau Po-yee), Pauline Wong Siu-fung (Wai-chui), Danny Lee Sau-yin (Inspector Cheung), Ko Chuen-hsiang (Chu Lo-tai), Yeung Kwan (Kit), Shing Fui-on (Luk), Lam Chung (Big Eye), Fan Mui-sang (Fan Tit-tau), Ng Hong-ning (Chuan), Chen Jing (Triad). 1.85:1. VHS: Tai Seng. 105 minutes.

A two part gangster film, this Mak Brothers/Win's coproduction does not do nearly as good a job at balancing its action and drama components as its obvious inspiration, **A Better Tomorrow**. When Tang Kat-yung forges a betting slip, his brother Kwok saves him from having his little finger cut off in punishment. When further troubles arise, the brothers enlist the aid of Li Ah-chai, a powerful opponent of their nemesis, and he smooths things out. The siblings join Ah-chai's gang and are betrayed during an exchange with one of Ah-chai's competitors. Further trouble arises when a Thai drug baron refuses to continue supplying his HK clients unless Ah-chai turns over the man's old enemy. Kat-yung's big mouth puts him out of favor with Ah-chai, prompting the former to accept a contract to murder the dealer under the latter's protection. This is done and Ah-chai quickly surmises Kat-yung's guilt, but Kwok intercedes for him again. Ah-chai spares Kat-yung but orders them both away, prompting Kat-yung to join up with Ah-chai's adversary.

While it compares well to many of the post-**A Better Tomorrow** triad films, **Rich and Famous** is not as bold and compelling as it clearly wishes to be. This is partially because the dramatic conflicts remain unresolved at the end (the story continues in **Tragic Hero** which, ironically, was released first, as the producers deemed it to be more commercial) but mainly due to the fact that the characters are largely interchangeable and never expand beyond genre stereotypes. Fans of continuity errors: Watch Danny Lee's hairstyle change dramatically in the few seconds it takes for him to walk from a police vehicle to the steps of a church.

832. Rich Man

(1992; Bright Films Production/Ko Chi Sum Films Co.) ★: 4/10. *Hoh yat gam joi loi* (Cantonese), *He ri jin zai lai* (Mandarin): "What Day Will Money Come Again." Cinematographer: Paul Yip Pak-ying; Art Director: Choi Man-chong; Music: Wong Bong; Writers: Joe Ma Wai-ho, Philip Kwok Wai-chung, Lee Wing-hung; Producer: Clifton Ko Chi-sum; Action Directors: Woo Chi-lung, So Ying-sang; Director: Joe Ma Wai-ho. Cast: Tommy Wong Kwong-leung (Wong Kwong), James Wong Jim (Peter Chow), Shing Fui-on (Chiu), Elaine Lui Siu-ling (Ling), Lau Kar-wing (Lawyer Lau), Vincent Wan Yeung-ming (Boss Ming), Miu Kiu-wai (The Banker), William Ho Kar-kui (Ming, the Waiter), Ng Chi-hung (Wong On-shek), Clifton Ko Chi-sum (Otto Chan), Vincent Kok Tak-chiu (Fat Guy in Car). 1.85:1. VHS: Tai Seng. Import LD/VCD: Universe. 79 minutes.

Deadbeat triad Wong Kwong gets tossed into jail following a gangfight. There he meets sleazy millionaire Peter Chow, and the two become fast friends. Both are soon back on the streets, and upon seeing firsthand just how broke Wong is, Chow offers him a job collecting debts. He also authorizes a bank loan that allows Wong to open his own sauna house. Soon the triad has more money than he ever dreamed of but finds that his old mobster buddies no longer treat him the same way. By the same token, Wong's crass demeanor makes him stand out like a sore thumb in his new social circle. Gangster or not, Wong still has his principles, and when he discovers just how much of a rat his benefactor is, he puts his foot down.

The premise is about as old as cinema itself and the writers are unable to come up with any fresh gags to reinvigorate it. The ending is also pretty weak; this is one instance where a comical revenge scheme, however familiar, would have been more satisfying. Joe Ma's directorial debut, **Rich Man**'s coarse language earned it the Category III rating, though the English translation is comparatively mild.

833. Righting Wrongs

(1986; Golden Harvest/Bo Ho Films Co.) ★: 7/10. *Chap faat sin fung* (Cantonese), *Zhi fa xian feng* (Mandarin): "Vanguard Enforcing the Law." Cinematographer: Tom Lau Moon-tong; Art Director: Raymond Lee King-man; Music: Romeo Diaz, Sing Kam-wing; Writers: Barry Wong Ping-yiu, Roy Szeto Cheuk-hon; Producer: Leonard Ho Koon-cheung; Action Directors: Yuen Biao, Corey Yuen Kwai, Mang Hoi, Hsu Hsia; Director: Corey Yuen Kwai. Cast: Yuen Biao (Hsia), Cynthia Rothrock (Cindy Si), Melvin Wong Kam-sun (Sgt. Wong Jing-wai), Roy Chiao Hung (Magistrate), Corey Yuen Kwai (Bad Egg), Fan Siu-wong (Yu Chi-wen), Wu Ma (Uncle Tsai), James Tien Chun (Chow Ting-kwong), Tai Po (Cop), Karen Shepherd (Karen), Peter Cunningham (Black Assassin), Chung Fat (Cop), Lau Siu-ming (Yu's Grandfather). Dolby Digital (DVD only). 1.85:1. VHS: Tai Seng (Remastered for English market; subtitled or dubbed). Import LD: Star Entertainment (No Subtitles). Import VCD: Mei Ah. 92 minutes (Subtitled version). Import DVD: Universe. Also known as **Above the Law** (UK video title).

We have had all manner of cinematic vigilantes over the years, from Charles Bronson's businessman in **Death Wish**, to Tom Skerritt's deli owner in **Fighting Back**, to Jack Palance's cop in **One Man Jury**, to Robert Forster's blue collar worker in the frankly-named **Vigilante**. This Golden Harvest actioner from Corey Yuen (who also co-stars) presents a most appropriate avenging angel: the vigilante *prosecutor*. Hsia Ling-ching is the frustrated lawyer who starts closing the book permanently on high-profile felons who evade justice. Pursued by tough lady cop Cindy (Cynthia Rothrock, wearing so much make-up she looks ready to go out on hooker patrol for the vice squad), Hsia must also dodge contract killers sent by Sgt. Wong, a crooked cop whose casual ruthlessness unnerves even his triad partners.

The screenplay follows all of the rules for this subgenre, serving up the obligatory soliloquies about how justice is dead and the police are ineffectual, and offering no genuine insights or solutions while killing off the most likeable characters in brutal ways. While the action is always given center stage, director Yuen mixes in some amusing transitions and keeps the expository sequences interesting by peopling them with a variety of familiar faces (including Roy Chiao Hung, Wu Ma, and Tai Po). The real star, however, is Yuen Biao: Whether scaling a highrise, leaping over speeding cars, hanging from an airplane, or just engaging in hand-to-hand combat, his physical prowess never ceases to amaze. Rothrock (working with far better martial arts choreographers than the ones on her later American and Indonesian pictures) comes off favorably, holding her own against Yuen in their inevitable bout. The cast also includes an almost unrecognizably young Fan Siu-wong (**Stone Age Warriors**) as a thief who can help Hsia out of his predicament, and martial artists Peter Cunningham and Karen Shepherd as the assassins on Wong's payroll. Jacky Cheung Hok-yau sings the memorable theme song. The English dubbed edition is different in a number of ways, including the fates of two main characters. Both versions are included on the DVD, though the alternate cut is presented with a Mandarin track rather than English.

Riki-Oh: The Story of Ricky *see* **Story of Ricky**

834. The Roar of the Vietnamese

(1991) ★: 5/10. *Yuet ching* (Cantonese), *Yue qing* (Mandarin): "Vietnam Youth." Cinematographer: Cheung King-nin; Art Director: Cheung Yuk-yu; Music: Au San-ming; Writers: Abe Kwong Man-wai, Cheng Wing-chiu; Producer: Chan Wai-chi; Action Director: Sit Chun-wai; Director: Cheng Wing-chiu. Cast: Sibelle Hu Hui-chung (Wai Yin), Waise Lee

Chi-hung (Tian San), Kara Hui Ying-hung (Yuen Wan-yin), Lau Ching-wan (Fan Wan-tin), Cheung Kwok-leung (Kuo), Kwan Lai-kit (Yuen Nan). 1.85:1. VHS: Tai Seng. Import LD/VCD: Universe. 86 minutes.

Prior to the 1997 handover, overcrowded Vietnamese refugee camps were a real problem in HK. Gangs of rootless Vietnamese thugs became the reason behind a rise in violent crime in both HK and the West. This film posits that Chinese triads often employed such refugees to do their dirty work in exchange for smuggling them to America and freedom. One such group of expatriates (including Lau, Hui, Cheung, and Kwan), acting on the orders of a corrupt police officer, is used for several missions to assassinate a series of rival gangsters. Not surprisingly, the triads have no intention of keeping their end of the deal, and after all of the targets have been eliminated, they set the refugees up for extermination.

In contrast to the norm, more attention is devoted to character than action here, and there is an interesting, if repetitive, score; but the premise and the climactic events are much too predictable for this to have any real impact. The performances are better than the material requires, and Lau, in particular, shows some of the charisma that brought him fame later in the decade (though he did not dub his own voice here). For another actioner with a similar theme, try **Phantom War**; for a more serious look at the refugee situation, seek out Ann Hui's **Boat People** and/or **The Story of Woo Viet**.

Roboforce *see* I Love Maria

835. Robotrix

(1991; Golden Harvest/Shochiku/Paragon Films) ★: 3/10. *Nui gei haai yan* (Cantonese), *Nu ji xie ren* (Mandarin): "Female Robot." Cinematographer: James Yeung Jim; Art Director: Bill Lui Cho-hung; Music: Jibson Yeung Siu-hung, James Yeung Jim; Writers: Jamie Luk Kim-ming, So Man-sing; Producer: Chua Lam; Action Director: Yuen Tak; Director: Jamie Luk Kim-ming. Cast: Chikako Aoyama (Selina Lam), Amy Yip Chi-mei (Ann), David Wu Tai-wai (Joe Chow), Hui Hiu-dan (Dr. Sara), Billy Chow Bei-lee (Sakamoto's Robot), Woo Fung (The Commissioner), Yung Sai-kit (Lucky John), Lam Chung (Ryuichi Sakamoto). 1.85:1. VHS: Tai Seng (No Subtitles). Import LD: Star Entertainment (No Subtitles). 97 minutes.

This tacky, softcore sci-fi-action-comedy has developed a cult following over the years but isn't really all that much fun. Japanese mad scientist/sexual sadist Ryuichi Sakamoto transfers his consciousness into one of his robots, becoming a seemingly indestructible killing machine. While kidnapping the son of a visiting oil sheik, he shoots and gravely wounds HK policewoman Selina Lam. Although she dies on the operating table, Selina is brought back from the dead by the brilliant Dr. Sara, who transfers the woman's consciousness into a robot of identical appearance. After some understandable anger on Selina's part, she accepts her fate and joins with Sara and the police to try and capture the murderous robot (who has been leaving a trail of dead prostitutes all over HK).

In addition to buxom Japanese adult film star Chikako Aoyama, the film also features HK's reigning breast fetish queen, Amy Yip, as Ann, a second mechanical sex bomb. Ann has never experienced sex, which leads to a tired subplot where she poses as a hooker to try and catch the killer. In fact, it is precisely this sort of padding that makes the film so disappointing: The pace is too slow and the inspired bits few and far between. There are also two instances of nasty sexual violence that further detract from the fun. Aoyama and Taiwanese actor David Wu would appear together again the same year in Golden Harvest's **Finale in Blood**. Subtitled video versions of **Robotrix** have been released in Australia and Taiwan. The latter is heavily censored but does feature some extra comic hijinks in a police station that is not included in HK prints.

836. Rock 'n Roll Cop

(1994; Sky Point Film Investment) ★: 8/10. *Saang Gong yat ho tung chap faan* (Cantonese), *Sheng Gang yi hao tong ji fan* (Mandarin): "South China's Public Enemy #1." Cinematographer: Ko Chiu-lam; Art Director: Eddie Ma Poon-chiu; Music: Danny Chung Teng-yat; Writer: Lu Bing; Action Director: Bruce Law Lai-yin; Producer-Director: Che-Kirk Wong Chi-keung. Cast: Anthony Wong Chau-sang (Hung), Wu Hsin-kuo (Wong Kun), Yu Rongguang (Shum Chi-hung), Carrie Ng Kar-lai (Hou-yee), Chen Ming-chen (Cindy Lam). 1.85:1. VHS: Tai Seng. Import LD/VCD/DVD: Ocean Shores. 92 minutes.

A stirring police procedural, **Rock 'n Roll Cop** finds the HK police joining forces with their Mainland counterparts to smash the Chun Lu Red Scarf gang, a vicious group of well-armed thieves operating on both sides of the border. When the gang brutally murders his superior, straight-laced Beijing cop Wong Kun collaborates with HK O.C.T.B. Inspector Hung, who has been sent to China to provide the local authorities with assistance, following a Red Scarf robbery in Kowloon. Although they are able to determine the gang's whereabouts, the fugitives manage to evade the police, taking Hung hostage in the process. Wong's men are able to effect a rescue, but the criminals manage to obtain fake passports from prostitute Hou-yee, the girlfriend of leader Shum Chi-hung. Hou-yee is no stranger to Wong, having been his lover a decade earlier, and he still has feelings for her and she for him.

Che-Kirk Wong's strengths as a director really shine through here via a meticulously staged and shot stakeout sequence in Shenzhen, and the climactic chase, which features no grandiose action but is still consistently exciting and perfectly paced. The storyline's romantic triangle is one of its weaker aspects, but the portions covering police method and the contrasting styles of HK and Mainland officers are effectively delivered (though no longer quite as relevant, now that HK and China have reunited), and the film is scored by composer Danny Chung (**As Tears Go By**) in a simple but striking manner. **Rock 'n Roll Cop** is very much in the style of Wong's previous procedurals, **Crime Story** and **Organized Crime and Triad Bureau**, and the three remain among the best local productions of their type to be produced in the '90s. Ocean Shores has released two different laserdisc versions: The one bearing catalogue number OL-395 is uncut, but the one numbered OL-395N is a censored version that greatly alters the film's climax. The DVD also contains this abbreviated version, despite the fact that it carries a Category III symbol on the cover. The company's VCD and Tai Seng's tape version are uncut.

837. The Romance of Book and Sword

(1987; Sil-Metropole Organisation/Yeung Tse Kong Movie Enterprises) ★: 6/10. *Sue gim yan sau luk* (Cantonese), *Shu jian en chou lu* (Mandarin): "Book Sword Gratitude Revenge Record." Cinematographer: Bill Wong Chung-bo; Art Directors: James Leung Wah-sang, Pok Yeuk-muk; Music: Law Wing-fai, Gu Guanren, Zhou Jie; Writer: Chun Sai-sam; Producers: Guo Fengqi, Shen Min-hui; Action Director: Hu Jianqiang; Director: Ann Hui On-wah. Cast: Zhang Duofu (Chen Jalo), Chang Dashi (Emperor Qian Long), Liu Jia (Huo Chingtong), Lu Yongquan (Daozhang), Ding Cuihua (Luo Bing), Yu Li (Yu Ruyi), Guo Bichuan (Wen Tailai), Ha Chier (Mu Cherlun), Wang Hangtao (Yu Wanting). 1.85:1.

VHS: World Video. Import LD: Star Entertainment. 88 minutes.

Released theatrically and on video in two parts, this is the first installment of director Ann Hui's epic adaptation of a famous Jin Yong period kung fu novel known in English as *Legend of the Book and Sword: Gratitude and Revenge*. Qian Long, emperor of The Ching Dynasty, may actually be a Han by birth and not a true Manchurian. The Red Flower Society, a rebel group which opposes the Manchus, confronts Qian about his origins and claims to have additional evidence that will weaken his grasp on power. Their deal: join with them and undermine the Manchu empire from the inside or face being exposed. Red Flower fighter Chen Jalo helps to foil a plot by the Chings to steal the holy Koran. The Manchurians had hoped that two Islamic tribes would attack each other as a result of the theft, thus reducing their numbers and the number of enemies the state faces. In gratitude for his assistance, Wei tribe chief Mu Cherlun pledges to aid Chen and the other Han fighters in the battle against the government. It is discovered that Qian and Chen are actually brothers who were separated at birth, and once the two men learn this, Chen, naturally, wants his brother to help restore the Han people to the level of power they possessed during The Ming Dynasty. Qian (whose real name is Chen Ronglee), however, is unwilling to endanger the people of his kingdom to attain that goal and orders that all Red Flower members, save Chen, be captured and executed.

A handsome and reverent reworking of the source material, **The Romance of Book and Sword** has an interesting premise and much in the way of refined verbal jousting, in addition to the usual martial arts combat (presented mostly in a traditional, down-to-earth fashion). However, both the presentation and the performances are a bit too staid for the film to really come across, and the multitude of lead characters will leave those unfamiliar with the novel a bit confused at times. It's all fairly captivating for as long as it unfolds but disappears quickly from memory shortly thereafter. The storyline continues in **Princess Fragrance**.

838. The Romance of the Vampires

(1994; Sunton Films Production) ★: 6/10. *Kap ngo yat goh man* (Cantonese), *Xi wo yi ge wen* (Mandarin): "Inhale My One Kiss." Cinematographer: Philip Ma Kam-cheung; Art Director: Chan Suk-han; Music: Lee Kai-cheong; Writer: Nam Yin; Producers: Victor Yeung Kar-on, Yip Wing-cho; Action Directors: Cho Wing, Yuk Shu; Director: Ricky Lau Koon-wai. Cast: Yvonne Yung Hung (Rainbow), Mondi Yau Yuet-ching (Moon), Ben Lam Kwok-bun (Ching Fung), Louie Yuen Siu-cheung (Cheung), Yuen King-tan (Pill), Billy Chow Bei-lee (Kwai Chung). 1.85:1. VHS: Tai Seng. Import LD/VCD/DVD: Ocean Shores. 93 minutes.

A Category III softcore horror film that would have been worthwhile even without the sex, **The Romance of the Vampires** is, along with **Doctor Vampire, Exorcist Master**, and **Vampire vs. Vampire**, one of the very few HK films to revolve around bloodsuckers of the Western variety. Yvonne Yung plays Rainbow, a blind prostitute who works for a phone sex/escort agency in order to save up enough money to pay for an operation to restore her sight. One evening, the gangster who spent five years in jail for causing her disability shows up, looking to exact revenge. She is saved by the intervention of handsome vampire Ching Fung, whose first mate looked exactly like Rainbow (a cliche dating back at least as far as Dracula himself). The vampire becomes hopelessly enamoured of Rainbow, but she is not safe from the murderous intentions of Fung's current mate, Moon, who reminds Fung that "cats can't be friends with fish."

The opening third is devoted almost entirely to softcore groping and all manner of low humor (Fung and Moon sleep in a glass coffin filled with dry ice fog, and have "The Clapper" in their bedroom!). However, once these obligatory commercial concessions subside, the humor retreats into the background, serving instead as occasional respite from the drama. Much of the film's effectiveness can be attributed to Yung, a sweet-looking and reasonably adept actress who has become typecast as a victim in rape/torture fantasies like **Don't Stop My Crazy Love for You** (1993), **Sex and the Emperor** (1995), and **Spike Drink Gang** (1995), but who handles the requirements of this role very well. Director Ricky Lau (who inaugurated the *gyonsi* hopping vampire craze with his Golden Harvest blockbuster **Mr. Vampire**), directs with an overabundance of derivative MTV stylistics, but screenwriter Nam Yin (brother of Ringo Lam and author of a number of his films) incorporates some effective allusions to other vampire movies, like **Count Dracula's Great Love** (1972) and **Near Dark** (1987). However, character motivation is not always clear and the ending (which unfolds amid a barrage of cheesy opticals) is awfully heavy handed. The balance is surprisingly watchable, and a subplot about the relationship between Rainbow and her landlord/protector (well-played by Louie Yuen) is genuinely touching. Veteran comedian and co-producer Yip Wing-cho has a cameo.

839. Romance of the West Chamber

(1997; Cameron Entertainment/Sum Yi Distributions/Hung Choi Productions) ★: 3/10. *Sai seung yim taam* (Cantonese), *Xi xiang yan tan* (Mandarin): "West Wing Steamy Talk." Cinematographer: Chim Pak-hung; Art Director: Law Lai-si; Producers: Eddie Wong Hon-wah, Wong Chi-hung; Action Director: Cheung Ping-chan; Director: Lam Yee-hung. Cast: Jimmy Wong Shu-kei (Chiang Chuen-sui), Keung Kar-ling (Hung), Elvis Tsui Kam-kong (Faben), Teresa Mak Kar-kei (Chunto). 1.85:1. VHS: World Video. Import LD/VCD/DVD: Mei Ah. 93 minutes.

This Category III period softcore entry lacks the invention and production values of the **Sex and Zen** and **Erotic Ghost Story** films and is quite dull, even when stacked up against a similarly low-rent entry like **Yu Pui Tsuen III**. Scholar Chiang Chuen-sui decides that a local monastery is the perfect place to continue his studies, especially as several beautiful maidens are residing there temporarily. After much persuading, he is given permission to stay by head monk Faben, and has his way with the beautiful Ann-ann. A gang of bandits soon appear on the scene and demand that Ann-ann be turned over to them. The girl's mother announces that anyone who can save her daughter from being taken will be granted Ann-ann's hand in marriage. Chuen-sui is able to come up with a plan to foil the miscreants, but his lover's mother was never serious about keeping her word, due to the scholar's low status. In defiance, Ann-ann and Chuen-sui continue to meet in secret, with handmaiden Hung acting as their go-between. Eventually, the girl's mother relents and gives her blessing, but a jealous suitor (to whom Ann-ann was already promised) sets out to preempt the nuptials.

You know you are in trouble when HK sex film king Elvis Tsui is cast as an honorable monk and is not even involved in any of the erotic sequences. Said encounters are routine and, coupled with the tedious, awkwardly structured storyline and largely somnambulant performances, mark this as highly avoidable, even for fans of the genre.

840. Romantic Dream

(1995; Cheung Man Movie Production Co.) ★: 4/10. *Jui nui jai 95 ji yi mung* (Cantonese), *Zhui nui zi 95 zhi qi meng* (Mandarin): "Chasing Girls '95: Dream of

Desire." Cinematographer: David Chung Chi-man; Art Director: Jason Mok Siu-kei; Music: Marco Wan Ho-kit, Anthony Lee Hon-kam; Writers: Lee Lik-chi, Vincent Kok Tak-chiu; Producer: Jimmy Heung Wah-sing; Director: Lee Lik-chi. Cast: Lau Ching-wan (Hung Chi-lung, aka Dino Sau), Sharla Cheung Man (Mandy Tan), Lawrence Cheng Tan-shui (Yip Hoi), Michael Wong Man-tak (Ko Kwan), Manfred Wong (Uncle Ken), Wong Kam-kong (Master Yim), Leo Koo Kui-kei (Peter), Cheng Cho (God of Cars), Yuen King-tan (Florist). 1.85:1. VHS/LD: Tai Seng. Import LD/VCD/ DVD: Mei Ah. 99 minutes.

Before proceeding any further, read the review for **Dream Lover. Romantic Dream** is Sharla Cheung Man's second version of the same story, this time with Cheung herself playing the female lead instead of producing. As before, the plot tells of the burgeoning love affair between a mechanic/inventor (called "Dino" here) and a beautiful rich girl ("Mandy"), but it opens in the 1960s, both are car enthusiasts, and Vivian is a lot more assertive and outgoing. A Japanese car company makes Dino rich beyond his wildest dreams, and he is drawn into a scheme to cheat him out of his new fortune. However, this time there is less emphasis on the fantastic, the premise is presented with a lighter hand, and the film is largely devoid of the sappiness that sunk **Dream Lover**. Unfortunately, the humor is just as uninspired, and Nat Chan does a conspicuously better job as the comic sidekick in the other film than Lawrence Cheng does here.

841. A Roof with a View

(1993; Golden Harvest/Paragon Films) ★: 5/10. *Tin toi dik yuet gwong* (Cantonese), *Tian tai de yue guang* (Mandarin): "The Moonlight from Heaven's Windowsill." Cinematographer: Bill Wong Chung-bo; Art Director: Mok Kwan-kit; Music: Violet Lam Man-yee; Writer: Yip Kwong-kim; Producer: Raymond Chow Man-wai; Director: Tony Au Ding-ping. Cast: Tony Leung Kar-fai (Lau Ching-man), Veronica Yip Yuk-hing (Yip Hiu-tung), Ray Lui Leung-wai (Screwball), Anita Lee Yuen-wah (Salon Girl), Ruth Winona Tao Kwun-mei (Ching-man's ex), Lindzay Chan Ling-chi (Hiu-tung's Sister-in-Law), Kent Cheng Chuk-see (Fat Ho), Kwan Hoi-shan (Uncle Bill). 1.85:1. VHS: Tai Seng. Import LD/VCD: Universe. 102 minutes.

In one of her first breakout roles following a brief sojourn in softcore porn, Veronica Yip is charming as Hiu-tung, a sweet, gullible single mother trying to stay afloat in a sea of (male) sharks. Her neighbor, Ching-man, is a cop trying to deal with the suicide of his partner. Polar opposites, the two soon become attracted to each other, and Ching-man acts as a surrogate father to the woman's young son. However, just when their relationship is about to cross over into genuine love, Hiu-tung's gangster husband returns from Taiwan, and Ching-man's doubts start to get the better of him.

While its heart is in the right place, **A Roof with a View** (terrible title) is just too calculated and artificial (is there *anyone* longing for another love story that ends with the man trying to catch the woman before she gets to the airport?). It is not without its pleasures, however. In addition to Yip's winning performance, Leung is warm and appealing, and the film's low-key approach is endearing. However, the quality of the cast and director Au's past track record can't help but leave one wishing for a better and more original movie. Sync sound recording and excellent subtitles help. Carina Lau Kar-ling has a cameo in the final reel.

842. Rosa

(1986; Golden Harvest/Bo Ho Films Co./Paragon Films) ★: 6/10. *San yung seung heung paau juk jaap* (Cantonese), *Shen yong shuang xiang pao xu ji* (Mandarin): "Godly Courageous Double Sound Pow Sequel." Cinematographer: Tom Lau Moon-tong; Art Directors: William Cheung Suk-ping, Tony Au Ding-ping; Music: Chow Kam-cheung; Writers: Barry Wong Ping-yiu, Wong Kar-wai; Producer: Sammo Hung Kam-po; Action Directors: Yuen Biao, Lam Ching-ying, Yuen Wah; Director: Joseph Cheung Tung-cho. Cast: Yuen Biao (Hsia, aka "Little Monster"), Lowell Lo Kwun-ting (Lei Kung), Luk Siu-fan (Rosa), Kara Hui Ying-hung (Lei's Sister), Paul Chun Pui (Paul Tien), James Tien Chun (Wang Ping-tang), Charlie Cho Cha-lei (Li Wei-feng), Dick Wei (Thug in Suit), Chung Fat (Assassin), Tai Po (Moore), Peter Chan Lung (Tsai's Son), Blackie Ko Shou-liang (Bad Driver). 1.85:1. VHS: Tai Seng (No Subtitles). Import VCD: Mega Star. 92 minutes.

This entry in the **Pom Pom** series casts Yuen Biao and Lowell Lo, standing in for Richard Ng and John Sham, as bumbling cops who somehow manage to crack cases in spite of themselves. After they inadvertently annoy their smarmy superior, rookie Hsia and hot-tempered Lei are paired together on a case involving an informant who took pictures of a mob rubout. Unable to track the man down, the partners decide to work on his girlfriend Rosa instead. Lei turns on the charm in order to romance her, while Hsia and Lei's sister develop their own relationship. When the gangsters kidnap the girls and demand the incriminating negative in exchange, Hsia and Lei must use their skills to save the day.

With Yuen Biao and many of his associates in the cast, this entry seems patterned as much after the **Lucky Stars** films as the earlier **Pom Pom** outings. The pace lags at times and the jokes run hot and cold, but the climax features some terrific hand-to-hand combat (particularly the fight between Yuen Biao and Dick Wei, which ends up with them trapped in a meat locker), and the sequence in which Rosa fulfil's Lei's "dying wish" is a gem.

Rose (1986) *see* **The Story of Rose**

843. Rose

(1992; Magic Productions Co./Fitto Film Company) ★: 6/10. *Baak mooi gwai* (Cantonese), *Bai mei gui* (Mandarin): "White Rose." Cinematographer: Nico Wong Man-wan; Art Director-Action Director: Mario Law Pui; Music: Richard Lo Sai-kit; Writers: Candy Cheng, Samson Chiu Leung-chun, Ng Kin-chi; Producer: Fitto Film Company; Director: Samson Chiu Leung-chun. Cast: Maggie Cheung Man-yuk (Rose Chin), Roy Cheung Yiu-yeung (Roy Cheung), Veronica Yip Yuk-hing (Lotus), Kelly Yiu Wai (Rose's Mother), Michael Wong Man-tak (Brian), Woo Fung (Lotus' Father), Norman Tsui Siu-keung (Roy's Friend in Macau). 1.85:1. VHS: Tai Seng. Import LD/VCD: Ocean Shores (Poor Subtitles). 99 minutes. Also known as **Blue Valentine**.

Two of HK's most popular genres, the romantic drama and the gangster thriller, are wedded in this novel effort. Rose Chin is an unhappy insurance agent who discovers that she is three months pregnant...the day after she broke up with her boyfriend. She manages to set up a lucrative policy for a notoriously uncooperative client, but just as he is about to sign the document, the man is scared away by Roy, a triad who promises to kill him. Furious over the money she has lost, Rose demands compensation from Roy. That evening the triad makes a proposal: He will buy a $US 1 million policy and make Rose the beneficiary if she agrees to spend three weeks with him. Before she can make up her mind, a gang fight breaks out and Roy is gravely injured. Forced to nurse him back to health, Rose quarrels with him and accidentally loses her baby. As she saved his life, Roy insists on nursing her back to health, in spite of Rose's undisguised contempt for him. The pronounced personality clash soon gives way to love (doesn't it always?), but fate intervenes when Roy's boss turns against him.

The project's intentions are revealed early on when Roy first proposes his deal. Rose points out their obvious incompatibility by saying, "Have you ever seen Maggie Cheung acting with Roy Cheung?" to which he replies, "Who knows? We haven't tried?" (Not entirely true: the pair appeared together for a couple of scenes in 1986's **The Story of Rose**). Samson Chiu and his fellow writers are trying to have it both ways, knowingly winking at the audience while also striving to fulfil their expectations. As contrived and artificial as the proceedings get, the film has a quirky, infectious appeal which can largely be attributed to its creative casting. While Roy Cheung plays triads better than anyone, it is Maggie Cheung who gives the more charming and natural performance. She is always credible, even when the script is not (which is most of the time). In one of the first "straight" roles she received after ending her brief softcore career, Veronica Yip gives a solid dramatic performance as Rose's suicidally lonely friend.

844. Rose Rose I Love You

(1993; Regal Films Company) ★: 6/10. *Mooi gwai mooi gwai ngoh oi nei* (Cantonese), *Mei gui mei gui wo ai ni* (Mandarin): "Rose Rose I Love You." Cinematographer: Chan Yuen-kai; Art Director: James Cheung Ying-wah; Music: Lowell Lo Kwun-ting; Writer: Chan Kai-ming; Producer: Jeff Lau Chun-wai; Action Directors: Corey Yuen Kwai, Yuen Tak; Director: Jacky Pang Yee-wah. Cast: Tony Leung Kar-fai (Keith Lui), Carina Lau Kar-ling (Pearl), Kenny Bee (Leung Sing-bo), Veronica Yip Yuk-hing (Beauty), Simon Yam Tat-wah (Micky), Charine Chan Kar-ling (Lulu), Ku Feng (Angry Father), Bowie Lam Bo-yee (Tam Tak-cheung). 1.85:1. VHS/LD: Tai Seng. Import LD/VCD: Universe. Running time unknown.

English speaking viewers will find this follow-up to **92 Legendary La Rose Noire** a bit more accessible, though a few of the jokes are still out of reach. Feuding policemen Lui and Leung both have their eye on schoolteacher Pearl and proceed to all but wage war in their effort to seduce her. In the meantime, Lui also has his hands full with mystery girl Beauty, who appears out of nowhere one day and enters his life. Also tossing his hat into the fray is escaped con Micky, who stole a valuable gem called The Malay Star and framed Black Rose for the crime. The masked heroine is about to enact ven-geance on Micky but is interrupted by White Rose, an equally skilled female avenger, who allows the convict to escape. Lui and Leung deduce that Pearl is Micky's old girlfriend and decide to stake her out, but, of course, neither she nor Beauty are really who they seem.

The humor is just as broad this time out but most of the sight gags need no explanation or context to be enjoyed, and Tony Leung Kar-fai again provides a great deal of fun with his high-pitched parody of Lui Kei. **Black Rose II** followed next.

845. Rouge

(1987; Golden Harvest/Golden Way Films/Paragon Films) ★: 10/10. *Yin chi kau* (Cantonese), *Yan zhi kou* (Mandarin): "Rouge Hook" ("Hook," in this instance, means "box" or "case"). Cinematographer: Bill Wong Chung-bo; Art Directors: Pok Yeuk-muk, Horace Ma Kwong-wing; Music: Michael Lai Siu-tin; Writers: Yau Tai On-ping, Lillian Lee Pik-wah; Producer: Jackie Chan; Director: Stanley Kwan Kam-pang. Cast: Anita Mui Yim-fong (Fleur), Leslie Cheung Kwok-wing (Chen Chen-pang), Alex Man Chi-leung (Yuan Ting), Emily Chu Bo-yee (Chu), Irene Wan Pik-ha (Shu-hsien), Lau Kar-wing (Movie Director), Kara Hui Ying-hung (Actress Playing Ghost). Dolby Digital (DVD only). 1.85:1. VHS: Tai Seng (Subtitles on Mandarin version only). LD: Media Asia. Import LD: Star Entertainment (No Subtitles). Import VCD: Mei Ah (No Subtitles). Import DVD: Mega Star. 95 minutes.

Jackie Chan produced this touching, beautifully composed drama which won five HK Film Awards prizes, including Best Picture. In 1934 the dashing Chen Chen-pang falls for Fleur, a cultured prostitute, after hearing her sing Cantonese opera one evening. He pampers her with gifts and affection, and the two are soon deeply in love. At this point the film shifts to 1987, with Fleur (looking unchanged after over half a century) arriving at a newspaper office one evening. She seeks to place a classified ad addressed to Chen-pang, asking for him to meet her at their usual place, but lacks the necessary money to pay for it. Yuan Ting, the classifieds editor, is followed by Fleur for the rest of the night, with the woman constantly turning up in unexpected places. While he initially thinks that this demure lady in a flowered *cheongsam* is a harmless (if slightly creepy) lunatic, Ting soon realizes that she is actually a ghost. Fleur explains to him that, after she was rejected by Chen-pang's family, the two of them committed suicide with an overdose of opium and sleeping pills, planning to join together forever in Hell. However, after waiting more than five decades, she has been unable to find him and has returned to Earth two days before the 53rd anniversary of their deaths. Pitying Fleur and her plight, Ting and his reporter girlfriend, Chu, agree to take the spirit into their home and aid her in finding Chen-pang. Along the way, they find their faltering relationship regaining the strength and passion it had when they first started dating. When Chen-pang fails to show up for the appointed rendezvous, Ting and Chu learn something surprising about Chen-pang's fate.

Told without special FX of any kind, **Rouge** is one of the most seductive films in memory, drawing the viewer into its spell from the opening image and maintaining that hold right through to the end. At the time of its production, Anita Mui was known in the pop music world for her flamboyance and everchanging persona, and in the movie world for her brassy, independent characters. For **Rouge**, she completely submerged herself into the role of a 1930s courtesan: unfailingly polite, timid, and willowy, with a hint of sadness and reservation in her eyes, even when smiling. While seemingly a one-note character, it is actually quite a difficult role, as Fleur's dispositions are as delicate as her demeanour. Much of the story's dramatic effect is drawn from the small hints of emotion in Mui's face (beautifully photographed in all manner of ways by **Zu** cinematographer Bill Wong), and the entire film employs this same subtlety, from the thoughtful, sincere script (co-authored by novelist Lillian Lee, who would later write **A Terracotta Warrior** and **Green Snake**) to Michael Lai's gentle, arresting score. Mui rightfully received the Best Actress awards in both HK and Taiwan, and her title song (heard during the finale) also won at the former ceremony. A story about the convergence of two very different eras in the history of Hong Kong and their contrasting outlooks on love and life, **Rouge** is refined and gratifyingly genuine, and this insight, coupled with its exquisite technical artistry, makes it one of the very best films of the 1980s.

846. The Royal Scoundrel

(1991; Cinema City Co./Paka Hill Film Production Co.) ★: 4/10. *Sa Tan-chai yue Chau Si-nai* (Cantonese), *Sha Tanzi yu Zhou Shihnai* (Mandarin): "Sa Tan-chai and Chow Si-nai" or "Sha Tan-chi and Chou Shi-nai." Cinematographer: Horace Wong Wing-hang; Art Director: Danny Yuen Ching-yeung; Music: William Woo Wai-lap; Writer: Sammy Tsang Kan-cheung; Producer: Raymond Wong Pak-ming; Action Director: Yuen Bun; Director: Johnny To Kei-fung. Cast: Tony

Leung Chiu-wai (Beach Boy), Jacqueline Wu Chien-lien (Yuk), Ng Man-tat (Chow), Waise Lee Chi-hung (Lee Nam), Wong Yat-fei (Rusty). 1.85:1. VHS: World Video. Import LD: Golden Cinema City. 89 minutes. Also known as **Son of the Beach** (World Video title).

A lesser work from director Johnny To (**The Heroic Trio**), **The Royal Scoundrel** makes for pleasant but unsatisfying viewing. Beach Boy and Chow are cops staking out a drug store (from inside a *mailbox* across the street!), in order to keep tabs on an underworld figure who frequents the place. Beach Boy soon falls for Yuk, the pretty young girl who works there, and is horrified by the abuse she endures at the hands of her sadistic stepfather. It is later determined that the stepfather is part of a stolen credit card ring, and when he takes Yuk hostage, the man is shot dead by Inspector Lee Nam. As if having their investigation taken away from them wasn't enough, Beach Boy and the bumbling Chow (whom everyone calls "Mrs. Chow" because he has seven children and no wife) discover that the sadistic Lee is their new superior. With nowhere to stay, Yuk accepts Beach Boy's invitation to move in with him, a lucky break for Beach Boy since he has to look after Chow's army of kids when the latter gets shot and hospitalized. To Beach Boy's horror, Lee starts wooing Yuk, and soon she has moved out of his home and into Lee's arms. The inspector then proceeds to frame Boy and Chow for robbery and murder, which puts a mob of very angry Taiwanese triads on their trail.

Tony Leung Chiu-wai and Jacqueline Wu (in her second film) have an appealing, natural chemistry, but the script is riddled with contrivances (for example: Beach Boy and Chow are able to escape a group of heavily armed attackers thanks to the former's homemade "Super Bullet") and Ng Man-tat's cowardly cop act gets old fast. Also, Leung and Wu's break-up is not staged in a believable fashion, and the film falters badly when she disappears for most of the second half. The climax, which takes place onboard a packed commuter train, is very nicely staged, however, and more in keeping with what To is capable of than anything else here.

847. Royal Tramp

(1992; Win's Movie Production) ★: 7/10. *Luk ting kei* (Cantonese), *Lu ding ji* (Mandarin): "The Legend of Mount Deer." Cinematographers: David Chung Chi-man, Henry Chan Chun-kit; Art Director: Jason Mok Siu-kei; Music: William Woo Wai-lap; Producers: Jimmy Heung Wah-sing, Stephen Siu Yeuk-yuen; Action Director: Ching Siu-tung; Writer-Director: Wong Jing. Cast: Stephen Chiau Sing-chi (Wilson Bond), Sharla Cheung Man (The Empress Dowager), Ng Man-tat (Hoi Tai-fu), Chingmy Yau Suk-ching (Kin-ning), Damian Lau Chung-yan (Chan Kan-nam), Elvis Tsui Kam-kong (O'Brian), Deric Wan Siu-lun (Emperor Hong Hay), Nat Chan Pak-cheung (Duran), Fennie Yuen Kit-ying (Twin #1), Vivian Chan Tak-yung (Twin #2), Sandra Ng Kwan-yu (Wai Chun-fa). Dolby Digital (Mega Star DVD Only). 1.85:1. VHS: Tai Seng. Import LD: Mei Ah. Import VCD/DVD: Mei Ah, Mega Star. 106 minutes.

848. Royal Tramp II

(1992; Win's Movie Production) ★: 6/10. *Luk ting kei II ji san lung gaau* (Cantonese), *Lu ding ji II zhi shen long jiao* (Mandarin): "The Legend of Mount Deer II: Godly Dragon Clan." Cinematographers: David Chung Chi-man, Henry Chan Chun-kit; Art Director: Jason Mok Siu-kei; Music: William Woo Wai-lap; Producers: Jimmy Heung Wah-sing, Stephen Siu Yeuk-yuen; Action Director: Ching Siu-tung; Writer-Director: Wong Jing. Cast: Stephen Chiau Sing-chi (Wilson Bond), Brigitte Lin Ching-hsia (Loneer), Chingmy Yau Suk-ching (Kin-ning), Damian Lau Chung-yan (Chan Kan-nam), Deric Wan Siu-lun (Emperor Hong Hay), Nat Chan Pak-cheung (Dor Lung), Yam Sai-kwoon (Fung Shek-fan), Kenneth Tong Chun-yip (Ng Ying-hung), Paul Chun Pui (Ng Sam-kwai), Michelle Lee Kai-yan (Or), Fennie Yuen Kit-ying (Twin #1), Vivian Chan Tak-yung (Twin #2), Sandra Ng Kwan-yu (Wai Chun-fa), Helena Law Lan (Dragon Sect Leader). Dolby Digital (Mega Star DVD only). 1.85:1. VHS: Tai Seng. Import LD: Mei Ah. Import VCD/DVD: Mei Ah, Mega Star. 93 minutes.

Among the most successful entries in the HK period fantasy craze, the **Royal Tramp** films are a send-up of the classic swordplay/fantasy novel *The Duke of Mount Deer* (1969), by Louis Cha Leung-yung, writing under his pen name "Jin Yong." One of the most prolific writers in the genre, a large percentage of Cha's work has been adapted for either TV or film. The founder-editor of the highly respected HK newspaper *Ming Pao* and its magazine offshoot, *Ming Pao Weekly*, Cha retired from the fiction field after completing the aforementioned novel. It was first adapted as a television miniseries in 1985, with newcomer Tony Leung Chiu-wai essaying the hero, "Wai Siu-bo." A major success, the program made Leung an overnight star. He would reprise the role a few years later in the theatrical feature **Hero Beyond the Boundary of Time**, an ill-conceived time travel comedy produced not only to exploit Leung's identification with the role but also to cash in on the preceding year's **Royal Tramp**, which found wide audience approval by allocating the lead to comedy superstar Stephen Chiau. Wai Siu-bo (anglicized to *Wilson Bond* in the preposterous English subtitles) is a brothel storyteller who likes to spin yarns about Chan Kan-nam, the legendary leader of "The Heaven and Earth Society." A rebel group, H & E is committed to toppling the evil Ching Dynasty and killing its traitorous military commander, Ngou Bai (called *O'Brian* in the subs). Acting on a tip, Imperial troops invade the brothel one day and find Chan, who has been in hiding there, unbeknownst to Siu-bo. Honored to meet his hero in the flesh, Siu-bo saves Chan when he is temporarily blinded and whisks him away to safety. In gratitude, Chan makes him a member of the group and assigns Siu-bo to infiltrate The Forbidden City. Once inside, he must steal four books which reveal the location of the Manchurians' treasure trove of plundered loot. After accidentally signing up to become a eunuch, he is aided by the head eunuch, Hoi Tai-fu, who, unbeknownst to Siu-bo, is also an H & E undercover operative. Hoi suspects that The Empress Dowager has been replaced with a double and is able to prove his suspicions by forcing her to use martial powers she couldn't possibly have. Meanwhile, Siu-bo has also become a confidant of The King, and he must juggle his various loyalties while making a not very concerted attempt to ward off the advances of the empress' cute daughter, Kin-ning.

As noted above, the translation is less than eloquent, but the storyline is coherent and most of the jokes survive. Anyone under the impression that toilet humor is unique to Western comedy has obviously never seen a Stephen Chiau film. In addition to endless jokes about castration and penis size, Chiau trots out that obligatory kung fu comedy stance, "Monkey Grabs the Peach" (you figure it out). One of the main plot elements even concerns the villain's penis. His (for lack of a better anatomical term) Achilles' Heel, he can retract it deep inside his body, making him invulnerable to attack! However, both Chiau and director Wong Jing execute these shopworn gags with so much zeal and enthusiasm, it's easy to lower one's defences and enjoy the ride. Suspension wires are visible at times but the action choreography is always impressive. The final battle, which finds the combatants duelling with razor sharp cymbals, is particularly enjoyable. The novel consists of five volumes, so, naturally, many subplots have been dropped. However, the film reportedly retains most of the characters, the basic plotline, and the original ending...up until the final shot, that is. In a clever set-up for the simultaneously-produced sequel (which hit theaters two months later), Cheung's character declares that she will return once more to face off against Siu-bo, but in her true form this time. She then changes into...*Brigitte Lin Ching-hsia*!

In **Royal Tramp II**, Lone-er (now played by Lin) is ordered to protect Ng Sam-kwai (the infamous traitor played by Eddy Ko Hung in **The Bride with White Hair** films), the King of Ping-si. The Emperor announces that Kin-ning will marry Ng's son, Prince Ng Ying-hung, as part of his plan to vanquish Sam-kwai, whose loyalty is in doubt. Wilson Bond is selected to kill Sam-kwai, an assignment which is complicated by the machinations of the H & E sect, to which Bond is also still loyal. Betrayed and poisoned by Ying-hung, Lone-er is saved by none other than Bond, who is coerced into making love to the stricken woman. While this successfully diffuses the toxins, it also causes 80% of her powers to transfer into his body. Bond's attempt to kill Sam-kwai fails, but Kin-ning makes the prince impotent. An enraged Sam-kwai declares war and dispatches his troops (led by the great warrior Fung Shek-fan) to attack the Emperor's palace.

Although she is eager for revenge at the end of the first film, Lone-er ends up as Bond's woman, a storyline concession seemingly made to put popular stars Lin and Chiau on the same side. Not surprisingly, it is their scenes together that provide the most entertainment (particularly "the seduction," which unfolds inside what appears to be a giant cocoon), though Lin's participation in the storyline is diminished in the final third. Chiau takes the opportunity to also poke fun at Lin's unmatched "Invincible Asia" character from **Swordsman II** and **The East Is Red** by playing (you guessed it) the effeminate "Vincible West!" Not quite on par with its forerunner, this entry still makes for engaging entertainment and also delivers the expected quota of high-flying martial combat. Damian Lau would play Chan Kan-nam once again in Wong Jing's **The New Legend of Shaolin**.

849. Royal Warriors

(1986; D & B Films Co.) ★: 7/10. *Wong ga jin si* (Cantonese), *Huang jia zhan shi* (Mandarin): "Royal Warriors." Cinematographers: Derek Wan Man-kit, Ma Chan-wah; Art Directors: Oliver Wong Yui-man, Yank Wong Yan-kwai, Dominique Lo Kar-yiu; Music: Romeo Diaz; Writer: Sammy Tsang Kan-cheung; Producer: Dickson Poon Dik-sun; Action Director: Mang Hoi; Director: David Chung Chi-man. Cast: Michelle Yeoh Chu-kheng (Michelle Yip), Hiroyuki Sanada (Yamamoto), Michael Wong Man-tak (Michael), Pak Ying (Bandana), Lam Wai (Bull), Kenneth Tsang Kong (Captain Lau Chi-shing), Michael Chan Wai-man (Harvey Lee, aka "Tiger"), Kam Hing-yin (Hijacker), Reiko Niwa (Yukiko), Chen Jing (Lou), Paul Chun Pui (Cop), Dennis Chan Kwok-san (Reporter), Lau Siu-ming (Yip), Woo Fung (Nightclub Patron), Eddie Maher (Thug), Blackie Ko Shou-liang (Bus Driver). Dolby Digital (DVDs only). 1.85:1. VHS/LD: Tai Seng (Remastered for the English market; subtitled or dubbed), Cinepix (Dubbed). Import LD: Mei Ah. Import DVD: Universe, Mega Star. 96 minutes. Also known as **In the Line of Duty** (International title and Cinepix title) and **Police Assassin** (UK video title).

One of the best films Michelle Yeoh Chu-kheng did for D & B, **Royal Warriors** boasts sensational action setpieces which more than compensate for its ordinary storyline. After teaming up to foil a hijacking meant to free criminal Harvey Lee before he could be extradited to HK, law enforcement officers Michelle Yip (a HK policewoman), Yamamoto (a former police officer in his native Japan), and airline security officer Michael find themselves the targets of Lee's old war buddies (Pak Ying and Lam Wai), who swore to live and die together. Yamamoto's wife and baby daughter are (predictably) killed by a car bomb, leading to a shootout in a nightclub that eliminates one of the attackers but also many innocent civilians. Ignoring the suspension issued by her by-the-book superior, Michelle teams up with Michael and the vengeful Yamamoto to end the threat to their lives.

Cinematographer-turned-director David Chung Chi-man (**Magnificent Warriors, I Love Maria**) keeps the proceedings moving at near warp speed throughout, and Mang Hoi's action choreography is so back-breakingly spectacular it induces sympathy pains. Yeoh is charming, graceful, and deadly in turns, and Sanada is nearly as impressive, hemmed in only by his stereotypical hardboiled character. In fact, the only liability here is Michael Wong (an extremely limited actor who has enjoyed an unaccountably long career in HK cinema), whose character is so obnoxious you wish that Michelle and Yamamoto will kill him themselves. The climax, in which chainsaw and a sledge hammer-wielding the villain squares off against the unarmed Yeoh, is so impressively staged that it raises one's admiration for Yeoh's abilities even higher, if that is possible. Known in some markets as **In the Line of Duty**, this should actually be called **In the Line of Duty 2**, as it followed the series' first entry, **Yes, Madam** (much of the music here was previously used in that film). Be that as it may, **In the Line of Duty 3** came next, with Cynthia Yang replacing Yeoh in the lead.

850. Rumble in the Bronx

(1995; Golden Harvest/Paragon Films) ★: 5/10. *Hung faan au* (Cantonese), *Gong fan ou* (Mandarin): "Red Indian Territory." Cinematographer: Jingle Ma Cho-shing; Art Director: Oliver Wong Yui-man; Music: Wong Chung-yin (HK version), J. Peter Robinson (US version); Writers: Edward Tang King-sang, Fibe Ma Mei-ping; Producer: Barbie Tung Wan-sze; Action Directors: Jackie Chan, Stanley Tong Kwai-lai; Director: Stanley Tong Kwai-lai. Cast: Jackie Chan (Jackie), Anita Mui Yim-fong (Elena), Francoise Yip Fong-wah (Nancy), Bill Tung Biu (Bill Chu), Marc Akerstream (Tony), Garvin Cross (Angelo), Morgan Lam (Danny Chan), Kris Lord (White Tiger), Emil Chow Wah-kin (Ice Cream Vendor), Alex To Tak-wai (Ice Cream Customer), Jamie Luk Kim-ming (Friend with Limo). Dolby Stereo. 2.35:1. VHS/DVD: New Line (89 minutes). LD: Image (89 minutes). Import LD/VCD: Star Entertainment (No Subtitles, 106 minutes). Import DVD: China Star (No Subtitles, 106 minutes).

The film that finally made Jackie Chan a star in America, **Rumble in the Bronx** is actually far from his best work, but a terrific promotional campaign by New Line Cinema helped it nab the number one spot on opening weekend and a solid final gross of over $30 million. Chan plays Keung, a martially adept HK police officer in the Bronx on vacation to visit his Uncle Bill, who is selling his grocery store. Elena, the new owner, soon finds that Bill's protection arrangement with the local thugs does not apply to her, and Keung must intervene when some of them try to steal merchandise. The gang later lures Keung into a trap and severely injures him. At this point, a second plot thread involving some missing diamonds comes into play, as the gems end up stashed in the wheelchair cushion of a young boy Keung has befriended. Murderous gangsters looking for the stones make Keung's life hell, prompting him to work with the local police. The climax finds Keung pursued by, and eventually pursuing, a huge hovercraft that ends up demolishing much of the surrounding area.

Unlike virtually everything Chan has done since, the film was not produced with Western markets in mind. Most of the

Caucasian actors are simply stuntmen (some are dubbed with new voices in the American version, but the voice actors are no better, making the exercise pretty pointless), and Vancouver makes a laughably unconvincing stand-in for New York City (watch for the Canadian mailboxes, and since when are there *mountains* in the NYC area?). Additionally, the story is nonsense, even for a Chan picture, and the ridiculous street gang wouldn't last five minutes in the real Big Apple. Still, there's Jackie, his incredible footwork, and a steady stream of action and stunts to keep things perking. Chan broke his ankle while leaping onto a hovercraft during the finale and, as always, the accident has been preserved for posterity in the outtakes. A delightful scene stealer in **Drunken Master II**, poor Anita Mui is given little to do here, and her role is substantially cut back in New Line's edition.

851. Run

(1994; Golden Harvest/Odeon Productions/Paragon Films) ★: 3/10. *Sin yan cheung* (Cantonese), *Xian ren zhang* (Mandarin): "Cactus." Cinematographer: John Yeung Hok-leung; Art Director: Yeung Chau-wing; Music: Denise Tam, Vili Chen, Leo Chan Wing-ming; Writers: Fung Wai-lam, Au Pui-ying; Producer: Chua Lam; Action Director: Tony Leung Siu-hung; Directors: Derek Chang Man-gon. Cast: Leon Lai Ming (Lam Man-fai), Veronica Yip Yuk-hing (Ho Ying), Eric Kot Man-fai (Leung), Jan Lam Hoi-fung (Tai), Chin Ho (The Killer), Peter Chan Lung (Roy). 1.85:1. VHS: Tai Seng. Import LD/VCD: Universe. 96 minutes.

HK films often copy their Western counterparts, but would you believe a HK version of **El Mariachi**?! This was even shot in Mexico, possibly even on some of the same locations as its model. While the Robert Rodriguez film is a classic example of low budget efficiency, **Run** is simply a monotonous and shameless exercise in plagiarism. Lam Man-fai is a broke musician wandering in Mexico with nothing but a guitar to his name. At the same time, a local hoodlum named Carlos has ordered his men to liquidate a former partner (Chin Ho), who is Chinese and carries his weapons in a guitar case. Naturally, the goons mistake Man-fai for their real target and almost succeed in icing him. Man-fai meets up with Ho Ying, a saloon owner whose brother was killed under mysterious circumstances. While visiting her sibling's grave, Ying encounters Carlos' real target, who reveals the fate of her brother. In love with one another, Man-fai and Ying try to flee Mexico and Carlos before the vicious hoodlum ends their lives.

While this has been put together with some style (Derek Chang made a name for himself as a music video director), it remains an empty and superficial endeavour that even the attractive leads cannot revive. At least the Mexican characters actually speak Spanish instead of post-synched Cantonese. Eric Kot and Jan Lam provide limp comic relief as Yip's two helpers.

852. Run and Kill

(1993; Come On Film Co.) ★: 3/10. *Woo sue* (Cantonese), *Wu shu* (Mandarin): "Crow Rat." Cinematographer: Tony Miu Kin-fai; Art Director: Vincent Lam Wai-sam; Music: Wong Bong; Writer: Bryan Cheung Wai-hung; Producers: Kimmy Suen King-on, Ng Kwok-kuen; Action Directors: Wong Pui-kei, Chan Siu-wah; Director: Billy Tang Hin-sing. Cast: Kent Cheng Chuk-see (Ng Kau-cheung, aka Fatty Cheung), Simon Yam Tat-wah (Ching Fung), Danny Lee Sau-yin (Inspector Man), Melvin Wong Kam-sun (Tong Man-ho, aka Panther), Esther Kwan Wing-ho (Fanny), Johnny Wang Lung-wei (Gang Leader), Lily Lee Li-li (Ng's Wife). 1.85:1. VHS: World Video. Import LD/VCD: Universe. 90 minutes.

Another repulsive entry in the short-lived "True Crime" craze, this Category III thriller contains scenes of sadism and violence that will go beyond the tolerance level of some viewers. Fed up with his cheating wife, Ng Kau-cheung goes to a bar to drown his sorrows. In the midst of a drunken stupor, he tells a fellow patron that he wants his wife dead. His unconscious wish comes true when thugs brutally murder the woman and her lover. Not surprisingly, the police suspect that Ng committed the crime; and if that were not enough, he is contacted by the Vietnamese killers, who demand $800,000 in payment for the job. Desperate to extricate himself from this increasingly dangerous misunderstanding, Ng travels to China, where he is advised by his Vietnamese gangster neighbor, Wah, to let his gang help him out. The plan goes disastrously wrong, resulting in the man's gruesome death. Blaming Ng for his younger brother's demise, Fung, Wah's demented sibling, swears vengeance upon Ng and his family.

One of the more infamous HK productions of the '90s, **Run and Kill** is undeniably effective when it comes to disturbing the viewer. However, as its storyline is unconvincing (the misunderstanding in the bar is ludicrously contrived), it possesses little dramatic power, making the violence seem especially gruesome and mean-spirited (there is a sequence involving the fate of a minor that would never be depicted as graphically in a Western feature). Dashes of black humor do little to alleviate this (see **The Underground Banker** for a more effective mixture of over-the-top gore and blacker-than-black comedy).

853. Run Don't Walk

(1989; Dennis Yu Film Production Co./Big Bright Investment Co.) ★: 3/10. *Lo foo chut gaam* (Cantonese), *Lao hu chu jian* (Mandarin): "Tiger Goes to Prison." Cinematographers: Abdul M. Rumjahn, Ardy Lam Kwok-wah; Music: Bobby Chan Dik-hong; Writer: Shum Kwok-wing; Producer: Dennis Yu Wan-kong; Action Director: Tony Leung Siu-hung; Director: Wong Chung. Cast: Ti Lung (Lok Pui), Richard Ng Yiu-hon (Ng Shing-choi), Lui Sau-ling (May), Kent Cheng Chuk-see (Sgt. Leung), Lam Chung (Sing). 1.85:1. VHS: Tai Seng. Import LD: Mei Ah. 92 minutes.

This starts off as a fairly amusing send-up of the Ti Lung thriller **People's Hero** (with Ti essentially portraying the same character), but then goes rapidly down the drain. On the day he is released from prison, reformed criminal Lok Pui goes to a bank to cash a check. In barges hapless, first-time robber Ng Shing-choi, who muffs the job and takes Lok hostage. Naturally, the suspicious Sgt. Leung believes that Lok was actually the mastermind and plans to send him up the river for another twenty years. The understandably annoyed ex-con plans on turning Ng over to the police but can't when he looks into the eyes of the man's adorable little girl. A mute, she can only be cured with an expensive operation, which is why Ng was robbing the bank. Lok arranges for Ng and his daughter to be smuggled to Thailand, but the pair become separated and the girl ends up in an orphanage. Ng manages to get the girl out but his and Lok's troubles are far from over, particularly as Lok's former boss is out to settle a score with him.

There are dollops of heavy-handed sentimentality but precious few laughs, unless you consider the sight of Richard Ng in a dress or disguised as an East Indian an intrinsically hilarious.

854. Run Tiger, Run

(1985; Cinema City Co.) ★: 3/10. *Leung ji lo foo* (Cantonese), *Liang zhi lao hu* (Mandarin): "Two Tigers." Cinematographer: Lam Chan-ting; Art Director: Lau Chi-wah; Music: Cheung Hung-yee; Writer: Raymond Wong Pak-ming; Producer-Director: John Woo Yu-sen. Cast: Teddy Robin Kwan (Teddy), Siu Bin-bin (Benny/Babe Steak), Pan Yin-tze (Mary Lee), Tsui Hark (Grandpa Steak). 2.35:1. VHS: Tai Seng (Poor Subtitles). 90 minutes.

Raymond Wong wrote this Cinema City farce which, like his **Happy Ghost** series, is aimed at the younger set. However, those films almost seem like high art compared to this manic, headache-inducing variation on **The Prince and the Pauper**, which is something producer-director John Woo probably leaves off his resume. Bosom buddies Teddy and Benny are poor but happy and carefree, using their wiles to get by. Meanwhile, Benny's exact lookalike, Babe Steak, is rich and terminally unhappy, despite the fact that he is spoiled rotten by his loving grandpa (played, in outrageously over-the-top fashion, by Tsui Hark). The old man drops dead one evening and his will reveals that he has left all of his vast fortune to Babe. It will be held in a trust until he is an adult, but if anything should happen to him before then, the money will go to the man's evil son. Naturally, the son dispatches goons to take care of Babe, but they snatch Benny and Teddy instead. The two vagabonds smell a potential score in the making and decide to hang around, a plan that also allows Teddy to court Mary, Babe's cute tutor.

Western viewers will enjoy spotting the numerous visual gags patterned closely after classic Warner Brothers and MGM cartoons, and there are several moments that border on the delectably surreal. However, what might have been fun as a one reel short becomes really hard to take at five times that length. Best left to John Woo completists; everyone else need only watch a few minutes from any sequence.

855. Runaway Blues

(1989; Tomson Film Co./Grandview Entertainment International/Impact Films Distribution Co.) ★: 5/10. *Piu sing* (Cantonese), *Biao cheng* (Mandarin): "City of Violent Winds." Cinematographer: Mark Lee Ping-bing; Art Director: Jason Mok Siu-kei; Music: Law Wing-fai; Writer: Lai Kit; Producer: Wallace Cheung Kwok-chong; Action Director: Blackie Ko Shou-liang; Director: David Lai Tai-wai. Cast: Andy Lau Tak-wah (Lam Kwong), Kelvin Wong Siu (Wah), Lui Sau-ling, Ngok Ling, Fong Kong, Blackie Ko Shou-liang (Triad in Race). 1.85:1. VHS: Tai Seng. Import LD/VCD: Ocean Shores. 96 minutes.

This brutally violent crime thriller was one of the first movies to receive HK's Category III rating. Low level Taiwanese triad Kwong must flee to HK after his self defence killing of a fellow gangster who blamed Kwong for the death of his girlfriend. Instructed by his boss to stay with Sue and her young son, Kwong proceeds to befriend rival triad Wah from Guangzhou, who deals in Rolexes and has had a falling out with Kwong's gang. Blackmailed into being an informer for the police, Kwong decides to take Sue (whom he now has feelings for) to the Mainland, where he runs into his old lover. The trio return to HK, but the police, tired of not getting the goods on top members of the gang, put a warrant out for Kwong, who hightails it to Macau. There, he and Wah join forces to protect themselves from extermination.

Terrific stuntwork (courtesy of ace choreographer Blackie Ko, who faces off against Andy Lau in a memorable moped race) and Kelvin Wong's commanding, charismatic performance help elevate this a bit above the usual triad thriller fare, though the storyline is convoluted and the characters are underdeveloped.

856. Saga of the Phoenix

(1990; Golden Harvest/Paragon Films) ★: 4/10. *A sau law* (Cantonese), *A xiu luo* (Mandarin): "Ah Sau-lo" or "A Xiuluo." Cinematographer: Kwan Chi-kan; Art Director: Eddie Ma Poon-chiu; Music: Phil Chan Fei-lap; Writers: Wong Chui-wah, Edward Leung Yiu-ming; Producer: Chua Lam; Action Director: Yuen Bun; Directors: Nam Nai-choi, Lau See-yu. Cast: Yuen Biao (Peacock), Gloria Yip Wan-yee (Ashura), Lau Sek-yin (Tan), Loletta Lee Lai-chun (Tan's Sister). Dolby Digital (DVD only). 1.85:1. VHS: Tai Seng (No Subtitles). Import LD: Star Entertainment (No Subtitles). Import VCD: Mega Star. Import DVD: Universe. 93 minutes.

An inferior follow-up to **Peacock King**, this tiresomely juvenile fantasy finds Earth threatened by another disaster when Ashura uses her previously dormant magical powers to save Peacock and Lucky Fruit (played this time by a different Japanese actor who is about a foot taller than Hiroshi Mikami) from a group of demons. Deemed a threat to mankind, Ashura is ordered to spend the rest of eternity sealed inside a giant Buddha, but after she and the monks plead for leniency, the girl is granted seven days on Earth before her spirit will be dispersed. In an attempt to lure Ashura down into the netherworld, the powerful Hell Concubine has her minion trap the girl's imp friend, Genie (a rubbery, E.T.-like creature that is only remotely convincing during the moments when it is presented using stop-motion animation). Peacock journeys down to Hell to save Genie but, after a duel of magic, is frozen solid by the Concubine. However, before being immobilized, he was able to send Genie back to Earth, where it was discovered by a tourist. Lucky Fruit and Ashura follow the girl back home to HK, but the Concubine is undaunted and spins new schemes to capture Ashura.

While there are scattered moments that rank with its forerunner, the fantasy elements here too often take a back seat to uninspired fish-out-of-water gags and other dull material. Yuen Biao receives star billing but little screen time, while far too much of the film is spent charting the nauseatingly precious antics of Genie. The Chinese titles are Ashura's name in Cantonese and Mandarin.

857. The Saint of Gamblers

(1995; Wong Jing's Workshop/Kotewall) ★: 4/10. *Do sing 2 gaai tau do sing* (Cantonese), *Du sheng 2 jie tou du sheng* (Mandarin): "Saint of Gamblers 2: The Street Corner Saint of Gamblers." Cinematographer: Andrew Lau Wai-keung; Art Director: Raymond Kwok Siu-keung; Music: Anthony Lee Hon-kam, Marco Wan Ho-kit; Action Director: Dion Lam Dik-on; Producer-Director: Wong Jing. Cast: Eric Kot Man-fai (Got), Chingmy Yau Suk-ching (Yuen-fan), Ng Man-tat (Uncle Tat), Ben Lam Kwok-bun (Ray Thai), Donnie Yen Chi-tan (Lone Seven), Sik Siu-lung (Siu-loong), Diana Pang Dan (Hokei), Shing Fui-on (Assassin), John Ching Tung (Tung), Nat Chan Pak-cheung (Announcer), Manfred Wong (Dwarf), Corey Yuen Kwai (Mahjong Player). 1.85:1. VHS: Tai Seng. Import LD: Cameron Entertainment. Import VCD: Mei Ah. 98 minutes.

The "official" sequel to Stephen Chiau's surprise hit **All for the Winner** (1990), this disjointed, infantile comedy is put together with such cartoonish zeal it remains fairly entertaining despite never really being genuinely funny. Eric Kot takes over the lead role this time, playing Got (short for "God Bless You"), Uncle Tat's latest supernatural discovery. Bringing Got over from China, Tat plans on entering him in The World Gambling Competition, where the boy will use his mental powers against reigning champion Ray Thai, the Gambling Saint of Macau. As Thai's underhanded dealings with Japanese mobsters have him under the scrutiny of Interpol agent Lone Seven (the brother of Lung Ng, the God of Gamblers' bodyguard), he plans on using Got as a decoy, thus taking the spotlight off of him. After winning their respective elimination rounds, Got and Thai face off for the championship.

A less gifted comedian than Stephen Chiau, Kot relies largely on energy to sell the weak material, but a good portion of his jokes involve local products and personalities that will not mean much to Western viewers, and the hit and miss ratio for the other humor is quite low. While this film suggested that Wong had finally run out of ideas, he managed to revitalize the gambling formula the following year with the surprisingly entertaining **God of Gamblers 3: The Early Stage**.

858. Satan Returns

(1996; Upland Film Corporate) ★: 4/10. *666 moh gwai fuk woot* (Cantonese), *666 mo gui fu huo* (Mandarin): "666: Satan Reborn." Cinematographer: Cheng Siu-keung; Art Director: Raymond Kwok Siu-keung; Music: Tommy Wai Kai-leung; Writer: Wong Jing; Producers: Yang Teng-kuei, Wong Jing; Action Director: Donnie Yen Chi-tan; Director: Lam Wai-lun (billed as "Ah Lun"). Cast: Chingmy Yau Suk-ching (Chan Shou-ching), Donnie Yen Chi-tan (Mo Ti-nam), Francis Ng Chun-yu (Judas), Dayo Wong Chi-wah (Ka-ming), Yuen King-tan (Rose), Spencer Lam Sheung-yee (The Reverend). 1.85:1. VHS/LD: World Video. Import LD/VCD: Mei Ah. 95 minutes.

This hackneyed thriller finds HK under seige by Judas, a Satanic serial killer who is kidnapping women born on 6/6/69. He then cuts out their hearts, a test to determine if they are the daughter of the devil. As she attended missionary school as a child, internal affairs policewoman Chan Sau-ching is chosen to join with the brutal officer Mo in his investigation of the killings, despite the fact that she is investigating Mo to determine if he is psychologically fit for duty (just one of many lapses in logic here). Judas begins to stalk Sau-ching, and, amid laughably overproduced visuals, there are torrents of blood, "double" nightmares, an exploding vending machine, an autopsy patient springing to life on the morgue table, and all manner of other supernaturally-induced mayhem.

One character makes reference to **The Silence of the Lambs** and **Se7en**, but there is the proverbial snowball's chance in Hell that **Satan Returns** will ever be held in the same regard as those Hollywood thrillers. In fact, it barely even rates as schlock entertainment, tendering one tired genre cliche after another as if they were the height of innovation. Dayo Wong provides ineffectual comic relief as one of the stupidest cops in the history of HK cinema, while Spencer Lam essentially reprises his priest character from the **Young and Dangerous** films.

859. Satin Steel

(1994; Mandarin Films/Ko Chi Sum Films) ★: 3/10. *Chung kam juk* (Cantonese), *Chong jin shu* (Mandarin): "Heavy Metal." Cinematographer: Sander Lee Kar-ko; Music: Anthony Lee Hon-kam; Writers: Roman Cheung Siu-lun, Vincent Kok Tak-chiu; Producers: Clifton Ko Chi-sum, Ronny Yu Yan-tai; Action Director-Director: Tony Leung Siu-hung. Cast: Jade Leung Ching (Jade Leung), Anita Lee Yuen-wah (Ellen Cheng), Russell Wong (Ken), Kenneth Chan Kai-tai (John Paul Belmondo). 1.85:1. VHS: Tai Seng. Import LD/VCD: Universe. 85 minutes.

Shot in Singapore and Indonesia, this brainless actioner stars Jade Leung as a like-named police officer with suicidal tendencies, clearly patterned after Mel Gibson's character in **Lethal Weapon**. She is sent to Singapore as part of a joint HK police/FBI operation to nab a gang of arms dealers. Paired up with fellow policewoman Ellen (who is tougher than she looks), Jade tracks the suspects to Indonesia, where she successfully solicits help from Ken, the head villain's lawyer. Dodging everything from bullets to seemingly indestructible native henchmen, Jade and Ellen trudge through the jungle to bust up their quarry's latest transaction.

The script (co-authored by the usually reliable Vincent Kok) strives for the heavy action/lightweight fun appeal of a live action comic book, but an overabundance of lame comedy, frivolous characters, ridiculous asides (one of the bad guys inexplicably has a *bionic hand*), and slipshod editing sink the production. A few impressive stunts (including Leung hanging from a helicopter) and some nice locations are all there is to be had in this self-consciously shoddy effort.

860. Saviour of the Soul

(1991; Team Work Production House) ★: 6/10. *'91 san diu hap lui* (Cantonese), *'91 shen diao xia lu* (Mandarin): "'91: The Mystical Condor Hero and His Companion." Cinematographer: Peter Pau Tak-hei; Art Director: Hai Chung-man; Music: Anthony Lun Wing-leung; Writer: Jeff Lau Chun-wai; Producers: Chan Pui-wah, David Lai Tai-wai; Action Director: Yuen Tak; Directors: David Lai Tai-wai, Corey Yuen Kwai. Cast: Andy Lau Tak-wah (Ching-lan), Anita Mui Yim-fong (May-chun), Aaron Kwok Fu-shing (Silver Fox), Gloria Yip Wan-yee (Hwa-shang), Carina Lau Kar-ling (Pet Lady), Kenny Bee (Koo), Henry Fong Ping (Fox's Master). Dolby Stereo (Laserdisc and DVD). 1.85:1. VHS: Tai Seng. Import LD/VCD/DVD: Universe. 93 minutes.

This flashy, in-name-only adaptation of Jin Yong's period novel ***San diu hap lui*** ("God Eagle Hero Couple") boasts eye candy visuals reminiscent of futuristic *manga*. However, if the design reveals a Japanese inspiration, the execution is distinctly Chinese and offers a rare foray in HK science fiction. In an unspecified future, a powerful assassin named Silver Fox targets law enforcer May-chun to avenge her blinding of his master. His first attempt on her life results in the death of May-chun's subordinate, Koo, but May-chun is able to save herself by gouging out one of Fox's eyes. May-chun then goes into hiding for a year, leaving her other assistant, Ching-lan, to care for Koo's younger sister, Hwa-shang. Seeking to find May-chun, the love-lorn Ching-lan accidentally arouses the ire of the powerful "Pet Lady," after forcing his way into her all-female stronghold. Eventually discovering May-chun's whereabouts, Ching-lan must come to her rescue when she is attacked and poisoned by Silver Fox. Desperate to save her, he takes his dying love to the Pet Lady for a cure but is rebuked, even after obeying the Lady's command to crawl across broken glass. Returning home, the pair are again attacked by Silver Fox, who uses his power over the ailing May-chun to turn her against Ching-lan.

Co-directed by Corey Yuen Kwai (**Fong Sai Yuk I & II**) and David Lai Tai-wai (**Operation Scorpio**), **Saviour of the Soul** has developed a cult following for its sensational action sequences, which feature wild futuristic weapons like "The Breathless Bullet," a projectile that sucks all the atmosphere out of rooms (an effect accomplished by having all the color drain out of the image). There are also a number of interesting and bizarre FX sequences, the most memorable of which is Fox's "Terrible Angel" spell. After filling his body with poison, he flings himself right *through* his victims, leaving the toxins behind in their bodies. The storyline is less satisfying, sagging in the middle and lacking clear transitions (largely the fault of the dreadful subtitles). Some of the comedy is rather broad (which can no doubt be attributed to writer Jeff Lau, who specializes in that sort of humor), especially sequences involving May-chun's twin sister, who is also played by Mui and dubbed by a male actor using a fey voice. Additionally, some of the film's sentiments will seem rather sappy to Western viewers. Still, the mix of fantasy, science fiction, and horror elements is consistently intriguing, and there is no faulting the film's technical achievements. The cinematography by Peter Pau delivers consistently dazzling imagery, and there is an arresting score by Anthony Lun. Kwok would go on to play Silver Fox one more time (for comedic effect) during the climax of **Millionaire Cop** (1993). Don't bother with the unrelated **Saviour of the Soul II** (1992), which plays far too broad and loose and lacks the necessary imagination and thrills to compensate.

861. Saviour of the Soul II

(1992; Team Work Production House) ★: 4/10. *92 san diu chi chi sam ching cheung gim* (Cantonese), *92 shen diao zhi chi xin qing chang jian* (Mandarin): "'92 The Mystical Condor Hero and His Companion: Crazy Heart Enduring Love Sword." Cinematographers: Lee Tak-wai, Tom Lau Moon-tong, Jimmy Leung Chi-ming; Art Director: Raymond Lee King-man; Music: To Chi-chi; Writers: Yip Kwong-kim, John Chan Kin-chung; Producer: Chan Pui-wah; Action Director: Yuen Tak; Directors: Corey Yuen Kwai, David Lai Tai-wai. Cast: Andy Lau Tak-wah (Ching-yan), Rosamund Kwan Chi-lam (The Ice Woman), Richard Ng Yiu-hon (The Devil King), Corey Yuen Kwai (Doc). 1.85:1. VHS: Tai Seng. Import LD/VCD: Universe. 92 minutes.

A disappointing follow-up, **Saviour of the Soul II** bears no direct connection to its forerunner but magnifies its worst qualities: namely, an overabundance of puerile humor and scattershot plotting. Ching-yan, Tim, and Doc are adventurers searching for the mythical Snowy Mountain. Ching-yan has dreamt of the place for years and these dreams always show him falling for the beautiful Ice Woman who resides on the mountain. The trio travel to an alternate world at the bottom of the sea (which looks like an old western movie set), where they must evade a lovelorn female casino owner infatuated with Ching-yan. The men discover a block of the mythical "Virgin Ice," which can engender eternal life through its "Essence Air." Their lives are then threatened by the monstrous Devil King, who seeks immortality for himself, but they have a powerful ally in the form of the Ice Woman.

While most viewers will find the humor unbearably juvenile, the action is appropriately boisterous and the production makes excellent use of frozen Canadian locales. On the meager plus side, some of the comedic devices are fun (particularly the super magnifying glass that enlarges objects for real) and the special effects have a surreal, demented brilliance to them (particularly Richard Ng's omnivorous devil and his harpy-like minions).

862. Scarred Memory

(1996; Media Asia Group/Media Asia Film Partners I) ★: 3/10. *Biu gip king ching* (Cantonese), *Bao jie qing qing* (Mandarin): "Sudden Disaster: Outpouring of Love." Cinematographer: Tony Miu Kin-fai; Art Director: Ken Chiu Kin-san; Music: Anthony Lee Hon-kam, Marco Wan Ho-kit; Writers: Ray Leung Kar-hei, Wong Sa-fei, Au Kin-cheung, Hsu Jen-to; Producer: Ma Fung-kwok; Action Director: Benz Kong To-hoi; Director: Ray Leung Kar-hei. Cast: Veronica Yip Yuk-hing (Ivy Yip), Simon Yam Tat-wah (Lee Yuen-lung), Fari-ni Cheung Yui-ling (Cat), Almen Wong Pui-ha (Flora). VHS: Tai Seng. Import LD/VCD: Mei Ah. 90 minutes.

This romantic thriller aspires to be something more than a run-of-the-mill production but, laudable ambitions aside, it fails pretty miserably. Doctor Ivy Yip is attacked and raped one evening by an assailant whose face she could not see. The experience causes her relationship to collapse and also begins to affect her performance on the job. She becomes obsessed with the case of Lee Yuen-lung, a Wanchai triad boss who suffered a severe head injury that has reduced his mental capacity to the level of a child. Ivy was the doctor-in-charge when he was brought in and hesitated during his initial emergency treatment, so she feels responsible for his current state. Leaving her job, Ivy relocates to Macau and encounters Lee there one day. While better than before, the man still possesses limited faculties and Ivy resolves to help him. Under the doctor's care, Lee gradually improves, and when she leaves for HK, he follows her there. However, the triad's criminal past comes back to haunt them both.

Never more than moderately interesting, **Scarred Memory** is further burdened by aggressively showy cinematography and editing that do nothing to heighten the drama they are supporting and are merely tiresome distractions. The identity of Ivy's attacker is never in the least bit of doubt and the final reel is simply ludicrous. Cinematographer Peter Ngor Chi-kwan has a supporting role.

School Commandos *see* **Truant Heroes**

863. School on Fire

(1988; Cinema City Co.) ★: 8/10. *Hok gaau fung wan* (Cantonese), *Xiao jiao feng yun* (Mandarin): "School Turbulence." Cinematographer: Joe Chan Kong-hung; Art Director: Luk Chi-fung; Music: Lowell Lo Kwun-ting; Writer: Nam Yin; Producer: Karl Maka; Action Directors: Chu Kai-sang, Lau Chi-ho; Director: Ringo Lam Ling-tung. Cast: Fennie Yuen Kit-ying (Chu Yuen-fong), Sarah Lee Lai-yui (Kwok Siu-chun), Roy Cheung Yiu-yeung (Brother Smart), Damian Lau Chung-yan (Wan), Lam Ching-ying (Hoi), Tommy Wong Kwong-leung (Chuen-ngor), Victor Hon Kwan (Chu Man-hung), William Ho Kar-kui (Brother Happy), Ng Chi-hung (Tin-chiu). 1.85:1. VHS: Tai Seng. Import LD: Golden Cinema City. Import VCD: Mega Star. 101 minutes.

This triad thriller is brutal and intense even by director Ringo Lam's standards. From its opening shot of the school (situated right next to an airstrip!), it is clear that this is one troubled institution. Triad gangs openly recruit and extort protection money from the students, most of whom regard their teachers as little more than objects of ridicule. The police, meanwhile, seem unable to control or protect anyone. Kwok Siu-chun and Chu Yuen-fong are schoolgirls from dysfunctional families who are dating triads from their age group. When Yuen-fong witnesses a murder, she is warned by triad boss Smart not to identify the guilty party. Listening to the advice of her teacher Mr. Wan, Yuen-fong decides to help the police. She is then humiliated by Smart and his men and ordered to come up with $30,000 as a penalty. Siu-chun helps her friend raise money by working as a prostitute, but the girl's temper, poor grades, and drug use lead to her downfall. Succumbing to the pressures of her life, Yuen-fong gets high and torches the school library. Although the school does not press charges, her actions still have disastrous consequences.

The film paints an incredibly bleak picture of the HK school system, and this turns out to be both its weakness *and* its strength. The storyline incorporates so many grim and violent events into such a short time frame, its plausibility can be questioned in some respects. On the other hand, this compact structure also allows Lam to craft one of the most intense and unrelenting films of his career; the climax borders on hair-raising. He also manages to coax uniformly excellent performances out of his cast. Sarah Lee (who won the year's Best Supporting Actress award) and Fennie Yuen are both very good, and Roy Cheung gives what might be termed his definitive "evil triad" performance. Damian Lau is also noteworthy as Wan, a man so frustrated by his inability to get through to his students because of a few triad troublemakers and his boss' unwillingness to help him that it all but drives him over the edge. The film ran into substantial problems with censors in both HK and Taiwan, and while the cuts are only noticeable on a handful of occasions in the HK version, the Taiwanese edition reportedly runs only about one hour and is missing all of the sequences in the school!

864. S.D.U.: Mission in Mission

[*sic*] (1994; Long Shong Pictures/Rising Sun Pictures) ★: 5/10. *Fei foo hung bye chi gik do chin si* (Cantonese), *Fei hu xiong shi zhi ji dao zhan shi* (Mandarin): "Flying Tiger Heroic Master: Extreme Warrior." Cinematographer: Chan Tung-

chuen; Music: Anthony Lee Hon-kam, Marco Wan Ho-kit; Writers: Dick Cho Kin-nam, Power Lee King-chu; Producer: Wong Ying-hung; Action Director-Director: Power Lee King-chu. Cast: Chan Kwok-bong (Bond), Peter Yung Kam-cheung (Cheung), Vincent Wan Yeung-ming (Chung-bing), Michael To Tai-yu (Yuk Fai), Kent Cheng Chuk-see (Chin), Jay Lau Kam-ling (May), Peter Chan Lung (Officer Cheung), Bobby Yip King-sang (Coconut). 1.85:1. VHS: World Video. Import LD/VCD: Universe. 92 minutes.

A quickie knockoff of **The Final Option**, this production even goes so far as to use two of that film's stars, Chan Kwok-bong and Peter Yung. A group of SDU candidates undergo a rigorous training regimen in order to earn a spot in the squad. Midway through the course, the men are ordered to help save hostages being held in a school, but some casualties ensue. When one of the criminals is assassinated in a police van by a sniper, it is suspected that the execution was carried out by a SDU member. On the squad's next assignment, an unseen shooter eliminates all of the culprits they manage to capture alive. The team leader begins to suspect that an old friend (who has never gotten over the way in which his brother was murdered in cold blood by robbers) is behind the vigilante-style executions.

The action sequences are diverting but a good portion of the running time is devoted to the commander's private life (which isn't all that interesting), and the identity of the killer is obvious almost from the moment he appears onscreen.

865. S.D.U. '97

(1997; Sharp Production) ★: 2/10. *Dak jung fei foo* (Cantonese), *Te zhong fei hu* (Mandarin): "Exceptional Flying Tigers." Cinematographer: Cheung King-nin; Art Director: Angelo Bernardo Castilho; Music: Not Original; Writer: Ricky Ng Kwok-shing; Producers: Victor Yeung Kar-on, Robin Yeung Kar-wah; Action Directors: Cho Wing, Wong Ming-kin, Wong Chor-wah; Director: Cho Wing. Cast: Jimmy Wong Kar-lok (Wong Kar-lok), Hilary Tsui Ho-ying (Mandy), Joe Junior (Godfather), Yu Rongguang (Yu), Law Kar-ying (Wong Yan-kwai). 1.85:1. VHS: Tai Seng. Import LD/VCD/DVD: New City. 89 minutes.

When his Mainland-trained commander orders him to fire, injuring a civilian during a hostage-taking incident, SDU officer Wong Kar-lok is unfairly disciplined by a police tribunal. In response, he quits the force and accepts a $500,000 offer from a HK millionaire to rescue the man's daughter, who was kidnapped in The Philippines. In Manila, Wong and some allies locate the hostage but are outnumbered and unable to get her to safety. Acquiring better weapons, the team takes another shot while time quickly runs out for the captive.

This is very cheap and very dull (a bad combination), and an inauspicious directorial debut for veteran stuntman/action coordinator Cho Wing. In what is unquestionably the worst scene, gunshot victim Joe Junior sings "I Just Called to Say I Love You" as he (slowly) expires, with the song then reprised in full over his wake!

866. Sea Root

(1995; Art Concept International) ★: 7/10. *Hoi gan* (Cantonese), *Hai gen* (Mandarin): "Sea Root." Cinematographer: Mark Lee Ping-bing; Art Director: Jessy Lam Chak-chi; Music: Chin Kin-tak, Lee Shun-ming, Ng Kwok-yan; Writer: Raymond To Kwok-wai; Producers: Michel Mak Shun-ming, Katie Chan Fuk-sun; Direction: The Art Concept Creative Group. Cast: Lau Ching-wan (Sea Root), Alice Lau Ar-lai (Lotus), Woo Fung (Father Fok), Yip Chun, Lee Fung. 1.85:1. VHS: Tai Seng. Import LD/VCD: Mei Ah. 96 minutes.

Opening with clips from vintage HK romantic dramas, this pleasant, low-key effort concerns the poor Tang family who live aboard their fishing vessel (which causes them to be referred to as "Boat People"). When one son decides to go to the city and find work, the family decides to buy a female helper from China. They end up with flaky motormouth Lotus, who has no experience at this sort of thing and cannot do anything right to save her life. Although he is in love with a childhood acquaintance in Canada, eldest son Sea Root gradually begins taking a liking to Lotus, though she does nothing but take advantage of the withdrawn, stuttering man at first. The pair complement each other: Lotus helps Root come out of his shell, while the attention he pays to her helps Lotus overcome the sadness she experiences upon learning that her old love (who came to HK earlier) has married someone else.

Alice Lau and Lau Ching-wan are both charming, and their appealing performances help one to forget the more trite aspects of the story.

867. Sea Wolves

(1991; D & B Films Co.) ★: 5/10. *Hoi long* (Cantonese), *Hai lang* (Mandarin): "Sea Wolves." Cinematographer: Ko Chiu-lam; Art Director: Ken Yip Kwok-kin; Music: Jonathan Wong Bong-yin; Writer: Leung Hung-wah; Producer: Stephen Shin Kei-yin; Action Director: Phillip Kwok Tsui; Director: Cheng Siu-keung. Cast: Cynthia Yang Li-ching (Inspector Yeung), Simon Yam Tat-wah (John Lam), Gary Chow King-yeung (Gary), Norman Tsui Siu-keung (Keung), Phillip Kwok Tsui (Chui), Eddie Maher (Smuggler), Tai Po (Inspector Song). 1.85:1. VHS: Tai Seng. Import LD/VCD: Universe. 90 minutes.

This run-of-the-mill D & B actioner concerns the efforts of some smugglers to get their vessel and its cargo past HK customs officers by hiding drugs in oil barrels with false bottoms. Before their ship reaches its destination, they run across a boat filled with Vietnamese refugees, one of whom is a friend of crew member John Lam. John's reunion with buddy Gary is short lived, however, as his partners proceed to brutally slaughter the Vietnamese. In the ensuing carnage, Gary is bashed on the head and knocked unconscious. John hides his friend (who has developed amnesia) in the ship's cargo hold, telling him that he is a wanted murderer who must stay out of sight. When the vessel reaches port, Gary is noticed by the inspectors and escapes, but the crew is not allowed to remove their cargo until the illegal immigrant is captured. When John's brother is murdered by the frustrated smugglers (who must deliver the contraband within a certain time period or lose their deal), he and Gary team up with female supercop Yeung to put the killers behind bars.

Compared to other entries in the company's exploitation line, the plotting here is a bit more intricate, but neither the characters nor the action setpieces are particularly interesting.

868. Secret Signs

(1993; Fu Ngai Film Production Co.) ★: 2/10. *Jing yan* (Cantonese), *Zheng ren* (Mandarin): "Corrupted Witness." Cinematographers: Abdul M. Rumjahn, Ko Chiu-lam; Art Director: Ringo Cheung Sek-wah; Music: Joseph Yip Kai-tat, Jim Knettle; Writers: Irene Au Lim-chi, Kit Man; Producer: Jim Choi Chi-ming; Action Director: Stephen Tung Wai; Director: Dick Cho Kin-nam. Cast: Max Mok Siu-chung (Yung Wing-kam), Gigi Lai Chi (Jackie), Lam Wai-hung, Lo Kin, Hon Chun. 1.85:1. VHS: Tai Seng. Import LD/VCD: Mei Ah. 96 minutes.

This film opens with an introductory crawl about the worldwide publicity resulting from the HK celebrity protest on January 5th, 1992 against triad involvement in the local film industry. While certainly an unusual beginning for a gangster thriller, it is an appropriate one, as this picture's producer, Jim Choi, himself a triad, was murdered by underworld assassins outside of his production company office on April 16, 1992. It is not clear how far along in production **Secret Signs** was at that point, but the final result certainly has all the earmarks of an unfinished project desperately padded out to feature length by investors hoping to get some kind of return on their money. After the aforementioned crawl and fifteen minutes of highly dubious documentary footage detailing the extent of Chinese gang crime in America, Australia, England, and The Netherlands, a story finally emerges. Illegal immigrant Yung Wing-kam joins a triad society and quickly demonstrates his superior combat skills during a knife fight. After helping his boss dispose of a rival gang leader and a corrupt cop, Yung meets pretty boutique owner Jackie and the two fall in love. However, vengeance-seeking hitmen and a vigilant police department (out to force Yung to testify against his boss) threaten the couple's happiness.

Routine in every department, it is doubtful that this would have been of much interest even if it had been made under normal circumstances. As it stands, **Secret Signs** is strictly for triad movie completists, and even they will be put off by how utterly lifeless it is. There is one unforgettable moment, however: Drugged by police, Yung imagines himself under attack from a band of cartoonish ghosts! Gigi Lai fans should note that the actress does not appear until almost an hour into the movie.

869. Security Unlimited

(1981; Golden Harvest) ★: 7/10. *Moh dang bo biu* (Cantonese), *Mo deng bao biao* (Mandarin): "Modern Bodyguards." Cinematographer: Tom Lau Moon-tong; Art Director: David Chan Chi-wai; Music: Sam Hui Koon-kit; Writers: Michael Hui Koon-man , Sam Hui Koon-kit; Producer: Raymond Chow Man-wai; Director: Michael Hui Koon-man. Cast: Michael Hui Koon-man (Chou Sai-cheong), Sam Hui Koon-kit (Sam), Ricky Hui Koon-ying (Bruce Tang), Stanley Fung Shui-fan (Fan), Lee Hoi-sang (Armored Car Robber). Dolby Digital (DVD only). 2.35:1. VHS: Tai Seng (No Subtitles). Import VCD: Mega Star (Poor Subtitles). Import DVD: Universe. 87 minutes.

One of the Hui Brothers most popular outings, **Security Unlimited** casts Michael as the incompetent captain of Wong's Security, who is known to his men as "The Crab" because he walks like Charles Bronson! Charged with training the company's recruits, he instructs them in all manner of bizarre and potentially fatal methods of enforcing the law and defending themselves from perpetrators. Sam and Ricky are two of his favorite whipping boys, but the tables are turned when Sam apprehends a bank robber and becomes Michael's superior.

As with most of the brothers' comedies, there is not much in the way of story and the gags are hit and miss, but even in the sequences that don't completely work, there are always one or two instances of physical comedy that generate a chuckle. Highlights include Michael trying to eat with broken arms while Ricky sneaks food to some illegal immigrants hidden under the table; Ricky imagining himself as Superman; the boys guarding the body of a dead millionaire whose $2 million platinum kidneys(!) are sought by a gang of thieves; and the climax, in which Michael and Sam must deal with a gang of robbers out to loot a display of priceless antiques from a skyscraper. Bill Tung Biu has a cameo as a befuddled racetrack announcer. Following this film, Sam left the team and signed on at Cinema City; the three brothers would not appear together again until 1990's **Front Page**.

870. Seeding of a Ghost

(1983; Shaw Brothers) ★: 6/10. *Chung gwai* (Cantonese), *Zhong gui* (Mandarin): "Seed Ghost." Writers: Wong Kam-ba, Lam Yee-hung; Producer: Mona Fong Yat-wah; Director: Yeung Kuen. Cast: Phillip Ko Fei (Chau), Norman Tsui Siu-keung (Anthony Fang Ming), Wong Yung, Yuen Chi-wai, Chuan Chi-hui. 2.35:1. VHS: World Video (Poor Subtitles). Import LD: Ocean Shores (Poor Subtitles). 90 minutes.

A dark and amusingly gruesome horror tale, this opens with cab driver Chau accidentally running down a mysterious old man. After getting out to check on the victim and finding nothing, Chau returns to find the man sitting, unharmed, in the back seat. The unearthly passenger is a wizard who warns the cabbie that tragedy lays ahead for him. Meanwhile, handsome philanderer Anthony Fang Ming is fooling around with Chau's wife, beautiful casino dealer Irene, but balks at her insistence that he divorce his spouse. The two argue and Fang abandons the girl in the countryside. Chased by a pair of hoods out to rape her, Irene runs into a dilapidated mansion and, during a scuffle, falls to her death. Anxious for vengeance, Chau enlists the aid of the wizard, and Irene's attackers are soon suffering the supernatural consequences. A special fate is reserved for Fang: His wife becomes possessed and impregnated with something ... not human.

The first half sets up the plot and then mixes in dollops of full frontal nudity and softcore sex before turning into an offshoot of the Shaws' infamous **Black Magic** films from the 1970s. There are plenty of crude but enthusiastically applied splatter FX, a victim vomiting up worms, elements of necrophilia, a toothy tentacled creature inspired by the monster from **Alien** (there is also a musical cue swiped from that film), and a wild climax set at a mahjong party. *Seeding of a Ghost* is an obvious must for fans of Eastern horror and those who enjoy HK cinema for its excesses.

Semi-Gods and Semi-Devils *see* **Dragon Chronicles: The Maidens of Heavenly Mountain**

871. Sentenced to Hang

(1989; Golden Harvest/Johnny Mak Production) ★: 7/10. *Saam long kei on* (Cantonese), *San lang qi an* (Mandarin): "Strange Case of the Three Wolves." Cinematographer: Herman Yau Lai-to; Art Director: Lau Sai-wan; Music: Joseph Chan Wing-leung; Writers: Stephen Siu Yeuk-yuen, Johnny Mak Dong-hung; Producer: Stephen Siu Yeuk-yuen; Director: Taylor Wong Tai-loi. Cast: Tony Leung Kar-fai (Li Wai), Kent Cheng Chuk-see (Ma Yee-charn), Elvis Tsui Kam-kong (Tang Chi-king), Tien Feng (Wong Kam-shek), Carrie Ng Kar-lai (Lai), Yung Sai-kit (Kau). 1.85:1. VHS: Tai Seng (No Subtitles). Import LD: Star Entertainment (No Subtitles). Import VCD: Mega Star. 105 minutes.

One of the first films to receive the adults-only Category III rating (though it would likely only receive IIB now), **Sentenced to Hang** is based on a real-life kidnapping and murder case and is the most accomplished effort to date by director Taylor Wong (**Tragic Hero**). Tired of the petty abuse continually heaped upon him by Wong (his rich, tyrannical boss), Wai and his friends kidnap the man's equally obnoxious son. They intend to demand a $2 million ransom but accidentally kill their captive. They proceed with their plan anyway and mail the dead man's ear, but Wong refuses to pay a cent. Next, they kidnap the old man himself and are able to collect money from his family. However, they commit the cardinal sin of men in this situation: They spend the cash openly and are soon threatened with blackmail by an associate.

While the ending is more or less a foregone conclusion and the final reel is a bit drawn out, this is a worthwhile thriller that offers up some potent suspense in its second act. The acting is effective all around, with Cheng, as the reluctant member of the trio, giving the standout performance. As with most of Johnny Mak's productions, the authority figures are depicted in a less than complimentary fashion, with the criminals and their plight far more likely to gain audience approval and sympathy. The Chinese title refers to the wolf masks the men wear to hide their identities.

872. A Serious Shock! Yes Madam!

(1992; New Treasurer Films Co.) ★: 2/10. *Moot lo kong fa* (Cantonese), *Mo lu kuang hua* (Mandarin): "Cornered Wild Flower." Cinematographer: Lee Yao-tong; Art Director: Chung Fat; Music: Not Original; Writer: Chan Bo-wai; Producer: Chung Wai-sing; Action Director: Fung Hark-on; Director: Lai Kin-kwok. Cast: Moon Lee Choi-fung (May), Cynthia Yang Li-ching (Hsie Wan-chin), Yukari Oshima (Coco), Waise Lee Chi-hung (Brother Boy), Wong Chi-yeung (Kent Chiang Siu-chi), Lawrence Ng Kai-wah (Wilson Tsiang), Ku Feng (Wang), Eric Tsang Chi-wai (Wan-chin's Foster Father), Fung Hark-on ("Possessed" Man). 1.85:1. Import LD: Universe. 98 minutes.

This girls-with-guns actioner may well be a serious shock for fans of Moon Lee, as the cute kung fu dynamo is cast against type as a ruthless villainess; other viewers will just be taken aback by the movie itself. Policewoman Hsie Wan-chin is preparing to marry fellow cop Wilson Tsiang. However, her best friend and fellow officer, May, has secretly been seeing Wilson and isn't prepared to accept that he no longer wants to continue with the affair. When she learns that Wilson plans on taking Wan-chin to England, May snaps completely and murders him. Working together with fellow policeman Kent, who has desired May for some time, May frames Wan-chin for the crime. The latter manages to flee the scene and is aided in her quest for revenge by flaky car thief Coco, whose involvement in Wan-chin's plight puts her life on the line as well.

While the premise is unique for this subgenre, it is hardly revolutionary and provides insufficient material for a feature film. Consequently, the running time is padded out with several odd digressions, including a bizarre flashback sequence that does nothing more than provide a bit of gratuitous nudity (the only reason this is rated Category III). Blithely illogical and poorly directed, this cheap effort has nothing to offer anyone who isn't infatuated with its female leads.

873. Seven Warriors

(1989; Maverick Films) ★: 5/10. *Chung yee kwan ying* (Cantonese), *Zhong yi qun ying* (Mandarin): "A Loyal and Faithful Group of Heroes." Cinematographer: Gary Ho Bo-yiu; Art Director: Oliver Wong Yui-man; Music: Lo Tai-yau, Richard Lo Sai-kit; Writer: Sammy Tsang Kan-cheung; Producers: Wang Ying-hsiang, John Sham Kin-fun, John Chan Koon-chung; Action Directors: Benz Kong To-hoi, Tony Poon Kin-kwan; Director: Terry Tong Kei-ming. Cast: Adam Cheng Siu-chau (Commander Chi), Tony Leung Chiu-wai (Wong Way-wu), Max Mok Siu-chung (Yung), Jacky Cheung Hok-yau (Ching), Ben Lam Kwok-bun (Mao), Wu Ma (Ghost), Shing Fui-on (Karl), Lo Lieh (Piu), Sammo Hung Kam-po (Hung), Phillip Kwok Tsui (Au), Shum Wai (King), Chen Jing (Hang), Fung Hark-on (Wolf). 1.85:1. VHS: Tai Seng (Poor Subtitles). Import LD/VCD: Ocean Shores (Poor Subtitles). 94 minutes. Also known as **Enforcers**.

The Seven Samurai HK-style: Threatened by a gang of well-armed thugs, a village enlists the aid of seven mercenaries (including a hawker, a blacksmith, a career soldier, and a drunken officer) to defend them. After training the inhabitants as best they can in various offensive and defensive skills, they prepare for the inevitable onslaught by an enemy of greatly superior numbers, led by the vicious Piu. When a cowardly man in the village betrays them, the warriors voluntarily leave, as part of a bargain with Piu, to preserve the lives of those they were hired to protect. However, when Piu's men rape and pillage the community in their absence, the seven return and fight to the last man.

Adam Cheng and Lo Lieh turn in solid performances as the opposing leaders, but nothing seems fresh here. American films like **The Magnificent Seven** and, to a lesser extent, **Battle Beyond the Stars**, were able to work within this outline but offer some new wrinkles via their settings and dramatic situations. **Seven Warriors** just feels like a retread, which is a shame, considering the calibre of the personnel involved. Those merely looking for action, and not context, will come away more satisfied. The stunts are not eye-popping but there are plenty of them, as well as a more than generous helping of gunplay and hand-to-hand combat.

874. The Seventh Curse

(1986; Golden Harvest/Paragon Films) ★: 8/10. *Yuen Chun-hup yue wai si lee* (Cantonese), *Yuan Zhenxia yu wei si li* (Mandarin): "Yuen Chun-hup and Wai Si-lee." Cinematographer: Lam Chiu; Art Director: Oliver Wong Yui-man; Music: Sing Kam-wing; Writers: Wong Jing, Yuen Kai-chi; Producer: Raymond Chow Man-wai; Action Director: Yuen Bun; Director: Nam Nai-choi. Cast: Chin Siu-ho (Dr. Yuan Chen-hsieh), Maggie Cheung Man-yuk (Tsai-hung), Chow Yun-fat (Wei), Sibelle Hu Hui-chung (Su), Dick Wei (Heh Lung), Tsui Sau-lai (Betsy), Elvis Tsui Kam-kong (Aquala, the Sorcerer), Ken Boyle (The Professor), Wong Jing (Would-be Playboy), Chor Yuen (Chu), Yasuaki Kurota (Captain Ho), Johnny Wang Lung-wei (Head Terrorist), Kara Hui Ying-hung (Inspector Chiang), Derek Yee Tung-sing (SDU Officer), Nina Li Chi (Party Guest). Dolby Digital (DVD only). 1.85:1. VHS: Tai Seng (Poor Subtitles). Import LD: Star Entertainment (No Subtitles). Import VCD: Mei Ah. Import DVD: Universe. 78 minutes.

If you are the type of person who enjoys HK cinema for its excesses, do not miss this incredible horror-action-gore-softcore hybrid, which is one of the wildest and most action-packed exploitation films from any territory. After aiding in the rescue of hostages held by a terrorist group, the dashing Dr. Yuan heads to Thailand to find a cure for a blood spell cast upon him one year earlier. Through flashbacks we see how Yuan encountered Betsy(!), a voluptuous girl from the neighboring "Worm Tribe," and intruded upon one of that clan's sacred rituals. Betsy was about to be sacrificed to "The Old Ancestor," a hyperactive, flesh-eating skeleton which transforms into a monstrous bat creature upon ingesting human tissue. For his punishment, local sorcerer Aquala poisoned Yuan, causing veins in his body to randomly burst. In spite of his condition, Yuan escaped and was saved by Betsy, who feeds him a chunk of breast tissue containing her personal "charm." This decidedly offbeat remedy has worked up until now, but twelve months later, the curse has begun manifesting itself again and Yuan will die when it finally reaches his heart. Aided by heroic tribesman Heh Lung and doggedly pursued by spoiled girl reporter Tsai-hung, Yuan strikes out to find a way to end his affliction. He also vows to save the local village's children, whom the sorcerer has kidnapped, using their blood to nourish "Little Ghost" (a vicious handpuppet thingie resembling a bug-eyed sperm cell), which likes to tear out its victims' spinal chords. Radioing for assistance from his esteemed colleague, witchcraft expert Dr. Wei, Yuan sets out to see whether black magic is a match for some good old fashioned heavy artillery.

In classic HK tradition, **The Seventh Curse** packs in more exploitable elements than ten comparable Western movies: gunplay, kung fu battles, **Raiders of the Lost Ark**-style adventure set-pieces, jungle warfare, torrents of blood, black magic spells, and enough grue and maggots to garner any gorehound's approval (as the sorcerer puts it, "The worms are highly prolific"). Add some clumsy subtitles ("Take my advice or I'll spank you without pants") and cameos by half of the actors on the Golden Harvest lot, and you have got a pretty amazing 78 minutes. Chin and Chow's characters are derived from a very popular series of science fiction novels by the prolific and talented writer Ngai Hong, who appears briefly as himself, introducing the story in Mandarin. Director Nam Nai-choi went on to helm **Erotic Ghost Story** and the even more excessive **Story of Ricky**.

875. Sex and the Emperor

(1994; Win's Entertainment) ★: 4/10. *Moon ching gam gung gei ngon* (Cantonese), *Man qing jin gong ji an* (Mandarin): "Manchurian Forbidden Hall Case." Cinematographer: Tony Miu Kin-fai; Art Director: Wong Kar-lung; Music: Marco Wan Ho-kit; Writer: Cheuk Bing; Producers: Wong Jing, Lee Siu-kei; Action Director: Chan Wai-to; Director: Sherman Wong Ching-wah. Cast: Yvonne Yung Hung (Guilian), Jimmy Wong Shu-kei (Li Lianying), Yung Sai-kit (Little On Dehai), Julie Lee Wah-yuet (Hongyi), Yuen King-tan ("Eight Semi-Devils"), Wong Yat-fei (The Emperor's Teacher). 1.85:1. VHS: Tai Seng. Import LD/VCD: Mei Ah. 92 minutes.

Another of Wong Jing's predictably sordid and repulsive period sex films that followed in the wake of the comparatively classy **Lover of the Last Empress**, this stars Yvonne Yung, who was also the main victim in **Chinese Torture Chamber Story**. During China's final dynasty, The Forbidden City was (if events here are to be believed) an unrivalled den of inequity, as eunuch Li Lianying (a real historical figure) soon discovers. Unlike his fellows, Li's parents bribed the castration master to remove only one of his testicles, leaving him sexually functional. While carrying on a secret affair with one of the young emperor's concubines, Li befriends the monarch, whose actions are being observed by the sinister head eunuch Little On. Of the literally thousands of women he has to choose from, the Emperor's favorite is chambermaid Guilian, but she is of too low a rank in society to be his Queen. Little On has Guilian expelled from the palace and, after torturing her unmercifully, sells the girl to a brothel. This launches the monarch on a sexual rampage that has disastrous consequences.

Like **Torture Chamber**, this is an unsavory mix of smarmy sex gags (on the level of **Porky's**) with the kind of sexual violence rarely encountered in Western cinema. While not as aggressively unpleasant as its companion piece, there is still much here that average viewers will find difficult to stomach, particularly as said sequences are photographed in a leering manner and lack a tenable sense of dark humor. There is also a depiction of various venereal diseases that looks like something out of an old army training film. One of the few enjoyable bits finds the whorehouse Madam (played by HK porn queen Julie Lee) demonstrating the "Eight Semi-Devil" sexual skills (which include stances like "Double Slut Foot" and "Super Sexual Pressure"), which provides a wild display of carnal kung fu!

876. Sex and Zen

(1991; Golden Harvest/Johnny Mak Productions) ★: 7/10. *Yuk po tuen chi tau ching biu gaam* (Cantonese), *Yu pui tsuan zhi tou qing bao jian* (Mandarin): "The Prayer Mat of Flesh: The Treasured Almanac of Secretive Affairs." Cinematographer: Peter Ngor Chi-kwan; Art Director: Raymond Lee King-man; Music: Joseph Chan Wing-leung; Writer: Lee Ying-kit; Producer: Stephen Siu Yeuk-yuen; Action Director: Tony Leung Siu-hung; Director: Michael Mak Dong-kit. Cast: Lawrence Ng Kai-wah (Mei Yeung-sheng), Kent Cheng Chuk-see (Doctor Tin Chan), Elvis Tsui Kam-kong (Wong Chut), Amy Yip Chi-mei (Huk-yeung/Chau-yin), Carrie Ng Kar-lai (Mistress Ku), Isabella Chow Wang (Shui Chu), Rena Murakami (Fa Sun), Lo Lieh (Chor Kun-lun), Tien Feng (Master Iron Doors). 1.85:1. VHS: Tai Seng, Indigo Media (Subtitled or Dubbed, R and unrated versions). Import LD/VCD/DVD: Universe (Two DVD versions). 93 minutes.

This Category III period sex fantasy was a major hit on its home turf and even garnered theatrical play in many Western specialty theatres. Based on an infamous 17th century novel (previously adapted in 1988 as **Yu Pui Tsuen**), it is the story of avaricious scholar Mei Yeung-sheng, whose sexual appetites far outweigh even those of his seemingly insatiable wife Chau-yin. Dissatisfied with the size of his small organ, Mei undergoes a riotous operation that leaves him with the penis of a horse! Eager to put his new member to the test, Mei seduces the abused wife of local shop owner Wong Chut. He then moves on to the beautiful, bisexual Shui Chu, whose cousin/lover does not take kindly to the fact that Chu is hiding Mei from her. Meanwhile, a revenge-minded Wong has taken up with Mei's wife, and the scholar's hedonistic ways eventually lead to his downfall.

A superior adult film, **Sex and Zen** is styled along the lines of the period fantasies being produced at the time and incorporates examples of humor that amuse through their sheer shock value (the horse organ transplant is only one example!). The story is pretty much non-existent, doing little more than setting up each sex scene, and the moralistic ending (which is probably true to the original work) doesn't exactly jibe with the filmmakers' campy approach to the material. The myriad couplings unfold amid lush, colorful surroundings, though much of the sex has elements of rape and/or S & M which, while tame by the standards of Asian pornography, may still offend some viewers. This is the only film to date in which local breast fetish queen Amy Yip exposes her nipples, something she reportedly did under triad coercion. Two sequels followed and a picturebook was released by Penthouse. Beware of Indigo Media's R-rated version, which is cut by 20 minutes!

877. Sex and Zen II

(1996; Golden Harvest/Jing's Production/Golden Movie International) ★: 6/10. *Yuk po tuen II yuk lui sam ging* (Cantonese), *Yu pui tsuan II yu nu xin jing* (Mandarin): "The Prayer Mat of Flesh II: Virgin Sutra of the Heart." Cinematographer: Cheung Man-bo; Art Director: Andrew Cheuk Man-yiu; Music: Music Sense Limited; Writer: Sai Moon-kin (pseudonym); Producer: Wong Jing; Action Director: Dion Lam Dik-on; Director: Chin Man-kei. Cast: Loletta Lee Lai-chun (Yiau), Hsu Chi (Mirage Lady/Siu-tsui), Elvis Tsui Kam-kong (Sai Moon-kin), Ben Ng Ngai-cheung (Ironman), Lok Tak-wah (Fa), Wong Yat-fei (Monk). 1.85:1. VHS: Tai Seng. Import LD/VCD: Mei Ah. 88 minutes.

Wong Jing produced this outrageous period sex fantasy, which won't disappoint fans of the Mak Brothers' 1991 cult favorite. While not a direct continuation of that film, this lower budget production (which outgrossed imported fare like **Ace Ventura: When Nature Calls**, **12 Monkeys**, and **Casino**) is certainly in the same vein. Former teen movie star-turned-Category III favorite Loletta Lee stars as Yiau, a chaste girl who is appalled by the non-stop sexual antics of her incredibly horny father (Elvis Tsui, the only cast member to return from part one), who practices the "Iron Dick" stance and uses his penis to smash watermelons and punch holes in boards. While Yiau is away attending school disguised as a boy (a send-up of Tsui Hark's **The Lovers**), the supernaturally gifted "Mirage Lady" appears in the province. Pursued by the demon fighter

Ironman, she engages a Taoist to change her form and adopts the name "Siu-tsui." She then marries into Yiau's family, quickly becoming the father's favorite sexual plaything. With him distracted, she is able to sleep with and kill every female member of the household, drawing life from their sexual outpourings. Siu-tsui later kills both the father and Ironman, then transforms into an incredible yin yang hybrid with a giant penis and a male/female voice. During the inevitable sexual encounter that follows, Yiau and the creature fight to bring each other to orgasm first because, as prophesied in the sacred text "The Secret of Virginity," the loser will be drained of all sexual energy and lifeforce.

As in his wacky **The Eternal Evil of Asia**, director Chin Man-kei thumbs his nose at good taste in an ingratiating "What, Me Worry?" fashion and largely avoids the sexual violence that cropped up in that film and Wong Jing's other Category III productions from the period. The sex is spirited and Lee and Hsu (who went on to become a major star in mainstream films) are certainly easy on the eyes. Oh, and yes, there is also a penis transplant and it's even more ridiculous than the horse penis from part one! The writer's credit is an obvious pseudonym, being the name of Elvis Tsui's character! As with the original, a hardcover picture book tie-in was released. In what may just be a publicity stunt, Lee complained that it included more explicit pictures of her than she had agreed to allow. It is certainly an odd charge, considering that her nude shots are all frame enlargements from the film. **Sex and Zen III** followed in 1998.

878. Sexy and Dangerous

(1996; Jing's Production/Golden Movies International) ★: 5/10. *Goo waak lui chi kuet chin gong woo* (Cantonese), *Gu huo nu zhi jue zhan jiang hu* (Mandarin): "Wise Girls Battling the Underworld Again." Cinematographer: Tony Miu Kin-fai; Art Director: Vincent Lam Wai-sam; Music: Wong Bong; Writers: Philip Kwok Wai-chung, Film Youth Scriptwriters' Group; Producer: Wong Jing; Action Director: Dion Lam Dik-on; Director: Billy Tang Hin-sing. Cast: Loletta Lee Lai-chun (Marble), Karen Mok Man-wai (Van), Mariane Chan Miu-ying (Fai Chick), Teresa Mak Kar-kei (Little Star), Francis Ng Chun-yu (George Wong), Ben Ng Ngai-cheung (Lurcher), Lily Chung Suk-wai (Aids), Maria Cordero (Fatty), Shing Fui-on (Brother Saur), Spencer Lam Sheung-yee ("Fly Head"), Mimi Chu Mi-mi (George's Mother), Wong Yat-fei (George's Father), Ng Chi-hung (Triad), Vincent Kok Tak-chiu (Hooker Client), Manfred Wong (Hooker Client), Johnny Wang Lung-wei (Uncle Ping), Bobby Yip King-sang (Ugly Triad). 1.85:1. VHS: Tai Seng. Import LD/VCD/DVD: Mei Ah. 91 minutes.

One of the more unusual **Young and Dangerous** ripoffs, this typical Wong Jing production benefits immensely from Francis Ng's marvellously entertaining performance as George, a cowardly but loveable would-be hood no one respects. Marble, Van, Fai Chick, and Little Star are triad tough girls (the *goo wak lui* of the Chinese title) operating on the streets and in the clubs of Causeway Bay. Marble loves handsome gang boss Brother One, for whom she spent a year in prison after taking the rap for gun possession. While inside, she becomes enemies with Aids, One's old girlfriend. Upon her release, Aids comes looking to settle her score with the girl, but Marble and her friends are saved by the quick thinking George, who is hopelessly infatuated with Marble. Teaming up with psychotic triad Lurcher, Aids sets traps for Marble's girls, while Lurcher has his own plans for One.

While the gender of the leads may be different, the formula is not, save for a bit more humor. Ng is a lot of fun, and Karen Mok is perfect as the female equivalent of Jordan Chan's "Chicken" character from the **Young and Dangerous** series. *Sexy and Dangerous* is passable fare and certainly one of director Billy Tang's better efforts to date.

879. Shadow Cop

(1993; New Treasurer Films Co.) ★: 4/10. *San taam gon sap lui* (Cantonese), *Shen tan gan shi lu* (Mandarin): "Mystical Detective Dry Wet Dressed." Cinematographer: Poon Tak-yip; Art Director: Lai Kin-kwok; Music: Johnny Yeung Kei-cheung; Writer: Ella Chan Bo-wah; Producers: Cheung Bo-wing, Chung Wai-sing; Action Director: Yuen Po; Director: Lai Kin-kwok. Cast: Carina Lau Kar-ling (Witty), Waise Lee Chi-hung (Chiu Chi-hsiong), Ben Lam Kwok-bun (Man Sin), Kenneth Tsang Kong (Chang), Angile Leung Wan-yui (The Medium), Chung Fat (Fat), Shing Fui-on (Maddie), Chen Kuan-tai (Tai), Gabriel Wong Yat-san (Taxi Driver), David Wu Tai-wai (2nd Ghost), Charlie Cho Cha-lei (Sleazeball). 1.85:1. VHS: Tai Seng. 91 minutes.

An unusually good cast gives this offbeat cop actioner a lift but not enough of one to counter its weaknesses. Narcotics cop Chiu is not having a good day. The morning after getting stoned on an undercover case, he wakes up to find hooker Witty in bed with him. Insisting that he was a client, she demands $2000 from him. When he can't pay, she handcuffs him to his door and storms off with his TV and VCR. That evening, on another undercover assignment, Witty waltzes in and blows his cover. Naturally, these two polar opposites attract, but just when the film is settling into that old familiar pattern, things take a striking turn: Chiu is killed while pursuing a drug runner and is framed for the disappearance of $10 million in cash. So now we have a rip-off of the Hollywood hit **Ghost**: Chiu can communicate with a friend of Witty and forces the woman (a bogus medium like Whoopi Goldberg's character) to help him and he can also move objects or people in moments of extreme anger.

While the change of direction in the second half helps to retain one's interest, the plagiarism and strained attempts at humor quickly relegate this to the scrap heap. The David Wu listed above is the actor/director, not the Taiwan-born star of **Full Throttle**.

880. Shanghai Blues

(1984; Film Workshop) ★: 8/10. *Seung hoi chi yau* (Cantonese), *Shang hai zhi ye* (Mandarin): "Shanghai Nights." Cinematographer: Peter Ngor Chi-kwan, Bill Wong Chung-po, David Chung Chi-man, Lau Hung-chuen; Art Director: Au Yeung Hing-yee; Music: James Wong Jim; Writers: John Chan Koon-chung, Raymond To Kwok-wai, Szeto Cheuk-hon; Producer-Director: Tsui Hark. Cast: Sylvia Chang Ai-chia (Shu-shu), Kenny Bee (Tung Kwok-man), Sally Yeh Chian-wen (Stool), Loletta Lee Lai-chun (Shu-shu's Assistant), Shing Fui-on (Dummy), Woo Fung (Club Manager), Ken Boyle (Rude Caucasian), Tsui Hark (Pedestrian Who Gets Soaked). 1.85:1. VHS: Tai Seng. Import LD: Golden Cinema City. 103 minutes.

Shanghai 1937: With the Japanese army poised to move in, singer Shu-shu and clown Tung Kwok-man meet briefly when they both seek shelter from falling bombs. Thanks to a power failure, the two are unable to get a good look at one another but, regardless, they pledge to meet again at that same spot when the war finally ends. The story then picks up ten years later with the arrival of Stool, an exceedingly clumsy girl who is soon robbed and ends up sharing Shu-shu's apartment. Residing above them is none other than Kwok-man, though, naturally, he and Shu-shu do not realize that they have met before. Thanks to both misunderstandings and accidental timing, Stool ends up in a beauty contest, Kwok-man sells one of the songs he has written, and the two women fall in love with the same man (guess who!).

Made in the spirit of vintage Hollywood screwball comedies and musicals, **Shanghai Blues** takes director Tsui Hark's gangster parody **All the Wrong Clues (...for the Right Solution)** to the next level by staging the charming shenanigans amid dazzling artificial vistas, gorgeous applications of color, and excellent period detail. Sylvia Chang and Sally Yeh give delightful performances (the latter boasts the facial expressions of a Warner Brothers cartoon character come to life), while Kenny Bee is equally appealing as the rather bumbling but upstanding male lead. Tsui stages the light-hearted chaos with impeccable comic timing, and the film just sails along, displaying more energy and congeniality than one usually finds in ten such efforts. This and the unrelated but even more wonderful **Peking Opera Blues** are the first two entries in a planned trilogy which, unfortunately, Tsui has yet to finish.

The Shanghai Encounter *see* **Shanghai Shanghai**

881. Shanghai Grand

(1996; Win's Entertainment/Film Workshop) ★: 4/10. *San seung hoi taan* (Cantonese), *Xin shang hai tan* (Mandarin): "New Shanghai Beach." Cinematographer: Poon Hang-sang; Art Director: Bruce Yu Kar-on; Music: William Woo Wai-lap; Writers: Sandy Shaw, Matt Chow Hoi-kwong, Poon Man-kit; Producer: Tsui Hark; Action Director: Stephen Tung Wai; Director: Poon Man-kit. Cast: Leslie Cheung Kwok-wing (Hui Man-keung), Andy Lau Tak-wah (Ting Lik), Ning Jing (Fung Ching-ching), Lau Shun (Uncle Lau), Wu Hsin-kuo (Fung King-yiu), Amanda Lee Wai-man (Laiman), Almen Wong Pui-ha (Female Assassin). 1.85:1. Dolby Stereo. VHS: Tai Seng. Import LD/VCD/DVD: Mei Ah. 95 minutes.

The Bund was the most memorable HK TV miniseries of the 1970s, captivating audiences and catapulting Chow Yun-fat to superstar status. The program is not available with English subtitles, but even so, it is a safe bet that this lavish but empty-headed theatrical remake would pale in comparison. This time out, Leslie Cheung has the Chow role, while Andy Lau essays the part originally played by Ray Lui Leung-wai. The story opens in the 1940s and unfolds in three parts, the first told from the point of view of Ding Lik, a sanitation man who dreams of respectability. He is well on the way to achieving that goal after saving the affluent Fung Ching-ching (daughter of powerful triad Fung King-yiu) from an attempted kidnapping. Ding befriends Taiwanese revolutionary Hui Man-keung, and together they eliminate a gangster out to take revenge on Ding for the latter's interference in the kidnapping plot. As a reward, Fung King-yiu grants Ding control over the dead man's territories. Ding then proceeds to romance Ching-ching but inadvertently catches her and Hui in a compromising position. The second part is told from Ching-ching's perspective and charts how she first met up with Hui and fell in love with him. The final third details how Hui's mission to avenge the death of some fellow rebels takes an unexpected turn that results in Ding wanting him dead.

The costumes and period re-creation are exceptional, but the film has been given a desaturated, sepia-toned look that, while aiming for the nostalgic, usually just devalues much of the work put into the production design. In contrast to many HK gangster sagas, there is far *too much* story here, the result of trying to cram a miniseries into a single feature, and the writing alternates between creaky melodrama (the love triangle) and genre cliches. (There is also a scene involving a giant rubber snake that is too ridiculous for words.) This also hardly seems like the sort of film that cries out for music video-style montages, yet they are used to elucidate important moments. Cheung and Lau acquit themselves well, but Mainland-born actress Ning Jing (**Red Firecracker, Green Firecracker**) is badly miscast, and even the formidable Wu Hsin-kuo (who barely looks old enough to be Ning's brother, let alone her father) fails to endow his gangster kingpin with the intensity he brings to his best performances. All in all, *Shanghai Grand* is a major disappointment.

882. Shanghai Heroic Story

(1992; Golden Power Productions) ★: 7/10. *Jing hung dei ji siu do wui* (Cantonese), *Ying xiong di zhi xiao dao hui* (Mandarin): "Hero's Turf: Dagger Club." Cinematographer: Shum Miu-wing; Art Director: Raymond Fung Yuen; Music: Mak Chun-hung; Writers: Nam Yin, Victor Hon Kwan, Candy Cheng; Producer: Nam Yin; Action Director: Lai Sing-kwong; Director: Chris Lee Kin-sang. Cast: Roy Cheung Yiu-yeung (Wong Tai-kwong), Damian Lau Chung-yan (Ngai Ting-yim), Nadia Chan Chung-ling (Wong Yuk-yu), Vincent Wan Yeung-ming (Lok Chi-hing), Yu Li (Nancy, aka Pearl), Victor Hon Kwan (King Kau-ling), William Ho Kar-kui (Lai Chi-ying), Lau Kar-wing (Lau), Manfred Wong (Lee). 1.85:1. Import LD/VCD/DVD: Ocean Shores. 96 minutes.

This handsome period actioner unfolds in the divided and crime-ridden Shanghai of WWII. Rising triad Wong Tai-kwong comes to Shanghai with the intention of buying back his lover, Nancy, from high-ranking mobster Ngai Ting-yim. Wong's courage and fighting prowess come to Ngai's attention and the two strike a deal: Wong will take care of Ngai's enemy and, if he lives, he can then take Nancy with him. Wong succeeds and Nancy is released from Ngai's control, prompting the two crime bosses to form an allegiance. Along the way, Wong has become tangentially involved with The Daggers and their fight to oppose the Japanese. On the day that the Daggers make a failed attempt to eliminate Ngai (now in league with the Japanese), Wong is betrayed by him, prompting Wong to join forces with the rebels for a second assault on their common enemy.

Little has been written about **Shanghai Heroic Story**, which is a shame, because it is definitely one of the better films of its type. The costumes and production design are first rate, the action scenes are invigorating, and the performers are laudable (in particular, Nadia Chan, who gives an engaging turn as Wong's tomboy sister). The main themes of loyalty and bonding between men of opposing views is not new, but solid work on both sides of the camera help to lend them new credence.

Shanghai Killer *see* **Goodbye, My Friend**

883. Shanghai 1920

(Fu Ngai Films; 1991) ★: 5/10. *Seung hoi 1920* (Cantonese), *Shang hai 1920* (Mandarin): "Shanghai 1920." Cinematographers: Walter Gregg, Joe Chan Kong-hung; Art Directors: Mok Kwan-kit, Ringo Cheung Sek-wah, Sin Ngai-lung; Music: Cho To-lung; Writers: Timothy R. Long, Michael Laughlin; Producer: Jim Choi Chi-ming; Action Director: Chris Lee Kin-sang; Director: Leung Po-chi. Cast: John Lone (Billy Fung), Adrian Pasdar (Dawson Cole), Fennie Yuen Kit-ying (Mei), Loletta Lee Lai-chun (Billy's Wife), Lau Siu-ming (Pao), Wong Kam-kong (Tso), Che-Kirk Wong Chi-keung (Triad). 1.85:1. VHS: Tai Seng. Import LD/VCD: Mei Ah. 114 minutes.

Gorgeous production design and attractive cinematography give this big budget production a slick veneer that makes it well worth catching. Regardless, from a cinematic standpoint, it is less satisfying and is notable mainly for the fact that it was produced by Jim Choi, a

Mainland-born triad who was murdered a year later. Set in the late '30s, the storyline tells of two old friends who first met in 1920: Billy, a young Chinese criminal, and Dawson, an American in Shanghai with his family. The two bond when Dawson's father is murdered by a psychotic triad (played by an amusingly beastly Che-Kirk Wong), an act for which Billy helps Dawson exact revenge. In 1937 Dawson returns to Shanghai to set up a shipping business and again crosses paths with Billy, who has spent several years in the "Bamboo House" (prison). When Dawson's business is ruined by a dock boss he would not split his profits with, Billy sneaks into the man's home and murders him. The friends go into partnership, but Billy's ambitions prompt him to use the company ships for smuggling opium, a betrayal of Dawson's trust that drives a serious wedge between them.

The plot does not offer one single surprise, and the second half contains some embarrassingly puerile and overwrought moments (particularly the sequence where an inebriated Dawson humiliates himself at Billy's wedding). Fennie Yuen and Loletta Lee are used merely as "flower vases," living and breathing scenery to complement the manufactured eye candy. A major box office flop, **Shanghai 1920** is a passable time killer but far from what it should have been, considering the talents involved.

884. Shanghai Shanghai

(1990; Golden Harvest/Bo Ho Films Co./Paragon Films) ★: 6/10. *Luen sai ngai lui* (Cantonese), *Luan shi er nu* (Mandarin): "Chaotic World's Sons and Daughters." Cinematographer: Wong Po-man; Art Directors: Yank Wong Yan-kwai, Fu Chi-chung; Music: Joseph Chan Wing-leung; Writers: Poon Yuen-leung, Raymond To Kwok-wai; Producer: Corey Yuen Kwai; Action Directors: Yuen Tak, Dion Lam Dik-on; Director: Teddy Robin Kwan. Cast: Yuen Biao (Little Tiger), George Lam Chi-cheung (Big Tiger), Anita Mui Yim-fong (Mary Sung Chia-pi), Sandy Lam Yik-lin (Pao), Sammo Hung Kam-po (Chin Hung-yun), Mang Hoi (Hai), Tien Niu (Ting-ting), Lo Lieh (Pai), Che-Kirk Wong Chi-keung (Chiang), Lawrence Cheng Tan-shui (Chen Ta-wen). 1.85:1. VHS: Tai Seng (No Subtitles). Import LD: Star Entertainment (No Subtitles). Import VCD: Mega Star. Import DVD: Universe. 87 minutes. Also known as **The Shanghai Encounter** (Title for dubbed version).

Set in the first half of the 20th century, this all-star production boasts excellent production values, slick cinematography, and plenty of excitingly choreographed action but still does not quite live up to its potential. Bumpkin Little Tiger's first day in Shanghai finds him landing in the middle of a gangland rubout at a ritzy nightclub. Setting a fire as a diversion, the killers manage to make off with $5 million that was earmarked for The Revolutionary Party. Eventually, the lad is able to track down his older brother, Big Tiger, a steadfastly ethical police officer saddled with a corrupt superior. Quickly determining that a cop's life is not for him, Little Tiger hooks up with The Swallow Acrobatic Troop and helps them when they are brutalized by men in the employ of powerful triad Chin Hung-yun. He then decides to infiltrate Chin's gang and, thanks to his incredible martial skills, is quickly accepted into their ranks. Big Tiger, meanwhile, is suffering over the fact that he is attracted to the beautiful Mary. An old flame who has just returned from America, Mary is part of the underground and this creates a major conflict for Big Tiger, whose job and conscience require that he arrest all revolutionaries. Complicating matters further, Mary is also Chin's goddaughter and she is secretly trying to undermine his operations from the inside, a fact that eventually becomes known to the crimelord (who is behind the theft of the $5 million).

The storyline is functional but never especially engaging, and the finale strains credulity a bit too far. The short running time and choppy plotting also indicate post-production trimming. Those weaknesses aside, the film is still quite entertaining, with frequent action and gunplay, plus some amusing asides. Anita Mui's dancing skills serve her very well here and that (plus some skilful editing) allows the actress to come off almost as well in the fight sequences as seasoned pros like Yuen Biao and Sammo Hung. Mui's increasingly combative but graceful dance with Yuen during one of the nightclub scenes is a classic example of "clandestine kung fu" and the highlight here.

885. The Shanghai Thirteen

(1983; Tai Tai Film Co.) ★: 5/10. *Sap saam taai bo* (Cantonese), *Shi sam tai bao* (Mandarin): "Thirteen Warlords." Cinematographer: Ng Kwok-yun; Art Director: Koo Ling-yuen; Music: Not Original; Action Directors: Chiang Sheng, Lu Feng, Wong Kwok-chu, Ching Tin-chi; Producer-Director: Chang Cheh. Cast: Ti Lung (No. 1), David Chiang Da-wei (Yeh), Chen Kuan-tai (Shen Gan-fuh), Leung Kar-yan (Tau Tah-yeh), Lu Feng (Tiger), Chi Kuan-chun (Yuan Hai, The Big Leopard), Chiang Sheng (Fon Jin-bang), Wong Ching (Shiun Lih), Jimmy Wang Yu (Black Hat), Chen Sing (Black Eagle), Danny Lee Sau-yin (Sheau-yang), Andy Lau Tak-wah (The Student). 1.85:1. VHS: Ocean Shores. 90 minutes.

Following his departure from Shaw Brothers, director Chang Cheh assembled many of the martial artists from his earlier features for this Taiwanese production, set during World War II. When it becomes clear that an upcoming treaty signing with Japan will have disastrous repercussions, Minister Gau sets out to inform the people. To ensure his safety, he employs a group of talented fighters called "The Thirteen Rascals" who defend him from all manner of government-hired assassins.

Aside from its cast of old favorites and some fine kung fu, there is little here to engage the viewer. Most of the stars do little more than appear onscreen for a few minutes, help Gau along to the next stage of his mission, and then get killed. The story has no sense of urgency or suspense, and the sentimental passages are especially heavy-handed. With a cast like this, every Shaw Brothers martial arts fan will still want to see the film, but even they had best approach it with low expectations.

886. Shaolin and Wu Tang

(1983) ★: 7/10. *Siu lam yue mo dong* (Cantonese), *Shao lin yu wu dang* (Mandarin): "Shaolin and Wu Tang." Music: Not Original; Writer: Wong Pak-king; Producer: Tang Shi-leung; Action Direction: The Lau Brothers; Director: Gordon Lau Kar-fai. Cast: Gordon Lau Kar-fai (Hung Yung-kit), Adam Cheng Siu-chau (Chou Fong-wu), Idy Chan Yuk-lin (Yen Lan), Johnny Wang Lung-wei (The Lord), Kwan Hoi-shan (Master Law), Lee Hoi-sang (Brother Fa-chi), Elvis Tsui Kam-kong (Reverend Fa-chau). 2.35:1. VHS: Arena/Xenon (Dubbed *and* Poor Subtitles), Tai Seng (Poor Subtitles). 87 minutes.

Martial arts star Gordon Lau made his directorial debut with this period kung fu yarn, which plays very much like the Shaw Brothers productions he is best known for. The film even opens with a bravura martial arts display under the credits, like several Shaw productions helmed by his brother, Lau Kar-leung. Shaolin student Hung Yung-kit and Wu Tang pupil Chou Fong-wu are best buddies, despite the fact that they are from competing schools. When an evil Ching lord demands to be instructed in the Wu Tang sword technique, he is politely refused. Deciding to take the Wu Tang sword manual instead, he poisons the clan chief and imprisons Fong-wu, telling him that Shaolin is responsible for his master's death. Yung-kit helps his friend escape, but when Yung-kit's sister is murdered, he mistakenly believes that Wu Tang is responsible for the crime. The Lord decides to have Shaolin and Wu Tang eliminated, and a contest between the two schools seems to be the best way to achieve that goal. One fighter is chosen by each side: Yung-kit for Shaolin and Fong-wu for Wu Tang.

The storyline is incredibly contrived, but the martial arts are first rate (the training sequences are patterned after those in **The 36th Chamber of Shaolin** and compare favorably), and the cast includes a number of old Shaw favorites. While presented in a straightforward manner, the film is well made and emerges as a highly entertaining entry in the genre. Character names are from the English dubbed version.

887. Shaolin Avengers

(1994; New Great Walls Film Company/Filmswell International) ★: 2/10. *Fong Sai-yuk yu Hung Hei-kwun* (Cantonese), *Feng Shiyu yu Hong Zhiguan* (Mandarin): "Fong Sai-yuk and Hung Hei-kwun" or "Feng Shi-yu and Hong Zhiguan." Music: Not Original; Director: Lee Chiu. Cast: Chin Kar-lok (Feng Shi-yu), Lam Ching-ying (Hong Zhi-guan), Kwan Hoi-shan (Feng's Father), Wu Ma (Yu Chi). 1.85:1. VHS/DVD: Tai Seng (Dubbed). 86 minutes.

Not to be confused with the 1976 Chang Cheh film, this low-budget Taiwanese production (possibly shot in tandem with **Martial Art Master: Wong Fai Hung** [*sic*]) is set shortly after the time when Ching soldiers set fire to Shaolin Temple. Young hero Fong Sai-yuk (identified in the English version by his Mandarin name) is an impetuous lad whose superb kung fu is about all that keeps him from getting beaten to death. One day it looks like Sai-yuk has finally met his match, but he is saved from death, thanks to the intervention of legendary Shaolin fighter Hung Hei-kwun (also identified in Mandarin form). Sai-yuk's mom is an old acquaintance of Hei-kwun and she agrees to hide a secret name list for him, but Manchu troops invade their home, slaughtering most of the inhabitants, and Hei-kwun is incapacitated by some poison needles. Sai-yuk and Hei-kwun concoct an elaborate plan that will allow the former to avenge the murder of his loved ones.

Chin Kar-lok's interpretation of Fong Sai-yuk is overly broad, but that is just one problem among many here. A poor scenario, mediocre martial arts, and lame humor make this painfully reminiscent of the worst 1970s chopsockies. The soundtrack includes music lifted from **Mad Max**.

Shaolin Challenges Ninja *see* **Heroes of the East**

Shaolin Executioner *see* **Executioners of Shaolin**

888. Shaolin Mantis

(1978; Shaw Brothers) ★: 7/10. *Tong long* (Cantonese), *Tang lang* (Mandarin): "Mantis." Cinematographer: Arthur Wong Ngok-tai; Art Director: Johnson Tsao; Music: Not Original; Writer: Szeto On; Producer: Mona Fong Yat-wah; Action Directors: Lau Kar-leung, Tang Wei-cheng; Director: Lau Kar-leung. Cast: David Chiang Da-wei (Wei Fung), Wong Hang-sau (Tien Chi-chi), Lau Kar-wing (Chi-chi's Grandad), Lily Li Li-li (Chi-chi's Mother), Norman Tsui Siu-keung (Fourth Uncle), Ha Ping (Chi-chi's Great Aunt), Gordon Lau Kar-fai (Monk), Lee Hoi-sang (Mongol Fighter). 2.35:1. No official domestic video release. 103 minutes. Also known as **The Deadly Mantis** (US title).

This is an unusual Shaw Brothers period kung fu thriller in that the hero is a member of The Ching Dynasty, almost without exception the villains in these films. Proficient kung fu fighter Wei Fung is ordered to spy on the Tien family, which is suspected of having ties with Ming revolutionaries. He gains access to the Tien home by getting hired on as a teacher for Chi-chi, a bratty young girl who has driven away more than her share of instructors. After the expected period of adversity, Chi-chi becomes fond of Fung, and when his identity is compromised, she claims to be his lover. Against his better judgment, the Tien patriarch decides to spare the teacher's life, on the condition that he never leave the village. The pair are married, but unless Fung can gather the required intelligence information and report back within a year, his family will be executed. Chi-chi decides to stand by her husband's side and the pair attempt to escape, but this means they will have to defeat the Tien family's most powerful fighters.

The martial arts are not as spectacular as those commonly found in Lau's films from this period, but kung fu is not the only point of interest here. The screenplay offers up a number of interesting twists, as well as some interesting ruminations on loyalty. There is the obligatory third act sequence in which the hero masters a special skill in order to defeat the powerful enemy (in this case, Fung creates the "Mantis" fighting style by observing a real praying mantis), but even the final outcome of this is not exactly as one would expect, incorporating one last, ironic revelation into a refreshingly offbeat scenario. The character names listed above are from the English-dubbed version.

Shaolin Master Killer *see* **The 36th Chamber of Shaolin**

889. Shaolin Rescuers

(1979; Shaw Brothers) ★: 7/10. *Gaai si ying hung* (Cantonese), *Jie shi ying xiong* (Mandarin): "Street Market Hero." Cinematographer: Tsao Hui-chi; Art Director: Johnson Tsao; Music: Not Original; Writers: Ngai Hong, Chang Cheh, Tsai Nai-pin; Producer: Mona Fong Yat-wah; Action Directors: Chiang Sheng, Lu Feng, Tai Chi-hsieh; Director: Chang Cheh. Cast: Phillip Kwok Tsui (Ying Cha-po), Lo Mang (Chun Ah-chin), Sun Chien (Chu Tsai), Lu Feng (Kau Ching-cheung), Chiang Sheng (Han Chi), Cho Tat-wah (Chun's Teacher). 2.35:1. No official domestic video release. Running time unknown. Also known as **Avenging Warriors of Shaolin** (US title).

There is a great deal of humor in this period martial arts yarn, which is much lighter in tone than most of Chang Cheh's films. Lazy restaurant workers Ying and Chun would risk their lives for a bit of fame and a chance to put their kung fu skills to the test. They befriend Chu Tsai, another martial arts master, and the three become inseparable. The traitorous priest Pai Mei (who is responsible for the burning of Shaolin Temple) and his minions trap and murder Chi San and Feng Shi-yu (or Fong Sai-yuk, as he is better known in Cantonese), as part of Pai's campaign to slay every single remaining rebel. His next target is Hong Si-kwun (Hung Hei-kwun in Cantonese) who has been badly injured in a fight with Pai's associates. The stricken man is discovered by the three friends and they nurse him back to health with a special (expensive) prescription. However, Hong's hiding place is discovered, leading to a deadly stand-off.

The effectively droll script (which still manages to come through in the dubbed version) gives extra resonance to what is a pretty routine scenario by genre standards. Phillip Kwok and Lo Mang do an excellent job of mixing their comedic and athletic abilities, and Sun Chien does some especially impressive work on the Shaolin Poles. Character names are from the English edition.

890. She Shoots Straight

(1990; Golden Harvest/Bo Ho Films/Paragon Films) ★: 6/10. *Wong fung lui cheung* (Cantonese), *Huang gu nu jiang* (Mandarin): "Huang Family Female Soldiers."

Cinematographers: Tom Lau Moon-tong, Jimmy Leung Chi-ming; Art Director: Raymond Lee King-man; Music: Lowell Lo Kwun-ting, Chow Kam-cheung; Writers: Yuen Kai-chi, Barry Wong Ping-yiu; Producers: Sammo Hung Kam-po, Chan Pui-wah; Action Directors: Corey Yuen Kwai, Mang Hoi, Yuen Tak; Director: Corey Yuen Kwai. Cast: Joyce Godenzi (Mina Kao), Tony Leung Kar-fai (Huang Tsung-pao), Carina Lau Kar-ling (Huang Chia-ling), Tang Pik-wan (Huang Matriarch), Yuen Wah (Yuan Hua), Angile Leung Wan-yui (Huang Chia-jui), Sandra Ng Kwan-yu (Huang Chia-ju), Sarah Lee Lai-yui (Youngest Huang Sister), Agnes Aurelio (Yuan Ying), Sammo Hung Kam-po (Hung), Lau Chi-wing (Superintendent Liu). Dolby Digital (DVD only), Stereo Sound (on Star laserdisc only). 1.85:1. VHS: Tai Seng (No Subtitles). LD: Media Asia. Import LD: Star Entertainment (No Subtitles). Import DVD: Universe. 91 minutes. Also known as **Lethal Lady**.

Terrific action punctuates this average HK police actioner, which also benefits significantly from the talent and intensity of its beautiful star, Eurasian actress Joyce Godenzi. She plays Mina, a decorated police officer who marries Huang Tsung-pao, another in a long line of law enforcers, which also include his mother and four sisters. The eldest sister, Chia-ling, takes an immediate dislike to Mina and is angered by the way she is close to out-ranking both her and Tsung-pao in the department. When a raid by a Vietnamese gang on a ritzy club results in several casualties, Chia-ling is saddled with the blame for exposing her identity as an undercover operative. Mina is forced by her arrogant superior to sign a report recommending that Chia-ling be suspended, which simply makes matters worse. Having had one of his men killed by Mina, the leader of the Vietnamese targets her for revenge, but the trap results in the death of Tsung-pao. This tragedy prompts Mina and Chia-ling to put their personal differences aside and avenge his death.

Several sequences are too melodramatic for their own good, and Lau Chi-wing's character is excessively banal, even for the action genre. Fortunately, Godenzi has a compelling presence and performs with tremendous vigour, adding a sense of realism to the action even when she is clearly being aided by wirework. The film's director, Corey Yuen, has an eye-blink cameo as a boatman, and co-producer Sammo Hung has a supporting role as a friend of the family. In real life, Hung and Godenzi tied the knot in 1995. Michael Dinga, Chung Fat, Yip Wing-cho, and Amy Yip Chi-mei also appear. Footnote: This film is a modern retelling of The Sung Dynasty story about The Yeung Family Female Soldiers. The Yeung clan lost their patriarch and six sons while defending against the Turkish tribes in the north. One grandson was left to carry on the family name. The lad in question, Yeung Chong-bo (see the name of Tony Leung Kar-fai's character above for a partial Mandarin equivalent), married a woman that everyone in the family did not accept, with the sole exception of the Yeung matriarch. Eventually Chong-bo, too, died in battle, but not before fathering a son to carry on the family name. Chong-bo's wife, Mok Gwi-ying, became renowned as the Yeung clan's fiercest fighter. As the story goes, the remaining Yeung women formed a female army to fight the Turkish tribes, with Gwi-ying as their leader. The banquet scene in the film (where the women learn about Tsung-pao's death) is identical to the manner in which the Yeung women are told of Chong-bo's passing.

891. She Starts the Fire

(1992; Jing's Production). ★: 1/10. *Fan feng lui long* (Cantonese), *Pen huo nu lang* (Mandarin): "Spray Fire Girl." Cinematographers: Jingle Ma Cho-shing, Henry Chan Chun-kit; Art Director: Horace Ma Kwong-wing; Music: Phil Chan Fei-lap; Writers: Wong Jing, Gordon Chan Kar-seung; Producer: Lam Pai-yan; Director: Lawrence Cheng Tan-shui. Cast: Chingmy Yau Suk-ching (Wendy), Lawrence Cheng Tan-shui (Charles Siu), Deanie Yip Tak-han (Big Beer), Carol Cheng Yu-ling (Tracy Siu), Paul Chu Kong (Kwok Lap), John Ching Tung (Brother Bo), Yuen King-tan (Blackjack Dealer). 1.85:1. VHS: Tai Seng (No Subtitles). Import LD: Star Entertainment (No Subtitles). 88 minutes.

This painfully unfunny comedy stars Chingmy Yau as a girl who was cursed by an Indonesian sorcerer as a child. This left her with both telekinetic and *pyro*kinetic abilities, the latter involuntarily coming into play whenever she gets excited or falls in love. After accidentally killing her family, she moves in with her one surviving relative (Deanie Yip), who is sharing a flat with nerdy Lawrence Cheng and his bitchy sister (Carol Cheng). Various parties try to take advantage of her powers, with thoroughly predictable results.

The writers never take proper advantage of the premise's comedic potential, opting for one obvious joke after another, and director/co-star Lawrence Cheng allows Deanie Yip and Carol Cheng to go so far over the top they're practically unbearable. Damian Lau Chung-yan has a cameo in the final minutes, though it is doubtful that many viewers will make it that far. As of this writing, only the Taiwanese tape version from Vidi Video has English subtitles, and this turkey is definitely not worth the effort involved in acquiring it.

892. Shogun & Little Kitchen

(1992; Hoventin Films) ★: 6/10. *Foh tau fuk sing* (Cantonese), *Huo tou fu xing* (Mandarin): "Meal Head Lucky Star." Cinematographer: David Chung Chi-man; Art Director: William Szeto Wai-yung; Music: Richard Yuen Cheuk-fan; Writers: James Yuen Sai-sang, Raymond To Kwok-wai; Producer: Laura Fau Lok-lin; Action Director: Yuen Cheung-yan; Director: Ronny Yu Yan-tai. Cast: Leon Lai Ming (Lam Feng), Yuen Biao (Tang Tai-chi), Ng Man-tat (Bo-bo), Maggie Siu Mei-kei (Ko Tin-oi), Monica Chan Fat-yung (Miss Kwok), Jimmy Wang Yu (Lin Ton), Leung Kar-yan (Tong), Lui Fong (Chao Wai-cheng), Josephine Koo Mei-wah (Feng's Mother). 1.85:1. VHS: World Video. Import LD/VCD/DVD: Mei Ah. 93 minutes.

Ronny Yu directed this middling comedy-drama which stars Leon Lai as disgruntled youth Lam Feng, who leaves his posh home after an argument with his father. He hooks up with Bo-bo, a charitable but poverty-stricken landlord/would-be master chef, and his limber aide Tai-chi. Bo-bo's struggling outdoor restaurant gets a shot-in-the-arm when Tai-chi's colorful, acrobatic cooking draws in scores of patrons, while romantic sparks soon begin to fly between Lam and Bo-bo's daughter Tin-oi. Conflict arises when a large corporation woos Tai-chi away with a lucrative contract and one of Bo-bo's tenants is blackmailed by gangsters in the employ of Lam's father to try and force the crotchety owner to sell his lucrative property for a pittance.

Considering the talent in front of the camera and behind the scenes, this ends up being a surprisingly ordinary affair. Still, the solid cast makes viewing worthwhile, with Yuen Biao (getting ample opportunity to display his impressive dexterity with every food item and culinary utensil imaginable) coming off best. Yu's directorial skills only really surface during a mostly superfluous but well-filmed climax, centred around and inside a burning building, which briefly includes the "step frame" technique he would later use to excellent effect during the action scenes in **The Bride with White Hair**. The storyline was originally to have revolved around Yuen Biao's character, but he left the production after only a few days of shooting because the producer defaulted on his payments. The script was quickly rewritten to make Leon Lai's character the protagonist, and, all things considered, the changes are not really evident in the final product. Even though this well-intentioned film is ultimately something of a disappointment, the lovingly filmed cooking sequences are guaranteed to have you on the phone to your favorite Chinese restaurant.

893. The Shootout

(1992; Golden Harvest/Golden Way Films/Paragon Films) ★: 4/10. *Aau him ching yan* (Cantonese), *Wei xian qing ren* (Mandarin): "Dangerous Lovers." Cinematographer: Eric Chu Kwok-fai; Art Director: Dominique Lo Kar-yiu; Music: Joseph Chan Wing-leung; Writer: Edward Tang King-sang; Producer: Anthony Chow Ting-on; Action Director: Leung Kar-hung; Director: Michael Mak Dong-kit. Cast: Aaron Kwok Fu-shing (Wang Chia-hui), Fennie Yuen Kit-ying (Min), Leung Kar-yan (Ma), Lau Ching-wan (Liu), Elvis Tsui Kam-kong (Han), Yuen King-tan (Hsi). 1.85:1. VHS: Tai Seng (No Subtitles). Import LD: Star Entertainment (No Subtitles). 95 minutes.

Jackie Chan's Golden Way Films is responsible for this lackluster actioner, which should have been better, considering the talent involved. In the wake of an armored car heist, the police select four officers to serve together as a team to solve the case. One of the men, inexperienced patrolman Wang, falls in love with Min, a karaoke hostess, who just happens to be the girlfriend of the robbers' leader, Han. After witnessing the criminal abuse Min, Wang becomes determined to rescue her. He and his partners disguise themselves as burglars and break into Han's house in order to find his gun and link him to two murders, but the plan goes awry when the suspect returns home unexpectedly.

Aaron Kwok's character is insufferably earnest, but comedienne Yuen King-tan is effective in a change-of-pace role as one of the robbers, and Leung and Lau have their moments as feuding officers with very different styles. However, too much of the running time is spent on Wang and Min's budding romance, and their characters are just not interesting enough to hold one's attention for such a lengthy detour. The storyline is strictly by-the-numbers, and even the acrobatic gunplay seems stale. Only the Taiwan video release has English subtitles.

894. Shyly Spirit

[*sic*] (1993) ★: 3/10. *Pa sau gwai* (Cantonese), *Pa xiu gui* (Mandarin): "Bashful Ghost." Cinematographer: Hsu Peng-ping; Music: Lam Shun-lung; Writer: Cheung Man-wah; Producer: Lee Yiu-ting; Action Director: Law Cheung-on; Director: Chong Yan-kin. Cast: Ngai Sing (Sing), Eric Tsang Chi-wai (Long-life Ko), Chung Fat (Wang), Peter Chan Lung (Ko), Stanley Fung Shui-fan (Captain Hao), Wong Sum (Sen), Dick Wei (Llama). 1.85:1. VHS/LD: World Video. 93 minutes.

Looking like a production from the early '70s, this shabby, anachronistic horror-comedy stars Eric Tsang as a young man in the 1930s, who is doomed to age before his time and not live to see his 24th birthday. Desperate to marry him off, his father arranges a wedding, only to have a rival use sorcery to scotch the nuptials. While peeping at his bride-to-be, Tsang accidentally falls through the bath house ceiling and kills the girl, sucking out her lifeforce in the process. After a corrupt lawman refuses to arrest the guilty party, the girl's mother decides not to bury her body until the daughter has exacted revenge. This leaves her a wandering (and for a time naked) spirit who cannot enter into the afterlife. Desperate to prolong his life, Tsang hires a llama to protect him from both spiritual and earthly perils.

While not completely without interest, this earnest effort is undone by weak direction and poverty row production values. The cheap sets wobble like there is no tomorrow, and the final reel is a mind-numbing assemblage of shoddy wirework and fighters crashing through breakaway furniture. On the plus side, how often do you get to see Peter Chan and Eric Tsang playing father and son? Lam Ching-ying makes a brief appearance in his trademark role of a Taoist priest.

895. Silent Love

(1986; D & B Films Co.) ★: 5/10. *Ting bat do dik suet wa* (Cantonese), *Ting bu dao de shuo hua* (Mandarin): "The Unheard Talk." Cinematographer: Wilson Chan Pui-kai; Art Director: Eric Lam Sai-kan; Music: The Melody Bank; Writers: Siu Kwok-wah, On Sai; Producer: Sammo Hung Kam-po; Director: David Chiang Da-wei. Cast: Season Ma Si-san (Heung Gite), Lau Ching-wan (Kelly Mak), Ronald Wong Pan (Leopard), Fan Siu-wong (Little Dragon), Chen Jing (Tong), Roy Cheung Yiu-yeung (Robert). 1.85:1. VHS: Tai Seng. Import LD: Mei Ah. 91 minutes.

A minor but interesting drama, **Silent Love** concerns a group of deaf pickpockets who are lead by Heung Gite, who can hear but is mute. One day she is saved from some rival street kids by young triad Kelly, who has just been released from prison. Kelly becomes friends with the youths (who live on a houseboat with a friendly hooker) and protects them when they have another run-in with the same hoods. When the man Kelly went to prison for refuses to reimburse him for the years he wasted behind bars, Gite steals his wallet. Through a series of events, the police become involved and the teens are forced to go into hiding.

The dramatic conflicts are simplistic and the repetitive musical score is grating, but the protagonists are refreshingly unique and the presentation is earnest. The performers playing the deaf teenagers are quite convincing, and the sequence in which Season Ma dances and signs the lyrics to a George Lam song is delightful. This was Lau Ching-wan's film debut, though he is dubbed by another actor here.

896. Sisters of the World Unite

(1991; Unique Films/Paka Hill Films Production Co.) ★: 4/10. *Sa-sa Ga-ga jaam hei loi* (Cantonese), *Shasha Jiajia zhan qi lai* (Mandarin): "Sa-sa and Ga-ga Step Up" or "Shasha and Jiajia Step Up." Cinematographer: Jingle Ma Cho-shing; Art Director: William Cheung Suk-ping; Music: Jonathan Lee Chung-shing, Ken Shima; Writers: Sylvia Chang Ai-chia, Maisy Choi Mei-see, Brenda Lo Yip-mei, Eveline Au Siu-hung; Producer: Sylvia Chang Ai-chia; Director: Maisy Choi Mei-see. Cast: Sylvia Chang Ai-chia (Sylvia Lau), Sally Yeh Chian-wen (Sally), John Sham Kin-fun (Yiu Bo-bo), Derek Yee Tung-sing (Johnny), David Wu Tai-wai (Ray). 1.85:1. VHS: Tai Seng. Import LD: Universe. 95 minutes.

This exceedingly mild comedy concerns the romantic exploits of housewife Sylvia and commercial producer Sally, sisters who have no luck in love. Timid Sylvia's husband, Bo-bo, is a philandering lout who doesn't appreciate her; and Sally's love, Johnny, refuses to divorce his sickly wife. Sylvia strikes out on her own, becoming a cooking teacher, while Sally becomes attracted to handsome Ray, who is several years younger and likes to take her out for "youthful activities" (i.e. roller coaster rides, racquetball, and other things she no longer has the energy for). Her confidence increased, Sylvia insists that Bo-bo go through the process of courting her all over again; only then will she decide if they will get back together. Sally, meanwhile, is going through all manner of anguish over whether she and Ray are really compatible, a process complicated by the fact that he wants to get married.

The two actresses are convincing, but the material is so slight, the film is rarely engaging. The situations are too predictable for the humor to hit the mark, and Maisy Choi's direction is overly self-conscious. Idy Chan Yuk-lin, Phillip Chan Yan-kin, Raymond Wong Pak-ming, Billy Lau Nam-kwong, Lau Siu-ming, Kenny Bee, and director Johnny To Kei-fung appear briefly.

897. The Six Devil Women

(1996; Cheung Sing Movie Co.) ★: 2/10. *Sam jan gung lo cheung che saat yan on ji luk moh nui* (Cantonese), *Shenzhen gong lu qiang che sha ren an zhi liu mo nu* (Mandarin): "Shenzhen Carjack Murder Case: Six Evil Women." Cinematographer: Wong Po-man; Art Director: Ma Lei-ou; Music: Sam Leung Yiu-san, Barry Cheung Fu-ling; Action Directors: Ko Man-dik, Ching Kwok-leung; Producer-Director: Ma Tin-yiu. Cast: Diana Pang Dan (Man Nap), Lee Suet-man (Cheung Fung), William Ho Kar-kui (Victim), Jimmy Wong Shu-kei, Leung Yuen-man. 1.85:1. VHS: Tai Seng. Import LD/VCD: Universe. 89 minutes.

This slapdash Category III yarn concerns a gang of male and female robbers preying on dimwitted men in Mainland China. Opening with an excerpt from the gang's trial, the film jumps back and forth from the court proceedings to the events leading up to the criminals' capture. The gang uses the following plan: Two of the women are picked up by a man, who takes them "home," on the promise of sex. Soon after their arrival, the male criminals show up, kill the victim, and take his belongings. The women are all from poor families in the country and soon get over their initial apprehension when presented with all manner of money and jewellery. However, the men take the majority of the booty and, fed up with being shortchanged, the girls decide to try and strike out on their own but barely escape alive when one victim (played by C-III regular William Ho) proves much harder to kill than expected. Their male partners are none too happy about this newfound display of independence, leading to dissension and the entire gang's downfall.

Whatever promise is inherent in the premise is quickly negated by weak performances, unbelievable situations, and a director more concerned about prolonged slow motion shots of wet, jiggling breasts, unmotivated sex scenes, and shirt-ripping catfights than anything else. The lack of a screenwriter credit tells you everything else you need to know.

The Six-Fingered Strings Demon *see* **Deadful [*sic*] Melody**

898. Sixty Million Dollar Man

(1995; Win's Entertainment) ★: 6/10. *Baak bin sing gwan* (Cantonese), *Bai bian xing jun* (Mandarin): "Hundred Changing Star Person." Cinematographer: Andrew Lau Wai-keung; Art Director: Cyrus Ho Kim-hung; Music: Anthony Lee Hon-kam, Marco Wan Ho-kit; Writer-Producer: Wong Jing; Action Director: Dion Lam Dik-on; Director: Raymond Yip Wai-man. Cast: Stephen Chiau Sing-chi (Lee Chak-sing), Ng Man-tat (Tat), Gigi Leung Wing-kei (Chung-chung), Paulyn Suen Kai-kwun (Bonnie), Elvis Tsui Kam-kong (Professor Chang Sze), Wong Yat-fei (Lee Yat-fai), Manfred Wong (Principal). 1.85:1. VHS/LD: Tai Seng. Import LD/VCD/DVD: Mei Ah. 90 minutes.

Partially shot in Hawaii, this Stephen Chiau outing is only genuinely funny when it parodies Hollywood films, but those parts generate enough laughs to make the whole film worthwhile. Chiau plays an obnoxious college student who is blown up by Japanese *yakuza* after he goes out with the gang leader's girlfriend. All that remains are his brain and his lips (shades of Woody Allen's **Sleeper**), but mad scientist Elvis Tsui (sporting an Einstein wig) gives him a whole new set of cheap electronic body parts (powered by regular household batteries!). With a special computer chip implanted in his brain, Chiau can change his limbs or his entire body into giant-sized household items (like a tube of toothpaste, a talking toilet, a spatula, a microwave oven, etc.), a talent which comes in handy when he gets a job as a biology teacher at a school full of murderous students. When the villain discovers that Chiau is still alive, he has one of his henchmen converted into a decidedly more expensive opponent.

The best gags come during a terrific, extended parody of **Pulp Fiction** (with Chiau and Paulyn Suen filling the John Travolta and Uma Thurman roles) which recreates the dance contest and overdose sequences. The second half is mainly a knockoff of Jim Carrey's **The Mask**, with amusing digital FX changing Chiau into all manner of weird creations. The balance consists largely of jokes recycled from the star's earlier, superior films, and the utter lack of plot and uneven pacing are rather trying. This works much better on video than it did in theatres, as the special effects are more convincing and you can fast forward through the slow portions in order to savor the jokes that do work.

899. Skin Striperess

[*sic*] (1992) ★: 5/10. *Lat pei gwai* (Cantonese), *Shuai pi gui* (Mandarin): "Ghost Throws Out Skin." Cinematographer: Chan Tung-chuen; Art Directors: Fred Chan Chi-chung, Fung Lok-ban; Music: Not Original; Writer: Johnny Lee King-kai; Producer: Kam Cheung-kuen; Action Director: Power Lee King-chu; Director: Billy Chan Wui-ngai. Cast: Chan Wing-chi (Chi), Lam Ching-ying (The Old Man), Billy Lau Nam-kwong (Lau), Peter Chan Lung (Chan), Yung Sai-kit (Yung). 1.85:1. Import LD/VCD: Mei Ah. 95 minutes.

This horror cheapie is yet another imitation of the French horror classic **Eyes Without a Face** (1959) mixed with Eastern horror tenets. Crooked developer Lau aims to buy a permit that will allow him to build a resort on a peaceful, untouched island. His bribe: a night with beautiful movie star Chi, whom Lau has control over, as he aided her poverty-stricken family in the Mainland. Before this "transaction" can occur, Chi is horribly disfigured by fallen power lines, and simple plastic surgery is not going to be enough. Lau learns from an evil priest that he can restore Chi's face if Lau provides a female victim who fits certain requirements. The developer finds such a woman and murders her, with the priest then skinning the corpse and performing a ritual that will cause the discarded flesh to fuse with Chi's damaged tissue. The flayed body is then buried, but the possibility exists that the victim may return as a ghost, which is precisely what happens when a stupid teenager (are there any other kind in these movies?) urinates on the grave. The understandably peeved spirit comes back for revenge, removing her victims' flesh in a less than surgically precise manner. Luckily, a powerful Taoist priest (played, of course, by Lam Ching-ying) is nearby to battle the evil.

This is a competent but forgettable enterprise whose main accomplishment is that it provides the dubious novelty of seeing horror comedy veterans Lam Ching-ying, Billy Lau, and Peter Chan in a sleazy Category III flick. Some atmospheric cinematography and a couple of imaginative touches keep it moderately entertaining.

900. Skinny Tiger and Fatty Dragon

(1990; Cinema City Co./Cinema Capital Entertainment) ★: 7/10. *Sau foo fei lung* (Cantonese), *Shou hu fei long* (Mandarin): "Skinny Tiger, Fat Dragon." Cinematographer: Gary Ho Bo-yiu; Art Director: Jessy Lam Chak-chi; Music: Richard Lo Sai-kit; Writer: Tsang Kwok-chi; Producers: Andrew Yau Teng-hon, Wellington Fung Wing; Action Directors: Ridley Tsui Bo-wah, Xiong Xinxin; Director: Lau Kar-wing. Cast: Sammo Hung Kam-po (Dragon), Karl Maka (Tiger Mak Tai-fu),

Carrie Ng Kar-lai (Lai), Woo Fung (Wu), Lau Kar-wing (Wing), Tai Po (Johnny), Gabriel Wong Yat-san (Burglar), Xiong Xinxin (Robber). 1.85:1. VHS: Tai Seng. LD: World Video. Import LD: Golden Cinema City. 105 minutes. Also known as **Nutty Kickbox Cops**.

Sammo Hung and Karl Maka team up for this amiable outing, which makes prime use of their talents. Known as "The 7-11 Cops" (because they provide 24 hour service), partners Dragon and Tiger set their sights on some drug traffickers. While trying to arrest a transvestite suspect, they accidentally molest Lai, a *real* woman and another of the criminals, who proceeds to press charges against them. The pair concoct a plan to frame Lai, making her seem to be Tiger's girlfriend, and also end up apprehending Tak, her boss, at the same time. However, they destroy their superior's wedding reception in the process and are ordered out of HK. After cooling their heels in Singapore, they decide to resign from the force and run a Karaoke bar, but fate intervenes when Tak is released on bail and sets out to avenge his humiliation. A pair of transvestite assassins kill Lai and then seek out Tiger and Dragon, but the pair manage to turn the tables on them. Realizing that they and their families will never be at peace until Tak is out of commission, the partners cook up a plan to finish him and his gang once and for all.

The storyline follows the buddy cop formula to the letter, the cross dressing attackers are right out of **Twinkle, Twinkle Lucky Stars**, Hung reprises his Bruce Lee imitation from **Enter the Fat Dragon**, and the detour to Singapore brings the proceedings to a screeching halt. Regardless, the action is terrific (Hung is a true master with nun-chucks), the comedy is painless, and all of the genre bases are covered in very satisfying fashion.

901. Slave of the Sword

(1993; Chang Hong Channel Film and Video Co.) ★: 3/10. *Gim no* (Cantonese), *Jian nu* (Mandarin): "Sword Slave." Cinematographer: Chen Chong-yuan; Music: Fu Hsuan; Writer: Chang Kuang-dou; Producer: Jessica Hsu Pei-rong; Action Director: Lin Wan-chang; Director: Chu Yen-ping. Cast: Pauline Chan Po-lin (Mu-lin), Joyce Ngai Suk-kwan (Yin), Jackson Liu Hsiu-hsien (Kin), Max Mok Siu-chung (The Eunuch). 1.85:1. VHS: Tai Seng (No Subtitles), SYS/Youngtze Video (Dubbed). Import LD: Star Entertainment (No Subtitles). 79 minutes.

A rather dull Taiwanese entry in the Category III softcore sweepstakes, this period drama concerns Mu-lin, a beautiful dancer whose father was murdered by mysterious assailants. Alone and without money, Mu-lin is kidnapped and taken to a brothel, where she becomes the new plaything of the madam, Yin. The woman's brother, Kin, falls in love with Mu-lin and she sets about turning him against Yin, as they were the parties responsible for her father's demise. Meanwhile, a shadowy figure is lurking in the background, crushing men's necks with his bare hands.

There is some very nice imagery here, patterned after the Mak Brothers' highly successful **Sex and Zen**, but the storyline is routine, the pacing deadening (a great deal of footage is repeated to pad the running time to feature length), and the sexual encounters routine. Most of the costumes and sets, and the majority of the action footage, is recycled from the far superior **Butterfly & Sword**. The character names above are from the English dubbed version.

A Slice of Death *see* **Abbot of Shaolin**

902. Slickers vs. Killers

(1991; Golden Harvest/Bojon Films Company) ★: 5/10. *Chi sin cham bin yan* (Cantonese), *Chi xian zhen bian ren* (Mandarin): "Sticky Thread Pillow Side Person." Cinematographer: Jimmy Leung Chi-ming; Art Director: Yank Wong Yan-kwai; Music: Lowell Lo Kwun-ting; Writers: Barry Wong Ping-yiu, Roy Szeto Cheuk-hon; Action Direction: Brandy Yuen Chun-yeung, Yuen Mo, Sammo Hung Stuntmen Association; Producer-Director: Sammo Hung Kam-po. Cast: Sammo Hung Kam-po (Success Hung), Carol Cheng Yu-ling (Miss Cheng/Ling's Mom), Joyce Godenzi (Dr. Ko), Yu Li (Lisa Yu), Jacky Cheung Hok-yau (Bat), Lam Ching-ying (Owl), Ngai Sing (Ai), Yip Wing-cho (Yip), Richard Ng Yiu-hon (Chow), Tommy Wong Kwong-leung (Murder Victim), Clifton Ko Chi-sum (Robert), Billy Lau Nam-kwong (Mainland Hick). 1.85:1. VHS: Tai Seng (Poor Subtitles). Import LD: Mei Ah. 97 minutes.

A lesser vehicle for Sammo Hung, this comedy-thriller has some effective moments and a quality cast but still never quite hits the mark. Success Hung is a great salesman, but his reign at the top may soon be over if newcomer Miss Cheng has her way. One evening Hung witnesses a triad rubout, but because of his penchant for telling tall tales, no one believes him. To make matters worse, a friend of the deceased believes that Hung helped to commit the murder. As a result, the cell phone salesman now has two groups of killers out to eliminate him. Through a series of misunderstandings, Hung soon has Miss Cheng, his wife, and his female psychiatrist involved. Cheng ends up in the hospital, while Hung, the two women, and a junior officer (who has a not-so-secret attraction to Mrs. Hung) go to a safe house. There, following many petty arguments and some comic pratfalls, all of the various hitmen converge to finish off eternal fall guy Hung.

There is some fine action (in the time-honored Sammo Hung tradition) and appealing performances from both Hung and Cheng (playing her "beautiful but repressed bitch" trademark character to a tee), but the marital conflicts and romantic misunderstandings are the stuff of bad sitcoms.

903. Snake and Crane Arts of Shaolin

(1978; Lo Wei Motion Picture Co.) ★: 5/10. *Se hok baat bo* (Cantonese), *She he ba bu* (Mandarin): "Snake Crane Eight Step." Cinematographer: Chan Chung-yuen; Art Director: Chow Chi-leung; Music: Not Original; Writer: Cheung San-yee; Producer: Hsu Li-hwa; Action Directors: Jackie Chan, To Wai-wor; Director: Chen Chi-hua. Cast: Jackie Chan (Hsu Ying-fung), Nora Miao Ker-hsiu (Tang Pin-er), Kam Kong (Chien Tse), Kim Chin-lin. 2.35:1. VHS: All Seasons (Dubbed), UAV (Dubbed), Simitar (Dubbed). DVD: Simitar (English and Cantonese tracks). Import VCD: Ocean Shores (Poor Subtitles). 92 minutes.

Those put off by the humor in Jackie Chan's work might enjoy this early period film in which the star largely plays it straight. Eight Shaolin martial arts masters invent a new form of kung fu called "The Eight Steps of the Snake and Crane" and record all of the training techniques in a book. Shortly thereafter, all eight of the masters and the book disappear. It turns up in the hands of Hsu Ying-fung, a cocky lad who has mastered all of its secrets. Representatives from various clans try to steal the book, but this is actually all part of a plan devised by Hsu's master, the sole surviving member of the original eight, who seeks to find the man who killed his peers.

Chan gets to display his proficiency in various styles here, most notably during an exciting climactic fight against three spear-wielding killers and, then, the main villain. Unfortunately, the storyline is grindingly routine and no more than an adequate framework for the kung fu. The stock music includes a cue some viewers might remember from **Monty Python and the Holy Grail**!

904. Snake Deadly Act

(1980; Million Film Co.) ★: 6/10. *Sau ying chui bo* (Cantonese), *She xing zui bu* (Mandarin): "Move Drunk Like a Snake." Cinematographer: Woo Fai-shen; Music: Not Original; Producer: Lee Ching; Action Director-Director: Wilson Tong Wai-shing. Cast: Ng Kun-lung (Master Kuo Chung), Wilson Tong Wai-shing (Mr. Kuo), Fung Hark-on (Yueh I), Angela Mao Ying (Brothel Madam), Michael Chan Wai-man (Casino Manager), Phillip Ko Fei (The Kuo Housekeeper), Peter Chan Lung (Chen), Bolo Yeung (The Giant). 2.35:1. VHS: Arena/Xenon. 91 minutes.

This low-budget period martial arts outing would probably be long forgotten had not the Eastern Heroes magazine in England given it much publicity as an exceedingly rare treasure. Fortunately, unlike many rediscovered "gems," this one does have merit, though it falls short of classic status. The episodic plot concerns Kuo Chung, the honorable son of a revered community leader, whose father rewards the poor people in his village with free food. However, the elder Kuo has a decidedly villainous past, having previously committed rape and other crimes. One of his old enemies, Yueh I, has returned after having lost to him in a duel several years before. One day the younger Kuo encounters a girl being harassed by some rascals. Learning that she has been sold to the local brothel, Kuo pledges to acquire her contract from the madam, only to discover that the latter is an adept swordswoman. Just when he is on the verge of losing, Chung is saved by Yueh, who proves himself a master of the snake fist style. When Chung and an associate try to swindle a casino, they find themselves at the mercy of the manager, a deadly proponent of the "No-Shadow Kick." Once again, Yueh intercedes and saves Chung from certain death; after much cajoling, Yueh agrees to take the youth on as his pupil. After a long and painful training session, Yueh instructs Chung to find the masked thief who has stolen some valuable antiques in the village. When Chung learns the identity of the felon, he is shocked, but he has an even greater surprise in store.

The pacing is rather slack at times, and there are ample digressions from the main story to provide additional fights, but **Snake Deadly Act** works well as a traditional revenge drama. The training sequences are brief but convincingly gruelling, and Fung Hark-on once again provides both a strong characterization and impressive kung fu. The fighting styles include the ever popular "Drunken Fist" stance and a new form practised by Wilson Tong's character which is based on the lobster claw (evidently a good way to counter the "snake head" utilized in the snake fist technique). One only wishes that Angela Mao, Peter Chan, and Michael Chan could have been afforded more screen time.

905. Snake in the Eagle's Shadow

(1978; Seasonal Film Corporation) ★: 7/10. *Se ying diu sau* (Cantonese), *She xing diao shou* (Mandarin): "Snake Form Tricky Hand." Cinematographer: Chang Hai; Art Director: Ting Yuen-tai; Music: Not Original; Writers: Ng See-yuen, Siu Lung, Clifford Choi Kai-kwong; Producer: Ng See-yuen; Martial Art Directors: Yuen Woo-ping, Hsu Hsia; Director: Yuen Woo-ping. Cast: Jackie Chan (Chien Fu), Simon Yuen Siu-tien (Pai Chang-tien), Hwang Jang-li (Shangkuan I-yun), Dean Shek Tien (Teacher Li), Peter Chan Lung (Substitute Instructor), Fung Hark-on (Master of the Snake Fist School), Roy Horan (Priest). 2.35:1. VHS: Arena/Xenon (Dubbed), World Video (Subtitled or Dubbed). Import VCD: Mei Ah (Poor Subtitles). 92 minutes. Also known as **Eagle's Shadow** (US theatrical title and World Video title).

A box office hit that helped to establish Jackie Chan's new persona, this terrific period kung fu comedy is an excellent vehicle for the fighting and performing styles of Jackie Chan and Simon Yuen. Shangkuan I-yun has used his deadly eagle claw technique to wipe out almost all of the proponents of the Snake Fist style, save for the lazy master, Pai Chang-tien. Put-upon orphan Chien Fu saves Pai's life one day, and as a reward, the old *sifu* instructs him in some Snake Fist style basics. When Pai is attacked and gravely injured by two Eagle Claw assassins, Chien nurses him back to health; in return, the old man teaches him everything he needs to know about the Snake Fist. Although Pai orders him not to use his skills in public, Chien disobeys and is seen by Shangkuan. However, when he sees his cat kill a cobra, Chien creates an even deadlier style that mixes snake with a new cat's claw style.

Some of the comedy is extremely broad, but the proceedings are consistently engaging and the fight sequences are meticulously choreographed. Only one complaint: Considering the skills of the antagonists, the final battle is disappointingly short. In light of the film's success, Jackie Chan, Simon Yuen, and director Yuen Woo-ping were quickly reteamed for the same year's **Drunken Master**, which is even better. The names listed above are from the dubbed version.

Soldier of Love *see* **Love Soldier of Fortune**

906. Somebody Up There Likes Me

(1996; Long Shong Pictures/Milestone Pictures) ★: 3/10. *Long maan fung bou* (Cantonese), *Lung man feng bao* (Mandarin): "Romantic Storm." Cinematographer: Arthur Wong Ngok-tai; Art Director: Alfred Yau Wai-ming; Music: Danny Wong Dan-yee; Writer: Chan Hing-ka; Producer: John Woo Yu-sen; Action Director: Yuen Tak; Director: Patrick Leung Pak-kin. Cast: Aaron Kwok Fu-sheng (Ken Wong), Carman Lee Yeuk-tung (Gloria Chan), Sammo Hung Kam-po (Black Jack Hung), Michael Tong Man-lung (Rocky Chan), Hilary Tsui Ho-ying (Pam), Law Koon-lan (Ken's Mother), Ann Hui On-wah (Teacher), Clifton Ko Chi-sum (Pao), Vincent Kok Tak-chiu (Obnoxious Spectator), Lawrence Ah Mon (Fight Official). Dolby Digital. 1.85:1. VHS: World Video. Import LD/VCD/ DVD: Universe. 111 minutes.

Bearing no connection to the like-named Robert Wise film from the 1950s, this kickboxing movie is an ill-conceived mix of genre cliches, hoary melodrama, and overproduced visuals, all of which have the cumulative effect of pummelling the viewer into a state of complete apathy. Young ex-con Ken Wong ruthlessly pursues beautiful Gloria Chan, with his advances eventually angering the girl's brother, Rocky. HK's kickboxing champ, Rocky pummels Ken in a bar, prompting the latter to dedicate himself to becoming a first-rate competitor. Under the tutelage of respected trainer Black Jack Hung, Ken gradually improves and defeats a series of other fighters. He then proceeds to challenge Rocky to a bout, causing predictable friction between him and Gloria (who has just discovered that she is pregnant). During their subsequent match, Ken accidentally kills Rocky. When Gloria refuses to have anything more to do with him, Ken begins to participate in brutal, bare knuckle underground matches that begin to take a toll on his health. When he decides to take a shot at the Asian championship, Ken shrugs off a blood clot he has developed, with predictable consequences.

Fans of Aaron Kwok and Carman Lee will be in seventh heaven, as the beautiful leads are granted enough close-ups here for ten movies. Such attention, however, does not make one care any more about their one-dimensional characters in a film that is nothing more than a parade of pretty images propping up overwrought, simplistic writing. The fight sequences are well-staged (Kwok comes off more convincing in the ring than out of it), but even they wear thin through repetition.

Son of the Beach *see* **The Royal Scoundrel**

907. Song of the Exile

(1990) ★: 6/10. *Haak to chau han* (Cantonese), *Ke tu qiu hen* (Mandarin): "Exile and Autumn Sorrow." Cinematographer: David Chung Chi-man; Art Director: Hai Chung-man; Music: Chan Yeung; Writer: Ng Lim-chan; Producers: Nai Chung-chou, Teng Fei-lin; Director: Ann Hui On-wah. Cast: Maggie Cheung Man-yuk (Cheung Hueyin), Lu Hsiao-fen (Aiko), Waise Lee Chi-hung (Mr. Cheung), Tien Feng (Hueyin's Grandfather). 1.85:1. VHS: Kino on Video, Tai Seng. LD: Laserlink International, Media Asia. 99 minutes.

Director Ann Hui grew up not knowing that her mother was Japanese, a fact she did not learn until she was a teenager. **Song of the Exile** is her largely biographical depiction of how alienation and distance (both literal and emotional) lead to a seemingly irreparable rift between a mother and daughter. It opens in London in the early '70s as Cheung Hueyin graduates from college with a Master's Degree and decides to return to HK for her sister's wedding. Shortly after her arrival, it becomes clear that the rift between Hueyin and her mother, Aiko, not only still exists, it has actually become even more pronounced. Already a widow, Aiko is now losing her favorite daughter to marriage and stills harbors resentment towards Hueyin for leaving her and going off to England. Through flashbacks, we learn Hueyin was spoiled by her grandparents, who treated Aiko with open disdain because of her nationality. This fuelled Aiko's negative feelings and turned her into the self-pitying, loathsome woman that Hueyin finds upon her return. Hueyin decides to accompany her mother on a trip to Japan, and there, totally out of her element, the girl begins to understand what it was like for Aiko living in Macau, away from everything that was a part of her heritage.

A filmmaker who always gets the best out of her actors, Hui elicits moving performances from both Maggie Cheung and Lu Hsiao-fen. However, in spite of its flashback-laden structure (which even occasionally places flashbacks within flashbacks), the story progresses along seemingly inescapable lines; no matter what dramatic friction arises, the resolution never really seems in doubt. **Song of the Exile** remains a laudable endeavor, earnestly presented and beautifully photographed, but is also a somewhat tedious and stifling one that never quite reaches its full potential.

908. The Soong Sisters

(1997; Golden Harvest/Fuji Television Network/Pony Canyon/More Team International Ltd. Production) ★: 6/10. *Sung ga wong chiu* (Cantonese), *Song jia huang chao* (Mandarin): "The Sung Family Dynasty" or "The Song Family Dynasty." Cinematographer: Arthur Wong Ngok-tai; Art Director: Eddie Ma Poon-chiu; Music: Kitaro, Randy Miller; Writer: Alex Law Kai-yui; Producers: Ng See-yuen, Alex Law Kai-yui; Director: Mabel Cheung Yuen-ting. Cast: Maggie Cheung Man-yuk (Soong Ching-ling), Michelle Yeoh Chu-kheng (Soong Ai-ling), Vivian Wu Kwan-mui (Soong May-ling), Wu Hsin-kuo (Chiang Kai-shek), Winston Chao Wen-hsuan (Dr. Sun Yat-sen), Jiang Wen (Charlie Soong), Elaine Kam Yin-ling (Madam Soong), Niu Zhenhua (H.H. Kung). Dolby Digital. 2.35:1. Import LD/VCD/DVD: Mei Ah. 135/146 minutes.

Cut by Mainland censors (who held back the film's release for almost three years), this sweeping epic is entertaining as melodrama, yet remains a strangely empty and passionless endeavour. It tells the respective life stories of Ching-ling, Ai-ling, and May-ling, daughters of the brilliant and charming Charlie Soong, the financial backer of Sun Yat-sen's revolt against the Qin government. While a Chinese patriot, Soong feels that the key to resurrecting his country lies in following the American example set by Abraham Lincoln. To that end, he sends his young girls to the United States for their education. Upon the sisters' return to China, Ching-ling falls in love with Sun (residing in Japan after the failure of his revolutionary government), much to the dismay of her father, who regards their union as a betrayal by both his child and his friend. Ai-ling marries millionaire H.H. Kung, while May-ling falls in love with Sun's top military man, Chiang Kai-shek. Following Sun's death, Chiang begins to stray from Sun's original doctrines, violently suppressing the communist factions of the Nationalist Party. This betrayal of her husband's ideals, and May-ling's subsequent marriage to Chiang, alienates Ching-ling, who leaves the family and travels to Russia. However, upon hearing that her mother has grown terminally ill, she returns to China and leads the forces opposing Chiang in order to unify the various factions against their common enemy, the Japanese, who are taking military advantage of China's internal strife.

Outstanding on a technical level, **The Soong Sisters** is a grand epic of the old school, with a multitude of extras, lavish sets, and splendid costumes. Beautiful cinematography and dynamic montages (particularly a sequence that intercuts between Chiang reading aloud from the bible and his men ruthlessly slaughtering communist supporters) are also plentiful. However, it presents history in such a formal, sober fashion, there is no place for the complex characterizations and stirring emotions that make for great drama. In spite of this, Maggie Cheung gives another astonishingly good performance as the unyielding Ching-ling, and Jiang Wen lights up the screen as the stern but loveable Soong patriarch. While competent, Vivian Wu is too young to be fully convincing as May-ling, and her performance lacks the authority the role requires. Michelle Yeoh is given virtually nothing to do as the materialistic Ai-ling, and Wu Hsin-kuo's Chiang (thanks to the censors' removal of scenes that showed his tender side) is merely menacing and malevolent; the man's great charisma is not in evidence here. In addition to the changes demanded by China, the film was reedited for its video release by Mei Ah, without Mabel Cheung's consent (she subsequently sued). The laserdisc set runs 135 minutes, about 11 minutes less than HK theatrical prints. The company's VCD and DVD versions are reportedly even shorter.

909. Soul

(1986; Molesworth/Quality Images) ★: 7/10. *Lo neung gau so* (Cantonese), *Lao niang gou sao* (Mandarin): "Old Woman Upheaves the Dogs." Cinematographer: Christopher Doyle; Art Director: Tony Au Ding-ping; Music: Danny Chung Teng-yat; Producer: Hsu Feng; Writer-Director: Shu Kei. Cast: Deanie Yip Tak-han (Lee Yip-cheong), Elaine Kam Yin-ling (Gigi), Dennis Chan Kwok-san (Wai-wai), Jacky Cheung Hok-yau (Jacky Cheong), Hou Hsiao-hsien (Boy-Boy), Manfred Wong (Insurance Agent), David Chiang Da-wei (Lee Kai-yeung), Alfred Cheung Kin-ting (Ticket Booth Attendant). 1.85:1. Import LD/VCD: Ocean Shores. 95 minutes.

Film critic Shu Kei's take on John Cassavetes' **Gloria, Soul** benefits from Shu's offbeat approach to the material and Deanie Yip's persuasive performance as a woman whose entire world goes to pieces in a matter of minutes. Not long after a trio of very stupid hoods kill a neighbor and threaten her life, Lee Yip-cheong learns that her police officer husband Kai-yeung has inexplicably jumped to his death from the roof of the station house. The authorities suspect that Kai-yeung must have been involved in underworld dealings, even though they have no proof, and the man's insurance company refuses to honor his policy because he has not paid his premiums for several months. On top of all this, Yip-cheong is obliged to look after the dead woman's bratty three-year-old boy. When the child is kidnapped by the gangsters (who want some mysterious book that was in Kai-yeung's possession), and it's clear that she will receive no help from the police, Yip-cheong takes matters into her own hands.

Filled with absurdist humor and a dream-like ambiance, **Soul** starts off beautifully, loses some of its focus in the second half, and then rebounds for a satisfying climax. The film has been referred to as a "feminist crime story," and there is certainly no arguing that the women here are far more intelligent, resourceful, and resilient than the men. While it may not have been his intention, Shu's decidedly non-glamorous depiction of gangsters and the workings of the mob is an effective contrast to the route most HK filmmakers would take following the runaway success of **A Better Tomorrow** (which opened seven weeks prior to this production). Acclaimed Taiwanese director Hou Hsiao-hsien appears in a supporting role as an old flame Yip-cheong enlists to help her. Christopher Doyle's stylish camerawork netted him the Best Cinematography prize at the 1987 HK Film Awards.

Spartan X *see* **Wheels on Meals**
The Spearman of Death *see* **Flag of Iron**

910. Spider Woman

(1995; Production Plaza/Good Standard International) ★: 2/10. *Ji jue nui* (Cantonese), *Zhi zhu nu* (Mandarin): "Spider Woman." Cinematographer: Joe Chan Kong hung; Art Director: Alex Mok Siu-on; Music: Chan Kwong-wing; Writers: Roy Szeto Cheuk-hon, Lo Kin; Producer-Director: Lo Kin. Cast: Jade Leung Ching (Kenny/Ken), Michael Wong Man-tak (Edwin), Chan Kwok-bong (Dr. Wong Fat-lok), Valerie Chow Kar-ling (Carman), Lowell Lo Kwun-ting (Malone), Dayo Wong Chi-wah ("Golden Corpse"), Leung Wing-chung (Gordon), Emily Kwan Bo-wai (Assistant Coroner). 1.85:1. VHS: Tai Seng. Import LD/VCD: Universe. 96 minutes.

This Category III thriller seemingly wants to be the local equivalent of glossy Hollywood trash like **Basic Instinct** but it only inspires snickers and groans in equal proportions. Undercover cop Edwin gets an assistant's position at a gallery run by Kenny, a woman with some obvious problems. He is investigating a series of brutal murders which are clearly the work of one killer. Could it be Kenny's lookalike sister, Ken, who mistrusts all men but is a nymphomaniac? Her psychiatrist, who violates every code of professional ethics in the book? Or maybe Edwin himself, who is ready to kill his soon-to-be ex-wife?

Peopled by ridiculous characters with exaggerated eccentricities (the worst being Dayo Wong's blatantly insane coroner who engages in violent sex and death games with his submissive assistant), the film tries much too hard at generating erotic subplots, forgetting to bother with a feasible framework. Situations are implausible, coincidences pile up, and no one behaves with any degree of sense. While adept at physical roles, Leung is not a good enough actress to pull off this sort of involved part, and it certainly doesn't help that she must act opposite Michael Wong, giving a performance here that is deficient even by his amateurish standards. There is also the question of sex, or lack thereof: Virtually everyone is connected to someone, but when they do finally get into bed, they never get naked (the adults-only rating is earned primarily for a handful of bloody murders). A better plan would have been to simply cast this with Category III regulars and make it an out-and-out softcore exploitation thriller. At least then it would have delivered on some level.

911. Spike Drink Gang

(1995; Jing's Production) ★: 1/10. *Mai wan dong* (Cantonese), *Mi hun dang* (Mandarin): "Love Potion Gang." Cinematographer: Tony Miu Kin-fai; Art Director: Wong Ting-hong; Music: Marco Wan Ho-kit, Anthony Lee Hon-kam; Producer: Lee Siu-kei; Writer-Director: Bosco Lam Hing-lung. Cast: Yvonne Yung Hung (Mrs. Tsui), Lo Mang (Chan Chi-hung), Elvis Tsui Kam-kong (Tsui), Chan Kwok-bong (Ho Siu-sun). 1.85:1. VHS: Tai Seng. Import LD/VCD: Universe. 92 minutes.

One of the milder entries in the "True Crime" subgenre, **Spike Drink Gang** is played largely for laughs but doesn't garner any. Not one. In a scenario based on a real-life case, a gang of robbers inject juice boxes with ether, sneak them onto store shelves, and then wait for a woman to purchase and drink the drugged beverage. When the victim is half unconscious, they rob, abduct, and rape her. Yvonne Yung is their first patsy, the scatterbrained wife of an equally dense butcher, and policeman Chan Kwok-bong enlists her services to apprehend the gang by having her undergo the whole ordeal again. Remarkably, this brainless idea actually works, allowing the authorities to nab two of the gang members while their leader (played by Shaw Brothers veteran Lo Mang) tries to evade capture.

In order to compensate for the fact that there is only about ten minutes worth of plot, the film stops dead in its tracks on several occasions for protracted and unfunny comic relief from Elvis Tsui as the honorable but vengeance-obsessed butcher. Even by the relaxed standards of Category III fare, this is utter swill.

912. Spirit of Love

(1993; Golden Harvest/Paragon Films) ★: 4/10. *Oi dik cheng leng* (Cantonese), *Ai de jing ling* (Mandarin): "Love Spirit." Cinematographer: Cheung King-nin; Art Director: Jon Hau Wing-choi; Music: Simon Leung Chi-wah, Tony Tam Chan-hung; Writers: Jamie Luk Kim-ming, So Man-sing; Producer: Chua Lam; Director: Jamie Luk Kim-ming. Cast: Loletta Lee Lai-chun, Vincent Lam Wai, Tom Poon Chun-wai, Joanna Chan Pui-san. 1.85:1. VHS: Tai Seng (No Subtitles). Import LD/VCD: Star Entertainment (No Subtitles). 99 minutes.

Difficult to locate in subtitled form, this Loletta Lee softcore outing will probably still appeal to those interested enough to seek it out in the first place. The storyline (rather nonsensical even by genre standards) concerns the spirit of an infant accidentally released from an amulet owned by Lee (playing a fashion model). Flashbacks reveal that Lee was once pregnant, but after she caught her boyfriend (husband?) fooling around, he kicked her in the stomach, which caused her to fall down a flight of stairs. After she loses the baby, a Taoist priest presents her with a locket containing the child's spirit. Following some nightmarish images (torrents of bloods issuing from a shower head and bedroom walls), the ghost of the baby (now looking to be about five years old) appears to Lee and she quickly accepts the cute little boy. During a fashion shoot, the child appears to her but cannot be seen by any of the crew. However, the ghost *does* appear in the developed film footage. With some magical assistance, the sadistic boyfriend is able to capture the boy, hoping to use the spirit's powers to win at gambling. The erotic sequences aren't bad, but the abuse directed towards the child (ghost or not) is a bit disquieting. The Lam Wai listed above is not the Mainland-born character actor best known for **Long Arm of the Law** and **Project A II**.

913. Spiritual Kung Fu

(1978; Lo Wei Motion Picture Co.) ★: 5/10. *Kuen jing* (Cantonese), *Quan jing* (Mandarin): "Fist Spirit." Cinematographer: Chen Rong-shu; Art Director: Chou Chi-liang; Music: Not Original; Writer: Poon Lui; Producers: Lo Wei, Hsu Li-hwa; Action Director: Jackie Chan; Director: Lo Wei. Cast: Jackie Chan (Yi-lang), James Tien Chun (Luk), Dean Shek Tien (Shaolin Student), Wong Ching (Luk's

Man). 2.35:1. VHS: All Seasons (Dubbed), Simitar (Dubbed), UAV (Dubbed). Import LD/VCD/DVD: Ocean Shores (Poor Subtitles). 90 minutes. Also known as **Karate Ghostbuster** (UK video title).

A close second to **Half a Loaf of Kung Fu!** as the oddest of Jackie Chan's '70s films, **Spiritual Kung Fu** casts him as Yi-lang, a consistently naughty pupil at Shaolin Temple. One evening a thief breaks into the temple and steals "The Book of The Deadly Fists," an irreplaceable kung fu manual. Anyone who masters this technique could use it to rule the martial world, precisely the goal of the villainous Wei-wu, who sets about using his improved skills to wipe out his enemies. To make matters worse, five really silly looking ghosts have appeared and none of the monks are able to drive them away. While dealing with the mischievous spirits, Yi-lang discovers the long-lost manual for the "Five Fists" fighting style, which just happens to be the spirits' home. Eager to improve his kung fu, Yi-lang takes lessons from the ghosts, and the new techniques he masters allow him to take on Wei-wu.

The special FX date back to the silent era, but the storyline (which includes a murder mystery) is interesting and there is a steady stream of action. Those, however, who are bothered by the goofier extremes of Chan's films should definitely avoid this one. The Chinese video versions are from a TV print which is missing some of the more off-color humor.

914. Spiritual Love

(1987; Golden Harvest/Johnny Mak Production/Paragon Films) ★: 6/10. *Gwai san neung* (Cantonese), *Gui xin niang* (Mandarin): "Ghost Bride." Cinematographers: Jingle Ma Cho-shing, Derek Wan Man-kit; Art Director: Fong Ying; Music: Joseph Chan Wing-leung; Writer: Stephen Siu Yeuk-yuen; Producer: Johnny Mak Dong-hung; Directors: David Lai Tai-wai, Taylor Wong Tai-loi. Cast: Chow Yun-fat ("Double Circle" Pu), Cherie Chung Cho-hung (Wei Hsiao-tieh), Deanie Yip Tak-han (Chin-hua), Pauline Wong Siu-fung (May), Paul Chun Pui (Pu's Boss), Ng Hong-ning (Big Guy). Dolby Digital (DVD only). 1.85:1. VHS: Tai Seng (No Subtitles). Import LD: Star Entertainment (No Subtitles). Import VCD: Universe (No Subtitles). Import DVD: Universe. 87 minutes.

In exchange for three years of his life, good-for-nothing Pu is able to save spirit Wei Hsiao-teh from having to spend all eternity with an ugly ghost for a husband. It doesn't take Pu long to fall head over heels for Hsiao-teh, especially after she helps him get even with his shrewish ex-girlfriend May and saves him from some murderous triads. When Hsiao-tieh's spirit is weakened by Taoist priests, Pu voluntarily sacrifices another ten years of his life to prevent her from fading away. The ritual only allots her another 49 days on earth, however; and there is another problem: May has committed suicide and come back as a vengeance-seeking ghost!

Fairly routine as ghost comedies go, **Spiritual Love** is still very watchable, thanks to a quality cast and a bravura finale in an abandoned disco. Chow Yun-fat is not used to best advantage here, being allowed to go a bit too far over-the-top during the comic bits; even a send-up of his famous "restaurant hit" scene from **A Better Tomorrow** falls pretty flat. He handles the sentimental and dramatic aspects of the role well, though. In an offbeat bit of casting, actress/singer Deanie Yip plays a female Taoist with a male hairstyle who carries a torch for Pu. She and Cherie Chung participate in an opera send-up, the effectiveness of which will depend on how much exposure the viewer has had to this uniquely Chinese art. The Universe VCD has no subtitles, despite claims to the contrary on the packaging. Character names above are taken from the subtitled version that aired on Channel 4 in the UK.

915. Spiritual Trinity

(1991; Hatract Films) ★: 5/10. *Yan gwai san* (Cantonese), *Ren gui shen* (Mandarin): "Human, Ghost, God." Cinematographer: Raymond Lam Fai-tai; Art Director: Fred Chan Chi-chung; Music: Wong Chi-hung; Writer: Johnny Lee King-kai; Producers: Kent Cheng Chuk-see, Kam Cheung-kuen; Action Directors: Hsiao Hou, Power Lee King-chu; Director: Ng Min-kan. Cast: Kent Cheng Chuk-see (Tien Kuei), Pauline Wong Siu-fung (Mun), Lam Ching-ying (Tien Lung), Gigi Lai Chi (Hsiu-shuan), Bonnie Fu Yuk-ching (Shu-wen), Peter Chan Lung (Shau), Chung Fat (Wizard). Stereo Sound (Laserdisc only). 1.85:1. VHS: World Video (No Subtitles). Import LD: Focus Entertainment (No Subtitles). 93 minutes.

A follow-up of sorts to the wonderful **Spooky Family**, with some of the same cast, this lightweight horror-comedy is, alas, not in the same league. The family depicted in this entry gets an unexpected visit from benevolent female ghost Shu-wen when one of son Yuen-kao's bizarre inventions inadvertently snares the wandering spirit, who was on her way to Hell. Shu-wen is taken into their home as a welcome guest, but trouble arises in the form of uncle Tien Lung, an expert ghost-hunter, who insists that humans and spirits can never live in harmony. Unfortunately, at this point, the proceedings get side-tracked and too much time is spent on patriarch Kuei's jealousy and worry that his brother might woo his wife away. Things pick up again in the final reel when a vicious demon Lung had imprisoned gets loose and possesses Shu-wen, leading to the sort of wild supernatural combat that made the first film so memorable. The soundtrack includes music lifted from **Aliens** and **Prince of Darkness**. The Taiwanese video version has English subtitles.

916. Split of the Spirit

(1987; Good Year Movie Co.) ★: 6/10. *Lai gwai chin sun* (Cantonese), *Li gui chan shen* (Mandarin): "Powerful Ghost Binds to Body." Cinematographer: Yang Wei-han; Art Director: Tu Hui-yan; Music: Peter Chang Hong-yi; Producer: Lo Wei; Writer-Director: Fred Tan Han-chang. Cast: Pauline Wong Siu-fung (Lu Ling), Hsu Shu-yuan, Wu Shao-gang, Ku Kuan-chung, Cynthia Yang Li-ching (Kao Pi-liang). 1.85:1. Import LD/VCD: Ocean Shores. 89 minutes.

Despite the success of her new show, "Split of the Spirit," high strung choreographer Lu Ling attempts suicide, due to the break-up of her relationship. Shortly after recovering, Ling accidentally bumps into an old woman carrying the ashes of socialite Jennifer Chung, who was murdered by her calculating husband. Ling cuts her finger on a shard of the smashed container, which allows Jennifer's spirit to enter into her. Ling is now, unknowingly, a vessel for Jennifer to take revenge on those involved in her demise. A photographer takes a picture of Ling that reveals her unusual condition, prompting him to try and help the understandably confused woman.

This flawed but intriguing Taiwanese production is included here not only because it stars Pauline Wong but also because it presents an interesting contrast to analogous HK pictures. While there are definite similarities in the way some sequences are presented, for the most part, **Split of the Spirit** tends to approach the material with a bit more artistry. Until the climax, special effects are kept to a minimum in favor on-set atmospherics, with effective results. However, the attempt to link Ling's situation with the plot of her show is a bit labored, and the story's resolution is not entirely satisfying. Director Fred Tan made only two other films, **Dark Night** (1986) and **Rouge of the North** (1988). He succumbed to AIDS-related hepatitis in 1990 at the young age of 35.

917. The Spooky Bunch

(1980; Hi-Pitch Co.) ★: 4/10. *Jong do jing* (Cantonese), *Zhuang dao zheng* (Mandarin): "Bumped to Propriety." Cinematographer: Anthony Ho Tung-lei; Art Director: Lee Ngok-see; Music: The Melody Bank, Tong Poon-kai; Writer: Joyce Chan Wan-man; Producer: Josephine Siao Fong-fong; Action Director: Ching Siu-tung; Director: Ann Hui On-wah. Cast: Josephine Siao Fong-fong (Chi), Kenny Bee (Dick), Olivia Cheng Man-ar, Lau Hark-sun, Kwan Chung. 1.85:1. VHS: Tai Seng (Poor Subtitles). 92 minutes.

Although it is regarded as one of the pivotal films of "The New Wave," time has not been kind to this ghost comedy, and most Western viewers will find it obscure and tiresome. A run-down Peking Opera troupe is hired to give a performance on Cheung Chau Island, right at a time when activity in the spirit world is especially high. The male lead is possessed by a female ghost named "Cat Shit," which leads to all manner of trouble. Flighty actress Chi temporarily makes friends with Cat Shit, but she and handsome young Dick are threatened by a gang of dead soldiers (killed by poisoned medicine) out for revenge. The platoon of bloodthirsty spirits proceed to possess the performers and have dastardly plans for Dick, but he is saved just in time by Chi. The soldiers demand a midnight performance with Chi as the star, but it may turn out to be her last role unless a powerful monk can vanquish the ghosts to the netherworld.

Josephine Siao gives an endearing performance and her playful tomfoolery is ceaselessly watchable. However, so many of the films that followed this surpass it, both in terms of technique and scripting. **The Spooky Bunch** will only be of interest to those studying the genre and/or director Ann Hui's output.

Spooky Encounters *see* **Encounter of the Spooky Kind**

918. Spooky Family

(1990) ★: 7/10. *Chuk gwai gap fung foon* (Cantonese), *Zhuo gui he gu huan* (Mandarin): "Capture Ghost United Joyful Family." Cinematographer: Chan Tung-chuen; Art Director: Fred Chan Chi-chung; Music: James Yeung Jim, Jibson Yeung Siu-hung; Writer: Johnny Lee King-kai; Producers: Charles Heung Wah-keung, Billy Chan Wui-ngai; Action Director: Power Lee King-chu; Director: Chin Yuet-sang. Cast: Kent Cheng Chuk see (Hung Ping), Pauline Wong Siu-fung (Hung's Wife), Nina Li Chi (Colleague Sister), Billy Lau Nam-kwong (The Top Wizard), Alvina Kong Yan-yin (Fa), Peter Chan Lung (Ghost Servant), Sandra Ng Kwan-yu (Customer), Shing Fui-on (Customer), Chung Fat (Wizard). 1.85:1. VHS: World Video. Import LD: Star Entertainment (No Subtitles). Running time unknown.

A terrific period horror-comedy, **Spooky Family** stars big Kent Cheng as bumbling restaurateur Hung Ping, who hasn't had a customer in a year. His wife and daughter use their psychic powers to tell fortunes, allowing the family to make ends meet. Hung makes use of his ample spare time by playing around in a makeshift lab with his bumbling son and an Uncle Fester lookalike called "Ghost Servant." His latest invention is the "Human and Corpse Linking Machine" which, if successful, will allow him to control (via mental telepathy) the dusty old *gyonsi* he has stashed in the lab. Using his son as a guinea pig, the experiment works, leading to some fun slapstick as the boy inadvertently causes the vampire to beat up his old man. Hung's fortunes seem to pick up a bit when he is hired to catch the mythical, all-powerful "Copper Vampire." Unfortunately, fate isn't going to give him a break here either: Jealous competitors get to the creature first and increase its power by feeding it potions and fresh blood. After a lengthy battle (which features Hung and son being bounced around like human pinballs), the monster is finally subdued with coffin nails and fifty-year-old chicken blood. Following this triumph, Hung receives a visit from the egotistical "Top Wizard." Anxious to defeat this blowhard during their inevitable magic duel, Hung has Ghost Servant enter his body so that they can combine their powers. The bizarre tag team is on the verge of triumphing when the Wizard slips Hung a supernatural mickey, causing the Ghost to get too drunk to help. The dimwitted Wizard unleashes the Copper Vampire, which then drinks his blood, causing its strength to increase even more. The family soon finds their house besieged by an army of the undead, and the only hope is for Hung to call on the beautiful "Colleague Sister" for help.

Even by the energetic standards of most HK comedies, **Spooky Family** offers more back-breaking slapstick bits than you've probably ever seen in one movie. This one ranks with the best of Sammo Hung's knockabout supernatural farces and is definitely recommended to both fans and the uninitiated. There is even an **Addams Family**-type theme song! Much of the same team re-assembled the next year for **Spiritual Trinity**.

919. Spooky, Spooky

(1988; Golden Harvest/Bojon Films Company/Paragon Films) ★: 7/10. *Gwai maang geuk* (Cantonese), *Gui meng jiao* (Mandarin): "Ghost Fierce Foot." Cinematographer: Jimmy Leung Chi-ming; Art Director: Raymond Lee King-man; Music: The Melody Bank; Writer: Roy Szeto Cheuk-hon; Producer: Leonard Ho Koon-cheung; Action Director: Yuen Wah; Director: Sammo Hung Kam-po. Cast: Alfred Cheung Kin-ting (Wang Hsiao-ming), Anthony Chan Yau (Chen), Wu Ma (Lu Hsien), Joyce Godenzi (Sgt. Pai), Chung Fat (Chen Ta-wen, aka "Queency"), Yuen Wah (East Bay Sgt.), Corey Yuen Kwai (Hen Egg), Richard Ng Yiu-hon (East Bay Station Commander), Yip Wing-cho (Village Head), Billy Lau Nam-kwong (Four Eyes), Feng Sing (East Bay Cop), James Tien Chun (Master Tien). 1.85:1. VHS: Tai Seng. LD: Winson Entertainment. 95 minutes.

Sammo Hung directed this terrific genre hybrid which mixes HK ghost movie conventions with components from **Jaws**, "dead teenager" movies, **Evil Dead II**, **The Thing**, and **Ghostbusters**! In olden times, a pair of adulterers are caught in the act and executed for their crime. Jump to 1988: A female swimmer is pulled underwater to her death by an unseen force. Rookie cop Wang, his lazy superior Lu, belligerent Inspector Chen, and the beautiful, man-hating Sgt. Pai are assigned to investigate, but the corpses continue to mount. The murderous nix is actually the female adulterer, and her quest for vengeance takes a bizarre turn when she falls for the noble but cowardly Wang. After a fierce battle, the spectre is dispersed, thanks to some handy vermilion bullets, but the still-skeptical Chen gets pulled underwater to *his* death, returning as a blue and bloated zombie. With the aid of coroner/ghosthunter *Queency* (Chung Fat, looking like Christopher Lloyd's "Doc" from **Back to the Future**) and their counterparts at the East Bay station, the officers try to survive the night until more help can arrive.

Filled with more energy and genuine laughs than any five Hollywood horror-comedies, **Spooky, Spooky** provides fresh spins on familiar setpieces (in a great send-up of the "blood test" scene from John Carpenter's **The Thing**, the cops test to see which of them is possessed by determining who has the saltiest sweat!) while also including the action quota demanded of any Sammo Hung project. Who could ask for anything more?

920. Spy Games

(1990; Film Workshop) ★: 4/10. *Jung yat naam bak woh* (Cantonese), *Zhong ri nan bei he* (Mandarin): "China Japan North South Cooperation." Cinematographer: Ardy Lam Kwok-wah; Art Director: Andy Lee Yiu-kwong; Music: Kou Otani; Writers: Ng Man-fai, Philip Cheng Chung-tai, Lam Kei-to, Lau Tai-muk; Producer: Tsui Hark; Director: David Wu Tai-wai. Cast: Kenny Bee (Ken Chung), Noriko Izumoto (Takako), Joey Wang Tsu-hsien (Joey Wong), Saburo Tokito (Kudo), Waise Lee Chi-hung (Lee Chi-hung), Liu Wai-hung (Ken's Cameraman), Phillip Chan Yan-kin (Ken's Boss), Michael Chan Wai-man (Lau), Lam Chung (CIA Man). 1.85:1. VHS: Tai Seng. Import LD: Mei Ah. 92 minutes.

An intriguing idea that just doesn't come off, this Film Workshop production mixes HK and Japanese talent together in a comic spy caper that is all but sunk by an abundance of unfunny comedy and contrived situations. As part of a practical joke gone awry, Japanese pop star Takako is convinced that her father is being held by murderous spies in HK. She immediately gets on a plane and lands bumbling TV anchorman Ken in a heap of trouble by stealing (and subsequently destroying) his station's camera van. Takako's belief that spies are after her actually turns out to be true: She has gotten caught in the middle of a battle between the KGB and CIA, and eternal fall guy Ken ends up in even more trouble when he tries to help her. In the meantime, Takako's boyfriend and manager join up with policewoman Joey to find her.

Director David Wu (**The Bride with White Hair 2**) and cinematographer Ardy Lam give the proceedings an attractive, glossy veneer, but that is not enough to compensate for the ennui that ensues when one realizes that the film is never going to be as challenging or entertaining as it could be. On the other hand, you do get to hear veteran tough guy Michael Chan sing, which may be enough for some viewers.

Stagedoor *see* **Hu-Du-Men**

921. Starry Is the Night

(1988; Shaw Brothers/Tomson Film Co./Popsight) ★: 5/10. *Gam ye sing gwong chaan laan* (Cantonese), *Jin ye xing guang can lan* (Mandarin): "Tonight's Starlight Is Splendid." Cinematographer: Henry Chan Chun-kit; Art Director: Daniel Lee Yan-kong; Music: Danny Chung Teng-yat; Writer: Leung Suk-wah; Producers: Hsu Feng, Mona Fong Yat-wah; Director: Ann Hui On-wah. Cast: Brigitte Lin Ching-hsia (To Cai-mei), George Lam Chi-cheung (Dr. Y.C. Cheung), David Wu Tai-wai (Cheung Tien-on), Derek Yee Tung-sing (Poon Chung-lung), John Woo Yu-sen (Father Fan), Maria Tung Ling (Mary), John Sham Kin-fun (Man at Rally). 1.85:1. VHS: Tai Seng. Import LD: Ocean Shores. 97 minutes.

39-year-old social worker To Cai-mei journeys to Macau in order to help a troubled client. While there, she encounters handsome 18-year-old scam artist Cheung Tien-on, who fled from HK owing over a million dollars following the stock market crash. Even though he is not one of her cases, Cai-mei's superior asks her to try and convince him to come back and face up to his responsibilities. However, the more time Cai-mei spends with Tien-on, the more she relishes his company, although she cannot come close to matching his pace when it comes to drinking and acts of irresponsible fun. Cai-mei's job is soon threatened by her actions, but in spite of deep reservations, she is not happy without Tien-on. Sprinkled throughout the present day footage are flashbacks to 1967 in which we see Cai-mei during her days as a university student and her budding relationship with faculty member Dr. Cheung. While in love with Cai-mei, Cheung refuses to leave his pregnant wife, and the emotional scars left by their inevitable break-up influence the pair's lives for years to come.

Starry Is the Night has a fine performance from Brigitte Lin and some beautifully staged, affecting sequences but is fatally compromised by the sort of melodramatic excesses (especially the narrative twist in the final third, which is simply unforgivable) typical of the Taiwanese Qiong Yao adaptations that made Lin a star in the early '70s. It has been suggested that director Ann Hui undertook this project so that she could complete her contract with Shaw Brothers, and move on, but portions of the film are so good, one cannot help but feel that Hui's heart was largely in her work here. David Wu (the Taiwanese actor, not the HK actor/director) won the Best Newcomer prize for his work here.

922. The Sting

(1992; Wong's Film Company) ★: 4/10. *Hap sing* (Cantonese), *Xia sheng* (Mandarin): "Chivalrous Saint." Cinematographer: Yuen Wai-kwok; Art Director: Ganni Ma Chi-ming; Music: Anthony Lee Hon-kam, Marco Wan Ho-kit; Writers: Lee Ying-kit, Johnny Lee King-kai; Producer: Billy Chan Wui-ngai; Action Director: Power Lee King-chu; Director: Nico Wong Man-wan. Cast: Andy Lau Tak-wah (Simon Tam), Rosamund Kwan Chi-lam (Yvonne), Simon Lui Yu-yeung (Joe), Bowie Lam Bo-yee (Michael Lam), Michael Dinga (Beardy), Fong Ying (Baddy), Chin Ho (Officer from Commercial Crimes Unit), Shing Fui-on (Tak), Pau Fong (Simon's Master). 1.85:1. LD: Network Kingdom. Import LD/VCD: Universe. 93 minutes.

This blithely eccentric comedy concerns the exploits of Simon Tam, a fast-talking but impoverished private investigator on a case involving over $1 billion in diamonds. At the center of the mystery is Yvonne, the gorgeous widow of a drug dealer/arms smuggler, who is up against triads out to claim the huge fortune her husband embezzled from a finance company. Simon seeks to help the girl out of her predicament but she lies to him at every turn, putting his life in danger repeatedly. A pushover for a beauty, Simon keeps coming back for more and just may convince Yvonne to trust him...if he survives.

Lots of wordplay and cartoonish action but not much in the way of comic inspiration here; the finale is particularly weak. Simon Lui garners a few chuckles as Simon's fey, acid-tongued assistant but the most notable aspect of this production is the stylish theatrical poster. **The Sting II** has no connection to this film.

923. The Sting II

(1993; Win's Movie Production) ★: 6/10. *Ji juen jau luk gai ji tau tin woon yat* (Cantonese), *Zhi zun zhou liu ji zhi tou tian huan ri* (Mandarin): "Most Respected Caper: Gigantic Deception." Cinematographers: Andrew Lau Wai-keung, Tony Miu Kin-fai; Art Director: Andrew Cheuk Man-yiu; Music: Phil Chan Fei-lap; Producer: Jimmy Heung Wah-sing; Action Director: Dion Lam Dik-on; Writer-Director: Wong Jing. Cast: Andy Lau Tak-wah (Mandy Chin), Tony Leung Kar-fai (Chung Chor-hung), Anita Lee Yuen-wah (Mona), Kwan Hoi-shan (Robinson), Yuen King-tan (Turkey Chu), Liu Kai-chi (Gold-finger Chi), Nat Chan Pak-cheung (Chan Chung-ming), Christy Chung Lai-tai (Lily), Johnny Wang Lung-wei (Lau), Yip Wing-cho (Chung's Dad), Tommy Wong Kwong-leung (Big Eye Kwong), William Ho Kar-kui (Inmate). 1.85:1. VHS: Tai Seng. Import LD/VCD/DVD: Mei Ah. 104 minutes. Also known as **Perfect Exchange**.

Even by Wong Jing's standards, this action comedy is too silly for its own good. It does have its moments, though, and Tony Leung Kar-fai gives one of his best comic performances to date. Mandy and Gold-finger are card sharks who bilk gangster Lau out of $6 million in a rigged game. One of their other dupes is prison guard Chung Chor-hung (no relation to Cherie

Chung), whom they also beat up for good measure. When the triad catches up with the two hucksters, he demands that Mandy get himself sent to prison in order to learn the location of some bonds from Robinson, a rival. Of course, the institution in question just happens to be the one where Chung is the Senior Inspector. Mandy gets to know Robinson and learns that he was framed by Lau for the murder of his own daughter. Lau managed to get all of Robinson's fortune, with the exception of the aforementioned securities. Mandy strikes a deal with Chung to avenge Robinson and take down Lau.

Penis jokes abound, but there are also clever references to **Prison on Fire I & II** (complete with Tommy Wong reprising his role from those films) and Leung's role in **The Lover**, making this moderately enjoyable pop entertainment from a man who has made more than his share. A clip from Wong's **Royal Tramp** can be spotted playing on a computer. This has no connection to the other Andy Lau film called **The Sting**, and the Chinese title's attempt to tie this into another Lau hit, **Casino Raiders**, is just as misleading. *The Sting II* was Christy Chung's first film.

924. Stone Age Warriors

(1991, Golden Gate Film Production) ★: 7/10. *Moh wik fei lung* (Cantonese), *Mo yu fei long* (Mandarin): "Magic Territory Flying Dragon." Cinematographers: Nico Wong Wan-man, Wong Wing-lung; Art Director: Chan Chi-yeung; Music: Richard Lo Sai-kit; Producers: Chan Wing-fu, Lui Wai-wah; Writer-Director: Stanley Tong Kwai-lai. Cast: Nina Li Chi (Lucy), Elaine Lui Siu-ling (Eko), Fan Siu-wong (Lung Fei), Dick Wei (First Guide), Shum Wai (Wong). 2.35:1. VHS/LD: World Video. Import LD/VCD: Ocean Shores (Poor Subtitles). 91 minutes.

Stanley Tong was hired to direct Jackie Chan's **Police Story III: Supercop** on the basis of what he was able to accomplish with this ambitious adventure, which was impressively mounted under very adverse conditions. After having issued a large policy to a Japanese client who subsequently disappeared in the wilds of Indonesia, insurance investigator Lucy is forced by her snivelling boss to check out the legitimacy of the claim. Pretending to be pregnant, Lucy cons the man's daughter, a movie star named Eko, to take her to where the latter suspects that her father may be found. After nearly getting trapped between two warring tribes, Eko and Lucy hook up with handsome Lung Fei, who agrees to act as their guide. After encountering the secret base of some mercenary drug runners, the women are separated from Lung and endure all the perils of the jungle, including scorpions, komodo dragons, and rapids which end with a plunge down a waterfall. After more perils, the two learn that Eko's father is a captive of the mercenaries and, along with Lung's help, set about trying to rescue him.

The first half is marred somewhat by lame sexual humor, and the cinematography is often substandard. However, more often than not, the film is excitingly staged, with nearly non-stop, well-edited action and martial arts. The actresses deserve special credit for undergoing the sort of perils that their Hollywood counterparts wouldn't dream of. *Stone Age Warriors* is definitely recommended to action fans and especially those who are tired of the typical cop and kung fu fare. Be sure to catch the outtakes under the end credits.

925. Stooge, My Love

(1996) ★: 5/10. *Mong jai doh ching* (Cantonese), *Wang zi duo qing* (Mandarin): "Susceptible Clueless Guy." Cinematographer: Li Hsin-yeh; Art Director: Ho Kim-seng; Music: Lee Kai-cheong; Writer: Raymond To Kwok-wai; Producer: Lawrence Wong Kar-hei; Action Director: Wong Chui-man; Director: Sherman Wong Ching-wah. Cast: Carrie Ng Kar-lai (Hua Tien-qiao), Wong Hei (Biscuit), Chin Siu-ho (Lone Kwan), Yuen King-tan (Sister Kwan), Leung Kar-yan (Mr. Man), Tai Po (Pimp), Derek Yee Tung-sing (Police Commissioner), Dennis Chan Kwok-san (Wong). 1.85:1. Import LD/VCD/DVD: New City. 95 minutes.

"Scar-Faced" Qiao, a fifty-something stripper without a penny to her name, takes it upon herself to look after Biscuit, a retarded man less than half her age. Her affection for him arises from the fact that she bore a son but had the baby almost immediately taken away from her. After vice cops raid the Kowloon Walled City, the two find themselves out on their own, desperately trying to make ends meet. Flashbacks reveal how Qiao was in love with handsome bouncer Kwan but was disfigured during a fight that broke out during her act. Qiao comes up with a plan that initially works like a charm: show up at wedding receptions as an anonymous relative from overseas and steal all the "Red Pockets" (envelopes containing monetary gifts). However, when Qiao lifts a socialite's necklace, she and Biscuit must relocate to another part of town. After meeting up with some of Kwan's old colleagues, Qiao is able to learn the location of her son.

Ng is excellent in a plum role that allows her to enact every emotion under the sun but Raymond To's heavy-handed screenplay never strays beyond the formulaic, and the dramatic conflicts do not have the intended resonance. Wong Hei is also effective, despite the fact that his performance suggests a bizarre cross between Jordan Chan and Eric Kot. Completed in 1995, the film spent over a year on the shelf before getting a perfunctory six day run in theatres.

The Story of CIA—First Strike [*sic*] *see* **First Strike**

926. The Story of Movie

[*sic*] (1996) ★: 8/10. *Din ying goo si* (Cantonese), *Dian ying gu shi* (Mandarin): "Movie Story." Cinematographer: Yuen Chan-wah; Music: Marco Wan Ho-kit, Anthony Lee Hon-kam; Writer: Sharun Hui Sa-long; Producers: Shum Yee-yee, Sam Shum Yeng; Action Directors: Dion Lam Dik-on, Mak Wai-cheung; Director: Si Mei-yee. Cast: Alice Lau Ar-lai (Lorna), Amanda Lee Wai-man (Cat), Moses Chan Ho (Brother Man), Ken Lo Wai-kwong (Chun), Victor Hon Kwan (Uncle Kwan), Peter Chan Lung (Kwong), Yip Wing-cho (Uncle Ya). 1.85:1. Video distributor unknown. 97 minutes. Also known as **The Movie Story**.

Fed up with her irresponsible parents and a dead end job in the family bar, brassy Lorna sees an escape in the form of handsome, soft-spoken trucker Chun. A former boxer, Chun is thinking of participating in an illegal fight, against his better judgment, for a big cash prize. Unsure of whether he will survive the match, Chun entrusts Lorna with his one and only possession: his truck. Meanwhile, in a parallel storyline, hooker Cat is tired of both her eccentric clients and her loan shark boss. It's apathy at first sight for Cat and her incredibly lazy protector, Brother Man, but the two gradually develop affection for one another. When he proposes that they elope, she refuses; but Man's gambling debts and careless skimming of mob money necessitate that he leave town post haste, and Cat just may decide to go with him after all.

The two couples' stories actually intersect at the very beginning, with the balance of the film presented in flashback. Even though you know that they will end up together, nothing else about the scenario is predictable, making this an unexpected, quirky treat. The female leads are both excellent, and Ken Lo acquits himself well in what is for all intents and purposes a non-action role. A terrific, imaginative score and offbeat supporting characters add to the fun. Wu Ma has an eyeblink cameo.

927. Story of Ricky

(1992; Golden Harvest/Diagonal Pictures/Paragon Films) ★: 6/10. *Lik wong* (Cantonese), *Li wang* (Mandarin): "King of Strength." Cinematographer: Mak Hoiman; Art Director: Ho Kim-seng; Music: Phil Chan Fei-lap; Producer: Chow Chantung; Action Director: Phillip Kwok Tsui; Writer-Director: Nam Nai-choi. Cast: Fan Siu-wong (Ricky Ho), Fan Mui-sang (The Assistant Warden), William Ho Kar-kui (The Warden), Yukari Oshima (Huang Chuan), Gloria Yip Wan-yee (Ying), Frankie Chin Chi-leung (Hai), Phillip Kwok Tsui (Kuang), Chen Jing (Bald Inmate). 1.85:1. VHS: Tai Seng (No Subtitles), Tokyo Shock (Dubbed). Import LD: Star Entertainment (No Subtitles). 90 minutes. Also known as **Riki-Oh: The Story of Ricky** (Tokyo Shock title).

If cinematic excess is what you treasure, you definitely need to see this adaptation of the **Riki-Oh** *manga* which is, without question, the goriest film the HK film industry has produced to date. By the year 2001, capitalist countries have privatized all government organizations, including their prisons. The institution depicted here is run by an incredibly corrupt warden, his equally evil assistant, and the various cell block leaders (called, amusingly enough, "The Gang of Four"). Musclebound new fish Ricky Ho (who is so tough he refused to let doctors remove the five bullets imbedded in his chest so he could keep them as "souvenirs") has been sent to prison for brutally murdering the thug whose lecherous advances drove his girlfriend to commit suicide. Ricky quickly makes all the wrong enemies by helping an old man being brutalized by one of the toughs in his cellblock. Rightfully suspecting that his authority will be challenged, the assistant warden orders gangleader Hai to kill the newcomer, but Ricky proves too powerful, disembowelling his opponent. Further attempts are made on Ricky's life and he is even buried alive at one point, but it would seem that nothing can stop his bloody crusade to vanquish evil and defend his fellow prisoners.

Director Nam Nai-choi (**The Seventh Curse**) does a fairly good job of bringing the grotesque, no-holds-barred world of Japanese comics to the screen, though the proceedings would have benefitted from more visual style, and one suspects that the *manga* sports far more intricate and involving storylines. Handsome Fan Siu-wong (who closely resembles his comic book counterpart) is a perfect, stoic lead, and the casting director deserves some sort of award for choosing actress Yukari Oshima to play one of the *male* gangleaders. The gore is hilariously excessive: Heads are shattered like cantaloupes, holes are punched through flesh, eyes are gouged out, legs and limbs are snapped like celery sticks, and razor blades are shoved into one victim's mouth (who is then repeatedly punched in the face). One character tries to strangle another, *using his own intestines*, and there is even a reprisal of the infamous "X-Ray Skull Punch" from Sonny Chiba's **The Street Fighter**! The make-up FX are not very convincing, adding to the intended *grand guignol* atmosphere, which is effective if approached with the right frame of mind. Unfortunately, the film is mainly content to be a collection of these splatter setpieces, and even the most spectacular of them (like one character's transformation into a mutant and his subsequent demise in a giant meat grinder) eventually generate ennui through repetition. Japanese actor Tetsuro Tamba appears briefly.

928. The Story of Rose

(1986; Molesworth/Gala Film Distribution) ★: 4/10. *Mooi gwai dik goo si* (Cantonese), *Mei gui de gu shi* (Mandarin): "The Story of Rose." Cinematographer: Chan Kwan-kin; Art Director: Fong Ying; Music: Chung Siu-fung; Producer: Teresa Woo San; Writer-Director: Yeung Fan. Cast: Chow Yun-fat (Charles Wong/Gaming), Maggie Cheung Man-yuk (Rose Wong), Roy Cheung Yiu-yeung (Alex), Alfred Cheung Kin-ting (Simon), Ha Ping (Nanny). 1.85:1. VHS: World Video. 92 minutes. Also known as **Rose** (1986).

Flighty teenager Rose has so many boys courting her that she thinks nothing of toying with their emotions and even has her maid lie to them on the phone. When she is discarded by a man named Tony (who proceeds to marry another woman), Rose travels to France, with the intention of continuing her studies. Her protective brother, Charles (Rose's only guardian, as their parents are dead), visits her in Paris and strongly urges her to come home to HK. She decides to stay, marries one of her classmates, and has a daughter. When Charles dies after a prolonged illness, Rose gets divorced and returns to her old home. One day she encounters Ga-ming, who is the spitting image of Charles. A mutual attraction develops, but Rose has never been able to get Tony out of her mind, and when he comes to see her out of the blue, she seems even more unsure of what to do. There is also the matter of yet another man who has fallen hopelessly in love with her.

As with writer-director Yeung Fan's other work, this deliberately paced drama is beautifully composed and photographed, with many pretty shots of French scenery, underscored by equally attractive but melancholy music. Unfortunately, look and mood are all the film has going for it, as the story is trivial melodrama (there are two achingly contrived developments in the final reel that strain credibility well past the breaking point), and Chow and Cheung have surprisingly little chemistry. In 1999 Yeung announced plans to issue a reedited version of the film, with a new score by composer Pau Pei-tak and a title song by popular singer Cass Phang Ling.

929. The Story of Woo Viet

(1981; Pearl City Films) ★: 8/10. *Woo Yuet dik goo si* (Cantonese), *Hu Yue de gu shi* (Mandarin): "Woo Yuet's Story." Cinematographer: Bill Wong Chung-bo; Art Director: Tony Au Ding-ping; Music: Violet Lam Man-yee; Writer: Alfred Cheung Kin-ting; Producer: Teddy Robin Kwan; Director: Ann Hui On-wah. Cast: Chow Yun-fat (Wu Yuet), Cherie Chung Cho-hung (Shum Ching), Lo Lieh (Sarm), Cora Miao Qian-ren (Li Lapquan), Dave Brodett (Migual). 1.85:1. VHS: Arena/Xenon (Poor Subtitles). Import LD: Winson Entertainment. 92 minutes. Also known as **God of Killers** (Arena/Xenon title).

While this is Chow Yun-fat's twelfth film, it is the first one of any real value, and his performance is a preview of what he would deliver on a consistent basis later on. South Vietnamese soldier-turned-refugee Wu Yuet escapes from Saigon and is taken to a refugee camp in HK. One evening a man makes an attempt on his life, but Wu kills him and escapes from the camp. With the help of a social worker he has been in touch with for some time, Wu contacts a snakehead who can have him smuggled to America. The price is $100,000: $30,000 in advance, the rest he earns working in Chinatown after his arrival. He meets Shum Ching, a Vietnamese girl with the same goal, and the two are issued phony Japanese passports. However, the set-up is a scam: During a stopover in Manila, Ching and the other women are taken to the local Chinatown and sold as prostitutes. Wu steals a gun from a policeman and sets off in search of Ching. After a two hour standoff, Wu makes a deal with the local Chinese ganglord: He will work for him until he has enough money to redeem Ching, and they will guarantee her safety in return. Wu does what he is told but, naturally, the arrangement is not so cut and dried.

Chow gives an excellent, low-key turn here, and the location shooting in The Philippines gives this a documentary quality that adds to the considerable dramatic realism Ann Hui achieves. Downbeat and unflinching, the film's nasty, realistic violence will turn off some viewers but is an integral part of the story and is not glamorized in any way. Be warned: This is definitely not an action film, as the blatantly fraudulent Arena/Xenon packaging portrays it (they have retitled the movie **God of Killers**, a meaningless and misleading combination of two of Chow's best known films, **God of Gamblers** and **The Killer**). The actor went on to play a Vietnamese assassin the next year in the exploitation picture **The Head Hunter**, while Hui made the popular and acclaimed **Boat People**.

930. Street Angels

(1996; BOB & Partners Company) ★: 4/10. *Hung dang kui* (Cantonese), *Hong deng qu* (Mandarin): "Red Light District." Cinematographer: Tony Miu Kin-fai; Art Director: Andrew Cheuk Man-yiu; Music: Wong Bong; Writer: Manfred Wong; Producers: Andrew Lau Wai-keung, Manfred Wong; Action Director: Dion Lam Dik-on; Director: Billy Tang Hin-sing. Cast: Chingmy Yau Suk-ching (Tung Yen), Michael To Tai-yu (Yip Sen-man, aka "Playboy Man"), Hsu Chi (Ming-ming), Simon Yam Tat-wah (Walkie Pi), Elvis Tsui Kam-kong (Moro), Valerie Chow Kar-ling (Karen), Linda Cheung Lan-ying (Pidan, aka "Black Beauty"), Spencer Lam Sheung-yee (Barrister Lam), Maria Cordero (Singer in Number One Club). 1.85:1. VHS/LD: Tai Seng. Import LD/VCD/DVD: Universe. 91 minutes.

A minor entry in the "young rascals" subgenre, **Street Angels** has a certain empty-headed appeal, thanks primarily to the attractive cast, a cool theme song, and some flashy visuals. When gang leader Walkie Pi murders a rival in a bowling alley, he manages to avoid the police but his girl, Tung Yen, is arrested. Upon her release from prison nine months later, Yen is hired as a *mamasan* in the "Number One" nightclub owned by the handsome millionaire "Playboy Man." The changes she introduces quickly make the club the top hotspot in Mongkok. The opposition retaliates by hiring someone who will do anything for the right amount of money: Walkie Pi. Pi's ruthless tactics and psychotic behavior prompt Yen to take desperate action against her ex.

The film aims to repeat the formula that made **Young and Dangerous** so successful, right down to having comic book panel drawings of the main characters. However, the plotting and direction are too simplistic for this to be anything other than low rent exploitation, in spite of Elvis Tsui's amusing turn as Playboy Man's perpetually horny bodyguard and Hsu Chi's wonderfully appealing performance as a flighty masseuse turned high class hostess.

931. Street of Fury

(1996; The Good Fellas Film Co.) ★: 4/10. *Lung foo boot laan gaai* (Cantonese), *Long hu bo lan jie* (Mandarin): "Dragon Tiger Portland Street." Cinematographer: Tony Miu Kin-fai; Art Director: Andrew Cheuk Man-yiu; Music: Wong Bong; Producer: Lee Siu-kei; Action Director: Tsui Chung-san; Director: Billy Tang Hin-sing. Cast: Louis Koo Tin-lok (Chen Yu-long), Gigi Lai Chi (Yi), Teresa Mak Kar-kei (Shan), Michael Tse Tin-wah (Hu), Elvis Tsui Kam-kong (King), Simon Lui Yu-yeung ("Short-Sighted"), Ben Lam Kwok-bun (Brother Beast), Jerry Lam Hiu-fung (Xiao-xiang), Wong Yat-fei (Hu's Uncle). 1.85:1. VHS: Tai Seng. Import LD/VCD: Universe. 95 minutes.

One of the weakest entries in the *goo wak jai* craze, this wearisome thriller concerns brothers Hu and Yu-long, two uneducated teens from the Nam Tin housing project who are hassled by gang leader Short-Sighted (more appropriately called "Four Eyes" by everyone onscreen). They join a rival triad faction, run by the demented Boss King, after Hu's girlfriend Yi is raped by Short-Sighted and his men. The hyper-aggressive Hu makes a name for himself when he takes revenge on Short-Sighted by chopping off one of the triad's hands. In the meantime, Yi, fed up with the poor treatment she has received from Hu, takes up with the obnoxious leader "Brother Beast," while Yu-long is none-too-subtly wooed by Shan, an old classmate who has racked up some major debts. When Short-Sighted's boss shaves Shan's head and tattoos her, King is able to get her freed, but the one-handed criminal takes Yi hostage and demands Hu in exchange.

Hemmed in by genre conventions, **Street of Fury** serves up the usual street battles (with lots of people in the background staring at the camera), romantic angst, and tit-for-tat reprisals. It will all seem like old news to aficionados, and the numerous "colorful" characters (particularly Elvis Tsui's would-be humorous, seemingly brain-damaged boss and Teresa Mak's feisty massage girl) just don't work.

932. A Sudden Love

(1995) ★: 2/10. *Ngau yue* (Cantonese), *Ou yu* (Mandarin): "Chance Meeting." Art Director: Andy Lee Yiu-kwong; Music: Lau Yee-tat; Writer: Wai Sam; Producers: Chan Chi-shun, Law Kwok-keung, Pauline Chan Po-lin; Cinematographer-Director: Shui Wu-tin. Cast: Pauline Chan Po-lin (Pauline), Dick Lau Dik-chi (Ken Wong Ka-keung). 1.85:1. VHS: Tai Seng. Import LD/VCD: Star Entertainment. 85 minutes.

Only the most devoted Pauline Chan fans need bother with this softcore travelogue which is one of the dullest Category III films in memory. Chan plays Pauline, a photographer vacationing on a tropical island. While taking pictures and soaking up the local color, she encounters Ken, the handsome cousin of Angie, an uninhibited florist. Angie develops a not-too-subtle lust for Ken and, after several attempts, finally manages to seduce him. However, Ken has his eye on Pauline and is not about to let Angie's immature attempts to separate them change his mind.

There are three sexual interludes in all but only one with Chan (and that is not until the very end of the film). The remainder of the running time is spent showing her taking pictures, riding a bicycle, swimming, playing darts: essentially, doing everything except what the target audience would want to see her do.

933. Summer Lover

(1992; Regal Films Co./Ko Chi Sum Films Co.) ★: 4/10. *Ha yat ching yan* (Cantonese), *Xia ri qing ren* (Mandarin): "Summer Sun Lovers." Cinematographer: Joe Chan Kong-hung; Art Director: Choi Man-chong; Music: Anthony Lee Hon-kam, Marco Wan Ho-kit; Writers: Roman Cheung Siu-lun, Joe Ma Wai-ho, Vincent Kok Tak-chiu; Producers: Clifton Ko Chi-sum, Ronny Yu Yan-tai; Director: Clifton Ko Chi-sum. Cast: Alfred Cheung Kin-ting (Ting), Max Mok Siu-chung (Chung), Vivian Chow Wei-man (Liza), Veronica Yip Yuk-hing (Siu-yuk), Loletta Lee Lai-chun (Janet), Russell Wong (Zeniger), James Wong Jim (Uncle Wah), Tommy Wong Kwong-leung (Ugly Guy in Supermarket), Paul Fonoroff (Laserdisc Shop Clerk). 1.85:1. VHS: Tai Seng. Import LD/VCD: Universe. 80 minutes.

Nerdy lifeguard Ting and his handsome buddy Chung happen upon a new laserdisc shop one evening and decide to check out a couple of titles from a special line designed for "lonely guys." Ting's disc stars beautiful "Laser Lady" Siu-yuk, who promises to honor and obey him and comes to three-dimensional life when lightning strikes Ting's television set! Siu-yuk can stay with him for one month's time, at which point she will vanish. However, Siu-yuk will disappear sooner than that if she happens to fall in love with him. While most men would be quite happy to be with this arrangement, Ting remains obsessed with Liza, a beautiful girl he sees sunbathing every morning. She only regards the 98-pound-weakling as a friend, preferring the considerably more masculine Zeniger, who does not return her affections. Siu-yuk offers to help Ting score with Liza, but she definitely has her work cut out for her. Meanwhile, Chung has released his Laser Lady, Janet, and is having the time of *his* life...what's left of it.

A HK imitation of **Video Girl Ai** (a Japanese *manga* that later became a feature film and made-for-video *anime* series), **Summer Lover** is aimed at young teenage males and features humor on the level of what you would expect for that age group (the broadest gags are punctuated with sound effects lifted from old Hollywood cartoons). Little of interest is done with the premise, but a few instances of satire (including parodies of **The Lover, The Last Emperor**, and **Rouge**) provide mild amusement. About the only surprise here is that Vivian Chow (who really looks like an *anime* character come to life) wasn't cast as Siu-yuk! Sync sound recording (only New York-born Russell Wong is post-dubbed) helps a little.

934. Summer Snow

(1995; Golden Harvest/Harvest Crown) ★: 5/10. *Nui yan sei sap* (Cantonese), *Nu ren si shi* (Mandarin): "Woman, Forty." Cinematographer: Mark Lee Ping-bing; Art Director: Yank Wong Yan-kwai; Music: Yoshihide Otomo; Writer: Chan Man-keung; Producer-Director: Ann Hui On-wah. Cast: Josephine Siao Fong-fong (May Sun), Roy Chiao Hung (Mr. Sun), Law Kar-ying (Bing), Law Koon-lan (Lan), Allen Ting Chi-chun (Allen), Ha Ping (Mrs. Han), Pau Fong (Pang), Lau Shun (Mr. Lo), Manfred Wong (Fish Vendor). 1.85:1. Import LD/VCD: Star Entertainment. Import DVD: China Star. 100 minutes.

One of the most inconsequential Best Picture winners in memory, Ann Hui's drama about Alzheimer's Disease has two fine lead performances but no more depth or dramatic resonance than an American TV Movie of the Week. Middle-aged May lives a hectic and unhappy life, having to get by on a small salary while also caring for her mother and father, the latter now almost entirely out of his mind. When the mother dies, things only become worse, as May and her timid husband find that their relatives will not help them. They are forced to put the father (who is 70 years old but still as strong as a bear) in a managed care facility during the day, and he does show some improvement. However, he wanders away one day and is ejected, forcing May to relocate him to a home which provides far less humane treatment. After seeing the sad effect this has on her father, May moves him back home, but the old man's health begins to deteriorate.

Once again, the great Josephine Siao can do no wrong, and Roy Chiao earned a richly deserved Best Actor nod for his superb performance (which he would somewhat cheapen the next year by parodying the role in the mediocre **Blind Romance**) as the proud but deluded patriarch. In addition, there are a few amusing and genuine moments along the way, but they add up to little in a storyline as routine and predictable as this (right down to the painfully obvious closing reel). A major disappointment.

The Sunset Warrior *see* **Heroes Shed No Tears**

935. Super Lady Cop

(1992; Golden Harvest/Try Ease/P.U. Production/Paragon Films) ★: 4/10. *Kong fung mat ling* (Cantonese), *Kuang feng mi ling* (Mandarin): "Wild Phoenix Secret Orders." Cinematographer: Cheung Fai-cho; Art Directors: Chong Chi-leung, Hadd Ng Kwok-hung; Music: Ng Kwok-king; Writers: Lam Kei-to, Lam Chiu-wing; Producer: Wellson Chin Sing-wai; Action Director: Tsui Chung-sun; Director: Yuen Chun-man. Cast: Cynthia Yang Li-ching (Nieh Ling), Alex Man Chi-leung (Chiu Shui), Athena Chu Yan (Yoki), Yuen Wah (Coach), Peter Lai Bei-tak (Kao). 1.85:1. Import LD/VCD: Universe. 93 minutes.

Not to be confused with **Lady Super Cop**, this unabashedly ridiculous sci-fi action-comedy stars Cynthia Yang as Nieh Ling, a cyborg from China, dispatched on a clandestine mission to HK to capture fugitive Chun and his two cohorts. The men are also super-powered machines but have started experiencing malfunctions that are scrambling their physical and mental processes. Thanks to a misunderstanding, inept local cop Chiu Shui shoots Ling with an "amnesia bullet" from her special gun, which leaves the cyborg confused and child-like. With the help of Chiu and street urchin Yoki (likeably played by Athena Chu), Ling is able to regain her memory in time to confront Chun at their creator's laboratory.

There is no shortage of stunts and undercranked, cartoonish action here (including a fun parody of the Street Fighter II video game with Yang playing "Chun Li"), but the film is more obnoxious than amusing and Alex Man's shameless overacting is largely to blame for that.

Super Ninjas *see* **Five Element Ninja**

Supercop *see* **Police Story III: Supercop**

Supercop 2: Super Plan *see* **Project S**

Sure Fire *see* **Tiger Cage**

936. Switch-Over

(1994; Artview Investment Co.) ★: 5/10. *San chiu long gwan* (Cantonese), *Xin qiao lang jun* (Mandarin): "New Cute, Bright Gentleman." Cinematographer: Philip Ma Kam-cheung; Art Director: Liu Kin-ming; Music: Wong Chi-hung; Writers: On Dik, Mo Kong; Producer: Chan Yam-sin; Director: Leung Cho-chi. Cast: Jacqueline Law Wai-kuen (Chuk Ying-choi), Wu Ma (Chuk), Chin Kar-lok (Wah), Ellen Chan Ar-lun (Monie), Gabriel Wong Yat-san (Little Ghost), William Ho Kar-kui (Tom), Charlie Cho Cha-lei (Servant of Hell). 1.85:1. VHS: Tai Seng. 92 minutes.

This mild comedy draws its premise from **Victor/Victoria**, though it does inadvertently walk the same path as the far more successful **He's a Woman, She's a Man**, which hit HK theatres six months later. Heeding the warning of a fortune teller, martial arts instructor Chuk insists that his daughter Ying-choi live her life as a man. Monie, the new girl next door, falls head-over-heels for Ying-choi, while the love of the latter's heart, kung fu student Wah, only has eyes for Monie. Predictable complications and sexual identity problems ensue. However, just when Ying-choi decides to give up her ruse and the story seems headed for a resolution, the plot takes a 180 degree turn and transforms into a ghost movie (see **Shadow Cop**)! After inadvertently offending an effeminate spirit called "Little Ghost," the spectre possesses half of Ying-choi, leading to a multitude of tired physical comedy showcasing the two inhabitants' inability to properly control the body (**All of Me** anyone?). Things pick up a bit in the last reel, as a "Servant of Hell" (Charlie Cho as an undead policeman) comes to take Little Ghost back to the netherworld. Master Chuk and an inept Taoist must figure out how to get the spirit out of Ying-choi's body in order to save her from being dragged down to Hell as well.

Jacqueline Law makes a convincing boy, but the formulaic plotting, misfired gags, and a terrible score make this only fair entertainment at best. Naming Law's character "Chuk Ying-choi" is a jokey reference to "Chuk Ying-toi," a character from folklore played by Charlie Yeung in **The Lovers** (also 1994).

937. The Sword

(1980; Golden Harvest) ★: 8/10. *Gim* (Cantonese), *Jian* (Mandarin): "Sword." Cinematographer: Bill Wong Chung-bo;

Music: Joseph Koo Kar-fai; Writers: Patrick Tam Kar-ming, Wong Ying, Lau Tin-chi; Producer: Raymond Chow Man-wai; Action Directors: Ching Siu-tung, Teng Te-hsiang; Director: Patrick Tam Kar-ming. Cast: Adam Cheng Siu-chau (Li Mak-yin), Norman Tsui Siu-keung (Lin Wan), Tien Feng (Wah), Eddy Ko Hung (Lin's Man), Lee Hoi-sang (Bald Swordsman), Lau Siu-ming (Caretaker). 2.35:1. VHS: Tai Seng (Poor Subtitles). Import VCD: Mega Star. 84 minutes.

An excellent period swordplay drama, **The Sword** tells the story of skilled swordsman Li Mak-yin, who is wandering the countryside in search of someone. Along the way he meets sprightly maiden Ying-chi and helps her ward off an attacker. At an inn he encounters his childhood sweetheart, Hsiao-yue, who has married a cruel nobleman named Lin Wan. Although he puts up a polite front, Lin does not trust Li's motives and orders his subordinate to murder him. Li survives the attack but is gravely injured. Nursed back to health by the beautiful Yuen Chi, Li learns from her that Ying-chi is about to be killed. After receiving a sword from Ying-chi, he is able to save the girl from a mob of assassins. Upon bringing Ying-chi to her home, he discovers that her father is the very man he seeks: Wah, the greatest swordsman in the land. The sword Li now possesses is the Chi Mud sword, a weapon reputed to be infused with great evil. Wah was advised to dispose of it but couldn't bear to part with the handsome weapon, giving it instead to Ying-chi for safe keeping but keeping her in the dark about its heinous reputation. Li defeats Wah in their subsequent duel, and that evening the latter is murdered by Lin's man, who makes it look like Wah died from injuries he received from Li. Now that he has Wah's prized Hon Sing sword in his possession, Lin also seeks the Chi Mud and will stop at nothing to get it.

Directed by Patrick Tam (one of the leading young directors credited with starting the "HK New Wave" movement, and one of the few who never quite found his niche), **The Sword** is shot and edited with an invigorating sense of style and composition. While it remains faithful to the emotion and traditions of the classic Chinese swordplay film, modern technique instills the storyline with an extra degree of resonance and excitement. There is also superb action choreography by future director Ching Siu-tung that is very much in the style that would become the norm for the genre (it was Ching's fine work here that prompted producer Raymond Chow to offer him his directorial debut, **Duel to the Death**). A key feature in its genre, **The Sword** has been difficult to see (in more ways than one) over the years, resulting in it being little known among Western aficionados. The Mega Star VCD presentation is far from pristine, but it is a disc that everyone who has an interest in HK swordplay films should seek out.

938. The Sword of Many Loves

(1993; Golden Harvest/Johnny Mak Production/Paragon Films) ★: 8/10. *Fei woo ngoi juen* (Cantonese), *Fei hu wai zhuan* (Mandarin): "The Story of Flying Fox." Cinematographers: Wong Po-man, Chiu Fu-keung; Art Director: Ho Kim-seng; Music: William Woo Wai-lap; Writers: Lee Ying-kit, Johnny Mak Dong-hung, Stephen Siu Yeuk-yuen; Producers: Johnny Mak Dong-hung, Stephen Siu Yeuk-yuen; Action Directors: Ma Yuk-shing, Yuen Cheung-yan; Director: Poon Man-kit. Cast: Leon Lai Ming (Wu Fei), Sharla Cheung Man (Purple Yuen), Michelle Lee Kar-yan (Ching Ling-ling), Elvis Tsui Kam-kong (Fung Nam-tin), Yuen King-tan (Mo-yung), William Ho Kar-kui (Sit Hei). 1.85:1. VHS: Tai Seng. Import LD/VCD: Universe. 111 minutes.

This is something of a ringer in the late '80s/early '90s wave of period fantasies, presenting its parable of revenge, romantic tragedy, and the supernatural with a greater emphasis on character and a less ornate (at times downright earthy) visual style. However, like other works by noted fantasy/swordplay author Louis Cha/Jin Yong (including such disparate films as **Swordsman** and **Ashes of Time**), the plot consists of plausible circumstances and conflicts affecting characters possessing mystical skills, creating a remarkable hybrid world. Footloose swordsman Wu Fei finds trouble awaiting him in Nanking when he crosses paths with Fung Nam-tin, an elder statesman whose obsessive love for his homicidal idiot son brings about the death of Wu's partner. Soon joining Wu in his quest for vengeance is Purple Yuen, a disguised nun who is actually Fung's daughter-by-rape. She seeks to avenge her dead mother but is distracted by her increasing attraction to Wu. Completing this romantic triangle-in-the-making is Ching Ling-ling, a callow Poison Mistress who is determined to have Wu, even if she has to transform him into a pig!

As always, the action choreography cheerfully defies all known laws of gravity and is rendered here with rousing ingenuity. Lensed on fresh Mainland locales, the film eschews the fairytale vistas of recent HK productions in favor of a deglamorized, naturalistic look more akin to the 1960s Taiwanese films of director King Hu Chin-chuan. Bracketing the central romance is an abundance of broad but often clever humor that reaches its zenith during Wu and Ling-ling's duel with two rival poisoners (played with zeal by Yuen King-tan and William Ho), a marvellous combination of exotic spells and accomplished FX trickery. Pop superstar Leon Lai is expressive and likeable, but it is Michelle Lee who really shines in a much weightier role than the decorative characters she generally essays. Sharla Cheung and Elvis Tsui (the ubiquitous leading lady and villain of the genre) do well by roles that allow them to expand on character types they have played numerous times in the past. While the script displays unexpected degrees of tenderness, the film's violence quotient runs an uneasy gamut from comical exaggeration (there are more giant lumps on display than in ten Warner Brothers cartoons!) to ferocious intensity (in particular, the evisceration of a little boy). A handful of other gory moments have been abbreviated in HK prints.

Sword of the Serpent *see* **The Sword Stained with Royal Blood**

939. The Sword Stained with Royal Blood

(1993; Production Line Films Co.) ★: 6/10. *San bik huet gim* (Cantonese), *Xin bi xue jian* (Mandarin): "New Azure Blood Sword." Cinematographers: Lau Hung-chuen, Philip Ma Kam-cheung, Poon Tak-yip; Art Director: Sze Mei-yee; Music: James Wong Jim, Mark Lui Chung-tak; Writers: Cheung Hoi-ching, Wai San; Action Directors: Austin Wai Tin-chi, Hsu Hsia; Producer-Director: Cheung Hoi-ching. Cast: Yuen Biao (Yuen Shing-chi), Sharla Cheung Man (Princess Kau), Danny Lee Sau-yin (Ha Suet-yee, aka "The Golden Snake Man"), Elizabeth Lee Mei-fung (Siu-yi), Anita Yuen Wing-yee (Jade Ho), Ng Man-tat (Sun Su-kuei), Elvis Tsui Kam-kong (Lord Wan), Wu Ma (General Suen), Yeh Chuan-chen (Ching-ching), Lung Fong (Wan's Brother), Tai Po (Wan's Brother), Melvin Wong Kam-sun (San), Peter Chan Lung (Fat Wan Clansman). 1.85:1. VHS: SYS/Youngtze (Dubbed *and* subtitled), World Video. LD: World Video. Import LD/VCD: Star Entertainment. Import DVD: China Star. 96 minutes. Also known as **Sword of the Serpent** (SYS/Youngtze title).

Based on a Jin Yong story (previously adapted in the 1981 Shaw Brothers film of the same name by director Chang Cheh), this is an enjoyable venture which stacks up well against the other recent remakes of swordplay classics. The storyline (which is interrupted by a few too many goofy asides) revolves around Ha

Suet-yee, an all-powerful swordsman known as "The Golden Snake Man," and the mission he undertakes to avenge his slaughtered kin and reclaim his wife, Siu-yi, from the stronghold of powerful warlord Wan. Numerous supporting characters figure into the action, including a heroic constable, a bratty princess and her dumpy *sifu*, a blind soothsayer, and a blood-drinking Poison Clan Mistress. Almost all of them want to get their hands on Ha's weapon (called, appropriately enough, "The Golden Snake Sword"), which is the key to his supernatural powers. The plot proper is an intricate web of loyalty and intrigue, which the English subtitles do a rather nebulous job of recounting, but it all becomes clear upon a repeat viewing.

The action scenes are well staged and often exciting, but the most interesting aspect of the film is Danny Lee's powerful anti-hero: a man bound by the codes of the martial world but torn apart by guilt and love for his long-suffering wife. This extra depth of character helps retain viewer interest whenever the scenario becomes too convoluted. The SYS/Youngtze tape runs a few minutes shorter than the original; it is also horribly dubbed *and* subtitled!

940. Swordsman

(1990; Golden Princess/Long Shong Pictures/Newport Distribution/Film Workshop) ★: 7/10. *Siu ngo gong wu* (Cantonese), *Xiao ao jiang hu* (Mandarin): "Smiling Proud Warrior." Cinematographers: Ardy Lam Kwok-wah, Peter Pau Tak-hei; Art Director: James Leung Wah-sang; Music: James Wong Jim, Romeo Diaz; Writers: Kwan Man-leung, Wong Ying, Lam Kei-to, Lau Tai-muk, Edward Leung Yiu-ming, Tai Fu-ho; Producer: Tsui Hark; Action Directors: Ching Siu-tung, Lau Chi-ho; Director: King Hu Chin-chuan, plus uncredited: Tsui Hark, Ann Hui On-wah, Ching Siu-tung, Andrew Kam Yeung-wah, Raymond Lee Wai-man. Cast: Sam Hui Koon-kit (Ling Wu-chung), Cecilia Yip Tung (Kiddo), Sharla Cheung Man (Ying), Jacky Cheung Hok-yau (Au Yeung), Lau Shun (The Eunuch), Yuen Wah (Zhor), Fennie Yuen Kit-ying (Blue Phoenix), Lau Siu-ming (Ngok), Lam Ching-ying (Kuk), Wu Ma (Lau). Dolby Digital (DVD only). 1.85:1. VHS: Tai Seng. Import LD: Golden Cinema City. Import VCD: Mei Ah. Import DVD: Mega Star (Coded for Region 3 only). 117 minutes.

In The Ming Dynasty, an invaluable scroll called "The Sacred Volume," containing secret writings about an all-powerful martial arts technique, is stolen from the Imperial Library in The Forbidden City. A recently retired official is fingered by the evil Imperial eunuch for the crime, and troops prepare to lay siege to his villa. Requesting help from the leader of the Wah Mountain School, the man instead finds himself with Ling Wu-chung and his female assistant Kiddo, who explain that their master has been delayed. The nobleman dies in the subsequent battle with the opposition (now led by powerful killer Zhor), prompting Ling and Kiddo to go and reunite with their Wah compatriots. Along the way, they strike up a temporary alliance with a member of the rival Sun Moon Sect, who is also an enemy of Zhor. Ling accidentally reveals the hiding place of The Sacred Volume to an Imperial spy, who then poisons him. The swordsman is saved by Sun Moon Sect chief Ying, who then joins forces with Ling. Subsequent events find Ling caught in the middle of various intrigues and forced to battle both the eunuch and his own master.

A lavish but troubled enterprise, **Swordsman** began production with acclaimed Taiwanese director King Hu (**A Touch of Zen**) at the helm, but he was dismissed early on by producer Tsui Hark when it became clear that Hu was not delivering the sort of film Tsui desired. After some cast changes and the contributions of several uncredited directors, the film finally wrapped at a much higher than planned cost of HK$30 million. Based on a novel by Jin Yong, the screenplay assumes that the viewer has a certain familiarity with the clans depicted, thus making the film a rather bewildering experience upon initial viewing. The second time through, however, the allegiances become clear and one is able to easily comprehend the story. While accomplished, neither the visuals nor the action sequences are quite on par with Film Workshop's best productions, though it is to the credit of everyone involved that the behind-the-scenes problems are not readily evident in the finished product. While he is able to project the amiable aspects of Ling's personality quite well, one is never convinced that Sam Hui is a kung fu master; the supporting characters are more interesting and engaging (particularly Fennie Yuen's mischievous "Blue Phoenix," who shoots live snakes at her enemies). If the film never quite reaches its potential, it is not for lack of trying, and the mixture of conspiracy and supernaturally enhanced kung fu is diverting and absorbing enough to make **Swordsman** well worth catching. It was followed by **Swordsman II** and **The East Is Red**.

941. Swordsman II

(1992; Golden Princess/Long Shong Pictures/Film Workshop) ★: 9/10. *Siu ngo gong woo ji Dung Fong Bat Baai* (Cantonese), *Xiao ao jiang hu zhi Dong Fang Bu Bai* (Mandarin): "Smiling Proud Warrior: Invincible Asia." Cinematographer: Tom Lau Moon-tong; Art Directors: William Cheung Suk-ping, Bruce Yu Kar-on; Music: Richard Yuen Cheuk-fan; Writers: Tsui Hark, Chan Tin-suen, Elsa Tang Pik-yin; Producer: Tsui Hark; Action Directors: Ching Siu-tung, Yuen Bun, Ma Yuk-shing, Cheung Yiu-sing; Director: Ching Siu-tung. Cast: Jet Li Lianjie (Ling Wu-chung), Brigitte Lin Ching-hsia (Invincible Asia), Michelle Lee Kar-yan (Kiddo), Rosamund Kwan Chi-lam (Ying), Fennie Yuen Kit-ying (Blue Phoenix), Yam Sai-kwoon (Master Wu), Lau Shun (Zen), Candice Yu On-on (Cici), Waise Lee Chi-hung (Hattori), Chin Kar-lok (Saru), Cheung Kwok-leung (Eunuch Hong), Wong Chi-yeung (Interpreter). 1.85:1. VHS: Tai Seng. Import LD: Golden Cinema City. Import VCD: Mei Ah (No Subtitles). DVD: Mei Ah. 108 minutes (HK version)/112 minutes (Taiwan version).

The original **Swordsman** was a problematic production that ended up being a box office disappointment in relation to its immense cost. Regardless, producer Tsui Hark pressed on with a sequel but made some fundamental changes up front. In addition to a smaller scale and budget, he replaced the entire cast, with the sole exception of Fennie Yuen (who reprises her role as "Blue Phoenix"). Taking over the lead role of "Ling Wu-chung" is Mainland martial arts dynamo Jet Li, who brings greater energy and presence to the part, almost entirely eclipsing one's memories of Sam Hui Koon-kit's interpretation. As the film opens, a new and powerful threat has appeared in the martial world: Invincible Asia. Following instructions found in The Sacred Volume, the ambitious villain castrated himself and is gradually transforming into a woman, a normal side effect of this ritual which gives the subject great supernatural powers. In league with Japanese ninjas, Asia plans on having the Sun Moon Sect rule the country and has kidnapped Chief Wu (father of Highlander Ying, played this time by Rosamund Kwan) as the first stage in this plan. While fleeing from a platoon of army scouts, Ling encounters Asia on a beach, practising his/her newly acquired abilities. Pretending to be mute, Asia (who had crossed paths with Ling briefly once before) flirts with the swordsman rather than killing him. Joining forces with Ying, Ling and his fellow Wah Mountain swordsmen set out to find Chief Wu, and Ling is eventually able to liberate him from one of Asia's prisons. However, Wu has changed during his incarceration and now, lusting after domination himself, has his own plans for The Sacred Volume. After so much death and treachery, Ling would like nothing more than to leave the turmoil of the martial world behind, but events necessitate that he intervene in this power struggle one more time.

Brigitte Lin cuts a dazzling figure in one of her most memorable Yin Yang roles; the character's sexual confusion adds a wonderful, atypical undercurrent to the proceedings, taking the traditional lovers-on-opposing-sides story element to an entirely new dimension. While involved, the plotting here is easier to comprehend (avoid the Taiwanese version, which is so badly translated it is incoherent) and the visuals are consistently arresting. The action choreography in period fantasies is almost always exciting, but the combat in **Swordsman II** features some of the most fluid and impressive wirework you will ever see and is an absolutely thrilling blend of mystical and traditional (i.e. earthbound) combat. This is required viewing for fans of both HK swordplay epics and ambitious, genre defining filmmaking. It was followed by **The East Is Red**.

942. The Tai-Chi Master

(1993; Eastern Production) ★: 8/10. *Taai gik Cheung Sam-fung* (Cantonese), *Tai ji Zhang Sanfeng* (Mandarin): "Tai Chi: Cheung Sam-fung" or "Tai Chi: Zhang Sanfeng." Cinematographer: Tom Lau Moon-tong; Art Director: Raymond Lee King-man; Music: William Woo Wai-lap; Writer: Yip Kwong-kim; Producer: Jet Li Lianjie; Action Directors: Yuen Woo-ping, Yuen Cheung-yan, Kok Hin-ming; Director: Yuen Woo-ping. Cast: Jet Li Lianjie (Shang Junbao), Michelle Yeoh Chu-kheng (Qiuxue), Chin Siu-ho (Dong Tianbao), Fennie Yuen Kit-ying (Little Melon), Yuen Cheung-yan (Reverend Ling), Lau Shun (Master Jueyuan). 1.85:1. VHS: Tai Seng. Import LD/VCD/DVD: Universe. 95 minutes.

While any film pairing Jet Li and Michelle Yeoh should automatically be of interest, this period kung fu entry by Yuen Woo-ping also sports some fine work by the talented Chin Siu-ho (**Fist of Legend**). It is a pleasing and dramatically sound spin on the age-old "childhood friends on opposite sides of the law" hook. Junbao and Tianbao are young Buddhist monks who have been ejected from their order following an altercation during a martial arts contest. After struggling to survive as beggars, the two take different roads in life: The ambitious Tianbao joins an army lorded over by the evil eunuch Liu Jing, while Junbao allies himself with female kung fu master Qiuxue and a group of villagers opposing Liu's tyranny and the eunuch's brutal tax collectors. Tianbao's ruthless nature allows him to rise quickly through the ranks, leading to murderous conflict and an inevitable showdown with Junbao and Qiuxue.

As with all of the director's recent films, the martial arts are enhanced with wirework but the trickery is successful more often than not, and the pole fight in the opening reel is among the most spectacular that Yuen has ever staged. The numerous other setpieces are also accomplished, with the three stars' skills consistently shining through. Cinema City ingenue Fennie Yuen and the director's brother, Yuen Cheung-yan, add some romance and humor in supporting roles; and while Li and Yeoh are as personable as ever, it is Chin who really impresses here. Cast against type in a role reportedly intended for Donnie Yen Chi-tan, he tackles his part with zeal and intensity, making Tianbao a venomous and thoroughly despicable scoundrel and a model of kung fu movie villainy. **Tai Chi II** has no connection to this film. Trivia note: Jet Li and Michelle Yeoh were originally to have been paired one year earlier for a remake of **Dragon Inn**, but the production was scrapped when producer Jim Choi Chi-ming was murdered. A rival remake, produced by Tsui Hark and starring Brigitte Lin Ching-hsia and Tony Leung Kar-fai, went ahead as scheduled.

943. Tai Chi II

(1995; Film Can Production Limited) ★: 5/10. *Tai gik kuen* (Cantonese), *Tai ji quan* (Mandarin): "Tai Chi Fist." Cinematographer: Chow Pak-ling; Art Directors: Edia Tsui Yim-ngai, Lin Chi-fu; Music: Not Original; Writer: Sze Yeung-pin; Producer: Anthony Wong Him; Action Director: Yuen Woo-ping; Directors: Yuen Woo-ping, Cheung Yam-yin. Cast: Jacky Wu Jing (Hawkman, aka Jacky), Christy Chung Lai-tai (Tsao Yeung-wan, aka Rose), Sibelle Hu Hui-chung (Jacky's Mother), Mark Cheng Ho-nam (Lam Wing), Lau Shun (Officer Tsao), Yu Hai (Yeung Shan-wu), Billy Chow Bei-lee ("The Great Kick of the North"), Darren Shahlavi (Smith), Chi Chuen-hua (Bald Villain). 1.85:1. VHS/LD/DVD: Tai Seng (Remastered for the English market; subtitled or dubbed). Import LD/VCD: Universe. 96 minutes.

Despite the Roman numeral in the English title and the participation of celebrated martial arts director Yuen Woo-ping, this modest, old-fashioned period entry bears no direct relation to Yuen's **The Tai Chi Master** (1993), aside from its hero's proficiency in the eponymous skill. When he's not driving his conservative father around the bend, Hawkman (newcomer Wu) spends his time receiving instruction in English and picking up romantic tips from his mom (veteran Taiwanese actress Hu, in a role patterned after Anita Mui Yim-fong's feisty stepmom from **Drunken Master II**). The object of his infatuation: American-educated Rose (gorgeous, Quebec-born Chung), whose quest to bring science and democracy to China is a serious embarrassment to her boyfriend Lam Wing, a Qing officer. When Wing is murdered by British opium smuggler Smith, Hawkman is framed for the crime and must use his talents to exonerate himself and save his fellow countrymen from the foreign scourge.

Although Yuen used to specialize in films that touted traditional skills, he utilizes too much cartoonish, undercranked wirework here, and that, coupled with the routine plot and weak stock score, makes this something of a disappointment. The film is more effective during the comic exchanges between Hawkman and his doting mom and the boy's rather charming attempts to ingratiate himself with Rose. Their interplay makes for pleasant, if not essential, viewing. Tai Seng's new translation on their English market version increases the accessibility of the humor, particularly during the hero's English lessons. A prime example: Jacky Wu's incredulous reaction upon learning that his mother's English name is "Diana"; he misinterprets it as *Di wan na*, which is Cantonese for "big windpipe"! In what is presumably his first lead role, Wu displays considerable physical dexterity; he's got the deadliest "flying braid stance" since Angela Mao Ying in **Hapkido** (U.S. title: **Lady Kung Fu**, 1973)!

944. Take Me

(1991) ★: 3/10. *Ching bat ji gam* (Cantonese), *Qing bu zi jin* (Mandarin): "Uncontrollable Love." Cinematographer: Poon Tak-yip; Art Director: Ring Law Chi-keung; Writer: Chung Kai-cheung; Action Director: Ridley Tsui Bo-wah; Producer-Director: Cha Chuen-yee. Cast: Veronica Yip Yuk-hing (Milk), Kenneth Tong Chun-yip (Wai), Maria Tung Ling (Mary), Charlie Cho Cha-lei ("The Human Dick"). 1.85:1. VHS: World Video. Import LD/VCD/DVD: Ocean Shores. 89 minutes.

One of Veronica Yip's softcore outings, **Take Me** casts her as the comely "Milk," whose wedding night turns out to be one she'll never forget: Her middle-aged husband dies of a heart attack before they can consummate the marriage. While he may be gone in body, the man's ghost remains to keep a watchful (and jealous) eye on the men Milk takes up with. Her next boyfriend, Ronald, meets an untimely fate when a pair of robbers toss him into the sea. The same pair of criminals soon appear at an art gallery that Milk happens to be patronizing. After forcing their victims to strip, they tie Milk to Wai, a penniless artist. The two hit it off and are soon in bed together, but there is one big problem: Ronald isn't dead after all. Milk tries to keep the two men from discovering each other, while deciding which one is the best for her.

Aside from the not insubstantial pleasure of seeing Veronica Yip and some of her co-stars *au naturel*, this is typical, brainless softcore, served up in standard fashion. Charlie Cho recreates the "Human Penis" exhibition from Ken Russell's **Crimes of Passion** and later joins Maria Tung for some **9 1/2 Weeks**-inspired "fun with food."

945. Takes Two to Mingle

(1990; Hatract Films) ★: 6/10. *Moh dang chan ga* (Cantonese), *Mo deng chen jia* (Mandarin): "Modern Living Family." Cinematographers: Derek Yee Tung-sing, Gigo Lee Chi-hang; Art Director: Andy Lee Yiu-kwong; Music: Richard Lo Sai-kit; Writer: Clarence Yip Wai-chung; Producers: Kam Hoi, Tsui Chung-lam; Action Director: James Ha Chim-see; Director: Dick Cho Kin-nam. Cast: Danny Lee Sau-yin (Lee), Wu Ma (Godfather Wong), Fennie Yuen Kit-ying (Lee Tung), Ricky Yee Fan-wai (Vicky), Lam Wai (Thai), Shing Fui-on (Thug), Blackie Ko Shou-liang (Thug). 1.85:1. Import LD: Star Entertainment (No Subtitles). 92 minutes.

This lightweight Danny Lee cop actioner takes part of its premise from, of all things, *Romeo and Juliet*. When Lee Tung falls in love with KK Wong, sparks fly in but for all the wrong reasons: Tung's brother is an ultra-righteous cop and KK's dad is a triad boss. The two men have a long history of adversity and nearly come to blows when Lee is inadvertently invited to Wong's birthday party. Lee and his men begin a campaign of harassment, shutting down Wong's bars and mahjong parlours. In response, Vicky, Wong's headman (yes, *man*), frames Lee and gets him in trouble with Internal Affairs. However, when Wong discovers that Vicky has extorted four million dollars from the organization and is running drugs, he reluctantly collaborates with Lee in order to set things right.

No surprises here but this remains a passable timewaster, helped in no small part by amusing performances from Lee and Wu (looking like Tung Chee-hwa!) and an exciting climactic shootout. The English title is a real head-scratcher and does not make any more sense even after one views the film. The Taiwanese video version from Scholar Films has English subtitles.

946. A Tale from the East

(1990) ★: 6/10. *Maan wa kei hap* (Cantonese), *Man hua qi xia* (Mandarin): "Comic Book Amazing Hero." Cinematographer: Michael Ma Koon-wah; Art Director: Tsui Chi-chung; Music: Wong Yiu-kwong; Producer: Phillip Chan Yan-kin; Action Directors: Tony Poon Kin-kwan, Benz Kong To-hoi; Writer-Director: Manfred Wong. Cast: Joey Wang Tsu-hsien (Kot-yee), Billy Lau Nam-kwong (Chu Tai-lit), David Wu Tai-wai (Huang Zhin), Jan Lam Hoi-fung (Electrician #1), Eric Kot Man-fai (Electrician #2), Ngai Hong (Wesley), Lawrence Cheng Tan-shui (Dunn), Alfred Cheung Kin-ting (Director), Manfred Wong (Uncle). VHS: World Video. Import LD: Ocean Shores. 89 minutes.

A group of campers find their evening under the stars ruined by a thunderstorm. While fleeing the rain, Tai-lit and his sister Kot-yee encounter Huang Zhin, a royal guard from the Ching Dynasty. He has revived after spending 200 hundred years in suspended animation and seeks to find the child princess he was ordered to guard. The princess, meanwhile, has also reawakened in the present day and is discovered by a pair of goofy electricians. The Mandarin-speaking misfits are eventually reunited, but they are not the only visitors from the 18th century: Their arch-enemy, a monstrous swordsman called "The Blood Devil," is also on the loose and seeks a magical pearl found in the princess' amulet which will give eternal life to the person who consumes it.

While not as imaginative or amusing as the best films of this type, **A Tale from the East** is lively, well-paced fun. The final battle (in an amusement park, of all places) is a nice change of pace, but this one really deserves points for recruiting legendary writer Ngai Hong (aka Ni Kuang) to play his own literary creation, Wai See-lei, better known in English as "Wisely" but called "Wesley" here. When one character asks him how he developed his theories on time travel, Ngai produces the laserdiscs for **Back to the Future** and **Somewhere in Time**! Amy Yip Chi-mei, Money Lo Man-yee, and Simon Lui Yu-yeung have cameos as themselves.

947. Tamagotchi

(1997; Film City/P.U. Productions) ★: 4/10. *Sei yuet sei yat* (Cantonese), *Si yu si ri* (Mandarin): "April 4th" Cinematographer: Tsang Tat-sze; Art Director: Mario Law Pui; Music: Van Lok Yik-chong; Writer: Lau Jun-wai; Producers: Daniel Lam Siu-ming, Danny Wong Lung-wai; Action Director: Bruce Mang Fan-lung; Director: Wellson Chin Sing-wai. Cast: Dayo Wong Chi-wah (Wan), Ruby Wong Cheuk-ling (Sam), Helena Law Lan (Miss Tsui), Wong Man-yee, Joseph Cheung Tung-cho. 1.85:1. VHS: Tai Seng. Import LD/VCD/DVD: Universe. 88 minutes.

In spite of the English title, this disappointing horror thriller has nothing at all to do with the hugely popular Japanese toy. Primary school teacher Miss Tsui goes to the home of perpetual absentee student Tintin Wang, only to be attacked and driven crazy by some unseen force. Tintin is traumatized and catatonic, but also quite creepy and in control of some form of supernatural power. Social worker Sam and her bumbling cop boyfriend Wan take a special interest in Tintin's case, which grows progressively weirder by the day. Sent to a school for orphans, the girl causes a number of strange occurrences, culminating in the death of the caretaker, an accident for which Sam is blamed. Although she is subsequently cleared, the bodies continue to mount up and Sam seems to be the only one who can solve the ongoing mystery.

While never genuinely frightening, the film remains moderately engrossing, thanks in large part to an engaging performance by Ruby Wong. However, the resolution is a complete letdown, failing to resolve the story in satisfying fashion, resorting instead to an unimaginative and completely predictable "twist" ending.

948. The Tantana

(1991; Bao Shiung Film & Communication Co.) ★: 3/10. *Bei jung sing lung* (Cantonese), *Mi zong cheng long* (Mandarin): "Secret Sect Becomes Dragon." Cinematographer: Ng Man-teng; Art Director: Wong Tung; Music: Lowell Lo Kwun-ting; Writer: Sharun Hui Sa-long; Producer: Jimmy Wang Yu; Action Directors: Mang Hoi, Siu Tak-fu; Director: Mang Hoi. Cast: Sammo Hung Kam-po (Gai-lap), Wu Ma (Chek-fei), Lam Ching-ying (Mud-yuet), Chin Kar-lok (Dragon), Mang Hoi (Ling-hoi), Ken Lo Wai-kwong (Against-Nature Boy), Tai Po (Hiu Wan). 1.85:1. Import LD/VCD: Universe. 91 minutes.

Eighteen years after he was vanquished from this world, the evil Against-Nature Boy returns, proclaiming his intention to destroy the palace of heaven. Llama Mud-yuet seeks out his old adversary, Chek-fei, in an attempt to locate The Sharp-Witted Buddha, whose powers are needed to repel the evil force that is about to ascend. After much squabbling, the pair accidentally discover that Mud-yuet's new pupil, Dragon, is actually the Buddha, but The Evil One appears and Mud-yuet is mortally wounded in the ensuing battle. Dragon seeks out the reclusive Master Gai-lap so that the learned old man will teach him how to utilize and properly control his new abilities in time for his appointed battle with Against-Nature Boy.

This Taiwanese period fantasy looks about ten years older than it is and, despite its cast of genre veterans, barely holds one's attention. Slack pacing, low production values, and poor editing make it a chore to sit through. Sammo Hung does not even appear until the final third of the film and is only afforded about ten minutes of screen time.

949. Task Force

(1997; Golden Harvest/Golden Icon Entertainment/Harvest Crown) ★: 8/10. *Yit huet jui keung* (Cantonese), *Re xue zui qiang* (Mandarin): "Hot Blood Is the Strongest." Cinematographer: Mark Lee Ping-bing; Art Director: Chris Wong Hoi-kwong; Music: Danny Wong Dan-yee; Writer: Chan Hing-ka; Producer: Amy Chin Siu-wai; Action Director: Chin Kar-lok; Director: Patrick Leung Pak-kin. Cast: Leo Koo Kui-kei (Rod Lin), Charlie Yeung Choi-nei (Fanny Chan), Eric Tsang Chi-wai (LuLu), Karen Mok Man-wai (Shirley Lau), Edmond So Chi-wai (Scar-Faced Triad), Waise Lee Chi-hung (Triad Boss), Lawrence Ah Mon (Hardy), Clifton Ko Chi-sum (Doctor at Hospital), Chin Kar-lok (Robber). Dolby Digital. VHS: Tai Seng. Import LD/VCD/DVD: Universe. 100 minutes.

Young, straight-arrow cop Rod Lin gets involved with flaky hooker Fanny (who is up to her ears in trouble and faces death if some loansharks manage to get their hands on her) in this offbeat effort that juggles genres surprisingly well. Difficult to summarize, the film mainly looks at the above two characters while also devoting some time to LuLu, Rod's perpetually horny co-worker, whose marriage disintegrated when his wife caught him fooling around; Rod's co-worker Shirley, whom he has unrequited feelings for; and a killer who may or may not be a fantasy figure in one of Fanny's elaborate lies.

Almost entirely unpredictable, the film slides back and forth between comedy and drama in surprisingly effective fashion, mixing tone and emotions far more satisfactorily than director Patrick Leung's previous effort, **Beyond Hypothermia**. Along the way, there are worthwhile insights about memories, relationships, and parents, winning performances from Koo and Yeung (her last on-camera role to date), plus send-ups of John Woo's **Face/Off** (Woo himself cameos as a police officer in the final reel) and the Bruce Lee/Chuck Norris fight in **Return of the Dragon**. There is also some rather witty casting (would you believe art film director Lawrence Ah Mon as Fanny's street-smart pimp?). While there are some similarities to Wong Kar-wai's work (particularly **Fallen Angels**), **Task Force** transcends this and emerges as a highly satisfying work in its own right from a director who had previously shown a shrewd grasp of the medium but little ability to tell a story or involve the viewer. John Lone also appears.

950. A Taste of Killing and Romance

(1994; 100th Century International Entertainment) ★: 3/10. *Saat sau dik tung wa* (Cantonese), *Sha shou de tong hua* (Mandarin): "Assassin's Fairy Tale." Cinematographer: Tony Fan Chuen-kam; Art Director: Ganni Ma Chi-ming; Music: Mark Lui Chung-tak; Writer: Cheuk Bing; Action Director: Stephen Tung Wai; Producers: Lee Lo-fu, Fung Chi-kar; Director: Veronica Chan Ching-yee. Cast: Andy Lau Tak-wah (Ko Sau), Anita Yuen Wing-yee (Yu-feng), Mark Cheng Ho-nam (Wong Cheong), Christine Ng Wing-mei (Ice), Waise Lee Chi-hung (Tung), John Ching Tung (Doomed Hit-man). 1.85:1. VHS/LD: World Video. Import LD/VCD. Star Entertainment. Import DVD: China Star. 93 minutes.

This hackneyed thriller proves that HK's female directors are capable of crafting an action film that is just as nasty as those created by men. Beyond that, its accomplishments are very limited, alternating as it does between sadistic violence and insipid drama. Andy Lau plays Ko, a tough but ethical killer who accidentally stumbles into a contract killing with which he has no involvement. Anita Yuen is miscast (and does not dub her own voice) in the role of Yu-feng, the rookie hitwoman (with *asthma*, yet) who takes Ko hostage in order to make a clean getaway from the scene of the crime. Before long, the two have fallen for each other, unaware that they both work for the same boss: Ice, who uses her art gallery as a front. However, not surprisingly, Ice soon assigns Yu-feng the task of killing Ko, and both are soon targeted by Wong Cheong, a killer who redefines the term "ruthless."

Director Veronica Chan doesn't shy away from showing the gory aftermath of her characters' actions, but the film goes overboard in its depiction of violence toward the defenceless (particularly in the sequence where a toddler has a bottle of Dettol poured down her throat). One murder even concludes with a strong intimation of necrophilia, which does not fit in here at all. There are plenty of stylistic devices on display but they are far from fresh (slow motion, black and white, etc.), having been utilized to better effect elsewhere. Chan also not only lifts the bullet p.o.v. shots from **Full Contact**, she all but restages the dragon boat ceremony assassination from **The Killer**. The ending, meanwhile, is right out of another Chow Yun-fat vehicle, **Flaming Brothers**. Even the score, from the usually dependable Mark Lui, sounds recycled (although they are not lifted directly, a couple of cues are conspicuously similar to music in **Terminator 2: Judgment Day**). Add this dearth of originality to the hokey and unconvincing love story and you've got a wearisome misfire that is strictly for die-hard fans of the two stars. Gratuitous in-joke: A bride and groom are named after Leon Lai Ming and Michelle Lee Kar-yan, two stars who might have been better cast as the leads here.

951. Taxi Hunter

(1993; Galaxy Films) ★: 5/10. *Dik si poon goon* (Cantonese), *Di shi pan guan* (Mandarin): "Taxi Judge." Cinematographer: Yu Kwok-bing; Art Director: Danny Yuen Ching-yeung; Music: Wong Bong; Writers: Lau Yin, Ray Mak Kai-chung, Herman Yau Lai-to, Leung Hung-wah; Producer: Steven Po Yu-chung; Action Director: James Ha Chim-see; Director: Herman Yau Lai-to. Cast: Anthony Wong Chau-sang (Kin), Yu Rongguang (Yu Kai-chung), Ng Man-tat (Gao), Athena Chu Yan (Mak Suet-yan), Woo Fung (Chan). 1.85:1. VHS/LD: World Video. Import LD/VCD: Universe. 89 minutes.

HK taxi drivers are not known for their politeness, choosing their passengers based on their destinations, sometimes demanding extra money for late night trips, and refusing to perform basic services. This thriller (which reunites Anthony Wong with **Untold Story** director Herman Yau) takes the problem to cartoonish extremes but remains fairly engrossing. Kin is a mild-mannered but highly successful insurance agent whose wife is expecting a baby any day. When she goes into labour and he tries to get her to the hospital in a cab, the driver refuses to take them, as she has started bleeding. While trying to leave the vehicle, the woman's dress gets caught in the car door and she is dragged behind the cab, killing both her and the baby. The subsequent mental strain causes Kin to begin to lose his faculties. In a drunken rage, he murders a belligerent cabbie but, upon trying the same approach on a similar hack a few nights later, ends up being beaten and robbed. Undaunted, Kin gets his hands on a gun (leading to an amusing recreation of the famous "You Talkin' to Me?" scene from **Taxi Driver**) and shoots a driver who refused to give an old lady a ride. He later slays another cabbie who was trying to rape his teenage passenger. The police decide to have officers pose as drivers to lure Kin out, and when the latter unknowingly assaults one such cop (Ng Man-tat at his most obnoxious), that is the beginning of his downfall.

Supposedly inspired by a real-life taxi driver strike that crippled HK, **Taxi Hunter** is saved from mediocrity by Anthony Wong's terrific, darkly comic performance. The character may be one-dimensional but Wong endows Kin with a believable degree of sorrow and rage, and the writers deserve credit for coming up with a reasonably fresh and satisfying conclusion. The film received the Category III rating, though the violence is actually quite tame, certainly when compared to other Wong/Yau collaborations like **The Untold Story** and **Ebola Syndrome**.

952. Tears and Triumph

(1994; Mandarin Films) ★: 3/10. *Jok ye cheung fung* (Cantonese), *Zuo ye chang feng* (Mandarin): "Last Night, Long Wind." Cinematographer: Abdul M. Rumjahn; Art Director: Bill Lui Cho-hung; Music: John Wong Sai-cheung; Writer: Raymond Wong Pak-ming; Producers: Raymond Wong Pak-ming, Li Ning; Director: David Lam Tak-luk. Cast: Anita Yuen Wing-yee (Sai Ming-jun), Lau Ching-wan (Xie Shi-wen), Frankie Lam Man-lung (Zuo Se-cheng), Mui Siu-wai (Xu Yu-yuan), Donna Chu Kit-yee (Shi-yi), Jamie Luk Kim-ming (Ye Zhan-kuen). 1.85:1. VHS: Tai Seng. Import LD: Cameron Entertainment. Import VCD: Mei Ah. 96 minutes.

The weakest of the Anita Yuen/Lau Ching-wan vehicles, this heavy-handed drama is attractively designed but stodgy and much too predictable. Sales Manager Sai Ming-jun discovers, much to her chagrin, that her company has changed hands and that Zuo Se-cheng, the man who dumped her when she became pregnant years before, is now her superior. After a problem involving a sales clerk arises, Se-cheng is about to fire her when she is backed up by Xie Shi-wen, who is a member of the affluent family that are the new owners. Ming-jun and Shi-wen begin to date, despite Se-cheng's desperate attempts to get back together with her. Although she is an intelligent and successful woman, Ming-jun is unable to see which of these two men is right for her, worrying about the complications that will arise in Xie's family because she is "a woman with a past." When she refuses to becomes Se-cheng's mistress, he sets out to ruin her.

Yuen and Lau are as appealing as always but even their customary chemistry cannot salvage this simple-minded and hackneyed scenario which features some of the most jaw-dropping contrivances in memory. Frankie Lam's character is such a broad and laughable caricature, one half expects him to be spending his free time torturing small animals and popping children's balloons.

953. Teenage Master

(1995; Win's Entertainment/The Young Filmmakers) ★: 2/10. *Siu fei hap* (Cantonese), *Xiao fei xia* (Mandarin): "Little Flying Hero." Cinematographer: Cheng Siu-wai; Art Director: Raymond Kwok Siu-keung; Music: Marco Wan Ho-kit, Anthony Lee Hon-kam; Writers: Lau Jun-wai, Cheuk Bing; Producer: Wong Jing; Action Director: Yuen Tak; Director: Lam Wai-lun. Cast: Xie Miao (Tse Fai), Ng Man-tat (Fung), Ken Lo Wai-kwong (Master Tse), Ngai Sing (Shek), Jacqueline Law Wai-kuen (Shun), Frankie Chin Chi-leung (Phys Ed Teacher), Vincent Kok Tak-chiu (Hospital Cop). 1.85:1. VHS: Tai Seng. Import LD/VCD: Mei Ah. 88 minutes.

Xie Miao, the pint-sized kung fu dynamo, paired with Jet Li in **The New Legend of Shaolin** and **My Father Is a Hero**, is the star of this lame kiddie comedy which will be all but unbearable to anyone whose age is in the double digits. When they learn that their master has taken ill, Mainland martial arts expert Tse and his equally adept son Fai sneak into HK. While escaping from a murderous thief, the pair are inadvertently blamed for his crimes and become separated. Fai makes off with a bag of loot and is taken in by the Fung family, whose greedy patriarch wants to get his hands on the jewels. Fai enrols in the local school, where he falls in love with a pretty young student and pulverizes a gang of bullies (who look about ten years older than everyone else), while his dad and the thief travel around HK trying to find him.

The kung fu is fairly well staged and the first reel isn't *too* bad, but once Xie meets up with Ng Man-tat and we segue into the school scenes, the film grows unbearably insipid. On the other hand, you *do* get to see Ken Lo play a good guy for a change.

954. Temptation of a Monk

(1993; Tedpoly Films) ★: 8/10. *Yau jang* (Cantonese), *You seng* (Mandarin): "Seduction of a Monk." Cinematographer: Andrew Lesnie; Art Directors: Timmy Yip Kam-tin, Yang Zhanjua, William Lygratte; Music: Lau Yee-tat; Writers: Eddie Fong Ling-ching, Lillian Lee Pik-wah; Producer: Teddy Robin Kwan; Director: Clara Law Cheuk-yiu. Cast: Wu Hsin-kuo (General Shi Yan-sheng), Joan Chen Chong (Princess Scarlet/Violet), Zhang Fengyi (General Huo Da), Michael Lee Ming-yeung (The Abbott), Lisa Lu Yan (Shi's Mother). Dolby Stereo. 1.85:1. VHS/DVD: Fox Lorber. Import LD/VCD/DVD: Ocean Shores. 118 minutes.

Tang Dynasty, 626 A.D.: Generals Shi Yan-sheng and Huo Da join forces to instigate a non-violent coup which will overthrow the latter's master. However, Shi has been deceived, and the action is anything but bloodless. Implicated in the murder of the prince, and with his battalion now eradicated by Huo's men, Shi goes into exile with his five remaining soldiers. Leaving behind the beautiful Princess Scarlet, Shi and his followers become monks but are predictable failures when it comes to fulfilling Buddha's commandments. Scarlet discovers their whereabouts, but after a night of revelry at a brothel, the party is ambushed and almost everyone is killed. Shi takes refuge at a remote and all-but-abandoned monastery, watched over by a 100-year-old abbot. While there, the now-humbled man reevaluates his life and beliefs, but the past is not easily escaped.

Rarely used to best advantage in his HK roles, Taiwanese dancer/actor Wu Hsin-kuo is excellent here, bringing the right amount of intensity and passion to his part. Joan Chen is luminous (though somewhat under-utilized) in a dual role, and Michael Lee is wonderful as the senile but still occasionally shrewd abbot. A film of stunning, resonant images, **Temptation of a Monk** boasts beautiful cinematography (by Australian cameraman Andrew Lesnie, who would go on to shoot **Babe** and **Babe: Pig in the City**), superb production design, striking costumes, and picturesque Mainland locales. Deliberately paced, the story's tempo is in keeping with Shi's increasingly meditative and self-aware state, and the film serves as a highly satisfying examination of a warrior's search for inner peace and spiritual redemption following a lifetime of violence. The film received the Category III rating for its battlefield bloodshed, brief nudity, and mild sexual content, though none of these elements are dwelled upon unnecessarily.

955. Ten Brothers

(1995; Win's Entertainment/Chang-Hong Film & Video Co.) ★: 6/10. *Sap fong dai* (Cantonese), *Shi xiong di* (Mandarin): "Ten Brothers." Cinematographer: Horace Wong Wing-hang; Art Director: Horace Ma Kwong-wing; Music: William Woo Wai-lap; Writers: Lee Lik-chi, Vincent Kok Tak-chiu, Cheng Man-fai, Li Mu-chiung; Producers: Jimmy Heung Wah-sing, Mark Wu Dan; Director: Lee Lik-chi. Cast: Sharla Cheung Man (Mrs. Ha), Kenny Bee (Ha), Law Kar-ying (Wonderful Eyes), Sik Siu-lung (Powerful Three), Kok Siu-man (Five), Elvis Tsui Kam-kong (Big Mouth Wu), Yuen King-tan (San), Wong Yat-fei (Ford), Shih Kien (Old Storyteller). 1.85:1. Dolby Stereo. VHS/LD: World Video. Import LD/VCD/DVD: Mei Ah. 100 minutes.

Lee Lik-chi (**Flirting Scholar**) directed this incredibly daffy period fantasy-comedy which is just about the craziest children's film you will ever see and a guilty pleasure of the first order. Kenny Bee and Sharla Cheung Man star as a bickering couple who inherit a small farm surrounded by magic soil. After growing a crop of giant vegetables, they come into possession of ten pearls that contain the spirits of enchanted fairies. When their farm is invaded by the forces of the evil warlord Big Mouth Wu, they swallow five pearls each, causing the ten fairies to be reborn as bizarre looking "children" with supernatural powers (elastic arms, super hearing, etc.). However, the first batch (headed up by child stars Kok Siu-man and Sik Siu-long) are taken by Wu and treated like dogs (literally, of course), so the other five (led by Law Kar-ying) and their mom must come to their rescue.

Ten Brothers is sure to be an unparalleled endurance test for those with little patience for outlandish culture clash humor and the lowest of scatological jokes, but for fans of **Flying Dagger** and **Holy Weapon** it is required viewing of the first order, with truly outrageous wire-work, complemented by some decent digital FX.

956. Ten Tigers of Kwangtung

(1979; Shaw Brothers) ★: 6/10. Chinese Titles Unknown. Music: Not Original; Writer: Ngai Hong; Producer: Mona Fong Yat-wah; Director: Chang Cheh. Cast: Ti Lung (Li Chen-chau), Alexander Fu Sheng (Tan Min), Phillip Kwok Tsui (Beggar Su Chan), Johnny Wang Lung-wei (Liang), Lo Mang (Iron Fingered Chen Ta-chuen), Lu Feng (Su Hei-hu), Sun Chien (Wang Yin-lin), Chiang Sheng (Cho Yu-sheng), Chin Siu-ho (Lin Fu-cheng), Wei Pai (Wang Chu-ying), Ku Feng (Tsai/Chu), Wang Li (Tung Chi), Dick Wei (Ching Kei), Jamie Luk Kim-ming (Manchu Soldier), Mai Te-lo (Fighter), Lam Wai (Casino Doorman). 2.35:1. VHS: Vista (Dubbed). 90/94 minutes.

While the lousy dubbing deserves a modicum of the blame, this period kung fu yarn suffers from awkward story construction. The film opens with a pair of killers out to eliminate the members of the title group as an act of vengeance. After they manage to kill one of their targets, the movie jumps back in time a few years. In this segment, The Tigers help Ming rebel Chu (who goes by the name Tsai) escape from the Manchu government troops who have a warrant out on him. Pawn broker Li Chen-chau hides the fugitive in the back room of his shop and makes a pact with some other kung fu experts to protect him. Looking for a way to ruin Li, one of his competitors notices all of the strange comings and goings from Li's place and alerts Manchu official Liang. With the unwitting help of some martial experts (including Beggar Su), Liang and his troops try to capture Chu, but Li is able to convince the rival fighters that the Manchus are just using them. Realizing their mistake, they join up with Li and help Chu escape, bringing about the death of Liang in the process. The film then switches back to the other plotline, revealing that the killers introduced in the opening reel seek to destroy Li and The Tigers to avenge the death of Liang.

Muddled storyline aside, this is an efficient and engaging period yarn with a can't-miss cast of Shaw Brothers favorites utilizing all manner of weapons and styles. Phillip Kwok steals the show as the gleefully alcoholic Beggar Su, who lives for wine and performs the most amazing acrobatics. In the now famous finale, one of the villains gets his head kicked...off! Character names above are from the dubbed version.

957. Teppanyaki

(1984; Golden Harvest/Paragon Films) ★: 8/10. *Tit baan siu* (Cantonese), *Tie ban shao* (Mandarin): "Iron Board Burn." Cinematographer: Larry Siu Yuen-chi; Art Director: David Chan Chi-wai; Music: Chris Babida; Producer: Raymond Chow Man-wai; Action Director: Yuen Tak; Writer-Director: Michael Hui Koon-man. Cast: Michael Hui Koon-man (Johnny Huang), Sally Yeh Chian-wen (Sisi), Michael Lai Siu-tin (Pierre), Frances Yip Lai-yi. Dolby Digital (DVD only). 1.85:1. VHS: Tai Seng. Import VCD: Mega Star. Import DVD: Universe. 89 minutes.

Most of the jokes hit the mark in this amusing Michael Hui effort, which is one of his best solo vehicles. Put-upon chef Johnny Huang is at the end of his rope: His wife is a corpulent shrew and his father-in-law/boss is a sadistic bully who likes to shave people's eyebrows off. Both make his life a living hell, and his only joy comes during the brief moments he can daydream about lovely calendar model Sisi. When his dream girl walks into the restaurant one day, Johnny seeks to win her favor by defeating her arrogant, tennis champion friends in a match (which he does, after trading his racquet for a frying pan). When Sisi suggests that the two go off to The Philippines on vacation, Johnny is ecstatic...until his wife, father-in-law, and 103-year-old grandfather tag along. After ditching the relatives, Johnny and Sisi charter a less-than-reliable plane and end up in the ocean, but the real horror is yet to come.

Some of the gags lose their effectiveness through repetition, and a good portion of them are simply variations on ones from classic Western comedies. Regardless, Hui's timing and physical comedy skills are as sharp as ever and that helps to keep one smiling throughout. Action director Yuen Tak is credited here as Hon Yee-sang.

958. A Terracotta Warrior

(1989; Art & Talent Groupe) ★: 8/10. *Chin yung* (Cantonese), *Qing yong* (Mandarin): "Chin's Terracottas." Cinematographers: Peter Pau Tak-hei, Li Hsin-yeh; Art Director: Hai Chung-man; Music: Joseph Koo Kar-fai, James Wong Jim, Romeo Diaz; Writer: Lillian Lee Pik-wah; Producers: Chu Muk, Hon Pui-chu, Tsui Hark; Action Director-Director: Ching Siu-tung. Cast: Gong Li (Snow/Lily), Zhang Yimou (Mong Tienfong), Yu Rongguang (Burt). Dolby Stereo. 2.35:1. Import LD/VCD: Star Entertainment (No Subtitles). 106 minutes.

In addition to his work on the **A Chinese Ghost Story** and **Swordsman** series, action specialist Ching Siu-tung also found time to helm this Hong Kong production (shot in Mainland China and reportedly financed largely by Chinese-Canadian businessmen), which has never received the attention that Western writers have afforded its Film Workshop counterparts. Acclaimed actor/director Zhang Yimou (**Raise the Red Lantern**) stars as Mong Tienfong, a Qin Dynasty chamberlain who makes the mistake of falling in love with Snow, one of his emperor's concubines. Both perish as a result of their indiscretion, with Snow committing suicide while Mong is transformed into a terracotta warrior and sealed inside the royal tomb. Thanks to an alchemist's experimental compound, Mong is preserved and is reawakened 3000 years later in the 1930s by Lily, a ditzy actress appearing in what the English subtitles identify as a Chinese adaptation of **Gone with the Wind**! Recognizing her to be the reincarnation of his lost love, Mong seeks to win over the dubious girl and adapt to the new alien world. Standing in his way is the movie-within-the-movie's tyrannical leading man, Burt, who has his eye on the royal mausoleum's store of priceless terracotta statues, which Mong is duty bound to protect.

The screenplay (by novelist Lillian Lee) derives some of its ingredients from previous Chinese fantasies and restages a pair of highlights from **Raiders of the Lost Ark**. However, what it lacks in originality, it more than makes up for in amiability, managing some clever observational humor amidst the expected fish-out-of-water elements. Gong and Zhang make a charming couple (aided, no doubt, by their offscreen relationship at the time), and much pleasure can be had watching Gong try her hand at screwball comedy. After playing the doomed lead in **Red Sorghum**, she seems to relish the chance to cut loose and have some fun. Despite being a smash hit in both HK and Taiwan, the film has never had an official video release in North America, and only the Taiwanese tape has English subtitles.

959. Thanks for Your Love

(1996; Team Work Production House/Centro/Scholar Films) ★: 5/10. *1/2 chi tung chun* (Cantonese), *1/2 ci tong chuang* (Mandarin): "1/2 Time Sharing Bed." Cinematographers: Lau Hung-chuen, William Yim Wai-lun; Art Directors: Jessy Lam Chak-chi, Yim Chi-lam; Music: Henry Lai Wan-man; Writers: Lee Chi-yin, Kei On (pseudonym for Jeff Lau Chun-wai); Producers: David Lai Tai-wai, Norman Law Man; Directors: Norman Law Man, Daniel Yu Wai-kwok. Cast: Andy Lau Tak-wah (Wah), Rosamund Kwan Chi-lam (Li Lam-lam), Michael To Tai-yu (Michael), Anita Lee Yuen-wah (Michael's New Girlfriend), Deanie Yip Tak-han (Mrs. Li), Sheila Chan Sak-lan (Nancy), Yuen King-tan (Yuen King-dan), Kong Suet-fa (Ben's wife). 1.85:1. VHS/LD: World Video. Import LD/VCD/DVD: Mei Ah. 94 minutes.

This unabashedly corny romantic comedy pulls out all the stops, even throwing in some gratuitous computer animation. However, it gets by mainly on the appeal of its two attractive leads. Lam-lam is a woman with a very odd problem: She gets violent whenever a man touches her. Michael, her boyfriend of seven years, decrees that he has endured enough beatings for one lifetime and walks out on her. Deciding that she needs some experience, Lam-lam allows herself to be picked up by Wah, a handsome layabout. Before being able to consummate their lust, both manage to knock themselves unconscious. Waking up the next morning, Lam-lam is sure that the two had sex, much to her chagrin. Wah, meanwhile, gets tossed out of his apartment and moves into Lam-lam's now vacant home. She returns from a business trip to find that he has not only settled in, but also told her parents that they are engaged! Although Wah tries everything he can think of to win her over, Lam-lam's heart still belongs to Michael, despite the fact that he is already seeing someone else. Even though he cannot win her hand, Wah still decides to help Lam-lam overcome her affliction. Naturally, things don't work out quite as planned. *Thanks for Your Love* is pleasant fluff, burdened by a needlessly contrived finale.

960. Theft Under the Sun

(1997; Media Asia Film Partners I/Concept Link Productions) ★: 4/10. *Ho ching koi tin* (Cantonese), *Hao qing gai tian* (Mandarin): "Passion Covers the Sky." Cinematographer: Peter Ngor Chi-kwan; Art Director: Vincent Lam Wai-sam; Music: Johnny Yeung Kei-cheung; Writers: Chung Kai-cheung, Lam Chiu-wing; Producer: John Chong Ching; Action Directors: Ma Yuk-shing, Bruce Law Lai-yin; Director: Cha Chuen-yee. Cast: Julian Cheung Chi-lam (Leung Ka-ho), Michael Wong Man-tak (Dan Peterson), Gigi Lai Chi (Fai-fai), Francis Ng Chun-yu (Mo). Dolby Stereo. 1.85:1. VHS: Tai Seng. Import LD/VCD/DVD: Mega Star. 101 minutes.

After three years in a triad gang, undercover cop Leung Ka-ho receives orders to prepare a mission that will trap his boss, the notorious fugitive Dan Peterson. However, things go wrong and not only does Peterson escape, Leung's superiors believe that he helped him to do so. Since he is under suspicion, Leung is not allowed to return to duty. After he hooks up again with Peterson, the two travel to Mongolia, where Peterson plans on purchasing stolen Russian missiles. In the mountains of Northern China, the pair pick up their cargo but lose one missile in an accident. As they face bandits and public security officers together, the bond between Leung and Peterson grows into genuine respect and friendship, thus threatening to make Leung forget that he is a law enforcement officer.

The first half serves up some fine action, and the location work in Russia provides a novel backdrop for a HK production. Unfortunately, that is not nearly enough to compensate for the predictable narrative, terrible digital effects work, and numerous implausibilities. Francis Ng gives the best performance, in a supporting role as a police psychologist who desperately tries to convince his superiors of Leung's innocence.

961. Their Private Lives

(1978; Goldig Films) ★: 2/10. *Oi yuk kong chiu* (Cantonese), *Ai yu kuang chao* (Mandarin): "Love Longing Mad Movement." Writer: Leung Lap-yan; Producers: Alex Gouw, Hendrick Gozali; Director: Yeung Kuen. Cast: Chow Yun-fat (Ko Ming-chung), Liao Yung-hsiang, Chen Hsi-lien. 2.35:1. Video distributor unknown. 77 minutes.

This early Chow Yun-fat feature is of far more interest for its curiosity value than its artistic merit. Chow (billed here as Aman Chow Yun-fat) plays Ko Ming-chung, an award-winning movie star voted the most popular in the land, who begins an affair with his female counterpart, Chiang Ai-ling. Ai-ling's husband is jealous, violent, and middle-aged; Ming-chung's wife is affluent and willing to put up with his indiscretions as long as he stays with her. When a reporter manages to get a picture of Ming-chung and Ai-ling together, their relationship is dragged through the press, and Ming-chung's wife sets out to ruin the girl's reputation.

While supposedly based on real events, this is still trite and heavy-handed, lacking both interesting characters and convincing dramatics. Many viewers would give up on it long before the finale, if not for the fact that at least one edition features elements that just might shock them out of their slumber. The original cut of the film featured brief nudity and some very mild sexual content, but the print previewed contained *hardcore* sex scenes! The performers in these inserts are obviously doubles, and this version was apparently cobbled together solely for play in the United States. It remains a terrible movie but is now an incredibly strange hybrid of two very different genres and a dubious highlight of Chow's filmography! The above running time applies only to this alternate cut, which lacks production credits.

962. They Came to Rob Hong Kong

(1989; Cinema City Co.) ★: 3/10. *Baat bo kei bing* (Cantonese), *Ba bo qi bing* (Mandarin): "Eight Treasure Ingenious Military Move." Cinematographer: Ardy

Lam Kwok-wah; Art Director: Fong Ying; Music: Lowell Lo Kwun-ting; Writers: Dean Shek Creative Unit; Producer: Dean Shek Tien; Action Director: Kwok Chan-fai; Director: Clarence Fok Yiu-leung. Cast: Dean Shek Tien (Sherlock False), Roy Cheung Yiu-yeung (Mao Yiu-tung), Chingmy Yau Suk-ching (Jenny Tung), Sandra Ng Kwan-yu (Comrade Monroe), Eric Tsang Chi-wai (Ken), Stanley Fung Shui-fan (Yuen), Liu Wai-hung (Leslie Cheung), Chin Siu-ho (Bruce Hung), Charlie Cho Cha-lei (Biggy), Kara Hui Ying-hung (Inspector Shang), Chen Jing (Rooster), Shing Fui-on (Brother Dean), Yeung Ching-ching (Shang), Yammie Nam Kit-ying (May), Ann Bridgewater (Policewoman). 1.85:1. VHS: Tai Seng. Import LD: Golden Cinema City. 98 minutes.

After a terrific action sequence in the opening reel, this Chinese New Year offering transforms into an outright comedy and falls completely apart. Mao Yiu-tung, a vicious robber from the Mainland, manages to elude police after they launch a surprise raid on his HK hideout. Sneaking back into China, he assembles a squad of local dimwits for a "Big Circle" robbery. After smuggling them back across the border, Mao has coach Jenny put them through a rigorous training regimen. Naturally, the Mainland hicks are nothing but dupes, with Mao really planning to kidnap a councilwoman and take revenge on the cop who organized the earlier attack on him.

Despite the presence of several fine comedians, the film has no rhythm and precious few laughs, consisting almost entirely of age-old sight gags and weak verbal humor. Still, how often do you get to hear Shing Fui-on sing a Cantonese version of The Knack's "My Sharona"? Among the more obscure jokes are a send-up of **A Better Tomorrow** and Chen Jing reprising his "Rooster" character from **Long Arm of the Law**.

963. They Don't Care About Us

(1996; Uniart Films Company) ★: 3/10. *Siu nin 15/16 si* (Cantonese), *Shao nian 15/16 shi* (Mandarin): "Teenage 15/16 Time." Cinematographer: Chim Pak-hung; Art Director: Angelo Bernardo Castilho; Music: Wong Bong; Writers: Anna Lee Yee-wah, Lau Wing-kin, Sharun Hui Sa-long; Producer: Benny Chan Muk-sing; Director: Lo Kim-wah. Cast: Theresa Lee Yee-hung (Brenda Lee), Carlo Ng Kar-lok (Chi), Wong Kwan-yuen (Kwok Man-sing), Jerry Lam Hiu-fung (Ken), Vincent Kok Tak-chiu (The Director), Annabelle Lau Hiu-tung (Bell), Wong Yat-fei (Uncle Choi), Lee Siu-kei (Mr. Ken). 1.85:1. VHS: Tai Seng. 88 minutes.

Unintentionally prophetic, the English title just about sums up how most viewers will react to this one-note drama. When her school teacher friend has a nervous breakdown, Brenda Lee offers to fill in for the next three months. The class, naturally, turns out to be filled with budding juvenile delinquents, and things get so bad Brenda has to hose them down at one point. After this extreme measure earns her a warning from the principal, Brenda decides to use different tactics, showing some of the girls that their popstar idol is really an egotistical rat, giving a shy student the courage to ask his secret love for a date, proving to another that he should shun his triad friends, etc.

Lee and some of the teen actors are personable (particularly Wong Kwan-yuen, who got his start as a child actor in films like **All About Ah Long** and **Blue Lightning**), but this trite exercise has little basis in reality, simplifying the problems of adolescence to distinct shades of black and white. Even the least discriminating members of the teenage target audience would be hard pressed to find much of value from the lessons taught here.

964. The Third Full Moon

(1994; Golden Harvest/Try Ease/P.U. Production/Paragon Films) ★: 6/10. *Jing yuet sap ng ji yat sang yat sai* (Cantonese), *Zheng yue shi wu zhi yi sheng yi shi* (Mandarin): "A Lifetime on the 15th Day of the First Month." Cinematographer: Jimmy Wong Kam-ching; Art Director: James Cheung Ying-wah; Music: Tommy Wai Kai-leung, Red Cat Entertainment; Writers: Abe Kwong Man-wai, Taures Chow Yin-han; Producers: Wellson Chin Sing-wai, Abe Kwong Man-wai; Action Directors: Yee Fei, Yee Bo; Director: Wellson Chin Sing-wai. Cast: Michael Chow Man-kin (Chou), Lau Ching-wan (Chou's Partner), Ivy Leung Si-man (Chau's Wife), Yu Rongguang (Chuen Sun), Lau Yee-tat (Lau), Jamie Luk Kim-ming (Cop), Helena Law Lan (Madam Lung), Dennis Chan Kwok-san (Man with Head Wound). 1.85:1. VHS: Tai Seng. Import LD/VCD: Universe. 95 minutes.

A follow-up to **Thou Shalt Not Swear**, this middling comic scarefest reteams Lau Ching-wan and Michael Chow and works best when it concentrates on the their antics. Following a dangerous scuffle with a berserk hospital patient, Lau's character (who is, once again, not given a name in the subtitles) decides it's time to leave the force and heads off to Africa. Three years later, Chou's wife discovers a body in a carpark, and since her story is contradictory, the police suspect her of somehow being involved in the case. They become doubly suspicious when the man she identifies as being on the scene is someone the police killed in a previous case. Another murder occurs and seems to be the work of the same mysterious assailant, who is in relentless pursuit of a ring found at the scene of the crime. Chau sets out to make sense of it all, aided by his partner, who has finally returned from overseas.

The horror elements are largely ineffectual but the developing story remains intriguing. Not all of the humor works, but Lau and Chow give pleasing performances (particularly Lau, who shows that he is just as adept as an eccentric as he is at playing straight-laced characters), and much of their interplay is inspired. Helena Law has a fun cameo as a coroner based on her character in the previous film.

965. The Thirty Million Rush

(1987; Cinema City Co.) ★: 6/10. *Wong choi sam chin man* (Cantonese), *Heng cai san qian wan* (Mandarin): "Thirty Million Dollars of Ill-Gotten Wealth." Cinematographers: Bob Thompson, Andrew Lau Wai-keung; Art Director: Suzy Cheung Kai-san; Music: Alvin Kwok Siu-lam; Writers: Karl Maka, Wellington Fung Wing, Tsang Kwok-chi; Action Director: Lau Kar-leung; Producer-Director: Karl Maka. Cast: Karl Maka (Baldy), Brigitte Lin Ching-hsia (Sister Maria), Paula Tsui Siu-fung (Siu-fung), Eric Tsang Chi-wai (Fatty), Angile Leung Wan-yui (Tomboy), Mark Cheng Ho-nam (Mark), Lau Kar-leung (Liang), Wong Ching (Inspector "Big Mouth"), Wong Jing (Tak the Pimp), John Woo Yu-sen (Man in Bed). 1.85:1. VHS: Tai Seng. Import LD: Golden Cinema City. 93 minutes.

This is an uneven but largely amusing Cinema City farce quite obviously patterned after the Hollywood hit, **It's a Mad, Mad, Mad, Mad World**. Tsang plays a worker at the HK mint who discovers that thirty million dollars worth of old bills that were scheduled to be burned made it through the shredder intact. Teaming up with Cheng and Leung, the three recruit experienced but bumbling con Maka to mastermind the break-in and theft of the cash. Complications arise in the form of Lin (as a kung fu fighting nun!) and Wong Ching (as a less-than-righteous cop out to nail Maka at any cost).

Not all of the humor works, but there are some terrific stunts (watch a car drive over Maka's *real* legs!) and the whole enterprise is consistently energetic and congenial. Furthermore, while **Mad World** knockoffs are a dime a dozen, this may be the only one where the avaricious participants actually get the money! Directors Wong Jing and John Woo have fun cameos, and Sam Hui Koon-kit sings the very catchy theme song.

966. The 36th Chamber of Shaolin

(1978; Shaw Brothers) ★: 9/10. *Siu lam sa luk fong* (Cantonese), *Shao lin sa liu fang* (Mandarin): "Shaolin 36th Chamber." Cinematographer: Huang Yeh-tai; Art Director: Johnson Tsao; Music: Not Original; Writer: Ngai Hong; Producer: Mona Fong Yat-wah; Action Director-Director: Lau Kar-leung. Cast: Gordon Lau Kar-fai (Liu Yu-te/San Te), Lo Lieh (General Tien), Wong Yue (Old Ground Rice), Norman Tsui Siu-keung (Liu Tsai), Lee Hoi-sang (The Senior Monk), Lau Kar-wing (General Yin), Simon Yuen Siu-tien (Teacher). 2.35:1. VHS: Crash Cinema (Dubbed), Embassy (Dubbed), Fox Lorber (Dubbed). DVD: Crash Cinema (Dubbed). 115 minutes. Also known as **Master Killer** (US theatrical and video title), **Shaolin Master Killer** (Crash Cinema title).

Often cited as the greatest kung fu movie of all time, this Shaw Brothers favorite features outstanding martial arts and fascinating training sequences. After his family and friends are massacred by Manchu soldiers, ethics student Liu Yu-te journeys to Shaolin Temple and becomes a monk, so that he may learn kung fu and exact revenge. Renamed San Te, he spends the next year doing menial tasks before beginning his martial training. He must pass through 35 chambers, in which he will be instructed (through torturous tests of endurance) on how to increase speed and improve his balance. After a year of instruction in these areas, he progresses on to weapons training. The most proficient and talented student in the history of Shaolin Temple, San Te masters every technique in only five years and even invents a new weapon: the three-section staff. Ejected from the temple because he wished to teach Shaolin techniques to the people (hence the 36th chamber of the title), San Te proceeds to recruit a group of students and take revenge on those who murdered his family.

While it does not fully dispense with the vengeance theme found in far too many period kung fu yarns, the emphasis on training here is a welcome departure, and the exercises are quite ingenious in form and function. With his angelic face, expressive eyes, and superb skills, Gordon Lau proved himself one of the greatest kung fu stars of the '70s and, thanks to this film's international success, all but found himself typecast as a monk from then on. Hsiao Hou and Peter Chan Lung can be glimpsed among the monks, and the latter also plays one of San Te's teachers. Character names are from the English dubbed version. It was followed by **Return to the 36th Chamber**.

This Day, Last Life *see* **The Reincarnation of Golden Lotus**

967. Those Were the Days...

(1995; Mandarin Films/Filmax Production Co.) ★: 4/10. *Chi wan saan sap saam taai bo* (Cantonese), *Ci yun shan shi san tai bo* (Mandarin): "Thirteen Gangsters of Chi Wan Shan." Cinematographer: Poon Yiu-ming; Art Director: Ringo Cheung Sek-wah; Music: Eric Moo Kai-yin, Wong Bong; Writers: Wong Ho-wah, Chan Wah, Raymond Lee Wai-man; Producers: Raymond Wong Pak-ming, Raymond Lee Wai-man; Action Director: Lau Chi-ho; Director: Billy Tang Hin-sing. Cast: Eric Moo Kai-yin (Chan Wah), Chan Kwok-bong (Safe-Box), Moses Chan Ho (Ko Fai), Kent Cheng Chuk-see (Chan's Father), Joey Maan Yee-man (Kiddy), Che-Kirk Wong Chi-keung (Big Nose), William Ho Kar-kui (Brother Wing, aka Devil Siu), Lee Siu-kei (Triad Boss), Victor Hon Kwan (Food Stall Proprietor), Bobby Yip King-sang (Ugly Guy). 1.85:1. VHS: Tai Seng. Import LD/VCD: Mei Ah. 91 minutes.

The first of four HK movies with the above English title released over a two year period, this one is the fact-based tale of Chan "Swindler" Wah (also one of the screenwriters here), a low-level gangster/junkie who was able to rise above his station and resume a normal life as a member of The Christian New Being Fellowship. Through flashbacks we are shown his days on the streets as a low-level triad boss battling with rivals and suffering at the hands of a particularly sadistic cop. Chan's life and health rapidly deteriorate and he seems destined to die in the gutter but the death of his father and the realization that only he can turn his life around finally convince Chan to make the first steps toward recovery.

Well-intentioned but too heavy-handed to come off, the film is further burdened by tedious action sequences that unfold almost entirely in slow motion, a stylistic approach that would have been much more effective in moderation. As with director Billy Tang's other work some imaginative visual touches manage to shine through, suggesting that he is capable of better work, if someone ever entrusts him with a good script. Eric Moo does an adequate job in the lead, but it is Kent Cheng's quiet but powerful turn as Chan's long-suffering father that one remembers.

968. Those Were the Days

(1996; Sam Po Entertainment Production Co.) ★: 4/10. *Wong gok dik tin hung 2 ji naam siu yi* (Cantonese), *Wang jiao de tian kong 2 zhi nan shao yi* (Mandarin): "Mongkok's Sky 2: Man Burns Clothing." Cinematographer: Mok Chat-yun; Music: John Wong Sai-cheung; Writer: Tam Oi-lai; Producer: Lau Chun-fai; Action Director: Ridley Tsui Bo-wah; Director: Lau Hung-chuen. Cast: Louis Koo Tin-lok (Yung), Cheung Yuk-san (Feng Yu-san), Cherie Chan Siu-ha (Yung's Girlfriend), Law Kar-ying (Feng Siu-tien), Roy Cheung Yiu-yeung (Fat), Helena Law Lan (Aunt Lan), Bobby Yip King-sang (Chin), William Ho Kar-kui (Loanshark Fu). 1.85:1. VHS: Tai Seng. 89 minutes.

Neither the English nor the Chinese titles (the latter trying to pass this off as a sequel to **Man Wanted**) have much of anything to do with what unfolds in this hard-to-swallow amalgamation of the triad and ghost movie genres. Mob enforcer Yung goes into hiding after assaulting a loanshark his boss only wanted him to frighten. He falls for his pretty, timid neighbor Yu-san, who makes funeral dolls (which are burned as offerings to the deceased) that all look remarkably like him. Yung's boss sells him out to the loanshark and the youth barely manages to escape a deadly trap that is set for him. During a subsequent attempt on Yung's life, Yu-san is mortally wounded trying to save him. At this point, the film takes a jarring detour into horror territory as Yu-san's ghost returns from the netherworld and Yung decides to be by her side forever.

The horror elements are a nostalgic throwback to the films of the '70s and '80s, while the gangster elements are all out of the '90s *goo wak jai* cycle, right on down to the excessive use of stylized slow motion during the streetfight sequences. The disparate approaches do not blend together well, making this of little interest beyond that of a curiosity. Veterans Law Kar-ying and Helena Law do the best work here as, respectively, Yu-san's blind grandfather and a friendly spiritualist.

969. Those Were the Days

(1996; United Filmmakers Organization) ★: 6/10. *Sei goh 32A woh yat goh heung jiu siu nin* (Cantonese), *Si ge 32A he yi ge xiang jiao shao nian* (Mandarin): "Four 32A's and a Banana Teenager." Cinematographer: Chan Siu-kwan; Art Director: James Cheung Ying-wah; Music: Ho Shung-chi; Writers: James Yuen Sai-sang, Wong Yuen-yin, Lam Ngoi-wah; Producer-Director: Eric Tsang Chi-wai. Cast: Loletta Lee Lai-chun (Minnie), Karen

Mok Man-wai (Patricia), Amanda Lee Wai-man ("Informant"), Linda Wong Hing-ping ("Bamboo"), Eric Tsang Chi-wai (Minnie's Father), Julian Cheung Chi-lam (Chan Yan-kin), Josie Ho Chiu-yee (Man-sze), Hilary Tsui Ho-yin (Heung), Jordan Chan Siu-chun (Super). 1.85:1. VHS: Tai Seng. 101 minutes.

Inspired by the Hollywood movie **Now and Then**, this well-intentioned but forgettable comedy-drama stars Loletta Lee, Karen Mok, Amanda Lee, and Linda Wong as twenty-something school friends who get together for Lee's wedding and reminisce about their days as teen schoolgirls in the mid–80s. The majority of the running time is devoted to flashbacks, with young newcomers (including Kong Lai-na and Choi Si-man) taking over the parts. The main focus is on Lee's character, "Minnie," her offbeat friendship with the school's tomboy, her puppy love crush on a handsome teacher, the facts of life, and her first real boyfriend.

The performers are personable (the young actresses are very well chosen, matching their adult counterparts in looks and personality), and some scenes are quite amusing and knowing, but the film is largely content to cover well trodden ground, albeit with greater frankness than comparable Western features, when it comes to things like menstruation. The "32A" in the Chinese title refers to bra size.

970. Those Were the Days

(1997; Brilliant Idea Group/The Young Filmmakers) ★: 6/10. *Jing jong nuan hing naan dai* (Cantonese), *Jing zhuang nan xiong nan di* (Mandarin): "Deluxe Two of a Kind." Cinematographer: Tony Miu Kin-fai; Art Director: Raymond Kwok Siu-keung; Music: Lincoln Lo Kin; Producer: Nat Chan Pak-cheung; Director: Dick Cho Kin-nam. Cast: Dayo Wong Chi-wah (Wong Ching-wai), Gallen Law Kar-leung (Li Kei), Francis Ng Chun-yu (Tse Yuen), Nat Chan Pak-cheung (Ngau Tat-wah), Hsu Chi (Shiu Fong-fong), Maggie Cheung Ho-yi (Ching Po-chu), Monica Chan Fat-yung (Chau), Teresa Mak Kar-kei (Woman in Bathtub), Alvina Kong Yan-yin (Cheung's Wife), Yuen King-tan (Po-chu's Mother), Law Kar-ying (Uncle Kin), Lawrence Cheng Tan-shui (Ko), Cheung Tat-ming (Cheung), Joyce Chan Yin-hang (Ka-yin), Vincent Kok Tak-chiu (Wang Tin-lam), Ricky Yee Fan-wai (Kwan Mak-kei), Ha Ping (Fong-fong's Mother), Lai Yiu-cheung (Law), Lee Siu-kei (The Director), Chor Yuen (Cho Wood Yau). 1.85:1. VHS/LD: World Video. Import LD/VCD/DVD: Mei Ah. 103 minutes.

Like **92 Legendary La Rose Noire**, this send-up of 1960s movies (inspired by the successful TVB series **Old-Time Buddies**) will probably leave most English-speaking viewers scratching their heads, but those with some knowledge of the performers being sent up here will find it moderately entertaining. The premise is terrific: Egomanical art movie director Wong Ching-wai (Dayo Wong, doing a brilliant impersonation of Wong Kar-wai) is sent back in time to 1967 as punishment for dissing old Cantonese movies. His sentence: make a movie, in this era, that one person likes. If he succeeds, he will be returned to his own time. After getting the stuffing beat out of him on the set of a Wong Fei-hung picture, Ching-wai allies himself with future stars Ngau Tat-wah, Li Kei, and Tse Yuen and gives them tips on what will make them famous. Then Ching-wai casts them in remakes of his films **Days of Being Wild**, **Happy Together**, and **Ashes of Time**! All three bomb but Ching-wai does finally find someone who liked his films: the young *Wong Jing*!

As mentioned above, not all of the jokes will be accessible and some are overly cruel (particularly at the expense of Lydia Shum Tin-ha, who is played here by a man in drag), but the **Back to the Future**-style premise is fun and a fair amount of the gags hit the mark. There are some particularly amusing jokes at the expense of junk movie king Wong Jing, as well as a look at how **Police Story**, **He's a Woman, She's a Man**, and **Young and Dangerous** would have turned out if cast with these 1960s idols (thinly veiled parodies of real stars like Lui Kei, Cho Tat-wah, Patrick Tse Yin, Josephine Siao Fong-fong, Kwan Tak-hing, Chan Po-chu, Nancy Sit Kar-yan, etc.).

971. Thou Shalt Not Swear

(1993; Golden Harvest/Try Ease/P.U. Production/Paragon Films) ★: 6/10. *Chat yuet sap sei* (Cantonese), *Qi yue shi si* (Mandarin): "July 14th." Cinematographer: Jimmy Wong Kam-shing; Art Director: Raymond Kwok Siu-keung; Music: Tommy Wai Kai-leung; Writers: Lau Jun-wai, Taures Chow Yin-han, Abe Kwong Man-wai; Producer-Director: Wellson Chin Sing-wai. Cast: Michael Chow Man-kin (Chou), Lau Ching-wan (Chou's Partner), Chen Ming-chen (Chia Chia-yi), Michael To Tai-yu (Chia-yi's Husband), Helena Law Lan (Lung), Ronald Wong Pan (Long Hair), Lau Yee-tat (Inspector Chung), Yuen King-tan (Nosy Woman at Apartment Building), Cheung Kwok-keung (Chen Te-kang), John Wakefield (Bartender). 1.85:1. VHS: Tai Seng. Import LD/VCD: Universe. 91 minutes.

The first of Wellson Chin and Abe Kwong's "date horror movies" (so-called because the Chinese titles are a date, either real or fictional), **Thou Shalt Not Swear** concerns a Chinese legend which states that on the 14th day of the seventh moon the gates of hell open, allowing ghosts to walk the earth for that evening. After a couple are sliced to pieces by a ceiling fan while in the middle of a heavy lovemaking session, a pair of seriously mismatched cops (played by Lau Ching-wan and Michael Chow) are assigned to the case. The chief suspect is Chen Ming-chen (**Rock 'n Roll Cop**), the wife of the deceased, who walked in on the couple when they were doing the nasty. While she claims to have left the scene before their deaths, none of her alibis check out. Nevertheless, the partners still believe her to be innocent. While following up various leads, it becomes painfully clear to the pair that this is no ordinary case, as each of the suspect's old friends turn out to be dead. Their demises can all be traced back to the day, many years ago, that they swore an oath together as children.

Lau and Chow play off each other well and their chemistry helps one to enjoy the less inspired bits (some of the humor revolves around the pair's terrible grasp of English, a gag that wears thin fast). The evolving mystery is interesting and Chin is able to makes the proceedings quite atmospheric, but the resolution and climactic action are a bit disappointing in light of such an effective build-up. Lau and Chow were re-teamed for the next year's **The Third Full Moon**.

Three Days of a Blind Girl *see* **Retribution Sight Unseen**

972. The Three Swordsmen

(1994; Wing Fat Film Production Co.) ★: 5/10. *Do gim siu* (Cantonese), *Dao jian xiao* (Mandarin): "Blade, Sword, Smile." Cinematographers: Chow Kim-ming, Chow Kei-seung; Art Director: Lau Sai-wan; Music: Alvin Kwok Siu-lam; Writers: Lee Sai-hung, Sze Mei-yee; Producers: Chan Chen-heng, Liu Chin-fat; Action Directors: Tony Leung Siu-hung, Yuen Bun; Director: Taylor Wong Tai-loi. Cast: Andy Lau Tak-wah (Siu Sam-siu), Brigitte Lin Ching-hsia (Ming Jian), Elvis Tsui Kam-kong (Wham Dao), Yu Li (Ku Choi-yi). 1.85:1. VHS: Tai Seng. Import LD/VCD: Universe. 86 minutes.

This extremely convoluted but agreeable period fantasy-comedy-adventure stars Andy Lau as the colorful warrior Siu Sam-siu, who is set to face noted opponent and compatriot Ming Jian (played by Brigitte Lin, with a dubbed male voice) in a showdown to decide who is the foremost swordsman in the martial world. The competition is put on hold when Siu is framed for murder and finds himself pursued by the resolute lawman Wham Dao (Elvis Tsui, on the right side of the law for a change). The Ming family comes to his aid but a traitor in their ranks hatches a plot that forces Siu and Ming Jian into a climactic duel to the death in order to facilitate the release of the former's fiancée.

A troubled project which was greatly altered in post production, the film suffers largely from a familiar downside of HK cinema: poorly translated English subtitles. That said, director Wong (**Deadly Dream Woman**) keeps things fast and funny enough to help retain the attention of English speaking viewers distanced by the muddled storyline. Lin is cast in a role that echoes "Invincible Asia" from **Swordsman II** (1992) and **The East Is Red** (1993) but also harkens back to one of her most unusual portrayals: male hero "Jia Baoyu" in Li Han-hsiang's adaptation of the Chinese literary warhorse **Dream of the Red Chamber**. This offbeat casting, and Lin's consistent success in such eccentric parts, heightens the interest level of both a throwaway character and a relatively minor film. A portion of the score has reportedly been lifted from Michael Mann's **Last of the Mohicans** (1992).

973. Thunder Cop

(1996) ★: 3/10. *San dip huet seung hung* (Cantonese), *Xin die xue shuang xiong* (Mandarin): "New Pair of Blood Splattering Heroes." Cinematographer: Lau Hung-chuen; Art Director: Ho Pik-wan; Music: Ng Kwok-king; Writer: Yuen Kam-lun; Producers: Victor Yeung Kar-on, Yuen Kam-lun, Norman Law Man; Action Director: Chan Chung-tai; Director: Clarence Fok Yiu-leung. Cast: Nicky Wu Chi-lung (Ng Chi-lone), Winston Chao Wen-hsuan (Chiu Kwok-ho), Rene Lau Yeuk-ying (Lau Mei-ying), Carrie Ng Kar-lai (Lai, aka Honey), Ivy Leung Si-man (Tung-tung), Ben Ng Ngai-cheung (Keung), Yuen King-tan (Fa). 1.85:1. VHS: Tai Seng. Import LD/VCD: Mei Ah. 92 minutes.

The Chinese title tries to pass it off as a sequel to **The Killer**, but this boring action-comedy doesn't deserve to be mentioned in the same breath. Hot-headed cop Ng Chi-lone is always in trouble with his superior and seems destined to be fired. Meanwhile, crime boss Chiu Kwok-ho decides he wants to retire after discovering that his partners are now dealing in drugs. One evening the two meet in a bar and, not realizing each other's identity, strike up a friendship. When some hitmen try to kill Chiu, Ng saves his life, an action that the police department finds more than a little suspicious. Suspended from the force, Ng's life is made even more complicated when he has to protect Chiu's girlfriend, who has also been targeted for termination.

The characters and their plights are uninteresting and the humor is very weak. Even colorful Carrie Ng can do little to enliven her supporting role as Ng's flighty relative. There is no shortage of gunplay but said sequences are so over-edited they are a pain to try and follow. On the other hand, it *is* fun to see Taiwanese star Winston Chao (who usually stars in much classier fare) leap around with two guns like Chow Yun-fat.

974. Thunder Cops II

(1989; Golden Flare Films Co.) ★: 6/10. *Lau man cha poh* (Cantonese), *Liu mang chai po* (Mandarin): "Hoodlum Police Woman." Cinematographer: Peter Ngor Chi-kwan; Art Director: Bill Lui Cho-hung; Music: Lowell Lo Kwun-ting; Producer: Wong Hoi; Action Director: Yuen Cheung-yan; Writer-Director: Jeff Lau Chun-wai. Cast: Sandra Ng Kwan-yu (Fong Ngoinam), Stephen Chiau Sing-chi (Sui Yien), Ann Bridgewater (Tsan), Shing Fui-on (Feitsat), Woo Fung (Sao Ko), Jeff Lau Chun-wai (Jeff Lau/Lofukao). 1.85:1. VHS: World Video. Import LD: Golden Flare. Import VCD: Panorama Entertainment. 102 minutes.

Right off the top, it should be noted that, despite the **II**, this film does not seem to be a follow-up to any other. Overly eager to nab criminal Feitsat, whom she has been tracking for a long time, policewoman Fong Ngoinam disobeys orders and intrudes on a sting operation, inadvertently allowing the man to escape. Soon afterwards, the informant and another female officer are killed and Ngoinam is framed on drug charges by her sadistic boss (played by director Jeff Lau), who is out to ruin her because Ngoinam's father had testified against him during an internal affairs investigation two years earlier. Escaping custody with the help of a sympathetic colleague, her only hope is, ironically, bartender Sui Yien, who is Feitsat's brother.

Certainly not the sort of fare one expects from Jeff Lau, **Thunder Cops II** is a remarkably grim and stylish police thriller with a strong dramatic performance by Sandra Ng. While the film defies some expectations, it also adheres to others, and none of the characters are especially endearing or even interesting. Still, there is some beautifully staged, slow motion combat, and this remains one of Lau's most consistent works to date. The Taiwanese video release on the New Ship label bears the Chinese title *Lai zi jiang hu* (or *Loi ji gong woo* in Cantonese), which translates into English as "Comes from the Triad."

975. Thunderbolt

(1995; Golden Harvest/Paragon Films) ★: 5/10. *Pik lik feng* (Cantonese), *Pi li huo* (Mandarin): "Thunderbolt Fire." Cinematographers: Horace Wong Wing-hang, Cheng Siu-keung, Joe Chan Kong-hung, Ardy Lam Kwok-wah, Lau Hung-chuen, Kwan Chi-kan. Art Director: Horace Ma Kwong-wing; Music: Kunihiko Ryo; Writers: Chan Hing-ka, Gordon Chan Kar-seung, Philip Kwok Wai-chung; Producer: Chua Lam; Action Directors: Jackie Chan, Frankie Chan Fan-kei, Sammo Hung Kam-po; Director: Gordon Chan Kar-seung. Cast: Jackie Chan (Jackie Chan), Anita Yuen Wing-yee (Amy Ip), Michael Wong Man-tak (Steve Cannon), Thorsten Nickel (Cougar), Chor Yuen (Tung), Dayo Wong Chi-wah (Lam), Ken Lo Wai-kwong (Cougar's Man), Corey Yuen Kwai (Doctor), Chin Kar-lok (Japanese Mechanic), Peter Yung Kam-cheung (Mechanic), Shing Fui-on (Obnoxious Customer at Garage). Dolby Stereo. 2.35:1. Import LD/VCD: Mei Ah. 110 minutes. Also known as **Dead Heat** (Japanese title).

A disappointing, ill-conceived Jackie Chan vehicle, **Thunderbolt** has some good kung fu action but not nearly enough to counter dull plotting, excessive use of slow motion, and some poorly staged racing sequences. Talented driver/mechanic Jackie helps the authorities nab road racers who have had their cars illegally modified. Thanks to Jackie's amazing driving skills, the HK police are able to apprehend Cougar, one of the world's most infamous bandit racers, who is also wanted on several counts of murder and other crimes. Cougar's thugs bust him out of jail and retaliate against Jackie, his family, and friends but Cougar stops short of killing him, demanding that Jackie compete against him in Japan at the Sendai Grand Prix. As insurance, he holds the mechanic's sisters hostage.

The first racing scene, which finds Jackie and Cougar going head-to-head in the streets, is exciting and quite well done. However, the later track sequences in Japan are so undercranked and blandly edited that they fall flat, and there is no spark at all between Chan and Anita Yuen. A terrific, prolonged battle in a *pachinko* parlor will satisfy fans, but the final bout between Chan and the villain never materializes. Considering how closely the screenwriters adhere to other conventions, they should have at least included that one, as the race wrap-up is a complete fizzle. Additionally, Chan is rarely allowed to display his exuberant personality, another fatal mistake. Not surprisingly, New Line Cinema passed on their option to release this in the North American market. In contrast to some of the star's early films, the Japanese version of this one runs a few minutes shorter.

Thunderbolt '91 *see* **Kung Fu vs. Acrobatic** [*sic*]

976. Tian Di

(1994; Win's Entertainment/Team Work Production House) ★: 3/10. *Tin yue dei* (Cantonese), *Tian yu di* (Mandarin): "Heaven and Earth." Cinematographer: Mark Lee Ping-bing; Art Director: Bill Lui Cho-hung; Music: Violet Lam Man-yee, Victoria Dolce Amore; Writer: David Chan Chi-wai; Producers: Charles Heung Wah-keung, Andy Lau Tak-wah; Action Director: Yuen Tak; Director: David Lai Tai-wai. Cast: Andy Lau Tak-wah (Cheung Ye-pang), Damian Lau Chung-yan (Tai Chai-man), Cherie Chan Siu-ha (Susu), King Shih-chien (Shantung Cat). 1.85:1. VHS: Tai Seng. Import LD/VCD: Universe. 103 minutes. Also known as **Chinese Untouchables** (UK video title), **Heaven and Earth**.

Easily the weakest of several HK knockoffs of Brian DePalma's **The Untouchables**, this action thriller unfolds in 1920s Shanghai, when members of the police department regularly turned a blind eye to sales of opium. Sent by the Nanking government, upstanding officer Cheung Ye-pang is given the task of cleaning up this "Paris of the Orient," a job he takes far more seriously than the openly corrupt city officials had expected. As with the Hollywood film, Cheung's initial attempts to battle the drug baron Tai Chai-man meet with failure, and he only begins to succeed after recruiting two loyal, equally incorruptible assistants. While Cheung is able to make great strides in his fight, Tai's social standing as a philanthropist proves to be a major obstacle, with tragedy soon pervading the law enforcer's life.

If it were just another run-of-the-mill formula picture, **Tian Di** would be much easier to dismiss. As a big budget production, it sports beautiful locations, some inventive action choreography, and lavish, authentic-looking sets and locales. Unfortunately, the storyline is so relentlessly predictable and the climax (which takes place inside the villain's lavish movie theater) is so utterly ridiculous, all of the attention to detail is for naught. Another detriment is the sepia-tinted photography, an overused technique intended to invoke nostalgia. While it has a magical effect on some movies, the altering of the image here only causes the tired proceedings to look murky and dreary, making it even harder to stay interested.

977. Tiger Cage

(1988; D & B Films Co.) ★: 6/10. *Dak ging to lung* (Cantonese), *Te jing tu long* (Mandarin): "Special Cop Slaughter Dragon." Cinematographers: Tomato Chan Man-to, Kin Lee Kin-keung; Art Director: Yim Ho-lam; Music: Donald Ashley; Writers: Anthony Wong Wing-fai, Yip Kwong-kim; Producer: Stephen Shin Kei-yin; Action Directors: Yuen Cheung-yan, Yuen Shun-yee, Yuen Yat-chor, Wong Kwan, Donnie Yen Chi-tan; Director: Yuen Woo-ping. Cast: Jacky Cheung Hok-yau (Fang Shun-yu), Carol Cheng Yu-ling (Shirley Ho Shih-ling), Simon Yam Tat-wah (Michael Huang), Donnie Yen Chi-tan (Terry), Ng Man-tat (Feng Chien-te), Irene Wan Pik-ha (Amy), Leung Kar-yan (Hsiu), Johnny Wang Lung-wei (Swatow Hsiung), Michael Woods (Black Thug), Fung Hark-on (Mechanic), Yuen Cheung-yan (Cop), Chen Jing (Pheasant). Dolby Digital (DVD only). 1.85:1. VHS: Tai Seng. Import LD: Mei Ah. Import VCD: Mega Star. Import DVD: Universe. 93 minutes. Also known as **Sure Fire** (UK video title).

There is action to spare in this conventional but entertaining police thriller. After successfully infiltrating a drug buy, Narcotics Squad officer Hsiu and his subordinates are able to capture all of the criminals, with the exception of their leader, Swatow. The next evening, Hsiu is murdered in cold blood by Swatow, prompting a desperate effort by the late officer's men to nab his killer. When they are finally able to apprehend the druglord, he is set up by Feng, a dirty cop working for American drug smugglers, and subsequently shot dead by officer Huang. When policeman Fang catches Feng and the foreign criminals together on video tape, he informs Huang; but, as subsequent events prove, there is more than one rat in the department.

As with the majority of D & B's action thrillers, **Tiger Cage** adheres entirely to formula, and the relentlessly brutal and protracted violence during the climax is numbing. The numerous chases and shootouts, however, are very well handled, and there is some fine kung fu, courtesy of Donnie Yen. One fight sequence, which unfolds in an apartment filled with propane gas, would be restaged a few years later in **The Bodyguard from Beijing** and again, with slight variation, in **Black Mask**. **Tiger Cage 2** and **Tiger Cage 3** are sequels only by way of the English titles.

Tiger Cage (1990) *see* **Tiger Cage 2**

978. Tiger Cage 2

(1990; D & B Films Co.) ★: 7/10. *Sai hak chin* (Cantonese), *Xi hei qian* (Mandarin): "Launder Dirty Money." Cinematographer: Mark Lee Ping-bing; Art Directors: Andy Lee Yiu-kwong, Leung Ping-kwan; Music: Richard Yuen Cheuk-fan; Writer: Patrick Yuen Yau-kwong; Producer: Stephen Shin Kei-yin; Action Directors: Yuen Shun-yee, Yuen Cheung-yan, Donnie Yen Chi-tan, Phillip Kwok Tsui; Director: Yuen Woo-ping. Cast: Donnie Yen Chi-tan (Dragon Yau), Rosamund Kwan Chi-lam (Mandy Chang), David Wu Tai-wai (David Ng), Robin Shou Wan-bo (Waise Chow), Gary Chow King-yeung (Ho Tak), Cynthia Yang Li-ching (Inspector Yeung), Carol Cheng Yu-ling (Petty Lee), Lo Lieh (Uncle Chiu), Michael Woods (Black Thug), John Salvitti (Caucasian Thug), Anita Lee Yuen-wah (Ann). 1.85:1. VHS: Tai Seng. Import LD: Universe. Import VCD: Universe, Mega Star. 95 minutes. Also known as **Tiger Cage** (UK video title).

While it has no direct connection to its forerunner, this remains a superior action adventure with invigorating gunplay and some outstanding martial arts, courtesy of Donnie Yen and Robin Shou. Quick tempered cop Dragon Yau is having the worst day of his life. First, his wife divorces him. A few minutes later he is almost killed trying to break up a robbery attempt. Later, after getting knocked out and dumped from a speeding ambulance, he is framed for murder and handcuffed to Mandy, the prim lawyer who effected his divorce. The two have inadvertently got themselves in the middle of a triad money laundering racket gone awry, and the perpetrators believe that Dragon and Mandy have their briefcase full of cash.

The scenario is flimsy and Rosamund Kwan's blithering coward is a bit much, but plotting and characterization are rarely better than competent in D & B productions anyway. Many films promise non-stop action but this one actually delivers. In fact, there is so much it is almost comical, as nary a minute goes by without a fight, chase, or painful stunt. After enjoying only a supporting role in the first film, Donnie Yen takes center stage and he is absolutely terrific, moving with such grace and lightning speed that only Robin Shou (who would later become known in America as the star of the awful but popular **Mortal Kombat**) is spry enough to really keep up with him. In addition to their expected bout, Yen also engages John Salvitti in a spectacular sword fight and battles huge Michael Woods while his hands are chained together! Cynthia Yang is wasted in a supporting role that almost seems like an afterthought, though she gets to do a bit more in the international version. That cut has her coming to Donnie Yen's rescue and doing her part to take out the bad guys.

979. Tiger Cage 3

(1991; D & B Films Co.) ★: 6/10. *Lang min chui gik sau* (Cantonese), *Leng mian ju ji shou* (Mandarin): "Cool-Faced Sniper." Cinematographer: Ko Chiu-lam; Art Director: Ho Chi-hang; Music: Schtung Music; Writer: Leung Kin; Producer: Dickson Poon Dik-sun; Action Directors: Yuen Shun-yee, Kuk Hin-chiu; Director: Yuen Woo-ping. Cast: Cheung Kwok-leung (James), Sharla Cheung Man (Suki), Michael Wong Man-tak (John), Wong Kam-kong (Lee Siu-pong), Woo Fung (Noble Liu), Michael Dinga (Alex). 1.85:1. VHS: Tai Seng. Import LD/VCD: Ocean Shores. 93 minutes.

The third and final entry in this "series" is the least successful but still makes for passable action fare. James is an investigator for the Commercial Crime Branch and is keeping tabs on Lee Siu-pong, an affluent player with obvious criminal intent. When Lee is threatened with blackmail by an associate, he orders his men to liquidate the extortionist, but a document detailing the scheme remains at large. Suspecting it has fallen into CCB hands, Lee has James' girlfriend, Suki, kidnapped. When James gives chase, he is badly burned in an explosion ignited by Lee. James survives the blast but his face and hands are horribly disfigured. After six months of recuperation, he sets out for revenge, sporting a silver mask to hide his mangled visage. In the interim, Suki did the only thing she could do to survive: She became Lee's mistress. However, fed up with being mistreated, she plots with one of Lee's competitors to bankrupt him.

Owing a small debt to Sam Raimi's **Darkman** (1990), **Tiger Cage 3** sports a fairly ambitious plot for the genre, but the two halves of the storyline don't meld especially well and the schmaltzy finale will satisfy no one. However, Yuen Woo-ping and his brother, Yuen Shun-yee, deliver a steady stream of terrific stunts (including a wild fight on some scaffolding that concludes with the opponents using flaming boards against each other) as compensation. Sharla Cheung's heroine is endowed with some welcome shades of grey, and this duplicity gives her more to do than just look sexy and/or scared like most of her counterparts in these films.

980. Tiger on the Beat

(1988; Cinema City Co.) ★: 7/10. *Liu foo chut gang* (Cantonese), *Lao hu chu geng* (Mandarin): "Tiger on the Beat." Cinematographers: Cho On-sun, Joe Chan Kong-hung; Art Director: Eric Lee Yiu-shing; Music: Teddy Robin Kwan; Writer: Tsang Kwok-chi; Producer: Karl Maka; Action Directors: The Lau Brothers; Director: Lau Kar-leung. Cast: Chow Yun-fat (Francis Li), Conan Lee Yuen-ba (Michael Cho), Nina Li Chi (Marydonna), Shirley Ng Ling (Mimi), James Wong Jim (Uncle Jim), Gordon Lau Kar-fai (Fai), Norman Tsui Siu-keung (Johnny Law), Phillip Ko Fei (Poison Snake Ping), Ti Lung (Loong), David Chiang Da-wei (The Commissioner), Shing Fui-on (Dummy), Lydia Shum Tin-ha (Clerk), Lau Kar-wing (Sour Puss). Dolby Digital (DVD only). 1.85:1. VHS: Tai Seng (Poor Subtitles). Import LD: Golden Cinema City. Import VCD: Mei Ah. Import DVD: Universe. 89 minutes.

Wild action and low humor dominate this entertaining knockoff of **Lethal Weapon**. Much to his consternation, lazy veteran cop Francis Li is partnered with musclebound upstart Michael Cho in order to investigate the murder of a Thai drug dealer who was doing business with the notorious gangster Johnny Law. The pair decide to lean on Marydonna, the buxom sister of smuggler "Poison Snake" Ping, who can tip them off about the location of Law's next drug buy. When Ping is murdered by Law's men, Marydonna cooperates, resulting in the arrest of Law and a much-needed promotion for Li. However, Law's men are not about to let her betrayal go unpunished.

Chow Yun-fat gives one of his most animated performances here, constantly bursting with energy and charm while not being the least bit afraid of making a fool of himself (at one point he even wets his pants!). Conan Lee (whom some might remember from his small roles in the American films **Eliminators** and **Armed Response**) performs some terrific stunts, and his gruff, by-the-book manner is a perfect contrast to Chow's clowning. The action scenes are thrilling and not just in the usual way: Chow comes up with an ingenious way to shoot around corners, while Lee and Gordon Lau engage in the wildest chainsaw duel ever filmed. Nina Li's presence results in more than a few breast gags and one politically incorrect plot turn you will never see in a Western film: When Li refuses to aid the investigation, Chow beats her up. Naturally, she is in love with him a few minutes later! *Tiger on the Beat* was followed by an in-name-only sequel.

981. Tiger on the Beat II

(1990; Cinema City Co.) ★: 7/10. *Liu foo chut gang II* (Cantonese), *Lao hu chu geng II* (Mandarin): "Tiger on the Beat II." Cinematographers: Paul Chan Chung-chau, Tony Fan Chuen-kam; Art Director: Barry Wong Ping-yiu; Music: Wong Kar-kui; Writers: Joyce Cheung Lai-ling, Wong Ho-yee; Producer: Karl Maka; Action Directors: The Lau Brothers; Director: Lau Kar-leung. Cast: Danny Lee Sau-yin (Lam Yick-lin), Conan Lee Yuen-ba (Buffalo), Ellen Chan Ar-lun (Sweet Dream), Gordon Lau Kar-fai (Fai), Roy Cheung Yiu-yeung (Fai's Man), James Wong Jim (Wong), Norman Tsui Siu-keung (Chui), Melvin Wong Kam-sun (Melvin), Maria Cordero (Maria), Mark Houghton (Mark), Phillip Ko Fei (Hood). 1.85:1. VHS: Tai Seng. Import LD: Golden Cinema City. Import VCD/DVD: Universe. 94 minutes.

Chow Yun-fat passed on appearing in this follow-up, which has no direct connection to the original, despite sharing many of the same actors (though only James Wong reprises his character). Lam Yick-lin is an agitated HK police officer whose miserable life quickly gets worse after he is forced to take in his muscular cousin, Buffalo. An A.B.C. (American Born Chinese), Buffalo has been sent to HK by his relatives, who are desperate that he find a wife. Buffalo gets involved with the lovely thief "Sweet Dream," who has witnessed a murder. She is wanted by gangster Fai and his men because she stole a ring they need to complete a drug deal with some foreigners. Being a gullible but good-natured person, Buffalo decides to help the girl, but when her constant claims of danger yield no tangible threat, he dismisses her as a crackpot. However, the threat is very real, as Buffalo, Lam, and policewoman Maria find out when they are attacked outside a nightclub by Fai's hoods. When a plot concocted by Lam ends up with Sweet Dream being kidnapped, Buffalo leads a valiant (and very ill-advised) one-man assault on Fai and his cronies.

The action is constant and quite impressively staged, though the plot contrivances (particularly the way in which no one ever believes Sweet Dream is really in danger) do start to pile up after a while. Chow Yun-fat's charismatic presence is also missed, and none of the characters or performances here stand out to the same degree. The best advice is to just sit back and enjoy the impeccably choreographed mayhem, which offers a terrific blend of martial arts and police action elements. Conan Lee was badly injured while jumping from a bridge to a lamp post, a stunt that remains in the film (you'll have no trouble understanding why it caused him to spend several months in the hospital). The sequence in which he fights barefoot on broken glass is often cited as a highlight, but praise should also be directed to Ellen Chan, who takes a lot of punishment in a physically demanding role.

982. The Tigers

(1991; Movie Impact) ★: 6/10. *Ng foo jeung ji kuet lit* (Cantonese), *Wu hu jiang zhi jue lie* (Mandarin): "The Five Tiger Officers Break Up." Cinematographer: Jingle Ma Cho-shing; Art Director: Lee Chingai; Music: Lau Yee-tat, Patrick Lui Yaufai; Writers: Nam Yin, James Yuen Sai-sang; Producer: Wallace Cheung Kwok-chong; Action Directors: Stephen Tung Wai, Tony Leung Siu-hung, Yuen Tak, Kar Lee; Director: Eric Tsang Chiwai. Cast: Andy Lau Tak-wah (Lau Chiming), Tony Leung Chiu-wai (Tau-pi), Felix Wong Yat-wah (Bong), Miu Kiu-wai (Wah), Kenneth Tong Chun-yip (Fong Heung-tung), Leung Kar-yan (Lam Hoitim), Irene Wan Pik-ha (Shirley), Chen Kuan-tai (Hon Wai), Lo Lieh (Chiu Chow), Phillip Chan Yan-kin (Tsao Siuping), Wong Kam-kong (Tam), Yammie Nam Kit-ying (Wah's Wife), Shing Fui-on (Shing Sha-pi), Michael Dinga (Defense Lawyer). 1.85:1. VHS: Tai Seng. Import LD/VCD: Ocean Shores. 110 minutes.

The TVB Network's top male stars (nicknamed the "Five Tiger Warriors") were brought together for the first time to appear in this theatrical crime thriller, but no one apparently felt the need to come up with an original or exciting storyline for them. Fortunately, the quality of the cast and some effective suspense keeps things hopping. Young hot shot CID officers Chi-ming, Tau-pi, Bong, and Wah are part of a raid on a drug smuggling operation co-run by psychotic criminal Fong. Officer Lam is able to apprehend Fong but ultimately lets the man escape because he is a relative. On top of that, Chi-ming and Tau-pi steal $1 billion of Fong's money rather than entering it into evidence. Instead of doing the intelligent thing and hiding the money away for a few years, some of the policemen spend it openly. There is also the matter of Fong, who threatens that, unless his boss (arrested in the raid) is released from prison, he will rat on Lam. To facilitate the release of Fong's boss, Bong intentionally botches his court testimony. However, the criminal isn't through with the officers just yet: He refuses to take the money back, and instead forces them to commit illegal acts for him. A plan concocted by Lam to double cross Fong fails, putting everyone's careers in serious jeopardy.

The trouble with this scenario is that all of the main characters must behave stupidly for there to be any story. One could certainly raise the question of how such police officers could possibly have lasted so long on the job when they seemingly don't even possess the smarts of your average rookie. If you can let that conceptual weakness slide, **The Tigers** remains compelling, thanks to some tense confrontations, an exciting climax, and a deliciously villainous, in-your-face performance by Kenneth Tong.

983. Till Death Do Us Laugh

(1996; Golden Harvest/BOB & Partners Company/Everwide) ★: 5/10. *Gwaai taam hip wooi* (Cantonese), *Guai tan xie hui* (Mandarin): "The Strange Tales Association." Cinematographers: Cheung Manbo, Chin Man-kei; Art Director: Stanley Cheung Sai-kit; Music: Yau Lung, Barry Chung Hing-hung; Writers: Wong Jing, Joe Ma Wai-ho, Matt Chow Hoi-kwong; Producers: Wong Jing, Manfred Wong, Andrew Lau Wai-keung; Directors: Joe Ma Wai-ho, Chin Man-kei, Yip Waiman. Cast: Anita Yuen Wing-yee (Yuen Siu-wen), Gigi Lai Chi (Mill), Hsu Chi (Yu Wai-kei), Liz Kong Hei-man (Flora), Cheung Tat-ming (Wang Kai-lang), John Tang Yat-kwan (Ball), Vincent Kok Takchiu (Wang's Boss), Lai Chun (Sau), Elvis Tsui Kam-kong (Father Chui), Guy Lai Ying-chau (The Chairman), Spencer Lam Sheung-yee (Yan). 1.85:1. VHS: Tai Seng. Import LD/VCD: Universe. 90 minutes.

This is yet another horror anthology that promises laughs and thrills but rarely delivers on either count. Reporter Yinyin is assigned to get a scoop on "The Strange and Unbelievable Experience Society," which meets once a year and is shrouded in mystery. Those who wish to join must tell a "horrible and unbelievable" story and are graded by the members. Story #1 (by director Joe Ma) stars Cheung Tat-ming as a put-upon accountant who has had about all he can take from his tyrannical boss. Purchasing a giant-sized kitchen knife, he plans on cutting his adversary into 18 pieces but inadvertently scares the man into a fatal heart attack instead. However, his new superior (Gigi Lai, with Bettie Page hair) is a knockout who has a new form of torture to inflict upon him. Vincent Kok gives an amusingly eccentric performance as the sweaty tyrant, but the first surprise can be spotted a mile down the road and the final twist is less than satisfying. Story #2 (by director Chin Man-kei) casts John Tang as a university freshman eager to score with the ladies. He finds his dream girl in the form of Liz Kong as a beautiful but decidedly unearthly student. Is she the "Lotus Pond Ghost" who is reputed to lure young men to their deaths? Does it all have something to with the "cursed" statue on the grounds that is making life hell for Tang's buddy? The ending for this one seems arbitrarily chosen and is a complete washout. Story #3 (by director Yip Wai-man) is the best, but that is more by default than anything else. Anita Yuen plays a housewife whose husband is away in Shanghai on business. Afraid of being all alone, she rents a room to a student (Hsu Chi), who turns out to be the ideal companion. However, when everyone begins to mistake her for her tenant, Yuen becomes convinced that Hsu is trying to "replace" her. The premise is not original, but the direction is stylish and the two leads are effective.

984. Till Death Do We Scare

(1982; Cinema City Co.) ★: 6/10. *Siu sang pa pa* (Cantonese), *Xiao sheng pa pa* (Mandarin): "Scared Kid." Cinematographers: Brian Lai Shui-ming, Abdul M. Rumjahn; Art Directors: Alex Ma Yiuping, Hai Chung-man; Music: Phil Chan Fei-lap; Writers: Raymond Wong Pakming, Clifton Ko Chi-sum; Producers: Karl Maka, Dean Shek Tien; Director: Lau Kar-wing. Cast: Alan Tam Wing-lun (Bruce Sit), Olivia Cheng Man-ar (Irene Leen), David Chiang Da-wei (Walter Fink), Wong Ching ("Butcher Man"), Raymond Wong Pak-ming (Stewart Pik), Eric Tsang Chi-wai (Bibot Tam). 1.85:1. VHS: Tai Seng. Import LD: Golden Cinema City. Import VCD: Mega Star. 91 minutes.

American make-up artist Tom Savini provided the basic but effective illusions for this mildly amusing horror-comedy. The lovely Irene Leen is a cursed woman: Three of her husbands have died on their wedding day. On the advice of several fortune tellers, she wisely decides to never marry again. However, the ghosts of the three men (played by David Chiang, Wong Ching, and Raymond Wong) decide to cure her depression by setting her up with another man. They choose Bruce, a nerdy radio announcer, to be their successor and set about helping him to win her over. Naturally, just when he is about to score, events arise that require the spectres to *prevent* him from getting lucky. To make matters worse, Bruce is tricked by another ghost into going to "Haunted Island" to retrieve the Ghost King's pearl. If that were not dangerous enough, he goes on the day of the Ghost Festival, when all of the spirits return from Hell and have a giant party!

Much more restrained than many of the efforts that would follow, the humor here is amiable and fairly inventive (including a great sequence in which Eric Tsang tries to deal with a haunted chair), and Savini's intentionally cartoonish make-up (face tearing, head stretching, etc.) fits the mood perfectly. Tsang, incidentally, is dubbed by another actor and it is quite strange to hear him yelling in terror without that familiar falsetto voice. Director Lau Kar-wing and co-writer Clifton Ko have cameos.

Till We Meet Again *see* **Au Revoir, Mon Amour**
Time Warriors *see* **The Iceman Cometh**

985. The Time You Need a Friend

(1985; Cinema City Co.) ★: 3/10. *Siu jeung* (Cantonese), *Xiao jiang* (Mandarin): "Joke Crafters." Cinematographers: Yip Ching-biu, Kan Wing-hing; Art Directors: To Man-ching, Lam Man-yam; Music: Lee Sou-chuen; Writer-Producer: Raymond Wong Pak-ming; Director: John Woo Yu-sen. Cast: Sun Yueh (Ku Ren), David Tao Tai-wai (Shen Bien), Lau Shui-kei, Kong Kwong. 2.35:1. VHS: Tai Seng (Poor Subtitles). 93 minutes.

Lensed in Taiwan, this melodramatic remake of **The Sunshine Boys** will exhaust the patience of all but the most devoted John Woo completists. Old-time comedians Ku Ren and Shen Bien ruled the movie screens for decades but parted company in the mid–60s on less than amicable terms. Now, years later, Ku has agreed to appear on a telethon to aid handicapped children and discovers that the organizer plans to also have him reunite with Shen on the program. The two meet prior to the event and spend the time playing cruel tricks on one another. A daughter that Ku never knew he had appears, and the program's sponsor deems this a threat to the actor's reputation and, by extension, the telethon. That, coupled with Shen's heart problems and their mutual animosity, makes it seem like the reunion will never come off. However, thanks to a little behind-the-scenes ingenuity by Shen's son and an assistant connected with the telecast, the pair are finally shamed into putting their differences aside for the sake of the children.

As subtle as a pie to the face and a double finger gouge to the eyes, **The Time You Need a Friend** is built almost entirely out of hackneyed precepts that were around long before its protagonists were said to be stars, the sort of creative laziness that characterizes most of Raymond Wong's scripts. The climactic sequence must be seen to be believed: When the pair's old-style routines are met with stony silence, they instead participate in a tacky "Solid Gold"-style song and dance number that goes over like gangbusters!

986. To Be No. 1

(1996; Colour Business Entertainment/Nam Yin Production Company) ★: 4/10. *Gam bong tai ming* (Cantonese), *Jin bang ti ming* (Mandarin): "Golden List of Signatures." Cinematographer: Peter Ngor Chi-kwan; Art Director: Chiu Chung-pang; Music: Mak Chun-hung; Writer: Nam Yin; Producer: Lam Ling-lam; Action Director: Lau Chi-ho; Director: Raymond Lee Wai-man. Cast: Julian Cheung Chi-lam (Fai Chuen), Allen Ting Chi-chun (Jose), Cheng Kar-lei (Apple), Simon Yam Tat-wah (Magic Lamp), Michael Chan Wai-man (Brother Piu), Ben Ng Ngai-cheung (Brother Paul), Danny Lee Sau-yin (Officer Kent), Ng Chi-hung (Ox), Wu Ma (Brother 19's Boss), Wong Chi-yeung (Brother 19), Peter Lai Bei-tak (Uncle Hoi), Lam Wai (Three), Victor Hon Kwan (Five), Vincent Wan Yeung-ming (Seven). 1.85:1. VHS: Tai Seng. Import LD/VCD/DVD: Ocean Shores. 96 minutes.

Not to be confused with the big budget Best Picture Winner **To Be Number One, To Be No. 1** is a thoroughly minor league attempt to ride the wave generated by the success of the **Young and Dangerous** series. Teenager Fai Chuen leaves his humble origins behind him and uses his resolve to rise quickly through the ranks of the Hung Lok Society, which is led by the famous boss Brother Piu. While Fai's violent and impulsive nature account for much of his success, they also, ultimately, spell his downfall when he kills the favorite lieutenant of a rival leader.

Singer Julian Cheung is a dull leading man, but the cast is loaded with genre veterans and their presence does much to keep the proceedings at least moderately interesting (how often do you get to see Wu Ma as a slick ganglord with a ponytail!). Still, when all is said and done, this adds nothing fresh or exciting to the cycle and is best left to completists.

987. To Be Number One

(1991; Golden Harvest/Johnny Mak Production/Dootson Investment Corporation) ★: 6/10. *Poh Ho* (Cantonese), *Bo Pao* (Mandarin): "Crippled Ho." Cinematographer: Peter Pau Tak-hei; Art Director: Jessy Lam Chak-chi; Music: Joseph Chan Wing-leung; Writers: Johnny Mak Dong-hung, Stephen Siu Yeuk-yuen; Producer: Stephen Siu Yeuk-yuen; Action Director: Tony Leung Siu-hung; Director: Poon Man-kit. Cast: Ray Lui Leung-wai (Ho), Kent Cheng Chuk-see (Ng Shing-kwan), Cecilia Yip Tung (Tse Yuen-ying), Amy Yip Chi-mei (May), Waise Lee Chi-hung (Chan Tai-man), Kenneth Tsang Kong (Chief Inspector Lui Ko-tin), Lawrence Ng Kai-wah (Ng Ming), Elvis Tsui Kam-kong (Chi), Tommy Wong Kwong-leung ("Loud" Hung), Lau Shun (Fung), Lo Lieh (Tin), Lau Kong (Lung), Ng Man-tat (Ping), Alvina Kong Yan-yin (Deranged Woman), Victor Hon Kwan (Kong), Frankie Chin Chi-leung (Little Hak), Chung Fat (Cham). Dolby Stereo (Laserdisc Only). 2.35:1. VHS: Tai Seng. Import LD/VCD: Universe. 137 minutes.

While undeserving of the Best Picture prize it collected, this Mak Brothers production is a moderately entertaining entry in the gangster genre. However, it was clearly supposed to be more than that and, as such, fails to deliver on its promise. The subject is real-life gangster "Crippled" Ho, and the film opens in 1963 with Ho's humble beginnings as a small-time criminal. He goes into a partnership with ganglord Ng Shing-kwan and dirty cop "Loud" Hung to control the local heroin trade. As the years pass, Ho's power base and wealth grow, incurring the wrath of Ng in the process. Crippled in an assassination attempt, Ho convinces Ng's disgruntled girlfriend to help him frame Ng on possession charges. This act makes him an enemy of top cop Lui Ko-tin (the man behind the rampant corruption in the HK police force and a partner of Ng), who retaliates against Hung and Ho. The latter is eventually able to strike a deal with Lui and is given all of Ng's old territories as a result. When Ng is released from Stanley Prison several years later, Lui gives him some of Ho's territories in an attempt to avert more internal fighting, but it is clear that the two are not ready to settle their differences. The creation of the Independent Commission Against Corruption in the '70s forces Lui to take early retirement. and Ho views this as his chance to eliminate Ng and rule the entire HK underworld. However, his followers have grown so complacent in the past few years his plan seems doomed to failure.

Ray Lui gives a typically flamboyant turn as Ho (and even gained weight for the part), though his scenery-chewing does not seem worthy of the Best Actor award he garnered. More impressive are Kent Cheng and Kenneth Tsang, as his uneasy partners/adversaries, and Cecilia Yip as Ho's ever-loyal wife. In spite of lavish production values and some show-stopping instances of gang warfare, this remains a curiously empty affair, lacking the passion and memorable characters found in the best triad thrillers. Regardless, it was a major box office success, prompting the Mak Brothers to re-team Lui and director

Poon for the two-part triad epic **Lord of East China Sea** (1993).

988. To Hell with the Devil

(1982; Golden Harvest/Paragon Films) ★: 5/10. *Moh dang tin si* (Cantonese), *Mo deng tian shi* (Mandarin): "Modern Exorcist." Cinematographer: Bill Wong Chung-po; Art Director: Alex Ma Yiu-ping; Music: Tang Siu-lam; Writers: John Woo Yu-sen, Roy Szeto Cheuk-hon, Shu Kei; Producer: Leonard Ho Koon-cheung; Director: John Woo Yu-sen. Cast: Ricky Hui Koon-ying (Bruce Lee), Stanley Fung Shui-fan (Flit), Hsu Jie (Peggy), Paul Chun Pui (Priest), Nat Chan Pak-cheung (Rocky), Chung Fat (The Devil), John Sham Kin-fun (Artist). 2.35:1. VHS: Tai Seng (Poor Subtitles). 92 minutes.

John Woo directed this frenetic HK horror-comedy which boasts a premise reminiscent of the Peter Cook/Dudley Moore vehicle **Bedazzled** (1967) but owes most of its creative inspiration to vintage Warner Brothers cartoons. Ricky Hui plays Bruce Lee(!), unsuccessful composer and hopeless schlub, who has finally bottomed out after a very long slide. Materializing to change his life is Flit, a minion of the devil (played by an almost unrecognizable Chung Fat, dubbed with a female voice) who prompts Lee to sell his soul in exchange for fulfilling his dreams of being a rock star and having Peggy, a Mandarin-speaking dancer, for his own. Naturally, things don't work out as planned, and when Lee tries to renege on the deal, Flit comes to collect the soul he is owed. Fortunately, the spirit of a deceased priest is in Lee's corner, leading to a frenzied battle between the forces of good and evil while Lee desperately tries to find and tear up his contract.

A large degree of patience is required to derive much pleasure from **To Hell with the Devil**. During the opening two-thirds, the humor ranges from mildly enjoyable (faithful recreations of horror parody standards) to downright excruciating (in particular, a lame soap opera parody that drags on and on), and Woo's frantic staging of virtually every sequence eventually becomes onerous. The energy does not let up in the final third, but the comedy sharpens appreciably, with the finale centering on a genuinely hysterical live-action parody of the old "Space Invaders" video game, complete with sound FX! While all of Woo's dramatic projects include perceptive uses of humor (sometimes of the darkest variety), full-length satire is just not his forte (Wong Jing and Chu Yen-ping are almost masters of tact in comparison). By the time he helmed the all-but-unbearable **Run Tiger, Run** (1985), his fortunes had deteriorated almost to the point of no return, and he was brought back from the brink only by the astronomical success of **A Better Tomorrow** (1986).

989. To Kill with Intrigue

(1977; Lo Wei Films) ★: 6/10. *Gim fa yin yue gong naam* (Cantonese), *Jian hua yan yu jiang nan* (Mandarin): "Sword Flower Mist Jiangnan." Cinematographer: Chen Chong-yuan; Art Director: Chou Tsu-liang; Music: Not Original; Writer: Ku Long; Producer: Hsu Li-hwa; Action Directors: Chen Hsin-I, Chen Wen-lung; Director: Lo Wei. Cast: Jackie Chan (Sau Lei), Hsu Feng (Ting Tan-yen), George Wang Kuo (The First Dragon), Shen Ie-lung, Yu Ling-lung. 2.35:1. VHS: All Seasons (Dubbed), Simitar (Dubbed), UAV (Dubbed). DVD: Simitar (English and Cantonese tracks). Import VCD: Ocean Shores (Poor Subtitles). 106 minutes.

On the evening of its patriarch's birthday, the Lei family faces destruction at the hands of a bandit gang with supernatural powers called "The Killer Bees," out to avenge events that unfolded fifteen years earlier. Worried about her safety, stoic Sau Lei sends away his pregnant girlfriend Chin-chin by pretending to have been unfaithful to her. His parents are killed but Sau Lei's life is spared by Ting Tan-yen, the scarred and bitter leader of The Killer Bees. Wandering the countryside in search of Chin-chin, Sau Lei joins forces with The Dragon Escort clan but is gravely injured while defending its leader. Chin-chin has been rescued by Chin Chun, who is both the Hunan governor and the secret leader of the villainous Bloody Rain clan, which seeks to vanquish all potential rivals. When Chin murders the Dragons' leader, Sau Lei seeks to avenge him but must first undergo the torturous whims of Ting Tan-yen, whose abilities he will need to succeed.

Scored with music lifted from Japanese swordplay films, this period costumer has its limitations (particularly if you are stuck watching the dubbed version) but remains effective, in spite of the highly melodramatic storyline and staging. Chan is quite good in one of his final, wholly serious portrayals, and the proceedings are boosted considerably by a compelling performance from the great Hsu Feng (the talented Taiwanese martial arts actress who would go on to become the successful producer of revered dramas like **Red Dust** and **Farewell My Concubine**). The kung fu is less impressive but adequate, and the locations (the story unfolds in the southern region of China) are gorgeous.

990. To Liv(e)

(1992; Riverdrive Productions) ★: 9/10. *Fau sai luen kuk* (Cantonese), *Fu shi lian qu* (Mandarin): "Love Song from a Floating World." Cinematographer: Wong Ping-hung; Art Director: Chin Yiu-hang; Music: Somei Satoh, Cui Jian, Tat Ming Pair, Lo Tai-yu; Producer: Willy Tsao Shing-yuen; Writer-Director: Evans Chan Yiu-shing. Cast: Lindzay Chan Ling-chi (Rubie), Josephine Koo Mei-wah (Teresa), Anthony Wong Yiu-ming (Tony), Fung Kin-chung (John), Suen Ming-chui (The Nuclear Goddess), Elsie Tu (Herself), Ha Ping (Rubie's Mom), Ma Pa-nu (Rubie's Dad). 1.85:1. VHS: Riverdrive Productions, World Video. Import LD: Mei Ah. 102 minutes.

Evans Chan's debut feature is an intriguing, politically-charged rumination on one of the most controversial topics in HK during the late 1980s: the forced repatriation of Vietnamese refugees. In December 1989, 51 of these people were secretly forced aboard a plane and flown back to Hanoi. When word of this leaked out, the action was condemned by a number of sources, including Norwegian actress/humanitarian Liv Ullmann. At the center of *To Liv(e)* is a series of letters written to Ullmann by magazine editor Rubie, who is angered by the way in which HK is being denounced by people who either do not know all of the facts or are conveniently forgetting the ones that would invalidate their appraisal of the situation. Rubie's artist boyfriend, John, doesn't want to emigrate, but her brother Tony does and has just been granted entrance into Australia. The reason for his leaving HK has nothing to do with the changes 1997 might bring: His girlfriend, Teresa, is 11 years older than he is, making their relationship a taboo one by traditional Chinese standards. Rubie's thoughts about the repatriation controversy (expressed in narration) intermingle with the problems in her daily life (her sometimes rocky relationship with John, Teresa's pronounced anxiety about the future, and her mother's violent dismissal of Tony's love for Teresa) to paint a portrait of what lay ahead for HK residents at that point in history and also the ideological gulf that exists between East and West.

A singular mixture of drama, dissertation, dance, and performance art, **To Liv(e)** also benefits from excellent lead performances and an eclectic selection of music that perfectly enhances the mood of each scene. Chan makes his points intelligently and convincingly, though the film falters when it tries to incorporate missionary/spokeswoman for the poor, Elsie Tu. While her life story is fascinating and relevant, she is not an actress, and the scene in which Rubie tries to elicit advice from her simply does not work. This, however, is a minor flaw in a compelling and fully assured debut. Lindzay Chan won the Best Actress prize and Josephine Koo the Best Supporting Actress award at the Taiwan Golden Horse Awards, and Chan also took Best Actress honors at the Portugal Sintra Festival of Cinema and Romanticism. The original screenplay and essays on **To Liv(e)** have been published in a book, available from the University of Hong Kong's Department of Comparative Literature.

991. To Live and Die in Tsimshatsui

(1994; Upland Film Corporate/Wong Jing's Workshop) ★: 7/10. *San bin yuen yan* (Cantonese), *Xin bian yuan ren* (Mandarin): "New Edge Man." Cinematographer: Cheung Man-bo; Art Director: Ring Law Chi-keung; Music: Wong Bong; Writer: Szeto Wai-cheuk; Producers: Yang Teng-kuei, Wong Jing; Action Director: Yik Tin-hung; Director: Andrew Lau Wai-keung. Cast: Jacky Cheung Hok-yau (Lik), Tony Leung Kar-fai (Milky Fai), Jacqueline Wu Chien-lien (Siu-bo), Roy Cheung Yiu-yeung (Hung Tai), Chan Kwok-bong (Bong), Kwong Wah (Ming), Gigi Lai Chi (Moon), Shing Fui-on (On), Parkman Wong Pak-man (Coffin Sing), Mimi Chu Mi-mi (Moon's Mother), Xiong Xinxin (Bald Triad), Bobby Yip King-sang (Ugly Triad). 1.85:1. VHS: Tai Seng. Import LD/VCD: Universe. 100 minutes.

Anticipating the sort of approach director Andrew Lau would bring to the **Young and Dangerous** series, this stylish thriller concerns Lik, an undercover policeman who has successfully infiltrated a triad gang. When his superior needlessly kills Lik's gangland boss, Coffin Sing, Lik (now suffering from intense guilt, and torn between his job and his underworld friends) sinks into depression and drinks excessively, alienating his girlfriend. The death of Sing leaves the leadership up for grabs, with the two main competitors being Hung Tai and "Father" Man. A major gang war erupts, with Lik on the side of Hung, while Lik's fellow undercover cop, Bong, keeps an eye on Man. Events come to a head when one of the cops is caught reporting in to the station and murdered, prompting the police to plan a decisive raid when Hung and Man are conducting negotiations.

While typical in the way it paints some (but not all) triads as being more honorable than their supposed moral opposites, the film very effectively portrays the mental anguish undercover officers face, and most of the characters transcend genre stereotypes. Jacky Cheung gives a strong performance in the lead, and Tony Leung Kar-fai is very good as a former undercover cop who lost everything but still tries to be a good father to his little boy. Jacqueline Wu is also notable as the uneducated girl from the wrong side of the tracks who recognizes Lik's tenderness and can't help but fall in love with him. The only missteps involve Lik's one-dimensional superior and Shing Fui-on's character, a veteran cop on the verge of retirement, a set-up that once again leads to the expected conclusion. Interestingly, the youngest triads in the film, who are usually fried on cough syrup, are little better than mindless animals, quite a contrast to how they would be depicted in Lau's **Young and Dangerous** series. **Modern Romance** can be seen playing during a sequence set in a movie theater.

992. To Miss with Love

(1992) ★: 2/10. *To hok ngoi juen* (Cantonese), *Tao xue wai zhuan* (Mandarin): "Escape from School Story." Cinematographer: Chen Rong-shu; Art Director: Lau Sai-wan; Music: Chow Kai-sang; Writer: John Chong Ching; Producer: Wong Jing; Action Director: Lam Moon-wah; Director: Chu Yen-ping. Cast: Dicky Cheung Wai-kin (Chang Yichien), Jimmy Lin Chi-ying (Lin Chi-yin), Sharla Cheung Man (Miss Chang), Athena Chu Yan (Lee Wen, aka Mudfish), Ng Man-tat (Director Ching Monta), Gabriel Wong Yat-san (Huang Yishang), Nicky Wu Chi-lung (Lone), Yuen King-tan (Fang), Chin Ho (Triad). 1.85:1. VHS: Tai Seng. Running time unknown.

This Taiwanese production unashamedly apes **Fight Back to School**, but star Dicky Cheung is no Stephen Chiau and the script does not even approach the comic invention found in that film and its two sequels. New teacher Miss Chang is assigned to take over Class D, the most rowdy and undisciplined brood in the school. She has some experience at handling students of this type but must also deal with the institution's horny director (Ng Man-tat, mugging virtually nonstop), who is not going to let her complete lack of interest deter him. When chief prankster Chang Yichien isn't driving The Director out of his mind, he is skipping school to pay off a $200,000 gambling debt. Miss Chang learns about his troubles and sets out to help him improve his grades, while also ironing out the romantic travails of her other students.

Aside from an amusing parody of **A Chinese Ghost Story** (with Athena Chu and Nicky Wu as the young lovers and Ng Man-tat as The Tree Devil!), there is nary a chuckle to be found here, and some token attempts at drama fail just as miserably.

993. To Spy with Love

(1990) ★: 2/10. *Siu sam gaan dip* (Cantonese), *Xiao xin jian die* (Mandarin): "Watch Out Spy." Cinematographer: Gigo Lee Chi-hang; Art Director: Patrick Tam Kar-ming; Writers: Roy Szeto Cheuk-hon, Raymond To Kwok-wai, Philip Cheng Chung-tai; Music/Producer: Teddy Robin Kwan; Action Directors: Yuen Tak, Chu Kai-sang; Director: Peter Mak Tai-kit. Cast: Teddy Robin Kwan (Terry), Sibelle Hu Hui-chung (Lee Ping), Nina Li Chi (Gigi Li Chi), Eric Kot Man-fai (Soft Fujiyama), Jan Lam Hoi-fung (Hard Fujiyama), Amy Yip Chi-mei ("Taiwan 72"), Maria Cordero (Drummer), Shing Fui-on (Cop). 1.85:1. VHS: Tai Seng (No Subtitles). Import LD: Mei Ah. Import VCD: Cameron Entertainment, Mega Star. 95 minutes.

This tiresome teen comedy steals a number of ideas from the Tom Hanks version of **The Man with One Red Shoe** (1985) and other spy spoofs, but is incapable of coming up with one single laugh on its own. Teddy Robin Kwan plays the manager of an all-girl rock group who are scheduled to compete in a battle of the bands. One evening a beautiful girl appears out of thin air and dies in his arms, but not before planting some microfilm in his van. He later discovers that she was a spy from the Taiwan secret service who was murdered by Japanese spies (Eric Kot and Jan Lam), who are operating out of a revamped transport truck. The intrigue (which includes the usual double crosses and disappearing bodies) centers on an attempt by the Taiwan agents (led by Sibelle Hu) to regain their country's treasures that were taken by Japanese invaders during WWII. Excruciating.

994. Today's Hero

(1991; Chun Sing Film Co.) ★: 3/10. *Ji joi chut wai* (Cantonese), *Zhi zai chu wei* (Mandarin): "Here Is Where Determination Appears." Cinematographer: Chan Yuen-kai; Art Director: Bill Lui Cho-hung; Music: Danny Chung Teng-yat; Writer-Producer: Jeff Lau Chun-wai; Action Director: Yuen Tak; Director: Thomas Yip Shing-hong. Cast: Kenny Bee (Mr. Smartie), Maggie Cheung Man-yuk (Annie), Meg Lam Kin-ming (Smartie's Sister), Shing Fui-on (The Cop), William Ho Kar-kui (Brother Tong), Jacqueline Law Wai-kuen (Mable), Chen Kuan-tai (Triad Boss). 1.85:1. Import LD: Ocean Shores. 95 minutes.

A weak and unappealing vehicle for Kenny Bee, this uninspired comedy casts him as Mr. Smartie, a bumbling, unemployed triad wannabe who mistakenly believes he only has one month to live. With the aid of his buddies, Smartie gets even with a policeman who had humiliated him in the past. With the cop now on a slow boat to China, Smartie takes his uniform and makes one last grasp at fame, solving crimes with the kind of flair the police department wouldn't dare display (he sneaks into a convenience store robbery nearly naked except for a gun stashed rather prominently in his underwear). He hooks up with TV reporter Annie, who decides to do an entire series of pieces on him. Although the police department would love to see Smartie behind bars, he is now such a hero in the eyes of the public they instead offer him a job that comes with a $10 million dollar insurance policy. Naturally, Smartie accepts and does his best to get killed in the line of duty so that his loyal sister can cash in.

Aside from a handful of amusing in-joke references to "The Goddess of Bust" [*sic*] Amy Yip Chi-mei, the humor alternates between tired shopworn gags and desperate scatological jokes. The same premise would be recycled for Leung Karyan's **Bogus Cops**, which is even worse.

995. Tom, Dick and Hairy

(1993; United Filmmakers Organization) ★: 8/10. *Fung chan saam hap* (Cantonese), *Feng chen san xia* (Mandarin): "Three World-Weary Heroes." Cinematographer: Bill Wong Chung-bo; Art Director: James Cheung Ying-wah; Music: Lowell Lo Kwun-ting; Writers: James Yuen Sai-sang, Lee Chi-ngai; Producers: Gordon Chan Kar-seung, Claudie Chung Chun; Directors: Peter Chan Ho-san, Lee Chi-ngai. Cast: Tony Leung Chiu-wai (Tom Chan), Tony Leung Kar-fai (Dick Ching), Lawrence Cheng Tan-shui (Giorgio Mao, aka "Hairy"), Ann Bridgewater (Cat), Anita Yuen Wing-yee (Fong), Michael Chow Man-kin ("Michelle"), Jay Lau Kam-ling (Joyce Lau), Athena Chu Yan (Pearl), Vivian Chow Wei-man (Francis). 1.85:1. VHS: Tai Seng. Import LD/VCD/DVD: Mei Ah. 99 minutes.

HK romantic comedies don't come any more engaging than this UFO production, which still ranks among the company's best. Roommates Tom, Dick, and Hairy could not be any more different: Tom is a reserved, financially strapped gentleman about to enter into a loveless marriage with icy, upper class bitch Joyce; Dick is an inveterate lady killer, nicknamed "Terminator," who has so many women throwing themselves at him that he has forgotten how to treat them courteously; and Hairy is a doltish weirdo who talks to plants and is obsessed with actress/singer Vivian Chow. Plagued with self-doubts about the marriage, Tom may be starting to crack up: He can see a giant version of "Little Tom" (i.e. his penis), and it even talks to him! His fortunes change when he meets beautiful, gregarious club girl Cat, who brings a new spark to his life; even his *car* seems to love her! Unfortunately, he eventually has to tell her about his forthcoming marriage. Dick, meanwhile, unknowingly picks up Tom's sister, Pearl, and pays the price for it. After joining a dating service and suffering through all manner of humiliating blind dates, Hairy meets his perfect match in Michelle. The only trouble is, Michelle is also a man.

While somewhat predictable (the storyline includes the usual quota of misunderstandings, unexpected arrivals, etc.), **Tom, Dick and Hairy** is overflowing with charm, and "The Two Tonys" are especially good here. The resolution to each of the romantic conflicts is a bit more imaginative than what is usually proffered by films of this ilk, and there are a lot of nice little throwaway comedic bits (like an in-joke reference to Tony Leung Chiu-wai's offscreen relationship with Carina Lau Kar-ling) that help to make the film very endearing. It also possesses a sense of spontaneity that is infectious; about midway through, a musical number breaks out and it's delightful!

Tongs *see* **Tongs: A Chinatown Story**

996. Tongs: A Chinatown Story

(1986; Pan Pacific Productions) ★: 4/10. *Tong hau gu si* (Cantonese), *Tang kou gu shi* (Mandarin): "Tong Story." Cinematographer: Michael Ma Koon-wah; Art Director: Ray Lam Chan-fai; Music: Joseph Chan Wing-leung; Writer: Stacey Asip; Producer: Jimmy Yang; Action Director: Hon Yee-sang; Director: Phillip Chan Yan-kin. Cast: Simon Yam Tat-wah (Mickey Lee), Tam Pak-pan (Paul Lee), Anthony Gioia (Detective Martinelli), Daisey Yong Ah-wan (Stacey), Stephen Leung (Johnny Young), Christopher O'Conner (Captain Silverman), Quitan Han (Chan Wing-leung), Ricky Yee Fan-wai (Communist Soldier on Boat). 1.85:1. VHS: Academy. Import LD: Ocean Shores. 87 minutes. Also known as **Tongs** (Academy title).

Lensed predominantly in New York City, with the actors mostly speaking English, this low-budget effort is earnestly produced but too cliched to make much of an impact. Arriving in NY from HK, brothers Mickey and Paul Lee are a study in contrasts. The former is mild mannered and simply wants to further his education, while the latter is a drug smuggler concerned only with making his fortune in America. Mickey inadvertently offends The Red Eagles, a local Chinese gang, while Paul joins up with their rivals, The Dragons. The Eagles attack Mickey one day and kill two of his friends. Mickey would also be dead were it not for the intervention of Paul, who fatally shoots one Eagle and then flees to Toronto. Mickey, meanwhile, realizes that he must take a stand and, with some friends to back him up, lays waste to one of the Eagles' hangouts. Impressed by his actions, the local Tong leader, Chan Wing-leung, grants Mickey a territory. However, in order to pacify the Eagles, Chan promises to give them Paul. When his brother is gunned down right before his eyes, Mickey realizes that he has been betrayed.

Mickey's transition from meek student to gang kingpin happens too quickly to be creditable, and the lion's share of the story proceeds along all too familiar lines. While one could argue that director Phillip Chan was going for a cinema *verite* look and feel, the film would have worked better had he been able to invest the material with the style and verve he brought to **Night Caller**. As is, it just looks cheap, underlit, and unprofessional. Simon Yam acquits himself fairly well in his first English-speaking part, and the mostly amateur cast is adequate. For all of the film's shortcomings, it is still much easier to take than Abel Ferrara's insipid Romeo and Juliet variation, **China Girl**, which was also shot in New York around the same time.

997. Too Many Ways to Be No. 1

(1997; Golden Harvest/Milkyway Image Production) ★: 8/10. *Yat kuo chi tau dik daan sang* (Cantonese), *Yi ge zi tou de dan sheng* (Mandarin): "The Birth of a Letterhead." Cinematographer: Horace Wong Wing-hang; Art Director: Silver Cheung Sai-wang; Music: Cacine Wong Kar-sin; Writers: Wai Kar-fai, Szeto Kam-yuen, Matt Chow Hoi-kwong; Producer: Johnny To Kei-fung; Director: Wai Kar-fai. Cast: Lau Ching-wan (Wong Ah-kau), Francis Ng Chun-yu (Matt Chan), Carman Lee Yeuk-tung (Prostitute), Cheung Tat-ming, Elvis Tsui Kam-kong, Matt Chow Hoi-kwong. 1.85:1. Import LD/VCD/DVD: New City. 90 minutes.

Just when the dominant *goo wak jai* (young rascals) trend was running out of creative and commercial might, along came this wild black comedy from John Woo *protege* Wai Kar-fai (**Peace Hotel**). The most singular gangster film in ages, **Too Many Ways to Be No. 1** reinvents the triad thriller in delightfully unexpected ways. It relays the misadventures of the Hung Lok Gang, the most pitifully inept criminals to ever walk the streets of HK. Relating the storyline would be counter productive, as much of the film's appeal lies in its inversion of traditional narrative and genre traditions. Suffice it to say, the central theme is fate and the consequences of seemingly trivial actions, as demonstrated through the decisions of gang member Wong Ah-kau: Should he go to China or to Taiwan? Along the way we are treated to some deliciously dark humor (when their leader is killed during a job, the men seal his corpse inside a wall but forget to remove his pager; it promptly starts beeping, and without it they cannot finish their job!), dollops of satire and absurdist happenstance (there is a definite European influence at work here, along with a nod or two to **Pulp Fiction**), and colorful protagonists whose inconsistent behavior perfectly mirrors that of the film. On the downside, the gambit eventually does run out of steam in the final reel, and the relentlessly nervous and showy camerawork (sequences unfold upside down, in darkness, through a fisheye lens, etc.) grows pretty wearisome. However, this remains one of the most daring and stimulating HK features of the '90s and should not be missed. It was rated Category III for brief nudity, very mild sexual content, and some fairly nasty violence. Much of the same creative team also worked on the equally pleasing **The Odd One Dies**.

998. Top Banana Club

(1996; Keen Pearl International) ★: 5/10. *Gam jong heung ji kui lok bo* (Cantonese), *Jin zhuang xiang jiao ju le bu* (Mandarin): "Golden Banana Club." Cinematographer: Tsang Chun-chung; Art Director: Tung Yao; Music: Edmund; Writers: Anthony Wong Chau-sang, Siu Kwok-wah, Dayo Wong Chi-wah; Director: Anthony Wong Chau-sang. Cast: Anthony Wong Chau-sang (Host/Inspector Wong/Mr. Shaw/John), Dayo Wong Chi-wah (Host/Kim Lin-kwan/May's Mother/Bar Geek), Jerry Lam Hiu-fung (Host/Cop/Dr. Lo), Siu Kwok-wah (Host/Triad Leader/Shaw/Bar Geek), Vivian Chow Wei-man (Jenny), Esther Kwan Wing-ho (May), Anita Lee Yuen-wah (May's Friend), Linda Cheung Lan-ying (Mrs. Shaw), Bobby Yip King-sang (Mainland Triad). 1.85:1. VHS: Tai Seng. Import LD/VCD: Universe. 101 minutes.

While this film bears no direct connection to **Banana Club**, it also concerns the smart aleck hosts of a talk radio show. However, this time out they are not the main characters and instead dispense relationship advice to callers. The actors playing the hosts do, however, also appear in the different segments as other characters (got all that?). In the opening story, Dayo Wong plays a triad obsessed with the beautiful Vivian Chow, who plays a good Christian girl with a stern police officer father (played by a lisping Anthony Wong). She convinces Dayo to go straight, but her dad is not convinced of his integrity, so Dayo takes rather dramatic steps to convince him. While this sounds like purely comedic material, it actually takes itself rather seriously in spots—a big mistake as it turns out. Story number two is about a geeky businessman (Siu Kwok-wah) who is unhappy with his wife's small breasts and tries to convince her to get them enlarged. The woman (Esther Kwan) goes through with the procedure, with decidedly unusual results. This one has some amusing moments (particularly Kwok's explanation as to why large breasts are a must in a capitalist society) but ultimately falls, uh, flat. The final story is the oddest: Anthony Wong plays a successful womanizer who tries to prove his mettle by seducing three different kinds of lesbians. His tactics and the outcome of each pursuit form the rest of the story.

If **Banana Club** can be deemed guilty of being a formulaic misfire, then **Top Banana Club** is guilty of going too far in the opposite direction, though that was clearly its intention. Just when it seems to be proceeding the way you expect it to, the film takes a sharp turn and heads down a different road altogether. In addition to the narrative twists, director Anthony Wong includes bizarre commercial breaks and alternate endings for two of the segments, the first of which appears midway through the second story. While this offbeat approach makes it a more interesting film than **Banana Club**, it doesn't really make it a more entertaining one, as **Top Banana Club** isn't as funny or hip as it clearly thinks it is. Regardless, Wong's ambition to deliver more than just the usual teen fodder is laudable, though one suspects that his backers were less than thrilled. Cheung Tat-ming appears briefly.

999. Top Borrower

(1997; Times Production/Canaan Film Production) ★: 1/10. *Je chin juan ga* (Cantonese), *Jie qian zhuan jia* (Mandarin): "Expert at Borrowing Money." Cinematographer: Wong Kar-fai; Art Director: Nelson Cheung Hok-yun; Music: Not Original; Writer: Times Production (individual writers not named); Producer: Leung Hung-wah; Director: Sherman Wong Ching-wah. Cast: Michael Chow Man-kin (Moron), Liz Kong Hei-man (Suzi), Max Mok Siu-chung (Dan Yiu/Sing/Priest/Food Critic). VHS: Tai Seng. Import LD/VCD: Panorama Entertainment. 87 minutes.

This shrill and tedious misfire strives to present a familiar premise in a fresh fashion but fails to come up with a single worthwhile moment or concept. Michael Chow (dubbed here by another actor) plays the aptly named "Moron," a cab driver who acquires a fortune in ransom money after a pair of dimwitted kidnappers kill each other. The film looks at the possible ways this newfound wealth could change his life. In one scenario, he takes half of the money and buys a new home for his family, but his wife learns that he is cheating on her and starts a relationship with their gay neighbor, Dan Yiu (aka "Damn You"—ha, ha). The second scenario has Moron taking all of the cash and buying the house, only to be tormented by both a cop (who suspects him of taking the money) and the dead men's partner (who *knows* that he took it). The third has him turning the loot over to the authorities, only to be deprived of a reward. *Top Borrower* offers no laughs, no suspense, and, most unforgivably of all, no point.

Top Squad *see* **The Inspector Wears Skirts**

1000. Touch and Go

(1991; Silver Medal/Born Top) ★: 6/10. *Yat chuk chik fat* (Cantonese), *Yi chu ji fa* (Mandarin): "One Touch Sent Promptly." Cinematographer: Ardy Lam Kwok-wah; Art Director: William Yam Wai-leung; Music: Noel Quinlan; Writers: Nam Yin, Candy Cheng; Producer: Nam Yin; Action Director: Yuen Tak; Director: Ringo Lam Ling-tung. Cast: Sammo Hung Kam-po (Fat Goose), Teresa Mo Shun-kwun (Angel), Vincent Wan Yeung-ming (Pitt), Irene Wan Pik-ha (May), Tommy Wong Kwong-leung (Lam Man-fu, aka "The God of Hell"), Ann Mui Ngoi-fong (Lulu), Lau Kong (Keung), Billy Chow Bei-lee (Hood). 1.85:1. VHS: Tai Seng. Import LD/VCD: Mei Ah. 97 minutes.

In interviews, director Ringo Lam has characterized this action-comedy as an assignment for hire he took in order to keep his hand in. There are certainly none of his usual trademarks on display, aside from the casting of Tommy Wong as the villain (though, in some ways, the finale does anticipate the conclusion of Lam's

Full Contact). That aside, if one views the film on its own terms, **Touch and Go** is a satisfying if overly familiar entry. After witnessing a triad murdering a police officer, restaurant worker Fat Goose is pursued by both the killers and the determined officer Pitt. When the killer, Lam Man-fu, is apprehended, Fat Goose agrees to testify against him, only to see Lam released on bail. Goose quickly develops second thoughts about helping the police when he sees his apartment go up in smoke. Lam and his cronies trick Pitt and Goose and are on the verge of killing them when Lam's girlfriend May intercedes and saves them. The hoods are after photos they secretly took of prominent figures (including Pitt's superior) carousing with prostitutes, part of a blackmail racket run by a crooked solicitor. When May is injured and Angel is kidnapped, Goose and Pitt prepare for a final showdown.

The scenario is old hat, the introduction of love interests for the men (May for Pitt and Angel, a reporter, for Goose) is awkward, and the comic asides involving Goose's mom are very weak. However, the stunt work is first rate throughout, and Hung performs an amazing bit where he bounces off the hood of a speeding car like a rubber ball. The violence is a bit nastier than necessary, but this remains good formula fare that will pass muster with most viewers.

1001. A Touch of Evil

(1995; Modern Producer/Joe Siu International Film) ★: 6/10. *Kong ye sang sei luen* (Cantonese), *Kuang ye sheng si lian* (Mandarin): "Crazy Wild Death Love." Cinematographer: Arthur Wong Ngok-tai; Art Director: Cheung Kar-fai; Music: Violet Lam Man-yee; Writers: Yip Kwong-kim, Poon Yuen-leung, Tony Au Ding-ping; Producer: Yip Kwong-kim; Action Director: Yuen Tak; Director: Tony Au Ding-ping. Cast: Tony Leung Kar-fai (Liang Shaolun), Rosamund Kwan Chi-lam (Coco Xu Liuxin), Michael Wong Man-tak (Yuan King), Elizabeth Lee Mei-fung (Leung's Girlfriend), Lung Fong (Long), Tai Po (Long's Man), Kwan Hoi-shan (Zhang Qiao). 1.85:1. VHS: Tai Seng. Import LD/VCD: Ocean Shores. 103 minutes.

A weak performance by Michael Wong almost sinks this otherwise accomplished thriller from the style-conscious director of **Dream Lovers**. Underhanded police officer Liang gives Coco Xu a choice: help him get the goods on drug dealer Yuan King or go to jail as an accessory to embezzlement. Her back against the wall, Coco reluctantly agrees. In the process, she begins to fall for King, who treats her and her flighty mother well and does not at all seem like a bad guy, making him a definite contrast to the brutish Liang. However, further exposure to the cop allows Coco to see that he does indeed have a softer side, and a love triangle develops. Ultimately, though, this makes Liang even more determined to get King, and his methods take on an even more sinister slant.

As is invariably the case with Tony Au's projects, the proceedings are invigoratingly stylish (even when viewed on the substandard Ocean Shores video transfer, which washes out the colors), and the director deserves credit for entrusting Rosamund Kwan (who is rarely given anything of interest to do in movies) with a significant and challenging role; she gives what is easily one of her best performances to date. Tony Leung Kar-fai is also effective but Michael Wong is unable to convey even the simplest emotions convincingly and this is a critical flaw. His character is supposed to be the more endearing male, but Leung ends up being far more interesting, in spite of the policeman's myriad flaws.

1002. Tragic Commitment

(1995; Shaw Brothers) ★: 2/10. *Moot yau lo gung dik yat ji* (Cantonese), *Mei you lao gong de ri zi* (Mandarin): "Days Without a Husband." Cinematographer: Li Hsin-yeh; Art Director: Ng Tin-sang; Music: Roel A. Garcia; Writers: Eileen Wu Ming-sun, Woman Wu Wo-men, Janet Lam Suk-lan; Producer: Lawrence Wong Kar-hei; Director: Frankie Chan Fan-kei. Cast: Anita Yuen Wing-yee (Lam Hiu-tung), Deanie Yip Tak-han (Ngank), Josie Ho Chiu-yee (Blacky), Julian Cheung Chi-lam (Alex Wong), Mimi Chu Mi-mi (Chat), Cammy Choi Mei-lan (Chillie), Shum Wai (Wei), Julie Lee Wah-yuet (Hooker), Dennis Chan Kwok-san (Museum Guard). 1.85:1. VHS: Tai Seng. Import LD: Cameron Entertainment. Import VCD: Mei Ah. 101 minutes.

A tiresome melodrama with broad, unlikeable characters, **Tragic Commitment** is not convincing—for even a moment. When her husband Alex Wong is badly burned while making a TV commercial, Hiu-tung learns that he fathered a child with a woman named Blacky. Alex dies shortly thereafter, prompting Hiu-tung to seek her out. Blacky turns out to be a crass, lower class woman from a bad family who has no desire to keep the baby. However, Alex's mother offers her a million dollars to have the child so that the Wong family line may continue. A legal contract is drawn up and, much to Hiu-tung's consternation, Blacky accepts the offer. Naturally, the pair's conflicting backgrounds lead to unpleasant situations and Blacky must be convinced once again to carry the baby to term. Further problems develop when it is discovered that she has a heart condition that threatens her life should she continue with the pregnancy (which, of course, she does).

One of those movies where the lazy screenwriters pile on the exposition through voiceovers and by having the main character bare her soul repeatedly on a talk radio show, **Tragic Commitment** is further proof that martial artist Frankie Chan has absolutely no business directing anything other than a kung fu bout.

1003. The Tragic Fantasy: Tiger of Wanchai

(1994; Regal Films Co.) ★: 5/10. *Jui sang mung sei ji waan jai ji foo* (Cantonese), *Zui sheng meng si zhi wan zi zhi hu* (Mandarin): "The Drunken Death Dream of the Wanchai Tiger." Cinematographer: Peter Ngor Chi-kwan; Art Director: Nelson Cheung Hok-yun; Music: Lau Yee-tat, Tommy Wai Kai-leung; Writers: Law Shing, Leung Yan-tung, Ng Lap-kwong; Producer: Steven Lo Kit-sing; Directors: Steven Lo Kit-sing, Joseph Chi Chong Chavez. Cast: Simon Yam Tat-wah (Chan Yiu-hing), Lau Ching-wan (Dee), Vincent Wan Yeung-ming (Hung), Roy Cheung Yiu-yeung (Chung), Marianne Chan Miu-ying (Mil Mil), Ben Lam Kwok-bun (Lam Kwok-yeung), Charine Chan Kar-ling (Fanny), Yvonne Yung Hung (Kitty), Lo Lieh (Kui), William Ho Kar-kui (Bill), Ku Feng (Kau). Dolby Stereo. 1.85:1. VHS: Tai Seng. Import LD/VCD/DVD: Universe. 103 minutes.

This glossy gangster yarn is the story of violent alcoholic Chan Yiu-hing, who goes from parking valet to powerful triad ganglord in a short period of time. When he and his buddies aren't using the patrons' expensive cars for impromptu races around Wanchai, they are getting into bloody scrapes with Lam, a local triad boss. After being severely beaten by Lam's men, Chan starts his own "legitimate" nightclub security service, which launches him on the way to the top. As his fame and fortune accumulate, Hing has a fling with trashy bar girl Kitty, but his heart really belongs to Mil Mil, a beauty whom he met while still a lowly street thug. Deep in love, he consents to Mil Mil's request that they should go to Canada and live a quieter life, but fate intervenes.

Flashy visuals and Dolby Stereo can do little to hide the fact that this triad crime drama has nothing new to offer, despite the fact that it strives to stand out from the pack by basing its protagonist on a real person. Simon Yam's character mirrors mobster Andely Chan Yiu-hing, aka "The Wanchai Tiger," a Sun Yee On triad enforcer who was indirectly involved in an incident where actress/singer Anita Mui was accosted by gangster Wong Long-wai at a nightclub (the episode is recreated here, with a fictional character named "Rose" standing in for Mui). Nineteen months later, Chan was murdered by killers on motorcycles. In spite of its ambitions, the film is really only noteworthy as an early example of the *goo wak jai* (young rascals) subgenre, that became extremely popular through the success of the **Young and Dangerous** series. *Tragic Fantasy* was rated Category III for some nasty violence, a brief sex scene, and, presumably, a rather glamorized depiction of gangster life.

1004. Tragic Hero

(1987; Johnny Mak Production/Win's Movie Production) ★: 5/10. *Ying hung hiu hon* (Cantonese), *Ying xiong hao han* (Mandarin): "Heroic Hero." Cinematographers: Abdul M. Rumjahn, Johnny Koo Kwok-wah; Art Directors: Chan Kwok-hei, Jessy Lam Chak-chi; Music: Joseph Chan Wing-leung; Writers: Stephen Siu Yeuk-yuen, Manfred Wong; Producer: Johnny Mak Dong-hung; Action Director: Tony Leung Siu-hung; Director: Taylor Wong Tai-loi. Cast: Chow Yun-fat (Chai), Alex Man Chi-leung (Yung), Andy Lau Tak-wah (Kwok), Ko Chuen-hsiang (Chu), Carina Lau Kar-ling (Poh-yee), Yeung Kwan (Kit), Pauline Wong Siu-fung (Chui), Shing Fui-on (Luk), Lam Chung (Big Eye), Danny Lee Sau-yin (Inspector Chang), Elvis Tsui Kam-kong (Chai's Man), Ng Hong-ning (Chuan). 1.85:1. VHS: Tai Seng. Import LD: Ocean Shores (No Subtitles). 96 minutes.

The follow-up to **Rich and Famous**, **Tragic Hero** (which actually came out first because the producers felt it was the more commercial of the two) opens a few years later, with Yung more determined than ever to kill Chai, now a successful businessman who seeks peace. Yung eliminates his competitors in the organization one by one until only he and his target retain any real hold on power. The two meet face to face and it is seems clear that a war is imminent. Kwok returns from self-imposed exile in Malaysia to try and convince Yung to spare Chai and apparently calms the waters. In the meantime, one of Chai's lieutenants tries to assassinate Yung on his own but is betrayed by a confederate. In light of this tragedy, Chai finally comes to the realization that the situation cannot be resolved without violence, a position that Kwok also adopts when Yung has his wife and children murdered.

Yung's actions and intent are so obvious that the relentless stalling on the part of Chai and Kwok is frustrating and illogical, making this even less dramatically sound than its predecessor. However, the final battle (which includes inordinate amounts of gunplay and destruction) is quite satisfying on a kinetic level, and Joseph Chan's score is among the most driving and memorable in the genre. The character names listed above are from the UK video version.

1005. The Trail

(1983; Golden Harvest/Paragon Films) ★: 6/10. *Jui gwai chat hung* (Cantonese), *Zhui gui qi xiong* (Mandarin): "Seven Heroes Chase Ghost." Cinematographer: James Chan Hau-ming; Art Director: David Chan Chi-wai; Music: Bobby Chan Dik-hong; Writers: Michael Hui Koon-man, Ronny Yu Yan-tai; Producer: Michael Hui Koon-man; Action Directors: Chung Fat, Feng Sing; Director: Ronny Yu Yan-tai. Cast: Ricky Hui Koon-ying (Ying), Kent Cheng Chuk-see (The Captain), Chung Fat (Flint), Anthony Chan Yau (Reader), Feng Sing (Fatty), Cho Tat-wah (Drunken Husband), Victor Hon Kwan (Thug with Knife). 2.35:1. VHS: Tai Seng (Poor Subtitles). Import VCD: Mega Star. 87 minutes. Also known as **The Trial** (Mega Star VCD title).

Xiang Xi Province, 1922: When a local official murders a travelling musician, he hires a gang of opium smugglers to dispose of the body. While travelling through a swamp, they accidentally drop the corpse into a sulphate spring and leave it, figuring that is as good a burial place as any. However, the dead man has other ideas and rises from the slimy grave to exact revenge, temporarily satiating its bloodlust by killing some pigs along the way. Desperate to rectify their error, the gang sets out to destroy the zombie, armed with virgin urine, charms, and other supernatural weapons.

While **The Trail** was co-written by comedian Michael Hui, it is mostly played straight, boasting highly atmospheric photography and superb production design (particularly the swamp, filled with gnarled undergrowth, and a tomb guarded by numerous terracotta warriors). One problem, though: There is just not enough storyline here for a feature length film. The epilogue sends up a certain Western horror classic in amusing fashion, and portions of the soundtrack are lifted from the Hollywood productions **The Thing** and **Sorcerer**.

1006. The Transmigration Romance

(1991; Hatract Films/Golden Sun Light Production Co.) ★: 3/10. *Fa gaai san nui* (Cantonese), *Hua jie shen nu* (Mandarin): "Flower Street Goddess." Cinematographer: Cheung Tak-wai; Art Director: Tsui Kwok-keung; Music: Not Original; Writer: Si Chun; Producer: Yuen Sin-kan; Action Director: Chris Lee Kin-sang; Director: Wong Shee-tong. Cast: Cynthia Yang Li-ching (Sis Chan), Huang Chia-da (Mo Tsai), Kwan Hoi-shan (The Judge), Frances Fong Ming, Ku Kwong-leung, Lam Wai (Inspector Lin), Sophia Crawford (Sofia). 1.85:1. VHS: Tai Seng. 92 minutes.

As punishment for the many evil deeds he committed while alive, Mo Tsai is not going to be reincarnated as a human being. However, after he defeats a netherworld judge at a game of cards, Mo is allowed a chance to alter his fate. Arriving back on earth, he must locate an exceedingly masculine man to house his spirit, because his family is too "feminine." Enlisting the aid of his recently deceased granddaughter Jo-Jo (who can remain in her body for another 49 days before her spirit disperses), Mo plots to take over the body of the girl's new human boyfriend. Kung fu fighting flower shop owner/Taoist Sis Chan steps in and saves him, but Mo is not vanquished yet.

An exceedingly odd combination of the ghost and action genres, **The Transmigration Romance** is so nutty one is never sure just where it is headed. Unfortunately, the proceedings are too inane, dull, and shoddily made to be much fun. The film also features one of the worst subtitling jobs ever, making the already nonsensical plot even harder to fathom. '70s kung fu star Huang Chia-da (aka Carter Wong) has never looked more bizarre onscreen, spending most of the running time buried under a white wig and eye patch. He even ends up in drag at one point!

1007. Treasure Hunt

(1994; Golden Princess/Eastern Renaissance Pictures) ★: 6/10. *Fa kei siu lam* (Cantonese), *Hua qi shao lin* (Mandarin): "American Shaolin." Cinematographer: Peter Pau Tak-hei; Art Director: Hai Chung-man; Music: Danny Chung Teng-yat; Writer: Kei On (pseudonym for Jeff Lau Chun-wai); Producer: Linda Kuk Mei-lai; Action Director: Phillip Kwok Tsui; Director: Jeff Lau Chun-wai. Cast: Chow Yun-fat (Jeff Chang Ching), Jacqueline Wu Chien-lien (Miss Mei), Gordon Lau Kar-fai (Abbot Hung Chi), Chin Han (Tong Ling/Captain Chiu), Phillip Kwok Tsui (Cab Driver), Roy Chiao Hung (Uncle Bill), Michael Wong Man-tak (Michael). 1.85:1. VHS/LD: Tai

Seng. Import LD: Golden Cinema City. Import VCD: Mei Ah (No Subtitles). Import DVD: Mei Ah. 105 minutes.

This typical Jeff Lau confection is all over the map but remains afloat thanks to the talents of its two stars, who manage to even make it out-and-out charming at times. CIA agent Jeff Chang is dispatched to China to steal a national treasure but does not know just exactly what it is. Meeting up with his contact, Tong Ling, Jeff hides out at Shaolin Temple, where he encounters Miss Mei. A prisoner of the monks, the girl possesses powers that allow her to pass objects through solid surfaces and can even make flowers grow...on people! After some initial friction, Jeff begins to hit it off with the monks, introducing them to new things and even teaching them to play baseball. Smitten with Miss Mei, Jeff wants to take her back to America but is unsure of what to say when she asks him to stay in China with her. In the meantime, he discovers his objective and also something about Tong that may pose a threat to the mission.

The comedy is mostly lowbrow, the sentiment is laid on with a trowel, and the violence causes a rather jarring change in tone (in other words, it's a typical Jeff Lau movie), but Chow and Wu are such an appealing couple that they transcend the pedestrian material. Shaw Brothers kung fu fans will get a major kick out of watching veteran favorites Gordon Lau (appropriately cast as the abbot of Shaolin Temple) and Phillip Kwok (amusing as an exceptionally rude cab driver) go at it with each other, and there is a fun in-joke reference to Chow's popular **Prison on Fire** movies.

1008. The Treasure Hunters

(1982; Shaw Brothers) ★: 7/10. Chinese Titles Unknown. Cinematographer: Chu Chien-hsiung; Music: Not Original; Writer: Wong Jing; Producer: Mona Fong Yat-wah; Action Director-Director: Lau Kar-yung. Cast: Alexander Fu Sheng (Chi Ta-po), Chan Chang-peng (Chau Chu-chi), Gordon Lau Kar-fai (Wu Sheung), Johnny Wang Lung-wei (Lord Mo Chung), Lau Kar-wing (Lu), Yeung Ching-ching (Mo's Woman), Lam Wai (Librarian). 2.35:1. No official domestic video release. 110 minutes. Also known as **Master of Disaster** (US title).

A Shaw Brothers period effort with a decidedly comic accent, this is the first film Alexander Fu did following an accident that broke both of his legs, but you would never know it from the graceful moves he utilizes throughout. Charming rogues Chi Ta-po and Chau Chu-chi decide to find the much sought-after treasure of the infamous pirate Chang Po-chu. The first step is to get their hands on Chang's letters, which are in the possession of a wily old antiques dealer who is no slouch when it comes to kung fu. The letters reveal the involvement of Fa Wah High Priest Wu Sheung, who has been blamed for a number of murders. The real culprit is actually the evil Lord "Double Daggers" Mo Chung, who is systematically eliminating anyone out to claim Chang's fortune, which is concealed somewhere inside Fa Wah Temple.

The kung fu is wonderful (particularly the "Five Monk Array" and "Flying Swallow" techniques) but the humor is a bit too broad (particularly a scene set in a library which goes on much too long); there are even a few examples of the sexual innuendo that would be prevalent in writer Wong Jing's later work. Regardless, this is enjoyable fare and one of the best showcases superb female fighter Yeung Ching-ching ever enjoyed. Too often relegated to minor supporting roles, she has ample screen time here and more than holds her own with the likes of Fu, Gordon Lau, and Johnny Wang. Lau Kar-wing participates in what has become a kung fu genre standard: the "fighting-amongst-valuable-antiques-while-desperately-trying-not-to-break-anything" scene. The soundtrack includes music lifted from **Mad Max**. Character names listed above are from the English dubbed version.

Triad Savagers [*sic*] *see* **Brotherhood**
Triad Savages *see* **Brotherhood**

1009. Triad Story

(1990; Film City Production) ★: 5/10. *Gong woo jui hau yat goh daai lo* (Cantonese), *Jiang hu zui hou yi ge da lao* (Mandarin): "Drifter: Last Big Man." Cinematographer: Cho On-sun; Art Director: Ken Yip Kwok-kin; Music: Not Original; Action Director: Siu Tak-fu; Producers: Lee Shing, Lam Kong; Writer-Director: Shum Wai. Cast: Stephen Chiau Sing-chi (Sin), Ko Chuen-hsiang (Feng), Wu Ma (Ma), Shing Fui-on (Maddy), Ng Man-tat (Tat), Shum Wai (Wai), Billy Chow Bei-lee (Chiang). 1.85:1. VHS: Tai Seng. Import LD/VCD: Universe. 95 minutes.

This minor crime drama is most interesting for the way in which it depicts the clash between the old guard and the young upstarts, thus serving as a bridge between the honor and tradition-bound "Hero" films of the '80s and the youth-oriented *goo wak jai* genre from the mid–90s. Feng, the aged head of a triad gang, has been released early from prison due to his poor health and good behaviour. He comes home and is distressed to find that his daughter has hooked up with a vicious and uncouth gang leader from America and will soon be going overseas with him. When discussions fail to resolve the conflict, two of Feng's old enforcers, Maddy and Tat, assault the young hood, who then has one of his men cripple Maddy. Feng and his cohorts steal a shipment of their adversary's drugs in retribution but must use them for an exchange when Feng's daughter is threatened with death.

While the early reels suggest that the storyline may take some offbeat turns, any such promise is gone by the mid-point, and everything wraps up with a standard, unimaginatively staged action finale. Despite his star billing, Stephen Chiau only has a supporting role and is dubbed by another actor. HK Censors gave this the Category III rating, but it must have been for the film's sympathetic portrait of triads, as the violence is quite tame.

1010. Triads: The Inside Story

(1989; Cinema City Co.) ★: 6/10. *Ngoh joi hak se wooi dik yat ji* (Cantonese), *Wo zai hei she hui de ri zi* (Mandarin): "My Days Inside the Underworld." Cinematographer: Herman Yau Lai-to; Art Directors: Kwan Kam-ming, Ho Chi-hang; Music: Lo Tai-yau, Richard Lo Sai-kit; Writer: Nam Yin; Producer: Richard Cheung Kuen; Action Director: Lam Moon-wah; Director: Taylor Wong Tai-loi. Cast: Chow Yun-fat (Li Man-ho), Roy Cheung Yiu-yeung (Yeung Kong), Michael Chan Wai-man (Tse Shing), Mak Kit-man (Jenny), Tien Feng (Uncle Kwan), Kenneth Tsang Kong (Sgt. Chan Tin-lok), Lam Kau (Uncle Ping), Kelvin Wong Siu (Little Ha), Shing Fui-on (Mad Keung), Lung Ming-yan (Coffin Rope), Wong Chi-yeung (Little Ha's Man), Pau Hon-lam (Chow Sai-lin), Robin Shou Wan-bo (Coffin Rope's Man), Chen Jing (Lunatic), Ng Hong-ning (Thug). Dolby Digital (DVD only). 1.85:1. VHS: Tai Seng. Import LD: Golden Cinema City. Import VCD: Mei Ah. Import DVD: Universe. 91 minutes. Also known as **The Inside Story**.

Li Man-ho finds himself with a terrible dilemma: His gangster father has been murdered and he is obliged to take his place as leader of the Hung Hing society. However, Man-ho has always distanced himself from the underworld and wants no part of it now. With Hung Hing in disarray, rival gangs plot to move in and take over their territories. Given the situation, Man-ho agrees to assume leadership and tries to negotiate his way out of trouble. However, one particular leader, Coffin Rope, is unwilling to play ball and causes the death of a Hung Hing man. When the gang captures him for revenge, Man-ho refuses to kill him, a serious error in judgment that helps to alienate top Hung Hing lieutenant Yeung Kong. His subsequent actions set the stage for the complete ruin of the gang.

While unique in that it devotes a good portion of the running time to character development (in particular, the men's relationships with their wives), **Triads** suffers from a predictable scenario (it is not a question of will Man-ho follow in his father's footsteps but when) that hinders its success somewhat. Chow Yun-fat has little of interest to do, leaving Roy Cheung to walk away with the picture. This sort of role is nothing new for him, but Cheung is completely convincing as a man with no choices in life other than to continue following the path he has been on since childhood. While not especially violent as these films go, HK censors slapped this with Category III anyway, apparently due to the film's depiction of triad initiation rituals.

The Trial *see* **The Trail**

1011. Tricky Brains

(1991; Win's Movie Production) ★: 5/10. *Jing goo juen ga* (Cantonese), *Zheng gu zhuan jia* (Mandarin): "Tricky Expert." Cinematographer: Peter Pau Tak-hei; Art Director: Raymond Lee King-man; Music: Lowell Lo Kwun-ting; Producer: Jimmy Heung Wah-sing; Action Director: Benz Kong To-hoi; Writer-Director: Wong Jing. Cast: Stephen Chiau Sing-chi (Jing Koo), Andy Lau Tak-wah (Chi Man-kit), Rosamund Kwan Chi-lam (Lucy Ching), Ng Man-tat (Yan-chi), Waise Lee Chi-hung (Macky Kam), Chingmy Yau Suk-ching (Banana Fung), Wong Jing (Chiu), Shing Fui-on (Chu), John Ching Tung (The Ultimate Expert), Charlie Cho Cha-lei (Drug Store Clerk). 1.85:1. VHS: Tai Seng. Import LD/VCD/DVD: Mei Ah. 107 minutes.

Practical joke king Jing Koo is unparalleled in his field, demanding and getting outrageously high fees for his services. His latest assignment comes via the shifty Macky Kam, who wants Jing to fool his coworker Chi Man-kit into thinking that he is a long lost sibling. The plan is to destroy Man-kit's relationship with the beautiful Lucy, whom Macky desires for himself. The scheme ends up working too well, causing Man-kit and his father to lose their jobs in the process. A guilt-ridden Jing decides to help set everything right, but there is a new trickster in town, called "The Ultimate Expert," out to challenge him for the title of number one prankster.

Tricky Brains follows the usual Wong Jing pattern of setting up the premise in the first reel and then casting it aside for the next three. For all of the bits that really hit the target (like a wonderful Peking Opera send-up and the climactic battle between Jing and The Ultimate Expert), one must also endure sophomoric routines featuring aphrodisiac pills, itching powder, super glue, or AIDS jokes. Also, a good number of the verbal jests (particularly some rhyming schtick between Chiau and Lau) don't really survive translation. Seasoned Chiau fans will want to take a look anyway, but those who are not familiar with the comedian won't understand his full appeal by only watching this picture.

1012. Tricky Business

(1995; Good Standard International) ★: 4/10. *Jing gong woo* (Cantonese), *Zheng gu wang* (Mandarin): "King of Pranks." Cinematographer: Kin Lee Kin-keung; Art Director: Cheuk Man-fai; Music: Marco Wan Ho-kit, Anthony Lee Hon-kam; Writers: Lee Lik-chi, Vincent Kok Tak-chiu; Producer: Wong Jing; Action Director: Dion Lam Dik-on; Director: Lee Lik-chi. Cast: Lau Ching-wan (Ko Hing), Anita Yuen Wing-yee (Moon), Eric Kot Man-fai (Lau-huet), Jan Lam Hoi-fung (Bat-chi), Law Kar-ying (Lau Kar-lin), Linda Cheung Yan-ling (Lin), Ha Ping (Hospital Orderly), Wyman Wong Wai-man (Shi Chung), Cheng Cho (Joe Yeung). 1.85:1. VHS: Tai Seng. Import LD/VCD: Mei Ah. 93 minutes.

Inspired by Wong Jing's **Tricky Brains**, this opens with a wonderfully zany sequence that sets one up to expect a comedy along the lines of classic Warner Brothers cartoons. Alas, the balance of the film is not nearly as inspired. Practical joke king Ko Hing is so proficient at his job, he has made a fortune hiring his services out to high paying clients. He does have his principles (which date back to the practical jokers of the Ming Dynasty, no less), however, and will not fool anyone he feels is undeserving of humiliation. When he turns down one such job, the disgruntled client hires Lau Kar-lin (aka "The Handsome and Charming Tricky Emperor") to take revenge. While fighting off one of Lau's ruses, Ko accidentally knocks blind girl Moon down a flight of stairs. Feeling sorry for the destitute girl, Ko lets her move in with him and love soon blossoms.

Aside from a handful of clever bits (like an attack by remote controlled banana peels!), this runs out of ideas fast and really bogs down whenever Eric Kot and Jan Lam are given center stage. The film's main deception turns out exactly as you would expect, and the final duel between Ko and Lau is distinctly underwhelming, thanks to some shoddy special FX.

1013. Trilogy of Lust

(1995; Good Standard International) ★: 3/10. *Huet luen* (Cantonese), *Xue lian* (Mandarin): "Blood Love." Cinematographers: Kwan Chi-kan, Cheng Chuk-ming; Art Director: Ken Chiu Kin-san; Producers: Julie Lee Wah-yuet, Tsai Lan; Writer-Director: Julie Lee Wah-yuet. Cast: Julie Lee Wah-yuet (Chi), Chan Wai-dik (Un), Siu Kwok-chu, Wan Sheung-lam, Yau Wai-fong. 1.85:1. Import LD/VCD: Universe. 83 minutes.

After starring in other people's Category III films, Julie Lee decided to produce one on her own, and the result certainly stands out from the pack (though not necessarily in a good way). Yik-sang is a would-be doctor who was dismissed from medical school after cheating on a test. Sporting a considerable chip on his shoulder, he makes his living on Tai O (an island off HK) as a fisherman. In search of a wife, Yik-sang travels to China and buys Chi, a young "intellectual" who is haunted by memories of repression during The Cultural Revolution. Chi soon finds her new life less than desirable once she is subjected to Yik-sang's "medical exams" and flagrant temper tantrums. She finds solace in the arms of Un, a young vegetable delivery boy, and the two begin a torrid affair. When Yik-sang's aunt catches the pair in the midst of one of their trysts, she tries to blackmail Chi, but Un kills her and disposes of the body at sea. Subsequent events result in more murders, causing the lovers to flee the police in a desperate attempt to reach the border and disappear into China.

Trilogy of Lust tries to tell a genuine story free of the sneering, juvenile humor so prevalent in these films. Unfortunately, said plotline offers nothing at all new but does provide for some of the most unpalatable images in memory (particularly Yik-sang tormenting Chi by covering her with fish blood, and Chi and Un making love amidst a mass of writhing *eels*). The sex (cut in numerous spots) is underscored with a bizarre collection of library cues that run the gamut from the sort of sleepy "la-la-la-la" fluff heard in European softcore to jagged heavy metal. Unless you desire an impromptu lesson in sexual positions like "Hanging the Drum on the Dragonhead," "Push the Boat Along the River," and "Hit the Cow Between the Mountains," take a pass. A XXX version of the film has been released on video in Germany. It was followed by an unrelated, but even more extreme, sequel.

1014. Trilogy of Lust II

(1995; Dens) ★: 3/10. *Huet luen II* (Cantonese), *Xue lian II* (Mandarin): "Blood Love II." Art Director-Writer-Producer: Julie Lee Wah-yuet; Director: Jirou Ishikawa. Cast: Julie Lee Wah-yuet (Linda Li), Elvis Tsui Kam-kong (Philip Chen), Chin Kwan, Chow Man-ho, Thomas Freitag (First Victim). 1.85:1. VHS: World Video. Import LD/VCD: Mei Ah. 88 minutes.

Julie Lee (billed here as "Julie Riva") is back with another of her self-produced adult thrillers. This one bears no connection to its forerunner but manages to be even more depraved and peculiar. Forty-something Linda spends her nights picking up unsuspecting men and murdering them in outlandish ways, following a round of S & M-tinged sex. She then severs a body part, like an ear or a nose, to keep as a souvenir. By day, Linda is the exceptionally nasty boss of a toy company, who is known among the employees as "The Spinster." Her continued cruel treatment of one female employee prompts the woman to convince a fellow male worker to seduce Linda as part of a plan to swindle her (a subplot that never really goes anywhere but provides for even more sex and death). In addition to being an unrepentant murderer, Linda is also a masochist, burning herself with cigarettes and masturbating with a hair brush. Her homicidal hatred of men can be traced back a number of years when she was gang raped by a relative and his perverted friends. After seducing and murdering a man in his twenties, Linda learns from a TV report that the victim was infected with AIDS but continues on with her macabre routine nevertheless.

In addition to the horror angle, the sexual acts depicted here tend to differ from the male-oriented fantasy fare that makes up the vast majority of HK adult cinema, leaning more towards the strange perversity of Japanese adult films (this perhaps explains Lee's choice of director for this entry). We are meant to feel some sympathy for Linda because of the extreme trauma of her past, and her story does end in a manner that is far removed from the norm for this sort of female vengeance material. Unfortunately, the film is just too bizarre, brutal, and puerile for it to succeed on any meaningful level. Regardless, *Trilogy of Lust II* is difficult to forget and leaves one convinced that Lee must have issues in her past that she is working out through these dark and disturbing features (she reportedly tried to commit suicide after this one came out). The sex scenes feature numerous cuts, indicating that this, too, had some hardcore footage at one point.

1015. Tristar

(1996; Mandarin Films/Cinema City Motion Picture/Film Workshop) ★: 5/10. *Daai sam yuen* (Cantonese), *Da san yuan* (Mandarin): "Big Three Round." Cinematographers: Arthur Wong Ngok-tai, Christopher Doyle; Art Director: Bill Lui Cho-hung; Music: Lowell Lo Kwun-ting; Writers: Philip Cheng Chung-tai, Tsui Hark, To Wan; Producer: Raymond Wong Pak-ming; Action Director: Xiong Xinxin; Director: Tsui Hark. Cast: Leslie Cheung Kwok-wing (Father Zhong Guoqiang), Anita Yuen Wing-yee (Bai Xuehua), Lau Ching-wan (Fa), Sunny Chan Kam-hung (Fa's Partner), Alvina Kong Yan-yin (Dongdong), Catherine Hung Yan (Mary), Chung King-fai (Dinosaur), Shing Fui-on (Father Robin), Moses Chan Ho (Chen Junnan), Xiong Xinxin (Loan Shark Tai), Raymond Wong Pak-ming (Superintendent Mai), Paul Fonoroff (Bearded Mormon). 1.85:1. VHS: Tai Seng. Import LD/VCD/DVD: Fitto Mobile. 106 minutes.

One of Tsui Hark's weakest efforts, this all-star farce was thrown together quickly so it would be ready for the lucrative Chinese New Year release window, and that hastiness shows in the final product. Flaky hooker Bai Xuehua owes gangster Dinosaur $200,000 but hasn't got the money. He suggests she agree to ply her trade in the Middle East for five years, but, not surprisingly, Xuehua isn't exactly keen on the idea. Eluding Dinosaur's thugs, she hides inside a church, where she confesses her predicament to the dashing Father Zhong. Moving into the girl's sleazy digs, Zhong (whose face was hidden from Xuehua in the confessional) makes it his mission in life to save Xuehua and her "coworkers" (who all dress like drag queens on a night out) while keeping his true identity a secret. Recently dumped by her parasitic boyfriend, Xuehua begins to fall for her benefactor, and he starts to feel some rather dangerous longings for her, too. However, Xuehua's troubles with Dinosaur are not over...

The first couple of reels are promising but **Tristar** quickly starts to lose focus and drifts into dullness. Rather than serve up a fresh twist or turn in the predictable scenario, the film is content to merely coast along on star appeal while mining whatever laughs it can from garish fashions and make-up (which actually suit Anita Yuen rather well), outlandish sets, and a pair of exceedingly vapid cops (played by Lau Ching-wan and Sunny Chan, the latter looking like a young Chow Yun-fat). Impromptu music video-style segments and a climactic sequence (set in an unbelievably garish karaoke lounge and reminiscent of Tsui's early gangster farce **All the Wrong Clues...For the Right Solution**) are jarring and desperate. On the other hand, you *do* get to see Leslie Cheung dressed up like Elvis and veteran tough guy Shing Fui-on as a priest with bleach blonde hair, so it's not a total loss. The Chinese title refers to a type of hand one can get in mahjong.

1016. Trouble Couples

(1987; Cinema City Co.) ★: 6/10. *Hoi sam mat yue* (Cantonese), *Kai xin wu yu* (Mandarin): "Happy, No Talking." Cinematographer: Joe Chan Kong-hung; Art Director: Kong Hoi-ming; Music: T and T; Producers: Raymond Wong Pak-ming, Alan Tam Wing-lun; Director: Eric Tsang Chi-wai. Cast: Anita Mui Yim-fong (Mui Tai-heung), Eric Tsang Chi-wai (Tsang Jo-choy), Fennie Yuen Kit-ying (Mui Sai-heung), Ann Bridegwater (Mui Yee-heung), Charine Chan Kar-ling (Mui Sarm-heung), Matthew Wong Hin-mung (Joe Kam Tze-mon), Edmond So Chi-wai (Boyfriend), Calvin Choi Yat-chi (Short-Sighted), Remus Choi Yat-kit (Boyfriend), Sandra Ng Kwan-yu (Oi-chee), Shing Fui-on (Mark), Helena Law Lan (Oi-chee's Mother), Charlie Cho Cha-lei (Chan), Lau Kar-wing (Godfather), Wong Jing (Teacher), Ha Ping (Woman on TV), Woo Fung (Man on TV). 1.85:1. VHS: Tai Seng. Import LD: Golden Cinema City. 88 minutes.

This conventional but agreeable farce finds the three youngest Mui girls agonizing over what to do with their nasty older sister Tai-heung. Family custom states that the girls can only start dating once the eldest is married. Their hope for freedom lies in the short and fat form of Tsang Jo-choy, a bumbling nebbish who seeks to get married within one month's time in order to slight his ex-girlfriend. After much cajoling on Jo-choy's part, Tai-heung agrees to marriage...with three very humbling conditions. Despite that fact that all of them essentially rob Jo-choy of his manhood, he agrees and undergoes a crash course in learning how to please his bride-to-be. He succeeds and the wedding goes without a hitch...until the reception, when Tai-heung learns the reason why Jo-choy courted her.

Anita Mui is not exactly convincing as a shrewish spinster but is a lot of fun to watch in the role. She and Eric Tsang make for one of the greatest odd couples to be found in HK cinema, and just watching the two of them interact is enough to invoke laughs. Edmond So, Calvin Choi, and Remus Choi make up the rock band Grasshopper, but it is Mui who is granted the requisite music video-style interlude here.

1017. Troublesome Night

(1997; Colour Business Entertainment/Nam Yin Production Company) ★: 5/10. *Yam yeung lo* (Cantonese), *Yin yang lu* (Mandarin): "Yin Yang Road." Cinematographer: Joe Chan Kong-hung; Art Director: Jason Mok Siu-kei; Music: Mak Chun-hung; Writers: Lau Hau-wai, Candy Cheng, Yeung Woon-choi; Producer: Nam Yin; Directors: Cheng Wai-man, Tam Long-cheung, Herman Yau Lai-to. Cast: Simon Lui Yu-yeung (Peter Butt, The Host/Mr. Big Mole), Louis Koo Tin-lok (Ken Ni Chi-keung), Jason Chu Wing-tong (Bee), Allen Ting Chi-chun (Guy with Long Hair), Christy Chung Lai-tai (Mrs. To), Sunny Chan Kam-hung (Jogger/To Ka-ming), Ada Choi Siu-fan (Horny Girl in Story #1), Teresa Mak Kar-kei (Virginal Girl in Story #1/Jojo), Helena Law Lan (Spooky Old Lady), Pak Kar-sin (Fat Girl), Ng Chi-hung (Ng Tai-hung), Christine Ng Wing-mei (May), Kenix Kwok Ho-ying (May), Yuen King-tan (Miss Yuen), Lee Siu-kei (Dr. Ho), Lee Lik-chi (The Director). 1.85:1. VHS: Mecapro. Import LD/VCD/DVD: Mei Ah. 98 minutes.

This horror anthology consists of four stories, none of which are especially creative but remain watchable thanks to a quality cast. Story #1 (*Chau mo pai* or "Speculating in Grave Stories," directed by Cheng Wai-man) concerns a trio of guys (led by Louis Koo) spending the night in the woods who run across three female campers (including Ada Choi and Teresa Mak). They break off into couples in order to play a rather macabre game: Each will copy the writings off as many tombstones as possible. But Koo keeps seeing ghosts and later discovers one girl's picture on a grave marker. Story #2 (*Yum yeung lo* or "Dark Bright Road," directed by Tam Long-cheung) stars Christy Chung as a woman driving in a heavy downpour who experiences some weird occurrences. Her husband (Sunny Chan) is also out in the same storm and is unable to find Chung, even when they are both standing in front of the same restaurant at the same time. Story #3 (*Hung dong dong* or "Red All Over," directed by Herman Yau) stars Teresa Mak as a girl who is ravaged by some invisible force and develops a distinct affinity for the color red. Her friends enlist the aid of a goofy exorcist named Mr. Big Mole (Tom Cruise's personal *feng shui* advisor, no less) to save her. The final story (*Tou dei wai* or "Turf," also directed by Yau) stars Ng Chi-hung as an egotistical movie star attending the premiere of his new film who unknowingly takes a seat reserved for a powerful ghost.

HK horror movies are very often funny or disgusting but are rarely scary, and '90s horror anthologies like this one will not be the least bit frightening to anyone over the age of 12. Still, there are a few clever touches (like characters recurring throughout some of the stories and a parody of **A Moment of Romance**) to help hold your attention. A box office success, this spawned several sequels.

1018. Troublesome Night II

(1997; China Star Entertainment Group/Win's Entertainment/Nam Yin Production Co.) ★: 5/10. *Yam yeung lo ji ngoh joi nei joh yau* (Cantonese), *Yin yang lu zhi wo zai ni zuo you* (Mandarin): "Yin Yang Road: I Am by Your Side." Cinematographer: Joe Chan Kong-hung; Art Director: Ho Chi-hang; Music: Mak Chun-hung; Writers: Tsang Kwok-chi, Lau Hau-wai; Producer: Nam Yin; Action Director: Chan Kai-tong; Director: Herman Yau Lai-to. Cast: Simon Lui Yu-yeung (Chai), Louis Koo Tin-lok (Sam), Allen Ting Chi-chun (Fai), Chin Kar-lok (Chuen), Amanda Lee Wai-man (Anita), Ng Chi-hung (Wah), Cheung Tat-ming (Dan), Lai Yiu-cheung (Curry), Christine Ng Wing-mei (Miu), Liz Kong Hei-man (Girl in Water), Vincent Kok Tak-chiu (Station Manager), Mang Fai (Sam's Opponent). 1.85:1. VHS: Mecapro. Import LD/VCD: Carnival. 96 minutes.

Three more ghost tales are presented in this initial sequel, which was directed entirely by Herman Yau this time and arrived in theaters only four months after its forerunner. In the first story, DJ Allen Ting (one of three hosts of a radio phone-in show called "One O'Clock Terror") callously advises a suicidal Amanda Lee that the best way for her to get over her boyfriend's death is to jump off a building...which she proceeds to do. Ting is then haunted by her apparition, prompting him to take drastic measures. In the second story, Simon Lui (as another of the DJs) joins nerdy buddies Cheung Tat-ming and Lai Yiu-cheung on a pleasure cruise with Christine Ng and boatman Ng Chi-hung (who accidentally killed Amanda Lee's boyfriend in the first story and has been suffering from paranoia ever since). Shortly after seeing a pig carcass floating in the water, Lui spots a half dead Liz Kong, whose presence is apparently the reason behind a number of strange and disgusting occurrences. Story #3 finds Louis Koo (the third DJ) plagued by weird visions and consumed by anxiety, which is made worse by the repeated appearances of a female ghost dressed in red.

The second story is easily the best, with Simon Lui, Cheung Tat-ming, and Lui Yu-yeung providing some solid laughs. Unfortunately, it drags on too long and the ending is weak. The remaining two thirds of the film are merely passable, and nothing here is ever genuinely scary, despite the fact that the gore quotient has been increased over the original film.

1019. Truant Heroes

(1992; Jing's Prod.) ★: 7/10. *To hok ying hung juen* (Cantonese), *Tso xue ying xiong zhuan* (Mandarin): "Escape from School Hero Story." Cinematographer: Tam Chi-wai; Art Director: Andrew Cheuk Man-yiu; Music: Lowell Lo Kwun-ting; Action Director: Sherman Wong Ching-wah; Producer-Director: Wong Jing. Cast: Alfred Cheung Kin-ting (Hou Shui-ken), Aaron Kwok Fu-shing (Ace), Chingmy Yau Suk-ching (Kwan Tak-hing/Ng Siu-yuen), Sharla Cheung Man (Lam Moon-shang, aka Dreamy), Gabriel Wong Yat-san (Turtle), Ng Man-tat (Blackie Tat), Michael Chan Wai-man (Chan Wai-ha), Dennis Chan Kwok-san (Headmaster), Barry Wong Ping-yiu (Police Commissioner Wong), Sarah Lee Lai-yui (2nd in Command), Yam Sai-kwoon (Ti), Yuen Cheung-yan (Doggie). 1.85:1. VHS: Tai Seng. Import VCD: Mega Star. 86 minutes. Also known as **School Commandos**.

Obviously inspired by the success of Stephen Chiau's **Fight Back to School** series, this amusing farce (which, oddly, has no writer credit) has Alfred Cheung taking the Chiau role as an undercover cop in a high school. Posing as a teacher, Hou Shui-ken is assigned to locate a student with a dog-shaped birthmark on his backside(!), in order to protect him from triad assassins. The timid Hou is quickly run ragged by his unruly charges, and to make matters worse, his ex-fiancée is also working undercover as a student in one of his classes. His biggest test comes later on, when a squad of Taiwanese killers invades the school prom.

In addition to Wong Jing's usual politically incorrect humor (some of which really hits the mark here), there are also some clever in-jokes (Sarah Lee sending up her tough girl **School on Fire** role, Chingmy Yau's mean character being called "Kwan Tak-hing" after the famous kung fu star, etc.). Some of the pranks the students inflict on Cheung are genuinely creative and Michael Chan has a great time poking fun at his usual gangster image by playing a former triad turned teacher who cannot quite give up his old ways.

1020. True Colours

(1986; Cinema City Co.) ★: 5/10. *Ying hung jing juen* (Cantonese), *Ying xiong zheng zhuan* (Mandarin): "A Hero's True Story." Cinematographer: Chan Chun-wai; Art Director: Andy Lee Yiu-kwong; Music: Danny Chung Teng-yat; Writer-Producer: Raymond Wong Pak-ming; Director: Che-Kirk Wong Chi-keung. Cast: Ti Lung (Ho Lung), Raymond Wong Pak-ming (Robert), Brigitte Lin Ching-hsia (May), Lam Chung (Inspector Cho). 1.85:1. VHS: Tai Seng. Import LD: Golden Cinema City. Import VCD: Mega Star. 90 minutes.

A weak remake (set in 1955) of Michael Curtiz's 1938 classic **Angels with Dirty Faces**, this features Ti Lung in the James Cagney role, Raymond Wong in the Pat O'Brien part, and Brigitte Lin (not getting a chance to be anything more than decoration) as the female lead. When he appears to slay a policeman during a gang war, triad member Ho Lung flees HK, leaving behind his girlfriend May and fellow two-bit gangster Robert. Five years pass and Lung returns to find Robert, now a minister, in charge of a home for troubled boys. At first Lung is put off by Robert's charges but soon warms up to them. May, meanwhile, is stuck in a loveless, abusive marriage with gangster tycoon Kuk, who has Lung beaten when he catches him with his old flame. In retaliation, Lung steals Kuk's ledger, which has enough incriminating dealings in it to put the man behind bars forever. In exchange for its return, he demands May and $1 million, but the plan fails and May is killed, prompting Lung to leave HK once more. One of Robert's boys sets out to avenge Lung and fails, prompting Robert to toss aside his religious beliefs and try the same thing.

Ti Lung does fine work as always, the period costumes and locations are nicely rendered, and some set-ups are quite stylish. Regardless, the film is severely crippled by Raymond Wong's inability to be the least bit convincing as a tough guy, and the dramatic content is feeble.

1021. The True Hero

(1994; New Prima Film Production) ★: 3/10. *Bo yue giu yeung* (Cantonese), *Bao yu jiao yang* (Mandarin): "Violent Rain, Intense Sun." Cinematographer: Wong Sai-kit; Art Director: Raymond Lam Chi-wai; Music: Dik Lok; Writers: Joseph Cheung Tung-cho, Patrick Yuen Yau-kwong, Jimmy Sin Chi-wai; Action Directors: Stephen Tung Wai, Benz Kong To-hoi, Tony Poon Kin-kwan; Producer-Director: Joseph Cheung Tung-cho. Cast: Simon Yam Tat-wah (Cheung Chi-wing), Anita Yuen Wing-yee (Hung), John Tang Yat-kwan (Kit), Derek Yee Tung-sing (Principal Chun), Lawrence Cheng Tan-shui (Joe), Austin Wai Tin-chi (Brother Four), John Ching Tung (Brother Tiger), Dennis Chan Kwok-san (Chan), Manfred Wong (Mr. Man), Jamie Luk Kim-ming (Teacher), Jacqueline Law Wai-kuen (Miss Ho). 1.85:1. VHS: Tai Seng. Import LD/VCD: Ocean Shores. 97 minutes.

A dismal blend of triad movie conventions and the sort of classroom comedy found in films like **Fight Back to School** and **Truant Heroes**, **The True Hero** also has more than its share of flimsy dramatics and hackneyed situations. When a school bus full of children is inadvertently blown up because of his actions, ruthless triad Cheung Chi-wing decides to reform and becomes a teacher at Pui Tak College. His new direction in life does not sit well with his girlfriend, bar hostess Hung, whose only objective in life is making money. He gets stuck with a class full of delinquents but eventually begins to get through, boosting their confidence and their grades in the process. However, Chi-wing's shady past comes back to haunt him, thanks to his students' triad connections. Caught in the wrong place at the wrong time, he is severely hurt defending one of them and must face off with two drug-dealing lieutenants.

Devotees of the **Young and Dangerous** series and its imitations might want to take a look at this, as it pre-dates them in its depiction of teen triads, but it is not in their league and there is little else here of value, save for an action-packed finale. The ending is particularly insipid. Watch **School On Fire** instead.

1022. Twenty Something

(1994; United Filmmakers Organization) ★: 6/10. *Maan 9 jiu 5* (Cantonese), *Wan 9 zhao 5* (Mandarin): "9PM 5AM." Cinematographer: Apple Kwan Pak-suen; Art Directors: Ben Luk Man-wah, James Cheung Ying-wah; Music: Clarence Hui Yuen, Joseph Wong Nai-nin; Writer: James Yuen Sai-sang; Producer: Peter Chan Ho-sun; Director: Teddy Chan Tak-sum. Cast: Farini Cheung Yui-ling (Jennifer), Jordan Chan Siu-chun (Bo Lam), Valerie Chow Kar-ling (Alice), Moses Chan Ho (Tom Chang), Yau Chau-yuet (Sue), Nelson Cheung Hok-yun (Nelson), Cheung Hung-on (Mick). 1.85:1. VHS: Tai Seng. Import LD/VCD/DVD: Mei Ah. 98 minutes.

This Category III feature is an interesting attempt by the United Filmmakers Organization to craft an adult drama that would be emotionally and dramatically effective while also being more sexually frank than is allowed under the guidelines of the Category II rating. The story looks at several men and women from the title age bracket who frequent a particular bar: Bo is a party animal who sleeps around with reckless abandon; Jennifer suffers from a hormone disorder that gives her an insatiable appetite for sex; Alice is the requisite "good girl" who is unsure of her new relationship; Sue is emotionally overwrought and constantly on the verge of tears and/or suicide; Pat, obnoxious and overweight, is constantly trying to insinuate herself into the crowd; etc. Interspersed throughout the feature are interviews with the characters in which they discuss their views on sex and relationships.

The performances are fine (particularly Jordan Chan in one of his breakout roles as the sort of hedonistic, insensitive clod who gives all single guys a bad name), and the dramatic situations, while occasionally exaggerated and simplistic (the fact that one couple should break up is illustrated by a vignette in a supermarket where one person chooses Coke while the other chooses Pepsi), present a good cross section of the problems these people might really face. However, the characters themselves are largely types and do not change much by the time the film has concluded, leaving the whole exercise feeling a bit empty.

1023. 24 Hours Ghost Story

(1997; Everwide) ★: 6/10. *Maang gwai tung siu pooi chu lei* (Cantonese), *Meng gui tong xiao pei zhu ni* (Mandarin): "Fierce Ghost Spends All Night with You." Cinematographer: Jimmy Wong Kam-shing; Art Director: Ken Chiu Kin-san; Music: Tommy Wai Kai-leung; Writers: Abe Kwong Man-wai, Danny Ko Lam-pau, Wellson Chin Sing-wai; Producers: Wong Jing, Wellson Chin Sing-wai, Abe Kwong Man-wai; Action Director: Yi Fei; Director: Wellson Chin Sing-wai. Cast: Francis Ng Chun-yu (Mo Tai-ho), Dayo Wong Chi-wah (Charlie Chan), Chin Kar-lok (Ah-ah), Gigi Lai Chi (Siu-wan), Simon Lui Yu-yeung (Frankie Ng), Liz Kong Hei-man (Apple), Yuen King-tan (Lotus), Lam Wai (River Wang), Jerry Lam Hiu-fung (Wang's Assistant). 1.85:1. VHS: Mecapro. Import LD/VCD/DVD: New City. 95 minutes.

The team behind some of HK's most successful ghost films returns with this opus, set in a haunted 24 hour convenience store! Clerk Mo Tai-ho thinks he's losing his sanity because only he can hear Peking opera issuing from telephones, a freezer, the stockroom, etc. Later on, he begins to experience weird, ghoulish dreams as well. The only person who believes him is eccentric cop Charlie Chan (Dayo Wong, reprising his role from **The Day that Doesn't Exist**), whose mother recommends such traditional weapons as a child's urine (which prevents a ghost from reincarnating) and the tail of a black dog. The former fails when a ghost forces Tai and Chan to drink the urine, and the latter cannot help because neither man has the heart to slice the tail off of a cute puppy. They enlist the services of a famous Taoist, but he ends up bouncing off the walls like a pinball. Chan learns that a tragedy occurred in the store seven years ago and seems destined to repeat unless he and Mo can keep everyone out of the building until after midnight on the seventh day of the seventh month.

The first half is too mild for its own good but the second half delivers a few chuckles (there is a great running joke about the way Gigi Lai's character expresses fear) and a handful of atmospheric moments. While it is never outright scary, **24 Hours Ghost Story** comes closer than most films of this type and makes for diverting viewing. Michael Chow Mankin has a rather unique cameo.

1024. The Twilight of the Forbidden City

(1992; Movie Impact) ★: 5/10. *Go bit ji gam sing* (Cantonese), *Gao bie zi jin cheng* (Mandarin): "Farewell Purple Forbidden City." Cinematographer: Mark Lee Ping-bing; Art Director: Jessy Lam Chak-chi; Music: William Woo Wai-lap; Writers: Manfred Wong, Johnny Lee King-kai, Lee Sai-hung, Ngai Chun; Producers: Kent Cheng Chuk-see, Clarence Yip Wai-chung; Action Director: Stephen Tung Wai; Director: Manfred Wong. Cast: Max Mok Siu-chung (Lau Loy-hay), Norman Law Man (Little Tak Cheung), Felix Wong Yat-wah (Wu Chung), Carrie Ng Kar-lai (Chiu Feng), Kent Cheng Chuk-see (General Cheung), Irene Wan Pik-ha (Chiu Ti), Shing Fui-on (General Tuen). 1.85:1. VHS: Tai Seng. Import LD/VCD: Ocean Shores. Running time unknown.

Set early in the century, this period drama covers the adult life of imperial eunuch Lau Loy-hay who, following the conclusion of his duties in The Forbidden City, lived as a surrogate husband and father. One day he saves the life of the revolutionary Wu Chung, who is being sought by soldiers for an assassination he committed. Lau agrees to work undercover with Wu in order to steal the royal seal, possession of which is key to ruling the country. The two manage to get close to General Cheung, the official charged with protecting the seal, but their attempt to purloin the object fails. Wu manages to escape but Cheung, upon learning that Lau is a eunuch, decides to make the youth his 13th wife! Rescued after he had already been defiled by Cheung, Lau is brought to the ruthless head eunuch, Little Tak Cheung (played by singer Norman Law), and takes a position in his household. Tak is in league with the Japanese to revive the Qing Dynasty, and Lau finds himself caught in the middle as a helpless pawn, pushed one way by Tak and another by his revolutionary friends.

A handsome but empty film, **The Twilight of the Forbidden City** strives to be a respectable historical drama but places so much emphasis on cruelty and sexual deviance that, truthful account or not, it operates on virtually the same level as unabashed exploitation items like **Sex and Zen** and **Lover of the Last Empress**. Cast in a role of much greater depth than he is generally offered, Max Mok does a good job of reflecting the anguish of this tragic figure, but his efforts are largely for naught in a production that creeps toward its predetermined conclusion with little conviction. Mok essayed a similar role four years earlier in **Lai Shi, China's Last Eunuch**.

1025. The Twin Bracelets

(1991; Cosmopolitan Film Productions Co.) ★: 7/10. *Seung juk* (Cantonese), *Shuang zhuo* (Mandarin): "Twin Bracelets." Cinematographer: Bob Thompson; Art Director: Lee Kwok-kwong; Music: Lo Tai-yau, Fabio Carli; Writer: Suki Yip Suk-wah; Producer: Lau Tin-chi; Director: Wong Yuk-san. Cast: Winnie Lau Siu-wai (Hsiu), Vivian Chan Tak-yung (Hui-hua), Roger Kwok Chun-on (Kuang), Michael To Tai-yu (Hui-hua's Brother), Wong Yat-fei (Singing Man). 1.85:1. VHS: World Video. Import LD/VCD/DVD: Mei Ah. 99 minutes.

The Mainland village of Hui An not only still observes the ancient custom of arranged marriages, it even forces the brides to see their husbands only three times a year until the woman has given birth to a son. Carefree teenage girls Hsiu and Hui-hua (who have sworn a vow of eternal friendship) are approaching adulthood, but the latter vehemently rejects the idea of being forced into marriage (based on the actions of her sadistic brother, who beats and cheats on his loyal, compliant wife for no reason at all) and hopes that she and Hsiu can always be together. Hsiu's parents marry her off to Kuang, a kind sculptor; Hui-hua's parents betroth her to a violent lout. The girl insists on a divorce but her family refuses to return the dowry her husband paid. Ostracized, Hui-hua leaves home and moves in with Hsiu, but the latter wishes to join her husband in Shenzhen and plans to secretly leave. Distressed by the thought that even Hsiu is now abandoning her, Hui-hua becomes desperate, setting the stage for tragedy.

A somber, engrossing drama, **The Twin Bracelets** is marred only by the sheer inevitability of its narrative. It does, however, make some very valid points about how some village traditions rob women of all their rights while giving men absolute freedom to mistreat them. The rural scenery is beautiful, and the lovely, traditional costumes are of a sort not often seen in HK cinema.

1026. The Twin Dragons

(1992; Golden Harvest/Hong Kong Film Directors' Guild/Paragon Films) ★: 5/10 (All versions). *Seung lung wooi* (Cantonese), *Shuang long hui* (Mandarin): "Twin Dragons Meet." Cinematographers: Horace Wong Wing-hang, Arthur Wong Ngok-tai; Art Directors: Bill Lui Cho-hung; Music: Liu Koon-ting (HK version), Michael Wandmacher, Phe Loung (US version); Writers: Barry Wong Ping-yiu, Tsui Hark, Joseph Cheung Tung-cho, Wong Yik; Producer: Teddy Robin Kwan; Action Directors: Jackie Chan, Ching Siu-tung, Stephen Tung Wai, Chris Lee Kin-sang, Yuen Woo-ping, Tsui Siu-ming; Directors: Tsui Hark, Ringo Lam Ling-tung. Cast: Jackie Chan (Ma Yu/Wan-ming), Maggie Cheung Man-yuk (Barbara), Nina Li Chi (Tang Hsin), Teddy Robin Kwan (Tarzan), David Chiang Da-wei (Sgt. Chiang/Hotel Staff Member), Anthony Chan Yau (Chen), Johnny Wang Lung-wei (Wei), Jamie Luk Kim-ming (Frankie Lo, aka Rocky), Che-Kirk Wong Chi-keung (Crazy Bull), Phillip Chan Yan-kin (Hotel Manager), Alfred Cheung Kin-ting (Yung), James Wong Jim (Yu and Wan-ming's Father), Sylvia Chang Ai-chia (Yu and Wan-ming's Mother), Guy Lai Ying-chau (Tsao), Feng Sing (Goon), Lau Kar-leung (Doctor), Eric Tsang Chi-wai (Man on Phone), Dennis Chan Kwok-san (Man with Boat), John Woo Yu-sen (Priest at Wedding), Tsui Siu-ming (Priest with Letter), Chor Yuen (Uncle Tang), Wong Jing (Supernatural Doctor), Clifton Ko Chi-sum (Clerk in Sports Section), David Wu Tai-wai (Waiter), Jacob Cheung Chi-leung (Waiter), Tsui Hark, Ringo Lam Ling-tung, Ng See-yuen (Card Players), Ching Siu-tung, Gordon Chan Kar-seung, Yip Wing-cho, Lau Kar-wing (Musicians)...and many more! Dolby Digital (US version and Universe DVD only), Sony Dynamic Digital Sound (US version only). 2.35:1. VHS: Tai Seng (No Subtitles), Dimension (Dubbed official US version), Ace Video (Dubbed), Bull Dog Entertainment (Dubbed), Front Row Entertainment (Dubbed). LD/DVD: Dimension (Dubbed official version). Import LD: Star Entertainment (No Subtitles). Import VCD: Star Entertainment

(No Subtitles), Mega Star. Import DVD: China Star (No Subtitles), Universe. 89 minutes (Dimension version)/104 minutes (HK version & English export version)/107 minutes (Taiwan version).

Jackie Chan does his take on Jean-Claude Van Damme's **Double Impact** (1991) in this action-comedy which was produced to benefit the Hong Kong Film Director's Guild and features an army of cameo appearances by filmmakers, all of whom worked for free to help keep the budget down to just over $1 million in US funds. Accidentally separated at birth, twin brothers Ma Yu and Wan-ming spend their formative years in very different environments. Yu is taken to New York and becomes a world famous pianist/conductor while, back in HK, Wan-ming grows up to be a street-smart mechanic with tremendous fighting abilities. Like the Corsican Brothers, each sibling can experience what the other does (a gag that is not applied with any degree of consistency). Their paths finally cross, at age 28, when Yu arrives in HK for a concert. In addition to hopelessly confusing their girlfriends (both of whom unknowingly prefer the other brother), Yu and Wan-ming end up in each other's predicaments: Yu has to deal with gangsters after his brother's head, while the talentless Wan-ming ends up having to fill in at a concert. After finally revealing to everyone involved that there are indeed two of them, the brothers team up to rescue Wan-ming's diminutive buddy, Tarzan, who has been kidnapped by the criminals.

Most of the jokes fall flat, and the contrived manner in which the twins are kept apart for so long shows just how lacking the screenplay is in the kind of comic invention that one expects from this sort of screwball comedy. The primitive blue screen twin effects are none too convincing either. There are at least three spots where one Chan "crosses the line" and dissolves into the other; and during a sequence set in a washroom, the matte line jittering around one Chan is so distracting that it's impossible to pay attention to anything else. Fortunately, the usual Jackie Chan action is in abundance, and with five first-rate action choreographers at the helm, the various stunts (particularly Chan's nimble acrobatics in a car testing lab during the finale), fights, and chases provide ample fun and make this worth catching, at least on video (where one can quickly dispense with the weaker elements). Note: Prior to Dimension's official North American English market release (known simply as **Twin Dragons**) in April 1999, several small companies released a dubbed bootleg version (derived from the UK video release on the Video Programme Distributors label). While they run longer than the Dimension cut, these tapes have poor picture quality and should be avoided.

1027. Twinkle Twinkle Lucky Star

(1996; Jing's Production) ★: 4/10. *Wan choi ji lek sing* (Cantonese), *Yun cai zhi li xing* (Mandarin): "Fortune Most Talented Lucky Star." Cinematographer: Tony Miu Kin-fai; Art Director: Raymond Kwok Siu-keung; Music: Danny Chung Teng-yat; Writer-Producer-Director: Wong Jing. Cast: Nat Chan Pak-cheung (The Windfall God/Chiu Tak-nak), Anita Yuen Wing-yee (Beautiful), Christy Chung Lai-tai (The Angel of Nine Heavens/Christie Lee), Michael Wong Mantak (St. Michael/Shing Shing), Francis Ng Chun-yu (Ugly Kwan), Law Kar-ying (Cup Noodle), Elvis Tsui Kam-kong (The God of Match Makers), Yuen King-tan (Masseuse), Mimi Chu Mi-mi (Masseuse), Shing Fui-on (Saur), John Ching Tung (The God of Wealth/Choi Sun), Alan Tam Wing-lun (King of Heaven), Wong Yat-fei (The God of Bad Luck), Eric Tsang Chi-wai (Himself), Manfred Wong (Chun), Norman Law Man (Policeman), Kenny Bee (The God of Yee Long), Joe Junior (Fairy), Edmond Leung Hon-man (Fairy), Miu Kiu-wai (Fairy), Danny Chung Teng-yat (Fairy), Bobby Yip King-sang (Gambling Contest Competitor), Anita Mui Yim-fong (Herself), Wong Jing (Man at Race Track). 1.85:1. VHS: World Video. Import LD/VCD/DVD: Mei Ah. 94 minutes.

This goofy fantasy-comedy goes down too many familiar avenues to be much fun, despite its incredible, star-laden cast. The Windfall God has the hots for the gorgeous Angel of Nine Heavens, but she is already interested in St. Michael; and besides, it is forbidden to fall in love in Heaven. When The King of Heaven learns of their transgression, both Angel and Michael are banished to Earth, but Windfall is determined to do whatever it takes to get his love back through The Pearly Gates. With the aid of human worshipper Beautiful, Windfall is able to find Angel. Now a 20-year-old named Christie Lee, Angel does not remember Windfall and will have nothing to do with him. To make matters worse, Christie is in love with singer Shing Shing who is (you guessed it) the reincarnation of St. Michael. Every attempt to woo his love fails miserably, prompting Windfall to enter a gambling competition Christie's company is sponsoring. Windfall prevails in the first eight rounds, but The King of Heaven, having learned of his subordinate's forbidden plans, sets out to stop him by sending down Windfall's arch-enemy, The God of Wealth.

Like most of Nat Chan's comedies, this is content to simply rehash old gags and send-ups that have worked before (often for other performers) without coming up with anything fresh. Occasional inventive bits and a multitude of star cameos (most memorably, Francis Ng reprising his "Ugly Kwan" character from **Young and Dangerous**) at least keep it watchable.

1028. Twinkle, Twinkle, Lucky Stars

(1985; Golden Harvest/Bojon Films Company/Paragon Films) ★: 6/10. *Ha yat fuk sing* (Cantonese), *Xia ri fu xing* (Mandarin): "Summer Sun Lucky Stars." Cinematographers: Arthur Wong Ngok-tai, Johnny Koo Kwok-wah; Art Director: Eddie Ma Poon-chiu; Music: Anders Nelsson; Writer: Barry Wong Ping-yiu; Action Direction: Sammo Hung Stuntmen Association, Yuen Biao, Lam Ching-ying, Yuen Wah, Chin Kar-lok; Producer-Director: Sammo Hung Kam-po. Cast: Sammo Hung Kam-po (Kidstuff), Jackie Chan (Muscles), Yuen Biao (Fung), Eric Tsang Chi-wai (Roundhead), Richard Ng Yiu-hon (Sandy), Stanley Fung Shui-fan (Rawhide), Miu Kiu-wai (Pagoda), Rosamund Kwan Chi-lam (Wang Yi-ching), Sibelle Hu Hui-chung (Woo Ba-wah), John Sham Kin-fun (Wormgrass), James Tien Chun (Lau), Anthony Chan Yau (Lotta), Kara Hui Ying-hung (Tour Girl), Sandra Ng Kwan-yu (Tour Girl), Season Ma Si-san (Tour Girl), Chung Fat (Assassin with Moustache), Richard Norton (Caucasian Assassin), Yasuaki Kurota (Japanese Assassin), Charlie Chin Hsiang-lin (Herb), Cho Tat-wah (Tsao), Michelle Yeoh Chu-kheng (Judo Teacher), Wu Ma (Black Magic Teacher), Billy Lau Nam-kwong (Play Director), Dick Wei (Thug), Phillip Ko Fei (Thug), Lau Kar-wing (Thug), Lee Hoi-sang (Thug), Melvin Wong Kam-sun (Ma). Dolby Digital (DVD only). 1.85:1. VHS: Tai Seng. Import LD: Media Asia. Import DVD: Universe. 94 minutes.

The third entry in the *ng fuk sing* series finds Kidstuff and the gang on vacation in Thailand for a little R & R, courtesy of the HK police department. Along to keep an eye on the boys, Chief Inspector Woo receives orders to obtain a list of drug traffickers from police informant Ma. However, before Ma can turn over the list, he is murdered by three assassins in the employ of a Thai druglord. With his dying breath, Ma tells Woo that he mailed the list to his friend Wang Yi-ching back in HK. Meanwhile, Muscles, Fung, and an associate (played by Andy Lau) are leaning on Lau, a local drug kingpin, who just happens to be the target of the same killers that liquidated Ma. When the murderers are able to eliminate Lau, Muscles and Fung aid the lucky stars in protecting Yi-ching.

The omnipresent sexual humor is especially tiresome this time out, but some solid action and a multitude of Golden Harvest stars make this worth the watch. Jackie Chan, Yuen Biao, and Andy Lau apprehend Dick Wei, Phillip Ko, Lau Kar-wing, and a dozen henchmen in an exciting battle, while Chan and Yuen later team up with Sammo Hung to give the contract killers a good thrashing (Hung makes creative use of tennis rackets to ward off Yasuaki Kurota's deadly *sais*). A sequence in which Rosamund Kwan evades one of the killers by pretending to be blind would be restaged by Carina Lau Kar-ling's character in Wellson Chin Sing-wai's **Naughty Boys**, a Golden Harvest production that followed the next year. In addition to the formidable line-up listed above, a couple dozen more stars can be spotted during the end crawl. **Lucky Stars Go Places** came next.

1029. Twist

(1995; Magnum/Uniden Investments) ★: 3/10. *Chaak wong* (Cantonese), *Zei wang* (Mandarin): "Thief King." Cinematographer: Ko Chiu-lam; Art Director: Raymond Lee King-man; Music: Wong Bong; Writers: Law Kam-fai, To Chi-kit; Action Director: Yee Tin-hung; Producer-Director: Danny Lee Sau-yin. Cast: Danny Lee Sau-yin (Lee Tin-kin), Simon Yam Tat-wah (John Yam Ka-wah), Suki Kwan Sau-mei (Ann Kwan Oi-ling), Michael Chow Man-kin (Michael Lam, aka "Doctor Lam"), Parkman Wong Pak-man (Man), Emily Kwan Bo-wai (May), Fan Siu-wong (Smarty), Melvin Wong Kam-sun (Melvin), Eric Kei Kar-fat (Eric Kei), Shing Fui-on (Mao Dong), Tommy Wong Kwong-leung (Mao Xi), Lau Siu-ming (Chan), Jamie Luk Kim-ming (Third Mao Brother). 1.85:1. VHS: Tai Seng. Import LD/VCD: Star Entertainment. 92 minutes.

This Category III rated Danny Lee police thriller is meant to be an outrageous send-up of the genre, but it is far too broad and simple-minded to work. Slick armored car thief John Yam makes off with $170 million using inside information provided by his girlfriend Ann Kwan. Thanks to various slip-ups by his partners, the Organized Crime and Triad Bureau is able to pick up Yam's trail, but he constantly leaves them looking like fools. When they do finally arrest and detain the pair, OCTB is unable to get their partners to testify against them or get the witnesses to conclusively identify them. Only able to keep Yam and Kwan for 48 hours under HK law, the police resort to increasingly desperate measures to obtain a confession before time runs out. Meanwhile, Yam and his lawyer exploit every loophole in the system.

Twist starts off like **Organized Crime and Triad Bureau**, albeit with a much more straightforward case and blander direction. However, from the time that the interrogations start, the proceedings become so cartoonishly exaggerated that the film's satirical intent is nullified. Unable to use "conventional" methods of torture because they will leave marks, the team resorts to hosedowns, tooth drilling, high-pressure enemas, and, ultimately, a condom filled with ice cubes. By this point, our sympathies have shifted from the law enforcers to the law breakers, and Lee's gleeful depiction of these sequences (during the condom bit the camera focuses on Kwan's jiggling breasts from both high and low angles) makes you wonder about his political sympathies. One could argue that the shift in audience favor is by design and a clever ploy to show the thin line between the two opponents, but such a view is showing far more imagination than the screenwriters did. This is strictly for those who are only interested in HK cinema for its excesses.

Two Champions of Death *see* **Two Champions of Shaolin**

1030. Two Champions of Shaolin

(1980; Shaw Brothers) ★: 5/10. *Siu lam yue mo dong* (Cantonese), *Shao lin yu wu dang* (Mandarin): "Shaolin and Wu Tang." Cinematographer: Tsao Hui-chi; Art Director: Johnson Tsao; Music: Not Original; Writers: Ngai Hong, Chang Cheh; Producer: Mona Fong Yat-wah; Action Directors: Phillip Kwok Tsui, Lu Feng, Chiang Sheng; Director: Chang Cheh. Cast: Lo Mang (Tung Chien-chen), Chin Siu-ho (Wei Sing-hung), Sun Chien (Chin Tai-lei), Chiang Sheng (Hu Wei-chen), Cho Tat-wah (Feng Te). 2.35:1. VHS: Southgate (Dubbed). 105 minutes. Also known as **Two Champions of Death** (US title).

A lesser effort from veteran director Chang Cheh, this period entry delivers fine martial arts but is run-of-the-mill in all other respects. Tung Chien-chen (aka "The Shaolin Hercules") was born a Manchu but was accepted at Shaolin Temple regardless because his father and mother were murdered by Manchurians. Shaolin is presently at war with the Wu Tang clan, a significant problem as the Wu Tangs are affiliated with the ruling Chings. When Tung is injured by some Wu Tang men, he is given refuge at the home of knife-throwing experts Chin Tai-lei and his sister Pei. They instruct the guest in their art, and, teaming up with fellow Shaolin fighter Hu Wei-chen, Tung is able to take revenge on his attackers. Pei and Tung marry but Wu Tang forces invade the wedding reception, capturing Tung and killing Pei and Tai-lei. However, Shaolin has an important ally in the form of Wu Tang man Wei Sing-hung, who opposes his clan's alliance with the Chings.

This lacks the humor and dramatic resonance of Chang Cheh's best works, and the story proceeds in such a linear fashion that there is little in the way of suspense or intrigue here either. The kung fu is fine but without an absorbing plot to contain them, the various setpieces are only interesting as displays of technique. Character names above are from the English version.

1031. The Ultimate Vampire

(1991; Eagle Film Production Co.) ★: 7/10. *Geung si ji juen* (Cantonese), *Jiang shi zhi zun* (Mandarin): "Stiff Corpse Extreme Respect." Cinematographer: Tony Miu Kin-fai; Art Director: Danny Yuen Ching-yeung; Music: Phil Chan Fei-lap; Writer: Lo Tse-chi; Producers: Wong Ying, Leung Wai-fan, Mak Tak; Action Director: Lau Chau-sang; Director: Andrew Lau Wai-keung. Cast: Lam Ching-ying (Lin Chiu), Chin Siu-ho (Charleson), Ronald Wong Pan (Wanchi), Carrie Ng Kar-lai (Li), Lau Shun (Shek Kin), Wong Chi-yeung (Shek's Pupil), Ku Feng (Chin), Joanna Chan Pui-san (Mary). 1.85:1. VHS: Tai Seng. Import LD/VCD: Ocean Shores. 88 minutes.

Lunar July is the month of ghosts in Chinese mythology, and on the 15th day of that month the gates of Hell open and stray ghosts can wander out. This occurrence is an important one for Lin Chiu, as he is the authorized printer of the Hell Bank Notes ghosts use as currency in the Netherworld. As part of their earthly daytrip, the ghosts get to attend their own private Peking Opera performance, during which they are monitored by the Hell Police. Lin's bumbling assistants Charleson and Wanchi attend the show, meeting up with a Tinkerbell-like sprite named Li. In order to help her escape her confines, they incapacitate the Hell Cops, allowing all the ghosts to disperse. Desperate to rectify this foul-up, Lin enlists help from Shek Kin, a powerful but disreputable magician. The spirits are corralled and turned over to the Hell Police, who force Lin to burn them a huge amount of Hell currency to keep the incident quiet. Meanwhile, Shek's pupil performs a spell allowing him to leave his body so that he can seduce a girl he has designs on. As a prank, Charleson and Wanchi hide his uninhabited body, only to have it be chewed apart by wild dogs. Eager for revenge, Shek makes Lin and his assistants procure a "coffin mushroom," which can only be obtained by kissing a slumbering vampire. Predictable complications ensue, as a group of hopping vampires are accidentally awakened and must be dealt with. When this fails to dispatch his enemies, Shek revives his increasingly monstrous apprentice, who proceeds to emulate Western bloodsuckers and drains several villagers. Lin is able to weaken the creature with a splash of the debilitating "Hundred Precious Soup" (the ingredients of which include a variety of vegetables and a portion of dog shit). Shek pretends to kill the monster but brings him back yet again, this time with an army of the undead to assist.

Arguably the best of the **Mr. Vampire** spinoffs, **The Ultimate Vampire** didn't have a lot in its production coffers (the work of the Hell Police perhaps?) but works wonderfully all the same, anchored by another terrific performance from the underappreciated Lam Ching-ying. The opticals are simple and the camera tricks date back to the beginning of the century, but director Andrew Lau knows what his audience wants and delivers the goods with energy and an invigorating sense of fun. Over the course of 88 minutes, jaded Western horror addicts can learn all about how important magic staples like "Pungent Tofu," "Hundred Precious Soup," "Coffin Mushrooms," and "Trunk Tactics" are in repelling evil, not to mention the benefits to be gained from eating mud. The end credits include outtakes which demonstrate that the often ballet-like grace onscreen isn't always captured on the first take, with the extensive wirework usually the main cause.

Ultra Force *see* **Killer Angels**
Ultra Force 2 *see* **Devil Hunters**

1032. The Umbrella Story

(1995; Golden Harvest/Golden Centro Pictures/Ko Chi Sum Films) ★: 6/10. *Yan gan yau ching* (Cantonese), *Ren jian you qing* (Mandarin): "Humanity Has Love." Cinematographer: Sander Lee Kar-ko; Art Directors: Bill Lui Cho-hung, Ring Lee Chi-keung, Ken Chiu Kin-san; Music: Anthony Lee Hon-kam, Marco Wan Ho-kit; Writer: Raymond To Kwok-wai; Producer-Director: Clifton Ko Chi-sum. Cast: Law Koon-lan (Mrs. Leung), Alice Lau Ar-lai (Miss Chan), Chow Chi-fai (Leung So), So Yuk-wah, Kiu Hon-man, Tse Kwan-ho. 1.85:1. VHS: Tai Seng. Import LD/VCD: Mei Ah. 98 minutes.

The one hundred year history of the Leung So Kee umbrella shop is traced in this insignificant put pleasant comedy-drama. Opening in the late 19th century, the film shows how Leung So ended up with his first foreign umbrella and decided to switch from selling cooking utensils to repairing and manufacturing umbrellas. Offering a lifetime guarantee, his shop is an instant success. Unfortunately, since steel ribs don't damage easily and it doesn't rain every day, business becomes sporadic and unpredictable. The Leungs run into some trouble initially when they try to marry off eldest son Tin-chi to the daughter of the local fireworks maker. However, the two are finally wed and become an ideal couple. Everyone's welfare becomes a concern when the Japanese army invades during the late '30s, but dimwitted younger brother Tin-yau drops a real bomb when he comes home from Shanghai with a Mandarin-speaking bride. Master Leung decides to expand by opening additional branches of the business, sending Tin-chi to Macau and Tin-yau to Hong Kong. In the years following WWII, the company faces serious competition in the form of cheap, mass-produced Japanese umbrellas but remains dedicated to the sort of hand crafted excellence that Leung So always insisted on.

Essentially a collection of vignettes, **The Umbrella Story** has rich, pleasing characters and that helps more than anything to win the viewer over. Taking a cue from **Forrest Gump**, characters are digitally inserted into vintage footage of HK and also share the screen with notables like Chiang Kai-shek and a really young Bruce Lee. However, these bits are mostly technically unconvincing and little more than a distraction in a narrative that is sketchy to begin with.

1033. Undeclared War

(1990; Cinema City/Cinema Capital Entertainment) ★: 5/10. *Sing jin fung wan* (Cantonese), *Sheng zhan feng yan* (Mandarin): "Holy War Turbulence." Cinematographer: Lau Hung-chuen; Art Director: Bill Lui Cho-hung; Music: Noel Quinlan; Writers: Timothy R. Long, Nam Yin, Louis Roth, Deborah Grant; Action Director: Chris Lee Kin-sang; Producer-Director: Ringo Lam Ling-tung. Cast: Peter Liapis (Gary Redner), Danny Lee Sau-yin (Inspector Bong), Vernon Wells (Hannibal), Rosamund Kwan Chi-lam (Ann Chang), Olivia Hussey (Rebecca Ecke), Tommy Wong Kwong-leung (Lieutenant Tang), Dean Harrington (Callahan), Louis Roth (Vladovich), Victor Hon Kwan (Arms Dealer), Feng Sing (Tiger), David Hedison (US Ambassador). 2.35:1. VHS: Imperial. Import LD: Golden Cinema City. 103 minutes.

Cinema City tried to crack the international market with this elaborate action thriller that mixes HK stars with third-string imported actors and offers an authentic combination of English and Cantonese dialogue. The end result is disappointingly routine, playing out like so many undistinguished Western genre films and giving director Ringo Lam no opportunities to display any of his trademark touches. After an American ambassador and his family are murdered by the World Liberation Army terrorist group (which is under the leadership of the notorious assassin "Hannibal"), belligerent CIA agent Gary Redner strikes up an uneasy alliance with HK cop Bong to put an end to the group's reign of terror. After murdering his nominal partner, Hannibal assumes leadership of the W.L.A. and plans to blow up the American Business Delegation meeting in HK.

While competently made, **Undeclared War** has little to distinguish it, aside from some attractive location work in HK, China, and Poland. Liapis is one of the least appealing heroes in memory, but Danny Lee remains engaging, in spite of the largely insipid dialogue he is forced to mouth. In fact, for many viewers, the major attraction here will be the opportunity to hear Lee, Rosamund Kwan, Tommy Wong, and Victor Hon speaking English. The film's poor showing in HK and inability to get a theatrical release in America was no doubt a contributing factor in Cinema City's eventual demise.

Under Police Protection *see* **Princess Madam**

1034. The Underground Banker

(1994; Wong Jing's Workshop) ★: 5/10. *Heung Gong on ji kap huet gwai lei wong* (Cantonese), *Xiang Gang qi an zhi xi xue gui li wang* (Mandarin): "Hong Kong Strange Case: The Bloodsucking Wealthy King." Cinematographer: Tony Miu Kin-fai; Art Director: Wu Ching-mo; Music: Marco Wan Ho-kit; Writer: Tsui Tat-cho; Producer: Wong Jing; Action Director: Lee Chung-chi; Director: Bosco Lam Hing-lung. Cast: Anthony Wong Chau-sang (Tong Chi-ming), Wong Chi-yeung (Canner), Lawrence Ng Kai-wah (Lam Kuo-jen), William Ho Kar-kui (Black Chao). 1.85:1. VHS: Tai Seng. Import LD/VCD: Mei Ah. 91 minutes. Also known as **Physical Weapon**.

This Category III outing is a typically uneven mixture of base humor and graphic carnage, with something to offend just about everyone. Regardless, it has a bit more going for it than most and may please those with the stomach for this type of brazen excess. Truck driver Tong Chi-ming has not had a good day: First he is harassed by triads, and then a highrise jumper splatters herself (and Tong's lunch) right before his eyes. However, things are looking up now that his application for public housing has finally been approved and he can move his family out of the flea trap they currently reside in. However, Tong's troubles are actually just starting: His new neighbor is none other than "reformed" serial killer Lam Kuo-jen (Lawrence Ng as an amusing caricature of the infamous, real-life murderer played by Simon Yam in **Dr. Lamb**), and his wife Chun has secretly accumulated a huge debt and must work as a hooker for gangsters in order to make even a dent in her interest payments. Tong sells his truck and everything else he has to pay back the loan, but the money is stolen and triads set fire to his apartment, killing Chun and horribly disfiguring his young son. Humiliated and at the end of his rope, Tong sets out for revenge...with a little help from his understanding friend next door.

While it showcases all of the customary exploitation elements (bracketed by the undisguised misogyny prevalent in Asian exploitation films) in the expected fashion, the film's warped sense of humor is more appreciable than that found in similar items like **The Untold Story** (which is made fun of here) and **Run and Kill**. You know there is demented genius at work when a viewer cannot help but cheer on a serial killer as he blinds and/or disembowels gangsters while the protagonist hacks the rest apart with meat cleavers. The final sequence, which finds the lead villain on the receiving end of a very painful comeuppance, is gallows comedy taken to its darkest shade of black.

1035. Underground Express

(1990; Golden Harvest/Johnny Mak Production) ★: 3/10. *Saang gang chi shi ti sze chi dei ha tung do* (Cantonese), *Sheng gong qi shi di si ji di xia tong dao* (Mandarin): "Hong Kong Flag Soldier Part 4: Underground Path." Cinematographer: Eric Chu Kwok-fai; Art Director: Dominique Lo Kar-yiu; Music: Joseph Chan Wing-leung; Writers: Johnny Mak Dong-hung, Stephen Siu Yeuk-yuen; Producer: Stephen Siu Yeuk-yuen; Action Director: Chin Yuet-sang; Director: Michael Mak Dong-kit. Cast: Elvis Tsui Kam-kong (Bing), Chen Jing (Doggy), Jacqueline Ng Suet-man (Wong Siu-wai), Frankie Chin Chi-leung (Shik). 1.85:1. VHS: Tai Seng. 100 minutes. Also known as **Long Arm of the Law IV**.

One of the more novel of the Mak Brothers' heroic gangster thrillers, this outing concerns events that might have transpired in the wake of the Mainland government's violent crackdown against protesting students in June of 1989. Pro-democracy concerns hire a triad gang to smuggle wanted student leaders across the border into HK. The trip is filled with danger, as overzealous security men threaten to detain and hand the fugitives over to their superiors unless they are bribed accordingly. When the border is closed before they can make their escape, the gangsters must solicit help from some villagers, using their smuggling boat to flee. They finally manage to reach HK, but a vicious, top-ranking Communist officer travels to the colony and illegally pursues them there. The gang finds themselves caught between the Mainland government and the HK police, who are after them for their previous crimes.

While the foundation is solid, the characters and situations are too simplistic to generate much interest, and the final reel (which finds the triads taking on a tanker filled with Red Army soldiers) is painfully ridiculous.

1036. The Unmatchable Match

(1990; Magnum) ★: 6/10. *Fung yue tung lo* (Cantonese), *Fung yu tong lu* (Mandarin): "Wind Rain Same Road." Cinematographers: Andrew Lau Wai-keung, Tony Miu Kin-fai; Art Directors: Andy Lee Yiu-kwong; Music: Phil Chan Fei-lap; Writers: Parkman Wong Pak-man, James Fung Shui-hung, Andy Liu Chi-keung; Producer: Danny Lee Sau-yin; Action Director: Sam Wong Ming-sing, James Ha Chim-see; Director: Parkman Wong Pak-man. Cast: Stephen Chiau Sing-chi (Cheung Lon, aka "Cockroach"), Michael Chan Wai-man (Fei), Vivian Chow Wei-man (Mandy), Shing Fui-on (Guts), Ricky Yee Fan-wai (Ricky), Danny Lee Sau-yin (Inspector Lee), Kwan Hoi-shan (Uncle Kin), Wong Chi-yeung (Mandy's Cousin). 1.85:1. VHS: Tai Seng. Import LD: Golden Cinema City. Import VCD/DVD: Universe. 98 minutes.

A fast paced and reasonably amusing buddy comedy patterned after **48 Hrs.**, this pairs up a pre-superstardom Stephen Chiau with veteran tough guy Michael Chan. Undercover cop Cheung Lon is ordered to get close to Fei, a triad boss on the run after a botched deal involving hot diamonds. They soon find themselves on the run, not only from the hoods who stole the stones, but from another group who blames Fei for the death of their leader. In asides that do little to enhance the narrative, both men experience trouble with their better halves: Cheung cannot tell bartender Mandy about his undercover assignment, and Fei yearns for the wife who walked out on him five years earlier. Naturally, as the two escape from various scrapes, they develop a friendship, making Cheung's job all the more difficult.

The plot proceeds strictly by the book, but Chiau and Chan (the latter quite appealing in a rare lead role) are an effective team and help one to forgive the narrative weaknesses. There are well-staged action setpieces sprinkled throughout, the best being a climactic gun battle in a dilapidated apartment building.

1037. The Untold Story

(1993; Uniden Investment) ★: 3/10. *Baat sin faan dim chi yan yuk cha siu baau* (Cantonese), *Ba xian fan dian zhi ren rou cha shao bao* (Mandarin): "The Eight Immortals Restaurant's BBQ Human Pork Buns." Cinematographer: Rudolf Chiu Wai-kei; Art Director: Horace Ma Kwong-wing; Music: Wong Bong; Writer: Law Kam-fai; Producer: Danny Lee Sau-yin; Director: Herman Yau Lai-to. Cast: Anthony Wong Chau-sang (Wong Chi-hang/Chan Chi-leung), Danny Lee Sau-yin (Inspector Lee), Emily Kwan Bo-wai (Bo), Julie Lee Wah-yuet (Pearl), Shing Fui-on (Cheng Poon). 1.85:1. VHS/LD/DVD: Tai Seng (Director's cut; remastered for the English market). Import LD: Golden Cinema City (Cut version). 96 minutes (Director's cut).

The most infamous entry in the (thankfully) short-lived trend of HK "True Crime" films, **The Untold Story** is based on a real-life murder case in Macau during the mid–80s. Anthony Wong stars as psychopath Wong Chi-hang, who flees HK in 1976 after burning alive a Mahjong player who owed him money. Ten years later in Macau, a bag of severed limbs washes up on a beach. The bumbling local police (headed up by the film's producer, Danny Lee) launch an investigation which eventually leads them to The Eight Immortals Restaurant, which Wong just happens to run. After being tortured and beaten repeatedly by both the police and his fellow prisoners, Wong confesses that he acquired the eatery by slaughtering the owner and his family. Later, he murdered and dismembered his cook (disposing of the evidence by using his remains to make pork buns), as well as a female employee, in order to cover his tracks.

Nothing is out of bounds in this film, and director Herman Yau revels in presenting all manner of grossout devices: rotting limbs, splattering blood, interrogation torture, urine drinking, people unknowingly munching on human flesh…you name it. In an interesting parallel to **The Silence of the Lambs**, Wong won the Best Actor prize at the HK Film Awards for his performance here, though he has done better work in mainstream roles and the film itself is never better than competent. Like the other "True Crime" films, there is really no point to the enterprise other than to serve as a catalogue of gory atrocities mixed with inane black humor, making this one strictly for sleaze fans. In light of the film's success, Wong and Yau reteamed for two other Category III thrillers: the almost respectable **Taxi Hunter** (1993) and the revolting **Ebola Syndrome** (1996), the latter a virtual remake of this film. Tai Seng's English market version contains some extra carnage that was snipped from HK prints by local censors and is definitely not for those with weak stomachs (in other words, if you think it probably isn't a good idea for you to watch it, then it isn't). **The Untold Story II** (which features Anthony Wong as a cop and Paulyn Suen Kai-kwun as the killer) followed in 1998. Bearing no connection to this film, it is somewhat more tasteful but no more effective.

1038. Usurpers of Emperor's Power

[*sic*] (1983; Shaw Brothers) ★: 5/10. *Fung san gip* (Cantonese), *Feng shen jie* (Mandarin): "Mystical Thief of Feudal Titles." Cinematographer: Nico Wong Man-wan; Art Director: Ho Kim-seng; Music: Not Original; Writer: Shaw's Writing Team; Producer: Mona Fong Yatwah; Action Directors: Wong Pui-kei, Yuen Bun, Yuen Wah; Director: Wah San. Cast: Lau Wing, Lau Suet-wah (Hsiang Ling), Lung Tin-cheung, Max Mok Siuchung (Prince Te Chao), Lam Wai (Soldier). 2.35:1. VHS: World Video (Poor Subtitles). Import LD: Ocean Shores (Poor Subtitles). 89 minutes.

This is yet another case where a widescreen Shaw Brothers epic has been released on video with the sides of the picture lopped off, making it extremely difficult for English-speaking viewers to read the subtitles and follow the plot. When Prince Kuang-yi and his men rape a young woman, they have a painter capture the event for posterity. The picture falls into the hands of the emperor, who proceeds to castigate the prince for his crime. In the meantime, Prince Te Chao and others who share his beliefs have enlisted the aid of assassin Li Lang to eliminate Kuang-yi. Te stages his own death as part of a plan to frame Kuang-yi and his supporters, and goes into hiding on Tiger Mountain with Li and his followers. Te is soon drugged and kidnapped by Kuang-yi's men, but Li is able to get the stricken prince away from his assailants before he can be taken off the mountain. However, the poison administered to Te has left him with the mind of a child, and Li soon discovers that one of his principal allies is not what he seems.

The customary Shaw visuals and production values are in place but the combat is choppy and would probably be difficult to follow, even if the entire frame was visible. That, coupled with the difficulty one has in appreciating anything beyond the major themes in the story, makes this best passed over until it is presented on video at its proper dimensions.

1039. Vampire Buster

(1989; In-Gear Film Production Co./Foo Ong Film) ★: 6/10. *Juk gwai daai si* (Cantonese), *Zhuo gui da shi* (Mandarin): "Capture Ghost, Great Master." Cinematographers: Tom Lau Moon-tong, Raymond Lam Fai-tai, Peter Ngor Chi-kwan; Art Director: Raymond Lee King-man; Music: Anders Nelsson; Writers: Barry Wong Ping-yiu, Yuen Kai-chi, Wong Jing; Producer: Rover Tang Kwong-chow; Action Directors: Stephen Tung Wai, Benz Kong To-hoi; Directors: Stanley Siu Kar-wing, Norman Law Man. Cast: Kent Cheng Chuk-see (Cheung Sap-yat), Jacky Cheung Hok-yau (Jackie), Stanley Fung Shui-fan (Councillor Stephen Kay), Nat Chan Pak-cheung (Chan), Elsie Chan Yik-si (Cat), Angile Leung Wan-yui (Mable), Shum Wai (Man Betting on Horse Race), Manfred Wong (Bo), Austin Wai Tin-chi (Cheung's Ancestor). 1.85:1. VHS: World Video. Import LD: Ocean Shores. 93 minutes.

Councillor Stephen Kay buys an antique vase at a charity auction, not realizing that the item contains an evil spirit. Imprisoned inside for hundreds of years, the creature is accidentally released by a phony spiritualist and proceeds to possess Kay. Arriving from China to save the day is Taoist master Cheung Sap-yat, whose ancestor was the priest who originally caught the demon. Unfortunately, all of Kay's relatives think that Cheung is crazy, making his task even more difficult. The creature leaves Kay and enters into his daughter, proceeding to wreak havoc in a hospital. To make matters worse, the police arrest Cheung and hold him as an illegal immigrant, leaving it up to Kay and his family to vanquish the evil.

While it adheres to genre conventions, **Vampire Buster** is a bit darker than most films of this type and benefits from a plethora of high-flying action and terrific stuntwork. Kent Cheng steals the show as the determined priest who is incredibly limber for his size.

1040. Vampire Family

(1993; Chang-Hong Channel Film & Video Co.) ★: 2/10. *Yut uk siu ah gwai* (Cantonese), *Yi wu shao ya gui* (Mandarin): "A House of Whistling Tooth Ghosts." Cinematographer: Cheung Tung-leung; Art Director: Cyrus Ho Kim-hung; Music: Lam Man-chung, Lam Chi-hang; Writer: Ella Chan Bo-wah; Producer: Hui Pui-yung; Action Director: Lam Manchung; Directors: Eric Tsang Chi-wai, Dick Cho Kin-nam. Cast: Eric Tsang Chiwai (Chung-ping Vamp), Jimmy Lin Chiying (David Vamp), Sandra Ng Kwan-yu (Chap-lay Vamp), Dicky Cheung Wai-kin (Delon), Athena Chu Yan (Julie May Chu), Alvina Kong Yan-yin (Tong Vamp), Michael Chow Man-kin (Wolf), Leung Kar-yan (Master Man Vamp). 1.85:1. VHS: Tai Seng. Import LD/VCD: Star Entertainment. 88 minutes.

This obnoxious comedy concerns The Vamps, a brood of (you guessed it) vampires who are gradually losing their powers with each successive generation. Bloodsuckers of the Western variety, the family lives a happy if unconventional existence (they can walk around in the daylight and no longer drink human blood). The most normal member is son David, an aspiring surgeon who develops a crush on pretty hospital worker Julie. Unfortunately, like his sister, David will sprout fangs whenever he gets sexually excited, something he is hard-pressed to explain to Julie.

The premise could allow for some reasonably amusing riffs on horror movie cliches but is simply used as window dressing for what is, in reality, just another lame vehicle for pretty boy pop star Jimmy Lin. Most of the comedy is left to Dicky Cheung, the poor man's Stephen Chiau Singchi, who relies on verbal jests that mostly do not translate and lame sight gags that do not generate so much as a smirk, let alone a chuckle. Eric Tsang, Sandra Ng, Alvina Kong, Leung Kar-yan, and Michael Chow (playing The Vamp's butler, who is half man and half wolf) mug and ham it up like there is no tomorrow, but with no decent material to work from, they are unable to keep this dud afloat.

1041. Vampire Settle (*sic*) on Police Camp

(1990) ★: 6/10. *Yat mei do goo* (Cantonese), *Yi mei dao gu* (Mandarin): "One Eyebrow Taoist Nun." Cinematographer: Cheung Yiu-cho; Art Director: Lee Yuk-chan;

Music: Wong Chi-hung; Writers: Chan Wah, Chan Wai-chi; Producers: Chung Kam-kwai, Ng Kan-yan; Action Directors: Hsiao Hou, Siu Pang, Pan Ma-chai; Director: Chen Chi-hua. Cast: Sandra Ng Kwan-yu (Madam Lee), Alvina Kong Yan-yin (Ma Siao-ling), Billy Lau Nam-kwong (Woodpecker), Angile Leung Wan-yui (Lung Fei-fung), Alex To Tak-wai, (Wong), Charlie Cho Cha-lei (Chao), Eddy Ko Hung (Chan), Woo Fung (Tong), Yip Wing-cho (Hwa). 1.85:1. VHS: World Video. Import LD/VCD: Mei Ah. Import DVD: Widesight. 86 minutes.

One of the best of the "Police Academy Meets the Monsters" hybrids inspired by **Haunted Cop Shop**, this lively outing finds a quartet of ghosts haunting police instructor Chan as retribution for the murderous acts of a distant ancestor. Following instructions received from a wizard, suitable male and female candidates are chosen from the rank and file. These recruits then spend their days learning all of the appropriate offensive and defensive stances, and their nights partying and playing practical jokes. There is the usual collection of sophomoric sex gags, drinking, dancing, and kung fu (of both the earthbound and magic variety), as well as some decidedly unusual ways to deal with the undead (e.g. possession by a ghost can be thwarted by placing a pair of soiled panties on the victim's head!). The climactic battle features every weapon in the Taoist arsenal, and Sandra Ng gets to play the female equivalent of Lam Ching-ying's ever-popular "One Eyebrow Priest" character.

As with many HK films, the presence of ghosts and the supernatural is taken entirely for granted (when Chan first reports the problem to his British superior, the man simply takes his word for it and orders him to vanquish the ghosts), a refreshing change from Western cinema, which always serves up at least one sceptic. *Vampire Settle on Police Camp* is fast moving fun from veteran director Chen (who helmed some of Jackie Chan's early work) that is a good bet for both newcomers and completists.

1042. Vampire vs. Vampire

(1989; Golden Harvest/Paragon Films) ★: 7/10. *Yat mei do yan* (Cantonese), *Yi mei dao ren* (Mandarin): "One Eyebrow Taoist." Cinematographer: Cho On-sun; Art Director: Ho Kim-seng; Music: The Melody Bank; Writers: Si Mei-yee, Sam Chi-leung, Chan Kam-cheung; Producer: Chua Lam; Action Directors: Stephen Tung Wai, Lee Chi-kit; Director: Lam Ching-ying. Cast: Lam Ching-ying (The One Eyebrow Priest), Chin Siu-ho (Ho), Lui Fong (Fong), Billy Lau Nam-kwong (The Captain), Sandra Ng Kwan-yu (The Captain's Cousin), Maria Cordero (Mother Superior), Regina Kent (Nun), Joanna Chan Pui-san (Nun), Chen Jing (Pimp). 1.85:1. Import LD: Mei Ah. Import VCD: Mei Ah, Mega Star. 86 minutes. Also known as **The One Eyebrow Priest**.

After starring in numerous horror comedies, Lam Ching-ying tries his hand at directing one, and the result is among the best in this subgenre. This time out, The One Eyebrow Priest and his pupils must rescue the local villagers when a nest of bats is discovered nearby. The creatures have poisoned the local water supply, and when the priest seeks out an alternate source, the bats secretly move his location marker. Consequently, the workmen then unearth the body of a powerful caucasian vampire. After feasting on blood, the creature lays siege to the countryside, and the priest's Eastern magic proves to be ineffectual against it. He is aided and abetted by a group of Chinese Catholic nuns and a tame baby *gyonsi* (who, unlike his annoying counterpart in **Mr. Vampire II**, is an imaginative asset to the story) the priest keeps around the house.

Lam's first and best stint behind the camera, this is a wonderful, fast paced combination of Chinese horror conventions and Western gothic thrills. While there are numerous instances of acrobatic action, the climactic duel between Lam and the creature in a forest at the stroke of midnight is edge-of-your-seat exciting!

1043. Vampire's Breakfast

(1987; Cinema City Co./Dennis Yu Film Production Co.) ★: 5/10. *Ling san maan chaan* (Cantonese), *Ling chen wan can* (Mandarin): "Before Dawn Supper." Cinematographers: Gary Ho Bo-yiu, Arthur Wong Ngok-tai; Art Director: Wong Chong-wah; Music: Phil Chan Fei-lap; Writer: Chan Hing-ka; Producer: Dennis Yu Wan-kong; Action Directors: Law Keung, Tony Leung Siu-hung; Producer: Dennis Yu Wan-kong; Director: Wong Chung. Cast: Kent Cheng Chuk-see (Liao Chi-piao, aka Fat Piao), Emily Chu Bo-yee (Angie Lin), Parkman Wong Pak-man (Inspector Chen), Keith Kwan Chiu-chung (Mao), Wu Ma (The Editor). 1.85:1. VHS: Tai Seng. Import LD: Golden Cinema City. Import VCD: Mega Star. 86 minutes.

This mild horror-comedy bears a number of similarities to the pilot feature for **The Night Stalker**, a short-lived American TV series. While out driving one evening, Angie Lin hits a man with her car, but when she gets out to check on him, he is nowhere to be found. Reporter Fat Piao is following a series of murders where the victims are found with little or no blood left in them. Teaming up with petty thief Mao, Piao discovers a gruesome caucasian ghoul with superhuman abilities draining the local blood bank. When the police arrive and are unable to apprehend the fiend, they try to frame Piao and Mao for the break-in. The former is later able to snap a picture of the monster, but the authorities successfully discredit his story, forcing Piao to try and vanquish the creature on his own.

It's always nice to see excellent character actor Kent Cheng in a lead role, and the atmospheric photography and locales are also a plus. Still, too much of the running time is spent on Piao's romantic pursuit of Angie, and (aside from a brief bit during the climax) there is not much here that one wouldn't find in a typical Western horror thriller.

1044. Velvet Gloves

(1996; Kuo Tai Film Co.) ★: 3/10. *Pik lik fung wong* (Cantonese), *Pi li feng huang* (Mandarin): "Thunder Phoenix." Cinematographer: Wong Fu-hung; Art Director: Wong Chien; Music: Not Original; Writer: Shen Wai; Producer: Chow Nai-sung; Action Directors: Lai Sheng-kuang, Han Chun; Director: Billy Chan Wui-ngai. Cast: Jade Leung Ching (Feng Tin), Zhang Fengyi (Chui Chiang), Farini Cheung Yui-ling (Mindy Li), Eddie Maher (Thug), Chien Pei-pei, Han Chun. 1.85:1. VHS: World Video. Import LD/VCD: Universe. 94 minutes.

The trials and travails of several young women seeking to graduate from a Mainland Special Unit police academy form the basis of this limp action drama (essentially a straight version of **The Inspector Wears Skirts**), which is slim on both plot and excitement. We follow the candidates as they undergo obstacle courses, endurance tests, target practice, and other standard training exercises. The main character is steely Feng Tin, who joined up in order to impress her male chauvinist father. The man took great pride in the accomplishments of his son—a soldier like himself—only to lose him in battle. As her father has never fully recovered from that loss, Tin believes that her success in this endeavour will lift him out of his depression (the English title refers to the keepsake she remembers her brother by). Of course, the whole film is just a lead-in to the climax wherein the graduating students are sent out on their first mission to subdue a gang of heavily-armed hooligans.

The hand-to-hand combat is competently staged but rarely convincing (particularly when the girls are able to easily subdue a mob of construction workers armed with clubs!); even the finale is lackluster. The storyline (what there is of it) is equally feeble, constructed around the sort of cliched situations and cardboard characters one would encounter in the worst TV fodder. And what is an actor the calibre of *Zhang Fengyi* (**Farewell, My Concubine**) doing in this? The Andy Lau vehicle **Proud and Confidence** [*sic*] (which was co-produced by this film's director, Billy Chan) does a somewhat better job with similar material.

1045. Vengeance Is Mine

(1988; D & B Films Co.) ★: 4/10. *Huet yi tin si* (Cantonese), *Xue yi tian shi* (Mandarin): "Blood Covered Angel." Cinematographer: Wilson Chan Pui-kai; Art Director: Eric Lam Yau-sang; Music: Phil Chan Fei-lap; Producer: Stephen Shin Kei-yin; Action Director: Tony Leung Siu-hung; Writer-Director: Lee Chi-ngai. Cast: Rosamund Kwan Chi-lam (Jane Li Su-ching), Derek Yee Tung-sing (Ko Wing-keung), Pat Ha Man-chik (Amy Wong), Kenneth Tong Chun-yip (Pi Kee), Tom Poon Chun-wai (Tom Tam), Kam Hing-yin (Tom's Brother), Ronald Wong Pan (Short Thug). 1.85:1. VHS: Tai Seng. Import LD: Mei Ah. Import VCD: Mega Star. 92 minutes.

Best known for UFO productions like **Doctor Mack** and **Lost and Found**, director Lee Chi-ngai made his directorial debut with this brutal, formulaic rape/revenge thriller. While driving home from work one evening, nurse Jane Li is kidnapped and raped by a gang of car thieves. She is saved from further harm by the intervention of taxi driver Ko. Even though he is willing to act as her witness, the woman refuses to report the attack to police. Three weeks later the hoods turn up again and brutally assault Jane's boyfriend, Tom. During the struggle, Jane accidentally kills one of the attackers but is acquitted during the subsequent court case. However, the police lack sufficient evidence to charge the attackers, and Tom, obeying the wishes of his publicity-shy family, abandons her. Eager to avenge their dead friend, the gang sets their sights not only on Jane but also Ko and Jane's friend Amy, whom they feel are in league with their target.

While it boasts a better grade of talent both in front of and behind the camera, **Vengeance Is Mine** is little more than an upscale version of American exploitation films like **I Spit On Your Grave** (1978) and **Sudden Death** (1985). Offering no insight or fresh thoughts on the subject, the film simply proceeds through the entire catalogue of genre cliches with tiresome predictability. Action director Tony Leung Siu-hung is billed here with the English name "Alex."

1046. The Victim

(1980; Graffon Films Co.) ★: 8/10. *San bat yau gei* (Cantonese), *Shen bu you ji* (Mandarin): "Fate Is Not Determined by Self." Music: Frankie Chan Fan-kei; Writer: Lau Tin-chi; Producer: Wong Fung; Action Director-Director: Sammo Hung Kam-po. Cast: Sammo Hung Kam-po (Chan-wing), Leung Kar-yan (Leung Chun-yau), Fanny Wang (Wen Yuet-yi), Chang Yi (Jo-wing), Peter Chan Lung (Yuet-ming), Chung Fat (Choy Fan-tan), Wilson Tong Wai-shing (Tong), Karl Maka (The Shaolin Abbot). 2.35:1. VHS: Ocean Shores (Dubbed). 93 minutes.

The undisciplined Chan-wing chooses kung fu master Leung Chun-yau to be his new teacher, and the fact that Chun-yau wants nothing to do with him is but a minor bump in the road as far as Chan is concerned. Chun-yau already has enough trouble on his hands: His big brother, Jo-wing, tried to rape Chun-yau's wife, Wen Yuet-yi, on their wedding night. On the run ever since, Chun-yau and Yuet-yi cannot seem to escape an inevitable confrontation between the two siblings. When their father takes ill, the two brothers join him at his bedside as he passes away. Jo-wing takes advantage of the situation to lay a trap for his rival, but Yuet-yi saves her husband's life by pretending to spurn him, under the condition that Jo-wing and his men let Chun-yau live. Devastated, Chun-yau finally agrees to teach Chan-wing his kung fu so that the two may take revenge.

A terrific old school kung fu film, **The Victim** opens on a comic note but grows progressively darker in its second half, though the mood is still lightened by an occasional gag (like when Chan-wing disguises himself as *Dracula* to scare some of Jo-wing's men). The storyline's central mystery (about a killer hired to eliminate Chun-yau) is really no mystery at all, but the climax does serve up an effective twist. Sammo Hung and Leung Kar-yan are at the top of their form here, and the martial arts training sequences and fights are outstanding, putting this far above most independently produced genre films of its era. Yuen Biao, Lam Ching-ying, and Billy Chan Wui-ngai are the assistant martial arts directors, and the latter also has a small role.

1047. Victory

(1994; Tedpoly Films/Newscope Productions) ★: 6/10. *Ching chun foh fa* (Cantonese), *Qing chun huo hua* (Mandarin): "Youthful Spark." Cinematographer: Poon Hang-sang; Art Director: Stanley Cheung Sai-kit; Music: Tree; Writer: Erica Lee Man; Producers: Teddy Robin Kwan, Andy Chin Wing-keung; Action Director-Director: Andy Chin Wing-keung. Cast: Derek Yee Tung-sing (Ma Chi), Carman Lee Yeuk-tung (So Yau-may), Cherie Chan Siu-ha (Spring), Farini Cheung Yui-ling (Gun), Hilary Tsui Ho-yin (Tung), Annabelle Lau Hiu-tung (Wu), Josie Ho Chiu-yee (Disappearance), Ng Ching-ching (Lee Kar-po, aka Broom), Fan Yik-man (Mary Chong). Dolby Stereo. 1.85:1. VHS: Tai Seng. Import LD/VCD: Fitto Mobile. 106 minutes.

The new coach of the Wah Shui University girls volleyball team is a ruthless dictator whose no-nonsense, win-at-all-costs approach is not what his players are used to. When Wah Shui loses a match to a team of extremely tall girls (called "The Devil Women," no less), the coach and some of the players quit and the school chancellor seems ready to close down the team. The girls' only hope is nerdy science teacher Ma Chi, who takes over the coaching duties, despite the fact that he doesn't even know the rules of the sport. However, after reading a few books and watching a few videos, Ma comes up with a way to defeat The Devil Women's seemingly invincible defensive line. In the requisite unnecessary subplot, team captain Yau-may develops a crush on her new coach and gets jealous when Ma runs into an old girlfriend.

A rare example of the HK sports movie, **Victory** adheres to the usual genre formula but is so amiably presented you cannot help but like it, at least a little. Above average music, a terrific Dolby Stereo mix, and excellent cinematography give the matches an extra level of excitement, helping to alleviate the fact that the resolution is never in doubt. Linda Wong Hing-ping sings the very catchy theme song.

1048. Viva Erotica

(1996; Golden Harvest/Film Unlimited/Golden Movies International) ★: 5/10. *Sik ching nam nui* (Cantonese), *Se qing nan nu* (Mandarin): "Sex Man Woman." Cinematographer: Jingle Ma Cho-shing; Art Director: Ringo Fung Kai-fai; Music: Clarence Hui Yuen; Producer: Raymond Chow Man-wai; Writers-Directors: Derek Yee Tung-sing, Law Chi-leung. Cast: Leslie Cheung Kwok-wing (Sing), Karen Mok Man-wai (Sing's Girlfriend), Hsu Chi (Mango), Law Kar-ying (Chung), Elvis Tsui Kam kong (Wah), Paul Chun Pui (Boss Wong), Lau Ching-wan (Derek

Yee), Anthony Wong Chau-sang (Wong). Dolby Digital (DVD only). 1.85:1. VHS: World Video. Import LD/ VCD/DVD: Universe. 99 minutes.

The buzz prior to the release of **Viva Erotica** was almost unparalleled: Derek Yee, acclaimed director of **C'est La Vie, Mon Cherie** and **Full Throttle**, was now going to collaborate with an unknown on *a Category III sex comedy*?! A scant few months away from the handover, the project appeared to be a last ditch attempt by HK filmmakers to churn out a classy adult film with a quality cast before the July 1st return to China and the threat of possible censure. The film that finally did emerge is disheartening: a sporadically witty, seemingly authentic look at the controlled insanity of the HK movie business, hobbled by an ill-conceived storyline and a desire to correspond to audience expectations, two of the sins it pretends to criticize. Sing is an art film director so down on his luck he agrees to make a Category III sex film in order to pay the bills. The situation he walks into recalls both the old Jayne Mansfield movie **The Girl Can't Help It** (1956) and Woody Allen's **Bullets Over Broadway** (1994): The producer is a gangster who will only finance the film if his gorgeous but conspicuously untalented girlfriend has the lead. The struggle to stay true to his own vision while also adhering to the regulations of the genre (unmotivated sex scenes, simplistic plots, overlit cinematography) prove to be both devastating and ultimately therapeutic for Sing, dispelling his cynicism and reawakening his creativity.

The satire that clicks here is actually fairly obvious, from the digs at industry giants Wong Kar-wai and Wong Jing (the latter embodied in a thinly-disguised cameo by Anthony Wong Chau-sang) and the triad influence to the frustrated craftsmen who just want to make the sort of movies that inspired them to be in the business in the first place. Then there is the satire that is *much* too obvious, like Lau Ching-wan's character, a depressed director named *Derek Yee* (whose background contains more than a few similarities to the real man), who throws himself off a building when his latest film bombs! As with analogous Hollywood "Movie Movies," one of the main satirical points here is that the public is so lazy, apathetic, and just plain stupid that it gets precisely the low level of cinema it deserves, a rather spurious stance for a film that is using elementary commercial draws like sex and the Category III rating to sell itself. The sex scenes themselves have the sort of hyper-stylized look of music videos and perfume commercials; they're flashy but not erotic, a grievous drawback here. However, the biggest miscalculation is the inclusion of Sing's relationship with his girlfriend: They make love, she gets jealous, they fight, they get back together again. The scenes between Leslie Cheung and Karen Mok ultimately add nothing other than a central relationship; it is not a factor in the development of Sing or the progression of the storyline. Hsu Chi is ideally cast (and won Best Supporting Actress for her efforts), but in actuality the most memorable performance here is by the reigning king of HK softcore, Elvis Tsui. Embodying a character largely based on himself, he gives a restrained and dignified performance (the sync sound recording allows one to hear his real voice, which is far more gentle than the actor who regularly dubs him) as a family man just trying to make a living in a business that demands him to be something that he is not. What a shame that the writers chose to base **Viva Erotica** around caricatures instead. There are a number of cameos by industry veterans, including directors Joseph Cheung Tung-cho and Teddy Chan Tak-sum, and Vincent Kok Tak-chiu, as well as cinematographers Peter Ngor Chi-kwan, Gigo Lee Chi-hang, and Arthur Wong Ngok-tai. The movie that Leslie Cheung and Law Kar-ying go to see is none other than the infamous **Chinese Torture Chamber Story** by director Bosco Lam Hing-lung, who is credited with creating the story for this film.

1049. Walk In

(1997; Colour Business Entertainment/Nam Yin Production Company) ★: 7/10. *Duet se* (Cantonese), *Duo she* (Mandarin): "Robbing Residence." Cinematographer: Peter Ngor Chi-kwan; Art Director: James Cheung Ying-wah; Music: Mak Chun-hung; Writer: Tsang Kwok-chi; Producer: Nam Yin; Action Directors: Dion Lam Dik-on, Bruce Law Lai-yin; Director: Herman Yau Lai-to. Cast: Danny Lee Sau-yin (Chicken Wong Tai-kit), Jacqueline Wu Chien-lien (Li Yi-wah), Dayo Wong Chi-wah (Tommy Cheung Chi-lik), Yu Li (Laura), Ada Choi Siu-fan (May), Vincent Wan Yeung-ming (Lo Bill), Yvonne Yung Hung (2nd Concubine), Law Koon-lan (Chicken's Wife), Ng Chi-hung (Triad with Cancer), Shing Fui-on (Saur), Frankie Chin Chi-leung (Ah Man). 1.85:1. Import LD/VCD/ DVD: Mei Ah. 101 minutes.

At the stroke of midnight, Lee Yi-wah jumps off the top of a building in front of several dozen witnesses, hits the concrete, then gets up and walks away with nothing more than a split lip. Meanwhile, a gang of criminals trying to rob an office building are interrupted by police. During the subsequent gun battle, one of the perpetrators (stammering simpleton Chicken Wong) and one of the cops (Tommy Cheung) are severely injured, leaving the former a vegetable and the latter a cripple. Cheung's girlfriend Laura remembers that, just before she jumped, Yi-wah said she would be reborn via a secret Taoist method called "walk in." After much convincing, Yi-wah (whose twenty-something body now houses the spirit of a bitter old man and is revered as an almost holy figure because of his/her mystic abilities) agrees to tell Cheung how to undergo the process, which will allow his soul to enter into Wong's comatose shell. Cheung commits suicide at 12 a.m. and the transference is a success, with him taking over Chicken's now-healthy body. However, he also inherits all of the man's problems: premature ejaculation, two different sets of triads out to kill him, gambling debts, and a wife, two mistresses, and a mother who hate him. Then there is also Chicken's bizarre sister, who, when she finds out that her brother now has a much higher I.Q. and far greater confidence, falls in love with him. There is also Laura, who is no longer attracted to Tommy since he is now twenty years older and not nearly as handsome. Finally, there is Chicken himself, whose spirit has started to re-assert itself.

A clever and surprisingly restrained work from the less-than-dependable Herman Yau (**The Untold Story**), **Walk In** starts serious but grows more comedic as it progresses, and the change in tone is handled with more success than is often the case with HK horror-comedies. In light of the intriguing premise and several genuinely funny moments, it is a shame that the narrative falls back on an action finale, though, admittedly, it is not often that you get to see a chase involving double decker buses. Typecast as a cop for so many years, Danny Lee gets a chance to shine in a real-change-of-pace role(s), and Jacqueline Wu also registers in an offbeat part, though one wishes that her character had been afforded more screen time. Singer/actor Emil Chow has an amusing cameo.

1050. Walk on Fire

(1988; Seasonal Film Corporation) ★: 6/10. *Lip ying gai waak* (Cantonese), *Lie yingji hua* (Mandarin): "Hunt Eagle Plan." Cinematographer: Horace Wong Wing-hang; Music: Not Original; Writer: Wong Kar-wai; Producer: Ng See-yuen; Action Director: Tony Leung Siu-hung; Director: Norman Law Man. Cast: Andy Lau Tak-wah (Lau Kwok-wah), Cherie Chung Cho-hung (Miss Chung), Kent Cheng Chuk-see (Tang), Ray Lui Leung-wai (Inspector Li), Dick Wei (Lung), Lau

Siu-ming (Officer Chan), Shum Wai (Chiu, aka "Cuttle Fish"), Maria Cordero (Anti-Drug Squad Officer), Yip Wing-cho (Chan), Big Al (Himself). 1.85:1. VHS: World Video. Import LD: Far East Music. Import VCD: Mei Ah. 104 minutes.

Scripting by future director Wong Kar-wai helps to elevate this cop actioner slightly above the pack. Andy Lau and Ray Lui play brothers working together on the police force. When Lui is murdered by gang leader Dick Wei (as retribution for his killing of the criminal's associates), Lau teams up with Lui's partner (Kent Cheng) and an informer (Cherie Chung). To facilitate the capture of the mobsters, Lau impersonates a jewellery store owner and hires the men to rob it, with the intention of arresting them in the act.

Even without make-up, Chung is too glamorous to be convincing as a junkie, but rotund Kent Cheng gets a good showcase for his comedic talents. The scene where he tries to get methadone for Chung by convincing the workers at a drug therapy clinic that he is a heroin addict is particularly amusing. Everything is not wrapped up neatly at the end, which, for this genre at least, is a welcome bit of innovation. Incidentally, if you happen to see the Far East Music laserdisc version of this, don't be surprised when a *commercial* appears right before the side change! That was a standard practice with this label.

1051. War of the Underworld

(1996; BOB & Partners Company) ★: 4/10. *Hung hing chai chi gong woo daai fung bo* (Cantonese), *Hong xing zai zhi jiang hu da feng bao* (Mandarin): "Hung Hing Guys: Violent Storm in the Underworld." Cinematographer: Yu Kwok-bing; Art Director: Ho Chi-hang; Music: Mak Chun-hung; Writers: Wong Jing, Candy Cheng; Producer: Wong Jing; Action Director: Yuen Bun; Director: Herman Yau Lai-to. Cast: Tony Leung Chiu-wai (Hong Fei), Carman Lee Yeuk-tung (Tong), Jordan Chan Siu-chun (Siu-chun), Ku Feng (Hong Sheng), Simon Lui Yu-yeung (Zhi-wei), Ng Chi-hung (Brother B), Victor Hon Kwan (Lei Bao), Ngai Sing (Scum), Lo Mang (Brother Monster), Spencer Lam Sheung-yee (Mao). 1.85:1. VHS: Tai Seng. Import LD/VCD/DVD: Mei Ah. 96 minutes.

A disappointing entry in the *goo wak jai* craze, this brings together a quality cast and then gives them nothing of interest to do. Set in the Causeway Bay area, the film opens with a shameless plug for **Young and Dangerous 3** via a gangfight that just happens to break out at a theater showing that BOB-produced hit. Hung Hing loudmouth Siu-chun is about to be chopped by a rival tough guy from the Tong Sheng gang named "Scum" (Ngai Sing, sporting a silly blonde wig) when he is saved by the legendary fighter Hong Fei. Siu-chun's sister, Tong, is a reporter, and she becomes obsessed with Fei after he lets her ride with him during an illegal road race. Fei's father, Hong Sheng, is the leader of the Hung Hing gang and wants his son to succeed him, but Fei still blames the old man for the death of his mother and sister. When Sheng suffers a stroke and brain damage, Hung Hing rapidly goes to pieces, resulting in the usual street fights and back stabbing, all captured with more tilted, off-kilter camera angles than the old *Batman* TV series.

One of HK's most dynamic performers, Tony Leung Chiu-wai is completely wasted here, and Jordan Chan is simply going through the motions (albeit with a high energy level) as the film's comic relief. Carman Lee's opening narration draws parallels between the youth gangs of modern times and the heroic swordsmen that inhabit Louis Cha's period adventures, setting one up for an ambitious and original saga. Instead, we get just another cliched scenario that is concerned only with incorporating as many exploitable elements as possible.

Warrior from Shaolin *see* **Carry on Wise Guy**

1052. A Warrior's Tragedy

(1993; Frankie Film Co.) ★: 5/10. *Bin sing long ji* (Cantonese), *Bian cheng lang zi* (Mandarin): "Edge City Wanderer." Cinematographer: Ng Wing-kit; Art Director: David Lo Kin-ming; Music: Roel A. Garcia; Action Director: Fung Hark-on; Writer-Producer-Director: Frankie Chan Fan-kei. Cast: Ti Lung (Fu Hung-suet), Frankie Chan Fan-kei (Yip Hoi), Fennie Yuen Kit-ying (Ma Fong-ling), Anita Yuen Wing-yee (Ting Ling-lam), Fung Hark-on (Siu Bee-lei), Julian Cheung Chi-lam (Lu Siu-kai). 1.85:1. LD: Long Shong. Import LD: Golden Cinema City. 89 minutes. *See* **A Warrior's Tragedy II**.

1053. A Warrior's Tragedy II

(1993; Frankie Film Co.) ★: 5/10. *Bin sing long ji II* (Cantonese), *Bian cheng lang zi II* (Mandarin): "Edge City Wanderer II." Same crew and cast credits as above. 1.85:1. LD: Long Shong. 84 minutes.

Released theatrically as a single, muddled feature and on video in two complete parts, this period fantasy is one of the strangest to be found in the recent cycle. It centers on two contrasting male protagonists: Yip Hoi, a carefree rogue, and Fu Hung-suet, a crippled and epileptic swordsman whose mother has trained him to be a cold-blooded killer to avenge the slaughter of their kin. The two men cross paths in a small village, where Fu falls in love with a kind-hearted prostitute whose love he initially rebukes. Fu's quest to kill the despot Ma Hung-kwan ends in failure, but the pursuit continues in Part II, with subsequent events resulting in a surprise revelation from Fu's mother about the lineage of her son and Yip Hoi.

Filled with humor that invariably falls flat and, in its complete form, too long by at least a third, the film manages the unique feat of seeming endlessly complicated while not really being about anything substantial. The storyline (which plays like a TVB serial that is missing all of the middle episodes) dutifully trots out all of the character types and battle sequences that genre convention requires, but the proceedings remain curiously uninvolving. Aside from the two leads, the only characters of interest are Anita Yuen's bubbly comic sidekick and Fung Hark-on's legless martial arts master who battles on stilts. Oddly, the film's biggest misstep is the one component that should have been done right: the fight choreography. While Frankie Chan's previous films have sported some of the best kung fu around, this entry is all but ploughed under by an overabundance of undercranking and silly wirework. The chintzy score (far below Roel A. Garcia's usual standards) doesn't help matters either, incorporating slightly re-orchestrated cues lifted from the Western films **Powaqqatsi** and **Terminator 2: Judgment Day**. Gorgeous costumes and picturesque Mainland settings keep it watchable, if not compelling, viewing. The import Golden Cinema City laserdisc is the edited version.

1054. Warriors Two

(1978; Golden Harvest) ★: 8/10. *Jaan sin sang yue jaau chin wa* (Cantonese), *Zan xian sheng yu zhao qian hua* (Mandarin): "Mr. Tsan and Banker Wah." Cinematographer: Ricky Lau Koon-wai; Music: Not Original; Writer: Szeto On; Producer: Raymond Chow Man-wai; Action Director-Director: Sammo Hung Kam-po. Cast: Sammo Hung Kam-po (Fei Chun), Casanova Wong (Chan Hua), Leung Kar-yan (Liang Tsan), Fung Hark-on (Mo), Lau Kar-wing (The Chief's Man), Lee Hoi-sang (Ya Chao), Lam Ching-ying (Thug), Dean Shek Tien (Mentor Chiu), Chung Fat (Tramp), Peter Chan Lung (Con Man). 2.35:1. VHS: Tai Seng (Poor Subtitles). Import LD: Star Entertainment (No Subtitles). 95 minutes.

One evening after work, bank cashier Chan Hua overhears his boss Mo discussing how he plans to murder the chief of their town. When Chan confides this knowledge to the devious Mentor Chiu, he is betrayed and almost killed by Mo's lackeys. Hiding at the home of his friend Fei (or "Fat") Chun, Chan is unaware that his boss' henchmen have murdered his mother as a way of luring him out into the open. In the meantime, Mo carries out his original plan and is soon elected head of the town. Chun then finally tells his friend about the killing, prompting Chan to request instruction in Wing Chun from the esteemed martial arts master Liang Tsan. After much practice, Chan has come close to mastering the various techniques and will receive ample opportunities to put them into practice when the time comes for him to try and avenge his mother's death. However, before he can face Mo, Chun, Chan, and Liang's niece must first take care of his ruthless fighters, who have each mastered a different, formidable skill.

The plot of this period yarn is no different than a hundred other films, but **Warriors Two** leads the pack when it comes to its martial arts sequences. Sammo Hung's accurate depiction of Wing Chun techniques has received much praise (see also **The Prodigal Son**), and the training sequences, in particular, are first rate. Hung gives one of his customarily likeable performances, and Leung Kar-yan is utterly convincing as the strict, humorless master. Leung's fight against a dozen attackers (after having stepped into a bear trap!) is one of the highlights here, but top honors must go to the extended final duel, which is a real showstopper.

1055. Watch Out

(1986; Tony Film Production Co.) ★: 3/10. *Gwai gaam yau yuen* (Cantonese), *Gui gan you yuan* (Mandarin): "Ghost So Very Predestined." Cinematographer: Wong Wang-fai; Music: Not Original; Writer: Edward Leung Yiu-ming; Producer-Director: Tony Leung Tung-lei. Cast: Stanley Fung Shui-fan (Lulu's Grandfather), Cher Yeung Suet-yee (Stella), Lee Kwok-lun (Peguin's Partner), Chan Kwok-kuen (Peguin). 1.85:1. VHS: World Video. 88 minutes.

When police officer Peguin is killed in the line of duty, he makes a deal in the afterlife that will allow him to possess the body of a millionaire. He then proceeds to aid the poor and romance pretty Stella, who is surprised by his change in outlook and demeanour. Stella eventually becomes pregnant, a problem—as the father is not of this earth. This sits well with another ghost (played by Stanley Fung), who seeks to be reincarnated through the newborn, a plan he hatched with Peguin's spirit at the outset of the film. While Peguin regrets his part in the scheme and faces death when it comes to fruition, Stella tries to "lose" the baby (she pays a judo instructor to beat her and tries to provoke robbers into kicking her!), but the ghost will not let any harm come her way. The couple decide to have the child and try to figure out a way to thwart the persistent spirit before it can act.

The first half is a complete washout, padding out the running time with a "dance fight," a little softcore sex, and a barrage of puerile gay jokes which are made more unpalatable by annoyingly overstated "comic" music cues (tracks from **Halloween, Mad Max**, and **Firestarter** are used during other sequences). The remainder of the film has some enjoyably depraved ambitions but never really capitalizes on them.

1056. Way of the Lady Boxers

(1992) ★: 3/10. *Laai hoi tit mok* (Cantonese), *La kai tie mu* (Mandarin): "Pull Open the Iron Curtain." Cinematographer: Lau Yip; Music: Not Original; Producer: Lai Ching-lam; Action Director: Woo Chi-lung; Director: Wong Wai-yip. Cast: Sibelle Hu Hui-chung (Chiang Hung), Sharon Yeung Pan-pan (Li Tong), Huang Chia-da (Chiu Chie), Jeff Falcon (Caucasian Villain). 1.85:1. VHS: Tai Seng. Import LD: Star Entertainment. 93 minutes. Also known as **Madam the Great** (Star LD title).

Female HK supercop Li Tong journeys to China in pursuit of drug traffickers in this low-budget actioner which is strictly for viewers with time on their hands. Ostensibly working together with her Mainland female counterpart, Chiang Hung, Li is actually pursuing her investigation under the guise of being a simple tourist. Hung keeps a close eye on her, however, which is fortunate, as she is able to save Li from some killers. When Li's partner is shot and left for dead by the main felon, she decides to cooperate openly with Chiang in order to close the case.

The action is fairly constant, but much of it is routine and distractingly undercranked. Yeung's obvious superiority over Hu as a martial artist doesn't help matters, and the portions where people are not kicking or shooting each other are deadly dull. On the plus side, excellent use is made of archaic, rusted-out refineries and factories as backdrops for the combat, and it is a pleasure to see '70s kung fu star Huang Chia-ta (aka Carter Wong) in action, even if only in a supporting capacity.

1057. Web of Deception

(1989; Cinema City Co./Film Workshop) ★: 6/10. *Geng wan gei* (Cantonese), *Jing hun ji* (Mandarin): "Thrilling Diary." Cinematographers: David Chung Chi-man, Eric Chu Kwok-fai; Art Director: Fong Ying; Music: Chiu Man-hoi; Writer: Lui Tat; Producer: Tsui Hark; Director: David Chung Chi-man. Cast: Brigitte Lin Ching-hsia (Jane Lin), Pauline Wong Siu-fung (May), Joey Wang Tsu-hsien (Queenie/Catherine), Elizabeth Lee Mei-fung (Mimi), Waise Lee Chi-hung (Inspector Li). 1.85:1. VHS: Tai Seng. Import LD: Golden Cinema City. 94 minutes. Also known as **Deception** (Tai Seng title).

Here is a film that sets out to be both a *homage* to Hitchcock thrillers and a mystery thriller on the level of those created by The Master. It is not entirely successful on either front but still well worth a look. Lawyer Jane Lin has been receiving blackmail letters from someone threatening to expose some financial double-dealing she did to get herself out of debt. Jane is planning on emigrating to Canada but is not taking her assistant May. Because of this, she suspects that May is the one who has been sending the letters. When Jane confronts May with her suspicions, the latter destroys all evidence of her crime but also learns that Jane has been secretly recording conversations with Mimi, her stockbroker. Suspecting that Jane believes Mimi to be the blackmailer, she witnesses her boss stashing over a million dollars in her home. Meanwhile, May's friend Queenie has met up with Catherine, her twin sister, who has just gotten out of jail. Owing $300,000 to the underworld, Catherine is in serious danger and needs money fast. When Queenie informs May of the situation, the latter comes up with a source for a lot of quick cash.

There are some nice twists in the storyline and director-cinematographer David Chung gives the proceedings a polished look, utilizing some effective deep focus compositions. However, despite good performances all round, the film is never quite as suspenseful or involving as it should be, and the idea of having twins Queenie and Catherine be such moral opposites is a pretty tired one, *homage* or not. Completed in 1988, the film did not open until October of the following year.

1058. Web of Deception

(1997; Martini Film Company/Million Sense) ★: 2/10. *Sup ng yik saat yan mong lok* (Cantonese), *Shi wu yi sha ren wang luo* (Mandarin): "$1.5 Billion Murder Network." Cinematographer: Ko Chiu-lam; Art Director: Vincent Lam Wai-sam; Music: Not Original; Writer: Takkie

Yeung Yat-tak; Producers: Kimmy Suen King-on, Wu Kee-charm; Action Director: Ma Yuk-shing; Directors: Billy Tang Hin-sing, Takkie Yeung Yat-tak. Cast: Francoise Yip Fong-wah (Fion Wong), Michael Chow Man-kin (Donson Woo), Diana Pang Dan (Jessica), Money Lo Man-yee (Candy). 1.85:1. VHS: Mecapro. Import LD/VCD/DVD: Ocean Shores. 87 minutes.

Plagued by problems during the Indonesian portion of its shoot, this action thriller is so utterly implausible it was doomed from the start anyway. Investment manager Fion Wong deals heavily in Japanese stocks and finds herself in dire straits when the Kobe earthquake causes the local market to take a nosedive. Without getting permission from her superiors, Fion enters into a takeover deal with corporate exec Donson Woo to acquire an Indonesian corporation using $US100 million of her company's money. The next day she wakes up to discover that the man claiming to be her partner was a fake and the money is gone. After she contacts the real Donson, he discovers that his company has also been fleeced. When the two team up to investigate, Donson finds himself framed for the murder of his secretary, Jessica. Not surprisingly, Jessica turns out to be alive, part of an elaborate scheme that is not as clear cut as it appears.

The scenery is nice but as far as imagination and (especially) credibility goes, this one is completely bankrupt. Francoise Yip (best known in the west for **Rumble in the Bronx**) looks far more like a fashion model than a respected investment manager, and even the usually reliable Michael Chow is not up to par here. During production, Chow, Yip, producer Suen, and eight crew members were arrested by Indonesian immigration authorities for allegedly having invalid work permits. After spending over 24 hours in jail, they were released when Suen greased a few palms.

1059. Wedding Bells, Wedding Belles

(1981; Golden Harvest/Paragon Films) ★: 3/10. *Gung ji giu* (Cantonese), *Gong zi jiao* (Mandarin): "Spoiled Young Master." Cinematographer: David Chung Chi-man; Music: Chow Siu-lung; Writer: Edward Tang King-sang; Producer: Raymond Chow Man-wai; Director: Yim Ho. Cast: Yee Lui (Kiu), Suet Lei (Tai Shui), Lau Hark-sun, Wong Yat-fei (Government Housing Man). 2.35:1. VHS: Tai Seng (Poor Subtitles). 92 minutes.

This obnoxious romantic comedy was celebrated director Yim Ho's third film and one suspects it is something he would like to forget. When his elderly boss, Mr. Chow, almost kills homely teenage girl Tai Shui with his car, TV personality Alexander Ha helps to mediate on the man's behalf. While Shui's family of fishermen are all too happy to take the appliances and electronic components being offered as compensation, they are none too pleased with the old man's plans to also marry the girl. Shui is especially unhappy, as she has already fallen in love with Alexander. While he is not in the least attracted to her, Alexander comes to Shui's rescue when she's about to be married off to Kiu, a dimwitted clam fryer who dresses like a ten year old and has a personality to match. Alexander tries to trick Shui into marrying Chow, but she is kidnapped by Kiu before this can happen. Eventually, all of the parties involved try to work out a compromise, as prompted by some even bigger bribes from Chow; but Shui comes to realize that Kiu is not such a bad catch after all.

The comedy consists almost entirely of broad, repetitive slapstick, and aside from a handful of instances (like a send-up of **The Exorcist**), the laughs are just not there. Yim keeps things moving along at a good clip, but the material is too weak for any director to have made much out of it. The film opens with music lifted from the disco version of the **Star Wars** soundtrack!

1060. The Wedding Days

(1997; Golden Harvest/United Filmmakers Organisation) ★: 6/10. *Yuen chuen git fan sau chaak* (Cantonese), *Wan quan jie hun shou ce* (Mandarin): "Complete Marriage Handbook." Cinematographers: Jingle Ma Cho-shing, Joe Chan Kong-hung, Cheung Man-bo; Art Director: James Cheung Ying-wah; Music: Clarence Hui Yuen; Producer: Eric Tsang Chi-wai; Writer-Director: James Yuen Sai-sang. Cast: Anita Yuen Wing-yee (Rachel Lam), Charlie Yeung Choi-nei (Janet Lee), Jordan Chan Siu-chun (Wong Chi-wei), Michael Wong Man-tak (Sam Wong), Alex To Tak-wai (Matt), Eric Tsang Chi-wai (Paul Kwan), Law Koon-lan (Mrs. Wong), Christine Ng Wing-mei (May), Sharon Kwok Sau-wan (Sam's ex), Emily Kwan Bo-wai (Liu), Simon Lui Yu-yeung (Shi), Vincent Kok Tak-chiu (Picky Customer), Dayo Wong Chi-wah (Vain Customer). 1.85:1. VHS: Mecapro. Import LD/VCD/DVD: Mei Ah. 109 minutes.

Talented screenwriter James Yuen (**He's a Woman, She's a Man**) made his directorial debut with this unadventurous but pleasant relationship comedy, which he also scripted. Childhood friends Rachel and Janet meet up again at the wedding of a mutual friend and find that they are still both single. Rachel is hopelessly in love with Sam, a divorced father of one, who does not want to be married again; while Janet's would-be husband refuses to divorce his current spouse. Much of the film unfolds in Janet's bridal shop, with her occupation a constant reminder of the void she feels in her life. Staff photographer Wei loves her but Janet doesn't know it because he cannot bring himself to vocalize his affection. Rachel, meanwhile, finally convinces Sam to make their relationship legal but must find a way to sell him on her desire to go the "church and banquet" route. Instead of using Wei, Rachel hires flaky "art" photographer Matt to take her wedding pictures, and Janet is soon attracted to him and his irreverent views, much to the consternation of Wei.

In many ways, this is a typical UFO film, placing numerous colorful characters into an intertwined storyline that allows for plenty of asides about life and relationships. The half devoted to Anita Yuen's character has several charming moments but sputters badly when it comes time for the requisite dramatic conflict. Blessed with a far more interesting character, Charlie Yeung gives a mature and affecting performance which makes the material seem more relevant than it really is, and Jordan Chan is engagingly guileless in the kind of role that brought him fame. The law of diminishing returns dictates that **The Wedding Days** cannot impart the same degree of warmth and vivacity found in earlier UFO efforts, but it remains largely pleasurable.

1061. We're Going to Eat You!

(1980; Seasonal Film Corporation) ★: 6/10. *Dei yuk mo moon* (Cantonese), *Di yu wu men* (Mandarin): "No Door in Hell." Cinematographer: Lau Hung-chuen; Art Director: Ting Yuen-tai; Music: Not Original; Writers: Tsui Hark, Roy Szeto Cheuk-hon; Producer: Ng See-yuen; Action Directors: Corey Yuen Kwai, Chin Yuet-sang; Director: Tsui Hark. Cast: Norman Tsui Siu-keung (Agent #999), Eddy Ko Hung (The Chief), Melvin Wong Kam-sun (Rolex), David Wu Tai-wai (Bisected Victim). 2.35:1. VHS: World Video (Tiny Subtitles). Import VCD: Mei Ah (Poor Subtitles). 90 minutes.

Tsui Hark's second film is a gory but wacky horror-comedy that is circulating on video in various versions, some of which are drastically censored. To make matters worse, each sports a dark, badly cropped image and poor subtitles. Despite these drawbacks, the film remains exciting and largely accessible, thanks to its fast pacing and basic storyline. Agent #999, a civil servant, is sent to arrest nortorious thief Rolex, who makes his home on an island.

What 999 doesn't know (but soon finds out) is that the place is populated almost entirely by *cannibals*, and he barely escapes with his life after foolishly entering the local slaughterhouse. Rolex, who wants to leave the island but cannot because of orders from the colony's leader (appropriately named "The Chief"), reveals himself to 999 in the hopes that they can join forces to escape. When that plan fails, Rolex tries to murder The Chief but ends up dead himself, leaving 999 and another unfortunate traveller to battle the hordes of hungry killers themselves.

Some critics have identified the island of flesh eaters as a metaphor for Communist China, but such a parallel seems fairly labored (The Chief's motto, "If you don't eat people, they'll eat you!" sounds more akin to capitalist dogma than communism). It is more likely that the project takes its inspiration from 1970s Italian horror pictures like **Man from Deep River**, **Cannibal Holocaust**, and **Zombie** (for its US release, the latter film was advertised with the tagline "We Are Going to Eat You!"), mixing their central ideas and images with uniquely Chinese situations and humor (including jokes about everyone from Wong Fei-hong to Abraham Lincoln!). The comic kung fu battles and a subplot involving a love-stricken transvestite provide a preview of the slapstick that would figure in Tsui's next picture, the marvellous gangster movie spoof **All the Wrong Clues...for the Right Solution**. However, this time out the non-stop barrage of chases, low humor, and manic editing eventually grows wearisome through repetition. Regardless, **We're Going to Eat You!** is a one-of-a-kind venture that should definitely be seen by horror fans and students of Tsui's work, in whatever form they can get it. Part of the score is lifted from Dario Argento's Italian horror thriller **Suspiria**.

1062. We're No Bad Guys

(1997; Golden Harvest/BOB & Partners Company) ★: 3/10. *Oi seung 100% ying hung* (Cantonese), *Ai shang 100% ying xiong* (Mandarin): "Loving 100% Heroes." Cinematographer: Tony Miu Kin-fai; Art Director: Stanley Cheung Sai-kit; Music: Chan Kwong-wing; Producers: Manfred Wong, Andrew Lau Wai-keung; Action Director: Kuk Hin-chiu; Writer-Director: Wong Jing. Cast: Dior Cheng Yee-kin (Plane), Jordan Chan Siu-chun (Turkey Chu), Gigi Leung Wing-kei (Carrie/Mandy Chan), Vivian Hsu Ruo-hsuan (Tinny Chung), Alex Fong Chung-sun (Angel), Law Kar-ying (Bond Chu, aka Jade Dragon), Lee Siu-kei (Chan Chi-fook, aka Dirty Fook), Ricky Yee Fan-wai (Flirty Tim), Michael Chan Wai-man (Mike), Meg Lam Kin-ming (Plane's Mother, aka Crab Beauty), Spencer Lam Sheung-yee (Bomb Squad Man). 1.85:1. VHS: Tai Seng. 101 minutes.

This typically uneven Wong Jing concoction (supposedly his answer to the **Aces Go Places** films) centers on a team of police officers (including temperamental hotshot Plane and his more level-headed girlfriend, Carrie) assigned to guard triad Dirty Fook, who is serving as a witness against his boss, Golden Teeth. While Plane is out getting food, high tech hitman Angel bursts in the safe house and annihilates everyone, including Carrie. The film picks up one year later, with Plane now the most violent and undisciplined cop on the force. His new partner, goofy Turkey Chu, turns out to be a good match, helping the moody Plane get back on track. However, just when he finally seems to be getting over Carrie, Plane meets computer expert Mandy, who is her spitting image. Turkey, meanwhile, gets to meet his idol, singer Tinny Chung, right before she is kidnapped by thugs working for Golden Teeth. While in the latter's hands, she witnesses his murder at the hands of Angel...or does she?

Insanely contrived (even by Wong's standards), **We're No Bad Guys** tries to be too many things at once. While this is more the norm than the exception with many HK features, some are able to perform that sort of juggling act better than others. This one has enough trouble keeping one ball in the air, let alone three or four. Jumping back and forth between screwball comedy (Jordan Chan making silly noises, and Law Kar-ying playing an idiot who thinks he's James Bond), scatological jokes (exploding toilets, no less), teen idol romance (Dior Cheng and Gigi Leung making goo goo eyes at each other), and gory action (bloody bullet hits, knifings, and throat slittings), the film is never at a loss for ideas, but none of them are especially clever and the end result is not only forgettable but not even all that interesting as it unfolds.

1063. What a Small World

(1989; Golden Harvest/Paragon Films) ★: 5/10. *Ngoh oi tong yan gaai* (Cantonese), *Wo ai tang ren jie* (Mandarin): "I Love Chinatown." Cinematographer: Jingle Ma Cho-shing; Art Director: David Chau Chi-wah; Music: Anders Nelsson; Producers: Anthony Chow Ting-on, Calvin Ng Wing-hei; Writer-Director: Jamie Luk Kim-ming. Cast: Ray Lui Leung-wai (Cheung Chi-hung), Nina Li Chi (Nina Lee), Rosamund Kwan Chi-lam (Michelle), Lawrence Ng Kai-wah (Franco Wong), Alex Fong Chung-sun (Chan), Woo Fung (Michelle and Franco's Boss), Jamie Luk Kim-ming (Bill). 1.85:1. VHS: Tai Seng (No Subtitles). Import LD: Mei Ah. 96 minutes.

When executive Michelle tries to surprise her nerdy husband Franco with a trip to Paris for their third anniversary, her well-laid plans go down the drain as Franco mistakenly thinks she has been flirting with their boss. Michelle flies out of HK by herself, followed a day later by Franco, who has realized the error of his ways. However, she has decided to go to London instead, where she meets up with Chi-hung, an old boyfriend/triad leader. Soon afterward, Franco's lonely trudge through the streets of Paris is curtailed by Nina, a girl he knew from his childhood days in the country. When Franco discovers Michelle's whereabouts, he and the rather dimwitted Nina fly to London. The couples eventually meet up and, to put it mildly, things do not go well. When an attempt is made on Franco's life, he blames Chi-hung, but it is actually the work of men employed by Nina's triad boss lover, who believes that she is cheating on him. Events are further complicated by the fact that Nina's sugar daddy is a drug dealer who just happens to be Chi-hung's mortal enemy.

A passable hybrid of the romantic comedy and action genres, **What a Small World** squeaks by on the strength of its attractive cast and even more attractive location work in France and the UK. It's a pleasant time if you don't ask for too much; this movie's idea of creativity is having Ray Lui play a *nice* triad!

1064. What a Wonderful World

(1996; Movie Impact/Impact Films Investment) ★: 4/10. *Kei yi lui ching ji jan sam oi sang ming* (Cantonese), *Qi yi lu cheng zhi zhen xin ai sheng ming* (Mandarin): "Fantastic Voyage: True Heart Loves Life." Cinematographer: Jacky Tang Hon-bong; Art Director: Eddie Ma Poon-chiu; Music: Lowell Lo Kwun-ting; Writers: Samson Chiu Leung-chun, Tang Kit-ming, Wong Ho-wah; Producer: Wallace Cheung Kwok-chong; Action Director: James Ha Chim-see; Director: Samson Chiu Leung-chun. Cast: Andy Lau Tak-wah (Sun Chung-wah), Kenny Bee (Gump Chung-shun), Theresa Lee Yee-hung (Chu), Louis Yuen Siu-cheung (Obnoxious Reporter), Kent Cheng Chuk-see (Doctor), Paul Fonoroff (Reporter Going to Canada). 1.85:1. VHS: Tai Seng. Import LD/VCD/DVD: Mei Ah. 100 minutes.

Diagnosed with a terminal blood disease, CCN reporter Sun Chung-wah decides that he must finish his life with a big, important assignment. He flies off to Singapore in search of Gump Chung-shun (first identified in the subtitles as Kim Chung-sun), a stock trader who ruined his company through speculation and is now the subject of a massive manhunt. By sheer luck, Sun stumbles across Gump in a hotel washroom, and when police arrive, he ends up being the fugitive's (willing) hostage. The pair disappear into the jungle with a belligerent local cop coordinating efforts to capture them. Sun and Gump (who is a very nervous and scared individual perplexed by all of the attention now thrust upon him) become separated, and the latter ends up dead. As Sun composes both his story and a statement for the police, we see flashbacks presenting the (ludicrous) circumstances that brought about Gump's death. After being harassed by reporters himself, Sun visits Chu, an incredibly bubbly prostitute (who keeps pictures of her 499 clients to date) whom Gump had visited on four occasions and held in great esteem. Two-and-a-half months pregnant with what might be his baby, Chu helps Sun to more fully understand both Gump and himself.

What a Wonderful World starts off serious and fairly credible, transforms into a broad farce with absolutely no credibility, and then ends up somewhere in between. Director Samson Chiu's message that one should make the most of life and live every day to its fullest only really comes across when Theresa Lee is given center stage in the final third. Absolutely charming in her film debut, Lee single-handedly reinvigorates the contrived and listless proceedings, offering a three-dimensional characterization of a woman with a truly unique view of life. Her performance and the incredible location scenery almost make this mess worth catching.

1065. What Price Survival

(1994; Hoventin Films Creativity) ★: 4/10. *'94 duk bei do ji ching* (Cantonese), *'94 du bi dao zhi qing* (Mandarin): "'94 Only Arm Sword's Love." Cinematographer: Cheung Tung-leung; Music: Chan Yeung; Writers: Daniel Lee Yan-kong, Chan Siu-cheung; Producer: Laura Fau Lok-lin; Action Director: Tang Tai-wo; Art Director-Director: Daniel Lee Yan-kong. Cast: Wu Hsin-kuo (Wang Ning), Charlie Yeung Choi-nei (Hsiao-lian), Jack Gao Jie (Jie), Norman Tsui Siu-keung (Wang Ching-kuo), Damian Lau Chung-yan (Wu An-kuo), David Chiang Da-wei (Pai Fu-kuo). 1.85:1. VHS: Tai Seng. Import LD/VCD/DVD: Ocean Shores. 96 minutes.

This swordplay yarn (set in the early part of the 20th century) has so much going for it that one cannot help but be disappointed by its utter lack of resonance. When he loses a duel to Yi Tao Hui swordmaster Wang Ching-kuo, Tsuo Chien Tang leader Pai Fu-kuo forfeits baby son Ning to his opponent. Over the intervening years, Wang passes on his skills to Ning and the youth is soon a master of the sword as well. Having brought up Ning with the idea that he must kill Pai, and having kept from the boy all knowledge of his real heritage, Wang plans to use him as a way of gaining the top position in the Tsuo Chien Tang society. As planned, Ning confronts Pai and the pair have their duel. Thanks to the intervention of Pai's subordinate, the devious Wu An-kuo, the master loses and dies at the hands of Ning. Learning that he has unknowingly slaughtered his real father, Ning leaves Yi Tao Hui behind but is destined to face off against both his old friend, Jie, and Master Wang before he can find peace.

The swordplay is adeptly staged, and the wintry locales are gorgeous. Unfortunately, it only takes one a few minutes to realize that look and style is really all that art director-director Daniel Lee was concerned about. Despite the presence of charismatic martial arts veterans David Chiang, Norman Tsui, and Damian Lau, none of the characters are memorable. As the nominal hero, Wu Hsin-kuo brings a lot of anger but no real passion or charisma to his role, and Charlie Yeung, while game, is not at all convincing as a swordswoman. As a result, too much of the film comes across as empty pageantry, and the final confrontation between Ning and Wang is ill-conceived and anti-climactic. With no dynamic personalities to carry it out, the story is no better than functional, and that makes its genre tenets seem especially tired. The best thing about the film is the thrilling action montage during the opening credits (also used as the movie's trailer); once you have watched that, you have seen everything of value on offer here.

1066. Whatever You Want

(1994; Shaw Brothers) ★: 5/10. *Jue gwong bo hei* (Cantonese), *Zhu guang bao qi* (Mandarin): "Pearl Light Treasure Vapors." Cinematographer: Cheng Siu-keung; Art Director: Raymond Kwok Siu-keung; Music: Marco Wan Ho-kit, Anthony Lee Hon-kam, Lee Kai-cheong; Producer: Mona Fong Yat-wah; Writer-Director: Wong Jing. Cast: Anita Yuen Wing-yee (Ko Sau-ping), Michael Wong Man-tak (Bolobolo), Christy Chung Lai-tai (Pearl Ko), Jordan Chan Siu-chun (Yam Kin-fai), Mimi Chu Mi-mi (Sau-ping's Mom), Sheila Chan Sak-lan (Julianna), Woo Fung ("Hercules"), Law Kar-ying (Keanu/Kwok-wing/Actor on TV), Sin Lap-man (Wong Jing-wai), Wong Yat-fei (Sau-ping's Boss), Bobby Yip King-sang (Obnoxious Movie Patron). 1.85:1. VHS: Tai Seng. Import LD: Cameron Entertainment. Import VCD: Mei Ah. 97 minutes.

An uneven comedy, **Whatever You Want** works best when it puts its tired "magic genie with three wishes" plotting aside and sends up both local and Hollywood movies. Gangly Ko Sau-ping is a nerdy girl who escapes from her displeasures in life by watching an endless supply of movies. While out obtaining exotic props for a commercial shoot, she acquires three exquisite pearls that house the genie Bolobolo. In exchange for releasing him from his confinement, he grants her the requisite three wishes. Although she comes to love the genie (who she nicknames "Bo"), Sau-ping uses one of her wishes to set him up with her gorgeous, bisexual half-sister Pearl, a decision she soon regrets when Pearl takes steps to ensure that Sau-ping will never see Bo again.

As with several of Wong Jing's pictures, this is absolutely merciless when it comes to trashing both Wong Kar-wai and his films (Sin Lap-man plays the satirical "Wong Jing-wai" character here, later essayed by Dayo Wong in the Nat Chan vehicle **Those Were the Days**), and the various other parodies (including **Speed** and **Chinese Torture Chamber Story**) are great fun too. While it does mine comedic gold on several occasions, a significant portion of **Whatever You Want** is tiresomely inane. The solution is to listen to the opening speech given by Yuen's character, in which she advises that the best way to watch Wong Jing's films is on fast forward. It is certainly the way to watch this one.

1067. Wheels on Meals

(1984; Golden Harvest/Paragon Films) ★: 6/10. *Faai chaan che* (Cantonese), *Kuai can che* (Mandarin): "Fast Food Car." Cinematographers: Arthur Wong Ngok-tai, Cheung Yiu-cho; Art Director: Fung Yuen-chi; Music: Keith Morrison; Writers: Edward Tang King-sang, Johnny Lee King-kai; Producer: Leonard Ho Koon-cheung; Action Directors: Kar Lee, Chin Kar-lok, Feng Sing, Chow Yan-kin, Wong Kam-kwan, Lai Keung-kuen, Shigeru Ishihara; Director: Sammo Hung Kam-po. Cast: Jackie Chan (Thomas), Sammo Hung Kam-po (Moby), Yuen Biao (David), Lola Forner (Sylvia), Benny "The Jet" Urquidez (Thug), Keith Vitali (Thug), Wu Ma (The Human Clock), Richard Ng Yiu-hon (Brilliant Patient), John Sham Kin-fun (Laughing Patient), Herb Edelman (Matt). Dolby Digital (DVD only).

1.85:1. VHS/LD: Tai Seng (Remastered for the English Market; subtitled or dubbed). Import LD: Star Entertainment (No Subtitles). Import DVD: Universe. 108 minutes. Also known as **Spartan X** (Japanese title).

Shot in Spain, this Jackie Chan/Sammo Hung/Yuen Biao outing is not one of their best efforts but the action sequences and beautiful scenery are sufficiently diverting. Thomas and David run a successful lunch wagon business in Barcelona. One day David's wandering eyes settle on the beautiful Sylvia (**The Armour of God**'s Lola Forner) and it is love at first sight, despite the fact that she is a pickpocket. Meanwhile, bumbling private eye Moby has been hired to find a long lost girl who, naturally, turns out to be Sylvia. The illegitimate child of a deceased Count, Sylvia stands to inherit his fortune if she turns up within two weeks of his death; otherwise, the money will go to the count's evil brother. As you would expect, the latter hires a number of goons to try and dispose of the girl, so it is up to Thomas, David, and Moby to protect her.

While studios like New Line and Dimension needlessly whittle down Chan's recent films, **Wheels on Meals** is one effort that would actually benefit from some judicious pruning. The generic plotting in the first half is so bland and predictable that even the best efforts of the stars cannot help one from wishing that the film would pick up speed and progress to the large-scale action. The back alleys and grand, Olde World buildings and squares of Barcelona provide a lovely backdrop for the martial arts and car stunts, and some of the numerous pratfalls generate legitimate laughs. During the big finale, Chan and Yuen square off against American martial artists Benny "The Jet" Urquidez (**Force: Five**) and Keith Vitali (**Revenge of the Ninja**); the Chan/Urquidez match-up is rightfully considered to be among the best around and gives Chan an opponent that is arguably his equal. Reportedly, the English title was originally *Meals on Wheels* but Golden Harvest chairman Raymond Chow Man-wai, having lost a bundle on the Hollywood bomb **Megaforce** (1982), declared that the company would no longer use titles starting with "M," hence the last minute switch! The Japanese title is **Spartan X**, whatever that means.

1068. When Fortune Smiles

(1990; Golden Harvest/Paragon Films) ★: 7/10. *Mo dik hang wan sing* (Cantonese), *Wu di xing yun xing* (Mandarin): "Unmatched Lucky Star." Cinematographers: Derek Wan Man-kit, Joe Chan Kong-hung; Art Director: Andy Lee Yiu-kwong; Music: Richard Yuen Cheuk-fan; Writer: Raymond To Kwok-wai; Action Directors: Tony Leung Siu-hung, Leung Mo-hung; Producer-Director: Anthony Chan Yau. Cast: Stephen Chiau Sing-chi (Vincent Han), Sandra Ng Kwan-yu (Rubbish Feng/Chao Fei-fei), Anthony Chan Yau (Detective Huang), Anthony Wong Chau-sang (Wei), Lam Kau (Chao), Shing Fui-on (Chao's Son), Mui Siu-wai (Wei's Wife), Yung Sai-kit (Simon), Billy Chow Bei-lee (Kickboxer). 1.85:1. VHS: Tai Seng (No Subtitles). Import LD: Star Entertainment (No Subtitles). Import VCD: Mega Star. 90 minutes.

Small-time crook Vincent Han is hired by a triad to steal a will made out by the gangster's deceased boss. Meanwhile, Wei, another triad, has hired garbage-woman Rubbish Feng to pose as his sister, Fei-fei, so that *she* can steal the will. Ultimately, Vincent comes up with a better idea: He will romance and marry "Fei-fei," thus allowing him easy access to the money. The pair actually do fall in love and reveal the truth to one another before the wedding. However, Wei interrupts the ceremony at its height and kidnaps them. Pocketing the family diamonds and beating a hasty retreat on his ship, the gangster thinks he has it made, but Vincent is not out of the action yet and sets out to make up for his earlier misdeeds by thwarting Wei.

This fast-paced farce has some terrific physical comedy bits, particularly a kick-boxing sequence that allows Chiau to trot out his Bruce Lee imitation, and an extended bit of pantomime between the comedian and Mui Siu-wai. Director Anthony Chan (who co-stars as a vain but bumbling private eye) keeps the energy level high right on up to the climax: a prolonged fight on a boat which finds Chiau using an inflated wetsuit to cushion himself against villain Billy Chow's punches and kicks! Not generally mentioned when Chiau films are discussed, **When Fortune Smiles** is a lot of fun and more worthwhile than some of the comic's best known titles.

1069. Where's Officer Tuba?

(1986; D & B Films Co.) ★: 3/10. *Pik lik daai la ba* (Cantonese), *Pi li da la ba* (Mandarin): "Thunderbolt Big Loud-speaker." Cinematographers: Andrew Lau Wai-keung, Michael Ma Koon-wah; Art Directors: Tony Au Ding-ping, Eric Lam Sai-kan; Music: Danny Chung Teng-yat; Writer: Barry Wong Ping-yiu; Producer: Sammo Hung Kam-po; Action Direction: The Sammo Hung Stuntmen Association; Directors: Ricky Lau Koon-wai, Phillip Chan Yan-kin. Cast: Sammo Hung Kam-po (Tuba), Jacky Cheung Hok-yau (Cheung), Joey Wang Tsu-hsien (Joanne), David Chiang Da-wei (Rambo Chow). 1.85:1. VHS: Tai Seng. Import VCD: Mega Star. 88 minutes.

This slow-moving, unfocused action comedy stars Sammo Hung as Tuba, a timid policeman who is so named because he plays that instrument in the police band. Hotshot cop Rambo Chow gets Tuba involved in an extortion case that ends up costing Chow his life. Soon thereafter, Chow's ghost returns to force Tuba to make good on a frivolous promise to avenge his death and bring the criminals to justice. In a series of tediously unfunny scenes, he proceeds to embarrass Tuba in front of his friends by forcing him to make lewd gestures and weird sounds. When he finally agrees to help Chow, Tuba and his gung ho beat partner, Cheung (who is unaware of Chow's spirit), set out to apprehend the bad guys.

This is a real disappointment considering the parties involved; the climactic action scenes are not up to Hung's usual standards, and there isn't even an explanation of why Chow can manipulate Tuba's body but cannot exact revenge on his own. There's lots of familiar faces in small roles to hold one's interest, including Melvin Wong Kam-sun, Stanley Fung Shui-fan, Paul Chun Pui, Woo Fung, Hwang Jang-li, Yuen Wah, Tai Po, Yip Wing-cho, Dennis Chan Kwok-san, John Sham Kin-fun, Alfred Cheung Kin-ting, Chen Jing, and Lam Ching-ying. Footage from this film was later used to pad out the English dubbed version of **Yes, Madam**.

The White-Haired Swordswoman II *see* **The Bride with White Hair 2**

1070. Who's the Woman, Who's the Man?

(1996; Golden Harvest/United Filmmakers Organization) ★: 6/10. *Gam chi yuk yip 2* (Cantonese), *Jin qi yu she 2* (Mandarin): "Golden Branch, Jade Leaf 2." Cinematographer: Henry Chan Chun-kit; Art Director: Hai Chung-man; Music: Clarence Hui Yuen; Writers: James Yuen Sai-sang, Lam Ngoi-wah; Producer-Director: Peter Chan Ho-sun. Cast: Anita Yuen Wing-yee (Lam Chi-wing), Leslie Cheung Kwok-wing (Sam), Anita Mui Yim-fong (Fan-fan), Jordan Chan Siu-chun (Fish), Theresa Lee Yee-hung ("O"), Eric Tsang Chi-wai ("Auntie"), Carina Lau Kar-ling (Rose). 1.85:1. VHS: Tai Seng. Import LD/VCD/DVD: Mei Ah. 109 minutes.

This rather prosaic follow-up to **He's a Woman, She's a Man** picks up right where the original ended, with transvestite pop star Chi-wing (spelled "Gee-wing" in the first film) and master songwriter Sam together at last and madly in love. Things start to unravel when reclusive pop sensation Fong Yim-mui (fittingly played by pop sensation Anita Mui Yim-fong) returns to Hong Kong after ten years of self-exile and quickly inserts herself into both Sam and Chi-wing's lives.

Like most sequels, this is content to replay the original concept, adding only a few marginal embellishments that won't upset the formula or alienate fans. Thus, since Sam had the sexual confusion before, Chi-wing has it now, and there is a superfluous but somewhat amusing subplot in which Chi-wing's goofy friend Fish sets out to seduce Yim-mui's cheerfully lesbian assistant "O." So good last time out, Cheung and Yuen are not used to best effect here. Sam's anxiety was an amusing component before, but his character is now so consumed with homophobia he loses all his dignity. Much of Yuen's appeal resides in the irresistible energy she brings to roles such as this, but she can get out of hand if not properly reined in. Perhaps in deference to the "Best Actress" honors she garnered last time out, Chan lets her play some of the more emotional moments too broadly, and as a result, Chi-wing is now more grating brat than wide-eyed innocent. The screenplay is also wanting, falling back on the old Hollywood genre adage that all problems will resolve themselves once everyone has slept together. The writers seemingly strive to make honest observations about homosexuality, but they are more convenient than convincing, particularly when presented in a scenario where the genuinely gay characters are not far enough removed from their mincing counterparts in older HK films. Mui, however, is perfectly utilized, dominating almost every scene she graces. The effeminate male/exquisitely female personas her character flits between are a clever allusion to the sort of image re-creation she indulges in as HK's top female singer. In addition to her regal and commanding presence, there are a number of wonderfully funny moments sprinkled throughout, allowing this sequel to remain a couple of notches above the generally weak crop of pictures produced in HK during the mid–90s. However, as the follow-up to a truly wonderful pop confection like **He's a Woman, She's a Man**, it finishes a distant second. As before, some knowledge of the local entertainment industry is really essential in order to fully appreciate all the humor and spot the many celebrity cameos (including director Ann Hui On-wah, Cheung Tat-ming, and actor/singer Emil Chow Wah-kin). Eric Tsang Chi-wai and Carina Lau Kar-ling briefly reprise their characters from the original to good effect. Subtitle translation is much improved over the first film, but the humor in calling Mui Yim-fong "Fong Yim-mui" will be lost on some English speaking viewers, as her character is inexplicably transcribed as "Fan-fan."

1071. Why Me?

(1985; Cinema City Co.) ★: 5/10. *Hoh bit yau ngoh* (Cantonese), *He bi you wo* (Mandarin): "Why Me?" Art Director: Andy Lee Yiu-kwong; Music: Chris Babida; Writers: Raymond Wong Pak-ming, Kent Cheng Chuk-see, Philip Cheng Chung-tai; Producer: Raymond Wong Pak-ming; Director: Kent Cheng Chuk-see. Cast: Kent Cheng Chuk-see (Fat Cat), Olivia Cheng Man-ar (Koko Cheng), Chow Yun-fat (Chow), Paul Chu Kong (Kong), Shing Fui-on (Ken), Eric Tsang Chi-wai (Eric), Kara Hui Ying-hung (Woman Whose Husband Gambles), Lau Kar-wing (Man Doing Lion Dance), Jamie Luk Kim-ming (Thug). 1.85:1. VHS: Tai Seng. Import LD: Golden Cinema City. Import VCD: Mega Star. Import DVD: Universe. 92 minutes.

Kent Cheng won the Best Actor prize for his impressive performance in this uneven but occasionally perceptive drama. While on assignment in a village, optimistic social worker Koko Cheng encounters Fat Cat, a large retarded man who lives with his elderly, poverty-stricken mother. After much cajoling, Koko is able to convince the woman that Fat Cat should be allowed to enroll in a community center, where he will learn a trade and interact with others like himself. However, there is a three year waiting list, and Koko's other attempts to help Fat Cat run into unexpected obstacles. To make matters worse, his mother is suffering from a seriously debilitating illness.

Fatally overplotted, **Why Me?** would have worked fine had it concerned itself merely with the relationship between Koko, Fat Cat, and the latter's mother. Instead, we are also served up a wholly superfluous romance between Olivia Cheng's character and her boss at work (Chow Yun-fat, completely wasted here), as well as the various problems plaguing the woman's family (divorced mother with a new husband, unemployed father addicted to gambling, and a grandmother to look after), presented with the sort of overstatement one expects from any script Raymond Wong had a hand in creating. The film is further trivialized by a barrage of distracting star cameos that add nothing of value. Fortunately, Kent Cheng is excellent, and some good points are raised about how poorly the mentally disturbed are often treated. Fat Cat's story continues in a sequel, produced by the rival Movie Impact company, called **The Beloved Son of God**.

1072. Why Wild Girls

(1994; Prairie Productions Co.) ★: 6/10. *Fung chan saam nui hap* (Cantonese), *Fung chen san nu xia* (Mandarin): "Wind Dust: Three Female Heroes." Cinematographer: Poon Hang-sang; Art Director: Jon Hau Wing-choi; Music: Wong King-wai; Writer: Cheung Cho-yee; Producers: Jon Hau Wing-choi, Norman Law Man; Director: Andy Chin Wing-keung. Cast: Loletta Lee Lai-chun (Jane Ma), Ellen Chan Ar-lun (Gigi Chan), Ivy Leung Siman (Bobo), Dior Cheng Yee-kin (Mike), Chan Kwok-bong (Hung), Kenneth Chan Kai-tai (Roger), Yuen King-tan (Fei-fei), Jamie Luk Kim-ming (Smart Leung). 1.85:1. VHS: Tai Seng. Import LD/VCD/DVD: Ocean Shores. 82 minutes.

The wild girls of the misleading English title are roommates Gigi (an actress/barmaid), Jane (looking for secretarial work), and Bobo (a voice artist for a movie production company), and their romantic pursuits make up the bulk of this likeable effort. The bombshell of the trio, Gigi is an inveterate partier who drinks too much and is out to advance her career. Meek Hung wants to date her but she won't give him the time of day. Instead, Bobo is interested in Hung and pursues him herself, while Gigi considers a marriage proposal from nerdy but rich businessman Roger. Jane is intrigued by the handsome Mike, who has just moved into the apartment building across the street. However, if she is to make any headway, Jane will have to do something about his domineering girlfriend, Frankie, who once denied her a secretarial job.

There is some brief nudity, but this is not the softcore tease the poster makes it out to be. While the plotting is conventional, the leads all give very natural and appealing performances (sync sound recording is an asset and rare for this sort of film), and while their characters do adhere to certain stereotypes, they display more maturity than the norm. The dramatic conflicts are also plausible, making this a nice little sleeper. What is with that incredibly abrupt ending, though?

1073. The Wicked City

(1992; Golden Princess/Film Workshop/Edko Films) ★: 4/10. *Yiu sau do si* (Cantonese), *Yao shou du shi* (Mandarin): "Monster City." Cinematographers: Andrew Lau Wai-keung, Joe Chan Kong-hung; Art

Director: Eddie Ma Poon-chiu; Music: Richard Yuen Cheuk-fan; Writers: Tsui Hark, Szeto Wai-cheuk; Producer: Tsui Hark; Action Directors: Chris Lee Kin-sang, Cheung Yiu-sing; Director: Peter Mak Tai-kit. Cast: Leon Lai Ming (Taki), Jacky Cheung Hok-yau (Ken Kai), Michelle Lee Kar-yan (Windy), Roy Cheung Yiu-yeung (Shudo), Tatsuya Nakadai (Daishu), Carman Lee Yeuk-tung (Orchid), Yuen Woo-ping (Sergeant Kayama). 1.85:1. VHS: Fox Lorber (Subtitled or Dubbed), Tai Seng. LD/DVD: Image. Import LD/VCD: Mei Ah. 90 minutes.

A tiresome live action remake of the like-named Japanese *anime*, this features some imaginative special FX but suffers from visual overkill, a dearth of interesting characters, and an ill-conceived approach to the source material. It also owes as much to the Hollywood movie **Alien Nation** as it does to its reputed source. Earth is infested with alien beings called Rapters (*sic*) that can assume human form. Ken and Taki are agents for the "Anti-Rapter Bureau," a secret group with telekinitic abilities tracking the aliens' movements and trying to eradicate them. Some of the creatures are going mad from consuming a drug called "Happiness," which increases body strength but causes the user to evaporate once he stops taking it. Taki is assigned to investigate multi-billionaire Daishu, whom the bureau has learned is at least 150 years old, making him an obvious candidate to be a rapter. Ken is not allowed to go on the mission because the agency knows that his mother was an alien and believe that he has been leaking secret information to the enemy. Daishu and a good number of his fellow creatures seek to coexist peacefully with humans, but a rival rapter faction, led by Daishu's power crazed son Shudo, opposes them, wanting to take the Earth for themselves.

While occasionally impressive, some of the FX are just plain silly (Shudo and his lover have sex while the latter is configured into a mutant pinball machine!), and the visuals are laid on so thick they do not have much resonance after a while, especially when the story surrounding them is so hackneyed. There is also some none-too-subtle symbolism (one of the rapters assumes the form of a deadly clock, an obvious reference to the then-approaching reunification with China), and an uncharacteristically weak score by talented composer Richard Yuen (**The Bride with White Hair**) does nothing to make the delirious action any more exciting or the emotional conflicts any more interesting. However, the film's undoing lies in its weak narrative. The Japanese feature was filled with adult overtones that gave the proceedings an extra layer of interest; this version is geared towards a more general audience, perhaps explaining why elements from **Alien Nation** have been incorporated to flesh out the story. This is also true of an unsuccessful subplot involving Taki's past and present relationship with Windy, Daishu's beautiful companion, that periodically brings things to a dead halt while adding nothing of value in return.

1074. Widow Warriors

(1990; Maverick Films) ★: 5/10. *Fu daam nui yi hung* (Cantonese), *Hu dan nu er gong* (Mandarin): "Tiger Courage Daughter Red." Cinematographer: Yu Chik-lim; Art Director: Hadd Ng Kwok-hung; Music: Not Original; Writer-Producer: Manfred Wong; Action Directors: Sun Chien, Johnny Wang Lung-wei; Director: Johnny Wang Lung-wei. Cast: Elizabeth Lee Mei-fung (Ching-ching), Tien Niu (Nan), Kara Hui Ying-hung (Sister-in-Law), Michiko Nishiwaki (Chieko), Winnie Lau Siu-wai (Wai), Shih Kien (Liu Lung), Phillip Chan Yan-kin (Liu Chuan-hau), Michael Chan Wai-man (Ma-yee), Ken Lo Wai-kwong (Yong), Dennis Chan Kwok-san (Hung), Cho Tat-wah (Yong's Father), Ha Chi-chun (Female Triad in Health Club), Ng Hong-ning (Bull). 1.85:1. VHS: Tai Seng. Import LD: Mei Ah. 92 minutes.

Good premise, weak execution. When their triad husbands are murdered by the rival Yim gang, the women of the Liu family decide to strike back before the Yims can seize their assets. However, a poorly thought out raid on a Yim stronghold goes disastrously wrong, and two of the women are killed while another is left paralysed. Pretending to cooperate with their rivals, the remaining Liu women and their male henchmen set about destroying the Yims.

There is no dearth of action and violence but also no real style or tension, save for the climactic unveiling of the traitor who brought about all the death and tragedy. Tien Niu (**City War**) gives the best performance here as a woman who grew up on the wrong side of the tracks but, even after falling into the lap of luxury, has not lost the resolve that allowed her to survive on the streets as a teenager. This was pop star Winnie Lau's film debut.

1075. Wild

(1996; Martini Film Company) ★: 6/10. *Kwong yau saam chin heung* (Cantonese), *Kuang ye san qian xiang* (Mandarin): "Crazy Wild 3000 Police." Cinematographer: Cheung Man-bo; Art Director: Vincent Lam Wai-sam; Music: Kam Pau-lin, Simon Lui Yu-yeung; Writer: Ng Man-fai; Producer: Kimmy Suen King-on; Director: Billy Tang Hin-sing. Cast: Francoise Yip Fong-wah (The Girl), Bowie Lam Bo-yee (The Leader), Simon Lui Yu-yeung (Hood with Lighter), Leung Yat-ho, Law Kwok-fai. 1.85:1. VHS: Tai Seng. Import LD/VCD: Fitto Mobile. 84 minutes.

Technique is everything in this crime thriller, which is based on a true Mainland case where 3000 rounds of ammunition were expended during the authorities' final battle with their targets. When a minor traffic accident results in the murder of the Public Security Bureau commander's son, four bodyguards hit the road, accompanied by a seductive hooker from Xinjiang. As they work their way south towards HK (hijacking buses and narrowly avoiding capture), the girl and the leader develop a heated attraction for one another.

The plot sets one up to expect "Natural Born Killers in China," but the violence and sexual content are actually pretty mild, particularly by director Billy Tang's standards. Relying extensively on long takes and photographed with great artistry, **Wild** serves as an even more potent example of the hypnotic visual style that gave some aesthetic validity to Tang's otherwise reprehensible rape/revenge yarn **Red to Kill**. Most of the film takes place in arid locales, giving it an unexpected visual connection to numerous Hollywood road movies, which always seem to unfold in the desert. A superficial exercise, to be sure, but *Wild* holds a viewer's attention nonetheless and stays in the memory afterwards. The English subtitles are very good, which is ironic, as no one really says anything of much consequence.

1076. The Wild Couple

(1996; Wing Wing Productions) ★: 4/10. *Foh yuen yeung* (Cantonese), *Huo yuan yang* (Mandarin): "Fiery Lovebirds." Cinematographer: Chiu Siu-tung; Art Director: Law Lai-si; Music: Not Original; Writer: Jimmy Leung Chi-ming; Producer: Leung Kwok-wing; Action Director: Mak Wai-cheung; Director: Ridley Tsui Bo-wah. Cast: Roy Cheung Yiu-yeung (Yue Hwa), Lily Chung Suk-wai (Hwang Mei-soo), Hugo Ng Toi-yung (Pang Chen), Ben Ng Ngai-cheung (Hai). 1.85:1. VHS: Tai Seng. Import LD/VCD: New City. 92 minutes.

Competent action scenes are all this low-budget production has to offer. Lovers from HK on the loose in China, Yue Hwa and his trashy girlfriend Hwang Mei-soo are a pair of brazen thieves. Along with their partner, they steal $6 million from Mainland mobster Pang Chen (Hugo Ng in a shamelessly over-the-top performance) and horribly disfigure him in the process. On the run from both Pang and the Public Security forces, the three kidnap the young daughter of a rich couple, ordering them to pay $10 million for the child's safe return. When they are betrayed by one of their contacts, Pang is able to discover their hideout, leading to a heated gun battle. However, the thieves are able to escape and set about trying to collect on their ransom demand, a task made difficult by a particularly determined police officer.

As befitting the new sense of caution regarding the depiction of Mainland officials in HK cinema, the Public Security men here are so righteous one half expects them to sprout wings and halos. Despite being flamboyant, uninhibited performers, Cheung and Chung have no real chemistry together, and the formula-bound script gives them few opportunities to breathe life into these cardboard characters. However, the only person one should feel any sympathy for is the poor little girl playing the hostage. She gets smacked around and abused to a degree that would never have been permitted in a Western production.

1077. The Wild Ones

(1989; Ko Chi Sum Productions) ★: 5/10. *Ngoh mei sing nin* (Cantonese), *Wo wei cheng nian* (Mandarin): "I Have Not Grown Up." Cinematographer: Lau Hung-chuen; Art Director: Bill Lui Biu; Music: Jonathan Wong Bong-yin; Writer: Nam Yin; Producer: David Lam Tak-luk; Action Director: Tony Leung Siu-hung; Directors: Francis Sung Ho-fai, David Lam Tak-luk. Cast: Olivia Cheng Man-ar (Sandy Kwong), Fennie Yuen Kit-ying (Kam), Loletta Lee Lai-chun (Mildred Lo), Irene Wan Pik-ha (Jane Chan), Charine Chan Kar-ling (Smart Ass), Tommy Wong Kwong-leung (Messy), Lau Siu-ming (Mildred's Father), Victor Hon Kwan (Jane's Father), Simon Yam Tat-wah (John). 1.85:1. VHS: Tai Seng. Import LD: Mei Ah. Import VCD: Mega Star. 94 minutes. Also known as **I Am Green**.

Disappointed by her lack of progress with Toronto youths, social worker Sandy Kwong goes back to HK and accepts a position at The Ma Tau Wei Girls' Home. She is assigned four girls: Mildred Lo (a rich girl with a vicious temper), Jane (a crippled mute with an abusive father), dimwitted prostitute Smart Ass, and Kam, the latter's "pimp." By adopting a different approach from that utilized by her superiors, Sandy is able to make some progress with her charges and tries to get them to face their problems. At the same time, Sandy tries to reacquaint herself with her disreputable mother, whom she has not seen in several years. In the process, she discovers that Kam is actually her younger sister.

Nam Yin's script bears some resemblance to his screenplay for **Prison on Fire**, though it lacks the power and suspense of that film; the situations here are mostly formulaic and unconvincing. Regardless, **The Wild Ones** does offer a strong central performance by Olivia Cheng and appealing ones from the girls, who have worked together on previous movies, albeit in different combinations.

1078. A Wild Party

(1993; Lotus Cinevision Co.) ★: 3/10. *Yin doi ching yuk pin ji woon chai dong on* (Cantonese), *Xian dai qing yu pian zhi huan qi dang an* (Mandarin): "Modern Lust Writing: Exchange Wife File" Cinematographer-Producer: King Hoi-lam; Art Director: Tin Chun; Music: Not Original; Writer-Director: Wong Pak-chi. Cast: Pauline Chan Po-lin (Susan), Chim Bing-hei, Ying Siu-lu. 1.85:1. VHS: Tai Seng (Poor Subtitles). Import LD/VCD: Ocean Shores (Poor Subtitles). 89 minutes.

A wife-swapping group called "The Happy Pal Club" is at the center of this Category III drama which is somewhat better produced and acted than most of its ilk. Unfortunately, while its goals may be loftier (presenting an actual storyline with fairly plausible conflicts and characters), the resulting film is just not very interesting and akin to a mediocre TV program spiced up with softcore interludes. It tells the overlapping stories of three protagonists: lonely cab driver Lee Keung, disenchanted divorcee Susan, and Siu-ying, a Mainland-born nurse who has only been in HK a month. The two women are under the influence of Dr. Poon, a most unconventional psychiatrist: He advises Susan that the best way for her to forget her ex is to watch him make love to another woman (of course, Poon has to be there observing as well, strictly for professional reasons), while he forces Siu-ying (who works at his practice) to pose as his spouse and participate in the circle's carnal activities. We also spend time with Szeto Tak, the leader of the club, his uninhibited wife, and their willing partners. Lee and Siu-ying eventually become more than friends, transcending the empty bacchanalian lifestyle practised by the club members, in the story's rather unconvincing resolution. Fans of Pauline Chan will be disappointed to learn that she stays clothed throughout, even during her one sex scene.

1079. Wild Search

(1989; Silver Medal/Born Top) ★: 7/10. *Boon ngoh chong tin ngaai* (Cantonese), *Ban wu chuang tian ya* (Mandarin): "Let's Face the World Together." Cinematographer: Andrew Lau Wai-keung; Art Director: Luk Chi-fung; Music: Lowell Lo Kwun-ting; Writer: Nam Yin; Producer-Director: Ringo Lam Ling-tung. Cast: Chow Yun-fat (Lau, aka Mew Mew), Cherie Chung Cho-hung (Cher), Tommy Wong Kwong-leung (Nam), Roy Cheung Yiu-yeung (Bullet), Paul Chun Pui (Hung), Ku Feng (Lee), Lau Kong (Leong), Ng Chi-hung (Cheong), Elaine Kam Yin-lung (Elaine Lee), Vincent Wan Yeung-ming (Cop). Dolby Digital (DVD only). 1.85:1. VHS: Tai Seng. Import LD: Golden Cinema City. Import VCD: Mei Ah (No Subtitles). Import DVD: Mei Ah. 95 minutes.

Ringo Lam has openly admitted that this thriller is an unabashed imitation of Peter Weir's **Witness**. However, it is different enough for this creative laziness to be forgiven and is a well-crafted and entertaining film on its own terms. Police officers Mew Mew and Nam lead a raid on some gun runners. In the subsequent shootout, a female suspect is killed, leaving her three-year-old daughter, Ka-ka, without a guardian. Mew traces the deceased to a country farm where he encounters her sister Cher. Lau and Cher get off on the wrong foot immediately, but gradually begin to develop affection for one another. She reveals to Mew that Ka-ka is the illegitimate offspring of Hung, a wealthy businessman/gangster who wants nothing to do with his daughter. When Mew confronts him, Hung has his men beat the officer up, getting him into trouble with his superiors. He then sends a brutal Vietnamese hitman named Bullet to terminate Mew in a bar. The attempt fails and Bullet is wounded, prompting him to swear vengeance. Meanwhile, the growing romance between Mew and Cher is threatened by Leong, the woman's ex-husband, who has returned to the farm from China and expects Cher to still care for him. This situation comes to a head just as Bullet arrives from the city looking to kill Mew.

Chow Yun-fat and Cherie Chung are both effective, endowing stock characters Mew (the functioning alcoholic with a heart of gold buried under his brusque exterior) and Cher (the simple but loyal country woman) with enough personality and vulnerability to make the viewer care about them. The action scenes are used more sparingly here than in Lam's other collaborations with Chow, though they are no less brutal, which is a bit distracting in a film dedicated largely to character development (in addition to the romantic subplot, a good portion of the running time is devoted to Cher's father and his animosity towards the child). Regardless, the suspense sequences are well mounted, particularly the climax, and effective use is made of a lovely song by the late Taiwanese singer Teresa Teng Li-chun which is heard several times in the film (including a cover version sung by Anita Mui Yim-fong).

1080. Will of Iron

(1991; D & B Films Co.) ★: 2/10. *Hak suet* (Cantonese), *Hei xue* (Mandarin): "Black Snow." Cinematographer: Wilson Chan Pui-kai; Art Director: Jonathan Cheung Hoi-kei; Music: Lowell Lo Kwun-ting; Writer: Law Tai-man; Producer: Stephen Shin Kei-yin; Action Director: James Ha Chim-see; Director: David Chiang Da-wei. Cast: Maggie Cheung Man-yuk (Maggie), Jacky Cheung Hok-yau (Jacky), Michael Wong Man-tak (Michael), Crystal Kwok Kam-yan (Carol), Woo Fung (Maggie's Uncle), David Chiang Da-wei (Jacky's Uncle), Lawrence Ah Mon (Lau), Mark Houghton (Mark). 1.85:1. VHS: Tai Seng. Import LD: Universe. 89 minutes.

Drug addicted cartoonist Jacky owes $180,000 to the mob, but buddy Michael saves his life when some hoods come to beat him to death. Michael, however, is no knight in shining armour: He is a drug dealer himself, in league with the very criminals Jacky owes the money to. With his back against the wall and time quickly running out, Jacky agrees to smuggle drugs to Holland in order to help erase his debt. However, when he learns that his distraught wife has attempted suicide, he backs out of his promise. Trying to help her friends, Michael's girlfriend Maggie gets involved, setting the stage for more tragedy.

Utterly unconvincing from start to finish, **Will of Iron** is written and directed in such a heavy-handed fashion it eventually becomes outright comical; the climax is especially ludicrous. A portion of the score would be recycled in the next year's **Handsome Siblings**.

1081. Wind Beneath the Wings

(1995; Golden Harvest/Paragon Films) ★: 2/10. *Hung jung siu je* (Cantonese), *Kong zhong xiao jie* (Mandarin): "Air Hostess." Cinematographers: William Yim Wai-lun, Gavin Liew; Art Director: Stanley Cheung Sai-kit; Music: Tommy Wai Kai-leung; Writers: Ivy Lee Mo-king, Pang Chi-lai; Producer: Barbie Tung Wan-sze; Director: Andy Chin Wing-keung. Cast: Valerie Chow Kar-ling (Lo Ka-ling), Moses Chan Ho (Chan Kai-ming), Dayo Wong Chi-wah (Kwok Ching-man), Yu Rongguang (Yu Sai-wing). 1.85:1. VHS: Tai Seng. Import LD: Cameron Entertainment. Import VCD: Mei Ah. 96 minutes.

Fresh from playing a stewardess in **Chungking Express**, Valerie Chow (who has since relocated to America and adopted the professional name "Rachel Shane") took to the skies again for this ill-conceived drama which depicts the ongoing trials and tribulations of a student attending stewardess school. Ling tries to keep up her studies while fending off an obnoxious male classmate and a rich patriarch who wants her to marry his timid son (kung fu star Yu Rongguang—as a bespectacled nerd!). Will Ling manage to find true love in the arms of Ming, a struggling musician with a low sense of self-worth?

With all the depth of a romance novel and all the excitement of a 22-hour flight, this is a very long slog through well-mapped terrain that will only pass muster with teenage girls and (perhaps) ardent Valerie Chow fans. One of 1995's biggest flops, *Wind* winged its way out of theaters after only four days.

1082. Wing Chun

(1994; Sil-Metropole Organisation/Wo Ping Films Company) ★: 7/10. *Wing Chun* (Cantonese), *Yong Chuan* (Mandarin): "Wing Chun." Cinematographer: Mark Lee Ping-bing; Art Director: Andy Lee Yiu-kwong; Writers: Anthony Wong Wing-fai, Elsa Tang Pik-yin; Action Directors: Yuen Woo-ping, Yuen Shun-yee, Donnie Yen Chi-tan; Producer-Director: Yuen Woo-ping. Cast: Michelle Yeoh Chu-kheng (Yim Wing-chun), Donnie Yen Chi-tan (Leung Pok-to), Waise Lee Chi-hung (Wong Hok-chow), Yuen King-tan (Abacus Fong), Catherine Hung Yan (Charmy), Norman Tsui Siu-keung ("Flying Chimpanzee"). 1.85:1. VHS/LD/DVD: Tai Seng (Remastered for the English market: subtitled or dubbed). Import LD/VCD: Star Entertainment. 95 minutes.

Lensed at picturesque Taiwan locales, **Wing Chun** is an enjoyable throwback to such Lau Kar-leung/Shaw Brothers productions as **Shaolin Challenges Ninja** (1979) and **My Young Auntie** (1980) in the way it eschews bloodshed in favor of honor and martial technique, with a healthy dose of comedy included to humanize the combatants. Kung fu expert Yim Wing-chun has no prospective suitors, as men are more than a little intimidated by her abilities. When a band of horse thieves kidnap her friend Charmy, Wing-chun is coerced into fighting two duels with bandit chieftain "Flying Chimpanzee" in order to secure her release.

While a subplot involving mistaken identity is contrived (in typical HK movie fashion, one character mistakes Wing-chun for a man simply because she wears men's clothes!) and some of the comedy laboured, the kung fu is consistently inventive and exciting, despite a heavy emphasis on wirework. Yeoh possesses poise and flexibility all but unmatched among contemporary martial arts stars, and it is a particular pleasure to see her face off against Shaw Brothers veteran Norman Tsui (**Duel to the Death**). Donnie Yen's supporting role as Wing-chun's childhood sweetheart allows him to do relatively little fighting, but '60s kung fu queen Cheng Pei-pei has a cameo as her erudite *sifu*. Incidentally, while the Wing-chun character is presumably based on the inventor of that martial arts style, it has no bearing on the plot here. Avoid the dubbed version at all costs.

1083. Winners & Sinners

(1983; Golden Harvest/Paragon Films) ★: 5/10. *Kei mau miu gai ng fuk sing* (Cantonese), *Qi mou miao ji wu fu xing* (Mandarin): "Strange Plan, Brilliant Idea: Five Lucky Stars." Cinematographer: Ricky Lau Koon-wai; Art Director: Jon Hau Wing-choi; Music: Chris Babida; Writers: Sammo Hung Kam-po, Barry Wong Ping-yiu; Producer: Leonard Ho Koon-cheung; Action Directors: Yuen Biao, Lam Ching-ying, Billy Chan Wui-ngai; Director: Sammo Hung Kam-po. Cast: Sammo Hung Kam-po (Teapot), John Sham Kin-fun (Curly Jack So), Richard Ng Yiu-hon (Windpipe), Charlie Chin Hsiang-lin (Lin, aka Vaseline), Stanley Fung Shui-fan (Ranks), Cherie Chung Cho-hung (Curly's Sister), James Tien Chun (Chan Chiu), Jackie Chan (7086), Phillip Chan Yan-kin (7086's Superior), Pat Ha Man-chik (Chan's Daughter), Tai Po (Chai), Cheung Chung (Ho Man), Cecilia Yip Tung (Ceci), Yuen Biao (CID Officer), Moon Lee Choi-fung (Girl), Lam Ching-ying (Housekeeper Chan), Dick Wei (Henchman), Feng Sing (Robber), Fung Hark-on (Pat), Peter Chan Lung (Henchman), Chung Fat (Henchman), Cho Tat-wah (Medicine Man), Wu Ma (Mailman), Barry Wong Ping-yiu (Announcer). Dolby Digital (DVD only). 1.85:1. VHS: Tai Seng (Remastered for the English Market; subtitled or dubbed). Import VCD: Mei Ah. Import DVD: Universe. 108 minutes (Subtitled), 102 minutes (Dubbed).

The first entry in the successful *ng fuk sing* action comedy series, **Winners & Sinners** sets the trend for later entries by offering up fights and stunts that are more inspired than the jokes. After having served time together, career miscreants Teapot, Curly Jack, Windpipe, Vaseline, and Ranks remain good buddies and form a cleaning company. In between making plays for Curly's beautiful sister, the boys bumble their way through a series of set-pieces that are only marginally connected to the main narrative (about a counterfeit deal between two gangsters that goes awry when the Lucky Stars accidentally make off with the printing plates).

Director Sammo Hung allows several comic sequences to drag on well after all possible laughs have been harvested; even Richard Ng's famous "invisibility trance" (where he walks around naked, thinking that no one can see him) would have garnered twice the laughs at half the length. You know comedic bankruptcy has set in when a film resorts to a fifty car pile-up. The proceedings only really come alive when co-star Jackie Chan executes the most amazing stunts ever performed on roller skates (including skating under a speeding tanker truck on a busy roadway!). As usual with the series, there are a multitude of familiar faces in small roles to keep one interested. **My Lucky Stars** came next.

1084. Witch from Nepal

(1985; Golden Harvest/Paragon Films) ★: 6/10. *Kei yuen* (Cantonese), *Qi yuan* (Mandarin): "Strange Destiny." Cinematographer: Tom Lau Moon-tong; Art Director: James Leung Wah-sang; Music: Violet Lam Man-yee, Chow Kam-cheung; Writer: Tsui Ching-hong; Producer: Raymond Chow Man-wai; Action Directors: Ching Siu-tung, Phillip Kwok Tsui, Lau Chi-ho, Tsui Chung-san; Director: Ching Siu-tung. Cast: Chow Yun-fat (Joe Wong), Emily Chu Bo-yee (Sheila), Yammie Nam Kit-ying (Ida Yuen), Dick Wei (The Warrior). 1.85:1. VHS: Tai Seng. LD: Media Asia. Import LD: Star Entertainment (No Subtitles). Import VCD: Mega Star. Import DVD: Universe. 89 minutes. Also known as **The Nepal Affair**.

This wonderfully preposterous Ching Siu-tung action fantasy stars Chow Yun-fat as architect Joe Wong, who takes a vacation in Nepal with his girlfriend Ida. While there, Joe is haunted by visions of a mysterious, veiled woman. Thrown from an elephant and badly injured, he is sent back to Hong Kong for treatment, only to find that same strange woman now a patient at the hospital. Possessing amazing powers and abilities, she heals his seriously infected leg, allowing him to leave the facility. Unable to get her out of his mind, he drives back to the hospital right at the moment immigration arrives to throw the illegal alien out of the country. Escaping with Joe, the woman (whose name is anglicized in the subs as *Sheila*) demonstrates some of her powers to Joe and teaches him to do a few rudimentary telekinetic tricks. After he bonds both mentally and physically with Sheila, Joe discovers that he has been selected to be the new leader of her tribe and the defender of Nepal. However, he has some formidable opposition in the form of a beastly warrior with considerable powers who has come to HK for a fight to the death.

Witch from Nepal is one of those distinctively HK enterprises that offers up a veritable shopping list of disparate components that somehow manage to transpire in the same film. To wit: a sappy love scene that climaxes with a fallen power line blasting two electrically charged hearts into the air; a hospital with a staff of about five orderlies that magically swells to ten times that number when an intruder breaks in; an attack by an entire graveyard full of muddy, mentally resurrected zombies; a runaway elevator that explodes through the roof of a building; a car accident that sends driver and vehicle on a voyage through time and space; a climactic battle in the *deserted* streets of HK (the place hasn't looked this empty since the Japanese invaded!), where an opponent is sent careening out of one skyscraper and through the window of another; and a villain who screeches like a bobcat and wields a giant bone as his weapon of choice. To Chow Yun-fat's eternal credit, he plays his role with complete conviction, and his belief in the material is *almost* enough to actually sell it. The important thing, though, is that **Witch from Nepal** fulfills the two primary commandments of exploitation cinema: It never lags and it is undeniably entertaining. Chow and Chu would appear together again the next year in **A Better Tomorrow**.

1085. With or Without You

(1992; Carrianna Film Production) ★: 3/10. *Ming yuet jiu jim dung* (Cantonese), *Ming yue zhao jian dong* (Mandarin): "Bright Moon Illuminates Tsimshatsui East." Cinematographer: Herman Yau Lai-to; Art Director: Ho Chi-hang; Music: Lau Yee-tat; Writers: Lam Chiu-wing, Lam Kei-to; Producer: Richard Cheung Kuen; Action Director: Lam Moon-wah; Director: Taylor Wong Tai-loi. Cast: Leon Lai Ming (Ming), Rosamund Kwan Chi-lam (Joey), Jacky Cheung Hok-yau (Prince), Ng Man-tat (Tat), John Ching Tung (Tung). 1.85:1. VHS/LD: World Video. 86 minutes.

Jacky Cheung is a ruthless hitman, Leon Lai is a determined rookie cop, and Rosamund Kwan is the woman caught between them in this stylish but utterly superficial thriller. After breaking up with his girl, Ming goes on a drunken binge and loses his gun at some point in the evening. He and his more experienced partner, Tat, desperately search for the missing weapon, which has fallen into the hands of a street urchin in the employ of high class club girl Joey. Ming gets his gun back and strikes up a relationship with Joey, but Prince, a very dangerous man from her past, is about to come back into her life and put an end to their romance.

While consistently watchable, this foolish drama is never the least bit creditable and features an annoyingly large number of time-killing "hit single" montages, which are evidently supposed to also function as character development. The stars are attractive and the action sequences are well-staged, however, so rabid fans may want to take a look regardless. The film's box office success led to an equally vapid prequel, **No More Love, No More Death**.

The Witness *see* **In the Line of Duty IV**

1086. Women's Prison

(1988; D & B Films Co./Alan and Eric Films) ★: 2/10. *Nui ji gaam yuk* (Cantonese), *Nu zi jian yu* (Mandarin): "Women Prison." Cinematographer: Lau Hung-chuen; Art Directors: Jon Hau Wing-choi, Luk Chi-fung; Music: Traditional; Writer: Nam Yin; Producers: Alan Tam Wing-lun, Eric Tsang Chi-wai, Teddy Robin Kwan; Action Director: Tam Lap-fai; Director: David Lam Tak-luk. Cast: Pat Ha Man-chik (Kelly Ho), Carol Cheng Yu-ling (Lynn), Petrina Fung Bo-bo (Jean), Charine Chan Kar-ling (Mendy), Elsie Chan Yik-si (Rose), Ha Chi-chun (Phys Ed Teacher), Maria Cordero (East Indian Guard), Simon Yam Tat-wah (Wayne Lau), Tommy Wong Kwong-leung (Jean's Husband). 1.85:1. VHS: Tai Seng. 92 minutes.

This is another tired, utterly routine women-in-prison drama, a subgenre that needs to be put out of its misery, and fast. On her wedding day, Kelly Ho kills a loan shark, earning herself eighteen months behind bars. Once inside she has the usual trouble adjusting to the staff and her fellow inmates. Her actions almost instantly make her an enemy of Fatty, a sadistic "Big Sister," and the cartoonishly mean phys ed instructor (played by Ha Chi-chun, eyeballs popping and riding crop at the ready). After days of abuse, Kelly escapes inside the back of a garbage truck but must surrender herself because a child made his way inside as well. The young boy (born at the institution) belongs to Jean, a friendly prisoner who works with Kelly in the kitchen. After humiliating Fatty, Kelly learns that she is pregnant. She joins up with Big Sister Lynn for protection, but the warden keeps the latter drugged up and in the infirmary, a lead-in to the inevitable riot.

Aside from another solid performance by the underrated Pat Ha and the novelty of seeing Carol Cheng in a very atypical part, this is a complete waste of time and celluloid.

1087. Wonder Seven

(1994; China Entertainment Films Production) ★: 5/10. *7 gam gong* (Cantonese), *7 jin gong* (Mandarin): "7 Golden Strong." Cinematographers: Poon Hang-sang, Peter Ngor Chi-kwan; Art Director: James Leung Wah-sang; Music: Lo Tai-yau, Barry Chung Hing-hung, Fabio Carli; Writers: Charcoal Cheung Tan, Elsa Tang Pik-yin, Ching Siu-tung; Producer: Catherine Hun Kar-chun; Action Directors: Ching Siu-tung, Lau Chi-ho, Dion Lam Dik-on, Xiong Xinxin; Director: Ching Siu-tung. Cast: Michelle Yeoh Chu-kheng (Ying), Li Ning (Fei), Kent Cheng Chuk-see (Nanny), Andy Hui Chi-on (Superman), Hilary Tsui Ho-ying (Tiny Archer), Xiong Xinxin (Shaolin Monk), Elvis Tsui Kam-kong (Coach), Chin Ho (Tsun), Wong Kam-kong (Colonel Yim), Bobby Yip King-sang (Head of Mainland Thieves). 1.85:1. VHS: Tai Seng. Import LD/VCD/DVD: Universe. 90 minutes.

A lesser effort from talented directoraction choreographer Ching Siu-tung, this muddled actioner never hits its stride, despite some stirring chases and hand-to-hand combat. The "Wonder Seven" are a group of orphans turned motorcycle-riding fighters, who battle evil for the Mainland government. After dealing with some thugs who had perpetrated a "Big Circle" robbery, the team is dispatched to HK to acquire two special cards which will allow access to a Swiss Bank Account containing millions of dollars in diamonds. They are opposed by Tsun and Ying, partners who do not see eye-to-eye on how they should conduct their missions. The beautiful Ying and Wonder Seven leader Fei (well-played by Olympic gymnast Li Ning) develop a strong attraction for one another, with Fei even sparing her life at one point. The increasingly deranged Tsun and his men (including a traitorous Mainland officer who used to work with Wonder Seven) soon target the orphans in their attempts to get the card they don't possess.

The film was reportedly restructured in post-production to make the plot more coherent, but the story still does not play out in a smooth and easily discernible fashion. With the exception of the leads, none of the characters are well-defined, and it even becomes difficult at times to tell who is who. However, **Wonder Seven** remains fairly enjoyable if one just approaches it as a fanciful action and stunt display, forgets about context, and just goes along for the ride. One bit, featuring a runaway elevator exploding through the roof of a skyscraper, is a restaging of a similar sequence in Ching's 1985 film **Witch from Nepal**.

Wong Fei-hung '92 *see* The Master

1088. Working Class

(1985; Cinema City Co./Film Workshop) ★: 6/10. *Da gung wong dai* (Cantonese), *Da gong huang da* (Mandarin): "King of the Working Stiffs." Cinematographer: Henry Chan Chun-kit; Art Director: Yiu Yau-hung; Music: Teddy Robin Kwan; Writer: Chan Kam-kuen; Producer: Shun Kar-chun; Director: Tsui Hark. Cast: Sam Hui Koon-kit (Yan), Joey Wang Tsu-hsien (Amy), Teddy Robin Kwan (Hing), Tsui Hark (Sunny), Ng Man-tat (Factory Foreman), David Wu Tai-wai (Factory Supervisor), Shum Wai (Wu), Angile Leung Wan-yui (Jane), Kwan Hoi-shan, Wong Wan-si (Factory Workers), Ken Lo Wai-kwong (Kickboxer), Bolo Yeung (Giant Kickboxer). 1.85:1. VHS: Tai Seng. Import LD: Golden Cinema City. Import VCD: Mega Star. 98 minutes.

Critics of Tsui Hark like to condemn him for "selling out" by abandoning his roots (i.e. his television work and films like **The Butterfly Murders** and **Dangerous Encounter—1st Kind**), ignoring the fact that Tsui often brings something more to the material even on his lesser works. On the other hand, **Working Class** is one movie that probably could have been made by just about anybody and turned out pretty much the same way. Regardless, it is not without its pleasures and is very much an archetypal Cinema City comedy. The perpetually unemployed Yan falls head-over-heels for gorgeous Amy, not knowing that she is actually from an affluent family. Amy keeps up this ruse, realizing that Yan has a bias against rich people. Meanwhile, Yan finally manages to find employment...at the noodle factory owned by Amy's father! When he finally does find out who Amy is, Yan is horrified, and all of his and Amy's various lies soon get hopelessly tangled together, leading to some amusing misunderstandings. Complicating matters is the plant's evil manager who has embezzled a huge sum and hatched a scheme to evade prosecution that has potentially deadly consequences.

While resolutely predictable, **Working Class** is amiable, lightweight fun. Sam Hui and Joey Wang are fine as the leads, but most of the laughs are provided by Teddy Robin Kwan and Tsui himself as Yan's layabout buddies. The best bit finds them trying to help Yan impress Amy by taking her to a luxurious villa; the one they steal the keys to turns out to be her parents' house!

1089. The Wrath of Silence

(1994; Golden Harvest/Good Standard International/Paragon Films) ★: 2/10. *Cham mak dik goo neung* (Cantonese), *Chen mo de gu niang* (Mandarin): "Silent Girl." Cinematographer: Michael Ma Koon-wah; Art Director: Edward Tang King-sang; Music: Roel A. Garcia; Writers: Frankie Chan Fan-kei, Lee Ping-kwong, Lee Wan-hang; Producer: Anthony Chow Ting-on; Director: Frankie Chan Fan-kei. Cast: Anita Yuen Wing-yee (Kwong Mei-chi), Takeshi Kaneshiro (Dr. Patrick Ko), Sin Lap-man (Pal), Maggie Siu Mei-kei (Lawyer Pao), Emily Kwan Bo-wai (The Policewoman), Frankie Chan Fan-kei (Yee), Ha Ping (Mei-chi's Boss), Feng Sing (Cop at Station). 1.85:1. VHS: Tai Seng. Import LD/VCD: Universe. 98 minutes.

Anita Yuen and Takeshi Kaneshiro are badly miscast in this ill-conceived and hopelessly contrived black comedy-thriller, which is a washout in both of those categories. Kwong Mei-chi is a morose and increasingly deranged funeral parlor worker who must take care of her retarded sister Mei-yee. When a psychopathic rapist/murderer molests Mei-yee and throws her off a building, Mei-chi's psychiatrist, Dr. Ko, is mistakenly blamed for the crime, even though he was actually trying to apprehend the real culprit. Mei-chi makes several attempts on Ko's life, only to be hit by a car before she can kill him. The driver is none other than the maniac (whose name is "Pal," like the TV system), who takes Mei-chi to the hospital and convinces her that he is a nice guy. In the meantime, Ko desperately tries to prove his innocence to Mei-chi.

Bereft of logic, thrills, and laughs, this is a strain from beginning to end. Some of the more misogynistic violence has been trimmed from the video version.

1090. Yes, Madam

(1985; D & B Films Co.) ★: 7/10. *Wong ga si je* (Cantonese), *Huang jia shi jie* (Mandarin): "Royal Hong Kong Policewoman." Cinematographer: Bill Wong Chung-bo; Art Directors: Ma Chun-kit, Wong Ching-kong; Music: Romeo Diaz;

Writer: Barry Wong Ping-yiu; Producer: Sammo Hung Kam-po; Action Directors: Corey Yuen Kwai, Mang Hoi; Director: Corey Yuen Kwai. Cast: Michelle Yeoh Chu-kheng (Inspector Ng), Cynthia Rothrock (Inspector Carrie Morris), Tsui Hark (Panadol), Dick Wei (Dick), Mang Hoi (Asprin), John Sham Kin-fun (Strepsil), Wu Ma (Beat Cop), James Tien Chun (Tin), Melvin Wong Kam-sun (Wong), Tai Po (Cop), Eddie Maher (Thug with Fake Passport), Chung Fat (Mad-dog), Sammo Hung Kam-po (Old Master), Richard Ng Yiu-hon (Old Master's Roommate), David Chiang Da-wei (Old Master's Roommate), Billy Lau Nam-kwong (Parking Meter Attendant), Shum Wai (Tin's Lawyer), Dennis Chan Kwok-san (Bartender), Lam Wai (Armored Car Robber), Chen Jing (Armored Car Robber). Dolby Digital (DVD only). 1.85:1. VHS: J & M Chevalier. Import LD: Mei Ah. Import VCD: Mega Star. Import DVD: Universe. 87/93 minutes. Also known as **Police Assassin 2** (UK video title).

Yes, Madam is noteworthy as being both the first entry in D & B's **In the Line of Duty** series and Michelle Yeoh's first outing in a lead role. Following the obligatory opening reel action sequence (which features Yeoh single-handedly nabbing some armored car hijackers), the film segues into the main storyline. Triad leader Tin's accountant decides to sell him out and takes pictures of a forged business contract. The traitor is liquidated but the hitman is unable to locate the microfilm, which has inadvertently been stolen by petty hotel thieves Asprin [*sic*] and Strepsil. When the dead man's passport is used by a fleeing criminal, HK police Inspector Ng lets the man go, as a means of tracking down Panadol, the forger who sold him the document. Teaming up with her Cantonese-speaking Scotland Yard counterpart, Inspector Carrie Morris, Ng sets out to get the goods on Tin. However, when legal means fail, the policewomen turn in their badges and confront Tin and his goons on their own turf.

Like virtually all of the D & B genre pictures that followed, the storyline is routine but the action certainly isn't. The final reel features some spectacular fighting, and Michelle Yeoh performs an amazing stunt where she flips backwards over a rail and through plate glass! The English export version (which runs 87 minutes) is missing the opening scene where Yeoh literally closes the book on a library flasher. Instead, it opens with a sequence recycled from **Where's Officer Tuba?** (featuring David Chiang Da-wei, who turns up later in **Yes, Madam** playing a completely different character) that has absolutely no bearing on the story presented here! This version also gives Eddie Maher third billing, though he is only in the film for a few minutes! Romeo Diaz is credited with the soundtrack, but a good portion of the music here has been lifted from **Halloween**.

Yes Madam '92: A Serious Shock *see* **A Serious Shock! Yes Madam!**

1091. Yesteryou, Yesterme, Yesterday

(1993; Movie Impact) ★: 6/10. *Gei dak...heung jiu sing suk si* (Cantonese), *Ji de...xiang jiao cheng shou shi* (Mandarin): "Remember...Banana Ripening Time." Cinematographer: Jingle Ma Cho-shing; Art Director: Ben Luk Man-wah; Music: Richard Lo Sai-kit; Writer: Lee Chi-ngai; Producer: Peter Chan Ho-sun; Director: Samson Chiu Leung-chun. Cast: John Tang Yat-kwan (Yeung Shing-bo), Eric Tsang Chi-wai (Yeung Kui-ting), Petrina Fung Bo-bo (Yeung Kong Po-chiu), Ellen Lo Oi-lun (Ting-ting), Ann Bridgewater (Lo Mo-zen, aka "Sensitive Plant"), Miu Kiu-wai (Fong), Barry Wong Ping-yiu (James Wong, aka The Killer). 1.85:1. VHS: Tai Seng. 93 minutes.

A charming coming-of-age comedy set in 1981, this is derivative of similar efforts but still pleasing on its own terms. On the very day that 14-year-old Yeung Shing-bo feels the first stirrings of manhood, he sees his old friend Ting-ting without glasses and realizes that she is not just one of the guys after all. His raging hormones are not helped by the fact that Ting-ting is already seeing an older boy, his family's new boarder is a beautiful cabaret performer, and a would-be triad schoolmate is willing to loan him his hooker girlfriend for a little initiation. On top of that, Shing-bo also must deal with wet dreams, his first kiss, the humiliation of his mom getting a job at the school, and the fact that the only girl who likes him is 11 years old.

Newcomer John Tang gives a natural, appealing performance and the film is a bit more forthright about sex than its Western counterparts, giving it an extra level of interest. However, other aspects are a bit too predictable and pat, keeping this from being any more than a pleasant diversion. It was followed by **Over the Rainbow, Under the Skirt** (1994) and **Yesterday You, Yesterday Me** (1997).*

1092. Young and Dangerous

(1996; Jing's Production/Art Top Movie Productions) ★: 6/10. *Goo waak jai ji yan joi gong woo* (Cantonese), *Gu huo zi zhi ren zai jiang hu* (Mandarin): "Young Rascals: Man of the World." Art Director: Lee Pik-kwan; Music: Clarence Hui Yuen; Writer-Producer: Manfred Wong; Cinematographer-Director: Andrew Lau Wai-keung. Cast: Dior Cheng Yee-kin (Chan Ho-nam), Jordan Chan Siu-chun (Chicken Chiu), Gigi Lai Chi (Smartie, aka Stammer), Francis Ng Chun-yu (Ugly Kwan), Ng Chi-hung (Brother B), Simon Yam Tat-wah (Chiang Tin-sung), Michael Tse Tin-wah (Dai Tin-yee), Jason Chu Wing-tong (Chou-pan), Jerry Lam Hiu-fung (Pou-pan), Suki Chan Sau-yu (Ho Yan), Spencer Lam Sheung-yee (Father Lam), Shing Fui-on (Brother Saur), Johnny Wang Lung-wei (Master Wai), Lee Siu-kei (Key), Cheng Cho (Ba-bai), Ha Ping (Mrs. Lee). 1.85:1. VHS/LD: World Video. Import LD/VCD/DVD: Mei Ah. 100 minutes.

A surprise hit, this triad thriller (adapted from a comic book by Niu Lo, aka "Cow Man," who has a cameo) spawned four sequels, a prequel, and a boatload of imitations (some of which turned out to be decidedly more interesting). When several youths in the Hung Hing Society execute a triad who owes him several millions dollars, psychotic gangster Ugly Kwan targets members Chan Ho-nam and Chicken Chiu. The Hung Hing guys are sent to Macau but are ambushed by Kwan's men, who kill Ho-nam's friend, Chou-pan. Ho-nam survives but is drugged and taped while having sex with Chicken's girlfriend. Devastated by this "duplicity," Chicken leaves for Taiwan, while Ho-nam must face "family punishment" and is thrown out of the gang. Kwan also uses the occasion to take control of Hung Hing and brutally kills Ho-nam's mentor, Brother B.

The storyline is thoroughly routine (if cast entirely with actors in their '30s and up, this would be virtually no different than the "Hero" films spawned by the success of **A Better Tomorrow**) but the manner of presentation is not: The action is stylized, the cinematography makes the neon-drenched streets glisten, and comic book panels are used as transitions between scenes. Dior Cheng is a handsome mannequin in the lead, but Jordan Chan is a joy, stealing every scene he is in, and Francis Ng gives a mannered, highly entertaining performance as the mumbling, egomanical Kwan (he would reprise the character in **Young and Dangerous: The Prequel** and gives a very similar turn in **Once Upon a Time in a Triad Society**). **Young and Dangerous 2** hit theaters only two months later.

*Yesterday You, Yesterday Me *was unavailable for review.*

1093. Young and Dangerous 2

(1996; BOB & Partners Company) ★: 6/10. *Goo waak jai 2 ji maang lung gwoh gong* (Cantonese), *Gu huo zi 2 zhi meng long guo jiang* (Mandarin): "Young Rascals II: Mighty Dragon Crosses River." Art Director: Cyrus Ho Kim-hung; Music: Clarence Hui Yuen, Ronald Ng Luk-sing; Writers: Manfred Wong, Sharon Hui Sa-long; Producers: Manfred Wong, Andrew Lau Wai-keung; Action Director: Dion Lam Dik-on; Cinematographer-Director: Andrew Lau Wai-keung. Cast: Jordan Chan Siu-chun (Chicken Chiu), Dior Cheng Yee-kin (Chan Ho-nam), Gigi Lai Chi (Smartie, aka Stammer), Chingmy Yau Suk-ching (Ting Siu-yiu), Anthony Wong Chau-sang (Tai Fai), Simon Yam Tat-wah (Chiang Tin-sung), Michael Tse Tin-wah (Dai Tin-yee), Jerry Lam Hiu-fung (Pou-pan), Halina Tam Siu-wan (KK), Spencer Lam Sheung-yee (Father Lam), Blackie Ko Shou-liang (Blackie Koh Chi-wah), Moses Chan Ho (Ko Chi). 1.85:1. VHS: Tai Seng. Import LD/VCD/DVD: Mei Ah. 103 minutes.

Jordan Chan is given center stage for this second installment in the popular "young rascals" series. Now that their conflict with Ugly Kwan is resolved, Chan Ho-nam and the rest of the Hung Hing boys open a nightclub in Causeway Bay. During his stay the previous year in Taiwan, Chicken joined up with the San Luen gang and courted his boss' exotic mistress, Ting Siu-yiu. In return for assassinating one of the gang's rivals, Chicken was made head of Poisonous Snake Hall. Meanwhile, back in HK, Ho-nam is competing with Tai Fai (an unkempt, nose-picking slob) to see who will get the territory previously controlled by Brother B. The San Luen group courts Hung Hing with a partnership offer in a Macau casino, but the latter group declines, leading to several violent acts on the part of the Taiwanese gangsters (including one that puts Ho-nam's girlfriend, Smartie, in a coma). Left in a very awkward position, Chicken decides to quit San Luen and support his old friends. However, Siu-yiu strikes a deal with Tai behind her boss' back, leading to his murder (for which Ho-nam and Chicken are framed) and an attack on the Hung Hing leaders.

About on par with its forerunner, this entry has a more compelling and involved storyline, but the climax (set at the grand opening of the casino) has no dramatic punch, lessening the movie's overall impact. Anthony Wong gives a typically colorful performance as Tai but the character is overly cartoonish and not nearly as memorable as Francis Ng's Kwan. The film is notable mainly for its depiction of how triads operate in Taiwan, spending great amounts of money to win seats in the government as a way of consolidating their power (this scenario is also examined in **Island of Greed**). **Young and Dangerous 3** arrived in theaters three months later.

1094. Young and Dangerous 3

(1996; Golden Harvest/BOB & Partners Company/Golden Movies International) ★: 7/10. *Goo waak jai 3 ji jek sau je tin* (Cantonese), *Gu huo zi 3 zhi zhi shou zhe tian* (Mandarin): "Young Rascals 3: Single Hand Covers the Sky." Art Director: Cyrus Ho Kim-hung; Music: Clarence Hui Yuen, Ronald Ng Luk-sing; Writers: Manfred Wong, Candy Cheng; Producers: Manfred Wong, Andrew Lau Wai-keung; Action Director: Dion Lam Dik-on; Cinematographer-Director: Andrew Lau Wai-keung. Cast: Dior Cheng Yee-kin (Chan Ho-nam), Jordan Chan Siu-chun (Chicken Chiu), Gigi Lai Chi (Smartie, aka Stammer), Karen Mok Man-wai (Shuk-fan), Roy Cheung Yiu-yeung (Crow), Anthony Wong Chau-sang (Tai Fai), Simon Yam Tat-wah (Chiang Tin-sung), Ng Chi-hung (Tiger), Michael Tse Tin-wah (Dai Tin-yee), Jerry Lam Hiu-fung (Pou-pan), Michael Chan Wai-man (Camel Lok), Halina Tam Siu-wan (KK), Spencer Lam Sheung-yee (Father Lam), Blackie Ko Shou-liang (Blackie Koh Chi-wah), Victor Hon Kwan (Uncle Eight Fingers), Lee Siu-kei (Key), Helena Law Lan (Granny). 1.85:1. VHS: Tai Seng. Import LD/VCD/DVD: Universe. 99 minutes.

Series newcomers Roy Cheung and Karen Mok steal this above average entry in the popular *goo wak jai* series. While attending a meeting of various gang members, Chan Ho-nam has a run-in with Crow, a thoroughly deranged killer who is one of Tung Sing boss Camel Lok's enforcers. When Tung Sing opens a bar right beside one of Hung Hing's clubs in Wanchai, trouble begins. During a visit to Holland, Hung Hing leader Chiang is murdered, and Ho-nam is made the scapegoat (once again). Crow makes his play for leadership by liquidating Lok, with the intention of using the man's funeral as an opportunity to wipe out all of his remaining opponents. In the various subplots, Chicken is allowed back into Hung Hing but must start from the bottom of the ladder, Smartie comes out of her coma but with severe amnesia, and Chicken falls head over heels for Father Lam's foul-mouthed daughter, Shuk-fan.

The film sags when the action shifts to Holland (the sequence is also poorly directed; during a shootout, dozens of locals can be seen in the background calmly watching the carnage unfold), but Karen Mok gives an energetic and appealing performance and Roy Cheung is wonderfully bizarre as the supremely evil Crow. Cheung had played triad villains in at least a dozen movies prior to this one but had never embodied a depraved madman quite so memorably as he does here. Halina Tam passed on appearing in the next instalment, so her "KK" character is played there by Pinky Cheung Man-chi.

1095. Young and Dangerous 4

(1997; Golden Harvest/BOB & Partners Company/Everwide) ★: 4/10. *97 goo waak jai jin mo bat sing* (Cantonese), *97 gu huo zi zhan wu bu sheng* (Mandarin): "97 Young Rascals: Have Battle, Will Win." Art Director: Ken Chiu Kin-san; Music: Clarence Hui Yuen, Ronald Ng Luk-sing; Writer-Producer: Manfred Wong; Action Director: Lee Chung-chi; Cinematographer-Director: Andrew Lau Wai-keung. Cast: Dior Cheng Yee-kin (Chan Ho-nam), Jordan Chan Siu-chun (Chicken Chiu), Michelle Lee Kar-yan (Lee Yan-yan), Karen Mok Man-wai (Lam Suk-fan, aka Wasabi), Alex Man Chi-leung (Chiang Tin-yeung), Roy Cheung Yiu-yeung (Lui Yiu-yeung, aka Thunder Tiger), Anthony Wong Chau-sang (Tai Fai), Ng Chi-hung (Tiger), Michael Tse Tin-wah (Dai Tin-yee), Jerry Lam Hiu-fung (Pou-pan), Jason Chu Wing-tong (Banana Skin), Pinky Cheung Man-chi (KK), Sandra Ng Kwan-yu (Sister Thirteen), Vincent Wan Yeung-ming (Ben Hon), Ken Lo Wai-kwong (Prince), Lee Siu-kei (Key), Spencer Lam Sheung-yee (Father Lam), Ronald Wong Pan (Superman). 1.85:1. VHS: Mecapro. Import LD/VCD/DVD: Mei Ah. 105 minutes.

Roy Cheung, so effective as the villain of the previous instalment, is back again as a different character in this disappointing entry. With Chiang Tin-sung now dead, his followers journey to Thailand to try and convince the man's brother, Tin-yeung, to take his place. Meanwhile, upstart triad Lui Yiu-yeung of the Tung Sing Society stirs up trouble by throwing boss Dinosaur off a building in Chan Ho-nam's territory. When a replacement for the dead man is discussed, Ho-nam fails to back up Chicken's bid for the position, creating a rift between the two friends. It is decided that Chicken will compete with dimwitted thug Barbarian, to see who earns the title of leader. Dai Tin-yee tries to take out Barbarian, on his own and is murdered by Lui and his men, while his new wife KK is raped. This leads to a showdown of words between the respective parties when it comes time for the members to elect the new leader.

Thoroughly uninspired, this sequel seems to have been concocted merely to keep the series going, and almost everyone—both in front of and behind the camera—is simply going through the motions. Writer-producer Manfred Wong is at a loss here, simply filling the storyline with components from earlier entries and padding the running time with enough subplots for two other movies. The pacing is slack and none of the new characters introduced here are at all interesting, with the lone exception of Sandra Ng as lesbian gang boss Sister Thirteen (the character would be spun off into her own movie, 1998's **Portland Street Blues**). **Young and Dangerous V** and **Young and Dangerous: The Prequel** followed in 1998.

1096. The Young Master

(1980; Golden Harvest) ★: 7/10. *Si dai chut ma* (Cantonese), *Shi di chu ma* (Mandarin): "Little Brother's Turn to Shine." Cinematographer: Chen Ching-chueh; Music: Not Original; Writers: Lau Tin-chi, Tung Lu, Edward Tang King-sang, Jackie Chan; Producer: Raymond Chow Man-wai; Action Directors: Jackie Chan, Fung Hark-on; Director: Jackie Chan. Cast: Jackie Chan (Lung), Wei Pai (Keung), Shih Kien (Sam Kung), Yuen Biao (Fourth Brother), Lily Li Li-li (Sister Sue), Whang Ing-sik (Kim), Tien Feng (Master Tien), Fung Hark-on (Kim's Man), Lee Hoi-sang (Kim's Man), Fan Mui-sang (Brother Bill). Dolby Digital (DVD only). 2.35:1. VHS/LD: Tai Seng (Remastered for the English market; subtitled or dubbed), Magnum (Poor Subtitles), Video Gems (Dubbed). Import VCD/DVD: Universe. 102 minutes (Subtitled version).

Jackie Chan directed and starred in this old-fashioned period martial arts outing which recreates the comedic tone found in the later films he did for director Lo Wei. Chan stars as Lung, an orphan brought up in a martial arts school by a strict, humorless master. During the annual Lion Dance competition, Lung's martially skilled friend Keung fakes an injury and secretly joins the competing school, allowing them to win. When his duplicity is discovered by the master, Keung is banished from the school and Lung sets off to find him. Looking for work, Keung joins up with two goons to rescue the other school's evil master, Kim, while he is being transported to prison. Mistaken for his friend, Lung soon finds himself on the run from resolute district marshall Sam Kung. Lung is able to best the old man's limber son but is eventually caught and handcuffed. Through a nice bit of trickery, Lung is able to elude Sam but must also cope with his daughter, who turns out to be a formidable martial artist in her own right. Striking a deal with Sam, Lung agrees to nab Kim on his own if the marshall agrees to drop all charges against Keung.

Running for an entire reel, the final duel is a bit too drawn out, with a climactic twist more than a little reminiscent of Chan's earlier blockbuster **Drunken Master** (1978). These are only minor complaints, however, as the majority of **Young Master** is a perfect reminder of how good traditional kung fu films can be when they are done right. The skirmish between Chan and Yuen Biao (the latter wielding a *bench* as his weapon of choice) is a highlight (you can imagine them practising such a sequence while they were in Peking Opera school together), but the showstopper is Chan's marvellous, farcical battle with Fung Hark-on and Lee Hoi-sang. Disguised as an old beggar, he manages to convince onlookers that the pair are beating a defenceless opponent while, in reality, it is *he* who is cleaning *their* clocks. Frankie Chan Fan-kei is credited with the music, but the majority of it is not original. The English dubbed version runs about 15 minutes shorter, so there is little reason to bother with it. Be sure to avoid Magnum Video's version of the film, which crops the image to dead center fullscreen and renders the subtitles illegible.

Young Master in Love *see* **Dragon Lord**

1097. Yu Pui Tsuen

(1987) ★: 6/10. *Juk boon yuk po tuen* (Cantonese), *Zu ben yu pu tuan* (Mandarin): "The Complete Prayer Mat of Flesh." Cinematographer: Ho Ming; Art Director: James Cheung Ying-wah; Music: Phil Chan Fei-lap, Tang Siu-lam; Writer: Manfred Wong; Producer: Wong Kiu-lap; Director: Ho Fan. Cast: Tang Yiu-fai (Mei Yeung-sun), Cheng Yuen-man (Ti Yuk-xiang), Sun Chien (Kuan Low-si), Chow Ying-ko, Hui Chi-wai. 1.85:1. VHS: World Video (No Subtitles). Import LD: Citimax, Jumbo Plain. Import VCD/DVD: Jumbo Plain. 91 minutes.

Four years before **Sex and Zen**, this film took a more sober approach in adapting the same source material. Scholar Mei Yeung-sun marries maiden Ti Yuk-xiang, but their sex life is a serious disappointment to the groom. However, with the help of the family sex manual they learn some new positions and Yuk-xiang responds more favorably to their lovemaking. In fact, they begin spending practically all of their free time having sex, much to the chagrin of the girl's father. Eventually, Mei leaves home for the city, ostensibly to become a government official. His real plan is to travel around and sample the countryside's women. On the advice of master thief/satyr Tsoi Kwun-lung, Mei visits a physician and leaves with a much bigger penis. With this new self-confidence, Mei soon seduces maiden Yim-fong and, with Tsoi to back him up, buys the woman from her inattentive husband, Kuan Low-si. Kuan, however, is not about to let this defeat go unavenged. Travelling to Mei's country home, he gets hired on as a workman and proceeds to seduce and impregnate the lonely and vulnerable Yuk-xiang. Meanwhile, Mei continues with his sexual exploits, but he has an unhappy surprise ahead of him.

Produced on a smaller budget than **Sex and Zen**, this remains a handsome production that is a definite step above most of the period softcore yarns that followed in its wake. The sex scenes are erotic and imaginatively staged, leaning more towards the sensual than the later film's furious bump and grind sessions, and there are some stylish nightmare sequences. Still, the original story's heavy-handed "you reap what you sow" moral is pretty hard to take, and this version's conclusion is far too abrupt.

1098. Yu Pui Tsuen III

(1996; My Way Film Company) ★: 5/10. *Daai noi mat taam ji ling ling sing sing* (Cantonese), *Da nei mi tan zhi ling ling xing xing* (Mandarin): "Big Inside Secret Cop: OO-Sex." Cinematographer: Sung Kong; Art Director: Tai Song; Music: Siu San; Producer: Cheung Kai-ping; Writer-Director: Lai Kai-keung. Cast: Elvis Tsui Kam-kong (Agent 000 May Yeung-sung, aka Lightning), Emily Kwan Bo-wai (Yim-fong), Wong Yat-fei (Koo Fung), Spencer Lam Sheung-yee (Sun Ng-hung, aka Lam Sheung-yee), William Ho Kar-kui (Choi Kwun-lun). 1.85:1. VHS: Tai Seng. Import LD/VCD/DVD: Jumbo Plain. 96 minutes.

Bearing no direct connection to any other film, this Category III period sex comedy is a moderately enjoyable send-up of Stephen Chiau's **Forbidden City Cop**. Bumbling secret agent 000 is assigned to go undercover in the Ying Chun Brothel, which is exuding such an influence on all of the area's men that the population is starting to decline. Armed with China's only fountain pen and his "electric eyes" stance, the underendowed 000's mission gets off to a successful start when he is able to win the confidence of the hookers by pretending to be a writer. However, things quickly take an inauspicious turn when his domineering wife shaves his head and forces him to wear a frightening chastity belt (if he gets an erection, blades clamp down on his penis!). With naked beauties constantly trying to seduce him, 000 must endure the tortures of hell, but it is only a matter of time before his natural urges will burst forth and set him free.

Lacking the production values and visual flare of the **Sex and Zen** series, **Yu Pui Tsuen III** compensates with some amusing sexual sight gags and several diverting erotic sequences, making it one of the better films in this subgenre. Soft-core veteran Elvis Tsui (who seems to star in every '90s adult film) gives a marvellous comic performance as the long-suffering agent.

1099. Zen of Sword

[*sic*] (1992; Citimedia) ★: 5/10. *Hap nui chuen kei* (Cantonese), *Xia nu chuan qi* (Mandarin): "Chivalrous Woman Legend." Cinematographers: Ko Chiu-lam, Wong Po-man, Cheng Siu-keung; Art Director: Ben Lau Man-hung; Writers: Lee Man-choi, Leung Kim-ho; Producer: Stephen Shin Kei-yin; Action Director: Phillip Kwok Tsui; Director: Yu Ming-sang. Cast: Cynthia Yang Li-ching (General Choi Siu-ching), Michelle Lee Kar-yan (Princess Choi Siu-ling), Lau Sek-ming (Prince Ha Hou), Waise Lee Chi-hung (General Lau Qun-hung), Lau Shun (The Royal Wizard of Yin), Kara Hui Ying-hung (Ha Hou's Aunt), Phillip Kwok Tsui (The God of War), Lau Siu-ming (Governor Tak Hong). Dolby Stereo. 1.85:1. VHS: Tai Seng. Import LD: Mei Ah. 89 minutes.

Quality cast aside, this medium-budget period swordplay fantasy (partially inspired by "Romeo and Juliet") hasn't much to offer that one cannot find in superior productions of this sort. The Chun Dynasty and the Ha Hou Dynasty both seek to restore themselves to their former glory. Chun princess Choi Siu-ling and the Ha Hou prince (who is named after his kingdom) are supposed to be mortal enemies but fall in love instead. Naturally, this does not go over well with Ha's vicious aunt, who cares only about the family name and honor. One of Princess Choi's protectors, General Lau Qun-hung, tries to steal her magic jade pipe, under orders from the malevolent Wizard of Yin. However, he ends up taking a fake, planted as a test of loyalty by his wife, General Choi Siu-ching. When Yin's forces slaughter almost all of the remaining Ha Hou troops, Princess Choi is mistakenly blamed for the tragedy, and the prince's aunt pushes him into pledging vengeance. Meanwhile, forces claiming to be loyal to the princess merely hope to get their hands on a vast treasure, which is to meant to reestablish the Chun kingdom.

The cinematography and settings are beautiful (though the HK video versions look inexplicably drab compared to their Taiwan counterpart), and the supernatural action quite plentiful, but the storyline is too routine to retain one's interest and the musical score is not always well suited to the visuals.

Zero Mark *see* **Conduct Zero**

1100. Zodiac Killers

(1991; Golden Harvest/Paragon Films) ★: 5/10. *Gik do jui jing* (Cantonese), *Ji dao zhui zong* (Mandarin): "Chasing to the Ends of the Earth." Cinematographer: David Chung Chi-man; Art Director: Hai Chung-man; Music: Schtung Music; Writers: Raymond To Kwok-wai, Ng Lim-chan; Producer: Eric Tsang Chi-wai; Action Director: Tang Tak-wing; Director: Ann Hui On-wah. Cast: Andy Lau Tak-wah (Ben Li), Cherie Chung Cho-hung (Meng Tieh-lan), Suen Fook (Ming), Tou Chung-wah (Chang Chih), Yasuaki Kurota (Ishikawa). 1.85:1. VHS: Tai Seng. Import LD/VCD: Mei Ah. 97 minutes.

Not entirely the exploitation film suggested by the English title, this middling drama has laudable ambitions but is curiously uninvolving much of the time. Impoverished, hot-tempered Chinese student Ben tries to get by in Japan by working as a tour guide. One evening, at a nightclub, he meets fellow student Meng Tieh-lan. He likes her immediately but she does not have the same feelings for him. When the girl's loutish sponsor tries to take advantage of her, Tieh-lan hooks up with another man, Asano, who turns out to be a *yakuza* on the run from both the police and his fellow gangsters. When the latter catch up to him, Asano gives Tieh-lan a tape and asks her to deliver it to mobster Ishikawa, the leader of a rival gang. Ishikawa's drugs were ripped off by Asano's boss several years earlier, and the latter's men also murdered Ishikawa's superior in the process; the tape contains the details of those incidents. Desperate for help and with nowhere to turn, Tieh-lan enlists the aid of Ben, who tries to help her deliver the tape and escape back to China.

Beautiful location photography is the main attraction of the film, which tries to walk the line between art and exploitation and does not really succeed on either front, thanks largely to indifferent scripting. A pair of painfully melodramatic twists (regarding an old girlfriend of one Chinese student and the fate of another) in the final few minutes don't help either. Nobuhiko Obayashi's Japanese film **Beijing Watermelon** (1990) does a much better job exploring the subject of Chinese students struggling to make ends meet in Japan. This was Cherie Chung's last screen appearance to date.

1101. Zu Time Warrior

(1985; Golden Harvest/Paragon Films) ★: 5/10. Same cast and crew as *Zu: Warriors from the Magic Mountain*. VHS: Tai Seng (Dubbed). 96 minutes.

1102. Zu: Warriors from the Magic Mountain

(1983; Golden Harvest/Paragon Films) ★: 8/10. *Suk san sun suk san geen hap* (Cantonese), *Zuo shan shen zuo shan jian xia* (Mandarin): "Zu Mountain: New Legend of the Zu Mountain Swordsmen." Cinematographer: Bill Wong Chung-bo; Art Director: William Cheung Suk-ping; Music: Kwan Sing-yu; Writer: Roy Szeto Cheuk-hon; Producer: Leonard Ho Koon-cheung; Action Directors: Corey Yuen Kwai, Mang Hoi, Yuen Biao, Fung Hark-on; Director: Tsui Hark. Cast: Yuen Biao (Ti Ming-chi), Adam Cheng Siu-chau (Ting Yin), Damian Lau Chung-yan (Abbot Hsiao Yu), Mang Hoi (Yi Chen), Brigitte Lin Ching-hsia (The Countess), Moon Lee Choi-fung (Leader of the Guards), Sammo Hung Kam-po (East Zu Soldier/Long Brows), Judy Ong (Lady Li I-chi), Ha Guang-li (Chi Wu-shuang), Norman Tsui Siu-keung (Heaven's Blade), Fung Hark-on (Evil Disciple). Dolby Digital (DVD Only). 1.85:1. VHS/LD: Tai Seng (Remastered for the English market). Import LD: Star Entertainment (No Subtitles). Import VCD: Universe (No Subtitles). Import DVD: Universe. 98 minutes.

Tsui Hark's exciting and exquisitely designed fantasy epic (the obvious inspiration for John Carpenter's **Big Trouble In Little China**) is often remembered as being the film that broke new technical ground for HK cinema. However, to cite **Zu** merely for its special FX is to sell short one of the grandest and most influential productions in the history of Chinese fantasy cinema. Set in 5th. century China, the involved storyline charts the adventures of Ti Ming-chi, a naive young soldier from the West Zu army, who strays from the battlefield and into a dark and dangerous world of mystical swordsmen and ravenous monsters. Saved from death by the noble warrior Ting Yin, Ti joins forces with him, the Abbot Hsiao Yu, his bumbling pupil Yi Chen, and the powerful old wizard Long Brows, in a quest to save mankind from the ravaging Blood Demon. Although Long Brows is able to temporarily subdue the creature, it manages to poison and possess

Hsiao. Ting takes the stricken monk to the mysterious Countess of Jade Pond in the hopes that she will cure him. The Countess obliges, but when the demon takes over Ting's body soon after, she is unable to help, and freezes her fortress solid in an attempt to subdue him. The creature still manages to escape, prompting Ting, Yi, and one of The Countess' guards (played by Moon Lee) to journey to Heaven's Blade Peak and seek out the all-powerful Twin Swords, which are in the possession of the enigmatic Lady Li I-chi. The united power of the swords is the only force strong enough to destroy the demon.

Adapted from Lee Sau-man's colossal 64 volume novel, "The Legend of the Zu Mountain Warriors," the $HK30 million production barrels along with the bold velocity that would become one of Tsui's trademarks. Some aspects of the storyline seem vague upon first viewing, especially since Tsui (who has a cameo in the final scene as a West Zu soldier) rushes through the expository passages like a kid rifling through a comic book to get to the next battle. The visuals have lost some of their sheen over the years but are still quite eye-catching and convey the fantasy milieu well. Knowing that the local industry lacked the technical know how to pull off the sort of FX he planned, Tsui lured **Star Wars** veterans Robert Blalack and Peter Kuran to HK, and had them instruct the local craftsmen. The result is the first ever merger of Chinese fantasy and Western technique. While the design and trappings are distinctly Eastern, the American influence is apparent at times, particularly in the Twin Swords (which resemble light sabers) and the cave demons which attack Ti early on (they look like mummified Jawas).

In typical Golden Harvest fashion, the dubbed version differs from the original. Bearing the onscreen title **Zu Time Warrior**, this version deletes about a half hour from the original, substituting new footage (shot in 1985) of Yuen Biao and Moon Lee in the present day. In addition, there are two other scenes set in the past, as well as a new epilogue back in the future. Reportedly, Tsui had always intended for **Zu** to be structured in this manner but, because he was over-budget and behind schedule, Golden Harvest assembled the footage that was finished and released the film as is, in order to make its promised Chinese New Year opening. Frankly, it is good that Tsui was not allowed to do the film as he had planned, since the alternate edition (released only in English dubbed form) significantly dumbs down the premise, making for a far less absorbing narrative. While there are lapses in continuity and spots where transitional shots are missing, Golden Harvest's cut remains vastly superior, whatever Tsui's feelings about it may be.

Hong Kong Video Resources

The VHS videotapes from Hong Kong are in the PAL format and will not work on North American NTSC television systems. However, almost all HK releases are available on NTSC VHS from domestic companies like Tai Seng, which are also the authorized distributors of import HK laserdiscs, VCDs, and DVDs. Orders should be addressed to these companies rather than the distributors in HK, which generally do not deal directly with the public. All Hong Kong LDs and DVDs are NTSC, and the vast majority of the latter are not region coded; VCDs will playback on North American systems, though some have compatibility problems with NTSC equipment (for example: Some VCDs playback on domestic Sony DVD players with the picture vertically elongated). As with North America, the laserdisc market in HK is all but extinct, so all of the LDs listed here are probably no longer available. As for the listings in each review, I have included all of the video distributors that offered the film in question at one time. To confirm availability, contact the companies in question.

Cameron Entertainment Co. Ltd.
Now markets all of its productions on video through Mei Ah; see listing for that company

Carnival Home Entertainment Ltd.
Unit 604, Taikoktsui Centre
11-15 Kok Cheung Street
Kowloon, Hong Kong
Phone: (852) 2787-5503
Fax: (852) 2787-4367

China Star Entertainment Group
Website: http://www.chinastar.com.hk/
E-Mail: video@chinastar.hk

Fitto Mobile Laser Distribution Co. Ltd.
Unit 20
8/F Metro Centre, Tower 1
32 Lam Hing Street
Kowloon Bay, Kowloon, Hong Kong
Phone: (852) 2751-2200
Fax: (852) 2756-3329

Golden Cinema City Video Distribution Ltd.
Defunct

Golden Flare Films
Defunct

J & M Chevalier
Defunct

Jumbo Plain Laser & Video Co.
B-03, Summit Insurance Building
789 Nathan Road
Kowloon, Hong Kong
Phone: (852) 2397-7632
Fax: (852) 2397-2167

Laserlink International
Defunct

Mecapro
Defunct

Mega Star Video Distribution (HK) Ltd.
Room 401-402, World Commerce Centre
11 Canton Road
TST, Kowloon, Hong Kong
Telephone: (852) 2317-4118
Fax: (852) 2317-4318

Mei Ah Laser Disc Co. Ltd.
Multimedia Division
Units 15-28, 17/F
Metro Centre Phase 1
32 Lam Hing Street
Kowloon Bay, HK
Telephone: (852) 2754-2855
Fax: (852) 2799-3643
http://www.meiah.com/centernf.htm
E-Mail: meiah@meiah.com

Network Kingdom Video & Audio Inc.
Defunct

New City Laser & Video Co. Ltd.
19/F, Wharf Cable Tower,
9 Hoi Shing Road
Tsuen Wan, New Territories

Hong Kong
Phone: (852) 2412-1388

Ocean Shores Group
Room 1505-1518, 15/F
Leader Industrial Centre
57-59 Au Pui Wan Street,
Fo Tan, Shatin, New Territories
Hong Kong
Phone: (852) 2577-9325
Fax: (852) 2890-8779
Website: http://www.ocean-shores.com/

Panorama Entertainment
16 Granville Road, I/F
Kowloon, Hong Kong
Website: http://www.panorama.com.hk/

Riverdrive Productions Ltd.
280 Riverside Drive, #10K
New York, NY 10025 USA
Phone: (212) 222-7350
Fax: (212) 865-6983
E-Mail: evanschan@aol.com

Star Entertainment Co. Ltd.
Now called China Star Entertainment Group; see listing for that company

Tai Seng Video Marketing Inc.
170 South Spruce Avenue, Suite 200
South San Francisco, CA 94080, USA
Phone: (800) 888-3836, (650) 871-8118, (888) 668-8338
Fax: (650) 871-2392
Website: http://www.taiseng.com/
E-Mail: webstaff@taiseng.com

Universe Laser & Video Co.
Room 3503-3505
Wharf Cable Tower
9 Hoi Shing Road
Tsuen Wan, New Territories
Hong Kong
Phone: (852) 2416-3008
Fax: (852) 2414-7207

Wide Sight Entertainment
Telephone: (852) 2380-3802
Fax: (852) 2393-6936

Winner's Workshop Production Co. Ltd.
Telephone: (852) 2774-2838
Fax: (852) 2356-9482

World Video & Supply Co.
150 Executive Park Blvd, Suite 1200
San Francisco, CA 94134
Telephone: (415) 468-6218
Fax: (415) 468-1381
Website: http://www.worldvideo.com
E-Mail: webmaster@worldvideo.com

GLOSSARY

Anime

Japanese animation.

Category I

A HK film rating that means the film in question is suitable for general audiences.

Category II, IIA, IIB

Category II is a HK film rating that means anyone may attend the movie in question but the examiners feel that it is "Not Suitable for Children." In the mid-90s, the rating was split into IIA ("Not Suitable for Children") and IIB ("Not Suitable for Children or Teenagers").

Category III

A HK film rating that means the film in question is restricted to those 18 years of age and over.

Cheongsam

A traditional Chinese dress.

CID

Short for the Criminal Investigation Division of the Hong Kong police force. The equivalent of a detective squad in a Western law enforcement agency. Members of the CID are usually referred to as "CIDs," rather than *chai yan* (Cantonese for "cops").

Feng shui

Feng shui or "wind water" is a Chinese practice based on geomantic principles that determine, configure, or repair the harmony which exists between a given location and the metaphysical forces that reside in it.

Fuk sing

Fuk sing (or *Fook sing*) is Cantonese for "Lucky Stars" (see ng fook sing).

Giallo

Giallo is Italian for "yellow" and refers to a type of mystery/thriller (usually Italian in origin) characterized by its stylish cinematography, brutal violence, and sexual content.

Ging fei pin

Cantonese for "Police and Robber Film."

Goo wak jai/Goo wak jai genre

Goo wak jai or "Devious Kid" is Cantonese vernacular for a male who has fallen in with a criminal gang. The term is related to *hung goo wak* or "Walk Deviously." The *goo wak jai* genre is primarily a mid-90s phenomena, spawned by the success of **Young and Dangerous**.

Goo wak lui

Goo wak lui or "Devious Woman" is Cantonese vernacular for a female who has fallen in with a criminal gang. **Sexy and Dangerous** is a film centered around *goo wak lui.*

Gweilo

Gweilo (or *gwai lo*) is Cantonese for "Ghost Man," a reference to Caucasians that has lost most of its derogatory meaning over the years.

Gyonsi

Hopping vampires are usually referenced to English as "*Gyonsi.*" More accurate Romanizations would be *Geung si* (Cantonese) and *Jiang shi* (Mandarin).

The Hong Kong Film Awards

The HK equivalent of The Academy Awards.

LD

Laserdisc, a 12 inch video format that is now almost entirely defunct.

Mamasan

A *mamasan* is the female manager of the hostesses at a hostess bar. At the more disreputable establishments, a *mamasan* may also serve as a pimp or a loan shark to her young charges.

Manga

Japanese comic books.

Mao shan

Mao shan is Cantonese for Mao Mountain which, legend has it, was home to many sorcerers and hermits. Their knowledge of the occult became well known and a school was established, at the mountain, for those interested in learning the magical martial arts techniques they specialized in.

Mo lei tau

Mo lei tau is Cantonese for "nonsense." Stephen Chiau Sing-chi became a huge star, thanks to his trademark *mo lei tau* verbal humor, which is difficult to translate successfully into English.

New Wave

A period, beginning at the end of the 1970s, when a new breed of young directors (including Tsui Hark, Ann Hui On-wah, and Patrick Tam Karming) brought new energy and creativity to HK cinema.

Ng fook sing

Cantonese for "Five Lucky Stars." The *ng fook sing* (or *ng fuk sing*) films were a series of highly successful action comedies, beginning with **My Lucky Stars** (1985).

Pachinko

Pachinko is a hugely popular Japanese game. One drops small steel balls (which are purchased from the establishment, usually in lots of several hundred at a time) into the machine and the object is to get them through a maze of pins and into small cups at the bottom. If you are successful, the machine then releases more balls for you to play with. The player wins or loses depending on how many balls he has left when he decides to stop.

Sais

A traditional martial arts weapon.

SDU

Special Duty Unit, HK's version of SWAT. SDU is also known as *Fei foo* or "The Flying Tigers" in Cantonese.

Seppuku

Japanese term for a ritualistic form of suicide performed by disgraced warriors.

Sifu

Cantonese for "Martial Father." In the old days, the relationship between a martial arts teacher and his students was taken very seriously because, once a teacher accepted a pupil, he treated this individual as if he or she were his own flesh and blood. In the English dubbed versions of most kung fu films, *sifu* (or *si fu*) is usually translated as "teacher," which is actually *lo si* in Cantonese and really only conveys the basic extent of the Chinese term.

Triads

Chinese gangsters.

TVB

TVB is HK's leading television network.

VCD

Video Compact Disc, the most popular video format in HK. VCDs are similar to DVDs but have a much lower storage capacity and offer considerably inferior picture and sound quality.

Yakuza

Japanese gangsters.

Bibliography

Program Guides

The China Factor in Hong Kong Cinema. Hong Kong: The 14th Hong Kong International Film Festival, 1990.

Fifty Years of Electric Shadows. Hong Kong: The 21st Hong Kong International Film Festival, 1997.

Hong Kong Cinema in the Eighties. Hong Kong: The 15th Hong Kong International Film Festival, 1991.

Hong Kong Panorama. Hong Kong: The 22nd Hong Kong International Film Festival, 1998.

Phantoms of the Hong Kong Cinema. Hong Kong: The 13th Hong Kong International Film Festival, 1989.

A Study of the Hong Kong Swordplay Film (1945-1980). Hong Kong: The 5th Hong Kong International Film Festival, 1981.

Books

Wood, Miles. *Cine East: Hong Kong Cinema Through the Looking Glass.* Guilford, Surrey, U.K.: FAB Press, 1998

Dannen, Frederic, and Barry Long. *Hong Kong Babylon: An Insider's Guide to the Hollywood of the East.* New York: Hyperion/Miramax Books, 1997.

Periodicals

Cineraider. Ed. Richard Akiyama, 1993–

Martial Arts Movie Associates. Eds. William Connolly (1985–), Rick Meyers (1985–1993), 1985– .

SKAM. Ed. Richard Akiyama, 1988–1992.

Websites

Hong Kong Cinema. Joseph M. Fierro, (This site was temporarily off-line, as of this writing, and no new URL was available.

Hong Kong Entertainment News in Review. Sanney Leung, http://www.hkmdb.com/hkentreview/

Hong Kong Films on DVD. Matthew Muldoon, http://www.public.asu.edu/~muldoon/hk/index3.htm.

Hong Kong Movie Database. Ryan Law, http://www.hkmdb.com/

Movieworld Hong Kong. Tong Chen, http://www.movieworld.com.hk/index.shtml

The Special Administrative Region (Hong Kong) Film Top Ten Box Office Home Page. Anonymous, http://www.geocities.com/Tokyo/Towers/2038/

Index

All names in the index are presented with the family first. For example, Brigitte Lin Ching-hsia is listed as "Lin Ching-hsia, Brigitte," as "Lin" is the actress' surname, "Ching-hsia" is her Chinese first name and "Brigitte" is her Western first name. If the person is only listed in the text via a Western name, then it is presented in standard form; for example, Johnny Chen is listed as "Chen, Johnny." Japanese performers are also listed in this manner; for example, Yasuaki Kurota is included as "Kurota, Yasuaki." Finally, actor Dick Wei can be found under "D," rather than "W," because "Dick" is an anglicized form of the actor's surname "Tik" and "Dick Wei" is the manner in which he is almost always credited. References are to entry numbers.